Y0-DOK-176

West's Law School
Advisory Board

JESSE H. CHOPER
Professor of Law,
University of California, Berkeley

DAVID P. CURRIE
Professor of Law, University of Chicago

YALE KAMISAR
Professor of Law, University of Michigan

MARY KAY KANE
Chancellor, Dean and Distinguished Professor of Law,
University of California,
Hastings College of the Law

WAYNE R. LaFAVE
Professor of Law, University of Illinois

ARTHUR R. MILLER
Professor of Law, Harvard University

GRANT S. NELSON
Professor of Law,
University of California, Los Angeles

JAMES J. WHITE
Professor of Law, University of Michigan

CASES, TEXT AND PROBLEMS ON

FEDERAL INCOME TAXATION

Fifth Edition

By

Alan Gunn

John N. Matthews Professor of Law
University of Notre Dame

Larry D. Ward

Dykstra Professor of Law
University of Iowa

AMERICAN CASEBOOK SERIES®

WEST
GROUP

A THOMSON COMPANY

Mat #40013547

West Group has created this publication to provide you with accurate and authoritative information concerning the subject matter covered. However, this publication was not necessarily prepared by persons licensed to practice law in a particular jurisdiction. West Group is not engaged in rendering legal or other professional advice, and this publication is not a substitute for the advice of an attorney. If you require legal or other expert advice, you should seek the services of a competent attorney or other professional.

American Casebook Series, and the West Group symbol
are registered trademarks used herein under license.

COPYRIGHT © 1981, 1988, 1992 WEST PUBLISHING CO.
COPYRIGHT © 1998 By WEST GROUP
COPYRIGHT © 2002 By WEST GROUP

                    610 Opperman Drive
                    P.O. Box 64526
                    St. Paul, MN 55164–0526
                    1–800–328–9352

All rights reserved
Printed in the United States of America

ISBN 0–314–26195–8

 TEXT IS PRINTED ON 10% POST CONSUMER RECYCLED PAPER

To Bertha Gunn and Curt Ward

*

Preface

In debate on the Income Tax Bill of 1861, Senator Simmons urged that no attempt be made to specify how a taxpayer's income was to be computed; adding detail to the bill would, he said, "only make it more confused than it is now."[1] Congress has never paid much attention to this advice, and the enactment of major, detailed tax legislation has now become almost an annual event. We have tried here, as in the previous editions, to prepare materials that will help students cope with a confusing mass of legislation by seeing the minutiae of the Code as reflections of the basic concepts and recurring problems of income taxation.

In this edition, we have engaged in the usual updating, including the important changes made by the Economic Growth and Tax Relief Reconciliation Act of 2001. We have also included several new principal cases and rulings and added a host of problems. Our organization remains largely unchanged, except for the addition of a new section on personal exemptions and child tax credits in Chapter Three. With considerable regret, we have eliminated most of the material on the income taxation of trusts in Chapter Seven. As in earlier editions, questions of "exclusions from gross income" and "deductions" are not rigidly separated, as both exclusions and deductions are means to the same end—the determination of taxable income. We continue to treat the income and deduction aspects of particular kinds of payments—especially interest—together, a technique we see as essential if students are to understand what is at stake in particular controversies.

In editing cases and other materials we have eliminated repetitive citations, references to "the Internal Revenue Code," "26 U.S.C.A.," "Treasury Regulations," and the like, footnotes, internal cross-references, and citations to the record, and we have corrected obvious typographical errors. These changes are not indicated. Other omissions and changes are marked in the usual ways. All numbered footnotes are from quoted materials, and they have not been renumbered; our own footnotes are lettered. References to pre-1954 section numbers have been updated except for cases in which the form of the old law bears on the outcome or importance of a decision. Citations to Tax Court memorandum opinions are to the Commerce Clearing House "Tax Court Memorandum Decisions." Letter rulings are cited by number only. For rulings issued before 2000, the first two digits of a letter ruling's number show the year in which it was issued. For those issued after 1999, the first four digits designate the year of issuance.

1. J. Seidman, Legislative History of Federal Income Tax Laws 1938-1861, p. 1043 (1938).

We thank Matthew J. Barrett, Calvin H. Johnson, Carolyn Jones, Michael S. Kirsch, Philip D. Oliver, Peter Van Zante and Pat Cain for valuable comments on this or earlier editions. All errors are ours.

Professor Ward would also like to acknowledge the extraordinary assistance provided on this edition by Mary McConnell Caruso and Diana DeWalle, without whose unflagging support he could never have completed this work. Professor Gunn thanks research librarian Dwight B. King, Jr., for assistance far beyond what what a faculty member should reasonably expect.

This edition is current as of February, 2002.

ALAN GUNN

LARRY D. WARD

February, 2002

Acknowledgments

We thank those who have given permission to reprint excerpts from the following:

Corneel, Guidelines to Tax Practice Second, 43 The Tax Lawyer 297 (1990). Reprinted by permission of the American Bar Association and Frederic G. Corneel. Copyright © 1990 American Bar Association.

Johnson, The Case for Taxing Fringe Benefits, 9 Tax Notes 43 (1979). Reprinted by permission of Tax Analysts. Copyright © 1979 by Tax Analysts.

*

Summary of Contents

*

Table of Contents

Table of Cases

The principal cases are in bold type. Cases cited or discussed in the text are roman type. References are to pages. Cases cited in principal cases and within other quoted materials are not included.

Table of Internal Revenue Code Sections

*

Table of Treasury Regulations and Rulings

*

CASES, TEXT AND PROBLEMS ON

FEDERAL INCOME TAXATION

Fifth Edition

*

Chapter One

INTRODUCTION

A. THE CONSTITUTION AND THE INCOME TAX

Article I, § 8, of the Constitution allows Congress to "lay and collect Taxes, Duties, Imposts and Excises * * *." This power is limited in three ways: (1) "direct" taxes must be apportioned among the states, (2) bills for "raising revenue" must originate in the House of Representatives, and (3) taxes must be "uniform throughout the United States." Since 1913, the Sixteenth Amendment has allowed Congress to tax "incomes" without apportionment, making moot the question whether an income tax is a "direct" tax.

1. APPORTIONMENT OF DIRECT TAXES

Two provisions of Article I require that direct taxes be apportioned among the states on the basis of population.

Article I, § 2:

* * *

Representatives and direct Taxes shall be apportioned among the several States * * * according to their respective Numbers, which shall be determined by adding to the whole Number of free Persons, including those bound to Service for a Term of Years, and excluding Indians not taxed, three fifths of all other Persons. * * *

Article I, § 9:

* * *

No Capitation, or other direct, Tax shall be laid, unless in Proportion to the Census or Enumeration herein before directed to be taken.

Are some or all income taxes "direct"? Unfortunately, the term "direct tax" has never had a settled meaning. The requirement that direct taxes be apportioned appears in the Constitution because of a dispute over how slaves were to be counted in fixing a state's representation in Congress. In order to induce the southern delegates to the

1

constitutional convention to agree to counting only three-fifths of slaves in determining representation, the requirement that taxes be apportioned was adopted. What the South lost in votes would be offset by a tax benefit. But in order to insure that the Federal government would not be prevented from collecting the kinds of taxes normal for the time, the apportionment requirement was limited to "direct" taxes, so as not to apply to "indirect taxes on exports and imports, and on consumption."[a] The fourth clause of Article One, § 9 (quoted above), was adopted to assure the southern delegates that no "capitation" tax on slaves would be enacted and that the population figures used to apportion any direct tax would be those determined by the census, not arbitrary figures fixed by Congress.

The history of the direct-tax provisions shows only that taxes on imports, exports, and consumption were not "direct." No settled concept of "direct taxation" existed when the Constitution was adopted. Some writers classified only real property taxes as "direct," others thought poll taxes "direct" too, some thought that "direct" taxes were those taxes (if any) that could not be shifted to others by the person liable for payment, and some thought income taxes, but not consumption taxes, to be "direct." As Seligman puts it, "there are almost as many classifications of direct and indirect taxes as there are authors," so that "[a]ny appeal to the usage, or lack of usage, among economists is * * * of no value in solving the question as to what is meant by the term in the constitution."[b] James Madison's Journal of the Constitutional Convention contains the following entry for August 20, 1787:

> Mr. King asked what was the precise meaning of *direct* taxation? No one answered.

Although Congress did occasionally enact apportioned taxes, an apportioned income tax would be almost inconceivable, as it would burden taxpayers in poor states more heavily than those in wealthier states. The answer to the question whether an income tax was direct therefore determined whether Congress could enact it. Over the years, the Supreme Court held that taxes on carriages, inheritance taxes, taxes on bank notes, and taxes on the gross receipts of businesses were "indirect." And in Springer v. United States, 102 U.S. (12 Otto) 586 (1880), the Court held that the Civil War income tax was not direct, saying that the only direct taxes are real property taxes and poll taxes.

Although *Springer* seemed clearly to have established that an income tax is not "direct" in the constitutional sense, the Supreme Court held in Pollock v. Farmers' Loan & Trust Co., 157 U.S. 429 (1895), that the Federal income tax imposed in 1894 was unconstitutional as applied to income from rent. It reasoned that, since a real-property tax is concededly a "direct" tax, a tax on the income from real property is also "direct" because it is, in substance, the same thing as a tax on real

a. This language, used by Gouverneur Morris, is quoted in E.R.A. Seligman, The Income Tax 551 (2d ed. 1914).

b. E.R.A. Seligman, op. cit., at 540.

property. The Court held also that the tax violated fundamental principles of federalism by treating interest on state and municipal bonds as income.[c] On rehearing, the Court decided that the tax was "direct" as applied to the income from personal as well as real property, and that the entire 1894 income-tax law was invalid because the unconstitutional portions were inseparable from the valid provisions; 158 U.S. 601 (1895).

The one thing about the distinction between "direct" and "indirect" taxes that is not unclear is that the distinction depends on the form of the tax. Therefore, the Court's conclusion in *Pollock* that a tax on income from property is direct because it is "in substance" a tax on the property itself is unconvincing, even assuming that the Court was right about the substantial equivalence of the two kinds of tax. Stanton v. Baltic Mining Co., 240 U.S. 103 (1916), described income taxes as "inherently" belonging to the class of indirect taxes and called the argument that a tax on the product of property is necessarily a tax on the property "wholly fallacious." The real reasons for the result in *Pollock* may be suggested by Justice Field's description of the tax as "class legislation" (because it applied only to annual incomes in excess of $4000). Justice Field felt that exempting even the poor from the operation of the tax would cause them to "lose their manliness and self-respect"; 157 U.S. at 597.

Chief Justice Fuller's opinion for the *Pollock* Court on rehearing observed that the direct-tax provisions of the Constitution were subject to amendment, so that if, on the "sober second thought of every part of the country," an income tax was thought desirable, it could be obtained. The Sixteenth Amendment, ratified in 1913, provides:

> The Congress shall have power to lay and collect taxes on incomes, from whatever source derived, without apportionment among the several States, and without regard to any census or enumeration.

Since the adoption of the Sixteenth Amendment there has been no serious doubt about the power of Congress to impose income taxes without apportionment, and very little doubt about its broad power to define income and to draw whatever distinctions it sees fit in devising the tax. Only one Supreme Court case[d] has held an income-tax provision unconstitutional on the ground that it sought to tax as income something that could not be called "income" within the meaning of the Sixteenth Amendment, and that case's authority today is most doubtful.

2. THE ORIGINATION CLAUSE

In practice, the requirement of Article I, § 7, that "Bills for raising Revenue shall originate in the House of Representatives" has become a

---

c. See p. 157, below.

d. Eisner v. Macomber, p. 99 below. In Edwards v. Cuba R. Co., p. 152 below, the Court held that the statute did not require including "contributions to capital" in income, and said that a statute that did so would be unconstitutional. The Court said in Helvering v. Independent Life Ins. Co., 292 U.S. 371 (1934), that a tax on the rental value of a building owned and used by the taxpayer would be unconstitutional unless apportioned. The Court went on to find that the statute in question did not impose such a tax.

formality. The House originates and passes dozens of tax measures every year. If the Senate wants to launch a major piece of tax legislation it has only to approve "amendments" to one of these bills, deleting whatever it finds undesirable. For example, the Tax Equity and Fiscal Responsibility Act of 1982 ("TEFRA"), an important tax statute, began in the House as a minor tax-reduction measure. When the bill reached the Senate, all of the provisions passed by the House (except for the bill number and the enacting clause) were deleted, the bill received a new name, and an extensive set of provisions aimed at increasing revenues by some one hundred billion dollars over three years was substituted.

Origination Clause challenges to the validity of TEFRA and other tax legislation have failed. Flint v. Stone Tracy Co., 220 U.S. 107 (1911), approved the Senate's replacement of an inheritance-tax provision with a corporate tax, and several courts of appeals have held TEFRA constitutional; see, e.g., Wardell v. United States, 757 F.2d 203 (8th Cir.1985). In Texas Ass'n of Concerned Taxpayers, Inc. v. United States, 772 F.2d 163 (5th Cir.1985), cert. denied 476 U.S. 1151 (1986), the Fifth Circuit ruled that TEFRA's constitutionality was a nonjusticiable political question. The District of Columbia Circuit upheld the dismissal of a challenge to TEFRA by several members of the House on the ground that the district court properly exercised its "remedial discretion" to withhold relief in a case involving a dispute among members of Congress; Moore v. United States House of Representatives, 733 F.2d 946 (D.C.Cir.1984), cert. denied 469 U.S. 1106 (1985).

3. THE UNIFORMITY CLAUSE

The requirement of Article I, § 8, that taxes be "uniform throughout the United States" does not prohibit a progressive tax or a tax that distinguishes between different sources or uses of income. The "uniformity" required is that taxes be "geographically uniform" in the sense that "whatever plan or method Congress adopts for laying the tax in question, the same plan and the same method must be made operative throughout the United States"; Knowlton v. Moore, 178 U.S. 41, 84 (1900) (inheritance tax); see also Brushaber v. Union Pacific R. Co., 240 U.S. 1, 24 (1916) (income tax).

The Crude Oil Windfall Profit Tax Act of 1980 imposed an excise tax on domestic oil production, exempting most oil from wells north of the Arctic Circle. A unanimous Supreme Court held in United States v. Ptasynski, 462 U.S. 74 (1983), that the exemption did not create a Uniformity Clause violation even though nearly all the exempt production was from wells in Alaska (indeed, the Act itself referred to "exempt Alaskan Oil"). Noting the "disproportionate costs" of producing Arctic oil, the Court held that "[t]he Uniformity Clause gives Congress wide latitude in deciding what to tax and does not prohibit it from considering geographically isolated problems"; 462 U.S. at 84. *Ptasynski* has been described as leaving the Uniformity Clause "virtually an empty shell"; Comment, The Uniformity Clause, 51 U.Chi.L.Rev. 1193 (1984).

B. INCOME TAX LEGISLATION AND REGULATIONS

The Revenue Act of 1913 imposed a progressive tax on individual[e] incomes. The tax's marginal rates reached a maximum of seven percent on incomes over $500,000. The first $3000 ($4000 for a married taxpayer) of income was excluded. Until 1939, the tax law consisted of the "revenue acts" adopted at regular intervals (typically every two years). In 1939 the first Internal Revenue Code (the "Internal Revenue Code of 1939") was adopted. Since the adoption of the 1939 Code, tax enactments (often called "Revenue Acts" or "Tax Reform Acts") have amended particular provisions of the Code instead of re-enacting the entire body of tax law.[f] In 1954, the Code was revised extensively and re-enacted as the "Internal Revenue Code of 1954." Since 1954, the Code has been amended many times, including major revisions in 1969, 1976, 1981, 1982, 1984, 1986, 1993, 1997, and 2001. The far-reaching Tax Reform Act of 1986 renamed the internal-revenue title of the United States Code (Title 26) the "Internal Revenue Code of 1986."

Today, the income tax (including the corporate income tax) is the Federal government's major source of revenue, as the following table shows.

TREASURY DEPARTMENT GROSS TAX COLLECTIONS
BY SOURCE: 2000
[in billions of dollars]

(IRS Statistics of Income Bulletin, Summer 2001)

Source	Amount	Percent of Total
Individual Income Tax	$1117.1	53.38
Corporate Income Tax	235.7	11.26
Employment Taxes (Mostly Social Security)	639.7	30.57
Estate & Gift Taxes	29.7	1.4
Excise Taxes	70.6	3.4

Much of today's tax law is found in regulations promulgated by the Treasury Department. These regulations are published in Title 26 of the Code of Federal Regulations. Part One of that title contains the income-tax regulations, which are numbered to correspond to the Code provisions which they implement: thus, Treas.Reg. § 1.61–14(a) interprets § 61 of the Code.

Under the Administrative Procedure Act, regulations first appear in proposed form. After public comment, and sometimes hearings, a pro-

---

e. A tax on the incomes of corporations was adopted in 1909. It was held to be an "indirect" tax in Flint v. Stone Tracy Co., 220 U.S. 107 (1911).

f. The principal practical effect of the change from regular re-enactment to a more-or-less permanent "code" has been to dampen somewhat the enthusiasm of counsel for a once-common argument that Congress, by re-enacting a tax provision without change, meant to endorse every court decision and administrative ruling interpreting that provision (the "re-enactment doctrine").

posed regulation may be adopted (with or without changes) or withdrawn. "Temporary regulations," which are issued without a comment period, are used in situations in which the Treasury Department considers immediate authoritative guidance important. (Recent tax legislation has imposed so heavy a drafting burden on the Treasury Department that "temporary" regulations are nearly as likely as ordinary regulations to be permanent.) Section 7805(e)(1) requires that all temporary regulations be issued as "proposed" regulations as well. Section 7805(e)(2) provides that "[a]ny temporary regulation shall expire within 3 years of the date of issuance of such regulation," but nothing prevents the Treasury Department from reissuing expired temporary regulations.

Regulations are either "legislative" or "interpretative." A legislative regulation is a regulation issued under a specific statutory grant of authority to the Treasury Department to make rules on a particular subject. The classic example of this process is the rules governing consolidated income-tax returns for related corporations, which take up some 150 pages in the Code of Federal Regulations; they are authorized by a six-page statute. Interpretative regulations are issued under § 7805(a), which authorizes the Treasury Department to "prescribe all needful rules and regulations."

Regulations are "the law" unless they are invalid. The Supreme Court has said that regulations must be upheld if they "implement the congressional mandate in some reasonable manner" (United States v. Correll, 389 U.S. 299, 307 (1967)), and that regulations "must be sustained unless unreasonable and plainly inconsistent with the revenue statutes" (Commissioner v. South Texas Lumber Co., 333 U.S. 496, 501 (1948), rehearing denied 334 U.S. 813 (1948)). Special deference is said to be given to legislative regulations; Rowan Cos., Inc. v. United States, 452 U.S. 247, 253 (1981). Despite these statements, courts which are convinced that they know the "right answer" to a question of statutory interpretation sometimes find it easy to persuade themselves that regulations requiring a different answer are invalid. See Wolfman, Foreword, 35 The Tax Lawyer 443 (1982).

C. TAXPAYERS AND TAX RATES

Income taxes are imposed upon individuals, trusts, estates, and corporations. Corporations which have 75 or fewer shareholders and which meet other requirements can elect (with unanimous shareholder consent) to have their incomes taxed to their shareholders, rather than to themselves. Corporations which have made valid elections to do this are called "S corporations," after subchapter S of the Code (§§ 1361–1379). Corporations which are not S corporations are often called "C corporations" (after subchapter C, which governs many aspects of the taxation of corporate-shareholder transactions). Income earned by a partnership is taxed to the partners, except in the case of some publicly traded partnerships, which are taxed as if they were corporations; § 7704.

1. THE PROGRESSIVE RATE SYSTEM

Income-tax rates for individuals and corporations have almost always been "progressive" in the sense that the tax on a high income is a larger percentage of the income than the tax on a low income. (A "proportional" tax takes the same percentage of all incomes—for example, a tax of "15 percent of all income" would be proportional. A "regressive" tax would take a larger percentage of low incomes than of higher incomes; thus, a tax of "20 percent of the first $100,000 of income plus 10 percent of the amount of income over $100,000" would be regressive.) In the past, the highest rates applicable to individuals have exceeded 90 percent. Tax rates were reduced considerably in the 1980s and increased somewhat in the '90s. Under current law, the top marginal individual income-tax rate for 2002 and 2003 is 38.6 percent. Section 1(i) provides for rate reductions over the next several years; by 2006, the maximum individual rate will be 35 percent. "Phaseouts" (discussed below) increase the effective rate for some taxpayers. The highest marginal rate for corporations is now 39 percent.

The tax rates imposed by § 1 (individuals, trusts, and estates) and § 11 (corporations) are *marginal* rates. To see how a system using marginal rates works, consider the following hypothetical progressive-rate structure:

Income	Tax
Not over $10,000	0
$10,000–$30,000	10% of the excess of income over $10,000
$30,000–$50,000	$2,000 plus 20% of the excess over $30,000
Over $50,000	$6,000 plus 50% of the excess over $50,000

Under this schedule, a taxpayer with an income of more than $50,000 is "in the 50–percent bracket." This does not mean that the tax is half of total income: the 50–percent rate applies only to the amount of income in excess of $50,000. Therefore, a taxpayer with a cash income of $50,001 would not have been better off after tax if that income had been $50,000, putting the taxpayer in a "lower bracket." The one-dollar loss of before-tax income would have reduced the tax by only 50 cents, because the 50–percent rate applies only to the one dollar of income in the highest bracket. As a general rule, if A's before-tax income is higher than B's before-tax income, A's after-tax income will also be higher than B's.[g]

The actual tax-rate system differs in important respects from the hypothetical rate structure presented above. The tax-rate schedules of § 1 apply to the taxpayer's *taxable income*. Taxable income is computed by subtracting from the taxpayer's gross income (defined in § 61) any allowable deductions. But the Code reduces ("phases out") certain

---

g. A minor exception to this rule can occur in the case of people who compute their taxes by using the "tax tables" authorized by § 3. Because the tax tables are less precise than the rate schedules of § 1, a difference of a dollar or two of income can produce a difference of several dollars in tax, but the amounts involved are small.

deductions as the taxpayer's income increases. In such cases, an additional dollar of gross income may increase taxable income by more than one dollar, thus increasing the *actual* marginal tax rate to an amount exceeding the *nominal* statutory maximum. For example, suppose that a taxpayer whose income is subject to tax at the nominal maximum rate of 31 percent earns an additional $100. If the additional $100 of income results in the disallowance of $3 in deductions that would otherwise have been allowable, the taxpayer's *taxable* income increases by $103 ($100 of additional income plus $3 of deductions that are no longer allowable at the higher level of income), and the tax increases by $31.93 (31% of $103). The *actual* marginal rate on the additional $100 of income is therefore 31.93 percent ($31.93/$100).[h] For criticisms of Congress's use of phaseouts to increase actual tax rates while leaving nominal rates low, see Coven, Congress as Indian–Giver: "Phasing–Out" Tax Allowances Under the Internal Revenue Code of 1986, 6 Va.Tax Rev. 505 (1987); Thomas, Phase out the Phaseouts, 69 Tax Notes 1689 (1995).

Many individual taxpayers who have "long-term capital gains" are taxed much more lightly on some or all of those gains than on other kinds of income; § 1(h). These gains include most gains from the sale of investment property, such as stocks and bonds, if the property was held for more than six months before being sold. The intricacies of capital-gains taxation will be covered in Chapter 10.

The corporate rate structure contains two "bubbles," by means of which some firms face a higher marginal rate than firms with higher incomes. Under § 11, the corporate income tax takes 15 percent of the first $50,000 of a corporation's income, 25 percent of the next $25,000 of income, 34 percent of income in excess of $75,000 up to $10 million, and 35 percent of taxable income over $10 million. A 5–percent surtax is then imposed upon taxable income in excess of $100,000, up to a maximum surtax of $11,750. A 3–percent surtax is imposed upon taxable income in excess of $15 million, up to a maximum surtax of $100,000. Therefore, actual corporate income-tax rates are as follows:

Taxable Income	Marginal Rate
Not over $50,000	15 percent
$50,001–$75,000	25 percent
$75,001–$100,000	34 percent
$100,001–$335,000	39 percent
$335,001–$10,000,000	34 percent
$10,000,001–$15,000,000	35 percent
$15,000,001–$18,333,333	38 percent
Over $18,333,333	35 percent

The $11,750 maximum 5–percent surtax equals the additional tax a corporation with $335,000 or more in taxable income would have paid under a flat rate of 34 percent, as compared with the tax computed at

h. We consider the details of these phaseout rules in connection with the deductions to which they relate.

the 15–, 25–, and 34–percent rates. Thus, the surtax is a phasing-out of the "benefits" a corporation can be thought of as receiving by having the "first layers" of its income taxed at less than the 34–percent rate.[i] The $100,000 maximum 3–percent surtax equals the additional tax that would have been paid on the first $10,000,000 of income if the rate of tax had been 35 percent, rather than 34 percent. "Qualified personal service corporations," as defined in § 448(d)(2), are taxed at a flat rate of 35 percent; § 11(b)(2).

The rate tables for individuals, estates, and trusts are adjusted annually to take account of inflation; § 1(f). That section requires the Service to issue "tables," which supplant the statutory figures. Corporate tax rates are not adjusted for inflation.

Although the Code provides for indexing of the tax rates (and of some other Code provisions containing references to fixed dollar amounts), it falls far short of dealing with inflation in a comprehensive way. Imposing taxes on incomes that are "real" in the sense that they measure actual purchasing power would entail adjusting the tax base, as well as the tax rates, for inflation. Consider, for example, a taxpayer who buys vacant land for $5000 and who sells it several years later for $10,000. The Code treats the $5000 difference between the purchase price and the sale price as income, but if inflation caused prices to double while the taxpayer held the land, the venture did not actually enrich the taxpayer at all. Congress has not yet shown serious interest in adjusting the tax base for inflation, in part, perhaps, because of the complexity of such adjustments and in part because exempting inflationary gains from taxation would require an increase in the tax rates for real gains.

Some taxpayers whose income taxes would be quite small in comparison with their "economic" or "accounting" incomes (in a very loose sense) are subject to minimum taxes, which are examined in Chapter 6.

Because the rates of §§ (1)(a) through (1)(e) are adjusted from time to time both to reflect inflation and because of the rate reductions called for by § 1(i), the use of examples and problems based on the actual rates in effect each year would be very cumbersome. To provide a reasonably realistic yet stable basis for examples and problems, we present, in

---

i. The benefit of having the first $50,000 of the firm's taxable income taxed at 15 percent (instead of 34 percent) is $9500 ($50,000 × [34% − 15%]); and the benefit of having the next $25,000 of taxable income taxed at 25 percent (instead of 34%) is $2250 ($25,000 × [34% − 25%]). The total savings from the use of the lower brackets is therefore $11,750. In order to recover this benefit by means of a 5–percent surtax, the surtax must apply to $235,000 of the firm's taxable income (because 5 percent of $235,000 is $11,750). The rate-phaseout surtax, which begins at taxable income of $100,000, extends to $335,000 ($100,000 + $235,000) of taxable income.

The curious idea that high-income taxpayers get a "benefit" from having less than all of their incomes taxed at the highest rate has led to recommendations that provisions like the personal exemption and the standard deduction be replaced with tax credits. In 1976, Congress replaced fixed-amount deductions under the estate and gift taxes with a "unified credit," ostensibly because credits are "fairer" than deductions or exclusions since credits benefit taxpayers in all brackets equally. As applied to deductions or credits for fixed dollar amounts, this is wrong. See Turnier & Kelly, The Economic Equivalence of Standard Tax Credits, Deductions and Exemptions, 36 U. Fla.L.Rev. 1003 (1984).

Appendix B, §§ 1(a) through 1(e) as they would read for the years 2002 and 2003 if they incorporated the reductions called for by § 1(i).

Problems

Problem (1). S, a single person, has a taxable income of $100,000. Use the tax rates of § 1(c) (Appendix B) to answer the following questions.

    (a) What is S's tax liability?

    (b) What is S's marginal tax rate?

    (c) What is S's average tax rate?

Problem (2). You are a congressional staff member. Congress is considering a substantial increase in the excise tax on alcoholic beverages. You have been asked whether the proposed tax will be progressive, regressive, or proportional with respect to income. What information would you need to answer that question?

2. PROGRESSIVITY IN PRINCIPLE

Now that we have seen what it means to call a tax-rate schedule "progressive," let us briefly examine some reasons for having progressive rather than proportional taxation. (No one ever publicly advocates regressive tax systems, though they are sometimes adopted. The Social Security tax, for instance, is an important and highly regressive tax, though its regressivity may be offset by the fact that the Social Security benefits financed by the tax are progressive.)

The simplest and probably the most popular argument for progressive taxes is that they tend to make after-tax incomes more nearly equal than pre-tax incomes. If A earns $100,000 a year before tax, while B earns $20,000, A's income is five times B's before tax. A proportional income tax—such as a tax of 20 percent of all income—would leave A with $80,000 after tax and B with $16,000. Although this tax would reduce the dollar difference between A's and B's incomes, it would still leave A with five times as much income as B. A progressive tax would reduce that relative difference. If, for example, the tax rates were 0% on the first $5000 of income, 5% on the next $5000, 10% on income from $10,000 to $50,000, and 50% on the excess of income over $50,000, A's tax would be $29,250; B's would be $1250. A's after-tax income of $70,750 would be about 3.8 times B's after-tax income of $18,750. Many see this kind of change as desirable social policy.

Arguments for progressivity that go beyond the simple approach sketched above focus on the declining marginal utility of the money that taxpayers take in each year. Not every dollar a taxpayer makes has the same value to that taxpayer. The first dollars, which buy the necessities of survival, are extremely important; the last dollars, which (for high-income persons) buy luxuries, could be given up without much pain. If we are willing to make plausible guesses about the "utility" of money earned by different people, we might also say that $20,000 earned by someone who earns only $20,000 is likely to be of more value than the last $20,000 earned by someone who has earned another $80,000. A flat-rate 50–percent income tax might devastate a family capable of earning only $20,000; a family that can earn $100,000 would probably not enjoy paying half of its income in taxes, but it could manage to live without hardship on what was left. This suggests that one's ability to pay a tax may increase by more than twice when one's income doubles, so that someone making $40,000 a year has more than twice the taxpaying capacity of someone making $20,000 a year.

If carried to an extreme, the notion of "ability to pay" might support a 100–percent tax on all incomes over a certain level, with no tax on incomes below that level. For instance, if *A* has an annual income of $20,000 and *B* has an income of $30,000, one could argue that *A* should pay no tax until *B* has paid a tax of $10,000. Few advocates of progressive taxation go that far, in part, perhaps, because at some point very high tax rates do serious economic harm by affecting incentives to engage in productive activity. Furthermore, the behavior of the rich may be more affected by tax rates than that of the poor. The very notion of declining marginal utility which is invoked to justify progressive taxation on grounds of fairness suggests that it is the high-income taxpayer, rather than someone struggling to make ends meet, who will turn to leisure rather than intensified money-making activity in response to high marginal tax rates.

Those who emphasize declining marginal utility in advocating progressive taxation often refer to the "sacrifices" made by paying taxes. It is interesting to note, in this context, that even a proportional income tax probably exacts a greater sacrifice from high-income taxpayers than from others. Consider, for instance, a flat-rate 20–percent tax as applied to one person who earns $50,000 a year and another who earns $100,000. The tax takes $10,000 from the first taxpayer and $20,000 from the second. Unless marginal utility declines *very* steeply, the high-income person is likely to dislike paying $20,000 more than the low-income person dislikes paying $10,000.[j] In addition to the usual assumptions about marginal utility, this guess is supported by the observation that one of the many reasons why some persons have higher earnings than others is that those who place a high value on wealth will exert more effort to make a lot of money than those whose values are less focused upon material goods. One reason why Donald Trump makes more money than Mother Teresa ever did is that he cares a lot more about making money than she did. An "equal-sacrifice" approach to taxation, with sacrifice measured according to the supposed pain inflicted by the tax, might support a regressive tax. (By way of analogy, consider an "equal-sacrifice" version of a military draft: such a draft

j. Under the usual assumptions about marginal utility, a $20,000 payment by a $100,000 earner would not hurt that person *twice* as much as a $10,000 payment by a $50,000 earner. But a guess that the high-income earner is hurt more by paying $20,000 than the low-income earner is hurt by paying $10,000 is plausible.

might require longer service from low-income persons than from those with higher incomes, on the ground that high-income draftees suffer greater opportunity costs from having to serve.)

Most analyses of progressivity have assumed, as we have so far, that high-income and low-income taxpayers are different persons. But income differences exist not only between different persons at any one time but also between the same person at different times. A particular taxpayer may have a low income for many years (while attending college and law school, for instance) and a high income in later years. The choice between progressive and proportional taxation has implications for that kind of taxpayer. Declining-marginal-utility notions, applied on a year-by-year basis, suggest that such a person might favor a progressive tax. That is, one might well be willing to accept the prospect of a high tax in one's high-income years in exchange for a very low tax in one's low-income years, even if the total lifetime tax is higher under a progressive tax than it would have been for the same person under a proportional tax. In effect, a progressive tax system allows those whose incomes will fluctuate to "borrow" during their low-income years (by paying very low taxes), repaying (with "interest" in the form of higher taxes) when their incomes rise. See McCaleb, Public Choice Perspectives on the Flat Tax Follies, 5 Cato J. 613 (1985).

Strong views about progressivity are held by many who have little specific knowledge of or interest in the workings of the tax system. One's beliefs about the steepness with which marginal utility declines, the relation between that matter and the ideal progressivity of a tax, and the desirability of using the tax system to change pre-tax income differences are unlikely to depend upon whether one has mastered the technicalities of income taxation. Indeed, although lawyers often think of themselves as uniquely suited to address all sorts of social problems, it seems doubtful that anything learned in the course of a legal education helps one to cope with questions of whether progressivity is, in principle, a good thing. On matters like this, an intelligent engineer, kindergarten teacher, or machinist is at least as well qualified as a lawyer to opine. Knowledge of and experience with the tax law can, however, furnish some understanding of how progressivity works in practice. One point in particular deserves emphasis: The tax rates of § 1 are a very poor guide to how progressive our tax system is in fact.

Over the past twenty years, changes in the rate schedules of § 1[k] seem to reflect a great reduction in the progressivity of the income tax until 1993, and some increase after that date. The highest marginal rates for individuals were 70 percent (on "unearned" income) as recently as

k. Section 11 also presents a progressive rate structure, though many service corporations face a flat-rate 35–percent tax. Whatever the merits of progressive rates for individual taxpayers, progressive rates for corporations make absolutely no sense. Suppose that a corporation having a million shareholders earns a million dollars, while a second corporation, with only one shareholder, earns $100,000. Ignoring non-corporate sources of income, the shareholder of the second corporation is doing much better financially than the shareholders of the first; yet a progressive corporate income tax taxes the income of the first corporation more heavily.

1981. For 2002 and 2003, the highest marginal rate listed in § 1 is 38.6 percent. Studies of the percentage of taxes paid by those in different income classes show, however, little change. Although the rate schedules have become much less progressive, the income tax is about as progressive today as it was in 1980. This has occurred because the amount of tax one pays depends not only upon the tax rates, but also upon the tax base. When marginal rates were very high, the Code provided countless opportunities for high-income taxpayers to reduce their taxable incomes (without corresponding reductions in their real wealth). Rate reduction has been accompanied by a narrowing of the opportunities to engage in tax-sheltering. Furthermore, lowering rates has tended to make some high-income taxpayers less eager to seek tax-favored investment opportunities and to incur the legal and other costs of exploiting those opportunities. Tax lawyers well know that the tax rates of § 1 are a very poor guide to how the tax works in practice.[l]

In principle, a taxpayer's income for a year is supposed to reflect the amount by which the taxpayer became richer during that year. In fact, any practical system of income measurement must fall far short of accuracy. Income from the ownership of property, in particular, is hard to measure accurately. For example, our tax system does not treat someone whose investments have doubled in value as having any income at all, unless the investments are sold. Furthermore, a variety of tax provisions subject various kinds of income to lighter-than-normal taxation, to further non-tax policies favored by legislators. Our tax system's inability to measure incomes accurately suggests caution about attempts to impose the very high marginal rates needed to implement a seriously redistributive system. Before taking much more from *A* than from *B*, we should be reasonably confident that *A* is richer than *B*. Those who understand the practical and political difficulties of measuring income may be more likely than others to doubt that the "taxable incomes" reported on Form 1040 tell us much about taxpayers' relative well-being.

Discussions of progressivity which, like this one, limit themselves to the income tax are incomplete. One standard argument for progressive income taxation is that that kind of taxation offsets the regressivity of such taxes as the retail sales tax and the Social Security tax. And even if the analysis is extended to all taxes, considering taxes without examining what is done with tax revenues can present a misleading picture. If the money raised by a progressive tax system is spent in a way that favors the rich, the overall result may be more regressive than a flat, low tax with less government spending.

l. As a dramatic example of the meaninglessness of tax rates, considered by themselves, consider what happened to the corporate income tax in 1986. Before the Tax Reform Act of 1986, the highest tax rate for many corporations was 46 percent. The 1986 act made the rate 34 percent for the highest-income corporations. Looking at the rate schedule alone would suggest that the 1986 Act amounted to a major reduction in corporate taxation. In fact, that act created a very large increase in corporate income taxes. The rate reductions were more than offset by measures which broadened the tax base for nearly all corporations.

Note and Question

1. *Progressivity and the long-run tax burden.* Consider a very simple progressive tax system: a tax of 0% of the first $25,000 a year of income plus 10% of the amount by which the taxpayer's income exceeds $25,000. *A* earns $50,000 a year for ten years. *B*, whose income fluctuates wildly, earns nothing in years 1, 3, 5, 7 and 9 and $100,000 in each of years 2, 4, 6, 8, and 10. Which of them pays more tax over the ten-year period?

2. *References.* McCombs, An Historical Review and Analysis of Early United States Tax Policy Scholarship: Definition of Income and Progressive Rates, 64 St.John's L.Rev. 471 (1990); Bankman & Griffith, Social Welfare and the Rate Structure: A New Look at Progressive Taxation, 75 Cal.L.Rev. 1905 (1987); Kornhauser, The Rhetoric of the Anti–Progressive Income Tax Movement: A Typical Male Reaction, 86 Mich.L.Rev. 465 (1987); Blum & Kalven, The Uneasy Case for Progressive Taxation (2d ed. 1963).

D. THE INTERNAL REVENUE SERVICE

The Internal Revenue Service (formerly the "Bureau of Internal Revenue") consists of those Treasury Department employees under the Commissioner of Internal Revenue. When the Code empowers the Service to do something, it does so by granting the power in question to "the Secretary," a term which includes any Treasury Department employee or agency to whom the Secretary of the Treasury has delegated authority. See §§ 7701(a)(11) & (12). One of the Service's major functions is seeing to it that taxes are collected.[m] Another important I.R.S. function is interpretation. Each year, the Service issues hundreds of published "Revenue Rulings" and "Revenue Procedures," which can be relied on by taxpayers as guides to the Service's view of the law.[n] In principle, a published ruling is nothing more than the Service's opinion about how a question should be answered; unlike a regulation, it exerts no authoritative force on judges. Some courts have begun to defer to rulings, however, much as they defer to regulations; Galler, Judicial Deference to Revenue Rulings: Reconciling Divergent Standards, 56 Ohio St.L.J. 637 (1996).

In addition to published rulings, the Service issues "letter rulings" in response to taxpayer requests for rulings on contemplated transactions. Because tax considerations play a large part in many business decisions, obtaining a favorable letter ruling from the Service is often

---

m. As § 7601 puts it, "[t]he Secretary shall, to the extent he deems it practicable, cause officers or employees of the Treasury Department to proceed, from time to time, through each internal revenue district and inquire after and concerning all persons therein who may be liable to pay any internal revenue tax * * *."

n. They should be relied on with considerable caution, however. Rulings are not binding on the courts, and the Service itself has been known to ignore its rulings or to "distinguish" them on rather tenuous grounds.

made a condition precedent to the consummation of a transaction. Although letter rulings are made public,[o] and are printed and distributed to lawyers and accountants by non-governmental publishers, they are meant to have no precedential status; indeed, under § 6110(k)(3), they cannot even be cited as precedent.[p] However, in Rowan Cos., Inc. v. United States, 452 U.S. 247, 261 n. 17 (1981), the Supreme Court cited and discussed a series of letter rulings as "evidence" that the Service viewed a ruling published in 1940 as good law even after the adoption of the 1954 Code. In principle, lawyers read letter rulings only to gain insight into the Service's thinking; in practice, many lawyers will treat these rulings in much the same way as if they were authoritative and will cite them in court, if they are helpful, as "evidence of administrative practice" rather than as "precedent."

From time to time the Service issues Revenue Procedures, which describe the Service's practices in dealing with particular kinds of

---

o. See § 6110.

p. The answer to the question whether, in administering the tax system, the Commissioner has a legally enforceable duty to "treat equally situated taxpayers equally" has, in general, been "no." The one case in which a taxpayer prevailed solely on "equal-treatment" grounds is International Business Machines Corp. v. United States, 343 F.2d 914 (Ct.Cl.1965). I.B.M.'s sole competitor in the manufacture, sale, and leasing of large computers was Remington Rand, which obtained a private ruling that its computer sales and leases were exempt from a certain Federal excise tax. I.B.M. learned of Remington Rand's ruling and sought one for itself. Some two years later, the Service denied I.B.M.'s ruling request and revoked Remington Rand's ruling. Pursuant to § 7805(b), the revocation of Remington Rand's ruling was made prospective, so that Remington Rand's sales and leases from 1952 to 1958 remained tax-exempt. The Court of Claims held that I.B.M. was entitled to a refund of its excise taxes for the period during which Remington Rand was exempt from the tax, emphasizing the unfairness and the effect on competition of taxing I.B.M. but not its sole competitor.

Although some of the language in the *I.B.M.* opinion could be read as supporting a sweeping "equal treatment of equals" rule, the Court of Claims itself read the decision narrowly, no doubt because of the chaos a broad "equal treatment" requirement would create. Bornstein v. United States, 345 F.2d 558 (Ct.Cl.1965), involved the shareholders of two of six related corporations formed to build apartment buildings. The lawyer for all six of the corporations sought and obtained a ruling on behalf of one of the corporations that certain distributions to shareholders would be taxed as capital gains rather than ordinary income. No ruling was sought for the other corporations because an I.R.S. employee had told the lawyer that, as the same legal principle was involved in the case of all the corporations, a ruling for one corporation would suffice. The Court of Claims upheld the Commissioner's determination that distributions to the shareholders of the corporations that had not obtained rulings were ordinary income. The employee's misrepresentation did not estop the Service because he had no authority to make representations of that sort, and the taxpayers could not rely on a ruling not issued to them. In a footnote, the court distinguished *I.B.M.* on the ground that I.B.M. had applied for a ruling of its own upon learning of Remington Rand's ruling, while the taxpayers in *Bornstein* had never asked for a ruling.

Justice Frankfurter's concurring opinion in United States v. Kaiser, 363 U.S. 299, 308 (1960), observed that "[t]he Commissioner cannot tax one and not tax another without some rational basis for the difference." However, in no case except *I.B.M.* has a taxpayer prevailed solely on the basis of a private ruling issued to someone else. Treas.Reg. § 601.201(*l*)(1) provides: "A taxpayer may not rely on an advance ruling issued to another taxpayer."

A few opinions dealing with retroactive revocations of *published* rulings have invoked "equal treatment" arguments to support findings that the Commissioner's failure to make the revocation prospective was an abuse of discretion; e.g., Baker v. United States, 748 F.2d 1465 (11th Cir.1984), rehearing denied 756 F.2d 885 (1985).

questions. (For an example, see Rev.Proc. 72–18, p. 406, below.) Each year, the Service issues Revenue Procedures listing issues on which the Service will not issue rulings or determination letters. Many of these issues involve factual questions; in addition, the Service will not rule on matters being litigated, on questions arising under legislative regulations which have not yet been issued, and on other specified matters. A ruling request must contain a complete statement of the facts relating to the transaction in question and copies of relevant documents. The Service will rule on proposed transactions, but not on hypothetical ones.

For many years, the Service was organized geographically, with District Offices handling most of the Service's audit, collection, and taxpayer-service functions, while Regional Offices handled appeals from the decisions of District Directors and the National Office issued rulings and technical advice. The IRS Restructuring and Reform Act of 1998 directed the Commissioner to reorganize the Service along functional, rather than geographic, lines; this restructuring has begun but has not yet been completed. The goal is to establish "organizational units serving particular groups of taxpayers with similar needs"; Act § 1001(a).

Problem

A has won a trip to the Sandwich Islands on a television game show. *A* wants to know how much income to report on his return. Would you advise *A* to request a ruling on the value of the prize?

———

Reference: Rogovin, The Four R's: Regulations, Rulings, Reliance and Retroactivity, 43 Taxes 756 (1965).

E. TAX CONTROVERSIES

Under the "self-assessment" system, taxpayers are required to file returns and pay the taxes due.[q] Taxpayers who (like nearly all individuals) report on a calendar-year basis must file returns and pay tax by April 15 of the year after the year in question (extensions of the date for filing can be obtained). Returns are checked for mathematical and other routine errors. Some returns are selected for audit, a process involving investigation (varying greatly in thoroughness from case to case) of a return's accuracy. (An extensive system of information reporting, which requires banks, employers, real-estate brokers, and others who engage in

q. Wage-earners pay most of their income taxes through the withholding system (§§ 3401–06 and 3501–10); over- or under-withholding is corrected by filing a return requesting a refund of amounts overwithheld or accompanied by the balance due. Most taxpayers for whom withholding does not adequately approximate the tax due (partners, self-employed taxpayers, corporations, trusts, and taxpayers with large amounts of investment income) must file estimated-tax returns and make quarterly payments of their estimated taxes for the year.

financial transactions to report payments to the Service, has in recent years greatly enhanced the Service's audit capability.) Most disputes which arise at the audit level are settled by agreement between the taxpayer and the Revenue Agent. If agreement is not reached, the Service will normally send the taxpayer a "30–day letter" explaining its determination. The taxpayer who wishes to pursue the matter further without paying the tax has thirty days to file a written protest[r] and appeal the proposed determination. If the taxpayer takes no action within thirty days, or if agreement is not reached on appeal, the taxpayer will be sent a deficiency notice, or "90–day letter." The taxpayer then has ninety days to pay the tax or file a petition with the Tax Court.[s] If the taxpayer does neither, the Service will assess the tax and demand payment by a date set by the District Director; if the taxpayer still does not pay, the Service will seize the taxpayer's assets.

The statute of limitations for filing a refund claim is the latest of: (1) three years from the date on which the return was filed; (2) three years from the due date for that return; or (3) two years from the date on which the tax was paid; §§ 6511(a), 6513. The Service may assess a tax within three years of the due date or the actual filing date of a return, whichever is later; §§ 6501(a), 6501(b). If a return omits an item of gross income greater in amount than 25 percent of the gross income shown on the return, the Service has six years, rather than three years, in which to assess the tax; § 6501(e). If the taxpayer files no return, or files one that is "false or fraudulent * * * with intent to evade tax," there is no statute of limitations on assessment; § 6501(c).

Income-tax disputes not settled can be litigated in the Tax Court (if the tax has not been paid) or by a suit for a refund in a Federal district court or the Court of Federal Claims.[t] Before enactment of the IRS Restructuring and Reform Act of 1998, the burden of proving facts was nearly always on the taxpayer in a civil proceeding. The 1998 Act shifted the burden of proof to the government if the taxpayer presents credible evidence and (1) complies with the substantiation and recordkeeping requirements of the Code and regulations; (2) exhausts administrative remedies within the Service and cooperates in satisfying reasonable requests by the government for witnesses and information; and (3) meets certain net-worth requirements; § 7491. Even if these conditions are complied with, the taxpayer still has the burden of "going forward" but the burden of persuasion shifts to the government. Few attorneys believe that the legislation will have much effect in income-tax cases. It

---

r. No written protest need be filed if the case involves a dispute of $2500 or less, or if the case is an "office interview" case (an audit conducted at a district office, rather than at the taxpayer's premises) or a "correspondence examination" (an audit conducted by mail). If the amount in question is more than $2500 but not more than $10,000, a "brief written statement" may be used instead of a formal protest. See Treas.Reg. § 601.105(d)(2).

s. This discussion has assumed that the tax has not been paid. If the tax was paid and the taxpayer is seeking a refund, the settlement procedure begins with the taxpayer's filing a claim for refund.

t. A claim for refund must have been denied or not acted on for six months in order for the taxpayer to bring a tax case in a district court or the Court of Federal Claims.

will often be expensive and burdensome for the taxpayer to comply with the various conditions, and few tax cases hinge on the burden of persuasion.

The Tax Court is an Article I court,[u] which has only "deficiency" jurisdiction (apart from some declaratory-judgment cases), and so cannot be availed of by a taxpayer who has paid the tax in full. Most Tax Court cases are decided by a single judge (jury trial is not available in the Tax Court); a few decisions are reviewed by the full court. Tax Court "memorandum decisions"—in cases involving only issues of fact or well-settled law—are not officially published. Tax Court "regular" decisions are published officially. The government is represented by lawyers in the Office of the Chief Counsel for the Internal Revenue Service in Tax Court cases.

Refund cases can be brought in a Federal district court or the Court of Federal Claims; jury trial is available in the district court. The government is represented by Justice Department lawyers in these cases, and in appellate tax cases.

District court and Tax Court decisions are appealable to the Courts of Appeals for the First through Eleventh and District of Columbia Circuits. Appeal of a Tax Court decision involving an individual taxpayer normally lies in the circuit in which the taxpayer lived when the petition in the Tax Court was filed. Decisions of the Court of Federal Claims are appealable to the Court of Appeals for the Federal Circuit. (The Court of Claims, which wrote several of the opinions in this book, was a predecessor of the Court of Federal Claims; it was replaced by the United States Claims Court and the Court of Appeals for the Federal Circuit in 1982, and the name of the United States Claims Court was later changed to the "Court of Federal Claims.") Decisions of the courts of appeals are reviewable by the Supreme Court, which seldom grants certiorari in tax cases. The Tax Court has adopted a practice, known as the "*Golsen* rule,"[v] of following decisions of a court of appeals to which the case before it is appealable.

The Service sometimes announces the Commissioner's "acquiescence" or "non-acquiescence" in court decisions (other than decisions of the Supreme Court, which the government must follow). These announcements were originally notices to the petitioner in the case of whether the Commissioner would appeal a Board of Tax Appeals decision. Originally limited to Tax Court decisions, the acquiescence program was extended to the decisions of other courts in 1993. Acquiescences and non-acquiescences are used to inform tax lawyers and government em-

u. The Tax Court (until 1942, the Board of Tax Appeals) was originally an administrative agency; it became a court in 1969. The Tax Court's full name from 1942 to 1969 was "The Tax Court of the United States"; today, it is "The United States Tax Court," which leaves the Supreme Court as the only court with the phrase "of the Unit-

ed States" in its name. For a detailed history of the Tax Court, see Dubroff, The United States Tax Court: An Historical Analysis (1979).

v. Named for Golsen v. Commissioner, 54 T.C. 742 (1970), affirmed 445 F.2d 985 (10th Cir.1971), cert. denied 404 U.S. 940 (1971).

ployees of the Service's position. It has been held that the Commissioner's acquiescence does not bar the government from assessing a tax even though the taxpayer would not owe the tax under the holding of the case in which the Commissioner acquiesced; Quinn v. Commissioner, 524 F.2d 617 (7th Cir.1975) ("the acquiescence program is not intended to substitute for the ruling or regulation program").

Because the taxpayer has a free choice of forum in tax cases, and because the tax decisions of courts other than the Supreme Court are not always binding on other courts,[w] questions of tax law often remain unsettled for many years after they first arise in litigation. The tax lawyer must evaluate reported cases, not merely find them; a favorable decision by a court to which the taxpayer does not have access means very little. For a proposal to streamline the tax-litigation system and provide a mechanism for obtaining definite answers to tax questions without waiting for Supreme Court review, see Griswold, The Need for a Court of Tax Appeals, 57 Harv.L.Rev. 1153 (1944); Popkin, Why a Court of Tax Appeals Is So Elusive, 47 Tax Notes 1101 (1990). Proposals to create one court to hear all appeals in tax cases have been resisted strongly by the organized tax bar.

Section 7430 provides for the award of attorneys' fees, expert witness fees, and the costs of studies, engineering reports, and analyses to taxpayers who "substantially prevail" with respect to either the amount in controversy or "the most significant issue or set of issues presented." In order to recover under this section, the taxpayer must have exhausted administrative remedies. If the government establishes that its position was "substantially justified," the taxpayer will not be treated as having "substantially prevailed"; § 7430(c)(4)(B). Awards of attorneys' fees under § 7430 cannot ordinarily exceed $125 an hour (indexed for inflation). Awards at a higher rate can be justified by a variety of reasons, including the difficulty of the issues in the case and the local availability of tax specialists. No award under § 7430 can be made "with respect to any portion of the * * * proceeding during which the prevailing party has unreasonably protracted such proceeding." If a taxpayer makes a "qualified offer" to settle a case and the Service declines it, the taxpayer will normally be treated as the "prevailing party" if subsequent litigation results in an award to the government equal to or less than the amount offered by the taxpayer; § 7430(c)(4)(E). The requirements of an offer's being "qualified" are set out in § 7430(g).

---

w. A court of appeals decision binds the district courts in that circuit, the Court of Federal Claims must follow decisions of the Court of Appeals for the Federal Circuit, and the Tax Court, under the *Golsen* rule, will follow the decisions of the court of appeals to which the case before it is appealable. Otherwise, however, the courts are free to disagree with each other over the law, and the Commissioner and taxpayers need not follow any decision other than one by the Supreme Court. In Dobson v. Commissioner, 320 U.S. 489 (1943), the Supreme Court established a doctrine requiring the courts of appeals to affirm Tax Court decisions unless the Tax Court had made a "clear-cut mistake of law." Today, Tax Court decisions on questions of fact are reviewed in the same manner as district court cases; see § 7482(a), which limits *Dobson*.

Awards under § 7430 cannot be made to individuals whose net worth exceeds $2,000,000 or to corporations with more than 500 employees and a net worth of over $7,000,000; § 7430(c)(4)(A)(ii) and 28 U.S.C.A. § 2412(d)(2)(B).

Although the government cannot recover attorneys' fees under § 7430, Tax Court petitioners (or their lawyers) who institute proceedings "primarily for delay," whose positions are "frivolous or groundless," or who have "unreasonably failed to pursue available administrative remedies" are subject to paying a penalty of up to $25,000 in damages to the United States; § 6673(b). Other courts may sanction litigants financially; when they do so in tax cases, the penalties may be collected as if they were taxes; § 6673(b).

F. INTEREST AND PENALTIES

1. INTEREST

Under § 6621, those who pay their taxes after the due date must pay interest at rates determined by a formula based on interest rates for short-term government obligations. The government pays interest to taxpayers when it makes untimely refunds. For individual taxpayers, interest received on refunds is includable in income; interest paid on deficiencies is not deductible. Corporate taxpayers can deduct interest on deficiencies but must pay an additional two-percent interest on "large" underpayments; § 6621(c). Generally, underpayments of more than $100,000 are "large."

2. CRIMINAL PENALTIES

Simply requiring taxpayers to pay interest on late payments would do little to discourage some taxpayers from taking extreme return positions, filing late, or paying taxes late. Accurate and timely filing and prompt payment are therefore encouraged by an array of criminal and civil penalties. Tax crimes include:

Tax evasion, a felony (§ 7201);

Willful failure to collect, account for, or pay a tax, a felony (§ 7202);

Willful failure to file returns, to keep required records, or to pay a tax, a misdemeanor (§ 7203); and

Willful filing of a false or fraudulent document, a misdemeanor (§ 7207).

3. CIVIL PENALTIES

Civil tax penalties are too numerous and too complex to describe in detail here. The principal civil penalties can usefully be thought of as falling into two categories: (1) penalties designed to deter inaccurate reporting and (2) penalties designed to encourage promptness in reporting and payment.

Penalties related to accuracy

Few income-tax returns are audited; in recent years the audit rate for individuals has been less than one percent. This encourages some taxpayers to file fraudulent returns and others to take "aggressive" return positions—positions which, while not so baseless as to be fraudulent, have very little chance of being upheld if contested.

Underpayments of tax attributable to fraud subject the taxpayer to a penalty of 75 percent of the underpayment; § 6663.

The Service's principal weapon against underpayments resulting from aggressive reporting which falls short of fraud is the *accuracy-related penalty* of § 6662. This penalty is 20 percent of any underpayment attributable to any of five kinds of error or misconduct. The three kinds of misconduct relevant to the basic course are:

> (1) Negligence or disregard of rules or regulations;

> (2) "Substantial understatement" of income-tax liability; and

> (3) Substantial overstatement of the value or the income-tax basis of property. (In some cases, the penalty for overstatements can be 40 percent, rather than 20 percent, of the understatement.)

In the context of the accuracy-related penalty, "negligence" includes "any failure to make a reasonable attempt to comply with" the law. "Disregard of rules or regulations" will trigger the penalty if it is "careless, reckless, or intentional"; § 6662(c).

An understatement of tax liability is "substantial" if it exceeds the greater of 10 percent of the tax required to be shown on the return or $5000 ($10,000 for most corporations). In most cases, portions of understatements can be ignored in applying these rules if (1) the taxpayer's position was supported by "substantial authority," or (2) the facts regarding the item in question were adequately disclosed. However, disclosure will not help if the item in question was not "reasonable" or was attributable to a tax shelter, and even "substantial authority" for a position taken on a tax-shelter item won't help unless the taxpayer also reasonably believed that the return position was "more likely than not the proper treatment"; § 6662(d)(2)(C).

The "authorities" which can be amassed to defend a return position against the substantial-understatement penalty are not limited to authorities of the conventional kind such as cases, statutes, regulations, and legislative history. They also include such things as proposed regulations, private letter rulings, IRS notices, and the Joint Committee Staff's explanations of new tax legislation (commonly called "Bluebooks").

The accuracy-related penalty and the fraud penalty are alternatives; the same understatement cannot trigger both penalties.

Today's tax law is so complex that many taxpayers cannot prepare their own returns. (The problem is by no means limited to taxpayers whose financial affairs are complex—routine events like moving, renting out one's house or apartment, or even earning a small amount of income (especially if the taxpayer has young children) can require the completion of tax forms with which many college graduates cannot cope.) As a result, recent enforcement efforts have tended to focus on tax-return preparers, rather than on taxpayers. Return preparers can be penalized under § 6694(a) if a return takes an undisclosed position "for which there was not a realistic possibility of being sustained on its merits." Preparer penalties will be discussed in more detail below.

Penalties related to timeliness

Section 6651 imposes a penalty of 5 percent a month (up to a total penalty of 25 percent) for failure without reasonable cause to file a return when due. It also imposes a penalty of one-half (sometimes one) percent a month (with a 25–percent maximum) for failure to pay a tax when due. If a return is not filed within 60 days of the due date, the late-filing penalty is at least $100 or 100 percent of the tax, whichever is less.

If failure to file a return is fraudulent, the late-filing penalty is 15 percent a month up to a maximum total penalty of 75 percent; § 6651(f).

———

The penalties described above are only a few of the hundreds of penalties contained in the Internal Revenue Code. Revenues from penalties are now so high that some writers have speculated that Congress has been using the penalty system as a revenue measure, much as some local governments have used speed limits to balance their budgets. Whether this is true or not, the availability of revenues from penalties does at least give revenue-conscious legislators some incentive to refrain from efforts to simplify the Code.

G. PROFESSIONAL RESPONSIBILITY IN TAX MATTERS

The ordinary rules of professional conduct to which all lawyers are subject have proved to be less than adequate as guides for tax practitioners in many situations. For one thing, state regulations based on the ABA's Model Rules of Professional Conduct and Model Code of Professional Responsibility deal largely with problems that arise in handling controversies before courts. Tax practitioners typically devote much of their efforts to planning transactions and advising their clients about how their affairs should be reported to the government, matters on which the ordinary state standards governing professional responsibility offer little useful guidance. Furthermore, official standards of professional responsibility tend to try to do two things at once: to lay out minimum standards beneath which lawyers cannot fall without being disciplined and to present models of conduct for practitioners who want to sleep well at night. Too often, the rules blur this distinction, implying at times that anything not forbidden is desirable. And sometimes, one suspects, the drafters of the rules have shied away from facing up to hard questions.

Authoritative guidance for tax lawyers is found not only in the usual state-law rules, but also in "Circular 230." This is a set of regulations issued under 31 U.S.C.A. § 330, which authorizes the Treasury Department to regulate practice before the Internal Revenue Service. Furthermore, some of the work tax lawyers do constitutes tax-return preparation (which can include conduct not involving filling out tax forms). For example, a lawyer who tells a client's accountant that a particular return position is acceptable is a "preparer," even though the lawyer never sees the return. The Code's "preparer penalties" (§ 6694) are therefore important to the tax lawyer.

1. AGGRESSIVE RETURN POSITIONS

For many years, lawyers were free to advise taxpayers to take any return position for which there was a "reasonable basis." Just what this meant has never been very clear, but it was not a demanding standard. Some people interpreted the "reasonable basis" standard as allowing any return position that would not, if detected, subject the taxpayer to the negligence penalty. The standard has been described, only partly in jest, as amounting to a "giggle test," so that any position that can be described without laughter is good enough. In private conversation, tax lawyers have been known to say that a position with a 10–percent, or even 5–percent, chance of success if litigated is good enough for reporting purposes.

An important early effort to raise the standard was the American Bar Association's Formal Opinion 85–352, which we would reproduce here but for difficulties in obtaining permission to reprint from the ABA, which seems to regard the issuance of ethical guidance as a money-making venture. The opinion concludes that lawyers may advise tax-return positions that are "warranted in existing law" or if there is "some realistic possibility of success" should the issue be litigated.

Notes

1. *"Some realistic possibility of success."* An American Bar Association Task Force Report has attempted a sort of quantification of the "realistic possibility" standard of Formal Opinion 85–352. The report concluded that a position with a "5% or 10% likelihood of success, if litigated," would not meet the standard; a position having a "likelihood of success closely approaching one-third" would. The report is reprinted in 39 The Tax Lawyer 635 (1986).

A one-third-chance standard, if that is what the ABA has really proposed, is high indeed. Except for cases in which the substantial-understatement penalty applies, no rule requires taxpayers to apply so high a standard to themselves. The prospect of a taxpayer's being sanctioned for taking a return position with, say, a one-fifth chance of being upheld is remote, perhaps nonexistent, except for cases involving tax shelters. Thus, Formal Opinion 85–352 may be saying that lawyers are not free to advise clients to take positions which the clients themselves are quite free to take. Apparently, however, the client with the gumption to ask the lawyer about the consequences of taking a position against which the lawyer has advised is entitled to an honest answer. And perhaps the lawyer should volunteer that answer even if the client does not ask.

The Task Force Report on Formal Opinion 85–352 says that a lawyer whose client declines to follow advice against taking a position "must counsel the taxpayer not to assert the position, and, unless this advice is accepted by the client, the lawyer may not prepare the return, and * * * must withdraw from further representation involving advice as to the position taken on the return"; 39 The Tax Lawyer at 639.

2. *Disclosure as an alternative.* Formal Opinion 85–352 does not prevent helping taxpayers litigate non-frivolous positions which fall short of the "realistic possibility of success" standard. Taxpayers who wish to do that can file a return not taking the position in question, file a claim for refund, and then sue for a refund in a district court or the Court of Federal Claims. But what of a taxpayer who wants to litigate a questionable but non-frivolous position in the Tax Court? Formal Opinion 85–352, unlike some other proposals for dealing with aggressive positions, does not expressly allow a lawyer to advise that a weak but non-frivolous position be taken on a return if the return discloses that a questionable position has been taken. However, the ABA Tax Section has said that lawyers should be allowed to advise the taking of nonfrivolous positions that do not meet the standards of Formal Opinion 85–352 if the return adequately discloses what is going on. See Wolfman, Holden & Harris, Standards of Tax Practice § 204.2.4.2 (1995).

3. *References.* Durst, The Tax Lawyer's Professional Responsibility, 39 U.Fla.L.Rev. 1027 (1987); Falk, Tax Ethics, Legal Ethics, and Real Ethics: A Critique of ABA Formal Opinion 85–352, 39 The Tax Lawyer 643 (1986); Rowen, When May a Lawyer Advise a Client That He May Take a Position on a Tax Return?, 29 The Tax Lawyer 237 (1976).

———

An ABA Formal Opinion binds no one. Formal Opinion 85–352 interprets the ABA's Model Rules of Professional Conduct and Model Code of Professional Responsibility, versions of which, when adopted by states,[x] do bind lawyers. Conceivably, Formal Opinion 85–352 could be regarded as persuasive by state authorities interpreting their states' versions of the Model Rules or Model Code, but it is hard to imagine a state bar sanctioning a lawyer for advising a client to take a weak but non-fraudulent return position. Indeed, even lawyers who encourage (or who themselves take) extremely aggressive reporting positions do not seem in practice to incur the displeasure of state bar authorities. Furthermore, much return preparation is done by persons who are not

x. The Tax Court has adopted the Model Rules for those who practice before it.

lawyers. Effective control of substandard tax-return advice requires action at the Federal level.

Circular 230 has adopted a version of the "realistic possibility of success if litigated" standard; see 31 C.F.R. § 10.34(a). As of this writing, no case of a practitioner's being disciplined for violating this standard is known to exist.

The main legal sanction for advising taxpayers to take unjustifiable positions is provided by § 6694, which penalizes tax-return preparers for understatements due to positions lacking a "realistic possibility of being sustained on [the] merits" (§ 6694(a)) or which result from the "willful" attempt to understate liability or from "reckless or intentional disregard of rules or regulations" (§ 6694(b)). Unlike the rather similar standard of Formal Opinion 85–352, the preparer penalties apply to positions taken in claims for refund, as well as on returns. The preparer penalty for unrealistic positions applies if the preparer "knew (or reasonably should have known)" of the position and if the position was not adequately disclosed or was frivolous; §§ 6694(a)(2) & (3).

In financial terms, the preparer penalties are not heavy: they are $250 for the unrealistic-position penalty (unless there was "reasonable cause for the understatement" and the preparer "acted in good faith"); $1000 for the willful-or-reckless penalty. Nevertheless, return preparers have strong incentives not to incur these penalties. Under § 7407, the Service can seek to enjoin preparers whose conduct has been subject to the preparer penalties from engaging in more of that conduct. A preparer who has "continually or repeatedly engaged" in various kinds of misconduct can be enjoined from acting as a return preparer. Repeated violations of the preparer rules may lead to referral to the Director of Practice of the IRS for consideration of suspension or disbarment from practice before the Service. The Service can follow up the imposition of the preparer penalty by identifying and examining other returns prepared by that preparer.[y] This could well lead to further penalties against the preparer, as well as to the assessment of deficiencies and penalties against the preparer's clients. Finally, and perhaps most important, the imposition of preparer penalties will almost certainly harm the preparer's reputation for integrity and competence.

Most lawyers—even most tax lawyers—seldom prepare income-tax returns in the way that H & R Block and many accountants and enrolled agents do. Nevertheless, lawyers will often be return preparers for purposes of § 6694. Section 7701(a)(36)(A) defines "income tax return preparer" so broadly that one who receives compensation for providing tax advice relevant to the reporting of specific return entries can be a "preparer" with respect to that portion of the return. Curiously, the regulations exclude advice about future transactions, even though that

---

y. Under § 7602, the Service can use a summons to obtain a list of the preparer's clients from the preparer. Furthermore, some (but not all) preparers must put their Taxpayer Identification Numbers on the returns they prepare. Even the Service's fairly primitive computer system should be able to use these numbers to pull returns prepared by a preparer whose conduct has attracted the Service's attention.

kind of advice necessarily contemplates the filing of a return taking specific positions; Treas.Reg. § 301.7701–15(a)(2)(i). Even giving oral advice can make one a preparer; Treas.Reg. § 1.6694–1(b)(2).

Problem and Notes

1. *The one-preparer-per-firm rule.* The regulations under § 6694 provide that only one individual associated with any one firm can be a preparer with respect to any one return (the firm itself can also be a preparer). This does not mean that there can be only one preparer per return: if a firm of accountants gets an opinion from a law firm about a specific item, the accounting firm, one of its members, the law firm, and one of its partners or associates may all be preparers. A "signing preparer" who receives advice from partners or employees is "the" preparer. If no partner or employee is a "signing preparer," the person with "overall supervisory responsibility" for the matter in question is the one individual preparer from that firm.

2. *Disclosure to avoid the penalty for unrealistic positions.* A signing preparer will not be subject to the penalty for unrealistic positions if the position in question is disclosed by filing Form 8275 with the return. Nonsigning preparers are treated as satisfying the disclosure requirement if the advice in question was accompanied by advice that disclosure is necessary. (Recall, however, that disclosure will not suffice if the position is frivolous.) See Treas.Reg. § 1.6694–2(c).

Note the peculiar difference between the preparer standards and the standards for taxpayers concerning positions that can be taken if they are disclosed. Disclosure on a return will shield the taxpayer from the substantial-understatement penalty only if the return position was "reasonable." Disclosure will shield the preparer if the position was "not frivolous." So, at least for now, the penalty for unrealistic positions will not be imposed on a preparer who advises a taxpayer to take an unreasonable but not frivolous return position with disclosure, though taking that position can expose the taxpayer to a penalty if the resulting understatement is substantial.

3. *Unrealistic positions.* According to the regulations, a position has "a realistic possibility of being sustained on the merits if a reasonable and well-informed analysis by a person knowledgeable in the tax law would lead such a person to conclude that the position has approximately a one in three, or greater, likelihood of being sustained on its merits"; Treas.Reg. § 1.6694–2(b)(1). The regulations say that the "authorities" provided in Treas.Reg. § 1.6662–4(d)(3)(iii), dealing with the "substantial understatement" component of the accuracy-related penalty, are "the authorities considered in determining whether a position satisfies the realistic possibility standard"; Treas.Reg. § 1.6694–2(b)(2). These authorities include proposed regulations and letter rulings, but not treatises or articles.

Legal positivism in the "law is what courts do" sense seems to have prevailed at Treasury, despite its generally unfavorable reception in jurisprudential circles. The regulations' emphasis on the existence of "authority" for a position is also worthy of note.

4. *Problem.* A newly enacted statute is completely ambiguous about an issue, a private letter ruling takes a pro-government position supported by absurdly unpersuasive reasoning, and a consideration of the purposes behind the enactment of the statute supports a pro-taxpayer interpretation. Thus, the only "reasonable" interpretation of the statute favors the taxpayer, but the only "authority" supports the government. Can the taxpayer take a favorable return position without disclosure? Can the taxpayer's lawyer recommend that course of conduct?

5. *References.* Symposium on Tax Ethics, 20 Capital U.L.Rev. 325 (1991); Wolfman, Holden & Harris, Standards of Tax Practice.

"RAISING STANDARDS": SOME RESERVATIONS

The unrealistic-position penalty and the very similar standard proposed in Formal Opinion 85–352 are attempts at raising an "ethical" standard for tax lawyers. Raising standards of ethics is the sort of thing that sounds self-evidently good, and it is quite true that the taking of absurdly unreasonable return positions has created serious problems for the tax system. Nevertheless, the wisdom of this kind of change can be doubted. For one thing, as noted above (pp. 23–24), the changes may subject tax advisers to a higher standard than taxpayers themselves must meet. Most of those who have addressed this issue directly have concluded that lawyers can advise clients to take any legal steps, though lawyers are certainly free to urge their clients to go beyond the minimum that the law requires.[z] Mandating that lawyers advise clients to do more than they must is a step that should not be taken without analysis of how that kind of rule will affect relations between lawyers and their clients. This is an analysis the Treasury and the ABA have not undertaken.[a] Furthermore, if the real problem is that unscrupulous tax advisers urge clients to play the "audit lottery" by taking unjustifiable positions, the new rules aim at the wrong target: they resemble trying to keep people from driving at 80 miles an hour in a 50–mile zone by lowering the speed limit to 25. Making more conduct "unlawful" helps little, if at all, in detecting and deterring conduct that is already prohibited.

z. See Holden, Constraining Aggressive Return Advice: A Commentary, 9 Va. Tax Rev. 771, 773 (1990)("the client's rights and duties neither expand nor contract by reason of the interjection of an adviser").

a. Klepper, Mazur & Nagin, Expert Intermediaries and Legal Compliance: The Case of Tax Preparers, XXXIV J.L. & Econ. 205 (1991), offers empirical data and theoretical arguments to show that the participation of professional preparers encourages compliance with the law with respect to issues on which the law is clear, but encourages aggressive positions when the law is ambiguous. The authors conclude that increasing penalties on preparers for noncompliance may, by raising the cost of employing a preparer, discourage the use of preparers and "dilute the procompliance influence of preparers on taxpayers as a whole. Thus, a policy of tighter preparer regulations could backfire and actually reduce aggregate compliance."

It is worth remembering that even a position with only a one-in-five chance of success will ultimately prevail 20 percent of the time, by definition. Clients who follow their lawyers' advice not to take particular positions will be justifiably annoyed when they learn that others who have taken those very positions have prevailed. As a specific example of this phenomenon, consider the Canadian experience with "surplus stripping." Surplus stripping was a method of taking money out of closely held corporations without (or so those who devised and used it hoped) making the shareholders liable for the tax on dividends. The more-conservative Canadian tax advisers told their clients not to engage in these transactions, which have been described as "blatantly transparent devices."[b] Inevitably, some advisers exercised less restraint. When Revenue Canada did not even challenge the surplus-stripping schemes, those who had been advised not to risk them "attacked their tax advisors for tendering bad advice"; this, in turn, generated "cries of outrage . . . from the more conservative members of the accounting and legal professions engaged in tax practice."[c] The immediate result of this outrage was the interesting though politically unsuccessful Carter Commission Report, but repeated experiences of that sort are more likely to inspire scorn for the tax system than to generate reform proposals, of which there is in any event no shortage.

Some of those concerned with the tax lawyer's professional obligations have insisted that the lawyer owes a greater duty to the government than would be owed to a private opponent. The oldest, simplest, and most clearly wrong version of the claim that the lawyer must balance the taxpayer's interests against the government's is Randolph Paul's assertion that the duty arises because the adversary is the government, which represents the public interest.[d] The idea that the public interest is always served by helping government employees do what they would like to do is itself controversial, to say the least. Furthermore, it is strange to claim that the public interest has no place in the litigation of private-law controversies; the rules of contract, tort, and property which emerge from litigation have at least as much to do with the health of our society as do most tax issues.

A more-attractive argument for requiring the taxpayer or the tax lawyer to attend to the government's interest in revenue-raising as well as to the taxpayer's interest in contributing as little as possible to that effort invokes the supposed imbalance of power between the government and the taxpayer. The taxpayer's decision whether to report a particular item will often determine tax liability, for the government can audit only one or two percent of all returns. Therefore, the argument proceeds, the tax system really does ask most taxpayers to assess their own taxes, and this can be done accurately only if taxpayers take the government's

b. Hartle, Some Analytical, Political and Normative Lessons from Carter, in N. Brooks (ed.), The Quest for Tax Reform 396, 401 (1988).

c. Id.

d. Paul, The Responsibilities of the Tax Adviser, 63 Harv.L.Rev. 377, 381–82 (1950).

interests into account more fully than they would the interests of someone who is suing, or being sued by, them.

The "balance of power" concern, though legitimate, can be overstated. While the government's ability to detect unusually optimistic returns is indeed small, the government's ability to extract concessions from many of those whose returns do attract the Service's attention is substantial. Most small taxpayers and their advisers do not relish a fight with the Service. A system that did succeed in causing taxpayers to report in much more favorable ways than they do today would not just create a "balance" between the taxpayer and the tax collector, it would in many cases give the tax collector a decided edge.

As an argument for raising the standard for tax advisers, without raising the taxpayer standard, the balance-of-power position says, in effect, that because the government cannot afford to audit everyone who gets legal or accounting advice in connection with a return, those taxpayers' representatives should perform the auditing function themselves, as a matter of professional responsibility. Were it not so expensive, some system in which every taxpayer's return had to survive scrutiny by an unbiased expert would have considerable appeal. It does not follow, however, that the taxpayer's lawyer or accountant can reasonably be asked to provide that kind of supervision. An adviser trying to act both as the taxpayer's representative and as an impartial auditor is unlikely to do either job well.

2. REPRESENTING TAXPAYERS BEFORE THE SERVICE

It is now generally accepted that Service personnel conducting an audit are the taxpayer's adversaries, not an impartial "tribunal" like a court or an administrative law judge. It follows that, although lawyers dealing with audits cannot advance positions that are completely without merit and cannot lie to revenue agents, they need not disclose legal authority adverse to their positions.

As we noted earlier, official "rules of conduct" for practitioners necessarily deal in large part with the minimum standards with which practitioners must comply to avoid being disciplined. The very promulgation of this kind of standard risks creating the impression that lawyers need not worry about doing anything more than they need do to avoid being penalized. Instead of describing more of those official standards here, we offer an excerpt from Frederic G. Corneel's "Guidelines to Tax Practice Second." These Guidelines are an example of the kinds of standards a firm might adopt for its own lawyers. They attempt to present standards of decent, responsible professional conduct, not just rules to obey to keep from being disbarred. Here are the portions of Corneel's suggested guidelines dealing with two matters of concern when dealing with the Service: (1) what to do when the lawyer discovers that a client has filed erroneous returns, and (2) how to handle the many issues that can arise in the course of an audit.

CORNEEL, GUIDELINES TO TAX PRACTICE SECOND[e]
43 The Tax Lawyer 297, 307–311 (1990).

IV. ADVICE CONCERNING TAX REPORTING

* * *

F. Prior Years' Returns

If we discover an error in a prior year's return that is not barred by the statute of limitations, whether or not of our own creation, we must advise the client of the error.[33] We should explain that present law does not mandate the filing of an amended return, but that a tax that is owed is a debt that should be paid and, therefore, in general an amended return should be filed to correct any clear and material errors.[34]

1. Although there is no legal obligation to file an amended return, the implications of an uncorrected error on future years' returns must be considered. An uncorrected error having an effect on future returns cannot knowingly be carried forward.

2. If correction gives rise to risk of penalty, we must describe the risk and explore ways of paying the tax due that will minimize exposure to the penalty. In any situation involving potential fraud charges, however, we should carefully explain to the taxpayer the benefits and hazards of the various options available, including any constitutional right not to cooperate with the Service. A lawyer who does not have criminal tax practice experience should consult with one who has such experience.

a. When a clear and material error was made on a return prepared by this firm or in an audit in which we acted as the client's representative, we should explain to the client our own interest in an appropriate correction, and suggest that if the client wants advice not colored by such interest, the client should consult another adviser. Indeed, we may be required to insist that the client consult another advisor, where our own interest is sufficiently disparate from that of the client.

b. When we were preparers of a return that we subsequently learned contains a clear and material error, and the client decides not to amend the return, we should consider whether the circumstances are such that we should no longer represent the client either in tax matters in general or, specifically, in any audit of the return.

c. * * * [I]f we should ever learn that a client asked us to assist in the preparation of a fraudulent return, we would immediately terminate all further representation.

e. From Frederic G. Corneel, Guidelines to Tax Practice Second, 43 The Tax Lawyer 297 (1990). Copyright © 1990 American Bar Association. Reprinted by permission of the American Bar Association.

33. 31 C.F.R. § 10.21 (1988). * * *

34. See generally Ronan, Do Clients Have a Duty to File Amended Tax Returns?, 33 Prac.Law. 25 (1987); * * *. A failure to correct a clear and material error in a refund claim before the refund is paid appears particularly serious.

3. If a client has failed to file returns for prior years and pay the taxes due, he is under a clear legal obligation to do so and usually the best advice is to report and pay. * * *

4. When we must respond to an independent auditor's letter and know of a clear error on a prior year's return that is not barred by the period of limitations, we must carefully consider whether this is a "contingent liability" to be disclosed by the client to the auditors. In that connection, it is relevant whether we believe it more likely than not that the claim will be asserted by the Service. Nevertheless, we must be certain that, by our silence, we do not mislead the auditors as to our client's situation, particularly since our client's refusal to correct a return containing a clear and substantial error may have a bearing on the auditor's reliance on the client's statements generally.

V. AUDIT REPRESENTATION

A. *Nature of Proceeding*

1. A tax audit is the first step and often also the last step in a potentially adversarial legal proceeding.

The following recommendations address audits when either the taxpayer has the burden of proof or when the Service may reasonably infer that we do not know the taxpayer's position to be clearly wrong. Obviously, when the audit is tending toward the direction of fraud charges, the client is entitled to take a position of "prove it" toward the Service and our role becomes pretty much that of an advocate in an adversarial proceeding.

2. Some lawyers handle audits on a superficial basis, in the hope that with only a little effort they can convince the agent to drop whatever questions the agent may have raised. Our firm's general approach is to persuade the client to authorize us to do a thorough and first class job. While at times the result may be an unnecessary expenditure of time and money, far more often a thorough preparation of the client's case will permit an earlier termination of the audit and a settlement of the controversy on terms favorable to the client. Superficial work, on the other hand, frequently leads to inconsistencies, as facts and legal theories developed in later stages of a proceeding do not coincide with earlier communications to the Service. Such inconsistencies undermine the lawyer's credibility and persuasiveness, thereby reducing the client's prospects for success.

Where the matter is small or the client's funds are limited, it may make sense to do less than a "full court press." Within the limits of our professional responsibility, the decision is the client's.

3. The Service representatives will have substantial knowledge and experience, while the client may not be aware of all the legal aspects of his particular situation. Unlike lawyers who are usually barred from having contact with the opposing party except through the opposing party's lawyer, Service agents are not similarly restricted. Clients, how-

ever, need and are entitled to the same protection as in other proceedings when the other side possesses legal expertise that they lack.

While a lawyer or other representative need not be present at all stages of an audit, we should at the outset seek to review with the client the legal aspects of the audit, particularly any weak spots in the client's situation.

4. Frequently we can do a better job representing a client at an appeals conference if the client is not present. When we believe this to be the case, we should point this out to the client, leaving the final decision to the client.

5. Both we and the client should cooperate with the Service, where this can be done without harm to the client's situation. We must remember, however, that it is not the Service but the courts that have the last word in determining what information—including information relating to third parties—the Service has a right to obtain from the client. In a particular case, there is nothing wrong with politely informing an agent that a summons will be required or that the propriety of a summons that has been issued will be tested in court.

6. Taxpayers have a right to periodically eliminate from their files papers no longer needed under applicable record keeping requirements, including memoranda and drafts regarding tax planning. Once an audit has started, however, any destruction of potentially relevant documents is improper.

B. *Truthfulness in Dealings With the Service*

1. We must at all times be truthful with the Service and use our best efforts to ensure that the client is also truthful.

a. To preserve our reputation for integrity and reliability we must, in communications to the Service, be clear as to the source of any facts we assert. "The corporation made all relevant elections on a timely basis" is a legitimate statement if we know it to be a fact. If we do not know it, we should say, "We are informed by John Jones, Treasurer of the corporation, that it made all relevant elections on a timely basis."

b. When we become aware of a clear and material error on the client's return, we should generally urge the client to permit disclosure, particularly when the proceeding involves the general correctness of the return rather than focusing on a specific issue. * * * (For instance, we should do so if we find during the course of an audit that a deduction was taken for a particular expenditure that was clearly non-deductible). Also, any mathematical mistakes whether made by ourselves, the client, or the Service, should be disclosed to the Service.

c. If, in an appropriate case, the client refuses to make the necessary correction or disclosure, in general, we should withdraw from further representation; the need to withdraw is particularly strong when we were the preparers of what is now known to be an erroneous return or when we may otherwise be understood by the Service to have participated in a misrepresentation by the client.

(i) Withdrawal from the engagement must be carefully undertaken so as to balance the desire or obligation to withdraw against the requirements that confidences not be disclosed and the client's interest not be otherwise prejudiced.

(ii) It may be helpful to remind the client that, during the course of an audit, it is customary for the auditing agent to ask whether the taxpayer or taxpayer's representative is aware of any matters requiring adjustment. If there is an undisclosed problem, and we have decided to continue representation in spite of the client's refusal to authorize disclosure, we must provide a truthful answer.

2. Difficult questions occasionally arise whether, in order to avoid misleading the Service, the lawyer should disclose information not known to the Service. Generally, in an audit, as in other adversarial proceedings, our obligation to tell the truth does not require disclosure of all relevant facts and law.

a. Excepting only the situations referred to in part V.B.1.b. above, we are under no legal or ethical obligation to volunteer to the Service information adverse to the client or to urge the client to do so. Nevertheless, in our dealings with the Service, we can often serve our client most effectively by frank recognition of the problems with our client's case and then explaining why, in spite of these problems, our client should prevail.

b. There is no obligation to call the attention of the Service to apparent legal or factual inconsistencies in a settlement that was arrived at fairly. A settlement is an agreement between the taxpayer and the Service relating to "the bottom line," and inconsistencies with facts or rules of law not agreed to are irrelevant. Nor must the settlement agreement be followed in future years unless it specifically so provides.

Note

1. *References.* Harris, On Requiring the Correction of Error Under the Federal Tax Law, 42 The Tax Lawyer 515 (1989); Popkin, Client–Lawyer Confidentiality, 59 Texas L.Rev. 755 (1981).

3. TAX PLANNING

CORNEEL, GUIDELINES TO TAX PRACTICE SECOND[f]
43 The Tax Lawyer 297, 311–314 (1990).

VI. TAX PLANNING

A. *Complexities of Tax Law*

Tax law has grown to the point where no one can possibly know all of the rules and approaches to various business and personal planning problems. Research, continuing education, the use of checklists, and consultation with others are all essential to prevent harm to our clients and malpractice exposure to the firm. We should not hesitate to suggest to the client consultation with experts outside our office whenever that appears in the client's best interest.

* * *

C. *Plans Must Be Conditioned on Compliance With Tax Law*

A tax plan should not be suggested without taking into consideration how the transaction should be reported and what the consequences of an audit of the return are likely to be. We will not suggest and we should counsel against plans that are bound to fail if all of the facts become known to the Service. We will not participate in transactions entirely lacking in economic substance and intended solely to conceal or mislead.

1. It is unethical to assist the client in the preparation of evidence designed to mislead the Service, such as a bill to a corporate client that includes, without disclosing, the cost of personal services to the owner of the corporation. On the other hand, it is entirely proper to advise clients on the best ways of documenting legitimate positions.

2. At times the client in ignorance of the tax law has taken steps resulting in adverse tax consequences or has failed to take steps to prevent such consequences. It is not unethical to make every effort to correct this result, provided that this can be done without destruction of existing documents, backdating of new documents or other steps intended to mislead the Service as to what in fact happened.

D. *Borderline Plans*

We should remember that our objective in tax planning is to produce a good tax plan, a plan that works. A plan that is not sustained on audit or by litigation was not a good plan, no matter how brilliantly conceived, unless the client desired to consummate the transaction despite the possibility or probability of adverse tax consequences. The decision

f. From Frederic G. Corneel, Guidelines to Tax Practice Second, 43 The Tax Lawyer 297 (1990). Copyright © 1990 American Bar Association. Reprinted by permission of the American Bar Association.

whether to risk the adverse consequences of borderline plans should be the client's, based upon our advice.

Clients are less well-informed than we are as to whether a proposed plan involves ethical but risky "skating on thin ice" or whether it involves "walking on water," that is, a breach of law. We must make the difference clear to them, and explain that being on the right side of this line is vital to our working with them on their tax plans. Lawyers' lectures to clients on morality are likely to be resented and useless, but clients can understand that we do not want to jeopardize continuing to make our living in our accustomed way. Further, it is often helpful to tell clients that if they do something clearly wrong, they can never thereafter be comfortable, that they will always be hostage to all who know or may come to know of their breach of law.

1. It would be unusual for us to suggest or recommend a plan which in our view would more likely than not result in negligence or similar penalties to the client if all the facts became known to the Service. Indeed, in planning, our standards are likely to be higher than in planning returns, since there will usually be opportunities in planning to reduce the risk of challenge.

2. Clients contemplating proceeding with a highly aggressive tax plan should make certain in advance that their tax return preparer will be willing to sign the return.

3. Sometimes we are blinded by our own brightness. If we have devised what we consider to be a particularly clever tax plan, we should remember the maxim, "If it is too good to be true, it isn't," and view each aspect and the overall plan through the eyes of an ambitious Service agent, determined to collect as much as possible. Finally, we should ask another experienced tax practitioner to review our plan and opinion carefully, both as to the technical details and as to the overall concept.

E. Tax Shelter Plans

We will not assist in the offering of a tax shelter program in which the tax benefits are important to the success of the investment unless it is substantially more likely than not that the material tax benefits will, in fact, be available to the investors. The degree of assurance we require as to the availability of the tax benefits depends upon the importance of the tax benefits to the success of the investment.

1. We should decline to participate in a tax opinion on a shelter program unless this firm also handles the balance of the legal work or has confidence in the other counsel involved and has adequate opportunity to explore any matters considered potentially troublesome. Familiarity with all of the facts is vital to such an opinion.

F. Following Up

A perfectly good tax plan may be spoiled in its implementation: there may be a failure to execute the proper documents, to make a timely filing of notices or elections, or to pay the amount necessary to avoid a gift or a dividend. We should make every effort to have our engagement in a tax planning matter also cover the implementation.

The desirability of assuring proper implementation of a plan that we helped create is very different from assuming any obligation to advise with respect to future changes in the law that may have a bearing on plans we have devised or on the repetition in future years of acts that we have previously approved. Most clients understand that nothing is less constant than the tax law and that what is right today may be wrong tomorrow. But it is a truth worth repeating both to our clients and ourselves.

Notes

1. *Backdating documents.* The rule here is as simple as rules get: Backdating documents is illegal and dishonest, and decent lawyers do not do it or tolerate their clients' doing it. The practical problem is one of client relations: a client who has missed a deadline may feel that the date on a document is a silly technicality, and that a lawyer who refuses to help is being stuffy. Some clients may assume, out of ignorance, that backdating is "the way things are done"; these clients may acquiesce when informed that this is not the case. Others will urge the lawyer to help them prepare fraudulently dated documents. This is a matter that will eventually arise in everyone's practice.

2. *State-of-mind issues.* Requests for rulings on contemplated transactions must usually contain a statement of the taxpayer's "business reasons" for engaging in the transaction. Often enough, the main reason for engaging in the transaction is to reduce taxes, but giving that as a "business reason" will not likely generate a favorable ruling. In practice, tax lawyers who would not dream of lying about anything else counsel their clients about the desirability of having a non-tax "business purpose" for a contemplated deal and send the clients off to think of something suitable. In fact, as we shall see (p. 424), "business purpose" or the absence of a "tax avoidance motive" seems not to provide a useful test for whether a transaction will (or should) succeed. Instead, the distinction between "shams" and legitimate tax-saving devices tends to turn on whether the transaction has real non-tax substance. The routine assertion of specious "business purposes" in requests for rulings may fairly be described as a fiction, rather than as a lie, as these assertions deceive no one. Making them is a formality, like the assertion in the old ejectment action that the plaintiff had leased the land in question to someone who now wants the defendant out.

3. *Reference.* Cooper, The Avoidance Dynamic: A Tale of Tax Planning, Tax Ethics and Tax Reform, 80 Colum.L.Rev. 1553 (1980).

———

We have not presented this extensive discussion of professional responsibility in tax matters because we think that tax lawyers need more guidance than other kinds of lawyers. On the contrary, our impression is that tax lawyers are, on the whole, very decent people. One bit of evidence of this is the tendency of tax lawyers to devote extensive attention in their writings to issues of ethics and professional responsibility. Ours is the only field of legal specialization in which there is a casebook devoted entirely to the ethics of practice in that field.[g] For many years, tax practitioners have reflected in print, thoughtfully and at length, on the ethical problems of tax practice. Tax Notes and The Tax Lawyer, two publications which all tax lawyers read regularly, publish many articles on ethics. For those who wish to read further in this field, we recommend Bittker, Professional Responsibility in Federal Tax Practice (1970), a somewhat-dated but still engaging collection of essays, and Wolfman, Holden & Harris, Standards of Tax Practice, a looseleaf publication which is updated regularly.

H. AN EXPENDITURE TAX?

Although an income tax has been the major source of revenue in the United States and most other industrialized countries for many years, some economists and lawyers have argued that a progressive tax on personal consumption would be preferable. Such a tax would, in essence, be an income tax with a deduction for amounts added to the taxpayer's savings during the year (amounts withdrawn from savings would be includable in income). Although detailed consideration of an expenditure tax is beyond the scope of this book, you may want to consider, as you encounter the problems that arise under the income tax, whether they would be as troublesome under an expenditure tax. Most academic discussions of the expenditure tax proposal begin with Andrews, A Consumption–Type or Cash Flow Personal Income Tax, 87 Harv.L.Rev. 1113 (1974). Political proposals, which have become fairly common in recent years, abound.

I. SELECTED BIBLIOGRAPHY

History. Paul, Taxation in the United States (1954).

Statutory Interpretation. Articles on the interpretation process in tax cases include Livingston, Congress, the Courts, and the Code: Legislative History and the Interpretation of Tax Statutes, 69 Tex.L.Rev. 819 (1991); Zelenak, Thinking about Nonliteral Interpretations of the Internal Revenue Code, 64 No.Car.L.Rev. 623 (1986); Brown, The Growing "Common Law" of Taxation, 1961 U.So.Cal.Tax Inst. 1; and Griswold, An Argument against the Doctrine That Deduc-

---

g. Wolfman, Holden & Schenk, Ethical   1995).
Problems in Federal Tax Practice (3d ed.

tions Should Be Narrowly Construed as a Matter of Legislative Grace, 56 Harv.L.Rev. 1142 (1943). The body of literature dealing with statutory interpretation in general is too extensive for even very selective citation here, except to note that Fuller, Positivism and Fidelity to Law—A Reply to Professor Hart, 71 Harv.L.Rev. 630 (1958), is a classic demolition of the idea that particular words can have a "plain meaning" divorced from their context.

Taxation and the Political Process. Doernberg & McChesney, Doing Good or Doing Well?: Congress and the Tax Reform Act of 1986, 62 N.Y.U.L.Rev. 891 (1987); Witte, The Politics and Development of the Federal Income Tax (1985); Surrey, Pathways to Tax Reform (1973).

Economics. Bradford, Untangling the Income Tax (1986); Goode, The Individual Income Tax (rev. ed. 1976); Kaldor, An Expenditure Tax (1955); Vickrey, Agenda for Progressive Taxation (1947).

Treatises. Bittker & Lokken, Federal Taxation of Income, Estates and Gifts, is a five-volume treatise which is regularly updated. A popular basic text for student use is Chirelstein, Federal Income Taxation (9th ed. 2002).

Miscellany. The Bureau of National Affairs publishes a series of "Tax Management Portfolios," each of which deals in some depth with a particular area. Tax Notes, a weekly magazine, contains descriptions of all important cases and rulings (including letter rulings) as well as news about current tax events and articles on tax policy.

Tax Services. Effective tax research requires the use of a looseleaf service such as the Standard Federal Tax Reporter (Commerce Clearing House) or the RIA United States Tax Reporter (Research Institute of America). Both Westlaw and Lexis have extensive tax libraries.

Chapter Two

THE CONCEPT OF INCOME

A. BASIC TAX COMPUTATIONS

For most taxpayers, the income tax is imposed by § 1 (individuals, estates, and trusts) or § 11 (corporations). In the case of some low- and middle-income taxpayers, tax tables authorized by § 3 substitute for the tax-rate schedules; the tables are easier to use than the rate schedules and provide for almost exactly the same tax liability. The tax on a given amount of *taxable income* is the amount determined under the appropriate schedule or table, less the amount of any *tax credits* (§§ 21 through 51).

"Taxable income" is calculated by subtracting the taxpayer's *deductions* from gross income. If gross income is $200,000 and deductions are $50,000, taxable income equals $150,000. Many deductions correspond to expenditures made by the taxpayer, such as business expenses, state and local income and property taxes, most charitable contributions, and most interest on home mortgages. A few deductions, however, are not tied to actual outlays. For example, most individual taxpayers get at least one deduction for a *personal exemption* (a married couple gets two of these, as even if they file a joint return they are two taxpayers). The statutory personal exemption is normally $2000, but this figure is adjusted annually for inflation: for 2002 it is $3000. Taxpayers with dependents (defined in § 152) get a personal exemption for each dependent as well. Therefore, a low-income or middle-income married couple with two dependent children will ordinarily deduct $12,000 (in 2002) in personal exemptions. (The special rules for upper-income taxpayers will be discussed later.)

For individual taxpayers, the calculation of taxable income involves two steps. First, some deductions—those listed in § 62—are subtracted from gross income, yielding a figure called *adjusted gross income*, or *AGI.* This figure is important because many sections of the Code require taxpayers to make calculations based on their AGI. (Many sections now require calculations based on *modified adjusted gross income*, which is AGI with minor adjustments. There is no one definition of modified AGI: each section that uses modified AGI contains its own definition. For many taxpayers, modified AGI is the same as AGI.) The deductions listed in § 62 are often called *above-the-line deductions*.[a] Next, the taxpayer subtracts deductions for personal exemptions and either (1) *itemized deductions* or (2) the *standard deduction* from AGI to determine taxable income. Itemized deductions are all deductions other than above-the-line deductions, personal exemptions, and the standard deduction. The statutory amount of the standard deduction is usually $5000 for a married couple filing a joint return and $3000 for an unmarried individual.[b] These figures are adjusted annually for inflation.

The system described above means that all taxpayers will deduct their above-the-line deductions and their personal exemptions. Taxpayers whose itemized deductions exceed their standard-deduction amounts will deduct their itemized deductions; those whose itemized deductions come to less than the standard deduction will take the standard deduction instead. Itemized deductions include things like charitable contributions, many state and local tax payments, and most home-mortgage interest. This system enables many low- and middle-income taxpayers to file simple tax returns, and it spares them the record-keeping burden of keeping track of things like charitable contributions.

Low- and middle-income parents are allowed *child tax credits*, as well as personal exemptions, for their dependent children who are U.S. citizens under the age of seventeen; § 24. As a rule, this is a tax credit of $600 for each "qualifying child." (The $600 amount is for years until 2004; after that, it is scheduled to increase to $1000 by 2010.) The credit is phased out for taxpayers whose "modified adjusted gross incomes" exceed $75,000 (for unmarried taxpayers) or $110,000 (married taxpayers filing joint returns). For each $1000 (or fraction of $1000) by which the taxpayer's modified AGI exceeds the statutory amount, the total credit is reduced by $50. For example, consider a married couple filing a joint return. The couple has two qualifying children. If their modified AGI is $110,000 or less, their child credit is $1200. If their modified AGI is $115,200, their credit is reduced by $300, to $900. If their modified AGI is $134,000 or more, they are not entitled to the credit. For some taxpayers, a portion of the child tax credit is refundable (that is, it is payable even to taxpayers who would owe no tax even without the credit). Special (and somewhat complex) rules apply to some taxpayers with more than three children.

The following diagram illustrates the computation of income tax for an individual or a married couple filing a joint return.

---

a. There are above-the-line deductions not listed in § 62. E.g., under certain circumstances, a taxpayer receiving alimony whose alimony payments decline substantially gets a deduction, meant to offset the previous inclusion of alimony in income. This deduction is allowed by § 71(f)(1)(B), which makes it "a deduction in computing adjusted gross income." It is not listed in § 62, though it should be.

b. The standard deduction for a taxpayer who can be claimed as a dependent on another person's return cannot exceed the greater of the following amounts: (1) $500, or (2) the taxpayer's earned income plus $250. § 63(c)(5). This rule limits the amount of a dependent's standard deduction that can be used against investment income.

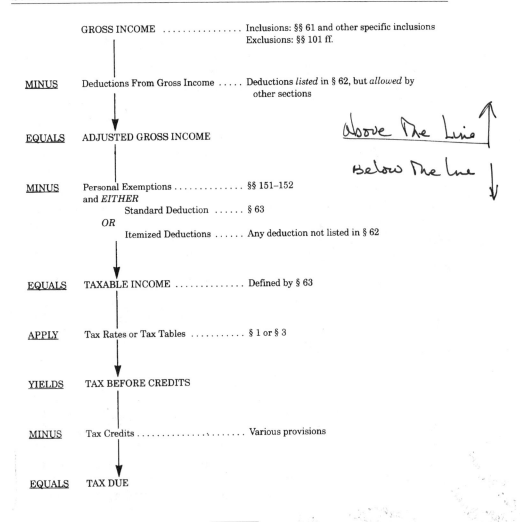

GROSS INCOME .... Inclusions: §§ 61 and other specific inclusions
Exclusions: §§ 101 ff.

MINUS   Deductions From Gross Income ..... Deductions *listed* in § 62, but *allowed* by other sections

EQUALS   ADJUSTED GROSS INCOME

above The Line

Below The line

MINUS   Personal Exemptions .... §§ 151–152
and *EITHER*
         Standard Deduction ...... § 63
    OR
         Itemized Deductions ...... Any deduction not listed in § 62

EQUALS   TAXABLE INCOME .... Defined by § 63

APPLY   Tax Rates or Tax Tables .... § 1 or § 3

YIELDS   TAX BEFORE CREDITS

MINUS   Tax Credits .... Various provisions

EQUALS   TAX DUE

By way of example, suppose a married couple with two dependent children has $60,000 gross income and the following deductions:

(1) $2000 loss on the sale of business property (§ 165(c)(1)),

(2) $8000 mortgage interest on principal residence (§ 163(a)),

(3) $1000 charitable contributions (§ 170(a)),

(4) $4000 state and local income taxes (§ 164(a)(3)), and

(5) $2000 property taxes on principal residence (§ 164(a)(1)).

Assume that the couple will file a joint return, and that they are entitled to a tax credit of $960 under § 21 for the costs of day care for the children while the parents worked. Because the couple's only above-the-line deduction is the deduction for loss on the sale of business property (§§ 62(a)(1) & (3)), their adjusted gross income ("AGI") is $58,000. From this figure, they will subtract itemized deductions (§ 63(d)) of $15,000 and personal-exemption deductions of $2000 each (we ignore inflation adjustments) for themselves and their two dependent children, or $8000. Therefore, their taxable income is $35,000. At the 2002–2003 statutory rates, the tax on $35,000 is $4650. From this amount the couple subtracts their $960 credit for child-care expenses and a $1200 child tax credit, yielding a tax of $2490. If the couple's itemized deductions had been $5000 or less, they would have taken the standard deduction instead of itemizing. This example used the statutory tax rates and dollar amounts for personal exemptions; the actual tax burden for this couple, using inflation-adjusted figures, would be considerably lower.

Two points about the computations described above merit special mention. First, § 62, which defines adjusted gross income, does not itself allow any deductions; it simply lists deductions authorized by other Code sections. The practical importance of AGI is that several Code sections use AGI in determining specific items. For example, § 213 allows a deduction for medical expenses in the amount by which the medical expenses for the year exceed 7.5 percent of AGI. Second, an above-the-line deduction will be worth more to many taxpayers than an identical itemized deduction would be worth, because only those taxpayers whose total itemized deductions exceed their standard deductions will claim itemized deductions on their returns.

Problem

In working this problem, use the amounts set forth in the Code (before inflation adjustments) for the standard deduction (§ 63) and the personal and dependency exemptions (§ 151).

A, age 67, has $40,000 of gross income, $4000 of deductions from rental property (see § 62(a)(4)), $1000 of property taxes on her home, and $2650 of state income taxes. Compute her adjusted gross and taxable incomes.

So far, we have examined tax computations for low- and middle-income taxpayers. Taxpayers with higher incomes face two additional complications, both of which were introduced in 1990 to raise revenues. These are (1) the "phaseout" of personal exemptions for high-income taxpayers and (2) a limit on the deductibility of some itemized deductions for those having high adjusted gross incomes. The 2001 tax act calls for the eventual elimination of these phaseouts, but they are scheduled to remain fully in place until 2005, and they will not be completely eliminated until 2010.

Section 151(d) phases out the personal exemption for taxpayers whose adjusted gross incomes exceed "threshold amounts." For joint returns, the statutory threshold amount is $150,000; this figure is adjusted for inflation. The personal-exemption deduction for a taxpayer with AGI over the threshold amount is reduced by 2 percent for each

2500^c (or fraction thereof) of AGI over the threshold. For example, if a married couple filing a joint return has AGI of $250,000, their AGI exceeds their threshold by $100,000. Their personal exemptions are therefore reduced by 80 percent. (The $100,000 by which AGI exceeds the threshold is 40 times $2500, and the reduction is two percent for each of those 40.)

The calculations described above create both (1) a very cumbersome way of calculating personal exemptions and (2) a system which imposes higher marginal tax rates on taxpayers with many dependents than upon those with the same incomes but few or no dependents. The Revenue Reconciliation Act of 1990 was unusual in being a tax-increase measure adopted just two weeks before Congressional elections. Congress wanted to increase taxes on the relatively wealthy without explicitly raising the tax rates very much; it therefore raised effective tax rates indirectly by phasing out personal exemptions and by limiting itemized deductions (as explained in the next paragraph). If its purpose was to adopt tax increases which would take voters more than two weeks to figure out, Congress did well; no member of the House Ways and Means Committee or the Senate Finance Committee was defeated in the 1990 elections.

Section 68, which was adopted in 1990, limits the deductibility of itemized deductions by taxpayers having AGI in excess of a $100,000 threshold ($50,000 for married taxpayers filing separate returns). The threshold amount rises with inflation. Generally, the total amount of the taxpayer's otherwise-deductible itemized deductions is reduced by 3 percent of the excess of AGI over the threshold. However, the reduction cannot be more than 80 percent of total itemized deductions. For purposes of § 68, deductions for medical expenses, casualty losses, investment interest, and wagering losses are not treated as itemized deductions. In other words, no matter how high a taxpayer's AGI, itemized deductions of the four specified kinds plus 20 percent of other itemized deductions will be allowed. Section 68 is only one of two provisions limiting itemized deductions. The other is § 67, which allows "miscellaneous itemized deductions" (§ 67(b)) to be deducted only to the extent that their total amount exceeds 2 percent of AGI. Section 67 applies first; that is, one applies § 68 to whatever itemized deductions are left after § 67 has done its work.

Like the phaseout of personal exemptions, § 68 was designed to raise taxes without raising tax rates.

In most cases, the amount of the extra tax imposed by the phaseout of itemized deductions does not depend at all on the amount of the taxpayer's itemized deductions. Consider an example of an unmarried taxpayer with AGI of $120,000, itemized deductions of $20,000 (before calculating the phaseout), and one personal exemption of $2000. Her AGI of $120,000 exceeds the $100,000 threshold by $20,000. She must therefore reduce the amount of her itemized deductions by 3 percent of $20,000, or $600. This increases the amount of her taxable income by

c. $1250 for married taxpayers filing separate returns.

$600, which will add $180 (30 percent of $600) to her tax bill, as she is in the 30–percent marginal bracket. If the amount of her itemized deductions had been $25,000 or $15,000, rather than $20,000, the increase in her taxable income would still have been $600, and the increase in her tax liability would still have been $180: for most taxpayers, the only figures used to calculate the phaseout are AGI and the statutory threshold. Why, then, does the statute call this a phaseout "of itemized deductions"? There are two reasons. First, because the taxable income added by § 68 is accomplished by reducing the amount of the itemized deductions the taxpayer can take, it does not affect those who take the standard deduction rather than itemizing. Second, the total amount of the increase in taxable income is limited to 80 percent of the taxpayer's itemized deductions (other than those for medical expenses, casualty losses, investment interest, and wagering losses). Therefore, the maximum amount by which § 68 can increase a taxpayer's taxable income does depend on the amount of the taxpayer's itemized deductions. Some high-income taxpayers with few itemized deductions will therefore be less affected by the phaseout than equally high-income taxpayers with more itemized deductions.

All of these calculations are considerably easier to make mechanically on the tax forms than to grasp by reading the Code or our description. Still, adding steps like these to the tax-computation process creates more ways than ever for taxpayers to go astray in the course of filing.

Problems

In working these problems, use the dollar figures set out in §§ 68 and 151 and the tax rates set out in Appendix B.

Problem (1). H and W, who are married and file a joint return, have AGI of $200,000 for the current year. They are entitled to four dependency exemptions (for their children) under § 151. They have $30,000 of itemized deductions that are subject to the limits of § 68.

    (a) Compute their taxable income.

    (b) By how much would their taxes increase if they earned an additional $100 of income during the year?

Problem (2). Before consideration of the charitable contribution described below, *M,* a single person, expects to have AGI of $150,000 and itemized deductions (subject to § 68) of $20,000. She is considering whether to make an additional charitable contribution (deductible as an itemized deduction under § 170) of $1000 before the end of the year. Does § 68 diminish the tax incentive for making the year-end contribution?

In most of the cases in this chapter the controversy ultimately involves the determination of taxable income. Sometimes the issue is whether an item is included in gross income, sometimes it concerns a deduction.

B. "ACCESSIONS TO WEALTH"

1. IN GENERAL

COMMISSIONER v. GLENSHAW GLASS CO.

Supreme Court of the United States, 1955.
348 U.S. 426, 75 S.Ct. 473, 99 L.Ed. 483.

Mr. Chief Justice Warren delivered the opinion of the Court.

This litigation involves two cases with independent factual backgrounds yet presenting the identical issue. The two cases were consolidated for argument before the Court of Appeals for the Third Circuit and were heard en banc. The common question is whether money received as exemplary damages for fraud or as the punitive two-thirds portion of a treble-damage antitrust recovery must be reported by a taxpayer as gross income under § 22(a) of the Internal Revenue Code of 1939 [now § 61]. In a single opinion, 211 F.2d 928, the Court of Appeals affirmed the Tax Court's separate rulings in favor of the taxpayers. 18 T.C. 860; 19 T.C. 637. Because of the frequent recurrence of the question and differing interpretations by the lower courts of this Court's decisions bearing upon the problem, we granted the Commissioner of Internal Revenue's ensuing petition for certiorari. 348 U.S. 813.

The facts of the cases were largely stipulated and are not in dispute. So far as pertinent they are as follows:

Commissioner v. Glenshaw Glass Co.—The Glenshaw Glass Company, a Pennsylvania corporation, manufactures glass bottles and containers. It was engaged in protracted litigation with the Hartford–Empire Company, which manufactures machinery of a character used by Glenshaw. Among the claims advanced by Glenshaw were demands for exemplary damages for fraud and treble damages for injury to its business by reason of Hartford's violation of the federal antitrust laws. In December, 1947, the parties concluded a settlement of all pending litigation, by which Hartford paid Glenshaw approximately $800,000. Through a method of allocation which was approved by the Tax Court, 18 T.C. 860, 870–872, and which is no longer in issue, it was ultimately determined that, of the total settlement, $324,529.94 represented payment of punitive damages for fraud and antitrust violations. Glenshaw did not report this portion of the settlement as income for the tax year involved. The Commissioner determined a deficiency claiming as taxable the entire sum less only deductible legal fees. As previously noted, the Tax Court and the Court of Appeals upheld the taxpayer.

Commissioner v. William Goldman Theatres, Inc.—William Goldman Theatres, Inc., a Delaware corporation operating motion picture houses in Pennsylvania, sued Loew's, Inc., alleging a violation of the federal antitrust laws and seeking treble damages. * * * Goldman reported only $125,000 of the recovery as gross income and claimed that the $250,000 balance constituted punitive damages and as such was not taxable. The Tax Court agreed, 19 T.C. 637, and the Court of Appeals, hearing this with the *Glenshaw* case, affirmed. 211 F.2d 928.

It is conceded by the respondents that there is no constitutional barrier to the imposition of a tax on punitive damages. Our question is one of statutory construction: are these payments comprehended by § 22(a)?

The sweeping scope of the controverted statute is readily apparent:

"§ 22. Gross income

"(a) General definition. 'Gross income' includes gains, profits, and income derived from salaries, wages, or compensation for personal service * * * of whatever kind and in whatever form paid, or from professions, vocations, trades, businesses, commerce, or sales, or dealings in property, whether real or personal, growing out of the ownership or use of or interest in such property; also from interest, rent, dividends, securities, or the transaction of any business carried on for gain or profit, *or gains or profits and income derived from any source whatever.* * * * "(Emphasis added.)

This Court has frequently stated that this language was used by Congress to exert in this field "the full measure of its taxing power." Helvering v. Clifford, 309 U.S. 331, 334; Helvering v. Midland Mutual Life Ins. Co., 300 U.S. 216, 223; Douglas v. Willcuts, 296 U.S. 1, 9; Irwin v. Gavit, 268 U.S. 161, 166. Respondents contend that punitive damages, characterized as "windfalls" flowing from the culpable conduct of third parties, are not within the scope of the section. But Congress applied no limitations as to the source of taxable receipts, nor restrictive labels as to their nature. And the Court has given a liberal construction to this broad phraseology in recognition of the intention of Congress to tax all gains except those specifically exempted. Commissioner v. Jacobson, 336 U.S. 28, 49; Helvering v. Stockholms Enskilda Bank, 293 U.S. 84, 87–91. Thus, the fortuitous gain accruing to a lessor by reason of the forfeiture of a lessee's improvements on the rented property was taxed in Helvering v. Bruun, 309 U.S. 461. [Further citations omitted.] Such decisions demonstrate that we cannot but ascribe content to the catchall provision of § 22(a), "gains or profits and income derived from any source whatever." The importance of that phrase has been too frequently recognized since its first appearance in the Revenue Act of 1913 to say now that it adds nothing to the meaning of "gross income."

Nor can we accept respondents' contention that a narrower reading of § 22(a) is required by the Court's characterization of income in Eisner v. Macomber, 252 U.S. 189, as " 'the gain derived from capital, from labor, or from both combined.' " The Court was there endeavoring to determine whether the distribution of a corporate stock dividend constituted a realized gain to the shareholder, or changed "only the form, not the essence," of his capital investment. Id., 252 U.S. at page 210. It was held that the taxpayer had "received nothing out of the company's assets for his separate use and benefit." Id., 252 U.S. at page 211. The distribution, therefore, was held not a taxable event. In that context—distinguishing gain from capital—the definition served a useful purpose. But it was not meant to provide a touchstone to all future gross income questions. [Citations omitted.]

Here we have instances of undeniable accessions to wealth, clearly realized, and over which the taxpayers have complete dominion. The mere fact that the payments were extracted from the wrongdoers as punishment for unlawful conduct cannot detract from their character as taxable income to the recipients. Respondents concede, as they must, that the recoveries are taxable to the extent that they compensate for damages actually incurred. It would be an anomaly that could not be justified in the absence of clear congressional intent to say that a recovery for actual damages is taxable but not the additional amount extracted as punishment for the same conduct which caused the injury. And we find no such evidence of intent to exempt these payments.

It is urged that re-enactment of § 22(a) without change since the Board of Tax Appeals held punitive damages nontaxable in Highland Farms Corp., 42 B.T.A. 1314, indicates congressional satisfaction with that holding. Re-enactment—particularly without the slightest affirmative indication that Congress ever had the *Highland Farms* decision before it—is an unreliable indicium at best. Helvering v. Wilshire Oil Co., 308 U.S. 90, 100–101; Koshland v. Helvering, 298 U.S. 441, 447. Moreover, the Commissioner promptly published his non-acquiescence in this portion of the *Highland Farms* holding and has, before and since, consistently maintained the position that these receipts are taxable. It therefore cannot be said with certitude that Congress intended to carve an exception out of § 22(a)'s pervasive coverage. Nor does the 1954 Code's legislative history, with its reiteration of the proposition that statutory gross income is "all-inclusive," give support to respondents' position. The definition of gross income has been simplified, but no effect upon its present broad scope was intended.[11] Certainly punitive damages cannot reasonably be classified as gifts, cf. Commissioner v. Jacobson, 336 U.S. 28, 47–52, nor do they come under any other exemption provision in the Code. We would do violence to the plain meaning of the statute and restrict a clear legislative attempt to bring the taxing power to bear upon all receipts constitutionally taxable were we to say that the

---

11. In discussing § 61(a) of the 1954 Code, the House Report states:

"This section corresponds to section 22(a) of the 1939 Code. While the language in existing section 22(a) has been simplified, the all-inclusive nature of statutory gross income has not been affected thereby. Section 61(a) is as broad in scope as section 22(a).

"Section 61(a) provides that gross income includes 'all income from whatever source derived.' This definition is based upon the 16th Amendment and the word 'income' is used in its constitutional sense." H.R.Rep. No. 1337, * * * at A18.

A virtually identical statement appears in S.Rep. No. 1622, * * * at 168.

payments in question here are not gross income. See Helvering v. Midland Mutual Life Ins. Co., supra, 300 U.S. at page 223.

Reversed.

MR. JUSTICE DOUGLAS dissents.[d]

MR. JUSTICE HARLAN took no part in the consideration or decision of this case.

Notes and Questions

1. *Other "windfall" cases.* The taxpayers in Cesarini v. United States, 296 F.Supp. 3 (N.D.Ohio 1969), affirmed 428 F.2d 812 (6th Cir.1970), bought a second-hand piano for $15. Seven years later they found $4467 in cash hidden in the piano. The court, relying on *Glenshaw Glass*, held that the windfall was income. What if the taxpayer finds a valuable object, rather than cash? Treas.Reg. § 1.61–14(a) has generally been read as requiring inclusion in income of the value of the found property. For a criticism of the regulation, noting that commercial fishermen, miners, and professional treasure hunters are not in fact taxed until they turn their "receipts" into cash, see McMahon & Zelenak, Baseballs and Other Found Property, 84 Tax Notes 1299 (1999).

Book reviewers and teachers are sent free books by publishers, who hope that the books will be reviewed or adopted for class use. The Service's position is that the value of the books is not income, except to recipients who display unseemly greed by giving the books to charity and taking a tax deduction for their value (p. 222, below).

2. *Realization.* A taxpayer who finds a gold coin worth $100 has "realized" that amount of income under Treas.Reg. § 1.61–14(a), but a taxpayer who buys a gold coin for $50 has no income when the coin increases in value to $150 (unless he sells it or exchanges it for something else). In each case the taxpayer's wealth has increased, but in the second case we would say that the gain in question has not been "realized." Suppose a taxpayer discovers a valuable natural gas deposit five thousand feet under his backyard. Has the gain been realized?

2. GROSS INCOME FROM SALES

Suppose a calendar-year taxpayer buys stock for $1000 on June 15 of the current year. By the end of the year, the stock has increased in value to $1500. The appreciation represents an increase in the taxpayer's wealth, and, in an ideal world, this increase might be subject to tax at year's end. But it is generally not administratively feasible to take account of appreciation or depreciation until the occurrence of a market transaction that fixes an asset's value. For this reason, the tax system usually does not tax appreciation (or allow a deduction for losses) until the taxpayer disposes of the property. (Until the property is disposed of,

---

d. See generally Wolfman, Silver & Silver, The Behavior of Justice Douglas in Federal Tax Cases, 122 U.Pa.L.Rev. 235 (1973)—Eds.

tax lawyers speak of the appreciation or depreciation as being "unrealized.")

Now suppose that the taxpayer sells the stock in the next year for $1700. The sale is a disposition (sometimes called a "realization event") which requires the taxpayer to reckon gain or loss on the transaction. Although the taxpayer receives $1700, he obviously does not have $1700 of "income." (The *Glenshaw Glass* Court's reference to taxable "receipts" is misleading: not everything that *comes in* is *income.*) The profit on the transaction is only the $700 excess of the amount received upon the sale ($1700) over the original investment in the stock ($1000); the taxpayer is entitled to offset the investment in the property against the sales proceeds in computing "income." Section 61(a)(3) provides that "*[g]ains* derived from dealings in property"[e] are included in gross income; the "gain" on the sale is the $700 of profit, not the $1700 sale price.[f] (If the taxpayer had sold the stock for less than its purchase price–say $900–the "gross income" upon the sale would have been zero: there is no such thing as "negative gross income." This taxpayer has realized a loss of $100 on the sale, and this loss will be dealt with by allowing the taxpayer a $100 deduction in calculating taxable income.)

Section 1001(a) tells us that a taxpayer's (realized) "gain" on the disposition of property is the excess of the "amount realized" over the "adjusted basis." In this case, the "amount realized" is simply the amount of cash for which the taxpayer sells the property, and the property's basis is its $1000 cost; § 1012. Later on, we shall look at cases in which property's basis must be adjusted and in which basis is something other than the cost of the property. For now, however, you can assume that basis is "cost" and that it need not be adjusted. Even with this simplification, the calculation of gains on sales may be far from obvious, as "cost" is a term of art; it does not always mean simply the amount of money the taxpayer pays to acquire property.

Problems and Notes

1. *Problems.*

(1) *A* finds and keeps a gold statue worth $10,000. If in a later year she sells the statue for $12,000, how much gain does she realize upon the sale?

(2) *B* buys a statue from an antique dealer for $4000; the statue's actual value is $14,000. Later, *B* sells the statue for $16,000. What is *B*'s gain on the sale?

(3) *C* receives a $500 Federal income-tax refund. Is this amount includable in *C*'s gross income?

e. Emphasis added.

f. One can imagine a tax system in which the entire sale price was treated as "gross income," with the amount paid for the property being allowed as a deduction. But that is not the way the Code deals with this problem.

2. *"Realization" and "recognition."* A realized gain is includable in gross income only if it is also *recognized*. Although Congress has provided for non-recognition of gain (or loss) in some situations, § 1001(c) prescribes that realized gains (or losses) are recognized unless some other section provides otherwise; § 1001(c). (An example of a non-recognition provision is § 1031, under which gain from the exchange of business or investment property for other business or investment property of "like kind" is not recognized.) The treatment of property dispositions is examined extensively in Chapters 8–11.

Although gain from a sale is "realized" (and usually "recognized") at the time of the sale, a sale itself does not ordinarily enrich the taxpayer. In the example in the text, the sale consisted of an exchange of property worth $1700 for $1700 in cash. The taxpayer's enrichment, or "accession to wealth," took place whenever the stock increased in value from $1000 to $1700.

3. *A definition of "income."* The "Haig–Simons" (or "Schanz–Haig–Simons") definition of income, which many economists use as a starting point in discussing tax-policy issues, is (Simons, Personal Income Taxation 50 (1938)):

> * * * the algebraic sum of (1) the market value of rights exercised in consumption and (2) the change in the value of the store of property rights between the beginning and end of the period in question. In other words, it is merely the result obtained by adding consumption during the period to "wealth" at the end of the period and then subtracting "wealth" at the beginning.

One major difference between Haig–Simons income and income under the Internal Revenue Code is that the Haig–Simons definition contains no realization requirement. A taxpayer who buys stock for $1000 on January 1 would have $700 in Haig–Simons income if the stock increased in value to $1700 by the end of the year, but such a taxpayer is not normally taxed unless the stock is sold or exchanged. The exemption of "unrealized appreciation" from taxation means that, if all else is equal, people will prefer investing in assets that will appreciate to investing in assets that will produce realized gains. Therefore, ignoring differences in risk, an investment in stock that will increase in value from $10,000 to $11,000 is preferable to an investment in $10,000 worth of stock expected to pay $1000 in dividends and to continue to sell for $10,000.

3. COMPENSATION FOR SERVICES

(a) Introduction

OLD COLONY TRUST CO. v. COMMISSIONER

Supreme Court of the United States, 1929.
279 U.S. 716, 49 S.Ct. 499, 73 L.Ed. 918.

MR. CHIEF JUSTICE TAFT delivered the opinion of the Court.

* * *

The facts certified to us are substantially as follows:

William M. Wood was president of the American Woolen Company during the years 1918, 1919, and 1920. In 1918 he received as salary and commissions from the company $978,725, which he included in his federal income tax return for 1918. In 1919 he received as salary and commissions from the company $548,132.87, which he included in his return for 1919.

August 3, 1916, the American Woolen Company had adopted the following resolution, which was in effect in 1919 and 1920:

"Voted: That this company pay any and all income taxes, State and Federal, that may hereafter become due and payable upon the salaries of all the officers of the company, including the president, William M. Wood; the comptroller, Parry C. Wiggin; the auditor, George R. Lawton; and the following members of the staff, to wit: Frank H. Carpenter, Edwin L. Heath, Samuel R. Haines, and William M. Lasbury, to the end that said persons and officers shall receive their salaries or other compensation in full without deduction on account of income taxes, State or Federal, which taxes are to be paid out of the treasury of this corporation."

This resolution was amended on March 25, 1918, as follows:

"Voted: That, referring to the vote passed by this board on August 3, 1916, in reference to income taxes, State and Federal, payable upon the salaries or compensation of the officers and certain employees of this company, the method of computing said taxes shall be as follows, viz.:

" 'The difference between what the total amount of his tax would be, including his income from all sources, and the amount of his tax when computed upon his income excluding such compensation or salaries paid by this company.' "

Pursuant to these resolutions, the American Woolen Company paid to the collector of internal revenue Mr. Wood's federal income and surtaxes due to salary and commissions paid him by the company, as follows:

Taxes for 1918 paid in 1919 .... $681,169.88
Taxes for 1919 paid in 1920 .... 351,179.27

The decision of the Board of Tax Appeals here sought to be reviewed was that the income taxes of $681,169.88 and $351,179.27 paid by the American Woolen Company for Mr. Wood were additional income to him for the years 1919 and 1920.

The question certified by the Circuit Court of Appeals for answer by this Court is:

"Did the payment by the employer of the income taxes assessable against the employee constitute additional taxable income to such employee?"

* * *

* * * Coming now to the merits of this case, we think the question presented is whether a taxpayer, having induced a third person to pay his income tax or having acquiesced in such payment as made in discharge of an obligation to him, may avoid the making of a return thereof and the payment of a corresponding tax. We think he may not do so. The payment of the tax by the employer was in consideration of the services rendered by the employee, and was a gain derived by the employee from his labor. The form of the payment is expressly declared to make no difference. Section 213, Revenue Act of 1918, c. 18, 40 Stat. 1065. It is therefore immaterial that the taxes were directly paid over to the government. The discharge by a third person of an obligation to him is equivalent to receipt by the person taxed. The certificate shows that the taxes were imposed upon the employee, that the taxes were actually paid by the employer, and that the employee entered upon his duties in the years in question under the express agreement that his income taxes would be paid by his employer. This is evidenced by the terms of the resolution passed August 3, 1916, more than one year prior to the year in which the taxes were imposed. The taxes were paid upon a valuable consideration, namely, the services rendered by the employee and as part of the compensation therefor. We think, therefore, that the payment constituted income to the employee.

* * *

Nor can it be argued that the payment of the tax in No. 130 was a gift. The payment for services, even though entirely voluntary, was nevertheless compensation within the statute. * * *

It is next argued against the payment of this tax that, if these payments by the employer constitute income to the employee, the employer will be called upon to pay the tax imposed upon this additional income, and that the payment of the additional tax will create further income which will in turn be subject to tax, with the result that there would be a tax upon a tax. This, it is urged, is the result of the government's theory, when carried to its logical conclusion, and results in an absurdity which Congress could not have contemplated.

In the first place, no attempt has been made by the Treasury to collect further taxes, upon the theory that the payment of the additional taxes creates further income, and the question of a tax upon a tax was not before the Circuit Court of Appeals, and has not been certified to this Court. We can settle questions of that sort when an attempt to impose a tax upon a tax is undertaken, but not now. United States v. Sullivan, 274 U.S. 259, 264; Yazoo & Mississippi Valley R. Co. v. Jackson Vinegar Co., 226 U.S. 217, 219. It is not, therefore, necessary to answer the argument based upon an algebraic formula to reach the amount of taxes due. The question in this case is, "Did the payment by the employer of the income taxes assessable against the employee constitute additional taxable income to such employee?" The answer must be "Yes."

Separate opinion of MR. JUSTICE MCREYNOLDS.

[Omitted.]

Problem, Notes and Questions

1. *Form of the receipt.* On similar facts the House of Lords held in Hartland v. Diggines, [1926] A.C. 289 (H.L.), that the employer's payment of an employee's income tax was income, saying at [1926] A.C. 292:

> It is true that the appellant did not receive cash in his hands, but he received money's worth year after year. This being so, I cannot resist the conclusion that the payment was in fact a part of his profits and emoluments as an officer of the company for which he has been properly assessed to tax.

What if an employer provides a suit, made by a tailor selected by the employer, to an employee? Is this as appealing a case for taxability as *Old Colony*? Would it matter whether the suit was of a "lower quality and cut" than the employee normally would buy, and that the employee wore the suit only to avoid offending the employer? If the employee does have income, is its amount what the employer paid the tailor for the suit, what the employee could have sold the suit for (secondhand) immediately after receiving it, or something else? In Wilkins v. Rogerson, [1961] 1 Ch. 133, 2 W.L.R. 102 (C.A.), the court held that the employee's income was £5, the value of the suit secondhand, rather than the £14, 15s. the employer paid for the suit, because the employee "received" only the suit, not the payment. What effect would you expect this decision to have on the pattern of compensation of employees in England?

2. *"A tax upon a tax."* Suppose the tax rate is 40 percent, and that an employee is paid $30,000 under an agreement like that in *Old Colony*. The employer then makes a tax payment of $12,000 on behalf of the employee. *Old Colony* holds that the $12,000 is income. Does it follow that if the company then pays $4800 more tax on behalf of the employee the additional payment is income? With a flat 40-percent tax, an employee who pays his own tax would have to be paid $50,000 gross salary to be left with $30,000 after taxes. If the government does not "collect further

taxes, upon the theory that the payment of the additional taxes creates further income," the employer would have to pay only $46,800. Since 1952, the government has in fact collected the "tax upon a tax," a practice approved in Safe Harbor Water Power Corp. v. United States, 303 F.2d 928 (Ct.Cl.1962).

How common is it for an employer to pay at least part of an employee's tax? Very common indeed: § 3402 requires "every employer making payment of wages" to "deduct and withhold upon such wages a tax * * *." An employee entitled to a "pre-tax" salary of $50,000 who has a tax of $11,000 "withheld" is economically identical to someone who has a nominal salary of $39,000, and whose employer also pays $11,000 of the employee's tax.

3. *The Old Colony principle in other contexts.* The principle that *A*'s payment of *B*'s obligation is tantamount to a payment from *A* to *B* (followed by *B*'s payment of the obligation) has widespread application in the tax law. For example, suppose a corporation pays its shareholder's indebtedness to a third party. How might the transaction be characterized for tax purposes? Suppose *C* transfers property with an adjusted basis of $40 and a value of $100 to *D* in exchange for $70 cash and *D*'s payment of *C*'s $30 debt to *E*. What result to *C* and *D*?

4. *Problem. E* is employed by *X* Corporation in a state which has no income tax. Last year, *E* accepted a temporary assignment for *X* in an adjoining state which imposes a 5–percent income tax on compensation earned within the state. *E* agreed to serve at his regular salary if *X* would pay any state income-tax liability incurred by *E* at the temporary post. *E* earned $10,000 while on the assignment. *X* paid the resulting $500 tax liability. Must *E* include the $500 in Federal gross income? (Does it matter whether the $500 is included? Consider § 164(a)(3).)

ACCOUNTING METHODS

Consider a taxpayer who in 2003 becomes entitled to receive a $10,000 payment for services and who receives the payment in 2004. Whether the payment is includable in the taxpayer's 2003 or 2004 income depends upon the taxpayer's accounting method. Generally speaking, an "accrual-method" taxpayer reports income upon acquiring a right to a payment; a "cash-method" taxpayer reports income when cash (or property, or a check) is received. Most employees use the cash method to report compensation for services. Business taxpayers often have a choice between cash-method and accrual-method accounting.

Cash-method taxpayers normally take deductions when they pay out money, while an accrual-method taxpayer becomes entitled to a deduction upon incurring a liability. (The many exceptions to these rules will be examined in Chapter 12.) Thus, someone who becomes liable in 2003 to pay a $10,000 business expense and who actually pays the expense in 2004 will deduct the expense in 2003 if the accrual method is used and in 2004 if the cash method applies.

(b) Transfers of Property as Compensation for Services: Section 83

COMMISSIONER v. LoBUE

Supreme Court of the United States, 1956.
351 U.S. 243, 76 S.Ct. 800, 100 L.Ed. 1142.

MR. JUSTICE BLACK delivered the opinion of the Court.

This case involves the federal income tax liability of respondent LoBue for the years 1946 and 1947. From 1941 to 1947 LoBue was manager of the New York Sales Division of the Michigan Chemical Corporation, a producer and distributor of chemical supplies. In 1944 the company adopted a stock option plan making 10,000 shares of its common stock available for distribution to key employees at $5 per share over a 3–year period. LoBue and a number of other employees were notified that they had been tentatively chosen to be recipients of non-transferable stock options contingent upon their continued employment. LoBue's notice told him: "You may be assigned a greater or less amount of stock based entirely upon your individual results and that of the entire organization." About 6 months later he was notified that he had been definitely awarded an option to buy 150 shares of stock in recognition of his "contribution and efforts in making the operation of the Company successful." As to future allotments he was told "It is up to you to justify your participation in the plan during the next two years."

LoBue's work was so satisfactory that the company in the course of 3 years delivered to him 3 stock options covering 340 shares. He exercised all these $5 per share options in 1946 and in 1947, paying the company only $1,700 for stock having a market value when delivered of $9,930. Thus, at the end of these transactions, LoBue's employer was worth $8,230 less to its stockholders and LoBue was worth $8,230 more than before. The company deducted this sum as an expense in its 1946 and 1947 tax returns but LoBue did not report any part of it as income. Viewing the gain to LoBue as compensation for personal services the Commissioner levied a deficiency assessment against him, relying on § [61] * * *.

LoBue petitioned the Tax Court to redetermine the deficiency, urging that "The said options were not intended by the Corporation or the petitioner to constitute additional compensation but were granted to permit the petitioner to acquire a proprietary interest in the Corporation and to provide him with the interest in the successful operation of the Corporation deriving from an ownership interest." The Tax Court held that LoBue had a taxable gain if the options were intended as compensation but not if the options were designed to provide him with "a proprietary interest in the business." Finding after hearings that the options were granted to give LoBue "a proprietary interest in the corporation, and not as compensation for services" the Tax Court held for LoBue. 22 T.C. 440, 443. Relying on this finding the Court of Appeals affirmed, saying: "This was a factual issue which it was the peculiar responsibility of the Tax Court to resolve. From our examination of the evidence we cannot say that its finding was clearly erroneous." 3 Cir., 223 F.2d 367, 371. Disputes over the taxability of stock option transactions such as this are longstanding. We granted certiorari to consider whether the Tax Court and the Court of Appeals had given § [61] too narrow an interpretation. 350 U.S. 893.

We have repeatedly held that in defining "gross income" as broadly as it did in § [61] Congress intended to "tax all gains except those specifically exempted." See, e.g., Commissioner of Internal Revenue v. Glenshaw Glass Co., 348 U.S. 426, 429–430. The only exemption Congress provided from this very comprehensive definition of taxable income that could possibly have application here is the gift exemption of § [102]. But there was not the slightest indication of the kind of detached and disinterested generosity which might evidence a "gift" in the statutory sense. These transfers of stock bore none of the earmarks of a gift. They were made by a company engaged in operating a business for profit, and the Tax Court found that the stock option plan was designed to achieve more profitable operations by providing the employees "with an incentive to promote the growth of the company by permitting them to participate in its success." 22 T.C. at page 445. Under these circumstances the Tax Court and the Court of Appeals properly refrained from treating this transfer as a gift. The company was not giving something away for nothing.

Since the employer's transfer of stock to its employee LoBue for much less than the stock's value was not a gift, it seems impossible to say that it was not compensation. The Tax Court held there was no taxable income, however, on the ground that one purpose of the employer was to confer a "proprietary interest." But there is not a word in § [61] which indicates that its broad coverage should be narrowed because of an employer's intention to enlist more efficient service from his employees by making them part proprietors of his business. In our view there is no statutory basis for the test established by the courts below. When assets are transferred by an employer to an employee to secure better services they are plainly compensation. It makes no difference that the compensation is paid in stock rather than in money. Section [61] taxes income derived from compensation "in whatever form paid." And in another stock option case we said that § [61] "is broad enough to include in taxable income any economic or financial benefit conferred on the employee as compensation, whatever the form or mode by which it is effected." Commissioner of Internal Revenue v. Smith, 324 U.S. 177, 181. LoBue received a very substantial economic and financial benefit from his employer prompted by the employer's desire to get better work from him. This is "compensation for personal service" within the meaning of § [61].

LoBue nonetheless argues that we should treat this transaction as a mere purchase of a proprietary interest on which no taxable gain was "realized" in the year of purchase. It is true that our taxing system has ordinarily treated an arm's length purchase of property even at a bargain price as giving rise to no taxable gain in the year of purchase. See Palmer v. Commissioner of Internal Revenue, 302 U.S. 63, 69. But that is not to say that when a transfer which is in reality compensation is given the form of a purchase the Government cannot tax the gain under § [61]. The transaction here was unlike a mere purchase. It was not an arm's length transaction between strangers. Instead it was an arrangement by which an employer transferred valuable property to his employees in recognition of their services. We hold that LoBue realized taxable gain when he purchased the stock.

A question remains as to the time when the gain on the shares should be measured. LoBue gave his employer promissory notes for the option price of the first 300 shares but the shares were not delivered until the notes were paid in cash. The market value of the shares was lower when the notes were given than when the cash was paid. The Commissioner measured the taxable gain by the market value of the shares when the cash was paid. LoBue contends that this was wrong, and that the gain should be measured either when the options were granted or when the notes were given.

It is of course possible for the recipient of a stock option to realize an immediate taxable gain. See Commissioner of Internal Revenue v. Smith, 324 U.S. 177, 181–182. The option might have a readily ascertainable market value and the recipient might be free to sell his option. But this is not such a case. These three options were not transferable and LoBue's right to buy stock under them was contingent upon his remaining an employee of the company until they were exercised. Moreover, the uniform Treasury practice since 1923 has been to measure the compensation to employees given stock options subject to contingencies of this sort by the difference between the option price and the market value of the shares at the time the option is exercised. * * *

It is possible that a bona fide delivery of a binding promissory note could mark the completion of the stock purchase and that gain should be measured as of that date. Since neither the Tax Court nor the Court of Appeals passed on this question the judgment is reversed and the case is remanded to the Court of Appeals with instructions to remand the case to the Tax Court for further proceedings.

Reversed and remanded.

Mr. Justice Frankfurter and Mr. Justice Clark, concurring.

[Omitted.]

Mr. Justice Harlan, whom Mr. Justice Burton joins, concurring in part and dissenting in part.

In my view, the taxable event was the grant of each option, not its exercise. When the respondent received an unconditional option to buy stock at less than the market price, he received an asset of substantial and immediately realizable value, at least equal to the then-existing spread between the option price and the market price. It was at that time that the corporation conferred a benefit upon him. At the exercise of the option, the corporation "gave" the respondent nothing; it simply satisfied a previously-created legal obligation. That transaction, by which the respondent merely converted his asset from an option into stock, should be of no consequence for tax purposes. The option should be taxable as income when given, and any subsequent gain through appreciation of the stock, whether realized by sale of the option, if transferable, or by sale of the stock acquired by its exercise, is attributable to the sale of a capital asset and, if the other requirements are satisfied, should be taxed as a capital gain. Any other result makes the division of the total gains between ordinary income (compensation) and capital gain (sale of an asset) dependent solely upon the fortuitous circumstance of when the employee exercises his option.

* * *

Problems, Notes and Questions

1. *Section 83.* Although § 83 applies to all cases of property transferred for services, its most difficult applications involve cases in which the taxpayer's rights to the property are subject to forfeiture. As in *LoBue*, officers or directors of corporate firms often receive part of their compensation in the form of stock (or options to purchase stock) in the firm. From the firm's viewpoint, the use of stock as compensation may more effectively harness the energies of management in making the firm profitable (and its stock price rise) because the managers share in the increased value of the firm through their stock ownership. The stock can also aid the firm in retaining a valued manager if it requires the manager to forfeit the property upon leaving the firm within some specified period of time. For instance, a firm might transfer stock to an officer, but require that she surrender the stock to the firm if she leaves her employment within the following five years. The possibility that the employee would have to forfeit the stock if she does not remain with the employer for five years diminishes the value of the stock to the manager. After all, who would pay the manager much for a share of stock that the buyer would have to forfeit if the manager left her job at any time in the next five years?

In 1969, Congress enacted § 83 to revise and clarify the tax treatment of compensatory grants of property. Notice how the provision synchronizes the timing and amount of the employee's income inclusion with the employer's business-expense deduction (§§ 83(a) and (h)).

2. *Problems.*

(1) On July 1, year 1, *E* receives, as compensation for services, stock of her employer, *X* Corporation. She must return the stock to *X* if she ceases to work for *X* before June 30, year 5. The restriction is noted on the stock certificate and is binding on any transferee. *E* may, however, transfer the stock (subject to the restrictions) by gift or sale. The stock is worth $50,000 on July 1, year 1, and $80,000 on June 30, year 5.

(a) E continues to work for X through June 30, year 5. E sells the stock on August 15, year 6, for $100,000. What result to E and X? See §§ 83(a), (c), and (h).

(b) Same as in (a), except that E makes a timely election under § 83(b).

(c) E makes a timely election under § 83(b), but resigns from X in year 2 and forfeits the stock. What result to E and X?

(d) Same as in (a), except that E sells the stock to F for $20,000 in year 2 and F sells the stock for $100,000 in year 6. What result to E, X, and F? See Treas.Reg. §§ 1.83–1(b) & (c).

(e) Same as in (a), except that the forfeiture will occur only if E is fired for cause. Treas.Reg. § 1.83–3(c)(2).

(2) A retiring employee is allowed to buy stock for $10,000. Stock of the same class sells on the market for $30,000. The employee or any transferee will forfeit the stock if the employee competes with the employer within the next five years. When does the employee have income? What more do you need to know? See Treas.Reg. § 1.83–3(c)(2).

(3) What result on the facts of *LoBue* under § 83? See § 83(e) and Treas.Reg. § 1.83–7.

3. *Options.* Suppose an employer's stock is actively traded on an established securities market at $50 a share. As compensation for services, an employee is given a non-forfeitable option to buy the stock at any time within the next two years at $45 a share. Such options are not actively traded on any established market. Why is it wrong to say that the option is worth exactly $5 a share? (Would an option to buy stock selling at $50 for $50 be worthless?) Must the employee attempt to value the option and include that value in income? See § 83(e)(3) and Treas. Reg. § 1.83–7(b).

There is no general rule of non-taxability for property lacking a "readily ascertainable" value. If an employee receives non-forfeitable stock of a closely held corporation as compensation for services, the stock must be valued and the value included in income even though stock that is not actively traded is very hard to value. Why does the rule for options (§ 83(e)(3)) differ from the rule for other kinds of property?

4. *The employer's deduction.* Most options are non-qualified stock options ("NQSOs"), as distinguished from the incentive stock options ("ISOs") discussed below. One reason for the popularity of options is that neither the grant nor the exercise of the option results in an expense for financial-accounting purposes. Yet, § 83(h) allows the employer to deduct the excess of the value of the stock over the exercise price of an NQSO. (This excess is called the "spread.") With the increasing popularity of NQSOs, and large increases in stock prices over the last decade, the tax deduction enables some large firms virtually to eliminate their tax liability without "booking" any compensation expense in reporting to shareholders. See Sullivan, Let the Good Times Roll: Options and Tax-free Profits, 87 Tax Notes 1185 (2000).

For an argument that the stock option is nevertheless an overly expensive way to compensate employees, see Johnson, Stock Compensation: The Most Expensive Way to Pay Future Cash, 85 Tax Notes, 351 (1999).

A divided Tax Court has held that the employer's deduction depends upon the employee's actually *including* the compensation in gross income; *includability* without inclusion is not enough; Venture Funding Ltd. v. Commissioner, 110 T.C. 236 (1998), affirmed 198 F.3d 248 (6th Cir. 1999), cert. denied 530 U.S. 1205 (2000).

5. *Incentive stock options.* From time to time, Congress has created tax incentives to encourage corporations to transfer stock to key employees. The current version is § 422, under which corporate employers may grant ISOs to employees. Neither the grant nor the exercise of an ISO is taxable to the employee. Therefore, if an employee receives an ISO allowing the purchase of employer stock for $50 a share and exercises the option when the stock has a value of $80 a share, the employee has no income, even if the employee's rights to the stock are vested. (Notice that this is the treatment Mr. LoBue argued for even before the enactment of § 422.)

At first glance, ISOs may appear to be superior to NQSOs because employees can receive unrestricted stock without becoming liable for income tax. However, the employer which sells stock to an employee who exercises an ISO cannot deduct the difference between the stock's value and the price the employee pays. (As noted above, employers which award stock taxable under § 83 can deduct the spread.) Therefore, the tax benefit (non-taxability) of ISOs to employees is offset by a tax detriment (non-deductibility) to employers. If an employer corporation faces a higher tax rate than its employees, the non-deductibility of compensation in the form of ISOs will cost the employer more in taxes than the employees gain by their tax exemption.

INCOME AND BASIS WHEN PROPERTY
IS RECEIVED FOR SERVICES

If *A* does some work for *B* and receives a $30,000 car as compensation, § 83(a) requires *A* to include $30,000 in gross income. This result is hardly surprising; it simply treats this case as being equivalent to one in which *A* was paid $30,000 in cash and used the cash to buy the car.

What happens if *A* then turns around and sells the car to *C* for $30,000? Under § 1001(b), *A*'s "amount realized" on selling the car to *C* for $30,000 is $30,000 (the amount of cash received). Whether *A* realizes gain on the sale depends upon *A*'s basis for the car. The only Code provision that purports to tell us *A*'s basis is § 1012, which says that property's basis is its "cost." But A has not paid any money for the car. Does it follow that *A*'s basis is zero? In the long run, *A* has done some work and ended up with $30,000 in cash, so A's total income must be $30,000. This, in turn, means that A's gain on selling the car to C must be zero. So, if A's gain on that sale is to be zero—the only answer that makes sense—A's basis for the car must have been $30,000. This is where some creative reading of the statute becomes essential. On these facts, A's "cost basis" has to be the $30,000 of income A recognized on receiving the car, not the amount of money (zero) A paid for the car. Again, we treat A as having received $30,000 of cash as compensation from B and used the $30,000 to purchase the car, thus obtaining a $30,000 basis.

In order to make clear that the word "cost" in § 1012 is a term of art, tax lawyers sometimes say that basis under that section is the "tax cost" of property. On the important principle that statutory language will not be given its "plain meaning" when doing so would produce results which are "absurd" or "plainly at variance with the policy of the legislation as a whole," see United States v. American Trucking Ass'ns, 310 U.S. 534, 543 (1940), rehearing denied 311 U.S. 724 (1940).

It is important to grasp that the taxpayer's basis for property received as compensation *does not* arise because the taxpayer "invested" $30,000 of his labor in earning the property. We cannot say that the taxpayer who gets a $30,000 car for performing services has a $30,000 basis for the car because the taxpayer "paid" $30,000 worth of work for the car: that argument would prove too much. The cost basis of § 1012 cannot include the value of the taxpayer's labor, which economists refer to as opportunity cost. A lawyer who charges a client $1000 to draft a will cannot offset against that amount the $800 the lawyer could have earned in her next-best income-earning opportunity. The lawyer was not required to include in her income the $800 of opportunity cost, and she therefore gets no basis credit for that amount. If taxpayers could obtain basis for their opportunity costs, little personal-service income would be taxable.

Problems and Note

1. *Problems.*

(1) A lawyer, who normally earns $100,000 a year, takes a one-year leave of absence without pay from her firm and uses the time to write a novel. By the end of the year she has finished the book, and at that time she sells all of her rights to the book to a publisher for $300,000. What is her gross income from the sale?

(2) A boatbuilder buys materials for $40,000 and builds a boat. The boatbuilder puts in his own labor, which has a market value of $20,000 in the sense that the builder would have earned that much if he had worked at his regular job instead of building the boat. He then sells the boat for $75,000. How much gain does the boatbuilder recognize on the sale?

(3) A and C are lawyers. Each performs work for a client and bills the client for $10,000. A uses the accrual method of accounting, and C

uses the cash method. If, before their clients pay, both *A* and *C* sell their "accounts receivable" (their rights to payment) for $10,000, how much gain or loss does each recognize upon the sale? (To put the same question in a somewhat different way, what were the bases of *A* and *C* in the accounts receivable they acquired upon billing their clients?)

2. *Reference.* Brown, The Growing "Common Law" of Taxation, 1961 U.So.Cal. Tax Inst. 1.

STATE–LAW DETERMINATIONS IN FEDERAL TAX CASES

Note that the determination of whether a taxpayer's rights to property are forfeitable or transferable depends upon the taxpayer's rights under non-tax law (in this case, the law of contracts and, perhaps, the law of securities regulation). What if a tax question turns upon a state-law matter and the law of the state is not clear? The Supreme Court has held that the court, in deciding the tax issue, should determine how the highest court of the state would rule. A decision of a state court other than the state's highest court is not controlling, even if the decision was reached in litigation involving the taxpayer and binds that taxpayer; Commissioner v. Estate of Bosch, 387 U.S. 456 (1967). However, an erroneous decision may have the effect of changing the taxpayer's rights when the decision becomes final; if it does, the change may affect tax liability.

As an example of the way in which even an erroneous decision by a state court can affect tax liability, consider a taxpayer who owns an income interest in a trust. Each year, the taxpayer receives and is taxed on $10,000. The taxpayer decides to assign this interest to her son, and in 2002 she executes documents purporting to do that. Let us suppose that this assignment is invalid under the state law, though this invalidity is not completely clear. Because of doubts about whether the assignment to her son was valid, the taxpayer seeks a decision on the matter from the local probate court. That court holds, incorrectly, that the assignment was valid, and its decision becomes final (that is, not appealable and not subject to collateral attack) in 2004. Who is taxable on the income in question? For 2002 and 2003, the taxpayer, not her son, must pay tax on the $10,000. The taxpayer was the owner of the interest, under state law, and the probate court's decision does not affect that conclusion because that decision was wrong. However, income paid by the trust after the probate court's decision became final is taxable to the son. Although the court's decision was based on a misunderstanding of state law, it effected a real change in the ownership of the interest in the trust. In other words, under state law as a court which made no mistakes would see it, the son became the owner of the interest in 2004, as a result of the probate court's erroneous decision, not in 2002. What the probate court *said* doesn't matter under *Estate of Bosch*. What the probate court *did* does matter, because its action transferred ownership of the interest from the mother to the son.

Problem

F, an employee of *Z* Corp., received stock of *Z* as compensation for services in year 1. Under a valid provision of *F*'s employment contract, *F*'s rights were forfeitable if he stopped working for *Z* Corp. before year 5. In a declaratory-judgment action brought by *F* against *Z* Corp., a state trial court erroneously held the forfeiture provision void. *Z* Corp. did not appeal, and the decision became binding on *F* and *Z* Corp. in year 2.

> (1) Does the trial court's erroneous (but now final) decision mean that *F* had income in year 1?

> (2) If not, when does *F* have income? If he quits his job before year 5 does he avoid income recognition altogether?

(c) Deferred Compensation: An Introduction to the Time–Value of Money

The question of *when* an income or deduction item should be taken into account in computing taxable income can be as important as the question whether a receipt is taxable or an expenditure deductible. Sometimes the importance of timing results from more-or-less accidental consequences of reporting income on a periodic basis. For example, a taxpayer may have a large deduction which will be wasted unless income is reported for the same period as the deduction, or tax rates may differ from one year to the next, or an income or deduction item may have been properly reportable in a year now closed by the statute of limitations. Even if none of these effects applies in a particular case, timing matters because tax liability now is more burdensome to the taxpayer than an equal dollar amount of liability later.

A dollar received today is usually worth more than a dollar to be received a year from now. This is because someone who receives a dollar today can invest it. If you can get a safe after-tax return of 10 percent (compounded annually) on your investments, you should prefer getting any amount over $1.00 today to getting $1.10 in one year. This principle underlies the "Present Value of One Dollar" table in Appendix A: the "present value" of one dollar to be received at some future time is the amount of money that would have to be invested today to generate a total of $1.00 (initial investment plus accumulated interest) at the end of the time period in question. For example, if the appropriate interest rate is 10 percent, compounded annually, the present value of $1.00 to be received five years from now is $.62, because an investment of $.62 at a return of 10 percent, compounded annually, will grow to $1.00 in five years.

Taxpayers can often take advantage of the time-value of money by arranging their affairs so as to postpone tax liability. Suppose, for example, that you would normally become liable for $1000 in income tax this year, and that you have an opportunity to put off this tax payment for nine years (without becoming liable for interest). If you can get a yearly after-tax return on your investment of 8 percent, compounded annually, this postponement would be worth as much to you as a forgiveness of half your liability: if you invest $500 at 8 percent, that investment will grow to $1000 in nine years. See Appendix A. Therefore, you should prefer a nine-year delay of your tax payment to a 49–percent (or smaller) reduction in your taxes without a delay. Note, though, that postponing your taxes while postponing the receipt of the economic benefit of your income-producing activities may accomplish nothing: the advantage of paying taxes later may be more than offset by the disadvantages of delaying the receipt of cash. Receiving $10,000 in cash, subject to a 30–percent tax, this year is better than receiving the same amount of cash, taxable at the same rate, a year from now. The objective of tax planning based on deferral is usually to delay taxes without delaying economic gains.

TAX–FAVORED SAVINGS

Because an income tax applies both to a taxpayer's earnings from working and to that taxpayer's investment returns, it is sometimes said that the income tax imposes a "double tax" on those who save some of the money they earn. To illustrate, consider a worker who, if there were no income tax, would save $2000 of this year's salary, invest it for 20 years at a return of 10 percent per year, compounded annually, and then spend the accumulated savings on retirement, a college education for the worker's child, or a new house. Two thousand dollars invested today at 10 percent will grow to $13,455 in 20 years. How would a 30–percent income tax, imposed on both the initial earnings and the annual investment return, change the amount the taxpayer would be able to spend after 20 years? The tax will take 30 percent of the $2000 of earnings, leaving $1400 to be invested. Then, as the investment earns an annual return of 10 percent, the tax will take 30 percent of that, so the annual after-tax return will be seven percent. An investment of $1400 at seven percent for 20 years will grow to $5418. Therefore, a 30–percent income tax will have taken almost 60 percent of what the taxpayer could have accumulated with no tax.

To encourage savings, Congress has enacted a wide (and ever-changing) variety of tax-favored savings programs, most of which are available only to those who earn income by performing services (as opposed to those having only income from investments, such as dividends, interest, and rent). The details of these many programs are well beyond the scope of a basic tax course: working with tax-favored savings is a specialty in itself. The tax principles behind the plans are very simple, however. There are basically two forms of benefit: (1) the earnings of the plan are not taxed at all, or (2) the money contributed to the plan is not taxed when it is earned and the return on the plan's investments is not taxed as it accrues, but the original investment and all accumulated savings are taxed when they are withdrawn from the plan. We shall illustrate these benefits by describing the Roth IRA,[g] which provides benefits by permanently exempting the plan's earnings from taxation, and the traditional IRA, which defers tax on contributions and earnings until they are withdrawn from the plan.

Title to investments made through IRAs is held by a trustee or custodian (a bank, insurance company, or mutual fund), but this has no important effects on the taxpayer's rights. One can establish an IRA simply by making a payment to a bank or mutual fund, which will invest the funds as the taxpayer directs, typically in stocks, bonds, or both, and which will act as the trustee or custodian for a small annual fee.

Roth IRAs (§ 408A)

Most individual taxpayers whose modified adjusted gross incomes do not exceed $95,000 ($150,000 for married taxpayers filing jointly) may contribute up to $3000 annually to a Roth IRA. The amount of the contribution is limited to the taxpayer's earned income, however. The $3000 contribution limit is phased out for taxpayers whose modified AGIs exceed the statutory threshold. Higher contribution limits apply to taxpayers over age 49. (The dollar figures are for the year 2002; they are scheduled to increase after that.)

Contributions to a Roth IRA are not deductible. But if the taxpayer takes only "qualified distributions" from the plan, the earnings of the plan are never taxed. Distributions from a Roth IRA made within the five-year period beginning with the taxpayer's *first* contribution to the Roth IRA cannot be qualified distributions; distributions after that time are qualified if they are made after the taxpayer reaches age 59½, or after the taxpayer's death, or because the taxpayer is disabled, or (up to $10,000) in connection with the purchase of the taxpayer's first home.

Consider our earlier example of a 30–percent taxpayer who, if there were no tax, would earn and save $2000, investing the savings for 20 years at 10 percent. If we assume that this taxpayer invests by contributing $1400 ($2000 less $600 in tax) to a Roth IRA, the investment will grow to $9418 in 20 years. At that time, if the taxpayer is over 59½ or is otherwise eligible to take a qualified distribution, the entire amount can be withdrawn without tax. Compare this result with that which would have obtained if the earnings had simply been invested: without the Roth IRA's tax exemption, the taxpayer would have accumulated only $5418 (after tax) by the end of the 20–year period.

Traditional IRAs (§ 219)

The eligibility rules for tax-favored contributions to and withdrawals from traditional IRAs resemble those for Roth IRAs, with two exceptions. First, withdrawals from traditional IRAs can be made without

---

g. "IRA" is short for "Individual Retirement Arrangement"(IRS Publication 590) or "Individual Retirement Account" (§ 408). The Code section that allows deductions for some contributions to IRAs is § 219, which uses the term "qualified retirement contributions," defined as including contributions to an "individual retirement plan." Section 7701(a)(37) defines "individual retirement plan" as an individual retirement account (§ 408(a)) or an individual retirement annuity (§ 408(b)).

losing tax benefits for a wider variety of purposes (including payment of some medical expenses and some educational costs for the taxpayer or the taxpayer's close relatives[h]). Second, the amount of modified AGI the taxpayer can have before losing eligibility for tax-favored contributions is considerably lower for traditional IRAs than for Roth IRAs, except for taxpayers who do not actively participate in their employers' tax-favored retirement plans: these taxpayers may make deductible contributions to traditional IRAs no matter how high their adjusted gross incomes.

Contributions to traditional IRAs are usually deductible, so money earned and contributed is not taxed at that time. Furthermore, the earnings of investments made through traditional IRAs are not taxed as they accumulate. Upon withdrawal, however, the original contributions and the earnings are fully taxable. (Withdrawals before the taxpayer reaches age 59½, or dies, or is disabled also trigger a 10–percent penalty tax unless made for one of the purposes listed in § 72(t).)

Because the contributions to and earnings of a traditional IRA are eventually subject to income tax, while the earnings of a Roth IRA are never taxed, the traditional IRA may seem at first glance to be inferior to the Roth IRA. This is an illusion, however. Consider again our 30–percent-bracket worker who has earned $2000 and plans to invest whatever is left after tax at 10 percent for 20 years. If the investment is made through a traditional IRA, the taxpayer's initial investment will be $2000 (as the investment is deductible, nothing need be kept back for taxes). In 20 years at 10 percent, this investment will grow to $13,455. If the taxpayer then withdraws the entire amount, the $13,455 withdrawal will be subject to a 30–percent income tax, leaving $9418 for the taxpayer to spend—exactly the same amount as if the taxpayer had used a Roth IRA. The traditional IRA's deferral of taxes on both the initial contributions and the annual earnings on those contributions yields the same tax benefit as the Roth IRA's forgiveness of taxes on the earnings (with no benefit for the initial contributions).[i]

If the taxpayer is subject to a lower marginal income-tax rate in the year of the contribution than in the year of withdrawal, the Roth IRA is better than the traditional IRA because the rate of tax applied to the initial contribution is lower than the rate that will be imposed at the end. Similarly, a traditional IRA is better than the Roth IRA (ignoring contribution limits) if the taxpayer expects to be in a lower marginal tax

h. Distributions from Roth IRAs for these purposes are taxable, but they do not trigger the special 10–percent penalty tax that normally attaches to distributions that are not qualified.

i. As the examples show, both kinds of tax benefit leave the taxpayer with the same amount of after-tax savings at the end if the tax rate for the year of the contribution is the same as the rate for the year of the withdrawal. A 30–percent tax, for instance, leaves the taxpayer with 70 percent of the amount that would have been accu-

mulated if there were no tax, whether the tax is imposed at the time of saving (as under a Roth IRA) or at the time of withdrawal (as under a traditional IRA). This happens because a reduction of the taxpayer's initial investment by 30 percent, with no further tax, means that the final accumulation will be 30 percent less than if no tax had ever been imposed—the same as if the 30–percent tax had been imposed only on the final accumulation.

bracket when funds are withdrawn than when funds are contributed. As a rule, therefore, the Roth IRA should be a better choice than the traditional IRA for younger workers. Furthermore, for taxpayers who can afford to set aside—for both contributions and taxes—more than the $3000 annual contribution limit, the Roth IRA in effect allows larger contributions. The $3000 limit in the case of a Roth IRA is an *after-tax* limit: a 30–percent taxpayer can earn $4286, pay $1286 in tax, and contribute the $3000 balance to a Roth IRA. The $3000 limit for a traditional IRA is a *pre-tax* limit: Someone who earns $4286 cannot use that entire amount in a traditional IRA to generate future funds and provide for the taxes that will eventually become due.

As a rule, the Roth IRA and the traditional IRA are alternatives. A taxpayer whose annual limit on IRA contributions is $3000 can contribute a total of $3000 to a Roth IRA, a regular IRA, or both. Taxpayers ineligible to make deductible contributions to traditional IRAs because they participate in employer plans and have adjusted gross incomes over the statutory limit can still contribute to traditional IRAs: although their contributions are not deductible, the earnings on contributions are not taxed until they are withdrawn.

Notes

1. *Other tax-favored savings plans.* Although we have used traditional IRAs and Roth IRAs to illustrate tax-favored savings, the real action (in terms of money) involves plans having much higher contribution limits and allowing contributions even for high-income taxpayers. Estimates of the total value of assets held by retirement plans range from $8 trillion to $10 trillion, as of 2001. Widely used forms of statutory deferred compensation include "qualified" pension and profit-sharing plans for employees and "Keogh plans," which are qualified plans for self-employed taxpayers (including partners, who are self-employed for tax purposes). A popular kind of qualified plan for employees is the "section 401(k) plan," which allows employees to make elective contributions (some employers will "match" all or part of an employee's contributions to a 401(k) plan). These plans confer benefits in the same way as traditional IRAs, but the limits on annual contributions are much higher. Earnings contributed to the plans are not taxed (sometimes by being excluded from the workers' incomes, sometimes by being deductible), earnings on contributions are not taxed as they accumulate, and withdrawals from the plans are taxable in full. Although employees are not taxed on the compensation that goes into these plans, the employer may deduct the compensation in full (contrast § 83(h)). These plans (like IRAs) are commonly called "retirement plans," but none of them requires the taxpayer to retire in order to get tax benefits; the rules for penalty-free withdrawals resemble those for IRAs.

Until 1982, the limits on deductible contributions to employee pension and profit-sharing plans were much more generous than the limits for Keogh plans. As a result, many doctors, dentists, and other professionals incorporated their businesses so that they could become employees of their corporations. Since 1982, there have been no significant differences between employee plans and Keogh plans.

2. Tax credit for IRA contributions and voluntary contributions to other retirement plans. For 2002 through 2006, § 25B gives many low-income taxpayers a non-refundable tax credit for contributions to IRAs and for voluntary contributions to some other retirement plans. For married couples filing joint returns, the credit can be as much as half of the first $2000 a year of contributions if the couple's modified AGI is $30,000 or less. So, in theory, a low-income couple contributing $2000 to an IRA can get a tax credit of $1000 for the contribution. However, many taxpayers with incomes that low will owe less than $1000 in income tax before taking the credit into account. As the credit is not refundable, any excess of the credit as calculated under § 25B over the pre-credit tax liability does the taxpayer no good. The credit is a smaller percentage of the first $2000 in contributions for couples with modified AGI over $30,000; no credit is allowed couples with modified AGI over $50,000. The AGI limits for most unmarried taxpayers are half those for couples.

3. Tax-free "rollovers." Suppose that an employee who participates in a qualified pension or profit-sharing plan retires, changes jobs, or is laid off. The employee may want to withdraw the funds from the employee plan so that the employee can direct future investments, and the employee who resigns or is laid off may have to withdraw the funds. Ordinarily, a distribution from the plan would trigger an income tax on the entire amount. Furthermore, if the employee is under age 59½, the 10–percent additional penalty tax on premature distributions may apply. However, if the funds are transferred to a traditional IRA (or to another qualified plan[j]) within 60 days,[k] the distribution is not taxable; § 402(c). Timing is of the essence: if the transfer to the IRA or other employer plan takes place 61 days after the distribution, the distribution is taxable in full unless the Service grants additional time, as it may in hardship cases.

As a rule, funds to be rolled over from one plan to another should be rolled over directly to the receiving plan, rather than being distributed to the taxpayer and then transferred. Advance planning is essential: once the worker receives a check from the employer's plan it is too late to make a direct rollover. If the rollover is not made directly from one plan to the other, the distribution is subject to a 20–percent withholding tax; § 3405(c). Because a completely tax-free rollover must consist of the entire amount of the distribution, the imposition of the withholding tax means that the taxpayer will have to come up with some other source of funds to avoid being taxed on part of the distribution. For example,

j. For instance, someone changing jobs may want to transfer funds from the former employer's plan to a plan maintained by the new employer. Not all plans will accept rollovers, however.

k. There are minor exceptions to the 60–day rule.

suppose that the employee's distribution from a qualified plan is $1 million, all of which would be includable in the employee's income if distributed and not rolled over. If the $1 million is transferred directly to the employee's IRA, no tax is owed. If it is paid to the employee, who then transfers the funds to the IRA, the withholding tax will take $200,000, so the employee will receive only $800,000 from the plan and will have to come up with $200,000 from some other source to reinvest the full $1 million to the IRA. (The withheld amount will be credited to the employee, who will therefore get it all back the next year, on filing a tax return for the year of the distribution. The problem created by the withholding tax is not that it takes $200,000 from the employee permanently, but that it may leave the employee with insufficient funds to effect a complete rollover. When that happens, the employee has income equal to the amount that was not rolled over, and the amount of money earning currently untaxed income in the employee's retirement plan is reduced.)

Rollovers from one traditional IRA to another are also tax free. Rollovers from one Roth IRA to another are allowed. Taxpayers with relatively low adjusted gross incomes may transfer funds from traditional IRAs to Roth IRAs without triggering the penalty tax on premature IRA distributions. These transfers will be taxable, but the Roth IRA rules will apply to the transferred funds and to the future earnings from those funds, which will not be taxed again when withdrawn from the Roth IRA. Transfers from a traditional IRA to a Roth IRA are particularly attractive for those whose incomes are temporarily very low. For example, someone who made deductible contributions to a traditional IRA while working, and who then stops working for a few years to attend law school, would be well advised to roll over the amounts in the traditional IRA to a Roth IRA during the low-bracket law-school years.

Some plans (including some IRAs) contain after-tax contributions, the distribution of which is not taxable to the recipient. Rollovers from plans containing after-tax contributions present special problems.

4. *Inalienability of employee plans and the special problem of divorce.* ERISA (see Note 5 below) requires pension and profit-sharing plans for employees to contain a provision making the employees' rights inalienable; among other things, this keeps employees' creditors from getting at their retirement benefits. There is an exception for divorce, and almost necessarily so: many middle- and even upper-income workers have few substantial assets other than their retirement plans. The court granting a divorce cannot simply award all or part of an employee's benefits to that employee's spouse, however. The state court must enter a decree that is a "qualified domestic relations order," or "QDRO," if the transfer is to be valid. Among other things, this means that divorcing couples cannot simply assign rights to benefits under pension or profit-sharing plans by agreement; a QDRO must be established by judicial decree. The details of this process are beyond the scope of the basic tax course. One still sees occasional examples of divorce courts that have not gotten the word, and which simply order one spouse to transfer an

interest in an employee plan to a spouse: this kind of order is not enforceable.

5. *Non-tax aspects of statutory deferred compensation.* In the past, some employees who had expected benefits from pension and profit-sharing plans received nothing because of inadequate funding, loss of benefits when employment ceased before rights became vested, and mismanagement of plan assets. The Employee Retirement Income Security Act of 1974 ("ERISA") established an extremely complicated set of rules regarding vesting, discrimination against low-wage employees, minimum funding requirements, government insurance, liability for mismanagement, and other matters. Deferred compensation has now become a major field of specialization for lawyers.

Investing for retirement by buying the stock of one's employer is usually a bad idea: if the employer's business turns bad, the employee risks not only the loss of a job but the loss of retirement savings as well. This lesson was recently learned the hard way by many Enron employees whose 401(k) plans were funded with Enron stock. One reform effected by ERISA was a limit on the investment of qualified plan assets in securities of the employer corporation. These limits do not apply to 401(k) plans, however, and employers often structure these plans to encourage investment in employer stock. Nor do the limits apply to employee stock ownership plans ("ESOPs"), as defined in § 4975(e)(7). Indeed, an ESOP is a qualified plan "designed to invest primarily in qualifying employer securities"; § 4975(e)(7). ESOPs, 401(k) plans containing heavy concentrations of employer stock, and "KSOPs" (401(k) plans combined with ESOPs) expose their employee-beneficiaries to the very risks that the general investment restrictions of ERISA were intended to prevent. The relaxation of the rules regarding transactions between plan and employer may, however, be useful to the employer and its principal shareholders. It is far from unusual for employee retirement plans to have as much as 80 percent of their investments in employer stock, a ratio that no investment advisor would recommend. (Few, if any, of the executives of these companies are so undiversified.) As this is written, Congress is preparing to hold hearings on the advisability of requiring 401(k) plans to allow employees to diversify their holdings. Thorough reform in this area would entail eliminating ESOPs, a prospect that seems unlikely.

The ESOP concept was invented by Louis O. Kelso, an investment banker who wrote a book called "How to Turn Eighty Million Workers into Capitalists on Borrowed Money." Mr. Kelso's opinion that ESOPs would lead to the "creation" of vast amounts of capital seems to have had some influence on Senator Russell Long, who was Chairman of the Senate Finance Committee when the first ESOP provisions were enacted. Senator Long retired many years ago, but ESOPs continue to thrive; indeed, they now qualify for more generous tax treatment than standard pension plans. See generally Doernberg & Macey, ESOPs and Economic Distortion, 23 Harv.J. on Legis. 103 (1986); Carlson, ESOP and Universal Capitalism, 31 Tax L.Rev. 289 (1976).

6. *Tax-favored savings for education.* Taxpayers who establish "Coverdell education savings accounts" ("education IRAs") may contribute up to $2000 a year (subject to the usual sort of phaseout for taxpayers with high AGIs). These accounts closely resemble Roth IRAs: contributions are not deductible, but the earnings are never taxed if they do not exceed the amount of "qualified education expenses" of the account's beneficiary in the year of withdrawal. Except for beneficiaries with "special needs," contributions cannot be made after the beneficiary turns 18. The details can be found in § 530.

Section 529 authorizes "qualified tuition programs," called "QTPs" or "section 529 plans." These programs, which can be established by state agencies and by colleges, receive non-deductible contributions, typically from parents who expect their children to attend college. Earnings on the contributions are never taxed if used for "qualified higher education expenses." Plans established by colleges must take the form of prepayments of tuition: for example, a parent could pay $2000 today to purchase a semester's worth of tuition (expected to cost perhaps $10,000) for some future year. State plans (the only kind allowed until 2002) are not limited in this way: in effect, they resemble Coverdell education savings accounts except that tax-free distributions may be made only for "higher education expenses" (Coverdell accounts can be used for elementary and secondary education expenses, as well as for college costs). There are no dollar limits on contributions to QTPs, nor is eligibility limited to those with relatively low adjusted gross incomes.

7. *Reference.* Kaplan, The Curious Evolution of Individual Retirement Accounts, 87 Tax Notes 671 (2000); Halperin, Retirement Security and Tax Equity: An Evaluation of ERISA, 17 B.C.Ind. & Comm.L.Rev. 739 (1976).

NON–QUALIFIED DEFERRED COMPENSATION

If a 50–percent–bracket employer pays a cash salary to a 50–percent–bracket employee, the transaction neither generates nor reduces income-tax revenues if the employer can deduct the payments. Whatever tax the government gets from the employee is exactly offset by the tax saved by the employer. But suppose the employer can get a deduction today for a payment that will be taxable to the employee only in the future. In that case, the payment costs the government money because the employer's deduction today benefits the employer by more than the employee's delayed tax costs the employee. If the ordinary rules of tax accounting were allowed to operate, it would be easy to generate a "tax float" in the case of payments for services. An accrual-method employer's promise to pay $100,000 in five years to a cash-method employee would give the employer a $50,000 tax saving today, at a cost (to the employee) of $50,000 in tax five years from now.

In extreme cases, the tax benefit of deferred-compensation transactions could outweigh the non-tax cost of paying compensation. Suppose, for instance, that a 50–percent–bracket employer which can get a 7–percent after-tax return (compounded semi-annually) were to incur a binding obligation to pay a cash-method employee $100,000 in 20 years. The employer's deduction would save it $50,000 in taxes in the year in which the employer made the promise. This amount, invested for 20 years, would grow to $197,962.99. At that time, the employer could pay the employee $100,000 and pocket $97,962.99. The employee would have $50,000 after tax. The overall result is more favorable to the employer (and to the employee) than if the employee had agreed to work for nothing. Note, too, that if the employer had agreed to pay the employee $200,000, rather than $100,000, the employer would have made an additional $97,962.99 from the tax system. This kind of situation would, among other things, take a lot of the fun out of bargaining.

Two provisions of the Code limit abuses of the kind described above. If the employer and employee are "related" (as defined in § 267(b)), the employer's deduction is allowable only when the payment is includable in the employee's income; § 267(a)(2). And even if the employer and employee are not "related," § 404(a)(5) will deny the employer a deduction until the taxable year in which the employee has income if the compensation is "paid or accrued under a [non-qualified] plan deferring the receipt of such compensation."

"Matching" rules like those of § 267(a) and § 404(a)(5) take the tax profit out of non-qualified deferred-compensation arrangements if the employer's tax bracket equals or exceeds that of the employee. (Note that the benefit of *qualified* plans depends upon the employer's getting a deduction upon making a payment under the plan, while the employee's tax is deferred until withdrawal.) But if the employer pays no income tax—if, for example, it is a tax-exempt organization—deferral of the employer's deduction imposes no tax detriment to offset the employee's tax benefit. Suppose, for example, that a university employee would like to invest $5000 of next year's salary for 10 years. If the going rate of return on investments is 10 percent, compounded semi-annually, the employee would be better off after tax (and the employer no worse off) if the university agreed to pay $13,266.49 in 10 years than if it paid $5000 today. In effect, if $5000 of the salary is left in the university's hands for 10 years, the employee's $5000 can grow at a tax-free rate of interest, while an investment by the employee would increase in value at an after-tax interest rate.

Section 457 limits the tax advantages of non-qualified deferred-compensation plans in the case of employees of states (and their political subdivisions or agencies) and of other tax-exempt organizations. Unless the plan for deferring compensation is an "eligible deferred compensation plan," employees of these organizations must include compensation in their incomes as soon as their rights are vested (i.e., not subject to substantial risk of forfeiture). Generally speaking, an "eligible deferred compensation plan" must limit each employee's annual deferred compensation to the lesser of total compensation or $11,000 in 2002 and increasing annually to $15,000 in 2006.

Problem and Notes

1. *Statutory approaches to time-value-of-money problems.* Congress often confers tax benefits by allowing taxpayers to take advantage of the time-value of money. The qualified pension and profit-sharing provisions illustrate this technique: Congress has encouraged employers to set up these plans by providing benefits in the form of tax deferral. Politically, it may sometimes be easier to enact benefits in the form of deferral than to enact benefits of equal value in the form of exemptions: recognizing and evaluating the advantages of deferral requires some sophistication, while the benefits of exemption are obvious to everyone.

In recent years, much tax legislation has been aimed at preventing taxpayers from using deferral to obtain unintended tax benefits. Section 457 is one example; others will be examined elsewhere in this book.

2. *Problem. D* and her employer enter into a contract under which the employer will pay *D* in year 2 for services which *D* will perform in year 1. *D* uses the cash method of accounting; the employer (who can deduct *D*'s compensation as a business expense) uses the accrual method. When does *D* have income and when does the employer take a deduction for *D*'s salary? See §§ 446(c) and 451(a) and Treas.Reg. §§ 1.446–1(c)(1)(i) and (ii); 1.451–1(a); 1.451–2; 1.461–1(a)(1) and (2). Note § 404(a)(5).

3. *Reference.* Halperin, Interest in Disguise: Taxing the "Time Value of Money," 95 Yale L.J. 506 (1986).

(d) Fringe Benefits

ADAMS v. UNITED STATES

United States Court of Claims, 1978.
585 F.2d 1060.

Before COWEN, SENIOR JUDGE, DAVIS and BENNETT, JUDGES.

PER CURIAM: The issue * * * is whether the fair rental value of a Japanese residence furnished the plaintiffs by the employer of plaintiff Faneuil Adams, Jr., is excludable from their gross income under § 119.

* * *

[Adams was president of Mobil Sekiyu Kabushiki Kaisha ("Sekiyu"), a subsidiary of Mobil Oil Corporation. Under a policy designed to prevent its overseas employees from suffering a hardship from overseas service, Sekiyu furnished Adams with a house in Tokyo, with a rental value of $20,000 for 1970 and $20,599.90 for 1971. Sekiyu subtracted from Adams' salary the amounts of $4,439 for 1970 and $4,824 for 1971, its estimates of the average housing cost in the United States of a person "similarly situated" to Adams. Adams reported as income the amounts subtracted from his salary. The government contended that the entire rental value of the house was includable in income.]

Plaintiff contends that the fair rental value of the residence supplied to him by Sekiyu in 1970 and 1971 is excludable from his gross income because of Section 119. Alternatively, plaintiff asserts that the excess of the fair rental value of the residence over the U.S. Housing Element amount represented a benefit to his employer and not a benefit to him, and therefore is not gross income to him. Finally, plaintiff contends that even if the fair rental value of the residence is income to him, it should be measured by the amount plaintiff would have spent for housing in the United States, rather than the fair rental value in Japan. Because we hold that the conditions of Section 119 and the Regulations promulgated thereunder have been met, we do not address the other arguments of plaintiff.

Section 119 provides in part:

There shall be excluded from gross income of an employee the value of any meals or lodging furnished to him by his employer for the convenience of the employer, but only if—

* * *

(2) in the case of lodging, the employee is required to accept such lodging on the business premises of his employer as a condition of his employment.

Thus, in order to qualify for the exclusion of Section 119, each of three tests must be met:

(1) the employee must be required to accept the lodging as a condition of his employment;

(2) the lodging must be furnished for the convenience of the employer; and

(3) the lodging must be on the business premises of the employer. [Treas.Reg. § 1.119–1(b).]

The Regulations further provide that the first test is met where the employee is "required to accept the lodging in order to enable him properly to perform the duties of his employment." Id.

It is clear that the first requirement of the statute has been met because the plaintiff was explicitly required to accept the residence provided by Sekiyu as a condition of his employment as president of the company. Sekiyu's goal was twofold: first, it wanted to insure that its president resided in housing of sufficiently dignified surroundings to promote his effectiveness within the Japanese business community. Secondly, Sekiyu wished to provide its president with facilities which were sufficient for the conduct of certain necessary business activities at home. Since at least 1954 Sekiyu had required that its chief executive officer reside in the residence provided to plaintiff, as a condition to appointment as president.

With respect to this first test of Section 119, then, this case is as compelling as United States Junior Chamber of Commerce v. United States, 334 F.2d 660 (1964). In that case, the court found that it was not necessary for the taxpayer-president to reside in the Chamber's "White House" during his term of office so long as he lived in the Tulsa area. But, as a practical matter, for the convenience of his employer and as a condition of his tenure, the president was required to live there. Therefore, it was held that the "condition of employment" test was met. The court noted that the "condition of employment" test is met if

> due to the nature of the employer's business, a certain type of residence for the employee is required and that it would not be reasonable to suppose that the employee would normally have available such lodging for the use of his employer. 334 F.2d at 664.

Here, because the size and style of one's residence had an important effect upon the Japanese business community, a certain type of residence was both required by Mobil and Sekiyu for the plaintiff and necessary for the proper discharge of his duties in Sekiyu's best interests.

In contrast, the Tax Court in James H. McDonald, 66 T.C. 223 (1976), found that the taxpayer was not expressly required to accept his accommodations as a condition of his employment in Tokyo. Moreover, the court noted that the apartment provided to the taxpayer was not integrally related to the various facets of the employee's position. In the present case, plaintiff was required to accept the housing, and the residence was directly related to plaintiff's position as president, both in terms of physical facilities and psychic significance. It is held, therefore, that plaintiff was required to accept the lodging in order to enable him properly to perform the duties of his employment.

As to the "for the convenience of the employer" test, in United States Junior Chamber of Commerce v. United States, 334 F.2d at 663, the court stated,

> "There does not appear to be any substantial difference between the * * * 'convenience of the employer' test and the 'required as a condition of his employment' test."

Since it has already been determined that the condition of employment test has been satisfied, on that basis alone it could be held that the convenience of the employer test has also been met.

In James H. McDonald, supra, 66 T.C. at 230, the court stated that the convenience of the employer test is satisfied where there is a direct nexus between the housing furnished the employee and the business interests of the employer served thereby. In *McDonald,* the taxpayer was a principal officer of Gulf who was furnished an apartment by his employer which totalled only about 1,500 square feet of living space. The taxpayer was not required to live in the apartment, and it was found that the only benefit Gulf received in maintaining the apartment was the flexibility it afforded Gulf in personnel transfers. There was no prestige consideration. The court held that there was an insufficient nexus between the apartment and the employer's business interests to meet the convenience of the employer test requirements. * * * Here there was a sufficiently direct relationship between the housing furnished the plaintiff by Sekiyu and Sekiyu's business interests to meet the convenience of the employer test. The lodging had been built and was owned by Sekiyu. It was specially identified with the business of Sekiyu, for the house had served as the home of its presidents since at least 1954. If Sekiyu's president had not resided in housing comparable to that supplied plaintiff, Sekiyu's business would have been adversely affected. The house had been designed for this purpose to accommodate substantial business activities, and therefore further served Sekiyu's business interests.

Moreover, the fact that Sekiyu subsidized plaintiff's use of the house was also in its best business interests. Sekiyu was interested in attracting a qualified person as its chief executive officer. Because of the unusual housing situation in Tokyo during the years in question, a person would have had to pay up to four times his U.S. housing costs to obtain comparable housing in Tokyo. Certainly, such a factor would have been a strong deterrent to any qualified person's interest in Sekiyu's presidency, absent a housing subsidy from Sekiyu. Furthermore, it was clearly in Mobil–Sekiyu's best business interests to maintain an equitable compensation relationship between its domestic employees and its American foreign-based ones. The housing subsidy was designed to accomplish that.

That the plaintiff also incurred a benefit from this residence and that it was, in part, a convenience to him, does not disturb the conclusion. As noted in William I. Olkjer, 32 T.C. 464, 469 (1959):

> No doubt the facilities furnished benefited the employee also. The test which the statute provides, however, is that of convenience to the employer. There is no provision to the effect that the employee is to be deprived of his right to exclude from gross income the value of food and lodging otherwise excludable because he, too, is convenienced.

See also United States Junior Chamber of Commerce v. United States, 334 F.2d 660 (1964); George I. Stone, 32 T.C. 1021, 1025 (1959).

The third and final test is whether the lodging was on the business premises of the employer. Observe first that "[t]he operative framework of [the clause 'on the business premises'] is at best elusive and admittedly incapable of generating any hard and fast line." Jack B. Lindeman, 60 T.C. 609, 617 (1973) (Tannenwald, J., concurring). This question is largely a factual one requiring a common-sense approach. The statute should not be read literally. As noted by the Tax Court in *Lindeman,* supra, 60 T.C. at 614:

> [T]he statutory language ordinarily would not permit any exclusion for lodging furnished a domestic servant, since a servant's lodging is rarely furnished on "the business premises of his employer"; yet the committee report * * * shows a clear intention to allow the exclusion where the servant's lodging is furnished in the employer's home.

In the original version of the 1954 Code, as enacted in the House, the term that was used in Section 119 was "place of employment." The Senate changed the wording to "business premises", which was accepted by the House. However, the change was without substance, for the House Conference Report stated that "[t]he term 'business premises of the employer' is intended, in general, to have the same effect as the term 'place of employment' in the House bill." H.Conf.Rep. No. 2543, 83d Cong., 2d Sess. 27, reprinted in [1954] U.S.Code Cong. & Admin.News, pp. 5280, 5286. The pertinent Treasury regulation similarly provides that "business premises" generally refers to the place of employment of the employee. Treas.Reg. Sec. 1.119–1(c)(1). The phrase, then, is not to be limited to the business compound or headquarters of the employer. Rather, the emphasis must be upon the place where the employee's duties are to be performed. See Comm'r of Internal Revenue v. Anderson, 371 F.2d 59, 64 (6th Cir.1966), cert. denied 387 U.S. 906 (1967). * * *

* * *

Interpretations of the phrase which are limited to the geographic contiguity of the premises or to questions of the quantum of business activities on the premises are too restrictive. But see Comm'r of Internal Revenue v. Anderson, 371 F.2d 59 (6th Cir.1966). Rather, the statutory language "on the business premises of the employer" infers [sic] a functional rather than a spatial unity. In Rev.Rul. 75–540, 1975–2 Cum.Bull. 53, it was determined that the fair rental value of the official residence furnished a governor by the state is excludable from the governor's gross income under Section 119 of the Code. The Ruling noted that the business premises test was met because the residence provided by the state enabled the governor to carry out efficiently the administrative, ceremonial, and social duties required by his office. The governor's mansion, thus, served an important business function in that it was clearly identified with the business interests of the state. It was, in short, an inseparable adjunct. * * *

We take cognizance of the admonition of Judge Raum to avoid "strained or eccentric" interpretations of the phrase "on the business premises." Gordon S. Dole, 43 T.C. at 708 (Raum, J., concurring), aff'd per curiam, 351 F.2d 308 (1st Cir.1965). However, we are persuaded that where, as here, (1) the residence was built and owned by the employer, (2) it was designed, in part, to accommodate the business activities of the employer, (3) the employee was required to live in the residence, (4) there were many business activities for the employee to perform after normal working hours in his home because of the extensive nature of the employer's business and the high-ranking status of the employee, (5) the employee did perform business activities in the residence,[2] and (6) the residence served an important business function of the employer, then

---

2. In addition to the consistent use of the den for work purposes, and the official phone calls, plaintiff used the house for gatherings of his staff with mixed business and social purposes and also for more extended business entertainment.

the residence in question is a part of the business premises of the employer.

The three statutory requisites for exclusion are met. Accordingly, pursuant to Section 119, the fair rental value of the residence is excludable from plaintiff's gross income. Plaintiffs are entitled to recover, and the amount will be determined under Rule 131(c).

Problems, Notes and Questions

1. *"On the business premises of the employer."* With the Court of Claims' "functional" approach to the "business premises" test, compare Commissioner v. Anderson, 371 F.2d 59 (6th Cir.1966), in which the taxpayer, a motel manager, lived in a house "two short blocks" from the motel in order to be on call twenty-four hours a day. The Tax Court found this to be close enough and allowed the exclusion, but the Court of Appeals reversed, saying at 371 F.2d 67:

> To make "two short blocks" or nearness to other business property of the employer the test is to disregard the word "on" as contained in the phrase "on the business premises of the employer", thereby rendering uncertain that which is certain and requiring litigation in each case to determine what may be sufficiently near under the circumstances of the particular case. Had Congress so intended, it would appear that it could readily have used the words "in the vicinity of" or "nearby" or "close to" or "contiguous to" or similar language, rather than say *"on"* the business premises.

In Dole v. Commissioner, 43 T.C. 697 (1965), affirmed 351 F.2d 308 (1st Cir.1965), the Tax Court held that houses a mile from the employer's mill were not on the premises because they were neither "an integral part of the business property" nor "premises on which the company carries on some of its business activities"; 43 T.C. at 707. The First Circuit affirmed on the basis of Judge Raum's concurring opinion for the Tax Court, which disapproved of the "two short blocks" exception the Tax Court had created in *Anderson* (43 T.C. at 709):

> [I]f "two short blocks" are not fatal, it is easy to see how one might be tempted to enlarge the distance to the 1 mile involved herein, or, for that matter, 2 miles or 5 miles. The real difficulty is that neither the residence in *Anderson* nor any single residence involved herein is "on the business premises" of the employer.

Suppose a college provides its president with a house several miles from campus. The president uses the house for entertaining prospective donors and does a considerable amount of paperwork at home on nights and weekends. Is the value of the house excludable under *Adams*? Under *Anderson* and *Dole*? Would the president lose the exclusion on the ground that he was not required to live in the house if his predecessor, the owner of a more stately house than the official residence, had refused to live in the house furnished by the college?

2. *"For the convenience of the employer."* Until § 119 was enacted in 1954, cases like *Adams* were dealt with under the predecessor of § 61. Meals and lodging furnished "for the convenience of the employer" were excludable, while meals and lodging furnished "as compensation" were not. Suppose that, in order to keep a valued employee from defecting to a competitor, an employer gives the employee a $50,000 raise. Is the payment excludable because it was made "for the convenience of the employer"? Would the case be any different if the employer let the employee live in a $500,000 mansion instead of giving him a raise?

3. *Section 107.* Look at § 107. Is this provision more or less similar to § 119 except for the absence(?) of a "business premises" requirement, or is it a subsidy to religious organizations? Section 107 has given rise to some interpretive problems. Consider these:

(1) Is a rabbi a "minister"? A minister "of the *gospel*"? Why?[l]

(2) Suppose an ordained minister becomes president of an oil company in Japan and is given the use of a furnished apartment. Does § 107 make inquiries into the "business premises" and "convenience of the employer" questions unnecessary? Why not?

4. *Is § 119 a "loophole"?* The taxpayer in *Adams* did include in income the amount by which his salary was reduced to reflect the estimated amount he would have spent for housing in the United States. Nothing in § 119 requires this inclusion. Should it? Consider a "conundrum" of the German tax theorist Kleinwächter, reported in H. Simons, Personal Income Taxation 53 (1938):

> * * * We are asked to measure the relative incomes of an ordinary officer serving with his troops and a *Flügeladjutant* to the sovereign. Both receive the same nominal pay; but the latter receives quarters in the palace, food at the royal table, servants, and horses for sport. He accompanies the prince to theater and opera, and, in general, lives royally at no expense to himself and is able to save generously from his salary. But suppose, as one possible complication, that the *Flügeladjutant* detests opera and hunting.
>
> The problem is clearly hopeless. To neglect all compensation in kind is obviously inappropriate. On the other hand, to include the perquisites as a major addition to the salary implies that all income should be measured with regard for the relative pleasurableness of different activities—which would be the negation of measurement. There is hardly more reason for imputing additional income to the *Flügeladjutant* on account of his luxurious wardrobe than for bringing into account the prestige and social distinction of a (German) university professor. * * *

5. *Meals.* Treas.Reg. § 1.119–1(f) gives several examples of cases in which meals are treated as furnished "for the convenience of the employer." Treas.Reg. § 1.119–1(e) (first sentence), following a statement in the Senate report on § 119, limits the exclusion to meals

l. We are indebted to Harold Dubroff for this question.

furnished "in kind." Despite this regulation, three courts of appeals had held cash "meal allowances" paid state troopers while on patrol excludable under § 119. In Commissioner v. Kowalski, 434 U.S. 77 (1977), the Supreme Court held that § 119 "does not cover cash payments of any kind." The Court also held that the payments could not be excluded on the ground that they were not income within the meaning of § 61, since such an exclusion would make cash payments "more widely excluded from income than meals in kind, an extraordinary result given the * * * obvious intent of § 119 to narrow the circumstances in which meals could be excluded"; 434 U.S. at 94. The only tie between the "meal allowance" payment in *Kowalski* and meals actually eaten by the taxpayer was that the payments were *called* "meal allowances." They were payable without regard to the cost of meals eaten by the troopers; indeed, they were payable even if the troopers skipped lunch.

In each of the following problems, the employee is a waiter or waitress who receives a cash salary of $150 a week. The meals in question are eaten on the employer's business premises, and they are furnished "for a substantial non-compensatory business reason of the employer" as that phrase is used in Treas.Reg. § 1.119–1(a)(2). In each case, compute the employee's gross income for the week under §§ 61 and 119.

Problem (1). An employee eats five meals, worth $5.00 each. He is not charged for the meals.

Problem (2). An employee eats five meals, worth $5.00 each. The employer charges the employee $1.00 for each meal the employee eats; employees are not charged for meals they skip.

Problem (3). An employee eats four meals, worth $5.00 each; on Friday he skips lunch. The employer charges each employee $5.00 a week for meals; this charge is payable whether or not the employee eats the meals furnished.

6. *Supper money.* Suppose a lawyer who works evenings buys supper in a restaurant and charges the firm for the meal. The value of the meal is not excludable under § 119 because the meal was not furnished "in kind" and because it was not consumed on the employer's business premises. Nevertheless, a revenue ruling issued in 1920[m]—long before § 119 was adopted—allowed the exclusion of "supper money," and the Service did not view § 119 as repealing this exclusion. The extent to which the "supper money" exclusion survives the enactment of § 132 (below), which purports to codify the tax treatment of fringe benefits, is unclear. The legislative history of § 132 said that "occasional" supper money and other reimbursed costs of overtime work may be excluded as a "de minimis" fringe benefit. Treas.Reg. § 1.132–6(d)(2) attempts to give some content to the word "occasional."

---

m. O.D. 514, 2 C.B. 90 (1920).

In 1984, Congress attempted to codify the tax treatment of employee fringe benefits. Until then, some fringe benefits were expressly made non-taxable by statute and some were excluded by regulation, ruling, or unwritten administrative practice. Section 61 now provides that gross income includes fringe benefits except as otherwise provided. The most-general exclusion provision is § 132, which provides that gross income does not include the value of any of these seven kinds of fringe benefits:

(1) *No-additional-cost services,* as defined in § 132(b). An everyday example of a no-additional-cost service is an airline employee's being allowed to travel free on a standby basis. This exclusion does not apply to benefits furnished a highly compensated employee unless the benefits are available on a non-discriminatory basis to a group of employees defined "under a reasonable classification" that does not discriminate in favor of highly compensated employees; § 132(j)(1).

(2) *Qualified employee discounts,* defined in § 132(c). Like the "no-additional-cost services" exclusion, this fringe benefit is excludable by a highly compensated employee only if offered on a non-discriminatory basis. A qualified discount cannot exceed the employer's gross profit (in the case of goods) or 20 percent of the employer's normal price (in the case of services). Employee discounts qualify for the exclusion only if offered with respect to goods or services normally sold to customers by the employer. Discounts on real property or personal property "of a kind held for investment" do not qualify. Generally speaking, the exclusion is available only to employees who work in the "line of business" dealing with the goods or services in question.

(3) *Working condition fringes,* defined in § 132(d) as property or services provided an employee under circumstances in which the employee's cost would have been deductible had the employee paid for the item.

(4) *De minimis fringes,* a category meant to cover benefits so small as to make the administrative costs of including the benefits in income outweigh the advantages of taxation. Section 132(e)(2) provides for treatment of some eating facilities for employees as de minimis fringes.

(5) *Qualified transportation fringes,* defined in § 132(f). Parking for employees, up to a value of $175 a month (indexed), can be a qualified transportation fringe. Unlike most fringe benefits, parking for employees and most other qualified transportation fringes can take the form of cash payments to reimburse employees who incur costs. For example, an employee who pays $150 a month to park in a commercial garage may exclude employer reimbursements of the payments under § 132.

Many fringe benefits must be provided "in addition to" other compensation. In other words, the employee must not be able to chose between the fringe benefit and cash. However, employers may offer employees a choice between taxable compensation and qualified transportation fringes. Employees who choose cash will be taxed on that cash; employees who choose parking will not be taxed. This change was adopted in the hope that it would increase tax revenues and employee use of mass transit by encouraging some employees to choose taxable cash and take the bus to work.

(6) *Qualified moving expense reimbursements,* defined in § 132(g);

(7) *Qualified retirement planning services*, defined in § 132(m).

Section 132 also excludes from income the value of automobiles used by automobile salesmen (§ 132(h)(3)) and "on-premises gyms and other athletic facilities" (§ 132(h)(4)).

Problem

E works for an international airline. As an employee of the airline, she is entitled to the following fringe benefits. To what extent do the benefits result in gross income to *E?*

(1) *E* may fly without charge on any of the airline's flights, provided she flies as a "special standby" passenger. Special standby passengers are admitted to a flight only if the plane has a seat available after all paying passengers have been seated.

(2) *E* may buy tickets for the use of any member of her family at a discount of 20 percent from the normal price.

(3) The airline reimburses *E* for the cost of parking in a commercial garage near *E*'s office.

(4) The airline maintains a cafeteria on its business premises. *E* and her dependents can buy meals in the cafeteria at a price much lower than prevailing prices for comparable meals in the area.

———

In addition to the exclusions allowed by §§ 119 and 132, fringe benefits that can be non-taxable include the following:

(1) Group-term life insurance purchased for employees. Generally, the exclusion cannot exceed the cost of the first $50,000 of coverage for each employee. See § 79.

(2) Reimbursements of medical expenses of an employee, an employee's spouse, or an employee's dependents, and of certain other health-related payments; § 105.

(3) Employer contributions to accident and health plans for employees; § 106.

(4) "Qualified tuition reductions." Section 117, which excludes some scholarship grants from the recipients' incomes, now makes clear that some tuition reductions for employees of schools and for employees' spouses and dependents are not income to the employees. A longstanding administrative practice had excluded free tuition for faculty children from faculty members' incomes, and the new provision (§ 117(d)) represents a considerable tightening up of the exclusion. Unlike the prior administrative practice, the statutory exclusion applies only to tuition

reductions for education "below the graduate level" (except for certain reductions given to graduate teaching or research assistants; § 117(d)(5)).

(5) Employer payments for "dependent care assistance" (within limits); § 129. Roughly speaking, dependent care assistance means day care for the employee's children while the employee works. The plan must meet a number of requirements spelled out in § 129.

(6) Employer reimbursements of an employee's costs of adopting a child may be excludable up to $10,000 per child under § 137. If the child has "special needs," the exclusion is $10,000 (even if the employee spends less than that amount in connection with the adoption, after 2002).

(7) Section 127 excludes employer payments under "educational assistance programs" for employees (up to a maximum of $5250 for each recipient).

Notes

1. *Nondiscrimination requirements.* Most employee fringe benefits must be provided on a basis which does not discriminate in favor of highly compensated employees if the fringe benefits are to retain their tax-free character. While non-discrimination may sound like an unquestionably good thing, non-discrimination requirements create serious problems for taxpayers. For one thing, low-income employees typically prefer cash to some kinds of fringe benefits (pensions being a classic example). When the law requires that fringe benefits actually be furnished to low-income as well as to high-income workers, it encourages compensation packages less attractive to employees—including low-income employees—than those employees would otherwise receive. Furthermore, non-discrimination rules are in practice very complicated; providing tax-free fringe benefits entails a good deal of red tape. This affects different employers in different ways. Large employers, with personnel offices staffed with experts, can often offer their employees tax-favored fringe benefits that are beyond the reach of smaller employers, for whom the costs of administering a fringe-benefit program can outweigh the tax savings.

2. *Cafeteria plans.* If an employer provides all of its employees with a particular benefit, whether or not individual employees ask for the benefit, it is easy to characterize the employer as providing "fringe benefits." Suppose, however, that individual employees can choose each year whether to take a fringe benefit or to take cash. In such a case, one can easily characterize the employees who elect fringe benefits as purchasing the benefits. Under § 125, many benefits retain their tax-free character even if offered under a plan which allows employees to choose between qualified benefits and cash. Therefore, employers can establish programs which pay for the (tax-free) day care, medical, or other expenses of employees who want those benefits, while paying cash to

employees who do not. In practice, "cafeteria plans" often simply offer employees an option to set aside part of their compensation to be used to reimburse them for the cost of medical expenses, day care, and group-term life insurance. As usual, non-discrimination requirements apply.

Cafeteria plans must contain a "use it or lose it" requirement, under which employees who have set aside part of their salaries for day care or medical costs may not get any of the money back if their actual costs turn out to be less than the amounts set aside. This encourages waste. Suppose, for instance, that an employee has agreed with her employer that $800 be set aside this year for medical and dental care not covered by the employee's health insurance. The employee will not be taxed on this $800, and if she actually incurs $800 in medical and dental bills, the $800 set aside will be used to pay those bills. But suppose that, late in December, the employee finds herself in the position of having spent only $600 all year for medicine and dentistry. She cannot get the other $200 back, so she may as well spend $200 on something medical, however frivolous the outlay. (One of your editors once owned seven pairs of glasses.)

———

Some fringe benefits are excludable because Congress wanted to encourage employers to provide particular benefits, such as educational plans. By excluding the value of these benefits from employees' incomes, Congress creates a form of subsidy. Other benefits may be excludable because measuring the recipients' benefits would entail serious administrative burdens. For example, if a lawyer who worked late were taxable on meals provided by the employer, the amount of the lawyer's income might in principle be the amount of money he saved by not having to buy his own meal, not necessarily the amount the employer paid for the meal. Valuation difficulties may account for some apparent anomalies, such as the difference between employee parking paid for by the employer (tax-free) and parking paid for by the employee with no employer reimbursement (taxable, because the employee cannot deduct the cost).

Although administrative considerations suggest that a wide variety of fringe benefits should be excludable, failure to tax fringe benefits in the same way as cash compensation creates undesirable incentives, as the following article shows.

JOHNSON, THE CASE FOR TAXING FRINGE BENEFITS[n]
9 Tax Notes 43 (1979).

I. THE PROBLEM

The undertaxation of fringe benefits, whether by law or merely lax enforcement, is causing permanent and continuing damage to the econo-

n. Copyright © 1979 by Tax Analysts. Reprinted by permission.

my of the country. When fringe benefits are exempt but cash is subject to tax, the tax incentive forces resources to be shifted toward meals, entertainment, travel and other noncash benefits, and makes it rational for a recipient to waste or destroy resources to avoid taxes.

Waste Caused by Exemption

Over time, an employer will always use the resources he is willing to devote to an employee in the form the employee wants. The tax system makes it rational for an employee to choose an untaxed noncash form.

For instance, a 50 percent tax bracket employee who receives $50 in cash compensation must pay $25 in tax and is left with $25. If the employer, on the other hand, pays $50 for a business lunch for the employee, the employee need not pay tax on the $50 worth of resources he consumes. The employee will prefer the tax exempt lunch over the cash as long as he gets $25 or more worth of pleasure out of the lunch. Thus the employee will demand lunches rather than cash compensation until such time as he is so satiated by lunches that he gets only $25 benefit out of every $50 consumed.

In consuming a $50 lunch which is worth only $25 to him, the employee wastes $25—as surely as if he had burned dollar bills. But as long as the lunch is exempt from tax the employee's choice is rational, because the resources he wastes are less than the tax he would pay on cash.[1]

While the private choice is for the lunch, society would benefit if the employee chose the cash and used his post-tax salary in a way that gave him his money's worth. The resources that went to make the lunch would be better used for a customer who gets $50 worth of pleasure from the expenditure. Few $50 lunches would be produced if they were sold only to customers who got $50 worth of benefit from them. The resources now devoted to luxury lunches would shift, once the distorting effect of the tax system is removed, to items for which there is greater utility.

Taxing the employee on the resources committed to him would end the waste caused by the exemption. Ending the exemption for lunches would not end lunches, but it would assure that the lunch is not a choice forced by the tax system.

Business lunches are used in this discussion because they provide a simple example, but the economic analysis is the same for such things as inventory or services provided at a discount to employee; company cars or airplanes; entertainment benefits such as sports or theater tickets, nightclubs, country clubs, resorts and hunting lodges; and other privileges such as a company apartment, executive gymnasiums, and personal financial counseling.

1. By spending $50 for a lunch, the employee generates restaurant jobs and restaurant taxes, but that is no advantage of the lunch, since the spending of the $50 cash by the employee and government also generates jobs and taxes.

In all these cases, the employee or customer is using resources for personal consumption. While all the benefits arise from business activities, they do not qualify as working conditions. Working conditions are tools of work. A flight to Paris by a flight attendant working on the flight is a working condition. Office space, air conditioning, and the joys of endeavor are similarly exempt from tax without possible challenge.

The Incentive to Consumption at the Top

Because the Federal tax system is progressive, most of the waste that accompanies the exemption for fringe benefits occurs in the highest tax brackets. An employee too poor to pay taxes on cash wages would not tolerate the loss of utility that noncash wages entail. It is rational to choose nontaxed benefits only when the loss of utility is less than the taxes avoided: Thus a 14 percent bracket taxpayer chooses the $50 lunch only if it entails waste of less than $7, a 25 percent taxpayer requires value of $37.50 from the lunch and tolerates waste of $12.50, a 50 percent taxpayer chooses the lunch if it is worth only $25 and tolerates waste of as much as $25.

* * *

Cost–Free Benefits

Taxing the employee or other recipient of a fringe benefit is justified because of the real resources consumed, and not because of the intangible pleasures the recipient gets. The intended impact of the federal income tax is to suppress the private consumption of resources to allow public government consumption. Where an employee is consuming resources in getting fringe benefits, those resources, like all consumption, are a positive target of federal taxation. Without tax, the resources are wasted in avoiding tax.

However, taxing truly cost-free benefits does have an economic detriment. The tax prevents use of a benefit that would otherwise be available. Thus a toll on a completed road reduces the public use of the road. Similarly, a seat in a movie theater that was built before television is a cost free asset if the seat is not filled. In such a case, taxing the theatre's ticket taker who sits in the back would just diminish the employee's enjoyment without shifting the seat to a higher user. Even where a tax wouldn't diminish use, taxing some free benefits would be frivolous—taxing air or [a] beautiful day, for instance, seems silly. If a benefit arises incidentally out of a use of resources that would have been undertaken even if there were no benefit to the recipient, that is like a cost-free benefit.

The argument that we shouldn't tax benefits that have no cost is much abused. While there is free air, there is, to quote a maxim, no such thing as a free lunch. "Cost to the economist is 'opportunity cost'—the benefit foregone by employing a resource in a way that denies its use to somebody else." Thus making a benefit available to an employee usually means that the benefit is denied to someone who would pay more. The measure of the cost is the price which the person who would pay the most for it would pay. Without the exemption, the entire economy will benefit as providers of fringe benefits undertake to locate and shift fringe benefit resources to the highest and best user of the resources instead of the tax-exempt beneficiary.

* * *

The fact that the provider of a noncash benefit uses his resources solely for business, does not mean the benefit should be exempt from tax. Cash compensation is provided by an employer for purely business motives, and yet the employee must be taxed on it. The argument that the benefit arises from non-compensatory use is often implausible: An employee, for instance, can meet any time in an office with a customer; the employee's meal with a customer is provided as a use of resources for the benefit of employee and customer. However, even if personal consumption is provided in a business context, the use of that resource should be taxed to prevent economic distortion. A lunch at which business is discussed is nonetheless a private consumption of resources which the tax is intended to suppress. One may meet for business purposes, but one eats for personal consumption and that consumption should bear its fair share of the federal tax burden.

Arm's length bargaining in the private sector will prevent an employee from being unfairly treated if he is taxed on the fair market value of resources he has consumed. The provider of benefits over time works to ensure that the recipient gets the maximum pleasure out of the resources or he shifts resources to some other form.

For instance, a customer's enjoyment provides the nexus between the cost of a sports or theater ticket for the customer and the return that the provider expects. For a large customer, the cost of any ticket for entertainment might seem small, but even there the provider will maximize the customer's enjoyment: no one would rationally provide professional wrestling tickets to a customer who would rather see opera. Similarly, where cash is an alternative, no provider would give a taxable benefit giving less utility or pleasure to the recipient than its cost. A recipient can spend cash in a way to ensure that its benefit is equal to its value. If fringe benefits are overtaxed, then employers would, over time, pay cash and the employee would buy the benefit.

The dangers of undertaxing fringe benefits are, thus, considerably larger and more realistic than the danger of overtaxing the benefits or taxing cost-free ones. Moreover, we do have tolls on roads even when they tax otherwise free use of the road—if only to raise revenue. If there is difficulty in administering a line between free and costly fringe benefits, then the answer is to draw the line where it is easiest and tax some "free" cases.

Tax Structure and Big Government

One should not confuse a tax increase which improves economic efficiency with an increase in the size of government or the level of taxes in general. There are, undoubtedly, people who believe that any tax preference, no matter how damaging to the economy, how irrational, or how inequitable, is still a blow struck for liberty. But the level of government is controlled by the deficit and by the budget process. For a given tax level, taxes not borne by fringe benefits must be borne by other people and other more beneficial economic transactions. Opposition to government is no reason to support government tax programs which distort private decision-making in such a pernicious way.

Most taxpayers pay for their meals, commuting, personal travel, and entertainment out of post-tax dollars. Yet the taxpayer sees other taxpayers getting the same benefits without tax. Our self-assessing system of taxation depends on [a] high level of morale and honesty by ordinary taxpayers. Any system that was not self-assessing would be an intolerable intrusion by the Internal Revenue Service in the affairs of individuals. Taxing everyone on the fringe benefits they receive is necessary to insure honest reporting by taxpayers who lack significant fringe benefits or who draw trivial benefits from the exemption.

In sum, the tax exemption for the consumption of resources in the form of fringe benefits is bad policy of such magnitude that it is worth devoting considerable administrative resources to reversing the incentive.

* * *

Notes

1. *Terminology.* The social waste which results when an employer spends $50 to provide an employee with a benefit which the employee values at $40 is sometimes called "deadweight loss."

2. *References.* Clotfelter, Equity, Efficiency, and the Tax Treatment of In–Kind Compensation, 32 Nat.Tax J. 51 (1979); Hickman, The Outlook for Fringe Benefits, 29 U.So.Cal.Tax Inst. 459 (1977); Bittker, The Individual as Wage Earner, 11 N.Y.U.Tax Inst. 1147 (1953).

WITHHOLDING, FICA, AND FUTA

As a practical matter, collection of significant amounts of tax on account of fringe benefits depends very much upon whether employers treat the benefits as "wages" for purposes of withholding tax under §§ 3401–3404. Section 3401 defines "wages" in a somewhat circular way as "all remuneration * * * for services performed by an employee for his employer, including the cash value of all remuneration paid in any medium other than cash * * *," with several specific exceptions. An argument could be made that any taxable benefit furnished an employee constitutes "wages" under this section, unless the benefit can be classified as a "dividend," or "interest," or "gain on the sale of property," or some other recognized kind of income other than "wages." The courts, however, have read the definition of "wages" more narrowly. For example, the Supreme Court held in Central Illinois Public Serv. Co. v. United States, 435 U.S. 21 (1978), that reimbursements of lunch expenses of employees on travel status were not "wages" under § 3401. Justice Blackmun's opinion for the Court said that a narrow interpretation of "wages" would promote simplicity and ease of administration.

Unlike most of those who pay "employees," people who purchase the services of independent contractors are not required to withhold. This makes it extremely important to know whether a worker is an employee or an independent contractor. In some cases, a withholding requirement for payments to independent contractors would obviously be impracticable; consider, for example, the problems of imposing withholding on the customers of plumbers, lawyers, or barbers. In other cases, however, drawing the line between "employees" and "contractors" borders on the absurd. For example, consider the commissions of a salesman who sells only the products of one company. Treas.Reg. § 31.3401(c)–1(b) adopts the common-law definition of "employee," so that the controlling factor is whether "the person for whom services are performed has the right to control and direct the individual who performs the services, not only as to the result to be accomplished * * * but also as to the details and means by which that [result] is accomplished." Therefore, whether a salesman is an "employee" under § 3401 may depend upon such trivia as whether the company or the salesman decides what customers are to be called on at particular times and how often the salesman stops off at the main office. Whatever the merits of the "right to control" standard as a test of tort liability under the doctrine of respondeat superior, its use in withholding cases breeds litigation and furthers none of the goals of the withholding system.

The existence of an employment relationship not only requires the employer to withhold income taxes in most cases, it may subject the employer to FICA (Social Security and Medicare) taxes and FUTA (Federal unemployment insurance) taxes. Self-employed taxpayers, who are not someone else's employee and whose work therefore does not generate FICA and FUTA taxes, must pay a "self-employment tax," which is roughly the equivalent to both the employer's and the employee's share of FICA taxes.

Note

1. *Payments for domestic service.* In 1993, President Clinton's first nominee for Attorney General withdrew her name after it was disclosed that she and her husband had failed to pay employment taxes for a couple they employed as domestic servants. The couple were illegal aliens, and so employing them was itself illegal. A second candidate withdrew after it became known that she had once employed an illegal alien, even though doing so was not illegal at the time and the candidate had paid all employment taxes due. These events—widely referred to as "Nannygate"—generated considerable interest in the extent of the employer's obligation with regard to taxes and other obligations on account

of such domestic workers as baby-sitters, cleaning people, and gardeners. In 1994, Congress simplified the rules for Social Security and Medicare taxes for domestic employees. It was widely believed that the earlier rules, which required quarterly returns for any employee who received $50 or more in wages for any calendar quarter, imposed so heavy a paperwork requirement that liberalization would improve compliance. Whether it has actually had that effect is a question on which the jury is still out.

Payments for "domestic service in a private home" are not "wages" for purposes of income-tax withholding; § 3401(a)(3). So those who employ domestic help need not concern themselves with withholding income taxes, unless both employer and employee agree to do so. However, FICA and FUTA taxes must be paid on the wages of many domestic workers who are employees (rather than independent contractors).

In the case of domestic service, an annual return must be filed and the FICA tax must be paid on cash remuneration if the employer pays the employee $1000 or more in cash during any calendar year. The $1000 figure will be adjusted for inflation. (If the employee is under age 18 at any time during the year, no FICA tax is owed unless the employee is someone who is not a student and whose principal business is the provision of household services). The employer's FICA tax consists of a 6.2 percent Social Security tax and a 1.45 percent Medicare tax; the employee's taxes (which must be paid by the employer but may be withheld by the employer from the employee's wages) are the same. The portion of the FICA tax consisting of Social Security tax does not apply to wages in excess of the "wage base," which is $84,900 for 2002. (Most workers not subject to the FICA tax, such as independent contractors, must pay a self-employment tax. The amount of this tax is roughly the same as the sum of the employer's and employee's FICA taxes that would have been paid had the worker been an employee.)

An employer who must withhold income taxes or pay Social Security taxes must furnish the employee with a W–2 form.

The FUTA tax, imposed upon employers by § 3301, is 6.2 percent of the first $7000 of wages paid to any employee. In the case of domestic service, the tax is due from any employer who pays $1000 or more in wages in any calendar quarter.[o] Most states also impose an unemployment-insurance tax; a credit against most of the Federal tax is allowed for payments of state unemployment taxes. The FUTA tax is reported on an annual return.

Employers of domestic help may also have to pay the earned-income credit (described at p. 244) in advance to employees who request it, and

o. Payment of $1000 in wages for domestic service in any calendar quarter subjects the employer to the FUTA tax not only for the year in question, but also for the following year; § 3306(a)(3). For example, an employer who pays sitters total wages of $1000 during the second quarter of year 1 must pay the FUTA tax on the first $7000 of wages paid to any person for domestic service in year 1 or year 2, even if the employer's payments do not reach the $1000 threshold in any other quarter.

employers must notify their employees that they may qualify for this credit.

Federal taxes are not the domestic employer's only burden. State income-tax withholding may be required, and state workers' compensation and unemployment compensation systems may require payments from those who employ domestic workers. Furthermore, many employers must obtain documentation to show that the employees in question may legally work in the United States and must complete Form I–9, issued by the Immigration and Naturalization Service. Form I–9 need not be submitted for household employees hired intermittently, such as most baby-sitters.

The obligations discussed above make it important to determine whether a worker is an "employee" or an "independent contractor." Nearly all nannies and baby-sitters should be employees, as it is very common in these situations for the employer to have the right to tell the employee exactly what should be done and how to do it. Gardeners—at least those who come just once a month or so—are a different matter; many of them set their businesses up as corporations or partnerships, and even those who don't tend to insist on considerable independence with respect to what they will do, and how, and when. Cleaning people may be a borderline case, with their classification turning upon such matters as whether they bring their own equipment and supplies, whether they run their businesses as corporations, partnerships, or sole proprietorships which have their own employer identification numbers, and whether their arrangement with the homeowner calls for the homeowner to supervise their work closely.

4. ILLEGAL GAINS

JAMES v. UNITED STATES

Supreme Court of the United States, 1961.
366 U.S. 213, 81 S.Ct. 1052, 6 L.Ed.2d 246.

MR. CHIEF JUSTICE WARREN announced the judgment of the Court and an opinion in which MR. JUSTICE BRENNAN and MR. JUSTICE STEWART concur.

The issue before us in this case is whether embezzled funds are to be included in the "gross income" of the embezzler in the year in which the funds are misappropriated under § 22(a) of the Internal Revenue Code of 1939 and § 61(a) of the Internal Revenue Code of 1954.

The facts are not in dispute. The petitioner is a union official who, with another person, embezzled in excess of $738,000 during the years 1951 through 1954 from his employer union and from an insurance company with which the union was doing business. Petitioner failed to report these amounts in his gross income in those years and was convicted for willfully attempting to evade the federal income tax due for each of the years 1951 through 1954 in violation of § 145(b) of the Internal Revenue Code of 1939 and § 7201 of the Internal Revenue Code of 1954. He was sentenced to a total of three years' imprisonment. The Court of Appeals affirmed. 273 F.2d 5. Because of a conflict with this Court's decision in Commissioner of Internal Revenue v. Wilcox, 327 U.S. 404, a case whose relevant facts are concededly the same as those in the case now before us, we granted certiorari. 362 U.S. 974.

In *Wilcox,* the Court held that embezzled money does not constitute taxable income to the embezzler in the year of the embezzlement under § 22(a) of the Internal Revenue Code of 1939. Six years later, this Court held, in Rutkin v. United States, 343 U.S. 130, that extorted money does constitute taxable income to the extortionist in the year that the money is received under § 22(a) of the Internal Revenue Code of 1939. In *Rutkin,* the Court did not overrule *Wilcox,* but stated:

> "We do not reach in this case the factual situation involved in Commissioner of Internal Revenue v. Wilcox, 327 U.S. 404. We limit that case to its facts. There embezzled funds were held not to constitute taxable income to the embezzler under § 22(a)." Id., 343 U.S. at page 138.

However, examination of the reasoning used in *Rutkin* leads us inescapably to the conclusion that *Wilcox* was thoroughly devitalized.

The basis for the *Wilcox* decision was "that a taxable gain is conditioned upon (1) the presence of a claim of right to the alleged gain and (2) the absence of a definite, unconditional obligation to repay or return that which would otherwise constitute a gain. Without some bona fide legal or equitable claim, even though it be contingent or contested in nature, the taxpayer cannot be said to have received any gain or profit within the reach of Section 22(a)." Commissioner of Internal Revenue v. Wilcox, supra, 327 U.S. at page 408. Since Wilcox embezzled the money, held it "without any semblance of a bona fide claim of right," ibid., and therefore "was at all times under an unqualified duty and obligation to repay the money to his employer," ibid., the Court found that the money embezzled was not includible within "gross income." But, Rutkin's legal claim was no greater than that of Wilcox. It was specifically found "that petitioner had no basis for his claim * * * and that he obtained it by extortion." Rutkin v. United States, supra, 343 U.S. at page 135. Both Wilcox and Rutkin obtained the money by means of a criminal act; neither had a bona fide claim of right to the funds. Nor was Rutkin's obligation to repay the extorted money to the victim any less than that of Wilcox. The victim of an extortion, like the victim of an embezzlement, has a right to restitution. Furthermore, it is inconsequential that an embezzler may lack title to the sums he appropriates while an extortionist may gain a voidable title. Questions of federal income taxation are not determined by such "attenuated subtleties." Lucas v. Earl, 281 U.S. 111, 114; Corliss v. Bowers, 281 U.S. 376, 378. Thus, the fact that Rutkin secured the money with the consent of his victim, Rutkin v. United States, supra, 343 U.S. at p. 138, is irrelevant. Likewise unimportant is the fact that the sufferer of an extortion is less likely to seek restitution than one whose funds are embezzled. What is important is that the right to recoupment exists in both situations.

Examination of the relevant cases in the courts of appeals lends credence to our conclusion that the *Wilcox* rationale was effectively vitiated by this Court's decision in *Rutkin.* * * *

When a taxpayer acquires earnings, lawfully or unlawfully, without the consensual recognition, express or implied, of an obligation to repay and without restriction as to their disposition, "he has received income which he is required to return, even though it may still be claimed that he is not entitled to retain the money, and even though he may still be adjudged liable to restore its equivalent." North American Oil Consolidated v. Burnet, supra, 286 U.S. at page 424. In such case, the taxpayer has "actual command over the property taxed—the actual benefit for which the tax is paid," Corliss v. Bowers, supra [281 U.S. 376]. This standard brings wrongful appropriations within the broad sweep of "gross income"; it excludes loans. * * *

But, we are dealing here with a felony conviction under statutes which apply to any person who "willfully" fails to account for his tax or who "willfully" attempts to evade his obligation. In Spies v. United States, 317 U.S. 492, 499, the Court said that § 145(b) of the 1939 Code embodied "the gravest of offenses against the revenues," and stated that willfulness must therefore include an evil motive and want of justification in view of all the circumstances. Id., 317 U.S. at page 498. Willfulness "involves a specific intent which must be proven by independent evidence and which cannot be inferred from the mere understatement of income." Holland v. United States, 348 U.S. 121, 139.

We believe that the element of willfulness could not be proven in a criminal prosecution for failing to include embezzled funds in gross income in the year of misappropriation so long as the statute contained the gloss placed upon it by *Wilcox* at the time the alleged crime was committed. Therefore, we feel that petitioner's conviction may not stand and that the indictment against him must be dismissed.

Since Mr. Justice Harlan, Mr. Justice Frankfurter, and Mr. Justice Clark agree with us concerning *Wilcox,* that case is overruled. Mr. Justice Black, Mr. Justice Douglas, and Mr. Justice Whittaker believe that petitioner's conviction must be reversed and the case dismissed for the reasons stated in their opinions.

Accordingly, the judgment of the Court of Appeals is reversed and the case is remanded to the District Court with directions to dismiss the indictment.

It is so ordered.

Reversed and remanded with directions.

Mr. Justice Black, whom Mr. Justice Douglas joins, concurring in part and dissenting in part.

* * *

[Justices Black and Douglas would have held that embezzled funds are not includable in income.]

MR. JUSTICE CLARK, concurring in part and dissenting in part as to the opinion of THE CHIEF JUSTICE.

Although I join in the specific overruling of Commissioner of Internal Revenue v. Wilcox, * * * I would affirm this conviction on either of two grounds. I believe that the Court not only devitalized *Wilcox,* by limiting it to its facts in Rutkin v. United States, * * * but that in effect the Court overruled that case *sub silentio* in Commissioner of Internal Revenue v. Glenshaw Glass Co., 1955, 348 U.S. 426. Even if that not be true, in my view the proof shows conclusively that petitioner, in willfully failing to correctly report his income, placed no bona fide reliance on *Wilcox.*

MR. JUSTICE HARLAN, whom MR. JUSTICE FRANKFURTER joins, concurring in part and dissenting in part as to the opinion of THE CHIEF JUSTICE.

I fully agree with so much of The Chief Justice's opinion as dispatches *Wilcox* to a final demise. But as to the disposition of this case, I think that rather than an outright reversal, which his opinion proposes, the reversal should be for a new trial.

I share the view that it would be inequitable to sustain this conviction when by virtue of the *Rutkin–Wilcox* dilemma it might reasonably have been thought by one in petitioner's position that no tax was due in respect of embezzled moneys. For as is pointed out, *Rutkin* did not expressly overrule *Wilcox,* but instead merely confined it "to its facts." Having now concluded that *Wilcox* was wrongly decided originally, the problem in this case thus becomes one of how to overrule *Wilcox* "in a manner that will not prejudice those who might have relied on it." 366 U.S. at page 221.

* * *

* * * [W]here the defendant is charged in a case like this with having "willfully" violated the law, I believe that both reason and authority require no more than that the trier of fact be instructed that it must take into account in determining the defendant's "evil motive and want of justification," Spies v. United States, 317 U.S. at page 498, his possible reliance on *Wilcox,* which not until now has this Court explicitly stated was wrongly decided. As far as fairness to this petitioner is concerned, I do not see why that is not amply accorded by the disposition which *Spies* itself exemplifies. * * * On the other hand, if the trier of fact, properly instructed, finds that the petitioner did not act in bona fide reliance on *Wilcox,* but deliberately refused to report income and pay taxes thereon knowing of his obligation to do so and not relying on any exception in the circumstances, I do not see why even the strictest definition of the element of "willfulness" would not have been satisfied. Willfulness goes to motive, and the quality of a particular defendant's

motive would not seem to be affected by the fact that another taxpayer similarly situated had a different motive.

* * *

* * * [I]t might be argued that petitioner at the time he failed to make his return was not under any misapprehension as to the law, but indeed that at the time and under the decisions of this Court his view of the law was entirely correct. The argument not only seems to beg the question, but raises further questions as to the civil liability of one situated in the circumstances of this petitioner. Petitioner's obligation here derived not from the decisions of this or any other court, but from the Act of Congress imposing the tax. It is hard to see what further point is being made, once it is conceded that petitioner, if he was misled by the decisions of this Court, is entitled to plead in defense that misconception. Only in the most metaphorical sense has the law changed: the decisions of this Court have changed, and the decisions of a court interpreting the acts of a legislature have never been subject to the same limitations which are imposed on legislatures themselves, United States Constitution, Art. I, §§ 9, 10, forbidding them to make any *ex post facto* law[3] and in the case of States to impair the obligation of a contract. Ross v. State of Oregon, 227 U.S. 150; New Orleans Water–Works Co. v. Louisiana Sugar Refining Co., 125 U.S. 18.

The proper disposition of this case, in my view, is to treat as plain error, Fed.Rules Crim.Proc. 52(b), 18 U.S.C.A., the failure of the trial court as trier of fact to consider whatever misapprehension may have existed in the mind of the petitioner as to the applicable law, in determining whether the Government had proved that petitioner's conduct had been willful as required by the statute. On that basis I would send the case back for a new trial.

Mr. Justice Whittaker, whom Mr. Justice Black and Mr. Justice Douglas join, concurring in part and dissenting in part.

[Justice Whittaker's opinion argued that an embezzler's loot could not be considered income under the Sixteenth Amendment.]

Problems, Notes and Question

1. *Tax crimes.* Sections 7201 to 7216 define various tax crimes, of which § 7201 (willful attempt to evade tax; a felony) and § 7203 (willful

---

3. Aside from problems of warning and specific intent, the policy of the prohibition against *ex post facto* legislation would seem to rest on the apprehension that the legislature, in imposing penalties on past conduct, even though the conduct could properly have been made criminal and even though the defendant who engaged in that conduct in the past believed he was doing wrong (as for instance when the penalty is increased retroactively on an existing crime), may be acting with a purpose not to prevent dangerous conduct generally but to impose by legislation a penalty against specific persons or classes of persons. That this policy is inapplicable to decisions of the courts seems obvious: their opportunity for discrimination is more limited than the legislature's, in that they can only act in construing existing law in actual litigation. Given the divergent pulls of flexibility and precedent in our case law system, it is disquieting to think what perplexities and what subtleties of distinction would be created in applying this policy, which so properly limits legislative action, to the decisions of the courts.

failure to file a return, supply information, or pay a tax; a misdemeanor) are two of the most important in practice. Use of these provisions to enforce the tax laws resembles the enforcement of traffic laws in the sense that the government makes no serious attempt to detect and convict every tax criminal. Instead, only the most flagrant offenders are prosecuted, in the hope that newspaper accounts of convictions will encourage compliance with the law. Although some of those convicted of tax evasion are also "non-tax" criminals like James, many others are people whose only criminal activities were violations of the tax law. Doctors, lawyers, and accountants are often objects of criminal tax investigations.

2. *The tax law and "non-tax" criminals.* Justice Black's dissenting opinion in Rutkin v. United States, 343 U.S. 130, 139 (1952), charged that the government's motive in seeking to make the proceeds of extortion taxable was "to give Washington more and more power to punish purely local crimes such as embezzlement and extortion"; 343 U.S. at 141. It is certainly true that decisions like *Rutkin* and *James* do give the Federal government that power, and that the government has not hesitated to use it. Is this consideration relevant in evaluating the soundness of the result reached in *James?* It has always been clear that some illegal gains are income. No one, for example, has ever argued that the profits of a business engaged in violating the antitrust laws should be tax exempt.

Although illegal gains are taxable, they are very often not taxed; consider the problems of devising an effective withholding system for payments to bookmakers or muggers. Because income taxes cannot be collected from criminals in significant amounts, the income tax encourages crime. For example, even if state lotteries provided expected pre-tax returns as great as those of illegal gambling ventures, some people would prefer illegal gambling because their receipts would not be reported. See generally Blakey & Kurland, The Development of the Federal Law of Gambling, 63 Cornell L.Rev. 923, 994–1011 (1978).

3. *Self-incrimination and tax returns.* Willful failure to file a return, or to pay a tax, is a crime, and an accurate return must disclose both the amount and the source of the taxpayer's income. This suggests that a non-tax criminal who wants to avoid becoming a tax criminal too should file a tax return reporting income from illegal activities and describing those activities, at least briefly. This course of conduct would lead to an investigation of the taxpayer, and the statements on the return could be used as evidence in criminal proceedings: by making the statements, the taxpayer would have waived his Fifth Amendment right not to incriminate himself; Garner v. United States, 424 U.S. 648 (1976). But the Fifth Amendment cannot be used to justify failure to file on the theory that filing by a criminal would be incriminatory; United States v. Sullivan, 274 U.S. 259 (1927).

The courts of appeals have held that the privilege against self-incrimination can be asserted on a return and used to excuse disclosing the source of income; e.g., United States v. Edwards, 777 F.2d 644 (11th Cir.1985), cert. denied 475 U.S. 1123 (1986). Whether assertion of the privilege can excuse disclosing the amount of income from illegal activities is doubtful. Justice Holmes' opinion in *Sullivan* described as "extreme if not * * * extravagant" the view that the Fifth Amendment can excuse failure to report the amount of income because the income was earned illegally, and several courts of appeals have agreed; e.g., United States v. Verkuilen, 690 F.2d 648, 654 (7th Cir.1982).

For a survey of the law and some practical suggestions for advising criminals about filing, see Rosenblatt, The Reporting of Illicit Income and the Fifth Amendment: An Illusion or Protection from Self–Incrimination?, 65 Taxes 288 (1987).

4. *Problems.*

(1) *T* is trustee of a family trust which is not subject to court supervision. *T,* in breach of trust, sells to himself for $4000 a trust asset worth $10,000. What tax result to *T*?

(2) *A* and *B* each own 50 percent of *X* Corporation. Two years ago, *A* embezzled $100,000 from the corporation. When the defalcation was discovered in the current year, *A* repaid the funds. What result to *A*? And *X* (see § 165(a))?

C. RECOVERY OF CAPITAL

Measuring "income" in the sense of "gain" or "profit" requires making an allowance for the costs of earning income. Thus, a taxpayer who spends $1000 to get $1500 has "income" of $500. This section will survey the methods by which the tax law accounts for the fact that not all "receipts" are "gains."

1. SALES

Recall that someone who sells property computes realized gain on the sale by subtracting the property's adjusted basis from the amount realized upon the sale (p. 49). So, someone who buys corporate stock for $3000 and sells it for $3700 realizes and recognizes a $700 gain, which is the taxpayer's gross income from the sale.

The importance of "basis" in the case of a sale or exchange is that it (together with the "amount realized") determines the amount of gain. In doubtful cases, therefore, the proper "cost" basis of property can be determined by working backward from the gain that should be realized when the property is sold to the basis figure that will produce that result. We have already seen some examples of this; review the materials at p. 60. Here is another example: a contestant in a television game show wins a $20,000 car. The taxpayer's gross income on receiving the car is $20,000 (see § 74). What is the taxpayer's "cost" basis for the car under § 1012? What must that basis be if the taxpayer is not to have additional income upon selling the car for $20,000 cash?

In the case of a sale, the taxpayer's "recovery of capital" takes place at the stage of calculating gross income. This is the simplest form of capital recovery. As we shall see, there are instances in which capital recovery is accomplished by reducing taxable income, rather than gross income, to account for the taxpayer's costs.

2. DIVIDENDS, INTEREST AND RENT

Suppose a taxpayer spends $100,000 to buy a tract of farm land, which the taxpayer then leases to a farmer for $8000 a year. The $8000 rent is includable in the taxpayer's gross income each year. The taxpayer's $100,000 investment in the income-producing property—the taxpayer's basis—does not enter into the calculation of either the gross income from the property or the taxpayer's taxable income; instead, it is left for use when the taxpayer sells the land. Similarly, someone who buys corporate stock for $100,000 cannot use any of the stock's $100,000 basis to offset the receipt of cash dividends: as in the case of unimproved land, the use of basis must await the disposition of the stock. And a taxpayer who buys $100,000 worth of corporate bonds includes in income all the interest received; as with stock and land, the basis will be used when the property is sold.

If the tax system's only concern were with getting the right figure for the taxpayer's long-run income, other methods of taxing dividends, interest, and rent could be used. For instance, under a "recover basis first" approach, a taxpayer would exclude all receipts from income until the total amount excluded equaled the basis of the property; further receipts would be fully taxable. Thus, the taxpayer in the previous paragraph who bought $100,000 worth of stock would exclude from income the first $100,000 in dividends and would treat as income any dividends in excess of that amount and the entire sale price. This approach would be simple, but it would allow excessive deferral of income in the sense of increases in the taxpayer's wealth. If the value of an income-producing asset remains constant, the annual receipts from that property measure the annual increase in the taxpayer's wealth. Ideally, this increase in wealth should be taxed as it occurs.

One shortcoming of our present system for taxing dividends is that the tax is, as a practical matter, elective. Corporations are fairly free to invest their earnings in expansion or new ventures, rather than to distribute them as dividends. When that happens, the shareholders still experience increases in wealth when the corporation does well, but because no dividends have been distributed the shareholders pay no tax. The existence of a separate tax on the incomes of corporations can probably best be justified as a surrogate for taxes on corporate shareholders' unrealized wealth increases.

EISNER v. MACOMBER

Supreme Court of the United States, 1920.
252 U.S. 189, 40 S.Ct. 189, 64 L.Ed. 521.

MR. JUSTICE PITNEY delivered the opinion of the Court.

This case presents the question whether, by virtue of the Sixteenth Amendment, Congress has the power to tax, as income of the stockholder and without apportionment, a stock dividend made lawfully and in good faith against profits accumulated by the corporation since March 1, 1913.

It arises under the Revenue Act of September 8, 1916 (39 Stat. 756 et seq., c. 463), which, in our opinion (notwithstanding a contention of the government that will be noticed), plainly evinces the purpose of Congress to tax stock dividends as income.

The facts, in outline, are as follows:

On January 1, 1916, the Standard Oil Company of California, a corporation of that state, out of an authorized capital stock of $100,000,000, had shares of stock outstanding, par value $100 each, amounting in round figures to $50,000,000. In addition, it had surplus and undivided profits invested in plant, property, and business and required for the purposes of the corporation, amounting to about $45,000,000, of which about $20,000,000 had been earned prior to March 1, 1913, the balance thereafter. In January, 1916, in order to readjust the capitalization, the board of directors decided to issue additional shares sufficient to constitute a stock dividend of 50 per cent. of the outstanding stock, and to transfer from surplus account to capital stock account an amount equivalent to such issue. Appropriate resolutions were adopted, an amount equivalent to the par value of the proposed new stock was transferred accordingly, and the new stock duly issued against it and divided among the stockholders.

Defendant in error, being the owner of 2,200 shares of the old stock, received certificates for 1,100 additional shares, of which 18.07 per cent., or 198.77 shares, par value $19,877, were treated as representing surplus earned between March 1, 1913, and January 1, 1916. She was called upon to pay, and did pay under protest, a tax imposed under the Revenue Act of 1916, based upon a supposed income of $19,877 because of the new shares; and an appeal to the Commissioner of Internal Revenue having been disallowed, she brought action against the Collector to recover the tax. In her complaint she alleged the above facts, and contended that in imposing such a tax the Revenue Act of 1916 violated article 1, § 2, cl. 3, and article 1, § 9, cl. 4, of the Constitution of the United States, requiring direct taxes to be apportioned according to population, and that the stock dividend was not income within the meaning of the Sixteenth Amendment. A general demurrer to the complaint was overruled upon the authority of Towne v. Eisner, 245 U.S.

418; and, defendant having failed to plead further, final judgment went against him. To review it, the present writ of error is prosecuted.

The case was argued at the last term, and reargued at the present term, both orally and by additional briefs.

We are constrained to hold that the judgment of the District Court must be affirmed: First, because the question at issue is controlled by Towne v. Eisner, supra; secondly, because a re-examination of the question with the additional light thrown upon it by elaborate arguments, has confirmed the view that the underlying ground of that decision is sound, that it disposes of the question here presented, and that other fundamental considerations lead to the same result.

[The Court's discussion of Towne v. Eisner, which held that a stock dividend was not taxable under the Revenue Act of 1913, is omitted.]

* * *

The Sixteenth Amendment must be construed in connection with the taxing clauses of the original Constitution and the effect attributed to them before the amendment was adopted. In Pollock v. Farmers' Loan & Trust Co., 158 U.S. 601, under the Act of August 27, 1894 (28 Stat. 509, 553, c. 349, § 27), it was held that taxes upon rents and profits of real estate and upon returns from investments of personal property were in effect direct taxes upon the property from which such income arose, imposed by reason of ownership; and that Congress could not impose such taxes without apportioning them among the states according to population, as required by article 1, § 2, cl. 3, and § 9, cl. 4, of the original Constitution.

Afterwards, and evidently in recognition of the limitation upon the taxing power of Congress thus determined, the Sixteenth Amendment was adopted, in words lucidly expressing the object to be accomplished:

"The Congress shall have power to lay and collect taxes on incomes, from whatever source derived, without apportionment among the several states, and without regard to any census or enumeration."

As repeatedly held, this did not extend the taxing power to new subjects, but merely removed the necessity which otherwise might exist for an apportionment among the states of taxes laid on income. Brushaber v. Union Pacific R.R. Co., 240 U.S. 1, 17–19; Stanton v. Baltic Mining Co., 240 U.S. 103, 112 et seq.; Peck & Co. v. Lowe, 247 U.S. 165, 172, 173.

* * *

The fundamental relation of "capital" to "income" has been much discussed by economists, the former being likened to the tree or the land, the latter to the fruit or the crop; the former depicted as a reservoir supplied from springs, the latter as the outlet stream, to be measured by its flow during a period of time. For the present purpose we require only a clear definition of the term "income," as used in common speech, in order to determine its meaning in the amendment, and, having formed also a correct judgment as to the nature of a stock dividend, we shall find it easy to decide the matter at issue.

After examining dictionaries in common use (Bouv.L.D.; Standard Dict.; Webster's Internat. Dict.; Century Dict.), we find little to add to the succinct definition adopted in two cases arising under the Corporation Tax Act of 1909 (Stratton's Independence v. Howbert, 231 U.S. 399, 415; Doyle v. Mitchell Bros. Co., 247 U.S. 179, 185), "Income may be defined as the gain derived from capital, from labor, or from both combined," provided it be understood to include profit gained through a sale or conversion of capital assets, to which it was applied in the *Doyle* Case, 247 U.S. 183, 185.

Brief as it is, it indicates the characteristic and distinguishing attribute of income essential for a correct solution of the present controversy. The government, although basing its argument upon the definition as quoted, placed chief emphasis upon the word "gain," which was extended to include a variety of meanings; while the significance of the next three words was either overlooked or misconceived. *"Derived— from—capital"*; *"the gain—derived—from—capital,"* etc. Here we have the essential matter: *not* a gain *accruing to* capital; not a *growth* or *increment* of value *in* the investment; but a gain, a profit, something of exchangeable value, *proceeding from* the property, *severed from* the capital, however invested or employed, and *coming in*, being *"derived"*— that is, *received* or *drawn by* the recipient (the taxpayer) for his *separate* use, benefit and disposal—*that* is income derived from property. Nothing else answers the description.

The same fundamental conception is clearly set forth in the Sixteenth Amendment—"incomes, *from* whatever *source derived*"—the essential thought being expressed with a conciseness and lucidity entirely in harmony with the form and style of the Constitution.

Can a stock dividend, considering its essential character, be brought within the definition? To answer this, regard must be had to the nature of a corporation and the stockholder's relation to it. We refer, of course, to a corporation such as the one in the case at bar, organized for profit, and having a capital stock divided into shares to which a nominal or par value is attributed.

* * *

A "stock dividend" shows that the company's accumulated profits have been capitalized, instead of distributed to the stockholders or retained as surplus available for distribution in money or in kind should opportunity offer. Far from being a realization of profits of the stockholder, it tends rather to postpone such realization, in that the fund represented by the new stock has been transferred from surplus to capital, and no longer is available for actual distribution.

The essential and controlling fact is that the stockholder has received nothing out of the company's assets for his separate use and benefit; on the contrary, every dollar of his original investment, together with whatever accretions and accumulations have resulted from employment of his money and that of the other stockholders in the business of the company, still remains the property of the company, and subject to business risks which may result in wiping out the entire investment. Having regard to the very truth of the matter, to substance and not to form, he has received nothing that answers the definition of income within the meaning of the Sixteenth Amendment.

* * *

We are clear that not only does a stock dividend really take nothing from the property of the corporation and add nothing to that of the shareholder, but that the antecedent accumulation of profits evidenced thereby, while indicating that the shareholder is the richer because of an increase of his capital, at the same time shows he has not realized or received any income in the transaction.

It is said that a stockholder may sell the new shares acquired in the stock dividend; and so he may, if he can find a buyer. It is equally true that if he does sell, and in doing so realizes a profit, such profit, like any other, is income, and so far as it may have arisen since the Sixteenth Amendment is taxable by Congress without apportionment. The same would be true were he to sell some of his original shares at a profit. But if a shareholder sells dividend stock he necessarily disposes of a part of his capital interest, just as if he should sell a part of his old stock, either before or after the dividend. What he retains no longer entitles him to the same proportion of future dividends as before the sale. His part in the control of the company likewise is diminished. Thus, if one holding $60,000 out of a total $100,000 of the capital stock of a corporation should receive in common with other stockholders a 50 per cent. stock dividend, and should sell his part, he thereby would be reduced from a majority to a minority stockholder, having six-fifteenths instead of six-tenths of the total stock outstanding. A corresponding and proportionate decrease in capital interest and in voting power would befall a minority holder should he sell dividend stock; it being in the nature of things impossible for one to dispose of any part of such an issue without a proportionate disturbance of the distribution of the entire capital stock, and a like diminution of the seller's comparative voting power—that "right preservative of rights" in the control of a corporation. Yet, without selling, the shareholder, unless possessed of other resources, has not the wherewithal to pay an income tax upon the dividend stock. Nothing could more clearly show that to tax a stock dividend is to tax a capital increase, and not income, than this demonstration that in the nature of things it requires conversion of capital in order to pay the tax.

* * *

Conceding that the mere issue of a stock dividend makes the recipient no richer than before, the government nevertheless contends that the new certificates measure the extent to which the gains accumulated by the corporation have made him the richer. There are two insuperable difficulties with this: In the first place, it would depend upon how long he had held the stock whether the stock dividend indicated the extent to which he had been enriched by the operations of the company; unless he had held it throughout such operations the measure would not hold true. Secondly, and more important for present purposes, enrichment through increase in value of capital investment is not income in any proper meaning of the term.

* * *

The government's reliance upon the supposed analogy between a dividend of the corporation's own shares and one made by distributing shares owned by it in the stock of another company, calls for no comment beyond the statement that the latter distributes assets of the company among the shareholders while the former does not, and for no citation of authority except Peabody v. Eisner, 247 U.S. 347, 349, 350.

* * *

Thus, from every point of view we are brought irresistibly to the conclusion that neither under the Sixteenth Amendment nor otherwise has Congress power to tax without apportionment a true stock dividend made lawfully and in good faith, or the accumulated profits behind it, as income of the stockholder. The Revenue Act of 1916, in so far as it imposes a tax upon the stockholder because of such dividend, contravenes the provisions of article 1, § 2, cl. 3, and article 1, § 9, cl. 4, of the Constitution, and to this extent is invalid, notwithstanding the Sixteenth Amendment.

Judgment affirmed.

MR. JUSTICE HOLMES, dissenting.

I think that Towne v. Eisner, 245 U.S. 418, was right in its reasoning and result and that on sound principles the stock dividend was not income. But it was clearly intimated in that case that the construction of the statute then before the Court might be different from that of the Constitution. 245 U.S. 425. I think that the word "incomes" in the Sixteenth Amendment should be read in "a sense most obvious to the common understanding at the time of its adoption." Bishop v. State, 149 Ind. 223, 230, 48 N.E. 1038, 1040; State v. Butler, 70 Fla. 102, 133, 69 South. 771. For it was for public adoption that it was proposed. McCulloch v. Maryland, 4 Wheat. 316, 407. The known purpose of this Amendment was to get rid of nice questions as to what might be direct taxes, and I cannot doubt that most people not lawyers would suppose when they voted for it that they put a question like the present to rest. I am of opinion that the Amendment justifies the tax. See Tax Commissioner v. Putnam, 227 Mass. 522, 532, 533, 116 N.E. 904.

MR. JUSTICE DAY concurs in this opinion.

Mr. Justice Brandeis delivered the following [dissenting] opinion:

* * *

Hitherto powers conferred upon Congress by the Constitution have been liberally construed, and have been held to extend to every means appropriate to attain the end sought. In determining the scope of the power the substance of the transaction, not its form has been regarded. [Citations omitted.] Is there anything in the phraseology of the Sixteenth Amendment or in the nature of corporate dividends which should lead to a departure from these rules of construction and compel this court to hold, that Congress is powerless to prevent a result so extraordinary as that here contended for by the stockholder?

First. The term "income," when applied to the investment of the stockholder in a corporation, had, before the adoption of the Sixteenth Amendment, been commonly understood to mean the returns from time to time received by the stockholder from gains or earnings of the corporation. A dividend received by a stockholder from a corporation may be either in distribution of capital assets or in distribution of profits. Whether it is the one or the other is in no way affected by the medium in which it is paid, nor by the method or means through which the particular thing distributed as a dividend was procured. If the dividend is declared payable in cash, the money with which to pay it is ordinarily taken from surplus cash in the treasury. But (if there are profits legally available for distribution and the law under which the company was incorporated so permits) the company may raise the money by discounting negotiable paper; or by selling bonds, scrip or stock of another corporation then in the treasury; or by selling its own bonds, scrip or stock issued expressly for that purpose. How the money shall be raised is wholly a matter of financial management. The manner in which it is raised in no way affects the question whether the dividend received by the stockholder is income or capital; nor can it conceivably affect the question whether it is taxable as income.

Likewise whether a dividend declared payable from profits shall be paid in cash or in some other medium is also wholly a matter of financial management. If some other medium is decided upon, it is also wholly a question of financial management whether the distribution shall be, for instance, in bonds, scrip or stock of another corporation or in issues of its own. * * *

* * *

Second. It has been said that a dividend payable in bonds or preferred stock created for the purpose of distributing profits may be income and taxable as such, but that the case is different where the distribution is in common stock created for that purpose. Various reasons are assigned for making this distinction. One is that the proportion of the stockholder's ownership to the aggregate number of the shares of the company is not changed by the distribution. But that is equally true where the dividend is paid in its bonds or in its preferred stock.

Furthermore, neither maintenance nor change in the proportionate ownership of a stockholder in a corporation has any bearing upon the question here involved. Another reason assigned is that the value of the old stock held is reduced approximately by the value of the new stock received, so that the stockholder after receipt of the stock dividend has no more than he had before it was paid. That is equally true whether the dividend be paid in cash or in other property, for instance, bonds, scrip or preferred stock of the company. The payment from profits of a large cash dividend, and even a small one, customarily lowers the then market value of stock because the undivided property represented by each share has been correspondingly reduced. The argument which appears to be most strongly urged for the stockholders is, that when a stock dividend is made, no portion of the assets of the company is thereby segregated for the stockholder. But does the issue of new bonds or of preferred stock created for use as a dividend result in any segregation of assets for the stockholder? In each case he receives a piece of paper which entitles him to certain rights in the undivided property. Clearly segregation of assets in a physical sense is not an essential of income. The year's gains of a partner is taxable as income, although there, likewise, no segregation of his share in the gains from that of his partners is had.

* * *

Mr. Justice Clarke concurs in this opinion.

Problem, Notes and Questions

1. *Income and enrichment.* Did the *Macomber* Court hold that stock dividends could not be taxed because their receipt did not make the taxpayer wealthier? If so, it would follow that cash dividends should not be taxed. A taxpayer who holds all the stock of a corporation whose assets consist solely of $50,000 in cash becomes no wealthier when the corporation declares and pays a $10,000 cash dividend.

Even if *Macomber* had gone the other way, the tax in question would have raised very little revenue. Just as corporations and their shareholders avoid the tax on cash dividends by not paying cash dividends, corporations could easily have avoided a tax on stock dividends by not making them. Perhaps for this reason, Congress has never again tried to tax a simple common-on-common stock dividend.

2. *Realization and the Constitution.* Does Eisner v. Macomber mean that Congress could not constitutionally tax as income unrealized increases in the value of stock (note that the statute in the *Macomber* case did *not* attempt to do that)? The taxpayers in Prescott v. Commissioner, 561 F.2d 1287 (8th Cir.1977), had elected under § 1361 to have their businesses taxed as corporations, although they were not actually incorporated. When Congress repealed § 1361 in 1966, it provided that all § 1361 elections not voluntarily revoked would be automatically terminated on January 1, 1969. In upholding a regulation which treated the automatic termination of a § 1361 election as a taxable event,

requiring the taxpayers to realize gain equal to the appreciation in business assets, the Eighth Circuit read Helvering v. Bruun (p. 118, below) as having abandoned any "severance" requirement for realization (561 F.2d at 1293):

> If *Eisner* stood undiminished by subsequent decisions, it would offer strong support to taxpayers' position. However, the Supreme Court has found it necessary to abandon the attempt at an all-inclusive definition of income which it had undertaken in *Eisner*. See 1 J. Mertens, Law of Federal Income Taxation, § 5.03 (1974). In Helvering v. Bruun, 309 U.S. 461 (1940), the Court held that a lessor realized income on the termination of a lease in the value of any improvements to the land made by the lessee, notwithstanding the improvements were not severed from the land. The Court thus abandoned the idea that gain must be severed from capital to be taxable. See also Commissioner v. Glenshaw Glass Co., 348 U.S. 426, 431 (1955) (noting this change).
>
> In place of the concept of severance, the Court, in determining whether there has been income, now looks to determine if there has been a "taxable event." United States v. Davis, 370 U.S. 65, 67 (1962); Commissioner v. Glenshaw Glass Co., supra, 348 U.S. at 431. The question asked is whether some event has occurred which marks an appropriate time to tax the increase in value of assets. United States v. Davis, supra.
>
> The requirement of a taxable event has been satisfied here. The action of Congress, as a result of which the taxpayers' businesses, which had fictional corporate status, returned to taxation as proprietorships, created an event upon which it was appropriate to tax the increase in value of those businesses. We conclude therefore that the tax was protected from Article I, § 9 by the income exception contained in the Sixteenth Amendment.

Accord, O'Dowd v. Commissioner, 595 F.2d 262 (5th Cir.1979).

Under §§ 951–64, some of the income of "controlled foreign corporations" is taxed to the corporations' shareholders even if the corporations distribute nothing. The "mark-to-market" rule of § 1256 requires that taxpayers holding some kinds of futures contracts, foreign currency contracts, and options be taxed as if they had sold those assets on the last business day of the taxable year. Under § 475, gains and losses on most securities held by securities dealers are also taxed on a mark-to-market basis. No serious commentator believes that these provisions are unconstitutional in failing to require a realization transaction.

Proposals for taxing increases in the value of property, even when those increases are not dramatized by a sale of the property or other realization event, have become fairly popular in recent academic literature. Some writers advocate measuring value increases directly at regular intervals. Others suggest that taxation can await disposition of the asset, with failure to tax wealth increases as they occur being made up for by imposing an interest charge at the time of sale. For example, a taxpayer who holds an asset for ten years and then realizes a $100,000 gain on the disposition of the asset might pay not only a tax on $100,000 income but also an interest charge, on the assumption that the gain accrued over the ten-year period. For an analysis and a review of the literature, see Blum, New Role for Treasury: Charging Interest on Tax Deferral Loans, 25 Harv.J.on Leg. 1 (1988).

3. *Problem.* A and B are employed by X Corporation, 50 percent of the stock of which is owned by each of them. Anticipating that X Corporation may be short of funds, A and B are thinking about reducing their cash salaries for next year by $100,000 and having X issue to each of them $100,000 worth of its stock as compensation for their services. They ask your advice as to whether the value of the stock would be (1) includable in their gross incomes and (2) deductible by X Corporation. What say you? Does the proposal make any non-tax sense?

3. DEPRECIATION

A taxpayer who pays $50,000 for an asset which will be used to produce income for five years, and which will then be worthless, must at some point deduct $50,000 from receipts if only "gain" is to be taxed. If the simplest kind of depreciation, or "cost recovery," is used, the mechanics of the procedure are as follows: the taxpayer deducts one-fifth ($10,000) of the asset's cost each year for five years. Unlike the case of computing gain from the sale of property, the money the taxpayer paid for the asset does not affect the determination of gross income (§ 61); instead, the taxpayer deducts the cost (over a five-year period) in computing taxable income (§ 63).

HAMPTON PONTIAC, INC. v. UNITED STATES

United States District Court, District of South Carolina, 1969.
294 F.Supp. 1073.

DONALD RUSSELL, DISTRICT JUDGE.

[Samuel W. Jones, Sr., the controlling shareholder and manager of the taxpayer corporation, wanted the corporation to acquire a Pontiac dealership in Columbia, South Carolina. Conversations with the management of the Pontiac Division of General Motors convinced Jones that the corporation could acquire a Pontiac franchise only if King Pontiac, the existing Pontiac dealer in Columbia, surrendered its franchise. Jones and the taxpayer made an agreement with King Pontiac and with Matthews, King Pontiac's controlling shareholder. King Pontiac and Matthews agreed "to procure the termination of" King Pontiac's franchise and to obtain a new franchise for Jones; Jones and the taxpayer agreed to pay $15,000 to King Pontiac and to pay a portion of the taxpayer's profits to Matthews for five years.]

* * *

With the surrender by King Pontiac of its franchise, the plaintiff was promptly awarded the Pontiac franchise in Columbia. By mutual consent, it was renewable indefinitely. The record shows that, at the termination of the initial franchise, it was renewed by the parties for another term. This seems to have been the normal pattern for General Motors dealership[s], as is hereafter noted. The franchise agreement included, also, specific provisions granting General Motors the right to terminate immediately the franchise in the event of the death or withdrawal of the dealership's controlling stockholder and/or manager.

After receiving the franchise, plaintiff commenced making the payments provided under the agreement with King Pontiac and Matthews. During 1962, plaintiff paid Matthews, pursuant to the agreement, $8,040.89. This sum it deducted as salary expense on its federal tax return for that year. Such deduction was disallowed. After making the tax payment required by the disallowed deduction, plaintiff filed this action for refund, contending that the payments made are deductible as ordinary and necessary business expense[s] or, in the alternative, are amortizable over the life of its franchise. The defendant denies that plaintiff is entitled to a deduction on either basis. The issues thus posed by this action are:

(1) Were the payments "ordinary and necessary business expenses"?

(2) If not, and if they represented capital investments, are they amortizable under Section 167?

The payments to Matthews were capital investments, not deductible as "ordinary and necessary business expenses." Plaintiff's agreement with Matthews, under which the payments were made, was executed by the plaintiff because plaintiff believed, based on information secured by it from Pontiac, that an agreement for the voluntary cancellation of King's franchise was an essential preliminary step to the award to it of the Pontiac franchise. Matthews, in turn, would only have agreed to the cancellation, payment for which to him and King Pontiac was contingent on plaintiff's securing a franchise, because he had some assurance that, upon the filing of the cancellation, Pontiac would award the new franchise to plaintiff. * * * That all payments under the agreement were only to be made if and after the plaintiff acquired the franchise demonstrates indisputably that the payments were directly related to the acquisition of the franchise. The contract with Matthews, and the obligations thereby undertaken by the plaintiff, were thus an integral part of plaintiff's expense in acquiring its Pontiac franchise. Payments made thereunder represent accordingly items includible in plaintiff's invested capital and are not deductible as business expense. [Citations omitted.]

Though the payments to Matthews should be capitalized, the issue remains whether such payments, so capitalized, may be amortized and, if so, on what basis. Under a Treasury Regulation, first adopted under the Revenue Act of 1918 and remaining substantially unchanged through successive reenactments, thereby acquiring the force of law, intangible assets may only be depreciated if the useful life of the asset is of limited duration, capable from experience of being "estimated with reasonable accuracy." Section 1.167(a)–3 [further citations omitted].

It is plaintiff's position that if the payments made as a part of the costs of securing the franchise are to be capitalized, they should be amortizable over the fixed life of the franchise (i.e., five years), the renewal provision of the franchise agreement being too uncertain and speculative to be regarded as giving added duration or import to the franchise. In support of this contention, plaintiff emphasizes that both parties must agree to a renewal and that whether each will so agree depends on the profitability of the franchise from the standpoint of each. * * *

The defendant, on the other hand, insists that the experience of General Motors dealerships, as developed in the record herein, shows that the renewal of the franchise, both by the manufacturer and the distributor, is normally routine or automatic and that it is wholly unrealistic to disregard such probability of renewal in arriving at the practical life of the franchise. Under this theory of the defendant, adopted by the Commissioner, the franchise had an indeterminate useful life and accordingly was not depreciable under Regulation 1.167(a)–3. It primarily relies, in support of its contention, upon C.I.R. v. Indiana Broadcasting Corporation (7th Cir.1965) 350 F.2d 580 and Richmond Television Corporation v. United States (4th Cir.1965) 354 F.2d 410.

The position of the plaintiff is contrary to the weight of the testimony. The record will not permit disregard of the renewal provisions of the franchise. The plaintiff has clearly failed to bear the burden of establishing the amortizable character of his payments on the basis of the fixed life of the franchise. See, Curry v. United States (4th Cir.1962) 298 F.2d 273, 275. The hearings before the Subcommittee of the Committee on the Judiciary, United States Senate, held in October and November, 1967, and incorporated by agreement of the parties in the record herein (hereafter cited as "Hearings"), established that, certainly in recent years, there had been among General Motors dealerships "relatively few nonrenewals upon expiration of the 5–year term agreements." No doubt this almost automatic renewal of franchise resulted from the demands of the distributors for protection against denial of renewals that culminated in the enactment in 1956 of the "Dealer's Day in Court Act" (Sections 1221–1225, 15 U.S.C.). General Motors has, however, gone beyond the requirements of the Act and given its dealers administrative protection in the exercise of their right of renewal. It provides a right of appeal by any dealer who is denied renewal of his franchise to an impartial "GM dealer relations umpire," who, if he finds the nonrenewal without just cause, may order the franchise renewed; and this decision of the impartial "umpire" is to be accepted as binding by General Motors, though not on the dealer. The present umpire is Honorable Charles Whittaker, formerly a justice of the United States Supreme Court. That these safeguards, given both by statute and by agreement, have given practical meaning to the renewal provision in General Motors' franchises is proven by the record of nonrenewals of such franchises. Thus, with

12,800 dealers, there was not one nonrenewal of franchise in 1964, there were 62 in 1965, 9 in 1966, and only 8 in the first nine months of 1967. More particularly, so far as this record shows, there was not one single instance in which, during the period covered by the franchise involved in this proceeding, a Pontiac Franchise in South Carolina was not renewed by both the manufacturer and the dealer.

The testimony that there had been a small drop in the number of franchised dealerships in South Carolina in the last decade, I regard as largely meaningless. There was no attempt in such testimony to identify and separate the types of franchises involved in the abandoned dealerships. * * *

It is plain from the language of the Court in Richmond Television Corporation v. United States (4th Cir.1965) 354 F.2d 410, 412, that renewal rights are not to be ignored or disregarded in determining the useful life of a contract or franchise under Section 167 but are to be weighed on the basis of the probability of renewal, arrived at in the light of actual "experience." Measured by this standard and giving due weight to the actual record of nonrenewals of General Motors' franchises, it cannot be said that the enjoyment of this franchise "may with reason be expected to end" in five years (354 F.2d 410, 413); on the contrary, the record would indicate quite clearly that the franchise was reasonably certain of renewal indefinitely.

* * *

Neither Helvering v. Kansas City American Ass'n Baseball Co. (8th Cir.1935) 75 F.2d 600, nor Bonwit Teller & Co. v. Commissioner (2d Cir.1931) 53 F.2d 381, on both of which plaintiff relies, is in point. The first involved the personal contract of a professional baseball player. Naturally, such a contract would not be routinely renewed. Its renewal would depend on the salary offered, the past record of the player, the present state of his health, whether the player was traded, and many other factors not typical of other agreements. The second dealt with a renewal option, to be exercised at the end of a twenty-year lease at a rental then to be agreed upon. Again, the renewability of such a lease at such an extended date at a purely speculative rental would not be a routine matter. In this case, on the contrary, as we have seen, the possibility of renewal of franchise is so likely and so near routine, the right of renewal so safeguarded by effective remedies, the record of almost automatic renewal so clearly established, that it would be unrealistic to hold that the useful life of this franchise was limited to five years.

There is, however, one contingency, real and not imaginary, that could terminate this franchise. It is one that would apply both to the original terms of the franchise and to any renewal thereof. It arises out of the very nature of the franchise agreement itself, as spelt out in the agreement. By the express terms of Paragraph "Third," the franchise is "a personal service contract, * * * entered into * * * in reliance upon and in consideration of the personal qualifications of * * * the following named person or persons who, it is agreed, will substantially participate in the ownership * * * and/or will actively participate in the operation of Dealer's Pontiac dealership: Sam W. Jones, Sr." To give force to this specific provision, the franchise states that, "Pontiac may terminate this Agreement immediately * * * in the event of * * * Removal, resignation, withdrawal or elimination from Dealer for any reason of any person named in Paragraph THIRD of this Agreement." The reasons for such provisions in the franchise were explained by the Marketing Vice–President of General Motors, in the Congressional hearings, already referred to, as follows:

"GM for many years has recognized that the degree to which a dealership will operate successfully in the performance of its functions and responsibilities is directly dependent upon the qualifications, abilities, and personal character of the individual or individuals who actually operate and own the dealership.

"For this reason all car division selling agreements provide that the relationship established by the selling agreement is expressly conditioned upon active participation in the operation, as well as the ownership of the dealership by the individual or individuals specifically named in the selling agreement. This is designed to bring competent management to the dealership operations. * * *

"Essentially, we rely on individuals, persons who we think have the energy, ability and character to make the association mutually profitable."

That the right of termination given by these provisions is rigorously exercised is manifested by a comparison of the record of involuntary franchise termination[s] and those caused by the death of the participating stockholder and manager under "Paragraph Third." In the Congressional hearing already referred to, it was established that, among GM dealers, 185 franchises were terminated in 1964 under the terms of "Paragraph Third" and only 8 for poor performance, in 1965, 201 were terminated under "Paragraph Third" and 1 for poor performance, and in 1966, 156 were terminated under "Paragraph Third" and not one for poor performance. It seems clear from such record that the death of the participating owner designated in "Paragraph Third" will normally occasion the termination of the franchise. The most that apparently the widow of a deceased participating manager can expect upon such event is "the opportunity to participate financially in the *successor dealership*" (Italics added). The very reference to "successor dealership" is consistent only with the conclusion that the former franchise had been terminated.

Tucker v. Commissioner (8th Cir.1955) 226 F.2d 177, while involving a Ford franchise, shows that this requirement that the manager of an automobile agency must be its controlling stockholder and that the death or withdrawal of such manager will call for the termination of the franchise is exactingly enforced by automobile manufacturers.

It seems plain, therefore, that the death of Mr. Jones will normally result in the termination of the franchise. Termination, under such circumstance, is not theoretical; it can, with reasonable probability, be expected. When that unfortunate event may occur cannot, of course, be predicted with absolute accuracy but, based on experience, the Treasury has established certain mortality tables, which can be utilized in determining when the termination of the franchise on account of Jones' death may reasonably be determined.[10] Such tables can be properly used in calculating the reasonable life of this franchise, as fixed by the terms of "Paragraph Third" of the franchise agreement. After all, calculations of useful life need not be "absolute"; all that is required for their use as a basis for depreciation under Section 167 is that the estimations or approximations be "reasonable" in the light of normal experience. Commonwealth Natural Gas Corp. v. United States (4th Cir.1968) 395 F.2d 493; Northern Natural Gas Co. v. O'Malley (8th Cir.1960) 277 F.2d 128, 135–6; Shell Pipe Line Corp. v. United States (D.C.Tex.1967) 267 F.Supp. 1014, 1021–2. Such tables represent "reasonable" estimations.

CONCLUSION

To sum up, I am of opinion: (1) that the payments by the taxpayer to Matthews must be capitalized and may not be expensed, (2) that such payments may not be amortized over the initial fixed term of the franchise agreement (i.e., five years) but, (3) that such payments may be amortized over the life expectancy of Samuel W. Jones, Sr., as computed by the mortality tables issued under the Treasury Regulation.

Let the parties agree upon and submit a judgment in accordance with the foregoing conclusions.

Problem, Note and Question

1. *No cash?* The owner of a professional sports franchise is allowed to depreciate the contracts of the players. A series of newspaper articles criticized this allowance as a tax loophole, which subsidizes professional sports. The arguments made were: (1) the owner's depreciation deduction is a deduction for an "imaginary" expense, since the owner does not part with any cash in the years in which depreciation is taken; (2) the owner gets a "double benefit" by deducting both depreciation and the player's salary (a business expense under § 162); and (3) if anyone should get a deduction for depreciation it is the players themselves, as it is their bodies that wear out. Are any of these criticisms sound?

2. *Problem.* A taxpayer buys a truck for $10,000, takes straight-line depreciation of $4000, and sells the truck for $7000. What is the taxpayer's gain on the sale? Sections 1001, 1011, 1016.

3. *Section 197.* It is often hard to determine the useful life of "intangible" assets such as franchises. Under § 197, which will be examined in Chapter 4, many purchased intangibles are depreciated (or "amortized") over 15 years, without regard to their actual expected lives. Under this provision, the amounts paid to Matthews in *Hampton*

---

10. Treas.Reg. § 1.72–9.

Pontiac would be amortized over fifteen years, rather than over Jones's life expectancy.

4. ANNUITIES

An annuity is a series of payments, often for a period measured by the life of the recipient (or the joint lives of the recipient and another person, such as the recipient's spouse). An individual can buy an annuity from an insurance company for a lump-sum payment; a contract like this assures the recipient of a lifetime source of funds. Pension payments over the life of the retiree are another common kind of annuity. Some annuities provide fixed monthly payments. Others tie the amount of the payment to the performance of an investment, such as a portfolio of securities; annuities that do this are called "variable annuities."

The simplest kind of annuity is a series of fixed payments for the life of the recipient. To see how the annuitant's costs are reflected in determining income, work out the following problems under § 72 and the regulations.

Problems

Problem (1). A, who was 65 years old on January 1, year 1 pays an insurance company $144,000 for an annuity of $1000 a month for A's lifetime, payments to begin on January 31, year 1. How much of each payment must A include in income? The actuarial tables referred to in § 72(c)(3)(A) are found in Treas.Reg. § 1.72–9 (in this case, Table V).

Problem (2). In January, year 3, A died. A had received $24,000 in annuity payments in year 1 and year 2, and nothing in year 3. Compute A's deduction for year 3. See § 72(b)(3).

Problem (3). If A had lived for more than 20 years, how much of A's $12,000 payment for year 21 would have been includable in A's income? See § 72(b)(2).

Notes

1. *Other methods of taxing annuities.* Until 1934, an annuitant treated all payments as a non-taxable recovery of basis until the sum of the payments equalled the amount paid for the contract; further payments were income in full. Until 1987, this method applied to employee annuities if the employee would recover basis within three years—in practice, this meant retired government employees. From 1934 to 1954, only the amount of each payment in excess of three percent of the amount paid for the contract was treated as a return of capital, and once capital was recovered further payments were fully taxable. Between 1954 and 1987, annuity computations were made as under current law except that neither an annuitant's death before recovery of his investment in the contract nor an annuitant's outliving his life expectancy had any tax effect. Under this system, annuitants who lived longer than the tables

predicted recovered more than their capital tax free, while those who did not survive for the expected period recovered less.

2. *Deferred annuities.* Consider a taxpayer who pays $50,000 today for an annuity contract which will be worth $200,000 in eighteen years. When the contract matures, the taxpayer can either withdraw the $200,000 as a lump sum or begin receiving periodic payments. Economically, this investment is identical to depositing $50,000 in a bank account, receiving interest at a rate of 8 percent, leaving each year's interest on deposit (also at 8 percent), and withdrawing the deposit plus accumulated interest after eighteen years. The bank depositor will be taxed each year on that year's interest. The annuitant, however, will not be, unless it is "a person who is not a natural person" (usually, a corporation); § 72(u). Because the annual increase in the value of an annuity contract is not taxed to an individual investor, these contracts provide an opportunity to defer taxes on investment income. Some deferred annuity contracts grow in value at a fixed rate, some provide for periodic rate adjustment, and some allow the investor to switch the funds among different investments.

One drawback to using annuity contracts to defer taxes on investment income is that most taxpayers who withdraw lump sums before reaching the age of 59½ become subject to an extra "early withdrawal tax" of 10 percent of the income portion of the withdrawals; § 72(q). Many of the companies which issue deferred annuity contracts also impose surrender charges for early withdrawals. Note that the tax benefit of investing in a deferred annuity contract is the same as the benefit of making a non-deductible contribution to a traditional IRA (p. 67, above). The most important difference between these investments is that there is no statutory limit on the amount that can be invested in an annuity contract.

5. BUSINESS EXPENSES

Lawyer *A*, a sole proprietor, takes in $200,000 in legal fees this year, while lawyer *B* receives $500,000 in fees. Which lawyer is doing better? Plainly, you cannot tell: if *A*'s costs for the year for things like rent, phone bills, and the salary of a secretary come to $50,000, while *B*'s expenses amount to $450,000, *A*'s practice is much more profitable than *B*'s, and *A* should pay more tax. In this kind of case, the taxpayer's "recovery of capital" does not involve the calculation of gross income: *A*'s gross income is $200,000; *B*'s is $500,000. The lawyers' costs of earning their incomes are taken into account by giving them deductions (under § 162(a)) for the expenses of their businesses.

Compare the way in which the income of a sole proprietor whose business involves selling goods is calculated. Suppose that *C* owns a small store, and sells merchandise that cost $180,000 for $380,000. *C* also incurs expenses like rent, utility bills, and salary, of $150,000. *C*'s gross income is $200,000, because gross income from sales is the taxpayer's gain on the sale, not the sale price (see p. 49, above). From that gross income, C will deduct business expenses of $150,000, leaving $50,000 of taxable income.

The line between business costs that affect the calculation of gross income and those taken into account (as deductions) in calculating taxable income is not always clear. For instance, is the cost of heating the factory in which the taxpayer manufactures widgets for sale part of the cost of the widgets—to be taken into account in calculating gain on the sale of the widgets—or is it just one more deductible business expense? Questions like this are addressed in detail in the regulations under § 471 (and, in some cases, § 263A); the details are well beyond the scope of the basic tax course. One point worth knowing, though, is that the costs of making sales—such as the costs of shipping or of operating delivery trucks—are treated as business expenses, not as part of the costs of the goods that have been sold.

Because the income tax is imposed on taxable income, rather than gross income, some taxpayers will not care whether a particular cost is used to calculate gross income or is a deduction, affecting taxable income but not gross income: what usually matters is that the cost somehow or other ends up being taken into account. As the following opinion shows, however, the distinction can be important.

DIXIE DAIRIES CORP. v. COMMISSIONER

United States Tax Court, 1980.
74 T.C. 476 (Acq.).

DRENNEN, JUDGE: In these consolidated cases, respondent determined the following deficiencies in, and additions to, petitioners' Federal corporate income taxes * * *.

Due to concessions by the parties, * * * the issues for our decision are:

> (1)(a) Whether certain payments made by each of the petitioners to its customers are to be excluded in determining gross income or are to be treated as deductions from gross income subject to the limitations of section 162(c)(2).

* * *

FINDINGS OF FACT

[The Alabama Dairy Commission established minimum prices at which milk could be sold. Petitioners circumvented the minimum-price regulations by purporting to sell milk at the minimum price and then giving the buyers cash "rebates." This practice was clearly illegal under Alabama law, but it was "widespread throughout the milk industry during the years here involved." The Dairy Commission's enforcement efforts were minimal: no sanctions were imposed upon any violator during the years involved in this case.

The taxpayers argued that their gross incomes from selling milk should be determined by subtracting the cost of the milk sold from the *net* sale price (i.e., the sale price nominally charged less the rebate paid in connection with the sale).]

* * *

In the case of each of the petitioners, respondent determined that section 162(c) precluded the cash rebates from being excluded in determining gross income or from being deducted from gross income.

* * *

OPINION

Cash Rebates

Each petitioner, pursuant to oral agreements between it and its retail customers entered into prior to the sale of the milk and milk products which generated the cash rebates in issue, paid cash rebates to those customers based on a percentage of the dollar volume of the purchases of the milk and milk products. The cash rebates were utilized as a means to circumvent the minimum prices set for such products by the Alabama Dairy Commission. The initial question to be decided is whether the cash rebates are to be excluded in determining gross income, as petitioners argue, or whether they are to be treated as deductions from gross income subject to the limitations of section 162, as respondent argues. In the various statutory notices of deficiency, respondent determined that the cash rebates could neither be excluded in determining gross income nor be deducted from gross income.[14]

The proper treatment to be accorded similar payments made by sellers of milk and milk products to retailers has been previously decided by this Court. Pittsburgh Milk Co. v. Commissioner, 26 T.C. 707 (1956); Atzingen–Whitehouse Dairy, Inc. v. Commissioner, 36 T.C. 173 (1961). In each of these cases, the Court determined that the payments were to be excluded in determining gross income, in effect, concluding that the milk and milk products were sold for an agreed net price which equaled the set minimum price less the cash rebates. The rationale underlying the decisions reached in *Pittsburgh Milk Co.* and *Atzingen–Whitehouse Dairy, Inc.,* has recently been reconsidered and approved by this Court. Max Sobel Wholesale Liquors v. Commissioner, 69 T.C. 477 (1977) (Court reviewed), [affirmed 630 F.2d 670] (9th Cir. [1980]); Haas Brothers, Inc. v. Commissioner, 73 T.C. 1217 (1980).

Respondent does not argue that the above-cited cases are factually distinguishable from the instant case, nor does he argue that the rationale of those decisions is inapplicable herein. Rather, he asserts that *Pittsburgh Milk Co.* and its progeny were incorrectly decided, and he urges us to reconsider and overrule those decisions.

---

14. Respondent does not argue that the manner in which the petitioners originally accounted for the cash rebates on their tax returns has any effect on whether the rebates can be excluded in determining gross income.

Respondent's argument that the cash rebates are not to be excluded in determining gross income has two components. The first component is that Congress, by enacting section 162(c)(2) in its present form, intended to prohibit taxpayers from benefiting from illegal payments such as these cash rebates. [Treas.Reg. §§] 1.61–3(a) and 1.471–3(d) were promulgated to prevent the congressional intent from being circumvented, by prohibiting an exclusion from income for any amount that would be nondeductible under section 162(c)(2). Therefore, the cash rebates are not excludable since section 162(c)(2) would preclude their deduction. In essence, respondent's argument is that the expression of public policy in section 162(c)(2), and the Treasury regulations enacted in furtherance of that policy, are subsequent to, and overrule the holdings of, *Pittsburgh Milk Co.* and *Atzingen–Whitehouse Dairy, Inc.*

The second component of respondent's argument is that, regardless of [Treas.Reg. §§] 1.61–3(a) and 1.471–3(d), the cash rebates are not excludable in determining gross income; rather, they are business expenses. Respondent contends that the agreements between petitioners and retailers were in contradiction of state law and unenforceable. Petitioners thus received the purchase price of the milk under claim of right with no obligation to pay the cash rebates. If petitioners did pay the cash rebates, such payments were unilateral and legally gratuitous acts and not part of the initial milk sales. They were, therefore, in substance, sales and promotional expenses governed by section 162. Thus, respondent argues that, contrary to this Court's holding in *Max Sobel,* there is no distinction "*between* a discount or rebate to which the customers became entitled at the time of sale *and* costs incurred in the form of illegal payments, or payments to the third parties, which were not made pursuant to agreement between the buyer and the seller." Max Sobel Wholesale Liquors v. Commissioner, supra at 482–483. Emphasis in original. See Alex v. Commissioner, 70 T.C. 322 (1978), [affirmed 628 F.2d 1222 (9th Cir.1980)].

We find neither component of respondent's argument persuasive. The effect of the enactment of section 162(c)(2) in its present form and of [Treas.Reg. §§] 1.61–3(a) and 1.471–3(d) on the rationale of *Pittsburgh Milk Co.* was addressed by this Court in Max Sobel Wholesale Liquors v. Commissioner, supra at 484–485. Therein, the Court held that if Congress had intended to overrule *Pittsburgh Milk Co.* by the enactment of section 162(c)(2), it would have been more specific in doing so. We agree with that assessment.

The second component of respondent's argument is likewise unpersuasive. We are convinced, as was the case in *Pittsburgh Milk Co.,* that the price at which the petitioners sold milk to retailers was an agreed net price comprised of the minimum set price less cash rebate, and it is only such net price that is includable in gross income. The purchase of the milk and the payment of the purchase price thereon, and the payment of the cash rebates are part of a single transaction. See Haas Brothers, Inc. v. Commissioner, supra at note 3.

Accordingly, the proper treatment for the cash rebates in issue is to exclude them in determining gross income. Furthermore, having reached this conclusion, we need not address the issues raised with respect to section 162(c).[20]

* * *

Notes

1. *Reduction of gross income vs. deduction from gross income.* The principal use of "gross income" in the tax law is as a starting point in computing the "taxable income" to which the tax rates of § 1 or § 11 apply. In most cases, it will not matter to a taxpayer whether an expenditure reduces the gross-income figure or is deducted from gross income. If, for example, an employer reimburses an employee for costs incurred in performing services, the payment might be treated as: (1) gross income to the employee, which is offset by a deduction for the employee under § 162, or (2) the repayment of a "loan" the employee made to the employer by spending money on the employer's behalf, in which case the payment is not includable in the employee's gross income. In either case, the taxable income is the same (assuming the payment and reimbursement take place in the same taxable year). As the principal case shows, however, there are times when the distinction matters. Some other sections under which the distinction can be important are §§ 6501(e) (note that this section contains its own special definition of "gross income") and 151.

2. *Business expenses.* Chapter 4 will examine the tax treatment of business costs in some detail. At this point, two matters worth thinking about are: (1) the variety of methods by which taxpayers take the costs of earning income into account—offsets to gross income, immediate deductions from gross (or adjusted gross) income, and delayed deductions—and (2) the distinction between the costs of producing revenues, which must almost always be taken into account in computing taxable income, and the costs of consumption and (some) savings, which generally do not enter into the computation of income.

D. REALIZATION AND RECOGNITION

HELVERING v. BRUUN

Supreme Court of the United States, 1940.
309 U.S. 461, 60 S.Ct. 631, 84 L.Ed. 864.

Mr. Justice Roberts delivered the opinion of the Court.

The controversy had its origin in the petitioner's assertion that the respondent realized taxable gain from the forfeiture of a leasehold, the

---

20. Petitioners argued that the milk-pricing regulations were not a "law of a state" within the sphere of sec. 162(c)(2), and also, that if they were the law of a state, the law was not generally enforced. Petitioner Pure Milk Co. also raised several constitutional arguments which we need not consider.

tenant having erected a new building upon the premises. The court below held that no income had been realized. Inconsistency of the decisions on the subject led us to grant certiorari. 308 U.S. 544.

The Board of Tax Appeals made no independent findings. The cause was submitted upon a stipulation of facts. From this it appears that on July 1, 1915, the respondent, as owner, leased a lot of land and the building thereon for a term of ninety-nine years.

The lease provided that the lessee might, at any time, upon giving bond to secure rentals accruing in the two ensuing years, remove or tear down any building on the land, provided that no building should be removed or torn down after the lease became forfeited, or during the last three and one-half years of the term. The lessee was to surrender the land, upon termination of the lease, with all buildings and improvements thereon.

In 1929 the tenant demolished and removed the existing building and constructed a new one which had a useful life of not more than fifty years. July 1, 1933, the lease was cancelled for default in payment of rent and taxes and the respondent regained possession of the land and building.

The parties stipulated "that as at said date, July 1, 1933, the building which had been erected upon said premises by the lessee had a fair market value of $64,245.68 and that the unamortized cost of the old building, which was removed from the premises in 1929 to make way for the new building, was $12,811.43, thus leaving a net fair market value as at July 1, 1933, of $51,434.25, for the aforesaid new building erected upon the premises by the lessee."

On the basis of these facts, the petitioner determined that in 1933 the respondent realized a net gain of $51,434.25. The Board overruled his determination and the Circuit Court of Appeals affirmed the Board's decision.

The course of administrative practice and judicial decision in respect of the question presented has not been uniform. In 1917 the Treasury ruled that the adjusted value of improvements installed upon leased premises is income to the lessor upon the termination of the lease. The ruling was incorporated in two succeeding editions of the Treasury Regulations. In 1919 the Circuit Court of Appeals for the Ninth Circuit held in Miller v. Gearin, 258 F. 225, that the regulation was invalid as the gain, if taxable at all, must be taxed as of the year when the improvements were completed.

The regulations were accordingly amended to impose a tax upon the gain in the year of completion of the improvements, measured by their anticipated value at the termination of the lease and discounted for the duration of the lease. Subsequently the regulations permitted the lessor to spread the depreciated value of the improvements over the remaining life of the lease, reporting an aliquot part each year, with provision that, upon premature termination, a tax should be imposed upon the excess of the then value of the improvements over the amount theretofore returned.

In 1935 the Circuit Court of Appeals for the Second Circuit decided in Hewitt Realty Co. v. Commissioner, 76 F.2d 880, that a landlord received no taxable income in a year, during the term of the lease, in which his tenant erected a building on the leased land. The court, while recognizing that the lessor need not receive money to be taxable, based its decision that no taxable gain was realized in that case on the fact that the improvement was not portable or detachable from the land, and if removed would be worthless except as bricks, iron, and mortar. It said, 76 F.2d at page 884: "The question as we view it is whether the value received is embodied in something separately disposable, or whether it is so merged in the land as to become financially a part of it, something which, though it increases its value, has no value of its own when torn away."

This decision invalidated the regulations then in force.

In 1938 this court decided M.E. Blatt Co. v. United States, 305 U.S. 267. There, in connection with the execution of a lease, landlord and tenant mutually agreed that each should make certain improvements to the demised premises and that those made by the tenant should become and remain the property of the landlord. The Commissioner valued the improvements as of the date they were made, allowed depreciation thereon to the termination of the leasehold, divided the depreciated value by the number of years the lease had to run, and found the landlord taxable for each year's aliquot portion thereof. His action was sustained by the Court of Claims. The judgment was reversed on the ground that the added value could not be considered rental accruing over the period of the lease; that the facts found by the Court of Claims did not support the conclusion of the Commissioner as to the value to be attributed to the improvements after a use throughout the term of the lease; and that, in the circumstances disclosed, any enhancement in the value of the realty in the tax year was not income realized by the lessor within the Revenue Act.

The circumstances of the instant case differentiate it from the *Blatt* and *Hewitt* cases; but the petitioner's contention that gain was realized when the respondent, through forfeiture of the lease, obtained untrammeled title, possession and control of the premises, with the added increment of value added by the new building, runs counter to the decision in the *Miller* case and to the reasoning in the *Hewitt* case.

The respondent insists that the realty,—a capital asset at the date of the execution of the lease,—remained such throughout the term and after its expiration; that improvements affixed to the soil became part of the realty indistinguishably blended in the capital asset; that such improvements cannot be separately valued or treated as received in exchange for the improvements which were on the land at the date of the execution of the lease; that they are, therefore, in the same category as improvements added by the respondent to his land, or accruals of value due to extraneous and adventitious circumstances. Such added value, it is argued, can be considered capital gain only upon the owner's disposition of the asset. The position is that the economic gain consequent upon the enhanced value of the recaptured asset is not gain derived from capital or realized within the meaning of the Sixteenth Amendment and may not, therefore, be taxed without apportionment.

We hold that the petitioner was right in assessing the gain as realized in 1933.

We might rest our decision upon the narrow issue presented by the terms of the stipulation. It does not appear what kind of a building was erected by the tenant or whether the building was readily removable from the land. It is not stated whether the difference in the value between the building removed and that erected in its place accurately reflects an increase in the value of land and building considered as a single estate in land. On the facts stipulated, without more, we should not be warranted in holding that the presumption of the correctness of the Commissioner's determination has been overborne.

The respondent insists, however, that the stipulation was intended to assert that the sum of $51,434.25 was the measure of the resulting enhancement in value of the real estate at the date of the cancellation of the lease. The petitioner seems not to contest this view. Even upon this assumption we think that gain in the amount named was realized by the respondent in the year of repossession.

The respondent can not successfully contend that the definition of gross income in Sec. 22(a) of the Revenue Act of 1932 is not broad enough to embrace the gain in question. That definition follows closely the Sixteenth Amendment. Essentially the respondent's position is that the Amendment does not permit the taxation of such gain without apportionment amongst the states. He relies upon what was said in Hewitt Realty Co. v. Commissioner, supra, and upon expressions found in the decisions of this court dealing with the taxability of stock dividends to the effect that gain derived from capital must be something of exchangeable value proceeding from property, severed from the capital, however invested or employed, and received by the recipient for his separate use, benefit, and disposal. He emphasizes the necessity that the gain be separate from the capital and separately disposable. These expressions, however, were used to clarify the distinction between an ordinary dividend and a stock dividend. They were meant to show that in the case of a stock dividend, the stockholder's interest in the corporate assets after receipt of the dividend was the same as and inseverable from that which he owned before the dividend was declared. We think they are not controlling here.

While it is true that economic gain is not always taxable as income, it is settled that the realization of gain need not be in cash derived from the sale of an asset. Gain may occur as a result of exchange of property, payment of the taxpayer's indebtedness, relief from a liability, or other profit realized from the completion of a transaction. The fact that the gain is a portion of the value of property received by the taxpayer in the transaction does not negative its realization.

Here, as a result of a business transaction, the respondent received back his land with a new building on it, which added an ascertainable amount to its value. It is not necessary to recognition of taxable gain that he should be able to sever the improvement begetting the gain from his original capital. If that were necessary, no income could arise from the exchange of property; whereas such gain has always been recognized as realized taxable gain.

Judgment reversed.

THE CHIEF JUSTICE[p] concurs in the result in view of the terms of the stipulation of facts.

MR. JUSTICE MCREYNOLDS took no part in the decision of this case.

Problems, Notes and Questions

1. *Sections 109 and 1019.* Look at § 109, the predecessor of which was enacted just two years after the *Bruun* decision.

The principal interpretive problem under § 109 arises from the limitation of the exclusion to income "other than rent." Was the income in *Bruun* "rent"? In what kind of case would the value of a tenant's improvements clearly be "rent"? The regulations' treatment of the "rent" issue is not entirely clear. See Treas.Reg. §§ 1.109–1(a) & 1.61–8(c).

One practical objection to taxing Bruun is that the transaction held to produce income gave the taxpayer no money with which to pay the tax. But it is certainly true, as the Court notes, that "realization" does not require that *cash* be realized. Thus, a taxpayer who receives a valuable painting as compensation for services realizes income. Why is the "lack of cash with which to pay the tax" argument more persuasive on facts like those of *Bruun* than in the case of an employee who receives non-cash compensation?

2. *Problems.* In year 1, *L* leased unimproved land (with a value and basis of $500,000) to *T* for a term of 50 years at $100,000 a year. The lease required *T* to erect an office building on the land and provided that all improvements made by *T* would become the property of *L* on termination of the lease by forfeiture or otherwise. In year 15, *T* forfeited the lease for non-payment of rent, and the land and building reverted to *L*. At that time, the building was worth $1,000,000 (and the land $750,000).

(1) What was *L*'s basis in the property in year 15?

p. Charles Evans Hughes, who had represented the taxpayer in Eisner v. Macomber.—Eds.

(2) In year 18, *L* sold the land and building for $2,000,000. What result to *L*?

(3) What results in (1) and (2) if § 109 were not in the Code?

3. *References*. Surrey, The Supreme Court and the Federal Income Tax: Some Implications of the Recent Decisions, 35 Ill.L.Rev. 779 (1941); Simons, Personal Income Taxation 196–204 (1938) (describing Eisner v. Macomber as "that engaging metaphysical treatise on the quiddity of income"); Note, The Supreme Court's Apparent Abandonment of a Definitive Concept of Taxable Income, 45 Harv.L.Rev. 1072 (1932).

E. CANCELLATION OF INDEBTEDNESS

UNITED STATES v. KIRBY LUMBER CO.

Supreme Court of the United States, 1931.
284 U.S. 1, 52 S.Ct. 4, 76 L.Ed. 131.

MR. JUSTICE HOLMES delivered the opinion of the Court.

In July, 1923, the plaintiff, the Kirby Lumber Company, issued its own bonds for $12,126,800 for which it received their par value. Later in the same year it purchased in the open market some of the same bonds at less than par, the difference of price being $137,521.30. The question is whether this difference is a taxable gain or income of the plaintiff for the year 1923. By the Revenue Act of 1921, c. 136, § 213(a), 42 Stat. 238, gross income includes "gains or profits and income derived from any source whatever," and by the Treasury Regulations * * * that have been in force through repeated re-enactments, "If the corporation purchases and retires any of such bonds at a price less than the issuing price or face value, the excess of the issuing price or face value over the purchase price is gain or income for the taxable year." Article 545(1)(c) of Regulations 62, under Revenue Act of 1921. [Further citations omitted.] We see no reason why the Regulations should not be accepted as a correct statement of the law.

In Bowers v. Kerbaugh–Empire Co., 271 U.S. 170, the defendant in error owned the stock of another company that had borrowed money repayable in marks or their equivalent for an enterprise that failed. At the time of payment the marks had fallen in value, which so far as it went was a gain for the defendant in error and it was contended by the plaintiff in error that the gain was taxable income. But the transaction as a whole was a loss, and the contention was denied. Here there was no shrinkage of assets and the taxpayer made a clear gain. As a result of its dealings it made available $137,521.30 [in] assets previously offset by the obligation of bonds now extinct. We see nothing to be gained by the discussion of judicial definitions. The defendant in error has realized within the year an accession to income, if we take words in their plain popular meaning, as they should be taken here. Burnet v. Sanford & Brooks Co., 282 U.S. 359, 364.

Judgment reversed.

Problems, Notes and Questions

1. *The "insolvency exception."* Suppose that a taxpayer who has no assets and who owes $50,000 to creditors has $10,000 of the debt cancelled. Does the rationale of the *Kirby Lumber* case support an exception to the rule that cancellation of debt is a "gain"? There is no general rule that the income of insolvent taxpayers is exempt from taxation, and the salary, interest, and other income of an insolvent is taxed. Nevertheless, the courts created a doctrine under which cancellation-of-indebtedness income is taxed only to the extent that the taxpayer is solvent after the cancellation. See Lakeland Grocery Co. v. Commissioner, 36 B.T.A. 289 (1937).

Sections 108(a)(1)(B) and 108(a)(3) now codify the insolvency exception. Section 108(a)(1)(A) creates a "bankruptcy exception," which excludes from income the amount of debt extinguished in bankruptcy. Note that the bankruptcy exception goes further than the insolvency exception by excluding cancellations of debt in bankruptcy in full, even if the debtor becomes solvent as a result of the proceedings.

The bankruptcy exception furthers bankruptcy-law goals. To say that a discharge in bankruptcy creates income would frustrate the "fresh start" policy of the Bankruptcy Act. Finding a justification for the insolvency exception, as applied to taxpayers who do not go through bankruptcy, presents problems. The cancellation of a debt creates an increase in the debtor's net worth even if the debtor remains insolvent after the cancellation: someone who is $20,000 in the hole has a greater net worth than someone who is $50,000 in the hole. Perhaps, given a system in which bankruptcy does not produce cancellation-of-indebtedness income, cancellation outside of bankruptcy should also not create income to an insolvent taxpayer. A less-favorable rule for insolvent taxpayers who do not go bankrupt would encourage bankruptcy while raising little, if any, revenue. See generally Wright, Realization of Income through Cancellations, Modifications, and Bargain Purchases of Indebtedness: I, 49 Mich.L.Rev. 459 (1951).

2. *Who is insolvent?* Suppose an individual taxpayer owes $100,000 in debts and has two assets, each worth $75,000. One of the assets (such as the taxpayer's principal residence) is exempt from the claims of the taxpayer's creditors; the other asset is not. Is the taxpayer insolvent? Before the enactment of the Bankruptcy Tax Act of 1980, which codified the insolvency exception, the answer was clearly "yes"; the cases held that exempt assets are not to be counted in determining and measuring insolvency. The rationale was that the income a taxpayer recognizes when a debt is canceled corresponds to the value of assets that are freed from the claims of the taxpayer's creditors. However, § 108(d)(3) defines insolvency as the excess of liabilities over "assets," without qualifying the term, and modern notions of why a debt reduction generates income do not depend on a "freeing of assets" rationale (see p. 138 below). The first case to consider the issue under current law is Carlson v. Commis-

sioner, 116 T.C. 87 (2001), which held that the term "assets" in § 108(d)(3) includes all of the taxpayer's assets, not just non-exempt assets.

3. *Reduction of basis following exclusion of cancellation-of-indebtedness income.* Section 108(b) requires that exclusions under § 108(a) reduce "tax attributes" of the taxpayer. One "tax attribute" is the basis of property held by the taxpayer at the beginning of the year following the year of the discharge. However, the basis of exempt property (under the Bankruptcy Act) will not be reduced. Section 1017 contains directions for calculating basis reductions. Another important tax attribute is a net-operating-loss carryover (a loss from an earlier year which, because its deduction in that year would provide no benefit, can be "carried over" to future years and deducted against those years' incomes); § 172.

To the extent that an exclusion of income under § 108(a) results in the reduction of the basis of property, the exclusion becomes a deferral, rather than a complete exemption. Lowering basis generally leads to more income later because of reduced depreciation deductions or increased gain when the property is sold.

4. *The Kerbaugh–Empire case.* Although the Supreme Court has never expressly overruled Bowers v. Kerbaugh–Empire Co., that decision is almost surely not the law today. In Burnet v. Sanford & Brooks Co., p. 702, below, the Court held that one year's income is not exempt from taxation merely because it is produced as part of a transaction that generated losses in a different year. The Ninth Circuit held in Vukasovich, Inc. v. Commissioner, 790 F.2d 1409 (9th Cir.1986), that *Kerbaugh–Empire* had been effectively overruled by later Supreme Court holdings, particularly *Sanford & Brooks*. The Ninth Circuit said at 790 F.2d 1416:

> Following an obviously outdated Supreme Court decision gives effect to an old decision only at the cost of ignoring more recent decisions. It forces the Supreme Court to reverse lower court decisions following the older law, burdening both the Supreme Court and litigants. It also deprives the Supreme Court of the benefit of a contemporary decision on the merits.

5. *Problems.*

(1) *D* owes *C* $100,000. *D* owns a single asset with a basis of $70,000 and a value of $40,000. *D* also has $60,000 in cash. *C* accepts $60,000 in cash from *D* in full satisfaction of the debt. What result to *D*?

(2) Same as (1) except that *D* also owes *E* $30,000. *D's* debt to *E* is not cancelled.

(3) *F*, a cash-method lawyer, owes *G* $500 for services *G* has performed for *F*. *F* would be entitled to a $500 deduction upon paying for these services. Although *F* is solvent, *G* cancels $300 of the debt because of doubts about *F*'s ability to pay it. What result to *F*? See § 108(e)(2). Why this rule?

DEBT WITHOUT RECEIPT: THE *RAIL JOINT* PRINCIPLE

Most debtors received cash or property when they became indebted. The tax imposed when a creditor cancels a debt can therefore be thought of as a tax on the proceeds of the loan. No tax was imposed when the taxpayer borrowed, because of the offsetting obligation to repay, but when the obligation to repay is cancelled, the funds received by the debtor and spent or saved become taxable. As the Supreme Court put it in United States v. Centennial Savings Bank, 499 U.S. 573, 582 (1991):

> Borrowed funds are excluded from income in the first instance because the taxpayer's obligation to repay the funds offsets any increase in the taxpayer's assets; if the taxpayer is thereafter released from his obligation to repay, the taxpayer enjoys a net increase in assets equal to the forgiven portion of the debt, and the basis for the original exclusion evaporates.

What if a taxpayer incurs an obligation without receiving cash or property, and the creditor cancels the obligation? Suppose, for instance, that in 2002 *A* promises to pay $10,000 to the University of Notre Dame in Fremantle, Australia. *A* will not receive a deduction for the payment if he makes it, because the donee is a foreign organization. *A*'s obligation is binding under local law, despite the absence of consideration in the usual sense. In 2003, *A* asks the university to let him off the hook, and the university cancels *A*'s debt. Does *A* have $10,000 in cancellation-of-indebtedness income in 2003? Probably not.

The "delayed tax on the loan proceeds" rationale of *Centennial Savings Bank* would not support taxing *A*. Unlike the case of a borrower, there are no "proceeds" to include in *A*'s income. Ordinarily, income corresponds to some receipt of money or property by the taxpayer (though income is often realized at some time other than the time of receipt). A tax on *A* would not be a tax on any money received by *A* at any time.

The inappropriateness of taxing someone like *A* can be seen by comparing *A* with *B*, who borrowed $10,000 in 2002, spent the money on personal consumption, and then had her $10,000 debt cancelled in 2003. If we look only at the events of 2003, we might be tempted to say that each taxpayer has become richer by $10,000 in 2003 and that each should therefore have $10,000 income. Looking at each taxpayer's entire transaction, however, we can see that *B* has received and spent $10,000 more than *A* in the long run (assuming all other aspects of their lives to be the same). Requiring both *A* and *B* to pay tax on $10,000 cancellation-of-indebtedness income would overtax *A* relative to *B*.

Several courts have held that cancellation of a debt gives rise to income only if incurring the debt gave the taxpayer money, property, or services. The leading case is Commissioner v. Rail Joint Co., 61 F.2d 751 (2d Cir.1932). The Rail Joint Company distributed its own bonds to its shareholders as a dividend, then bought back some of the bonds for less than face value. The court held that the taxpayer corporation, having received nothing when it issued the bonds, had no income when it bought them back for less than face value. As a more-recent example, consider Whitmer v. Commissioner, 71 T.C.M. 2213 (1996). Whitmer owned all the stock of Midwest, a corporation in the life-insurance business. Midwest owed ITT Life $237,000 on account of payments received by Midwest; Midwest was bound to repay this amount because policies had lapsed. Whitmer had guaranteed this payment, making him liable to ITT if Midwest failed to pay. In 1987, ITT forgave $212,000 of this debt. The Tax Court held that this cancellation did not result in income to Whitmer, as he had received no cash or property when he became "indebted" (71 T.C.M. at 2216):

> Midwest obtained a nontaxable increase in its assets on account of its debt to ITT. Petitioner did not. To be sure, petitioner intended as Midwest's sole shareholder to derive some benefit from the arrangement with ITT. The hard fact remains, however, that the * * * loan proceeds that were the subject of the debt went to Midwest, and they did not go into petitioner's pocket. ITT's forgiveness of its debt to Midwest also did not increase petitioner's net worth. It merely prevented petitioner's net worth from being decreased.

The Second Circuit in *Rail Joint* distinguished *Kirby Lumber* by saying that the Kirby Lumber Company's assets "were increased by the cash received for the bonds." In fact, some of the bonds in *Kirby Lumber* were issued to satisfy dividend arrearages on preferred stock. See Bittker, Income from the Cancellation of Indebtedness: A Historical Footnote to the *Kirby Lumber Co.* Case, 4 J.Corp.Tax 124 (1977). In other words, *Kirby Lumber* was itself a *Rail Joint* case. This fact did not appear in the record of the *Kirby Lumber* case, and both parties argued the case in the Supreme Court on the assumption that the nature of the consideration received for the bonds did not matter.[q] In view of this history, the *Kirby Lumber* opinion need not be read as holding that no *Rail Joint* exception can be created: appellate opinions apply the law to the facts as disclosed in the record, not to facts that might have been in the record but were not. See Gunn, Reconciling *United States Steel* and *Kirby Lumber,* 42 Tax Notes 851 (1989).

Problems and Notes

1. *Reduction of purchase price.* The taxpayer in Hirsch v. Commissioner, 115 F.2d 656 (7th Cir.1940), bought real estate for $29,000, paying $10,000 down and assuming a $19,000 mortgage debt. Several years later, when the unpaid balance of the mortgage was $15,000 and

---

q. An assertion that the bonds were not issued for cash first appeared in the Kirby Lumber Company's motion to remand the case to the Court of Claims for findings on this issue. The government opposed the motion on several grounds, including the immateriality of the nature of the consideration; Bittker, Income from the Cancellation of Indebtedness: A Historical Footnote to the *Kirby Lumber Co.* Case, 4 J.Corp. Tax. at 127–28 (1977).

the value of the property had fallen to $8000, the mortgagee agreed to take $8000 in full satisfaction of the debt. The court held that the $7000 in debt that was cancelled was a "reduction in the purchase price" and not income: "To say that anything of value has moved to [the taxpayer] is contrary to fact"; 115 F.2d at 657. See also Dallas Transfer & Terminal Warehouse Co. v. Commissioner, 70 F.2d 95, 96 (5th Cir.1934), holding that cancellation of a lessee's debt for unpaid rent did not produce income:

> Taxable income is not acquired by a transaction which does not result in the taxpayer getting or having anything he did not have before. Gain or profit is essential to the existence of taxable income. A transaction whereby nothing of exchangeable value comes to or is received by a taxpayer does not give rise to or create taxable income.

Section 108(e)(5) now codifies the reduction-of-purchase-price rule.

2. *Problems.*

(1) *G* borrows $100,000 from *H* and uses the money to buy a machine from *J*. *H* cancels $10,000 of *G*'s debt. *G* is solvent at all times. Does *G* have $10,000 income?

(2) Same as (1) except that the $100,000 indebtedness was a purchase-money obligation incurred when *G* bought the machine from *H*.

3. *Qualified real property business indebtedness.* The statutory reduction-of-purchase-price rule applies only in the case of a debt owed to the seller of the property. If, for example, *A* buys a building from *B* and pays for the building with money borrowed from *C*, a reduction of the debt *A* owes to *C* is not ordinarily covered by § 108(e)(5). (The Service has ruled, however, that the cancellation of a debt owed to a non-seller can be excluded under § 108(e)(5) if the cancellation "is based on an infirmity that clearly relates back to the original sale," as when fraud by the seller resulted in a higher purchase price; Rev.Rul. 92–99, 1992–2 C.B. 35.)

Sections 108(a)(1)(D) and 108(c) create an exclusion for discharge of "qualified real property business indebtedness." This exclusion, which is available only to taxpayers other than C corporations, applies only to the extent that the amount of the debt before the cancellation exceeds the value of the property which secures the debt. If, for example, a taxpayer incurs a $200,000 debt to buy or build a building used in a trade or business, and if the value of the building falls to $180,000, a cancellation of $30,000 of the debt will produce income of only $10,000. The basis of the property must be reduced by the amount of debt-cancellation income excluded under § 108(a)(1)(D).

REVENUE RULING 84–176
1984–2 C.B. 34.

ISSUE

Is the amount owed by a taxpayer, that is forgiven by a seller in return for a release of a contract counterclaim, income from discharge of indebtedness pursuant to section 61(a)(12) and thereby subject to exclusion under section 108?

FACTS

The taxpayer, a domestic corporation, is a wholesale distributor. In 1981, it entered into two contracts with an unrelated seller under which the taxpayer agreed to purchase various quantities of goods. The goods were to be shipped in six lots between March and August, 1982. The seller subsequently shipped all of lot 1 and part of lot 2, and then refused to ship the rest of the order. At the time of this refusal, the taxpayer had an outstanding account payable to the seller of 1,000x dollars for goods actually shipped.

After the seller failed to ship the remaining goods, the taxpayer refused to pay the 1,000x dollars already owed. The seller then filed suit against the taxpayer in U.S. District Court for such payment. The taxpayer later filed a counterclaim for breach of contract, claiming damages for lost profits.

In December, 1982, the parties settled the suit. The taxpayer agreed to pay the seller 500x dollars of the 1,000x dollars outstanding indebtedness. The remaining 500x dollars was "forgiven" by the seller in return for executing a release of the breach of contract counterclaim.

On its federal income tax return for 1982, the taxpayer excluded the 500x dollars from income pursuant to section 108 of the Code and reduced the basis of its assets by that amount as required under section 1017. [Under the version of § 108 in effect for 1982, a corporate taxpayer could elect to exclude cancellation-of-indebtedness income. Taxpayers who made the election had to reduce the basis of their assets by the amount of income excluded. This elective exclusion was repealed in 1986.]

LAW AND ANALYSIS

Section 61(a) provides that gross income means gross income from whatever source derived. Section 61(a)(12) provides that gross income includes income from discharge of indebtedness. [Treas.Reg. §] 1.61–12(a) provides that a taxpayer may realize income by the payment of obligations at less than their face value.

* * *

The Supreme Court in United States v. Kirby Lumber Co., 284 U.S. 1 (1931), established the principle that the gain or saving that is realized by a debtor upon the reduction or cancellation of the debtor's outstanding indebtedness for less than the amount due may be "income" for federal tax purposes. The taxpayer-corporation in *Kirby Lumber* had purchased its own bonds at a discount in the open market. Holding that the difference between the issue price and the price at which the bonds were subsequently acquired represented taxable income to the corporation, the Court said that as a result of these purchases, the taxpayer made available $137,521.30 of assets previously offset by the obligation of bonds now extinct. The taxpayer had realized within the year an accession to income.

Not every indebtedness that is cancelled results in gross income being realized by the debtor "by reason of" discharge of indebtedness within the meaning of section 108 of the Code. If a cancellation of indebtedness is simply the medium for payment of some other form of income, section 108 does not apply. For example, if an employee owes his employer $100 and renders $100 worth of services to the employer in return for cancellation of the debt, the employee has received personal services income, rather than income from cancellation of indebtedness within the meaning of section 108. In such a case, the full amount of the indebtedness is satisfied by the performance of services having a value equal to the debt. Since the debt cancellation is only the medium of paying the personal services income, section 108 is inapplicable. See Spartan Petroleum Co. v. United States, 437 F.Supp. 733 (D.S.C.1977). See also [Treas.Reg. §] 1.1017–1(b)(5) (no reduction of basis of property is allowed under sections 108 and 1017 to the extent of the value of property transferred to a creditor in connection with a debt cancellation), and Rev.Rul. 83–60, 1983–1 C.B. 39.

The Senate Finance Committee Report regarding the amending of section 108 of the Code in the Bankruptcy Tax Act of 1980 [Pub.L. 96–589, 1980–2 C.B. 607], discusses the exceptions to the general rule of income realization when indebtedness is forgiven or otherwise cancelled. That report acknowledges the proposition set forth in *Spartan Petroleum* that income from cancellation of indebtedness does not automatically fall within the scope of the debt discharge rules. It states in a footnote that debt discharge that is only a medium for some other form of payment, such as a gift or salary, is treated as that form of payment rather than under the debt discharge rules. Footnote 6, S.Rep. No. 1035, 96th Cong., 2d Sess. 8 (1980), 1980–2 C.B. 624.

In this situation, the settlement should be analyzed as if the taxpayer actually received compensation for damages arising out of the seller's breach of contract and then paid the full amount of the account payable. There is no requirement that money be actually exchanged in order for taxation to result. The amount received by the taxpayer for the breach of contract is ordinary income because the facts demonstrate that the taxpayer was reimbursed for lost profits and income. Therefore, the 500x dollars not paid by the taxpayer to the seller was the medium through which income from the damages for breach of contract arose. This amount is to be treated as a payment for lost profits rather than a discharge of indebtedness.

HOLDING

The amount owed by the taxpayer that is forgiven by the seller in return for a release of a contract counterclaim is not income from discharge of indebtedness under section 61(a)(12) and therefore is not subject to exclusion under section 108.

Problems, Notes and Question

1. *Problems.*

(1) *D* borrows $1000 from *C*. *C* cancels the debt because *C* is *D*'s parent and it is *D*'s birthday. Does *D* have income? See § 102(a).

(2) *L*, a recent medical school graduate, owes the St. Stephen's University Medical School $40,000 for amounts borrowed from the school to finance *L*'s education. If the school hires *L* to teach a clinical course and compensates her by cancelling half her debt, does *L* have income? Does it matter if *L* is insolvent at the time of the cancellation? (Note that insolvency and poverty are not necessarily the same thing: most recent professional-school graduates are insolvent; few are poor.)

2. *Loan-forgiveness programs.* Many schools have adopted programs designed to encourage their graduates to take low-paying public-interest jobs. Under many of these programs, the schools lend a graduate taking an approved job some or all of the money needed to make payments on student loans and then forgive the loans from the school as the graduate works at the public-interest job. Section 108(f) had previously provided an exclusion from income for state and Federal government programs. It was expanded in 1997 to cover programs of educational organizations as well. Under § 108(f)(3), the exclusion does not apply to loan-forgiveness on account of services performed for the educational organization itself.

3. *One more wrinkle.* Banks sometimes charge depositors early-withdrawal penalties if the depositors withdraw their funds prematurely. In form, these penalties involve the cancellation of debt, because a bank pays a depositor who incurs the penalty less than the amount the bank would otherwise owe. Is the income a bank realizes when it charges early-withdrawal penalties income from the discharge of indebtedness, which can be excluded from income if the bank is insolvent? According to the Supreme Court, it is not, because a debt reduced according to the terms of the original loan agreement has not been "discharged." United States v. Centennial Savings Bank, 499 U.S. 573 (1991). The Court saw the insolvency exception as intended to encourage failing businesses to acquire their debts at less than face value whenever possible. Without the exception, the prospect of taxable income without cash to pay the tax might cause some troubled businesses to pass up opportunities to have their debts reduced. But "[a] debtor who negotiates in advance the circumstances in which he will liquidate the debt for less than its face value is in a position to anticipate his need for cash * * * and can negotiate the terms of the anticipated liquidation accordingly"; 499 U.S. at 583.

4. *References.* Bittker & Thompson, Income From the Discharge of Indebtedness: The Progeny of United States v. Kirby Lumber Co., 66

Calif.L.Rev. 1159 (1978); Wright, Realization of Income through Cancellations, Modifications, and Bargain Purchases of Indebtedness, 49 Mich. L.Rev. 459 (Part I) and 667 (Part II) (1951).

———

The following opinion may be useful for review of cancellation-of-indebtedness income, as it involves the application of some fundamental principles to a fact situation in which the right answers are far from obvious.

ZARIN v. COMMISSIONER

United States Court of Appeals, Third Circuit, 1990.
916 F.2d 110.

Before STAPLETON, COWEN AND WEIS, CIRCUIT JUDGES.

COWEN, CIRCUIT JUDGE: David Zarin ("Zarin") appeals from a decision of the Tax Court holding that he recognized $2,935,000 of income from discharge of indebtedness resulting from his gambling activities, and that he should be taxed on the income. * * * After considering the issues raised by this appeal, we will reverse.

I.

[David Zarin, an engineer, was a compulsive gambler. Resorts International, which operated a casino in Atlantic City, extended Zarin credit in excess of the amounts allowed under the rules governing casino gambling in New Jersey. Its willingness to do this may have resulted from the help that Zarin's extravagant bets gave the casino's business, as other patrons became excited by watching Zarin place large bets. During April of 1980, Resorts let Zarin have chips in the face amount of $3,435,000 on credit. Zarin lost all the chips gambling. Resorts finally cut off his credit on April 29, 1980.

After Zarin failed to pay the casino, Resorts sued him for $3,435,000 in a New Jersey court. The case was settled by Zarin's agreeing to pay Resorts $500,000. The Commissioner contended that the difference between the $3,435,000 that Zarin owed and the $500,000 he agreed to pay was cancellation-of-indebtedness income.

The Tax Court found that the Commissioner had not met his burden of proving that Zarin's gambling debts were enforceable under New Jersey law. The burden of proving this issue was on the Commissioner because he had raised the cancellation-of-indebtedness issue late in the proceedings—he had originally argued that Zarin had recognized income from larceny by trick and deception. Nevertheless, the Tax Court held, with several judges dissenting, that Zarin had recognized income from the discharge of indebtedness.]

* * *

II.

The sole issue before this Court is whether the Tax Court correctly held that Zarin had income from discharge of indebtedness.[6] * * *

Under the Commissioner's logic, Resorts advanced Zarin $3,435,000 worth of chips, chips being the functional equivalent of cash. At that time, the chips were not treated as income, since Zarin recognized an obligation of repayment. In other words, Resorts made Zarin a tax-free loan. However, a taxpayer does recognize income if a loan owed to another party is canceled, in whole or in part. §§ 61(a)(12), 108(e). The settlement between Zarin and Resorts, claims the Commissioner, fits neatly into the cancellation of indebtedness provisions in the Code. Zarin owed $3,435,000, paid $500,000, with the difference constituting income. Although initially persuasive, the Commissioner's position is nonetheless flawed for two reasons.

III.

Initially, we find that sections 108 and 61(a)(12) are inapplicable to the Zarin/Resorts transaction. Section 61 does not define indebtedness. On the other hand, section 108(d)(1), which repeats and further elaborates on the rule in section 61(a)(12), defines the term as any indebtedness "(A) for which the taxpayer is liable, or (B) subject to which the taxpayer holds property." § 108(d)(1). In order to come within the sweep of the discharge of indebtedness rules, then, the taxpayer must satisfy one of the two prongs in the section 108(d)(1) test. Zarin satisfies neither.

Because the debt Zarin owed to Resorts was unenforceable as a matter of New Jersey state law, it is clearly not a debt "for which the taxpayer is liable." § 108(d)(1)(A). Liability implies a legally enforceable obligation to repay, and under New Jersey law, Zarin would have no such obligation.

Moreover, Zarin did not have a debt subject to which he held property as required by section 108(d)(1)(B). Zarin's indebtedness arose out of his acquisition of gambling chips. The Tax Court held that gambling chips were not property, but rather, "a medium of exchange within the Resorts casino" and a "substitute for cash." Alternatively, the Tax Court viewed the chips as nothing more than "the opportunity to gamble and incidental services * * *." *Zarin*, 92 T.C. at 1099. We agree with the gist of these characterizations, and hold that gambling chips are merely an accounting mechanism to evidence debt.

Gaming chips in New Jersey during 1980 were regarded "solely as evidence of a debt owed to their custodian by the casino licensee and

---

6. Subsequent to the Tax Court's decision, Zarin filed a motion to reconsider, arguing that he was insolvent at the time Resorts forgave his debt, and thus, under § 108(a)(1)(B), could not have income from discharge of indebtedness. He did not, however, raise that issue before the Tax Court until after it rendered its decision. The Tax Court denied the motion for reconsideration. By reason of our resolution of this case, we do not need to decide whether the Tax Court abused its discretion in denying Zarin's motion.

shall be considered at no time the property of anyone other than the casino licensee issuing them." N.J. Admin. Code tit. 19k, § 19:46–1.5(d) (1990). Thus, under New Jersey state law, gambling chips were Resorts' property until transferred to Zarin in exchange for the markers, at which point the chips became "evidence" of indebtedness (and not the property of Zarin).

Even were there no relevant legislative pronouncement on which to rely, simple common sense would lead to the conclusion that chips were not property in Zarin's hands. Zarin could not do with the chips as he pleased, nor did the chips have any independent economic value beyond the casino. The chips themselves were of little use to Zarin, other than as a means of facilitating gambling. They could not have been used outside the casino. They could have been used to purchase services and privileges within the casino, including food, drink, entertainment, and lodging, but Zarin would not have utilized them as such, since he received those services from Resorts on a complimentary basis. In short, the chips had no economic substance.

* * *

Not only were the chips non-property in Zarin's hands, but upon transfer to Zarin, the chips also ceased to be the property of Resorts. Since the chips were in the possession of another party, Resorts could no longer do with the chips as it pleased, and could no longer control the chips' use. Generally, at the time of a transfer, the party in possession of the chips can gamble with them, use them for services, cash them in, or walk out of the casino with them as an Atlantic City souvenir. The chips therefore become nothing more than an accounting mechanism, or evidence of a debt, designed to facilitate gambling in casinos where the use of actual money was forbidden. Thus, the chips which Zarin held were not property within the meaning of § 108(d)(1)(B).

In short, because Zarin was not liable on the debt he allegedly owed Resorts, and because Zarin did not hold "property" subject to that debt, the cancellation of indebtedness provisions of the Code do not apply to the settlement between Resorts and Zarin. As such, Zarin cannot have income from the discharge of his debt.

IV.

Instead of analyzing the transaction at issue as canceled debt, we believe the proper approach is to view it as disputed debt or contested liability. Under the contested liability doctrine, if a taxpayer, in good faith, disputed the amount of a debt, a subsequent settlement of the dispute would be treated as the amount of debt cognizable for tax purposes. The excess of the original debt over the amount determined to have been due is disregarded for both loss and debt and accounting purposes. Thus, if a taxpayer took out a loan for $10,000, refused in good faith to pay the full $10,000 back, and then reached an agreement with the lend[e]r that he would pay back only $7000 in full satisfaction of the debt, the transaction would be treated as if the initial loan was $7000.

When the taxpayer tenders the $7000 payment, he will have been deemed to have paid the full amount of the initially disputed debt. Accordingly, there is no tax consequence to the taxpayer upon payment.

The seminal "contested liability" case is N. Sobel, Inc. v. Commissioner, 40 B.T.A. 1263 (1939). In *Sobel*, the taxpayer exchanged a $21,700 note for 100 shares of stock from a bank. In the following year, the taxpayer sued the bank for rescission, arguing that the bank loan was violative of state law, and moreover, that the bank had failed to perform certain promises. The parties eventually settled the case in 1935, with the taxpayer agreeing to pay half of the face amount of the note. In the year of the settlement, the taxpayer claimed the amount paid as a loss. The Commissioner denied the loss because it had been sustained five years earlier, and further asserted that the taxpayer recognized income from the discharge of half of his indebtedness.

The Board of Tax Appeals held that * * * the portion of the note forgiven by the bank "was not the occasion for a freeing of assets and that there was no gain * * *." [Citation omitted.] Therefore, the taxpayer did not have any income from cancellation of indebtedness.

There is little difference between the present case and *Sobel*. Zarin incurred a $3,435,000 debt while gambling at Resorts, but in court, disputed liability on the basis of unenforceability. A settlement of $500,000 was eventually agreed upon. It follows from *Sobel* that the settlement served only to fix the amount of debt. No income was realized or recognized. When Zarin paid the $500,000, any tax consequence dissolved.[10]

* * *

The Commissioner argues that *Sobel* and the contested liability doctrine only apply when there is a an unliquidated debt; that is, a debt for which the amount cannot be determined. See Colonial Sav. Ass'n v. Commissioner, 85 T.C. 855, 862–863 (1985) (*Sobel* stands for the proposition that "there must be a liquidated debt"), aff'd, 854 F.2d 1001 (7th Cir.1988). See also N. Sobel Inc. v. Commissioner, 40 B.T.A. at 1265 (there was a dispute as to "liability and the amount" of the debt). Since Zarin contested his liability based on the unenforceability of the entire debt, and did not dispute the amount of the debt, the Commissioner would have us adopt the reasoning of the Tax Court, which found that Zarin's debt was liquidated, therefore barring the application of *Sobel* and the contested liability doctrine. *Zarin*, 92 T.C. at 1095 (Zarin's debt "was a liquidated amount" and "there is no dispute about the amount [received].").

We reject the Tax Court's rationale. When a debt is unenforceable, it follows that the amount of the debt, and not just the liability thereon, is in dispute. Although a debt may be unenforceable, there still could be

---

10. Had Zarin not paid the $500,000 dollar settlement, it would be likely that he would have had income from cancellation of indebtedness. The debt at that point would have been fixed, and Zarin would have been legally obligated to pay it.

some value attached to its worth. This is especially so with regards to gambling debts. In most states, gambling debts are unenforceable, and have "but slight potential * * *," United States v. Hall, 307 F.2d 238, 241 (10th Cir.1962). Nevertheless, they are often collected, at least in part. For example, Resorts is not a charity; it would not have extended illegal credit to Zarin and others if it did not have some hope of collecting debts incurred pursuant to the grant of credit.

Moreover, the debt is frequently incurred to acquire gambling chips, and not money. Although casinos attach a dollar value to each chip, that value, unlike money's, is not beyond dispute, particularly given the illegality of gambling debts in the first place. This proposition is supported by the facts of the present case. Resorts gave Zarin $3.4 million dollars of chips in exchange for markers evidencing Zarin's debt. If indeed the only issue was the enforceability of the entire debt, there would have been no settlement. Zarin would have owed all or nothing. Instead, the parties attached a value to the debt considerably lower than its face value. In other words, the parties agreed that given the circumstances surrounding Zarin's gambling spree, the chips he acquired might not have been worth $3.4 million dollars, but were worth something. Such a debt cannot be called liquidated, since its exact amount was not fixed until settlement.

To summarize, the transaction between Zarin and Resorts can best be characterized as a disputed debt, or contested liability. Zarin owed an unenforceable debt of $3,435,000 to Resorts. After Zarin in good faith disputed his obligation to repay the debt, the parties settled for $500,000, which Zarin paid. That $500,000 settlement fixed the amount of loss and the amount of debt cognizable for tax purposes. Since Zarin was deemed to have owed $500,000, and since he paid Resorts $500,000, no adverse tax consequences attached to Zarin as a result.

* * *

STAPLETON, CIRCUIT JUDGE, dissenting: I respectfully dissent because I agree with the Commissioner's appraisal of the economic realities of this matter.

Resorts sells for cash the exhilaration and the potential for profit inherent in games of chance. It does so by selling for cash chips that entitle the holder to gamble at its casino. Zarin, like thousands of others, wished to purchase what Resorts was offering in the marketplace. He chose to make this purchase on credit and executed notes evidencing his obligation to repay the funds that were advanced to him by Resorts. As in most purchase money transactions, Resorts skipped the step of giving Zarin cash that he would only return to it in order to pay for the opportunity to gamble. Resorts provided him instead with chips that entitled him to participate in Resorts' games of chance on the same basis as others who had paid cash for that privilege. Whether viewed as a one or two-step transaction, however, Zarin received either $3.4 million in cash or an entitlement for which others would have had to pay $3.4 million.

Despite the fact that Zarin received in 1980 cash or an entitlement worth $3.4 million, he correctly reported in that year no income from his dealings with Resorts. He did so solely because he recognized, as evidenced by his notes, an offsetting obligation to repay Resorts $3.4 million in cash. See, e.g., Vukasovich, Inc. v. Commissioner, 790 F.2d 1409 (9th Cir.1986); United States v. Rochelle, 384 F.2d 748 (5th Cir.1967), cert. denied, 390 U.S. 946 (1968); Bittker and Thompson, Income From the Discharge of Indebtedness: The Progeny of United States v. Kirby Lumber Co., 66 Calif.L.Rev. 159 (1978). In 1981, with the delivery of Zarin's promise to pay Resorts $500,000 and the execution of a release by Resorts, Resorts surrendered its claim to repayment of the remaining $2.9 million of the money Zarin had borrowed. As of that time, Zarin's assets were freed of his potential liability for that amount and he recognized gross income in that amount. * * * United States v. Kirby Lumber Company, 284 U.S. 1 (1931) * * *. But see United States v. Hall, 307 F.2d 238 (10th Cir.1962).[2]

The only alternatives I see to this conclusion are to hold either (1) that Zarin realized $3.4 million in income in 1980 at a time when both parties to the transaction thought there was an offsetting obligation to repay or (2) that the $3.4 million benefit sought and received by Zarin is not taxable at all. I find the latter alternative unacceptable as inconsistent with the fundamental principle of the Code that anything of commercial value received by a taxpayer is taxable unless expressly excluded from gross income. Commissioner v. Glenshaw Glass Co., 348 U.S. 426 (1955); United States v. Kirby Lumber Co., supra. * * * .

* * *

Notes and Questions

1. *Good and bad analogies.* Think hard about the majority's example of a taxpayer who borrowed $10,000 in cash, refused in good faith to pay it back, and then agreed with the lender to repay $7000. The court says that the taxpayer would have no income because the debt was "contested." Did it have to go that far to keep Zarin from having income, or is Zarin's situation distinguishable? Judge Stapleton, like the majority, sees Zarin as equivalent to someone who borrowed cash. Is that right? If Zarin had borrowed $3.4 million from a bank, lost the money at the casino, and paid back only $500,000, he plainly would have had

2. This is not a case in which parties agree subsequent to a purchase money transaction that the property purchased has a value less than thought at the time of the transaction. In such cases, the purchase price adjustment rule is applied and the agreed-upon value is accepted as the value of the benefit received by the purchaser; see e.g., Commissioner v. Sherman, 135 F.2d 68 (6th Cir.1943); N. Sobel, Inc. v. Commissioner, 40 B.T.A. 1263 (1939). Nor is this a case in which the taxpayer is entitled to rescind an entire purchase money transaction, thereby to restore itself to the position it occupied before receiving anything of commercial value. In this case, the illegality was in the extension of credit by Resorts and whether one views the benefit received by Zarin as cash or the opportunity to gamble, he is no longer in a position to return that benefit.

income from cancellation of his debt. It may be worth noting, though, that few banks would have lent Zarin $3.4 million for gambling. In the Tax Court, Zarin pointed out that the only reason the casino let him have so many chips was that it knew that it would get them back very soon.

2. *Section 108(e)(5)*. Suppose the casino had agreed to sell Zarin chips for $500,000, rather than for $3.4 million. In that case, Zarin would have had no income. If the casino knew from the start that Zarin would be unable to repay the whole $3.4 million, did the series of transactions between Zarin and the casino differ in any important way from the casino's selling him chips at a discount?

If Zarin's debt had been incurred to buy property, rather than services, § 108(e)(5) would have provided expressly for nonrecognition of income upon a later reduction of the purchase-money debt. If this "reduction-of-purchase-price" rule had remained a caselaw exception to the principle that reduction of a debt creates income, extension of the exception to cases involving services—like *Zarin*—would have been easy. But Congress codified the exception in 1980. It did this, apparently, not to prevent further expansion of the exception, but rather just because it was there. One danger of codifying a judge-made doctrine is that courts may read Congress as freezing the doctrine in the form it had at the time of codification.

INCOME AS "FLOW" AND INCOME AS "GAIN"

Until the adoption of the income tax and that tax's intrusion into their professional and personal lives, lawyers thought of income primarily in connection with trusts. The kind of income to which the income beneficiary of a trust is entitled is easily thought of as a flow of wealth. Thus dividends, interest, and rent are income for trust-accounting purposes, but increases in the value of trust corpus, whether realized or not, are additions to corpus, not income. Some economists, too, once considered income as a flow or yield, as distinguished from the "capital" that produces that flow. E.R.A. Seligman, for example, defined income, "as contrasted with capital," as "that amount of wealth which flows in during a definite period."[r] Income, under this view, is something physical—something very like receipts.

The displacement of the concept of income (for tax purposes) as flow by a concept of income as gain can be shown by comparing the Supreme Court's opinion in Eisner v. Macomber with that in Commissioner v. Glenshaw Glass Co. In *Macomber*, income was something "derived from" capital or labor. It was analogized to fruit, crops, and the outlet from a reservoir (while "capital" was like trees, land, or the reservoir itself). By the time of *Glenshaw Glass*, it was enough to say simply that the taxpayers had realized "accessions to wealth."

Understanding that today's notions of the nature of income were not always held can help to explain the development of the law of cancellation-of-indebtedness income. The cancellation of a debt is not obviously

---

r. The Income Tax 19 (2d ed. 1914).

something that produces a flow of assets to the debtor, which shows why, until the *Kirby Lumber* decision, it was doubtful that a reduction of debt created income. The "insolvency exception" to the *Kirby Lumber* rule may also be a relic of the flow idea of income. Cancellation of a solvent taxpayer's debt can be thought of (with some effort) as producing a flow of things to a taxpayer by freeing some of the taxpayer's assets from the claims of creditors. But the stock of things an insolvent taxpayer has does not increase when a debt is cancelled; the taxpayer has gained by becoming less deeply in debt than before the cancellation, but the gain will not be reflected in a material way until some future time, if ever.

Modern tax writers tend to assume that any gain is, at least potentially, income, and to view the tax process as starting with all gains of whatever sort as income and then excluding whatever gains cannot or should not, for reasons of convenience, be taxed. Thus, it is said that unrealized increases in the value of property are "really" income, but are not taxed because of the administrative problems of valuing property regularly and the inconvenience to taxpayers of having to pay a tax despite not having done anything to produce the cash with which the tax must be paid. This reasoning may be useful, but it was not necessarily the reasoning of most of those who designed the income tax in 1913: they might have said simply that someone whose property has increased in value has not "received"[s] income because nothing new has "come in."

Do not assume that either the flow or the gain theory of income is right in some absolute sense. No simple definition of "income" can give satisfactory answers to all the practical questions of how people in particular circumstances should be taxed. Gain and flow concepts provide (at best) the starting points for thinking about tax problems, not the answers. The Supreme Court's most fundamental error in Eisner v. Macomber was its resort to the dictionary.

References. Lane, A Theory of the Tax Base: The Exchange Model, 3 Am.J.Tax Pol'y 1 (1984); Wright, The Effect of the Source of Realized Benefits upon the Supreme Court's Concept of Taxable Receipts, 8 Stan.L.Rev. 164 (1956); Kaldor, An Expenditure Tax 21–78 (1955); Simons, Personal Income Taxation (1938).

F. DAMAGES AND SOCIAL WELFARE PAYMENTS

1. DAMAGES, IN GENERAL

SAGER GLOVE CORP. v. COMMISSIONER

Tax Court of the United States, 1961.
36 T.C. 1173, affirmed 311 F.2d 210 (7th Cir.1962), cert. denied
373 U.S. 910, 83 S.Ct. 1298, 10 L.Ed.2d 411 (1963).

ATKINS, JUDGE: [Sager Glove Corp., which manufactured industrial safety material, sued Bausch & Lomb Optical Co. and others for viola-

s. Today, as a technical matter, it is improper to speak of "receiving" income, though saying "Smith has received $10,000 income" is a handy way of saying "Smith has received $10,000, and must include that amount in income."

tions of the antitrust laws. Its amended complaint alleged that Bausch & Lomb's refusal to supply it with lenses for safety goggles forced Sager to cancel a contract with General Motors, "losing thereby many thousands of dollars in profits," and caused Sager to refuse other orders, to lose many of its customers, and to be "destroyed completely as a competitor in the industrial goggle field." In its prayer for relief, Sager sought damages for loss of money spent on research, manufacturing, development, and sales, for the costs of fighting the defendants' "destructive competition tactics," for the loss of "valuable and profitable contracts and orders," including the General Motors contract, and other items.

After Sager had obtained a favorable verdict in the antitrust case, the trial court granted the defendants' motion for a new trial. The case was then settled for $478,142.]

* * *

OPINION

Of the amount of $478,142 received by the petitioner in the settlement of the antitrust suit, $132,000 was paid specifically as reimbursement for attorneys' fees. The parties are in agreement that to that extent the recovery constituted ordinary income and that such amount is deductible by the petitioner. The controversy relates to the remainder of the award, $346,142.

In its return for 1951 the petitioner reported one-third of $478,142, or $159,380, as ordinary income. It reported the balance, $318,762, as nontaxable income with the explanation that it represented punitive damages awarded in the antitrust suit. Thereafter, in Commissioner v. Glenshaw Glass Co., 348 U.S. 426, the Supreme Court held that the punitive two-thirds portion of a treble-damage antitrust recovery constitutes taxable income under § [61] * * *.

The present position of the petitioner is that no portion of the amount received in settlement constituted punitive damages and that the whole amount, aside from the attorneys' fees, should be regarded as a nontaxable return of capital. It argues that the gravamen of its action in the antitrust suit was the injury and damage to its business generally by the tortious tactics and actions of the defendants, that it was specifically alleged in the complaint that a portion of its business, namely, the goggles business, was destroyed, and that hence the capital invested in that business and the goodwill attaching thereto were injured and destroyed. It is contended, therefore, that the amount received should be regarded as payment in reduction of a loss of capital rather than as taxable income. The petitioner relies principally upon Farmers'

& Merchants' Bank v. Commissioner, (C.A.6) 59 F.2d 912, reversing 20 B.T.A. 622.

The respondent, on the other hand, determined that the full amount of the award constituted ordinary income under section [61]. On brief he argues principally that the amount received, aside from that received for attorneys' fees, was compensation for lost profits.

The taxability of the proceeds of a lawsuit, or of a sum received in settlement thereof, depends upon the nature of the claim and the actual basis of recovery. If the recovery represents damages for lost profits, it is taxable as ordinary income. However, if it represents a replacement of capital destroyed or injured, the money received, to the extent it does not exceed the basis, is a return of capital and not taxable. United States v. Safety Car Heating Co., 297 U.S. 88; Phoenix Coal Co. v. Commissioner, (C.A.2) 231 F.2d 420; Durkee v. Commissioner, (C.A.6) 162 F.2d 184; Raytheon Production Corp. v. Commissioner, (C.A.1) 144 F.2d 110, certiorari denied 323 U.S. 779. [Further citations omitted.]

The respondent's determination that the amount in controversy is taxable as ordinary income is presumptively correct, and the burden of proof was upon the petitioner to show what portion of the amount received, if any, constituted nontaxable income. [Citations omitted.]

In the instant case the antitrust suit was tried and damages awarded, but the court granted a motion for a new trial and the case was settled out of court by the parties. The general release which the petitioner signed specifically designates $132,000 of the lump sum of $478,142 as reimbursement of attorneys' fees. Therein the parties did not specify to what extent, if any, the balance of $346,142 might be allocable to recovery of lost profits, to compensation for injury to capital, or to punitive damages. However, reference was made therein to the fact that such balance was the amount of damages which, upon the trial, the plaintiff had claimed for the period January 1, 1936, through December 31, 1943. This amount was the amount which, at the antitrust trial, the petitioner's president, Sager, testified represented the estimated lost net profits from the goggles business over that period. This indicates strongly to us that the amount of $346,142 received in settlement represented compensation for lost profits. We note also that in filing its return for the year 1951, the petitioner made no claim that any portion represented a reimbursement for loss of capital.

The petitioner on brief makes much of the fact that the complaint in the antitrust suit alleged that there had been damage to its business and property generally through injury or destruction of the goggles business, and the fact that in his charge to the jury the District Court judge stated that the allegation had to do with damage to the petitioner's business or property and that the jury should award damages if it found that the petitioner was excluded from the goggles business. However, as we read the instructions to the jury they are of a general nature and could well contemplate a finding of damages for lost profits. The complaint itself specifically alleges damage for lost profits, in addition to the general allegation of damage to the business and property. In this respect the instant case is distinguishable from the case principally relied upon by the petitioner, Farmers' & Merchants' Bank v. Commissioner, supra, and from Durkee v. Commissioner, supra. In those cases the taxpayer did not seek reparation for loss of profits, but only for tortious injury to goodwill. In each of those cases, the allegation as to profits before and after the acts complained of was merely an evidential factor in determining actual loss and not an independent basis for recovery.

On brief the petitioner also contends that the testimony of Sager in the instant case is a basis for holding that the recovery to the extent of $346,142 constituted an amount received in reduction of loss of capital rather than ordinary income. Sager testified that the petitioner lost goodwill and patronage of customers in the goggles business, and he estimated the value thereof at $500,000. He also testified that the petitioner had invested an estimated amount of $50,000, including a part of his salary and a part of the salaries of others, in research, equipment, and advertising in the goggles business. He stated that in his opinion the amount received in settlement was not sufficient to compensate the petitioner for the injury and damage to its business and property. But irrespective of whether the petitioner did in fact sustain some damage to its goodwill or to other capital assets, the ultimate question to be determined here is whether the amount paid in settlement was, to any extent, for such damage. Sager himself testified that he did not participate in the settlement negotiations and the persons who did engage in such settlement did not testify. As stated above, the release itself does not indicate that any portion of the amount agreed upon was compensation for damage to capital.

Upon a consideration of the record as a whole, we cannot conclude that the petitioner has met its burden of showing that any portion of the amount received in settlement was paid as compensation for injury to goodwill or any other capital item. Neither the complaint, nor the release, nor the evidence as a whole provides a basis for making an allocation of the recovery and finding that all or any part represented a return of capital.[2] See Liebes & Co. v. Commissioner, [(C.A.9) 90 F.2d 932]; Ralph Freeman, supra; and Chalmers Cullins, [24 T.C. 322].

We hold that the respondent did not err in treating the full amount received by the petitioner in settlement as ordinary income.

Decision will be entered under Rule 50.

2. In this respect it should also be noted that although Sager testified that the goodwill and patronage of the goggles business which was lost had an estimated value of $500,000, there is no evidence whatever as to the cost or other basis thereof. Thus, even if some portion of the settlement was for damage to capital, such amount would constitute income. It should also be noted that although Sager testified that the estimated amount, including a part of his salary and a part of the salaries of others, which the petitioner had invested in equipment and for research and advertising was $50,000, and that this investment had been lost, there is no evidence to show that whatever amount was so expended, or a part thereof, had not been deducted by the petitioner. If so, any recovery thereof would constitute taxable income.

Notes and Questions

1. *Taxation of damages.* In Raytheon Production Corp. v. Commissioner, followed in the principal case, the First Circuit put the question to be resolved in deciding whether damages are taxable as: "In lieu of what were the damages awarded?" This test goes back at least to Lyeth v. Hoey, 305 U.S. 188 (1938), which held that damages received as the result of a will contest were non-taxable because inheritances are not taxed (see § 102).

Sometimes the "in lieu of" test is easily applied, as in Lyeth v. Hoey, where the damages are clearly tax free, or in the case of damages for breach of an employment contract, where payments in lieu of the salary the taxpayer would have earned are clearly taxable. But what of the principal case? How can one rationally distinguish compensation "for" an injury to "goodwill," which is non-taxable if less than the taxpayer's basis for the goodwill, from payments "for" loss of profits? If "goodwill" is merely a name given to the profitability of the taxpayer's business, "goodwill" and "profits" are the same thing. It is often suggested that the wording of the taxpayer's complaint in the suit for damages is controlling. The First Circuit relied on the complaint to hold in *Raytheon* that the suit was for damage to goodwill. See also State Fish Corp. v. Commissioner, 48 T.C. 465 (1967). In Agar v. Commissioner, 290 F.2d 283 (2d Cir.1961), the court affirmed a Tax Court finding that payments to a former employee were taxable severance pay rather than non-taxable damages for injury to personal reputation. The Tax Court's decision was based on the testimony of the *employer* as to the "basic reason" for the payment.

2. *Tort and contract.* In S.M. 2042, IV–1 C.B. 26 (1925), the Bureau ruled that amounts received in settlement of a claim for breach of promise to marry were income. An earlier ruling holding damages for alienation of affections and for "slander or libel of a personal character" non-taxable was distinguished on the ground that those damages arose from torts, and not from "a contract of which the benefits are due * * * to the exercise of the mental faculties." After McDonald v. Commissioner, 9 B.T.A. 1340 (1928) (Acq.), held damages for breach of promise to marry non-taxable, the Bureau revoked S.M. 2042.

3. *"Business" and "personal" injuries.* If the rule that damages are taxed like the items they replace were taken literally, damages for the destruction of property (including goodwill) would not be taxed, even if they exceeded the property's basis, since "freedom from destruction" is not a taxable event. Nevertheless, such damages are income, and must be so unless some clearly realized "accessions to wealth" are to be tax free. This is as true of personal as of business property; a taxpayer whose vacation home, with a basis of $20,000, is destroyed will have $10,000 income if he receives $30,000 in damages from a tortfeasor or in insurance payments. However, the courts have held that damages for injuries to one's "personal" as distinguished from "business" reputation

are tax free, perhaps in reliance on the "gain derived from labor or capital" approach of Eisner v. Macomber. See Hawkins v. Commissioner, 6 B.T.A. 1023 (1927); compare Agar v. Commissioner, 290 F.2d 283 (2d Cir.1961), hinting that the distinction is unrealistic. Justice Frankfurter's concurring opinion in United States v. Kaiser, 363 U.S. 299, 311 (1960), said:

> payment which compensates for a loss of something which would not itself have been an item of gross income is not a taxable payment. The principle is clearest when applied to compensation for the loss of what is ordinarily thought of as a capital asset, e.g., insurance on a house which is destroyed. * * * If a capital asset is sold for no more than its basis there is no taxable gain. The result, then, is the same if it is destroyed and there is paid in compensation no more than its basis. There are, to be sure, difficulties, not present where ordinary assets are involved, in applying this principle to compensation for the loss of something which has no basis and which is not ordinarily thought of as a capital asset, such as health or life or affection or reputation.

Can a distinction between damage to one's personal reputation and damage to one's vacation home be based on the fact that people ordinarily do not sell their personal reputations?

For many years, damages for injury to personal reputation were fully excludable from income under § 104(a)(2). Today, however, § 104(a)(2) excludes only damages on account of personal "physical" injuries, as explained below.

2. DAMAGES UNDER SECTION 104

Between 1918 and 1996, § 104(a)(2) provided that damages received "on account of personal injuries or sickness" were excludable from gross income. This rule was much better than the "in lieu of" test for taxpayers who recovered for personal injuries. Consider, for example, a taxpayer injured in an auto accident who recovered $50,000 for lost wages, $100,000 for pain and suffering, and $10,000 in punitive damages. Under the "in lieu of" test, the recoveries for punitive damages and lost wages would have been taxable; the balance of the damages would not have been. Under § 104(a)(2) as it existed until 1996, all of the compensatory damages—lost wages and pain and suffering—were excludable. Whether the punitive damages would have been excludable as well was a question on which the courts were divided.

In the 1980s and '90s, the scope of the exclusion from income of all "personal injury" recoveries was the subject of considerable litigation, which led to little in the way of reliable guidelines. The Supreme Court held that damages for discrimination on the basis of sex could not be excluded as "personal injury" damages: the Federal legislation on which the plaintiff's claim was based did not create a "tort-like" cause of action because it allowed recovery only for back pay, but not for pain and suffering, harm to reputation, or punitive damages, and because jury trial was not available; United States v. Burke, 504 U.S. 229 (1992). Most commentators read *Burke* as meaning that damages for age discrimination, and for sex-based discrimination after 1991, would be excludable, as the civil rights legislation involved in those cases did allow jury trials and punitive damages. But in Commissioner v. Schleier, 515 U.S. 323 (1995), the Court held that recoveries under the Age Discrimination in Employment Act were not excludable. It held not only that the cause of action created by the ADEA was not "tort-like"—its remedies, though broad, were not broad enough—but also that the injury inflicted by age discrimination was an "economic injury" (even if pain and suffering or embarrassment resulted), rather than a "personal injury."

Burke, Schleier, and a great many lower-court decisions left the scope of the personal-injury exclusion very unclear. In 1996 Congress rewrote the exclusion. Today, the statutory exclusion expressly covers only compensatory damages, and it applies only to recoveries for "personal physical injuries or physical sickness"; § 104(a)(2). Emotional distress is not a "physical injury or physical sickness," though recoveries for medical expenses in emotional distress cases remain excludable. Note the special rule of § 104(c): this provision was adopted because one state's wrongful-death statute, which allowed recovery of specified amounts in wrongful-death actions, was described by some courts as allowing only "punitive" damages.

Suppose a taxpayer recovers damages for a loss that is not a "physical injury" under § 104 but which would not be taxable under the "in lieu of" test: are the damages excludable? For many years—at least since the 1930s—the "in lieu of" test and the complete exclusion of § 104 have provided the only rules for taxing damages, so that recoveries not completely excluded by section 104 were either taxed or excluded by the "in lieu of" test. For example, a taxpayer cheated out of the interest on tax-exempt bonds who then recovered the lost amount from the tortfeasor could never have argued with a straight face that the recovery was excludable under § 104, but the recovery would certainly have been excludable under the common-law test. The recent narrowing of § 104 would therefore seem to mean that recoveries for "personal injuries" that are not "*physical* injuries" must be evaluated under the "in lieu of" test. Consider, for example, a taxpayer who is defamed and who, as a result, recovers $40,000 for lost earnings and $35,000 for mental suffering. Under the former version of § 104(a)(2), the taxpayer could exclude the entire recovery. Under the "in lieu of" test, which is how recoveries not within § 104 have always been taxed (or not taxed), the $40,000 for lost earnings is taxable; the $35,000 for mental suffering is not. This seems to be the right answer, but some commentators have assumed that recoveries formerly excludable under § 104(a)(2) but no longer covered by that section are taxed in full, and there are hints in the committee reports that the drafters of the 1996 amendments assumed that this was the case. If that view is correct, the defamation victim in the example would have gross income of $75,000.

Problems and Notes

1. *Problems.*

(1) *A* suffers serious physical injuries in an automobile accident caused by *B*. *A* sues *B* and recovers the following amounts: $30,000 for medical expenses (none of which *A* had deducted), $50,000 for lost wages, $20,000 for pain and suffering, and $100,000 in punitive damages. How much of the recovery is includable in *A*'s gross income? How much would have been includable if § 104(a)(2) were not in the Code?

(2) Same as (1) except that after *A* filed suit, seeking damages in the amounts listed above, *A* and *B* settled *A*'s claim for $100,000.

(3) *P*, the former friend of a famous movie actor, recovers $500,000 in settlement of a "palimony" claim; that is, a claim based on a promise that the actor would support her if she gave up her career and catered to his every whim. Of this amount, $300,000 is for *P*'s forgone earnings; the balance is for the loss of the support the actor promised her. How much, if any, of the $500,000 must *P* include in her gross income?

2. *Annuity payments.* An accident victim who receives a cash settlement of $100,000 from an insurance company and who uses the $100,000 to buy an annuity includes the "interest" portion of the annuity in income under § 72 (p. 113). But if the settlement takes the economically identical form of an award of an annuity to the victim, the victim can exclude all of the annuity payments (see the second parenthetical in § 104(a)(2)). This feature of § 104 accounts in part for the popularity of "structured settlements" in tort cases.

In Kovacs v. Commissioner, 100 T.C. 124 (1993), affirmed 25 F.3d 1048 (6th Cir.1994), cert. denied 513 U.S. 963, a divided Tax Court held that statutory interest on a personal-injury award is not excludable under § 104(a), even though the statute excludes the interest component of an annuity received as personal-injury damages. The distinction is between interest that is labelled as such and payments that are interest in substance, but not in name. See also Brabson v. United States, 73 F.3d 1040 (10th Cir.1996), holding pre-judgment interest taxable.

3. *Damages vs. earnings.* Dorothy Garber's blood contained a rare antibody useful in the preparation of diagnostic reagents. She agreed to sell her blood to laboratories for substantial sums, including a $25,000 bonus for signing one contract. In order to increase the concentration of antibodies in her blood, Garber agreed to painful "stimulation" and "plasmapheresis" processes, which produced such side effects as dizziness and headaches. In United States v. Garber, 589 F.2d 843 (5th Cir.1979), the Fifth Circuit affirmed Garber's conviction for tax evasion because of her failure to report the sums received from the laboratories.[t]

---

t. On rehearing *Garber* en banc, the Fifth Circuit reversed and remanded for a new trial, suggesting that Garber might be able to establish a colorable claim to a basis in the blood she sold, thus showing that the taxability of her gain was controversial and

Section 104(a)(2) was inapplicable as a matter of law because Garber had no tort claim against the hospitals; indeed, she did not even think she had one.

4. *Reference.* Wright, The Effect of the Source of Realized Benefits upon the Supreme Court's Concept of Taxable Receipts, 8 Stan.L.Rev. 164 (1956).

3. SOCIAL WELFARE PAYMENTS

REVENUE RULING 85–39
1985–1 C.B. 21.

ISSUE

Are "dividend payments" made by the State of Alaska pursuant to Alaska Statutes section 43.23 (1983) includible in gross income under section 61 of the Internal Revenue Code?

FACTS

Alaska adopted a constitutional amendment in 1976 that established a permanent fund into which the State must deposit at least 25 percent of its mineral income each year. Alaska Const., Art. IX, section 15. In 1980, the Alaska State legislature enacted a statute establishing a dividend program to distribute annually a portion of the fund's earnings directly to the State's adult residents. As stated in section 1 of the 1980 statute, the purposes of the statute are threefold. The statute is to provide a mechanism for equitably distributing to the people of Alaska a portion of the State's energy wealth, to encourage increased awareness and involvement by the residents of the State in the management and expenditure of the fund, and to encourage persons to maintain their residence in Alaska and to reduce population turnover. The Alaska legislature found that the constant turnover in the population led to political, economic, and social instability and was harmful to the State. They also found that it was in the public interest of the State to promote a stable population by providing an incentive to encourage Alaskans to maintain their residency in the State.

The legislature amended section 2 of the statute in 1982 to revise the eligibility requirements for receiving distributions. Section 1, stating the purpose of the Act, was not amended. The statute as amended provides a dividend payment each year to eligible individuals who apply prior to a specific date. Generally, eligible individuals are State residents who have resided in the State for at least six consecutive months immediately preceding the date of application for the dividend. A State resident is an individual who is physically present in the State with the intent to remain permanently in the State or, if the individual is not physically present in the State, intends to return to the State.

that her failure to report her income was not willful; 607 F.2d 92 (5th Cir.1979). The court's opinion on rehearing did not suggest that § 104 could apply.

Law and Analysis

Section 61 and the Income Tax Regulations thereunder provide that gross income means all income from whatever source derived unless excluded by law.

Section 102 provides that gross income does not include the value of property acquired by gift, bequest, devise, or inheritance.

Although certain payments made under legislatively provided social benefit programs for promotion of the general welfare are not includible in a recipient's gross income, Rev.Rul. 76–131, 1976–1 C.B. 16, holds that bonus payments received by Alaska residents under the Alaska Longevity Bonus Act are includible in the recipient's gross income pursuant to section 61 of the Code. That Act, the stated purpose of which was to provide an incentive to residents to continue uninterrupted residence in the State, is distinguishable from general welfare program payments because the bonus is payable to a State resident regardless of financial status, health, educational background, or employment status.

The United States Supreme Court in Commissioner v. Duberstein, 363 U.S. 278, 285 (1960), held that a gift, in the statutory sense, proceeds from a detached and disinterested generosity out of affection, respect, admiration, charity, or like impulses. Although the donor's intent is the most critical factor, the donor's characterization of his or her actions is not determinative. The determination must be based on the totality of the facts in each case. The absence of a legal or moral obligation to make a payment does not necessarily establish that the payment is a gift. However, if a payment does proceed from the constraining force of any moral or legal duty, or from the incentive of an anticipated benefit beyond the satisfaction that flows from the performance of a generous act, it does not constitute a gift.

The dividend payments made by the State of Alaska pursuant to section 43.23 of the Alaska statutes are not general welfare program payments. The payments are not restricted to those in need. There is no indication of a legislative intent that would support their characterization as gifts. As stated expressly in the statute, the State anticipates a benefit from making the payment, namely a reduced population turnover resulting in a more stable political, economic, and social environment.

Holding

Dividend payments made by the State of Alaska pursuant to section 43.23 of the Alaska statutes are includible in gross income under section 61.

Notes and Questions

1. *"Welfare program payments."* Could the Alaska Legislature have made payments under the Longevity Bonus Act exempt from Federal taxation by a carefully worded "statement of purpose" in the Act? Payments under the Social Security Act were held tax exempt in I.T.

3447, 1941–1 C.B. 191, which gave no reason for the exclusion. Payments to United States citizens or residents under foreign social security plans are taxable. Rev.Rul. 76–121, 1976–1 C.B. 24.

The Ninth Circuit rejected a taxpayer's contention that payments under the Alaska program described in the ruling were "gifts" in Greisen v. United States, 831 F.2d 916 (9th Cir.1987).

2. *Taxation of Social Security benefits.* Most Social Security benefits (and some tier 1 Railroad Retirement benefits) are partially includable in the incomes of upper- and middle-income recipients under § 86, which was added to the Code in 1984 and expanded in 1993. The portion of the benefits included in gross income depends on the taxpayer's "modified AGI," which for most taxpayers is the sum of AGI and tax-exempt interest. High-income taxpayers have to include as much as 85 percent of Social Security benefits; middle-income taxpayers include up to 50 percent; low-income taxpayers include nothing. The formulas used in § 86 are complex because of the need to make smooth transitions between these groups.

The complexities of § 86 are handled well by the tax forms, which reduce them to a series of simple, mechanical calculations. Nevertheless, this kind of complexity creates hardship for many taxpayers because it makes it almost impossible to plan intelligently. A low-income retiree deciding whether it would be worthwhile to take a part-time or temporary job might want to consider all of the following: (1) the income from the job will be subject to income and Social Security taxes; (2) the income from the job may reduce the amount of Social Security benefits the taxpayer will receive (some recipients get less from Social Security if they have other earnings); and (3) the income from the job may affect the amount of the taxpayer's Social Security benefits that are taxed, because it will increase the taxpayer's modified AGI. Few tax professionals (maybe none) can handle questions like this without pencil, paper, calculator, and constant reference to the Code. We doubt that many people other than tax professionals even try.

3. *Section 85.* Unemployment benefits are taxable under § 85, which was enacted because unemployment benefits replace taxable wages and because exclusion of unemployment benefits creates an incentive for unemployment. Are these reasons any less applicable to workers' compensation payments, which continue to be excluded under § 104, than to unemployment compensation?

G. IMPUTED INCOME

REVENUE RULING 79–24

1979–1 C.B. 60.

FACTS

Situation 1. In return for personal legal services performed by a lawyer for a housepainter, the housepainter painted the lawyer's personal residence. Both the lawyer and the housepainter are members of a barter club, an organization that annually furnishes its members a directory of members and the services they provide. All the members of the club are professional or trades persons. Members contact other members directly and negotiate the value of the services to be performed.

Situation 2. An individual who owned an apartment building received a work of art created by a professional artist in return for the rent-free use of an apartment for six months by the artist.

LAW

* * *

[Treas.Reg. §] 1.61–2(d)(1) provides that if services are paid for other than in money, the fair market value of the property or services taken in payment must be included in income. If the services were rendered at a stipulated price, such price will be presumed to be the fair market value of the compensation received in the absence of evidence to the contrary.

HOLDINGS

Situation 1. The fair market value of the services received by the lawyer and the housepainter are includible in their gross incomes under § 61.

Situation 2. The fair market value of the work of art and the six months fair rental value of the apartment are includible in the gross incomes of the apartment-owner and the artist under § 61.

Problem and Notes

1. *Imputed income from services.* The lawyer-housepainter exchange clearly creates taxable income, and would do so in principle even if the taxpayers were not members of a barter club. But just as clearly, a lawyer who paints his own house does not have taxable income. The benefits created when a taxpayer performs services for himself (or his family) are called "imputed income." No one has ever suggested that imputed income from services be measured and taxed. Its existence is worth noting not because it is a candidate for taxation but because the taxation of income other than imputed income gives the tax system a bias against exchange transactions. Thus, a parent considering whether to take a job and hire someone to care for his children, house, and garden in his absence might be induced by the income tax to decline the job even though, in the absence of taxation, he might have gone to work.[u]

A popular belief about taxation is that an income tax, by reducing the real (i.e., after-tax) return from working, encourages people to

u.   But see § 21.

reduce the amount of work they do and to choose more non-taxable leisure. This phenomenon, which economists call the "substitution effect," certainly exists for some taxpayers. (Compare a means test for welfare payments.) But an income tax may also increase some people's desire to work. By taking money the taxpayer otherwise could have spent or saved, the tax may spur the worker to greater efforts in order to maintain a standard of living or level of savings. This is called the "income effect."

A few cases have come very close to taxing some kinds of imputed income from services performed by the taxpayer. For example, Williams v. Commissioner, 64 T.C. 1085 (1975), held that a real-estate salesman employed by Dart Industries had to include in income a commission on his own purchase of real estate from Dart. The taxpayer argued that the "commission" was in fact a reduction in price, and that the commission was not "compensation for services" because, in the case of his own purchase, he did not have to go out and find a buyer. But the Tax Court found a "service" in the taxpayer's finding "a buyer (himself) willing and able to purchase property from his employer."

2. *Imputed income from property.* One kind of imputed income that has been taxed in Wisconsin and in a few foreign countries is imputed "rental" income from the taxpayer's ownership of a house. The taxpayer who owns a house is seen as being equivalent, economically, to another taxpayer who has a salary, or income from rents, interest, or dividends, and who uses some of that income to pay rent. In principle, the same sort of imputed income arises from ownership of any personal asset such as a car, a washing machine, or a ballpoint pen. In Helvering v. Independent Life Ins. Co., 292 U.S. 371 (1934), the Court said that "[t]he rental value of [a] building used by the owner does not constitute income within the meaning of the Sixteenth Amendment." This statement, of doubtful validity as a current rule of constitutional law, shows the persistence of the idea that income is a "flow" of "things."

3. *Problem.* Two taxpayers, L and M, are identically situated in almost every respect. Each earns $60,000 a year and each has accumulated $100,000 in savings. L invests his $100,000 in corporate bonds paying $12,000 in interest every year. He spends $12,000 a year for rent on the apartment in which he lives. M spends her $100,000 savings to buy an apartment across the street from the building in which L lives. Their apartments are identical in every respect except for minor details of interior decoration. How are L and M taxed?

4. *References.* Lane, A Theory of the Tax Base: The Exchange Model, 3 Am.J.Tax Pol'y 1, 34–41 (1984); Goode, The Individual Income Tax 52–57, 117–125 (rev. ed. 1976); Vickrey, Agenda for Progressive Taxation 17–52 (1947).

H. "ACCESSIONS TO WEALTH" REVISITED: CONTRIBUTIONS TO CAPITAL

EDWARDS v. CUBA RAILROAD CO.

Supreme Court of the United States, 1925.
268 U.S. 628, 45 S.Ct. 614, 69 L.Ed. 1124.

MR. JUSTICE BUTLER delivered the opinion of the Court.

Plaintiff, a New Jersey corporation, owns and operates a railroad in Cuba. In March, 1917, it made return of its income for 1916, and, in due time, paid the tax assessed on the basis of its return. Plaintiff had received in 1911 to 1916, inclusive, subsidy payments from the republic of Cuba, amounting in all to $1,696,216.20, but did not report any part of them as taxable income. * * *

An act of the Congress of the republic of Cuba of July 5, 1906, authorized the President to contract with one or more companies for the construction and operation of certain lines of railroad on designated routes between places specified. The republic granted a subsidy up to $6,000 per kilometer, payable in six annual installments, to the companies constructing and maintaining in use the specified lines. Any company having such a contract was entitled to receive subsidies for that part of the railroad constructed after the passage of the act, as well as for the part constructed after the making of the contract. March 25, 1909, the President of the republic and the plaintiff made a contract, by which the latter agreed, in consideration of $6,000 per kilometer to be paid by the republic as specified in the law of 1906, to construct and operate a railroad on the routes and between the places specified; and the plaintiff agreed to reduce by one-third the tariffs then in force for the transportation of permanent employees and troops of the government, and, in case of war or any disturbance of the public order, to transport troops in special trains at the rate of one cent per man per kilometer, and also agreed to reduce the fares for all first-class passengers. The entire line covered by this contract was completed in 1911. The subsidy payments amounted in all to $1,642,216.20, about one-third of the cost of the railroad.

An act of June 1, 1914, added to the law of 1906 an article which provided that the subsidy per kilometer for the construction of a railroad from Casilda to Placetas del Sur should be 6,000 pesos for a part and 12,000 pesos for the rest of the distance. June 30, 1915, in accordance with that act, the President of the republic and plaintiff made a contract for the construction of the railroad. It bound the company to carry public correspondence free of charge on the lines of this railroad, to carry small produce for 50 per cent. of the tariff, and to allow telegraph and telephone stations to be established by the government alongside the railroad. And there was handed over to the plaintiff certain land, buildings, construction and equipment then in the possession of the state, which theretofore had been acquired and built in an earlier effort to complete that line. The subsidy payment in 1916 was $54,000.

All the subsidy payments under both contracts were credited to a suspense account and, June 30, 1916, were transferred to the surplus account, and were used for capital expenditures. The cost of construction as carried on the books was not reduced by such payments.

* * * [The government argued that the payments were taxable under various statutes imposing taxes on the "net income" of a corporation.] Defendant insists that the subsidies were merely payments in advance on account of transportation service, later to be performed by the plaintiff for the government, and therefore are to be deemed income and taxable as such.

* * *

The Sixteenth Amendment, like other laws authorizing or imposing taxes, is to be taken as written, and is not to be extended beyond the meaning clearly indicated by the language used. The Cuban laws and contracts are similar to legislation and arrangements for the promotion of railroad construction which have been well known in the United States for more than half a century. Such aids, gifts and grants from the government, subordinate political subdivisions or private sources— whether of land, other property, credit or money—in order to induce construction and operation of railroads for the service of the public are not given as mere gratuities. Burke v. Southern Pacific R.R. Co., 234 U.S. 669, 679; Louisville & Nashville R.R. v. United States, decided March 2, 1925, 267 U.S. 395. Usually they are given to promote settlement and to provide for the development of the resources in the territory to be served. The things so sought to be attained in the public interest are numerous and varied. There is no support for the view that the Cuban government gave the subsidy payments, lands, buildings, railroad construction and equipment merely to obtain the specified concessions in respect of rates for government transportation. Other rates were considered. By the first contract, plaintiff agreed to reduce fares for first-class passengers and by the second, it agreed to reduce the rates on small produce. Clearly, the value of the lands and other physical property handed over to aid plaintiff in the completion of the railroad from Casilda to Placetas del Sur was not taxable income. These were to be used directly to complete the undertaking. The Commissioner of Internal Revenue, in levying the tax, did not include their value as income, and defendant does not claim that it was income. Relying on the contract for partial reimbursement, plaintiff found the money necessary to construct the railroad. The subsidy payments were proportionate to mileage completed; and this indicates a purpose to reimburse plaintiff for capital expenditures. All—the physical properties and the money subsidies— were given for the same purposes. It cannot reasonably be held that one was contribution to capital assets, and that the other was profit, gain or income. Neither the laws nor the contracts indicate that the money subsidies were to be used for the payment of dividends, interest or anything else properly chargeable to or payable out of earnings or income. The subsidy payments taxed were not made for services rendered or to be rendered. They were not profits or gains from the use or operation of the railroad, and do not constitute income within the meaning of the Sixteenth Amendment. See Stratton's Independence v. Howbert, 231 U.S. 399, 415; Eisner v. Macomber, 252 U.S. 189, 207; Merchants' Loan & Trust Co. v. Smietanka, supra.

Judgment affirmed.

Notes and Questions

1. *Rationale.* Having conceded that the value of the "lands and other physical properties" furnished by the Cuban government was not includable in income, the government had little left to argue. But why was it so clear that the value of the property was not income? Consider some analogies.

(1) Can the railroad company be viewed as acting, in some respects, as the Cuban government's agent, spending some of the government's money to produce benefits for the government? Note that there is little difference between (a) the government's building railroad tracks and letting the railroad use them for nothing, and (b) the government's giving the railroad money on the condition that it use the money to build tracks.

(2) Compare the Cuba Railroad Company with the (hypothetical) Kansas Railroad Company, which plans to build and operate a railroad in an area much less mountainous than Cuba. No one would suggest that the Kansas Railroad Company has income because of the ease with which track can be laid in Kansas. If the Cuban government makes Cuba roughly comparable to Kansas (from a railroading point of view) by paying for the extra costs of building a railroad in the mountains, could inclusion of those payments in the Cuba Railroad Company's income be reconciled with excluding the benefits of level terrain from the income of the Kansas Railroad Company?

2. *Depreciation aspects.* The basis of property contributed to the capital of a corporation and "not contributed by a shareholder as such," or of property purchased with money contributed to capital by a non-shareholder,[v] is zero; § 362(c). As a result, no depreciation is allowed in the case of non-shareholder contributions. The *long-run* effect of a non-shareholder contribution of property to a corporation's capital is, therefore, the same as if the value of the property were included in income and the taxpayer were then allowed depreciation on the property using its value at the time of the contribution as the basis (be sure you understand why).

Compare a corporation which receives a capital contribution from a local government in the form of a building with another taxpayer which

---

v. This statement, while true for many taxpayers, is an oversimplification of the rule of § 362(c), which you should examine with care.

is given money each year to rent a building. The latter plainly has no net income; even if we said that each year's subsidy payment was income, that income would be offset by a deduction for rent. One way of looking at the exclusion of capital contributions from income is to say that it serves to equalize the tax treatment of those who receive property and those who receive the use of property. Without the exclusion, those who receive property would normally be worse off, as they would have to pay a tax on the property's receipt and would get the tax back only in the future.

Until 1954, the basis of property received as a non-shareholder contribution to capital was the transferor's basis; Brown Shoe Co. v. Commissioner, 339 U.S. 583 (1950) (overruled by § 362). As a result, taxpayers receiving contributions to capital could not only exclude the contributions but also depreciate them. This rule means that, for pre–1954 contributions, the question whether the taxpayer received a "contribution" of property (as opposed to a mere right to use property) matters a great deal. See United States v. Chicago, Burlington & Quincy R. Co., 412 U.S. 401 (1973), holding that highway undercrossings and overcrossings paid for out of public funds were not contributed to the capital of a railroad company. This conclusion rested on findings that the money in question was spent primarily to benefit the public, not the railroad; that the facilities did not materially enhance the railroad's earning power; that the facilities "most likely would not have been constructed at all" but for governmental intervention; and that the payments were not "bargained for," since the railroad accepted, but did not seek, the crossing improvements.

3. *Scope of the exclusion.* Some aspects of the rule excluding non-shareholder contributions to the capital of a corporation from the corporation's income are codified in § 118.

*

Chapter Three

SOME EXCLUSIONS, DEDUCTIONS, AND CREDITS

This chapter continues the study of how taxable income is determined and adds the subject of tax credits. Unlike the Code provisions dealt with in Chapter 2, some of those examined here reflect Congress's practice of using the tax system to further non-tax goals. For example, interest on state and local bonds (Section A, below) is excludable from the recipient's income for revenue-sharing reasons, not because that kind of interest gives taxpayers any less "ability to pay" than other kinds of investment income. Some of the exclusions, deductions, and credits considered in this chapter are hard to classify as either "non-tax-purpose" or "tax-purpose" provisions: the deduction for extraordinary medical expenses (Section F), for instance, clearly does encourage spending on medical treatment, yet there may be sound tax reasons for allowing the deduction. Similarly, the partial tax credit for child-care expenses incurred by working parents (Section J) may be a compromise between allowing business-expense deductions for these costs (on the theory that child-care costs are a parent's cost of working) and denying any tax benefit (on the theory that the costs are the "personal" costs of having children).

A. TAX–EXEMPT INTEREST

In Pollock v. Farmers' Loan & Trust Co., 157 U.S. 429 (1895), the Supreme Court held the Income Tax Act of 1894 unconstitutional in taxing the interest on state and municipal bonds. The Court reasoned that such bonds are the means by which states carry out their governmental functions, that Congress could not tax the property or income of a state or one of its subdivisions, and that a tax on income derived from state or local securities was, in effect, a tax on a state's power to borrow. The Supreme Court overruled *Pollock* in South Carolina v. Baker, 485 U.S. 505 (1988), rehearing denied 486 U.S. 1062 (1988).

Although South Carolina v. Baker makes it very clear that Congress now has the power to tax interest on state and local bonds, Congress has shown no sign of wanting to exercise that power in a sweeping way.[a] Section 103, which provides that gross income does not include interest on any "state or local bond," is seen today as a form of revenue sharing. By giving up the taxes it could collect on state and local bond interest, the Federal government enables states and cities to borrow more cheaply than they could if that interest were taxed. In effect, the Federal government pays part of the states' borrowing costs.

KING v. COMMISSIONER

United States Tax Court, 1981.
77 T.C. 1113 (Acq.).

FEATHERSTON, JUDGE: Respondent determined the following deficiencies in petitioners' Federal income taxes:

Year	Amount
1971	$17,492
1972	4,941
1973	7,791
1974	4,108

The issue for decision is whether the interest, or any portion thereof, received by petitioner Virginia S. King on warrants issued to her by the Trinity River Authority is excludable from income for the years in controversy under section 103(a)(1).

FINDINGS OF FACT

[Petitioner owned an undivided one-fourth interest in the Smither Farm, a 4,928.35–acre tract of land. The Trinity River Authority of Texas ("TRA") bought the Smither Farm from petitioner and the other co-owners. Petitioner's share of the purchase price consisted of $122,048.70 in cash and warrants—negotiable, interest-bearing notes— with a face amount of $490,000. If petitioner and the other owners of the Smither Farm had refused to sell their interests, TRA could have condemned 22.14 acres of the land and a "flowage easement" over an additional 2,316.03 acres.]

* * *

During 1971, 1972, 1973, and 1974, petitioner received $33,692, $9,750, $13,686, and $6,500, respectively, from TRA as interest on the warrants outstanding during each of those years, and petitioners excluded the interest from gross income for Federal income tax purposes. Respondent determined that the warrants do not qualify as obligations

a. South Carolina v. Baker did not itself involve an attempt by Congress to prevent states from issuing tax-exempt bonds. The case involved the constitutionality of § 103(b)(3), which requires that bonds be registered to be tax exempt.

for which interest is excludable under section 103, and he increased petitioners' taxable income accordingly.

OPINION

Petitioner contends that the interest which she received on the warrants issued by TRA as part of the consideration for the purchase of her land is exempt from Federal income taxes as interest on "obligations" of a "political subdivision" of Texas within the meaning of section 103(a)(1).

Section 103(a)(1) in broad terms provides that the "gross income" of a taxpayer does not include "interest" on the "obligations" of "any political subdivision" of a State. It is stipulated that TRA is a political subdivision of the State of Texas, and it is clear that the warrants were "obligations" of TRA. But not every obligation is covered by the exemption prescribed by section 103(a)(1). Rather, the interest exclusion reflects a longstanding policy of the Federal Government to avoid imposing burdens or restraints on the exercise by the States and their political subdivisions of their power to borrow funds. The "purpose of the exclusion is to permit state and local governments to obtain capital at a low rate of interest." Fox v. United States, 397 F.2d 119, 122 (8th Cir.1968); see also Helvering v. Stockholms Enskilda Bank, 293 U.S. 84, 87 (1934). Interest is not excludable under section 103(a)(1) unless the obligation is incurred in the exercise of the political subdivision's borrowing power.

The path to the decision as to whether the warrants here in issue were "obligations" within the meaning of section 103(a)(1) has been illuminated by Drew v. United States, 551 F.2d 85 (5th Cir.1977), which also involved warrants issued by TRA in connection with the Lake Livingston project. In that case, the taxpayer owned land within the project site and was informed, along with other similarly situated landowners, of TRA's power of eminent domain. When TRA was unable to reach agreement with a landowner, condemnation proceedings were instituted. The taxpayer reached agreement with TRA on the sale of his land, elected to receive the consideration in the form of cash and warrants, and argued that the interest on the warrants was nontaxable under section 103(a)(1). The Court of Appeals, affirming a decision by the District Court, held that interest on the warrants was not excludable from the taxpayer's income because the interest was part of the award paid for the land under a threat of condemnation and not in a voluntary lending-borrowing transaction.

In reaching its conclusion, the Court of Appeals in *Drew* stated (551 F.2d at 87–88):

> It is evident that the obligation incurred by the governmental agency in condemnation award cases is under its power of eminent domain and not in the exercise of its borrowing power. The distinguishing feature between condemnation award cases and those in which the exemption is allowed, e.g., where the Government floats

bonds or securities, is the involuntary nature of the condemnation cases.

In this connection, the *Drew* court quoted (551 F.2d at 88) from United States Trust Co. of New York v. Anderson, 65 F.2d 575, 578 (2d Cir.1933), where it is pointed out that State and municipal bonds, if tax exempt, will command a better price in the market than if they are subject to taxation—

> "because the purchaser is not compelled to buy them and, being a free agent, may be induced by the tax exemption feature to prefer them to private bonds for investment. It disregards the whole purpose of the exemption to apply it to interest upon obligations of a state which it can *compel* a citizen to take in exchange for the fair value of his property."

See also Holley v. United States, 124 F.2d 909, 910 (6th Cir.1942).

* * *

We think the reasoning of *Drew* quite clearly denies the section 103(a)(1) interest exclusion claimed by petitioner in connection with the consideration received for the portion of the Smither Farm—the 22.14 acres of land and the flowage easement over 2,316.03 acres—that was subject to condemnation. The parties have stipulated that $465,361.24 represents the portion of the total consideration attributable to this land and easement which were acquired by TRA on terms and in circumstances basically similar to the properties involved in the *Drew* case. The interest on the warrants to the extent attributable to these properties was part of the just compensation for the properties sold under a threat of condemnation and is not excluded from petitioner's income by section 103(a)(1).

With respect to the properties which were not subject to condemnation—the 2,590.18 acres of land and the fee interest in the 2,316.03 acres covered by the flowage easement—we think the opposite answer is required. The parties have stipulated that the owners "were under no legal obligation to sell" these properties to TRA. They have also stipulated:

> Had Petitioner and the other owners of the Smither Farm refused to accept the offer of * * * [TRA] as outlined in the letter dated October 29, 1968, the * * * [TRA] would have restricted its purchase of the Smither Farm to that portion that was subject to * * * [TRA's] power of eminent domain—that is, 22.14 acres of land and a flowage easement over 2,316.03 acres of land.

The properties not subject to condemnation were thus acquired in a voluntary transaction. The portion of the consideration attributable to them represented payments on contracts or warrants calling for interest on deferred payments. We think the interest on the warrants, to the extent that they are attributable to these properties, is excludable from petitioner's income under section 103(a)(1).

* * *

To reflect the foregoing,

Decision will be entered under Rule 155.

Problem and Notes

1. *The "efficiency" of § 103(a) as a subsidy.* When tax rates were more progressive than they are today, it was generally thought that § 103 cost the Federal government more in lost revenues than the states gained in interest-expense savings. The reason for the gap between lost Federal revenues and savings for the states was that interest rates on tax-exempt bonds had to be set high enough to make the bonds attractive to buyers who were not in the highest Federal tax brackets. Suppose, for example, that tax-exempt bonds were sold only to investors subject to a 70–percent marginal rate. If that were the case, the bonds would pay only 30 percent of the interest paid on comparable taxable securities. A state that would have to pay $100 a year in interest to sell a $1000 taxable bond could sell a tax-exempt bond to a 70–percent taxpayer for $30 a year in interest. Section 103 would cost the Federal government $70 a year in taxes and the state would gain $70 a year by being able to market 3–percent (rather than 10–percent) bonds. The investor would gain nothing at all, and so the subsidy would be "efficient" in the sense that all of the lost Federal revenues would go to the states as interest-cost savings.

Unfortunately, there has always been a severe shortage of 70–percent taxpayers. In order to sell enough bonds to meet their needs, the states had to pay enough interest to make their bonds attractive to lower-bracket investors. If a state paid 5–percent interest on a bond that would have paid 10 percent if its interest were taxable, the Federal government lost $50 a year in taxes on each $1000 bond sold to a 50–percent taxpayer.[b] But 70–percent taxpayers also bought these bonds, and when that happened, the Federal government lost $70 a year in taxes for each bond, while the state saved only $50.

In the early 1990s, the highest marginal rate for most individuals was about 31 percent; in those days, the subsidy of § 103 may have been quite efficient. If the states could have found buyers for all of their bonds in the ranks of 31–percent taxpayers, the subsidy would have been completely efficient; even if bonds in those days were priced so as to sell to 28–percent taxpayers, the difference between 28 percent and 31

b. The figures in the text are approximations which ignore some of the effects of repealing § 103. For example, overall tax rates might be reduced somewhat, and investors deprived of access to tax-exempt bonds would not necessarily invest in taxable bonds; some at least would surely invest in other tax-favored areas instead. The phenomena indicated by the figures in the text are real, but their extent cannot be measured accurately.

percent is quite small. Today, though, the highest marginal rate is 38.6 percent, even before considering phaseouts of personal exemptions, itemized deductions, and other things. This change has increased the popularity, and reduced the efficiency, of tax-exempt bonds.

2. *Arbitrage bonds.* States themselves are exempt from tax under § 115. Were it not for § 103(b)(2), a state could issue bonds paying (say) 9 percent, invest the proceeds in taxable corporate bonds paying 10 percent, and generate revenues without taxing its residents. If the states were free to do this, they would undoubtedly issue a great quantity of tax-exempt arbitrage bonds, and in order to attract enough buyers the interest rates would have to approach those for taxable bonds. As long as the exempt bonds bore interest even slightly below that of taxable bonds it would pay the states to issue them, even though only a very small fraction of the revenues lost to the Federal government would end up in the state treasuries. Section 103(b)(2) denies the exemption of § 103(a) to arbitrage bonds, as defined in § 148.

3. *Private-activity bonds.* States and their political subdivisions have developed techniques for "selling" their power to issue tax-exempt bonds. As a simple example, suppose that a company which needs to borrow $1,000,000 to build a restaurant would have to pay 10 percent (taxable) interest to raise the money, while the state in which the restaurant is located can borrow at 7 percent. The state borrows the $1,000,000, uses the proceeds to build the restaurant, and then leases the restaurant to the company, at a rent sufficient to cover interest and amortization of principal. In effect, the company has borrowed the money to build the restaurant and the debt may be secured only by the building (i.e., the debt may not be a general obligation of the state), but in form, at least, the state is "the issuer" and the interest is tax exempt.

Over the years, states and cities have issued bonds to raise money for home mortgages, industrial development, college dormitories, and many other projects far removed from what one usually thinks of as "governing." Congress has responded by limiting the extent to which the power granted by § 103(a) can be used in this way. Section 103(b)(1) denies tax-exemption to interest on "private activity bonds" unless those bonds are "qualified bonds"; these terms are defined in §§ 141–145 and 147. In addition to restricting the use of particular kinds of bonds, the Code puts a "volume cap" on the amount that a state can raise each year by issuing private-activity bonds, although some kinds of private-activity bonds are exempt from the "cap"; § 146. Each state's annual volume limit is the higher of (1) $50 for each resident of the state, as determined by Census Bureau estimates, or (2) $150,000,000; § 146(d).

The Revenue Reconciliation Act of 1993 created a new kind of tax-exempt bond for use in financing the purchase of assets by "enterprise zone businesses." These are most businesses operating in "empowerment zones" or in "enterprise communities" chosen by the Secretary of Housing and Urban Development and the Secretary of Agriculture from areas nominated by state and local governments. The Taxpayer Relief

Act of 1997 authorized the creation of new empowerment and enterprise zones, provided for the issuance of new kinds of bonds to finance businesses in these areas, and adopted special rules for the District of Columbia, Alaska, and Hawaii. No useful purpose would be served by going into detail about any of this. The many details are spelled out in §§ 1391–1397D. The "empowerment zone" and "enterprise community" concepts are said to be experimental, and so their special tax provisions are currently scheduled to expire after a few years; few observers expect this to happen.

4. *Registration and reporting.* Quite apart from the advantage of paying no tax on interest income (an advantage which is partially or completely offset by the "implicit tax" in the form of receiving lower interest than taxable bonds pay), some people have found tax-exempt bonds useful in concealing income from governments, university financial-aid officers, and spouses. Sections 103(b)(3) and 149 now require that most bonds be registered to be exempt from tax, and § 6012(d) requires persons who file income-tax returns to report their tax-exempt interest.

5. *Problem.* T won a lottery sponsored by a state. T's prize was $1,000,000, payable in 20 installments of $50,000 each, plus interest at 7 percent on the unpaid balance. Can T exclude the interest from income?

6. *References.* Goode, The Individual Income Tax, 133–38 (rev. ed. 1976); Surrey, Pathways to Tax Reform 209–22 (1973); Rolph & Break, Public Finance 555–70 (1961).

B. TAX EXPENDITURES

Section 103 is an example of a "tax expenditure," a feature of the tax law which exists to further some non-tax goal (revenue sharing, in the case of § 103) rather than to measure "income" in some normative sense.

TAX EXPENDITURES

Committee on the Budget
United States Senate
March 17, 1976
Pages 1–4.

* * *

DEFINING TAX EXPENDITURES

Tax expenditures are revenue losses resulting from Federal tax provisions that grant special tax relief designed to encourage certain kinds of behavior by taxpayers or to aid taxpayers in special circumstances. These provisions may, in effect, be viewed as the equivalent of a simultaneous collection of revenue and a direct budget outlay of an equal amount to the beneficiary taxpayer.

Section 3(a)(3) of the Congressional Budget and Impoundment Control Act of 1974 specifically defines tax expenditures as:

> * * * those revenue losses attributable to provisions of the Federal tax laws which allow a special exclusion, exemption, or deduction from gross income or which provide a special credit, a preferential rate of tax, or a deferral of tax liability; * * *.

In the legislative history of the Congressional Budget Act, provisions classified as tax expenditures are contrasted with those provisions which are part of the "normal structure" of the individual and corporate income tax necessary to collect government revenues.

* * *

The listing of a provision as a tax expenditure in no way implies any judgment about its desirability or effectiveness relative to other tax or nontax provisions that provide benefits to specific classes of individuals and corporations. Rather, the listing of tax expenditures, taken in conjunction with the listing of direct spending programs, is intended to allow Congress to scrutinize all Federal programs—both nontax and tax—when it develops its annual budget. Only if tax expenditures are included will Congressional budget decisions take into account the full spectrum of Federal programs.

In numerous instances, the goals of these tax expenditures might also be achieved through the use of direct expenditures or loan programs. Because any qualified taxpayer may reduce tax liability through use of a tax expenditure, such provisions are comparable to entitlement programs under which benefits are paid to all eligible persons. Since tax expenditures are generally enacted as permanent legislation, it is important that, as entitlement programs, they be given thorough periodic consideration to see whether they are efficiently meeting the national needs and goals that were the reasons for their initial establishment.

Major Types of Tax Expenditures

Tax expenditures may take any of the following forms: (1) exclusions, exemptions, and deductions, which reduce taxable income; (2) preferential tax rates, which reduce taxes by applying lower rates to part or all of a taxpayer's income; (3) credits, which are subtracted from taxes as ordinarily computed; and (4) deferrals of tax, which result from delayed recognition of income or from allowing in the current year deductions that are properly attributable to a future year.

The amount of tax relief per dollar of each exclusion, exemption, and deduction increases with the taxpayer's marginal tax rate. Thus, the exclusion of interest income from state and local bonds saves [$31] in tax for every $100 of interest for the taxpayer in the [31] percent tax bracket, whereas the savings for the taxpayer in the [15] percent bracket is only [$15]. Similarly, * * * any itemized deduction is worth [more] in tax saving to a taxpayer in the [31] percent bracket [than] to one in the [15] percent bracket.

A tax credit is subtracted directly from the tax liability that would otherwise be due; thus the amount of tax reduction is the amount of the credit—which does not depend on the marginal tax rate.

The numerous tax expenditures that take the form of exclusions, deductions, and exemptions are relatively more valuable to * * * [higher-bracket than to lower-bracket] individuals. However, this fact should be viewed in the context of recent increases * * * in the standard deduction, which provide[s] more tax saving for certain low-middle income taxpayers than itemized deductions, thus reducing the number of them who itemize.

Moreover, even though some tax expenditures may provide most of their tax relief to those with high taxable incomes, this may be the consequence of overriding economic considerations. For example, tax expenditures directed toward capital formation may deliberately benefit savers who are primarily higher income taxpayers.

TAX EXPENDITURES

Stanley S. Surrey, an assistant secretary of the Treasury in the 1960s, developed and spread the idea that some tax provisions—those designed to subsidize particular activities rather than to measure people's taxable capacity—were functionally the same as spending programs and should be evaluated in the same way as spending programs. These provisions, known as "tax expenditures," are measures that award benefits (in the form of exclusions, deductions, or credits) to promote non-tax goals. Some resistance to this idea arose because, it was argued, viewing tax relief as equivalent to spending suggested that "everything belongs to the government." However, the tax-expenditure concept, properly applied, does not treat all failures to tax something as "expenditures." The deduction for business expenses, for example, is not a tax expenditure, because taxing people on their incomes necessarily requires a deduction for business expenditures: If we know that A's business took in $1,000,000 last year while B's took in only $50,000 we have no idea whether A should be taxed more heavily than B (if it cost A $1,000,000 to earn the $1,000,000 he took in, he has just broken even, and so should not have any taxable income). Nor are things like the personal exemptions or the fact that the maximum (nominal) rate of tax is 38.6 percent (in 2002–2003), rather than 50 percent, tax expenditures: they simply reflect decisions motivated by beliefs about what *tax* policy requires. Only tax provisions that exist to serve *non-tax* goals are properly thought of as tax expenditures.

In contrast to provisions like the deduction for business expenses, consider the tax credit for using alcohol as a fuel (§ 40). This credit was not adopted because there is some tax reason why those who use alcohol as fuel have less ability to pay than others, it was adopted to encourage the use of alcohol as a fuel. It is no different in principle, and little different in practice, from a government program that sends a check to taxpayers who use alcohol as fuels, with the amount of the check determined according to the proof (the higher the better) and the amount of alcohol used as fuel each year. The fact that the check the taxpayer gets is a tax-refund check, issued by the Internal Revenue Service, rather than a check issued by the Department of Energy, will not matter to the recipient or the taxpaying public, and therefore should not matter to Congress, either. In deciding whether the alcohol-fuels credit is a good thing, Congress would be well advised to consult experts on energy production and on the environment, not tax specialists, who have nothing relevant to say about the subject. (In practice, of course, much of the encouragement Congress gets to retain this credit comes from the producers of alcohol-based fuels.)

It is often hard to tell whether a particular provision should be seen as a tax expenditure or not. Consider the deduction for extraordinary medical expenses (§ 213). Some analysts have assumed that this is a tax expenditure, intended to subsidize medical care. But the deduction can be defended on tax-policy grounds. If both A and B earn $100,000 (after expenses) but A has to spend $50,000 on medical care while B spends nothing, A seems to have much less ability to pay than B, and the attractiveness of income as a tax base is often thought to be its correlation with ability to pay. Similarly, the deduction of "personal" interest, such as interest on a home-mortgage loan, is usually thought of as a tax expenditure to encourage homebuying, but it can be defended on tax-policy grounds alone. Some of the opposition to the tax-expenditure concept may exist because some tax-expenditure theorists have been too willing to label particular provisions as "expenditures."

The "tax expenditure budget" which follows estimates the revenue losses from many provisions which have been identified officially as "tax expenditures." In many of these cases, the designation of a provision as a tax expenditure is controversial. Furthermore, the list does not include some features of the tax law that most analysts see as tax expenditures: depreciation allowances that allow costs to be recovered more rapidly than the assets in question decline in value, for example. The United States has published tax-expenditure budgets since 1975. The governments of most other industrialized countries publish similar budgets.

ESTIMATES OF TOTAL TAX EXPENDITURES[c]

(In Millions of Dollars)

		Total from corporations and individuals						
	2001	2002	2003	2004	2005	2006	2007	2003-2007
National Defense								
1 Exclusion of benefits and allowances to armed forces personnel	2,160	2,190	2,210	2,240	2,260	2,290	2,310	11,310
International affairs:								
2 Exclusion of income earned abroad by U.S. citizens	2,450	2,540	2,660	2,690	2,760	2,810	3,170	14,090
3 Exclusion of certain allowances for Federal employees abroad	760	800	840	880	920	960	1,020	4,620
4 Extraterritorial income exclusion	4,490	4,820	5,150	5,510	5,890	6,290	6,730	29,570
5 Inventory property sales source rules exception	1,400	1,470	1,540	1,620	1,700	1,790	1,880	8,530
6 Deferral of income from controlled foreign corporations (normal tax method)	6,600	7,000	7,450	7,900	8,400	8,930	9,550	42,230
7 Deferred taxes for financial firms on certain income earned overseas	1,300	550	0	0	0	0	0	0
General science, space, and technology:								
8 Expensing of research and experimentation expenditures (normal tax method)	2,020	1,780	2,380	2,880	3,400	3,910	4,160	16,730
9 Credit for increasing research activities	5,370	6,010	4,590	4,020	2,330	990	410	12,350
Energy:								
10 Expensing of exploration and development costs, fuels	50	60	70	90	90	100	100	450
11 Excess of percentage over cost depletion, fuels	250	260	270	290	300	310	320	1,490
12 Alternative fuel production credit	900	850	410	130	130	130	130	930
13 Exception from passive loss limitation for working interests in oil and gas properties	20	20	20	20	20	20	20	100
14 Capital gains treatment of royalties on coal	100	100	110	120	120	130	140	620
15 Exclusion of interest on energy facility bonds	90	90	100	120	130	140	150	640
16 Enhanced oil recovery credit	310	360	440	530	640	760	910	3,280
17 New technology credit	60	80	100	100	100	90	90	480
18 Alcohol fuel credits [1]	30	30	30	30	30	30	30	150
19 Tax credit and deduction for clean-fuel burning vehicles	50	50	50	20	- 10	- 50	- 50	- 40
20 Exclusion from income of conservation subsidies provided by public utilities	70	70	70	70	70	70	60	340
Natural resources and environment:								
21 Expensing of exploration and development costs, nonfuel minerals	10	10	10	10	10	10	10	50
22 Excess of percentage over cost depletion, nonfuel minerals	250	260	270	290	300	300	310	1,470
23 Exclusion of interest on bonds for water, sewage, and hazardous waste facilities	400	420	440	480	530	580	630	2,660
24 Capital gains treatment of certain timber income	100	100	110	120	120	130	140	620
25 Expensing of multiperiod timber growing costs	360	360	370	380	390	400	410	1,950
26 Tax incentives for preservation of historic structures	180	200	210	220	230	240	250	1,150
Agriculture:								
27 Expensing of certain capital outlays	170	170	170	170	170	170	170	850
28 Expensing of certain multiperiod production costs	120	130	130	130	120	120	120	620
29 Treatment of loans forgiven for solvent farmers	10	10	10	10	10	10	10	50
30 Capital gains treatment of certain income	990	1,040	1,100	1,160	1,220	1,290	1,360	6,130
31 Income averaging for farmers	70	70	70	70	80	80	80	380
32 Deferral of gain on sale of farm refiners	10	10	10	10	10	10	10	50
Commerce and housing:								
Financial institutions and insurance:								
33 Exemption of credit union income	1,000	1,070	1,150	1,230	1,320	1,420	1,530	6,650
34 Excess bad debt reserves of financial institutions	60	50	30	20	10	0	0	60
35 Exclusion of interest on life insurance savings	16,290	17,710	19,250	20,940	22,780	24,790	26,930	114,690
36 Special alternative tax on small property and casualty insurance companies	10	10	10	10	10	10	10	50
37 Tax exemption of certain insurance companies owned by tax-exempt organizations	220	230	250	260	280	290	300	1,380
38 Small life insurance company deduction	100	100	100	100	100	100	100	500
Housing:								
39 Exclusion of interest on owner-occupied mortgage subsidy bonds	800	830	870	960	1,050	1,140	1,240	5,260
40 Exclusion of interest on rental housing bonds	160	170	180	200	220	240	260	1,100
41 Deductibility of mortgage interest on owner-occupied homes	64,510	64,190	66,110	68,070	70,870	73,560	76,870	355,480
42 Deductibility of State and local property tax on owner-occupied homes	22,410	22,680	23,580	23,210	20,330	16,300	14,410	97,830
43 Deferral of income from post 1987 installment sales	1,040	1,050	1,080	1,100	1,120	1,140	1,160	5,600
44 Capital gains exclusion on home sales	19,090	19,670	20,260	20,860	21,490	22,140	22,800	107,550
45 Exception from passive loss rules for $25,000 of rental loss	4,800	4,400	4,070	3,780	3,530	3,290	3,090	17,760
46 Credit for low-income housing investments	3,220	3,330	3,460	3,630	3,810	3,980	4,130	19,010
47 Accelerated depreciation on rental housing (normal tax method)	5,190	5,440	5,710	5,790	5,800	5,720	5,800	28,820
Commerce:								
48 Cancellation of indebtedness	30	30	30	40	40	40	40	190
49 Exceptions from imputed interest rules	80	80	80	80	80	80	80	400
50 Capital gains (except agriculture, timber, iron ore, and coal) (normal tax method)	67,800	61,810	60,200	56,990	56,180	50,670	49,880	273,920
51 Capital gains exclusion of small corporation stock	70	100	130	160	210	250	300	1,050
52 Step-up basis of capital gains at death	26,540	27,610	28,710	29,860	31,050	32,300	33,590	155,510
53 Carryover basis of capital gains on gifts	530	600	680	760	900	1,080	1,130	4,550
54 Ordinary income treatment of loss from small business corporation stock sale	40	40	40	50	50	50	50	240
55 Accelerated depreciation of buildings other than rental housing (normal tax method)	4,540	4,560	4,240	3,960	3,800	4,160	4,880	21,040

c. From Analytical Perspectives, Budget of the United States Government, Fiscal Year 2003, pp. 99–101.

		Total from corporations and individuals							
		2001	2002	2003	2004	2005	2006	2007	2003-2007
56	Accelerated depreciation of machinery and equipment (normal tax method)	37,860	37,130	36,480	36,790	37,430	38,520	40,930	190,150
57	Expensing of certain small investments (normal tax method)	1,670	1,430	1,420	1,390	1,360	1,480	1,720	7,370
58	Amortization of start-up costs (normal tax method)	130	160	200	240	250	270	270	1,230
59	Graduated corporation income tax rate (normal tax method)	4,940	5,590	6,210	6,580	7,120	7,450	7,880	35,240
60	Exclusion of interest on small issue bonds	310	310	330	360	390	430	470	1,980
	Transportation:								
61	Deferral of tax on shipping companies	20	20	20	20	20	20	20	100
62	Exclusion of reimbursed employee parking expenses	1,980	2,090	2,190	2,300	2,420	2,550	2,670	12,130
63	Exclusion for employer-provided transit passes	220	280	360	410	470	540	600	2,380
	Community and regional development:								
64	Investment credit for rehabilitation of structures (other than historic)	30	30	30	30	30	30	30	150
65	Exclusion of interest for airport, dock, and similar bonds	630	640	680	750	820	890	980	4,120
66	Exemption of certain mutuals' and cooperatives' income	60	60	60	60	70	70	70	330
67	Empowerment zones, Enterprise communities, and Renewal communities	380	730	1,130	1,170	1,280	1,410	1,580	6,570
68	New markets tax credit	10	90	190	290	430	610	830	2,350
69	Expensing of environmental remediation costs	80	100	100	20	- 20	- 10	- 10	80
	Education, training, employment, and social services:								
	Education:								
70	Exclusion of scholarship and fellowship income (normal tax method)	1,210	1,200	1,210	1,240	1,330	1,380	1,390	6,550
71	HOPE tax credit	4,130	4,110	3,520	2,680	2,930	2,730	2,900	14,960
72	Lifetime Learning tax credit	2,370	2,290	2,360	3,140	2,980	2,740	2,960	14,180
73	Education Individual Retirement Accounts	30	50	80	130	220	330	470	1,230
74	Deductibility of student-loan interest	390	450	640	660	680	700	720	3,400
75	Deduction for higher education expenses	0	430	2,290	2,960	3,710	3,010	0	11,970
76	State prepaid tuition plans	190	270	340	400	460	530	590	2,320
77	Exclusion of interest on student-loan bonds	230	230	240	260	290	310	350	1,450
78	Exclusion of interest on bonds for private nonprofit educational facilities	540	550	580	640	700	760	830	3,510
79	Credit for holders of zone academy bonds	30	50	70	80	90	90	90	420
80	Exclusion of interest on savings bonds redeemed to finance educational expenses	10	20	20	20	20	20	20	100
81	Parental personal exemption for students age 19 or over	1,010	1,070	1,120	1,170	1,230	1,280	1,340	6,140
82	Deductibility of charitable contributions (education)	3,830	3,980	4,200	4,440	4,600	4,840	5,030	23,110
83	Exclusion of employer-provided educational assistance	260	410	500	530	560	590	620	2,800
	Training, employment, and social services:								
84	Work opportunity tax credit	300	230	140	60	30	10	0	240
85	Welfare-to-work tax credit	90	70	40	20	10	0	0	70
86	Employer provided child care exclusion	720	740	770	810	930	1,020	1,080	4,610
87	Employer-provided child care credit	0	40	90	130	150	150	160	680
88	Assistance for adopted foster children	190	220	250	260	270	280	290	1,350
89	Adoption credit and exclusion	130	140	220	450	500	540	560	2,270
90	Exclusion of employee meals and lodging (other than military)	710	740	780	810	850	890	930	4,260
91	Child credit [2]	19,840	19,760	19,680	19,550	20,550	21,530	21,240	102,550
92	Credit for child and dependent care expenses	2,670	2,610	2,670	2,960	2,700	2,150	1,920	12,400
93	Credit for disabled access expenditures	50	50	50	50	60	60	60	280
94	Deductibility of charitable contributions, other than education and health	30,150	30,810	32,080	33,830	35,190	36,890	38,290	176,280
95	Exclusion of certain foster care payments	500	510	520	530	540	570	610	2,770
96	Exclusion of parsonage allowances	350	370	400	420	450	470	490	2,230
	Health:								
97	Exclusion of employer contributions for medical insurance premiums and medical care	82,800	90,910	99,260	106,940	115,380	124,050	134,960	580,590
98	Self-employed medical insurance premiums	1,520	1,730	2,420	3,570	3,870	4,170	4,430	18,460
99	Workers' compensation insurance premiums	4,730	4,870	5,080	5,230	5,410	5,570	5,790	27,080
100	Medical Savings Accounts	20	20	20	20	20	20	20	100
101	Deductibility of medical expenses	4,990	5,260	5,530	5,840	6,280	6,600	7,100	31,350
102	Exclusion of interest on hospital construction bonds	1,100	1,130	1,190	1,310	1,440	1,570	1,700	7,210
103	Deductibility of charitable contributions (health)	4,010	4,180	4,420	4,690	4,850	5,100	5,320	24,380
104	Tax credit for orphan drug research	140	150	170	190	220	240	270	1,090
105	Special Blue Cross/Blue Shield deduction	270	300	340	310	300	270	300	1,520
	Income security:								
106	Exclusion of railroad retirement system benefits	380	390	400	400	400	400	400	2,000
107	Exclusion of workers' compensation benefits	5,560	5,810	6,070	6,320	6,600	6,900	7,200	33,090
108	Exclusion of public assistance benefits (normal tax method)	370	380	400	410	430	450	470	2,160
109	Exclusion of special benefits for disabled coal miners	70	70	60	60	60	50	50	280
110	Exclusion of military disability pensions	110	120	120	120	130	130	140	640
	Net exclusion of pension contributions and earnings:								
111	Employer plans	42,070	48,070	53,080	54,500	55,630	58,980	63,320	285,510
112	401(k) plans	44,080	52,960	59,510	62,770	65,290	69,230	73,320	330,120

		Total from corporations and individuals							
		2001	2002	2003	2004	2005	2006	2007	2003-2007
113	Individual Retirement Accounts	18,680	18,090	18,660	19,050	18,930	19,230	18,330	94,200
114	Low and moderate income savers credit	0	550	1,960	1,940	1,900	1,800	1,280	8,880
115	Keogh plans	6,160	6,520	6,770	7,040	7,250	7,490	7,730	36,280
	Exclusion of other employee benefits:								
116	Premiums on group term life insurance	1,750	1,780	1,800	1,830	1,860	1,890	1,920	9,300
117	Premiums on accident and disability insurance	210	220	230	240	250	260	270	1,250
118	Small business retirement plan credit	0	20	50	90	120	130	150	540
119	Income of trusts to finance supplementary unemployment benefits	20	20	30	30	30	30	30	150
120	Special ESOP rules	1,290	1,340	1,420	1,490	1,570	1,640	1,730	7,850
121	Additional deduction for the blind	40	40	40	40	40	40	40	200
122	Additional deduction for the elderly	1,970	1,890	1,950	2,060	2,100	2,150	2,050	10,310
123	Tax credit for the elderly and disabled	30	30	30	30	30	30	30	150
124	Deductibility of casualty losses	210	250	310	360	410	450	490	2,020
125	Earned income tax credit [3]	4,940	4,370	4,800	4,930	5,100	5,180	5,390	25,400
	Social Security:								
	Exclusion of social security benefits:								
126	Social Security benefits for retired workers	17,830	18,000	18,180	18,560	18,850	19,720	20,890	96,200
127	Social Security benefits for disabled	2,690	2,930	3,240	3,630	4,020	4,470	5,020	20,380
128	Social Security benefits for dependents and survivors	3,720	3,870	4,060	4,320	4,560	4,820	5,170	22,930
	Veterans benefits and services:								
129	Exclusion of veterans death benefits and disability compensation	3,150	3,190	3,300	3,490	3,680	3,870	4,080	18,420
130	Exclusion of veterans pensions	70	80	80	80	90	90	100	440
131	Exclusion of GI bill benefits	90	90	90	100	100	110	110	510
132	Exclusion of interest on veterans housing bonds	40	40	40	40	50	50	60	240
	General purpose fiscal assistance:								
133	Exclusion of interest on public purpose State and local bonds	23,100	23,680	24,270	24,880	25,500	26,140	26,800	127,590
134	Deductibility of nonbusiness state and local taxes other than on owner-occupied homes	45,520	46,160	48,150	47,730	43,270	34,820	30,890	204,860
135	Tax credit for corporations receiving income from doing business in U.S. possessions	2,190	2,240	2,240	2,240	2,200	1,300	0	7,980
	Interest:								
136	Deferral of interest on U.S. savings bonds	290	300	310	330	330	350	360	1,680
	Addendum: Aid to State and local governments:								
	Deductibility of:								
	Property taxes on owner-occupied homes	22,410	22,680	23,580	23,210	20,330	16,300	14,410	97,830
	Nonbusiness State and local taxes other than on owner-occupied homes	45,520	46,160	48,150	47,730	43,270	34,820	30,890	204,860
	Exclusion of interest on State and local bonds for:								
	Public purposes	23,100	23,680	24,270	24,880	25,500	26,140	26,800	127,590
	Energy facilities	90	90	100	120	130	140	150	640
	Water, sewage, and hazardous waste disposal facilities	400	420	440	480	530	580	630	2,660
	Small-issues	310	310	330	360	390	430	470	1,980
	Owner-occupied mortgage subsidies	800	830	870	960	1,050	1,140	1,240	5,260
	Rental housing	160	170	180	200	220	240	260	1,100
	Airports, docks, and similar facilities	630	640	680	750	820	890	980	4,120
	Student loans	230	230	240	260	290	310	350	1,450
	Private nonprofit educational facilities	540	550	580	640	700	760	830	3,510
	Hospital construction	1,100	1,130	1,190	1,310	1,440	1,570	1,700	7,210
	Veterans' housing	40	40	40	40	50	50	60	240
	Credit for holders of zone academy bonds	30	50	70	80	90	90	90	420

[1] The determination of whether a provision is a tax expenditure is made on the basis of a broad concept of 'income' that is larger in scope than is 'income' as defined under general U.S. income tax principles. For tax reasons, the tax expenditure estimates include, for example, estimates related to the exclusion of extraterritorial income, as well as other exclusions, notwithstanding that such exclusions define income under the general rule of U.S. income taxation.

[2] In addition, the partial exemption from the excise tax for alcohol fuels results in a reduction in excise tax receipts (in millions of dollars) as follows: 2001 $990; 2002 $1,020; 2003 $1,050; 2004 $1,080; 2005 $1,080; 2006 $1,100; and 2007 $1,120.

[3] The figures in the table indicate the effect of the child tax credit on receipts. The effect of the credit on outlays (in millions of dollars) is as follows: 2001 $980; 2002 $7,390; 2003 $7,390; 2004 $7,210; 2005 $6,950; 2006 $9,380; and 2007 $9,200.

[4] The figures in the table indicate the effect of the earned income tax credit on receipts. The effect of the credit on outlays (in millions of dollars) is as follows: 2001 $26,120; 2002 $28,280; 2003 $30,630; 2004 $31,080; 2005 $31,720; 2006 $33,130; and 2007 $34,090.

Note: Provisions with estimates denoted normal tax method have no revenue loss under the reference tax law method. All estimates have been rounded to the nearest $10 million. Provisions with estimates that rounded to zero in each year are not included in the table.

Notes

1. *Tax expenditures.* One common objection to the use of the tax law to subsidize favored activities is that Congress sometimes enacts tax subsidies without critical scrutiny of the costs and benefits to be obtained. A compelling example is the House of Representatives' passage in 1976 of a tax credit for the purchase of garden tools (the credit was dropped by the Conference Committee). Another objection is that tax benefits in the form of deductions or exclusions from income benefit high-income taxpayers more than low-income ones; thus, the exclusion from income of a $1000 scholarship is worth nothing to a student with no other income but can save a high-income student as much as $386 (in 2002–2003). Tax subsidies in the form of tax credits do not have the "upside down" effect of deductions or exclusions. However, if a credit is equivalent to a payment that should be includable in income, the tax system's failure to treat the amount of the credit as income benefits high-bracket taxpayers more than low-bracket ones. See Edrey & Abrams, Equitable Implementation of Tax Expenditures, 9 Va.Tax Rev.

109 (1989). Furthermore, unless a credit is refundable it does nothing for a taxpayer whose income is so low that no tax would be due in any event. Few direct subsidy programs would be limited in this way.

Some people defend tax expenditures on the ground that they involve less bureaucratic interference with the recipients' affairs than direct subsidy programs. Surrey, Pathways to Tax Reform, pp. 130–33 (1973), points out that there is no necessary reason why direct spending should involve more red tape than a tax program: an agency charged with disbursing funds could be authorized to mail out checks with no more documentation from the recipient than people provide on tax returns. Furthermore, some tax-expenditure programs do condition tax benefits on compliance with very detailed requirements; see, e.g., Treas. Reg. § 1.190–2.

Tax expenditures also contribute significantly to the Code's complexity. Although legislators regularly lament the complexity of the Code, the enactment of new and the modification of old tax expenditures continue unabated.

2. *References.* There is a large body of literature on tax expenditures and on the related topic of a "comprehensive tax base." (A comprehensive tax base is, essentially, one without exclusions or deductions for tax expenditures.) Articles dealing with particular tax expenditures (or provisions which may or may not be tax expenditures) will be cited in connection with the discussions of those provisions. Here are a few general references: Bartlett, The End of Tax Expenditures As We Know Them?, 91 Tax Notes 413 (2001); Thuronyi, Tax Expenditures: A Reassessment, 1988 Duke L.J. 1155; Surrey & McDaniel, Tax Expenditures (1985); McIntyre, A Solution to the Problem of Defining a Tax Expenditure, 14 U.C. Davis L.Rev. 79 (1980); Surrey & McDaniel, The Tax Expenditure Concept and the Budget Reform Act of 1974, 17 B.C.Ind. & Comm.L.Rev. 679 (1976); Blum, Book Review, 1 J.Corp.Tax. 486 (1975); Surrey, Pathways to Tax Reform (1973).

SOME TAX EXPENDITURES FOR HIGHER EDUCATION

When the concept of tax expenditures was first developed, many of its advocates hoped that public understanding of the functional equivalence of many tax provisions and spending programs would lead to the replacement of some tax-expenditure provisions with direct subsidy programs, which would not suffer from the vices peculiar to tax subsidies. In practice, just the opposite seems to have happened: tax subsidies seem to have an almost irresistible political appeal. Those who dislike taxation support them because they seem to "reduce taxes"; those who favor government spending like them because they confer benefits in much the same way as formal spending programs. The Taxpayer Relief Act of 1997, an act that had an astonishing level of bipartisan support, created a variety of new tax-expenditure provisions ostensibly designed to help middle-income taxpayers cope with college costs, and the 2001 legislation expanded some of these provisions and added a deduction for some college-tuition payments. In form, these subsidies benefit students and parents who pay tuition (and sometimes other expenses), though it is inevitable that colleges will capture a portion of the benefits by raising tuition. We have already discussed two provisions that subsidize saving for education expenses: § 529 ("qualified tuition programs") and § 530 ("Coverdell education savings accounts"); p. 71 above. Here we shall look briefly at two tax credits and a deduction.

The *Hope Scholarship Credit*[d] of § 25A(b) is a tax credit equal to the first $1000 and half of the second $1000 in tuition and academic fees paid for the education of a student during the first two years of post-secondary education. The credit is phased out for upper-income taxpayers: the phaseout begins at a modified AGI of $40,000 ($80,000 for joint returns) and is completed when modified AGI reaches $50,000 ($100,000 for joint returns). This phaseout makes the credit unavailable to the wealthy. It is also unavailable to the poor, as the credit, being nonrefundable, gives no benefit to taxpayers who would have no income-tax liability in the first place. The credit is allowed for tuition paid for the taxpayer, the taxpayer's spouse, or a dependent of the taxpayer. Taxpayers making tuition payments for more than one student are entitled to a Hope Scholarship Credit for each student. (This brief and non-technical description does not begin to do justice to the many details of § 25A, which is replete with definitions and qualifications.)

The *Lifetime Learning Credit* of § 25A(c) is a credit equal to 20 percent of the "qualified tuition and related expenses" paid by the taxpayer up to a total of $5000 a year ($10,000 after 2003). Unlike the Hope Scholarship Credit, the Lifetime Learning Credit is calculated on a per-taxpayer basis, rather than per student. It is not limited to tuition for the first two years of post-secondary education. Like the Hope Scholarship Credit, the Lifetime Learning Credit is phased out for upper-income taxpayers and is of no value to low-income taxpayers. Tuition and fees paid for a student for whom a Hope Scholarship Credit is available cannot be counted in calculating the Lifetime Learning Credit. (For example, a taxpayer paying $10,000 in tuition for a dependent's first year of college can elect a Hope Scholarship Credit of $1500, but cannot also claim a Lifetime Learning Credit based on the tuition over $1500. If the same taxpayer also pays $20,000 in tuition for the graduate education of another dependent, a Lifetime Learning Credit of $1000 is allowed.)

The Hope Scholarship Credit and the Lifetime Learning Credit differ in some curious ways. For example, if the student in question has been convicted of a state or Federal drug offense, the Hope Scholarship Credit is not available but the Lifetime Learning Credit is. The dollar limits on the Hope Scholarship Credit and the phaseout amounts for

d. For reasons not explained in the committee reports, the names "Hope Scholarship Credit" and "Lifetime Learning Credit" are capitalized, unlike the names of other credits. This may reflect the profound importance of these credits, in comparison with all the others. Or it may not.

both credits will be adjusted for inflation, but the dollar limits on the Lifetime Learning Credit will not be indexed (though they double in 2003). Neither credit can be claimed by a married taxpayer unless a joint return is filed.

Section 222, enacted in 2001, allows an above-the-line deduction for "qualified tuition and related expenses." For 2002 and 2003, the maximum deduction allowed by this section is $3000; the deduction is phased out for taxpayers whose modified AGI exceeds $65,000 ($130,000 for married couples filing jointly). The deduction is not allowed for tuition paid for a student with respect to whom a Hope Scholarship or Lifetime Learning Credit is claimed, which means that students (and their families) eligible for more than one of these benefits will have to perform a fair amount of calculations to decide which benefit to take. The maximum deduction and the phaseout thresholds will increase in 2004 and 2005. Section 222 is "temporary" in the sense that it is scheduled to expire after 2005, but re-enactment seems very likely.

Problem

M and *F*, a married couple, have a daughter, *D*, age 21, and a son, *S*, 19. In the current year, *M* and *F* contribute $15,000 toward the cost of *D*'s tuition at Elite University, where *D* is a senior. The balance of *D*'s college costs are covered by a scholarship (excludable from income under § 117). *M* and *F* also pay *S*'s $5000 tuition at State University, where he is a sophomore. *S* lives with *M* and *F*, and pays the $1000 balance of his tuition by means of a part-time job. Both *D* and *S* are dependents of their parents. What education deductions and credits are the various parties entitled to if *M* and *F* file a joint return on which they report AGI (apart from any effect of the above payments) of:

    (1) $90,000?

    (2) $110,000?

C. GIFTS AND BEQUESTS

COMMISSIONER v. DUBERSTEIN

Supreme Court of the United States, 1960.
363 U.S. 278, 80 S.Ct. 1190, 4 L.Ed.2d 1218.

MR. JUSTICE BRENNAN delivered the opinion of the Court.

These two cases concern the provision of the Internal Revenue Code which excludes from the gross income of an income taxpayer "the value of property acquired by gift."[1] They pose the frequently recurrent question whether a specific transfer to a taxpayer in fact amounted to a "gift" to him within the meaning of the statute. The importance to decision of the facts of the cases requires that we state them in some detail.

---

1. The operative provision in the cases at bar is § 22(b)(3) of the 1939 Internal Revenue Code. The corresponding provision of the present Code is § 102(a).

No. 376, Commissioner v. Duberstein. The taxpayer, Duberstein, was president of the Duberstein Iron & Metal Company, a corporation with headquarters in Dayton, Ohio. For some years the taxpayer's company had done business with Mohawk Metal Corporation, whose headquarters were in New York City. The president of Mohawk was one Berman. The taxpayer and Berman had generally used the telephone to transact their companies' business with each other, which consisted of buying and selling metals. The taxpayer testified, without elaboration, that he knew Berman "personally" and had known him for about seven years. From time to time in their telephone conversations, Berman would ask Duberstein whether the latter knew of potential customers for some of Mohawk's products in which Duberstein's company itself was not interested. Duberstein provided the names of potential customers for these items.

One day in 1951 Berman telephoned Duberstein and said that the information Duberstein had given him had proved so helpful that he wanted to give the latter a present. Duberstein stated that Berman owed him nothing. Berman said that he had a Cadillac as a gift for Duberstein, and that the latter should send to New York for it; Berman insisted that Duberstein accept the car, and the latter finally did so, protesting however that he had not intended to be compensated for the information. At the time Duberstein already had a Cadillac and an Oldsmobile, and felt that he did not need another car. Duberstein testified that he did not think Berman would have sent him the Cadillac if he had not furnished him with information about the customers. It appeared that Mohawk later deducted the value of the Cadillac as a business expense on its corporate income tax return.

Duberstein did not include the value of the Cadillac in gross income for 1951, deeming it a gift. The Commissioner asserted a deficiency for the car's value against him, and in proceedings to review the deficiency the Tax Court affirmed the Commissioner's determination. It said that "The record is significantly barren of evidence revealing any intention on the part of the payor to make a gift. * * * The only justifiable inference is that the automobile was intended by the payor to be remuneration for services rendered to it by Duberstein." The Court of Appeals for the Sixth Circuit reversed. 265 F.2d 28, 30.

No. 546, Stanton v. United States. The taxpayer, Stanton, had been for approximately 10 years in the employ of Trinity Church in New York City. He was comptroller of the Church corporation, and president of a corporation, Trinity Operating Company, the church set up as a fully owned subsidiary to manage its real estate holdings, which were more extensive than simply the church property. His salary by the end of his employment there in 1942 amounted to $22,500 a year. Effective November 30, 1942, he resigned from both positions to go into business for himself. The Operating Company's directors, who seem to have included the rector and vestrymen of the church, passed the following resolution upon his resignation: "Be it resolved that in appreciation of the services rendered by Mr. Stanton * * * a gratuity is hereby awarded to him of

Twenty Thousand Dollars, payable to him in equal instalments of Two Thousand Dollars at the end of each and every month commencing with the month of December, 1942; provided that, with the discontinuance of his services, the Corporation of Trinity Church is released from all rights and claims to pension and retirement benefits not already accrued up to November 30, 1942."

The Operating Company's action was later explained by one of its directors as based on the fact that, "Mr. Stanton was liked by all of the Vestry personally. He had a pleasing personality. He had come in when Trinity's affairs were in a difficult situation. He did a splendid piece of work, we felt. Besides that * * * he was liked by all of the members of the Vestry personally." And by another: "[W]e were all unanimous in wishing to make Mr. Stanton a gift. Mr. Stanton had loyally and faithfully served Trinity in a very difficult time. We thought of him in the highest regard. We understood that he was going in business for himself. We felt that he was entitled to that evidence of good will."

On the other hand, there was a suggestion of some ill-feeling between Stanton and the directors, arising out of the recent termination of the services of one Watkins, the Operating Company's treasurer, whose departure was evidently attended by some acrimony. At a special board meeting on October 28, 1942, Stanton had intervened on Watkins' side and asked reconsideration of the matter. The minutes reflect that "resentment was expressed as to the 'presumptuous' suggestion that the action of the Board, taken after long deliberation, should be changed." The Board adhered to its determination that Watkins be separated from employment, giving him an opportunity to resign rather than be discharged. At another special meeting two days later it was revealed that Watkins had not resigned; the previous resolution terminating his services was then viewed as effective; and the Board voted the payment of six months' salary to Watkins in a resolution similar to that quoted in regard to Stanton, but which did not use the term "gratuity." At the meeting, Stanton announced that in order to avoid any such embarrassment or question at any time as to his willingness to resign if the Board desired, he was tendering his resignation. It was tabled, though not without dissent. The next week, on November 5, at another special meeting, Stanton again tendered his resignation which this time was accepted.

The "gratuity" was duly paid. So was a smaller one to Stanton's (and the Operating Company's) secretary, under a similar resolution, upon her resignation at the same time. The two corporations shared the expense of the payments. There was undisputed testimony that there were in fact no enforceable rights or claims to pension and retirement benefits which had not accrued at the time of the taxpayer's resignation, and that the last proviso of the resolution was inserted simply out of an abundance of caution. The taxpayer received in cash a refund of his contributions to the retirement plans, and there is no suggestion that he was entitled to more. He was required to perform no further services for Trinity after his resignation.

The Commissioner asserted a deficiency against the taxpayer after the latter had failed to include the payments in question in gross income. After payment of the deficiency and administrative rejection of a refund claim, the taxpayer sued the United States for a refund in the District Court for the Eastern District of New York. 137 F.Supp. 803. The trial judge, sitting without a jury, made the simple finding that the payments were a "gift," and judgment was entered for the taxpayer. The Court of Appeals for the Second Circuit reversed. 268 F.2d 727.

The Government, urging that clarification of the problem typified by these two cases was necessary, and that the approaches taken by the Courts of Appeals for the Second and the Sixth Circuits were in conflict, petitioned for certiorari in No. 376, and acquiesced in the taxpayer's petition in No. 546. On this basis, and because of the importance of the question in the administration of the income tax laws, we granted certiorari in both cases. 361 U.S. 923.

The exclusion of property acquired by gift from gross income under the federal income tax laws was made in the first income tax statute passed under the authority of the Sixteenth Amendment, and has been a feature of the income tax statutes ever since. The meaning of the term "gift" as applied to particular transfers has always been a matter of contention. Specific and illuminating legislative history on the point does not appear to exist. Analogies and inferences drawn from other revenue provisions, such as the estate and gift taxes, are dubious. See Lockard v. Commissioner, 1 Cir., 166 F.2d 409. The meaning of the statutory term has been shaped largely by the decisional law. With this, we turn to the contentions made by the Government in these cases.

First. The Government suggests that we promulgate a new "test" in this area to serve as a standard to be applied by the lower courts and by the Tax Court in dealing with the numerous cases that arise.[6] We reject this invitation. We are of opinion that the governing principles are necessarily general and have already been spelled out in the opinions of this Court, and that the problem is one which, under the present statutory framework, does not lend itself to any more definitive statement that would produce a talisman for the solution of concrete cases. The cases at bar are fair examples of the settings in which the problem usually arises. They present situations in which payments have been made in a context with business overtones—an employer making a payment to a retiring employee; a businessman giving something of value to another businessman who has been of advantage to him in his business. In this context, we review the law as established by the prior cases here.

The course of decision here makes it plain that the statute does not use the term "gift" in the common-law sense, but in a more colloquial sense. This Court has indicated that a voluntarily executed transfer of his property by one to another, without any consideration or compensa-

6. The Government's proposed test is stated: "Gifts should be defined as transfers of property made for personal as distinguished from business reasons."

tion therefor, though a common-law gift, is not necessarily a "gift" within the meaning of the statute. For the Court has shown that the mere absence of a legal or moral obligation to make such a payment does not establish that it is a gift. Old Colony Trust Co. v. Commissioner, 279 U.S. 716, 730. And, importantly, if the payment proceeds primarily from "the constraining force of any moral or legal duty," or from "the incentive of anticipated benefit" of an economic nature, Bogardus v. Commissioner, 302 U.S. 34, 41, it is not a gift. And, conversely, "[w]here the payment is in return for services rendered, it is irrelevant that the donor derives no economic benefit from it." Robertson v. United States, 343 U.S. 711, 714.[7] A gift in the statutory sense, on the other hand, proceeds from a "detached and disinterested generosity," Commissioner of Internal Revenue v. LoBue, 351 U.S. 243, 246; "out of affection, respect, admiration, charity or like impulses." Robertson v. United States, supra, 343 U.S. at page 714. And in this regard, the most critical consideration, as the Court was agreed in the leading case here, is the transferor's "intention." Bogardus v. Commissioner, 302 U.S. 34, 43. "What controls is the intention with which payment, however voluntary, has been made." Id., 302 U.S. at page 45 (dissenting opinion).

The Government says that this "intention" of the transferor cannot mean what the cases on the common-law concept of gift call "donative intent." With that we are in agreement, for our decisions fully support this. Moreover, the *Bogardus* case itself makes it plain that the donor's characterization of his action is not determinative—that there must be an objective inquiry as to whether what is called a gift amounts to it in reality. 302 U.S. at page 40. It scarcely needs adding that the parties' expectations or hopes as to the tax treatment of their conduct in themselves have nothing to do with the matter.

It is suggested that the *Bogardus* criterion would be more apt if rephrased in terms of "motive" rather than "intention." We must confess to some skepticism as to whether such a verbal mutation would be of any practical consequence. We take it that the proper criterion, established by decision here, is one that inquires what the basic reason for his conduct was in fact—the dominant reason that explains his action in making the transfer. Further than that we do not think it profitable to go.

Second. The Government's proposed "test," while apparently simple and precise in its formulation, depends frankly on a set of "principles" or "presumptions" derived from the decided cases, and concededly subject to various exceptions; and it involves various corollaries, which add to its detail. Were we to promulgate this test as a matter of law, and accept with it its various presuppositions and stated consequences, we would be passing far beyond the requirements of the cases before us, and would be painting on a large canvas with indeed a broad brush. The Government derives its test from such propositions as the following:

7. The cases including "tips" in gross income are classic examples of this. See, e.g., Roberts v. Commissioner, 9 Cir., 176 F.2d 221.

That payments by an employer to an employee, even though voluntary, ought, by and large, to be taxable; that the concept of a gift is inconsistent with a payment's being a deductible business expense; that a gift involves "personal" elements; that a business corporation cannot properly make a gift of its assets. The Government admits that there are exceptions and qualifications to these propositions. We think, to the extent they are correct, that these propositions are not principles of law but rather maxims of experience that the tribunals which have tried the facts of cases in this area have enunciated in explaining their factual determinations. Some of them simply represent truisms: it doubtless is, statistically speaking, the exceptional payment by an employer to an employee that amounts to a gift. Others are overstatements of possible evidentiary inferences relevant to a factual determination on the totality of circumstances in the case: it is doubtless relevant to the over-all inference that the transferor treats a payment as a business deduction, or that the transferor is a corporate entity. But these inferences cannot be stated in absolute terms. Neither factor is a shibboleth. The taxing statute does not make nondeductibility by the transferor a condition on the "gift" exclusion; nor does it draw any distinction, in terms, between transfers by corporations and individuals, as to the availability of the "gift" exclusion to the transferee. The conclusion whether a transfer amounts to a "gift" is one that must be reached on consideration of all the factors.

* * *

Third. Decision of the issue presented in these cases must be based ultimately on the application of the fact-finding tribunal's experience with the mainsprings of human conduct to the totality of the facts of each case. The nontechnical nature of the statutory standard, the close relationship of it to the data of practical human experience, and the multiplicity of relevant factual elements, with their various combinations, creating the necessity of ascribing the proper force to each, confirm us in our conclusion that primary weight in this area must be given to the conclusions of the trier of fact. [Citations omitted.]

This conclusion may not satisfy an academic desire for tidiness, symmetry and precision in this area, any more than a system based on the determinations of various fact-finders ordinarily does. But we see it as implicit in the present statutory treatment of the exclusion for gifts, and in the variety of forums in which federal income tax cases can be tried. If there is fear of undue uncertainty or over-much litigation, Congress may make more precise its treatment of the matter by singling out certain factors and making them determinative of the matter, as it has done in one field of the "gift" exclusion's former application, that of prizes and awards. Doubtless diversity of result will tend to be lessened somewhat since federal income tax decisions, even those in tribunals of first instance turning on issues of fact, tend to be reported, and since there may be a natural tendency of professional triers of fact to follow one another's determinations, even as to factual matters. But the question here remains basically one of fact, for determination on a case-by-case basis.

One consequence of this is that appellate review of determinations in this field must be quite restricted. Where a jury has tried the matter upon correct instructions, the only inquiry is whether it cannot be said that reasonable men could reach differing conclusions on the issue. * * * Where the trial has been by a judge without a jury, the judge's findings must stand unless "clearly erroneous." Fed.Rules Civ.Proc. 52(a), * * *.

Fourth. A majority of the Court is in accord with the principles just outlined. And, applying them to the *Duberstein* case, we are in agreement, on the evidence we have set forth, that it cannot be said that the conclusion of the Tax Court was "clearly erroneous." It seems to us plain that as trier of the facts it was warranted in concluding that despite the characterization of the transfer of the Cadillac by the parties and the absence of any obligation, even of a moral nature, to make it, it was at bottom a recompense for Duberstein's past services, or an inducement for him to be of further service in the future. We cannot say with the Court of Appeals that such a conclusion was "mere suspicion" on the Tax Court's part. To us it appears based in the sort of informed experience with human affairs that fact-finding tribunals should bring to this task.

As to *Stanton,* we are in disagreement. To four of us, it is critical here that the District Court as trier of fact made only the simple and unelaborated finding that the transfer in question was a "gift." To be sure, conciseness is to be strived for, and prolixity avoided, in findings; but, to the four of us, there comes a point where findings become so sparse and conclusory as to give no revelation of what the District Court's concept of the determining facts and legal standard may be. See Matton Oil Transfer Corp. v. The Dynamic, 2 Cir., 123 F.2d 999, 1000–1001. Such conclusory, general findings do not constitute compliance with Rule 52's direction to "find the facts specially and state separately * * * conclusions of law thereon." While the standard of law in this area is not a complex one, we four think the unelaborated finding of ultimate fact here cannot stand as a fulfillment of these requirements. It affords the reviewing court not the semblance of an indication of the legal standard with which the trier of fact has approached his task. For all that appears, the District Court may have viewed the form of the resolution or the simple absence of legal consideration as conclusive. While the judgment of the Court of Appeals cannot stand, the four of us think there must be further proceedings in the District Court looking toward new and adequate findings of fact. In this, we are joined by Mr. Justice Whittaker, who agrees that the findings were inadequate, although he does not concur generally in this opinion.

Accordingly, in No. 376 [*Duberstein*], the judgment of this Court is that the judgment of the Court of Appeals is reversed, and in No. 546 [*Stanton*], that the judgment of the Court of Appeals is vacated, and the case is remanded to the District Court for further proceedings not inconsistent with this opinion. It is so ordered.

* * *

MR. JUSTICE HARLAN concurs in the result in No. 376. In No. 546, he would affirm the judgment of the Court of Appeals for the reasons stated by MR. JUSTICE FRANKFURTER.

MR. JUSTICE WHITTAKER, agreeing with *Bogardus* that whether a particular transfer is or is not a "gift" may involve "a mixed question of law and fact," 302 U.S., at page 39, concurs only in the result of this opinion.

MR. JUSTICE DOUGLAS dissents, since he is of the view that in each of these two cases there was a gift under the test which the Court fashioned nearly a quarter of a century ago in Bogardus v. Commissioner, 302 U.S. 34.

MR. JUSTICE BLACK, concurring and dissenting.

I agree with the Court that it was not clearly erroneous for the Tax Court to find as it did in No. 376 that the automobile transfer to Duberstein was not a gift, and so I agree with the Court's opinion and judgment reversing the judgment of the Court of Appeals in that case.

I dissent in No. 546, Stanton v. United States. The District Court found that the $20,000 transferred to Mr. Stanton by his former employer at the end of ten years' service was a gift and therefore exempt from taxation under I.R.C. of 1939, § 22(b)(3) (now § 102(a)). I think the finding was not clearly erroneous and that the Court of Appeals was therefore wrong in reversing the District Court's judgment. * * *

MR. JUSTICE FRANKFURTER, concurring in the judgment in No. 376 and dissenting in No. 546.

* * *

Despite acute arguments at the bar and a most thorough re-examination of the problem on a full canvass of our prior decisions and an attempted fresh analysis of the nature of the problem, the Court has rejected the invitation of the Government to fashion anything like a litmus paper test for determining what is excludable as a "gift" from gross income. Nor has the Court attempted a clarification of the particular aspects of the problem presented by these two cases, namely, payment by an employer to an employee upon the termination of the employment relation and non-obligatory payment for services rendered in the course of a business relationship. While I agree that experience has shown the futility of attempting to define, by language so circumscribing as to make it easily applicable, what constitutes a gift for every situation where the problem may arise, I do think that greater explicitness is possible in isolating and emphasizing factors which militate against a gift in particular situations.

* * *

The Court has made only one authoritative addition to the previous course of our decisions. Recognizing Bogardus v. Commissioner, 302 U.S. 34, as "the leading case here" and finding essential accord between the Court's opinion and the dissent in that case, the Court has drawn from the dissent in *Bogardus* for infusion into what will now be a controlling qualification, recognition that it is "for the triers of the facts to seek among competing aims or motives the ones that dominated conduct." 302 U.S. 34, 45 (dissenting opinion). All this being so in view of the Court, it seems to me desirable not to try to improve what has "already been spelled out" in the opinions of this Court but to leave to the lower courts the application of old phrases rather than to float new ones and thereby inevitably produce a new volume of exegesis on the new phrases.

Especially do I believe this when fact-finding tribunals are directed by the Court to rely upon their "experience with the mainsprings of human conduct" and on their "informed experience with human affairs" in appraising the totality of the facts of each case. Varying conceptions regarding the "mainsprings of human conduct" are derived from a variety of experiences or assumptions about the nature of man, and "experience with human affairs," is not only diverse but also often drastically conflicting. What the Court now does sets fact-finding bodies to sail on an illimitable ocean of individual beliefs and experiences. This can hardly fail to invite, if indeed not encourage, too individualized diversities in the administration of the income tax law. I am afraid that by these new phrasings the practicalities of tax administration, which should be as uniform as is possible in so vast a country as ours, will be embarrassed. By applying what has already been spelled out in the opinions of this Court, I agree with the Court in reversing the judgment in Commissioner v. Duberstein.

But I would affirm the decision of the Court of Appeals for the Second Circuit in Stanton v. United States. I would do so on the basis of the opinion of Judge Hand and more particularly because the very terms of the resolution by which the $20,000 was awarded to Stanton indicated that it was not a "gratuity" in the sense of sheer benevolence but in the nature of a generous lagniappe, something extra thrown in for services received though not legally nor morally required to be given. This careful resolution, doubtless drawn by a lawyer and adopted by some hardheaded businessmen, contained a proviso that Stanton should abandon all rights to "pension and retirement benefits." The fact that Stanton had no such claims does not lessen the significance of the clause as something "to make assurance doubly sure." 268 F.2d 728. The business nature of the payment is confirmed by the words of the resolution, explaining the "gratuity" as "in appreciation of the services rendered by Mr. Stanton as Manager of the Estate and Comptroller of the Corporation of Trinity Church throughout nearly ten years, and as President of Trinity Operating Company, Inc." The force of this document, in light of all the factors to which Judge Hand adverted in his opinion, was not in the least diminished by testimony at the trial. Thus the taxpayer has totally failed to sustain the burden I would place upon him to establish that the payment to him was wholly attributable to generosity unrelated to his performance of his secular business functions as an officer of the corporation of the Trinity Church of New York and the Trinity Operating Co. Since the record totally fails to establish taxpayer's claim, I see no need of specific findings by the trial judge.

Problems and Notes

1. *Problem.* Your client is the president of a company which for some years has done business with the Tuscarora Metal Co. Tuscarora's president, one Furman, has done business (mostly over the telephone) with your client. Your client has known Furman "personally" for about seven years. From time to time your client has provided the names of potential customers to Furman. One day Furman telephoned your client, saying that the information about customers had proved so helpful that he wanted to give your client a present. Your client demurred, but at Furman's insistence finally accepted a new Mercedes–Benz. Advise your client whether he should report the value of the car as income on his return, and about his chances if he does not report it and the Service challenges the exclusion.

2. *"Gifts" to employees.* Section 102(c), which was enacted in 1986, overrules *Stanton.* Some non-cash employee achievement awards can be excludable by employees under § 74(c), and transfers of items so low in value that accounting for them would be "unreasonable or administratively impracticable" are excludable as "de minimis fringe benefits" under § 132(e).

3. *State law in Federal tax cases.* Note the *Duberstein* Court's recognition of the difference between "gifts" under § 102 and gifts "in the common-law sense." Some tax provisions incorporate state-law (or non-tax Federal-law) concepts expressly or by necessary implication. Recognition of income under § 83, for example, depends upon whether the property is transferable or subject to a substantial risk of forfeiture, which in turn depends upon the recipient's rights under local law. State-law labels, however, are usually irrelevant to questions of Federal taxation. A state statute declaring that state employees' salaries are gifts from the state would have no effect upon the taxability of those salaries.

In Burnet v. Harmel, 287 U.S. 103 (1932), the Supreme Court described the relationship between the tax law and non-tax law by saying: "state law creates legal interests but the federal statute determines when and how they shall be taxed." *Harmel* held that a transfer of property which was treated as a sale by the law of Texas was not a "sale" for purposes of the tax law.

4. *Problem.* Uncle promises Nephew that if Nephew will refrain from smoking, drinking, and specified other pleasures until he turns 21, Uncle will pay Nephew $5000. Nephew refrains and Uncle pays. Can Nephew exclude the payment from his income as a "gift"? Does it matter whether local law would enforce Uncle's promise, either on

promissory estoppel grounds or as supported by consideration (see Hamer v. Sidway, 124 N.Y. 538, 27 N.E. 256 (1891))?

5. *Strike benefits.* In United States v. Kaiser, 363 U.S. 299 (1960), a companion case to *Duberstein,* the Court held that the question whether benefits paid by a labor union to workers on strike were gifts was a question of fact. Since 1960 taxpayers have won some of the strike-benefits cases and lost others. IRS Publication 17 ("Your Federal Income Tax") deals with the problem by telling taxpayers:

> Benefits paid to you by a union as strike or lockout benefits * * * are usually included in your income as compensation. You can exclude these benefits from income only when the facts clearly show that the union intended them as gifts to you. [Publication 17, 2000, p. 93]

Similar language used to appear in the instructions to Form 1040. Today's instructions do not mention the matter.

6. *References.* Klein, An Enigma in the Federal Income Tax: The Meaning of the Word "Gift," 48 Minn.L.Rev. 215 (1963); Griswold, Foreword: Of Time and Attitudes—Professor Hart and Judge Arnold, 74 Harv.L.Rev. 81 (1960).

ESTATE OF HELLSTROM v. COMMISSIONER

Tax Court of the United States, 1955.
24 T.C. 916.

* * *

FINDINGS OF FACT

The stipulated facts are so found and are incorporated herein by this reference.

During the year in issue, petitioner was a resident of Chicago, Illinois. Petitioner's husband died on February 20, 1952. * * *

Petitioner's husband, together with others, organized the Hellstrom Corporation under the laws of the State of Illinois in 1944. * * * At the time of his death, he owned 426 of the 1,685 outstanding shares of the corporation's stock. Petitioner owned 175 such shares. Decedent's salary as president of the corporation for the year 1952 would have been $33,600. From January 1 until the date of his death, he received $4,666.68 of such sum, on which the corporation withheld tax in the amount of $815.30.

On March 1, 1952, ten days after the death of Arthur W. Hellstrom [petitioner's husband], the board of directors of Hellstrom Corporation met and passed the following resolution:

> RESOLVED, that in recognition of the services rendered to this corporation for many years by Arthur W. Hellstrom, its founder and late president, and in conformity with the policy of this corporation to make reasonable provision for the surviving dependents of its

deceased officers and employees, although it is under no obligation so to do, this Board of Directors does hereby authorize and direct the Treasurer of this corporation to pay monthly to Selma M. Hellstrom, the surviving wife of said Arthur W. Hellstrom, a sum equal to his last salary per month, said monthly salary to continue until this Board of Directors shall require the reduction or discontinuance of such payments.

At a subsequent meeting of the board of directors of Hellstrom Corporation, held on October 11, 1952, the question was raised as to the period for which such payments should continue. It was agreed by the directors that such payments should continue only until the end of the year 1952, and the following resolution was thereupon adopted:

RESOLVED, that the payments heretofore on March 1, 1952 directed to be made by the Treasurer of this corporation to Mrs. Selma Hellstrom in recognition of the services of Arthur W. Hellstrom be continued to include all payments due on and prior to December 31, 1952.

Hellstrom Corporation, pursuant to such resolutions, paid to petitioner during the calendar year 1952 the sum of $28,933.32. This sum represented the salary which petitioner's husband would have received for the remainder of 1952 had he lived. On its Federal income tax returns filed for its fiscal years ending July 31, 1952, and July 31, 1953, Hellstrom Corporation claimed as a deduction the amounts paid to petitioner in each respective fiscal year.

On the joint return which petitioner filed for the calendar year 1952, she reported the receipt of $28,933.32 "as gratuitous recognition of deceased Arthur W. Hellstrom's services. Said sum is not taxable."

Respondent determined that such sum constituted taxable income to petitioner under section [61].

The payments made to petitioner by the Hellstrom Corporation were a gift to her. * * *

Opinion

Rice, Judge. Petitioner claims that the sums paid to her by the Hellstrom Corporation in 1952 were a gift. As indicated by our findings, we agree that such sums were a gift and, hence, excludible from her gross income in that year.

The substance of the respondent's argument and the basis of his determination is his Ruling I.T. 4027, 1950–2 C.B. 9, 11, which states "that payments made by an employer to the widow of a deceased officer or employee, in consideration of services rendered by the officer or employee, are includible in the gross income of the widow for Federal tax purposes." He argues that the intent of the board of directors of the corporation was that the payments in question were "in recognition for the services rendered to this corporation for many years" by petitioner's husband, and that the words, "in recognition" are equivalent to "in consideration" within the meaning of his regulation. We think this argument is nothing more than an argument in semantics. Obviously, where a voluntary payment is made by a corporation to the widow of a deceased employee, the basic reason for the payment is because of the deceased employee's past association with the corporation. We think it makes little difference how the corporation formally expresses its motives for the payment. Where such payment is a gift, as the whole record here establishes that the payments in question were, it remains a gift regardless of the fact that the corporation may state its reasons for making the payment were "because of" or "in recognition of" or "in consideration of" the services of the deceased employee. This seems to us the only sensible construction of the Supreme Court's language in Bogardus v. Commissioner, 302 U.S. 34, 44 (1937), wherein it said that a gift is nonetheless a gift because inspired by gratitude for past faithful services.

* * *

In view of the other evidence in the record, we attach no particular significance to the fact that the corporation claimed deductions on its returns for the amount paid to petitioner. Nor do we attach any significance to the fact that the amount paid to her was the amount of salary her husband would have drawn had he lived. Alice M. MacFarlane, 19 T.C. 9 (1952). Gifts to widows of deceased employees are frequently determined by the amount of salary which the employee drew or would have drawn.

We think the controlling facts here which establish the payment in question as a gift are that the payment was made to petitioner and not to her husband's estate; that there was no obligation on the part of the corporation to pay any additional compensation to petitioner's husband; it derived no benefit from the payment; petitioner performed no services for the corporation and, as heretofore noted, those of her husband had been fully compensated for. We think the principal motive of the corporation in making the payment was its desire to do an act of kindness for petitioner. The payment, therefore, was a gift to her and not taxable income.

> *Decision will be entered that there is no deficiency and that there is an overpayment of tax in the amount of $113.54 for the year 1952.*

Problems, Notes and Questions

1. *The "gifts to widows" cases.* The principal case presents a fairly typical example of a situation that breeds litigation. Apparently, not all factfinders have had the same "experience with the mainsprings of human conduct," for the survivors of corporate executives have tended to lose cases like *Hellstrom's Estate* in the Tax Court and to win them in the district courts. Some courts of appeals have read *Duberstein* as requiring them to accept the trial courts' findings except in the clearest

cases or in cases where the trial courts have given improper reasons for their findings. However, in Carter's Estate v. Commissioner, 453 F.2d 61 (2d Cir.1971), the Second Circuit reversed a Tax Court "no gift" decision because of its belief that the taxpayer's chances of a victory in a district court would have been "overwhelming":

> If Mrs. Carter had paid the tax here at issue and sued for a refund, the odds that a district court would have found the payments constituted a gift would thus have been overwhelming. If it had done so, Fanning v. Conley, * * * 357 F.2d 37 [2d Cir.1966], is proof positive that we would have affirmed. Not content with reliance on the "unless clearly erroneous" rule, F.R.Civ.P. 52(a), we went to pains to point out for the guidance of the district courts that the very factors here principally relied upon by the Commissioner to negate the inference of gift—the references to salary continuation, the deduction of the payment as a business expense, although not as compensation, and the failure to investigate the widow's financial circumstances—"should not be the controlling or determinative factor," 357 F.2d at 41. Indeed, on the last item Mrs. Carter stands rather better than did Mrs. Fanning, in light of Salomon Bros.' knowledge of the heavy costs entailed by her husband's many hospitalizations. We cannot believe the Supreme Court intended that, at least in an area where, in contrast to the entire field of controversy with respect to gifts versus compensation, similar fact patterns tend to recur so often, the result should depend on whether a widow could afford to pay the tax and sue for a refund rather than avail herself of the salutary remedy Congress intended to afford in establishing the Tax Court and permitting determination before payment. The "mainsprings of human conduct," 363 U.S. at 289, do not differ so radically according to who tries the facts.

Note that § 274(b) now denies business-expense deductions for most substantial "gifts." As the question whether something is a gift is typically factual, however, this does not supply automatic answers in most cases.

2. *Problems.*

(1) *X* Corp. plans to pay $50,000 to the surviving spouse of a key executive who has recently died. How might the resolution authorizing the payment be drafted so as to promote:

　　(a) the payment's exclusion in full from the surviving spouse's income; or

　　(b) the payment's deductibility in full by *X* Corp.; or

　　(c) a sporting chance for both the exclusion and the deduction?

(2) *Y* Corp., acting solely out of "detached and disinterested generosity," gives $25 in cash to each of two of its customers, Herb and Mary, who are married to each other. Does § 274(b) limit *Y* Corp.'s deduction? Is it clear that *any* of the amount can be deducted as a business expense?

3. *The basis of property received as a gift.* How much income does the donee have upon selling corporate stock received as a gift in each of the following cases? See § 1015(a), and assume in each case that the donor paid no gift tax on account of the transfer.

(1) The donor bought the stock for $1000. When the stock was worth $1200 the donor gave it to the donee. Later, the donee sold the stock for $1250.

(2) The donor bought the stock for $1000. When the stock was worth $800, the donor gave the stock to the donee. Later on, the donee sold the stock for $900.

Section 1015 is examined more fully in Chapter 8.

4. *Transfers between spouses.* Most transfers of property between spouses are treated in much the same way as if they were gifts, whether or not they are gifts under *Duberstein;* see § 1041. Thus, if *H* sells stock with a basis of $20,000 to his wife, *W,* for $25,000, *H* recognizes no gain and *W* takes the stock with a basis of $20,000. In the case of transfers of property with a value less than basis, § 1041(b)(2) produces a different loss-basis figure than § 1015(a). In Problem (2) (note 3, above), what is the donee's gain or loss if the donor and donee are spouses?

Section 1041 is examined more fully in Chapter 8.

GIFTS AND "ASSIGNMENTS OF INCOME"

Donors get no deductions for gifts to friends or family members, and donees have no income. Overall, therefore, cash gifts have no income-tax effect: If *A* earns a salary or collects interest on a bond and then gives some of the salary or interest to *B, A* has income and *B* does not. Should this tax result change if the donor gives the money away before earning or receiving it? Suppose *A* agrees with his employer that half of *A*'s salary be paid to *A*'s children instead of to *A.* Or suppose *A* instructs his bank to pay this year's interest on *A*'s bank account to his brother. These cases differ very little from cases in which *A* collects his own salary and interest and then gives some of the money away, and so making a gift before recognizing the income in question does not shift taxation to the donee. See Lucas v. Earl (p. 435 below) (earned income); Helvering v. Horst (p. 457, below) (interest on coupon bonds); and § 83(a) (property transferred in connection with the performance of services).

Potential income in the form of unrealized appreciation in the value of property can be transferred by gift. If *A* holds stock with a basis of $10,000 and a value of $15,000, *A* can give to *B* $15,000 either by selling the stock and giving *B* the proceeds or by giving *B* the stock, which *B* then sells. If *A* sells the stock, the $5000 gain is *A*'s, but if *A* gives the stock away, the gain is taxable to *B;* § 1015(a).

Problem

In gratitude for *T*'s preparing her Uncle *M*'s income-tax return without charge, Uncle *M*, who owns a local used-car lot, gave *T*'s daughter *D* an old, somewhat rusty car, which Uncle *M* had had on his lot with a sign in the window saying "For Sale—$700." If someone is to be taxed, should it be *T*, *D*, or both?

BEQUESTS

Bequests, like gifts, are excluded from income by § 102. As with gifts, the exclusion does not extend to compensation that takes the form of a bequest, even if local law regards the compensation as a "bequest." The bequest exclusion may be somewhat broader than the exclusion for gifts, however. For one thing, the exclusion for bequests is plainly not confined to gratuities: a spouse's statutory share is not income even if the decedent tried to disinherit the surviving spouse. The Service once ruled that bequests to employees for "long and loyal service" were not income to the employees just because of that language; Rev.Rul. 57–398, 1957–2 C.B. 93. Section 102(c) now provides, however, that the exclusion of § 102(a) does not apply to "any amount transferred by or for an employer to * * * an employee."

The basis of inherited property or property acquired by way of several substitutes for testamentary transactions is the property's value at the date of the decedent's death (or at the alternate valuation date of § 2032); § 1014. Section 1014 is often described as the "stepped up basis at death" rule, although in the case of property worth less than the decedent's basis § 1014 steps the basis down. Section 1014 will be examined in some detail in Chapter 8.

The 2001 tax act provides that some property inherited from decedents who die in 2010 gets a limited step-up in basis; the details of this rule will be discussed in Chapter 8. Because the 2001 Act sunsets in 2011, this carryover-basis rule will be effective for only one year absent further legislation. Further legislation is certain; what form that legislation will take is anyone's guess.

Problems, Notes and Question

1. *Problems.* Would § 102(c) require the employee to recognize income in these cases? In addition to the statute itself, see Prop.Treas. Reg. § 1.102–1(f).

(1) *B*, an executive of *X* Corporation, left $10,000 by will to *S*, who had been *B*'s secretary for twenty years.

(2) Same as (1), except that *B* was a sole proprietor rather than an employee of a corporation.

(3) *C*, a lawyer in practice by herself, employed her teenage son, *T*, as a messenger. *T* worked about five hours a week after school. *C* died, leaving her entire estate of some $500,000 to *T*.

2. *Gifts and bequests of income from property.* Consider a donee who receives stock with a value of $1000 in 2002 and who, in later years, gets $700 in dividends on the stock. In a sense, the donee has received the dividends as well as the stock as a gift; yet § 102(b)(1) renders the exclusion inapplicable to the income from property acquired by gift or bequest. Compare § 1015, which makes a donee taxable on gain on the sale of gift property (including gain representing appreciation while the donor held the property) by limiting the donee's basis to that of the donor.

What of a gift or bequest in the form of a right to the income from property, as when *A* transfers property in trust to pay income to *B* for life? Irwin v. Gavit, 268 U.S. 161 (1925), held the bequest exclusion inapplicable to an income beneficiary, reading the exclusion as applying to bequests of "corpus" as distinguished from "income." The Irwin v. Gavit rule is now § 102(b)(2).

3. *References.* Compare Wolder, Bequest to an Attorney, 45 Taxes 411 (1967), with Wolder v. Commissioner, 493 F.2d 608 (2d Cir.1974), cert. denied 419 U.S. 828 (1974).

POLICY GROUNDS FOR EXCLUDING GIFTS AND BEQUESTS

Henry Simons found it "difficult to see why gifts should not be regarded as income to the recipient" (Personal Income Taxation 58 (1938)). Later writers have shared Simons' difficulty. For example, the Carter Commission Report, an ambitious Canadian examination of income-taxation principles, recommended that gifts and bequests be included in the recipients' incomes. The lack of a consensus about whether gifts and bequests should be excluded from income may be responsible in part for the somewhat unsatisfactory quality of judicial opinions interpreting § 102. Without a sense of the reasons for excluding gifts, a judge cannot interpret that section according to its purpose and so must fall back on "common sense" notions of what a gift is.

Before exploring possible reasons for the exclusion of § 102, let us be clear about what is at stake. If Smith earns $100 and gives the money to Jones, current law taxes Smith and not Jones. One can imagine a tax system that taxed Jones rather than Smith; this could be achieved by giving Smith a deduction for the gift to Jones and including the amount of the gift in Jones's income. The difference between that system and ours would be fairly minor—the $100 is taxed at Smith's rates under current law and would be taxed at Jones's rates under the alternative. Simons and the Carter Commission had in mind a much-more-fundamental departure from current practice: they would have taxed both Smith and Jones on $100. That is, they would have given no deduction to the taxpayer making a gift or bequest, but would nevertheless have included the amount in the recipient's income.

It may be tempting to brush aside the Simons proposal as imposing a "double tax," but the matter cannot be dismissed that easily. If Smith earns $100 and spends that $100 on haircuts, both Smith and the barber have $100 of income. There is, therefore, no principle that *money* can be included in the income of only one person, no matter how often it is spent. It may be useful here to recall Simons' own definition of income as the sum of savings and consumption (see p. 50). Smith's getting haircuts is consumption, and if the barber saves the $100 or spends it on consumption there has been a total of $200 in savings and/or consumption so far. The gift question can therefore be rephrased this way: if Smith earns $100 and gives it to Jones, who spends it, have both Smith and Jones spent $100 on consumption? Simons thought that the answer was "yes"; Smith consumed because giving money away (or leaving it at death) was one way of enjoying it; Jones consumed in the usual sense.

The question, then, comes down to whether there is $100 or $200 of consumption when Smith gives $100 to Jones, who spends it. And a case for excluding gifts and bequests from income can be developed by noting that the "enjoyment" one has from seeing one's friends and relatives consume cannot reasonably be treated as "consumption" for tax purposes in all cases. If Smith's pleasure at watching Jones spend $100 is "consumption" when Jones spends $100 received from Smith, it might equally count as "consumption" (to Smith) when Jones earns the money and spends it. Yet no one has ever argued that parents should be treated as having income when their children earn and spend money, just because the parents derive pleasure from their children's well-being. "Consumption," in the Haig–Simons sense, must consist of spending, not of "satisfaction."

As an illustration of the argument outlined above, suppose that Smith owns income-producing property worth $1 million. The property produces income (and cash) of $100,000 a year. If Smith lives for 50 years, receiving and spending $100,000 a year, there is $100,000 a year of consumption, and therefore of income, in Smith's corner of the world for each year of the 50–year period. Suppose now that Smith dies during year two, leaving the property to Jones, who receives and spends $100,000 a year in each of the next 48 years. To say that the case in which Smith dies is one in which there is $1 million more consumption and income (in year two) than there would have been if Smith had lived is unconvincing.

A very different argument for the gift and bequest exclusion rests on the observation that money received in a donative transaction is not earned, and so would not be counted in determining "national income" for the period in question. Those who drafted the early income-tax statutes may have excluded gifts and bequests simply for this reason. Simons' response to this argument seems persuasive. He pointed out the absurdity of assuming that "a good method for measuring the relative incomes of individuals must yield quantities which, summated, will in turn afford a satisfactory measure of * * * [what] we call social income."[e]

e. Personal Income Taxation, p. 58.

Notes

1. *Gifts and bequests of appreciated property.* Suppose A owns an asset with a basis of $1000 and a value of $1500. The $500 difference between the asset's value and its basis is potential income, which will be taxed to A if the asset is sold. If A gives the asset to B, who sells it, the $500 will be taxed to B, rather than to A, and if A dies, leaving the asset to C, the income will be taxed to nobody. Nothing in the discussion above justifies either of these results. For further discussion of the disappearance of income when the owner of appreciated property dies, see Chapter 8.

2. *The estate and gift taxes.* The Code imposes an estate tax (§ 2001) on the value of property left by a decedent and a gift tax (§ 2501) upon large lifetime gifts. Under the 2001 tax act, the estate tax (but not the gift tax) is scheduled for extinction in 2010 and for resurrection in 2011; we shall see.

The estate and gift taxes are not at all equivalent to including the value of bequests and gifts in the recipients' incomes. For one thing, only a tiny fraction of the population makes transfers that are taxable under the estate and gift taxes. There is a lifetime exemption[f] from these taxes for the first $1 million transferred ($2 million for a married couple) (2002 figures, increasing to $3.5 and $7 million by 2009); transfers to one's spouse and to charities are not taxed; and most donors who make lifetime gifts can exclude the first $10,000 a year given to each donee. More basically, the estate and gift taxes are taxes on decedents' and donors' transfers of accumulated wealth, not on the receipt of wealth by heirs and donees. If A dies, leaving $1000 each to 1001 donees, an estate tax will be imposed because A died wealthy (the standard justification for the tax is that it helps to reduce large concentrations of wealth). If B receives a total of $1,001,000 in bequests in small amounts from relatively low-wealth decedents, B will owe no tax. Unlike the income tax, which focuses on increases in wealth, the estate and gift taxes aim at those who have large fortunes. These taxes apply whether or not those amassing the fortunes paid income tax as they accumulated. Thus, someone who saves diligently out of a fully taxed salary and leaves an estate of $5,000,000 will pay the same estate tax as someone who bought a small amount of IBM stock in 1945 and watched that stock grow in value to $5,000,000, all without income tax (because unrealized appreciation is not taxed).

The income tax on the one hand and the estate and gift taxes on the other serve such different functions and operate in such different ways that they are usually viewed by tax theorists as having little to do with each other. The existence of estate and gift taxes provides no reason for

f. Technically, there is a tax credit equal to the amount of tax that would be payable under the Code's rate schedules on the first $1 million of transfers. This credit produces the equivalent of a $1 million exemption.

excluding bequests and gifts from income; the justification for that exclusion must be found in the policies underlying the income tax.

D. LIFE–INSURANCE PROCEEDS

Some kinds of life insurance receive very favorable tax treatment. This situation exists mainly because the tax rules devised for term insurance—the most basic kind of life insurance—have been applied to forms of insurance that involve a large "investment" component. For the most part, the tax law fails to deal adequately with the investment aspects of the transaction.

Life insurance takes many forms, but in substance all life insurance is either (1) term insurance, or (2) a combination of term insurance and some form of investment vehicle. An examination of the tax treatment of life insurance should therefore begin with a look at term insurance.

Term Insurance

Term life insurance in its simplest form provides death benefits if the insured dies during the coverage period, but no other benefits. It gives persons to whom others look for financial support a way to protect their dependents against the risk that the breadwinner will die prematurely. A simplified but essentially accurate way to look at term insurance is to imagine a group of thousands of people who face much the same (small) risk of early death—a group of healthy 35–year-olds, for example. These people can protect their dependents by contributing fairly small annual sums to a "pool," which will be used to pay large sums to the survivors of those few contributors who die during the period. For example, if there is one chance in 300 that a member of the group will die during the year, each member could in principle pay in $1000 for $300,000 of insurance protection. (In practice, the charge would have to be somewhat larger, as organizing the insureds, making sure that only healthy persons sign up, and handling the collection of contributions and the payment of benefits will cost something. Insurance companies exist to provide these services.)

Term insurance is usually written for a short period, often one year. Renewable term insurance allows the insured to purchase insurance for another term (at a higher rate, because the insured will be older) without taking a new physical exam. Some term-insurance policies may be converted by the insured to a more-elaborate kind of policy.

Term insurance is not an "investment" in the usual sense because the expected return for an insured is necessarily less than the amount of premiums paid. (A positive expected return would exist only if the pool created by the payment of premiums were expected to pay out more than it took in. As the pool's only important source of funds is the premiums, this would be impossible.)[g] People buy term insurance not because the

---

g. Term insurance does offer a very small investment return, because insurance companies invest the premiums they receive. The returns on those investments

odds of making a profit are in their favor, but because the financial costs to their survivors of early, uninsured death would be catastrophic. Many breadwinners prefer paying a relatively small sum annually to exposing their dependents to a small risk of great financial loss, even though the "expected return" from their outlays is negative.

Section 101(a) excludes from income life-insurance proceeds "paid by reason of the death of the insured." (In an apparent attempt to discourage speculative trading in insurance policies, § 101(a)(2) denies the exclusion in the case of many transfers of life-insurance contracts for "valuable consideration.") As applied to term insurance, this exclusion makes sense in a world in which bequests are excluded from income. Insureds as a group get back only their premiums less the insurance company's costs and profits. Taxing the insurance benefits of those few insureds who die during the coverage period would seriously overtax insureds, considered as a class. Those who buy term insurance do not experience an "accession to wealth" on an overall basis; it follows that they should not be taxed.

So far, so good. But many life-insurance policies combine term insurance with other things that are not really life insurance at all. When § 101(a) excludes the proceeds of these policies from income, the result is that investment returns, which would have been taxed if they had been earned on investments distinct from life insurance, fall within the insurance exclusion.

Life Insurance with an Investment Component

Picture a young, high-income lawyer with two children and few assets. She would ordinarily want to use some of her earnings to provide insurance protection for her dependents and to invest some of her earnings to provide for retirement, the children's education, and other future needs. One way to do this would be to buy term insurance with some of her earnings and to invest some of the balance, perhaps in mutual funds. The insurance companies, seeing an opportunity to expand their activities, have devised package deals for this kind of customer. In exchange for payments from the insured, the company agrees to provide death benefits if the insured dies young and to invest some of the payments to provide for future needs if the insured does not die young. In other words, the insurance company offers products which combine term insurance with investments.

Investments take many forms, from fixed-income products like bonds and certificates of deposit to riskier but generally more lucrative investments. For this reason, insurance policies that combine traditional life-insurance protection with investments come in a bewildering variety, which makes policies very hard to compare. Not only do different policies

cover a small part of the cost of the insurance. In a sense, therefore, insureds get an investment return because they would have to pay more for term insurance if the companies could not invest their premiums. But the amounts of money involved are so small that the text's treatment of term insurance as offering no investment return is accurate enough.

offer different kinds of investments, policies often vary the mix between term insurance and investment as time passes. For example, many buyers will prefer a large amount of insurance protection when their children are young and their salaries are their only source of support; as they age and become wealthier, they will often want less insurance and more investment. For that kind of buyer, a policy that offers a relatively large "insurance" component in its early years, with a shift away from insurance and toward investment in later years, will be best.

Today, most life insurance sold on an individual basis (as opposed to "group" insurance like that provided as a fringe benefit by many employers) has a large investment component. "Universal" life insurance is the current hot product, but the details of particular insurance products are unimportant. The key feature of all insurance other than term insurance is its blend of insurance and investment features.

Some combinations of products have an obvious common sense to them—cars usually come with tires, for instance. But why would someone who wants both to buy life insurance and to invest in the stock market want a package deal? Someone who needs a refrigerator and a pair of shoes would not search for a seller who offers that combination of goods. Why would someone who wants insurance protection and a mutual fund not simply buy the insurance from Allstate and the mutual fund shares from Vanguard? Some do, of course—the simplest approach to the insurance/investment matter is to "buy term and invest the difference." But many investors, often encouraged by commission salespersons, buy a blend of the two from an insurance company. The reason, in a word, is "tax." The exclusion from income of insurance proceeds payable at death and the favorable treatment of insurance benefits even if paid during the insured's life spill over from the insurance portion of a package deal to the investment return.

The Taxation of Life Insurance

When a policy combining term insurance and an investment has been in force for many years, one can look at the payment that will go to the survivor as consisting of two parts: (1) an insurance payment purchased with the portion of the premiums attributable to the term-insurance portion of the package and (2) the insured's investments over the years plus the return that those investments have earned. If the investments had been made separately, much of the return would have been taxed as dividends, interest, or gains from the sale of property.

In principle, the tax law might treat the term-insurance and investment components of an insurance policy separately, taxing the insured on investment returns as they accrue (or perhaps when the insured dies), but leaving mortality gains untaxed. In fact, it does not. Suppose, for example, that an insured dies at a time when the accumulated investment value of a policy is $200,000, and that the insured's survivors get $300,000 (consisting of $100,000 attributable to the insured's having died early and the $200,000 of accumulated investment). Section 101(a) excludes the entire $300,000 from the beneficiary's income. Furthermore, the insured paid no tax on whatever interest or other investment return is included in the $200,000 "accumulated investment" figure. This exclusion may represent a considerable tax saving.

A point worth emphasizing is that the tax advantages of making an investment through the purchase of life insurance would vanish if life-insurance companies were taxed as heavily on their investment returns as the insureds would have been taxed had they made their own investments. On an overall basis, whether the insurance company or the insured pays tax on investment income is a trivial detail. In theory, life-insurance companies, like corporations generally, are taxpayers. In practice, investments held by life-insurance companies are taxed at low effective rates.

Few investors are willing to tie up their investments for life; they may need cash for emergencies, to provide for retirement, or just to spend. Life-insurance policies that combine term insurance and investment provide ways in which the insured can withdraw the accumulated investment. One way is by cashing in the policy; policies like this develop "cash-surrender values" as time goes by (either according to a fixed schedule or according to the performance of the investments that make up the portfolio). Sometimes insureds will withdraw some, but not all, of the cash-surrender value. Some policies provide for the insured to begin receiving annuity payments upon reaching a designated age. And insureds may borrow against their policies (usually from the company that issued the policy). The tax treatment of payments made during the life of the insured is governed by § 72.

A common use of the return on the investment component of life insurance is to pay some of the premiums on the policy. This practice results in a complete tax exemption for the investment return because § 72(e)(4)(B) provides that "dividends" on insurance policies are tax free if retained by the insurer as premiums. (Contrast an insured who buys term insurance and pays the premiums with interest earned on a bank account.)

Investment returns withdrawn during the insured's life do not escape taxation completely. But the tax treatment of these returns is quite favorable, because the tax is not paid until the return is withdrawn, and because a recover-basis-first system is often used to determine when withdrawals are taxed. As a rule, lump-sum payments to an insured ("amount[s] not received as an annuity") are tax free until the total amount of the payments to the insured exceeds the total amount of premiums paid by the insured; § 72(e)(5). (By contrast, early withdrawals from annuity contracts are taxed under § 72(e)(2), which does not apply to most life-insurance contracts because of § 72(e)(5)(C).) The proceeds of loans against insurance policies are tax free because loan proceeds are not income. Annuity payments are taxed under the usual rules for annuities—the "investment in the contract" is excluded from gross income over the annuitant's life expectancy (see p. 113). As we have seen, paying a tax late can be of great financial benefit. An investor with a choice between paying tax annually on interest earned by an investment and deferring the tax until the investment is cashed in will come out ahead by choosing the latter course.

Notes and Questions

1. *Extreme cases.* If there were no limits on the extent to which life insurance and investments can be combined, few investments would be taxable. Banks, mutual funds, and stockbrokers could simply offer a few dollars of life insurance as part of whatever investments they sold. The Code attempts to control the use of the insurance exemption to shelter investment income in two ways.

First, § 7702 defines "life insurance." The definition is much too complex for detailed examination in a basic course, but its purpose is simple. A "life-insurance" policy must offer a decent amount of real insurance coverage in proportion to its investment elements if it is to be treated as providing life insurance for tax purposes. Section 7702 is not very restrictive; insurance policies containing substantial investment components can pass its tests. If a policy offers some life-insurance protection but falls short of meeting the requirements of § 7702, the policyholder may be taxed annually on part of the increase in cash-surrender value and § 101(a) will cover only the "insurance" portion of death benefits; § 7702(g).

Second, § 72(e)(10) treats some distributions (including loans) from "modified endowment contracts" as income to the recipient. Very non-technically, a "modified endowment contract" is an insurance policy which pays out too much money in the first seven years of its existence.

2. *Payment of death benefits to the terminally or chronically ill.* Some life insurance policies will pay death benefits to insureds who are still alive, but who are terminally ill. Even if a particular insured's policy will not do that, an insured with a terminal illness may be able to sell the policy. These techniques enable some persons with serious illnesses to use their term life insurance to pay medical and living expenses. The ordinary tax rules would discourage this practice, because they exempt death benefits but tax lifetime benefits and gains from selling policies. Therefore, Congress enacted § 101(g) in 1996. Ignoring technicalities, this provision allows terminally ill insureds to receive "accelerated death benefits" and the proceeds of selling life-insurance policies to a "viatical settlement provider" tax free. Some taxpayers who are chronically, but not terminally, ill may also exclude lifetime payments under life-insurance policies under this section.

3. *After-death earnings.* Section 101(a)'s exclusion for payments "by reason of the death of the insured" does not extend to interest paid when an insurance company holds the policy proceeds after the insured dies and pays interest to the beneficiaries; § 101(c). Section 101(d) taxes the "interest" component of deferred post-death payments such as annuities.

4. *Why doesn't everyone buy life insurance?* In view of the substantial tax advantages of savings combined with life insurance over conventional savings, why do any insurable investors put their money in banks or in the stock market?

5. *Reference.* Pike, Reflections on the Meaning of Life: An Analysis of Section 7702 and the Taxation of Cash Value Life Insurance, 43 Tax L.Rev. 491 (1988).

E. SCHOLARSHIPS AND PRIZES

Under the 1939 Code the taxability of scholarships and prizes was determined under the predecessor of § 102, with haphazard results. It may seem strange to you that grants to post-doctoral research fellows, quiz-show prizes, or athletic scholarships could have been held "gifts"; they are certainly not payments made because of the payors' "detached and disinterested generosity." But when the early scholarship and prize cases were decided, the scope of the "gift" exclusion was even less clear than it is today. The courts tended to focus upon whether a payment was made pursuant to an enforceable contract, particularly in "prize" cases;[h] and upon whether an employment or similar relationship between the taxpayer and "donor" was present. Today, the taxability of prizes and scholarships is determined under §§ 74 and 117.

1. SCHOLARSHIPS

From 1954 to 1986, degree candidates could exclude scholarship and fellowship grants from income. Non-degree candidates could exclude awards for incidental research and other expenses plus up to $300 a month, with a maximum lifetime exclusion of $10,800. The exclusion generated litigation over questions like whether payments to teaching assistants were taxable compensation or excludable scholarships and whether hospital interns and residents could exclude up to $300 a month of their salaries on the ground that their work gave them educational benefits.[i]

The Tax Reform Act of 1986 eliminated the scholarship exclusion for non-degree candidates and limited the exclusion for degree candidates to amounts paid for tuition and required fees, books, supplies, and equipment. Under § 117(c), even a tuition reduction is taxable if it "represents payment for teaching, research, or other services * * * required as a condition for receiving" the scholarship.

---

h. See Robertson v. United States, 343 U.S. 711 (1952), relying on Corbin on Contracts and the Restatement to hold that a prize for composing one of the "three best symphonies" was awarded "for consideration" and so was not a gift.

i. The interns and residents lost almost all of the reported cases. See Parr v. United States, 469 F.2d 1156, 1159 (5th Cir.1972) ("we sympathize with the District Court's lamentation that these facts, or facts nearly identical, have been litigated so often that one may wonder whether this is wise or what good it can do"). Nevertheless, interns and residents were remarkably litigious.

Section 117(d) was amended in 1988 to exclude from income "qualified tuition reductions" in the case of graduate teaching or research assistants; see § 117(d)(5). The statute and the committee reports make clear that the exclusion is subject to the "compensation" provision of § 117(c), so that a tuition reduction in exchange for services will still be taxable. In view of this insistence that compensation—even in the form of a tuition reduction—remains taxable, it is hard to see how the change has much effect. Such amounts may, however, be excluded by § 127, which was made permanent and extended to graduate and professional education in 2001.

Problem, Notes and Questions

1. *Athletic scholarships.* According to Rev.Rul. 77–263, 1977–2 C.B. 47, athletic scholarships are governed by § 117, at least if the recipient is "expected," rather than required, to play a particular sport and if inability to play does not cancel the scholarship. Although athletic scholarships awarded by schools which compete for national championships resemble salaries, and although it is doubtful that scholarship recipients at those schools are only "expected" to play if they want to keep their scholarships, the exclusion seems safe. Meddling with college sports is politically touchy, and the Service has bigger fish to fry.

2. *Problem.* S receives a $25,000 scholarship to Countryview University. S's total expenses for the year come to $28,000, consisting of:

Tuition	$18,000
Lab Fees	500
Required Textbooks	500
Books Recommended	250
Gym Uniform (Required)	50
Meals, Lodging, Travel	6000
Incidental Expenses	2700

How much of S's $25,000 scholarship is includable in her gross income?

3. *Policy issues.* Is the exclusion for scholarships a tax-expenditure provision? Does a scholarship award give the recipient any less "ability to pay" taxes than a salary? To the extent that a scholarship consists of cash, to be used to pay living expenses, a scholarship seems hardly distinguishable from any other source of funds, but tuition reductions may be a different matter. Students in low-tuition state schools and in private schools with "below-cost" tuition have no taxable income. Neither, for that matter, do people who have no interest in going to college. Should a student who receives an annual $5000 tuition scholarship to a private school be taxed like a student who attends a tuition-free public school or like a student with a $5000 annual income which is used to pay tuition?

4. *References.* Dodge, Scholarships Under the Income Tax, 46 The Tax Lawyer 697 (1993); Crane, Scholarships and the Federal Income Tax Base, 28 Harv.J. on Leg. 63 (1991).

2. PRIZES

TURNER v. COMMISSIONER

Tax Court of the United States, 1954.
13 T.C.M. 462.

* * *

Reginald, whose name had been selected by chance from a telephone book, was called on the telephone on April 18, 1948 and was asked to name a song that was being played on a radio program. He gave the correct name of the song and then was given the opportunity to identify a second song and thus to compete for a grand prize. He correctly identified the second song and in consideration of his efforts was awarded a number of prizes, including two round trip first-class steamship tickets for a cruise between New York City and Buenos Aires. The prize was to be one ticket if the winner was unmarried, but, if he was married, his wife was to receive a ticket also. The tickets were not transferable and were good only within one year on a sailing date approved by the agent of the steamship company.

The petitioners reported income on their return of $520, representing income from the award of the two tickets. The Commissioner, in determining the deficiency, increased the income from this source to $2,220, the retail price of such tickets.

Marie was born in Brazil. The petitioners had two sons. Reginald negotiated with the agent of the steamship company, as a result of which he surrendered his rights to the two first-class tickets, and upon payment of $12.50 received four round trip tourist steamship tickets between New York City and Rio de Janeiro. The petitioners and their two sons used those tickets in making a trip from New York City to Rio de Janeiro and return during 1948.

The award of the tickets to Reginald represented income to him in the amount of $1,400.

OPINION

MURDOCK, JUDGE: Persons desiring to buy round trip first-class tickets between New York and Buenos Aires in April 1948, similar to those to which the petitioners were entitled, would have had to pay $2,220 for them. The petitioners, however, were not such persons. The winning of the tickets did not provide them with something which they needed in the ordinary course of their lives and for which they would have made an expenditure in any event, but merely gave them an opportunity to enjoy a luxury otherwise beyond their means. Their value to the petitioners was not equal to their retail cost. They were not transferable and not salable and there were other restrictions on their use. But even had the petitioner been permitted to sell them, his experience with other more salable articles indicates that he would have had to accept substantially less than the cost of similar tickets purchased from the steamship company and would have had selling expenses. Probably the petitioners could have refused the tickets and avoided the tax problem. Nevertheless, in order to obtain such benefits as they could from winning the tickets, they actually took a cruise accompanied by their two sons, thus obtaining free board, some savings in living expenses, and the pleasure of the trip. It seems proper that a substantial amount should be included in their income for 1948 on account of the winning of the tickets. The problem of arriving at a proper fair figure for this purpose is difficult. The evidence to assist is meager, perhaps unavoidably so. The Court, under such circumstances, must arrive at some figure and has done so. Cf. Cohan v. Commissioner, 39 Fed.(2d) 540.

Decision will be entered under Rule 50.

Problems, Notes and Questions

1. *Valuation questions.* Would the *Turner* court's treatment of the valuation issue be appropriate in a case involving steamship tickets given an employee by an employer as a "prize" for selling impressive quantities of the employer's product? See Treas.Reg. § 1.61–21(b) for the valuation of non-cash fringe benefits.

2. *Problem.* A, a professional athlete, was awarded the "Hickock Belt." This is a large bejewelled belt worth some $10,000. A is pleased with winning the award, though his pleasure comes more from the recognition of his achievements than from owning the object itself. A has never spent any of his considerable salary on jewelry or trophies. How much income, if any, should A report? Would including $10,000 in A's income be "inequitable" in any way?

3. *Tax-exempt awards: section 74(b).* From 1954 to 1986, "prizes and awards made primarily in recognition of religious, charitable, scientific, educational, artistic, literary, or civic achievement" were excludable if the recipient did not enter a contest to receive the award and did not have to render substantial future services. In practice, this meant that Nobel prizes, Pulitzer prizes, and similar awards were tax exempt. Section 74(b)(2) now limits the exclusion to recipients who assign their prizes to a "governmental unit" or to certain kinds of educational or charitable organizations.

4. *"Employee achievement awards" under sections 74(c) and 274(j).* In order to "recognize traditional business practices of making awards of tangible personal property for length of service or safety achievement,"[j] § 74(c) excludes from income the value of an "employee achievement award" as defined in § 274(j). The Senate Finance Committee's report lists "engraved plaques, desk accessories, [and] emblematic jewelry that identify or symbolize the awarding employer or the achievement" and "items such as watches on retirement after lengthy service" as examples of excludable awards. Awards of more-useful items would presumably fail to qualify on the ground that the circumstances "create a significant

j. S.Rep. No. 99–313, 99th Cong., 2d Sess. 49 (1986).

likelihood of the payment of disguised compensation"; § 274(j)(3)(A)(iii). An excludable award must be "awarded as part of a meaningful presentation"; § 274(j)(3)(A)(ii).

Section 274(j) limits an employer's deduction for employee achievement awards to $400 for any one employee a year or, if the award is a "qualified plan award," to $1600 for any one employee a year. If the employer makes awards of property costing more than the deduction limits, the employer gets no deduction for the excess cost and the employee must include in income the excess cost or the excess of the award's value over the limit, whichever is more; § 74(c)(2).

5. *Problem.* P, a visiting professor at the Lakeside University Law School, receives a "gift" from the school at the end of the academic year. Must P include anything in income if the gift is:

(1) a framed picture of the law-school building, worth about $30.00 retail and probably not salable by P for more than $2.00?

(2) an expensive running suit emblazoned with the university's name and insignia?

F. EXTRAORDINARY MEDICAL COSTS

Under § 213(a), the medical expenses of the taxpayer, the taxpayer's spouse, and the taxpayer's dependents are deductible to the extent that they exceed 7.5 percent of the taxpayer's adjusted gross income (§ 62). Insurance premiums for medical and dental care are medical expenses (§ 213(d)(1)(C)), as are the costs of prescribed drugs and insulin (§ 213(b)). Some medical expenses paid by a decedent's estate are deductible on the decedent's final tax return (§ 213(c)).

FERRIS v. COMMISSIONER

United States Court of Appeals, Seventh Circuit, 1978.
582 F.2d 1112.

Before PELL, SPRECHER, and WOOD, CIRCUIT JUDGES.

PELL, CIRCUIT JUDGE.

In 1971, taxpayers Collins and Bonnie Ferris spent $194,660 to construct a swimming pool addition to their home in Maple Bluff, Wisconsin. The question in this litigation is how much of that sum may be deducted from the couple's 1971 income as a medical expense in computing their federal tax liability for that year.

Certain background facts are not disputed. Mrs. Ferris suffers from a degenerative spinal disorder which was, in 1970, causing her serious difficulty in walking or sitting. Her physician recommended that the Ferrises install a swimming pool at their residence and that Mrs. Ferris use it twice a day for the rest of her life to prevent the onset of permanent paralysis.

The Ferris residence was fairly described by Sherman Geib, taxpayers' expert appraiser, as "a luxury residence with highest quality materials and workmanship. Numerous special features and meticulous attention to details." The residence is a two and one-half story English Tudor style home, constructed of hand-cut, hand-laid stone, with servants' quarters, pantries, and other amenities befitting a home of its type. Geib estimated the market value of the home prior to the construction of the pool addition at $275,000, including therein the $160,000 value of the 3.8 acres on which the house is built.

The Ferrises, responding to the physician's suggestion, retained an architect to design an addition to their home to enclose a swimming pool. He designed a 20 by 40 foot pool with a hand-cut stone edge, Tudor style semi-circular ends, and a fountain. He recommended that the housing structure and the interior areas ought to be designed so as to use materials architecturally compatible with the main residence and of the same quality construction. The Ferrises agreed, and the exterior of the addition was constructed of hand-cut, hand-laid stone, with an expensive roof to match that of the residence. The interior featured more hand-cut stone for some walls, exposed cedar paneling for others, a cathedral ceiling with exposed wood paneling, and a ceramic tile pool deck area. All of these features, needless to say, were costly. The architect also proposed, and the Ferrises accepted, inclusion in the structure of a number of recreational entertainment facilities, such as a bar and cooking area, a sauna bath, an open terrace, a raised dining area, an indoor sunning area, and two dressing rooms. Geib, the appraiser, estimated that the swimming pool addition increased the value of the Ferris home by $97,330.

On their joint federal tax return for 1971, taxpayers claimed that $172,160 of the $194,660 spent on the pool addition were expenses for medical care within the meaning of § 213. Taxpayers had reduced the cost of the pool by the amount of money estimated to have been spent for some of the entertainment and recreational features included in the addition. Based on Geib's appraisal that the increase in the value of the residence would be roughly 50% of the cost of the addition, taxpayers claimed as deductible uncompensated expenses for medical care $86,000. The Commissioner of Internal Revenue took a different view, determining that the entire cost of a building to house the pool was not incurred primarily for medical purposes, and, using taxpayers' appraiser's 50% value added factor, allowing only a deduction of $6,500, roughly one-half of the $13,074 cost of the pool itself.

In the proceedings in the Tax Court, the Commissioner conceded that some sort of enclosure was medically necessary if Mrs. Ferris was to take twice-daily swims during the winter, and the battle shifted to the question of how much of the costs of the luxurious addition constructed by the Ferrises was properly deductible. The Commissioner contended that the expensive construction materials used were not medically necessary, and that a cost reduction should be made to account for the fact that the non-medical features built into the addition necessarily increased its size above what would have been medically necessary. He argued that an adequate pool with enclosure could have been built for $70,000 that would have increased the value of taxpayers' residence by $31,000, and thus that only $39,000 should be considered a medical expense.

The Tax Court found as a fact that "no doubt * * * a large portion of the total cost of the * * * addition was attributable to the need of having the structure architecturally and aesthetically compatible with petitioner's residence which is clearly a personal motivation." The court rejected the Commissioner's argument that the degree to which the addition's costs could be considered medical expenses should be accordingly reduced, however, because it was aware of "no case limiting a medical expense within the meaning of section 213 to the cheapest form of treatment." The court did agree with the Commissioner that a reduction to account for the enlarged size of the building due to the clearly nonessential features of the addition was appropriate, and reduced taxpayers' claimed medical expense by $4,000 (50% of the $8,000 it found allocable to the space for nonessentials). The court reasoned, alternatively, that the Commissioner's hypothetical $70,000 addition (with $10,000 of extra costs the court thought were medically necessary but which were not included in the Commissioner's hypothetical figures) would have added nothing to the value of taxpayers' residence, thus yielding virtually the same result the court had reached by its preferred approach. The Commissioner appeals.

As we have indicated, the Commissioner does not dispute that the reasonable costs of a swimming pool and enclosure, to the degree they are uncompensated by increased value in taxpayers' residence, are properly deductible as a medical expense within the meaning of § 213 in the circumstances of this case. It no doubt would startle the average taxpayer that the cost of an enclosed swimming pool facility, which would typically be erected for other than medical purposes and which, even given a medical motive for its construction, could receive substantial nonmedical use once built * * * could be deducted for federal income tax purposes. Even those with passing familiarity with federal tax principles might well be surprised that an expense like this, which is clearly capital in nature, could possibly be deducted in its entirety in the year in which incurred. See § 263(a).

Nonetheless, this is the approach Congress has chosen. Section 213 contains no ceiling limitation on the amount of deductible medical expenses, although all earlier formulations of the deduction did contain such a limitation. See Section 127 of the Revenue Act of 1942, ch. 619, 56 Stat. 798; Section 213 of the Internal Revenue Code of 1954, ch. 736, 68A Stat. 69; Section 1 of the Act of October 23, 1962, 76 Stat. 1141. When the ceiling limitations were removed by the Social Security Amendments of 1965, P.L. No. 89–97, 79 Stat. 286, Congress was responding to the hardship imposed when a taxpayer incurred extraordinary medical expenses but was obliged to pay income taxes on funds used to defray them. See H.Conf.Rep. No. 682, 89th Cong., 1st Sess., at

48 (1965); U.S.Code Cong. & Admin.News 1965, p. 1943. It nonetheless recognized that its choice would allow deductibility of expenses "for facilities, devices, services, and transportation which are of the types customarily used, or taken, primarily for other than medical purposes," id., U.S.Code Cong. & Admin.News 1965, p. 2243, and expressed its concern over the possibilities of abuse in such areas, swimming pools being specifically cited. Id. We believe the history of ceiling limitations on medical deductions and Congress' expressed concern over the abuse potential inherent in removing that limitation counsel against loose construction of § 213, but it does seem clear that even capital expenditures, to the extent they are uncompensated by increases in property value, may be considered medical expenses to the degree they are incurred "for medical care" within the meaning of § 213. See Oliver v. Commissioner, 364 F.2d 575, 578 (8th Cir.1966); Riach v. Frank, 302 F.2d 374 (9th Cir.1962); Wallace v. United States, 309 F.Supp. 748 (S.D.Iowa 1970), aff'd, 439 F.2d 757, 759 (8th Cir.1971), cert. denied, 404 U.S. 831; Gerard v. Commissioner, 37 T.C. 826 (1962).

The central question here is the degree to which the cost of taxpayers' swimming pool addition was an expense "for medical care." The Secretary of the Treasury has promulgated regulations on this point which taxpayers do not attack and which we find wholly consistent with § 213. [Treas.Reg.] § 1.213–1(e)(1)(ii) provides, in part:

> Deductions for expenditures for medical care allowable under section 213 will be *confined strictly to expenses incurred primarily for the prevention or alleviation of a physical or mental defect or illness.* (Emphasis added.)

* * *

We believe, in the light of the legislative history of § 213 and the Secretary's regulations, that the Tax Court erred as a matter of law in rejecting the Commissioner's argument that the substantial expense attributable to architectural and aesthetic compatibility was not incurred with the "primary purpose" of and "related directly to" the medical care of Mrs. Ferris. Section 213, by allowing complete deduction of capital expenditures even though they may receive substantial nonmedical use, is already quite generous in providing for medical expense deductions. We have no doubt that the 89th Congress which removed the ceiling on medical expenses, not to mention the average taxpayer, would be astounded to learn that this generosity allows deduction not only of a swimming pool and a building to house it, but also of a pool addition constructed in the grand and luxurious style employed here. This is not the law. Where a taxpayer makes a capital expenditure that would qualify as being "for medical care," but does so in a manner creating additional costs attributable to such personal motivations as architectural or aesthetic compatibility with the related property, the additional costs incurred are not expenses for medical care.

It is no answer to say, as the Tax Court did, that taxpayers are not limited to choosing the cheapest form of medical treatment available to them. A taxpayer with the means and the inclination to patronize a relatively expensive physician or to select a private room for his stay in a hospital will undoubtedly deduct more from his taxable income than a taxpayer with lesser means or more frugal tastes, but the fact remains that both taxpayers are incurring costs unquestionably directly related to medical care. That cannot be said here.

The task in cases like this one is to determine the minimum reasonable cost of a functionally adequate pool and housing structure. Taxpayers may well decide to exceed that cost and construct a facility more in keeping with their tastes, but any costs above those necessary to produce a functionally adequate facility are not incurred "for medical care." * * *

* * *

For the reasons stated herein, the judgment of the Tax Court is reversed and the cause is remanded for further proceedings consistent herewith.

Problem, Notes and Questions

1. *Payments to medical practitioners.* Nearly all payments to physicians, dentists, chiropractors, podiatrists, and other medical practitioners are payments for "medical care" under § 213(a). That section does not require that treatment be medically necessary, or even that the taxpayer be sick. Payments for abortions and sterilizations are deductible. The costs of facelifts and hair-transplants were made nondeductible by the enactment of § 213(d)(9) in 1990.

2. *Purchase of "non-medical" goods or services for medical reasons.* The principal case is fairly typical of those in which a taxpayer seeks a medical-expense deduction for a cost which is not a doctor's fee or the purchase price of medicine but which is incurred for medical reasons. In some cases, the costs produce no "personal" or "consumption" benefits and bear so close a relationship to medical treatment that they are routinely allowed; an example is the cost of transportation to and from a doctor's office. Treas.Reg. § 1.213–1(e)(1)(iv). The troublesome cases involve payments of the sort that healthy taxpayers incur to finance personal consumption. The most extreme reported example may be Rabb v. Commissioner, 31 T.C.M. 476 (1972), in which the taxpayer sought a medical-expense deduction for over $15,000 spent on tailored clothing, department-store charge accounts, furniture, payments on a lakeside cottage and a boat, and similar items. One of the taxpayer's psychiatrists testified that the taxpayer would have had to be institutionalized but for the "relief" this spending gave her, and another psychiatrist had recommended shopping trips as "milieu therapy." The court found an insufficiently "direct and proximate" relationship between the illness and the expenditures and disallowed the deduction. Other cases include Ochs v. Commissioner, 195 F.2d 692 (2d Cir.1952) (children's tuition in boarding school, to free their mother from "irritation and nervousness," which

might have caused a recurrence of throat cancer; non-deductible); Rev. Rul. 62–189, 1962–2 C.B. 88 (wig for taxpayer's daughter, who had lost all hair from disease, purchased on doctor's recommendation; deductible). Is it conceivable that expenses like those involved in these cases would be treated as medical expenses under a medical-insurance policy or a national health program?

The Conference Committee Report on the Tax Reform Act of 1986 confirms that some capital expenditures can be deducted under § 213; see H.R.Rep. No. 99–841, 99th Cong., 2d Sess., II–22:

> The conferees intend to reaffirm that the full costs of specified capital expenditures incurred to accommodate a personal residence to the needs of a physically handicapped individual, such as construction of entrance ramps or widening of doorways to allow use of wheelchairs, constitute medical expenses eligible for the deduction * * *.

Revenue Ruling 87–106, 1987–2 C.B. 67, lists expenditures (such as lowering cabinets, widening hallways, and installing railings) which "generally" do not increase the market value of a residence and so are generally deductible in full if incurred for the proper purpose.

3. *Travel expenses.* Section 213(d)(2) allows some lodging costs while away from home for medical care to be treated as medical expenses. Note the "no-smile rule" of § 213(d)(2)(B).

4. *Policy considerations.* Is the medical-expense deduction a "tax expenditure" (pp. 163–172, above)? If one views the deduction as a program under which Congress uses the tax system to subsidize medical care, the "subsidy" seems strange indeed, for it "pays for" a substantial portion of the medical costs of a taxpayer with a $300,000 annual income and little or none of the medical costs of low-income taxpayers. But the "subsidy" theory of the medical-expense deduction assumes that a "normative" tax system—one designed by someone indifferent to subsidizing health care—would not allow a deduction for medical expenses. Is this the case? See G. Break & J. Pechman, Federal Tax Reform 21–22 (1975):

> The major function of personal deductions is to adjust for unusual circumstances that have a bearing on an individual's capacity to pay income taxes. * * * Clearly, a family with heavy medical payments is less able to pay than a family with the same income and no medical expenses.

As originally enacted in 1942, the medical-expense deduction was limited to $2500. The ceiling was increased from time to time and finally eliminated in 1965.

5. *Problem.* Which of the following costs qualify for deduction under § 213?

(a) Attendance at a "stop smoking" clinic. *yes*

(b) A weight-loss program. *If general health no; for specific illness yes*

(c) Non-prescription flu remedies.   *no*

(d) Non-prescription insulin.   *yes*

(e) Transportation from the taxpayer's rural home to a tertiary-care hospital in University City (300 miles away).   *no*

(f) Meals ($75) and lodging ($160) incurred by the taxpayer while in University City to receive the medical treatment.   *yes*

(g) Meals ($75) and lodging ($160) paid by the taxpayer for a family member who accompanies her to University City for treatment.   *limited to $50*

(h) Medical-insurance premiums (paid by the taxpayer) on a policy covering the taxpayer and her dependent children.   *yes*

(i) Medical costs incurred by an organ donor in a transplant operation.

(j) Attendance at an alcoholism rehabilitation clinic.

(k) An elevator installed in the home of a heart patient so that he will not have to climb stairs.

(*l*) Hospitalization of the taxpayer's child. The taxpayer is divorced, and the child is a dependent of the taxpayer's former spouse.

6.   *References.* Newman, The Medical Expense Deduction: A Preliminary Postmortem, 53 So.Cal.L.Rev. 787 (1980); Andrews, Personal Deductions in an Ideal Income Tax, 86 Harv.L.Rev. 309 (1972).

G.   CHARITABLE CONTRIBUTIONS AND TAX–EXEMPT ORGANIZATIONS

WINN v. COMMISSIONER

United States Court of Appeals, Fifth Circuit, 1979.
595 F.2d 1060.

Before THORNBERRY, CLARK and RONEY, CIRCUIT JUDGES.

CHARLES CLARK, CIRCUIT JUDGE: * * *

[The Tax Court found the following facts relating to the taxpayers' claimed deduction under § 170 (67 T.C. 499, 506–07 (1976)):

On their 1967 Federal income tax return, petitioners claimed as a deduction a contribution made to the "Sara Barry Fund." Payment was made by check dated December 30, 1967, in the amount of $10,000. On the face of the check it was noted that the contribution was made for the Korean Presbyterian Mission. The check was endorsed "For Deposit Sara Barry Fund" and deposited in the personal account of Ms. Sara Barry at the Bank of Benoit, Benoit, Miss.

Ms. Sara Barry is petitioner's first cousin; she is the daughter of the brother of petitioner's mother. At the time the $10,000 gift was made, Ms. Barry was serving in the Korean mission field of the Presbyterian Church in the United States. She was sponsored in her mission work in South Korea by the Benoit Presbyterian Church, the First Presbyterian Church of Greenville, Miss., and by a Presbyterian church in Chattanooga, Tenn. Petitioner regarded Ms. Barry as an agent of the Presbyterian Church at the time the gift was made.

Ms. Barry established and worked primarily with a fellowship Bible study aimed at young college students in Korea. This work, authorized by the Presbyterian Church, was in need of funds, thus the Benoit Presbyterian Church would, at various times, sponsor a Sara Barry Day to initiate contributions from members of the community. Contributions to the Sara Barry Fund in Benoit, Miss., were handled by petitioner's uncle, Ms. Barry's father, who is an elder in the Benoit church. Funds channeled to Ms. Barry's father were deposited in her personal bank account in Benoit, Miss. Although on occasion petitioner made contributions to his local Presbyterian Church in Greenville, Miss., at the time of his gift to the Sara Barry Fund he was advised that contributions to the Greenville church could be expended for the World Council of Churches, a use which petitioner did not support. Thus, petitioner made his contribution to the fund because he felt the money would be put to purposeful evangelistic ends in Korea under the agency of the Presbyterian Church in the United States.]

* * *

The Tax Court denied the Winns['] claimed deduction in 1967 for a $10,000 check payable to the "Sara Barry Fund" to support Presbyterian mission work in Korea. * * *

Section 170(c) permits a taxpayer to deduct a contribution or gift "to or for the use of" a qualified charity. The [T]ax [C]ourt disallowed Winn's deduction under this section because it found that the Presbyterian churches, which were qualified charities, never received or had the use of the $10,000. The taxpayers, however, argue that the funds were actually given in a church-sponsored program and used in church-sponsored work and therefore were made "for the use of" that donee. The Winns rely on Bauer v. United States, 449 F.Supp. 755 (W.D.La. 1978), as authority for the proposition that donations ultimately used for charitable purposes are in fact made "for the use of" a charitable institution. *Bauer* held that a charity need not have full control of the donated funds to satisfy that test. The taxpayers in *Bauer* were permitted to deduct scholarship funds given to selected individual students attending qualified educational institutions. See also Sico Foundation v. United States, 295 F.2d 924 (Ct.Cl.1961); Morey v. Riddell, 205 F.Supp. 918 (S.D.Calif.1962). We also note that a donor can earmark a contribution given to a qualified organization for specific purposes without losing the right to claim a charitable deduction. See Phinney v. Dougherty, 307 F.2d 357 (5th Cir.1962). Such a contribution still would be "to or for the use of" a charitable entity despite the fact that the donor controlled which of the qualified entity's charitable purposes would receive the exclusive benefit of the gift.

Proof that the church in Benoit sponsored "Sara Barry Days" for the express purpose of collecting funds for this part of its work, that an officer of that church took the funds donated and dealt with them as the church wished, and that the funds went to the support of the work the church intended is sufficient to establish that the funds were donated for the use of the Benoit Presbyterian church. The [T]ax [C]ourt's contrary legal conclusion based on these undisputed facts is reversed.

Affirmed[k] in Part, Reversed in Part.

Problem, Notes and Question

1. *Winn today.* In Davis v. United States, 495 U.S. 472 (1990), the Supreme Court denied a deduction under § 170 for parents' payment of their children's living expenses while the children worked as Mormon missionaries. While *Davis* resembles *Winn, Davis* was a much stronger case for the government because the taxpayers in *Davis* paid the living expenses of their children, a standard kind of non-deductible payment, while Winn's payment bore no clear one-to-one relationship to Sara Barry's living expenses. The *Davis* decision held that the payments were not "for the use of" the church (§ 170(c)); that phrase, said the Court, referred to "donations made in trust or in a similar legal arrangement." Nor were the payments deductible as outlays incident to the performance of services for a charity under Treas.Reg. § 1.170A–1(g), because the taxpayers who made the payments performed no services. The Court did not decide whether the payments could be deducted as payments "to" the church on the theory that the children were acting as agents of the church when they received the payments. As the taxpayers had failed to raise that argument before the court of appeals, the Supreme Court declined to address it.

Where does *Davis* leave *Winn?* On the facts, *Winn* seems much the better case for deductibility. (An even stronger case would be one in which the contributor had no family tie to the missionary at all, but nevertheless gave the contribution to the missionary rather than to the organization, perhaps for reasons similar to Winn's or perhaps just because that seemed the simplest thing to do.) *Davis* disposes of the argument made by the Fifth Circuit that funds advanced with a charitable purpose and actually used for that purpose are given "for the use of" the organization under § 170(c). But the last paragraph of the *Winn* opinion suggests that the argument the *Davis* Court refused to address— that the contribution was made "to" the church because the money was given to an agent of the church—could be persuasive on facts like those of *Winn,* even though it might be weak when the agent of the church is the donor's child and the funds are used for living expenses. The last paragraph of *Winn* would lose little if any force if the word "to" were

k. On another issue.—Eds.

substituted for "for the use of." So a decent case for the proposition that *Winn* survives *Davis* can be constructed, though the matter is certainly not clear. Cautious donees will make their checks payable to the organization.

2. *Contributions with strings attached.* Deductible gifts with strings are common and often unquestioned. Gifts of funds to be used to build a specific building or of paintings to be hung in a particular museum are deductible. On the other hand, a "contribution" to a university, conditioned upon the university's using the funds to award a scholarship to the donor's child, surely does not qualify for a deduction under § 170. Transfers in exchange for anticipated (but not guaranteed) benefits raise serious enforcement problems. An example is Klappenbach v. Commissioner, 52 T.C.M. 437 (1986), denying a deduction for a "gift" to a retirement home on the ground that the payment was "induced by" an anticipated benefit in the form of care provided to the "donor's" mother by the home. See also Ltr. Rul. 9004030, concerning a church which announced that it would pay the tuition of its members' children who attended a particular private school. The church asked those members whose children attended the school to increase their contributions to the church by the amount of the tuition they were saving, and many (but not all) of the members did. The Service ruled that members could deduct only the excess of their contributions over the tuition the church paid for their children. While the principle involved in the ruling seems beyond controversy, cases in which the tie between a "contribution" and a "benefit" is not obvious will present serious enforcement difficulties.

Here is a somewhat more controversial example. The Church of Scientology conducts "auditing" and "training" sessions, for which it charges fees. In Hernandez v. Commissioner, 490 U.S. 680 (1989), the Supreme Court held that payments for these sessions were not deductible under § 170 because the members received a "quid pro quo"; this, according to the Court, meant that the payments were not "gifts." The Court compared the payments to tuition paid to parochial schools and to payments to hospitals for medical treatment, neither of which can be deducted under § 170. The Court also rejected the taxpayers' argument that denying their deductions violated the Establishment and Free Exercise clauses of the First Amendment. Justice O'Connor, dissenting, noted that fees paid to religious organizations for pew rents, church dues, Masses, and attendance at religious services have long been treated as deductible. She inferred from this practice that a "quid pro quo" in the form of a religious benefit does not make a payment to a church nondeductible. The *Hernandez* majority found the record inadequate to determine whether the kinds of cases described by Justice O'Connor actually involved mandatory payments.

In 1993 the Service and the Church of Scientology settled their differences, and the Service ruled the church tax exempt. The settlement agreement was leaked to the press and reprinted in a major newspaper. In the settlement, the Service conceded the issue on which it had won in *Hernandez*. In Sklar v. Commissioner, 279 F.3d 697 (9th Cir. 2002), the taxpayers, arguing that deductions for religious instruction should not be limited to Scientologists, claimed charitable-contribution deductions for the religious portion of their children's education. In a scathing critique of the Service's policy of allowing deductions for Scientology training, the court said in dicta that the policy "clearly contravenes" *Hernandez*, "grants an unconstitutional denominational preference," and should "be invalidated on the ground that it violates either the Internal Revenue Code or the Establishment Clause." Ultimately, however, the court refused to extend "the unlawful policy set forth in the [Scientology] closing agreement * * * to all religious organizations." It concluded that the taxpayers had not proven that they had paid any more than the market value of a secular education at a comparable school.

Section 170(*l*) deals with the particular problem of "donors" to universities whose contributions give them a right to buy tickets to sporting events.

A taxpayer who incurs out-of-pocket expenses in doing work for a charitable organization can deduct the expenses. Traveling expenses, however, are deductible only if the "no-smile rule" of § 170(j) is satisfied.

3. *Qualified donees.* Section 170(c) describes the organizations to which deductible contributions can be made. All of these organizations are exempt from income taxes (except for the tax on "unrelated business taxable income" imposed by § 511), but not all tax-exempt organizations are organizations to which deductible contributions can be made. For example, non-profit social-welfare organizations with extensive lobbying activities may be exempt from tax under § 501(c)(4), but not under § 501(c)(3). Contributions to such organizations are not deductible because of § 170(c)(2)(D). Similarly, contributions to labor unions, trade associations, and social clubs cannot be deducted under § 170 although § 501(c) exempts these and many other organizations from income taxation.

Section 6113 requires some tax-exempt organizations to which deductible contributions cannot be made to include in their fundraising solicitations conspicuous, express statements that contributions are not deductible. Section 6710 imposes a penalty for violating § 6113. The maximum penalty for unintentional violations is $10,000 a year.

4. *Limits on the charitable-contribution deduction.* An individual taxpayer's total annual deduction under § 170 is limited by § 170(b)(1)(A) to fifty percent of his "contribution base" (§ 170(b)(1)(F)); more-stringent limits apply to contributions to most "private foundations" (§ 170(b)(1)(B)), to corporate contributions (§ 170(b)(2)), and to contributions of "capital gain property" (§ 170(b)(1)(C)). Contributions in excess of the annual limits can be carried over to future years as provided by § 170(d).

Contributions of partial interests in property were once allowed in full, but they raised troublesome valuation and other problems. For example, a taxpayer who transferred property in trust to a relative for life, then to charity, could claim a deduction for the estimated value of the remainder interest even though a trustee's power to invade corpus for the income beneficiary might destroy the value of the remainder. Section 170(f) now limits the deductibility of contributions of partial interests in property.

5. *Problem.* This year *T* made the following cash contributions:

(1) $1000 to the Poors, a needy family.

(2) $5000 to *T*'s church.

(3) $2000 to the University Athletic Scholarship Fund. (Donors of $1500 or more can purchase tickets which entitle the holder to preferred seats at university basketball games.)

(4) $500 to the Amalgamated Sisterhood of Laborers, a labor union.

(5) $1000 to the Australian National University.

(6) $500 to the Republican Party.

T's adjusted gross income is $100,000. To what extent can *T* deduct these amounts under § 170?

6. *Policy issues.* Some commentators argue that § 170 should be replaced by a tax credit (or a direct "matching-grant" subsidy), so that the Code will not subsidize the contributions of upper-bracket taxpayers more heavily than those of low-income taxpayers. Since the wealthy tend to give relatively more to schools and less to churches than the poor, the change would have significant practical effects even if the amount of the credit or matching grant were set so as to keep total contributions at their current level.

Whether the deduction for contributions is a "subsidy" is controversial. For arguments that it is not, see Andrews, Personal Deductions in an Ideal Income Tax, 86 Harv.L.Rev. 309 (1972); Bittker, Charitable Contributions: Tax Deductions or Matching Grants?, 28 Tax L.Rev. 37 (1972).

BOB JONES UNIVERSITY v. UNITED STATES

Supreme Court of the United States, 1983.
461 U.S. 574, 103 S.Ct. 2017, 76 L.Ed.2d 157.

CHIEF JUSTICE BURGER delivered the opinion of the Court.

We granted certiorari to decide whether petitioners, nonprofit private schools that prescribe and enforce racially discriminatory admissions standards on the basis of religious doctrine, qualify as tax-exempt organizations under § 501(c)(3).

I

A

* * *

B

No. 81–3, Bob Jones University v. United States

Bob Jones University is a nonprofit corporation located in Greenville, S.C. Its purpose is "to conduct an institution of learning * * *, giving special emphasis to the Christian religion and the ethics revealed in the Holy Scriptures." Certificate of Incorporation, Bob Jones University, Inc., of Greenville, S.C. The corporation operates a school with an enrollment of approximately 5,000 students, from kindergarten through college and graduate school. Bob Jones University is not affiliated with any religious denomination, but is dedicated to the teaching and propagation of its fundamentalist Christian religious beliefs. It is both a religious and educational institution. Its teachers are required to be devout Christians, and all courses at the University are taught according to the Bible. Entering students are screened as to their religious beliefs, and their public and private conduct is strictly regulated by standards promulgated by University authorities.

The sponsors of the University genuinely believe that the Bible forbids interracial dating and marriage. To effectuate these views, Negroes were completely excluded until 1971. From 1971 to May 1975, the University accepted no applications from unmarried Negroes,[5] but did accept applications from Negroes married within their race.

Following the decision of the United States Court of Appeals for the Fourth Circuit in McCrary v. Runyon, 515 F.2d 1082 (1975), aff'd, 427 U.S. 160 (1976), prohibiting racial exclusion from private schools, the University revised its policy. Since May 29, 1975, the University has permitted unmarried Negroes to enroll; but a disciplinary rule prohibits interracial dating and marriage. That rule reads:

"There is to be no interracial dating.

    "1. Students who are partners in an interracial marriage will be expelled.

    "2. Students who are members of or affiliated with any group or organization which holds as one of its goals or advocates interracial marriage will be expelled.

    "3. Students who date outside of their own race will be expelled.

    "4. Students who espouse, promote, or encourage others to violate the University's dating rules and regulations will be expelled."

The University continues to deny admission to applicants engaged in an interracial marriage or known to advocate interracial marriage or dating.

Until 1970, the IRS extended tax-exempt status to Bob Jones University under § 501(c)(3). By the letter of November 30, 1970, that

---

5. Beginning in 1973, Bob Jones University instituted an exception to this rule, allowing applications from unmarried Negroes who had been members of the University staff for four years or more.

followed the injunction issued in Green v. Kennedy, 309 F.Supp. 1127 (DC 1970), the IRS formally notified the University of the change in IRS policy, and announced its intention to challenge the tax-exempt status of private schools practicing racial discrimination in their admissions policies.

* * *

Thereafter, on April 16, 1975, the IRS notified the University of the proposed revocation of its tax-exempt status. On January 19, 1976, the IRS officially revoked the University's tax-exempt status, effective as of December 1, 1970, the day after the University was formally notified of the change in IRS policy. * * *

The United States District Court for the District of South Carolina held that revocation of the University's tax-exempt status exceeded the delegated powers of the IRS, was improper under the IRS rulings and procedures, and violated the University's rights under the Religion Clauses of the First Amendment. 468 F.Supp. 890, 907 (1978). * * *

The Court of Appeals for the Fourth Circuit, in a divided opinion, reversed. * * *

C

No. 81–1, Goldsboro Christian Schools, Inc. v. United States

Goldsboro Christian Schools is a nonprofit corporation located in Goldsboro, N.C. Like Bob Jones University, it was established "to conduct an institution or institutions of learning * * *, giving special emphasis to the Christian religion and the ethics revealed in the Holy scriptures." Articles of Incorporation ¶ 3(a). The school offers classes from kindergarten through high school, and since at least 1969 has satisfied the State of North Carolina's requirements for secular education in private schools. The school requires its high school students to take Bible-related courses, and begins each class with prayer.

Since its incorporation in 1963, Goldsboro Christian Schools has maintained a racially discriminatory admissions policy based upon its interpretation of the Bible. Goldsboro has for the most part accepted only Caucasians. On occasion, however, the school has accepted children from racially mixed marriages in which one of the parents is Caucasian.

* * *

II

A

In Revenue Ruling 71–447, the IRS formalized the policy, first announced in 1970, that § 170 and § 501(c)(3) embrace the common-law "charity" concept. Under that view, to qualify for a tax exemption pursuant to § 501(c)(3), an institution must show, first, that it falls within one of the eight categories expressly set forth in that section, and second, that its activity is not contrary to settled public policy.

Section 501(c)(3) provides that "[c]orporations * * * organized and operated exclusively for religious, charitable * * * or educational purposes" are entitled to tax exemption. Petitioners argue that the plain language of the statute guarantees them tax-exempt status. They emphasize the absence of any language in the statute expressly requiring all exempt organizations to be "charitable" in the common-law sense, and they contend that the disjunctive "or" separating the categories in § 501(c)(3) precludes such a reading. Instead, they argue that if an institution falls within one or more of the specified categories it is automatically entitled to exemption, without regard to whether it also qualifies as "charitable." The Court of Appeals rejected that contention and concluded that petitioners' interpretation of the statute "tears section 501(c)(3) from its roots." 639 F.2d, at 151.

It is a well-established canon of statutory construction that a court should go beyond the literal language of a statute if reliance on that language would defeat the plain purpose of the statute:

> "The general words used in the clause * * *, taken by themselves, and literally construed, without regard to the object in view, would seem to sanction the claim of the plaintiff. But this mode of expounding a statute has never been adopted by any enlightened tribunal—because it is evident that in many cases it would defeat the object which the Legislature intended to accomplish. And it is well settled that, in interpreting a statute, the court will not look merely to a particular clause in which general words may be used, *but will take in connection with it the whole statute * * * and the objects and policy of the law. * * *"* Brown v. Duchesne, 19 How. 183, 194 (1857) (emphasis added).

Section 501(c)(3) therefore must be analyzed and construed within the framework of the Internal Revenue Code and against the background of the congressional purposes. Such an examination reveals unmistakable evidence that, underlying all relevant parts of the Code, is the intent that entitlement to tax exemption depends on meeting certain common-law standards of charity—namely, that an institution seeking tax-exempt status must serve a public purpose and not be contrary to established public policy.

This "charitable" concept appears explicitly in § 170 of the Code. That section contains a list of organizations virtually identical to that contained in § 501(c)(3). It is apparent that Congress intended that list to have the same meaning in both sections. In § 170, Congress used the list of organizations in defining the term "charitable contributions." On its face, therefore, § 170 reveals that Congress' intention was to provide tax benefits to organizations serving charitable purposes. The form of § 170 simply makes plain what common sense and history tell us: in enacting both § 170 and § 501(c)(3), Congress sought to provide tax benefits to charitable organizations, to encourage the development of private institutions that serve a useful public purpose or supplement or take the place of public institutions of the same kind.

* * *

When the Government grants exemptions or allows deductions all taxpayers are affected; the very fact of the exemption or deduction for the donor means that other taxpayers can be said to be indirect and vicarious "donors." Charitable exemptions are justified on the basis that the exempt entity confers a public benefit—a benefit which the society or the community may not itself choose or be able to provide, or which supplements and advances the work of public institutions already supported by tax revenues.[18] History buttresses logic to make clear that, to warrant exemption under § 501(c)(3), an institution must fall within a category specified in that section and must demonstrably serve and be in harmony with the public interest. The institution's purpose must not be so at odds with the common community conscience as to undermine any public benefit that might otherwise be conferred.

B

We are bound to approach these questions with full awareness that determinations of public benefit and public policy are sensitive matters with serious implications for the institutions affected; a declaration that a given institution is not "charitable" should be made only where there can be no doubt that the activity involved is contrary to a fundamental public policy. But there can no longer be any doubt that racial discrimination in education violates deeply and widely accepted views of elementary justice. Prior to 1954, public education in many places still was conducted under the pall of Plessy v. Ferguson, 163 U.S. 537 (1896); racial segregation in primary and secondary education prevailed in many parts of the country. See, e.g., Segregation and the Fourteenth Amendment in the States (B. Reams & P. Wilson eds. 1975). This Court's decision in Brown v. Board of Education, 347 U.S. 483 (1954), signaled an end to that era. Over the past quarter of a century, every pronounce-

---

18. The dissent acknowledges that "Congress intended * * * to offer a tax benefit to organizations * * * providing a public benefit," but suggests that Congress itself fully defined what organizations provide a public benefit, through the list of eight categories of exempt organizations contained in § 170 and § 501(c)(3). Under that view, any nonprofit organization that falls within one of the specified categories is automatically entitled to the tax benefits, provided it does not engage in expressly prohibited lobbying or political activities. The dissent thus would have us conclude, for example, that any nonprofit organization that does not engage in prohibited lobbying activities is entitled to tax exemption as an "educational" institution if it is organized for the " 'instruction or training of the individual for the purpose of improving or developing his capabilities,' " 26 CFR § 1.501(c)(3)–1(d)(3) (1982). As Judge Leventhal noted in Green v. Connally, 330 F.Supp. 1150, 1160(DC), summarily aff'd sub nom. Coit v. Green, 404 U.S. 997 (1971), Fagin's school for educating English boys in the art of picking pockets would be an "educational" institution under that definition. Similarly, a band of former military personnel might well set up a school for intensive training of subversives for guerrilla warfare and terrorism in other countries; in the abstract, that "school" would qualify as an "educational" institution. Surely Congress had no thought of affording such an unthinking, wooden meaning to § 170 and § 501(c)(3) as to provide tax benefits to "educational" organizations that do not serve a public, charitable purpose.

ment of this Court and myriad Acts of Congress and Executive Orders attest a firm national policy to prohibit racial segregation and discrimination in public education.

An unbroken line of cases following Brown v. Board of Education establishes beyond doubt this Court's view that racial discrimination in education violates a most fundamental national public policy, as well as rights of individuals.

* * *

Congress, in Titles IV and VI of the Civil Rights Act of 1964, Pub.L. 88–352, 78 Stat. 241, 42 U.S.C. §§ 2000c, 2000c–6, 2000d, clearly expressed its agreement that racial discrimination in education violates a fundamental public policy. Other sections of that Act, and numerous enactments since then, testify to the public policy against racial discrimination. [Citations omitted.]

The Executive Branch has consistently placed its support behind eradication of racial discrimination. * * *

* * *

C

Petitioners contend that, regardless of whether the IRS properly concluded that racially discriminatory private schools violate public policy, only Congress can alter the scope of § 170 and § 501(c)(3). Petitioners accordingly argue that the IRS overstepped its lawful bounds in issuing its 1970 and 1971 rulings.

Yet ever since the inception of the Tax Code, Congress has seen fit to vest in those administering the tax laws very broad authority to interpret those laws. In an area as complex as the tax system, the agency Congress vests with administrative responsibility must be able to exercise its authority to meet changing conditions and new problems. Indeed as early as 1918, Congress expressly authorized the Commissioner "to make all needful rules and regulations for the enforcement" of the tax laws. Revenue Act of 1918, ch. 18, § 1309, 40 Stat. 1143. The same provision, so essential to efficient and fair administration of the tax laws, has appeared in Tax Codes ever since, see § 7805(a); and this Court has long recognized the primary authority of the IRS and its predecessors in construing the Internal Revenue Code, see, e.g., Commissioner v. Portland Cement Co. of Utah, 450 U.S. 156, 169 (1981); United States v. Correll, 389 U.S. 299, 306–307 (1967); Boske v. Comingore, 177 U.S. 459, 469–470 (1900).

* * *

D

The actions of Congress since 1970 leave no doubt that the IRS reached the correct conclusion in exercising its authority. It is, of course, not unknown for independent agencies or the Executive Branch to misconstrue the intent of a statute; Congress can and often does correct such misconceptions, if the courts have not done so. Yet for a dozen years Congress has been made aware—acutely aware—of the IRS rulings of 1970 and 1971. As we noted earlier, few issues have been the subject of more vigorous and widespread debate and discussion in and out of Congress than those related to racial segregation in education. Sincere adherents advocating contrary views have ventilated the subject for well over three decades. Failure of Congress to modify the IRS rulings of 1970 and 1971, of which Congress was, by its own studies and by public discourse, constantly reminded, and Congress' awareness of the denial of tax-exempt status for racially discriminatory schools when enacting other and related legislation make out an unusually strong case of legislative acquiescence in and ratification by implication of the 1970 and 1971 rulings.

* * *

III

Petitioners contend that, even if the Commissioner's policy is valid as to nonreligious private schools, that policy cannot constitutionally be applied to schools that engage in racial discrimination on the basis of sincerely held religious beliefs.

* * *

[The court held that the government's "fundamental, compelling, overriding interest in eradicating racial discrimination in education" outweighed "whatever burden denial of tax benefits places on petitioners' exercise of their religious beliefs."]

* * *

The judgments of the Court of Appeals are, accordingly,

Affirmed.

JUSTICE POWELL, concurring in part and concurring in the judgment.

* * *

II

I * * * concur in the Court's judgment that tax-exempt status under §§ 170(c) and 501(c)(3) is not available to private schools that concededly are racially discriminatory. I do not agree, however, with the Court's more general explanation of the justifications for the tax exemptions provided to charitable organizations. The Court states:

"Charitable exemptions are justified on the basis that the exempt entity confers a public benefit—a benefit which the society or the community may not itself choose or be able to provide, or which supplements and advances the work of public institutions already supported by tax revenues. History buttresses logic to make clear that, to warrant exemption under § 501(c)(3), an institution must fall within a category specified in that section and must demonstrably serve and be in harmony with the public interest. The institution's purpose must not be so at odds with the common community conscience as to undermine any public benefit that might otherwise be conferred." (footnotes omitted).

Applying this test to petitioners, the Court concludes that "[c]learly an educational institution engaging in practices affirmatively at odds with [the] declared position of the whole Government cannot be seen as exercising a 'beneficial and stabilizing influenc[e] in community life,' * * * and is not 'charitable,' within the meaning of § 170 and § 501(c)(3)" (quoting Walz v. Tax Comm'n, 397 U.S. 664, 673 (1970)).

With all respect, I am unconvinced that the critical question in determining tax-exempt status is whether an individual organization provides a clear "public benefit" as defined by the Court. Over 106,000 organizations filed § 501(c)(3) returns in 1981. Internal Revenue Service, 1982 Exempt Organization/Business Master File. I find it impossible to believe that all or even most of those organizations could prove that they "demonstrably serve and [are] in harmony with the public interest" or that they are "beneficial and stabilizing influences in community life." Nor am I prepared to say that petitioners, because of their racially discriminatory policies, necessarily contribute nothing of benefit to the community. It is clear from the substantially secular character of the curricula and degrees offered that petitioners provide educational benefits.

Even more troubling to me is the element of conformity that appears to inform the Court's analysis. The Court asserts that an exempt organization must "demonstrably serve and be in harmony with the public interest," must have a purpose that comports with "the common community conscience," and must not act in a manner "affirmatively at odds with [the] declared position of the whole Government." Taken together, these passages suggest that the primary function of a tax-exempt organization is to act on behalf of the Government in carrying out governmentally approved policies. In my opinion, such a view of § 501(c)(3) ignores the important role played by tax exemptions in encouraging diverse, indeed often sharply conflicting, activities and viewpoints. As Justice Brennan has observed, private, nonprofit groups receive tax exemptions because "each group contributes to the diversity of association, viewpoint, and enterprise essential to a vigorous, pluralistic society." *Walz*, supra, at 689 (concurring opinion). Far from representing an effort to reinforce any perceived "common community conscience," the provision of tax exemptions to nonprofit groups is one indispensable means of limiting the influence of governmental orthodoxy on important areas of community life.[3]

3. Certainly § 501(c)(3) has not been applied in the manner suggested by the Court's analysis. The 1,100–page list of exempt organizations includes—among countless examples—such organizations as American Friends Service Committee, Inc., Committee on the Present Danger, Jehovahs Witnesses in the United States, Moral

Given the importance of our tradition of pluralism, "[t]he interest in preserving an area of untrammeled choice for private philanthropy is very great." Jackson v. Statler Foundation, 496 F.2d 623, 639 (C.A.2 1973) (Friendly, J., dissenting from denial of reconsideration en banc).

I do not suggest that these considerations always are or should be dispositive. Congress, of course, may find that some organizations do not warrant tax-exempt status. In these cases I agree with the Court that Congress has determined that the policy against racial discrimination in education should override the countervailing interest in permitting unorthodox private behavior.

* * *

Justice Rehnquist, dissenting.

The Court points out that there is a strong national policy in this country against racial discrimination. To the extent that the Court states that Congress in furtherance of this policy could deny tax-exempt status to educational institutions that promote racial discrimination, I readily agree. But, unlike the Court, I am convinced that Congress simply has failed to take this action and, as this Court has said over and over again, regardless of our view on the propriety of Congress' failure to legislate we are not constitutionally empowered to act for it.

In approaching this statutory construction question the Court quite adeptly avoids the statute it is construing. This I am sure is no accident, for there is nothing in the language of § 501(c)(3) that supports the result obtained by the Court. * * * With undeniable clarity, Congress has explicitly defined the requirements for § 501(c)(3) status. An entity must be (1) a corporation, or community chest, fund, or foundation, (2) organized for one of the eight enumerated purposes, (3) operated on a nonprofit basis, and (4) free from involvement in lobbying activities and political campaigns. Nowhere is there to be found some additional, undefined public policy requirement.

* * *

The Court suggests that unless its new requirement be added to § 501(c)(3), nonprofit organizations formed to teach pickpockets and

Majority Foundation, Inc., Friends of the Earth Foundation, Inc., Mountain States Legal Foundation, National Right to Life Educational Foundation, Planned Parenthood Federation of America, Scientists and Engineers for Secure Energy, Inc., and Union of Concerned Scientists Fund, Inc. See Internal Revenue Service, Cumulative List of Organizations Described in Section 170(c) of the Internal Revenue Code of 1954, pp. 31, 221, 376, 518, 670, 677, 694, 795, 880, 1001, 1073 (Revised Oct. 1981). It would be difficult indeed to argue that each of these organizations reflects the views of the "common community conscience" or "demonstrably * * * [is] in harmony with the public interest." In identifying these organizations, largely taken at random from the tens of thousands on the list, I of course do not imply disapproval of their being exempt from taxation. Rather, they illustrate the commendable tolerance by our Government of even the most strongly held divergent views, including views that at least from time to time *are* "at odds" with the position of our Government. We have consistently recognized that such disparate groups are entitled to share the privilege of tax exemption.

terrorists would necessarily acquire tax-exempt status. Since the Court does not challenge the characterization of *petitioners* as "educational" institutions within the meaning of § 501(c)(3), and in fact states several times in the course of its opinion that petitioners *are* educational institutions, it is difficult to see how this argument advances the Court's reasoning for disposing of petitioners' cases.

But simply because I reject the Court's heavyhanded creation of the requirement that an organization seeking § 501(c)(3) status must "serve and be in harmony with the public interest" does not mean that I would deny to the IRS the usual authority to adopt regulations further explaining what Congress meant by the term "educational." The IRS has fully exercised that authority in Treas.Reg. § 1.501(c)(3)–1(d)(3), which provides:

"(3) *Educational defined*—(i) *In general.* The term 'educational', as used in section 501(c)(3), relates to—

"(a) The instruction or training of the individual for the purpose of improving or developing his capabilities; or

"(b) The instruction of the public on subjects useful to the individual and beneficial to the community.

"An organization may be educational even though it advocates a particular position or viewpoint so long as it presents a sufficiently full and fair exposition of the pertinent facts as to permit an individual or the public to form an independent opinion or conclusion. On the other hand, an organization is not educational if its principal function is the mere presentation of unsupported opinion.

"(ii) *Examples of educational organizations.* The following are examples of organizations which, if they otherwise meet the requirements of this section, are educational:

"*Example (1).* An organization, such as a primary or secondary school, a college, or a professional or trade school, which has a regularly scheduled curriculum, a regular faculty, and a regularly enrolled body of students in attendance at a place where the educational activities are regularly carried on.

"*Example (2).* An organization whose activities consist of presenting public discussion groups, forums, panels, lectures, or other similar programs. Such programs may be on radio or television.

"*Example (3).* An organization which presents a course of instruction by means of correspondence or through the utilization of television or radio.

"*Example (4).* Museums, zoos, planetariums, symphony orchestras, and other similar organizations."

I have little doubt that neither the "Fagin School for Pickpockets" nor a school training students for guerrilla warfare and terrorism in other countries would meet the definitions contained in the regulations.

Prior to 1970, when the charted course was abruptly changed, the IRS had continuously interpreted § 501(c)(3) and its predecessors in accordance with the view I have expressed above. This, of course, is of considerable significance in determining the intended meaning of the statute. NLRB v. Boeing Co., 412 U.S. 67, 75 (1973); Power Reactor Development Co. v. Electrical Workers, 367 U.S. 396, 408 (1961).

* * *

I have no disagreement with the Court's finding that there is a strong national policy in this country opposed to racial discrimination. I agree with the Court that Congress has the power to further this policy by denying § 501(c)(3) status to organizations that practice racial discrimination.[3] But as of yet Congress has failed to do so. Whatever the reasons for the failure, this Court should not legislate for Congress.

Petitioners are each organized for the "instruction or training of the individual for the purpose of improving or developing his capabilities," 26 CFR § 1.501(c)(3)–1(d)(3), and thus are organized for "educational purposes" within the meaning of § 501(c)(3). Petitioners' nonprofit status is uncontested. There is no indication that either petitioner has been involved in lobbying activities or political campaigns. Therefore, it is my view that unless and until Congress affirmatively amends § 501(c)(3) to require more, the IRS is without authority to deny petitioners § 501(c)(3) status. For this reason, I would reverse the Court of Appeals.

Notes

1. *Congressional inaction.* The only Code provision conditioning tax benefits upon nondiscrimination is § 501(i), which denies tax-exempt status to social clubs which have written charter provisions or policy statements providing for discrimination on the basis of race, color, or religion (but only if a religious restriction is designed to further race or color discrimination). The *Bob Jones* Court refers to congressional disapproval of discrimination, but whether Congress would have legislated nondiscrimination requirements under §§ 501(c)(3) and 170 if *Bob Jones* had gone the other way is far from clear. Note that contributions to women's colleges and to churches that will not ordain women are tax deductible.

2. *Tax-expenditure analysis.* For an approach very different from that of *Bob Jones,* see McGlotten v. Connally, 338 F.Supp. 448 (D.D.C. 1972). *McGlotten* held that granting some forms of tax benefits to fraternal organizations was government action, which violated the constitutional rights of those against whom the organizations discriminated. The court also held that the tax deductibility of contributions to fraternal orders and the tax-exempt status of those organizations conferred

---

3. I agree with the Court that such a requirement would not infringe on petition-   ers' First Amendment rights.

"federal financial assistance," which subjected the organizations to the nondiscrimination requirements of the Civil Rights Act of 1964. Although none of the opinions in *Bob Jones* describe the tax benefits at issue there as "subsidies," the Court said in Regan v. Taxation with Representation of Washington, 461 U.S. 540 (1983), that §§ 501(c)(3) and 170 "are a form of subsidy," although they are not "in all respects identical" to cash subsidies.

3. *References.* Freed & Polsby, Race, Religion, and Public Policy: Bob Jones University v. United States, 1983 Sup.Ct.Rev. 1; Stephan, Bob Jones University v. United States: Public Policy in Search of Tax Policy, 1983 Sup.Ct.Rev. 33; Bittker & Rahdert, The Exemption of Nonprofit Organizations from Federal Income Taxation, 85 Yale L.J. 299 (1976).

HAVERLY v. UNITED STATES

United States Court of Appeals, Seventh Circuit, 1975.
513 F.2d 224, cert. denied 423 U.S. 912, 96 S.Ct. 216, 46 L.Ed.2d 140 (1975).

Before HASTINGS, SENIOR CIRCUIT JUDGE, SWYGERT and CUMMINGS, CIRCUIT JUDGES.

HASTINGS, SENIOR CIRCUIT JUDGE.

* * *

During the years 1967 and 1968 Charles N. Haverly was the principal of the Alice L. Barnard Elementary School in Chicago, Illinois. In each of these years publishers sent to the taxpayer unsolicited sample copies of textbooks which had a total fair market value at the time of receipt of $400. The samples were given to taxpayer for his personal retention or for whatever disposition he wished to make. The samples were provided, in the hope of receiving favorable consideration, to give taxpayer an opportunity to examine the books and determine whether they were suitable for the instructional unit for which he was responsible. The publishers did not intend that the books serve as compensation.

In 1968 taxpayer donated the books to the Alice L. Barnard Elementary School Library. The parties agreed that the donation entitled the taxpayer to a charitable deduction under § 170, in the amount of $400, the value of the books at the time of the contribution.

The parties further stipulated that the textbooks received from the publishers did not constitute gifts within the meaning of § 102 since their transfer to the taxpayer did not proceed from a detached and disinterested generosity nor out of affection, respect, admiration, charity or like impulses.

Taxpayer's report of his 1968 income did not include the value of the textbooks received, but it did include a charitable deduction for the value of the books donated to the school library. The Internal Revenue Service assessed a deficiency against the taxpayer representing income taxes on the value of the textbooks received. Taxpayer paid the amount of the deficiency, filed a claim for refund and subsequently instituted this action to recover that amount.

The amount of income, if any, and the time of its receipt are not issues here since the parties stipulated that if the contested issue of law was decided in the taxpayer's favor, his taxable income for 1968 as determined by the Internal Revenue Service would be reduced by $400.00.

Upon agreement of the parties, the case was submitted to the district court on the uncontested facts and briefs for decision without trial. The district court issued a memorandum opinion which held that receipt of the samples did not constitute income. Haverly v. United States, N.D.Ill., 374 F.Supp. 1041 (1974). The court subsequently ordered, in accordance with its decision, that plaintiffs recover from the United States the sum of $120.40 plus interest. The United States appeals from that judgment. We reverse.

* * *

The Supreme Court has frequently reiterated that it was the intention of Congress "to use the full measure of its taxing power" and "to tax all gains except those specifically exempted." James v. United States, 366 U.S. 213, 218–219 (1961). The Supreme Court has also held that the language of Section 61(a) encompasses all "accessions to wealth, clearly realized, and over which the taxpayers have complete dominion." Id. at 219; Commissioner v. Glenshaw Glass Co., 348 U.S. 426, 431 (1955).

* * *

The receipt of textbooks is unquestionably an "accession to wealth." Taxpayer recognized the value of the books when he donated them and took a $400 deduction therefor. Possession of the books increased the taxpayer's wealth. Taxpayer's receipt and possession of the books indicate that the income was "clearly realized." Taxpayer admitted that the books were given to him for his personal retention or whatever disposition he saw fit to make of them. Although the receipt of unsolicited samples may sometimes raise the question of whether the taxpayer manifested an intent to accept the property or exercised "complete dominion" over it, there is no question that this element is satisfied by the unequivocal act of taking a charitable deduction for donation of the property.

The district court recognized that the act of claiming a charitable deduction does manifest an intent to accept the property as one's own. It nevertheless declined to label receipt of the property as income because it considered such an act indistinguishable from other acts unrelated to the tax laws which also evidence an intent to accept property as one's own, such as a school principal donating his sample texts to the library *without* claiming a deduction. We need not resolve the question of the tax consequences of this and other hypothetical cases discussed by the district court and suggested by the taxpayer. To decide the case before us we need only hold, as we do, that when a tax deduction is taken for the donation of unsolicited samples the value of the samples received must be included in the taxpayer's gross income.

This conclusion is consistent with Revenue Ruling 70–498, 1970–2 Cum.Bull. 6, in which the Internal Revenue Service held that a newspaper's book reviewer must include in his gross income the value of unsolicited books received from publishers which are donated to a charitable organization and for which a charitable deduction is taken. This ruling was issued to super[s]ede an earlier ruling, Rev.Rul. 70–330, 1970–1 Cum.Bull. 14, that mere retention of unsolicited books was sufficient to cause them to be gross income.

The Internal Revenue Service has apparently made an administrative decision to be concerned with the taxation of unsolicited samples only when failure to tax those samples would provide taxpayers with double tax benefits. It is not for the courts to quarrel with an agency's rational allocation of its administrative resources.

In light of the foregoing, the judgment appealed from is reversed and the case is remanded to the district court with directions to enter judgment for the United States.

Reversed.

Problem, Notes and Questions

1. *Contributions of appreciated property.* The amount of the deduction allowed by § 170 in the case of non-cash contributions is often the property's value: basis is disregarded except for contributions which receive special treatment under § 170(e). Therefore, a taxpayer planning to sell appreciated stock held longer than the long-term holding period for capital gains and give the proceeds to a charity would be better advised to contribute the stock itself. The donation of the stock will give the same § 170 deduction as a donation of the sale proceeds, and the gift of the stock is not an event which requires the taxpayer to recognize the gain (contrast § 84). Does the tax treatment of gifts of appreciated stock provide a lesser degree of "double tax benefits" than Haverly sought?

Section 170(e)(1) limits the deduction to the property's basis in the case of most contributions of ordinary-income property, short-term capital gain property, and tangible personal property which the donee will not use in carrying out its exempt functions. In addition, deductions for contributions to most private foundations are limited to basis. Section 170(e) will be discussed further in Chapter 10.

2. *Substantiation requirements: non-cash contributions.* Most non-cash contributions to charity raise valuation questions. Valuation is often a "matter of opinion," and the high odds against being audited have encouraged taxpayers to err on the high side in claiming deductions for contributions of property. Treas.Reg. § 1.170A–13(c) requires most taxpayers who claim deductions in excess of $5000 for an item (or a set of "similar items") of property other than cash or publicly traded securities to support their claims by obtaining "qualified appraisals" of

the property and submitting "appraisal summaries" with their returns. The regulations' detailed requirements cannot be easily summarized, but a sense of their scope may be conveyed by noting that they concern themselves with the way in which an appraiser's fee was calculated, with the time when the appraisal must be performed, with the appraiser's qualifications and relationship to the donor, and—in some detail—with the information which the appraisal must contain.

In the case of contributions of property for which a deduction of $5000 or less is claimed, the donor must maintain "reliable written records" containing specified information. Except in cases in which obtaining a receipt would be "impractical," the donor must obtain and keep a receipt from the donee describing the property "in detail reasonably sufficient under the circumstances"; Treas.Reg. § 1.170A–13(b).

Section 6050L requires donees of "charitable deduction property" who dispose of the property within two years after receipt to report specified information to the Service and the donor. "Charitable deduction property" is property other than publicly traded securities for which the donor claimed a deduction of more than $5000.

3. *Substantiation requirements: all contributions.* Section 170(f)(8) disallows a deduction for any contribution of $250 or more, even if the contribution was a contribution of cash, unless the taxpayer obtains "substantiation" of the contribution by means of a "contemporaneous written acknowledgment of the contribution by the donee organization." The donor's canceled check is not adequate. Section 170(f)(8)(B) sets forth requirements for acknowledgments; the requirements include a description and valuation of any goods or services given by the organization in return for the contribution. The substantiation requirement need not be met if the donee itself reports the contribution, and the Treasury Department is given authority to prescribe regulations making substantiation unnecessary in "appropriate cases" (according to the committee reports, this may include contributions made by payroll deduction); §§ 170(f)(8)(D) & (E).

Suppose that Smith contributes $250 to a church and does not obtain substantiation. Jones contributes $249 to the same church; she does not obtain substantiation either. How much of their contributions can each deduct?

4. *Problem.* T has an adjusted gross income of $100,000. Which of the following can T deduct under § 170?

(1) T performed $5000 worth of free legal services for the community hospital. T spent $370 of his own funds in doing this work.

(2) T contributed publicly traded stock with a basis of $4000 and a value of $3000 to the University Law School.

H. STATE, LOCAL, AND FOREIGN TAXES

REVENUE RULING 79–180

1979–1 C.B. 95.

ISSUE

Is the New York State renters tax deductible by renters as a real property tax under section 164(a)(1)?

FACTS

On July 6, 1978, the State of New York amended the New York Real Property Tax Law (McKinney 1972) to provide that certain renters of residential property have an interest in real property, are personally liable for the real property taxes due on their interest, and are entitled to a federal itemized deduction for those taxes. Laws 1978, chapter 471. The effective date of the amendment is April 1, 1980. Laws 1979, chapter 41.

Section 304 of the New York Real Property Tax Law provides that all assessments shall be against the real property itself which shall be liable to sale pursuant to law for any unpaid taxes or special ad valorem levies.

However, where real property in whole or in part is rented for residential purposes pursuant to a lease or to the same occupant or occupants for twelve consecutive months or longer, or if the dwelling unit is subject to rent controls and regulation, a renter who pays $150 or more a month in rent (or less than $150, if the renter makes an election) is deemed to have an interest in the real property and is subject to state and local laws covering the levy and collection of taxes and the enforcement of collection of delinquent taxes. This provision does not, however, relieve the owner of real property from the obligation of paying all taxes due on the owner's property or vitiate the sale of the real property for unpaid taxes or special ad valorem levies. The owner of real property is obligated to apply the first money received each month from the renter to taxes due on the owner's real property.

The owner of the real property is required to file annually, on or before the tax status date, with the appropriate assessment department, the rent roll covering all units of the property, including names of those renters to whom section 304 applies. The schedule of rents must include all units whether rented or not and whether residential or not. An assessed valuation is assigned to each rental unit of the property by establishing the relationship of the yearly rent for the unit to the total yearly rent roll and applying this ratio to the assessment established for the rental property as a whole, less the assessment on that portion of the property that is determined not held for rental purposes. Taxes on the property not held for rental purposes are assessed solely against the owner and are not considered in determining the assessed valuation of each rental unit. In the event that the assessor reassesses the real property, the relationships established for the prior assessments shall be applied to the new assessments.

Section 926–a of the New York Real Property Tax Law provides that the owner of the real property is deemed an agent of the collecting officer for purposes of collecting taxes due from each renter to whom section 304 applies. The payments by the renter to the owner must be made in two separate amounts, consisting of basic rent (the rental amount less the amount of the real property tax designated for the rental unit) and the real property tax due from the rental unit. The annual real property tax must be paid to the owner in equal monthly installments. Tax payments to the owner discharge the renter's liability for taxes so paid, regardless of any subsequent disposition of the moneys made by the owner. If a renter fails to pay that portion of the rental charges attributable to taxes or is delinquent in payments to the owner so that less than all of the money due for real property taxes is paid to the owner, the owner is deemed to have assumed the renter's interest in the unit. Where a rental unit is vacant all or part of the taxing period, the owner is deemed to hold the renter's interest in that unit for the period of the vacancy and to assume the liability for taxes levied on that unit.

An owner of real property, where a renter who has an interest in real property pursuant to section 304 is an occupant, may not charge such a renter an amount in any rent period in excess of the rent reserved in the lease or the maximum rent permitted under rent controls and regulations, reduced by the renters tax allocated to the renter.

Law and Analysis

Section 164(a)(1) allows as a deduction, for the taxable year within which paid or accrued, state and local, and foreign, real property taxes.

[Treas.Reg. §] 1.164–3(b) provides that the term "real property taxes" means taxes imposed on interests in real property and levied for the general public welfare.

Under federal law, a tax is an enforced contribution, exacted pursuant to legislative authority in the exercise of the taxing power, and imposed and collected for the purpose of raising revenue to be used for public or governmental purposes, and not as a payment for some special privilege granted or service rendered. Rev.Rul. 77–29, 1977–1 C.B. 44.

Rev.Rul. 58–141, 1958–1 C.B. 101, states that the question of whether a particular contribution, charge, or burden is to be regarded as a tax depends on its real nature and, if it is not in its nature a tax, it is not material that it may have been so called.

Thus, the fact that the State of New York treats a portion of the total rental amounts paid by renters to owners of real property as real property tax payments does not establish that those payments are in fact real property tax payments, because the focus is on the nature of the transaction under federal law. See Lyeth v. Hoey, 305 U.S. 188 (1938).

The New York renters tax does not impose on the renter any economic burden that did not exist prior to the enactment of section 304 of the New York Real Property Tax Law. Rather, the renters tax merely divides the separately determined rental amount into a so-called rental payment and a so-called real property tax payment. The lack of an economic burden on the renter is further evidenced by the fact that the owner is not relieved from the obligation of paying all taxes due on the owner's property. Under section 926–a, the owner is deemed to assume the renter's interest in the unit if the renter is delinquent in making payment to the owner. In the event of the renter's nonpayment, section 304 looks to the owner for payment and the taxing authority may enforce payment against the owner's interest in the entire property.

Holding

The New York State renters tax paid by renters pursuant to sections 304 and 926–a of the New York Real Property Tax Law is not a tax on the renter for federal income tax purposes, but rather is part of the renters' rental payments.

Because the New York renters tax is not a tax on the renter for federal income tax purposes, it is not necessary to decide whether such a tax could qualify as a real property tax deductible under section 164(a)(1) by the renter. * * *

Problems, Notes and Question

1. *Deductible taxes.* Only those taxes described in §§ 164(a) and 164(b) and not excluded by § 164(c) are deductible under § 164. Section 275 lists some nondeductible taxes. Under some circumstances, a tax not deductible under § 164 may be deducted under some other section. A tax which is a business expense, for example, is deductible under § 162.

Until 1987, retail sales taxes were deductible under § 164. The Tax Reform Act of 1986 eliminated this deduction in order to make up for revenues lost because of other provisions of the Act. The change gives states an incentive to replace sales taxes with deductible taxes. In the long run, repeal of the sales-tax deduction may have more effect upon the form of state taxation than upon Federal revenues.

2. *Foreign income taxes.* Taxpayers can deduct foreign income taxes under § 164, but most people with foreign-source incomes will prefer to elect under § 901 to credit those taxes against their United States income tax. Why are payments of foreign income taxes treated more favorably than payments of state or local income taxes? Compare foreign real-property taxes, which are deductible but not creditable, and foreign personal-property taxes, which are not even deductible (unless they are business or investment expenses).

3. *Problems*. Which of the following taxes paid by *I*, an individual taxpayer, can be deducted? In the case of deductible taxes, indicate whether or not the deduction is above the line.

(1) Real-property taxes on *I*'s residence. *B*

(2) Real-property taxes on investment rental property owned by *I*.

(3) Real-property taxes on a laundry and dry-cleaning building owned by *I* and used only as *I*'s place of business.

(4) Sales tax on *I*'s personal automobile. NON DEDUCT.

(5) Sales tax on *I*'s business automobile. A

(6) Federal income tax. NON DEDUCT

(7) Non-resident state income tax paid on income from mineral royalties. personal deduct B

(8) City income tax. B

(9) Self-employment tax (note § 164(f)). A but only 50%

4. *References*. Kaplow, Fiscal Federalism and the Deductibility of State and Local Taxes under the Federal Income Tax, 82 Va.L.Rev. 413 (1996); Turnier, Evaluating Personal Deductions in an Income Tax—The Ideal, 66 Cornell L.Rev. 262 (1981).

I. PERSONAL EXEMPTIONS AND FILING STATUS

Section 151 generally allows taxpayers to deduct exemptions in the amount of $2000 for themselves, their dependents, and, sometimes, their spouses. The $2000 exemption amount is adjusted annually for inflation and is phased out (reduced) as the taxpayer's adjusted gross income increases beyond specified levels, depending upon his filing status;[l] § 151(d). The inflation-adjusted exemption amount for 2002 is $3000. If a taxpayer (or a dependent) dies during the year, the exemption is allowed in full, without proration to the date of death.

Although § 151(b) generally allows each taxpayer a personal-exemption deduction for himself, § 151(d)(2) denies a deduction to a person (regardless of age) for whom a dependency exemption is allowable to another. When a husband and wife file a joint return, each is a taxpayer, and each is entitled to an exemption, even if only one of them has gross income. In the unusual circumstance where only one of the spouses has gross income but they do not file a joint return, the filing spouse can claim the non-filing spouse's personal exemption; § 151(b).

Taxpayers are usually entitled to personal-exemption deductions for their dependents. A dependent is a person who is related to the taxpayer in one of the ways specified in the statute, or who (even if not a relative) lives with the taxpayer and is "a member of the taxpayer's household," and who receives over half of his support from the taxpayer; § 152(a).

l. See pp. 42–44, above.

(Note that a taxpayer's spouse can never be the taxpayer's dependent; § 152(a)(9).) The most-common dependents, of course, are the taxpayer's children (including the taxpayer's adopted and foster children and step-children) and parents; §§ 152(a) & (b)(2). "Support" includes the cost of food, shelter, clothing, medical and dental care and education; Treas. Reg. § 1.152–1(a)(2)(i). The amount of support is usually based upon the amount expended by the taxpayer, but support furnished in the form of lodging is based upon its value; id. In determining whether the taxpayer has furnished over half of a putative dependent's support, any amounts contributed by the dependent must also be taken into account in determining total support. In determining total support for the taxpay-er's child, scholarships (though not student loans) are excluded; § 152(d).

If the parents of a child are divorced, it is often difficult to deter-mine which parent furnishes over half the child's support (and which is therefore entitled to the dependency exemption). To avoid that difficulty, § 152(e) provides a special rule for the children of divorced parents. Where the child receives over half of his support from his two parents combined (and is in the custody of one or both parents for over half the year), the child is generally treated as having received over half his support from the parent who had custody for the greater portion of the year.[m] (If a parent has remarried, support received from the parent's spouse counts as support received from the parent; § 152(e)(5).) Never-theless, the custodial parent can assent to the noncustodial parent's claiming the exemption by executing a waiver, which must be attached to the noncustodial parent's tax return; § 152(e)(2). So, the statute gives the parents a choice as to which of them gets to claim the dependency exemption. The parents will usually minimize their combined taxes by assigning the dependency exemption to the parent who faces the higher tax rate. More than just the dependency exemption is at stake. The allocation of the exemption also determines which parent gets the child tax credit of § 24 and the Hope and Lifetime Learning credits of § 25A[n]. Since the divorce decree often specifies who is to receive the dependency exemption, allocation of the exemption becomes one of the many tax issues that must be negotiated in the divorce proceeding.

Suppose that three adult children contribute equal amounts toward the support of their aged parent. Each could claim the parent as a dependent, except that none of them furnished over half the parent's support. To provide relief in this situation, § 152(c) allows the three to enter into a *multiple-support agreement*, in which they can determine which of them will be treated as satisfying the support requirement.

---

m. That is, the parent having *physical* custody for a greater portion of the year; Condello v. Commissioner, 76 T.C.M. 460 (1998).

n. For some other purposes, however, allocation of the exemption is less impor-tant. For example, the child-care credit of § 21 (pp. 241–243, below) is allowed to the custodial parent even if she has relin-quished her claim to a dependency exemp-tion for the child; § 21(e)(5). And a child of divorced parents is considered to be a de-pendent of both parents for purposes of the medical-expense deduction of § 213 (pp. 200–206, above); § 213(d)(5).

Under a multiple-support agreement, the taxpayer is treated as having provided over half the support of a putative dependent if: (1) no one person furnished over half of the dependent's support; (2) over half of the support was provided by persons who would have been entitled to claim the dependency exemption but for the person's failing to satisfy the support test; (3) the taxpayer contributed over 10 percent of the support; and (4) each person contributing more than 10 percent of the support agrees not to claim the supportee as a dependent for the year; id.

Even if the taxpayer furnishes over half the support of another, a dependency exemption is usually not allowable if the supportee has gross income in excess of the exemption amount; § 151(c)(1)(A). This gross-income limit does not apply to a child of the taxpayer who is under age 19 or who is a full-time student under the age of 24. No dependency deduction is allowable for a dependent who is married and who files a joint return; § 151(c)(2).

FILING STATUS

The taxpayer's filing status determines the rates that apply to the taxpayer's income.[o] If a couple is married at the end of the year, they can either file separately or combine their income and deductions on a joint return under § 6013; §§ 1(a) & (d).[p] If one spouse has substantially higher income than the other, they can usually reduce their taxes by filing a joint return. Spouses with relatively equal incomes may be better off filing separately, depending upon what deductions and credits each is entitled to. Section 7703 prescribes rules for determining when a person is considered to be married for purposes of § 1.

Filing a joint return makes both spouses liable for the tax; 6013(d)(3). This can cause considerable hardship. If *H* and *W* file a joint return for year 1 and then divorce in year 2, either spouse can be made to pay a deficiency for year 1—even a deficiency attributable to the other spouse's earnings. One should not file jointly with an unreliable spouse if any serious possibility that the return significantly understates income exists.

Some relief for truly egregious cases is provided by § 6015(b), the so-called "innocent spouse" rule. A taxpayer who is divorced, legally separated, widowed, or living apart (for 12 months) from the person with whom a joint return was filed may elect separate liability under new § 6015(c). The statute goes into considerable detail about the timing of the election (generally, it may be made within two years of the time that the government begins trying to collect the tax), about the allocation of a deficiency when a taxpayer makes the election, and about circumstances in which the election is not valid. See also § 66, dealing with the similar

---

o. Other issues that depend upon the taxpayer's filing status include (1) whether a tax return must be filed; § 6012(a); and (2) the amount of the standard deduction; § 63(c).

p. Policy issues involving the taxation of married couples are discussed at pp. 451–455, below.

problem of the spouse in a community-property state who is regarded, for tax purposes, as "owning" half of the other spouse's earnings, even though the amount or even the existence of those earnings may have been kept secret by the spouse who earned them.

Even if a spouse fails to qualify for treatment as an innocent spouse and does not make a valid election out of joint liability, § 6015(f) provides that an individual may be relieved of tax liability, under procedures to be established by the Treasury, if it would be "inequitable to hold the individual liable for any unpaid tax or deficiency * * * ."

Single persons must usually calculate their tax under § 1(c), unless they are either surviving spouses or heads of households. A "surviving spouse" is an unmarried person whose spouse died during either of the two years immediately preceding the taxable year and who furnishes over half of the cost of a household (in which the surviving spouse lives) that constitutes the principal place of abode for a child with respect to whom the person is entitled to a dependency exemption; § 2(a). Although single, a surviving spouse gets the benefits of the joint-return rates of § 1(a).

Generally speaking, a "head of household" is an unmarried taxpayer (not a surviving spouse) who furnishes over half the cost of maintaining a household (in which the taxpayer lives) that constitutes the principal place of abode for one or more of the taxpayer's descendants or any other person for whom the taxpayer is entitled to a dependency exemption; § 2(b). Head-of-household status can also be based upon furnishing a home for the taxpayer's parent if the taxpayer is entitled to a dependency exemption for the parent; id. A head of household is taxed more lightly than a single person but not so lightly as a surviving spouse; compare §§ 1(a)-(c).

To qualify as either a surviving spouse or a head of household, the taxpayer must furnish over half the cost of maintaining the household. These costs include property taxes, mortgage interest, rent, utilities, maintenance, property insurance, and food consumed on the premises, but not education, medical treatment or vacations; Treas. Reg. § 1.44A–1(d)(3).

Problems

Problem (1). A and B, husband and wife, have one son, C (age 23), and an adopted daughter, D (age 19). C is a full-time law student, who expects to earn $10,000 doing part-time work during the year. He also receives $5,000 per year in scholarship grants. He expends both sums for his support. C is married and files a joint return with his wife. D dropped out of college after the spring term (January–May) to "find herself." D will earn approximately $10,000 this year, all of which is devoted to her support. A's father, F, is 84 years old. (His wife died many years ago.) F's only income is $6000 a year from a rental house; he incurs $4500 of expenses with respect to this house. A and B file a joint return.

(a) *A* and *B* contribute $12,000 a year toward the cost of *C*'s education. Are they entitled to a dependency exemption for *C*?

(b) *A* and *B* furnish $12,000 toward *D*'s support. Are they entitled to a dependency exemption for *D*? Is *D* entitled to a personal exemption?

(c) *A* and *B* furnish $15,000 toward *F*'s support. *F* furnishes $1500 of his own support. Are *A* and *B* entitled to a dependency exemption for *F*?

(d) Must *F* file a tax return? (Examine § 6012(a).)

Problem (2). *L* and *M* are divorced and share joint custody of their child *C*, who receives a majority of her support from *L*. *M* has physical custody of the child, except for *C*'s semi-monthly weekends with *L*. The divorce decree is silent as to which parent gets the dependency exemption for *C*. Neither *L* nor *M* has remarried.

(a) Who is entitled to the dependency exemption?

(b) What is *M*'s filing status? *L*'s?

(c) Assume that *L*'s income is considerably higher than *M*'s. What would you advise *M* to do?

Problem (3). *G* is divorced. She and her two children (ages 13 and 11) live with her partner, *H*, who furnishes over half their support and who maintains the home in which they live. How many dependency exemptions can *H* claim? What is *H*'s filing status? (Consider § 2(b)(3).)

Problem (4). *P*, *Q* and *R* contribute to the support of *S*, a single person. *P*, who contributes 40% of *S*'s support, is *S*'s adult child. *Q*, who contributes 15% of *S*'s support, is *S*'s adult grandchild. *R*, who contributes 35% of *S*'s support, is *S*'s long-time friend. *S* contributes 10% of her own support (from her savings). *S*'s gross income does not exceed the exemption amount. Who is entitled to the dependency exemption for *S*?

Problem (5). *W*'s husband, *H*, died on November 15, 2002. No executor is appointed for *H*'s estate. Can *W* file a joint return with *H* for 2002? See §§ 6013(a) & (c).

Problem (6). Same as (5), except that an executor is appointed for *H*'s estate on January 10, 2003.

Problem (7). Same as (5), except that an executor is appointed on May 10, 2003.

Problem (8). After her husband's death, *W*, (in Problem (5)) provided all the support for her child, *C*, who was 12 years old at *H*'s death. Which rate schedule should *W* use in computing:

(a) Her 2002 tax liability?

(b) Her 2004 tax liability?

J. ALIMONY AND RELATED ISSUES

Until 1942, alimony was not income to the spouse who received it and was not deductible by the payor; Gould v. Gould, 245 U.S. 151

(1917). Under the high tax rates needed to finance World War II this situation would have been intolerable, for a taxpayer's combined alimony and tax bills could have exceeded his income. Therefore, Congress enacted the predecessors of § 71, which makes "alimony or separate maintenance payments" taxable to the recipient, and § 215, which gives the payor a deduction for payments taxable to the recipient under § 71. Section 62(a)(10) makes alimony an "above-the-line" deduction. In 1984 Congress revised the tax treatment of alimony and child-support payments. The Code now allows divorcing spouses great flexibility in determining the tax consequences of payments in connection with divorce. As is typically the case with modern tax legislation, § 71 is highly technical, and errors in drafting a divorce settlement agreement can have costly tax consequences.[q]

If divorce-related payments to a spouse or former spouse are "alimony or separate maintenance" as defined in § 71, the recipient includes the payments in income and the payor deducts them. If the payments are not alimony, the recipient has no income and the payor no deduction.

A payment is alimony only if it meets all of the conditions of § 71(b) and is not "child support" within the meaning of § 71(c). (A further requirement, applicable to couples who are not divorced at the end of the taxable year, is that the spouses not file a joint return; § 71(e).) The requirements for "alimony" treatment under § 71 are as follows:

(1) The payment must be in cash (§ 71(b)(1)). Note that § 71(b)(1) does not require that the recipient *receive* cash: a cash payment "to a third party for the benefit of the payee spouse" can be alimony; H.R.Rep. No. 98–432, 98th Cong., 2d Sess. 1496 (1984).

(2) The payment must be received under a "divorce or separation instrument"; § 71(b)(1)(A). "Divorce or separation instrument[s]" include decrees, written separation agreements, and written instruments "incident to" decrees; § 71(b)(2).

(3) The "divorce or separation instrument" must not "designate" the payment as not includable in income under § 71 and not deductible under § 215; § 71(b)(1)(B).

(4) If the spouses are divorced or legally separated, they must not be members of the same household when the payment is made; § 71(b)(1)(C).

(5) The liability for payments must cease upon the death of the recipient; § 71(b)(1)(D). This requirement is intended to distinguish alimony from payments made to purchase property from the spouse receiving the payment. Under pre–1985 law, there was a great deal of litigation about the purpose for which particular payments were made. In the typical case, a husband would claim that payments he made were alimony, and therefore deductible, and the wife would insist that the

q. E.g., Goldman v. Commissioner, 112 T.C. 317 (1999), affirmed sub nom. Schutter v. Commissioner, 242 F.3d 390 (10th Cir. 2000) (payments of $20,000 monthly held not deductible because of an apparent drafting error in the agreement).

payments were for her share of community property or for some other asset, and therefore not income to her except to the extent, if any, that they exceeded the property's basis. Whether payments in lieu of a spouse's interest in property under an "equitable distribution" statute could be alimony was unclear. Under present law, transfers of property between spouses (and former spouses) are tax free. (See § 1041(b), discussed pp. 543–545.) The thought behind the termination-at-death rule seems to be that no one would agree to sell property for payments terminating at death; the rule is therefore a crude way of distinguishing payments "for property" (which should not be alimony) from other payments. Whether this assumption makes sense is doubtful; it is not unheard of for people to transfer property in exchange for lifetime annuities.

(6) The payments must not be "fixed" as child support by the decree or agreement; § 71(c). A payment is "fixed" for the support of the payor's children if the instrument calls it child support or if the payment is eliminated upon the happening of a "contingency specified in the instrument [and] relating to a child."

Current law does not require that payments be spread out over time in order to be alimony: a single payment can satisfy the definition. However, if payments decline substantially over the first three "post-separation years," § 71(f) requires "recomputations." A "recomputation" includes "excess alimony payments" in the payor's income for the third post-separation year, and gives the recipient a deduction for "excess alimony payments." For example, suppose that H pays W $100,000 alimony during the year in which H and W are divorced. H deducts this amount and W includes it in income. If H makes no payments in either of the next two years, § 71(f) treats H as having $85,000 income and gives W an $85,000 deduction in year three. Section 71(f)(5) describes two situations in which reduced alimony payments will not trigger recomputations.

Problems

Problem (1). R and E are divorced. The divorce decree requires R to pay E $40,000 a year for ten years "as alimony and child support." Upon the death or remarriage of E, the payments decrease by $10,000 a year. If the only child of R and E dies before all payments have been made, the payments decrease by $30,000 a year. How much of each year's payment is income to E and deductible by R?

Problem (2). Same as problem (1), except that the decree provides that "none of the amount is to be treated as alimony for Federal tax purposes."

Problem (3). R and E are divorced. An agreement incident to the decree requires R to pay E alimony of $50,000 a year for ten years, with payments to cease upon E's death. If E dies within ten years of the divorce, R is obliged to pay $40,000 a year in "child support" for the remainder of the ten-year period. These "child support" payments will go to a trust, which will support the couple's minor children. How much is taxable to *E*?

Problem (4). At the time of divorce, *R* agrees to pay *E* alimony of $50,000 a year for seven years, with payments to cease upon *E*'s death. In the first year, *R* makes the full $50,000 payment, in the second year he pays only $20,000, and in the third year and subsequent years he pays nothing. What are the income-tax consequences of these events to *R* and *E*? See § 71(f).

BRODERSEN v. COMMISSIONER

United States Tax Court, 1971.
57 T.C. 412.

STERRETT, JUDGE: The respondent determined a deficiency in the Federal income tax of the petitioners of $216.45 for the taxable year ended December 31, 1966.

The only issue for decision is whether a premium paid by petitioner for insurance on his life, purchased pursuant to a divorce decree and naming his former wife as owner-beneficiary, is deductible under § 215.

[The Tax Court's findings of fact are omitted.]

OPINION

Petitioner and Barbara were divorced on August 6, 1965. The judgement approved and adopted a property settlement denoted as a stipulation, which had been entered into by the parties in lieu of alimony. The stipulation contained a provision requiring petitioner to transfer to Barbara a $125,000 decreasing-term insurance policy, while at the same time paying the annual premiums. The sole question for our determination is whether the $555 premium paid in 1966 is deductible by petitioner under § 215 * * *.

It is evident from the [language of § 215] that petitioner's right to deduct the premium payment hinges upon the includability of such payment in Barbara's income within the purview of section 71. * * * The question of deductibility in the instant case then turns on whether Barbara constructively received income by reason of the payment by the petitioner of the insurance premium.

Our research into the question of the appropriate tax treatment to be accorded a payment, pursuant to a property settlement, by a former husband of insurance premiums on his life reveals two distinct strains of cases reaching opposing results due to two separate factual conclusions deemed controlling. First, there are the cases which find governing the fact that the policy was acquired for security purposes. For example it has been said: "It is well established that premiums paid by a former husband on a policy of insurance which merely provides security for continued alimony or support payments to his divorced wife in the event of his death are not includible in the gross income of the wife as additional alimony." [Citations omitted.]

The second strain finds dispositive the fact that the wife is the owner and beneficiary of the policy: "It is difficult to see on what theory it could be successfully contended that the payments of insurance premiums * * * did not constitute [the wife's] income * * *. The policies in question were her property and all payments made were at her instigation for her account, and designed to redound to her benefit." Anita Quinby Stewart, 9 T.C. 195, 198 (1947). [Further citations omitted.]

Respondent naturally urges the applicability of the first line of cases, contending that the facts here present require a conclusion that the policy was acquired solely to secure the amounts due under the settlement stipulation between petitioner and Barbara. Petitioner, on the other hand and equally naturally, emphasizes the fact that Barbara was the owner of the policy and contends accordingly that the premium payments must have redounded to her benefit, making said payments her income and deductible to him under the second line of cases.

At the outset we note our agreement with respondent that the policy in issue was purchased solely for security purposes. In support of this conclusion we emphasize the fact that a decreasing-term policy is involved here and that the amount payable upon death under the policy is reduced as the alimony obligation is fulfilled. Thus, in order to obtain any personal benefit Barbara would not only have to outlive petitioner but petitioner would have to die within a 12–year period. It is clear then that the policy carried with it no independent financial advantage to Barbara. It added nothing directly to her resources but rather merely assured her of the receipt of the payments already due from her former husband under their stipulation of settlement.

Our agreement with the respondent on this point means that the factual determinations underlying the aforenoted two strains of cases coexist in this controversy, apparently for the first time. Faced with the Rubicon we opt for the applicability of the first line of cases and hold that the theory underlying the second line is inapposite where pure term insurance is involved.

The cases cited by petitioner involved whole life policies and we find the difference between such policies and term life policies highly significant. As owner of a whole life policy the wife is entitled to surrender it for its cash value, borrow on it, etc., thereby obtaining an additional economic benefit, over and above any agreed-upon alimony payments. With a term policy however, there is only a contingent right to obtain a fixed amount of cash at the death of the insured which at the best most affords the wife peace of mind in knowing her payments are secured. Such peace of mind does not provide an additional economic benefit. As the Court of Appeals for the Seventh Circuit in Seligmann v. Commissioner, 207 F.2d 489, 494 (C.A.7, 1953), reversing a Memorandum Opinion of this Court, stated:

we are unable to discern how it can be thought that petitioner realized a taxable economic gain during the years in question. Certainly, as noted, she received no cash, either actually or constructively, and it would appear equally certain that she received no property capable of measurement or ascertainment. The most that can be said is that the right which she acquired at the time the separation agreement was executed was preserved to her from year to year, including those here involved, by the husband's payment of the premiums on his life insurance policies which he was obligated to make. After the payments were made she had no different or greater right than she had before. * * * *Mere peace of mind or the satisfaction which stems from knowledge that protection may be of benefit in the future does not constitute taxable economic gain.* [Emphasis supplied.]

In addition, we note again that as a decreasing-term policy the amount payable upon death is reduced as the alimony obligation is fulfilled.

* * *

Petitioner directs our attention to the Second Circuit's opinion in Stevens v. Commissioner, 439 F.2d 69 (C.A.2, 1971), reversing a Memorandum Opinion of this Court, wherein the Court of Appeals held that the premiums paid on a whole life insurance policy acquired as security for the payment of alimony owned by the wife were taxable to the wife. Particular attention is placed on that portion of the opinion where the court said:

> To deny constructive receipt of benefit whenever the wife's interest in the proceeds is contingent on her surviving her former spouse is to presume that an insurance policy's only value to the beneficiary lies in receipt of the face amount upon death of the insured. If this analysis were correct, premiums paid on a term insurance policy could never qualify as alimony payments because the protection of term insurance to an irrevocable beneficiary extends only for a specified period rather than over the life of the insured. See Note, Alimony Taxation of Indirect Benefits: A Critique and a Proposal, 66 Col. L. Rev. 1118, 1132–35 (1966). Rather the contingencies which will deny deductibility are those which might operate to thwart the wife's receipt of the economic benefit the premium payments conferred, that is, the protection, during a limited term, of the wife's right to receive alimony over the full alimony period. [439 F.2d at 72–73. Footnote omitted.]

This language petitioner maintains is dispositive of the question presented in the instant case. We cannot agree. The present case is distinguishable on its facts. In *Stevens,* the insurance policy acquired on behalf of the wife was a whole life policy, which as previously noted permitted her to receive certain additional benefits. Therefore, even though the policy was acquired as security, the wife, in substance, received additional alimony. Such additional benefits were not present in the instant case. Further, the policy acquired in the *Stevens* case was in the possession of the wife which afforded her the opportunity of discovering the available benefits. In the present case the petitioner was in possession of the policy and Barbara was unfamiliar with the provisions contained therein.

Finally, we note that the reference to term insurance is clearly dictum and we respectfully decline to follow it for reasons heretofore set forth. * * *

Reviewed by the Court.

Decision will be entered for the respondent.

TANNENWALD, J., dissenting: There is no escape from the fact that what the petitioner's wife bargained for was a *secured* obligation to make the payments which qualify under the statute. That a secured obligation has a value beyond that of an unsecured obligation similarly is beyond question. That increased value, in a very real sense, provided an indefeasible economic benefit to petitioner's wife and the amount of the premium paid is an appropriate measure of that value. See Stevens v. Commissioner, 439 F.2d 69 (C.A.2, 1971), reversing a Memorandum Opinion of this Court. The fact that petitioner's wife would not receive additional money beyond the amount of the direct payments which petitioner was obligated to pay is beside the point. Given the bargaining stance of the parties, it is clear that the insurance was an integral part of the provision made for the wife's support. Consequently, in my opinion, the premiums should be treated as part and parcel of petitioner's obligation arising out of the marital relationship within the meaning of sections 71 and 215. * * * See Raum, J., dissenting, in Florence H. Griffith, 35 T.C. 882, 894 (1961).

In the instant case, the petitioner's wife or her estate was the sole owner of the totality of rights and benefits provided by the policy. Neither her death nor her remarriage operated to defeat that ownership.

* * *

I would hold for petitioner.

RAUM, J., agrees with this dissent.

Notes

1. *Indirect alimony—insurance premiums.* Alimony does not cease to be alimony if the recipient uses some of the payments to carry insurance on the payor's life, but *Brodersen* and several other cases have held that a husband's payments of premiums on term insurance required by a decree or agreement were not "alimony" under § 71 because the wife gets "no benefit" from the payments unless the husband dies. In some of the cases, both the husband and the wife had some interest in the policy. For example, a couple might agree that the wife will get the policy proceeds if the husband dies within ten years of the divorce, but that all rights to the policy will revert to the husband if he survives. In

cases like that, premium payments benefit both spouses, and denying a deduction for the full amount of the payments makes sense. The Second Circuit, recognizing that insurance protection constitutes an economic benefit even to a beneficiary who never actually receives cash, held the cost of providing such protection deductible as alimony in Stevens v. Commissioner, 439 F.2d 69 (2d Cir.1971).

Temp.Treas.Reg. § 1.71–1T(a)(Q & A 6) may concede the issue on which the Commissioner prevailed in *Brodersen*. In response to a question whether alimony payments may be made in a form other than cash, A6 says, in part, "Premiums paid * * * for term or whole life insurance on the payor's life * * * will qualify as payments on behalf of the payee spouse to the extent that the payee spouse is the owner of the policy." Query whether the absence of a reference to the "security" wrinkle in *Brodersen* means that the government has now changed its mind, or whether the silence on this point means only that the drafter of the regulation was unaware of the wrinkle. One would ordinarily expect that a document abandoning a doctrine would mention that doctrine.

2. *Indirect alimony—payments related to housing.* Divorce decrees often provide that one spouse can occupy the family home and that the other spouse is to make the mortgage payments. If *H* makes mortgage payments on a house *owned* by *W*, the payments can be alimony (assuming that all of the requirements of § 71 have been met). Often, though, both spouses will have an ownership interest in the house, and both may be liable on the mortgage. This complicates things.

The Service held in Rev.Rul. 67–420, 1967–2 C.B. 63, that a husband's mortgage payments on a house held by him and his ex-wife as tenants by the entirety were alimony to the extent that they relieved the wife of personal liability for half of each payment. The wife lived in the house, but that was not controlling. Temp.Treas.Reg. § 1.71–1T(a)(Q & A 6) confirms that payment of the ex-wife's mortgage can be a "cash payment," without going into the details of ownership. If the spouse who does not make the payments has no personal liability, the Service takes the position that the payments cannot be alimony, even though they enable that spouse to continue living in the house. As in some of the cases involving insurance, mortgage payments made by one spouse when the other spouse lives in the house can benefit both parties: the payor builds up an equity in the house and the other spouse gets a place to live. The difficulties of figuring out how much a payment by one spouse benefitted the other may justify the holding of Rev.Rul. 67–420, which ignores the benefit of occupying the house and looks only to whether the "recipient" is relieved of personal liability to make a payment. See Judge Simpson's concurring opinion in Taylor v. Commissioner, 45 T.C. 120, 126 (1965) (Acq. in result).

Payments of utility bills on a house owned by the payor and occupied by the recipient—a cost of "current enjoyment" of the property—can be alimony; Rev.Rul. 62–39, 1962–1 C.B. 17.

3. *References.* Moran, Welcome to the Funhouse: The Incredible Maze of Modern Divorce Taxation, 26 Harv.J. on Leg. 117 (1989); Asimow, Alimony and Marital Property Divisions under the 1986 Act, 65 Taxes 352 (1987); Berman, The Alimony Deduction: Time to Slaughter the Sacred Cow, 5 Am.J. Tax Pol'y 49 (1986); Note, Alimony Taxation of Indirect Benefits: A Critique and a Proposal, 66 Colum.L.Rev. 1118 (1966).

TAX PLANNING FOR DIVORCE AND SEPARATION: RATE SCHEDULES AND DEPENDENCY EXEMPTIONS

A taxpayer who is divorced or legally separated[r] at the end of the taxable year pays taxes at the rates for single taxpayers (§ 1(c)) or, if the requirements of § 2(b) are met, at the lower rates for "heads of households" (§ 1(b)). If a couple is not divorced or *legally* separated at the end of the year, and if they are separated and there is: (1) a written separation agreement, or (2) a decree for support, the couple has a choice of tax rates. They can either file a joint return, paying taxes at the rates of § 1(a), or they can file separate returns, paying taxes at the rates of § 1(d). (For the one case in which a married taxpayer can file as a single taxpayer, see § 7703.) If separate returns are filed, alimony is taxed to the recipient and deducted by the payor under §§ 71 and 215; if a joint return is filed, alimony is ignored; see § 71(e).

The exemption for dependent children of divorced or separated parents is normally claimed by the parent who has custody for a greater portion of the taxable year than the other parent; § 152(e)(1). However, the custodial parent can assign the deduction to the non-custodial parent by executing a written declaration to be filed with the non-custodial parent's return; § 152(e)(2). If no one person provides more than half of a child's support, and if the other requirements of § 152(c) are satisfied, the dependency exemption can be assigned by a "multiple support agreement" to any person who provides more than 10 percent of the child's support.

For purposes of deducting a child's medical expenses, a child of divorced parents can be treated as a dependent of both parents; § 213(d)(5). In determining the credit for household and dependent care services (§ 21), a child can be a "qualifying individual" with respect to the custodial parent even if that parent assigns the dependency exemption to the non-custodial parent; § 21(e)(5).

K. PERSONAL TAX CREDITS

1. THE CREDIT FOR HOUSEHOLD AND DEPENDENT CARE SERVICES

An apparently insoluble problem of an income tax which allows deductions for "business" expenses but not for "personal" costs is how

r. I.e., separated under a "decree of divorce or of separate maintenance"; § 7703(a)(2).

the tax system should take account of the costs of caring for the taxpayer's children or other dependents while the taxpayer works. Because these costs are typically[s] incurred to enable the taxpayer to work, they are "business expenses" in the sense of being caused (in a "but for" sense) by the taxpayer's work; because the costs arise only for taxpayers who have children (or other dependents) they are also caused by the taxpayer's having children, which is about as "personal" as an activity can be.

Under the 1939 Code, which did not refer specifically to child-care costs, the courts denied a deduction on the ground that the costs were "personal"; see Smith v. Commissioner, p. 323, below. From 1954 to 1976, § 214 allowed a deduction for some of the costs of caring for certain dependents if the costs were incurred "to enable the taxpayer to be gainfully employed." Only low- and middle-income taxpayers could qualify for the deduction. In 1976, Congress replaced the deduction with a limited tax credit, which is now allowed by § 21. Beginning in 2003, the amount of the credit for household and dependent care is 35 percent of "employment-related expenses," as defined in § 21(b)(2), if the taxpayer's adjusted gross income is $15,000 or less. As AGI rises, the credit percentage declines until it reaches 20 percent for taxpayers with AGI in excess of $43,000; § 21(a)(2). The maximum amount of employment-related expenses which can be taken into account in computing the credit is $3000 if the taxpayer has one "qualifying individual" and $6000 if there are two or more; § 21(c). Thus, the maximum credit allowed by § 21 is $2100 (for a taxpayer with two or more "qualifying individuals" and AGI of $15,000 or less).

Section 21(d) limits the amount of employment-related expenses that qualify for the credit to the taxpayer's earned income for the year; in the case of a married taxpayer, the limit is whichever spouse's income is lower. Therefore, a couple with "personal" reasons for keeping their child in nursery school cannot take a credit based on $2400 in tuition if one spouse earns only $100 a year. However, § 21(d) treats many disabled spouses and spouses who are full-time students as having earned incomes of $200 or $400 a month.

Although no deduction can be taken for the costs of caring for dependents, the practical effect of a deduction for up to $5000 in child-

s. But what if the taxpayer's main reason for working is to earn money to provide care for a dependent? In principle, a distinction might be drawn between parents who would have placed their children in day care even if the parents did not work and parents whose children are in day care only (primarily?) to enable the parents to work. In practice, this kind of distinction could not be easily applied. See Brown v. Commissioner, 73 T.C. 156 (1979), which allowed a credit under an earlier version of § 21 for the costs of sending the taxpayer's child to a private school. The taxpayer preferred private school to public school for her child, but the court allowed a credit for part of the private-school costs because "one of" the taxpayer's reasons for sending the child to a boarding school "was to be able to take a job." Judge Tannenwald, dissenting, would have disallowed the credit on the ground that the taxpayer worked so that she could afford the private school.

care expenses can be obtained for employees if the employer establishes a "cafeteria plan" under § 125 and if one of the benefits available under the plan is work-related child care. For example, an employee who pays for day care can agree with her employer to a $5000 salary reduction each year in exchange for $5000 in reimbursements for the costs of day care. The reimbursement is excludable from the employee's income under § 129. Amounts excluded from an employee's income under § 129 cannot be used to compute the § 21 credit; § 129(e)(7). The administrative costs of establishing and maintaining cafeteria plans are so high that most of the benefits of § 129 will go to large organizations and their employees.

Problems, Notes and Question

1. *Problems.*

(1) *P*, a single parent, has two children, ages three and seven. *P*, who works full time, pays a neighbor $2000 a year to take care of the three-year-old and pays $1500 a year to send the seven-year-old to an after-school program run by a local church. The church-run school complies with all state and local laws and regulations for day-care programs; the neighbor, whose house has no smoke detectors, does not. Compute *P*'s credit under § 21 if:

> (a) *P*'s AGI is $15,000;

> (b) *P*'s AGI is $40,000.

(2) *Q* and *R*, who have two young children, support *Q*'s seventy-year-old mother, for whom they claim a personal exemption under § 151(c). Both *Q* and *R* work full time; *Q*'s mother takes care of the children while *Q* and *R* work. If *Q* and *R* pay *Q*'s mother for doing this, can they take the credit under § 21? See § 21(e)(6).

(3) *S* is a full-time law student; her husband, *T*, works full time. Are *S* and *T* entitled to a credit under § 21 for the costs of nursery school for their four-year-old twins? Work through § 21(d). What if both *S* and *T* are full-time students?

(4) *H* works full time and earns $35,000 a year; *W*, a lawyer, works for four hours a day and earns $30,000 a year. *W* also spends five hours every day doing pro bono work, for which she receives no pay. *H* and *W* pay a day-care center $5000 a year to care for their three-year-old child during the nine hours of each working day when neither *H* nor *W* is at home. Compute the couple's credit under § 21.

2. *Summer camp and § 21.* Can the cost of sending children to summer camp while their parents work qualify as employment-related expenses under § 21? In Zoltan v. Commissioner, 79 T.C. 490 (1982) (Acq.), the Tax Court allowed the credit, finding that the taxpayer's "principal purpose in sending her child away to camp was to provide for his well-being and protection" and noting that the summer camp was

"virtually as inexpensive as" alternative forms of care. Section 21(b)(2)(A) (last sentence), which was enacted in 1987, overrules *Zoltan*.

2. THE EARNED–INCOME CREDIT

The *earned-income credit* of § 32 differs from most other credits in that it is "refundable"—i.e., the amount by which the credit exceeds the taxpayer's tax liability before applying the credit is paid to the taxpayer. Thus, if tax liability would be $1500 without the credit, and if the amount of the credit is $1700, the taxpayer owes no tax and receives a $200 payment from the government.

The earned-income credit is a percentage of the taxpayer's earned income. The percentage varies according to the number of "qualifying children" in the taxpayer's household: 7.65 percent if there is no qualifying child; 34 percent if there is one; 40 percent if there are two or more. (Taxpayers with no qualifying child must meet other special requirements as well, such as being at least 25 years old and not more than 65.) Because the credit is intended to supplement the incomes of low-income working people, it is phased out as the taxpayer's income increases.

Few observers object to the earned-income credit in principle. It is intended to make work more attractive to low-income taxpayers, especially to low-income taxpayers who support minor children. (These taxpayers, though not subject to heavy income taxation, have to pay FICA taxes, which contain no exemptions for the poor; part of the idea behind the earned-income credit was to make up for this feature of payroll taxes.) In practice, though, the credit has been troublesome because it is complex, because it creates unfortunate incentives, and because it has been vulnerable to fraud.

The earned-income credit is complex, even for a tax provision. As a result, many of the low-income workers who benefit from the credit must obtain professional help with their returns. Furthermore, many of those eligible for the credit may not know of its existence. Because the credit is refundable, many of those who can claim it are people whose incomes are so low that they owe no tax, and who may have no reason to file a return other than to claim the credit.

While the credit does encourage some low-income persons to work, not all of the incentives it creates are benign. The phaseouts, which kick in as the taxpayer's earned income (or modified AGI) rises, create very high effective marginal rates. As a result, some part-time workers who receive an earned income credit will pocket little more by working full time, as their higher pretax earnings will be largely offset by the loss of some or all of the credit. And the credit typically provides much higher total benefits to two unmarried low-income workers, each supporting a child, than to a married couple with the same total income. (This is an example of a "marriage penalty"; for more on marriage penalties see p. 452.) This feature, together with other marriage penalties on low-income taxpayers, creates an incentive for low-income single parents not to marry. In 2001, the phaseout ranges for married taxpayers were modified to reduce the marriage penalty. The credit does not encourage savings: under § 32(i), the credit is not available to those whose "disqualified income"—essentially, income from investments—exceeds $2200 (adjusted for inflation after 1995).

The earned-income credit has been an invitation to tax fraud. Were it not for the credit, filing fraudulent returns for low-income taxpayers would be a low-stakes venture, as one's refund would not normally exceed the amount withheld. But because the credit is refundable, the refund potential is limited only by the size of the credit. Today, a taxpayer who wrongly claims the credit because of recklessness or intentional disregard of rules and regulations cannot claim the credit again for two years. Those who fraudulently claim the credit can get no further credit for ten years. Furthermore, a taxpayer who has been denied the credit for the two-year or ten-year period cannot claim it again, even after the period expires, until the Service has received evidence that the taxpayer qualifies for the credit and "certifies" the taxpayer's eligibility.

Notes

1. *Other personal tax credits.* Some low-income taxpayers who are at least 65 years old or who are retired because of permanent and total disability can take a nonrefundable *credit for the elderly and the permanently and totally disabled* under § 22. The credit is 15 percent of the taxpayer's "§ 22 amount," which is $5000 for a single taxpayer and $7500 for a married couple filing jointly if both spouses qualify for the credit because of age or disability. The "§ 22 amount" is reduced by non-taxable pensions, annuities, and disability benefits, so that taxpayers who receive substantial Social Security benefits cannot take the credit. Like the earned-income credit, the credit for the elderly and the permanently and totally disabled is phased out as income increases. The maximum amount of the credit is $750 for single taxpayers and $1125 for a married couple filing jointly if both spouses qualify for the credit.

A nonrefundable credit for adoption expenses incurred by low- and middle-income individuals was enacted in 1996 and revised in 1997 and 2001. Generally speaking, the credit is allowed for "qualified adoption expenses" up to $10,000 for an adopted child; § 23. The credit limit is gradually reduced for taxpayers whose adjusted gross incomes (with modifications) exceed $150,000; it reaches zero for AGI of $190,000. If a taxpayer's employer pays qualified adoption expenses of the taxpayer, the taxpayer can exclude the payments from gross income, subject to the same rules (i.e., phaseouts) as the taxpayer's AGI increases; § 137. For taxpayers who adopt a child with "special needs," the amount of the adoption credit (before the phaseout) is $10,000, even if the taxpayer's actual adoption expenses are less than that amount. Beginning in 2003, both the maximum dollar amount of the credit and the phaseout threshold will be adjusted for inflation.

If a state elects not to issue an amount of "qualified mortgage bonds" which it could issue under § 103, residents of that state can qualify for the *home mortgage interest credit* of § 25.

In the past, tax credits have been allowed for contributions to political candidates and for the costs of home insulation and other energy-saving services and products. In 1976, the House of Representatives passed a bill which would have allowed a tax credit for the purchase of garden tools; this provision did not become law. In the late 1990s, there was a time when the administration was proposing new tax credits at a rate of one proposal a week.

2. *References.* Alstott, The Earned Income Tax Credit and the Limitations of Tax–Based Welfare Reform, 108 Harv.L.Rev. 533 (1995); Yin & Forman, Redesigning the Earned Income Tax Credit Program to Provide More Effective Assistance for the Working Poor, 59 Tax Notes 951 (1993).

Chapter Four

BUSINESS AND INVESTMENT EXPENSES

A. DEPRECIATION AND RELATED MATTERS

Some costs of earning income are deducted when paid or accrued under § 162 (if the taxpayer is engaged in a "trade or business") or under § 212 (if the taxpayer is engaged in an income-producing activity, such as investing in securities, which is not a trade or business). But some business or investment costs, called "capital expenditures," are not deducted immediately; instead, they are included in the basis of an asset (i.e. "capitalized") and are normally recovered either through depreciation or by reducing gain (or increasing loss) when the taxpayer disposes of the asset. As a rough guide, you can think of "capital expenditures" as the costs of acquiring or improving assets expected to last substantially beyond the end of the taxable year in which the costs were incurred. See § 263 and the materials at pp. 269–293, below.

Some capital expenditures cannot be recovered through depreciation. For example, the cost of land purchased for a business use or of corporate stock, held as an investment, must be capitalized, but because the land or stock is not expected to suffer a reasonably predictable decline in value between purchase and disposition, land and stock are not depreciable. The costs of such personal assets as the taxpayer's house are capitalized in the sense of becoming the property's cost basis under § 1012, but because the assets are not used in a trade or business or held for the production of income, § 167(a) does not allow a depreciation deduction (compare § 262).

1. DEPRECIATION, OR COST RECOVERY

Although a taxpayer must usually capitalize (rather than immediately deduct) the cost of business or investment assets, many of those assets will eventually be "used up" in producing income. Consider, for example, a taxpayer who purchases a truck for use in a business. The entire cost of the truck cannot be deducted in the year of purchase because the truck will be useful in producing income over several years. The outlay represents in part a cost of producing income in the year of purchase and in part a cost of producing income in those future years in which the truck is used. But eventually the truck will wear out and will no longer be useful in generating income. If the taxpayer is to be taxed on only net income, the taxpayer must eventually be allowed to deduct the cost of the truck. Although Congress might have postponed any deduction for the cost of an asset until the asset was retired from service (or disposed of), that approach would result in taxing the taxpayer on more than net income in the years before the asset was retired. In an ideal world, the taxpayer might deduct in each year the amount by which the truck declined in value during the year. But the same practical considerations that prevent our taxing unrealized gains prevent our allowing deductions for the decline in an asset's value during the year. Congress has instead specified that the cost of an asset be deducted through *depreciation*; see § 167(a).

Before turning to the refinements of the present depreciation regime (the "Modified Accelerated Cost Recovery System," or "MACRS," for short), we consider the traditional approach to computing depreciation. In principle, depreciation refers to the systematic allocation of an asset's cost over its useful life. (Although depreciation has traditionally been based on the asset's useful life, we shall see below that Congress today allows depreciation over an arbitrary "recovery period" that may be shorter than the asset's productive life.) The useful life is the period over which the asset may reasonably be expected to be useful to the taxpayer in his business or investment activity; Treas.Reg. § 1.167(a)–1(b).

Under the *straight-line* method of depreciation, the cost (or other basis) of the asset (less its estimated salvage value) is deductible in equal annual amounts over its useful life; Treas.Reg. § 1.167(b)–1(a). For example, suppose that on January 1, year 1, the taxpayer purchased for $10,000 a business asset with an estimated useful life of five years and no salvage value. Under the straight-line method, the taxpayer can deduct depreciation of $2000 ($10,000/5) for each of the five years.

Under general principles, any salvage value is subtracted from the depreciable basis in computing depreciation under the straight-line method. (Salvage value refers to the estimated amount realizable upon the sale of the asset at the end of its useful life in the hands of the taxpayer; Treas.Reg. § 1.167(a)–1(c)(1).) For example, suppose that in the preceding example the asset was estimated to have a salvage value of $2000 at the end of its five-year useful life. The taxpayer's annual depreciation deduction under the straight-line method would be $1600 ($8000/5).

Another common method for computing depreciation is the *declining-balance method*. To illustrate, assume that the taxpayer in the preceding example uses the 200–percent (or "double") declining-balance method. Under this method, the taxpayer first determines the straight-line percentage rate for the asset. Under the straight-line method, the taxpayer could deduct 20 percent (⅕) of the cost of the asset in each year. This rate is multiplied by 200 percent to determine the 200–percent declining-balance rate, which in this case is 40 percent (200% × 20%). The depreciation deduction for each year is determined by multiplying the adjusted basis of the asset at the beginning of that year by this rate. Thus, the deduction for year 1 would be $4000 (40% of $10,000). At the beginning of year 2, the adjusted basis would be $6000 ($10,000 cost less $4000 depreciation for year 1), and the depreciation deduction for year 2 would be $2400 (40% of $6000). The deduction for year 3 would be $1440 (40% of $3600), etc. See Treas.Reg. §§ 1.167(b)–2(a) & (b), ex. (1). Under the declining-balance method, the depreciable basis is not reduced by the asset's salvage value before applying the applicable percentage; instead, the depreciation deduction is disallowed to the extent that it would result in reducing the adjusted basis below the salvage value; Treas.Reg. § 1.167(b)–2(a).

Under the 150–percent declining-balance method, the percentage rate is 150 percent of the straight-line rate. Thus, in the preceding example (where the straight-line rate was 20 percent), the 150–percent declining-balance rate is 30 percent (150% × 20%), and the depreciation deduction is $3000 (30% of $10,000) for year 1, $2100 (30% of $7000) for year 2, etc.

The following chart summarizes the timing of depreciation deductions under each of these methods for an asset with a $10,000 cost, five-year life, and no salvage value.

Year	Straight–Line	200% D.B.	150% D.B.
1	$ 2000	$ 4000	$ 3000
2	2000	2400	2100
3	2000	1440	1470
4	2000	864	1029
5	2000	1296	2401
Total	$10,000	$10,000	$10,000

In this example, the remaining cost of the asset has been deducted in the last year of the asset's life under the declining-balance methods. In practice, users of a declining-balance method usually shift to the straight-line method for the year in which the straight-line method would produce a larger deduction. Thus, in this example, the user of the 200–percent declining-balance method would probably shift to the straight-line method at the beginning of year 4 and recover the remaining $2160 of basis ratably over the remaining two years of the asset's life. This approach would result in depreciation of $1080 ($2160/2) for each of years 4 and 5. The user of the 150–percent declining-balance method would switch to straight-line at the beginning of year 3 and deduct $1633.33 ($4900/3) for each of years 3, 4, and 5. The following chart shows the effect of this switch from declining-balance to straight-line depreciation.

Year	Straight–Line	200% D.B.	150% D.B.
1	$ 2000	$ 4000	$ 3000
2	2000	2400	2100
3	2000	1440	1633
4	2000	1080	1633
5	2000	1080	1634
Total	$10,000	$10,000	$10,000

These examples assume that the taxpayer placed the property in service on the first day of the taxable year. If the property was placed in service after the first day of the year, general depreciation principles require that the deduction for the first and last years of the asset's life be prorated to reflect the number of days during those years that the asset was in service; Treas.Reg. § 1.167(a)–10(b). Rather than requiring (or permitting) the taxpayer to take account of the exact day on which an asset was placed in service, the Code today requires the use of a "convention" under which assets are (conclusively) presumed to have been placed in service at a certain point (or points) during the year.

Notice that the declining-balance method produces deductions in excess of those allowable under the straight-line method in the early years of the asset's life. For this reason, the declining-balance method is sometimes referred to as an "accelerated" method of depreciation. But since the total of the taxpayer's depreciation deductions with respect to the property cannot exceed the property's basis, the straight-line method generally produces larger deductions in the later years of the asset's life. Because of the time-value of money, taxpayers will generally prefer to deduct depreciation (and thus reduce taxes) sooner rather than later and will therefore usually prefer to use an accelerated method of depreciation whenever possible.

THE MODIFIED ACCELERATED COST RECOVERY SYSTEM

Under current law, depreciation schedules for most tangible assets held for investment or used in a trade or business are specified by § 168. That section treats the salvage value of all property as being zero, so that the entire basis of the property can be deducted if the property is held for the "recovery period."

In order to compute depreciation deductions, one needs to know the property's *recovery period*, the *method* of depreciation to be used, and the *convention* for determining when the property is treated as having been placed in service. See § 168(a).

Recovery periods

The first step in applying § 168 is to determine the property's "applicable recovery period" (§ 168(c)). These periods range from three years (for some racehorses, for example) to thirty-nine years (for nonresidential real property). As a general rule, an asset's recovery period depends upon the property's "class life" under the now-obsolete "Accelerated Depreciation Range" or "ADR" system. See § 168(e)(1), which translates ADR class lives into recovery periods. The Service establishes class lives by issuing revenue procedures: the most recent list of class lives can be found in Rev.Proc. 87–56, 1987–2 C.B. 674. The following excerpt from Rev.Proc. 87–56 should give you a sense of how property is classified for depreciation purposes.

Asset class	Description of assets included	Class Life (in years)	General Depreciation System	Alternative Depreciation System
			Recovery Periods (in years)	

SPECIFIC DEPRECIABLE ASSETS USED IN ALL BUSINESS ACTIVITIES, EXCEPT AS NOTED:

00.11	**Office Furniture, Fixtures, and Equipment:** Includes furniture and fixtures that are not a structural component of a building. Includes such assets as desks, files, safes, and communications equipment. Does not include communications equipment that is included in other classes.........	10	7	10
00.12	**Information Systems:** Includes computers and their peripheral equipment used in administering normal business transactions and the maintenance of business records, their retrieval and analysis. Information systems are defined as:			

1) Computers: A computer is a programmable electronically activated device capable of accepting information, applying prescribed processes to the information, and supplying the results of these processes with or without human intervention. It usually consists of a central processing unit containing extensive storage, logic, arithmetic, and control capabilities. Excluded from this category are adding machines, electronic desk calculators, etc., and other equipment described in class 00.13.

2) Peripheral equipment consists of the auxiliary machines which are designed to be placed under control of the central processing unit. Nonlimiting examples are: Card readers, card punches, magnetic tape feeds, high speed printers, optical character readers, tape cassettes, mass storage units, paper tape equipment, keypunches, data entry devices, teleprinters, terminals, tape drives, disc drives, disc files, disc packs, visual image projector tubes, card sorters, plotters, and collators. Peripheral equipment may be used on-line or off-line.

Does not include equipment that is an integral part of other capital equipment that is included in other classes of economic activity, i.e., computers used primarily for process or production control,

Asset class	Description of assets included	Class Life (in years)	General Depreciation System	Alternative Depreciation System
	switching, channeling, and automating distributive trades and services such as point of sale (POS) computer systems. Also, does not include equipment of a kind used primarily for amusement or entertainment of the user	6	5	5
00.13	**Data Handling Equipment, except Computers:** Includes only typewriters, calculators, adding and accounting machines, copiers, and duplicating equipment	6	5	6
00.21	**Airplanes (airframes and engines), except those used in commercial or contract carrying of passengers or freight, and all helicopters (airframes and engines)**................	6	5	6
00.22	**Automobiles, Taxis**	3	5	5
00.23	**Buses**................................	9	5	9
00.241	**Light General Purpose Trucks:** Includes trucks for use over the road (actual unloaded weight less than 13,000 pounds)	4	5	5
00.242	**Heavy General Purpose Trucks:** Includes heavy general purpose trucks, concrete ready-mix trucks, and ore trucks, for use over the road (actual unloaded weight 13,000 pounds or more)	6	5	6
00.25	**Railroad Cars and Locomotives, except those owned by railroad transportation companies**	15	7	15
00.26	**Tractor Units For Use Over–The–Road**	4	3	4
00.27	**Trailers and Trailer–Mounted Containers**	6	5	6
00.28	**Vessels, Barges, Tugs, and Similar Water Transportation Equipment, except those used in marine construction**	18	10	18

* * *

DEPRECIABLE ASSETS USED IN THE FOLLOWING ACTIVITIES:

01.1	**Agriculture:** Includes machinery and equipment, grain bins, and fences but no other land improvements, that are used in the production of crops or plants, vines, and trees; livestock; the operation of farm dairies, nurseries, greenhouses, sod farms, mushroom cellars, cranberry bogs, apiaries, and fur farms; the performance of agriculture, animal husbandry, and horticultural services	10	7	10
01.11	**Cotton Ginning Assets**	12	7	12
01.21	**Cattle, Breeding or Dairy**	7	5	7
01.22	**Horses, Breeding or Work**	10	7	10
01.221	**Any horse that is not a race horse and that is more than 12 years old at the time it is placed in service**	10	3	10

Asset class	Description of assets included	Class Life (in years)	Recovery Periods (in years) General Depreciation System	Alternative Depreciation System
01.222	**Any race horse that is more than 2 years old at the time it is placed in service**		3	12
01.23	**Hogs, Breeding**	3	3	3
01.24	**Sheep and Goats, Breeding**	5	5	5
01.3	**Farm buildings except structures included in Class 01.4**	25	20	25
01.4	**Single purpose agricultural or horticultural structures (within the meaning of section 48(p) of the Code)**	15	7	15
10.0	**Mining:** Includes assets used in the mining and quarrying of metallic and nonmetallic minerals (including sand, gravel, stone, and clay) and the milling, beneficiation and other primary preparation of such materials	10	7	10
13.0	**Offshore Drilling:** Includes assets used in offshore drilling for oil and gas such as floating, self-propelled and other drilling vessels, barges, platforms, and drilling equipment and support vessels such as tenders, barges, towboats and crewboats. Excludes oil and gas production assets	7.5	5	7.5
13.1	**Drilling of Oil and Gas Wells:** Includes assets used in the drilling of onshore oil and gas wells and the provision of geophysical and other exploration services; and the provision of such oil and gas field services as chemical treatment, plugging and abandoning of wells and cementing or perforating well casings. Does not include assets used in the performance of any of these activities and services by integrated petroleum and natural gas producers for their own account	6	5	6

* * *

In some cases, § 168 assigns property to a particular class without regard to the property's ADR class life. Sections 168(e)(2) and 168(c) give residential rental property a 27.5–year recovery period and assign a 39–year period to most buildings other than residential rental property. Section 168(e)(3) specifies recovery periods for a variety of assets.

Depreciation Methods

Property in the 3–year, 5–year, 7–year and 10–year classes will ordinarily be depreciated under a 200–percent declining-balance method, switching to straight-line when straight-line gives a larger deduction; § 168(b)(1). For 15–year and 20–year property, the normal method is 150–percent declining-balance, switching to straight-line; § 168(b)(2). Most real property must be depreciated on the straight-line method; §§ 168(b)(3)(A) & (B).

Most tangible property used predominantly outside the United States, property used by tax-exempt organizations, property financed with tax-exempt bonds, and some imported property must be depreciated under the alternative depreciation system of § 168(g), which uses straight-line depreciation over recovery periods which are longer for many assets than the usual periods. Taxpayers not required to use the alternative depreciation system may elect to use that system for particular items of real property or for other property on a class-by-class basis; §§ 168(g)(1)(E) & (g)(7).

Conventions

Personal property is usually depreciated by using a "half-year convention," which treats all of the personal property placed in service during any year as having been placed in service in the middle of the year; § 168(d)(1). Under this convention, the depreciation deduction for the first year is half of a full year's deduction. Section 168(d)(3) requires some taxpayers who place much of their property in service toward the end of the year to use a mid-quarter convention. Depreciation on real property is calculated by using a mid-month convention; §§ 168(d)(2) & (d)(4)(B). These conventions apply to depreciation in the year in which the property is disposed of as well as to depreciation for the first year of use.

––––––

The Service has issued tables incorporating the depreciation calculations described here. One can look up depreciation deductions in these tables, rather than calculate them. See Rev. Proc. 87–57, 1987–2 C.B. 687, and Rev. Proc. 89–15, 1989–1 C.B. 816.

Problems and Notes

1. *Expensing in lieu of depreciation.* Section 179 allows taxpayers who purchase tangible, personal, depreciable property for use in the "active conduct of a trade or business" to expense up to $25,000 (for 2003 and later years) of the cost of the property placed in service in any year. Section 179(b)(2) scales down this limit for taxpayers who place in service "§ 179 property" with a total basis of more than $200,000 in any one year. The amount of the deduction under § 179 cannot exceed the taxpayer's taxable income (computed without regard to § 179 itself) from the active conduct of a trade or business.

Under § 179(b)(3)(B), amounts the taxpayer cannot expense under § 179 because taxable income from a trade or business is less than the maximum annual deduction can be carried over to later years and deducted then (subject to the same limit).

Section 1397A allows the expensing of up to an additional $35,000 a year in the case of "qualified zone property." This is part of a set of tax-incentive provisions aimed at encouraging investment in "empowerment zones."

2. *Luxury automobiles.* The line between business and personal use of property is very hard to fix in the case of automobiles. Even if it is clear that a particular car is used by its owner or the owner's employee only for business, the fact that the car is a Cadillac rather than a Ford may give rise to a suspicion that the owner has bought some personal consumption or that the employee has been furnished a fringe benefit. In response to this concern, § 280F(a)(1) limits depreciation deductions on passenger automobiles. The limits do not apply to taxpayers in the business of leasing automobiles. In order to prevent taxpayers from circumventing § 280F(a)(1) by leasing, rather than buying, business vehicles, § 280F(c) authorizes regulations imposing limits upon deductions for rentals of cars leased for 30 days or more.

3. *Depreciation of improvements.* If the recovery periods assigned to property by § 168 were realistic, one would expect that the cost of improvements or additions to depreciable property would be recovered over the remaining life of the property improved, because improvements are not ordinarily designed to outlast the underlying property. In fact, however, § 168's recovery periods are sometimes unrealistically short, especially in the case of buildings. Section 168(i)(6) requires that depreciation on improvements of or additions to property be taken as if the property had been placed in service at the time of the improvement or addition. Therefore, a taxpayer who adds a new wing to an office building which has 10 years of depreciation remaining must recover the cost of the new wing over 39 years.

4. *Depreciation and basis.* Section 1016 requires that "proper adjustment" to the basis of property be made for (among other things) the amount allowed as depreciation if that amount reduced the taxpayer's income. See §§ 1016(a)(2)(A) & (B). Does this mean that the taxpayer's basis is not reduced if the taxpayer takes $10,000 in depreciation but gets no tax benefit from the deduction (because taxable income would have been zero even without the deduction)? Not necessarily, for § 1016(a) goes on to specify that the reduction is "not less than the amount allowable." Therefore, the "tax benefit" aspect of § 1016 comes into play only for taxpayers who take more depreciation than they should have taken, and who get less than full benefit from the excess deduction.

"Allowable" depreciation under § 1016 is depreciation allowable under the taxpayer's depreciation method. The basis of property depreciated on the straight-line method is reduced by straight-line depreciation, even if the taxpayer could have elected a faster method but chose not to do so.

5. *Problems.* On March 1 of year 1, *T* purchases equipment for use in her business at a cost of $35,000. The property has an ADR class life of 8 years. *T* expects to use the property for 7 years, after which time *T* expects it to have a salvage value of $2000. This is the only item of property that *T* places in service during the year. Assume that the maximum amount that can be expensed under § 179 is $25,000.

(1) How much of the cost can *T* deduct in year 1 and year 2 if she makes no § 179 election? What is her adjusted basis at the end of each year?

(2) Same as (1), except that the property was purchased on December 15.

(3) Same as (1), except that *T* makes a § 179 election.

(4) Same as (1), except that *T* makes an election under §§ 168(b)(3)(D) and (b)(5).

(5) Same as (1), except that *T* makes an election under §§ 168(g)(1)(E) and (g)(7).

(6) Same as (1), except that the property was an office building purchased for $440,000, of which $50,000 was allocable to the land and $390,000 to the building.

6. *Policy issues.* Depreciation deductions are necessary in order to measure taxpayers' net incomes, but it would be misleading to look at § 168 as being directed solely at this concern. Congress has often used the depreciation deduction to encourage both particular activities and investment in depreciable property in general. One way to "stimulate the economy" is to reduce taxes, and one way of reducing (some people's) taxes is to allow depreciation at a rate faster than the rate at which the assets in question decline in value.

The use of accelerated depreciation as a means of tax reduction reached a peak in 1981, when § 168 was enacted. The 1981 version of § 168 allowed the cost of buildings to be written off over 15 years, with the predictable effect of diverting resources to the construction of buildings. In 1986, Congress reduced depreciation deductions (and many other tax benefits), especially in the case of buildings. As applied to corporations, the 1986 legislation increased income taxes substantially, even though it reduced the highest corporate tax rate from 46 percent to 39 percent.

SIMON v. COMMISSIONER

United States Court of Appeals, Second Circuit, 1995.
68 F.3d 41 (Non-acq.).

Before OAKES, WINTER AND MAHONEY, CIRCUIT JUDGES.

WINTER, CIRCUIT JUDGE.

This appeal from the Tax Court raises the question whether professional musicians may take a depreciation deduction for wear and tear on antique violin bows under the Accelerated Cost Recovery System ("ACRS") of the Economic Recovery Tax Act of 1981 ("ERTA") * * *, although the taxpayers cannot demonstrate that the bows have a "determinable useful life."

The parties agree that under the pre-ERTA Internal Revenue Code of 1954 and the Treasury Department regulations interpreting that Code, the bows would be considered depreciable property only if the taxpayers could demonstrate a determinable useful life. The issue here is to what extent, if any, the ACRS modified the determinable useful life requirement.

BACKGROUND

The facts are essentially undisputed. Richard and Fiona Simon are highly skilled professional violinists. * * *

* * *

The business property at issue consists of two violin bows ("the Tourte bows") made in the nineteenth century by Francois Tourte, a bowmaker renowned for technical improvements in bow design. These bows were purchased by the Simons in 1985 and were in a largely unused condition at the time. The Tax Court found that "old violins played with old bows produce exceptional sounds that are superior to sounds produced by newer violins played with newer bows." [Citation omitted.] The Tax Court also found that violin bows suffer wear and tear when used regularly by performing musicians. With use, a violin bow will eventually become "played out," producing an inferior sound. [Citation omitted.] However, a "played out" Tourte bow retains value as a collector's item notwithstanding its diminished utility. The Simons' Tourte bows, for example, were appraised in 1990 at $45,000 and $35,000, even though they had physically deteriorated since their purchase by the Simons in 1985 for $30,000 and $21,500, respectively.

The Simons use the Tourte bows regularly in their trade. In 1989, the tax year in question, the Simons performed in four concerts per week as well as numerous rehearsals with the Philharmonic. Their use of the Tourte bows during the tax year at issue subjected the bows to substantial wear and tear. Believing that they were entitled to depreciate the bows under the ACRS, the Simons claimed depreciation deductions for the two bows on their 1989 Form 1040 in the amount of $6,300 and $4,515. The parties stipulated that these amounts represent the appropriate ACRS deductions if deductions are allowable.

The Tax Court agreed with the Simons and allowed the depreciation deductions. The Commissioner brought the present appeal.[1]

---

1. The Third Circuit has recently held for the taxpayers in a companion case raising the same issues presented here. *See* Liddle v. Commissioner, 65 F.3d 329 (3d Cir.1995), aff'g 103 T.C. 285 (1994).

DISCUSSION

This appeal turns on the interpretation of the ACRS provisions of § 168,[2] which provide a depreciation deduction for "recovery property" placed into service after 1980. Recovery property is defined by that section as "tangible property of a character subject to the allowance for depreciation" when "used in a trade or business, or ... held for the production of income." § 168(c)(1). The record establishes that the Simons' Tourte bows were tangible property placed in service after 1980 and used in the taxpayers' trade or business. The Commissioner contends, however, that the bows are not "property of a character subject to the allowance for depreciation."

The parties agree that Section 168's phrase "of a character subject to depreciation" must be interpreted in light of the § 167(a) allowances for "exhaustion, wear and tear, and ... obsolescence." The Simons and the Tax Court maintain that, when read in conjunction with the plain language of Section 167, Section 168 requires only that the Tourte bows suffer wear and tear in the Simons' trade to qualify as "recovery property." The Commissioner, on the other hand, argues that because all property used in a trade or business is necessarily subject to wear and tear, the Simons' construction of Section 168 would effectively render Section 168's phrase "of a character subject to the allowance for depreciation" superfluous, a result that Congress presumably could not have intended. * * * Therefore, Section 168's requirement that the property be "of a character subject to the allowance for depreciation" must include an element beyond wear and tear, namely the "determinable useful life" requirement embodied in Treas. Reg. § 1.167(a)–1, a Treasury regulation of pre-ERTA vintage.

We do not agree with the Commissioner's premise because some tangible assets used in business are not exhausted, do not suffer wear and tear, or become obsolete. For example, paintings that hang on the wall of a law firm merely to be looked at—to please connoisseur clients or to give the appearance of dignity to combative professionals—do not generally suffer wear or tear. More to the point, the Simons' Tourte bows were playable for a time precisely because they had been kept in a private collection and were relatively unused since their manufacture. Indeed, it appears that one had never been played at all. Had that collection been displayed at a for-profit museum, the museum could not have depreciated the bows under ERTA because, although the bows were

---

2. For purposes of this appeal, we apply the Internal Revenue Code as it existed prior to the Tax Reform Act of 1986. The relevant portions of Section 168 read as follows:

(a) *Allowance of deduction.* There shall be allowed as a deduction for any taxable year the amount determined under this section with respect to recovery property.

* * *

(c) *Recovery Property.* For purposes of this title—

(1) *Recovery property defined.* Except as provided in subsection (e), the term "recovery property" means tangible property of a character subject to the allowance for depreciation—

(A) used in a trade or business, or

(B) held for the production of income.

being used in a trade or business, they were not subject to wear and tear. The Tourte bows are not unlike numerous kinds of museum pieces or collectors' items. The Commissioner's textual argument thus fails because there are tangible items not subject to wear and tear.

The Commissioner next argues that Congressional intent and the notion of depreciation itself require that Section 168's statutory language be supplemented by reading into the word "character" a requirement that tangible property have a demonstrable useful life. To address that issue, we must briefly examine the history of the depreciation allowance.

The tax laws have long permitted deductions for depreciation on certain income-producing assets used in a trade or business. [Citations omitted.] The original rationale for the depreciation deduction was to allow taxpayers to match accurately, for tax accounting purposes, the cost of an asset to the income stream that the asset produced. * * * In its traditional incarnation, therefore, the pace of depreciation deductions was determined by the period of time that the asset would produce income in the taxpayer's business. As the Supreme Court noted in Massey [Motors, Inc. v. United States, 364 U.S. 92, 101 (1960)], "Congress intended by the depreciation allowance not to make taxpayers a profit thereby, but merely to protect them from a loss. * * * Accuracy in accounting requires that correct tabulations, not artificial ones, be used."

To implement this accurate tax accounting, the concept of a determinable useful life was necessary because, without such a determination, one could not calculate the proper annual allowance * * *. The regulation that the Commissioner now relies upon was promulgated under the 1954 Internal Revenue Code and reflects the rationale underlying the accounting scheme in effect just prior to ERTA. * * *

ERTA, however, altered the depreciation scheme for two reasons other than sound accounting practice that are not consistent with the Commissioner's argument. First, the ACRS introduced accelerated depreciation periods as a stimulus for economic growth. See H.R. Conf. Rep. No. 215, 97th Cong., 1st Sess. 206 (1981) * * * , S. Rep. No. 144, 97th Cong., 1st Sess. 47 (1981) * * *. Under ACRS, the cost of an asset is recovered over a predetermined period unrelated to—and usually shorter than—the useful life of the asset. Moreover, the depreciation deductions do not assume consistent use throughout the asset's life, instead assigning inflated deductions to the earlier years of use. *See* § 168(b). Therefore, the purpose served by the determinable useful life requirement of the pre-ERTA scheme—allowing taxpayers to depreciate property over its actual use in the business—no longer exists under the ACRS. See generally *Massey*, 364 U.S. 92. Because the ACRS is different by design, there is no logic in the Commissioner's suggestion that depreciation practice under the old Section 167 calls for the imposition of a determinable useful life requirement after ERTA.

A second congressional purpose embodied in ERTA also militates against reading a determinable useful life prerequisite into § 168. In addition to stimulating investment, Congress sought to simplify the depreciation rules by eliminating the need to adjudicate matters such as useful life and salvage value, which are inherently uncertain and result in unproductive disagreements between taxpayers and the Internal Revenue Service. S. Rep. No. 144 at 47. Indeed, the legislation specifically sought to "de-emphasize" the concept of useful life. * * *

* * *

The Commissioner's strongest support for her claim that Congress intended to maintain § 1.167(a)–1's determinable useful life requirement comes from the House Conference Report, which noted that

> Under present law, assets used in a trade or business or for the production of income are depreciable if they are subject to wear and tear, decay or decline from natural causes or obsolescence. Assets that do not decline in value on a predictable basis or that do not have a determinable useful life, such as land, goodwill, and stock, are not depreciable.

H.R. Conf. Rep. No. 215 at 206. The Simons unsuccessfully attempt to recharacterize this statement as an inartful catalogue of assets that are not subject to exhaustion, wear and tear, or obsolescence. The House report means what it says but gives us slight pause. In light of the overriding legislative intent to abandon the unnecessarily complicated rules on useful life, we cannot employ two sentences in a legislative report to trump statutory language and a clearly stated legislative purpose. Continued reliance on Treas.Reg. § 1.167(a)–1 is in sharp conflict with the overall legislative history of ERTA, which definitively repudiates the scheme of complex depreciation rules, including "current regulations." S. Rep. No. 144 at 47. We are thus not persuaded by the Commissioner's call for us to interpret a statute that abrogates a current regulatory regime as in fact incorporating the details of that scheme. In particular, we reject the argument that we should retain regulatory provisions now divorced from their functional purpose.

* * *

One should not exaggerate the extent to which our holding is a license to hoard and depreciate valuable property that a taxpayer expects to appreciate in real economic value.[7] * * *

For the foregoing reasons, we affirm.

OAKES, SENIOR CIRCUIT JUDGE, Dissenting:

I cannot believe that Congress, in changing the depreciation deduction from the Asset Depreciation Range System ("ADRS") for recovery

---

7. We note that our decision today is limited to "recovery property," a concept that was deleted from the statute in the Tax Reform Act of 1986. Moreover, ACRS' depreciation deductions first became available in 1981. Therefore, this opinion applies only to property placed in service between January 1, 1981 and January 1, 1987.

of assets placed in service after December 31, 1980, to the Accelerated Cost Recovery System ("ACRS") whereby the cost of an asset is recovered over a predetermined period shorter than the useful life of the asset or the period the asset is used to produce income, intended to abandon the concept underlying depreciation, namely, that to permit the deduction the property must have a useful life capable of being estimated. [Citation omitted.] I find no indication in either the changes of statutory language or the well-documented legislative history that Congress intended such a radical change as the majority of this panel, the Tax Court majority, and the Third Circuit in *Liddle* have held it did. Indeed, it seems to me that the statutory language and the legislative history— consistent with the dual congressional purpose of simplification and stimulating economic growth by permitting accelerated depreciation periods—retained the fundamental principle that, in order to depreciate, the asset involved must have a determinable useful life.

First, with respect to the statutory language, the question before us is whether antique violin bows constitute depreciable "recovery property" under section 168(c)(1) of the Internal Revenue Code effective during 1989, the year in issue. Section 168(c)(1) defined "recovery property" by saying:

> except as provided in subsection (e) the term "recovery property" means *tangible property of a character subject to the allowance for depreciation*—(A) used in a trade or business, or (B) held for the production of income.

Id. (emphasis added). * * * [T]he cases are legion that under § 167, taxpayers must establish that the property being depreciated has a determinable useful life. [Citations omitted.]

Under the majority's interpretation, however, the only criterion necessary to obtain a deduction under section 168(c) is that the property be subject to wear and tear. Thus, a car buff in the trade or business of buying, collecting, and selling antique automobiles, who drives his autos to auto shows may obtain a depreciation deduction, or the law office that buys fine Sheraton or Chippendale desks or chairs for office use can take a deduction, though in each case the auto or furniture is actually appreciating in value and has no determinable useful life.

As for legislative history, the majority candidly admits that House Conference Report 97–215, which states that "assets that do not decline in value on a predictable basis or that do not have a determinable useful life, such as land, goodwill, and stock, are not depreciable," "means what it says." The majority then adds that the Report "gives us slight pause."

* * * I agree with the Commissioner that [the majority's] interpretation renders meaningless the phrase in § 168(c)(1) "of a character subject to the allowance for depreciation," since all tangible property used in a business is necessarily subject to wear and tear. * * *

Since, concededly, taxpayers Richard and Fiona Simon have not established that the bows in question have determinable useful lives, the bows do not qualify for the depreciation deduction. It is a long way from the dual purpose of section 168 (to shorten the depreciation periods for property that would have been depreciable under section 167 in order to stimulate investment and to simplify the complex series of rules and regulations pertaining to useful lives by substituting a four-tier system of three-year, five-year, ten-year, and fifteen-year property), to abandonment of the underlying concept of depreciable property altogether. In my view, the decision of the Tax Court should be reversed and accordingly I hereby dissent.

Notes and Question

1. *Simon today.* Whether or not the *Simon* case made sense under ERTA, when § 168 itself allowed "cost recovery" deductions for "recovery property," does it apply today? As in pre-ERTA days, the depreciation deduction is allowed by § 167, which provides for a "reasonable allowance" for exhaustion, wear and tear, and obsolescence. (For the years involved in *Simon*, § 167 did not apply to "recovery property.") Section 168, however, still specifies recovery periods and depreciation methods for most tangible assets, and still provides that salvage values are ignored.

2. *Reference.* Polito, Fiddlers on the Tax: Depreciation of Antique Instruments Invites Reexamination of Broader Tax Policy, 13 Am.J. Tax Pol. 87 (1996).

DEPRECIATION COMPUTATIONS UNDER PROVISIONS OTHER THAN SECTION 168

Section 168 applies only to tangible property; § 168(a). Copyrights, patents, and some other depreciable intangibles must be depreciated under § 167(a), which provides for a "reasonable allowance." A "reasonable allowance" includes the straight-line method. The accelerated methods allowed by § 168(b) do not apply to intangible property; see § 168(a). This does not mean, however, that straight-line is the only acceptable method for depreciating intangibles. Although § 168 does not authorize accelerated depreciation for intangibles, accelerated methods may sometimes be justified as producing a "reasonable allowance" under § 167(a). See Treas.Reg. § 1.167(a)–1(a) ("reasonable allowance" is "not necessarily at a uniform rate"). As a general rule, taxpayers using an accelerated method under § 167(a) must justify the practice by showing that the asset's decline in value matches the pattern of deductions the method generates; see Computing & Software, Inc. v. Commissioner, 64 T.C. 223 (1975). Films, videotapes, and sound recordings are subject to the rules for intangible property because of §§ 168(f)(3) and 168(f)(4). Computer software must be depreciated under the straight-line method over thirty-six months; § 167(f)(1).

Section 168(f)(1) allows a taxpayer to elect out of § 168 in the case of property "properly depreciated" under most methods "not expressed in a term of years." Methods of this sort include:

(1) *The machine-hour method:* Suppose a $10,000 machine is expected to be usable for 2000 operating hours and then to have a scrap value of $2000. Under the machine-hour method, each year's depreciation would be the $8000 difference between basis and salvage value times a fraction with a numerator of the number of hours the machine was used in that year and a denominator of 2000. Thus, if the machine was used for 500 hours the first year, that year's depreciation deduction would be $2000 ($8000 × $\frac{500}{2000}$).

(2) *The income-forecast method:* A taxpayer who can estimate the total revenue to be produced by an asset can compute depreciation on the basis of the portion of total revenue earned during the taxable year. This method is sometimes used to depreciate films. Under § 167(g)(6), the income-forecast method can be used only for films, videotapes, copyrights, books, patents, and "other property specified in regulations."

Several Code provisions other than §§ 167 and 168 provide for recovering particular kinds of costs by depreciation or "amortization." (Amortization is the process of writing off costs ratably over some period: the terms "depreciation" and "amortization" are often used interchangeably, though "amortization" is not used in connection with tangible property.) Sections 248 and 709 allow the costs of organizing corporations and partnerships to be written off over five years (or longer, if the taxpayer so elects). Section 169 allows a five-year writeoff for some of the costs of "certified pollution control facilities." Some "start-up" costs of acquiring or creating an active trade or business can be deducted over five years (or longer) under § 195. Section 197 allows 15–year amortization of many intangible assets.

Problem

On July 1 of this year, *P* and *Q* formed *X* Corporation by filing articles of incorporation with the Secretary of State. The corporation began business immediately after the articles were filed. *X* Corporation paid *L,* a lawyer, $500 for drafting its articles of incorporation, by-laws, and minutes of the organizational meeting of the shareholders and directors. *X* Corporation also paid a $100 incorporation fee to the state. The certificate of incorporation provides that the corporation's existence will be perpetual. What amount, if any, can the corporation deduct this year? See § 248 and the regulations under that section.

2. DEPRECIATION: LEASED PROPERTY

M. DeMATTEO CONST. CO. v. UNITED STATES

United States Court of Appeals, First Circuit, 1970.
433 F.2d 1263.

Before ALDRICH, CHIEF JUDGE, McENTEE and COFFIN, CIRCUIT JUDGES.

ALDRICH, CHIEF JUDGE.

In 1926 the trustees under the will of one Eben Jordan, owning a parcel of land near Park Square, Boston, granted a ground lease on a net rental basis, the lease to expire, unless earlier for default or upon the payment of a substantial penalty by the lessee, 20 years after the death of certain lives in being, but in any event in 1990. The lessee thereafter erected a building known as the Motor Mart Garage. The taxpayer, M. DeMatteo Construction Co., purchased the property from the trustees in 1959. At this time the lease was in full force, and one of the named lives was still in being. The lease had, accordingly, not less than 20,[1] and not more than 31 years to run. In 1969, at the time of trial, the lease was still in effect, and the remaining named life still in being. Taxpayer's president, according to his testimony at the trial, initially allocated ten percent of its acquisition cost to the land, and ninety percent to the building. This latter percentage he intended to depreciate for tax purposes over the useful life of the building. To support the depreciation deduction taxpayer employed a qualified real estate expert, who advised it to apportion the cost at approximately two-thirds for the building and one-third for the land.

Taxpayer assumed a twenty-year life for the building from the date of purchase, and on this assumption took depreciation deductions on its income tax returns. * * *

The trial proceeded solely upon, and the evidence offered related solely to, taxpayer's first ground for relief, viz., its right to take depreciation in the building. In this court it seeks to argue, in addition, a premium lease amortization theory. We will not, however, consider this second alternative, which would require a different approach and different evidence.[2] This is an appeal asserting error at trial, not an opportunity to try some new theory.

The district court dismissed the complaint on alternate grounds, that taxpayer had no cost basis in the building which would reach the end of its useful life prior to its reversion to taxpayer at the expected termination of the lease, and that the taxpayer had, in any case, failed to meet its burden of proving the fair and reasonable value of its interest in the building. D.Mass.1970, 310 F.Supp. 1313.

The initial lessor was entitled to claim no depreciation with respect to the building constructed by the lessee for the obvious reason that it had made no investment in the improvement and therefore had no cost basis in it. [Citations omitted.] Taxpayer's assertion that the situation changed when it purchased the property, that because it acquired title to the building it obtained a cost basis in it, assumes the point in issue. It does not explain why the rationale underlying the denial of depreciation to the original lessor does not apply equally to the subsequent purchaser. It may be that taxpayer would present some sort of claim if, at the time of purchase, the anticipated life of the building had exceeded the term of the lease. Cf. Millinery Center Bldg. Corp. v. Commissioner of Internal Revenue, 1956, 350 U.S. 456. Where, however, as the trial court found to

---

1. No evidence was introduced as to the age or life expectancy of the named life in being.

2. Not the least of which would be the anticipated length of the lease. See n. 1, ante.

be the case here, the building's useful life will expire before the purchaser gains possession of it, and there is no indication the purchaser believes otherwise, the selling lessor has nothing to sell except the bare legal title, and the purchaser buys nothing more. We see no justification for allocating a portion of taxpayer's purchase price to, and thus establishing a cost basis in, the building when taxpayer purchased no interest of any substance in it.

Taxpayer places its reliance upon World Publishing Co. v. Commissioner of Internal Revenue, 8 Cir.1962, 299 F.2d 614, which holds that depreciation is available because the purchasing lessor acquires the building as income producing property. That decision has received considerable criticism, and we decline to follow it. It is the lease which produces the income, not a building which the lessee constructed and which is going to reach the end of its useful life before the taxpayer obtains possession. Taxpayer may have had an amortizable cost basis in the lease, but, as we have indicated, that question is not before us. Nor can we accept the distinction the Eighth Circuit draws in order to escape the force of the unanimous decisions reaching a contrary result where the lessor acquires the property by inheritance or devise. See the cases cited therein 299 F.2d at 618.[5]

Finally, taxpayer asserts that it had an interest in the building because the lessee, through default or otherwise, might prematurely terminate the lease before the expiration of the life of the building. The depreciable interest, if any, cf. Puerto Rico v. United States, 1 Cir.1942, 132 F.2d 220, cert. denied 319 U.S. 752, is a highly speculative one, and the taxpayer had failed to prove its worth. It is obviously considerably less than the full value of the building. In this respect the Commissioner's finding of no depreciable interest must be presumed to be correct.

Affirmed.

Problem, Notes and Questions

1. *The "premium lease amortization theory."* Suppose *L* leases property to *T* for twenty years in 2002, at an annual rental of $50,000. The property declines in attractiveness to tenants in 2003, perhaps because of general economic conditions or perhaps because a neighbor builds a smog factory next door. *L*'s lease has now become a "premium lease," since the rental *L* is entitled to receive is higher than the rental *L* could get a new tenant to pay. Because the tenant must pay higher

---

5. As the opinion in *World Publishing* recognizes, the depreciation provisions of the revenue laws make no distinction between purchased property and property acquired by inheritance or devise. § 167. The provisions for determining basis, on the other hand, are different. Purchased property has a basis of cost, while property taken by inheritance or devise has a basis of fair market value at the time of the trans-

fer. §§ 1012, 1014. However, an economically rational purchaser will pay the fair market value at the time of acquisition. If *World Publishing* is correct in distinguishing between persons acquiring by devise and by deed, both have acquired the same property, from the same type of predecessor, and have the same basis, but one can depreciate and the other cannot.

rentals than a new tenant would pay, a buyer of the land (subject to the lease) from *L* should be willing to pay more than would be paid for identical property without the lease. This difference is the "premium value."

In Friend v. Commissioner, 119 F.2d 959 (7th Cir.1941), cert. denied 314 U.S. 673 (1941), the court refused to let an heir depreciate the premium value of a lease on the ground that, because the decedent had no depreciable interest in the lease, as distinct from the land, the heir could have none. In Commissioner v. Moore, 207 F.2d 265 (9th Cir.1953), cert. denied 347 U.S. 942 (1954), the taxpayer inherited leased land on which stood a building with a shorter useful life than the term of the lease. The court denied depreciation on the *building,* but remanded the case for findings on whether the *lease* had a premium value. In most of the cases, the taxpayer either failed to advance the "premium lease" theory or failed to establish that the lease had a premium value. Section 167(c)(2) now prohibits allocating to the lease any of the property acquired subject to a lease.

2. *The World Publishing decision. World Publishing Co.,* which the First Circuit refused to follow in *DeMatteo,* involved a taxpayer who paid $700,000 for land subject to a long-term lease. On the land was a building, constructed by the tenant, which had a useful life stipulated to be shorter than the remaining term of the lease. The taxpayer had legal title to the building as well as to the land. The trial court found that the value of the land at the time of purchase was $400,000 and that the value of the building was $300,000. The Eighth Circuit held that, on these facts, it "clearly" followed that the taxpayer had a $300,000 depreciable basis in the building. Is this sound? Suppose that, just before the taxpayer agreed on a purchase price for the land and building, the value of the building increased by $200,000 because of a sudden increase in demand for buildings of that type. Bearing in mind that the building will not last longer than the lease, would you advise the buyer to increase his offer for the property by $200,000 over what he would have paid before the increase? See Note, 76 Harv.L.Rev. 1303 (1963).

3. *Depreciation of improvements by a lessee.* Smith leases Blackacre to Jones, and Jones spends $500,000 to construct a building on Black-acre. Before the Tax Reform Act of 1986, Jones depreciated the building in the usual way only if its expected useful life was less than the unexpired term of the lease. If the building's useful life exceeded the lease term, Jones took annual deductions over the term of the lease. Although these rules made some sense in principle, practical considerations made recovery over the unexpired term of a lease an unsatisfactory rule. For example, if the lease had five years to go but was renewable, disputes over whether the lease was likely to be extended arose. Even if the lease had no formal renewal option, renewal (or the making of a new lease) was always a possibility. Section 168(i)(8) now requires that buildings erected on leased property and improvements made to leased property be depreciated under the ordinary cost-recovery rules; in effect, the lease is ignored.

4. *Problem.* L owned land that was subject to a 20–year lease. L sold the land to P for $100,000, of which $70,000 was allocable to the remaining term of the lease and $30,000 to the reversion. If the land had not been subject to the lease, its value would have been only $80,000. Can P amortize any portion of the purchase price? See § 167(c)(2).

5. *Reference.* Morris & Glicklich, Some Incongruities in the Taxation of Leased Real Property, 40 The Tax Lawyer 85 (1986).

3. DEPLETION

(a) *Cost Depletion*

Section 611 allows a "reasonable allowance for depletion" as a deduction in computing taxable income in the case of "natural deposits" and timber. "Cost depletion," described in Treas.Reg. §§ 1.611–2 and 1.611–3, is closely analogous to depreciation and to the treatment of cost in determining gain or loss on the sale of property. A taxpayer who pays $1 million for a mineral deposit containing 500,000 "units" of minerals (tons of coal, cubic yards of sand, barrels of oil, etc.) must at some point use the deposit's $1 million basis in computing taxable income. Cost depletion works by allocating the cost or other basis to units sold during the year and units remaining after the end of the year. Thus, if the taxpayer sold 100,000 units in the first year of mining, and estimated at year's end that 400,000 units remained, the taxpayer's deduction for cost depletion would be $200,000 (20 percent of $1,000,000.)

(b) *Percentage Depletion*

Taxpayers have been allowed to use some form of cost depletion since 1913. In 1918, Congress allowed taxpayers who discovered mineral deposits on properties that had been unproven when purchased to use "discovery value depletion" in cases in which the value of the property after discovery was materially greater than the cost. Discovery depletion was computed like cost depletion, except that the basis used was the property's value at discovery (or within thirty days thereafter). By using this new method, a taxpayer who had bought a mineral interest and discovered a deposit could recover more than the property's cost tax free. The Senate Finance Committee Report hints, without saying so explicitly, that discovery value depletion was adopted to stimulate prospecting.

Discovery depletion was administratively unmanageable because there was no good way to measure discovery values. As a substitute for discovery depletion in the case of oil and gas wells, Congress adopted percentage depletion—a deduction of 27.5 percent of the gross income from the property, limited to 50 percent of the taxable income from the property—in 1926. Like discovery depletion, percentage depletion was not limited to basis. Unlike discovery depletion, percentage depletion was allowed taxpayers who had bought proven properties.

Between 1926 and 1954, Congress extended percentage depletion to various minerals other than oil and gas, and the 1954 Code allowed percentage depletion for nearly all minerals at the rates listed in

§ 613(b). Sections 613(b)(7)(C) and 613A, enacted in 1975, cut back considerably on percentage depletion for oil and gas.

Notes

1. *The "economic interest" concept.* Only those taxpayers with an "economic interest" in a mineral deposit can take percentage depletion. A contract coal miner hired on a day-to-day basis does not have an economic interest, even if compensated on a per-unit basis, but someone with a long-term right to mine coal and share in the sales proceeds does have an economic interest, even if the interest falls short of being "ownership" under local law. Much of the case law on economic interest can be summarized by saying that a taxpayer with a right to a share in the proceeds of a mine or well and either (1) an ownership interest in the deposit, or (2) an interest which is not technically ownership but which gives the taxpayer rights similar to the rights of owners or lessees, has an economic interest. Weaver v. Commissioner, 72 T.C. 594 (1979), described "economic interest" as "substantial bona fide ownership or leasehold interest in the minerals in place, or the economic equivalent thereof." But the Supreme Court has held that owners of lands along the California coast had economic interests in offshore deposits because state regulations prohibited offshore drilling, so that the owner of the deposits had to obtain the landowners' consent to drill from coastal lands; Commissioner v. Southwest Exploration Co., 350 U.S. 308 (1956). And in United States v. Swank, 451 U.S. 571 (1981), the Court held that a coal miner had an economic interest in a deposit even though his rights as lessee were subject to termination by the lessor on thirty days' notice.

2. *Percentage depletion and basis.* Although the taxpayer's basis does not enter into the computation of percentage depletion, § 1016 requires that basis be reduced by depletion allowed or allowable. The depletion deduction allowable in a given year is percentage or cost depletion, whichever is greater (see § 613(a), last sentence). Rev.Rul. 75–451, 1975–2 C.B. 330, holds that depletion deductions do not reduce basis below zero.

3. *Limits on percentage depletion for oil and gas.* Section 613A, adopted in 1975, denies percentage depletion on oil and most natural gas to taxpayers who sell oil or gas at retail (§ 613A(d)(2)) and to taxpayers engaged in refining on a large scale (§ 613A(d)(4)). Other taxpayers can take percentage depletion on oil and gas production up to the "depletable oil quantity" or "depletable natural gas quantity" as defined in § 613A(c). The rate of percentage depletion for most oil and gas is 15 percent.

4. *Reference.* Eisenstein, The Ideologies of Taxation 123–146 (1961).

4. BUSINESS TAX CREDITS

Over the years, Congress has subsidized a variety of activities by enacting tax credits for a portion of the money taxpayers spend in designated ways. The tax-credit system has been remarkably unstable. Major tax legislation typically extends the lives of some credits, terminates others, and changes the amounts of and eligibility requirements for existing credits. What follows is a very brief description of the current tax-credit menu.

The *energy credit* (§ 48) is allowed for a portion of the costs of "energy property" placed in service during the year. "Energy property" consists of equipment using solar or geothermal energy. Section 48 also allows a *reforestation credit*. The *orphan drug credit* of § 45C encourages clinical testing of drugs that treat rare diseases or conditions. The *Indian employment credit* (§ 45A) goes to those who employ enrolled members of Indian tribes, or the spouses of enrolled members, for work performed within an Indian reservation. Section 45 grants a credit for producing energy using wind or a closed-loop biomass, whatever that may be. An "eligible small business" that pays to make its facilities more accessible to the disabled may qualify for the *disabled access credit* of § 44. Other credits include the *enhanced oil recovery credit* (§ 43), the *low-income housing credit* (§ 42), the *credit for increasing research activities* (§ 41), the *alcohol fuels credit* (§ 40), the *credit for producing fuel from a nonconventional source* (§ 29), the *welfare-to-work credit* (§ 51A), the *work opportunity credit* (§ 51), the *credit for employer-provided child care expenses*, § 45F, the *credit for small employer pension plan startup costs*, § 45E, and the *credit for qualified electric vehicles* (§ 30).

Employers in "empowerment zones" are given an *empowerment zone employment credit* (§ 1396) for a portion of wages paid to "qualified zone employees." Those who conduct businesses in empowerment zones and "enterprise communities" get some other tax breaks as well, mostly in connection with the use of tax-exempt bonds for financing.

Tax credits have a strong appeal to politicians of both parties. They encourage various activities, some of which are desirable (though nobody except its recipients defends the alcohol fuels credit on the merits). They seem to take the form of "tax cuts" rather than "spending programs" (in political terms), making them attractive to some legislators who would not dream of supporting "spending" programs that would cost the same and have identical effects. In part, at least, because of this political appeal, the tax credit menu changes considerably from year to year. Some of the credits are "permanent"; others are "temporary"; all have an uncertain future.

B.   CAPITAL EXPENDITURES

1. ASSETS OTHER THAN INVENTORY

This section examines the borderline between business and investment "expenses," which are deducted as they are incurred, and "capital expenditures," which add to the basis of property. Although many Code sections deal with capitalization of particular costs, no general Code provision spells out rules for distinguishing capital expenditures from current expenses. Section 263(a) denies a deduction for amounts "paid out for new buildings or for permanent improvements or betterments made to increase the value of any property or estate" and for payments "restoring property or in making good the exhaustion thereof for which an allowance is or has been made." Sections 162 and 212, in allowing deductions for "ordinary * * * expenses," have been read as disallowing deductions for capital expenditures, which are neither "ordinary" nor "expenses."[a] A capitalization requirement can also be found in § 446(b), which requires that a taxpayer's accounting method "clearly reflect income," in § 1016(a)'s requirement of "proper adjustment" for expenditures "properly chargeable to capital account," and even in § 1012's definition of basis as "cost." Section 263A, which will be discussed further below, requires that the "proper share" of the "indirect" costs of producing property be capitalized.

PLAINFIELD–UNION WATER CO. v. COMMISSIONER

Tax Court of the United States, 1962.
39 T.C. 333 (Non-acq.).

FORRESTER, JUDGE: * * * [Petitioner was a public utility which supplied water through mains and pipes which it owned. In 1950 petitioner began using river water from the Elizabethtown water system in its Maple Avenue main. Unlike the well water previously carried by this main, the river water was acidic. This water caused petitioner's tar-lined pipes to clog because of a process called "tuberculation," and the Maple Avenue main had to be cleaned in 1954. By 1957 the main was clogged again, and in 1957 and 1958 petitioner spent $42,003.80 in cleaning the main and lining it with cement to prevent future clogging. Petitioner deducted most of this cost as a "repair."]

* * *

The cleaning and cement lining of the Maple Avenue main was a repair which restored the original water carrying capacity of the pipes in question. Such pipe was previously and thereafter continued to be used in the normal course of petitioner's operations as a water company. The repair did not form a part of an overall plan of improvement. The cleaning and lining did not materially increase the useful life, value, or structural strength of the pipes involved, nor did it render those pipes suitable for any new or additional use by petitioner.

---

a. One problem with attributing the capital-expenditure requirement to §§ 263, 162, and 212 is that these sections deal with deductions. A line between capital expenditures and current costs must be drawn even in cases in which no question of a deduction can arise, as when a taxpayer spends money to fix up a personal residence. If the fixing up is so extensive as to amount to an "improvement," the cost will be added to the property's basis; but if the cost is an "expense," it is not deductible because the requirements of §§ 162 and 212 are not satisfied (see also § 262).

Opinion

The issue before us is whether the cost of cleaning and cement lining the Maple Avenue main during 1957 is a deductible repair under section 162(a) and the regulations thereunder, or whether it is a capital expenditure.

The area of repair or capital expenditure is replete with innumerable decisions which struggle unsuccessfully to draw a clear and useful line of general applicability. An expenditure which returns property to the state it was in before the situation prompting the expenditure arose, and which does not make the relevant property more valuable, more useful, or longer-lived, is usually deemed a deductible repair. A capital expenditure is generally considered to be a more permanent increment in the longevity, utility, or worth of the property.

As the Board stated in Illinois Merchants Trust Co., Executor, 4 B.T.A. 103, 106:

> A repair is an expenditure for the purpose of keeping the property in an ordinarily efficient operating condition. It does not add to the value of the property, nor does it appreciably prolong its life. It merely keeps the property in an operating condition over its probable useful life for the uses for which it was acquired. Expenditures for that purpose are distinguishable from those for replacements, alterations, improvements or additions which prolong the life of the property, increase its value, or make it adaptable to a different use. The one is a maintenance charge, while the others are additions to capital investment which should not be applied against current earnings. * * *

The cost of keeping property "in an ordinarily efficient operating condition, may be deducted as an expense." [Treas.Reg. §] 1.162–4. If the repair does not "*materially* add to the value of the property nor appreciably prolong its life," it may be deducted as an expense. Ibid. (Emphasis supplied.) Petitioner asserts that the instant case comes within the purview of these criteria, and we agree.

Respondent contends that the value of the pipe to petitioner was materially increased by the expenditure and that it is, therefore, a capital expenditure. But any properly performed repair adds value as compared with the situation existing immediately prior to that repair. The proper test is whether the expenditure materially enhances the value, use, life expectancy, strength, or capacity as compared with the status of the asset prior to the condition necessitating the expenditure. Comparing the period before tuberculation and after expenditure, we see that the useful life of the Maple Avenue main was not increased by the cleaning and lining and that neither the strength nor the capacity of said main was enhanced.

Respondent is in error when he contends that the expenditure allowed petitioner to put the pipes to a new use. The main continued to be used in the normal course of petitioner's operations as a water company. It is true that water derived from rivers rather than water derived from wells was being used, but the substantial utilization of the pipes was the same, to wit, the conveyance of water to various homes.

Further, the river water could be, and was, used in the relevant pipes without the cement lining. Periodic cleanings, clearly deductible ordinary expenses, would allow petitioner to use the Maple Avenue main at full capacity without cement linings. The cement lining was not a permanent addition to the pipe. By lining the pipes, petitioner merely eliminated, temporarily, a maintenance problem. That petitioner chose a less expensive, nonpermanent method of eliminating the tuberculation and restoring the capacity does not establish a new use.

Indeed, respondent has stipulated that the expenditure in question did not establish a new or additional use:

> The cement lining of 16 inch cast iron pipe by petitioner in 1957 did not make the pipe suitable for any new or additional use by petitioner. Such pipe was previously and thereafter continued to be used in the normal course of petitioner's operations as a water company.

We hold that the expenditure in question did not result in a substantial new or additional use for the relevant pipes.

While an item which would otherwise be classified as a deductible repair may be held capital if it is part of an overall plan of general improvement, we hold that the relevant cleaning and cement lining comprised a very minor part of petitioner's operation and was not part of any general plan.

Respondent offers several cases which, in their factual context, hold that an expenditure should be capitalized. See e.g., Bonwit Teller & Co., 17 B.T.A. 1019, affirmed in part and reversed in part 53 F.2d 381 (C.A.2), certiorari denied 284 U.S. 690; Teitelbaum v. Commissioner, 294 F.2d 541 (C.A.7), affirming a Memorandum Opinion of this Court, certiorari denied 368 U.S. 987; Hotel Sulgrave, Inc., 21 T.C. 619.

We consider other cases, discussed immediately below, to be more in point.

In Midland Empire Packing Co., 14 T.C. 635, the continued operation of a meat packing plant was threatened by oil seepage from a neighboring refinery into the cellar of the plant. Taxpayer lined the basement walls and floors with concrete to restore normal operating condition. We held that the expenditure was a deductible expense, since it did not increase useful life or value to taxpayer, did not provide for changed or enlarged use of the premises, and did not materially add value when compared with the preseepage period. We said at page 641: "The repairs merely served to keep the property in an operating condition over its probable useful life for the purpose for which it was used."

In Illinois Merchants Trust Co., Executor, supra, a lowering of the water level of a river exposed part of the wooden pilings upon which a building rested. Dry rot set in which threatened collapse of the building.

Taxpayer sawed off the rotted parts and replaced them with concrete supports. The repair also entailed removal of a large part of the building's ground floor and the shoring up of a wall. The Board held the expenditure deductible.

In Regenstein v. Edwards, 121 F.Supp. 952 (M.D.Ga.), the floor of the third story of landlord's building sagged. After some temporary steps, steel columns and steel crossbeams were installed in order to permanently cure the defect. The court held that the entire expenditure was for the sole purpose of restoring the property to its former condition and allowed the deduction since neither use, value, nor life expectancy was increased.

* * *

Respondent argues that the need for an expenditure in the cases discussed above resulted from an unexpected happening or unusual circumstance. He asserts that the expenditure in the instant case was capital because the need for it arose from a management decision. We do not understand respondent to argue that the expenditure was not "ordinary" or "necessary" as used in section 162(a). We do not find that petitioner expected in 1950 that there would be a need for a cement lining. Indeed, in 1954 petitioner merely cleaned the relevant pipe, did not line it until 1957, and the tuberculation could have been removed by periodic cleaning.

We do not agree that the deduction in the instant case requires a relatively sudden, unexpected, or unusual external factor which results in casualty damage. In Kansas City Southern Ry. Co. v. United States, [112 F.Supp. 164 (Ct.Cl.1953)], a deduction was allowed for the elimination of water pockets under railroad tracks. The water pockets were not relatively sudden, unexpected, or unusual occurrences (Id. at p. 165):

> Water pockets developed from time to time in the subgrade of the railroad track at various locations. * * * If the nature of the soil is such that the water becomes trapped in the subgrade, the subgrade becomes and remains soft and yielding * * *.

* * *

We have given full consideration to the entire factual context of the instant case. The useful life, strength, value, and capacity of the cleaned and lined water pipes were not increased by the expenditure in issue. Said expenditure did not make the relevant water main suitable for any new or additional use. Said main continued to be used in the normal course of petitioner's operations as a water company. Viewing the record as a whole, we hold that the cleaning and cement lining of the Maple Avenue main in 1957 was a repair, the cost of which is deductible under section 162(a).

Decision will be entered under Rule 50.

Problems, Notes and Questions

1. *"Repairs" vs. "Improvements."* Compare the principal case with Mt. Morris Drive–In Theatre Co. v. Commissioner, 25 T.C. 272 (1955), affirmed 238 F.2d 85 (6th Cir.1956). The taxpayer's construction of a drive-in theater caused rain water to drain onto a neighbor's land. In settlement of a suit brought by the neighbor, the taxpayer constructed a drainage system. The majority of the Tax Court held the cost of the drainage system a capital expenditure because the need for drains should have been foreseen when the theater was built. A concurring opinion thought the foreseeability of the need for the drainage system irrelevant. Five dissenting judges thought the expenditures were for repairs, since they did not "improve, better, extend, increase, or prolong the useful life of the property."

Sometimes taxpayers are compelled by law to add to buildings features which do not increase the amount of money the buildings earn or add to their lives. For example, in Trenton–New Brunswick Theatres Co. v. Commissioner, 13 T.C.M. 550 (1954), an order of a city building inspector required the taxpayer to build a fire passageway in its theater. Accepting, arguendo, the taxpayer's contention that the "improvement" made the theater less profitable than it had been, the court nevertheless held the expenditure to be capital.

An expenditure which would be a "repair" if it had been the only such expenditure for the year in question may become part of a capital expenditure if the "repair" is made pursuant to a "general plan of rehabilitation." Thus, the cost of a new roof cannot be treated as "repairs" on the theory that the replacement of a shingle is a repair, so the replacement of a roof is "many repairs." The taxpayer in Moss v. Commissioner, 831 F.2d 833 (9th Cir.1987), spent $270,268 on repairs to a hotel. These amounts (plus an additional $132,140 spent in the previous year) were paid for painting, wallpapering, and other items which the Commissioner conceded "normally qualify as repair expense[s]." The Tax Court held that the outlays had to be capitalized because they were incurred as part of a general rehabilitation plan. The Ninth Circuit reversed, noting that the "rehabilitation doctrine" had been applied only in cases involving "substantial capital improvements and repairs to the same specific asset, usually a structure in a state of disrepair."

Airlines perform extensive maintenance on aircraft, including a "heavy maintenance visit" approximately every eight years of an aircraft's service. These heavy maintenance visits can cost several million dollars per plane; they involve completely disassembling the plane and, depending on what is found when the plane is taken apart, they may include replacement of major components. On older airplanes, extensive improvements may be added. Rev. Rul. 2001–4, I.R.B. 2001–3, 295, attempts to distinguish the cases in which some or all of the costs of a heavy maintenance visit must be capitalized from those in which they may be expensed. The ruling allows an immediate deduction for all the costs ($2 million) of a heavy maintenance visit that does not result in the replacement of major components. It holds that the costs of replacing a major part of an aircraft's skin panels must be capitalized, as must the costs of upgrades. If the work on a particular plane is so extensive that it materially increases the value and prolongs the life of the plane, all of the costs must be capitalized.

2. *Small items.* The regulations allow farmers to expense the costs of small tools (§ 1.162–12), and professional people can deduct amounts spent for "books, furniture, and professional instruments and equipment, the useful life of which is short" (§ 1.162–6). Why are these costs deductible? Are they at all analogous to repairs?

The taxpayer in Cincinnati, New Orleans & Texas Pacific Ry. Co. v. United States, 424 F.2d 563 (Ct.Cl.1970), was required by the ICC to expense most purchases of property costing less than $500. The Court of Claims upheld the taxpayer's use of this practice for tax purposes upon a showing that the government's approach, which required capitalizing all purchases of more than $100, would have increased the taxpayer's annual income by a relatively small amount. The court suggested that the Treasury Department adopt regulations under which similar rules would apply to other taxpayers.

3. *Problems. T* owns a laundry and dry-cleaning business. Last year he made the expenditures listed below. *T* has asked you whether and to what extent he can deduct the expenditures.

(1) *T* bought a second-hand delivery truck for $10,000.

(2) *T* repainted the interior of the building at a cost of $6000. This is a job *T* does every third year.

4. *References.* Shugerman, Basic Criteria for Distinguishing Revenue Charges from Capital Expenditures in Income Tax Computations, 49 Mich.L.Rev. 213 (1950); Note, Income Tax Accounting: Business Expense or Capital Outlay, 47 Harv.L.Rev. 669 (1934).

COMMISSIONER v. IDAHO POWER CO.

Supreme Court of the United States, 1974.
418 U.S. 1, 94 S.Ct. 2757, 41 L.Ed.2d 535.

MR. JUSTICE BLACKMUN delivered the opinion of the Court.

This case presents the sole issue whether, for federal income tax purposes, a taxpayer is entitled to a deduction from gross income, under § 167(a), for depreciation on equipment the taxpayer owns and uses in the construction of its own capital facilities, or whether the capitalization provision of § 263(a)(1) of the Code bars the deduction.

I

Nearly all the relevant facts are stipulated. The taxpayer-respondent, Idaho Power Company, is a Maine corporation organized in 1915, with its principal place of business at Boise, Idaho. It is a public utility engaged in the production, transmission, distribution, and sale of electric energy. The taxpayer keeps its books and files its federal income tax returns on the calendar year accrual basis. The tax years at issue are 1962 and 1963.

For many years, the taxpayer has used its own equipment and employees in the construction of improvements and additions to its capital facilities. The major work has consisted of transmission lines, transmission switching stations, distribution lines, distribution stations, and connecting facilities.

During 1962 and 1963, the tax years in question, taxpayer owned and used in its business a wide variety of automotive transportation equipment, including passenger cars, trucks of all descriptions, power-operated equipment, and trailers. Radio communication devices were affixed to the equipment and were used in its daily operations. The transportation equipment was used in part for operation and maintenance and in part for the construction of capital facilities having a useful life of more than one year.

On its books, the taxpayer used various methods of charging costs incurred in connection with its transportation equipment either to current expense or to capital accounts. To the extent the equipment was used in construction, the taxpayer charged depreciation of the equipment, as well as all operating and maintenance costs (other than pension contributions and social security and motor vehicle taxes) to the capital assets so constructed. This was done either directly or through clearing accounts in accordance with procedures prescribed by the Federal Power Commission and adopted by the Idaho Public Utilities Commission.

For federal income tax purposes, however, the taxpayer treated the depreciation on transportation equipment differently. It claimed as a deduction from gross income *all* the year's depreciation on such equipment, including that portion attributable to its use in constructing capital facilities. The depreciation was computed on a composite life of 10 years and under straight-line and declining-balance methods. The other operating and maintenance costs the taxpayer had charged on its books to capital were not claimed as current expenses and were not deducted.

To summarize: On its books, in accordance with Federal Power Commission–Idaho Public Utilities Commission prescribed methods, the taxpayer capitalized the construction-related depreciation, but for income tax purposes that depreciation increment was claimed as a deduction under § 167(a).

* * *

The taxpayer asserts that its transportation equipment is used in its "trade or business" and that depreciation thereon is therefore deductible under § 167(a)(1) of the Code. The Commissioner concedes that § 167 may be said to have a literal application to depreciation on equipment used in capital construction, Brief for Petitioner 16, but contends that the provision must be read in light of § 263(a)(1) which specifically disallows any deduction for an amount "paid out for new buildings or for permanent improvements or betterments." He argues that § 263 takes precedence over § 167 by virtue of what he calls the "priority-ordering" terms (and what the taxpayer describes as "housekeeping" provisions) of § 161 of the Code, and that sound principles of accounting and taxation mandate the capitalization of this depreciation.

* * *

II

Our primary concern is with the necessity to treat construction-related depreciation in a manner that comports with accounting and taxation realities. Over a period of time a capital asset is consumed and, correspondingly over that period, its theoretical value and utility are thereby reduced. Depreciation is an accounting device which recognizes that the physical consumption of a capital asset is a true cost, since the asset is being depleted. As the process of consumption continues, and depreciation is claimed and allowed, the asset's adjusted income tax basis is reduced to reflect the distribution of its cost over the accounting periods affected. The Court stated in Hertz Corp. v. United States, 364 U.S. 122, 126 (1960): "[T]he purpose of depreciation accounting is to allocate the expense of using an asset to the various periods which are benefited by that asset." See also United States v. Ludey, 274 U.S. 295, 300–301 (1927); Massey Motors, Inc. v. United States, 364 U.S. 92, 96 (1960); Fribourg Navigation Co. v. Commissioner of Internal Revenue, 383 U.S. 272, 276–277 (1966). When the asset is used to further the taxpayer's day-to-day business operations, the periods of benefit usually correlate with the production of income. Thus, to the extent that equipment is used in such operations, a current depreciation deduction is an appropriate offset to gross income currently produced. It is clear, however, that different principles are implicated when the consumption of the asset takes place in the construction of other assets that, in the future, will produce income themselves. In this latter situation, the cost represented by depreciation does not correlate with production of current income. Rather, the cost, although certainly presently incurred, is related to the future and is appropriately allocated as part of the cost of acquiring an income-producing capital asset.

The Court of Appeals opined that the purpose of the depreciation allowance under the Code was to provide a means of cost recovery, Knoxville v. Knoxville Water Co., 212 U.S. 1, 13–14 (1909), and that this Court's decisions, e.g., Detroit Edison Co. v. Commissioner of Internal Revenue, 319 U.S. 98, 101 (1943), endorse a theory of replacement through "a fund to restore the property." 477 F.2d, at 691. Although tax-free replacement of a depreciating investment is one purpose of depreciation accounting, it alone does not require the result claimed by the taxpayer here. Only last Term, in United States v. Chicago, B. &

Q.R. Co., 412 U.S. 401 (1973), we rejected replacement as the strict and sole purpose of depreciation:

> "Whatever may be the desirability of creating a depreciation reserve under these circumstances, as a matter of good business and accounting practice, the answer is * * * '[d]epreciation reflects the cost of an existing capital asset, not the cost of a potential replacement.' " Id., at 415.

Even were we to look to replacement, it is the replacement of the constructed facilities, not the equipment used to build them, with which we would be concerned. If the taxpayer now were to decide not to construct any more capital facilities with its own equipment and employees, it, in theory, would have no occasion to replace its equipment to the extent that it was consumed in prior construction.

Accepted accounting practice and established tax principles require the capitalization of the cost of acquiring a capital asset. In Woodward v. Commissioner of Internal Revenue, 397 U.S. 572, 575 (1970), the Court observed: "It has long been recognized, as a general matter, that costs incurred in the acquisition * * * of a capital asset are to be treated as capital expenditures." This principle has obvious application to the acquisition of a capital asset by purchase, but it has been applied, as well, to the costs incurred in a taxpayer's construction of capital facilities. [Citations omitted.]

There can be little question that other construction-related expense items, such as tools, materials, and wages paid construction workers, are to be treated as part of the cost of acquisition of a capital asset. The taxpayer does not dispute this. Of course, reasonable wages paid in the carrying on of a trade or business qualify as a deduction from gross income. § 162(a)(1). But when wages are paid in connection with the construction or acquisition of a capital asset, they must be capitalized and are then entitled to be amortized over the life of the capital asset so acquired. [Citations omitted.]

Construction-related depreciation is not unlike expenditures for wages for construction workers. The significant fact is that the exhaustion of construction equipment does not represent the final disposition of the taxpayer's investment in that equipment; rather, the investment in the equipment is assimilated into the cost of the capital asset constructed. Construction-related depreciation on the equipment is not an expense to the taxpayer of its day-to-day business. It is, however, appropriately recognized as a part of the taxpayer's cost or investment in the capital asset. The taxpayer's own accounting procedure reflects this treatment, for on its books the construction-related depreciation was capitalized by a credit to the equipment account and a debit to the capital facility account. By the same token, this capitalization prevents the distortion of income that would otherwise occur if depreciation properly allocable to asset acquisition were deducted from gross income currently realized. See, e.g., Coors v. Commissioner, 60 T.C., at 398; Southern Natural Gas Co. v. United States, 412 F.2d, at 1265.

An additional pertinent factor is that capitalization of construction-related depreciation by the taxpayer who does its own construction work maintains tax parity with the taxpayer who has its construction work done by an independent contractor. The depreciation on the contractor's equipment incurred during the performance of the job will be an element of cost charged by the contractor for his construction services, and the entire cost, of course, must be capitalized by the taxpayer having the construction work performed. The Court of Appeals' holding would lead to disparate treatment among taxpayers because it would allow the firm with sufficient resources to construct its own facilities and to obtain a current deduction, whereas another firm without such resources would be required to capitalize its entire cost including depreciation charged to it by the contractor.

Some, although not controlling, weight must be given to the fact that the Federal Power Commission and the Idaho Public Utilities Commission required the taxpayer to use accounting procedures that capitalized construction-related depreciation. Although agency-imposed compulsory accounting practices do not necessarily dictate tax consequences, Old Colony R. Co. v. Commissioner of Internal Revenue, 284 U.S. 552, 562 (1932), they are not irrelevant and may be accorded some significance. * * *

The presence of § 263(a)(1) in the Code is of significance. Its literal language denies a deduction for "[a]ny amount paid out" for construction or permanent improvement of facilities. The taxpayer contends, and the Court of Appeals held, that depreciation of construction equipment represents merely a decrease in value and is not an amount "paid out," within the meaning of § 263(a)(1). We disagree.

The purpose of § 263 is to reflect the basic principle that a capital expenditure may not be deducted from current income. It serves to prevent a taxpayer from utilizing currently a deduction properly attributable, through amortization, to later tax years when the capital asset becomes income producing. The regulations state that the capital expenditures to which § 263(a) extends include the "cost of acquisition, construction, or erection of buildings." Treas.Reg. § 1.263(a)–2(a). This manifests an administrative understanding that for purposes of § 263(a)(1), "amount paid out" equates with "cost incurred." The Internal Revenue Service for some time has taken the position that construction-related depreciation is to be capitalized. Rev.Rul. 59–380, 1959–2 C.B. 87; Rev.Rul. 55–252, 1955–1 Cum.Bull. 319.

There is no question that the cost of the transportation equipment was "paid out" in the same manner as the cost of supplies, materials, and other equipment, and the wages of construction workers.[11] The

---

11. The taxpayer contends that depreciation has been held not to be an expenditure or payment for purposes of a charitable contribution under § 170 of the Code, e.g., Orr v. United States, 343 F.2d 553 (C.A.5, 1965); Mitchell v. Commissioner, 42 T.C. 953, 973–974 (1964), or for purposes of a medical-expense deduction under § 213, e.g., Gordon v. Commissioner, 37 T.C. 986 (1962). Section 263 is concerned, however,

taxpayer does not question the capitalization of these other items as elements of the cost of acquiring a capital asset. We see no reason to treat construction-related depreciation differently. In acquiring the transportation equipment, taxpayer "paid out" the equipment's purchase price; depreciation is simply the means of allocating the payment over the various accounting periods affected. As the Tax Court stated in Brooks v. Commissioner, 50 T.C., at 935, "depreciation—inasmuch as it represents a using up of capital—is as much an 'expenditure' as the using up of labor or other items of direct cost."

Finally, the priority-ordering directive of § 161—or, for that matter, § 261 of the Code—requires that the capitalization provision of § 263(a) take precedence, on the facts here, over § 167(a). Section 161 provides that deductions specified in Part VI of Subchapter B of the Income Tax Subtitle of the Code are "subject to the exceptions provided in part IX." Part VI includes § 167 and Part IX includes § 263. The clear import of § 161 is that, with stated exceptions set forth either in § 263 itself or provided for elsewhere (as, for example, in § 404 relating to pension contributions), none of which is applicable here, an expenditure incurred in acquiring capital assets must be capitalized even when the expenditure otherwise might be deemed deductible under Part VI.

* * *

We hold that the equipment depreciation allocable to taxpayer's construction of capital facilities is to be capitalized.

The judgment of the Court of Appeals is reversed.

It is so ordered.

Judgment of Court of Appeals reversed.

Mr. Justice Douglas, dissenting.

[Omitted.]

Problem and Note

1. *Similar problems.* The *Idaho Power* court mentions the costs of tools used in construction and of construction workers' wages as examples of costs to be capitalized when property is built rather than bought. Another example is insurance during the construction period. Construction period interest and taxes, on the other hand, were long regarded as currently deductible, and *Idaho Power* was not generally read as changing the law in this area. But § 263A, which was enacted in 1986, now requires capitalization of the "proper share of those indirect costs (including taxes) * * * allocable to" real or tangible personal property

with the capital nature of an expenditure and not with its timing, as are the phrases "payment * * * within the taxable year" or "paid during the taxable year," respectively used in §§ 170 and 213. The treatment of depreciation under those sections has no relevance to the issue of capitalization here. See, e.g., Producers Chemical Co. v. Commissioner, 50 T.C. 940, 959 (1968).

produced by the taxpayer. Section 263A(f) provides for capitalization of some construction-period interest, including interest on indebtedness "allocable * * * to property used to produce [new] property."

2. *Problem. I* Corp. spends $100,000 for a truck and uses the truck in the construction of a natural gas pipeline, which *I* will operate. During the construction period, depreciation on the truck is $40,000. Under *Idaho Power,* all of this depreciation is capitalized as part of the cost of the pipeline. When the pipeline construction is completed, *I* Corp. sells the truck for $70,000. What result? (Consider § 1016.)

INDOPCO, INC. v. COMMISSIONER

Supreme Court of the United States, 1992.
503 U.S. 79, 112 S.Ct. 1039, 117 L.Ed.2d 226.

JUSTICE BLACKMUN delivered the opinion of the Court.

In this case we must decide whether certain professional expenses incurred by a target corporation in the course of a friendly takeover are deductible by that corporation as "ordinary and necessary" business expenses under § 162(a).

I

* * * Petitioner INDOPCO, Inc., formerly named National Starch and Chemical Corporation and hereinafter referred to as National Starch, is a Delaware corporation that manufactures and sells adhesives, starches, and specialty chemical products. In October 1977, representatives of Unilever United States, Inc., also a Delaware corporation (Unilever), expressed interest in acquiring National Starch, which was one of its suppliers, through a friendly transaction. National Starch at the time had outstanding over 6,563,000 common shares held by approximately 3700 shareholders. The stock was listed on the New York Stock Exchange. Frank and Anna Greenwall were the corporation's largest shareholders and owned approximately 14.5% of the common. The Greenwalls, getting along in years and concerned about their estate plans, indicated that they would transfer their shares to Unilever only if a transaction tax-free for them could be arranged.

Lawyers representing both sides devised a "reverse subsidiary cash merger" that they felt would satisfy the Greenwalls' concerns. * * *

In November 1977, National Starch's directors were formally advised of Unilever's interest and the proposed transaction. At that time, Debevoise, Plimpton, Lyons & Gates, National Starch's counsel, told the directors that under Delaware law they had a fiduciary duty to ensure that the proposed transaction would be fair to the shareholders. National Starch thereupon engaged the investment banking firm of Morgan Stanley & Co., Inc., to evaluate its shares, to render a fairness opinion, and generally to assist in the event of the emergence of a hostile tender offer.

* * *

[After some negotiations over price and the issuance of a favorable ruling by the Internal Revenue Service, Unilever acquired National Starch. Some of National Starch's shareholders received Unilever stock; the rest got cash. National Starch paid $2,225,586 to Morgan Stanley, $505,069 to Debevoise, and $150,062 for miscellaneous items such as accounting and printing. It claimed that all of these costs were deductible as business expenses. The Tax Court held that the outlays were capital expenditures, and the Third Circuit affirmed.] In [affirming], the Court of Appeals rejected National Starch's contention that, because the disputed expenses did not "create or enhance . . . a separate and distinct additional asset," see Commissioner v. Lincoln Savings & Loan Assn., 403 U.S. 345, 354 (1971), they could not be capitalized and therefore were deductible under § 162(a). We granted certiorari to resolve a perceived conflict on the issue among the Courts of Appeals.

II

Section 162(a) allows the deduction of "all the ordinary and necessary expenses paid or incurred during the taxable year in carrying on any trade or business." In contrast, § 263 of the Code allows no deduction for a capital expenditure—an "amount paid out for new buildings or for permanent improvements or betterments made to increase the value of any property or estate." 26 U.S.C. § 263(a)(1). * * * [T]he Code endeavors to match expenses with the revenues of the taxable period to which they are properly attributable, thereby resulting in a more accurate calculation of net income for tax purposes. See, e.g., Commissioner v. Idaho Power Co., 418 U.S. 1, 16 (1974); [further citations omitted].

In exploring the relationship between deductions and capital expenditures, this Court has noted the "familiar rule" that "an income tax deduction is a matter of legislative grace and that the burden of clearly showing the right to the claimed deduction is on the taxpayer." [Citations omitted.] The notion that deductions are exceptions to the norm of capitalization finds support in various aspects of the Code. Deductions are specifically enumerated and thus are subject to disallowance in favor of capitalization. See §§ 161 and 261. Nondeductible capital expenditures, by contrast, are not exhaustively enumerated in the Code; rather than providing a "complete list of nondeductible expenditures," *Lincoln Savings*, 403 U.S., at 358, § 263 serves as a general means of distinguishing capital expenditures from current expenses. See Commissioner v. Idaho Power Co., 418 U.S., at 16. For these reasons, deductions are strictly construed and allowed only "as there is a clear provision therefor." [Citations omitted.][4]

* * *

4. See also Johnson, The Expenditures Incurred by the Target Corporation in an Acquisitive Reorganization are Dividends to the Shareholders, 53 Tax Notes 463, 478 (1991) (noting the importance of "a strong law of capitalization" to the tax system).

National Starch contends that the decision in *Lincoln Savings* * * * announced an exclusive test for identifying capital expenditures, a test in which "creation or enhancement of an asset" is a prerequisite to capitalization, and deductibility under § 162(a) is the rule rather than the exception. We do not agree, for we conclude that National Starch has overread *Lincoln Savings*.

In *Lincoln Savings*, we were asked to decide whether certain premiums, required by federal statute to be paid by a savings and loan association to the Federal Savings and Loan Insurance Corporation (FSLIC), were ordinary and necessary expenses under § 162(a), as Lincoln Savings argued and the Court of Appeals had held, or capital expenditures under § 263, as the Commissioner contended. We found that the "additional" premiums, the purpose of which was to provide FSLIC with a secondary reserve fund in which each insured institution retained a pro rata interest recoverable in certain situations, "serv[e] to create or enhance for Lincoln what is essentially a separate and distinct additional asset." 403 U.S., at 354. "As an inevitable consequence," we concluded, "the payment is capital in nature and not an expense, let alone an ordinary expense, deductible under § 162(a)." Ibid.

Lincoln Savings stands for the simple proposition that a taxpayer's expenditure that "serves to create or enhance * * * a separate and distinct" asset should be capitalized under § 263. It by no means follows, however, that *only* expenditures that create or enhance separate and distinct assets are to be capitalized under § 263. We had no occasion in *Lincoln Savings* to consider the tax treatment of expenditures that, unlike the additional premiums at issue there, did not create or enhance a specific asset * * *.

Nor does our statement in *Lincoln Savings*, 405 U.S., at 354, that "the presence of an ensuing benefit that may have some future aspect is not controlling" prohibit reliance on future benefit as a means of distinguishing an ordinary business expense from a capital expenditure.[6] Although the mere presence of an incidental future benefit—"*some future aspect*"—may not warrant capitalization, a taxpayer's realization of benefits beyond the year in which the expenditure is incurred is undeniably important in determining whether the appropriate tax treatment is immediate deduction or capitalization. * * *

III

In applying the foregoing principles to the specific expenditures at issue in this case, we conclude that National Starch has not demonstrated that the investment banking, legal, and other costs it incurred in

---

6. Petitioner contends that, absent a separate-and-distinct-asset requirement for capitalization, a taxpayer will have no "principled basis" upon which to differentiate business expenses from capital expenditures. We note, however, that grounding tax status on the existence of an asset would be unlikely to produce the bright-line rule that petitioner desires, given that the notion of an "asset" is itself flexible and amorphous. See Johnson, 53 Tax Notes, at 477–478.

connection with Unilever's acquisition of its shares are deductible as ordinary and necessary business expenses under § 162(a).

Although petitioner attempts to dismiss the benefits that accrued to National Starch from the Unilever acquisition as "entirely speculative" or "merely incidental," the Tax Court's and the Court of Appeals' findings that the transaction produced significant benefits to National Starch that extended beyond the tax year in question are amply supported by the record. For example, in commenting on the merger with Unilever, National Starch's 1978 "Progress Report" observed that the company would "benefit greatly from the availability of Unilever's enormous resources, especially in the area of basic technology." * * * Morgan Stanley's report to the National Starch board concerning the fairness to shareholders of a possible business combination with Unilever noted that National Starch management "feels that some synergy may exist with the Unilever organization given a) the nature of the Unilever chemical, paper, plastics and packaging operations * * * and b) the strong consumer products orientation of Unilever United States, Inc."

In addition to these anticipated resource-related benefits, National Starch obtained benefits through its transformation from a publicly held, freestanding corporation into a wholly owned subsidiary of Unilever. The Court of Appeals noted that National Starch management viewed the transaction as " 'swapping approximately 3500 shareholders for one.' " Following Unilever's acquisition of National Starch's outstanding shares, National Starch was no longer subject to what even it terms the "substantial" shareholder-relations expenses a publicly traded corporation incurs, including reporting and disclosure obligations, proxy battles, and derivative suits. The acquisition also allowed National Starch, in the interests of administrative convenience and simplicity, to eliminate previously authorized but unissued shares of preferred and to reduce the total number of authorized shares of common from 8,000,000 to 1,000.

* * *

IV

The expenses that National Starch incurred in Unilever's friendly takeover do not qualify for deduction as "ordinary and necessary" business expenses under § 162(a). The fact that the expenditures do not create or enhance a separate and distinct additional asset is not controlling; the acquisition-related expenses bear the indicia of capital expenditures and are to be treated as such.

The judgment of the Court of Appeals is affirmed.

It Is So Ordered.

Notes

1. *Hostile takeovers.* In A.E. Staley Mfg. Co. v. Commissioner, 119 F.3d 482 (7th Cir.1997), the Seventh Circuit ruled that most of the costs

of resisting a hostile, though ultimately successful, takeover attempt did not have to be capitalized under *INDOPCO*. The Service had earlier held in a technical advice memorandum that costs of "directly resisting" a hostile takeover attempt were deductible if the attempt failed (even if the target was taken over by a "white knight"); T.A.M. 9043002. These decisions give a target's management some incentive to resist a takeover attempt, at least for a while, so as to be able to characterize the bid as hostile, bringing the case within *Staley* rather than *INDOPCO*.

2. *What costs of a friendly takeover must be capitalized?* The payments held in *INDOPCO* to be capital expenditures were payments to third parties. What of other costs associated with an acquisition, such as the salaries of corporate employees who work on the acquisition? Recall that, under *Idaho Power*, wages and depreciation associated with the construction of assets have to be capitalized. In Wells Fargo & Co. v. Commissioner, 224 F.3d 874 (8th Cir.2000), the Eighth Circuit held that salaries of corporate officers who worked on the acquisition of another corporation did not have to be capitalized because it is common to pay salaries to corporate officers; the payments were therefore "ordinary." The court did not cite *Idaho Power*. Although the *Wells Fargo* opinion asserts repeatedly that the Tax Court's reasoning in requiring capitalization of these costs was "illogical," the opinion fails to give reasons why salaries should be distinguished from other acquisition costs. Compare Lychuk v. Commissioner, 116 T.C. 374 (2001), in which the Tax Court ruled unanimously that wages and bonuses paid to employees for their work in acquiring installment contracts from automobile dealers had to be capitalized as part of the cost of those contracts. Several dissenting judges would also have required capitalization of a portion of the taxpayer's overhead; the majority ruled that these costs were not so closely related to the acquisitions that they had to be capitalized.

3. *Capitalization and basis.* Conventional capital expenditures give the taxpayer a basis in some asset. That basis will then be recovered through depreciation if the asset has a limited useful life (a truck, for instance). If the asset does not have a limited useful life (land, or corporate stock), the basis will be used to calculate gain or loss when the asset is sold. Therefore, in the ordinary case, outlays that are capitalized may affect tax liability someday. In *INDOPCO*, however, it is hard to see how the corporation gets a basis in anything. Perhaps it can treat the money as adding to the basis of its goodwill, which is depreciable over 15 years under § 197 (discussed below). However, "goodwill" is generally thought of as adhering to a business, rather than to a corporation itself. Query whether, if INDOPCO had sold one of its businesses as a going concern right after its acquisition by Unilever, it could have treated a portion of the takeover costs as being part of the basis of "goodwill" that it had sold. All of the "benefits" described by the Court would have remained with the corporation in this case, making goodwill treatment seem unsound.

The basis problem would not exist if the court had accepted Professor Calvin H. Johnson's argument (footnote 4 of the opinion) that the expenditures were made to benefit the corporation's shareholders. According to that view, the outlays would have been non-deductible by the corporation and income to the shareholders. The shareholders would then have had increased bases for their INDOPCO stock. Note that some of the costs were incurred to arrange a tax-free acquisition of stock by Unilever, rather than an outright purchase, which National Starch's principal shareholders did not want.

4. *"Substantial" future benefits.* The *INDOPCO* opinion offers nothing in the way of general rules for determining whether future benefits from a particular outlay are so substantial that capitalization is required. (The *Lincoln Savings* "asset" approach did offer a general rule, though not one that made much sense.) In response to the questions raised by *INDOPCO* the Service has ruled that advertising costs remain generally deductible, despite the prospect of future benefits (Rev.Rul. 92–80, 1992–2 C.B. 57) and that severance payments to former employees are generally deductible as well, even though the payments may produce "some future benefits, such as reducing operating costs and increasing operating efficiencies" (Rev.Rul. 94–77, 1994–2 C.B. 19).

Section 198 deals with one particular problem. It allows taxpayers who incur "qualified cleanup costs" in connection with removing "hazardous substances" from a "qualified cleanup site" to elect to expense the costs (all of the quoted phrases are technical terms defined in § 198).

When capitalization is undesirable because the period over which the benefits of the outlay will be received is uncertain, rules providing for the amortization of the costs over some arbitrary period may be an attractive compromise between a current deduction and capitalization with no prospect of recovery through depreciation. Section 197, discussed in the text that follows, does this for some "intangibles."

"INTANGIBLE" CAPITAL EXPENDITURES

Many outlays promise future benefits that cannot easily be allocated to particular years. A camera manufacturer incurs advertising expenses to promote a new product; if the campaign succeeds the product will sell well for many years. A candy wholesaler spends large sums studying and then putting into practice a plan to expand the business's operations into neighboring states. A bank trains hundreds of new employees to conduct a credit-card business. In all of these cases the expenditures in question relate to future years' profits, yet attempts to recover the costs through depreciation or amortization pose serious problems of assigning realistic lives to the benefits of the outlays. Economically, allowing taxpayers current deductions for costs like these would provide an undeserved benefit, but requiring capitalization could deny any tax effect to the costs until the business is sold or abandoned.

During the 1980s the government became more and more insistent that costs incurred to provide "intangible" future benefits be capitalized. For example, Rev.Rul. 89–23, 1989–1 C.B. 85, held that the costs of developing and designing packages for new products had to be capitalized. (The ruling was inspired by an audit dispute over the costs of designing packages for L'eggs panty hose.) The Service's position on package-design costs was rejected in RJR Nabisco, Inc. v. Commissioner, 76 T.C.M. 71 (1998)(Non-acq.), which held that these costs are just another form of advertising expense, deductible even though they may generate some long-term benefits.

While the government insisted upon capitalization of outlays that used to be routinely deducted, some taxpayers obtained amortization deductions for outlays that would traditionally have been viewed as buying "goodwill," which could not then be amortized for lack of an ascertainable useful life. For example, in Newark Morning Ledger Co. v. United States, 507 U.S. 546 (1993), the Supreme Court allowed a corporation which bought newspapers as going businesses to depreciate the portion of the purchase price allocable to "an intangible asset denominated 'paid subscribers'." Although the papers' total numbers of subscribers remained fairly constant, the taxpayer was able, with expert testimony, to determine the approximate rate at which subscribers who took the papers at the time of the purchase would cease subscribing. The government did not contest the taxpayer's estimates of the useful lives of the subscriber lists, but rather argued that the list of subscribers was an asset indistinguishable from goodwill, which was not depreciable. Although "goodwill" is often defined as including the expectation of continued patronage, the majority held that the subscriber lists' relationship to continued patronage did not make those lists non-depreciable, because the taxpayer's expert testimony had established that the lists had limited useful lives.

Section 197 now provides for the amortization of some intangible assets—including goodwill—over a 15–year period. "Section 197 assets," eligible for amortization under this provision, include goodwill, going-concern value, "information base" (which includes subscriber lists like those involved in *Newark Morning Ledger*), know-how (including patents and copyrights), covenants not to compete, franchises, trademarks, and other specified items. Generally speaking, § 197 applies to intangibles *purchased* by the taxpayer, but not to intangible assets *created* by the taxpayer. However, if the taxpayer creates an intangible asset "in connection with a transaction * * * involving the acquisition of assets constituting a trade or business or substantial portion thereof," the asset is amortizable under § 197. Most computer software is excluded from § 197; as a rule, software is depreciable over three years under § 168.

ECONOMIC EFFECTS OF ALLOWING AN IMMEDIATE DEDUCTION FOR A CAPITAL EXPENDITURE

Do not make the mistake of thinking that capitalization questions involve "mere timing" problems and so do not matter very much because most capitalized costs can be deducted later through depreciation, amortization, or depletion. In fact, allowing an immediate deduction for the cost of a long-lived income-producing asset produces the same effect as capitalizing the cost and exempting the income the asset earns from taxation, provided certain conditions are met.[b] Consider a taxpayer who pays $100,000 for a machine with a ten-year life and no salvage value. The machine will generate $20,000 in revenue each year (a 20–percent pre-tax return on the $100,000 cost), all of which (except for income taxes) the taxpayer will spend on consumption. Assume that the taxpayer has a large amount of other income, and that the taxpayer is subject to a flat-rate 40–percent income tax. If the taxpayer capitalizes the cost of the machine and takes straight-line depreciation, the taxpayer's decision to purchase the asset rather than to spend its purchase price on consumption amounts to a decision to give up $100,000 of consumption in the year the machine was bought in exchange for $16,000 annual consumption[c] over a ten-year period.

Now suppose the taxpayer is offered a tax exemption for the earnings from the machine. Because the machine produces no taxable income, no depreciation is allowed. The taxpayer will be able to spend $20,000 a year for ten years.

If, instead of an exemption for the machine's earnings, an immediate deduction for the purchase price of the machine (and of similar machines) were allowed, the taxpayer would still be able to spend $20,000 a year for ten years. We have assumed that the taxpayer was willing to give up $100,000 of current consumption to buy a non-deductible machine. If the cost of machines is deductible, the taxpayer can buy $166,666.67 worth of machines by giving up $100,000 of consumption (because the out-of-pocket cost of an immediately deductible $166,666.67 investment to a 40–percent taxpayer is $100,000). The gross return on this investment will be $33,333.33 (20 percent of $166,666.67) a year. This amount will be fully taxable (no depreciation being allowed because the cost of the machine was deducted at the time of purchase). Therefore, the taxpayer will be able to spend 60 percent of this sum, or $20,000, each year.

The equivalence between an immediate deduction and an exemption for return on investment holds for any constant rate of return and tax rate. Suppose a taxpayer has an amount, I, of pre-tax income to invest. The rate of return is R and the tax rate is T. If the investment is non-deductible and the return is non-taxable, the taxpayer can invest $(1-T) \times I$. The return (not taxed) will be $R \times (1-T) \times I$. If, on the other hand, the return is taxable but the investment is deductible, the taxpayer will invest I, for an after-tax return of $I \times (1-T) \times R$.

The equivalence between current deductibility and exemption of return was first noted in Brown, Business–Income Taxation and Invest-

___

b. The conditions are that rates of return on investments and tax rates are constant, and that the taxpayer has enough income so that deductions are not wasted.

c. The machine will generate a $20,000 annual cash return, but only $10,000 in

taxable income (because of the $10,000 annual depreciation deduction). Each year's income tax will be $4000, leaving the taxpayer $16,000 to spend.

ment Incentives; in L. Metzler et al., Income, Employment and Public Policy; reprinted in R. Musgrave & C. Shoup, Readings in the Economics of Taxation (1959).

Notes and Question

1. *"Economic depreciation."* The example in the text is somewhat misleading in suggesting that the income in question would have been subject to a 40–percent tax rate if straight-line depreciation had been used. In fact, even straight-line depreciation may be too fast if "proper" depreciation is an allowance that matches an asset's decline in value. An asset that will generate $10,000 a year in revenues for ten years declines in value by less than 10 percent in each of its early years, and by more than 10 percent in each of its later years. See Chirelstein, Federal Income Taxation 165–167 (9th ed. 2002), for a description and explanation of "economic" or "sinking fund" depreciation. Strictly speaking, the equivalence between expensing and a tax exemption holds true only if economic depreciation is used as a basis for the comparison.

In the case of an asset that does not decline in value—a bond, for example—proper depreciation is zero, and the equivalence between expensing and exempting investment return holds.

If depreciable assets can be depreciated at rates faster than the rates at which the assets decline in value, while non-depreciable assets cannot be depreciated at all, the tax system creates a bias in favor of investing in depreciable property as opposed to investing in non-depreciable property or in businesses that acquire no assets at all.

2. *Why should any expenditures be capitalized?* It is often said that capitalization is needed to "match" income and related expenditures. But this argument begs the question of *why* income and expenditures should "match" in this way. In contexts other than capitalization, the tax system generally makes little effort to match income and expenditures (see Chapter 12). A justification for "matching" in the capitalization context can be found by noting that expensing would in effect exempt savings from taxation: a taxpayer who earns $100,000 and uses those earnings to buy income-producing property has "saved" those earnings, and if the amount saved could be deducted the earnings would not be taxed. Whether the tax system should exempt savings from taxation is quite controversial: an "expenditure" or "consumption" tax (see p. 37, above) would allow an immediate deduction for all savings (with dissavings being taxable). Our present tax system is not a pure income tax, but rather is a blend of income and expenditure taxation because some savings are currently deductible, because most depreciable assets can be depreciated more rapidly than they decline in value, and because unrealized appreciation (a form of savings) is not taxed.

3. *Expensing provisions.* Several Code provisions allow immediate deductions for costs that would (or might) have to be capitalized under normal tax principles. In terms of revenue effect, the most important of

these is probably § 263(c), which allows a current deduction at the taxpayer's election for "intangible drilling and development costs" in the case of oil, gas, and geothermal wells. "Intangible" drilling and development costs are costs of such items as fuel, labor, and supplies used in drilling or developing wells. The scope of the deduction is outlined in Treas.Reg. § 1.612–4.

The option to expense intangible drilling and development costs was first allowed by regulation, perhaps because of a mistaken assumption that only the purchase price of an asset could be a capital expenditure. Congress enacted the predecessor of § 263(c) in response to F.H.E. Oil Co. v. Commissioner, 147 F.2d 1002 (5th Cir.1945), rehearings denied 149 F.2d 238, 150 F.2d 857 (1945), which held the regulations invalid.

Current deductions are specifically allowed by § 263(d) (certain costs of rehabilitating railroad rolling stock); § 173 (costs of establishing, maintaining, or increasing the circulation of a periodical); § 174(a) (research or experimental expenditures); § 175 (farmers' soil and water conservation expenditures); § 180 (farmers' costs of fertilizer); and § 190 (up to $15,000 a year of the costs of making the taxpayer's facilities or public transportation vehicles accessible to handicapped and elderly people).

Note also the treatment of traditional IRAs and qualified pension and profit-sharing plans described in Chapter 2. By allowing deductions or exclusions for amounts set aside for retirement, the Code exempts a form of savings from taxation.

4. *Reference.* Surrey, Pathways to Tax Reform 120–125 (1973).

2. INVENTORIES

"Inventory" refers to goods purchased or manufactured by a firm and held for sale as part of the firm's ordinary business operations. The cost of the units sold during the year must be offset against the selling price of those units if we are to tax only net income. But, just as the capitalization requirement denies current deductions for the costs of assets that will be used to produce income in future periods, so must we deny current deductions for amounts spent for goods that will not be sold until a future period.

If each unit of a particular good purchased for resale cost the same amount, we could easily determine the cost of the goods sold by multiplying the number of units sold by the cost of each unit. In reality, however, prices change. If, for example, a grocery store purchases cans of corn at varying prices throughout the year, how does it determine the cost of the units sold and the (nondeductible) costs of the units remaining in inventory at the close of the year? In most cases, it is not practicable to connect costs with receipts on an asset-by-asset basis.[d] Thus, when a

---

d. In the case of some high-priced goods (for example, automobiles held by a dealer), the cost of goods sold may be ascertained by specific identification of the item sold.

Land and buildings held for sale to the taxpayer's customers are not considered inventory: the taxpayer must offset receipts from a sale of land by the costs of acquiring and improving the particular tract sold.

grocery store sells a can of corn, it does not compute its gain by subtracting the cost of that particular can from the sale price. Instead, it adopts a method of inventory accounting based upon an arbitrary assumption about which goods are sold first.

Two common inventory-accounting methods are "first-in, first-out" ("FIFO"), which treats the first goods acquired as the first resold, and "last-in, first-out" ("LIFO"), which treats the last items acquired as the first resold. To illustrate, suppose that a taxpayer purchases two widgets, one for $1.00 in year 1 and the other for $2.00 in year 2, and suppose that one widget is sold in year 3 for $2.50. Under FIFO, the taxpayer is viewed as having sold the first widget purchased, at a gain of $1.50. Under LIFO, it is viewed as having sold the last widget purchased, at a gain of $.50.

	FIFO	LIFO
Sales	$2.50	$2.50
Cost of goods sold	1.00	2.00
Gross income (year 3)	$1.50	$ .50

When prices are rising, LIFO will show higher costs (hence lower profits) than FIFO, making LIFO more attractive for tax purposes. For non-tax purposes, however, some taxpayers will prefer FIFO, since FIFO inventories will result in higher profits (or smaller losses) on the financial statements shown to creditors and shareholders. The Wall Street Journal for February 10, 1971, reports that in 1970 the Chrysler Corporation changed its method of accounting for inventories from LIFO to FIFO at a cost of some $53 million in additional tax liability for years up to and including 1970 in order to improve the appearance of its financial statements. Why did Chrysler not simply change to FIFO for financial-accounting purposes while retaining LIFO for tax purposes? See § 472(c). What kinds of taxpayers are hurt by the conformity requirement of this section? What taxpayers will not care?

The usual justification for allowing LIFO inventory accounting is that the method tends to reduce "imaginary" gains attributable to inflation. The argument is that a taxpayer that buys a widget for $1.00 in year 1 and sells it for $1.10 in year 2 has not really made a profit if it must spend $1.10 to replace the widget sold, as will be the case if the price of widgets increased ten percent from year 1 to year 2 because of inflation. Is there any good reason for allowing taxpayers with "imaginary" inflationary gains to report only their "real" incomes when the gains result from using inventories while requiring taxpayers with other inflation-created gains to report the entire amounts? Most of the "gain" reported by a taxpayer with a savings account is attributable to inflation, and does not represent any increase in purchasing power, yet such a taxpayer cannot exclude any of the interest income.

A recurring problem involving manufacturers is "costing" (i.e., the assigning of costs to manufactured items). In principle, determining the cost of manufactured inventory items resembles determining the costs to be capitalized when a taxpayer builds assets to be used in its business, but as a historical matter the rules for capitalization developed independently of those concerned with costing of inventories. However, § 263A, enacted in 1986, applies the same "uniform capitalization rules" to inventory as to capitalization of the costs of self-constructed assets. Section 263A applies to purchased inventory only in the case of taxpayers whose annual gross receipts from sales average more than $10 million. Regulations providing for simplified costing procedures for purchased inventory are authorized by § 263A(i)(2).

The heart of § 263A is § 263A(a), which requires the inclusion in inventory costs of all "direct costs" of the property and of the "property's proper share of those indirect costs (including taxes) part or all of which are allocable to such property." The regulations go on at some length about the kinds of costs that may have to be allocated in full or in part to inventory.

Problems and Notes

1. *Farmers.* Farmers (other than those which are corporations or which are partnerships having at least one corporate partner) are subject to much-less-strict costing rules than other taxpayers. See, for example, § 263A(d)(3), which allows many farmers to elect out of the uniform capitalization rules. As a result, farming has become a business in which some people invest for tax reasons, and this has led to provisions like §§ 447, 448, and 263A(d)(3)(B), all of which are aimed at confining the major tax benefits of farming to "real" farmers.

2. *Lower of cost or market.* Inventories can be valued at the "lower of cost or market" except for LIFO inventories, which must be valued at cost; Treas.Reg. §§ 1.471–4 & 1.472–2(b). The effect of valuing inventory at the market price of the goods, when that price is less than cost, is to reduce the taxpayer's income when prices fall before the goods in question are actually sold at that lower price. This occurs because the cost of goods sold, for a taxpayer with inventories, is the sum of the amount included in inventory at the beginning of the year and additions to inventory during the year less the amount included in inventory at the end of the year. For example, if the taxpayer has an opening inventory of $10,000, produces an additional $1000 of inventory items during the year, and has an inventory of $10,100 at the end of the year, the cost of goods sold is $900 (opening inventory of $10,000 plus additions of $1000, less closing inventory of $10,100). If a decline in prices reduces the closing inventory (under a "lower of cost or market" system) to $9500, the taxpayer's cost of goods sold will be increased to $1500, reducing income (or increasing loss) by $600.

3. *Problems.* In year 1, *R* began the business of selling widgets at retail. In that year he purchased 1000 widgets at $1 and sold 750 at $3. In year 2, he purchased 2000 widgets at $2 and sold 1800 at $4.

(1) What is R's gross income from the widget business if R uses the FIFO method of accounting for inventory?

(2) Same as (1), except that R uses LIFO.

C. BUSINESS, INVESTMENT, AND PERSONAL EXPENSES

Three general provisions allow business and investment expenses to be deducted: Sections 162, 167, and 212. Section 262 denies deductions for "personal, living, or family expenses." Other sections allowing or denying deductions for particular expenses will be considered in the material that follows; most of these sections are refinements of the general rules of § 162 or § 212. Note that many taxes are deductible under § 164 even if they are not business or investment expenses. The deductibility of interest depends upon § 163 and other provisions dealing with interest; interest deductions will be examined in Chapter 5.

As a rough approximation, most non-capital costs of earning a profit (or of trying to earn a profit) can be deducted. Technically, however, the Code creates different classes of profit-making activities. If an activity is a "trade or business,"[e] depreciation on assets used in the activity can be deducted under § 167(a)(1) and other expenses are deductible under § 162(a); if property is held "for the production of income," depreciation is authorized by § 167(a)(2), and expenses of managing, conserving, and maintaining the property are deductible under § 212(2). Costs incurred "for the production or collection of income" are deductible because of § 212(1).[f]

Whether an activity is a trade or business or merely a profit-making activity that falls short of being a trade or business can be important for a variety of reasons. For example, many business expenses are above-the-line deductions because of § 62(a)(1), while expenses deductible under 212 are ordinarily itemized deductions (but see § 62(a)(4)). Section 67 allows deductions for "miscellaneous itemized deductions" only to the extent that the total of these deductions exceeds 2 percent of an individual's adjusted gross income; many business expenses will not be subject to this floor because they are not itemized deductions, while most § 212 expenses are "miscellaneous itemized deductions." Other sections which draw distinctions between a trade or business and lesser income-producing activities include §§ 172 (net operating loss carryovers and carrybacks), 1091 (losses on wash sales of securities), and 56 (the alternative minimum tax).

The line between "trade or business" and other for-profit activities was addressed by the Supreme Court in Commissioner v. Groetzinger,

---

e. The words "trade" and "business" seem to have no independent significance; that is, there are no "trades" that are not "businesses" and vice versa. Compare "damn Yankee," "law and order," and "cease and desist."

f. Section 212 does not apply to corporations because, historically, any income-producing corporate activity is treated as part of the corporation's "trade or business."

480 U.S. 23 (1987), which held that a full-time gambler who bet only for his own account and whose "intended livelihood source" was gambling was engaged in a trade or business for purposes of §§ 62(a)(1) and 162(a). Although the Court described its holding as being "confined to" those specific sections, the *Groetzinger* opinion is likely to be viewed as authoritative wherever the issue arises, if only because of the absence of other authority. *Groetzinger* and other cases establish the following points:

(1) The expenses of managing one's own investments are not business expenses even if management of the investments is the taxpayer's full-time activity. (The predecessor of §§ 212(1) and 212(2) was enacted in response to the Supreme Court's decision in Higgins v. Commissioner, 312 U.S. 212 (1941), which refused to overturn a Board of Tax Appeals finding that an investor's activities were not a trade or business "[n]o matter how large the estate or how continuous or extended the work required may be"; 312 U.S. at 218. Because the applicable revenue act contained no provision for deducting expenses other than those now allowed by § 162(a), Higgins could not deduct salaries and office expenses allocable to the securities trading. Section 212 now eliminates the distinction between "business" and "investment" when the issue is whether "ordinary and necessary" expenses are deductible.)

(2) An active "trader" in securities—someone who buys and sells securities in large quantities, and who typically holds securities for a short time—can be in a trade or business.[g] (For more on this point, see Estate of Yaeger v. Commissioner, which follows this note.)

(3) One "must be involved in the activity with continuity and regularity" if the activity is to be a trade or business; 480 U.S. at 35.

(4) The Code normally focuses on "a common-sense concept of what is a trade or business"; id.

(5) One need not hold one's self out as offering goods or services to others to be engaged in a trade or business (this was the principal issue in the *Groetzinger* case).

(6) The fact that one's livelihood derives from an activity is some indication that the activity is a trade or business.

ESTATE OF YAEGER v. COMMISSIONER

United States Court of Appeals, Second Circuit, 1989.
889 F.2d 29, cert. denied 495 U.S. 946, 110 S.Ct. 2205, 109 L.Ed.2d 531.

Before FEINBERG and NEWMAN, CIRCUIT JUDGES, and MISHLER, SENIOR DISTRICT JUDGE.

MISHLER, SENIOR DISTRICT JUDGE:

Petitioner appeals from a decision and order of the [T]ax [C]ourt * * * that found that Louis Yaeger, deceased, was not in the trade or

g. See Levin v. United States, 597 F.2d 760 (Ct.Cl.1979).

business of trading in securities and, therefore, that the interest he incurred in buying securities on margin was "investment interest" within the meaning of section 163(d) and ordered that there is a deficiency due from the taxpayer for taxable years 1979 and 1980. * * *

We affirm the [T]ax [C]ourt's order that there is a deficiency due from the taxpayer for taxable years 1979 and 1980. * * *

I. TRADE OR BUSINESS OF TRADING IN SECURITIES

A. *Background*

The facts as stipulated and found by the [T]ax [C]ourt are not in dispute. Yaeger graduated Phi Beta Kappa from Columbia University in 1921 having studied business and finance. Upon graduation he went to work as an accountant and subsequently became employed as an auditing agent for the Internal Revenue Service. He left this employ in 1923 and went to work as a bond salesman in New York City, eventually becoming an investment counselor.

Commencing in the mid–1920s, Yaeger began actively trading stocks and bonds on the stock market on his own account in addition to conducting his investment consulting business. In the 1940s, Yaeger gave up his investment consulting business because the management of his own account had grown so demanding. Thereafter, he devoted himself exclusively to trading on his own account, which was his sole occupation until the day he died.

Prior to 1979, Yaeger maintained accounts with several brokerage firms in New York, including H. Hentz & Co. His account at H. Hentz & Co. was the largest account that firm had maintained for a United States citizen. During the period between 1979 and his death, Yaeger maintained accounts with three brokerage firms and occasionally dealt with two others.

The following chart describes the trading activity in Yaeger's various accounts throughout the years in issue:

Year	Purchase Transactions	Sales Transactions	Number Shares Bought	Number Shares Sold
1979	1,176	86	1,453,555	822,955
1980	1,088	39	1,658,841	173,165

Yaeger maintained an office at H. Hentz & Co. from which he conducted most of his trading activity. For a brief period of time he also conducted his activity from another brokerage firm. H. Hentz & Co. provided Yaeger with an assistant, a telephone, use of the secretarial pool, and access to the research staff and facilities. Yaeger spent a full day at his office, researching investment opportunities and placing orders, and then returned home to read more financial reports late into the night. He worked every day of the week. When he was out of town, he maintained telephone contact with the brokers who handled his accounts. Yaeger was trading on the stock market the day before he died.

Yaeger subscribed to a distinct investment strategy. His trading strategy was to buy the stock of companies in which the stock prices were extremely undervalued and hold the stock until it reached a price that reflected the underlying value of the company. He rarely purchased "blue chip" stocks and many of the stocks he held did not pay dividends. Instead, Yaeger constantly looked for companies that were experiencing financial distress but whose underlying value was not recognized.

This strategy required thorough research that extended beyond the study of mainstream publications. He also poured [sic] over annual reports and brokerage house reports. Once Yaeger determined that the targeted company was experiencing temporary difficulties, he began to accumulate the stock. He would buy stock as it became available, although some of the stock was not frequently or actively traded and was difficult to acquire. He would initially buy small quantities of stock to avoid attracting attention from other investors. Once he obtained a sizeable amount of stock he would let his position be known. Yaeger took whatever steps he thought necessary to improve the position of the companies in which he invested, often supplying unsolicited business advice to the managers and occasionally attempting to arrange mergers or acquisitions.

In addition to selecting financially troubled companies in which to invest, Yaeger increased his gain on his investments by using margin debt.[h] Yaeger financed his purchases by borrowing to the maximum extent allowable under law and the custom of the brokerage houses, which was generally 50 percent. If the value of his stock rose he would use that increased value as equity to support more debt. From time to time Yaeger shifted accounts from one brokerage house to another in order to maximize the volume of margin debt he could carry. Once or twice during his career Yaeger was overleveraged and suffered substantial losses when he was forced to sell enough stock to maintain his margin debt.

During the years 1979 and 1980, the ratio of Yaeger's margin debt to portfolio value was 47 percent and 42 percent, respectively. Yaeger's total stock market related debt equalled $42,154,048 in 1979 and $54,968,371 in 1980. When he died, his portfolio was subject to debt in the amount of $70,490,018.

* * *

Of the stock which Yaeger sold in taxable years 1979 and 1980, the percentage of total sales of securities which he had held for twelve months or more was 88 percent and 91 percent, respectively. The purchase dates of the securities sold in 1980 ranged from March 1970 to December 1979. In 1979, Yaeger did not sell any security that had been

---

h. Buying securities on margin means that the buyer pays only a portion of the purchase price to the broker; the balance is a loan by the broker to the buyer. When the value of stock bought on margin falls, the buyer must pay the broker additional cash, because the amount of the debt cannot exceed more than a specified portion (say half) of the value of the stock in the buyer's account.

held for less than three months and, in 1980, did not sell any security that had been held for less than six months. On schedule C of the tax returns, Yaeger deducted interest expense in 1979 and 1980 in the amounts of $5,865,833 and $7,995,010, respectively.

The sole issue considered by the [T]ax [C]ourt was whether the claimed deductions of the interest expenses Yaeger incurred in purchasing securities on margin were subject to the limitation on the deductibility of investment interest set forth in section 163(d). This issue turned on whether Yaeger's stock market activities constituted investment activity or the activity of trading in securities as a trade or business. According to the [T]ax [C]ourt, the "pivotal inquiry" was "whether Yaeger was interested in deriving income from capital appreciation or from short-term trading." The court determined that Yaeger was an investor, not a trader, because Yaeger held his stocks and bonds for lengthy periods of time anticipating that they would appreciate in value. Thus, the interest expense he incurred was "investment interest" within the meaning of section 163(d) and subject to the deductibility restrictions of that section.

B. Discussion

Section 163 generally provides for the deduction of interest incurred on indebtedness. As defined in section 163(d)(3)(D), "investment interest" is "interest paid or accrued on indebtedness incurred or continued to purchase or carry property held for investment." Section 163(d) limits the deductibility of investment interest by a noncorporate taxpayer to the extent of the taxpayer's investment income, plus $10,000. [Current law limits deductibility to the taxpayer's "net investment income"— Eds.] * * * Section 163(d) does not apply to interest paid to buy property for personal use or property for trade or business use. See H.R.Rep. 413, pt. 1, 91st Cong., 1st Sess. 72, reprinted in 1969 U.S.Code Cong. & Admin.News 1645, 1719 ("interest on funds borrowed in connection with a trade or business would not be affected by the limitation").

The Internal Revenue Code does not define "trade or business." Determining whether a taxpayer's trading activities rise to the level of carrying on a trade or business turns on the facts and circumstances of each case. Higgins v. Commissioner, 312 U.S. 212, 217 (1941). In determining whether taxpayers who manage their own investments are traders, "relevant considerations are the taxpayer's investment intent, the nature of the income to be derived from the activity, and the frequency, extent, and regularity of the taxpayer's securities transactions." Moller v. United States, 721 F.2d 810, 813 (Fed.Cir.1983), cert. denied, 467 U.S. 1251 (1984).

Investors are engaged in the production of income. [Citation omitted.] Traders are those "whose profits are derived from the 'direct management of purchasing and selling.'" [Citations omitted.] Investors derive profit from the interest, dividends, and capital appreciation of securities. [Citations omitted.] They are "primarily interested in the long-term growth potential of their stocks." [Citation omitted.] Traders, however, buy and sell securities "with reasonable frequency in an endeavor to catch the swings in the daily market movements and profit thereby on a short term basis." [Citations omitted.]

Thus, the two fundamental criteria that distinguish traders from investors [are] the length of the holding period and the source of the profit. These criteria coincide with the congressional purpose behind the enactment of section 163(d) * * *. Congress was concerned with the prevalent use of borrowed money to purchase investment assets and the distortion of taxable income that often results when the investments produce long-term capital gain rather than ordinary income. As explained in the House Report accompanying the 1969 Act:

> The itemized deduction presently allowed individuals for interest makes it possible for taxpayers to voluntarily incur substantial interest expense on funds borrowed to acquire or carry investment assets. Where the interest expense exceeds the taxpayer's investment income, it, in effect, is used to insulate other income from taxation. For example, a taxpayer may borrow substantial amounts to purchase stocks which have growth potential but which return small dividends currently. Despite the fact that receipt of the income from the investment may be postponed (and may be capital gains), the taxpayer will receive a current deduction for the interest expense even though it is substantially in excess of the income from the investment.

[Citation omitted.]

The activity of holding securities for a length of time to produce interest, dividends, and capital gains fits the abuse targeted by section 163(d): investing for postponed income and current interest deduction.

The [T]ax [C]ourt properly concluded that Yaeger was an investor. It is true that Yaeger initiated over 2000 securities transactions in 1979 and 1980 and pursued his security activities vigorously and extensively. And there is no doubt, as the [T]ax [C]ourt stated, that Yaeger "maintained a margin of debt which would have caused a more faint-hearted investor to quail." However, "[n]o matter how large the estate or how continuous or extended the work required may be," the management of securities investments is not the trade or business of a trader. *Higgins,* supra, at 218.

More importantly, most of his sales were of securities held for over a year. He did not sell any security held for less than three months. He realized a profit on the securities through both dividends and interest. Most of his profit, however, came from holding undervalued stock until its market improved. This emphasis on capital growth and profit from resale indicates an investment motivated activity. [Citation omitted.] In addition, since the income came from long-term appreciation, Yaeger would receive the benefit of favorable capital gains treatment. To disregard the nature of the income and length of his holdings simply because

Yaeger was a vigorous investor would defeat the purpose of section 163(d).

* * *

Problem and Note

1. *Employee business expenses.* Working as an employee is a trade or business, and so an employee's business expenses are deductible under § 162(a). Union dues and subscriptions to professional journals are everyday examples of employee business expenses. Unlike the business expenses of people who are not employees, however, most employee business expenses are itemized deductions and are also "miscellaneous itemized deductions" for purposes of the 2–percent floor of § 67. See §§ 62(a)(1) & (2). Employee expenses reimbursed by the employer and the expenses of one who is a "qualified performing artist" are above-the-line deductions; §§ 62(a)(2) & (b). Some employment-related expenses of handicapped employees are exempt from the 2–percent–floor computations; §§ 67(b)(6) & (d).

Other limits on employees' deductions will be examined later on in this chapter.

2. *Problem. S,* a single person with no dependents, is employed by X Corp. as its full-time general counsel. S's gross income for the current year is $67,000. During the year S paid expenses as follows:

(1) $2000 incurred for air transportation while traveling on business for X Corp. (X Corp. reimbursed S for the $2000, and S included the $2000 reimbursement in gross income.);

(2) $800 for membership in various professional organizations (bar associations, etc.) (S was not reimbursed for these expenses.);

(3) $5000 expenses of a single rental residence which S actively manages. (S included the rent in gross income.);

(4) $500 for investment advice with respect to stock investments;

(5) $4000 of state income taxes;

(6) $3000 in charitable contributions.

Determine S's adjusted gross and taxable income.

As noted earlier, classifying a deductible expense as a "miscellaneous itemized deduction" hurts some taxpayers because those deductions are allowed only to the extent that they exceed two percent of AGI. Another drawback of miscellaneous itemized deductions is that they are not allowed at all in calculating the Alternative Minimum Tax (which will be examined briefly in Chapter 6). When a taxpayer incurs a very large miscellaneous itemized deduction in connection with the production of income, disallowing the deduction under the AMT can be a very serious matter. This issue has arisen fairly often in connection with legal fees incurred to get damages that are income to the taxpayer.

KENSETH v. COMMISSIONER

United States Court of Appeals, Seventh Circuit, 2001.
259 F.3d 881.

Before POSNER, KANNE and ROVNER, CIRCUIT JUDGES.

POSNER, CIRCUIT JUDGE.

Some years ago Mr. Kenseth filed an age-discrimination suit against his former employer. He had a contingent-fee contract with the law firm that represented him, pursuant to which the firm deducted 40 percent of the proceeds of the settlement that it obtained for him, remitting the balance to him. The Tax Court ruled that the entire proceeds, including the $91,800 deducted by the law firm as its fee, were part of Kenseth's gross income. The fee was (most of it anyway, as we'll see in a moment) a deductible expense—but only for purposes of the regular federal income tax; it is one of a long list of expenses ("miscellaneous expenses") that are not deductible from gross income in computing the alternative minimum tax, § 56(b)(1)(A)(i) [citation omitted], the purpose of which is "to make sure that the aggregating of tax-preference items [and of other expenses specified in §§ 56 [and] 58] does not result in the taxpayer's paying a shockingly low percentage of his income as tax." First Chicago Corp. v. Commissioner, 842 F.2d 180, 181 (7th Cir.1988). As a result of not being able to deduct the law firm's fee, Kenseth owed some $17,000 in alternative minimum tax that he would not have owed had the contingent fee been excludable from his gross income in computing his alternative minimum tax liability. He took a further hit because his deduction from gross income of the $91,800 pocketed by the law firm was reduced by $5,298 by reason of the 2 percent minimum for miscellaneous itemized deductions and by $4,694 because of the overall limitation on itemized deductions. §§ 67, 68.

In an effort to avoid these tax bites, Kenseth points out that under Wisconsin law (as under that of every other state, as far as we know), which is the law that governed his contract with the law firm, the firm had a lien on the proceeds of any settlement or judgment to the extent of the contingent fee. And the firm could even have enforced the lien if Kenseth had terminated the firm before the case went to judgment or settlement, provided the termination was not for cause. These facts show, he argues, that the part of the proceeds that went to pay the law firm's fee should not have been treated as income to him—in which event he would not have had to pay any alternative minimum tax on it.

The circuits are split on whether a contingent fee is, as the Tax Court held in this case, a part of the client's taxable income. [Citations omitted.] We have not yet had occasion to take sides in the controversy. But with all due respect to those who disagree, we think the Tax Court's resolution of the issue is clearly correct. Taxable income is gross income minus allowable deductions. § 63(a) [further citation omitted]. If a taxpayer obtains income of $100 at a cost in generating that income of $25, he has gross income of $100 and a deduction of $25, see § 162(a), yielding taxable income of $75; he does not have gross income of $75. If, therefore, for some reason the cost of generating the income is not deductible, he has taxable income of $100. See § 62(a)(1) and, with specific reference to legal fees incurred for the production of income, Alexander v. Commissioner, 72 F.3d 938, 944–46 (1st Cir.1995). That is Kenseth's situation under the alternative minimum tax.

He concedes as he must that had he paid the law firm on an hourly basis, the fee would have been an expense. It would have been a deduction from, not a reduction of, his gross income, as held in the *Alexander* case. We cannot see what difference it makes that the expense happened to be contingent rather than fixed. If a firm pays a salesman on a commission basis, the sales income he generates is income to the firm and his commissions are a deductible expense, even though they were contingent on his making sales. Of course there is a sense in which contingent compensation constitutes the recipient a kind of joint venturer of the payor. But the plaintiff concedes, as again he must, that Wisconsin law does not make the contingent-fee lawyer a joint owner of his client's claim in the legal sense any more than the commission salesman is a joint owner of his employer's accounts receivable. The lawyer has a lien, that is, a security interest. Wis. Stat. § 757.36. But the ownership of a security interest is not ownership of the security. A firm whose assets are secured by a mortgage can deduct the interest from its income, but it is not allowed to reduce its income by the amount of the interest. Interest on a secured obligation is just another expense. And, though this is just the icing on the cake, Wisconsin now (the rule may once have been different, see Mohr v. Harris, 118 Wis. 2d 407, 348 N.W.2d 599, 600–02 (Wis.App.1984); Wallach v. Rabinowitz, 185 Wis. 115, 200 N.W. 646, 647 (Wis. 1924)), prohibits lawyers from acquiring "a proprietary interest in the cause of action or subject matter of litigation the lawyer is conducting for a client." Wisconsin State Rules of Professional Conduct, Supreme Court Rule 20:1.8(j). The rule allows the lawyer to acquire a lien and to make a contingent-fee contract, but neither a lien nor a contractual right is "proprietary."

* * * In essence, Kenseth wants us to recharacterize this as a case in which he assigned 40 percent of his tort claim to the law firm. But he didn't. A contingent-fee contract is not an assignment [citation omitted]; and in Wisconsin the lawyer is prohibited from acquiring ownership of his client's claim. So what Kenseth really is asking us to do is to assign a portion of his income to the law firm, but of course an assignment of income (as distinct from the assignment of a contract or an asset that generates income) by a taxpayer is ineffective to shift his tax liability. [Citations omitted.]

* * *

[Kenseth] argues that his position would eliminate an inequity created by the much-criticized alternative minimum tax. As an original matter, in taxation's Garden of Eden, it would indeed be difficult to think of a reason why Kenseth should have been denied the normal privilege of deducting from his gross income 100 percent of an expense reasonably incurred for the production of taxable income. And nothing in the background of the alternative minimum tax law indicates why attorneys' fees were, along with other "miscellaneous expenses," lumped in with tax-preference items and denied the normal privilege. See generally Laura Sager & Stephen Cohen, "How the Income Tax Undermines Civil Rights Law," 73 So. Calif. L. Rev. 1075, 1090–93 (2000). But the idea behind the tax is of course to limit otherwise allowable deductions, so that, to put it crudely, everybody who has income pays some federal income tax. So rather than ask why attorneys' fees are not deductible for purposes of the alternative minimum tax, we should ask why those fees should be distinguished from other miscellaneous deductions that the tax disallows; no answer comes to mind.

Enough; for in any event it is not a feasible judicial undertaking to achieve global equity in taxation, see Benci–Woodward v. Commissioner, supra, 219 F.3d at 944, and cases cited there, especially when the means suggested for eliminating one inequity (that which Kenseth argues is created by the alternative minimum income tax) consists of creating another inequity (differential treatment for purposes of that tax of fixed and contingent legal fees). And if it were a feasible judicial undertaking, it still would not be a proper one, equity in taxation being a political rather than a jural concept. Indeed the cases that reject the Tax Court's position seem based on little more than sympathy for taxpayers. The granddaddy of those cases, Cotnam v. Commissioner, [263 F.2d 119 (5th Cir.1959)], a 2–1 opinion (so far as relates to the issue in our case) with Judge Wisdom dissenting, states its rationale as follows: "The amount of the contingent fee was earned, and well earned, by the attorneys. True, in a remote rather than a proximate sense, the entire amount of the judgment had also been earned by Mrs. Cotnam, but she could never have collected anything or have enjoyed any economic benefit unless she had employed attorneys, and to do so, she had to part with forty per cent of her claim long before the realization of any income from it." 263 F.2d at 126. This rationale badly flunks the test of neutral principles. It is often the case that to obtain income from an asset one must hire a skilled agent and pay him up front; that expense is a deductible expense, not an exclusion from income.

AFFIRMED.

INFORMATION REPORTING OF BUSINESS PAYMENTS AND RECEIPTS

Payments made by businesses are often includable in the gross incomes of the recipients. In order to enforce proper reporting by the recipients, the Code requires payors to report many business-related payments—including nearly all payments for services—made to any individual who receives $600 or more from the payor during the year; §§ 6041, 6041A. These payments are reported on Form 1099, which in the case of large businesses must be filed electronically. Copies of Form 1099 must be given to the persons who received the payments in question. Penalties for failure to file Form 1099 and for late filing or inaccurate reporting are imposed by §§ 6721 through 6724.

Sections 6041 and 6041A require reporting by persons "engaged in a trade or business," and by some government agencies, but not by those engaged in investment or personal activities. Contrast the requirements for reporting and withholding tax from wages (p. 88), which apply to most of those who pay wages, whether or not they are in "business."

A cash payment received by any person engaged in a trade or business must be reported if the payment (or a series of related payments) exceeds $10,000; § 6050I. The Service (as well as other government agencies) is likely to be curious about the affairs of those who use large amounts of cash in conducting their affairs.

1. PROFIT–MAKING ACTIVITIES

LARSON v. COMMISSIONER

United States Tax Court, 1991.
61 T.C.M. 2085.

MEMORANDUM FINDINGS OF FACT AND OPINION

PATE, SPECIAL TRIAL JUDGE. * * *

Respondent determined deficiencies of $2,932 and $3,333 in petitioners' Federal income taxes for 1984 and 1985. The sole issue for our decision is whether petitioners operated their dog kennel with an actual and honest profit objective.

FINDINGS OF FACT

* * *

During 1984 and 1985, Mr. Larson was employed full time as a pressman and Mrs. Larson was employed full time as a secretary. They reported $37,733 and $40,172 in total wages during those years. For the years 1982 through 1986, petitioners also bred and sold Shetland sheepdogs (hereinafter Shelties) under the pseudonym "Silva Wind Shelties" (hereinafter kennel). On their 1984 and 1985 income tax returns, petitioners reported receipts from their kennel of $1,050 and $2,050 for the years 1984 and 1985, respectively. After deducting expenses, they reported losses of $14,757 and $16,907, respectively.

* * *

[At the trial, the parties agreed to different dollar amounts for the expenses in question.]

Petitioners operated their kennel as "dog fanciers." As such, they were not required by Nevada to obtain a kennel license or health certificates for their dogs. However, as dog fanciers, they were limited to breeding five adult dogs. To breed any greater number would have required a license as a "dog breeder."

* * *

Petitioners were members of the American Kennel Club (hereinafter the AKC) and operated their kennel strictly in accordance with AKC rules. They believed in the ethical practices promoted by the AKC and, in fact, complained about a breeder violating such controls. Consequently, all of the Shelties handled by petitioners were both bred and raised in conformity with those standards.

Petitioners spent a great deal of their time with their Shelties. They provided them with the most intensive care because they felt that proper nurturing would "socialize" their animals and thereby make them better pets. Much of the record is devoted to a description of such care. Admittedly, they did this not only to improve the quality of their puppies, but because they derived personal gratification from handling them.

To house their Shelties, petitioners built an enclosed kennel adjacent to their home. In addition, they used a spare bedroom for birthing puppies and for keeping records.

Prior to starting their kennel, petitioners had no training or experience in breeding or caring for dogs. However, they took the time to educate themselves. They were interested in building up a renowned kennel with a reputation for quality Shelties. To pursue this goal, they entered several of their Shelties in dog shows in attempts to win championship status. In some instances, they were able to secure professional handlers to assist them. Although several of their dogs won ribbons and awards, none became champions.

Petitioners advertised in newspapers and magazines when they had puppies for sale. They also sent cards to prospective purchasers at Christmastime. During 1984, they offered approximately 20–25 puppies for sale, but sold only seven for $1,075. They sold eight puppies in 1985 for $1,805. Petitioners also reported income from fees charged for administering vaccinations to puppies that they sold. Prices for Shelties in the years in issue ranged from $100 to $350. Petitioners anticipated selling approximately 35 puppies per year with their present facilities and hoped to eventually expand their operations.

One of petitioners' major concerns when selling puppies was to place them in a good home. They remained in contact with purchasers to ensure that the puppies received proper care and allowed purchasers to return puppies that were not receiving proper care. They would often "dog sit" for dogs they sold, for free or for a nominal fee, when the purchasers went on vacation. When unable to sell a puppy, they gave it away to a good home.

Petitioners attempted to reduce their costs by grooming their own dogs, administering vaccinations, assisting in litter births, and other routine veterinarian duties. However, they compensated their sons (at the rate of $1.50 per day) when the boys cared for the dogs.

With regard to recordkeeping, petitioners did not maintain a separate checking account for their dog breeding activities; they used their personal checking account. However, they had business cards and stationery imprinted, pre-printed sales invoices, kept a ledger in which they recorded expenditures for various expenses (dog food, supplies, veterinary charges, etc.), and kept copies of sales invoices for the puppies they sold.

In 1986, after four years of operations, petitioners ceased selling dogs because they became convinced that they could not command the prices for their puppies which would enable them to realize a profit. They now keep their five dogs as pets.

OPINION

In order to deduct losses incurred in any activity, a taxpayer must show that he entered into the activity, or continued the activity, with the objective of making a profit from such activity. [Treas.Reg. §] 1.183–2(a). If the taxpayer engages in the activity without such profit objective, deductions attributable to such activity are allowed, but only to the extent of the income derived from the activity. § 183. The test under § 183 is whether the individual engaged in the activity with an actual and honest objective of making a profit. [Citations omitted.] In this context, profit means economic profit, independent of tax savings. [Citations omitted.] While a reasonable expectation of profit is not required, the taxpayer's profit objective must be bona fide. [Citations omitted.]

The burden of proof is on the taxpayer to show that he engaged in the activity with the objective of realizing an economic profit. Rule 142(a). In making this determination, all relevant facts and circumstance are to be taken into account. [Citations omitted.] Greater weight must be given to objective facts than to petitioner's mere statements of intent. [Treas.Reg. §] 1.183–2(a); [further citations omitted].

[Treas.Reg. §] 1.183–2(b) provides a nonexclusive list of factors which should normally be considered in determining whether an activity is engaged in with the requisite profit objective. The nine factors are: (1) The manner in which the taxpayer carries on the activity; (2) the expertise of the taxpayer or his advisors; (3) the time and effort expended by the taxpayer in carrying on the activity; (4) the expectation that assets used in the activity may appreciate in value; (5) the success of the taxpayer in carrying on other similar or dissimilar activities; (6) the taxpayer's history of income or losses with respect to the activity; (7) the amount of occasional profits, if any, which are earned; (8) the financial status of the taxpayer; and (9) whether elements of personal pleasure or recreation are involved. No single factor, nor the existence of even a majority of the factors, is controlling, but rather it is an evaluation of all the facts and circumstances in the case taken as a whole which is determinative. [Treas.Reg. §] 1.183–2(b); [further citations omitted].

In applying these criteria to petitioners' operations, we find that they operated in a businesslike manner. They built a kennel to adequately house their Shelties and acquired supplies and equipment suitable for raising them. They exhibited their dogs at shows in attempts to establish a good reputation for their kennel, thereby enhancing the prices their puppies would command. They advertised and sent cards to prospective customers to spur sales. In addition, they kept records necessary to keep track of the kennel's profitability.

Petitioners devoted a good deal of the time left free from their employment to their kennel. They obviously were interested in building up a quality operation, and personally spent a considerable amount of time birthing, grooming, feeding, exercising, and "socializing" their puppies.

Respondent argues that the five successive losses reported by petitioners show that they did not have a profit objective. He reasons that "where the taxpayer has substantial assets and sources of income outside of the activity, it is more probable that the activity is not profit motivated." Sampson v. Commissioner, [43 T.C.M. 1408 (1982)]. However, petitioners did not have "substantial" assets or "substantial" outside income. Although it is true that petitioners earned good wages, they were not "high income" in the sense that they had a lot of extra disposable income. In fact, financing their kennel created a hardship on them.

Respondent also argues that petitioners did not maintain a formal set of books and records or a separate checking account for their kennel and this indicates the lack of a profit objective. See [Treas.Reg. §] 1.183–2(b)(1). Although petitioners' records were not kept in a neat professional manner, when we factor in the newness of their venture and their lack of training in accounting, the records were adequate. Moreover, the absence of a separate checking account does not necessarily indicate an unbusinesslike manner. See Engdahl v. Commissioner, 72 T.C. [659,] at 667 [(1979)(Acq.)].

Finally, respondent points to the enjoyment petitioners got from raising dogs to show that it was a hobby. However, merely because a person might enjoy his business does not mean that it is a hobby or undertaken for personal reasons. As stated in [Treas.Reg. §] 1.183–2(b)(9):

> the fact that the taxpayer derives personal pleasure from engaging in the activity is not sufficient to cause the activity to be classified as not engaged in for profit if the activity is, in fact, engaged in for profit as evidenced by other factors * * *.

Therefore, as long as the activity was entered into with an actual and honest objective of making a profit, the deduction of a loss is not precluded by § 183.

Nor do we give much credence to respondent's position that the intensive care petitioners lavished on their puppies indicated that they were not concerned with making a profit. Petitioners were interested in building a quality operation, not a "puppy mill," and believed that the extra handling would "pay off" with better puppies for which they could charge a higher price. It was not until they had operated their kennel for some time that they became convinced that this concept would not produce the expected profits. They then discontinued operations.

We believe that petitioners started their kennel with the goal of producing a profit from an activity which they enjoyed. Due to their lack of experience at inception, they may not have fully realized the obstacles that they would have to surmount to accomplish that goal. They devoted their best efforts to the enterprise, but after a few years came to understand that the profits they anticipated had not been and were not likely to be realized. At that time, they discontinued their operations. This pattern is not unusual; it befalls many new entrepreneurs.

In summary, despite the absence of profits during the years in question, we think that the work which petitioners took on was just too arduous and the relative financial commitment too large, when compared with petitioners' outside income, to construe the operation of their kennel as a hobby. Moreover, petitioners ran their kennel in a manner befitting a small business. For these reasons, we find that petitioners had an actual and honest objective of profit, and accordingly, may deduct the losses they sustained in operating their kennel.

Due to the stipulations of the parties—

Decision will be entered under Rule 155.

Problems and Notes

1. *Problems. H,* who breeds horses, is held not to have engaged in the activity "for profit." The activity generates $10,000 gross income for the taxable year and the following expenses:

Deductible state and local taxes	$4000
Depreciation	5000
Feed, fuel, repairs, and other current expenses	6000

(1) How much of these expenses can *H* deduct?

(2) How much could *H* have deducted if the gross income from the activity had been $3000?

2. *Determining whether an activity is "engaged in for profit."* The absence of businesslike record-keeping counts heavily against the taxpayer in hobby-loss cases, but keeping adequate books is not, by itself, enough to show a profit motive. In Golanty v. Commissioner, 72 T.C. 411 (1979), affirmed without published opinion 647 F.2d 170 (9th Cir.1981), the Tax Court observed that "the keeping of books and records may represent nothing more than a conscious attention to detail." Further-

more, tax-conscious hobbyists may keep detailed records in the hope that enough business trappings will allow them to deduct their losses.

The Senate Finance Committee report on § 183 says that whether the taxpayer had a profit-making objective is to be determined according to "the facts and circumstances (without regard to the taxpayer's subjective intent)." It also says that the expectation of profit need not be "reasonable."

In cases involving "vacation homes" and "home offices," § 280A limits deductions to income from the activity without inquiring into the taxpayer's profit motive. In effect, the statute conclusively presumes the absence of a profit motive in these situations. Section 280A will be examined below at pp. 369–376.

3. *Reference.* Samansky, Hobby Loss or Deductible Loss: An Intractable Problem, 34 U.Fla.L.Rev. 46 (1981).

2. CONNECTING EXPENSES TO ACTIVITIES

(a) The Role of Motive

UNITED STATES v. GILMORE

Supreme Court of the United States, 1963.
372 U.S. 39, 83 S.Ct. 623, 9 L.Ed.2d 570.

Mr. Justice Harlan delivered the opinion of the Court.

In 1955 the California Supreme Court confirmed the award to the respondent taxpayer of a decree of absolute divorce, without alimony, against his wife Dixie Gilmore. Gilmore v. Gilmore, 45 Cal.2d 142, 287 P.2d 769. The case before us involves the deductibility for federal income tax purposes of that part of the husband's legal expense incurred in such proceedings as is attributable to his successful resistance of his wife's claims to certain of his assets asserted by her to be community property under California law. The claim to such deduction, which has been upheld by the Court of Claims, 290 F.2d 942, is founded on § [212(2)] * * *.

At the time of the divorce proceedings, instituted by the wife but in which the husband also cross-claimed for divorce, respondent's property consisted primarily of controlling stock interests in three corporations, each of which was a franchised General Motors automobile dealer. As president and principal managing officer of the three corporations, he received salaries from them aggregating about $66,800 annually, and in recent years his total annual dividends had averaged about $83,000. His total annual income derived from the corporations was thus approximately $150,000. His income from other sources was negligible.

As found by the Court of Claims, the husband's overriding concern in the divorce litigation was to protect these assets against the claims of his wife. Those claims had two aspects: *first,* that the earnings accumulated and retained by these three corporations during the Gilmores' marriage (representing an aggregate increase in corporate net worth of some $600,000) were the product of respondent's personal services, and not the result of accretion in capital values, thus rendering respondent's stockholdings in the enterprises *pro tanto* community property under California law; *second,* that to the extent that such stockholdings were community property, the wife, allegedly the innocent party in the divorce proceeding, was entitled under California law to more than a one-half interest in such property.

The respondent wished to defeat those claims for two important reasons. *First,* the loss of his controlling stock interests, particularly in the event of their transfer in substantial part to his hostile wife, might well cost him the loss of his corporate positions, his principal means of livelihood. *Second,* there was also danger that if he were found guilty of his wife's sensational and reputation-damaging charges of marital infidelity, General Motors Corporation might find it expedient to exercise its right to cancel these dealer franchises.

The end result of this bitterly fought divorce case was a complete victory for the husband. He, not the wife, was granted a divorce on his cross-claim; the wife's community property claims were denied in their entirety; and she was held entitled to no alimony. 45 Cal.2d 142, 287 P.2d 769.

Respondent's legal expenses in connection with this litigation amounted to $32,537.15 in 1953 and $8,074.21 in 1954—a total of $40,611.36 for the two taxable years in question. The Commissioner of Internal Revenue found all of these expenditures "personal" or "family" expenses and as such none of them deductible. [§ 262.] In the ensuing refund suit, however, the Court of Claims held that 80% of such expense (some $32,500) was attributable to respondent's defense against his wife's community property claims respecting his stockholdings and hence deductible under § [212(2)] as an expense "incurred * * * for the * * * conservation * * * of property held for the production of income." * * *

The Government does not question the amount or formula for the expense allocation made by the Court of Claims. Its sole contention here is that the court below misconceived the test governing § [212(2)] deductions, in that the deductibility of these expenses turns, so it is argued, not upon the *consequences* to respondent of a failure to defeat his wife's community property claims but upon the *origin* and *nature* of the claims themselves. So viewing Dixie Gilmore's claims, whether relating to the existence or division of community property, it is contended that the expense of resisting them must be deemed nondeductible "personal" or "family" expense under § [262], not deductible expense under § [212(2)]. For reasons given hereafter we think the Government's position is sound and that it must be sustained.

I

For income tax purposes Congress has seen fit to regard an individual as having two personalities: "one is [as] a seeker after profit who can deduct the expenses incurred in that search; the other is [as] a creature satisfying his needs as a human and those of his family but who cannot deduct such consumption and related expenditures."[11] The Government regards § [212(2)] as embodying a category of the expenses embraced in the first of these roles.

Initially, it may be observed that the wording of § [212(2)] more readily fits the Government's view of the provision than that of the Court of Claims. For in context "conservation of property" seems to refer to operations performed with respect to the property itself, such as safeguarding or upkeep, rather than to a taxpayer's retention of owner-ship in it. But more illuminating than the mere language of § [212(2)] is the history of the provision.

Prior to 1942 § [162] allowed deductions only for expenses incurred "in carrying on any trade or business" * * *. In Higgins v. Commission-er, 312 U.S. 212, this Court gave that provision a narrow construction, holding that the activities of an individual in supervising his own securities investments did not constitute the "carrying on of trade or business," and hence that expenses incurred in connection with such activities were not tax deductible. Similar results were reached in United States v. Pyne, 313 U.S. 127, and City Bank Farmers Trust Co. v. Helvering, 313 U.S. 121. The Revenue Act of 1942 (56 Stat. 798, § 121), by adding what is now § [212(1) & (2)], sought to remedy the inequity inherent in the disallowance of expense deductions in respect of such profit-seeking activities, the income from which was nonetheless taxable.

As noted in McDonald v. Commissioner, 323 U.S. 57, 62, the purpose of the 1942 amendment was merely to enlarge "the category of incomes with reference to which expenses were deductible." And committee reports make clear that deductions under the new section were subject to the same limitations and restrictions that are applicable to those allowable under § [162].[14] Further, this Court has said that § [212] "is comparable and *in pari materia* with § [162]," providing for a class of deductions "coextensive with the business deductions allowed by § [162], except for" the requirement that the income-producing activity qualify as a trade or business. Trust of Bingham v. Commissioner, 325 U.S. 365, 373, 374.

A basic restriction upon the availability of a § [162] deduction is that the expense item involved must be one that has a business origin. That restriction not only inheres in the language of § [162] itself, confining such deductions to "expenses * * * incurred * * * in carrying on any trade or business," but also follows from § [262], expressly rendering nondeductible "in any case * * * [p]ersonal, living, or family expenses." * * * In light of what has already been said with respect to

11. Surrey and Warren, Cases on Feder-al Income Taxation, 272 (1960).

14. H.R.Rep. No. 2333, 77th Cong., 2d Sess. 75: "A deduction under this section is subject, except for the requirement of being incurred in connection with a trade or busi-ness, to all the restrictions and limitations that apply in the case of the deduction under section [162] of an expense paid or incurred in carrying on any trade or busi-ness." See also S.Rep. No. 1631, 77th Cong., 2d Sess. 88.

the advent and thrust of § [212], it is clear that the "[p]ersonal * * * or family expenses" restriction of § [262] must impose the same limitation upon the reach of § [212]—in other words that the only kind of expenses deductible under § [212] are those that relate to a "business," that is, profit-seeking, purpose. The pivotal issue in this case then becomes: was this part of respondent's litigation costs a "business" rather than a "personal" or "family" expense?

The answer to this question has already been indicated in prior cases. In Lykes v. United States, 343 U.S. 118, the Court rejected the contention that legal expenses incurred in contesting the assessment of a gift tax liability were deductible. The taxpayer argued that if he had been required to pay the original deficiency he would have been forced to liquidate his stockholdings, which were his main source of income, and that his legal expenses were therefore incurred in the "conservation" of income-producing property and hence deductible under § [212(2)]. The Court first noted that the "deductibility [of the expenses] turns wholly upon the nature of the activities to which they relate" (343 U.S., at 123), and then stated:

> "Legal expenses do not become deductible merely because they are paid for services which relieve a taxpayer of liability. That argument would carry us too far. It would mean that the expense of defending almost any claim would be deductible by a taxpayer on the ground that such defense was made to help him keep clear of liens whatever income-producing property he might have. For example, it suggests that the expense of defending an action based upon personal injuries caused by a taxpayer's negligence while driving an automobile for pleasure should be deductible. Section [212(2)] never has been so interpreted by us. * * *

* * *

The principle we derive from these cases is that the characterization, as "business" or "personal," of the litigation costs of resisting a claim depends on whether or not the claim *arises in connection with* the taxpayer's profit-seeking activities. It does not depend on the *consequences* that might result to a taxpayer's income-producing property from a failure to defeat the claim, for, as *Lykes* teaches, that "would carry us too far" and would not be compatible with the basic lines of expense deductibility drawn by Congress. Moreover, such a rule would lead to capricious results. If two taxpayers are each sued for an automobile accident while driving for pleasure, deductibility of their litigation costs would turn on the mere circumstance of the character of the assets each happened to possess, that is, whether the judgments against them stood to be satisfied out of income or nonincome-producing property. We should be slow to attribute to Congress a purpose producing such unequal treatment among taxpayers, resting on no rational foundation.

* * *

II

In classifying respondent's legal expenses the court below did not distinguish between those relating to the claims of the wife with respect to the *existence* of community property and those involving the *division* of any such property. * * * Nor is such a break-down necessary for a disposition of the present case. It is enough to say that in both aspects the wife's claims stemmed entirely from the marital relationship, and not, under any tenable view of things, from income-producing activity. This is obviously so as regards the claim to more than an equal division of any community property found to exist. For any such right depended entirely on the wife's making good her charges of marital infidelity on the part of the husband. The same conclusion is no less true respecting the claim relating to the existence of community property. For no such property could have existed but for the marriage relationship. Thus none of respondent's expenditures in resisting these claims can be deemed "business" expenses, and they are therefore not deductible under § [212(2)].

In view of this conclusion it is unnecessary to consider the further question suggested by the Government: whether that portion of respondent's payments attributable to litigating the issue of the existence of community property was a capital expenditure or a personal expense. In neither event would these payments be deductible from gross income.

The judgment of the Court of Claims is reversed and the case is remanded to that court for further proceedings consistent with this opinion. It is so ordered.

Judgment of Court of Claims reversed and case remanded.

MR. JUSTICE BLACK and MR. JUSTICE DOUGLAS believe that the Court reverses this case because of an unjustifiably narrow interpretation of § [212] and would accordingly affirm the judgment of the Court of Claims.

Notes and Questions

1. *Applying the "origin of the claim" test.* Taxpayers charged with purely "personal" crimes, like murder or manslaughter while off duty, have occasionally tried to deduct their legal fees on the theory that a conviction would have been bad for business. The cases have been routinely decided against the taxpayer. See Johnson v. Commissioner, 37 T.C.M. 1645 (1978); Hylton v. Commissioner, 32 T.C.M. 1238 (1973). On the other hand, the costs of defending a criminal prosecution arising out of business activities are deductible; see Commissioner v. Tellier, 383 U.S. 687 (1966), in which the Commissioner conceded that the costs of resisting a criminal prosecution for mail fraud and Securities Act violations were ordinary and necessary expenses of carrying on the taxpayer's securities business, but argued, unsuccessfully, that a deduction should be denied on "public policy" grounds.

Suppose a wife suing a husband for divorce obtains a court order restricting the activities of a corporation, all the stock of which is owned by the husband, in order to prevent the husband's causing corporate assets to be concealed or dissipated. The corporation's costs of seeking a relaxation or clarification of the order have a "business" origin in the sense that they are incurred because of business necessity. But they can also be thought of as having an ultimately "personal" origin in the dispute between the husband and wife. Dolese v. United States, 605 F.2d 1146 (10th Cir.1979), cert. denied 445 U.S. 961 (1980), allowed a deduction under § 162.

United States v. Patrick, 372 U.S. 53 (1963), a companion case to *Gilmore,* held that the costs of carrying out a property-settlement agreement—including costs of transferring securities between the spouses, leasing real property owned by the couple to a corporation, and transferring the real property to a trust—were "personal" expenses under *Gilmore.* How far can this sort of reasoning be pushed? Does a taxpayer who goes into business in order to earn money to support a spouse or friend with expensive tastes get no deduction for the business's expenses because their "origin" was "personal"?

Suppose a lawyer buys an oriental rug which is always kept in the lawyer's office. It has generally been assumed that the costs of furnishing a business office are business costs, so that the lawyer can deduct depreciation on the rug under § 167(a)(1). But if the lawyer is an employee, this may not be the case. Henderson v. Commissioner, 46 T.C.M. 566 (1983), held that a South Carolina assistant attorney general could not deduct $70 spent on a framed print and a plant for her office. The court described the expenses as aiding "only tangentially, if at all," in the performance of the taxpayer's duties as an employee. An earlier case allowing a pediatrician to deduct the costs of furnishing an office was distinguished on the ground that the pediatrician had bought paintings "intended to be of interest to children."

The question whether tax consequences in a particular case turn upon what the taxpayer does or upon why he does it arises throughout the tax law. See generally Blum, Motive, Intent, and Purpose in Federal Income Taxation, 34 U.Chi.L.Rev. 485 (1967). Was *Gilmore* an exception to a general rule that expenses are classified as "business" or "personal" according to taxpayers' reasons for incurring them, or does it go deeper?

2. *Capital-expenditure aspects.* The Supreme Court has used an "origin of the claim" test to require capitalization of the costs of litigation arising out of the acquisition of an asset. The taxpayers in Woodward v. Commissioner, 397 U.S. 572 (1970), were the controlling shareholders of a corporation. Upon the approval of a perpetual extension of the corporation's charter, the taxpayers were required by local law to buy the stock of shareholders who had voted against the extension. After failing to reach agreement on the stock's value with the dissenters, the taxpayers brought an appraisal action in a state court. The taxpayers argued that the costs of bringing this action were deduct-

ible, and were not costs "of acquisition" of property under Treas.Reg. § 1.263(a)–2(a), since everyone agreed that the taxpayers were to get title. The Court, reading *Gilmore* as holding that the "origin and character of the claim" rather than the "consequences of the litigation" controls the tax treatment of litigation costs, required capitalization, observing that "nothing is more clearly part of the process of acquisition than the establishment of a purchase price." A companion case, United States v. Hilton Hotels Corp., 397 U.S. 580 (1970), required the surviving corporation in a merger to capitalize the costs of fixing the price to be paid dissenting shareholders for their stock, even though title to the dissenters' stock had passed to the corporation under local law when the merger was approved.

Woodward and *Hilton Hotels* left open the question whether a "primary purpose" test determines whether litigation costs can (or must) be capitalized as costs of "defending or protecting" (rather than "acquiring") title to property. Gilmore v. United States, 245 F.Supp. 383 (N.D.Cal.1965) ("*Gilmore No. 2*"), allowed the taxpayer in the principal case to include his legal fees in the basis of the property he kept his wife from getting.

The taxpayer in Spector v. Commissioner, 71 T.C. 1017 (1979), received cash and other property under an agreement settling his and his wife's claims to community property. The Commissioner conceded that *Gilmore No. 2* allowed capitalization of that portion of the costs allocable to stock and real estate, but argued that the costs allocable to the husband's receipt of cash could not be capitalized because cash cannot have a basis higher than its value, and could not be deducted because of *Gilmore No. 1*. The court agreed.

WILD v. COMMISSIONER

Tax Court of the United States, 1964.
42 T.C. 706 (Acq.).

OPINION

KERN, JUDGE: Respondent determined a deficiency of $1,541.90 in petitioner's Federal income tax for the year 1960. The only issue presented for our decision is whether respondent correctly determined that petitioner is not entitled to a claimed deduction of $6,000 for legal fees in obtaining monthly alimony payments incident to a divorce proceeding as an ordinary and necessary expense for the production or collection of income pursuant to section 212(1).

* * *

In 1959 petitioner sued her husband for a legal separation. Subsequently her action was changed to one of divorce. In 1960 a divorce was granted to the petitioner and a stipulation relative to child custody and support and property was made a part of the divorce decree.

* * *

Petitioner contends that the amount of the legal fees claimed as a deduction was an ordinary and necessary expense incurred for the production of income which is deductible under section 212(1). Respondent contends that such expense is not deductible pursuant to section 262 because it was a personal expense arising from the marital relationship and was thus "the product of her [petitioner's] personal and family life and not a profit-seeking activity." Respondent relies on United States v. Gilmore, 372 U.S. 39, and United States v. Patrick, 372 U.S. 53.
* * *

[Treas.Reg. §] 1.262–1(b)(7), which has never been withdrawn or modified by respondent, provides as follows:

§ 1.262–1 Personal, living, and family expenses.

(b) Examples of personal, living, and family expenses. Personal, living, and family expenses are illustrated in the following examples:

(7) Generally, attorney's fees and other costs paid in connection with a divorce, separation, or decree for support are not deductible by either the husband or the wife. However, the part of an attorney's fee and the part of the other costs paid in connection with a divorce, legal separation, written separation agreement, or a decree for support, which are properly attributable to the production or collection of amounts includible in gross income under section 71 are deductible by the wife under section 212.

In Jane U. Elliott, 40 T.C. 304 (filed May 15, 1963), acq. 1964–1 C.B. (Part 1) 4, we held that legal fees paid for the collection of alimony from the taxpayer's former husband were deductible under section 212(1). See also Estate of Daniel Buckley, 37 T.C. 664, 674; Barbara B. LeMond, 13 T.C. 670; and Elsie B. Gale, 13 T.C. 661, affirmed on other grounds 191 F.2d 79.

Respondent argues that these cases are no longer applicable in view of the Supreme Court's decisions in United States v. Gilmore, supra, and United States v. Patrick, supra (both decided on February 18, 1963). * * * In those cases it was held that expenses of husbands in connection with resisting money demands of their wives in divorce actions could not be deducted under section 212(2) as expenses paid for the management, conservation, or maintenance of property held for the production of income. In the instant case the deduction is claimed under section 212(1), which expressly provides for the deduction of expenses "paid or incurred * * * for the production or collection of income." Here the expenses were paid "for the production or collection" of alimony which was reported, when paid to petitioner, as her taxable income in conformity with the provisions of the Internal Revenue Code.

In view of the fact that respondent has never changed or modified his regulation as above quoted since the Supreme Court's decisions in the *Gilmore* and *Patrick* cases were handed down on February 18, 1963, the fact that we decided the case of Jane U. Elliott, supra, some 3 months after February 18, 1963, and the fact that respondent noted his acquiescence in that case on March 16, 1964, and has never withdrawn it, we would be disinclined to overrule our holding in the *Elliott* case and to disapprove respondent's pertinent and outstanding regulation unless we were compelled to do so by the decisions of the Supreme Court in the *Gilmore* and *Patrick* cases. Since those cases dealt with another subsection of the Internal Revenue Code in the context of another factual background, it is our opinion that we are not compelled by them to reach such a result.

On the authority of the cases and regulations referred to above, it is our conclusion that the legal fees in issue which represented the cost to petitioner of producing monthly alimony payments, which were included in her gross income, are deductible under section 212(1) as ordinary and necessary expenses paid or incurred during the taxable year for the production or collection of taxable income.

Reviewed by the Court.

Decision Will Be Entered for the Petitioner.

RAUM, J., dissenting: I think that a fair reading of United States v. Gilmore, 372 U.S. 39, and United States v. Patrick, 372 U.S. 53, calls for a result contrary to that reached in the prevailing opinion, and that the distinction between sections 212(1) and (2) relied upon by the majority is spurious.

Sections 212(1) and (2) of the 1954 Code, here involved, are merely fragmented parts of what was formerly section 23(a)(2) of the 1939 Code, the history of which was outlined in *Gilmore*. At one time section 23(a) provided merely for the deduction of expenses in carrying on a trade or business. It was then amended so as to add deductions for like expenses not connected with trade or business. The old trade or business deductions were continued in section 23(a)(1), and the new deductions were contained in section 23(a)(2). These new deductions were spelled out in section 23(a)(2) as follows:

> **(2) Non-trade or Non-business Expenses.**—In the case of an individual, all the ordinary and necessary expenses paid or incurred during the taxable year for the production or collection of income, or for the management, conservation, or maintenance of property held for the production of income.

The Supreme Court in *Gilmore* held that section 24(a)(1), which specifically denied any deduction for "personal" or "family" expenses, was a limitation upon section 23(a)(2), and that, accordingly, expenses incurred by a husband in a divorce action to protect his income-producing property were not deductible even though the situation were otherwise literally covered by section 23(a)(2). The theory of the decision in that case and in *Patrick* was that the claims in respect of which the expenses were incurred arose from the taxpayer's "marital relationship * * * and were thus the product of [his] * * * personal or family life * * *." 372 U.S. at 56.

That theory was plainly applicable to all parts of section 23(a)(2), which had the *identical* legislative history, and I can conceive of no justification for reaching a different result in respect of that portion of section 23(a)(2) that became section 212(1) of the 1954 Code from that portion which became section 212(2). Section 24(a)(1) is just as much a limitation upon that part of section 23(a)(2) which deals with deduction of expenses incurred "for the management, conservation, or maintenance of property held for the production of income" as it is upon that part which involves expenses "for the production or collection of income." If the fact that the claim grew out of the marital relationship required classification of the expenses as "personal" or "family" under section 24(a)(1) in the one situation, the same must obtain in the other. And there is no suggestion whatever that a contrary result must be reached merely because section 23(a)(2) was itself divided into two parts as section 212(1) and (2) of the 1954 Code, obviously for the purpose of drafting convenience only. Section 24(a)(1) of the 1939 Code became section 262 of the 1954 Code, and the limitations in respect of deductions for "personal" and "family" deductions in section 262 are just as much a gloss on section 212 as the corresponding provisions of section 24(a)(1) were a restriction on section 23(a)(2).

Gilmore and *Patrick* make it clear that such limitations are operative when the claim arises out of the marital relationship in a divorce proceeding, and I think it quixotic to reach a different result here. The mere fact that the Treasury has not withdrawn the regulation upon which the majority rely is of no controlling significance. The *Gilmore* and *Patrick* cases were decided only last year, and it is notorious that the wheels of administration often turn slowly.

Tietjens and Pierce, JJ., agree with this dissent.

Pierce, J., dissenting: I agree with the dissenting opinion of Judge Raum, but I wish to add a word about Jane U. Elliott, 40 T.C. 304, upon which the majority relies in part. I regard it as distinguishable. In the instant case, expenses were incurred in order to *establish* petitioner's right to alimony, plainly a "personal" or "family" right. In *Elliott,* on the other hand, the right to alimony had already been established, and the expenses were incurred merely in order to effect *collection* of a fixed obligation, just as they might have been incurred by a noteholder seeking to collect interest on his note or a lessor seeking to collect rent from his lessee. Since *Elliott* is distinguishable I see no reason to extend it to reach an unsound result.

Tietjens and Raum, JJ., agree with this dissent.

Problem, Notes and Questions

1. *Section 212(3).* Section 212(3) was enacted in 1954. The Service once argued that § 212(3) applied only to such costs as those of preparing tax returns and resolving tax controversies, but the Commissioner conceded in Merians v. Commissioner, 60 T.C. 187 (1973) (Acq.), that the

costs of tax planning are also deductible under that section. Deductions allowed by § 212 are "miscellaneous itemized deductions" under § 67. Therefore, the many taxpayers whose miscellaneous itemized deductions come to less than 2 percent of their adjusted gross incomes cannot deduct these costs.

2. *Deductible lawyers' fees on divorce.* Under *Wild,* costs allocable to getting an award of alimony are deductible under § 212(1), and the costs of advising the taxpayer about the divorce's tax consequences are deductible under § 212(3). But several cases have held that the costs of resisting a wife's alimony claims are not deductible under § 212(1), even though success in avoiding or reducing alimony increases the husband's taxable income (see § 215). Can this rule be reconciled with that of *Wild?*

United States v. Davis, 370 U.S. 65 (1962), held that a husband who paid his wife's legal expenses pursuant to a "customary practice" could not deduct that portion of the fees allocable to tax advice; § 212(3) covers "only the expenses of the taxpayer himself." Could the wife in *Davis* have deducted the tax-advice portion of the fees her husband paid for her? Jernigan v. Commissioner, 34 T.C.M. 615 (1975), implies that she could not. How should payment of the wife's legal fees be arranged so as to avoid "wasting" her § 212(1) and § 212(3) deductions?

3. *Capital expenditures and § 212.* Why weren't the fees involved in *Wild* non-deductible capital expenditures, amortizable over the period in which the taxpayer would receive alimony? A taxpayer who buys a right to future payments must capitalize the purchase price; were the expenses in *Wild* fundamentally different? Whatever the correct answer in principle, the current deductibility under § 212 of many costs incurred in connection with acquiring "income" (as opposed to an income-producing "asset") is well-established. See Treas.Reg. §§ 1.212–1(a)(1), 1.212–1(b), and 1.212–1(k).

Under Treas.Reg. § 1.263(a)–2(c), the "cost of defending or perfecting title to property" must be capitalized, while the costs of "management, conservation, or maintenance" of property are deductible under § 212(2) (or, if the property is used in a trade or business, under § 162). An expansive reading of Treas.Reg. § 1.263(a) might suggest that the costs of defending any action for damages must be capitalized, since the effect of losing the lawsuit will be to deprive the taxpayer of title to some property. But the courts have not been that strict, and capitalization has been required (or allowed) only in cases in which the issue in the lawsuit involved ownership of the property or (under the "origin of the claim" test) arose out of the acquisition of the property.[j]

The taxpayer in Southland Royalty Co. v. United States, 582 F.2d 604 (Ct.Cl.1978), cert. denied 441 U.S. 905 (1979), owned mineral property subject to a lease to the Gulf Oil Corp. The lease was for a maximum term of 50 years. Gulf sued the taxpayer, seeking a declarato-

j. See the *Woodward* and *Hilton Hotels* cases, p. 313, above.

ry judgment that the 50–year term should not include a twelve-year period for which production had been restricted by the Texas Railroad Commission. Ultimately, the issue in the declaratory-judgment action was whether the lease to Gulf would expire in 1975 or in 1987. Reasoning that the issue in the suit was whether Gulf or the taxpayer was "to have and control the leasehold for almost 12 additional years and to exploit the mineral estate during that time-span," the court required capitalization of the cost of defending the declaratory-judgment action. The dissent would have allowed a deduction (under § 162, since the taxpayer was in "business") because the "primary purpose" of defending the suit was to enable the taxpayer to operate the property after 1975 and to collect income from its operation after that date.

The *Southland Royalty* decision allowed the taxpayer to deduct the costs of bringing a lawsuit to establish its right to a royalty of ⅛ of the sale price of gas from certain wells. Since this litigation did not involve title to the gas, or whether Southwest was entitled to payment for it, but only the question of how much (income) Southwest was to get for its gas, the Court of Claims allowed a deduction.

4. *Problem. P,* an investor, agrees to buy Blackacre, a tract of unimproved income-producing real property, from *D* for $100,000. *D* breaches his contract to sell the property to *P*. *P* brings an action in which he obtains a decree of specific performance and a judgment for $30,000, the amount for which Blackacre was rented during the period between the scheduled closing and *P*'s recovery of the property. How should *P* treat the $20,000 in legal fees which the suit cost him? How should he have treated the fees if he had lost his suit?

PEVSNER v. COMMISSIONER

United States Court of Appeals, Fifth Circuit, 1980.
628 F.2d 467, rehearing en banc denied 636 F.2d 1106 (1981).

Before AINSWORTH, GARZA and SAM D. JOHNSON, CIRCUIT JUDGES.

SAM D. JOHNSON, CIRCUIT JUDGE:

This is an appeal by the Commissioner of Internal Revenue from a decision of the United States Tax Court. The [T]ax [C]ourt upheld taxpayer's business expense deduction for clothing expenditures in the amount of $1,621.91 for the taxable year 1975. We reverse.

Since June 1973 Sandra J. Pevsner, taxpayer, has been employed as the manager of the Sakowitz Yves St. Laurent Rive Gauche Boutique located in Dallas, Texas. The boutique sells only women's clothes and accessories designed by Yves St. Laurent (YSL), one of the leading designers of women's apparel. Although the clothing is ready to wear, it is highly fashionable and expensively priced. Some customers of the boutique purchase and wear the YSL apparel for their daily activities and spend as much as $20,000 per year for such apparel.

As manager of the boutique, the taxpayer is expected by her employer to wear YSL clothes while at work. In her appearance, she is expected to project the image of an exclusive lifestyle and to demonstrate to her customers that she is aware of the YSL current fashion trends as well as trends generally. Because the boutique sells YSL clothes exclusively, taxpayer must be able, when a customer compliments her on her clothes, to say that they are designed by YSL. In addition to wearing YSL apparel while at the boutique, she wears them while commuting to and from work, to fashion shows sponsored by the boutique, and to business luncheons at which she represents the boutique. During 1975, the taxpayer bought, at an employee's discount, the following items: four blouses, three skirts, one pair of slacks, one trench coat, two sweaters, one jacket, one tunic, five scarves, six belts, two pairs of shoes and four necklaces. The total cost of this apparel was $1,381.91. In addition, the sum of $240 was expended for maintenance of these items.

Although the clothing and accessories purchased by the taxpayer were the type used for general purposes by the regular customers of the boutique, the taxpayer is not a normal purchaser of these clothes. The taxpayer and her husband, who is partially disabled because of a severe heart attack suffered in 1971, lead a simple life and their social activities are very limited and informal. Although taxpayer's employer has no objection to her wearing the apparel away from work, taxpayer stated that she did not wear the clothes during off-work hours because she felt that they were too expensive for her simple everyday lifestyle. Another reason why she did not wear the YSL clothes apart from work was to make them last longer. Taxpayer did admit at trial, however, that a number of the articles were things she could have worn off the job and in which she would have looked "nice."

On her joint federal income tax return for 1975, taxpayer deducted $990 as an ordinary and necessary business expense with respect to her purchase of the YSL clothing and accessories. However, in the [T]ax [C]ourt, taxpayer claimed a deduction for the full $1381.91 cost of the apparel and for the $240 cost of maintaining the apparel. The [T]ax [C]ourt allowed the taxpayer to deduct both expenses in the total amount of $1621.91. The [T]ax [C]ourt reasoned that the apparel was not suitable to the private lifestyle maintained by the taxpayer. This appeal by the Commissioner followed.

The principal issue on appeal is whether the taxpayer is entitled to deduct as an ordinary and necessary business expense the cost of purchasing and maintaining the YSL clothes and accessories worn by the taxpayer in her employment as the manager of the boutique. This determination requires an examination of the relationship between Section 162(a), which allows a deduction for ordinary and necessary expenses incurred in the conduct of a trade or business, and Section 262 of the Code, which bars a deduction for all "personal, living, or family expenses." Although many expenses are helpful or essential to one's business activities—such as commuting expenses and the cost of meals while at work—these expenditures are considered inherently personal and are disallowed under Section 262. See, e.g. United States v. Correll, 389 U.S. 299 (1967); Commissioner v. Flowers, 326 U.S. 465 (1946).

The generally accepted rule governing the deductibility of clothing expenses is that the cost of clothing is deductible as a business expense only if: (1) the clothing is of a type specifically required as a condition of employment, (2) it is not adaptable to general usage as ordinary clothing, and (3) it is not so worn. Donnelly v. Commissioner, 262 F.2d 411, 412 (2d Cir.1959).[3]

In the present case, the Commissioner stipulated that the taxpayer was required by her employer to wear YSL clothing and that she did not wear such apparel apart from work. The Commissioner maintained, however, that a deduction should be denied because the YSL clothes and accessories purchased by the taxpayer were adaptable for general usage as ordinary clothing and she was not prohibited from using them as such. The [T]ax [C]ourt, in rejecting the Commissioner's argument for the application of an objective test, recognized that the test for deductibility was whether the clothing was "suitable for general or personal wear" but determined that the matter of suitability was to be judged subjectively, in light of the taxpayer's lifestyle. Although the court recognized that the YSL apparel "might be used by some members of society for general purposes," it felt that because the "wearing of YSL apparel outside work would be inconsistent with * * * [taxpayer's] lifestyle," sufficient reason was shown for allowing a deduction for the clothing expenditures.

In reaching its decision, the [T]ax [C]ourt relied heavily upon Yeomans v. Commissioner, 30 T.C. 757 (1958). In Yeomans, the taxpayer was employed as fashion coordinator for a shoe manufacturing company. Her employment necessitated her attendance at meetings of fashion experts and at fashion shows sponsored by her employer. On these occasions, she was expected to wear clothing that was new, highly styled, and such as "might be sought after and worn for personal use by women who make it a practice to dress according to the most advanced or extreme fashions." 30 T.C. at 768. However, for her personal wear, Ms. Yeomans preferred a plainer and more conservative style of dress. As a consequence, some of the items she purchased were not suitable for her private and personal wear and were not so worn. The [T]ax [C]ourt allowed a deduction for the cost of the items that were not suitable for her personal wear. Although the basis for the decision in *Yeomans* is not clearly stated, the [T]ax [C]ourt in the case *sub judice* determined that

> [a] careful reading of *Yeomans* shows that, without a doubt, the Court based its decision on a determination of Ms. Yeomans' lifestyle and that the clothes were not suitable for her use in such lifestyle. Furthermore, the Court recognized that the clothes Ms. Yeomans purchased were suitable for wear by women who customarily wore such highly styled apparel, but such fact did not cause the

---

3. When the taxpayer is prohibited from wearing the clothing away from work a deduction is normally allowed. See Harsaghy v. Commissioner, 2 T.C. 484 (1943). However, in the present case no such restriction was placed upon the taxpayer's use of the clothing.

court to decide the issue against her. Thus, *Yeomans* clearly decides the issue before us in favor of the petitioner.

[38 T.C.M. 1210, 1212 (1979)].

Notwithstanding the [T]ax [C]ourt's decision in *Yeomans,* the Circuits that have addressed the issue have taken an objective, rather than subjective, approach. Stiner v. United States, 524 F.2d 640, 641 (10th Cir.1975); Donnelly v. Commissioner, 262 F.2d 411, 412 (2d Cir.1959). An objective approach was also taken by the [T]ax [C]ourt in Drill v. Commissioner, 8 T.C. 902 (1947). Under an objective test, no reference is made to the individual taxpayer's lifestyle or personal taste. Instead, adaptability for personal or general use depends upon what is generally accepted for ordinary street wear.

The principal argument in support of an objective test is, of course, administrative necessity. The Commissioner argues that, as a practical matter, it is virtually impossible to determine at what point either price or style makes clothing inconsistent with or inappropriate to a taxpayer's lifestyle. Moreover, the Commissioner argues that the price one pays and the styles one selects are inherently personal choices governed by taste, fashion, and other unmeasurable values. Indeed, the [T]ax [C]ourt has rejected the argument that a taxpayer's personal taste can dictate whether clothing is appropriate for general use. See Drill v. Commissioner, 8 T.C. 902 (1947). An objective test, although not perfect, provides a practical administrative approach that allows a taxpayer or revenue agent to look only to objective facts in determining whether clothing required as a condition of employment is adaptable to general use as ordinary streetwear. Conversely, the [T]ax [C]ourt's reliance on subjective factors provides no concrete guidelines in determining the deductibility of clothing purchased as a condition of employment.

In addition to achieving a practical administrative result, an objective test also tends to promote substantial fairness among the greatest number of taxpayers. As the Commissioner suggests, it apparently would be the [T]ax [C]ourt's position that two similarly situated YSL boutique managers with identical wardrobes would be subject to disparate tax consequences depending upon the particular manager's lifestyle and "socio-economic level." This result, however, is not consonant with a reasonable interpretation of Sections 162 and 262.

* * *

Reversed.

Problem and Notes

1. *"Inherently personal" expenses.* On the cost of uniforms, see Treas.Reg. § 1.262–1(b)(8) (members of the armed forces), and Rev.Rul. 70–474, 1970–2 C.B. 35 ("police officers, firemen, letter carriers, nurses, bus drivers, and railway men who are required to wear distinctive types of uniforms while at work" may deduct costs of acquiring and maintain-

ing uniforms if they "are not suitable for ordinary wear"). For an unsuccessful attempt by a lawyer to deduct the cost of clothing, see Kosmal v. Commissioner, 39 T.C.M. 651 (1979), affirmed mem. 670 F.2d 842 (9th Cir.1982). The taxpayer was a deputy district attorney with ambitions of becoming a "big time Beverly Hills P.I. attorney."

Drake v. Commissioner, 52 T.C. 842 (1969) (Acq.), held the excess of an Army enlisted man's cost of required haircuts over what he would have spent on haircuts but for his employment nondeductible because "[e]xpenses for personal grooming are inherently personal in nature."

Another expense that has been held "inherently personal" is the cost of providing care for the taxpayer's children while the taxpayer works; Smith v. Commissioner, 40 B.T.A. 1038 (1939), affirmed mem. 113 F.2d 114 (2d Cir.1940). For many employees, the holding of *Smith* has been largely undone by the enactment of § 129, allowing the exclusion from employees' incomes of benefits under dependent care assistance programs. Compare the limited tax credit of § 21 (Chapter 3).

The ultimate case on "inherently personal expenses" may be Vitale v. Commissioner, 47 T.C.M. 1869 (1999), aff'd in an unpublished opinion 217 F.3d 843 (4th Cir. 2000). The taxpayer planned to write a book on prostitution. To gather data, he visited prostitutes and paid for their services. The Tax Court found that the taxpayer did actually hope to make a profit from the book and allowed him to deduct many of his costs. But not the payments for the services.

2. *Food, automobiles, housing, and similar items.* Drawing the line between business and personal costs has been extraordinarily difficult in the case of goods and services which many people buy as "personal consumption" but which some people buy for business reasons. Consider, for example, the costs of attending sporting events with prospective clients (who may also be friends), or of eating in restaurants with colleagues or customers, or of maintaining a room in a house which is used for working at home evenings. Congress has responded to a perceived excess of claimed deductions in this area by enacting very specific Code provisions which will be examined in some detail later on in this chapter: § 274 (travel, meals, and entertainment); § 280F ("listed property," such as automobiles and computers); and § 280A (home offices and vacation homes).

3. *Problem. M* is a professional musician. In the current year he spent $1000 for formal clothing (tuxedo, etc.), which he wore only during concert appearances. Is the cost of the clothing deductible?

4. *Reference.* Halperin, Business Deductions for Personal Living Expenses: A Uniform Approach to an Unsolved Problem, 122 U.Pa. L.Rev. 859 (1974).

(b) *"Ordinary and Necessary"*

WELCH v. HELVERING

Supreme Court of the United States, 1933.
290 U.S. 111, 54 S.Ct. 8, 78 L.Ed. 212.

Mr. Justice Cardozo delivered the opinion of the Court.

The question to be determined is whether payments by a taxpayer, who is in business as a commission agent, are allowable deductions in the computation of his income if made to the creditors of a bankrupt corporation in an endeavor to strengthen his own standing and credit.

In 1922 petitioner was the secretary of the E.L. Welch Company, a Minnesota corporation, engaged in the grain business. The company was adjudged an involuntary bankrupt, and had a discharge from its debts. Thereafter the petitioner made a contract with the Kellogg Company to purchase grain for it on a commission. In order to re-establish his relations with customers whom he had known when acting for the Welch Company and to solidify his credit and standing, he decided to pay the debts of the Welch business so far as he was able. In fulfillment of that resolve, he made payments of substantial amounts during five successive years. In 1924, the commissions were $18,028.20, the payments $3,975.97; in 1925, the commissions $31,377.07, the payments $11,968.20; in 1926, the commissions $20,925.25, the payments $12,815.72; in 1927, the commissions $22,119.61, the payments $7,379.72; and in 1928, the commissions $26,177.56, the payments $11,068.25. The Commissioner ruled that these payments were not deductible from income as ordinary and necessary expenses, but were rather in the nature of capital expenditures, an outlay for the development of reputation and good will. The Board of Tax Appeals sustained the action of the Commissioner (25 B.T.A. 117), and the Court of Appeals for the Eighth Circuit affirmed. 63 F.(2d) 976. The case is here on certiorari.

* * *

We may assume that the payments to creditors of the Welch Company were necessary for the development of the petitioner's business, at least in the sense that they were appropriate and helpful. McCulloch v. Maryland, 4 Wheat. 316. He certainly thought they were, and we should be slow to override his judgment. But the problem is not solved when the payments are characterized as necessary. Many necessary payments are charges upon capital. There is need to determine whether they are both necessary and ordinary. Now, what is ordinary, though there must always be a strain of constancy within it, is none the less a variable affected by time and place and circumstance. Ordinary in this context does not mean that the payments must be habitual or normal in the sense that the same taxpayer will have to make them often. A lawsuit affecting the safety of a business may happen once in a lifetime. The counsel fees may be so heavy that repetition is unlikely.

None the less, the expense is an ordinary one because we know from experience that payments for such a purpose, whether the amount is large or small, are the common and accepted means of defense against attack. Cf. Kornhauser v. United States, 276 U.S. 145. The situation is unique in the life of the individual affected, but not in the life of the group, the community, of which he is a part. At such times there are norms of conduct that help to stabilize our judgment, and make it certain and objective. The instance is not erratic, but is brought within a known type.

The line of demarcation is now visible between the case that is here and the one supposed for illustration. We try to classify this act as ordinary or the opposite, and the norms of conduct fail us. No longer can we have recourse to any fund of business experience, to any known business practice. Men do at times pay the debts of others without legal obligation or the lighter obligation imposed by the usages of trade or by neighborly amenities, but they do not do so ordinarily, not even though the result might be to heighten their reputation for generosity and opulence. Indeed, if language is to be read in its natural and common meaning (Old Colony R. Co. v. Commissioner, 284 U.S. 552, 560; Woolford Realty Co. v. Rose, 286 U.S. 319, 327), we should have to say that payment in such circumstances, instead of being ordinary is in a high degree extraordinary. There is nothing ordinary in the stimulus evoking it, and none in the response. Here, indeed, as so often in other branches of the law, the decisive distinctions are those of degree and not of kind. One struggles in vain for any verbal formula that will supply a ready touchstone. The standard set up by the statute is not a rule of law; it is rather a way of life. Life in all its fullness must supply the answer to the riddle.

The Commissioner of Internal Revenue resorted to that standard in assessing the petitioner's income, and found that the payments in controversy came closer to capital outlays than to ordinary and necessary expenses in the operation of a business. His ruling has the support of a presumption of correctness, and the petitioner has the burden of proving it to be wrong. Wickwire v. Reinecke, 275 U.S. 101; Jones v. Commissioner (C.C.A.) 38 F.(2d) 550, 552. Unless we can say from facts within our knowledge that these are ordinary and necessary expenses according to the ways of conduct and the forms of speech prevailing in the business world, the tax must be confirmed. But nothing told us by this record or within the sphere of our judicial notice permits us to give that extension to what is ordinary and necessary. Indeed, to do so would open the door to many bizarre analogies. One man has a family name that is clouded by thefts committed by an ancestor. To add to his own standing he repays the stolen money, wiping off, it may be, his income for the year. The payments figure in his tax return as ordinary expenses. Another man conceives the notion that he will be able to practice his vocation with greater ease and profit if he has an opportunity to enrich his culture. Forthwith the price of his education becomes an expense of the business, reducing the income subject to taxation. There is little difference between these expenses and those in controversy here. Reputation and learning are akin to capital assets, like the good will of an old partnership. Cf. Colony Coal & Coke Corp. v. Commissioner (C.C.A.) 52 F.(2d) 923. For many, they are the only tools with which to hew a pathway to success. The money spent in acquiring them is well and wisely spent. It is not an ordinary expense of the operation of a business.

Many cases in the federal courts deal with phases of the problem presented in the case at bar. To attempt to harmonize them would be a futile task. They involve the appreciation of particular situations, at times with border-line conclusions. Typical illustrations are cited in the margin.[1]

The decree should be Affirmed.

Problem and Notes

1. *"Ordinary" and "necessary" expenses.* Denying deductions for outlays that are not "ordinary" may help assure the nondeductibility of capital expenditures and may help to deny business deductions for personal outlays (a function served by the "necessary" requirement as well). See Harbor Medical Corp. v. Commissioner, 38 T.C.M. 1144 (1979), denying business-expense deductions for the costs of operating an airplane owned by a medical corporation. Flying was a hobby of the corporation's shareholder-employees, and use of the plane in the business made no business sense. The court held the expenses to be neither "ordinary" nor "necessary."

In Car–Ron Asphalt Paving Co., Inc. v. Commissioner, 758 F.2d 1132 (6th Cir.1985), a taxpayer was denied a deduction for "kickbacks"

---

1. Ordinary expenses: Commissioner v. People's Pittsburgh Trust Co. (C.C.A.) 60 F.(2d) 187, expenses incurred in the defense of a criminal charge growing out of the business of the taxpayer; American Rolling Mill Co. v. Commissioner (C.C.A.) 41 F.(2d) 314, contributions to a civic improvement fund by a corporation employing half of the wage earning population of the city, the payments being made, not for charity, but to add to the skill and productivity of the workmen (cf. the decisions collated in 30 Columbia Law Review 1211, 1212, and the distinctions there drawn); Corning Glass Works v. Lucas, 59 App.D.C. 168, 37 F.(2d) 798, donations to a hospital by a corporation whose employees with their dependents made up two-thirds of the population of the city; Harris & Co. v. Lucas (C.C.A.) 48 F.(2d) 187, payments of debts discharged in bankruptcy, but subject to be revived by force of a new promise. Cf. Lucas v. Ox Fibre Brush Co., 281 U.S. 115, where additional compensation, reasonable in amount, was allowed to the officers of a corporation for services previously rendered.

Not ordinary expenses: Hubinger v. Commissioner (C.C.A.) 36 F.(2d) 724, payments by the taxpayer for the repair of fire damage, such payments being distinguished from those for wear and tear; Lloyd v. Commissioner (C.C.A.) 55 F.(2d) 842, counsel fees incurred by the taxpayer, the president of a corporation, in prosecuting a slander suit to protect his reputation and that of his business; One Hundred Five West Fifty-Fifth Street v. Commissioner (C.C.A.) 42 F.(2d) 849, and Blackwell Oil & Gas Co. v. Commissioner (C.C.A.) 60 F.(2d) 257, gratuitous payments to stockholders in settlement of disputes between them, or to assume the expense of a lawsuit in which they had been made defendants; White v. Commissioner (C.C.A.) 61 F.(2d) 726, payments in settlement of a lawsuit against a member of a partnership, the effect being to enable him to devote his undivided efforts to the partnership business and also to protect its credit.

paid to a company official to obtain paving contracts on the ground that the payments were not "necessary." The kickbacks were not illegal, and so § 162(c) did not disallow the deductions. The Tax Court had found as a fact that the kickbacks were not necessary in the "appropriate and helpful" sense because the taxpayer had obtained other contracts without resorting to bribery. The Sixth Circuit held this finding "not clearly erroneous" and observed that the courts "should never construe general language in tax statutes in a manner which rewards graft and corruption * * *." A different panel of the Sixth Circuit had allowed a deduction on similar facts in Raymond Bertolini Trucking Co. v. Commissioner, 736 F.2d 1120 (6th Cir.1984). The *Car–Ron* panel distinguished *Bertolini* on the ground that the Commissioner had argued in that case that the kickbacks were not "ordinary" but had conceded that they were "necessary."

You may find it instructive to compare the *Car–Ron* and *Bertolini* cases with Brizell v. Commissioner, 93 T.C. 151 (1989). *Brizell* involved the deductibility of kickbacks paid by a printing company to purchasing agents who worked for the company's customers. Payments of this sort were widespread in the industry. By demanding the payments, the purchasing agents committed crimes, and several of them were eventually convicted. The Tax Court held that the payments were deductible as ordinary and necessary expenses of the corporation's business. Section 162(c)(2), which disallows deductions for some illegal kickbacks, did not apply here because, under New York law, only "voluntary" payments are illegal bribes, and the payments in question, having been extorted from the corporation, were not "voluntary." That is, although it was illegal for the agents to demand and receive the payments, it was not illegal for the Brizells' corporation to pay them—the corporation was a victim, not a perpetrator, under New York law.

For further exploration of the matter of disallowing deductions on non-tax "public policy" grounds see pp. 383–395, below.

2. *Problem.* R is a commission sales representative for a publisher of specialized law reports (tax, labor, etc.). R quoted L, a lawyer, a price of $700 on a looseleaf service, and L then executed the order form, which R submitted to the publisher for acceptance. The publisher rejected the order because R had mistakenly assumed that L was eligible for a 30 percent "library discount." When R told L that the true price was $1000, L was annoyed, but because she badly needed the looseleaf service in her practice she agreed to pay $1000. R, hoping to retain L as a customer in the future, personally reimbursed L for $150 of the "extra" expense. What, if anything, can R deduct? What can L deduct?

3. *References.* Whether *Welch* held the expenses in question to be "personal" or "capital," or whether it denied a deduction just because they were "unusual," is a much-debated question. For discussions, see Newman, On the Tax Meaning of "Ordinary": How the Ills of *Welch* Could Be Cured Through Christian Science, 22 Ariz.St.L.J. 231 (1990); Griswold, An Argument against the Doctrine That Deductions Should Be

Narrowly Construed as a Matter of Legislative Grace, 56 Harv.L.Rev. 1142 (1943).

3. "A REASONABLE ALLOWANCE FOR SALARIES"

One "cost of doing business" that is not deductible is a corporation's payment of dividends to shareholders. In cases in which a corporation's shareholders are also its employees, payments to shareholders must be classified as "dividends," or "salaries," or a mixture of both. Since both dividends and salaries are ordinary income to the recipient, but dividends are not deductible by the corporation, the owners of a closely held corporation have every incentive to pay high salaries and low dividends, or no dividends at all.

ELLIOTTS, INC. v. COMMISSIONER

United States Court of Appeals, Ninth Circuit, 1983.
716 F.2d 1241.

Before HUG, SKOPIL, and FLETCHER, CIRCUIT JUDGES.

HUG, CIRCUIT JUDGE:

Elliotts, Inc. ("Taxpayer"), challenges the Tax Court's determination of deficiencies in its 1975 and 1976 tax returns. It argues that the Tax Court erred in finding that part of the compensation paid Taxpayer's chief executive and sole shareholder during those years constituted a dividend distribution and thus was not deductible under section 162(a)(1) of the Internal Revenue Code. We reverse.

I. BACKGROUND

Taxpayer is an Idaho corporation that sells equipment manufactured by John Deere Co. and services equipment made by Deere and several other manufacturers. * * *

Taxpayer was incorporated in 1952. During its first year, it grossed $500,000 in agricultural equipment sales in the Burley area. It employed about eight people at that time. By 1975, Taxpayer was employing 40 people, selling both agricultural and industrial equipment throughout southeast Idaho, and achieving gross annual sales in excess of $5 million.

Edward G. Elliott has been Taxpayer's chief executive officer since its incorporation and he has also been its sole shareholder since 1954. He has always had total managerial responsibility for Taxpayer's business. In addition to being Taxpayer's ultimate decision and policy maker, he has performed the functions usually delegated to sales and credit managers. It is undisputed that he works about 80 hours each week.

For several years, Taxpayer has paid Elliott a fixed salary of $2000 per month plus a bonus at year's end. Since Taxpayer's incorporation, Elliott's bonus has been fixed at 50% of net profits (before subtraction of taxes and management bonuses).

On its return for the fiscal year ending February 28, 1975, Taxpayer claimed a $181,074 deduction for total compensation paid Elliott. It claimed a similar $191,663 deduction on its return for the fiscal year ending February 28, 1976. The Commissioner * * * found these deductions to be in excess of the amounts Taxpayer properly could deduct as reasonable salary under section 162(a)(1). * * *

* * * The [Tax C]ourt, after reviewing the testimony and statistical evidence, concluded that the payments to Elliott, in addition to providing compensation for personal services, were intended in part to distribute profits. Although the Tax Court acknowledged that it could not determine what amounts paid Elliott actually were dividends, it found that the total amounts paid him were in excess of reasonable compensation. It determined that $120,000 was reasonable compensation for the year 1975 and that $125,000 was reasonable for 1976. The deficiencies assessed to Taxpayer by the Commissioner were reduced accordingly. Taxpayer appeals the Tax Court's determination of reasonable compensation.

II.   THE SHAREHOLDER-EMPLOYEE PROBLEM

The issue presented by this case concerns the deductibility by a corporation of payments ostensibly made as compensation for services to an employee who is also a shareholder. If the payments are reasonable compensation for services rendered, the corporation may deduct them. § 162(a)(1). If, however, they are actually dividends, they are not deductible. Thus, it will normally be in a corporation's interest to characterize such payments as compensation rather than dividends.

The general problem is that of distinguishing between dividends and compensation for services received by a shareholder-employee of a closely held corporation. What makes this situation troublesome is that the shareholder-employee and the corporation are not dealing with each other at arm's length. It is likely to be in the interests of both the corporation and the shareholder-employee to characterize any payments to the shareholder-employee as compensation rather than dividends. For this reason, a taxpayer's characterization of such payments may warrant close scrutiny to ensure that a portion of the purported compensation payments is not a disguised dividend. [Citation omitted.]

The problem of determining whether compensation payments contain an element of disguised dividend is exacerbated in a case such as this one where the shareholder-employee is the corporation's sole shareholder. Not only is a sole shareholder likely to have complete control over the corporation's operations, he will also be the only recipient of its dividends. If a corporation has multiple shareholders, the existence of a plan which compensates shareholder-employees in proportion to their ownership interests may be evidence that compensation payments contain disguised dividends. In the case of a sole shareholder, such evidence is meaningless.

Section 162(a)(1) permits a corporation to deduct "a reasonable allowance for salaries or other compensation for personal services actually rendered." There is a two-prong test for deductibility under section 162(a)(1): (1) the amount of the compensation must be reasonable and (2) the payments must in fact be purely for services. Treas.Reg. § 1.162–7(a); [further citation omitted.]

Proof of the second prong, which requires a "compensatory purpose," can be difficult to establish because of its subjective nature. See Note, Reasonable Compensation and the Close Corporation: McCandless, the Automatic Dividend Rule, and the Dual Level Test, 26 Stan. L. Rev. 441, 447 (1974) (hereafter "Note, Reasonable Compensation"). The existence of a compensatory purpose can often be inferred if the amount of the compensation is determined to be reasonable under the first prong. For these reasons, courts generally concentrate on the first prong—whether the amount of the purported compensation is reasonable. * * *

One court has departed from this practice of restricting the inquiry in most cases to the reasonableness of the payments. In Charles McCandless Tile Serv. v. United States, 422 F.2d 1336 (Ct.Cl.1970), the Court of Claims held that ostensible compensation payments paid to two shareholder-employees, even though reasonable in amount, "necessarily" contained disguised dividends because the closely held corporation had been profitable and had not paid out any dividends since its formation. This has become known as the "automatic dividend rule," and has been subjected to much criticism. * * *

We reject the automatic dividend rule of *McCandless* for several reasons. First, there is no statute requiring profitable corporations to pay dividends. * * *

Second, the automatic dividend rule is based on the faulty premise that shareholders of a profitable corporation will demand dividends. See *McCandless*, 422 F.2d at 1339–40. Shareholders are generally concerned with the return on their investment. While some shareholders may prefer to see their return in the form of dividends, others will prefer to have the corporation reinvest its profits so that their return will be in the form of appreciation and the potential of greater future return. See, Note, Reasonable Compensation, 26 Stan. L. Rev. at 450–53. If the shareholders prefer to have their return in the form of appreciation rather than dividends, there is nothing in the law precluding the corporation from reinvesting its profits.

Third, it may well be in the best interests of the corporation to retain and reinvest its earnings. * * *

For these reasons, we will not presume an element of disguised dividend from the bare fact that a profitable corporation does not pay dividends.

In determining the deductibility of compensation payments paid to shareholder-employees, we will continue to concentrate on the reasonableness of those payments. In the rare case where there is evidence that an otherwise reasonable compensation payment contains a disguised dividend, the inquiry may expand into compensatory intent apart from reasonableness. But where, as here, the evidence focuses only on reasonableness and the failure to pay dividends, and there is no other evidence of an intent to hide dividends in compensation payments, our inquiry will be confined to the reasonableness issue. The inquiry into reasonableness is a broad one and will, in effect, subsume the inquiry into compensatory intent in most cases.

In evaluating the reasonableness of compensation paid to a shareholder-employee, particularly a sole shareholder, it is helpful to consider the matter from the perspective of a hypothetical independent investor. A relevant inquiry is whether an inactive, independent investor would be willing to compensate the employee as he was compensated. The nature and quality of the services should be considered, as well as the effect of those services on the return the investor is seeing on his investment. The corporation's rate of return on equity would be relevant to the independent investor in assessing the reasonableness of compensation in a small corporation where excessive compensation would noticeably decrease the rate of return.

Bearing in mind the preceding discussion, we now turn to the reasonableness of the compensation paid by Taxpayer to Elliott.

III. Reasonableness Determination

[The court found several errors in the Tax Court's application of various "factors." It had failed to consider Elliott's "extreme personal dedication and devotion to his work"; it ignored the fact that the corporation's average return on equity was 20%, which would "satisfy an independent investor and would indicate that Taxpayer and Elliott were not exploiting their relationship"; it looked only at the amount of compensation paid in two particular years, rather than on the reasonableness of the compensation plan on an overall basis; and it erred in ruling that the "bonus" portion of Elliott's compensation should be discounted because, as sole shareholder, he needed no bonus to give him an incentive to work hard.]

IV. Conclusion

We reverse and remand to the Tax Court for reconsideration in light of this opinion. On remand, the Tax Court should begin its analysis by looking at the reasonableness of the compensation payments and should consider the bonus payments in the context of the reasonableness of the formula used. It should not be assumed solely from Elliott's role as sole shareholder and the absence of dividends that the compensation payments necessarily contained disguised dividends. These are just two of many factors to be considered.

Problem, Notes and Questions

1. *Problem.* *S* is president and sole shareholder of *X* Corp. *S* anticipates that *X* Corp. will earn $200,000 (before taxes and before deduction of any salary paid to *S*) during the current year. *S* plans to withdraw $100,000 from the corporation (either as salary or as a dividend) and to leave the balance of the earnings in the corporation. If *S* is subject to a 30–percent income tax, what amount will *S* have left after tax if she receives a $100,000 salary payment? How much if she receives a $100,000 dividend? What amount will *X* Corp. have left after its tax in each case (assume that *X* Corp. is a "qualified personal service corporation," subject to a 35–percent tax under § 11(b)(2))?

2. *The "automatic-dividend rule."* The Service's position on the connection between failure to pay dividends and the reasonableness of compensation was set out in Rev.Rul. 79–8, 1979–1 C.B. 92, which concluded as follows:

> The failure of a closely held corporation to pay more than an insubstantial portion of its earnings as dividends on its stock is a very significant factor to be taken into account in determining the deductibility of compensation paid by the corporation to its share-holder-employees. Conversely, where after an examination of all of the facts and circumstances (including the corporation's dividend history) compensation paid to shareholder-employees is found to be reasonable in amount and paid for services rendered, deductions for such compensation under section 162(a) of the Code will not be denied on the sole ground that the corporation has not paid more than an insubstantial portion of its earnings as dividends on its outstanding stock.

Would the Ninth Circuit agree that failure to pay substantial dividends is "a very significant factor" in deciding whether compensation was reasonable? Although *Elliotts, Inc.*, rejected the automatic-dividend rule, something resembling that rule has resurfaced in the Ninth Circuit. O.S.C. & Associates, Inc. v. Commissioner, 187 F.3d 1116 (9th Cir.1999), cert. denied 529 U.S. 1097 (2000), affirmed the Tax Court's denial of a deduction for "incentive compensation" payments to shareholder-employees even though the Tax Court had found as a fact that the payments were reasonable in amount. Because the corporation had never paid dividends, had paid out nearly all of its earnings as compensation, and had limited participation in the incentive program to employees who were also shareholders, the court held that the payments were "intended" as distributions of profits to shareholders rather than as compensation.

3. *Determining "reasonable compensation."* It is usual for courts to decide whether compensation is reasonable in amount by considering a variety of factors. This approach was sharply criticized by Judge Posner in Exacto Spring Corp. v. Commissioner, 196 F.3d 833, 834–835 (7th Cir.1999):

In reaching its conclusion, the Tax Court applied a test that requires the consideration of seven factors, none entitled to any specified weight relative to another. The factors are, in the court's words, "(1) the type and extent of the services rendered; (2) the scarcity of qualified employees; (3) the qualifications and prior earning capacity of the employee; (4) the contributions of the employee to the business venture; (5) the net earnings of the employer; (6) the prevailing compensation paid to employees with comparable jobs; and (7) the peculiar characteristics of the employer's business." 75 T.C.M. at 2525. It is apparent that this test, though it or variants of it (one of which has the astonishing total of 21 factors, Foos v. Commissioner, 1981 T.C. Memo 61, 41 T.C.M. (CCH) 863, 878–79 (1981)), are encountered in many cases, [citations omitted], leaves much to be desired—being, like many other multi-factor tests, "redundant, incomplete, and unclear." Palmer v. City of Chicago, 806 F.2d 1316, 1318 (7th Cir.1986).

To begin with, it is nondirective. No indication is given of how the factors are to be weighed in the event they don't all line up on one side. And many of the factors, such as the type and extent of services rendered, the scarcity of qualified employees, and the peculiar characteristics of the employer's business, are vague.

Second, the factors do not bear a clear relation either to each other or to the primary purpose of section 162(a)(1), which is to prevent dividends (or in some cases gifts), which are not deductible from corporate income, from being disguised as salary, which is. E.g., Rapco, Inc. v. Commissioner, 85 F.3d 950, 954 n. 2 (2d Cir.1996). Suppose that an employee who let us say was, like Heitz, a founder and the chief executive officer and principal owner of the taxpayer rendered no services at all but received a huge salary. It would be absurd to allow the whole or for that matter any part of his salary to be deducted as an ordinary and necessary business expense even if he were well qualified to be CEO of the company, the company had substantial net earnings, CEOs of similar companies were paid a lot, and it was a business in which high salaries are common. The multifactor test would not prevent the Tax Court from allowing a deduction in such a case even though the corporation obviously was seeking to reduce its taxable income by disguising earnings as salary. The court would not allow the deduction, but not because of anything in the multi-factor test; rather because it would be apparent that the payment to the employee was not in fact for his services to the company. Treas. Reg. § 1.162–7(a); [further citation omitted].

Third, the seven-factor test invites the Tax Court to set itself up as a superpersonnel department for closely held corporations, a role unsuitable for courts, as we have repeatedly noted in the Title VII context, [citations omitted] * * * . The judges of the Tax Court are not equipped by training or experience to determine the salaries of corporate officers; no judges are.

Fourth, since the test cannot itself determine the outcome of a dispute because of its nondirective character, it invites the making of arbitrary decisions based on uncanalized discretion or unprincipled rules of thumb. The Tax Court in this case essentially added the IRS's determination of the maximum that Mr. Heitz should have been paid in 1993 and 1994 to what he was in fact paid, and divided the sum by two. It cut the baby in half. One would have to be awfully naive to believe that the seven-factor test generated this pleasing symmetry.

Fifth, because the reaction of the Tax Court to a challenge to the deduction of executive compensation is unpredictable, corporations run unavoidable legal risks in determining a level of compensation that may be indispensable to the success of their business.

Instead of applying "factors" to decide the reasonableness of compensation, Judge Posner's opinion suggested that salaries of executives should be "presumptively reasonable" if the shareholders of the corporation "are obtaining a far higher return than they had any reason to expect." Query: if the corporation is losing money at an alarming rate, are the officers presumptively entitled to no compensation?

4. *Golden-parachute payments.* A golden-parachute arrangement protects a corporation against hostile takeover attempts by providing for large cash payments to the corporation's managers if they are dismissed after a change in the ownership or control of the corporation. Section 280G denies deductions for "excess parachute payments," as defined at great length, and § 4999 subjects the recipient of an excess parachute payment to a 20–percent nondeductible excise tax. A payment is not an excess parachute payment to the extent that the payment is "reasonable compensation" for past or future services.

The legislative history of § 280G shows that Congress intended that section to be a "tax penalty." Congress was concerned that "in many instances golden parachute contracts do little but assist an entrenched management team to remain in control"; Explanation of Provisions Approved by the [Senate Finance] Committee on March 21, 1984, S.Prt. No. 98–169, Vol. I., 98th Cong., 2d Sess. at 195 (1984). Whether § 280G will deter "entrenched managements" from using golden-parachute arrangements to protect themselves against dismissal is uncertain; indeed, the tax penalties for excess parachute payments may make golden parachutes even more effective as deterrents. The point of a parachute arrangement is to make it expensive for outsiders to buy the stock of a corporation and dismiss the old guard. Adding a tax penalty to the nontax costs of taking over a corporation may tend to deter takeovers rather than to encourage them, as the Senate Finance Committee seems to have hoped. For a criticism of the golden-parachute provisions, see Wolk, The Golden Parachute Provisions: Time for Repeal?, 21 Va.Tax Rev. 125 (2001).

5. *"Unreasonable" payments other than salaries.* Although § 162 contains no express "reasonable allowance" limits on deductions other

than salaries, it is quite clear that the reasonableness of any purported "business expense" payment to someone closely related to the taxpayer must be considered in determining whether the payment was what it purported to be. The law could hardly be otherwise, for if the taxpayer's characterization were determinative the nondeductibility of dividends or gifts could not be enforced. Thus, excessive "rents" paid by a corporate lessee to shareholder-lessors may be nondeductible dividends, not because the statute requires that rents be "reasonable" but simply because it requires that they be "rents." Safway Steel Scaffolds Co. v. United States, 590 F.2d 1360 (5th Cir.1979).

6. *Are all "unreasonable" salaries nondeductible?* Suppose a corporation pays an employee a salary which, considered objectively, is unreasonably high. Should § 162(a)(1) limit the corporation's deduction if it is established that the payment is not a disguised dividend—that the employee is neither a shareholder nor a friend or relative of a shareholder? Patton v. Commissioner, 168 F.2d 28 (6th Cir.1948), disallowed a deduction for the "excessive" portion of a salary paid a non-owner of the business on the sole ground that the salary was excessive in amount. Judge McAllister's dissent argued that since the payments were "not a distribution of profits under the guise of a salary" they should have been deductible in full. Compare Treas.Reg. § 1.162–7(b)(3).

Dean Griswold has shown that Congress, in adding the "reasonable allowance for salaries" phrase to the statute, intended to allow a deduction even when no salary was actually paid, not to limit a deduction. Although a deduction for unpaid salaries would be almost unthinkable under the current income tax, it made sense in the case of the World War I Excess Profits Tax, since without it the tax would have discriminated against partnerships and sole proprietors, which usually do not (and in the case of sole proprietors cannot) pay "salaries" to the owners of the business. See Griswold, New Light on "A Reasonable Allowance for Salaries," 59 Harv.L.Rev. 286 (1945).

7. *Constructive dividends.* Some corporate taxpayers disguise dividends as something else to avoid taxation of the dividends to the shareholders. Such "constructive dividends" as bargain sales to shareholders and free shareholder use of company cars, airplanes, and vacation properties are easily dealt with in principle, but hard to police in practice. Particularly troublesome are purported "loans" to shareholders. The Tenth Circuit summed up the courts' attitude toward purported "borrowings" by shareholders in Dolese v. United States, 605 F.2d 1146, 1154 (10th Cir.1979), cert. denied 445 U.S. 961 (1980):

> Perhaps in recognition of human nature, the courts have been liberal in cases of shareholder borrowing from controlled corporations. * * * But whereas withdrawal of reasonable amounts are [sic] countenanced as a loan if other loan factors are present, excessive and continuous diversion of corporate funds into the controlling shareholder's pocket takes on a different character. There is a

principle of too much; phrased colloquially, when a pig becomes a hog it is slaughtered.

4. TRAVEL AND ENTERTAINMENT

(a) Commuting and Lunching Expenses

The basic rule for commuting expenses is very simple: they are not deductible. The Supreme Court confirmed this point in Commissioner v. Flowers, 326 U.S. 465 (1946), which held that a lawyer who lived in Jackson, Mississippi, could not deduct the costs of traveling to work in Mobile, Alabama. The Court described the expenses as incurred solely because of the taxpayer's decision to live in Jackson after taking the job in Mobile. Professor William Klein has pointed out the conclusory nature of this argument; it is as easy to say that the costs were incurred because of the "business" decision to work in Mobile as to say that they resulted from a "personal" decision to live in Jackson. Klein, Income Taxation and Commuting Expenses: Tax Policy and the Need for Nonsimplistic Analysis of "Simple" Problems, 54 Cornell L.Rev. 871, 875 (1969).

Although Treas.Reg. § 1.162–2(e) says simply that "[c]ommuters' fares are not considered as business expenses and are not deductible," the Service has ruled that a taxpayer who incurs "additional expenses" in getting tools to work can deduct those extra costs; Rev.Rul. 75–380, 1975–2 C.B. 59. But if the "additional" expense arises because the need to carry tools requires a more expensive mode of travel than the taxpayer otherwise would have used, it is not, in the Service's view, deductible. Thus, a musician who must carry a tuba to work cannot deduct the cost of taking a taxi rather than a bus, but an extra charge by the cab company for carrying the tuba is deductible. The courts have been less strict.

If the costs of getting the taxpayer to work are deemed "personal" costs of living far from work, does treating even the "additional" costs of getting the taxpayer's tools to work as deductible "business" expenses make sense? In a brief *per curiam* opinion, decided without oral argument, the Supreme Court held that an airline pilot who drove to work carrying a flight bag and an overnight bag, and who would have driven to work even if he had not had to transport this equipment, could take no deduction. But the Court added: "Additional expenses may at times be incurred for transporting job-required tools and material to and from work. Then an allocation of costs between 'personal' and 'business' expenses may be feasible. But no such allocation can be made here." Fausner v. Commissioner, 413 U.S. 838 (1973), rehearing denied 414 U.S. 882 (1973).

Another possible exception to the nondeductibility of commuting expenses may exist, at least in the Tenth Circuit, for taxpayers who are "on duty" while they are commuting. Pollei v. Commissioner, 877 F.2d 838 (10th Cir.1989), allowed police captains to deduct the costs of commuting to work in their personally owned unmarked cars. The court observed that the captains were on duty from the moment they left their homes. The Tax Court, in denying deductions, had noted that the captains were also on duty when running personal errands during their off hours. The Tenth Circuit thought that situation distinguishable because the captains' commuting trips were regularly scheduled, so that the department could "rely" on their exercising supervisory powers while they were commuting.

The costs of commuting to a distant, temporary job are deductible as travel expenses, and the costs of travel between one job site and another, as when a lawyer takes a cab from the office to the courthouse, are not commuting expenses and are therefore deductible. If the taxpayer works at home, the case is more complex, as the following ruling shows.

REVENUE RULING 99–7

1999–1 C.B. 361.

ISSUE

Under what circumstances are daily transportation expenses incurred by a taxpayer in going between the taxpayer's residence and a work location deductible under § 162(a)?

LAW AND ANALYSIS

Section 162(a) allows a deduction for all the ordinary and necessary expenses paid or incurred during the taxable year in carrying on any trade or business. Section 262, however, provides that no deduction is allowed for personal, living, or family expenses.

A taxpayer's costs of commuting between the taxpayer's residence and the taxpayer's place of business or employment generally are nondeductible personal expenses under [Treas.Reg.] §§ 1.162–2(e) and 1.262–1(b)(5). However, the costs of going between one business location and another business location generally are deductible under § 162(a). Rev. Rul. 55–109, 1955–1 C.B. 261.

Section 280A(c)(1)(A) * * * provides, in part, that a taxpayer may deduct expenses for the business use of the portion of the taxpayer's personal residence that is exclusively used on a regular basis as the principal place of business for any trade or business of the taxpayer. (In the case of an employee, however, such expenses are deductible only if the exclusive and regular use of the portion of the residence is for the convenience of the employer.) In Curphey v. Commissioner, 73 T.C. 766 (1980), the Tax Court held that daily transportation expenses incurred in going between an office in a taxpayer's residence and other work locations were deductible where the home office was the taxpayer's principal place of business within the meaning of § 280A(c)(1)(A) for the trade or business conducted by the taxpayer at those other work locations. The court stated that "we see no reason why the rule that local transportation expenses incurred in travel between one business location and another are deductible should not be equally applicable *where the taxpayer's principal place of business with respect to the activities in-*

volved is his residence." 73 T.C. at 777–778 (emphasis in original). Implicit in the court's analysis in Curphey is that the deductibility of daily transportation expenses is determined on a business-by-business basis.

Rev. Rul. 190, 1953–2 C.B. 303, provides a limited exception to the general rule that the expenses of going between a taxpayer's residence and a work location are nondeductible commuting expenses. Rev. Rul. 190 deals with a taxpayer who lives and ordinarily works in a particular metropolitan area but who is not regularly employed at any specific work location. In such a case, the general rule is that daily transportation expenses are not deductible when paid or incurred by the taxpayer in going between the taxpayer's residence and a *temporary* work site *inside* that metropolitan area because that area is considered the taxpayer's regular place of business. However, Rev. Rul. 190 holds that daily transportation expenses are deductible business expenses when paid or incurred in going between the taxpayer's residence and a *temporary* work site *outside* that metropolitan area.

Rev. Rul. 90–23, 1990–1 C.B. 28, distinguishes Rev. Rul. 190 and holds, in part, that, for a taxpayer who has one or more regular places of business, daily transportation expenses paid or incurred in going between the taxpayer's residence and *temporary* work locations are deductible business expenses under § 162(a), regardless of the distance.

Rev. Rul. 94–47, 1994–2 C.B. 18, amplifies and clarifies Rev. Rul. 190 and Rev. Rul. 90–23, and provides several rules for determining whether daily transportation expenses are deductible business expenses under § 162(a). Under Rev. Rul. 94–47, a taxpayer generally may not deduct daily transportation expenses incurred in going between the taxpayer's residence and a work location. A taxpayer, however, may deduct daily transportation expenses incurred in going between the taxpayer's residence and a *temporary* work location *outside* the metropolitan area where the taxpayer lives and normally works. In addition, Rev. Rul. 94–47 clarifies Rev. Rul. 90–23 to provide that a taxpayer must have at least one regular place of business located "away from the taxpayer's residence" in order to deduct daily transportation expenses incurred in going between the taxpayer's residence and a *temporary* work location in the same trade or business, regardless of the distance. In this regard, Rev. Rul. 94–47 also states that the Service will not follow the decision in Walker v. Commissioner, 101 T.C. 537 (1993). Finally, Rev. Rul. 94–47 amplifies Rev. Rul. 190 and Rev. Rul. 90–23 to provide that, if the taxpayer's residence is the taxpayer's principal place of business within the meaning of § 280A(c)(1)(A), the taxpayer may deduct daily transportation expenses incurred in going between the taxpayer's residence and another work location in the same trade or business, regardless of whether the other work location is regular or *temporary* and regardless of the distance.

For purposes of both Rev. Rul. 90–23 and Rev. Rul. 94–47, a *temporary* work location is defined as any location at which the taxpayer performs services on an irregular or short-term (*i.e.*, generally a matter of days or weeks) basis. However, for purposes of determining whether daily transportation expense allowances and per diem travel allowances for meal and lodging expenses are subject to income tax withholding under § 3402, Rev. Rul. 59–371, 1959–2 C.B. 236, provides a 1–year standard to determine whether a work location is *temporary*. Similarly, for purposes of determining the deductibility of travel away-from-home expenses under § 162(a)(2), Rev. Rul. 93–86, 1993–2 C.B. 71, generally provides a 1–year standard to determine whether a work location will be treated as *temporary*.

The Service has reconsidered the definition of a *temporary* work location in Rev. Rul. 90–23 and Rev. Rul. 94–47, and will replace the "irregular or short-term (i.e., generally a matter of days or weeks) basis" standard in those rulings with a 1–year standard similar to the rules set forth in Rev. Rul. 59–371 and Rev. Rul. 93–86.

If an office in the taxpayer's residence satisfies the principal place of business requirements of § 280A(c)(1)(A), then the residence is considered a business location for purposes of Rev. Rul. 90–23 or Rev. Rul. 94–47. In these circumstances, the daily transportation expenses incurred in going between the residence and other work locations in the same trade or business are ordinary and necessary business expenses (deductible under § 162(a)). [Citations omitted.] In contrast, if an office in the taxpayer's residence does not satisfy the principal place of business requirements of § 280A(c)(1)(A), then the business activity there (if any) is not sufficient to overcome the inherently personal nature of the residence and the daily transportation expenses incurred in going between the residence and regular work locations. In these circumstances, the residence is not considered a business location for purposes of Rev. Rul. 90–23 or Rev. Rul. 94–47, and the daily transportation expenses incurred in going between the residence and regular work locations are personal expenses (nondeductible under §§ 1.162–2(e) and 1.262–1(b)(5)). [Citations omitted.]

* * *

HOLDING

In general, daily transportation expenses incurred in going between a taxpayer's residence and a work location are nondeductible commuting expenses. However, such expenses are deductible under the circumstances described in paragraph (1), (2), or (3) below.

(1) A taxpayer may deduct daily transportation expenses incurred in going between the taxpayer's residence and a *temporary* work location *outside* the metropolitan area where the taxpayer lives and normally works. However, unless paragraph (2) or (3) below applies, daily transportation expenses incurred in going between the taxpayer's residence and a *temporary* work location *within* that metropolitan area are nondeductible commuting expenses.

(2) If a taxpayer has one or more regular work locations away from the taxpayer's residence, the taxpayer may deduct daily transportation expenses incurred in going between the taxpayer's residence and a *temporary* work location in the same trade or business, regardless of the distance. * * *

(3) If a taxpayer's residence is the taxpayer's principal place of business within the meaning of § 280A(c)(1)(A), the taxpayer may deduct daily transportation expenses incurred in going between the residence and another work location in the same trade or business, regardless of whether the other work location is *regular* or *temporary* and regardless of the distance.

* * *

Note

1. *Working couples.* Suppose that H and W, who are married to each other, work in cities 300 miles apart. In this kind of case, heavy commuting expenses for at least one of the spouses are inevitable, and it seems artificial to say that the expenses result from a "personal choice about where to live." Nevertheless, no exception for this kind of case has yet been created by statute, regulation, ruling, or caselaw. See footnote 11 to Hantzis v. Commissioner, p. 349, below.

MOSS v. COMMISSIONER

United States Court of Appeals, Seventh Circuit, 1985.
758 F.2d 211, cert. denied 474 U.S. 979, 106 S.Ct. 382, 88 L.Ed.2d 335 (1985).

Before CUMMINGS, CHIEF JUDGE, and BAUER and POSNER, CIRCUIT JUDGES.

POSNER, CIRCUIT JUDGE.

The taxpayers, a lawyer named Moss and his wife, appeal from a decision of the Tax Court disallowing federal income tax deductions of a little more than $1,000 in each of two years, representing Moss's share of his law firm's lunch expense at the Café Angelo in Chicago. 80 T.C. 1073 (1983). The Tax Court's decision in this case has attracted some attention in tax circles because of its implications for the general problem of the deductibility of business meals. See, e.g., McNally, Vulnerability of Entertainment and Meal Deductions Under the Sutter Rule, 62 Taxes 184 (1984).

Moss was a partner in a small trial firm specializing in defense work, mostly for one insurance company. Each of the firm's lawyers carried a tremendous litigation caseload, averaging more than 300 cases, and spent most of every working day in courts in Chicago and its suburbs. The members of the firm met for lunch daily at the Café Angelo near their office. At lunch the lawyers would discuss their cases with the head of the firm, whose approval was required for most settlements, and they would decide which lawyer would meet which court call that afternoon or the next morning. Lunchtime was chosen for the daily meeting because the courts were in recess then. The alternatives were to meet at 7:00 a.m. or 6:00 p.m., and these were less convenient times. There is no suggestion that the lawyers dawdled over lunch, or that the Café Angelo is luxurious.

The framework of statutes and regulations for deciding this case is simple, but not clear. Section 262 disallows, "except as otherwise expressly provided in this chapter," the deduction of "personal, family, or living expenses." Section 119 excludes from income the value of meals provided by an employer to his employees for his convenience, but only if they are provided on the employer's premises; and section 162(a) allows the deduction of "all the ordinary and necessary expenses paid or incurred during the taxable year in carrying on any trade or business, including * * * (2) traveling expenses (including amounts expended for meals * * *) while away from home. * * *" Since Moss was not an employee but a partner in a partnership not taxed as an entity, since the meals were not served on the employer's premises, and since he was not away from home (that is, on an overnight trip away from his place of work, see United States v. Correll, 389 U.S. 299 (1967)), neither section 119 nor section 162(a)(2) applies to this case. The Internal Revenue Service concedes, however, that meals are deductible under section 162(a) when they are ordinary and necessary business expenses (provided the expense is substantiated with adequate records, see section 274(d)) even if they are not within the express permission of any other provision and even though the expense of commuting to and from work, a traveling expense but not one incurred away from home, is not deductible. [Treas.Reg.] § 1.262–1(b)(5); Fausner v. Commissioner, 413 U.S. 838 (1973) (per curiam).

The problem is that many expenses are simultaneously business expenses in the sense that they conduce to the production of business income and personal expenses in the sense that they raise personal welfare. This is plain enough with regard to lunch; most people would eat lunch even if they didn't work. Commuting may seem a pure business expense, but is not; it reflects the choice of where to live, as well as where to work. Read literally, section 262 would make irrelevant whether a business expense is also a personal expense; so long as it is ordinary and necessary in the taxpayer's business, thus bringing section 162(a) into play, an expense is (the statute seems to say) deductible from his income tax. But the statute has not been read literally. There is a natural reluctance, most clearly manifested in the regulation disallowing deduction of the expense of commuting, to lighten the tax burden of people who have the good fortune to interweave work with consumption. To allow a deduction for commuting would confer a windfall on people who live in the suburbs and commute to work in the cities; to allow a deduction for all business-related meals would confer a windfall on people who can arrange their work schedules so they do some of their work at lunch.

Although an argument can thus be made for disallowing *any* deduction for business meals, on the theory that people have to eat whether they work or not, the result would be excessive taxation of people who spend more money on business meals because they are business meals than they would spend on their meals if they were not working. Suppose a theatrical agent takes his clients out to lunch at the expensive restaurants that the clients demand. Of course he can deduct the expense of their meals, from which he derives no pleasure or sustenance, but can he also deduct the expense of his own? He can, because he cannot eat more cheaply; he cannot munch surreptitiously on a peanut butter and jelly sandwich brought from home while his client is wolfing down tournedos Rossini followed by soufflé au grand marnier. No doubt our theatrical agent, unless concerned for his longevity, derives personal utility from his fancy meal, but probably less than the price of the meal. He would not pay for it if it were not for the business benefit; he would get more value from using the same money to buy something else; hence the meal confers on him less utility than the cash equivalent would. The law could require him to pay tax on the fair value of the meal to him; this would be (were it not for costs of administration) the economically correct solution. But the Government does not attempt this difficult measurement; it once did, but gave up the attempt as not worth the cost, see United States v. Correll, supra, 389 U.S. at 301 n. 6. The taxpayer is permitted to deduct the whole price, provided the expense is "different from or in excess of that which would have been made for the taxpayer's personal purposes." Sutter v. Commissioner, 21 T.C. 170, 173 (1953).

Because the law allows this generous deduction, which tempts people to have more (and costlier) business meals than are necessary, the Internal Revenue Service has every right to insist that the meal be shown to be a real business necessity. This condition is most easily satisfied when a client or customer or supplier or other outsider to the business is a guest. Even if Sydney Smith was wrong that "soup and fish explain half the emotions of life," it is undeniable that eating together fosters camaraderie and makes business dealings friendlier and easier. It thus reduces the costs of transacting business, for these costs include the frictions and the failures of communication that are produced by suspicion and mutual misunderstanding, by differences in tastes and manners, and by lack of rapport. A meeting with a client or customer in an office is therefore not a perfect substitute for a lunch with him in a restaurant. But it is different when all the participants in the meal are coworkers, as essentially was the case here (clients occasionally were invited to the firm's daily luncheon, but Moss has made no attempt to identify the occasions). They know each other well already; they don't need the social lubrication that a meal with an outsider provides—at least don't need it daily. If a large firm had a monthly lunch to allow partners to get to know associates, the expense of the meal might well be necessary, and would be allowed by the Internal Revenue Service. See Wells v. Commissioner, 36 T.C.M. 1698, 1699 (1977), aff'd without opinion, 626 F.2d 868 (9th Cir.1980). But Moss's firm never had more than eight lawyers (partners and associates), and did not need a daily lunch to cement relationships among them.

It is all a matter of degree and circumstance (the expense of a testimonial dinner, for example, would be deductible on a morale-building rationale); and particularly of frequency. Daily—for a full year—is too often, perhaps even for entertainment of clients, as implied by Hankenson v. Commissioner, 47 T.C.M. 1567, 1569 (1984), where the Tax Court held nondeductible the cost of lunches consumed three or four days a week, 52 weeks a year, by a doctor who entertained other doctors who he hoped would refer patients to him, and other medical personnel.

We may assume it was necessary for Moss's firm to meet daily to coordinate the work of the firm, and also, as the Tax Court found, that lunch was the most convenient time. But it does not follow that the expense of the lunch was a necessary business expense. The members of the firm had to eat somewhere, and the Café Angelo was both convenient and not too expensive. They do not claim to have incurred a greater daily lunch expense than they would have incurred if there had been no lunch meetings. Although it saved time to combine lunch with work, the meal itself was not an organic part of the meeting, as in the examples we gave earlier where the business objective, to be fully achieved, required sharing a meal.

The case might be different if the location of the courts required the firm's members to eat each day either in a disagreeable restaurant, so that they derived less value from the meal than it cost them to buy it, cf. Sibla v. Commissioner, 611 F.2d 1260, 1262 (9th Cir.1980); or in a restaurant too expensive for their personal tastes, so that, again, they would have gotten less value than the cash equivalent. But so far as appears, they picked the restaurant they liked most. Although it must be pretty monotonous to eat lunch the same place every working day of the year, not all the lawyers attended all the lunch meetings and there was nothing to stop the firm from meeting occasionally at another restaurant proximate to their office in downtown Chicago; there are hundreds.

An argument can be made that the price of lunch at the Café Angelo included rental of the space that the lawyers used for what was a meeting as well as a meal. There was evidence that the firm's conference room was otherwise occupied throughout the working day, so as a matter of logic Moss might be able to claim a part of the price of lunch as an ordinary and necessary expense for work space. But this is cutting things awfully fine; in any event Moss made no effort to apportion his lunch expense in this way.

Affirmed.

Problem and Notes

1. *Deduction and exclusion issues.* If Moss had been an employee of the firm, rather than a self-employed taxpayer (that is, a partner), the issue would have been whether the cost of the meals was includable in his income. In principle, includability of a meal in an employee's income raises the same question as the deductibility of the cost of a meal

purchased by a self-employed taxpayer: in each case, the issue is whether some or all of the meal's cost should be included in the tax base of the person who eats the meal. In the case of the employee, exclusion from the tax base can be achieved by allowing the employee to exclude a receipt from income. A self-employed taxpayer's meal will be "taxable" in the sense that the money the taxpayer earns and uses to buy the meal is includable in income if the cost of the meal is not deductible.

When one taxpayer pays for a business meal which another taxpayer eats, issues of both deductibility and includability arise. The person who eats the meal (an employee, for example) needs to determine whether the meal can be excluded under § 119 or as a de minimis fringe benefit (§ 132); the person who furnishes the meal (such as an employer) will usually treat the cost of the meal as a business expense under § 162(a).

2. *Section 274.* As the *Moss* opinion shows, even a properly deductible or excludable meal involves some element of personal consumption: at the very least, someone who eats a business meal has been spared the cost of buying a sandwich. In response to this concern and to a suspicion that many claimed "business" meals have little business connection, Congress amended § 274 in 1986. Food and beverage expenses are now subject to § 274(a)'s business-connection requirements, and the Conference Committee Report instructs the Treasury Department "to adopt stricter substantiation requirements for business meals"; H.R.Rep. No. 99–841, 99th Cong., 2d Sess. at II–27 (1986). Section 274(k) denies a deduction for food and beverage expenses subject to § 274(a) if the expense is "lavish or extravagant under the circumstances" or if "the taxpayer (or an employee of the taxpayer) is [not] present at the furnishing of such food or beverages." Furthermore, § 274(n) limits deductions for most meals that survive §§ 162, 274(a), and 274(k) to 50 percent of the amount which would ordinarily be deductible. For many transportation workers—bus and truck drivers, pilots and flight attendants, and so on—the deductible portion of a meal's cost will gradually rise to 80, rather than 50, percent over a ten-year period; § 274(n)(3).

3. *Problem.* Each Friday the Law School faculty has lunch in the meeting room of a nearby restaurant. Often a guest speaker makes a brief presentation at these affairs. Sometimes, however, the faculty holds an informal discussion of the school's problems or aspirations. The dean believes that the luncheons provide an excellent opportunity for informal interchange and getting acquainted with new or visiting faculty members. Each faculty member pays for lunch. To what extent, if any, are the meal costs deductible?

(b) "Away from Home"

Suppose a taxpayer takes a three-day business trip to another city. In a sense, the costs of the taxpayer's meals and hotel room are "personal"; they are incurred for the "personal" purpose of keeping the taxpayer alive and comfortable. But in a case like this, the expenses plainly represent some extra cost solely attributable to the business activity. The traveler will not save on mortgage payments or rent by being out of town for three days, and the restaurant meals the taxpayer eats may be much more expensive than eating at home would have been. For these reasons, § 162(a)(2) allows a deduction for meals and lodging "while away from home in the pursuit of a trade or business."

The reasons for allowing the § 162(a)(2) deduction do not extend to a case in which a taxpayer chooses to live far from work, as when an actor who works in Hollywood lives in Montana. Although a literal reading of § 162(a)(2) might support a finding that this actor, while working in Hollywood, is "away from home in the pursuit of a trade or business," the courts have denied the deduction. The Service and the Tax Court reason that the taxpayer's "home" for purposes of § 162(a)(2) is the taxpayer's "principal place of business," so that the taxpayer is not "away from home" while working; this is the "tax-home" concept. Other courts say that a taxpayer who chooses to live far from the site of a permanent job has made a "personal choice" to incur the expenses in question and so is not away from home "in the pursuit of a trade or business." For example, the Second Circuit rejected the "tax home" concept in Rosenspan v. United States, 438 F.2d 905 (2d Cir.1971), cert. denied 404 U.S. 864 (1971), holding that a taxpayer's "home" is his principal residence. But the court added that no deduction is allowed a taxpayer who maintains that home "in a locale apart from where he regularly work[s] as a matter of personal choice rather than business necessity." This approach has been followed by other courts of appeals.

The Supreme Court has passed up several opportunities to resolve the "tax home" controversy. See Commissioner v. Stidger, 386 U.S. 287 (1967), involving a Marine Corps captain assigned to a base in Japan who maintained a home for his family in California. The Court relied on statutes and military practices governing travel allowances for armed forces personnel to deny a deduction for the taxpayer's living costs in Japan, thus deciding the case in a way that gives no guidance for cases involving civilians.

Section 911, a relief provision for taxpayers working abroad, refers to the taxpayer's "tax home" in a context that makes it clear that "tax home" means "principal place of business"; see §§ 911(d)(1) & (c)(2)(B)(i). This Congressional endorsement of the tax-home concept may encourage the courts to use that concept in cases arising under § 162(a)(2).

Whatever the interpretative technique used to get there, it is clear that a taxpayer on a three-day business trip away from both home and principal place of work can deduct meals and lodging. At the other extreme, a taxpayer who takes a permanent job 500 miles from home cannot deduct meals and lodging at the job site even if this is "away from home" in a literal sense. There was once an extensive body of case law on how long one had to expect to be away if an away-from-home job was to be "temporary." Today, the Code draws the line at one year except for Federal employees investigating or prosecuting crime; see § 162(a)(last two sentences).

ROBERTSON v. COMMISSIONER

United States Court of Appeals for the Fifth Circuit, 1999.
190 F.3d 392.

Before REYNALDO G. GARZA, HIGGINBOTHAM and DAVIS, CIRCUIT JUDGES.

W. EUGENE DAVIS, CIRCUIT JUDGE:

James Lawton Robertson, a former Mississippi Supreme Court justice, and his wife, Lillian Janette Humber Robertson ("the Taxpayers"), appeal from an order of the United States Tax Court finding deficiencies in income tax due from the Taxpayers for the taxable years 1990, 1991, and 1992. Justice Robertson contends that the Tax Court erred in requiring him to declare as income the amounts that the State of Mississippi reimbursed him for travel, meals, and lodging incurred in attending court sessions in Jackson, Mississippi. More particularly, he contends that the Tax Court erred in finding that Jackson, Mississippi—where the court sits—was his "tax home" rather than Oxford, Mississippi, his place of residence. For reasons that follow, we affirm the Tax Court's order.

I.

Justice Robertson began practicing law in Greenville, Mississippi in 1965. In 1979, he became a full-time law professor at the University of Mississippi School of Law ("the law school"), which is adjacent to Oxford, Mississippi. Justice Robertson and his wife owned a home in Oxford, were registered to vote in Oxford, conducted their banking in Oxford, registered their automobiles in Oxford, enrolled their three sons in public schools in Oxford, paid real estate taxes and claimed a homestead exemption for their home in Oxford, attended church in Oxford, and were involved in several civic organizations in Oxford.

On January 17, 1983, the Governor of Mississippi appointed Justice Robertson to the Mississippi Supreme Court to fill a retired justice's unexpired term. The Mississippi Supreme Court * * * sits 157 miles away from Oxford in Jackson, Mississippi * * * . In November 1983, he was elected [for the remainder of the term] without opposition. Justice Robertson ran for reelection in 1984 and won a full eight-year term that expired on December 31, 1992.

While serving on the Mississippi Supreme Court, Justice Robertson continued to teach one course each semester at the law school. Because of the distance between Oxford and Jackson, he developed a weekly schedule to accommodate his two positions. On Sunday afternoons, Justice Robertson drove from Oxford to Jackson. He remained in Jackson from Monday through Thursday and attended to his duties on the Mississippi Supreme Court. While in Jackson, he resided in an apartment and paid monthly rent. On Thursday afternoons, Justice Robertson drove from Jackson to Oxford. He remained in Oxford from Thursday through Sunday, teaching his course at the law school on Friday afternoons and spending the weekends with Mrs. Robertson and their three sons at their Oxford home. Justice Robertson completed such round trips between Oxford and Jackson 48 times in 1990, 45 times in 1991, and 30 times in 1992.

Justice Robertson's duties as a Mississippi Supreme Court justice required him to be in Jackson at least two days out of each week that the Mississippi Supreme Court was in session—one day for panel hearings and one day for en banc hearings. At the Mississippi Supreme Court, Justice Robertson had an office, staff, and access to the state library. Nonetheless, he completed much of his judicial work at the law school library in Oxford during the weekends. He also performed various nonjudicial civic functions in Oxford, the purpose of which was in part to secure re-election.

Justice Robertson was reimbursed by the State of Mississippi for some of the travel, lodging, and meal expenses he incurred while attending Mississippi Supreme Court sessions in Jackson and returning to his residence in Oxford. The Taxpayers did not report this reimbursement as income on their federal joint income tax returns for 1990, 1991, and 1992. Moreover, the Taxpayers deducted those travel, lodging, and meal expenses that were not reimbursed by Mississippi.

* * * The Commissioner determined that the Taxpayers had underreported their income by the amount of travel, lodging, and meal expense reimbursements Justice Robertson had received from the State of Mississippi. The Commissioner also disallowed the deductions claimed by the Taxpayers for the unreimbursed travel, lodging, and meal expenses. The Taxpayers filed a petition in the Tax Court challenging the deficiencies. Following trial, the Tax Court sustained the deficiencies, with the exception of certain amounts conceded by the Commissioner.

II.

* * *

Gross income does not * * * include the amount of reimbursed trade or business expenses paid to a qualifying employee under an accountable plan. [Treas.Reg.] § 1.62–2(c)(2), (4). An accountable plan is one in which (1) the reimbursed expenses would otherwise be allowable as a deduction to the employee under * * * [§ 162] and are paid or incurred by the employee in connection with the performance of services as an employee of the employer; * * * .

Section 162(a) allows as a deduction ordinary and necessary expenses incurred during the taxable year in carrying on a trade or business. This deduction includes traveling expenses incurred while "away from home" in the pursuit of a trade or business. § 162(a)(2). To qualify under this provision, an expense must satisfy three conditions: "(1) the expense must be reasonable and necessary; (2) the expense must be incurred while 'away from home;' and (3) the expense must be incurred 'in the pursuit of business.' " Putnam v. United States, 32 F.3d 911, 916 (5th Cir.1994) (quoting Commissioner v. Flowers, 326 U.S. 465, 470 (1946)).

The word "home" for purposes of business deductions under § 162 "does not have its usual and ordinary meaning." Putnam, 32 F.3d at 917. This court has repeatedly recognized that the term "home" means "the vicinity of the taxpayer's principal place of business and not where his personal residence is located." Id. at 916. Thus, a taxpayer's "home" for purposes of Section 162 "is that place where he performs his most important functions or spends most of his working time." Id. at 916–17. If a taxpayer has two places of business or employment separated by considerable distances, the court applies an objective test in which it considers the length of time spent at each location, the degree of activity in each location, and the relative proportion of the taxpayer's income derived from each location. [Citations omitted.]

Here, the Tax Court applied the above test and determined that Justice Robertson's home for purposes of Section 162 was Jackson rather than Oxford. Accordingly, because Justice Robertson's traveling expenses were not incurred while "away from home," the Tax Court concluded that they were not eligible for deduction as ordinary and necessary business expenses. The Taxpayers challenge that conclusion on several grounds, which we consider below.

III.

* * *

The Taxpayers argue that the Tax Court erred in its determination that Justice Robertson's home for purposes of Section 162 was Jackson rather than Oxford. The Taxpayers observe that justices who maintain their residence outside of Jackson spend less than forty percent of the calendar year in Jackson, and that many of their duties (reading briefs and records and clerk memos, writing opinions, etc.) can be performed anywhere. The Taxpayers contend that Justice Robertson did not perform his duties as a justice of the Mississippi Supreme Court solely while in Jackson. Rather, he spent many weekends in Oxford reading briefs and writing opinions. Moreover, the Taxpayers point out that Justice Robertson's duties as an adjunct professor of law involved much more than just showing up in a classroom and teaching. He was also required to prepare for classes, to counsel students, to judge moot court arguments, to engage in discussion and conferences with faculty colleagues, to participate as an instructor in continuing legal education programs, to present papers on academic occasions, to prepare and publish scholarly articles, to grade exam papers, and to keep up with the literature in his field. These duties were far more time-consuming than the teaching itself, and the Taxpayers argue that they too were performed in Oxford.

Following a careful review of the record, we conclude that the Tax Court did not clearly err in finding that Justice Robertson's tax home was Jackson. In a typical work week, Justice Robertson spent four days in Jackson and three days in Oxford. While in Jackson, all four days were committed to Justice Robertson's work as a justice of the Mississippi Supreme Court. Even assuming that Justice Robertson spent a significant part of each weekend in Oxford performing his duties both as a justice and as an adjunct professor of law, the fact remains that the greater part of his typical work week was spent in Jackson. Justice Robertson's office and staff were located in Jackson, and his most important duties—holding panel and en banc hearings—were performed in Jackson. Justice Robertson earned $75,000 per year as a justice, and $15,000 per year as an adjunct professor, meaning that the greater relative proportion of his income was derived from his work in Jackson. In light of all these facts, we can find no clear error in the Tax Court's determination that Jackson rather than Oxford was Justice Robertson's tax home.

Additionally, the Taxpayers argue that the present case is analogous to this Court's decision in United States v. Le Blanc, 278 F.2d 571 (5th Cir.1960), in which we determined that the expenses incurred by a justice of the Louisiana Supreme Court while traveling between his home district and New Orleans during the court term were deductible as ordinary and necessary business expenses. In *LeBlanc*, we carefully explained that the Louisiana Constitution: (1) requires the justices of the Louisiana Supreme Court to be and to remain residents of their home districts; and (2) further requires the Louisiana Supreme Court to be in annual session from October through June in New Orleans. In light of this legal requirement, we concluded that it was "most certainly 'the exigencies of business'" rather than personal convenience that forced Justice LeBlanc to incur his traveling expenses. Id. at 575 (quoting Peurifoy v. Commissioner, 358 U.S. 59, 60, 79 S. Ct. 104, 105, 3 L. Ed. 2d 30 (1958)). Consequently, "mileage, travel, carrier fares, board and lodging during the absence were deductible." *Id*.

* * *

For these reasons, the decision of the Tax Court is AFFIRMED.

Question

1. *How much did Justice Robertson really lose?* If, as the court held, Justice Robertson's tax home is in Jackson, can he deduct his living costs while in Oxford, pursuing his other "trade or business" of being an adjunct professor?

HANTZIS v. COMMISSIONER

United States Court of Appeals, First Circuit, 1981.
638 F.2d 248.

Before CAMPBELL and BOWNES, CIRCUIT JUDGES, and KEETON, DISTRICT JUDGE.

LEVIN H. CAMPBELL, CIRCUIT JUDGE.

The Commissioner of Internal Revenue (Commissioner) appeals a decision of the United States Tax Court that allowed a deduction under

§ 162(a)(2) for expenses incurred by a law student in the course of her summer employment. The facts in the case are straightforward and undisputed.

In the fall of 1973 Catharine Hantzis (taxpayer), formerly a candidate for an advanced degree in philosophy at the University of California at Berkeley, entered Harvard Law School in Cambridge, Massachusetts, as a full-time student. During her second year of law school she sought unsuccessfully to obtain employment for the summer of 1975 with a Boston law firm. She did, however, find a job as a legal assistant with a law firm in New York City, where she worked for ten weeks beginning in June 1975. Her husband, then a member of the faculty of Northeastern University with a teaching schedule for that summer, remained in Boston and lived at the couple's home there. At the time of the Tax Court's decision in this case, Mr. and Mrs. Hantzis still resided in Boston.

On their joint income tax return for 1975, Mr. and Mrs. Hantzis reported the earnings from taxpayer's summer employment ($3,750) and deducted the cost of transportation between Boston and New York, the cost of a small apartment rented by Mrs. Hantzis in New York and the cost of her meals in New York ($3,204). The deductions were taken under § 162(a)(2) * * *.

The Commissioner disallowed the deduction on the ground that taxpayer's home for purposes of section 162(a)(2) was her place of employment and the cost of traveling to and living in New York was therefore not "incurred * * * while away from home." The Commissioner also argued that the expenses were not incurred "in the pursuit of a trade or business." Both positions were rejected by the Tax Court, which found that Boston was Mrs. Hantzis' home because her employment in New York was only temporary and that her expenses in New York were "necessitated" by her employment there. The court thus held the expenses to be deductible under section 162(a)(2).

In asking this court to reverse the Tax Court's allowance of the deduction, the Commissioner has contended that the expenses were not incurred "in the pursuit of a trade or business." We do not accept this argument; nonetheless, we sustain the Commissioner and deny the deduction, on the basis that the expenses were not incurred "while away from home."

I.

Section 262 of the Code declares that "except as otherwise provided in this chapter, no deductions shall be allowed for personal, living, or family expenses." Section 162 provides less of an exception to this rule than it creates a separate category of deductible business expenses. This category manifests a fundamental principle of taxation: that a person's taxable income should not include the cost of producing that income. See

Note, The Additional Expense Test: A Proposal to Help Solve the Dilemma of Mixed Business and Personal Expenses, 1974 Duke L.J. 636, 636. "[O]ne of the specific examples given by Congress" of a deductible cost of producing income is travel expenses in section 162(a)(2). Commissioner v. Flowers, 326 U.S. 465, 469 (1946). See Rev.Rul. 60–16, 1960–1 C.B. 58, 60.

The test by which "personal" travel expenses subject to tax under section 262 are distinguished from those costs of travel necessarily incurred to generate income is embodied in the requirement that, to be deductible under section 162(a)(2), an expense must be "incurred * * * in the pursuit of a trade or business." * * *

II.

The Commissioner has directed his argument at the meaning of "in pursuit of a trade or business." He interprets this phrase as requiring that a deductible traveling expense be incurred under the demands of a trade or business which predates the expense, i.e., an "already existing" trade or business. Under this theory, section 162(a)(2) would invalidate the deduction taken by the taxpayer because she was a full-time student before commencing her summer work at a New York law firm in 1975 and so was not continuing in a trade or business when she incurred the expenses of traveling to New York and living there while her job lasted. * * *

Such a reading of the statute is semantically possible and would perhaps expedite the disposition of certain cases. Nevertheless, we reject it as unsupported by case law and inappropriate to the policies behind section 162(a)(2).

* * *

III.

* * * *Flowers* construed section 162(a)(2) to mean that a traveling expense is deductible only if it is (1) reasonable and necessary, (2) incurred while away from home, and (3) necessitated by the exigencies of business. Because the Commissioner does not suggest that Mrs. Hantzis' expenses were unreasonable or unnecessary, we may pass directly to the remaining requirements. Of these, we find dispositive the requirement that an expense be incurred while away from home. As we think Mrs. Hantzis' expenses were not so incurred, we hold the deduction to be improper.

The meaning of the term "home" in the travel expense provision is far from clear. When Congress enacted the travel expense deduction now codified as section 162(a)(2), it apparently was unsure whether, to be deductible, an expense must be incurred away from a person's residence or away from his principal place of business. See Note, A House is not a Tax Home, 49 Va.L.Rev. 125, 127–28 (1963). This ambiguity persists and courts, sometimes within a single circuit, have divided over the issue. Compare Six v. United States, 450 F.2d 66 (2d Cir.1971) (home held to be residence) and Rosenspan v. United States, 438 F.2d 905 (2d Cir.), cert. denied, 404 U.S. 864 (1971) and Burns v. Gray, 287 F.2d 698 (6th Cir.1961) and Wallace v. Commissioner, 144 F.2d 407 (9th Cir.1944) with Markey v. Commissioner, 490 F.2d 1249 (6th Cir.1974) (home held to be principal place of business) and Curtis v. Commissioner, 449 F.2d 225 (5th Cir.1971) and Wills v. Commissioner, 411 F.2d 537 (9th Cir.1969). It has been suggested that these conflicting definitions are due to the enormous factual variety in the cases. See Bell v. United States, 591 F.2d 647, 649 (Ct.Cl.1979) ("We believe that much of the problem in differing definitions is the result of attempting to conceptualize the reasons for decisions which are based on widely varying factual situations."); Brandl v. Commissioner, 513 F.2d 697, 699 (6th Cir.1975) ("Because of the almost infinite variety of the factual situations involved, the courts have not formulated a concrete definition of the term 'home' capable of universal application."). We find this observation instructive, for if the cases that discuss the meaning of the term "home" in section 162(a)(2) are interpreted on the basis of their unique facts as well as the fundamental purposes of the travel expense provision, and not simply pinioned to one of two competing definitions of home, much of the seeming confusion and contradiction on this issue disappears and a functional definition of the term emerges.

We begin by recognizing that the location of a person's home for purposes of section 162(a)(2) becomes problematic only when the person lives one place and works another. Where a taxpayer resides and works at a single location, he is always home, however defined; and where a taxpayer is constantly on the move due to his work, he is never "away" from home. (In the latter situation, it may be said either that he has no residence to be away from, or else that his residence is always at his place of employment. See Rev.Rul. 60–16, 1960–1 C.B. 58, 62.) However, in the present case, the need to determine "home" is plainly before us, since the taxpayer resided in Boston and worked, albeit briefly, in New York.

We think the critical step in defining "home" in these situations is to recognize that the "while away from home" requirement has to be construed in light of the further requirement that the expense be the result of business exigencies. The traveling expense deduction obviously is not intended to exclude from taxation every expense incurred by a taxpayer who, in the course of business, maintains two homes. Section 162(a)(2) seeks rather "to mitigate the burden of the taxpayer who, *because of the exigencies of his trade or business, must* maintain two places of abode and thereby incur additional and duplicate living expenses." [Citations omitted.] Consciously or unconsciously, courts have effectuated this policy in part through their interpretation of the term "home" in section 162(a)(2). Whether it is held in a particular decision that a taxpayer's home is his residence or his principal place of business, the ultimate allowance or disallowance of a deduction is a function of the court's assessment of the reason for a taxpayer's maintenance of two homes. If the reason is perceived to be personal, the taxpayer's home will generally be held to be his place of employment rather than his residence and the deduction will be denied. See, e.g., *Markey,* supra, 490 F.2d at 1252–55; *Wills,* supra, 411 F.2d at 540–41; *Daly,* supra, 72 T.C. at 195–98; Lindsay v. Commissioner, 34 B.T.A. at 834–44. If the reason is felt to be business exigencies, the person's home will usually be held to be his residence and the deduction will be allowed. [Citations omitted.] We understand the concern of the concurrence that such an operational interpretation of the term "home" is somewhat technical and perhaps untidy, in that it will not always afford bright line answers, but we doubt the ability of either the Commissioner or the courts to invent an unyielding formula that will make sense in all cases. The line between personal and business expenses winds through infinite factual permutations; effectuation of the travel expense provision requires that any principle of decision be flexible and sensitive to statutory policy.

Construing in the manner just described the requirement that an expense be incurred "while away from home," we do not believe this requirement was satisfied in this case. Mrs. Hantzis' *trade or business* did not require that she maintain a home in Boston as well as one in New York. Though she returned to Boston at various times during the period of her employment in New York, her visits were all for personal reasons. It is not contended that she had a business connection in Boston that necessitated her keeping a home there; no professional interest was served by maintenance of the Boston home—as would have been the case, for example, if Mrs. Hantzis had been a lawyer based in Boston with a New York client whom she was temporarily serving. The home in Boston was kept up for reasons involving Mr. Hantzis, but those reasons cannot substitute for a showing by *Mrs.* Hantzis that the exigencies of *her* trade or business required *her* to maintain two homes.[11] Mrs. Hantzis' decision to keep two homes must be seen as a choice dictated by personal, albeit wholly reasonable, considerations and not a business or occupational necessity. We therefore hold that her home for purposes of section 162(a)(2) was New York and that the expenses at issue in this case were not incurred "while away from home."

We are not dissuaded from this conclusion by the temporary nature of Mrs. Hantzis' employment in New York. * * *

* * *

Reversed.

11. In this respect, Mr. and Mrs. Hantzis' situation is analogous to cases involving spouses with careers in different locations. Each must independently satisfy the requirement that deductions taken for travel expenses incurred in the pursuit of a trade or business arise while he or she is away from home. See Chwalow v. Commissioner, 470 F.2d 475, 477–78 (3d Cir.1972) ("Where additional expenses are incurred because, for personal reasons, husband and wife maintain separate domiciles, no deduction is allowed."); Hammond v. Commissioner, 213 F.2d 43, 44 (5th Cir.1954); Foote v. Commissioner, 67 T.C. 1 (1976); Coerver v. Commissioner, 36 T.C. 252 (1961). This is true even though the spouses file a joint return. *Chwalow,* supra, 470 F.2d at 478.

KEETON, DISTRICT JUDGE, concurring in the result.

Although I agree with the result reached in the court's opinion, and with much of its underlying analysis, I write separately because I cannot join in the court's determination that New York was the taxpayer's home for purposes of § 162(a)(2). In so holding, the court adopts a definition of "home" that differs from the ordinary meaning of the term and therefore unduly risks causing confusion and misinterpretation of the important principle articulated in this case.

In adopting section 162(a)(2), Congress sought "to mitigate the burden of the taxpayer who, because of the exigencies of his trade or business, must maintain two places of abode and thereby incur additional and duplicate living expenses." Kroll v. Commissioner, 49 T.C. 557, 562 (1968). See Rosenspan v. United States, 438 F.2d 905, 912 (2d Cir.), cert. denied, 404 U.S. 864 (1971); James v. United States, 308 F.2d 204, 206–07 (9th Cir.1962). In the present case, the taxpayer does not contend that she maintained her residence in Boston for business reasons. Before working in New York, she had attended school near her home in Boston, and she continued to do so after she finished her summer job. In addition, her husband lived and worked in Boston. Thus, on the facts in this case, I am in agreement with the court that the taxpayer's deductions must be disallowed because she was not required by her trade or business to maintain both places of residence. However rather than resting its conclusion on an interpretation of the language of section 162(a)(2) taken as a whole, which allows a deduction for ordinary and necessary expenses incurred "while away from home in the pursuit of trade or business," the court reaches the same result by incorporating the concept of business-related residence into the definition of "home," thereby producing sometimes, but not always, a meaning of "home" quite different from ordinary usage.

* * *

The court enters this conflict among circuits with a "functional" definition of home not yet adopted by any other circuit. I read the opinion as indicating that in a dual residence case, the Commissioner must determine whether the exigencies of the taxpayer's trade or business require her to maintain both residences. * * * If so, the Commissioner must decide that the taxpayer's *principal residence* is her "home" and must conclude that expenses associated with the secondary residence were incurred "while away from home," and are deductible. If not, as in the instant case, the Commissioner must find that the taxpayer's *principal place of business* is her "home" and must conclude that the expenses in question were not incurred "while away from home." The conclusory nature of these determinations as to which residence is her "home" reveals the potentially confusing effect of adopting an extraordinary definition of "home."

A word used in a statute can mean, among the cognoscenti, whatever authoritative sources define it to mean. Nevertheless, it is a distinct disadvantage of a body of law that it can be understood only by those who are expert in its terminology. Moreover, needless risks of misunderstanding and confusion arise, not only among members of the public but also among professionals who must interpret and apply a statute in their day-to-day work, when a word is given an extraordinary meaning that is contrary to its everyday usage.

The result reached by the court can easily be expressed while also giving "home" its ordinary meaning, and neither Congress nor the Supreme Court has directed that "home" be given an extraordinary meaning in the present context. * * *

In analyzing dual residence cases, the court's opinion advances compelling reasons that the first step must be to determine whether the taxpayer has business as opposed to purely personal reasons for maintaining both residences. This must be done in order to determine whether the expenses of maintaining a second residence were, "necessitated by business, as opposed to personal, demands," * * * and were in this sense incurred by the taxpayer "while away from home in pursuit of trade or business." Necessarily implicit in this proposition is a more limited corollary that is sufficient to decide the present case: When the taxpayer has a business relationship to only one location, no traveling expenses the taxpayer incurs are "necessitated by business, as opposed to personal demands," regardless of how many residences the taxpayer has, where they are located, or which one is "home."

In the present case, although the taxpayer argues that her employment required her to reside in New York, that contention is insufficient to compel a determination that it was the nature of her trade or business that required her to incur the additional expense of maintaining a second residence, the burden that section 162(a)(2) was intended to mitigate. Her expenses associated with maintaining her New York residence arose from personal interests that led her to maintain two residences rather than a single residence close to her work. While traveling from her principal residence to a second place of residence closer to her business, even though "away from home," she was not "away from home in pursuit of business." Thus, the expenses at issue in this case were not incurred by the taxpayer "while away from home in pursuit of trade or business."

In the contrasting case in which a taxpayer has established that both residences were maintained for business reasons, section 162(a)(2) allows the deduction of expenses associated with travel to, and maintenance of, one of the residences if they are incurred for business reasons *and that abode is not the taxpayer's home.* A common sense meaning of "home" works well to achieve the purpose of this provision.

In summary, the court announces a sound principle that, in dual residence cases, deductibility of traveling expenses depends upon a showing that both residences were maintained for business reasons. If that principle is understood to be derived from the language of section 162(a)(2) taken as a whole, "home" retains operative significance for determining *which* of the business-related residences is the one the expense of which can be treated as deductible. In this context, "home" should be given its ordinary meaning to allow a deduction only for expenses relating to an abode that is not the taxpayer's principal place of residence. On the undisputed facts in this case, the Tax Court found that Boston was the taxpayer's "home" in the everyday sense, i.e., her principal place of residence. Were the issue relevant to disposition of the case, I would uphold the Tax Court's quite reasonable determination on the evidence before it. However, because the taxpayer had no business reason for maintaining both residences, her deduction for expenses associated with maintaining a second residence closer than her principal residence to her place of employment must be disallowed without regard to which of her two residences was her "home" under section 162(a)(2).

Problems, Notes and Questions

1. *The "tax home" concept.* The Tax Court has added a "real home" requirement to the notion that a taxpayer's principal place of work is "home." Since § 162(a)(2) is meant to account for the "duplication" of living expenses by a taxpayer travelling on business, the deduction is not allowed to someone like an itinerant salesman who maintains no permanent residence. Compare Wirth v. Commissioner, 61 T.C. 855 (1974). Furthermore, the Tax Court has allowed deductions under § 162 to taxpayers with no "tax homes" (i.e. principal place of work) who are away from their "real homes" on temporary jobs. Rambo v. Commissioner, 69 T.C. 920 (1978).

An interesting variation on the "itinerant" cases is Henderson v. Commissioner, 143 F.3d 497 (9th Cir.1998), involving a taxpayer who spent most of the year working for a traveling ice show. When not at work, he stayed with his parents in Boise, Idaho. The Tax Court and the court of appeals denied the deduction, in part because Henderson had no actual home in Boise and therefore incurred no duplicate expenses; that much of the decision is routine. Both courts added, however, an observation that Boise could not have been Henderson's "tax home" because he had no "business reason" for living in Boise (citing *Hantzis*). Apparently, therefore, he would not have been able to deduct his expenses while on the road even if he had owned a house in Boise (or, perhaps, anywhere else). Judge Kozinski, dissenting, observed at 143 F.3d 502,

> Leave it to the IRS to turn a family reunion into a taxable event. Henderson is being hit with extra taxes because his lifestyle doesn't conform to the IRS's idea of normalcy. * * * In the name of family values, I respectfully dissent.

2. *The "sleep or rest" or "overnight" rule.* A lawyer who lives and works in New York goes to Washington on business, leaving in the morning and returning the same night. Is the lawyer "away from home," so that the cost of meals in Washington is deductible? No, because the Supreme Court, in United States v. Correll, 389 U.S. 299 (1967), approved the Commissioner's long-standing position that a taxpayer is not "away from home" unless the trip lasts long enough to require "sleep or rest." The Court thought that a purely "geographical"

definition of "away from home" would discriminate against intracity travelers and commuters, who cannot deduct the cost of lunch.

Does the "sleep or rest" rule mean that a New York lawyer who spends a day in Washington on business cannot deduct plane fare to and from Washington? Just what is it that § 162(a)(2) adds to the general rule of § 162(a)?

3. *"Temporary" vs. "indefinite" employment.* In deciding whether employment is "temporary" rather than "indefinite," the reasonably anticipated duration of the employment controls. As noted earlier, § 162(a) provides that "the taxpayer shall not be treated as being temporarily away from home during any period of employment if such period exceeds 1 year." This is not high-quality drafting. For example, what of the taxpayer who goes off on an 11–month assignment and then has the tour extended for three more months? Is this one 14–month "period of employment," making none of the taxpayer's expenses deductible, is it two separate periods, each shorter than twelve months, making all of the expenses deductible, or are expenses for the first eleven (or twelve?) months, but no more, deductible? What of a taxpayer who takes a 12–month position with employer *A* and then, without going home, signs on with employer *B* for another year in the same location? And how about visiting professors who accept permanent offers?

Rev.Rul. 93–86, 1993–2 C.B. 71, says that the one-year rule is applied by asking whether the employment is realistically expected to last, and does last, for no more than a year. If a trip expected not to last more than a year is extended beyond one year, expenses up to the time the expectation changed are deductible. According to the ruling, expenses of a trip expected to last more than a year are not deductible even if the trip does not actually last that long.

4. *Scope of the deduction.* As to the deductibility of particular items under § 162(a)(2), see Rev.Rul. 63–145, 1963–2 C.B. 86 (laundry and local transportation at the temporary job site deductible); Rev.Rul. 54–497, 1954–2 C.B. 75 (cost of trips home on weekends deductible up to the amount that would have been spent on food had the taxpayer remained at the site of the temporary job).

If a worker's family goes along on an away-from-home trip, living costs must be allocated between the worker's deductible costs and the other family members' costs, which are nondeductible unless those family members can qualify on their own under § 162(a)(2). The taxpayer in Cass v. Commissioner, 86 T.C. 1275 (1986), was an economics professor at the University of Pennsylvania who spent a year as a visiting scholar at Cal Tech. In allocating meal expenses among himself, his wife, and their two children (ages 17 and 11), Cass used "a formula based on the proportionate body weights of the members of his family." The court described this formula as "creative," noted that it ignored relative metabolic rates, mentioned the eating habits of teenage children, and concluded that the "simplest approach available"—dividing total food expenses (less the cost of dog food) by four—was best, "[i]n the absence of proof of a more precise method."

Section 274(m)(3) disallows deductions for the costs of a spouse, dependent, or other person who accompanies someone on a business trip. (There are some exceptions, as for a case in which two employees, who are married to each other, are sent on a trip together, and there is a business reason for sending both employees on the trip.) It is quite doubtful that the expenses disallowed by § 274(m)(3) would have been deductible under prior law; the provision seems to have been aimed at exceptionally optimistic return positions.

5. *Substantiation.* Section 274(d)(1) disallows deductions for traveling expenses unless the taxpayer "substantiates" the amount of the expenses and the time, place, and business purpose of the travel. Rather than claiming deductions for actual meal expenses, business travellers can use *per diem* rates published in the Federal Register. The *per diem* allowance system originally allowed one daily amount for meals for short trips and another, larger amount for longer trips. Today, however, the rules are complex, with amounts that vary from place to place and according to the type of work the taxpayer does. Taxpayers can find the rates for travel in the United States in IRS Publication 1542. The overseas rates can be found on the internet.

6. *Problems.*

(1) *P*, who teaches law in California, takes a leave of absence for a year. She spends that year as a visiting professor in New York City, where she pays $20,000 to rent a one-bedroom apartment occupied by *P* and her husband. *P*'s husband spends the year taking courses in cultural subjects. *P* asks you whether she can reasonably claim a deduction for any or all of the rent and utility bills for the apartment and whether, in view of the fact that she has not recorded the amounts she spent on meals, she can deduct anything for that. Respond.

(2) A lawyer travels (overnight) on business for her client. She pays meal costs of $100, for which she is reimbursed by her client. To what extent does § 274(n) allow a deduction by the lawyer for the cost of the meal? By the client?

(3) An employee, *E*, pays $60 for a meal and is reimbursed for the full $60 by his employer, *R*. *R* treats the reimbursement as "wages" for withholding purposes. Under §§ 61 and 162, and disregarding for the moment the effect of § 274, *E* would have to include the $60 reimbursement in income and could deduct the $60 expense; *R* could deduct the $60 reimbursement. How does § 274 affect *E*'s and *R*'s deductions? See § 274(n)(2)(A).

(c) Combined Business and Pleasure Trips

A taxpayer on a long business trip surely does not lose the deduction for even part of the plane fare or hotel bills because of a single weekend spent playing golf. A taxpayer on an extended vacation surely gets no deduction for the trip's cost by spending a day dealing with business matters (except for additional costs attributable to business activities). In between these cases fall many in which neither the purpose nor the function of the trip can be described as being "solely" or even, perhaps, "primarily" for business or for pleasure. Treas.Reg. § 1.162–2 attempts to deal with these problems. Consider carefully § 1.162–2(b)(2)'s example of the taxpayer who spends one week of a trip on business and an additional five weeks on personal activities. How, if at all, might a taxpayer make a "clear showing" that the trip was not "primarily personal in nature"? Compare Treas.Reg. § 1.162–5(e)(2), covering travel to take business-related courses. See generally Klein, The Deductibility of Transportation Expenses of a Combination Business and Pleasure Trip—A Conceptual Analysis, 18 Stan.L.Rev. 1099 (1966).

Foreign travel is subject to the special rules of § 274(c) and Treas. Reg. § 1.274–4.

The costs of attending foreign conventions can be deducted only as provided in § 274(h), which was added to the Code in 1976. The Senate Finance Committee's report on this provision expressed concern that taxpayers were taking "government-subsidized vacations," noting that some organizations had advertised "that they will find a convention for the taxpayer to attend in any part of the world at any given time of the year"; S.Rep. No. 94–938, 94th Cong., 2d Sess. 157 (1976). Special rules govern conventions on cruise ships and in Caribbean countries; §§ 274(h)(2) & (h)(6). Section 274(m) limits deductions for transportation by water.

If a taxpayer's employer pays the costs of a trip, the initial question is whether the trip's value is income to the employee. In Rudolph v. United States, 370 U.S. 269 (1962),[k] the taxpayer and the government apparently agreed that both the includability question and the question whether, if includable, the value of the trip was deductible by the employee under § 162 depended upon the taxpayer's " 'dominant motive and purpose' in taking the trip and the company's in offering it." Is it obvious that the taxability of an employer-financed trip and the deductibility of a trip paid for by the employee raise exactly the same issues? Consider parking spaces furnished by an employer. Their value has never been considered income to the employee, although an employee who pays for parking has incurred a non-deductible commuting expense.

If an employer pays for an employee's trip, and if the trip amounts to a social, entertainment, amusement, or recreational activity, see §§ 274(a) and 274(e) for the possibility of denying a deduction to the employer.

Problem

L is a sole practitioner who lives and practices law in Cleveland. On day 1, *L* flies to Los Angeles (arriving in the evening) to conduct a

---

k. The Court dismissed the writ of certiorari as improvidently granted.

negotiation on behalf of her client. Days 2, 3, and 4 are spent in negotiations. On day 5, *L* flies to San Diego, where she visits her sister on days 5 and 6. On day 7, she flies from San Diego back to Cleveland. To what extent is the cost of *L*'s meals, lodging and airfare deductible?

(d) Entertainment

MOORE v. UNITED STATES

United States District Court, E.D. Virginia, 1996.
943 F.Supp. 603.

MacKENZIE, DISTRICT JUDGE.

* * *

For a number of years in the 1980s, the Moores hosted an annual party in December for a few hundred business associates. The annual party typically included a cocktail hour, a seated dinner, dancing, and live entertainment by a nationally known performer. At some time during each party, Mr. Moore would typically address the attendees—the overwhelming majority of whom were real estate agents who had sold at least two homes constructed by the Moores during the calendar year—to thank them for their efforts to sell houses his company had constructed during the last year and to encourage them to sell houses his company would construct in the coming year. On their annual tax returns, the Moores made it their practice to deduct the costs associated with these annual parties as business-related entertainment expenses, pursuant to §§ 162 and 274.

The 1989 party took place in the grand ballroom of the Omni Waterside Hotel in Norfolk and featured a performance by singer Barbara Mandrell. The Moores claimed a business-related entertainment expense deduction of $347,000 for this party on their 1989 tax return * * *. The Government opposes the deduction, contending that the party is really a nondeductible goodwill expense, as opposed to a business-related entertainment expense.

* * *

* * * Although the Government did not contest the deductibility of the annual party in prior tax years, it now claims that the 1989 party constituted non-deductible goodwill expense because it was not directly related to the Moores' trade or business, as required by § 274(a)(1) and Treasury Regulation § 1.274–2. The Moores maintain that the party expenses were directly related to their business because the entertainment took place in a "clear business setting," as that term is defined in Treasury Regulation § 1.274–2(c)(4).

Generally, business expenses are deductible if they are shown to be "ordinary and necessary." See § 162. Business entertainment expenses are deductible, however, only if they are shown to be "ordinary and necessary" and they are shown to be either "directly related to" the active conduct of the taxpayer's trade or business, or, in the case of entertainment directly preceding or following a substantial and bona fide business discussion, "associated with" the active conduct of a taxpayer's trade or business. See § 274(a)(1)(A); Treas. Reg. § 1.274–2(a)(1). The Moores do not contend that the party presently at issue directly preceded or followed a substantial and bona fide business discussion so as to qualify for the less exacting "associated with" standard. Therefore, the Court need only decide whether the 1989 party was "directly related" to the active conduct of the Moores' business.

A business entertainment expense qualifies as "directly related"— and therefore deductible—if an active business discussion occurred during the entertainment activity or if the entertainment activity took place in a clear business setting. See Treas. Reg. § 1.274–2(c)(3) and (4); [further citation omitted]. The Moores do not contend that an active business discussion took place during the 1989 party. The Court will address, therefore, only whether the 1989 party qualifies as a clear business setting.

A taxpayer can show that entertainment occurred in a clear business setting by "clearly establishing that any recipient of the entertainment would have reasonably known that the taxpayer had no significant motive, in incurring the expenditure, other than directly furthering his trade or business." Treas. Reg. § 1.274–2(c)(4). Generally speaking, however, entertainment will not be considered to have occurred in a clear business setting if the entertainment is marked by substantial distractions, e.g., a meeting or discussion at a night club or during essentially social gatherings such as cocktail parties, or a meeting or discussion including persons other than the taxpayer's business associates at places such as cocktail lounges. See Treas. Reg. § 1.274–2(c)(4) and (7). Nonetheless, some entertainment which is accompanied by substantial distractions—such as the entertainment of business and civic leaders at the opening of a new hotel or theatrical production where the taxpayer's obvious intention is to obtain business publicity as opposed to maintaining goodwill—may be considered to have occurred in a clear business setting if there was no meaningful personal or social relationship between the taxpayer and the recipients of the entertainment See Treas. Reg. § 1.274–2(c)(4).

The Fourth Circuit Court of Appeals addressed the deductibility of business entertainment expenses in Berkley Machine Works & Foundry Co. v. Commissioner, 623 F.2d 898 (4th Cir.), cert. denied, 449 U.S. 919, 66 L. Ed. 2d 147, 101 S. Ct. 317 (1980). In that case, a Norfolk-based machine shop claimed a deduction of some $100,000 for business entertainment expenses incurred in connection with a hunting and fishing facility it maintained on Ocracoke Island, North Carolina for the purpose of entertaining customers and their families on weekends. *Berkley*, 623 F.2d at 900. Although business was invariably discussed during weekend trips to the hunting and fishing facility, the court found that the expense of maintaining the facility was not directly related to the company's active conduct of its business—and therefore not deductible—because no weekends were arranged with anything more than a general expectation of deriving some business benefit, other than the general business goodwill which Congress intended to eliminate as a deduction by means of the directly related test, at some indefinite future time. * * *

The Moores aver that the 1989 party occurred in a clear business setting because the attendees all knew that the only reason the Moores incurred the expense of the party was to promote the sale of their homes. The Government, on the other hand, maintains that the 1989 party did not occur in a clear business setting because distractions during the party were substantial. The Court agrees with the Moores that the expense of the 1989 party was incurred in a clear business setting, as that phrase has been defined in the Treasury Regulations and interpreted in the case law from this circuit.

The Moores have satisfied the requirements of the Treasury Regulations regarding business entertainment expenses incurred in a clear business setting in either of two ways. First, they have established that any attendee at the 1989 party would have reasonably known that the expense of the party was incurred only to further the Moores' business. See Treas. Reg. § 1.274–2(c)(4). At trial, two real estate agents who attended the Moores' 1989 party, Janice Walz and Janice Haworth, testified that from their perspective, the Moores' sole motivation in hosting the annual party was to promote the sale of their homes. * * * [T]he Government failed to give the Court any reason to believe that the perceptions of these two veteran professionals was anything other than reasonable. * * * The Court therefore CONCLUDES that the expense of the 1989 party was incurred in a clear business setting, as that term has been defined in the Treasury Regulations.

The Fourth Circuit's disposition of *Berkley* does not compel a different conclusion. The entertainment at issue in this case is similar to that in *Berkley* because it took place in a setting with substantial distractions and because it involved a fairly large number of people, some of whom were not business associates of the taxpayers. [Citation omitted.]. Nonetheless, the entertainment expense at issue in *Berkley* was incurred with no more than a general expectation of deriving some business benefit at some indefinite future time. In contrast, the Moores incurred the expense of their annual parties for the specific purpose of rewarding the real estate agents who had sold at least two (2) of their homes during the current fiscal year and encouraging those agents to sell at least two (2) additional homes to be built by the Moores in the succeeding fiscal year. In addition, Mr. Moore's uncontroverted testimony was that the sales of his homes tripled once he started having the annual party for real estate agents. Given the dramatic effect which the annual parties had on the Moores' business, this Court does not find it difficult to believe that the entertainment aspect of the 1989 party was clearly subordinate to the business purpose of promoting the sale of homes, as required by *Berkley*. The Court therefore FINDS that the expense of the 1989 party was incurred in a clear business setting, as that phrase has been interpreted in this circuit * * *.

The Moores have * * * satisfied the Court that the expense of the 1989 party was incurred in a clear business setting, as that phrase has been defined in the Treasury Regulations and interpreted in case law from this circuit. Any reasonable attendee of the 1989 party would have known that the Moores had no significant motive for throwing the party other than promoting the sale of their homes. In addition, the 1989 party occurred under circumstances where there was no meaningful personal or social relationship between the Moores and the attendees of the party. Lastly, the dramatic increase in the sale of homes constructed by the Moores which resulted from the annual parties establishes that the entertainment aspect of the 1989 party was clearly subordinate to the business aspect, as required by controlling case law from this circuit.

* * *

Problems and Notes

1. *Section 274 as applied to entertainment.* Although business-entertainment deductions have never involved large amounts of money, Congress has regularly amended § 274 to keep up with abuses in this area, which are thought to be important because of taxpayer morale. The concern here is that the practice of deducting entertainment costs as business expenses undermines respect for the tax system and encourages an "everybody else cheats so why shouldn't I" mentality even among those who have no opportunity to claim that their entertainment activities are business related. Efforts to tighten up on entertainment, travel, and food deductions usually meet with resistance from those who make their livings by supplying entertainment, travel, and food.

Section 274(*l*), which was enacted in 1986, limits deductions for most entertainment tickets to the face value of the tickets (thus denying deductions for premiums paid to "scalpers") and disallows most of the costs of a "skybox or other private luxury box leased for more than 1 event."

Section 274(a)(3) denies any deduction for membership fees in "any club organized for business, pleasure, recreation, or other social purpose."

Under § 274(n), only 50 percent of the cost of most business entertainment can be deducted.

2. *Entertainment "facilities."* Section 274(a)(1)(B) disallows deductions for any item "[w]ith respect to a facility used in connection with" the entertainment and other activities listed in § 274(a)(1)(A). The taxpayer in Ireland v. Commissioner, 89 T.C. 978 (1987), was a stockbroker who owned lakefront property. He used the property for meetings with investment advisors, clients, salespeople, and his partners. He and his family never used the property for vacations. However, the families of Ireland's business associates sometimes accompanied them to the meetings and enjoyed the taxpayer's beach. Holding that "any use of the facility, no matter how small, in connection with entertainment is fatal

to the claimed deduction," the Tax Court denied deductions for depreciation on the taxpayer's buildings.

3. *Problems.*

(1) A law firm pays $24,000 for four season tickets to the home games of the local major league baseball club. These tickets are usually lent to clients of the firm. Often, but not always, a member of the firm accompanies the clients to the games. Sometimes their spouses accompany them. When the tickets are not being used by clients, the firm's summer clerks and associates use the tickets. Can the firm deduct the cost of the tickets?

(2) The law firm in (1), above, also sponsors a retreat for its partners and associates each summer. The retreat is held at a resort which offers boating, hiking, golf, and tennis. The retreat begins on Friday morning and ends on the following Sunday evening. There is a three-hour meeting on each day, which all participants are expected to attend. At the meetings the participants discuss firm problems and long-range goals. Informal discussions of these matters usually continue throughout the day, as the participants enjoy the recreational activities offered by the resort. Although the firm pays the cost of the participants' meals and lodging, each participant is responsible for his own "extras," such as boat rental, greens fees, etc. During the current year the firm's share of the costs came to $10,000 ($6000 for meals and $4000 for lodging). What can the firm deduct?

4. *Substantiation.* George M. Cohan spent thousands of dollars entertaining actors, employees, and drama critics, and on business-related travel. He kept no records, and because it was impossible to tell how much had been spent the Board of Tax Appeals denied any deduction. The Second Circuit reversed and remanded, directing the Board to "make as close an approximation as it can, bearing heavily if it chooses upon the taxpayer whose inexactitude is of his own making"; Cohan v. Commissioner, 39 F.2d 540 (2d Cir.1930) (L. Hand, J.). Section 274(d) overrules the *Cohan* rule for travel and entertainment expenses, and for gifts.

5. LISTED PROPERTY

GENERAL EXPLANATION OF THE REVENUE PROVISIONS OF THE DEFICIT REDUCTION ACT OF 1984

Staff, Joint Committee on Taxation (1984).
pp. 559–560.

Congress believed that the investment incentives afforded by the investment tax credit[l] and accelerated cost recovery should be directed to

---

l. The investment tax credit was a credit of 10 percent (sometimes 6 percent) of the cost of most tangible, depreciable business or investment property other than buildings. It was repealed in 1986.—Eds.

encourage capital formation, rather than to subsidize the element of personal consumption associated with the use of very expensive automobiles. The transportation necessary for conducting a business can be obtained from a luxury car or another car. To the extent an automobile is required for this necessary transportation, the generally allowable tax benefits should be available. Beyond that point, however, the extra expense of a luxury automobile provides, in effect, a tax-free personal emolument which Congress believed should not qualify for tax credits or acceleration of depreciation deductions because such expenditures do not add significantly to the productivity which these incentives were designed to encourage.

Congress was also concerned that many taxpayers claimed the advantage of the investment tax credit and accelerated depreciation with respect to automobiles and other property used primarily for personal or investment use rather than in the conduct of a trade or business. The incentives of the investment credit and ACRS were designed to encourage investment in new plant and equipment rather than to subsidize the purchase of personal property that is used incidentally or occasionally in the taxpayer's business. Therefore, Congress decided not to allow the incentive portion of tax benefits for property whose predominant use is personal or investment-related, rather than in the conduct of a trade or business.

Congress was also concerned that some taxpayers acquired automobiles and other property very late in the taxable year and claimed a very high percentage of business use for that portion of the year. Business use in subsequent years would often be minimal. Taxpayers could nonetheless claim full ACRS deductions for that first year and not be subject to recapture by reason of greatly diminished business use in the subsequent years.

In addition, Congress was concerned with significant noncompliance under prior law resulting from the overstatement of deductions and credits related to the business use of automobiles and other property that typically is used for personal purposes. Specifically, some taxpayers had attempted to convert personal use to business use through a variety of arguments, such as that an employee's "on-call" status or need to work late rendered any use a business use; or that signs, special paint, personalized license plates, or unique hood ornaments made the car a constant advertisement so that all use was business-related. Further, many taxpayers overstated the percentage of business use by after-the-fact, optimistic estimates of that use based on inexact recollection. The requirement of prior law that adequate records be kept was not observed uniformly. Thus, Congress believed that it is appropriate to require that contemporaneous records must be kept as a condition of claiming deductions with respect to this property.

* * *

The concerns described by the Joint Committee Staff led Congress to enact § 280F, which subjects deductions under §§ 168 (depreciation) and 179 (expensing) to severe limits if the property is "listed property" as defined in § 280F(d)(4). One restriction—the annual dollar limits on depreciation deductions for a passenger automobile—has already been noted (p. 255, above).

The most important limit on deductions associated with listed property is found in § 280F(b)(1), which comes into play if listed property "is not predominantly used in a qualified business use for any taxable year." If listed property fails the "qualified business use" test, depreciation deductions for that property must be taken under the "alternative depreciation system" of § 168(g); this is usually straight-line depreciation over the property's ADR class life. Furthermore, § 280F(d)(1) provides that deductions under § 179 are considered depreciation deductions in applying § 280F. This means that expensing under § 179 is not allowed if the property in question fails the "qualified business use" test.

Section 280F(d)(3) provides that an employee's use of listed property in connection with employment shall be considered use in a trade or business only if the use is "for the convenience of the employer and required as a condition of employment." These tests will be very difficult to satisfy. Most employees can therefore take *no* deductions under § 168 on account of the use of listed property in connection with employment. That is, employee use not only cannot be "qualified business use" under § 280F(b), it is not even use "in a trade or business for purposes of determining the amount of any depreciation deduction"; § 280F(d)(3)(A).[m]

CADWALLADER v. COMMISSIONER

United States Tax Court, 1989.
57 T.C.M. 1030, affirmed on another issue 919 F.2d 1273 (7th Cir.1990).

MEMORANDUM FINDINGS OF FACT AND OPINION

CLAPP, JUDGE:

Respondent determined deficiencies in petitioners' Federal income taxes as follows:

---

m. As originally enacted, § 280F did not limit employee deductions calculated under a method not involving the property's useful life in years. Thus, employee deductions for the use of an automobile were not affected by § 280F if the employee used the standard mileage rate, even though that rate consists, in part, of depreciation (calculated according to miles driven, rather than according to the car's life in years). The statutory changes eliminating this qualification were adopted to remove obsolete terminology from § 280F and not, apparently, to prevent employees from using the standard mileage rate. The forms and instructions still allow employees who use their cars in business to use the standard mileage rate.

Year	Deficiency	Sec. 6651(a)(1)
1982	$ 315	$78.75
1983	345	
1984	1,626	

After concessions, the [issue is] whether section 280F prevents petitioners from deducting under section 179 the cost of computer equipment they purchased in 1984. [The Tax Court's discussion of Cadwallader's claimed deduction for the costs of a "home office" is omitted. The Seventh Circuit's opinion on the home-office issue is reproduced below, p. 372.]

FINDINGS OF FACT
* * *

During the years at issue, Cadwallader was a tenured psychology professor at Indiana State University (the university) in Terre Haute, Indiana, where he teaches psychology classes each semester. During the years in issue, the university class schedules showed petitioner as teaching an average of 13 hours per semester. Some of these classes were taught by both petitioner and another faculty member.

A tenured professor such as Cadwallader is expected to conduct research as a part of his job. Cadwallader conducts his research in the history of psychology. As a result of this research, Cadwallader has accumulated over the years an extensive amount of historical reference materials. Most of these materials are not available in the university library. Cadwallader could not conduct his research if he did not have access to his reference materials.

* * *

In September 1984, petitioners purchased a personal computer. Cadwallader uses the computer for storing information and for word processing in his academic research. He has given seminars on computer use. During the years in issue he did not have access to a computer at the university.

Douglas [Cadwallader's wife] used the computer in connection with her job at the West Central Indiana Economic Development District, where she was promoted to chief transportation planner in the spring of 1984. Her employer did not have a computer of its own and did not explicitly require her to purchase the computer as a condition of her employment.

OPINION
* * *

* * * Section 280F(d)(4)(A)(iv) provides that "any computer or peripheral equipment" is "listed property." "Employee use of listed property shall not be treated as use in a trade or business for purposes" of expensing under section 179 unless "such use is for the convenience of the employer and required as a condition of employment." Section 280F(d)(3)(A); [Temp.Treas.Reg. §] 1.280F–6T(a)(1).

In order for the "condition of employment" requirement to be satisfied, petitioners' employers need not explicitly require them to use a computer. [Temp.Treas.Reg. §§] 1.280F–6T(a)(2)(ii) and (a)(4) Ex. (2). Instead, it is only necessary that petitioners' use of the computer be required in order for them to properly perform the duties of their employment. [Temp.Treas.Reg. §] 1.280F–6T(a)(2)(ii). We conclude that this requirement is satisfied. Cadwallader's duties of employment included historical research that involved massive amounts of data and writing. This research was substantially aided by a computer. Under the instant facts, the computer was required in order for Cadwallader to properly perform the duties of his employment. Similarly, Douglas testified that her office was required to do planning which involved extensive number crunching. Much of this work previously had been done on a mainframe computer owned by the state, but the state eliminated access to this computer. The previous chief transportation planner had purchased a personal computer in order to be able to do his work. Her office lacked the funds to purchase a computer of its own. Thus, the computer was required in order for Douglas to properly perform the duties of her employment.

We also conclude that the "convenience of employer" requirement is satisfied. Here the computer purchase spared petitioners' employers the cost of providing them with suitable computer equipment with which to engage in their job responsibilities. See Weissman v. Commissioner, 751 F.2d [512] at 517 [(2d Cir.1984)].

Thus, section 280F does not prevent petitioners from deducting the cost of their computer equipment under section 179.

Decision Will Be Entered Under Rule 155.

Problems and Note

1. *Problems.*

(1) *P* is a partner in a law firm. She has a computer at her office and another at home. Each year, *P* uses the home computer 60% for work related to her practice, 30% for keeping track of her investments, and 10% for personal matters, such as writing letters to friends and family. The home computer cost *P* $4000. Over the computer's useful life, how much depreciation will *P* be allowed to deduct? Will her depreciation be limited to that allowed by § 168(g)?

(2) The facts and questions are the same as above except that *P*'s use of the home computer each year is 40% for work related to her practice, 50% for investments, and 10% personal.

(3) The facts and questions are the same as in *Problem (1),* except that the home computer is owned by *A*, a law-firm associate.

(4) *K*, a law professor, buys a computer to help him with his research and teaching. *K* tells you that because he will keep the comput-

er in his office at the law school at all times, he does not have to worry about whether his use is "for the convenience of the employer and required as a condition of employment." *K* cites § 280F(d)(4)(B), which he has read hastily. Is he right?

2. *Leased listed property.* Leasing property on a long-term basis differs little, if at all, from buying it. Section 280F(d)(3)(A), as "clarified" retroactively in 1986, denies rental deductions to employees who lease listed property unless the convenience-of-the-employer and condition-of-employment tests are satisfied.

6. SPECIAL LIMITS ON DEDUCTIONS RELATING TO REAL PROPERTY

The tax system has had a lot of trouble dealing with buildings. One source of difficulty is that buildings can be depreciated much more rapidly than they decline in value. Although a well-maintained building has an indefinite useful life in fact, the entire cost of a building used in a trade or business or held for investment can be recovered over 27.5 years (residential rental property) or 39 years (other buildings). In the past, even faster write-offs were allowed: the Economic Recovery Tax Act of 1981 established a 15-year useful life for most buildings. Not surprisingly, this generous depreciation system encouraged people to invest heavily in buildings.

By 1986, real estate (and other) "tax shelters" had gotten out of hand, and Congress adopted § 469, imposing limits on "passive-activity losses," which will be discussed in Chapter 8. Generally speaking, § 469 allows taxpayers to use deductions from "passive activities" (which include rentals of real estate) only against income from passive activities. Thus, a taxpayer whose real-estate rentals generate $50,000 in gross income and $200,000 in deductions cannot use the $150,000 "excess" deductions to offset income from salary, dividends, or interest. However, individual taxpayers with adjusted gross incomes (§ 62) of $100,000 or less can deduct up to $25,000 in losses from real-estate rental activities (in which they actively participate) against any kind of income. The $25,000 allowance is "phased out" for taxpayers with AGI over $100,000: each dollar of excess AGI reduces the $25,000 amount by fifty cents; see § 469(i).

The limits on passive-activity losses apply to all rental real estate (except some hotels). More-stringent limits, imposed by § 280A, apply to deductions "with respect to the use of a dwelling unit which is used by the taxpayer during the taxable year as a residence." One problem in this area—the "vacation home"—is in principle similar to the "hobby loss" situation (§ 183), and is dealt with in much the same way. Another matter—the use of a portion of the taxpayer's residence as a "home office"—causes concern because the taxpayer who works at home in the evening may do so more for personal convenience than out of business necessity, because claims of "business use" are easier to make than to verify, and because many of those who work at home part-time have not in fact spent any more on housing than they would have spent if they worked only in their offices.

(a) Vacation Homes

Consider a taxpayer who owns a summer cottage which is used each year for a 30–day vacation and is rented out for 60 days. One question this fact pattern presents is how to allocate expenses like maintenance and repairs between the "personal" vacation use and the "business" rental one. Section 280A(e) provides an allocation formula. In this case, since rental use is two-thirds of the property's total use, two-thirds of the costs of maintenance and repairs are allocable to the rental use.

Another issue is whether deductions allocable to rental use should be allowed in excess of rental income. Section 280A(c)(5) imposes limits similar to those applied to "hobby losses" by § 183. Unlike § 183, however, § 280A applies without regard to the taxpayer's intention to make a profit. As in the case of § 183, deductions which are allowed without regard to the taxpayer's intention to make a profit are not limited to the income from the property, but do count in applying the income limit to other deductions. Suppose, for instance, that rental income is $4000, that deductions for state taxes allocable to the rental period are $1000, and that depreciation, maintenance and repairs allocable to the rental period come to $5000. The taxpayer deducts all of the state taxes and $3000 of the other expenses.

The calculations described above require that a portion of the deductions allowable without regard to whether the taxpayer seeks a profit (taxes and casualty losses) be allocated to the rental use of the property. Even though these deductions are allowed in full, the more of them that are allocated to rental use, the smaller the amount of other deductions that will be allowed. In the above example, for instance, if state taxes allocable to the rental period had been $2000, rather than $1000, only $2000 of the other expenses would have been deductible. Unfortunately, § 280A(e) gives no allocation formula for deductions not "attributable to the rental of the unit." Proposed Treas.Reg. § 1.280A–3(d) applies the § 280A(e) formula to these deductions. But Bolton v. Commissioner, 694 F.2d 556 (9th Cir.1982), held that deductions for interest and property taxes had to be allocated to the rental period according to the ratio of the number of days of rental use to the number of days in the year. In other words, while expenses like maintenance, repairs, and depreciation are allocated either to the period of use or to the period of personal use, property taxes must be allocated among the rental period, the personal-use period, and the period during which the property is not used at all.

Two "de minimis" rules—§ 280A(d)(1) for cases in which personal use is minor, and § 280A(g) for cases in which a dwelling unit is rented out for fewer than 15 days in a year—put some trivial cases outside the reach of § 280A.

Problems and Notes

1. *Problems.*

(1) *O* owns a lakeside cottage, which he uses for personal purposes for 30 days in the current year and which he rents out to someone not related to *O* at an arm's length rental for 60 days. The rental produces $700 gross income. *O*'s annual expenses are as follows:

Real-property taxes	$650
Depreciation	300
Utilities, repairs, and maintenance	400

How much of the expenses can *O* deduct? Must the property's basis be adjusted for depreciation (Prop.Treas.Reg. § 1.280A–2(i)(5))?

(2) Same as above, except that *O* rents the property out for 14 days, receiving $300 in rent. See § 280A(g).

(3) Same as (1), except that *O* uses the cottage for personal purposes for only 10 days. See § 280A(d)(1).

2. *"Dwelling unit."* Although most taxpayers affected by § 280A own real property, a "dwelling unit" need not be realty. See § 280A(f)(1)(A).

3. *Rental of the taxpayer's principal residence.* Although the title of § 280A refers to "vacation homes," its limits apply to rentals of any dwelling unit used as a residence by the taxpayer during the year. Thus, a college teacher who rents out his home during a six-month sabbatic leave is subject to the limits of § 280A(e) and 280A(c)(5). Section 280A can also limit deductions otherwise allowable in cases in which a home-owner moves out and tries, unsuccessfully, to rent the house. Even if the house has been "converted" from personal to income-producing use, no deductions for depreciation, maintenance, or repairs will be allowable for the year of the conversion because of § 280A(e).

Section 280A(d)(4) calls off the (c)(5) "hobby loss" limits in the case of a rental for a "qualified rental period."

(b) Home Offices

Section 280A disallows all deductions under §§ 162, 167, and 212 attributable to the use of a portion of the taxpayer's residence as a "home office" unless the use falls within one of the exceptions of § 280A(c)(1), (2), or (4). And even if a particular home office does come within one of the exceptions, so that deductions for heat, light, depreciation, and so on are not completely disallowed, the "hobby loss" limits of § 280A(c)(5) apply. Furthermore, in applying those limits, deductions of the trade or business in question which are not allocable to the use of the home office must be subtracted from gross income derived from that use before deductions allocable to the use can be taken; see § 280A(c)(5).

An important reason for the enactment of § 280A in 1976 was that many employees claimed deductions for housing expenses "allocable" to space in a house used while working at home in the evening and on weekends. Although employees had little success in litigation, they were not clearly barred from claiming the deductions on their returns, and few taxpayers are audited. Section 280A, as applied to home-office deductions, has more to do with limiting return positions than with affecting the outcomes of litigated cases.

CADWALLADER v. COMMISSIONER

United States Court of Appeals, Seventh Circuit, 1990.
919 F.2d 1273.

Before CUMMINGS and POSNER, CIRCUIT JUDGES, and PELL, SENIOR CIRCUIT JUDGE.

POSNER, CIRCUIT JUDGE.

The question presented by this appeal from a decision by the Tax Court is whether Thomas Cadwallader, a professor of psychology at Indiana State University, is entitled to a deduction from income tax for the expense of maintaining an office in his home. Cadwallader has the exclusive use of two offices in the psychology department, one 11 feet by 13 feet and the other 12 by 12, plus a 4 by 7 storage room. But he does most of his research and writing in his home office. The statute, so far as relevant here, allows an employee to take a home office deduction only if the office is exclusively used on a regular basis for the convenience of his employer as the employee's principal place of business. § 280A(c)(1)(A). The Tax Court denied the deduction on the ground that the "focal point" of Cadwallader's work for the university was the campus, where he teaches thirteen hours a week, meets with students, attends faculty meetings, and keeps substantial research materials. 57 T.C.M. 1030 (1989).

* * * [L]ike the Second Circuit in Weissman v. Commissioner, 751 F.2d 512 (2d Cir.1984), we have rejected the "focal point" test. Meiers v. Commissioner, 782 F.2d 75, 79 (7th Cir.1986) (per curiam). The facts of *Weissman* show why. Weissman, a professor like Cadwallader, had a campus office, but he shared it with other professors and as a result did all his research and writing at home—in fact he spent eighty percent of his working time at home. The Tax Court thought, nevertheless, that the campus was the focus of his activities. Maybe so—"focus" is a vague word in this setting—but, reversing the Tax Court, the Second Circuit held that the home office was Weissman's principal place of business.

After the decision in the present case, the Tax Court abandoned the focal point test, at least for cases where the employer provides no office for the employee. Soliman v. Commissioner, 94 T.C. 20 (1990). Soliman was an anesthesiologist whose medical practice required that he spend thirty percent of his time working in an office and the rest in hospitals, none of which provided him with office space. The Tax Court held that he was entitled to a home office deduction. Although the focus of an anesthesiologist's activity is the hospital operating room where he administers anesthesia, the home office was Dr. Soliman's only office, and his work required that he have an office.

We should think about the purpose of the home office deduction and why it is so limited—for it must be either the taxpayer's principal place of business, or a place where he meets or deals with customers, clients, or patients, or a separate structure used in connection with the business; it must be used exclusively and on a regular basis for these things; and it must be for the exclusive convenience of the employer, if as here the taxpayer is an employee rather than an independent contractor. § 280A. Expenses incurred solely to produce income should in principle be deductible from income tax because otherwise the taxpayer would be taxed on his gross revenue, not on his income. The difficulty is that often expenses have a dual purpose—they produce income but they are also a form of consumption, producing not income but utility. Moss v. Commissioner of Internal Revenue, 758 F.2d 211, 212 (7th Cir.1985). The specific abuse to which the home office deduction conduced, before the deduction was narrowed in the current law, was that an employee could by transferring some of his work from the place of his employment to his home deduct from income tax a portion of his living expenses—expenses he would have incurred even if he had not been working at all. H.R. Rep. No. 658, 94th Cong., 2d Sess. 160 (1976); S. Rep. No. 938, 94th Cong., 2d Sess. 147 (1976). For under the former law, although "personal, living or family expenses" were disallowed as a deduction, "all the ordinary and necessary expenses paid or incurred * * * in carrying on any trade or business" were allowed, §§ 162(a), 262, and in harmonizing these provisions the Tax Court, with some judicial backing, had allowed home office expenses to be deducted provided they were "appropriate and helpful." [Citations omitted.] With so fuzzy a standard, taxpayers could claim the deduction on the flimsiest of grounds with no fear of a fraud penalty, and thus could pocket a tax savings except in the unlikely event of an audit.

The current statute guards against abuse in a variety of ways. The home office must be for the convenience of the employer; that is, it can't just be a place in which the employee chooses to do some of his work. It must be used exclusively for the employer's work, implying that it has no personal, no household, use. And unless it is distinctively furnished and equipped as an office—which is the implication of its being used for meetings with clients, customers, or patients—or, clearer still, it is a separate structure, the taxpayer must show that it is his principal place of business, not just a cozy den in which he grades exam papers in the evening. If the conditions in the statute are satisfied, then even if the home office is not a separate structure there is a reasonable probability that the taxpayer's house is actually larger than it would be if he did not imperatively require a home office. For the home office that satisfies the statutory conditions is one that not only is vital to the taxpayer's business or employment but also has no use but office use. In such a case the added expense of the office is incurred solely to produce income; it yields no, or at least very little, personal utility.

With the purpose behind the home office deduction and its limitations in mind, we can examine the application of the statutory term "principal place of business" to the facts of this case unencumbered by the vagaries of the focal point test or the "all relevant factors" laundry list that is its principal competitor. Soliman v. Commissioner, supra, 94 T.C. at 26–28. Research and writing are the principal work of most university (as distinct from college) professors, including Professor Cadwallader. If, therefore, the university failed to supply him with adequate office facilities, this would imply that it expected him to equip his home with a suitable office. If he did so, and used the home office exclusively and on a regular basis for his scholarly research and writing, then he would be entitled to the home office deduction. But if he is given adequate facilities on the campus to conduct the major part of his scholarly research and writing there, the fact that he chooses to work at home instead does not entitle him to a deduction. It is then not the convenience of the employer but the professor's own convenience, and perhaps his tax planning, that induces him to maintain a home office. The Tax Court found that the two and a half offices which the university furnishes Cadwallader are adequate, so he has no imperative need for a home office. Those findings, which are not clearly erroneous and therefore bind us, * * * compel us to affirm the denial of the deduction.

Affirmed.

Problems, Notes and Question

1. *Principal place of business.* Soliman v. Commissioner, discussed in the *Cadwallader* opinion, was affirmed by the Fourth Circuit but reversed by the Supreme Court in Commissioner v. Soliman, 506 U.S. 168 (1993). The Court held that the taxpayer's home office, however necessary it may have been for the business, was not his "principal place of business" because his activities in the operating room were both more important and more time-consuming than those he conducted in the office. This decision generated great uncertainty for many self-employed taxpayers, such as salespersons who run their businesses from home but spend much of their time on the road. The Taxpayer Relief Act of 1997 added a new last sentence to § 280A(c)(1) in an attempt to deal with this problem. If the taxpayer does not conduct "substantial administrative or management activities" of a trade or business at some other "fixed location," a place of business used by the taxpayer for those activities is a "principal place of business."

If read literally, the last sentence of § 280A(c)(1) is quite sweeping. For instance, the home office a textbook author whose only "administrative or management activities" consist of signing the publisher's form contract once every few years might qualify under this provision, even though the author does the bulk of his research and writing elsewhere.

In Popov v. Commissioner, 246 F.3d 1190 (9th Cir.2001), the Ninth Circuit found that the living room of the one-bedroom apartment in which the taxpayer, a concert violinist, lived with her husband and child was her "principal place of business" because she practiced there. (Among other things, the court had to find that the room was used "exclusively" for this purpose; Ms. Popov's husband and child must have led miserable lives, confined as they seem to have been to the bedroom.) The courts' willingness to allow deductions to classical musicians is noteworthy (recall the *Simon* case, p. 256.) But even the Ninth Circuit, which is developing a reputation for independence (to put it politely) in tax cases, refused to allow the Popovs to deduct their meals, long-distance phone bills, and clothing, which they had also claimed, so there are limits.

2. *Recurring problems under § 280A.* Teachers have lost nearly all of their home-office cases, but they continue to litigate; the statute has therefore failed as a deterrent to the taking of too-optimistic return positions.

Several cases have held that the "meeting or dealing with" condition of § 280A(c)(1)(B) requires face-to-face dealings: taking phone calls from clients is not enough. See Green v. Commissioner, 707 F.2d 404 (9th Cir.1983). Proposed Treas.Reg. § 1.280A–2(c) will codify this point.

What if a taxpayer who has two businesses uses a home office as the principal place of the business which is not the taxpayer's principal business? See § 280A(c)(1)(A).

Taxpayer persistence in claiming even clearly unwarranted deductions for home offices is shown by a number of cases in which deductions have been denied because the taxpayer had no income from the activity or because the space in question was not used exclusively for business.

3. *Special cases.* Note §§ 280A(c)(2)–(4), exempting storage, rental, and day-care activities from the home-office limits. Section 280A(c)(6) was added to the Code in 1986 to overrule Feldman v. Commissioner, 84 T.C. 1 (1985), affirmed 791 F.2d 781 (9th Cir.1986), which involved an employee who leased his home office to his employer, who in turn allowed the taxpayer to use the space as a home office. The courts held that the arrangement fell within the "rental" exception of § 280A(c)(3), even though the purported rent payments were functionally equivalent to compensation for services. From a non-tax point of view, neither the employer nor the employee will care whether the employer gives the employee a $2000 raise or "rents" the employee's study for $2000 a year.

4. *Problems.* Can the taxpayers in the following cases deduct the expenses of a home office?

(1) *T* devotes virtually all of his working time (50–60 hours a week) to the analysis, purchase, and sale of securities. He uses one room of his six-room apartment exclusively for this work. (He has no other employment.) In the current year, *T* engaged in approximately 300 purchase or sale transactions. (*T* typically holds securities for very short periods,

sometimes trading in and out of a security several times in a single day.) *T* realized $270,000 in gains from securities transactions and received $30,000 of dividends and interest from his securities holdings.

(2) *P* is a partner in a law firm. Although she spends most of each working day at her firm's downtown office, she uses one room of her ten-room house exclusively for performing professional work in the evenings and on weekends. Five or six times a year *P* meets with clients in her home office, and she frequently receives telephone calls there from clients and colleagues.

7. THE "CARRYING ON" REQUIREMENT

FRANK v. COMMISSIONER

Tax Court of the United States, 1953.
20 T.C. 511.

[After his discharge from the Navy in 1945, Frank and his wife (a lawyer) began a trip through the United States "to investigate and, if possible, acquire a newspaper or radio enterprise to operate." They paid $1000 to a lawyer for his services in connection with unsuccessful negotiations to purchase a newspaper in Delaware, and some $5000 for traveling, telephone, and telegraph expenses.

In November, 1946, the Franks bought a newspaper in Canton, Ohio, and began to publish it.

The Tax Court's Findings of Fact are omitted.]

Van Fossan, Judge: The only question presented is whether the petitioners may deduct $5,965 in the determination of their net income for the year 1946 as ordinary and necessary business expenses or as losses. The petitioners base their claim for deductions upon [§§ 162 and 212]. The evidence reasonably establishes that the petitioners expended the amount of expenses stated in our Findings of Fact during the taxable year in traveling, telephone, telegraph, and legal expenses in the search for and investigation of newspaper and radio properties. * * *

The travel expenses and legal fees spent in searching for a newspaper business with a view to purchasing the same cannot be deducted under the provisions of section [162]. The petitioners were not engaged in any trade or business at the time the expenses were incurred. The trips made by the taxpayers from Phoenix, Arizona, were not related to the conduct of the business that they were then engaged in but were preparatory to locating a business venture of their own. The expenses of investigating and looking for a new business and trips preparatory to entering a business are not deductible as an ordinary and necessary business expense incurred in carrying on a trade or business. George C. Westervelt, 8 T.C. 1248. The word "pursuit" in the statutory phrase "in pursuit of a trade or business" is not used in the sense of "searching for" or "following after," but in the sense of "in connection with" or "in the course of" a trade or business. It presupposes an existing business with which petitioner is connected. The fact that petitioners had no established home during the period of their travels further complicates the question and alone may be fatal to petitioners' case. If they had no home, how could they have expenses "away from home"? The issue whether all or part of the expenses so incurred were capital expenditures is not raised or argued and we do not pass judgment on such question.

Neither are the travel and legal expenses incurred by the petitioners in their attempt to find and purchase a business deductible under section [212], which allows the deduction of expenses incurred in the production or collection of income or in the management, conservation, or maintenance of property held for the production of income. There is a basic distinction between allowing deductions for the expense of producing or collecting income, in which one has an existent interest or right, and expenses incurred in an attempt to obtain income by the creation of some new interest. Marion A. Burt Beck, 15 T.C. 642, affd. 194 F.2d 537. Stella Elkins Tyler, 6 T.C. 135. The expenses here involved are of the latter classification. The traveling costs were incurred in an endeavor to acquire a business which might, in the future, prove productive of income. It might reasonably be said that petitioners were engaged in the active search of employment as newspaper owners, but that cannot be regarded as a business. It is much like the situation obtaining in Mort L. Bixler, 5 B.T.A. 1181, or like that found in McDonald v. Commissioner, 323 U.S. 57, where it was held that a Pennsylvania court of common pleas judge seeking reelection could not deduct under section [212] expenses of such campaign. The Supreme Court said " * * * his campaign contributions were not expenses incurred in being a judge but in trying to be a judge for the next ten years."

The petitioners contend finally that the expenses in question must be allowed as deductions as nonbusiness losses under section [165(c)(2)]. This subsection of the Code provides a deduction for losses incurred in transactions entered into for profit. The only transaction entered into for profit by the petitioners, as disclosed by the facts, was the purchase of a newspaper in Canton, Ohio. Other possible transactions were investigated and rejected or otherwise not entered into. It cannot be said that the petitioners entered into a transaction every time they visited a new city and examined a new business property. Nor can we hold that petitioners entered into such transactions and then abandoned them, as they here contend. Rather, they refused to enter into such transactions after the preliminary investigation. If the general search for a suitable business property itself be considered as a transaction entered into for profit, no abandonment of such project occurred in the taxable year so as to enable deduction of these expenses as losses. Travel and legal expenses, such as were incurred here by petitioners, are not deductible as losses. Robert Lyons Hague, 24 B.T.A. 288; cf. Charles T. Parker, 1 T.C. 709. The cases cited by the petitioners concern instances where transactions were actually entered into and losses were then sustained upon abandonment. We cannot find this situation here.

We conclude that the petitioners may not deduct the expenses claimed for 1946 under the applicable provisions of the Internal Revenue Code.

Decision will be entered for the respondent.

Problems, Notes and Questions

1. *"Start-up" and "expansion" costs.* Consider a taxpayer incurring business-related costs in years before business activities begin. Some of these costs will be non-deductible under § 162 because they are capital expenditures: for example, the costs of obtaining a license to carry on the business. Other costs—sometimes called "pre-opening" expenses—are non-deductible under § 162 because no business is being "carried on," but are not capital expenditures. These non-capital pre-opening expenses can now be written off over a five-year period under § 195(b) if the trade or business is an "active" one. Some courts, reading the capitalization requirement very broadly, have held that many, if not all, pre-opening costs are capital expenditures on the theory that they are costs of acquiring "the new business"; see Central Texas Savings & Loan Association v. United States, 731 F.2d 1181 (5th Cir.1984). Because § 195 does not authorize a five-year write-off for capital expenditures, these cases come close to reading § 195 out of the Code.

A taxpayer who incurs non-capital expenses in expanding an existing business (as opposed to "starting" a "new" business) can deduct the expenses currently. This distinction places considerable weight on the rather arbitrary line between different businesses. The issue has come up in a series of cases involving deductions by banks for the costs of setting up credit-card operations. The courts have held these costs to be deductible expenses of operating the banks' existing "consumer credit businesses," rather than non-deductible costs of starting new "credit card businesses." See, e.g., Colorado Springs Nat. Bank v. United States, 505 F.2d 1185 (10th Cir.1974); Note, 61 Cornell L.Rev. 618 (1976).

2. *Costs of seeking employment.* It is now settled that an employee who incurs expenses in seeking a new job in the same field can deduct those expenses under § 162. See Cremona v. Commissioner, 58 T.C. 219 (1972) (Acq.), allowing a taxpayer employed as an "administrator" by Isotopes, Inc., a deduction for fees paid for employment counseling and job referral services in an unsuccessful attempt to obtain a similar job elsewhere. The court characterized the employee's trade or business as "being an 'administrator.'" Why was his trade or business not "being an 'administrator' for Isotopes, Inc."? *Cremona* rejected a long-standing Service position that the costs of an unsuccessful job search are not deductible. The Service has acquiesced in *Cremona,* but continues to rule that the costs of seeking employment in a new trade or business are not within § 162 or § 212, irrespective of whether the attempt succeeds; Rev.Rul. 75–120, 1975–1 C.B. 55.

Consider a law student who pays for a trip to California to look for a job. The costs are not deductible under *Frank*. Does it follow that if a California law firm picks up the tab the student has income? Rev.Rul. 63–77, 1963–1 C.B. 177, holds without explanation that the reimbursement is not income except to the extent that it exceeds the job-seeker's actual expenses.

Letter Ruling 9641003 presents an interesting contrast to Rev. Rul. 63–77. The letter ruling dealt with airline tickets furnished by an employer to employees for travel to a remote work site and back home again. The site was one to which the employees could not have taken their families. Ruling that the "only possible exception" to the rule taxing fringe benefits was the exception for working condition fringes, and that that exception did not apply because the employees could not have deducted their airfares if they had paid for their own tickets, the Service concluded that the tickets were taxable fringe benefits. The letter ruling's insistence that excludability and non-deductibility are subject to the same tests is inconsistent with Rev. Rul. 63–77. Query whether the fact that the taxpayers in the letter ruling were employees and the law students were not can be used to distinguish the rulings. Anyone who gets a taxable fringe benefit is an "employee" for purposes of taxability; Treas.Reg. § 1.61–21(a)(4)(ii), which suggests that employee status does not matter. But see Rev. Rul. 80–99, 1980–1 C.B. 10, holding that a state government employee who attends a political convention at a political party's expense has no income. This ruling is careful to "distinguish" situations involving expenses paid by the taxpayer's employer, which may explain the Service's willingness to issue Ltr. Rul. 9641003 despite Rev. Rul. 63–77 (which was not cited in the letter ruling).

3. *Moving expenses.* Section 217 allows an above-the-line deduction for some of the costs of moving to a new job location, even in the case of an employee or self-employed person who had no job before the move. *above line*

4. *"Carrying on" someone else's business.* Suppose that *A*, who owns and operates a business, falls upon hard times. *A*'s sister, *S*, helps out by paying some of *A*'s current business expenses. *S* cannot deduct the payments because, as to her, they are gifts to *A*. See Deputy v. du Pont, 308 U.S. 488 (1940), holding that expenses must "proximately result" from the *taxpayer's* business to be deductible under § 162. Can *A* deduct the expenses?

5. *Problems.*

(1) *C*, a certified public accountant, paid an employment agency $5000 to assist her in obtaining a better-paying position. The agency arranged several interviews for *C*, and as a result of one interview she received an offer of a position as treasurer of a corporation. *C* turned down the offer because she felt that the salary offered was not commensurate with the job's responsibilities. Can she deduct the fee? *deductible*

(2) *S* graduates from law school and begins work as an associate with a firm in New York City, which is 200 miles from *S*'s home. *S*

works for this firm for eight months and then changes jobs, remaining in New York. *S* works at the new job for several years. Can *S* deduct any of the costs of moving to New York?

6. *Reference.* Lee, Start–Up Costs, Section 195, and Clear Reflection of Income: A Tale of Talismans, Tacked–On Tax Reform, and a Touch of Basics, 6 Va.Tax Rev. 1 (1986).

8. EDUCATIONAL EXPENDITURES

SHARON v. COMMISSIONER

United States Tax Court, 1976.
66 T.C. 515, affirmed 591 F.2d 1273 (9th Cir.1978), cert. denied
442 U.S. 941, 99 S.Ct. 2883, 61 L.Ed.2d 311 (1979).

SIMPSON, JUDGE: * * * [Sharon graduated from Brandeis University in 1961 and from Columbia University School of Law in 1964. He spent $175.20 for New York bar review courses and materials, and paid a $25.00 New York bar examination fee. He worked as a lawyer in New York until 1967, when he accepted a position with the Internal Revenue Service in California.

After moving to California, Sharon spent $230 for a California bar review course and $582 for other costs (registration, bar examination, and admittance fees) of obtaining admission to practice before the California courts and Federal courts in California. In 1970 he spent $313.35 on travel and miscellaneous expenses in connection with admission to practice before the U.S. Supreme Court.

The Tax Court's findings of fact and its discussion of an issue involving deductions for a "home office" are omitted.]

* * *

2. AMORTIZATION OF LICENSE TO PRACTICE LAW IN NEW YORK

The next issue to be decided is whether the petitioner may amortize the cost of obtaining his license to practice law in New York. The petitioner contends that he is entitled under section 167 to amortize the cost of such license over the period from the date of his admission to the bar to the date on which he reaches age 65, when he expects to retire. In his cost basis of this "intangible asset," he included the costs of obtaining his college degree ($11,125), obtaining his law degree ($6,910), a bar review course and related materials ($175.20), and the New York State bar examination fee ($25). As justification for including these education expenses in the cost of his license, he points out that, in order to take the New York bar examination, he was required to have graduated from college and an accredited law school.

The petitioners rely upon section 1.167(a)–3 of the Income Tax Regulations, which provides in part:

If an intangible asset is known from experience or other factors to be of use in the business or in the production of income for only a limited period, the length of which can be estimated with reasonable accuracy, such an intangible asset may be the subject of a depreciation allowance. * * *

There is no merit in the petitioner's claim to an amortization deduction for the cost of his education and related expenses in qualifying himself for the legal profession. His college and law school expenses provided him with a general education which will be beneficial to him in a wide variety of ways. See James A. Carroll, 51 T.C. 213, 216 (1968). The costs and responsibility for obtaining such education are personal. Section 1.262–1(b)(9) of the Income Tax Regulations provides that expenditures for education are deductible only if they qualify under section 162 and section 1.162–5 of the regulations. In the words of section 1.162–5(b), all costs of "minimum educational requirements for qualification in * * * employment" are "personal expenditures or constitute an inseparable aggregate of personal and capital expenditures." There is no "rational" or workable basis for any allocation of this inseparable aggregate between the nondeductible personal component and a deductible component of the total expense. Fausner v. Commissioner, 413 U.S. 838, 839 (1973). Such expenses are not made any less personal or any more separable from the aggregate by attempting to capitalize them for amortization purposes. David N. Bodley, 56 T.C. 1357, 1362 (1971); Nathaniel A. Denman, 48 T.C. 439, 446 (1967); Huene v. United States, 247 F.Supp. 564, 570 (S.D.N.Y.1965). Since the inseparable aggregate includes personal expenditures, the preeminence of section 262 over section 167 precludes any amortization deduction. Cf. Commissioner v. Idaho Power Co., 418 U.S. at 17; Bodzin v. Commissioner, 509 F.2d at 681. The same reasoning applies to the costs of review courses and related expenses taken to qualify for the practice of a profession. William D. Glenn, 62 T.C. 270, 274–276 (1974).

In his brief, the petitioner attempts to distinguish our opinion in *Denman* by asserting that he is not attempting to capitalize his educational costs, but rather, the cost of his license to practice law. Despite the label which the petitioner would apply to such costs, they nonetheless constitute the costs of his education, which are personal and nondeductible. Moreover, in his petition, he alleged that the capital asset he was seeking to amortize was his education.

There remains the $25 fee paid for the petitioner's license to practice in New York. This was not an educational expense but was a fee paid for the privilege of practicing law in New York, a nontransferable license which has value beyond the taxable years, and such fee is a capital expenditure. Cf. Arthur E. Ryman, Jr., 51 T.C. 799 (1969); Glenn L. Heigerick, 45 T.C. 475 (1966); S.M. Howard, 39 T.C. 833 (1963); O.D. 452, 2 C.B. 157 (1920). The Commissioner has limited his argument to the educational expenses and apparently concedes that the fee may be amortized. Since the amount of the fee is small, the petitioner might, ordinarily, be allowed to elect to deduct the full amount of the fee in the year of payment, despite its capital nature. Cf. sec. 1.162–12(a), Income Tax Regs., with respect to the treatment of inexpensive tools. However, since the fee was paid prior to the years in issue, we cannot allow a current deduction in this case. Therefore, in view of the Commissioner's concession and our conclusion with respect to the third and fourth issues, a proportionate part of such fee may be added to the amounts to be amortized in accordance with our resolution of the third issue.

3. LICENSE TO PRACTICE LAW IN CALIFORNIA

[The court held that practicing law in California was a "new" trade or business, so that the cost of the bar review course was neither deductible nor amortizable. The Commissioner did not argue that the other costs of obtaining a license to practice in California—bar examination and admittance fees—were not amortizable.

The court also held that by obtaining admission to practice before the United States Supreme Court Sharon acquired an amortizable intangible asset.

The amortization period for Sharon's California and Supreme Court licenses was held to be his life expectancy; his testimony that he would retire at sixty-five if financially able to do so did not suffice to establish a shorter useful life.]

[The dissenting opinions of Judges Dawson, Scott, Irwin, and Sterrett are omitted.]

Problems, Notes and Questions

1. *Personal expenditures?* The idea that the costs of law school or medical school are "personal" is often ridiculed; "surely," it is said, "most of those who spend money on training to enter a profession do so solely or primarily so that they can earn money by practicing that profession." Is it so clear? Parents often finance their children's professional educations for "personal" reasons. Do the reasons people pay for their own professional educations differ greatly from the reasons they have for paying their children's tuition?

2. *Deductible educational costs.* Under the version of Treas.Reg. § 1.162–5(a) in force from 1958 to 1967, educational expenses were deductible if incurred for the *purpose* of "maintaining or improving skills" used in an existing job. Non-deductible educational expenditures were those for the purposes of fulfilling "general education aspirations or other personal purposes" and "of obtaining a new position or substantial advancement in position." The current regulations apply an "objective" standard; in part, at least, in response to cases under the "purpose" test holding that accountants, revenue agents, and others had attended law school for reasons related to their employment even though, upon graduation, they had changed their minds and taken up the practice of law.

Much of the difficulty in applying the current regulations arises because of the need to decide whether the "trade or business" for which one qualifies because of schooling is a "new" one, or merely a branch of an existing one. Cooper v. Commissioner, 38 T.C.M. 955 (1979), held that an accountant who became a C.P.A. qualified for a new business. Examples in the regulations deal extensively with teachers who become certified to teach new subjects or to teach in different states.

3. *Problems.*

(1) *L*, a recent law-school graduate, plans to live and work in New York and to get an LL.M. degree in taxation from New York University. From the point of view of the deductibility of his expenses for tuition and books, does it matter whether *L* starts work immediately, attending LL.M. classes on a part-time basis, or spends a year in the full-time LL.M. program and then begins work?

(2) *A*, a certified public accountant, pays tuition for night classes at a local law school. *A* does not want to become a lawyer, but she thinks her legal studies will benefit her accounting career. Can she deduct her expenses if:

(a) She attends an LL.M. program (open to nonlawyers)?

(b) She takes the first year of a J.D. program?

(c) She takes all three years of a J.D. program and graduates, but does not take a bar exam?

4. *References.* Wolfman, The Cost of Education and the Federal Income Tax, 42 F.R.D. 535 (1966); Wolfman, Professors and the "Ordinary and Necessary" Business Expense, 112 U.Pa.L.Rev. 1089 (1964).

D. "PUBLIC POLICY" LIMITS ON DEDUCTIONS FOR BUSINESS AND INVESTMENT EXPENSES AND LOSSES

McDONALD v. COMMISSIONER

Supreme Court of the United States, 1944.
323 U.S. 57, 65 S.Ct. 96, 89 L.Ed. 68.

Mr. Justice Frankfurter announced the conclusion and judgment of the Court, and an opinion in which the Chief Justice, Mr. Justice Roberts and Mr. Justice Jackson concur.

This is a controversy concerning a deficiency in petitioner's income tax for 1939.

In December 1938, the Governor of Pennsylvania appointed petitioner to serve an unexpired term as Judge of the Court of Common Pleas of Luzerne County. Under Pennsylvania law such an interim judgeship is filled for a full term at the next election. McDonald accepted this temporary appointment with the understanding that he would contest both the primary and general elections. To obtain the support of his party organization he was obliged to pay to the party fund an "assessment" made by the party's executive committee against all of the party's candidates. The amounts of such "assessments" were fixed on the basis of the total prospective salaries to be received from the various offices. The salary of a common pleas judge was $12,000 a year for a term of ten years, and the "assessment" against petitioner was fixed at $8,000. The proceeds from these "assessments" went to the general campaign fund in the service of the party's entire ticket. In addition to this political levy, McDonald also spent $5,017.27 for customary campaign expenses—advertising, printing, travelling, etc. The sum of these outlays, $13,017.27, McDonald deducted as a "reelection expense." The Commissioner of Internal Revenue disallowed the item and notified him of a deficiency of $2,506.77.

In appropriate proceedings before the Tax Court of the United States that Court sustained the Commissioner, 1 T.C. 738, and its decision was affirmed by the Circuit Court of Appeals for the Third Circuit. 139 F.2d 400. We brought the case here, 321 U.S. 762, to give a definitive judicial answer to an important problem in the administration of the federal income tax.

* * *

"All the ordinary and necessary expenses paid or incurred during the taxable year in carrying on any trade or business" are allowed by § [162] as deductions in computing net income. According to tax law terminology * * * the performance by petitioner of his judicial office constituted carrying on a "trade or business" within the terms of § [162] of the Internal Revenue Code. He was therefore entitled to deduct from his gross income all the "ordinary and necessary expenses" paid during 1939 in carrying on that "trade or business." He could, that is, deduct all expenses that related to the discharge of his functions as a judge. But his campaign contributions were not expenses incurred in being a judge but in trying to be a judge for the next ten years. That is as true of the money he spent more immediately for his own reelection as it is of the "assessment" he paid into the party coffers for the success of his party's ticket. The incongruity of allowing such contributions as expenses incidental to the means of earning income as a judge is underlined by the insistence that payment of the "assessment" levied by the party as a prerequisite to being allowed to be a candidate is deductible as a "business" expense. If such "assessments" for future acquisition of a profitable office are part of the expenses in performing the functions of that office for the taxable year, then why should not the same deduction be allowed for "assessment" against office holders not candidates for immediate reappointment or reelection but who pay such "assessments" out of party allegiance mixed or unmixed by a lively sense of future favors?

In order to disallow them we are not called upon to find that petitioner's outlays come within the prohibition of § [262] in that they constituted "Personal * * * expenses." "Whether and to what extent deductions shall be allowed depends upon legislative grace; and only as there is clear provision therefor can any particular deduction be allowed." New Colonial Ice Co. v. Helvering, 292 U.S. 435, 440. For these campaign expenses to be deductible, it must be found that they can conveniently come within § [162]. To put it mildly, that section is not a clear provision for such an allowance. To determine allowable deductions by the different internal party arrangements for bearing the cost of political campaigns in the forty-eight states would disregard the explicit restrictions of § [162] confining deductible expenses solely to outlays in the efforts or services—here the business of judging—from which the income flows. Compare Welch v. Helvering, 290 U.S. 111, 115–116.

Petitioner next insists that inasmuch as he was defeated for reelection his campaign expenses constitute a loss incurred in a "transaction entered into for profit" and as such a deductible allowance by virtue of § [165(c)(2)]. Such an argument does not deserve more than short shrift. It suffices to say that petitioner's money was not spent to buy the election but to buy the opportunity to persuade the electors. His campaign contribution was not an insurance of victory frustrated by "an act of God" but the price paid for an active share in the hazards of popular elections. To argue that the loss of the election proves that the expense incurred in such election is a deductible "loss" under § [165(c)(2)] is to play with words.

* * *

It is not for this Court to initiate policies as to the deduction of campaign expenses. It is for Congress to determine the relation of campaign expenditures to tax deductions by candidates for public office, under such circumstances and within such limits as commend themselves to its judgment. But we certainly cannot draw intimations of such a policy from legislation by Congress increasingly restrictive against campaign contributions and political activities by government officials. The relation between money and politics generally—and more particularly the cost of campaigns and contributions by prospective officeholders, especially judges—involves issues of far-reaching importance to a democracy and is beset with legislative difficulties that even judges can appreciate. But these difficulties can neither be met nor avoided by spurious interpretation of tax provisions dealing with allowable deductions.

To find sanction in existing tax legislation for deduction of petitioner's campaign expenditures would necessarily require allowance of deduction for campaign expenditures by all candidates, whether incumbents seeking reelection or new contenders. To draw a distinction between outlays for reelection and those for election—to allow the former and disallow the latter—is unsupportable in reason. It is even more unsupportable in public policy to derive from what Congress has thus far enacted a handicap against candidates challenging existing officeholders. And so we cannot recognize petitioner's claim on the score that he was a candidate for reelection.

* * *

Affirmed.

MR. JUSTICE RUTLEDGE concurs in the result.

MR. JUSTICE BLACK, dissenting.

* * *

The Court's decision is * * * grounded upon its reference to congressional policy restricting campaign contributions and political activities by government officials. We are not dealing here, however, with campaign contributions made by one person to further the candidacy of another. Besides, Congress has not attempted to regulate expenditures of candidates for state office. I can hardly conceive that we should infer that it wanted to penalize through its tax laws, necessary campaign expenses, and thereby condemn a practice of campaigning that is as old as our country and which exists in every state of the Union. Unless our democratic philosophy is wrong, there can be no evil in a candidate spending a legally permissible and necessary sum to approach the electorate and enable them to pass an informed judgment upon his qualifications. This is not, of course, to be taken as denoting approval of corrupt campaign expenditures, or of any of the myriad abuses which beset our systems of election. But we ought not to eviscerate a revenue act, and deny this state official a deduction for expenses incurred in a state election campaign, because Congress has limited campaign contributions in federal elections, and passed restrictive legislation against political activities by federal employees.

* * *

State officials all over this nation have been subject to federal income taxes since 1939. When they run for office, they must necessarily spend some money to advertise their campaigns. We permit private individuals to deduct expenses incurred in advertising to get business. If this petitioner had owned a factory, the operations of which were suspended because of war contracts, and had advertised goods which he could not presently sell, the expenses of such advertising would have been deductible under Treasury rulings.

So long as campaign expenses spent by candidates are legitimate, ordinary, and necessary, I am unwilling to assume that Congress intended by the 1942 Act[n] to discriminate against the thousands of state officials subject to federal income taxes. The language Congress used literally protects petitioner's right to a deduction; nothing in the legislative history indicates an intent to deny it. Certainly there are abuses in campaign expenditures. But that is a problem that should be attacked squarely by the proper state and federal authorities, and not by strained

n. Which enacted the predecessors of §§ 212(1) & (2).—Eds.

statutory construction which permits a discriminatory penalty to be imposed on taxpayers who work for the states, counties, municipalities, or the federal government. I think we should reverse and remand this cause to the Tax Court with instructions to pass upon the factual questions which it did not previously determine.

MR. JUSTICE REED, MR. JUSTICE DOUGLAS, and MR. JUSTICE MURPHY join in this dissent.

Problem, Notes and Question

1. *The McDonald rule today.* The Tax Court followed *McDonald* in denying a deduction for expenses incurred by a labor union president in an unsuccessful reelection campaign; Carey v. Commissioner, 56 T.C. 477 (1971), affirmed mem. 460 F.2d 1259 (4th Cir.1972), cert. denied 409 U.S. 990 (1972). Although decisions rendered after *McDonald* had established that fees paid to an employment agency are deductible,[o] the majority thought "campaign" expenditures not so clearly "ordinary and necessary business expenses" as employment-agency fees. It added that "public policy" considerations "comparable" to those in *McDonald* should be taken into account, since "the presidency of a large international labor union is akin to a public office." Four dissenters argued that the legislative history of the specific "public policy" provisions enacted in 1969 (p. 394, below) meant that deductions should generally be disallowed on such grounds only at the express command of Congress.

In Mays v. Bowers, 201 F.2d 401, 403 (4th Cir.1953), cert. denied 345 U.S. 969 (1953), the court explained the disallowance of deductions for the costs of campaigning for public office as follows:

> If such deductions should be allowed, the government to the extent of the reduction in taxes thereby obtained would be paying the campaign expenses of the taxpayer, and would be paying a larger portion in the case of a wealthy taxpayer in the high income brackets than of a poor taxpayer in the lower brackets.

Is this sound, or does it assume the answer to the question to be decided—whether campaign costs are "business expenses"?

2. *Fines and penalties.* Section 162(f) codifies Tank Truck Rentals, Inc. v. Commissioner, 356 U.S. 30 (1958), which denied a deduction for fines imposed on the taxpayer and its drivers for violating state maximum weight laws. The Court felt that a deduction would "frustrate state policy," whether the violations were "innocent" or "deliberate."

The taxpayer in Hawronsky v. Commissioner, 105 T.C. 94 (1995), was a doctor who received a "scholarship" for medical school on the condition that he work for a particular period of time for the Indian Health Service. He didn't, and pursuant to the relevant statute he had to pay the government treble damages. The Tax Court rejected his deduction of most of the damages as a business expense on the grounds that

o. See Cremona v. Commissioner, p. 378 above.

the penalty was imposed by statute and was not shown to bear any close relationship to the government's damages; these features made it clear that it really was a penalty.

Section 162(g) disallows deductions for the "punitive" portion of antitrust damages paid by taxpayers who have been convicted in criminal antitrust proceedings, or who have entered guilty or nolo contendere pleas.

3. *Problem.* T Corp. operates a trucking business. Its trucks were found to be operating in violation of the weight limits imposed by state law. T Corp. was required to pay a criminal fine of $100 for each violation. In addition, it was required to pay a civil fine of five cents a pound for each pound of excess weight. The civil fine, which came to $250, was earmarked for the state road-improvement fund. Can T Corp. deduct the fines?

[handwritten margin note: Neither civil nor criminal fines are deductible]

MAX SOBEL WHOLESALE LIQUORS
v. COMMISSIONER

United States Tax Court, 1977.
69 T.C. 477 (Acq.), affirmed 630 F.2d 670 (9th Cir.1980).

[handwritten margin note: illegal rebates]

QUEALY, JUDGE: This proceeding involves the redetermination of deficiencies in income taxes of petitioner as follows:

FYE Jan. 31—	Deficiency
1973	$72,468
1974	59,487
1975	42,410

As a result of concessions by the parties, the sole question for decision is whether the petitioner is precluded from charging as cost or deducting under § 162(c)(2) the cost of liquor and wine transferred to selected customers in violation of the laws of the State of California.[p]

FINDINGS OF FACT

* * *

As a wholesaler of liquor and wine, the petitioner was required to file or to post each month the selling prices for the liquor and wine to be sold by it in accordance with §§ 24756 and 24862 of the California Business & Professions Code. Such price list became effective for sales made during the ensuing month. The prices posted by petitioner and its competitors, in most cases, were determined in the first instance by the producers or importers of such spirits. The producers or importers of liquor and wine supplied "suggested" monthly price lists to the petition-

p. In California Retail Liquor Dealers Ass'n v. Midcal Aluminum, Inc., 445 U.S. 97 (1980), the Supreme Court held that the California wine pricing system involved in this case constituted resale price maintenance in violation of the Sherman Act.— Eds.

er in order that such prices might be posted with the ABC. If the petitioner did not conform to the suggested prices, there was a risk that the supplier would terminate petitioner's right to distribute the brands of liquor and wine which the petitioner obtained from that source.

During the period involved in this proceeding, the petitioner evolved a procedure whereby certain selected customers might purchase liquor and wine from the petitioner on a basis more favorable than the selling prices for such liquor and wine posted by the petitioner with the ABC. An agreement was entered into with such customers pursuant to which, with each purchase of liquor or wine, the customer would be entitled to a credit of a stated percent of the total purchase, which amount would be available to be used by such customer in the purchase of additional quantities of liquor or wine. In other instances, the agreement provided that with the purchase of a case of certain liquors or wines, the purchaser would be entitled to receive an additional bottle of that liquor or wine.

The petitioner maintained a "black book" setting forth the name of the customer, the purchases by such customer, and the credit to which the customer was entitled. Periodically, such credits would be availed of by the customer to purchase additional liquor or wine or the customer would be supplied with the additional bottles to which the customer became entitled under the agreement of purchase.

When the petitioner received a regular order from its customers, the order was filled and delivered by the petitioner out of inventory. As a part of petitioner's accounting and billing system, a sales invoice was prepared with respect to each sales transaction which listed thereon the brand and quantity of the spirits sold and the sales price, along with any posted discount. The billing price for liquor and wine listed on such sales invoice conformed to the prices posted with the ABC as required by California law.

When the petitioner received an order for use of the "credit" from one of the selected customers to whom the petitioner had agreed to give such credit, a document was prepared identifying the retailer, the type of spirits, brand name, quantity, and amount. A copy of this document, referred to as a "drop tag," was transmitted to the employee in charge of maintaining the inventory records in order that he might remove the designated quantity from inventory. Another copy of the "drop tag" was sent to the warehouse in order that the goods would be released for pickup by the retailer or for delivery. The additional goods supplied to the customer were thus removed from inventory and automatically charged as a part of the cost of sales. The credits and deliveries made on account thereof were recorded in the "black book" but did not otherwise appear in the petitioner's accounting records.

The practice whereby the petitioner gave rebates, credits, or additional merchandise to selected customers, without reflecting such in the prices posted by petitioner with the ABC, was in violation of the laws of the State of California.

* * *

In his notice of deficiency, respondent increased petitioner's income as reported for the years ending January 31, 1973 and 1974, in the amounts of $121,218 and $13,757, on account of the additional spirits charged to the cost of goods sold.

OPINION

* * *

Sales of spirits were reflected on the books of the petitioner at invoice prices in conformity with the schedule of prices filed with the ABC. The additional spirits which the customers obtained by credits earned on such purchases were delivered out of inventory and the cost thereof was automatically reflected in the cost of sales. While respondent seeks to distinguish between the granting of a rebate payable in merchandise and a rebate payable in cash, the result is the same. In fact, the case of one of petitioner's competitors who granted cash rebates "under the table" is also before this Court. The basic question is whether such rebates, regardless of form, come within the scope of § 162(c).

* * *

Section 162(c)(2) * * * denies the *deduction* of certain payments, which might otherwise be deductible under § 162(a), on account of the illegality of such payments. The Court must first decide whether the agreement between petitioner and its selected customers, whereby the stated invoice price of the spirits was subject to a credit for the purchase of additional merchandise, constituted an "illegal bribe, illegal kickback, or other illegal payment" otherwise deductible under § 162(a).

The practice of illegally rebating did not originate with these San Francisco wholesale liquor dealers. This practice first came before the Tax Court in the case of rebates granted contrary to state law in the sale of milk. Pittsburgh Milk Co. v. Commissioner, 26 T.C. 707 (1956). The *Pittsburgh Milk* case was then invoked by the respondent to deny to the taxpayer, an Illinois liquor dealer, an adjustment in computing the World War II excess profit tax credit for an abnormal deduction for illegal rebates to its customers. Tri–State Beverage Distributors, Inc. v. Commissioner, 27 T.C. 1026 (1957).

In the *Pittsburgh Milk* case (and the cases which followed that decision), this Court distinguished *between* a discount or rebate to which the customers became entitled at the time of sale *and* costs incurred in the form of illegal payments, or payments to the third parties, which were not made pursuant to agreement between the buyer and the seller. Where the rebate was a part of the transaction of sale, this Court held that the deductibility of such payment was not the question. The rebate was a reduction in gross income. This principle was reaffirmed in

Atzingen–Whitehouse Dairy, Inc. v. Commissioner, 36 T.C. 173 (1961), wherein this Court said:

Raum, Judge: (1) We have concluded on the evidence that the actual prices at which petitioner sold its products were the invoice prices minus the discounts agreed upon between petitioner and its customers. Accordingly, the problem before us is not whether such discounts are deductible as "ordinary and necessary" business expenses from gross income in arriving at net income, cf. Tank Truck Rentals v. Commissioner, 356 U.S. 30; rather it is whether the discounts must be taken into account in determining the amount of gross income chargeable to petitioner in the first instance. Cf. Lela Sullenger, 11 T.C. 1076 acq. 1952–2 C.B. 3. We hold, following Pittsburgh Milk Co., 26 T.C. 707, which involved a virtually identical situation, that in computing gross income the amount of petitioner's sales must be based upon its actual prices and not upon the theoretical legal minimum prices. The present case is closer to the *Pittsburgh Milk Co.* case than to Boyle, Flagg & Seaman, Inc., 25 T.C. 43, relied upon by respondent.

Respondent urges that the decision in the *Pittsburgh Milk Co.* case be reconsidered. He made a similar contention in two other cases, in which the holding in the *Pittsburgh Milk Co.* case was reaffirmed and followed in memorandum opinions by this Court. Moreover, the theory of the *Pittsburgh Milk Co.* case has been applied, at the respondent's urging, in Tri–State Beverage Distributors, Inc., 27 T.C. 1026, 1030–1031. We are not disposed to reopen the question.

* * *

In his brief, respondent * * * contends that in accounting for the additional spirits supplied by petitioner to its customers pursuant to the illegal rebates, the cost of such spirits was treated as a part of the cost of sales by the petitioner and is, therefore, distinguishable from the rebates involved in the *Pittsburgh Milk* line of cases. Those cases did not, however, look to the manner in which the taxpayer entered the transaction in its books in order to conceal the illegal rebate. Bookkeeping entries were ignored. In the *Pittsburgh Milk* case, the illegal rebates were charged to "advertising" and deducted as such. In the *Rosedale Dairy* case, the illegal rebates were deducted as "freight and hauling." In the *Harmony Dairy* case, the payments were disguised as "advertising or other operational expenditures." In the *Atzingen–Whitehouse Dairy* case, the illegal rebates were charged to "selling expense-sales promotion."

Finally, there is the question whether subsequent amendment of § 162(c) might be construed as having overruled the *Pittsburgh Milk* line of cases. Section 162(c)(2) in its present form was added to the Internal Revenue Code by § 310 of the Revenue Act of 1971. The change in law was intended merely to define the degree of criminality or culpability which would vitiate the deduction. Section 162(c)(3) was added to the Code at the same time. In both cases, the statute reads that "No deduction shall be allowed under subsection (a)'' for the payments described in § 162(c)(2) and (3). Since the *Pittsburgh Milk* line of cases did not deal with the deductibility of the payment, but rather its exclusion from gross income, it would be difficult to infer that Congress intended to overrule prior law.

We must assume that Congress was aware of the decision of this Court in the *Pittsburgh Milk* case. At the time that the legislation was enacted, the respondent had acquiesced in that decision. If Congress had intended to overrule the *Pittsburgh Milk* case, it is only reasonable to expect that the amendment would have been more specific in so doing or that the congressional intent would find expression in the report of the Finance Committee accompanying the bill. S.Rept. 92–437, 92d Cong., 1st Sess. 72–73.

Notwithstanding, respondent has changed his position in an effort to extend the statute to exclude bribes, kickbacks, and other illegal payments which might otherwise be chargeable to the cost of goods sold. See Rev.Rul. 77–244, [1977–2 C.B. 58]. Section 1.61–3(a), Income Tax Regs., provides that amounts which are a type for which a deduction would be disallowed under § 162(c), (f), or (g) in the case of a business expense may not be deducted from gross receipts in order to arrive at gross income. Similarly, § 1.471–3(d), Income Tax Regs., provides that ''cost shall not include an amount which is of a type for which a deduction would be disallowed under § 162(c), (f) or (g) and the regulations thereunder in the case of a business expense.''

In our opinion, assuming the validity of the regulations, the rule stated would not apply in the case before the Court. Depending upon the nature of the business, the cost of goods sold may include material, labor, and overhead. There may be certain expenses of a dual character which may be chargeable either to overhead in the cost of goods sold or deducted as administrative or sales expense. In any event, the Court would limit the regulations as to preclude the deductibility of an illegal payment charged to overhead in the cost of sales *of the type* which might otherwise be deductible as administrative or sales expenses. A typical example would be a bribe given for the purpose of obtaining goods or for the purpose of expediting its delivery to the taxpayer for manufacture and resale.

In the case before the Court, we are not confronted with that type of expense. In effect, the petitioner's agreement with its selected customers provided for the sale of spirits priced at $102.50 for $100 or for the sale of 13 bottles of wine for the price of 12 bottles. The additional quantity supplied came out of inventory and was automatically reflected in the cost of sales. Such costs are not an overhead or indirect expense charged to the cost of sales and were not ''of a type'' for which a deduction would be disallowed under § 162(c)(3).

In view of the foregoing, it is the opinion of the Court that the *Pittsburgh Milk* line of cases has not been overruled either by subsequent decisions of this Court or any other court, and that no congressional intent to overrule that line of cases can be inferred from its legislative enactment of § 162(c)(2). The only logical inference would seem to be to the contrary. Accordingly, the respondent's position with respect to this issue must be rejected.

* * *

Decision will be entered under Rule 155.

Reviewed by the Court.

DRENNEN, J., dissenting: I do not disagree with the principles expressed in the majority opinion; nevertheless, I would reach the opposite conclusion in this case for a reason not discussed in the majority opinion. Stated briefly, I would reduce the cost of goods sold by the cost to the taxpayer of the "credit" merchandise which I conclude was not sold by the taxpayer.

A "sale" was defined by the Supreme Court in Commissioner v. Brown, 380 U.S. 563 (1965), to be "a transfer of property for a fixed monetary price or its equivalent." As I understand the facts in this case, Sobel sold wine and liquor to its preferred customers at list prices and entered the full amount of the list prices in sales. It then noted a credit in favor of the preferred customers in its "black book." Subsequently, according to the majority opinion, the customers were delivered additional merchandise "at no additional charge, in satisfaction of the credits recorded in the 'black book' " from its inventory and the cost of such merchandise to Sobel was charged to cost of goods sold. Presumably no further sale was recorded in Sobel's books. In my opinion this subsequent transaction did not constitute a sale of the credit merchandise under the above definition of "sale."

* * *

I doubt that the majority would allow this credit as a deduction under § 162(c)(2). Since petitioner included in sales the entire list price of the merchandise actually sold I do not believe the principle espoused in Pittsburgh Milk Co. v. Commissioner, 26 T.C. 707 (1956), should be involved.

FAY, DAWSON, and WILES, JJ., agree with this dissenting opinion.

Problems, Notes and Questions

1. *"Reduction of gross income" vs. "deduction."* The Service will follow *Max Sobel;* Rev.Rul. 82–149, 1982–2 C.B. 56. See also the *Dixie Dairies* case, p. 115, above.

2. *Bribes and other illegal payments.* Evaluate § 162(c) in light of Judge Wilbur's concurring opinion in Alex v. Commissioner, 70 T.C. 322, 332 n. 2 (1978), affirmed 628 F.2d 1222 (9th Cir.1980):

[Section 162(c)] imposes enormous financial penalties varying with the type of business and the taxpayer's marginal rate, frequently spelling financial ruin for an individual who would receive only a small financial penalty under state law. * * * The unexpected financial ruin, attributable to a tax burden wholly unrelated to his net income in an economic sense, is not required by the exigencies of federalism—indeed it is most likely counterproductive. It is tangential at best to the object of collecting taxes on net income and ability to pay, and undermines the self-assessment system.

3. *Lobbying.* From 1962 to 1993, some business costs associated with lobbying concerning legislation "of direct interest to the taxpayer" were deductible under former § 162(e)(1)(A). The Revenue Reconciliation Act of 1993 amended § 162(e) to deny deductions for most lobbying activities. A taxpayer whose business consists of lobbying can, of course, deduct the costs of carrying on that business (§ 162(e)(5)(A)), and § 162(e)(5)(B) creates a *de minimis* exception for certain "in-house" expenditures (not including payments to lobbyists). Under § 162(e)(2), the costs of lobbying a "local council or similar governing body" on legislation or proposed legislation of direct interest to the taxpayer remain deductible.

4. *Non-statutory public-policy limits on deductions.* The Tax Reform Act of 1969 rewrote much of the law on denial of deductions on public-policy grounds. S.Rep. No. 91–552, 91st Cong., 1st Sess. 274 (1969), says: "The provision for the denial of the deduction for payments in these situations which are deemed to violate public policy is intended to be all inclusive. Public policy, in other circumstances, generally is not sufficiently clearly defined to justify the disallowance of deductions." Does this history mean that nonbusiness deductions are not subject to "public policy" limits because the sections allowing those deductions do not expressly impose them? The taxpayer in Mazzei v. Commissioner, 61 T.C. 497 (1974), contributed $20,000 to a venture which he thought was a scheme to manufacture counterfeit money, but which was in fact a scheme to steal the $20,000 from the taxpayer. A divided Tax Court refused to allow a "theft loss" deduction under § 165(c)(3).

The courts' willingness to deny deductions on "public policy" grounds even when no statute disallows the deductions is shown by Wood v. United States, 863 F.2d 417 (5th Cir.1989). Wood, a dealer in marijuana, forfeited property to the government because his interest in the property was traceable to commissions from drug smuggling. The Fifth Circuit found it "easy to sustain a public policy rationale" for denying Wood a loss deduction under § 165. The court cited the Supreme Court's *Tank Truck Rentals* decision (p. 387) without noting that Congress had codified that decision in § 162 and that the codification was purportedly "exclusive."

With *Wood,* compare Stephens v. Commissioner, 905 F.2d 667 (2d Cir.1990), which allowed a criminal to deduct a restitution payment to his victim. Stephens, whose jail sentence for fraud was suspended on condition that he pay restitution, claimed a deduction under § 165(c)(2). The Tax Court held that the payment was comparable to a fine paid to a government, and should be nondeductible on the same "public policy" grounds that make fines nondeductible (§ 162(f)). The Second Circuit, quoting Commissioner v. Tellier (p. 312), noted that "the federal income tax is a tax on net income, not a sanction against wrongdoing" and pointed out that Stephens had paid tax on the funds he had stolen, so that denial of a deduction would, in a sense, impose a "double" tax. The court concluded that allowing Stephens a deduction would not "severely and immediately frustrate public policy."

5. *Problems.*

(1) L erected an apartment complex in University City at a cost of $1,000,000. A local ordinance required L to obtain a five-year occupancy permit from the University City Housing Authority before renting apartments. An occupancy permit can be issued only after an inspection by the Housing Authority indicates that the project complies with the local housing code.

After inspecting L's complex, the inspector from the Housing Authority told L that he had detected several minor, technical violations of the housing code. The inspector stressed that the violations would not impair tenant safety and that L could probably get a waiver of the violations if he appealed to the Housing Board. Unfortunately, he added, the appeal process would take several months, and the project could not be opened until the appeal was decided. L thereupon offered the inspector $5000 if he would not report the violations. The inspector accepted the payment and the Housing Authority issued an occupancy permit. Can L deduct the $5000 payment?

(2) L was indicted on charges arising out of the transaction described in (1). He was tried, convicted, and sentenced to six months in jail and a $10,000 fine. L paid a lawyer $3000 for defending the case. What, if anything, can L deduct? (Note Commissioner v. Tellier, p. 312, above.)

6. *Illegal drug sales.* Note § 280E. Suppose a drug dealer spends $100,000 to acquire a supply of his product, sells the goods at retail for $200,000, and pays salaries of $20,000 to employees or independent contractors who help to arrange the sales and deliver the drugs. What is the dealer's taxable income?

*

Chapter Five

INTEREST INCOME AND DEDUCTIONS

Interest is includable in the lender's income under § 61(a)(4) unless § 103 applies. As to deductibility by the borrower, § 163(a) seems to say that all interest can be deducted. However, several Code provisions limit or deny altogether the deductibility of many kinds of interest. Section 163(a) really means only that interest is deductible unless some other provision denies a deduction.

A. SOME FORMS OF INTEREST

The simplest form of interest is an explicit annual (or more frequent) charge of a percentage of a loan for the period in which the loan remains outstanding. But other ways of charging for the "use or forbearance of money" are common.

"Points." Banks often charge "loan processing fees," or "points," to borrowers. These fees serve to avoid statutory limits on interest charges and to enable banks to advertise interest rates that are lower than the true rates. The Service and the Tax Court treat points as interest unless they are paid for such "services" as preparing and reviewing documents, doing the paper work required for FHA and VA mortgage loans, and appraising the property that secures the loan. See Rev.Rul. 67–297, 1967–2 C.B. 87; Rev.Rul. 69–188, 1969–1 C.B. 54; Wilkerson v. Commissioner, 70 T.C. 240 (1978), reversed on other grounds 655 F.2d 980 (9th Cir.1981). This distinction is not a happy one; a lender who charges interest in the conventional way typically uses some of the money collected to cover costs of this sort, and the borrower pays the costs "for the use or forbearance of money" whether the payments take the form of points or conventional interest. See Asimow, The Interest Deduction, 24 U.C.L.A. L.Rev. 749, 763–67 (1977).

Most "points" on loans other than home-mortgage loans cannot be deducted when paid, but rather must be written off over the term of the loan under § 461(g).

"Carrying charges." Section 163(b) contains a formula for allocating carrying charges on installment-purchase contracts between interest and other payments ("finance charges" or "service charges").

"Imputed interest" under §§ 483 and 1274. If Seller sells property to Buyer for $10,000 to be paid five years after the transfer of the property, it makes sense to treat part of the $10,000 payment as interest, since sellers charge (and buyers pay) for delay in paying the purchase price. Under § 483 or § 1274, which will be examined at p. 677, below, both the seller and the buyer must treat part of the deferred purchase price on most sales as interest if the agreement does not provide for stated interest at an adequate rate.

B. THE TIMING OF INTEREST INCOME AND DEDUCTIONS: ORIGINAL–ISSUE DISCOUNT

Suppose A lends $10,000 to B Corp. today, with B to repay $26,532.98 in 10 years. The $16,532.98 difference between the stated redemption price at maturity of the instrument ($26,532.98) and the price at which it was issued to A ($10,000) is called "original issue discount" ("OID"); § 1273(a)(1). OID represents another form of interest. When should A report this interest as income, and when should B deduct[a] it?

The Code once required straight-line reporting by both lender and borrower, so that A would report $1653.30 in interest each year, and B would get an annual $1653.30 deduction. Straight-line reporting of OID bore little relation to economic reality. A loan which requires all interest to be paid at the end of the loan period—10 years, in the example—is economically equivalent to a loan which requires more frequent payment (every six months, say), with the lender then re-lending each interest payment to the borrower. Consider, for example, a case in which A lends $10,000 to B on January 1, 2003, with B to repay $26,532.98 to A on January 1, 2013. This loan is economically identical to a series of smaller loans (each requiring a payment of interest every 6 months, at a 10–percent annual rate), as follows:

(1) Original loan of $10,000 on January 1, 2003.

(2) A receives $500 in interest from B on July 1, 2003, and immediately lends that $500 to B.

(3) A receives $525 in interest from B on January 1, 2004, and lends that $525 to B. The reason that this interest payment is $525 rather than $500 is that it consists of $500 interest on the original $10,000 loan plus $25 interest on the second loan.

---

a. All the examples in this section will assume that the interest in question is fully deductible by the borrower.

(4) *A* receives $551.25 on July 1, 2004 ($500 on the first loan, $25 on the second loan, and $26.25 on the third loan), and lends *B* $551.25.

(5) Etc., for each 6–month period.

Note that if the parties had actually made the series of loans described above, the first year's interest would have been only $1025, not $1653.30. Straight-line reporting overstates interest in the early years of a loan and understates interest in later years. That is, straight-line reporting ignores the fact that interest is compounded.

Today § 1272 requires that OID be reported by both lender and borrower on a "constant-rate" basis. This means that the parties (regardless of their accounting methods) are taxed as if they had actually paid, received, and re-lent interest at regular intervals. The compounding period is 6 months; i.e., interest is treated as compounded semi-annually. The interest rate used for the calculations is whatever interest rate makes the total amount of interest over the term of the loan equal the amount of the discount. In the example above—a $10,000 loan on which the lender will receive $26,532.98 in 10 years—the interest rate is 10 percent, because an investment of $10,000 at 10 percent, compounded semi-annually, will grow to $26,532.98 in 10 years.[b]

Why did Congress think it necessary to change from the simple straight-line method to the much-more-complex constant-rate method? As noted above, the straight-line method overtaxes the lender in the early years of a loan, and undertaxes the borrower; in later years, these positions are reversed. If everyone were taxed at the same rate, the change would not have been worth making because overtaxation of one party would simply offset undertaxation of the other. But when a low-tax or tax-exempt lender (like a pension trust or a university) bought an OID obligation from a high-bracket issuer, the issuer was better off than if it had borrowed in a conventional way because it got its interest deductions earlier. The lender was little or no worse off, because it paid little or no tax. In short, straight-line reporting always produced a tax advantage (net to both parties) when the borrower was in a higher bracket than the lender, and always produced a tax detriment when the borrower was in a lower bracket than the lender. Well-advised people engaged in these transactions only when the borrower was subject to a higher rate of tax than the lender.

Notes

1. *Loans with low periodic interest payments.* The examples in the text assumed, for simplicity, that no interest was payable over the life of the loan. Suppose a loan calls for semi-annual payments of interest at one percent, with a large "balloon" payment at the end. This loan also

b. The future-value table in Appendix A is based on annual, rather than semi-annual, compounding. To derive correct results for semi-annual compounding from the table, divide the interest rate by two and double the number of years. That is, the future value of $1.00 after 10 years at 10 percent, compounded semi-annually, is the same as the future value of $1.00 after 20 years at 5 percent, compounded annually.

involves OID, but that discount is only a part of the interest; the stated interest is interest too. Suppose, for instance, that L lends $10,000 to B, who agrees to pay L $100 in interest every six months plus a final payment of $25,000 in 10 years. This debt has $15,000 of OID and $200 a year in interest in addition to that OID. Section 1272 applies to the OID.

2. *Exceptions.* Section 1272(a)(2) describes a number of obligations which involve OID but which are exempt from § 1272. Note particularly § 1272(a)(2)(C), excluding obligations with a maturity date of one year or less. If a cash-method investor buys a one-year certificate of deposit from a bank, paying $10,000 and receiving $10,500 in one year, no income need be reported until the certificate matures.

3. *Market-discount bonds.* The discussion above focuses on discount arising at the original issuance of a debt instrument. But what happens if an instrument, originally issued for its face (principal) amount, is later purchased at a lower price (maybe because of a general increase in interest rates)? For example, X Corp. issues a $1000 bond to A for $1000. Several years later, and after an increase in interest rates, B purchases the bond from A for $900 when the bond has a remaining maturity of ten years. The $100 difference between the bond's stated redemption price ($1000) and B's basis immediately after acquisition ($900) is "market discount" and the bond is a "market-discount bond"; § 1278(a). Unlike the taxpayer who buys a bond with OID, B can postpone the recognition of income until she disposes of the bond, but upon disposition the accrued market discount (computed under the straight-line method) is treated as ordinary income; § 1276(a). So, if B holds the bond until maturity, the $100 difference between her amount realized ($1,000) and her adjusted basis ($900) is ordinary income.

Suppose instead that B held the bond for five years and then sold it to C for $960, producing a gain of $60. At the time of sale, the accrued market discount would be $50 (5/10 of $100); § 1276(b)(1). B would thus have to recognize $50 of ordinary gain (equal to the accrued market discount) and $10 of capital gain.

Section 1276 applies only if a market-discount bond is disposed of at a gain. If the bond is sold at a loss, the loss is a capital loss; the holder is not required to recognize market discount as income, thus increasing her basis and generating a larger capital loss. So, in the above example, if B had sold the bond for $890, B would have had no ordinary income and a capital loss of $10.

Under § 1276(b)(2), the holder of a market-discount bond can elect to compute the accrued market discount on the basis of a constant interest rate instead of using the straight-line method. As the above discussion of OID suggests, the holder will often have less ordinary income if the election is made. (Even if an election is made, the accrued market discount is not includable in income until the bond is disposed of, though § 1278(b) permits a taxpayer to elect to include market discount (as interest) currently.)

4. *Interest on "junk bonds."* Debt instruments which pay very high interest—so-called "junk bonds"—are likely to be risky: that is why the interest is so high. If a particular loan carries a high risk that it will not be repaid, the loan may resemble an equity investment in the borrower's activity more closely than it does a normal loan, because the "lender's" chance of repayment depends a great deal on the success of the "borrower's" business. Section 163(e)(5), which was added to the Code in 1989, limits the deductibility of interest on some corporate "high yield obligations" in two ways. First, the "disqualified portion" of any OID on a high-yield obligation cannot be deducted at all. (Section 163(e)(5)(C) defines "disqualified portion"; non-technically, it might be described as the "most excessive" part of the interest.) Second, the issuer of a high-yield OID obligation cannot deduct even the deductible portion of the interest until payment (though the lender must still include the interest in income under the OID rules).

The definition of a high-yield obligation is complex. The basic notion is that long-term obligations bearing interest at rates exceeding the "applicable Federal rate" of § 1274(d) by more than five percent are suspect if the instrument has "significant" OID. See § 163(i) for the details.

The enactment of § 163(e) probably owes as much to a Congressional sense that paying very high interest is somehow "bad for the economy" as to concerns about sound tax policy. However, neither this concern nor a belief that very-high-yield obligations look more like equity than debt can explain why the new legislation is limited to OID obligations. That feature of the legislation probably stems from the fact that the obligations with which Congress was concerned typically are deeply discounted, rather than from any principled distinction between discount and other forms of interest.

5. *References.* Lokken, The Time Value of Money Rules, 42 Tax L.Rev. 1 (1986); Canellos & Kleinbard, The Miracle of Compound Interest: Interest Deferral and Discount After 1982, 38 Tax L.Rev. 565 (1983).

C. DEDUCTIBLE AND NONDEDUCTIBLE INTEREST

Under § 163(a), "interest paid or accrued within the taxable year on indebtedness" is deductible by the payor. But this general rule is limited by a number of Code provisions which deny deductibility to many kinds of interest:

(1) Interest on indebtedness "incurred or continued to purchase or carry" tax-exempt bonds cannot be deducted; § 265(a)(2).

(2) Interest which is treated as an expense of a "passive activity," such as renting property, is deductible only against income from passive activities if the taxpayer is an individual; § 469. (Passive activities will be examined in Chapter 8.)

(3) Interest on indebtedness "incurred or continued to purchase or carry" certain life-insurance and annuity contracts cannot be deducted because of § 264. Compare Knetsch v. United States, p. 418, below, which involved taxable years before the enactment of § 264(a).

(4) Investment interest, as defined in § 163(d)(3), can be deducted by a non-corporate taxpayer only to the extent of the taxpayer's "net investment income" for the year.

(5) Interest costs allocable to the construction of real property or other property with a long useful life must be capitalized if the property has an "estimated production period" of more than two years or if the estimated production period is more than one year and the property costs more than one million dollars; § 263A(f).

(6) "Personal interest" incurred by a non-corporate taxpayer is not deductible. Section 163(h) defines personal interest as all interest other than interest listed in §§ 163(h)(2)(A)–(F). Of particular importance to middle-income taxpayers is the deductibility of "qualified residence interest" as defined in § 163(h)(3).

The existence of Code sections which disallow deductions for some (but not all) interest payments creates serious problems of how to assign interest to activities. Because interest is a cost of obtaining current cash, a taxpayer who borrows money "to buy" a particular asset can be thought of not only as incurring the interest for the purpose of buying that asset, but also as incurring it for the purpose of keeping whatever other assets the taxpayer could have sold to raise the cash. Consider, for example, an interesting Canadian case, The Queen v. Bronfman Trust, 86 D.T.C. 5059 (Sup. Ct. of Canada 1987). The Canadian Income Tax act allowed a deduction for interest on "borrowed money used for the purpose of earning income from a business or property." The trustees wanted to make a large cash distribution to a beneficiary. They could have raised the money by selling some of the trust's securities, but they thought it wise to keep the securities and borrow money for the distribution. The Court of Appeal allowed the deduction because the borrowing enabled the trust to keep its income-producing assets. The Supreme Court reversed on the ground that keeping the securities was only an "indirect" use of the borrowed funds. The materials that follow will explore the ways in which Congress, the courts, and the Service have dealt with this problem under the Internal Revenue Code.

1. SECTION 265(a)(2)

WISCONSIN CHEESEMAN, INC. v. UNITED STATES

United States Court of Appeals, Seventh Circuit, 1968.
388 F.2d 420.

Before KILEY, SWYGERT and CUMMINGS, CIRCUIT JUDGES.

CUMMINGS, CIRCUIT JUDGE.

This lawsuit involves the proper construction of Section 265[(a)](2). The question for resolution is whether the taxpayer may deduct from its gross income the interest it paid on its mortgage and some of its short-term loans.

Taxpayer is located in Sun Prairie, Wisconsin, and is in the business of packaging fancy cheeses for sale as Christmas gifts. Its business is seasonal and is most active during the last three months of each calendar year. Its sales are solicited exclusively through a catalog mailed each October. It incurs high costs in the last three months of each calendar year. Funds are borrowed annually from September through early November to cover such costs.

During the three fiscal years ending July 31, 1960, 1961 and 1962, taxpayer obtained short-term bank loans to meet its recurring needs for working capital. These borrowings took place each fall and were repaid, from late November through January, out of the receipts of each year's sales. The balance of the receipts was used to purchase municipal bonds and treasury bills. The treasury bills were acquired with staggered maturity dates to meet the off-season needs of the business. They were reduced to cash by the middle of each July. The municipal bonds were used as collateral for the bank loans, enabling taxpayer to borrow almost 100% of their value. On August 1, 1959, taxpayer had municipal bond holdings of $138,168.29. By July 31, 1962, these holdings had increased to $218,542.70.

In the second of the fiscal years involved, in order to build a new plant, taxpayer borrowed $69,360 from a bank. This loan was secured by a mortgage upon its real estate. The proceeds of the loan were used to pay for construction and not directly to purchase municipal bonds.

For these taxable fiscal years, the Commissioner of Internal Revenue disallowed taxpayer's deductions of interest on the mortgage and on some of the short-term loans. The taxpayer paid the resulting assessments and later brought this refund suit against the United States.

The District Court held that taxpayer incurred the indebtedness to "carry obligations * * * the interest on which is wholly exempt" from Federal income tax within the meaning of Section 265[(a)](2). Therefore, judgment was entered for the United States. We agree as to the interest on the short-term loans but not as to the mortgage interest.

INTEREST ON SHORT-TERM LOANS

During each fall in the years in question, taxpayer used its municipal bonds as collateral for short-term bank loans for essential working capital. Instead of resorting to bank loans, taxpayer could have sold its municipals to meet the high cost seasonal needs of its business. Because this alternative was available to taxpayer, the Government argues that the short-term indebtedness was automatically incurred in order to enable taxpayer to "carry [tax-exempt] obligations," so that the interest on this indebtedness would be non-deductible under Section 265[(a)](2). The District Court construed Section 265[(a)](2) as forbidding the deduction of interest on indebtedness incurred or continued "in order to" or "for the purpose of" carrying tax-exempt obligations. We approve this construction but do not believe deduction is forbidden whenever taxpayer has an alternative of liquidating tax-exempts in lieu of borrowing.

The taxpayer contends that the short-term loans were incurred for the purpose of meeting its heavy fall seasonal financing needs, whereas the Government contends that the indebtedness was incurred for the purpose of making it possible for taxpayer to carry its municipal securities. In holding that the interest on the short-term loans could not be deducted, the District Court stated:

> "To accomplish the purpose of obtaining cash to meet plaintiff's seasonal needs, it was not a condition precedent that indebtedness be incurred. To accomplish the purpose of carrying the municipal securities, it was a condition precedent that indebtedness be incurred."

In reaching its conclusion that no refund was due, the District Court construed the Congressional intent as not to grant a deduction for interest payments by a taxpayer who holds securities, the interest from which is not taxable. This is the double benefit prohibited by Section 265[(a)](2). Stated another way, Congress sought to prevent a taxpayer from requiring the United States to finance its investments. United States v. Atlas Life Insurance Co., 381 U.S. 233, 247.

In our view, the taxpayer is not *ipso facto* deprived of a deduction for interest on indebtedness while holding tax-exempt securities. The Government has not convinced us that interest deduction can be allowed only where the taxpayer shows that he wanted to sell the tax-exempt securities but could not. For example, Congress certainly did not intend to deny deductibility to a taxpayer who holds salable municipals and takes out a mortgage to buy a home instead of selling the municipals. As the Court of Claims stated in Illinois Terminal Railroad Company v. United States, 375 F.2d 1016, 1021 (Ct.Cl.1967):

> "It is necessary [for the Commissioner] to establish a sufficiently direct relationship of the continuance of the debt for the purpose of carrying the tax-exempt bonds."

This construction flows from the use of "to" in Section 265[(a)](2). In this case, this nexus or "sufficiently direct relationship" is established by the fact that the tax-exempt securities were used as collateral for the seasonal loans. Under Section 265[(a)](2), it is clear that a taxpayer may not deduct interest on indebtedness when the proceeds of the loan are used to buy tax-exempts. 4A Mertens, Law of Federal Income Taxation (1966 ed.) § 26.13 and cases cited. Applying the rule that the substance of the transaction is controlling in determining the tax liability, the same result should follow when the tax-exempt securities are used as collateral for a loan. Surely one who borrows to buy tax-exempts and one who borrows against tax-exempts already owned are in virtually the same economic position. Section 265[(a)](2) makes no distinction between them.

In addition, our analysis of the statute and its legislative history convinces us that the deduction should not be allowed if a taxpayer could reasonably have foreseen at the time of purchasing the tax-exempts that a loan would probably be required to meet future economic needs of an ordinary, recurrent variety. This test would not permit this taxpayer to deduct the short-term loan interest, for its regular business pattern shows that it would have to go into debt each fall if it bought or kept municipals as a long-term investment. This established course of conduct is convincing proof that the underlying reason for these recurring loans was to carry the municipals.

To support its position, taxpayer relies on subsequent legislative history. However, subsequent legislative history is rarely of persuasive weight. United States v. United Mine Workers of America, 330 U.S. 258, 282. Furthermore, subsequent legislative history only indicates that Section 265[(a)](2) was not intended to operate as a "mechanical rule." Here we are not applying a mechanical rule but are insisting upon a connection between the tax-exempt securities and the loans before interest deductibility is disallowed.

* * *

INTEREST ON MORTGAGE

The $69,360 construction loan was secured by a ten-year 6% mortgage on taxpayer's real estate. No municipal bonds were put up as collateral. The mortgage was for a new plant to meet a growing demand. The entire $69,360 mortgage proceeds were used to pay for this plant. According to the uncontroverted testimony, if taxpayer had sold municipal bonds to pay for the plant, it would have had fewer liquid assets to meet seasonal needs and would have had difficulty in borrowing to meet those needs. Plant construction is undeniably a major, non-recurrent expenditure and is usually financed over a long term. We cannot say that a reasonable person would sacrifice liquidity and security by selling municipals in lieu of incurring mortgage debt to finance a new plant. Business reasons dominated the mortgaging of the property. Therefore, we are unwilling to accept the Commissioner's view that taxpayer should have liquidated municipals instead of obtaining a real estate mortgage loan. There is an insufficient relationship between the mortgage indebtedness and the holding of the municipal bonds to justify denial of deduction of the mortgage interest. For non-deductibility, we have seen that the Commissioner must establish a sufficiently direct relationship between the debt and the carrying of the tax-exempt bonds. That has not been done as to the mortgage, so that the mortgage interest deductions must be allowed under Section 163(a).

The judgment is affirmed in part and reversed in part and the cause is remanded.

REVENUE PROCEDURE 72–18

1972–1 C.B. 740.

Section 1. Purpose

The purpose of this Revenue Procedure is to set forth guidelines for taxpayers and field offices of the Internal Revenue Service for the application of section 265[(a)](2) * * * to certain taxpayers holding state and local obligations the interest on which is wholly exempt from Federal income tax. * * *

* * *

Sec. 3. General Rules

.01 Section 265[(a)](2) of the Code is only applicable where the indebtedness is incurred or continued for the purpose of purchasing or carrying tax-exempt securities. Accordingly, the application of section 265[(a)](2) requires a determination, based on all the facts and circumstances, as to the taxpayer's purpose in incurring or continuing each item of indebtedness. Such purpose may, however, be established either by direct evidence or by circumstantial evidence.

.02 Direct evidence of a purpose to *purchase* tax-exempt obligations exists where the proceeds of indebtedness are used for, and are directly traceable to, the purchase of tax-exempt obligations. Wynn v. United States, 411 F.2d 614 (1969), certiorari denied 396 U.S. 1008 (1970). Section 265[(a)](2) does not apply, however, where proceeds of a bona fide business indebtedness are temporarily invested in tax-exempt obligations under circumstances similar to those set forth in Revenue Ruling 55–389, C.B. 1955–1, 276.

.03 Direct evidence of a purpose to carry tax-exempt obligations exists where tax-exempt obligations are used as collateral for indebtedness. "[O]ne who borrows to buy tax-exempts and one who borrows against tax-exempts already owned are in virtually the same economic position. Section 265[(a)](2) makes no distinction between them." Wisconsin Cheeseman v. United States, 388 F.2d 420, at 422 (1968).

.04 In the absence of direct evidence linking indebtedness with the purchase or carrying of tax-exempt obligations as illustrated in paragraphs .02 and .03 above, section 265[(a)](2) of the Code will apply only if the totality of facts and circumstances supports a reasonable inference that the purpose to purchase or carry tax-exempt obligations exists. Stated alternatively, section 265[(a)](2) will apply only where the totality of facts and circumstances establishes a "sufficiently direct relationship" between the borrowing and the investment in tax-exempt obligations. See *Wisconsin Cheeseman,* 388 F.2d 420, at 422. * * *

* * *

Sec. 4. Guidelines for Individuals

* * *

.04 Generally, a purpose to carry tax-exempt obligations will be inferred, unless rebutted by other evidence, wherever the taxpayer has outstanding indebtedness which is not directly connected with personal expenditures * * * and is not incurred or continued in connection with the active conduct of a trade or business * * * and the taxpayer owns tax-exempt obligations. This inference will be made even though the indebtedness is ostensibly incurred or continued to purchase or carry other portfolio investments.

Portfolio investment for the purposes of this Revenue Procedure includes transactions entered into for profit (including investment in real estate) which are not connected with the active conduct of a trade or business. Purchase and sale of securities shall not constitute the active conduct of a trade or business unless the taxpayer is a dealer in securities within the meaning of section 1.471–5 of the Income Tax Regulations. A substantial ownership interest in a corporation will not be considered a portfolio investment. For example, where a taxpayer owns at least 80 percent of the voting stock of a corporation that is engaged in the active conduct of a trade or business, the investment in such controlling interest shall not be considered to be a portfolio investment.

A sufficiently direct relationship between the incurring or continuing of indebtedness and the purchasing or carrying of tax-exempt obligations will generally exist where indebtedness is incurred to finance portfolio investment because the choice of whether to finance a new portfolio investment through borrowing or through the liquidation of an existing investment in tax-exempt obligations typically involves a purpose either to maximize profit or to maintain a diversified portfolio. This purpose necessarily involves a decision, whether articulated by the taxpayer or not, to incur (or continue) the indebtedness, at least in part, to purchase or carry the existing investment in tax-exempt obligations.

A taxpayer may rebut the presumption that section 265[(a)](2) applies in the above circumstances by establishing that he could not have liquidated his holdings of tax-exempt obligations in order to avoid incurring indebtedness. The presumption may be overcome where, for example, liquidation is not possible because the tax-exempt obligations cannot be sold. The presumption would not be rebutted, however, by a showing that the tax-exempt obligations could only have been liquidated with difficulty or at a loss; or that the taxpayer owned other investment assets such as common stock that could have been liquidated; or that an investment advisor recommended that a prudent man should maintain a particular percentage of assets in tax-exempt obligations. Similarly, the presumption would not be rebutted by a showing that liquidating the holdings of tax-exempt obligations would not have produced sufficient cash to equal the amount borrowed.

The provisions of this paragraph may be illustrated by the following example:

Taxpayer A, an individual, owns common stock listed on a national securities exchange, having an adjusted basis of $200,000; he owns rental property having an adjusted basis of $200,000; he has cash of $10,000; and he owns readily marketable municipal bonds having an adjusted basis of $41,000. A borrows $100,000 to invest in a limited partnership interest in a real estate syndicate and pays $8,000 interest on the loan which he claims as an interest deduction for the taxable year. Under these facts and circumstances, there is a presumption that the $100,000 indebtedness which is incurred to finance A's portfolio investment is also incurred to carry A's existing investment in tax-exempt bonds since there are no additional facts or circumstances to rebut the presumption. Accordingly, a portion of the $8,000 interest payment will be disallowed under section 265[(a)](2) of the Code.

* * *

SEC. 7.   PROCEDURES

.01 When there is direct evidence under sections 3.02 and 3.03 establishing a purpose to purchase or carry tax-exempt obligations (either because tax-exempt obligations were used as collateral for indebtedness or the proceeds of indebtedness were directly traceable to the holding of particular tax-exempt obligations) no part of the interest paid or incurred on such indebtedness may be deducted. However, if only a fractional part of the indebtedness is directly traceable to the holding of particular tax-exempt obligations, the same fractional part of the interest paid or incurred on such indebtedness will be disallowed. For example, if A borrows $100,000 from a bank and invests $75,000 of the proceeds in tax-exempt obligations, 75 percent of the interest paid on the bank borrowing would be disallowed as a deduction.

.02 In any other case where interest is to be disallowed in accordance with this Revenue Procedure, an allocable portion of the interest on such indebtedness will be disallowed. The amount of interest on such indebtedness to be disallowed shall be determined by multiplying the total interest on such indebtedness by a fraction, the numerator of which is the average amount during the taxable year of the taxpayer's tax-exempt obligations (valued at their adjusted basis) and the denominator of which is the average amount during the taxable year of the taxpayer's total assets (valued at their adjusted basis) minus the amount of any indebtedness the interest on which is not subject to disallowance to any extent under this Revenue Procedure.

Notes

1. *Policy issues.* Those who support § 265(a)(2) argue that it prevents taxpayers from obtaining the "double tax benefit" of both excluding income from an investment in tax-exempt bonds and also deducting a cost of making that investment. Another way of putting it is to say that

a taxpayer who borrows at 10 percent to buy tax-exempt bonds paying 7 percent has engaged in a transaction that loses money before tax, but which would produce an after-tax profit if the interest deduction were allowed (assuming a taxpayer subject to income tax of more than 30 percent). Were it not for § 265(a)(2), high-income wage earners could reduce their taxes by borrowing money and buying tax-exempt bonds with the borrowed funds. Allowing this would make the highest income-tax rates elective.

One weakness in the arguments outlined above can be illustrated by using a tax-expenditure analysis. The exclusion from income of interest on tax-exempt bonds creates a sort of revenue-sharing program. Because the bonds are tax exempt, they pay less interest than otherwise-identical taxable bonds, which hurts the investors who buy the tax-exempt bonds but helps the states and cities which issue them. The tax-exempt bond program is similar in principle and in practice to a program under which interest on state and local bonds is taxed and most of the taxes collected are paid to the issuers of the bonds. Under that kind of "direct" spending program, interest incurred to buy the bonds would be deductible. It can be argued that the "implicit tax" paid by those who buy tax-exempt bonds should not be treated differently from an actual tax. Both the implicit tax and an actual tax paid over to the issuers have similar effects on both issuers and buyers of the bonds.

Another argument against § 265(a)(2) is that the disallowance of the interest deduction discriminates arbitrarily against those who need to borrow to purchase tax-exempt bonds. Some taxpayers who hold taxable bonds paying 10 percent interest can make an after-tax profit by selling those bonds and buying tax-exempt bonds paying 7 percent; indeed, § 103 is intended to induce just that kind of behavior. In practice, therefore, §§ 103 and 265(a)(2) have the effect of giving a tax incentive for buying state and local bonds to people with incomes from property, but not to people with earned incomes.

For discussions of these and other issues, see Oliver, Section 265(2): A Counterproductive Solution to a Nonexistent Problem, 40 Tax L.Rev. 351 (1985), and Klein, Borrowing to Finance Tax–Favored Investments, 1962 Wis.L.Rev. 608.

2. *Section 265(a)(1).* Deductions under § 212 for costs other than interest which are "allocable to" tax-exempt interest are disallowed by § 265(a)(1). That section also disallows deductions for amounts allocable to tax-exempt income other than interest.

ATTRIBUTING INTEREST TO ACTIVITIES

As *Wisconsin Cheeseman* and Rev.Proc. 72–18 show, an income tax which allows deductions for some but not all interest payments must have rules for attributing indebtedness to particular activities. Current law uses four techniques for meeting this need: tracing, allocating, stacking, and looking to the property which secures the debt in question.

Tracing. Wisconsin Cheeseman shows how difficult it is to "trace" interest to particular activities on the basis of the taxpayer's purpose for incurring a debt. One problem with "purpose" tests is that most decisions to borrow are also decisions not to sell assets. A taxpayer who owns a debt-free house worth $100,000 and who borrows $100,000 "for the purpose of" buying tax-exempt bonds can be thought of as having a purpose of keeping the house as well: one way to buy the bonds would be to sell the house, and so the taxpayer's borrowing can be plausibly described as either "keeping the house" or "buying the bonds." In practice, it seems clear that a taxpayer who has owned a house outright for many years and who then borrows and buys tax-exempt bonds with the proceeds would be denied an interest deduction under § 265(a)(2). A taxpayer who has owned municipal bonds for several years, and who borrows and uses the proceeds to buy a house, would be allowed an interest deduction.

Some of the difficulties which arise in using "purpose" versions of tracing can be avoided by tracing on a flow-of-funds basis, but only at the cost of considerable arbitrariness. Consider, for example, a taxpayer who has $200,000 cash in the bank and who borrows another $200,000. The taxpayer then buys a $200,000 house and $200,000 worth of municipal bonds. One way to determine whether the debt was incurred to purchase the bonds or to purchase the house might be to find out whether the taxpayer used the money in the bank account or the borrowed money to pay for the bonds. Needless to say, this kind of tracing puts a premium on tax planning. The temporary regulations under § 163 use a form of flow-of-funds tracing to identify investment interest, personal interest, and interest associated with passive activities.

Allocating. Note Rev.Proc. 72–18's treatment of interest incurred to purchase portfolio investments. This technique—"allocating" the debt in question among the taxpayer's assets without regard to which funds went where or to the taxpayer's purpose—could in principle be used across the board. That is, a taxpayer's debt could be allocated among all assets held by the taxpayer either according to the assets' values or according to their bases. For a proposal along these lines, see Note, The Deductibility of Interest Costs by a Taxpayer Holding Tax–Exempt Obligations: A Neutral Principle of Allocation, 61 Va.L.Rev. 211 (1975).

Stacking. Stacking resembles allocation except that debt is assigned to particular assets (or activities) in some arbitrary order. For an example of stacking, see § 263A(f)(2)(A)(ii). Under this section, any interest cost which the taxpayer could have avoided by using money spent on "production expenditures" to pay off debt is "allocated" to the production of property. In other words, the taxpayer's debt is treated as being incurred to finance production expenditures to the extent of those expenditures.

Security. Under § 163(h), which will be examined in more detail below, interest on a debt secured by a mortgage on a "qualified residence" can be deducted (within limits, and subject to some exceptions).

In many cases, interest on a properly secured debt can be deducted without regard to the taxpayer's purpose for borrowing or use of the loan proceeds.

2. OTHER TAX–ARBITRAGE SITUATIONS

The kind of transaction which § 265(a)(2) sometimes prevents—paying deductible interest in order to obtain a non-taxable return—is an arbitrage transaction, which taxpayers would engage in even at a pre-tax cost in order to take advantage of differential tax rates on different kinds of income. Possibilities for this kind of arbitrage are not limited to tax-exempt bonds. The existence of any kind of favorably taxed investment will encourage some taxpayers with heavily taxed incomes, like salaries, to borrow (thus reducing their taxable incomes by deducting interest) and to use the borrowed funds to purchase assets which produce tax-favored income.

Section 163(d) limits deductions for "investment interest." The concern here is the same as in the case of borrowing to purchase or carry tax-exempt bonds: many investments produce gains in the form of unrealized appreciation. This kind of gain is at worst deferred and at best tax-free because of § 1014(a). For a useful discussion of Congress's reasons for limiting the deductibility of investment interest and for an application of those reasons to a particular problem, see Estate of Yaeger v. Commissioner, p. 294, above.

Sections 264(a)(2), (3) and (4) limit deductions for interest on debts incurred to obtain a particular kind of tax-deferred investment return: increase in the value of insurance and annuity contracts attributable to "inside buildup," which is not taxed to the policy holder.

In recent years, Congress has encouraged investment in tangible income-producing assets by allowing accelerated depreciation, and in some cases expensing, of the costs of the assets. Assets entitled to this tax treatment therefore produce a kind of tax-favored income, and some commentators have argued that interest incurred to purchase those assets should be made non-deductible. For discussions, see Hickman, Interest, Depreciation, and Indexing, 5 Va.Tax Rev. 773 (1986); Warren, Accelerated Capital Recovery, Debt, and Tax Arbitrage, 38 The Tax Lawyer 549 (1985); Johnson, Tax Shelter Gain: The Mismatch of Debt and Supply Side Depreciation, 61 Tex.L.Rev. 1013 (1983).

3. PERSONAL INTEREST

Until the enactment of the Tax Reform Act of 1986, interest was deductible under § 163(a) unless some other provision, such as § 265(a)(2), made it nondeductible. This meant that "personal" interest, such as interest on a loan taken out to finance a vacation trip, was fully deductible. Today, the statutory pattern is reversed in the case of taxpayers other than corporations. Section 163(h)(1) disallows deductions for "personal interest," which is defined as all interest other than the six kinds of interest listed in § 163(h)(2). The term "personal interest" can be misleading: some kinds of interest not closely related to personal consumption are nondeductible. For example, individuals, estates, and trusts cannot deduct interest on income-tax deficiencies because § 163(h)(2) does not list that kind of interest.[c]

Whether deductions should be allowed for interest on debt incurred for personal consumption—to buy a house or to take a vacation, for example—has been controversial. The case against the deduction rests on a belief that interest incurred "for consumption" is simply a cost of consumption, which should be nondeductible just like other consumption costs. Under this view, the deductibility of home-mortgage interest is a subsidy for home ownership. In one respect, however, interest differs from other consumption-type outlays. Unlike the purchase price of a house or a vacation trip, interest payments enable the borrower to have the house or trip earlier rather than later, but they do not pay for the house or the trip itself. One can look at "consumer interest" as a cost of pulling one's stream of future earnings into the present; viewed in that way, interest seems to be as much a cost "of earning later" as a cost "of consuming earlier."

Under the Schanz–Haig–Simons definition of income (p. 50, above), income is the sum of the taxpayer's "savings" and "consumption." Should a taxpayer who pays $100 in interest to take a $1000 vacation trip this year rather than next year be viewed as having "consumed" $1100 or $1000? If the taxpayer had been able to pay for the trip without borrowing, the consumption expense would have been $1000. Schanz himself thought that all interest should be deductible; see Simons, Personal Income Taxation 61 (1938).

One argument for allowing consumer interest to be deducted is that the deduction helps to equate the tax treatment of people with incomes from property with that of people with earned incomes. Someone who owns income-producing property can give up future (taxable) income in exchange for current consumption by selling the property and spending the proceeds. A wage-earner who borrows for current consumption also gives up future income, in the sense that some future earnings will go to pay off interest on the debt. If consumer interest cannot be deducted, the wage-earner will remain taxable on the forgone future earnings.

Although Congress decided in 1986 to make personal interest generally nondeductible, it felt compelled for political reasons to continue to allow deductions for most home-mortgage interest. Section 163(h)(2)(D) says that "qualified residence interest" is not "personal interest." "Qualified residence interest," defined in § 163(h)(3), consists of interest on "acquisition indebtedness" (§ 163(h)(3)(B)) and on "home equity indebtedness" (§ 163(h)(3)(C)). By drawing a line between these kinds of

---

c. Temp.Treas.Reg. § 1.163–9T(b)(2)-(i)(A). The Tax Court has held this regulation invalid and has allowed deductions as "business interest" for interest paid on deficiencies attributable to the income of unincorporated businesses. Every court of appeals to consider the issue has reversed. For an opinion which evaluates the arguments, see Kikalos v. Commissioner, 190 F.3d 791 (7th Cir.1999).

debt—which give rise to deductible interest—and other non-business debts, Congress has put a premium on careful tax planning.

In addition to the kinds of interest that are deductible under § 163, some interest on student loans can be deducted under § 221, which was added to the Code in 1997 and expanded in 2001. Interest deductions allowed by this section are above-the-line deductions; § 62(a)(17). Generally speaking, up to $2500 a year in interest payments on "qualified education loans"—loans to pay such "qualified higher education expenses" as tuition, room, board, books, and supplies of the taxpayer, the taxpayer's spouse, or a dependent of the taxpayer for post-secondary education—are deductible. The deduction is phased out for upper-income taxpayers: the phaseout begins at modified AGI of $50,000 ($100,000 for joint returns) and is completed at modified AGI of $65,000 ($130,000 for joint returns). Beginning in 2003, the income levels for the phaseouts will be indexed, but the dollar limits on the amount of interest that is deductible will not be. A taxpayer who is someone else's dependent cannot take the deduction.

Problems and Note

1. *Problems.*

(1) *A* owns a house which cost $100,000 to buy and which is now worth $200,000. *A* borrows $150,000. The loan is secured by a mortgage on the house, which is *A*'s principal residence. *A* uses the loan proceeds to buy an airplane (flying is *A*'s hobby). How much of *A*'s $15,000 annual interest payment is deductible?

(2) *B* borrows $1,125,000 to buy a new principal residence. The loan is secured by a mortgage on the residence. How much of the $112,500 in interest that *B* pays in the first year of the loan can *B* deduct?

(3) Fifteen years after buying the house described in Problem (2), *B* owes a balance of $800,000 on the mortgage principal. Interest rates have dropped, so *B* refinances her loan, taking out a new $800,000 loan and paying off the balance of the original loan. How much of the interest on the new loan, which is secured by a mortgage on *B*'s house, can *B* deduct?

(4) *C* borrows $50,000, secured by a mortgage on his principal residence, and uses the loan proceeds to buy tax-exempt bonds. The residence had no mortgage on it until the loan in question. Can *C* deduct the interest on the loan?

(5) Same as Problem (4), except that *C* uses the loan proceeds to buy Acme Widget Works stock. Can *C* deduct the interest if he has no investment income for the year? See § 163(d)(3)(B)(i).

(6) *D* borrows $50,000, which she uses to buy a large boat. The boat, which will be used only for recreation, is equipped with bunks, a kitchen ("galley"), and a toilet ("head"). The loan is secured by a mortgage on

the boat. Under what circumstances can *D* deduct the interest on the loan?

(7) *E* owns a house worth $500,000; the mortgage was paid off many years ago. *E*, who expects to incur some $300,000 in personal expenses this year, would like to borrow the $300,000 and to deduct all of the interest on the debt. *E* is fond of her neighborhood and would not want to move away, but she would be willing to move to another house (to the one across the street, for example, which has just gone on the market). Under § 121, *E* would exclude from income any gain if she sold her house. Advise *E* about how to proceed.

(8) *G*'s estate holds income-producing securities and no other assets. The estate owes $100,000 in income taxes for its first taxable year. If the estate borrows $100,000 to pay this tax, can it deduct interest on the debt up to the amount of its net investment income for the year?

(9) *K* and *L*, husband and wife, graduated from law school two years ago. This year, they paid $4000 of interest on indebtedness incurred by them in financing their law-school education. Their only source of income is their salaries, and they file a joint return on which they take the standard deduction. To what extent can they deduct the interest paid if each is employed at an annual salary of $57,500? $70,000?

(10) *M* has AGI of $100,000, comprising $6000 of dividends and interest and $94,000 of salary. She also incurred stock-market investment expenses of $3000 for items other than interest and $7500 for interest. To what extent can *M* deduct the $7500 of interest in the current year?

2. References. Koppelman, Personal Deductions Under an Ideal Income Tax, 43 Tax L.Rev. 679 (1988); Asimow, The Interest Deduction, 24 U.C.L.A. L.Rev. 749 (1977); Vickrey, Agenda for Progressive Taxation 22–24 (1947).

TRACING UNDER § 163

Temporary (and proposed) Treas.Reg. § 1.163–8T (1987) prescribes tracing rules for §§ 163(d) and (h). Under the regulations, debt is ordinarily assigned to activities on a flow-of-funds version of tracing, so that someone who borrows $100,000, uses the borrowed money to pay business expenses, and then uses $100,000 of previously accumulated cash to buy a personal-use airplane can deduct the interest on the debt.

What of a taxpayer who places borrowed funds in a bank account which also contains the taxpayer's own money? The regulations say that expenditures made from the account are treated as made from the borrowed funds first. The dates on which checks are written control. See Temp.Treas.Reg. § 1.163–8T(c)(4). Under a special exception, however, taxpayers can elect to treat any expenditure made from an account within 15 days of the deposit of borrowed funds as being made from the debt proceeds; Temp.Treas.Reg. § 1.163–8T(c)(4)(iii).

Suppose a taxpayer borrows $12,000, uses half the money to pay business expenses, and spends the other half on a vacation trip. So long as none of the debt has been repaid, half the interest is deductible and the other half is not. What if the taxpayer then repays half the debt? The regulations deal with this problem by supplying a set of ordering rules. Generally speaking, the taxpayer is treated as paying off the least desirable portion of the debt (here, the personal-expenditure portion) first; Temp.Treas.Reg. § 1.163–8T(d).

The tracing rules of Temp.Treas.Reg. § 1.163–8T do not override the tracing rules under "disallowance provisions" such as § 265(a)(2). Therefore, interest on debt that would be treated as having been used to pay a business expense under the § 163 regulations but which would be treated as incurred to purchase or carry tax-exempt bonds under *Wisconsin Cheeseman* and Rev.Proc. 72–18 is not deductible; Temp.Treas.Reg. § 1.163–8T(m).

Problems

In each of these problems determine how much of *T*'s annual interest payment is deductible as business interest. If deductibility depends upon whether *T* makes an election, assume that she makes whatever election allows the greatest interest deduction.

Problem (1). *T* borrows $100,000 and deposits the borrowed funds in her checking account, which had a balance of $50,000 before the deposit. Five days later, *T* writes a $75,000 check on the account to buy a new personal car. Six days after that, *T* writes another $75,000 check to pay business expenses. *T* pays $10,000 interest on the loan.

Problem (2). Same as (1), except that the check for the business expenses was written 20 days after the loan proceeds were deposited.

Problem (3). At the end of the year in which the loan in (2) was made, *T* repaid half of the principal, leaving a $50,000 balance. During the next year, *T* pays $5000 interest on that remaining $50,000 debt.

D. INTEREST–FREE LOANS

Section 7872 requires that many interest-free and low-interest loans be recharacterized as loans bearing interest at arm's-length rates. The need for this kind of recharacterization can be shown by an example involving a corporation and its sole shareholder. Suppose that *S* owns all the stock of *C,* a corporation, and that *C* has on hand $100,000 in cash, which it does not need for its business. One way for *S* to receive the use of this cash is for *C* to invest the money and use the earnings to pay dividends to *S*. If this is done, both *C* and *S* will have income. If, for example, *C* invests the money, earns a return of $8000 a year, and pays $8000 a year in dividends, *C* has investment income of $8000 each year and *S* has that much dividend income. Until the enactment of § 7872 in 1984, *C* and *S* could avoid this "double taxation" of corporate earnings by making an interest-free loan. If C had lent S the $100,000, charging no interest, and S had made the investment, S still would have had $8000 a year in income. But C would have had no income, because the maker of a loan was treated as taxable only on interest actually charged.

Under § 7872, the tax treatment of the interest-free loan from C to S depends on whether the loan is payable on demand or whether it has a fixed term. Suppose that the loan from C to S is a demand loan. Under § 7872(a), which applies to demand loans (and to gift loans, whether payable on demand or not), the tax treatment of C and S is as follows:

(1) Section 7872(a)(1)(A) treats both parties as if C had transferred the "forgone interest" on the loan to S. This interest is the amount of interest that would have been charged on an arm's length loan: it is calculated using rates announced by the Treasury department. Suppose that the forgone interest on a $100,000 demand loan is $7500 for one year. Section 7872 says that C and S are taxed as if C had paid this amount to S. Because S is C's only shareholder, and because C failed to charge interest for that reason, the payment would be treated as a dividend. C would get no deduction and S would have $7500 in dividend income. (If the loan had been made by an employer to an employee, the § 7872(a)(1)(A) payment would have been salary, taxable to the employee and often deductible under § 162 by the employer. If the loan had been between friends or relatives, with the absence of interest attributable to a gift motive, the payment would have been a gift, nondeductible by the lender and not income to the borrower.)

(2) Section 7872(a)(1)(B) says that S and C are treated as if S had paid the $7500 back to C "as interest." This payment gives C $7500 in interest income. Whether S can deduct the payment depends on the usual rules for deducting interest. In this particular case, the interest constructively paid by S would be investment interest, because S used the loan proceeds to buy investment property. S can therefore deduct the payment up to the amount of "net investment income" for the year; § 163(d).

If we assume that S has no investment income other than the $8000 earned from the investment made with the loan proceeds, the overall result of all this is as follows: C has $7500 in interest income and no deductions; S has $7500 in dividend income, a $7500 deduction for investment interest, and $8000 in investment income.

If the loan from C to S had been a term loan, the recharacterization would have been more complex. A portion of the loan—essentially, an amount equal to the present value of the right to use $100,000 for the term of the loan—would have been treated as a dividend to S. The balance would have been treated as an original-issue-discount transaction, on which C would report interest income and S would be treated as paying interest. See § 7872(b).

The idea underlying these recharacterizations is that not receiving interest is economically equivalent to receiving interest and then transferring it back to the borrower (as a dividend, compensation, or gift, depending on why the loan was interest-free). Recharacterization is necessary whenever simply ignoring the forgone interest produces tax results more favorable than those that would have applied to actual transfers.

For another illustration of the need for § 7872, consider a gift loan. Suppose that M has $300,000 in the bank, producing annual interest of $28,000. If M simply orders the bank to pay the interest to her daughter, D, for three years, M will have $28,000 annual interest income and D will have none. But suppose that M lends the $300,000 to D, without interest, for three years, and D puts the money in a bank, earning $28,000 a year. If this transaction were taken at face value, M would have no interest income over the three-year period; instead, D would have income. Under § 7872, the tax results of the interest-free gift loan will be identical to those of having the bank pay interest on M's money to D if interest at the applicable federal rate is $28,000: M will have $28,000 a year in interest income under § 7872(a)(1)(B); D will have $28,000 a year in interest income from the bank; and D's interest income will be offset by a $28,000 annual deduction for the investment interest D is deemed to have paid M (ignoring limits on deductibility). The § 7872(a)(1)(A) constructive payment from M to D has no income-tax effect on either M or D because it is a gift.

Section 7872 does not apply to all interest-free or low-interest loans. For example, if an automobile manufacturer lends money to car buyers at little or no interest to promote sales of slow-moving models, the transaction is not subject to § 7872. Section 7872(c)(1) lists the below-market loans to which § 7872 applies. Although § 7872 applies to gift loans, § 7872(c)(2)(A) and § 7872(d) contain some *de minimis* exceptions for small gift loans between individuals. It would be almost pointless, and very burdensome, to require § 7872 calculations whenever a friend or relative lends a small amount of money without charging interest. Section 7872(c)(3) provides a *de minimis* exception for compensation-related and corporate-shareholder loans of not more than $10,000.

Problems and Note

1. *Problems.* In each of these problems, assume that the "applicable Federal rate" is 10 percent, compounded semi-annually. At that rate, one year's interest on a $100,000 loan will be $10,250.

(1) On January 1, P lends his daughter, D, $200,000, at no interest. The purpose of the loan is to enable D to earn enough interest to pay her tuition and other expenses while attending law school. D uses the $200,000 to buy a three-year certificate of deposit ("CD") from a bank. D receives $18,000 in interest on the CD each year. Explain the income-tax consequences to P and D of these transactions.

(2) Same as (1), except that P lends D only $100,000; D's interest on the CD she buys is $9000 a year. See § 7872(d).

2. *References.* Keller, The Tax Treatment of Interest–Free Loans: A Two Transaction Approach, 1 Va.Tax Rev. 241 (1981); Note, The Income Tax Treatment of Interest–Free Loans, 1 Va.Tax Rev. 137 (1981).

E. "SHAM TRANSACTIONS" AND RELATED MATTERS

This section will introduce various "doctrines" having to do, in general, with "form" and "substance." Questions of whether transactions are shams, or whether they have a business purpose or a non-tax effect, arise throughout the tax law, not just in cases involving interest deductions. This material is examined here primarily because one of the leading Supreme Court decisions on the subject—Knetsch v. United States, below—involved the interest deduction.

KNETSCH v. UNITED STATES

Supreme Court of the United States, 1960.
364 U.S. 361, 81 S.Ct. 132, 5 L.Ed.2d 128.

MR. JUSTICE BRENNAN delivered the opinion of the Court.

This case presents the question of whether deductions from gross income claimed on petitioners' 1953 and 1954 joint federal income tax returns, of $143,465 in 1953 and of $147,105 in 1954, for payments made by petitioner, Karl F. Knetsch, to Sam Houston Life Insurance Company, constituted "interest paid * * * on indebtedness" within the meaning of * * * § 163(a) of the Internal Revenue Code of 1954. The Commissioner of Internal Revenue disallowed the deductions and determined a deficiency for each year. The petitioners paid the deficiencies and brought this action for refund in the District Court for the Southern District of California. The District Court rendered judgment for the United States, and the Court of Appeals for the Ninth Circuit affirmed, 272 F.2d 200. Because of a suggested conflict with the decision of the Court of Appeals for the Fifth Circuit in United States v. Bond, 258 F.2d 577, we granted certiorari, 361 U.S. 958.

On December 11, 1953, the insurance company sold Knetsch ten 30–year maturity deferred annuity savings bonds, each in the face amount of $400,000 and bearing interest at 2½% compounded annually. The purchase price was $4,004,000. Knetsch gave the Company his check for $4,000, and signed $4,000,000 of nonrecourse annuity loan notes for the balance. The notes bore 3½% interest and were secured by the annuity bonds. The interest was payable in advance, and Knetsch on the same day prepaid the first year's interest, which was $140,000. Under the Table of Cash and Loan Values made part of the bonds, their cash or loan value at December 11, 1954, the end of the first contract year, was to be $4,100,000. The contract terms, however, permitted Knetsch to borrow any excess of this value above his indebtedness without waiting until December 11, 1954. Knetsch took advantage of this provision only five days after the purchase. On December 16, 1953, he received from the company $99,000 of the $100,000 excess over his $4,000,000 indebtedness, for which he gave his notes bearing 3½% interest. This interest was also payable in advance and on the same day he prepaid the first year's interest of $3,465. In their joint return for 1953, the petitioners deducted the sum of the two interest payments, that is $143,465, as "interest paid * * * within the taxable year on indebtedness," under § [163].

The second contract year began on December 11, 1954, when interest in advance of $143,465 was payable by Knetsch on his aggregate indebtedness of $4,099,000. Knetsch paid this amount on December 27, 1954. Three days later, on December 30, he received from the company cash in the amount of $104,000, the difference less $1,000 between his then $4,099,000 indebtedness and the cash or loan value of the bonds of $4,204,000 on December 11, 1955. He gave the company appropriate notes and prepaid the interest thereon of $3,640. In their joint return for the taxable year 1954 the petitioners deducted the sum of the two interest payments, that is $147,105, as "interest paid * * * within the taxable year on indebtedness," under § 163(a).

The tax years 1955 and 1956 are not involved in this proceeding, but a recital of the events of those years is necessary to complete the story of the transaction. On December 11, 1955, the start of the third contract year, Knetsch became obligated to pay $147,105 as prepaid interest on an indebtedness which now totalled $4,203,000. He paid this interest on December 28, 1955. On the same date he received $104,000 from the company. This was $1,000 less than the difference between his indebtedness and the cash or loan value of the bonds of $4,308,000 at December 11, 1956. Again he gave the company notes upon which he prepaid interest of $3,640. Petitioners claimed a deduction on their 1955 joint return for the aggregate of the payments, or $150,745.

Knetsch did not go on with the transaction for the fourth contract year beginning December 11, 1956, but terminated it on December 27, 1956. His indebtedness at that time totalled $4,307,000. The cash or loan value of the bonds was the $4,308,000 value at December 11, 1956, which had been the basis of the "loan" of December 28, 1955. He surrendered the bonds and his indebtedness was canceled. He received the difference of $1,000 in cash.

The contract called for a monthly annuity of $90,171 at maturity (when Knetsch would be 90 years of age) or for such smaller amount as would be produced by the cash or loan value after deduction of the then existing indebtedness. It was stipulated that if Knetsch had held the bonds to maturity and continued annually to borrow the net cash value less $1,000, the sum available for the annuity at maturity would be $1,000 ($8,388,000 cash or loan value less $8,387,000 of indebtedness), enough to provide an annuity of only $43 per month.

The trial judge made findings that "[t]here was no commercial economic substance to the * * * transaction," that the parties did not intend that Knetsch "become indebted to Sam Houston," that "[n]o indebtedness of [Knetsch] was created by any of the * * * transactions," and that "[n]o economic gain could be achieved from the purchase of these bonds without regard to the tax consequences * * *." His conclusion of law, based on this Court's decision in Deputy v. du Pont, 308 U.S. 488, was that "[W]hile in form the payments to Sam Houston were compensation for the use or forbearance of money, they were not in substance. As a payment of interest, the transaction was a sham."

We first examine the transaction between Knetsch and the insurance company to determine whether it created an "indebtedness" within the meaning of * * * § 163(a), or whether, as the trial court found, it was a sham. We put aside a finding by the District Court that Knetsch's "only motive in purchasing these 10 bonds was to attempt to secure an interest deduction."[2] As was said in Gregory v. Helvering, 293 U.S. 465, 469: "The legal right of a taxpayer to decrease the amount of what otherwise would be his taxes, or altogether avoid them, by means which the law permits, cannot be doubted. * * * But the question for determination is whether what was done, apart from the tax motive, was the thing which the statute intended."

When we examine "what was done" here, we see that Knetsch paid the insurance company $294,570 during the two taxable years involved and received $203,000 back in the form of "loans." What did Knetsch get for the out-of-pocket difference of $91,570? In form he had an annuity contract with a so-called guaranteed cash value at maturity of $8,388,000, which would produce monthly annuity payments of $90,171, or substantial life insurance proceeds in the event of his death before maturity. This, as we have seen, was a fiction, because each year Knetsch's annual borrowings kept the net cash value, on which any annuity or insurance payments would depend, at the relative pittance of $1,000.[3] Plainly, therefore, Knetsch's transaction with the insurance company did "not appreciably affect his beneficial interest except to reduce his tax * * *." Gilbert v. Commissioner, 2 Cir., 248 F.2d 399, 411 (dissenting opinion). For it is patent that there was nothing of substance to be realized by Knetsch from this transaction beyond a tax deduction. What he was ostensibly "lent" back was in reality only the rebate of a substantial part of the so-called "interest" payments. The $91,570 difference retained by the company was its fee for providing the facade of "loans" whereby the petitioners sought to reduce their 1953 and 1954 taxes in the total sum of $233,297.68. There may well be single premium

2. We likewise put aside Knetsch's argument that, because he received ordinary income when he surrendered the annuities in 1956, he has suffered a net loss even if the contested deductions are allowed, and that therefore his motive in taking out the annuities could not have been tax avoidance.

3. Petitioners argue further than in 10 years the net cash value of the bonds would have exceeded the amounts Knetsch paid as "interest." This contention, however, is predicated on the wholly unlikely assumption that Knetsch would have paid off in cash the original $4,000,000 "loan."

annuity arrangements with nontax substance which create an "indebtedness" for the purposes of * * * § 163(a). But this one is a sham.[4]

The petitioners contend, however, that the Congress in enacting § 264 authorized the deductions. They point out that § 264(a)(2) denies a deduction for amounts paid on indebtedness incurred to purchase or carry a single-premium annuity contract, but only as to contracts purchased after March 1, 1954. The petitioners thus would attribute to Congress a purpose to allow the deduction of pre–1954 payments under transactions of the kind carried on by Knetsch with the insurance company without regard to whether the transactions created a true obligation to pay interest. Unless that meaning plainly appears we will not attribute it to Congress. "To hold otherwise would be to exalt artifice above reality and to deprive the statutory provision in question of all serious purpose." Gregory v. Helvering, supra, 293 U.S. at page 470. We, therefore, look to the statute and materials relevant to its construction for evidence that Congress meant in § 264(a)(2) to authorize the deduction of payments made under sham transactions entered into before 1954. We look in vain.

* * *

The judgment of the Court of Appeals is affirmed.

Affirmed.

MR. JUSTICE DOUGLAS, with whom MR. JUSTICE WHITTAKER and MR. JUSTICE STEWART concur, dissenting.

* * *

It is true that in this transaction the taxpayer was bound to lose if the annuity contract is taken by itself. At least the taxpayer showed by his conduct that he never intended to come out ahead on that investment apart from this income tax deduction. Yet the same may be true where a taxpayer borrows money at 5% or 6% interest to purchase securities that pay only nominal interest; or where, with money in the bank earning 3%, he borrows from the self same bank at a higher rate. His aim there, as here, may only be to get a tax deduction for interest paid. Yet as long as the transaction itself is not hocus-pocus, the interest charges incident to completing it would seem to be deductible under the Internal Revenue Code as respects annuity contracts made prior to March 1, 1954, the date Congress selected for terminating this class of deductions. § 264. The insurance company existed; it operated under Texas law; it was authorized to issue these policies and to make these annuity loans. While the taxpayer was obligated to pay interest at the

---

4. Every court which has considered this or similar contracts has agreed with our conclusion, except the Court of Appeals for the Fifth Circuit in the *Bond* case and one District Court bound by that decision, Roderick v. United States, 59–2 U.S.T.C. ¶ 9650. See Diggs v. Commissioner, 2 Cir., 281 F.2d 326, certiorari denied 364 U.S. 908; Weller and Emmons v. Commissioner, 3 Cir., 270 F.2d 294, certiorari denied 364 U.S. 908; Haggard v. United States, 59–1 U.S.T.C. ¶ 9299; Oliver L. Williams, 18 T.C.M. 205. See also Rev.Rul. 54–94, 1954–1 Cum.Bull. 53, and the dissenting opinion of Judge Wisdom in *Bond*.

rate of 3½% per annum, the annuity bonds increased in cash value at the rate of only 2½% per annum. The insurance company's profit was in that 1–point spread.

Tax avoidance is a dominating motive behind scores of transactions. It is plainly present here. Will the Service that calls this transaction a "sham" today not press for collection of taxes arising out of the surrender of the annuity contract? I think it should, for I do not believe any part of the transaction was a "sham." To disallow the "interest" deduction because the annuity device was devoid of commercial substance is to draw a line which will affect a host of situations not now before us and which, with all deference, I do not think we can maintain when other cases reach here. The remedy is legislative. Evils or abuses can be particularized by Congress. We deal only with "interest" as commonly understood and as used across the board in myriad transactions. Since these transactions were real and legitimate in the insurance world and were consummated within the limits allowed by insurance policies, I would recognize them taxwise.

Notes and Questions

1. *Some variations on the Knetsch pattern.* In order for *Knetsch*-type plans to produce after-tax gains, even if the interest deductions are allowed, the return on the transaction must be taxed more lightly than the income sheltered by the interest deductions. One simple example is that of a taxpayer who borrows at 10 percent and uses the loan proceeds to buy tax-exempt bonds paying 7 percent. What would the taxpayer's marginal rate have to be for such a transaction to produce tax benefits in excess of the 3–percent annual economic loss? Section 265(a)(2) disallows deductions for interest on debt "incurred or continued to purchase or carry" tax-exempt obligations.

The taxpayer in Goldstein v. Commissioner, 364 F.2d 734 (2d Cir.1966), cert. denied 385 U.S. 1005 (1967), won $140,000 in the Irish Sweepstakes in 1958. She then borrowed about $945,000 from banks, prepaying $81,000 interest. She used the loan proceeds to buy discounted notes, which paid taxable interest at a rate lower than that of the bank loans. The object of the transaction was to deduct $81,000 in "interest" in 1958 (a year in which the taxpayer's marginal rates without the interest deduction would have been very high) and to get in exchange a smaller amount of income spread over the years 1959, 1960, and 1961 (years in which her tax rates would have been lower than those of 1958). The loans from the banks were secured by the notes purchased with the loan proceeds. Goldstein was not personally liable on those notes, and she never had possession of either the notes (held by the lenders) or the loan proceeds. The Second Circuit found that the loans were not "shams," and that they created a "genuine indebtedness," but nevertheless denied the interest deduction because the taxpayer had anticipated no "economic" gain from the transaction.

Were the payments in *Knetsch* and *Goldstein* "interest" in the ordinary sense of amounts "paid for the use of money"?

2. *"Shams."* In a sense, "sham" is just a pejorative label given by a court to a transaction which the court has decided should not be given its intended effect. Nevertheless, most lawyers have a fair idea of what will and what will not be labeled a "sham," at least in the sense that some transactions clearly are shams, some clearly are not, and some are borderline. Consider a problem involving marital status. For reasons that will be explored in Chapter 7, two people whose incomes are approximately the same will often pay less tax if they are not married than if they are. As a rule, a taxpayer's marital status is determined at the end of the taxable year; § 7703(a). These rules give many two-earner married couples a tax incentive to be unmarried at the end of the year. Suppose that Harry and Wendy, a married couple who would pay less income tax this year if they were not married, take one of the following steps:

(1) Harry and Wendy get a divorce, which is fully effective under the law of the state in which they live. They continue to live together and share expenses, just as they did before they were divorced, but they do not remarry.

(2) Harry and Wendy fly to a Caribbean country on December 29. They get a divorce in that country on December 30, and on January 1 they remarry. Their divorce is recognized by the state in which they live, so if one of them should die on December 31, the other would not have a surviving spouse's property rights.

(3) Same as (2), except that the state where the couple lives would not recognize their Caribbean divorce.

(4) Harry and Wendy pay Harry's cousin Clifford, a notorious forger, to create documents purporting to show that Harry and Wendy are divorced.

For tax purposes, it seems clear that Harry and Wendy are not married in case (1) and that they are married in case (3) and case (4). Case (2) is borderline: it resembles case (1) because the divorce is valid and has some non-tax effects, but it also resembles cases (3) and (4) because the non-tax effects of the divorce are, and were intended to be, trivial.

The taxpayers in Boyter v. Commissioner, 74 T.C. 989 (1980), remanded 668 F.2d 1382 (4th Cir.1981), obtained Caribbean divorces late in the year and remarried in Maryland, where they lived, early the next year. The Tax Court held that the divorces were not valid under Maryland law, although no Maryland authority dealt explicitly with this question. Because marital status depends upon state law, the Tax Court held that the Boyters could not file tax returns as single persons. On appeal, the Fourth Circuit held that the Tax Court should have ruled on the Commissioner's contention that the Boyters' divorces were "shams" even if the Maryland courts would have recognized those divorces. The

Court of Appeals' opinion said that "the sham transaction doctrine may apply in this case if, as the record suggests, the parties intended merely to procure divorce papers rather than actually to effect a real dissolution of their marriage contract"; 668 F.2d at 1387.

3. *Tax-avoidance purpose.* Learned Hand's dissent in Commissioner v. Newman, 159 F.2d 848, 850–51 (2d Cir.1947), cert. denied 331 U.S. 859 (1947), summed up the law of "tax avoidance" as follows:

> Over and over again courts have said that there is nothing sinister in so arranging one's affairs as to keep taxes as low as possible. Everybody does so, rich or poor; and all do right, for nobody owes any public duty to pay more than the law demands: taxes are enforced exactions, not voluntary contributions. To demand more in the name of morals is mere cant.

On the other hand, the Service's ruling on the Caribbean-divorce issue says (Rev.Rul. 76–255, 1976–2 C.B. 40):

> The true nature of a transaction must be considered in light of the plain intent and purpose of the statute. Such transaction should not be given any effect for Federal income tax purposes if it merely serves the purpose of tax avoidance.

In Publication 1 ("Your Rights as a Taxpayer"), the Service once set forth a position similar to that of Judge Hand: "You have the right to plan your business and personal finances in such a way that you will pay the least tax that is due under the law" (Publication 1, 1988, p. 1). The current version of Publication 1 contains a watered-down version: "You are responsible for paying only the correct amount of tax due under the law—no more, no less" (Publication 1, 2000, p. 1).

The Service has sometimes referred to non-tax *effect,* rather than to non-tax *purpose,* in ruling on the validity of questionable transactions. For example, Announcement 87–3, I.R.B. 1987–2, 40, says that the Service will scrutinize arrangements designed to defer income from 1986 to 1987 (a year in which tax rates decreased) to see whether the arrangements have "business *substance*" (emphasis added). In view of the fact that almost all economically important transactions contain features designed to reduce taxes, the apparent shift in emphasis away from the taxpayer's "motive" or "purpose" and toward the question whether the transaction has "substance" seems wise.

Yosha v. Commissioner, 861 F.2d 494 (7th Cir.1988), involved deductions for losses supposedly resulting from trading option straddles and hedges. Judge Posner pointed out that "there is no rule against taking advantage of opportunities created by Congress or the Treasury Department for beating taxes," and observed that "[m]any transactions are largely or even entirely motivated by the desire to obtain a tax advantage." Nevertheless, the taxpayer lost, not because he was tax-motivated but because the Tax Court had found that the transactions in question "lacked economic substance"; 861 F.2d at 499.

4. *Reference.* Blum, Knetsch v. United States: A Pronouncement on Tax Avoidance, 1961 Sup.Ct.Rev. 135.

Chapter Six

THE ALTERNATIVE MINIMUM TAX

In the late 1960s the Treasury Department disclosed that hundreds of taxpayers with high "economic" incomes were paying little or no income tax. This disclosure led Congress to enact an array of Code provisions aimed at limiting the ability of wealthy taxpayers to avoid tax liability completely. Among these provisions was a "Minimum Tax for Tax Preferences," which was adopted in 1969. Over the years Congress has revised the minimum-tax provisions often and extensively. Today's version is the Alternative Minimum Tax ("AMT") of § 55, which was enacted in 1986 and revised in minor ways since then.

The Senate Finance Committee's report on the Tax Reform Bill of 1986 offered the following justifications for the minimum-tax provisions (S.Rep. No. 99–313, 99th Cong., 2d Sess. at 518–19):

> The committee believes that the minimum tax should serve one overriding objective: to ensure that no taxpayer with substantial economic income can avoid significant tax liability by using exclusions, deductions, and credits. Although these provisions may provide incentives for worthy goals, they become counterproductive when taxpayers are allowed to use them to avoid virtually all tax liability. The ability of high-income individuals and highly profitable corporations to pay little or no tax undermines respect for the entire tax system and, thus, for the incentive provisions themselves. In addition, even aside from public perceptions, the committee believes that it is inherently unfair for high-income individuals and highly profitable corporations to pay little or no tax due to their ability to utilize various tax preferences.

A. INDIVIDUALS

In practice, people think of the AMT as a tax payable instead of the regular tax if the minimum tax for the year is higher. Technically, however, a taxpayer subject to minimum-tax liability pays a minimum tax equal to the excess of the "tentative minimum tax for the taxable year" over the "regular tax for the taxable year"; see § 55(a). Because the taxpayer remains subject to the regular tax, the net effect is the same as if the taxpayer had to pay the tentative minimum tax in lieu of the regular tax whenever the tentative minimum tax is more. For example, if the "regular tax" is $50,000 and the "tentative minimum tax" is $80,000, the taxpayer pays the $50,000 regular tax plus a minimum tax of $30,000.[a] But it is easier to think of the taxpayer as paying the tentative minimum tax of $80,000 instead of the regular tax.

The tax base for the AMT is the excess of "alternative minimum taxable income" ("AMTI") over an "exemption amount," which is $49,000 for married couples filing jointly and surviving spouses, $35,750 for most unmarried individuals, and $24,500 for married individuals filing separately, until 2005; §§ 55(d)(1). (All of our problems and examples will use these figures.) The AMT rates are mildly progressive: 26 percent of the first $175,000 of AMTI in excess of the exemption amount; 28 percent on AMTI that exceeds the exemption amount by more than $175,000. In calculating the AMT, most long-term capital gains are subject to tax at the same rates as those of the regular tax; § 55(b)(3). The tax treatment of capital gains will be examined in Chapter 10.

To illustrate AMT calculations, consider an unmarried taxpayer with AMTI of $100,000. The taxpayer's tentative minimum tax is 26 percent of $64,250 ($100,000 AMTI less $35,750 exemption amount), or $16,705. If the taxpayer's regular tax exceeds $16,705, no AMT is due. If the regular tax is less than $16,705, the taxpayer owes the regular tax plus whatever AMT makes the total tax equal to $16,705.

Many non-refundable credits cannot be used against the alternative minimum tax; § 26(a).

If a taxpayer's AMTI exceeds a specified amount, the exemption amount is "phased out" at a rate of 25 cents for every dollar of excess; § 55(d)(3). For example, if a married couple filing a joint return has $190,000 in AMTI, the couple's exemption amount is reduced by $10,000 (25 percent of the excess of their AMTI over $150,000); § 55(d)(3)(A). This makes their exemption amount $39,000 rather than $49,000. Like other rate-bracket phaseouts, this feature puts a "bubble" into the minimum-tax rate structure. The effective marginal minimum-tax rates for someone with AMTI in the phaseout range are 32.5 percent and 35 percent.[b]

---

a. Strictly speaking, this description is true only for taxpayers not entitled to tax credits (most of which are not allowed against the AMT). For a taxpayer with credits, the AMT is the excess of the tentative minimum tax over the regular tax *before credits*. However, under § 26(a), most credits are allowable—even against the regular tax—only to the extent that the taxpayer's regular tax before credits exceeds the AMT. The description in the text is therefore true in substance even for many taxpayers with credits, though it is techni-

cally inaccurate. For example, consider a taxpayer with regular-tax liability before credits of $20,000, a tentative minimum tax of $30,000, and a credit (not allowable under the AMT) of $6000. Technically, the credit is disallowed *under the regular tax* because regular tax liability (before credits) is less than the tentative minimum tax. The taxpayer therefore owes $20,000 in regular tax and an AMT of $10,000.

b. An additional $1 of income will increase AMTI by $1 and will decrease the exemption amount by $.25. This increases

Problems

Problem (1). H and W, who will file a joint return, owe a regular tax of $20,000. Their AMTI is $110,000. They do not qualify for any tax credits. Compute the tax liability of H and W for the year.

Problem (2). Same as above, except that H and W have AMTI of $250,000.

Problem (3). Same as above except that H and W have AMTI of $260,000.

———

Section 55(b)(2) defines alternative minimum taxable income as: (1) taxable income, (2) computed with "adjustments" required by §§ 56 and 58, (3) plus the amount of "items of tax preference" defined in § 57. Although the statute calls some of the changes made to taxable income "adjustments" and others "items of tax preference," there is no functional difference between adjustments and preferences: preference items are for all practical purposes simply positive adjustments. One calculates AMTI in much the same way as one calculates taxable income: the only difference is that the AMT uses different (and usually more strict) rules for some exclusions and deductions.

Although § 55 calculates AMTI by starting with taxable income and adjusting that figure, most people think of AMTI as a sort of taxable income calculated using different measures of gross income and deductions.[c] Many income and deduction items dealt with previously in this book receive different treatment under the alternative minimum tax than under the regular tax. Examples are:

(1) *Depreciation.* Section 56(a)(1) provides minimum-tax depreciation rules which result in cost recovery that is slower for some assets than cost recovery under the regular tax. On assets for which the 200–percent declining-balance method is used for regular-tax purposes, the AMT requires the 150–percent declining-balance method; § 56(a)(1).

(2) *Miscellaneous itemized deductions.* Under the regular tax, miscellaneous itemized deductions (§ 67) are deductible to the extent that their total amount exceeds 2 percent of adjusted gross income. For purposes of the AMT, these deductions are disallowed; § 56(b)(1)(A)(i).

the tax by 26% or 28% of $1.25 (depending on whether the taxpayer's nominal AMTI marginal rate is 26% or 28%) for each dollar increase in AMTI. The tax on an additional dollar of AMTI is therefore $.325 or $.35.

For a married couple filing a joint return, this means that the real AMT marginal rates are:

AMTI	Rate
Not over $ 49,000	0%
Over $ 49,000 but not over $150,000	26%
Over $150,000 but not over $209,200	32.5%
Over $209,200 but not over $346,000	35%
Over $346,000	28%

c. However, adjusted gross income is not recomputed for AMT purposes; thus, references to AGI in both regular-tax and AMT provisions are references to AGI as defined in § 62.

(3) *Taxes.* State and local personal-property taxes and state, local, and foreign real-property taxes and income taxes can be deducted in determining AMTI only if they are above-the-line deductions under the regular tax; § 56(b)(1)(A)(ii).

(4) *Medical expenses.* For AMT purposes, medical expenses are deductible only to the extent that they exceed 10 (rather than 7.5) percent of adjusted gross income; § 56(b)(1)(B).

(5) *Tax-exempt interest.* The minimum-tax exclusion from income of tax-exempt interest is narrower than the exclusion under the regular tax. Interest on "private activity bonds" (other than bonds of organizations described in § 501(c)(3)) is included in AMTI; § 57(a)(5). (Under the regular tax, interest on some private-activity bonds is excludable under § 103.) If interest on a private-activity bond is subject to the minimum tax, interest incurred to purchase or carry that bond is deductible (up to the investment-interest limit) for AMT purposes even though § 265(a)(2) disallows deductions for the interest under the regular tax; § 56(b)(1)(C)(iii).

(6) *Interest deductions.* In lieu of a deduction for "qualified residence interest," the alternative minimum tax allows a deduction for "qualified housing interest," which is interest on debt incurred in "acquiring, constructing, or substantially rehabilitating" either the taxpayer's principal residence or a "qualified dwelling which is a qualified residence"; §§ 56(b)(1)(C) & (e). Unlike the regular tax, the minimum tax allows no deduction for a loan secured by a residence but used for some personal purpose not connected with that residence. A boat cannot be a "qualified dwelling," even though a sufficiently residential boat may be a "qualified residence." Compare § 56(e)(2) with § 163(h)(4)(A).

(7) *Standard deduction and personal exemptions.* These deductions are not allowed under the alternative minimum tax; § 56(b)(1)(E).

Problem

H and *W,* who will file a joint return, have a taxable income of $40,000, computed as follows:

Gross Income (salaries)		$85,000
Less: Alimony paid to *H*'s former spouse		20,000
Adjusted Gross Income		$65,000
Less: Personal Exemptions	10,000	
State & Local Taxes	8,000	
Miscellaneous Itemized Deductions	4,000	
Mortgage Interest	3,000	
Total:		25,000
Taxable Income		$40,000

W exercised an ISO (p. 60, above), paying $20,000 for stock worth $50,000. This $30,000 gain was not included in her gross income for regular-tax purposes (§ 421). The couple received $11,000 in tax-exempt interest on private-activity bonds which were not issued by a § 501(c)(3) organization. The mortgage interest is attributable entirely to loans which *H* and *W* took out to pay the college tuition of their dependent children. The couple has no tax credits. Compute their alternative minimum tax.

Notes and Questions

1. *The basis of property under the minimum tax.* Because some receipts and deductions which affect the basis of property receive special treatment under the minimum tax, the basis of property for minimum-tax purposes may differ from the property's regular-tax basis. Consider a taxpayer who deducts $50,000 in depreciation under §§ 167 and 168 in determining taxable income, and whose depreciation deduction for minimum-tax purposes is limited to $47,000. Under § 1016, the basis of the property is adjusted downward by the $50,000 of depreciation taken. For minimum-tax purposes, the downward adjustment is only $47,000. See § 56(a)(7).

The requirement that separate basis adjustments be made under the regular and minimum taxes has an important effect upon record-keeping. Suppose a taxpayer exercises an incentive stock option in year 1, purchasing stock worth $100,000 for $60,000. Under § 56(b)(3) the exercise of the option creates a $40,000 adjustment (in plain English, the exercise produces $40,000 in gross income for minimum-tax purposes only). Suppose also that the taxpayer owes enough regular tax for year 1 so that his minimum tax is zero. Does the fact that no minimum tax was owed mean that the taxpayer's exercise of the ISO has no minimum-tax consequences? No: if the taxpayer sells the stock in year 7 for $95,000, he will have a gain of $35,000 under the regular tax, but a loss of $5000 under the minimum tax; § 56(b)(3)(last sentence). Therefore, the taxpayer's minimum-tax liability for year 7 will depend in part upon the fact that the exercise of the ISO in year 1 produced a gain for minimum-tax purposes, even though that gain was taxed at a zero rate. This example shows that taxpayers must keep track of events having significance under the minimum tax even if they owe no minimum tax for the years in which the events took place.

2. *The minimum-tax credit.* The deductions and exclusions which create "adjustments" and "preferences" under the alternative minimum tax are of two kinds. Some, like the exclusion from income of interest on private-activity bonds, provide a permanent reduction in tax. Others, such as accelerated depreciation deductions, defer tax. In order to take account of the fact that a deferral of tax is less valuable than a complete forgiveness of the same amount of tax, Congress has created the minimum-tax credit of § 53.

The minimum-tax credit allows some taxpayers who pay minimum taxes to credit some or all of those taxes against their regular-tax liability in later years. In determining the amount of the credit for individual taxpayers, the tentative minimum tax is recomputed, using only "deferral preferences." "Deferral preferences" are adjustments and preferences other than the following four "exclusion preferences":

(1) adjustments required by § 56(b)(1) for miscellaneous itemized deductions, taxes, medical expenses, interest, the standard deduction, and personal exemptions;

(2) percentage depletion in excess of basis (§ 57(a)(1));

(3) tax-exempt interest on certain private-activity bonds (§ 57(a)(5)); and

(4) part of the exclusion for gain on the sale of certain small-business stock (§ 57(a)(7)).

In most[d] cases, the amount of the minimum tax as redetermined by using only deferral preferences becomes a credit against regular-tax liability in later years. Because reducing regular-tax liability in those later years below the point at which the tentative minimum tax in those years would exceed the regular tax would do the taxpayer no good, § 53(c) limits the credit for any year to the excess of the regular tax over the tentative minimum tax. This limit preserves the credit until its use can benefit the taxpayer.

3. *The effect of the minimum tax upon business tax credits.* Consider an individual taxpayer whose regular-tax liability before credits is $50,000. The taxpayer has non-refundable tax credits of $10,000, which would reduce this liability to $40,000. If the taxpayer's tentative minimum tax for the year is $46,000, only $4000 of the $10,000 in credits could be useful; the rest could produce no tax benefit because every dollar of reduction in regular-tax liability below $46,000 would create a dollar of minimum-tax liability. Congress has decided that the tax benefits of most credits should not be lost in this way. Section 26 provides that credits for a particular year are allowed only to the extent that they reduce regular-tax liability to the amount of the tentative minimum tax. Because most unused credits can be carried back or forward under § 39, this limit preserves tax credits which the minimum tax would eliminate.

4. *References.* Moran, Stargazing: The Alternative Minimum Tax for Individuals and Future Tax Reform, 69 Or.L.Rev. 223 (1990); Coven, The Alternative Minimum Tax: Proving Again That Two Wrongs Do Not Make a Right, 68 Cal.L.Rev. 1093 (1980).

A NOTE ON FLUCTUATING INCOMES

Roughly speaking, taxpayers subject to the AMT fall into two categories. Some of them pay little regular tax year after year; others have occasional years in which regular-tax liability is low while paying substantial regular taxes in most years. Someone whose regular-tax

d. For taxpayers who have taken tax credits allowable against the AMT, the rules are a bit more elaborate than those described in the text.

liability is low only occasionally presents a less-attractive target for the minimum tax than someone whose regular tax is low year after year. Suppose, for instance, that Smith's tentative minimum tax is $50,000 each year for ten years and that her regular tax is $10,000 in each of those years. Jones's tentative minimum tax is also $50,000 a year in each of the ten years, but his regular tax is $10,000 in year one and $90,000 in years two through nine. A minimum tax imposed on a strictly annual basis would treat Jones as being in the same position as Smith in year one, even though Jones's low regular-tax liability for that year may have been a fluke, attributable more to chance fluctuations than to systematic use of tax preferences.

Several features of the minimum tax operate to reduce the burden of that tax for taxpayers whose regular-tax liabilities sometimes exceed their tentative minimum taxes. The minimum-tax credit is one example: the credit is of use only to taxpayers who will have years in which they are not subject to the minimum tax. Similarly, § 26's preservation of tax credits which would be rendered valueless by the minimum tax can benefit only people who have some taxable years in which they pay only the regular tax. Finally, taxpayers can elect (under the regular tax) to write off some tax preferences over ten years, and they can elect to use the minimum-tax depreciation schedules for regular-tax purposes; see §§ 59(e) & 168(b)(2)(C). By exercising these elections, taxpayers substitute regular-tax liability for minimum-tax liability in early years and reduce regular-tax liabilities in later years.

HOW IMPORTANT IS THE ALTERNATIVE MINIMUM TAX?

The AMT was advertised as a tax affecting only a few wealthy taxpayers who used "loopholes" extensively. The one major regular-tax "loophole" that the AMT actually caught, however—the deduction for the full value of appreciated property contributed to charity—became part of the AMT as well, thanks largely to lobbying by universities and other charities. At about the same time, the AMT was amended to disallow the standard deduction and personal exemptions, deductions that play a minor part in the affairs of the truly wealthy, but which are important to many middle-income taxpayers, especially those with many children. Because the standard deduction and personal exemptions are indexed for inflation, they become larger every year. And because the AMT rates and exemption amounts are not indexed for inflation, more middle-income people, even those who have no tax preferences or adjustments other than the standard deduction and personal exemptions, have become subject to the AMT. Furthermore, because miscellaneous itemized deductions and most state taxes are not allowed at all under the AMT, taxpayers with large employee business expenses, those with heavy costs of producing non-business income (recall the *Kenseth* case, p. 300), and those who live in high-tax states can easily run afoul of the AMT. This problem has become even more serious than it used to be because the 2001 legislation reduced tax rates under the regular tax while leaving the AMT untouched except for trivial increases in the AMT exemption amounts for individuals. Today, it is not at all unusual for wage earners making less than $150,000 a year and who have no investments at all, let alone investments in "tax shelters," to face AMT liability. And the AMT increases the cost of compliance for many taxpayers who do not actually owe it. Many taxpayers must complete the AMT form to determine whether they owe the tax or not, and taxpayers who may be close to AMT liability have to fill out worksheets to determine whether the AMT will limit their credits. In addition, tax planning requires attention to the AMT. Unless something is done about these matters, the regular-tax rates for many middle-income taxpayers will become largely meaningless. Reform may be hard to accomplish, as the AMT retains its undeserved image as a tax imposed on people who are abusing the system.

B. CORPORATIONS

Corporations, like other taxpayers, are subject to the alternative minimum tax. Some minimum-tax adjustments apply only to individuals: for example, individuals cannot deduct most state and local taxes in computing AMTI; corporations can. See generally § 56(b). A corporation's exemption amount is $40,000, and the exemption amount is phased out for AMTI in excess of $150,000. The minimum-tax rate for corporations is 20 percent.

The most important minimum-tax difference between corporations and other taxpayers is that corporations are subject to the adjusted-current-earnings adjustment of § 56(g). This adjustment creates a sort of "minimum minimum tax" in the sense that it is an adjustment to AMTI, rather than to taxable income directly. A corporation first computes its AMTI in the usual way and then adjusts that AMTI to reflect the difference between AMTI and adjusted current earnings.

The adjustment for adjusted current earnings (which may be negative) is 75 percent of the difference between a corporation's AMTI (determined before the adjusted-current-earnings adjustment and without regard to the AMT net-operating-loss deduction) and its "adjusted current earnings," as defined in § 56(g)(3). The "adjusted current earnings" figure is itself derived by adjusting AMTI: most of the adjustments have the effect of making AMTI (as adjusted) resemble the corporation's "earnings and profits," a term used (but never defined) in subchapter C of the Code. For example, most items that are not deductible in computing earnings and profits are also non-deductible in computing adjusted current earnings, and items excludable in computing AMTI but includable in computing earnings and profits—tax-exempt interest, for example—increase adjusted current earnings.

Some "small" corporations are exempt from the AMT. Very roughly, a corporation is "small" if, in its first three years of existence, its average annual gross receipts do not exceed $5 million. After qualifying under this test, a corporation's average annual gross receipts can increase to $7.5 million without loss of small-corporation status. See § 55(e).

*

Chapter Seven

WHO IS THE TAXPAYER?

The concept of income is inherently personal. One cannot even think of any of the forms of income listed in § 61, for example, without thinking of some individual or other entity whose income is under consideration. Except for income from property held in trust or by an estate, for which detailed provisions tie income to particular taxpayers, the Code is almost silent on the subject of choosing the person to be taxed as a result of income-producing events. Yet this subject is important; in part because some person or organization must be made responsible for paying a tax, in part because a progressive tax extracts more from one person with a $20,000 annual income than from two with incomes of $10,000 each, but mainly because the concept of income is meaningless except as a concept of someone's income. This chapter will present the efforts of the courts (and, occasionally, Congress) to give meaning to the question-begging formulations of §§ 1 and 11, which impose tax on the incomes "of" individuals, trusts, estates, and corporations, and § 61, which defines "gross income" without reference to any person.

A. PERSONAL SERVICE INCOME

LUCAS v. EARL

Supreme Court of the United States, 1930.
281 U.S. 111, 50 S.Ct. 241, 74 L.Ed. 731.

MR. JUSTICE HOLMES delivered the opinion of the Court.

This case presents the question whether the respondent, Earl, could be taxed for the whole of the salary and attorney's fees earned by him in the years 1920 and 1921, or should be taxed for only a half of them in view of a contract with his wife which we shall mention. The Commissioner of Internal Revenue and the Board of Tax Appeals imposed a tax upon the whole, but their decision was reversed by the Circuit Court of Appeals, 30 F.(2d) 898. A writ of certiorari was granted by this court.

By the contract, made in 1901, Earl and his wife agreed "that any property either of us now has or may hereafter acquire * * * in any way,

435

either by earnings (including salaries, fees, etc.), or any rights by contract or otherwise, during the existence of our marriage, or which we or either of us may receive by gift, bequest, devise, or inheritance, and all the proceeds, issues, and profits of any and all such property shall be treated and considered, and hereby is declared to be received, held, taken, and owned by us as joint tenants, and not otherwise, with the right of survivorship." The validity of the contract is not questioned, and we assume it to be unquestionable under the law of the State of California, in which the parties lived. Nevertheless we are of opinion that the Commissioner and Board of Tax Appeals were right.

The Revenue Act of 1918 approved February 24, 1919, c. 18, §§ 210, 211, 212(a), 213(a), 40 Stat. 1057, 1062, 1064, 1065, imposes a tax upon the net income of every individual including "income derived from salaries, wages, or compensation for personal service * * * of whatever kind and in whatever form paid," § 213(a). The provisions of the Revenue Act of 1921, c. 136, 42 Stat. 227, 233, 237, 238, in sections bearing the same numbers are similar to those of the above. A very forcible argument is presented to the effect that the statute seeks to tax only income beneficially received, and that taking the question more technically the salary and fees became the joint property of Earl and his wife on the very first instant on which they were received. We well might hesitate upon the latter proposition, because however the matter might stand between husband and wife he was the only party to the contracts by which the salary and fees were earned, and it is somewhat hard to say that the last step in the performance of those contracts could be taken by anyone but himself alone. But this case is not to be decided by attenuated subtleties. It turns on the import and reasonable construction of the taxing act. There is no doubt that the statute could tax salaries to those who earned them and provide that the tax could not be escaped by anticipatory arrangements and contracts however skilfully devised to prevent the salary when paid from vesting even for a second in the man who earned it. That seems to us the import of the statute before us and we think that no distinction can be taken according to the motives leading to the arrangement by which the fruits are attributed to a different tree from that on which they grew.

Judgment reversed.

THE CHIEF JUSTICE took no part in this case.

Problems, Note and Question

1. *"Attenuated subtleties."* Did the result in *Earl* turn upon the fact that Mrs. Earl was not a party to the contracts between Earl and those for whom he performed services? In United States v. Basye, 410 U.S. 441 (1973), a portion of payments for medical services furnished by doctors practicing as a partnership was paid (pursuant to contract) to a retirement trust, established to benefit the partnership's doctors (i.e., both present and future partner and non-partner doctors). The Court,

relying on Lucas v. Earl, held the fees to be income of the partnership, rather than the trust.

2. *Problems.*

(1) *C*, age 14, won a cereal box-top contest. The prize was a one-week session at a soccer camp for *C* and nineteen friends chosen by *C*. The contest sponsor paid the cost of the participants' tuition, meals, lodging and transportation. What result to *C*?

full value to winner

(2) Each child of an executive at Generous Industries, Inc., is entitled to a scholarship (of up to $10,000 a year) to defray the tuition at a private elementary or secondary school. *E* is an executive at Generous Industries. In the current year *E*'s child *C* receives from Generous Industries an $8000 scholarship to attend a private school. What result?

addition of $8,000 to E

(3) Each child of a faculty member at Metropolitan University is entitled to a scholarship (of up to $10,000 a year) to defray the tuition at a private elementary or secondary school. *P* is a professor at Metropolitan University. In the current year *P*'s child *C* receives from the University an $8000 scholarship to attend a private school. What result? See § 117(d). In interpreting this section, it is worth noting that its legislative history says that "qualified tuition reductions" may be in the form of cash grants.

exception under § 117(d)

POE v. SEABORN

Supreme Court of the United States, 1930.
282 U.S. 101, 51 S.Ct. 58, 75 L.Ed. 239.

Mr. Justice Roberts delivered the opinion of the Court.

Seaborn and his wife, citizens and residents of the State of Washington, made for the year 1927 separate income tax returns as permitted by the Revenue Act of 1926, c. 27, § 223.

During and prior to 1927 they accumulated property comprising real estate, stocks, bonds and other personal property. While the real estate stood in his name alone, it is undisputed that all of the property real and personal constituted community property and that neither owned any separate property or had any separate income.

The income comprised Seaborn's salary, interest on bank deposits and on bonds, dividends, and profits on sales of real and personal property. He and his wife each returned one-half the total community income as gross income and each deducted one-half of the community expenses to arrive at the net income returned.

The Commissioner of Internal Revenue determined that all of the income should have been reported in the husband's return, and made an additional assessment against him. Seaborn paid under protest, claimed a refund, and on its rejection, brought this suit.

The District Court rendered judgment for the plaintiff (32 F.(2d) 916); the Collector appealed, and the Circuit Court of Appeals certified to us the question whether the husband was bound to report for income tax the entire income, or whether the spouses were entitled each to return one-half thereof. This Court ordered the whole record to be sent up. 281 U.S. 704.

The case requires us to construe sections 210(a) and 211(a) of the Revenue Act of 1926 (44 Stat. 21), and apply them, as construed, to the interests of husband and wife in community property under the law of Washington. These sections lay a tax upon the net income of every individual. The Act goes no farther, and furnishes no other standard or definition of what constitutes an individual's income. The use of the word "of" denotes ownership. It would be a strained construction, which, in the absence of further definition by Congress, should impute a broader significance to the phrase.

The Commissioner concedes that the answer to the question involved in the cause must be found in the provisions of the law of the State, as to a wife's ownership of or interest in community property. What then, is the law of Washington as to the ownership of community property and of community income including the earnings of the husband's and wife's labor?

The answer is found in the statutes of the State, and the decisions interpreting them.

These statutes provide that, save for property acquired by gift, bequest, devise or inheritance, all property however acquired after marriage, by either husband or wife, or by both, is community property. On the death of either spouse his or her interest is subject to testamentary disposition, and failing that, it passes to the issue of the decedent and not to the surviving spouse. While the husband has the management and control of community personal property and like power of disposition thereof as of his separate personal property, this power is subject to restrictions which are inconsistent with denial of the wife's interest as co-owner. The wife may borrow for community purposes and bind the community property. Fielding v. Ketler, 86 Wash. 194, 149 P. 667. Since the husband may not discharge his separate obligation out of community property, she may, suing alone, enjoin collection of his separate debt out of community property. Fidelity & Deposit Co. v. Clark, 144 Wash. 520, 258 P. 35. She may prevent his making substantial gifts out of community property without her consent. Parker v. Parker, 121 Wash. 24, 207 P. 1062. The community property is not liable for the husband's torts not committed in carrying on the business of the community. Schramm v. Steele, 97 Wash. 309, 166 P. 634.

The books are full of expressions such as "the personal property is just as much hers as his" (Marston v. Rue, 92 Wash. 129, 159 P. 111, 112); "her property right in it [an automobile] is as great as his" (Id., 92 Wash. 133, 159 P. 111, 113); "the title of one spouse therein was a legal title, as well as that of the other" (Mabie v. Whittaker, 10 Wash. 663, 39 P. 172, 175).

Without further extending this opinion it must suffice to say that it is clear the wife has, in Washington, a vested property right in the community property, equal with that of her husband; and in the income of the community, including salaries or wages of either husband or wife, or both. A description of the community system of Washington and of the rights of the spouses, and of the powers of the husband as manager, will be found in Warburton v. White, 176 U.S. 484.

The taxpayer contends that if the test of taxability under Sections 210 and 211 is ownership, it is clear that income of community property is owned by the community and that husband and wife have each a present vested one-half interest therein.

The Commissioner contends, however, that we are here concerned not with mere names, nor even with more technical legal titles; that calling the wife's interest vested is nothing to the purpose, because the husband has such broad powers of control and alienation, that while the community lasts, he is essentially the owner of the whole community property, and ought so to be considered for the purposes of sections 210 and 211. He points out that as to personal property the husband may convey it, may make contracts affecting it, may do anything with it short of committing a fraud on his wife's rights. And though the wife must join in any sale of real estate, he asserts that the same is true, by virtue of statutes, in most States which do not have the community system. He asserts that control without accountability is indistinguishable from ownership, and that since the husband has this, quoad community property and income, the income is that "of" the husband under sections 210, 211 of the income tax law.

We think in view of the law of Washington above stated this contention is unsound. The community must act through an agent. This Court has said with respect to the community property system (Warburton v. White, 176 U.S. 494) that "property acquired during marriage with community funds became an acquet of the community and not the sole property of the one in whose name the property was bought, although by the law existing at the time the husband was given the management, control, and power of sale of such property. This right being vested in him, not because he was the exclusive owner, but because by law he was created the agent of the community."

In that case, it was held that such agency of the husband was neither a contract nor a property right vested in him, and that it was competent to the legislature which created the relation to alter it, to confer the agency on the wife alone, or to confer a joint agency on both spouses, if it saw fit—all without infringing any property right of the husband. See, also, Arnett v. Reade, 220 U.S. 311, at page 319.

The reasons for conferring such sweeping powers of management on the husband are not far to seek. Public policy demands that in all ordinary circumstances, litigation between wife and husband during the life of the community should be discouraged. Law-suits between them would tend to subvert the marital relation. The same policy dictates that third parties who deal with the husband respecting community property shall be assured that the wife shall not be permitted to nullify his transactions. The powers of partners, or of trustees of a spendthrift trust, furnish apt analogies.

The obligations of the husband as agent of the community are no less real because the policy of the State limits the wife's right to call him to account in a court. Power is not synonymous with right. Nor is obligation coterminous with legal remedy. The law's investiture of the husband with broad powers, by no means negatives the wife's present interest as a co-owner.

We are of opinion that under the law of Washington the entire property and income of the community can no more be said to be that of the husband, than it could rightly be termed that of the wife.

* * *

The Commissioner urges that we have, in principle, decided the instant question in favor of the Government. He relies on United States v. Robbins, 269 U.S. 315; Corliss v. Bowers, 281 U.S. 376, and Lucas v. Earl, 281 U.S. 111.

In the *Robbins* Case, we found that the law of California, as construed by her own courts, gave the wife a mere expectancy and that the property rights of the husband during the life of the community were so complete that he was in fact the owner. Moreover, we there pointed out that this accorded with the executive construction of the Act as to California.

The *Corliss* Case raised no issue as to the intent of Congress, but as to its power. We held that where a donor retains the power at any time to revest himself with the principal of the gift, Congress may declare that he still owns the income. While he has technically parted with title, yet he in fact retains ownership, and all its incidents. But here the husband never has ownership. That is in the community at the moment of acquisition.

In the *Earl* Case a husband and wife contracted that any property they had or might thereafter acquire in any way, either by earnings (including salaries, fees, etc.), or any rights by contract or otherwise, "shall be treated and considered, and hereby is declared to be received, held, taken, and owned by us as joint tenants. * * * "We held that assuming the validity of the contract under local law, it still remained true that the husband's professional fees, earned in years subsequent to the date of the contract were his individual income, "derived from salaries, wages, or compensation for personal service," under sections 210, 211, 212(a) and 213 of the Revenue Act of 1918 (40 Stat. 1062–1065). The very assignment in that case was bottomed on the fact that the earnings would be the husband's property, else there would have been nothing on which it could operate. That case presents quite a different question from this, because here, by law, the earnings are never the property of the husband, but that of the community.

Finally the argument is pressed upon us that the Commissioner's ruling will work uniformity of incidence and operation of the tax in the various states, while the view urged by the taxpayer will make the tax fall unevenly upon married people. This argument cuts both ways. When it is remembered that a wife's earnings are a part of the community property equally with her husband's it may well seem to those who live in states where a wife's earnings are her own, that it would not tend to promote uniformity to tax the husband on her earnings as part of his income. The answer to such argument, however, is that the constitutional requirement of uniformity is not intrinsic, but geographic. Billings v. United States, 232 U.S. 261; Head Money Cases, 112 U.S. 580; Knowlton v. Moore, 178 U.S. 41. And differences of state law, which may bring a person within or without the category designated by Congress as taxable, may not be read into the Revenue Act to spell out a lack of uniformity. Florida v. Mellon, 273 U.S. 12.

The District Court was right in holding that the husband and wife were entitled to file separate returns, each treating one-half of the community income as his or her respective incomes, and its judgment is affirmed.

THE CHIEF JUSTICE and MR. JUSTICE STONE took no part in the consideration or decision of this case.

Notes and Questions

1. *The basis of the Seaborn decision.* Article 5.22 of the Texas Family Code now provides that "each spouse has the sole management, control, and disposition of the community property that he or she would have owned if single." Does Poe v. Seaborn still require that community income in Texas be taxed half to the husband and half to the wife? Why?

Consider the deference to local law in *Seaborn.* Why was the "owner" label applied by Washington law to Mrs. Seaborn controlling? Was half of the income in *Seaborn* taxed to Mrs. Seaborn because the law gave her ownership rights, or because it described her as an owner? And in any event, why should "ownership" matter, given Lucas v. Earl? Indeed, is it even possible for state law to make someone an "owner" of *income*? Is income money? Would "income" in the sense in which that term is used in Federal tax cases even exist if the Internal Revenue Code were repealed?

With *Seaborn,* compare Corliss v. Bowers, 281 U.S. 376 (1930). In 1922, the taxpayer had created a trust to pay the income to his wife for life, with remainder to their children, but retained the power to revoke the trust. The Revenue Act of 1924 taxed the income of revocable trusts (including those created before passage of the Act) to their grantors. The taxpayer argued that Congress could not constitutionally tax him on the trust's 1924 income (which had been paid to the taxpayer's wife) because he had neither legal nor equitable title to the trust property when the 1924 Act was passed. In upholding the constitutionality of taxing the grantor, Justice Holmes said:

But taxation is not so much concerned with the refinements of title as it is with actual command over the property taxed * * *. If a man directed his bank to pay over income as received to a servant or friend, until further orders, no one would doubt that he could be taxed upon the amounts so paid. It is answered that in that case he would have a title, whereas here he did not. But from the point of view of taxation there would be no difference. * * * The income that is subject to a man's unfettered command and that he is free to enjoy at his own option may be taxed to him as his income, whether he sees fit to enjoy it or not.

281 U.S. at 378.

Seaborn is sometimes distinguished from *Earl* on the ground that the "assignment" in *Seaborn* was "imposed by law." Is a state's community property system more "law" than its law of contracts?

2. *The other edge of the sword.* Suppose a wife in a community property state is deserted by her husband, who then proceeds to earn and squander a great deal of money. The state law regards half the husband's income as "belonging" to the wife, which, as a practical matter, means at best that she can prevent some of his spending if she can find him, and perhaps only that she can get some of what has not been spent if her husband dies or if she gets a divorce. Does it make any sense at all to tax the wife on half of what the husband earns? Can this result be avoided, given Poe v. Seaborn? United States v. Mitchell, 403 U.S. 190 (1971), holds that it cannot.

Section 66, which was added to the Code in 1980 and which has since been expanded, alleviates the *Mitchell* problem for some cases in which taxing one spouse on "community" income earned by the other would make no sense at all.

Being deserted can create tax problems for a spouse even in noncommunity property states because the tax rates for married taxpayers not filing joint returns are higher than the rates for both married taxpayers filing jointly and unmarried taxpayers. Section 7703(b) helps in a few cases, but only if the deserted spouse maintains a household for his dependent children or stepchildren. Note that § 7703(b) can result in A's not being married to B for tax purposes even though B is married to A.

3. *"Elective" community property.* The inevitable result of Poe v. Seaborn was the adoption by a number of states of "community property" laws. The Supreme Court held in Commissioner v. Harmon, 323 U.S. 44 (1944), that Oklahoma's new community property system, which applied only to couples who so elected, did not effect a splitting of income. Does that make sense? At least some "traditional" community property states allow the parties to elect out of community property treatment, a feature that has never been thought to make Poe v. Seaborn inapplicable to couples who do not exercise the election. Justice Douglas, dissenting in *Harmon*, said that "the truth of the matter is that

Lucas v. Earl * * * and Poe v. Seaborn * * * state competing theories of income tax liability." (323 U.S. at 56.)

4. *The Uniform Marital Property Act.* Effective January 1, 1986, Wisconsin became the first state to adopt a community property system based upon the Uniform Marital Property Act, which was promulgated in 1984 by the Conference of Commissioners on Uniform State Laws. Unless the spouses otherwise agree, the Wisconsin law vests in each spouse an undivided half-interest in all marital property. Rev.Rul. 87–13, 1987–1 C.B. 20, holds that, where the spouses file separate returns, each must report as income half of the couple's total wages and half the income from marital property.

5. *"Tax avoidance."* The "assignment of income doctrine" is often justified by saying that it is "needed to prevent tax avoidance." Do statements like this say anything more than that income should be taxed to its earner, rather than to the person to whom the earnings in question are given? If earnings produced by *A*'s efforts are paid to *B*, and if the person who should be taxed on those earnings is *B*, there would be no unjustifiable "tax avoidance" if *B* were taxed. Therefore, to say that "*A* should not be able to avoid taxes by having his salary paid to *B*" is simply to say that salaries should be income to their earners, not to their earners' donees.

6. *Income of children.* Read § 73. Is this an exception to the rule of Lucas v. Earl or a confirmation of it? How would the income of a child be taxed without § 73?

Since 1987, some unearned income of children under the age of fourteen has been taxed at the marginal rate of the child's parents. See pp. 469–471.

7. *References.* Gunn, Tax Avoidance, 76 Mich.L.Rev. 733, 758–65 (1978); Swihart, Federal Taxation of New Mexico Community Property, 3 Natural Resources J. 104 (1963); Bruton, Taxation of Family Income, 41 Yale L.J. 1172 (1932).

REVENUE RULING 72–542

1972–2 C.B. 37.

Advice has been requested with respect to the treatment, for Federal income tax purposes, of proceeds, received by a race track on charity day, that are subsequently distributed to a charitable organization.

The taxpayer is a corporation engaged in the business of operating a pari-mutuel race track. The corporation is licensed, regulated, and supervised by the Racing Commission of the state where the track is operated. The corporation is licensed to operate the track a predetermined number of days, but elected under regulations of the Racing Commission to operate the track one additional day only for purposes of charity. Under such regulations, the corporation's election requires it to contribute all of the gross amount of that portion of gross receipts of all pari-mutuel wagers retained by it (i.e., a certain percentage of the pari-mutuel wagers less the state's tax thereon) from such charity day racing, to a charitable corporation, trust, fund or foundation. A foundation was formed by the corporation that qualifies as an organization described in section 170(c)(2). The taxpayer's portion of the pari-mutuel wagers from charity day racing was distributed to the foundation. There was no expectation of an economic return commensurate with the amount distributed.

There is no written or verbal [sic] lease between the taxpayer and the foundation concerning the use of the track facilities during charity day, and the provisions of the general insurance policy issued to the taxpayer provides [sic] public liability coverage on charity day. Advertising and promotional activities for charity day are provided by the taxpayer.

Section 61(a) defines gross income as all income, from whatever source derived, except as otherwise provided by law.

[Treas.Reg. §] 1.61–2(c) provides that the value of services is not includible in gross income when such services are rendered directly and gratuitously to an organization described in section 170(c). However, such section of the regulations also provides that if, pursuant to an agreement or understanding, services are rendered to a person for the benefit of an organization described in section 170(c) and an amount for such services is paid to such organization by the person to whom the services are rendered, the amount so paid constitutes income to the person performing the services.

It is a fundamental concept in tax law that there is realization of income to the person who has the right to receive it or the power to dispose of it, and payment directly to an exempt organization, at the direction of the person whose individual personal services earned it, constitutes an assignment of income that is disregarded for Federal income tax purposes. See Helvering v. Horst, 311 U.S. 112.

Revenue Ruling 68–503, C.B. 1968–2, 44, holds that when, at the request of a political fund-raising organization, an individual taxpayer gratuitously rendered professional services as a featured performer in entertainment programs planned, organized, promoted, and scheduled by the organization, no amount is includible in the individual taxpayer's gross income. The rationale of such holding is that the fund-raising organization was the promoter of the entertainment program.

In the instant case, the taxpayer and not the foundation is the promoter of charity day since only the taxpayer is licensed by the state to operate a pari-mutuel race track. Under the state's regulations, the taxpayer could operate the track an additional day over the predetermined number of days allotted to it only if the taxpayer contributes its portion of the pari-mutuel wagers to a charitable organization. The taxpayer is not an agent for the foundation and is in effect assigning to the foundation earnings derived by it from the operation of the charity day racing.

Accordingly, that portion of gross receipts of all pari-mutuel wagers retained by the taxpayer on charity day racing and subsequently distributed to the charitable foundation is income to the taxpayer within the meaning of section 61.

Section 162(a) allows as a deduction in computing taxable income all the ordinary and necessary expenses paid or incurred during the taxable year in carrying on any trade or business. Section 170(a) allows as a deduction any charitable contribution paid within the taxable year.

Section 162(b) and [Treas.Reg. §] 1.162–15(a)(1) provide, in pertinent part, that no deduction is allowable under section 162(a) for a contribution or gift by an individual or a corporation if any part thereof is deductible under section 170.

If a taxpayer makes a transfer of property to a charitable organization with a reasonable expectation of an economic return to himself in his trade or business, commensurate with the amount of the transfer, no deduction under section 170 is allowable with respect to such transfer and the transfer may constitute an ordinary and necessary business expense under section 162. See Revenue Ruling 72–314, C.B. 1972–1, 44: Conversely, if a taxpayer makes a voluntary transfer of property to a charitable organization without expectation of a commensurate economic return to him in his trade or business, the deductibility of the transfer is determined under section 170, and no deduction under section 162 is allowable with respect to such transfer.

Whether a particular transfer was made with a reasonable expectation of an economic return commensurate with the amount of the transfer is a question of fact. In the instant case, the taxpayer did not expect a commensurate economic return from the amount distributed to the foundation.

Accordingly, the amount of pari-mutuel wagers retained by the taxpayer on charity day racing and distributed to the charitable foundation is not deductible as an ordinary and necessary business expense by the taxpayer under section 162(a). However, such amount is deductible as a charitable contribution under section 170, subject to the conditions and limitations contained in section 170.

Note

1. *How to do it.* In Rev.Rul. 77–121, 1977–1 C.B. 17, the Service elaborated on Rev.Rul. 72–542. The 1977 ruling also concerned a race track's "charity day," but in that ruling the charity agreed to reimburse the track for any losses it suffered and to assume all responsibility for promoting the event. These facts, said the 1977 ruling, made the charity the event's promoter, and the income from the event was taxable to the charity, not the track.

KIRCHER v. UNITED STATES

United States Court of Appeals, Federal Circuit, 1989.
872 F.2d 1014.

Before RICH, SMITH, and NEWMAN, CIRCUIT JUDGES.

EDWARD S. SMITH, CIRCUIT JUDGE.

In these federal income tax cases, Father Jerome G. Kircher and Father Valens J. Waldschmidt (collectively referred to as taxpayers) appeal from decisions of the United States Claims Court dismissing their complaints and denying them a refund of income taxes assessed by and paid to the Internal Revenue Service (IRS). * * * We affirm.

ISSUE

The issue on appeal is whether the Claims Court erred in holding that the taxpayers had earned income as chaplains at public hospitals in their individual capacities and not as agents of their religious order.

BACKGROUND

A. The Taxpayers

* * * The taxpayers are ordained Roman Catholic priests and are members in good standing of the Province of St. John the Baptist of the Order of Friars Minor. This is an Ohio nonprofit corporation and is a subdivision of the Roman Catholic religious order commonly known as the Franciscans (Franciscan Order). A primary mission of the Franciscan Order is serving and administering to the poor and to the infirm. The Franciscan Order is, and was at all times during the tax years in question, an exempt organization as described in section 501(c)(3).

As members of the Franciscan Order, the taxpayers were required to subscribe to and to obey vows of poverty and obedience. Father Kircher, on August 16, 1935, and Father Waldschmidt, on August 16, 1942, testified to their final and solemn vows of poverty and obedience. In accordance with their vows, the taxpayers executed a declaration renouncing all interest in ownership of compensation received for services performed while members of the Franciscan Order.

1. Father Kircher and the Leper Hospital

Father Kircher, during the tax years in question, held the position of Roman Catholic chaplain at the National Leprosarium (now known as the National Hansen's Disease Center), Public Health Service, Department of Health, Education & Welfare in Carville, Louisiana (Leper Hospital). This position was a civil service position in the Federal Government. It was the practice of the Leper Hospital to have two chaplains in residence, one of whom was a Roman Catholic and the other a Protestant. Within the Roman Catholic Church, only an ordained priest may celebrate the Eucharist and administer the Sacraments according to its rites. Accordingly, only an ordained priest could serve as the Roman Catholic chaplain at the Leper Hospital.

All appointments to civil service positions at the Leper Hospital are made by the chief of the Personnel Office and are processed by the Personnel Office. The position of chaplain was under the general supervision of the chief of Rehabilitation Branch. This individual also evaluated Father Kircher's performance of his duties as described in his job description. Neither the Leper Hospital, the Public Health Service, nor the Civil Service Commission supervised the manner in which Father Kircher carried out his religious duties as chaplain. However, the Leper Hospital did establish the framework within which Father Kircher served. In addition, the Leper Hospital determined the manner and scope of Father Kircher's other activities which were not related to the actual conduct of religious rites or ceremonies or to his priestly function.

The Roman Catholic Diocese of Baton Rouge (Diocese) and its predecessor, the Roman Catholic Archdiocese of New Orleans (Archdiocese), have made Roman Catholic priests available to serve as chaplains at the Leper Hospital since 1896. Since 1959, the Franciscan Order has had an understanding with the Archdiocese, and subsequently the Diocese, that the Franciscan Order would provide from its members individuals to serve as chaplain at the Leper Hospital. The director of the Leper Hospital, the chief of the Rehabilitation Branch, and the chief of the Personnel Office had no knowledge of this understanding.

By letter dated June 7, 1971, the Franciscan Order advised Father Kircher that he had been assigned to the chaplaincy of the Leper Hospital. On June 15, 1971, using the Standard Form 171 of the United States Civil Service Commission, Father Kircher applied for the position. The Standard Form 171 submitted by Father Kircher was processed in accordance with the usual procedures of the Civil Service Commission and Father Kircher was interviewed by the chief of the Rehabilitation Branch at the Leper Hospital. During this process, Father Kircher understood that, although he had been assigned to the Leper Hospital by his religious superiors, he had not been hired as the chaplain and would not be unless the chief of the Personnel Office acted favorably upon his application form and appointed him to the position.

On or about June 30, 1971, Father Kircher was selected for the civil service position designated as Chaplain CA–494 IA. He entered duty on July 1, 1971. There was no written agreement between the United States and the Roman Catholic Church or any subdivision thereof regarding the employment of Father Kircher as a chaplain at the Leper Hospital.

Father Kircher was required by the Franciscan Order to assure that there was always a Roman Catholic chaplain available to patients of the Leper Hospital and, accordingly, was not permitted by the Franciscan Order to be absent from the hospital unless a replacement priest was available for the period of time he was to be absent. However, during Father Kircher's absences from the Leper Hospital, neither the Roman Catholic Church nor the Franciscan Order had any legal responsibility to provide a replacement. Father Kircher had an annual visitation by the Minister Provincial of the Franciscan Order, Father Kircher's religious superior, and various other visits by other members of the Franciscan Order. These occasions afforded the opportunity for these individuals to observe and to comment on Kircher's performance.

From July 1971 through November 1982, the Leper Hospital paid Father Kircher biweekly by means of a payroll check. These checks were made payable to Father Kircher, not to his religious order. Father Kircher endorsed and deposited his payroll checks in a checking account entitled "Franciscan Fathers, Chaplain P.H.S. Hospital, Carville, Louisiana." Father Kircher was the only individual authorized to sign checks on this account. On a regular basis, Father Kircher remitted to the Franciscan Order any amounts in the Franciscan Fathers checking account in excess of those retained for his daily living needs as permitted by the order. During his period of service as chaplain at the Leper Hospital, Father Kircher received paid annual leave, sick leave, and holidays.

2. Father Waldschmidt and the Mental Hospital

[Father Waldschmidt served as chaplain at a state mental hospital in Ohio. His appointment was obtained in a manner similar to that of Father Kircher's. Father Waldschmidt's arrangement with the mental hospital was similar to Father Kircher's arrangement with the Leper Hospital.]

B. The Federal Income Tax Returns

The taxpayers timely filed federal income tax returns for the tax years in question. On these returns, the taxpayers reported as gross income all amounts received for their chaplaincy services; however, the taxpayers excluded from adjusted gross income all of the amounts received for chaplaincy services. Upon audit, the IRS disallowed the exclusion from adjusted gross income of the taxpayers' salaries as chaplains. A timely claim for refund was filed but was denied. The taxpayers then commenced suits in the Claims Court.

The parties filed partial stipulations of facts and filed cross-motions for summary judgment. Both parties asserted that they were entitled to summary judgment based on this court's decision in Fogarty v. United States [780 F.2d 1005 (Fed.Cir.1986)]. Following a hearing on the parties' motions, the Claims Court held that the United States was entitled to summary judgment, concluding that the taxpayers had earned income as chaplains at the respective hospitals in their individual capacities and not as agents of the Franciscan Order. The taxpayers' complaints were dismissed.

ANALYSIS

* * *

The Internal Revenue Code imposes a tax on the taxable income of "*every*" individual (unless statutorily exempted or excluded) [§ 1], and it defines gross income as "all income from whatever source derived." [§ 61.] Thus, in considering whether the income of certain individuals is not taxable to those individuals, we are looking to depart from a thoroughfare heavily traveled in one direction and from which the exits are very few and extremely narrow.

The question whether a member of a religious order earns income in an individual capacity, or as an agent of his order, is one of law based on general principles of agency to be established by considering all of the underlying facts. There are no hard and fast rules. The unique facts in each case will inevitably lead the court to place more emphasis on one or more factors and less on others.

The taxpayers do not dispute that the legal principles set forth in *Fogarty* control the outcome of their cases. Rather, the taxpayers contend that the Claims Court's failure to consider and apply to the facts of their cases all "six factors" set forth in *Fogarty* to reach its decision is reversible error. We disagree.

In *Fogarty,* we addressed the issue whether a member of a religious order, who is subject to vows of poverty and obedience, earned income in an individual capacity or, alternatively, earned income as an agent of his religious order. In that case, we gave, by way of example only, some considerations that may be relevant to this legal issue. These included the following: (1) the degree of control exercised by the order over the member, (2) the ownership rights between the member and the order, (3) the purposes or mission of the order, (4) the type of work performed by the member vis-a-vis the purposes or mission of the order, (5) the dealings between the member and the third-party employer, and (6) the dealings between the employer and the order. However, we did not intend to formulate rigid standards. Rather, we adopted a flexible approach that would balance the diverse factual circumstances of each case against the basic principle of income taxation that income is taxable to the person who earns it. We reject all approaches that attempt to specify particular factors that must be considered in determining the issue at bar.

The taxpayers further argue that the Claims Court's analysis is flawed because it only recites the similarities between the taxpayers' cases and the facts set forth in *Fogarty*. The taxpayers contend that an examination of the significant differences involved between the taxpayers' cases and Father Fogarty's case necessarily leads to the conclusion that the taxpayers were acting as agents of the Franciscan Order in carrying out the mission of the order. We are unpersuaded.

Father Fogarty was a Roman Catholic priest and a member of the Society of Jesus religious order (Jesuit Order) who was instructed by his religious superiors to accept a teaching position at the University of Virginia's Department of Religious Studies. Teaching is an essential and traditional mission of the Jesuit Order. Although Father Fogarty's teaching duties were determined by the University of Virginia, Father Fogarty's acceptance and retention of the position was subject to the dictates of his religious superior. There was, however, no employment agreement between the University of Virginia and the Jesuit Order. Father Fogarty received monthly payroll checks made payable to him individually, which checks were deposited in a checking account in the name of Father Fogarty's religious order. Father Fogarty's entire salary went to his religious order and the order provided him with living expenses.

After a careful review of the record and of the arguments presented on appeal, we must conclude that the taxpayers' cases are not distinguishable from *Fogarty*. Both the taxpayers and Father Fogarty were directed by their religious superiors to pursue positions at secular institutions. Because of their vows of obedience and poverty, the taxpayers, like Father Fogarty, were required to accept those positions and were not entitled to keep the income earned as compensation. Instead, as in *Fogarty*, this income was turned over by the taxpayers to their religious order and their order provided them with living expenses.

Moreover, while occupying their positions, the taxpayers, as was Father Fogarty, were pursuing essential and traditional missions of their religious order. Here, the taxpayers pursued the Franciscan Order's mission of serving and administering to the poor and to the infirm, by serving as chaplains in federal and state hospitals whereas, in *Fogarty*, Father Fogarty pursued the Jesuit Order's mission of teaching by teaching courses on Catholic religious thought, development, and history at the University of Virginia.

Finally, we recognize no distinguishable difference in this case vis-a-vis *Fogarty* either as to the dealings between the taxpayers and the hospitals or as to the dealings between the hospitals and the Franciscan Order. Here, as in *Fogarty*, the contractual employment relationship existed solely between the individual taxpayers and the hospitals. The taxpayers' cases, like Father Fogarty's case, involved no agreement between the hospitals and the religious order. The sole dealing between the Franciscan Order and the hospitals was making the taxpayers available to fill the hospitals' openings in their chaplaincy positions.[14] Although the hospitals may have looked to the Franciscan Order as a source of candidates to fill their chaplaincy vacancies, all applications for those positions were processed in accord with the usual hiring procedures of the hospitals. The appointment or rejection of a candidate for a chaplaincy position rested within the exclusive discretion of the hospital authorities.

CONCLUSION

For the reasons discussed, the Claims Court's judgments, dismissing the taxpayers' complaints seeking a refund of income taxes paid for the tax years in question, are affirmed.

---

14. This is not to say that, as a requirement for agency status, the dealings between the employers (hospitals) and the third party (the Franciscan Order) need rise to the level of an oral or written agreement since, as previously discussed, we have rejected any so called "triangle theory" which requires contractual agreement between the employer and the third party. Such a relationship, however, would be objective evidence that may be considered. See *Fogarty*, 780 F.2d at 1012.

Problems, Notes and Questions

1. *Performance of services for a charity.* If contributions to a charity are deductible, why does it matter whether an individual or organization performing services for a charity must include the earnings in question in income?

2. *Other cases.* Rev.Rul. 74–581, 1974–2 C.B. 25, held that law school faculty and students representing litigants as part of a clinical program did not have to include in income fees for court-appointed appearances. The fees were paid to the faculty members and students, who turned them over to the law school. The Service explained the result by saying that the taxpayers were "working solely as agents of the law school." Is a student an "agent" of a school, or vice versa?

3. *Problems.*

(1) *F* is a member of a religious order that requires a vow of poverty from its members. Upon becoming a member, *F* agreed never to claim compensation for his services while a member of the order. With the permission of the order, *F* accepted a full-time teaching post at a public university. *F*'s vow required him to endorse his university salary checks over to the order. At no time after endorsing the checks did *F* exercise any control over the funds. *F* lived in an apartment rented for him by the order and was required to submit to the order a monthly budget of living expenses. If the order approved the budget, it paid *F*'s monthly living expenses. Must *F* include his university salary in gross income?

(2) *R*, a musician, has been asked to give a concert, with the proceeds from ticket sales going to a political fund-raising organization. *R* would not be paid for her performance. *R* asks you how the concert should be organized so as to avoid *R*'s being taxed on the proceeds. What do you advise?

B. MARRIAGE AND THE INCOME TAX

Many (but not all[a]) of the differences in the tax burdens of married couples in community property and common-law states were eliminated by the Revenue Act of 1948, which allowed married couples to "split" their incomes if they elected to file joint returns. Until 1969, the principal effect of filing a joint return was to make the tax on a given amount of a married couple's taxable income equal to twice the tax on one income of half the amount of income reported. Thus, the tax for a jointly filing couple with total taxable income of $20,000 was twice the

a. Suppose that one spouse has adjusted gross income of $100,000 and miscellaneous itemized deductions of $3000, and that the other spouse has $100,000 adjusted gross income and no miscellaneous itemized deductions. In a community property jurisdiction, each spouse would be allocated half of the miscellaneous itemized deductions (be- cause the amounts were paid from community funds), and so none of them would be deductible (recall that under § 67, these deductions are allowed only to the extent that they exceed 2 percent of AGI). In a common-law jurisdiction, if the spouses file separate returns, $1000 of the miscellaneous itemized deductions will be deductible.

tax payable by an unmarried taxpayer with an income of $10,000 (and less than the tax of a single taxpayer with an income of $20,000). This income-splitting feature not only reduced the tax differences between couples in community property and common-law states, it made irrelevant the distribution of income between spouses in common-law states. So long as a joint return was filed, a married couple, each member of which had $10,000 taxable income, paid the same tax as a family in which one spouse had $20,000 taxable income and the other had none.

One side effect of the 1948 legislation was this: An unmarried taxpayer with an income of $20,000 could reduce his tax by marrying someone with no income. Single taxpayers, understandably enough, complained; and in the Tax Reform Act of 1969 Congress tried to deal with this "discrimination" against the unmarried. The 1969 Act did not eliminate income splitting, but it raised the rates for married taxpayers who file joint returns. The act also raised the rates for married taxpayers who do not file joint returns. The 1969 Act made almost everyone unhappy. Single taxpayers still see themselves as victims of discrimination, because a single taxpayer can still come out ahead after tax by marrying someone with no income and filing a joint return. Married taxpayers also complain of discrimination, because two unmarried taxpayers with roughly equal incomes will often increase their tax burdens by marrying each other, whether or not they file joint returns.

A "marriage penalty" or "marriage bonus" can arise whenever the Code uses a dollar figure, such as a limit on the amount of an expense that can be deducted or an amount of adjusted gross income at which a tax benefit is phased out. The rate brackets of § 1 are one example. Consider another: the phaseouts of the child tax credit of § 24. An unmarried taxpayer begins to lose this credit when modified AGI passes $75,000; a married couple filing a joint return begins to lose it at modified AGI of $110,000. Two unmarried taxpayers, each with modified AGI of $75,000 and each of whom supports a "qualifying child," will get a child tax credit of $600 each (through 2004). If they marry and file a joint return, and if their modified AGI is $150,000, they will get no child tax credit. Apart from various other possible marriage penalties, marriage will cost this couple $1200 a year just because of the loss of the child tax credit.

The "marriage penalty" in the case of the child tax credit could be eliminated easily enough. If the phaseout numbers for a married couple filing jointly were twice the numbers for unmarried taxpayers, the couple in the previous paragraph would lose none of their child tax credit by marrying. This approach would, however, create a "marriage bonus" for some taxpayers. Suppose that an unmarried taxpayer starts to lose the child tax credit at a modified AGI of $75,000 and that a married couple filing jointly began to lose it at a modified AGI of $150,000. Under this system, an unmarried taxpayer with AGI of $125,000 would get no child tax credit, but such a taxpayer would qualify for the full credit by marrying someone with no income. For a taxpayer with two children, this would amount to a $1200 "marriage bonus."

The reductions in tax rates effected by the Tax Relief Act of 2001 were designed to reduce some marriage penalties. The standard deduction for a married couple will be twice the amount for single taxpayers in 2009 (smaller increases begin in 2005), the top amount of a married couple's income taxed at 15% will increase to twice the amount for unmarried taxpayers by 2008, and the phaseout range for the earned-income credit for a couple will increase gradually until 2007. Several other phaseout thresholds have been or will be raised for married taxpayers. These changes fall far short of eliminating marriage penalties and they increase marriage bonuses for many couples with unequal incomes. The general effect of the changes is to make being married less unattractive for some couples, and more attractive for others.

One fairly popular proposal for eliminating all "marriage penalties" is to allow (or require) married taxpayers to file as if they were unmarried. This approach has problems too. For one thing, unless Poe v. Seaborn were overruled by statute, it would revive the geographic discrimination that led to the 1948 legislation. Compare a married couple in Wisconsin with one in Indiana, and assume that, in each case, one spouse earns $100,000 a year and the other earns nothing. The Wisconsin couple could file as unmarried taxpayers and still have their incomes split, as the tax law treats each spouse as earning $50,000. The Indiana couple would get no income splitting if they filed as if single. Furthermore, even if the *Seaborn* problem were solved legislatively, the tax burden of a married couple with income of $100,000 would vary, depending on which spouse earned how much income. Some couples regard the earnings of either spouse as "theirs." For this kind of person, the idea that equal-income couples would pay different income taxes depending on the irrelevant (to them) detail of which spouse earned how much would seem unattractive.

Marriage penalties are by no means limited to the rich, or even to the relatively well off. Two low-income taxpayers with children who marry each other can easily lose several thousand dollars in earned-income credits (even if they have no income-tax liability).

A 1995 article on marriage penalties contained an example of two taxpayers with a combined tax liability of $8912 who would have a liability of $36,570 if they married each other; Maule, Tax and Marriage: Unhitching the Horse and the Carriage, 67 Tax Notes 539, 542 (1995). The example is artificial, but not unrealistic. The situation is even worse today, as the Taxpayer Relief Act of 1997 enacted a number of new deductions and credits subject to dollar limits and phaseouts. In the past, many people have assumed that few taxpayers actually decide whether or not to marry because of tax considerations. Today, it seems clear that many do, and that some of those who do not later regret their choices.

Problems, Notes and Questions

1. *Problems.* These problems are designed to illustrate the marriage penalties and bonuses created by a progressive rate structure. For

simplicity, we offer the following rate brackets for use in doing the problems. These rates affect married taxpayers in much the same way as the actual rates, but they are much simpler. Assume that there are no deductions (including personal exemptions).

§ 10000(a): (Rates for unmarried taxpayers)

If taxable income is:	The tax is:
Not over $10,000	10 percent of taxable income.
Over $10,000 but not over $30,000	$1000 plus 20 percent of the excess.
Over $30,000	$5000 plus 50 percent of the excess.

§ 10000(b): (Rates for married taxpayers filing jointly)

If taxable income is:	The tax is:
Not over $16,000	10 percent of taxable income.
Over $16,000 but not over $40,000	$1600 plus 20 percent of the excess.
Over $40,000	$6400 plus 50 percent of the excess.

§ 10000(c): (Rates for married taxpayers filing separately)

If taxable income is:	The tax is:
Not over $8000	10 percent of taxable income.
Over $8000 but not over $20,000	$800 plus 20 percent of the excess.
Over $20,000	$3200 plus 50 percent of the excess.

(1) Arnold and Barbara are unmarried. Each has $25,000 of gross income and $25,000 taxable income. What is their combined tax liability? See § 10000(a).

(2) Arnold and Barbara get married and file a joint return. Their gross income and taxable income is $50,000. What is their combined tax liability? See § 10000(b).

(3) Arnold and Barbara, distressed by the "marriage penalty" illustrated in (2), try to avoid it by filing separate returns. Each has gross income and taxable income of $25,000. will this help? See § 10000(c).

(4) Cora and Dave are unmarried. Cora has gross and taxable income of $45,000; Dave has $5000 gross and taxable income. What is their combined tax liability? See § 10000(a).

(5) Cora and Dave get married. The couple's gross and taxable income is $50,000. What is their combined tax liability if they file a joint return? See § 10000(b).

2. *Conflicting policy goals.* Is it possible to have a progressive income tax that is marriage-neutral and also imposes equal taxes on couples with equal incomes?

3. *The incremental tax on a second wage-earner's income.* Consider a married couple with one wage-earner making $100,000 a year. The spouse who does not work outside the home is thinking of taking a job which will pay $10,000 a year and which will cost $6000 in additional commuting expenses, lunches, and clothing, and in payments to plumbers, painters and cleaning people needed to do the work around the house that the spouse who is going to work used to do. These costs are not deductible. By how much will the couple's income (after the additional expenses and taxes) increase if the spouse takes the job? (Unless your instructor requests otherwise, use the rate schedule in Appendix B.)

Former § 221, enacted in 1981, allowed a married couple filing a joint return a deduction equal to ten percent of the lesser of (1) the earned income of the lesser-earning spouse or (2) $30,000. The provision was repealed in 1986.

4. *References.* Esenwein, Income Taxation of Married Couples: Background and Analysis, 90 Tax Notes 1081 (2001); Zelenak, Marriage and the Income Tax, 67 So.Cal.L.Rev. 339 (1994); Jones, Split Income and Separate Spheres: Tax Law and Gender Roles in the 1940s, 6 Law & History Rev. 259 (1988); Bittker, Federal Income Taxation and the Family, 27 Stan.L.Rev. 1389 (1975).

C. INCOME FROM PROPERTY

1. IN GENERAL

BLAIR v. COMMISSIONER

Supreme Court of the United States, 1937.
300 U.S. 5, 57 S.Ct. 330, 81 L.Ed. 465.

Mr. Chief Justice Hughes delivered the opinion of the Court.

This case presents the question of the liability of a beneficiary of a testamentary trust for a tax upon the income which he had assigned to his children prior to the tax years and which the trustees had paid to them accordingly.

* * *

[Blair was the life income beneficiary of a trust created under his father's will. In 1923, he irrevocably assigned to each of three children $9000 a year from the trust income. In later years, he assigned additional interests to his children. The trustees thereafter distributed the income directly to the children in accordance with the assignments. The Commissioner, sustained by the Court of Appeals, sought to tax the income to Blair, and the Supreme Court granted certiorari.

The Court's discussion of (1) a procedural issue and (2) the validity of the assignments under state law has been omitted.]

Third. The question remains whether, treating the assignments as valid, the assignor was still taxable upon the income under the federal income tax act. That is a federal question.

Our decisions in Lucas v. Earl, 281 U.S. 111, and Burnet v. Leininger, 285 U.S. 136, are cited. In the *Lucas* case the question was whether an attorney was taxable for the whole of his salary and fees earned by him in the tax years or only upon one-half by reason of an agreement with his wife by which his earnings were to be received and owned by them jointly. We were of the opinion that the case turned upon the construction of the taxing act. We said that "the statute could tax salaries to those who earned them and provide that the tax could not be escaped by anticipatory arrangements and contracts however skillfully devised to prevent the salary when paid from vesting even for a second in the man who earned it." That was deemed to be the meaning of the statute as to compensation for personal service and the one who earned the income was held to be subject to the tax. In Burnet v. Leininger, supra, a husband, a member of a firm, assigned future partnership income to his wife. We found that the revenue act dealt explicitly with the liability of partners as such. The wife did not become a member of the firm; the act specifically taxed the distributive share of each partner in the net income of the firm; and the husband by the fair import of the act remained taxable upon his distributive share. These cases are not in point. The tax here is not upon earnings which are taxed to the one who earns them. Nor is it a case of income attributable to a taxpayer by reason of the application of the income to the discharge of his obligation. Old Colony Trust Company v. Commissioner, 279 U.S. 716 [further citations omitted]. There is here no question of evasion or of giving effect to statutory provisions designed to forestall evasion; or of the taxpayer's retention of control. Corliss v. Bowers, 281 U.S. 376; Burnet v. Guggenheim, 288 U.S. 280.

In the instant case, the tax is upon income as to which, in the general application of the revenue acts, the tax liability attaches to ownership. See Poe v. Seaborn, supra; Hoeper v. Tax Commission, 284 U.S. 206.

The Government points to the provisions of the revenue acts imposing upon the beneficiary of a trust the liability for the tax upon the income distributable to the beneficiary. But the term is merely descriptive of the one entitled to the beneficial interest. These provisions cannot be taken to preclude valid assignments of the beneficial interest, or to affect the duty of the trustee to distribute income to the owner of the beneficial interest, whether he was such initially or becomes such by valid assignment. The one who is to receive the income as the owner of the beneficial interest is to pay the tax. If under the law governing the trust the beneficial interest is assignable, and if it has been assigned without reservation, the assignee thus becomes the beneficiary and is entitled to rights and remedies accordingly. We find nothing in the revenue acts which denies him that status.

The decision of the Circuit Court of Appeals turned upon the effect to be ascribed to the assignments. The court held that the petitioner had no interest in the corpus of the estate and could not dispose of the income until he received it. Hence it was said that "the income was *his*" and his assignment was merely a direction to pay over to others what was due to himself. The question was considered to involve "the date when the income became transferable." 83 F.2d 655, at page 662. The Government refers to the terms of the assignment—that it was of the interest in the income "which the said party of the first part now is, or may hereafter be, entitled to receive during his life from the trustees." From this it is urged that the assignments "dealt only with a right to receive the income" and that "no attempt was made to assign any equitable right, title or interest in the trust itself." This construction seems to us to be a strained one. We think it apparent that the conveyancer was not seeking to limit the assignment so as to make it anything less than a complete transfer of the specified interest of the petitioner as the life beneficiary of the trust, but that with ample caution he was using words to effect such a transfer. That the state court so construed the assignments appears from the final decree which described them as voluntary assignments of interests of the petitioner "in said trust estate," and it was in that aspect that petitioner's right to make the assignments was sustained.

The will creating the trust entitled the petitioner during his life to the net income of the property held in trust. He thus became the owner of an equitable interest in the corpus of the property. [Citations omitted.] By virtue of that interest he was entitled to enforce the trust, to have a breach of trust enjoined and to obtain redress in case of breach. The interest was present property alienable like any other, in the absence of a valid restraint upon alienation. [Citations omitted.] The beneficiary may thus transfer a part of his interest as well as the whole. See Restatement of the Law of Trusts, §§ 130, 132 et seq. The assignment of the beneficial interest is not the assignment of a chose in action but of the "right, title, and estate in and to property." [Citations omitted.]

We conclude that the assignments were valid, that the assignees thereby became the owners of the specified beneficial interests in the income, and that as to these interests they and not the petitioner were taxable for the tax years in question. The judgment of the Circuit Court of Appeals is reversed and the cause is remanded with direction to affirm the decision of the Board of Tax Appeals.

It is so ordered.

HELVERING v. HORST

Supreme Court of the United States, 1940.
311 U.S. 112, 61 S.Ct. 144, 85 L.Ed. 75.

MR. JUSTICE STONE delivered the opinion of the Court.

The sole question for decision is whether the gift, during the donor's taxable year, of interest coupons detached from the bonds, delivered to the donee and later in the year paid at maturity, is the realization of income taxable to the donor.

In 1934 and 1935 respondent, the owner of negotiable bonds, detached from them negotiable interest coupons shortly before their due date and delivered them as a gift to his son who in the same year collected them at maturity. The Commissioner ruled that under the applicable § 22 of the Revenue Act of 1934, 48 Stat. 680, 686, the interest payments were taxable, in the years when paid, to the respondent donor who reported his income on the cash receipts basis. The circuit court of appeals reversed the order of the Board of Tax Appeals sustaining the tax. 2 Cir., 107 F.2d 906; 39 B.T.A. 757. We granted certiorari, 309 U.S. 650, because of the importance of the question in the administration of the revenue laws and because of an asserted conflict in principle of the decision below with that of Lucas v. Earl, 281 U.S. 111, and with that of decisions by other circuit courts of appeals. See Bishop v. Commissioner, 7 Cir., 54 F.2d 298; Dickey v. Burnet, 8 Cir., 56 F.2d 917, 921; Van Meter v. Commissioner, 8 Cir., 61 F.2d 817.

The court below thought that as the consideration for the coupons had passed to the obligor, the donor had, by the gift, parted with all control over them and their payment, and for that reason the case was distinguishable from Lucas v. Earl, supra and Burnet v. Leininger, 285 U.S. 136, where the assignment of compensation for services had preceded the rendition of the services, and where the income was held taxable to the donor.

The holder of a coupon bond is the owner of two independent and separable kinds of right. One is the right to demand and receive at maturity the principal amount of the bond representing capital investment. The other is the right to demand and receive interim payments of interest on the investment in the amounts and on the dates specified by the coupons. Together they are an obligation to pay principal and interest given in exchange for money or property which was presumably the consideration for the obligation of the bond. Here respondent, as owner of the bonds, had acquired the legal right to demand payment at maturity of the interest specified by the coupons and the power to command its payment to others which constituted an economic gain to him.

Admittedly not all economic gain of the taxpayer is taxable income. From the beginning the revenue laws have been interpreted as defining "realization" of income as the taxable event rather than the acquisition of the right to receive it. And "realization" is not deemed to occur until the income is paid. But the decisions and regulations have consistently recognized that receipt in cash or property is not the only characteristic of realization of income to a taxpayer on the cash receipts basis. Where the taxpayer does not receive payment of income in money or property realization may occur when the last step is taken by which he obtains the fruition of the economic gain which has already accrued to him. Old Colony Trust Co. v. Commissioner, 279 U.S. 716; Corliss v. Bowers, 281 U.S. 376, 378. Cf. Burnet v. Wells, 289 U.S. 670.

In the ordinary case the taxpayer who acquires the right to receive income is taxed when he receives it, regardless of the time when his right to receive payment accrued. But the rule that income is not taxable until realized has never been taken to mean that the taxpayer, even on the cash receipts basis, who has fully enjoyed the benefit of the economic gain represented by his right to receive income, can escape taxation because he has not himself received payment of it from his obligor. The rule, founded on administrative convenience, is only one of postponement of the tax to the final event of enjoyment of the income, usually the receipt of it by the taxpayer, and not one of exemption from taxation where the enjoyment is consummated by some event other than the taxpayer's personal receipt of money or property. Cf. Aluminum Castings Co. v. Routzahn, 282 U.S. 92, 98. This may occur when he has made such use or disposition of his power to receive or control the income as to procure in its place other satisfactions which are of economic worth. The question here is, whether because one who in fact receives payment for services or interest payments is taxable only on his receipt of the payments, he can escape all tax by giving away his right to income in advance of payment. If the taxpayer procures payment directly to his creditors of the items of interest or earnings due him, see Old Colony Trust Co. v. Commissioner, supra; Bowers v. Kerbaugh–Empire Co., 271 U.S. 170; United States v. Kirby Lumber Co., 284 U.S. 1, or if he sets up a revocable trust with income payable to the objects of his bounty, §§ 166, 167, Revenue Act of 1934, Corliss v. Bowers, supra; cf. Dickey v. Burnet, 8 Cir., 56 F.2d 917, 921, he does not escape taxation because he did not actually receive the money. Cf. Douglas v. Willcuts, 296 U.S. 1; Helvering v. Clifford, 309 U.S. 331.

Underlying the reasoning in these cases is the thought that income is "realized" by the assignor because he, who owns or controls the source of the income, also controls the disposition of that which he could have received himself and diverts the payment from himself to others as the means of procuring the satisfaction of his wants. The taxpayer has equally enjoyed the fruits of his labor or investment and obtained the satisfaction of his desires whether he collects and uses the income to procure those satisfactions, or whether he disposes of his right to collect it as the means of procuring them. Cf. Burnet v. Wells, supra.

Although the donor here, by the transfer of the coupons, has precluded any possibility of his collecting them himself he has nevertheless, by his act, procured payment of the interest, as a valuable gift to a member of his family. Such a use of his economic gain, the right to receive income, to procure a satisfaction which can be obtained only by the expenditure of money or property, would seem to be the enjoyment of the income whether the satisfaction is the purchase of goods at the corner grocery, the payment of his debt there, or such non-material satisfactions as may result from the payment of a campaign or community chest contribution, or a gift to his favorite son. Even though he never receives the money he derives money's worth from the disposition of the coupons which he has used as money or money's worth in the procuring of a satisfaction which is procurable only by the expenditure of money or money's worth. The enjoyment of the economic benefit accruing to him by virtue of his acquisition of the coupons is realized as completely as it would have been if he had collected the interest in dollars and expended them for any of the purposes named. Burnet v. Wells, supra.

In a real sense he has enjoyed compensation for money loaned or services rendered and not any the less so because it is his only reward for them. To say that one who has made a gift thus derived from interest or earnings paid to his donee has never enjoyed or realized the fruits of his investment or labor because he has assigned them instead of collecting them himself and then paying them over to the donee, is to affront common understanding and to deny the facts of common experience. Common understanding and experience are the touchstones for the interpretation of the revenue laws.

The power to dispose of income is the equivalent of ownership of it. The exercise of that power to procure the payment of income to another is the enjoyment and hence the realization of the income by him who exercises it. We have had no difficulty in applying that proposition where the assignment preceded the rendition of the services, Lucas v. Earl, supra; Burnet v. Leininger, supra, for it was recognized in the *Leininger* case that in such a case the rendition of the service by the assignor was the means by which the income was controlled by the donor and of making his assignment effective. But it is the assignment by which the disposition of income is controlled when the service precedes the assignment and in both cases it is the exercise of the power of disposition of the interest or compensation with the resulting payment to the donee which is the enjoyment by the donor of income derived from them.

This was emphasized in Blair v. Commissioner, 300 U.S. 5, on which respondent relies, where the distinction was taken between a gift of income derived from an obligation to pay compensation and a gift of income-producing property. In the circumstances of that case the right to income from the trust property was thought to be so identified with the equitable ownership of the property from which alone the beneficiary derived his right to receive the income and his power to command disposition of it that a gift of the income by the beneficiary became effective only as a gift of his ownership of the property producing it. Since the gift was deemed to be a gift of the property the income from it was held to be the income of the owner of the property, who was the donee, not the donor, a refinement which was unnecessary if respondent's contention here is right, but one clearly inapplicable to gifts of interest or wages. Unlike income thus derived from an obligation to pay interest or compensation, the income of the trust was regarded as no more the income of the donor than would be the rent from a lease or a crop raised on a farm after the leasehold or the farm had been given away. Blair v. Commissioner, supra, 300 U.S. 12, 13 and cases cited. See also Reinecke v. Smith, 289 U.S. 172, 177. We have held without deviation that where the donor retains control of the trust property the income is taxable to him although paid to the donee. Corliss v. Bowers, supra. Cf. Helvering v. Clifford, supra.

The dominant purpose of the revenue laws is the taxation of income to those who earn or otherwise create the right to receive it and enjoy the benefit of it when paid. See, Corliss v. Bowers, supra, 281 U.S. 378; Burnet v. Guggenheim, 288 U.S. 280, 283. The tax laid by the 1934 Revenue Act upon income "derived from * * * wages, or compensation for personal service, of whatever kind and in whatever form paid * * *; also from interest * * * "therefore cannot fairly be interpreted as not applying to income derived from interest or compensation when he who is entitled to receive it makes use of his power to dispose of it in procuring satisfactions which he would otherwise procure only by the use of the money when received.

It is the statute which taxes the income to the donor although paid to his donee. Lucas v. Earl, supra; Burnet v. Leininger, supra. True, in those cases the service which created the right to income followed the assignment and it was arguable that in point of legal theory the right to the compensation vested instantaneously in the assignor when paid although he never received it; while here the right of the assignor to receive the income antedated the assignment which transferred the right and thus precluded such an instantaneous vesting. But the statute affords no basis for such "attenuated subtleties." The distinction was explicitly rejected as the basis of decision in Lucas v. Earl. It should be rejected here, for no more than in the *Earl* case can the purpose of the statute to tax the income to him who earns, or creates and enjoys it be escaped by "anticipatory arrangements * * * however skillfully devised" to prevent the income from vesting even for a second in the donor.

Nor is it perceived that there is any adequate basis for distinguishing between the gift of interest coupons here and a gift of salary or commissions. The owner of a negotiable bond and of the investment which it represents, if not the lender, stands in the place of the lender. When, by the gift of the coupons, he has separated his right to interest payments from his investment and procured the payment of the interest to his donee, he has enjoyed the economic benefits of the income in the same manner and to the same extent as though the transfer were of earnings and in both cases the import of the statute is that the fruit is not to be attributed to a different tree from that on which it grew. See Lucas v. Earl, supra, 281 U.S. 115.

Reversed.

The separate opinion of MR. JUSTICE McREYNOLDS.

The facts were stipulated. In the opinion of the court below [107 F.2d 907], the issues are thus adequately stated: "The petitioner owned a number of coupon bonds. The coupons represented the interest on the bonds and were payable to bearer. In 1934 he detached unmatured coupons of face value of $25,182.50 and transferred them by manual delivery to his son as a gift. The coupons matured later on in the same year, and the son collected the face amount, $25,182.50, as his own property. There was a similar transaction in 1935. The petitioner kept his books on a cash basis. He did not include any part of the moneys collected on the coupons in his income tax returns for these two years. The son included them in his returns. The Commissioner added the moneys collected on the coupons to the petitioner's taxable income and determined a tax deficiency for each year. The Board of Tax Appeals, three members dissenting, sustained the Commissioner, holding that the amounts collected on the coupons were taxable as income to the petitioner." The decision of the Board of Tax Appeals was reversed and properly so, I think.

The unmatured coupons given to the son were independent negotiable instruments, complete in themselves. Through the gift they became at once the absolute property of the donee, free from the donor's control and in no way dependent upon ownership of the bonds. No question of actual fraud or purpose to defraud the revenue is presented.

Neither Lucas v. Earl, 281 U.S. 111, nor Burnet v. Leininger, 285 U.S. 136, support petitioner's view. Blair v. Commissioner, 300 U.S. 5, 11, 12, shows that neither involved an unrestricted completed transfer of property.

Helvering v. Clifford, 309 U.S. 331, 335, 336, decided after the opinion below, is much relied upon by petitioner, but involved facts very different from those now before us. There no separate thing was absolutely transferred and put beyond possible control by the transferor. The court affirmed that Clifford, both conveyor and trustee, "retained the substance of full enjoyment of all the rights which previously he had in the property." "In substance his control over the corpus was in all essential respects the same after the trust was created, as before." "With that control in his hands he would keep direct command over all that he needed to remain in substantially the same financial situation as before."

The general principles approved in Blair v. Commissioner, 300 U.S. 5, are applicable and controlling. The challenged judgment should be affirmed.

THE CHIEF JUSTICE and MR. JUSTICE ROBERTS concur in this opinion.

Problems, Notes and Questions

1. *Timing.* Was Horst's transfer of the coupons a taxable event? If so, when would Horst have been taxed, and how much income would he have had? Compare Harrison v. Schaffner, 312 U.S. 579 (1941), in which a trust beneficiary assigned to a relative part of her income for the year after the year of the assignment. The court held that *Horst,* rather than *Blair,* controlled, and that the donor was taxable "when the gift is effectuated by payment." See also Helvering v. Eubank, p. 465.

A taxpayer holding "series E" or "series EE" government bonds can elect to report interest income annually or to report it all when the bond matures; § 454. Suppose a taxpayer who has not elected annual reporting makes a gift of the bond after holding it for a few years. The Service's view is that the taxpayer must report income accrued up to the date of the gift in the year of the gift. Rev.Rul. 54–327, 1954–2 C.B. 50; Rev.Rul. 55–278, 1955–1 C.B. 471. In Rev.Rul. 87–112, 1987–2 C.B. 207, a taxpayer who transferred U.S. savings bonds to a spouse in a transfer covered by § 1041 was taxed at the time of transfer on the accrued interest. The transferee assumed the transferor's basis, as increased by the interest taxable to the transferor.

How would Horst have been taxed if he had given his bond and all its coupons to his son between interest dates? See First Nat. Bank of St. Elmo, Ill. v. United States, 194 F.2d 389 (7th Cir.1952), in which a bank which owned mineral interests conveyed those interests to its shareholders as a dividend. The bank was held taxable on the royalty income attributable to production up to the time of the conveyance.

2. *Other cases.* In Braunstein v. Commissioner, 21 T.C.M. 1132 (1962), the holders of an Irish Sweepstakes ticket gave the ticket away before the race but after being notified that their ticket had been "assigned" a horse. The "assignment" meant that the taxpayers were assured of a small prize even if their horse lost the race. The Tax Court held the donors taxable on the guaranteed proceeds, but not on the remaining winnings and not on the fair market value of the ticket at the time of the transfer.

In Caruth Corp. v. United States, 865 F.2d 644 (5th Cir.1989), the controlling shareholder of a corporation gave shares of the corporate stock to a charity after the declaration of a dividend but before the record date. (Dividends are payable to those persons who own shares on the record date.) The court held that the dividend was not taxable to the donor. Contrast *Caruth* with Ferguson v. Commissioner, 174 F.3d 997 (9th Cir.1999). In *Ferguson*, the taxpayers gave stock to charities after a majority of the outstanding shares had been tendered to an acquirer pursuant to a tender offer, and then the charities tendered the stock. Finding that the merger was "practically certain" to go through, and that the stock had ripened into a fixed right to receive cash by the date the stock was transferred to the charities, the court held that the taxpayers were taxable on the gain. Was not the dividend in *Caruth* practically certain to go through after it had been declared?

3. *Section 1286.* Section 1286, enacted in 1982, raises some doubt about whether *Horst* is still the law. Section 1286(b) provides that a person who strips one or more coupons from a bond and then "disposes of the bond or such coupon" has income in the amount of interest accrued on the bond up to the time of disposition. Section 1286(f) gives the Treasury Department broad authority to issue regulations providing for the proper result if "the tax treatment under this section does not accurately reflect the income of the holder of a stripped coupon or stripped bond." Perhaps the new regulations will preserve (or change) *Horst*.

In view of the holding of *Horst,* as clarified by *Schaffner,* should a taxpayer who strips a coupon from a bond and gives the coupon to a relative be viewed as having "disposed of" the coupon?

4. *Interest-free loans.* One way for a taxpayer to shift income temporarily to a relative is to lend the relative money without charging interest. For example, suppose Horst lends his son $50,000 for two years, without interest, and the son puts the money in a savings account, receiving $5000 in interest in each of the two years. Economically, this transaction differs very little from one in which Horst invests the $50,000 himself and pays the interest to the son, but it was generally assumed that an interest-free loan did not generate taxable income to the lender. Today, the parties to "gift loans" at no interest or low interest are taxed as if the borrower had paid the lender interest at a market rate. See § 7872, discussed at pp. 415–418.

5. *Pattern and rationale.* The interests transferred in *Horst* and in Harrison v. Schaffner are called "carved-out" income interests. What factual difference between those cases and *Blair* led to the difference in result? Conceding that line drawing must be done everywhere in the law, why is the line drawn in this particular way? Suppose Horst had given his son the bond and the coupons; would (should) he have remained taxable on the interest as the coupons became due?

6. *Problems.*

(1) *P* owned real property that was subject to a lease with a remaining term of 25 years. Last year, *P,* intending to make a gift, irrevocably assigned his rights to future rental payments under the lease to his adult child, *C.* (*P* paid a gift tax on the transfer.) The lessee thereafter paid the rent to *C.* What result to *P* and *C*?

(2) Suppose instead that, on last December 31, *P* assigned to *C* the fee interest in the property (subject to the lease). At that time, the lessee owed $1000 rent for the month of December. The lessee paid the $1000 to *C* in January of this year. Both *P* and *C* are cash-method taxpayers.

(3) *P* was seriously injured in an automobile accident caused by *D's* drunken driving. *P* filed suit against *D* seeking compensatory and punitive damages. Immediately after filing suit, *P* irrevocably assigned her claim for punitive damages to her adult child, *C.* The assignment was permissible under state law. *P* was awarded $100,000 in punitive damages, which *D* paid to *C* in the current year after *D* lost an appeal to the state supreme court. What result to *P* and *C*?

(4) What result in (3) if instead *P* had assigned one-third of any recovery to her attorney?

7. *References.* Lyon & Eustice, Assignment of Income: Fruit and Tree as Irrigated by the P.G. Lake Case, 17 Tax L.Rev. 295 (1962); Surrey, The Supreme Court and the Federal Income Tax: Some Implications of the Recent Decisions, 35 Ill.L.Rev. 779 (1941).

2. PROPERTY OR SERVICES?

HELVERING v. EUBANK

Supreme Court of the United States, 1940.
311 U.S. 122, 61 S.Ct. 149, 85 L.Ed. 81.

Mr. Justice Stone delivered the opinion of the Court.

This is a companion case to Helvering v. Horst, 311 U.S. 112, decided this day, and presents issues not distinguishable from those in that case.

Respondent, a general life insurance agent, after the termination of his agency contracts and services as agent, made assignments in 1924 and 1928 respectively of renewal commissions to become payable to him for services which had been rendered in writing policies of insurance under two of his agency contracts. The Commissioner assessed the renewal commissions paid by the companies to the assignees in 1933 as income taxable to the assignor in that year under the provisions of the 1932 Revenue Act, 47 Stat. 169, § 22, of which does not differ in any respect now material from § 22 of the 1934 Revenue Act involved in the *Horst* case. The Court of Appeals for the Second Circuit reversed the order of the Board of Tax Appeals sustaining the assessment. 110 F.2d 737; 39 B.T.A. 583. We granted certiorari * * *. 311 U.S. 630.

No purpose of the assignments appears other than to confer on the assignees the power to collect the commissions, which they did in the taxable year. The Government and respondent have briefed and argued the case here on the assumption that the assignments were voluntary transfers to the assignees of the right to collect the commissions as and when they became payable, and the record affords no basis for any other.

For the reasons stated at length in the opinion in the *Horst* case, we hold that the commissions were taxable as income of the assignor in the year when paid. The judgment below is

Reversed.

The separate opinion of Mr. Justice McReynolds.

The cause was decided upon stipulated facts. The following statement taken from the court's opinion discloses the issues:

"The question presented is whether renewal commissions payable to a general agent of a life insurance company after the termination of his agency and by him assigned prior to the taxable year must be included in his income despite the assignment.

"During part of the year 1924 the petitioner was employed by The Canada Life Assurance Company as its branch manager for the state of Michigan. His compensation consisted of a salary plus certain commissions. His employment terminated on September 1, 1924. Under the terms of his contract he was entitled to renewal commissions on premiums thereafter collected by the company on policies written prior to the termination of his agency, without the obligation to perform any further services. In November 1924 he assigned his right, title and interest in the contract as well as the renewal commissions to a corporate trustee. From September 1, 1924 to June 30, 1927, the petitioner and another, constituting the firm of Hart & Eubank, were general agents in New York City for the Aetna Life Assurance Company, and from July 1, 1927, to August 31, 1927, the petitioner individually was general agent for said Aetna Company. The Aetna contracts likewise contained terms entitling the agent to commissions on renewal premiums paid after termination of the agency, without the performance of any further services. On March 28, 1928 the petitioner assigned to the corporate trustee all commissions to become due him under the Aetna contracts. During the year 1933 the trustee collected by virtue of the assignments renewal commissions payable under the three agency contracts above mentioned, amounting to some $15,600. These commissions were taxed to the petitioner by the commissioner and the Board has sustained the deficiency resulting therefrom." [110 F.2d 738.]

The court below declared: "In the case at bar the petitioner owned a right to receive money for past services; no further services were required. Such a right is assignable. At the time of assignment there was nothing contingent in the petitioner's right, although the amount collectible in future years was still uncertain and contingent. But this may be equally true where the assignment transfers a right to income from investments, as in Blair v. Commissioner, 300 U.S. 5, and Horst v. Commissioner, 2 Cir., 107 F.2d 906, or a right to patent royalties, as in Nelson v. Ferguson, 3 Cir., 56 F.2d 121, certiorari denied 286 U.S. 565. By an assignment of future earnings a taxpayer may not escape taxation upon his compensation in the year when he earns it. But when a taxpayer who makes his income tax return on a cash basis assigns a right to money payable in the future for work already performed, we believe that he transfers a property right, and the money, when received by the assignee, is not income taxable to the assignor."

Accordingly, the Board of Tax Appeals was reversed; and this, I think, is in accord with the statute and our opinions.

The assignment in question denuded the assignor of all right to commissions thereafter to accrue under the contract with the insurance company. He could do nothing further in respect of them; they were entirely beyond his control. In no proper sense were they something either earned or received by him during the taxable year. The right to collect became the absolute property of the assignee without relation to future action by the assignor.

A mere right to collect future payments, for services already performed is not presently taxable as "income derived" from such services. It is property which may be assigned. Whatever the assignor receives as consideration may be his income; but the statute does not undertake to impose liability upon him because of payments to another under a contract which he had transferred in good faith, under circumstances like those here disclosed.

As in Helvering v. Horst just decided, the petitioner relies upon opinions here; but obviously they arose upon facts essentially different from those now presented. They do not support his contention. The general principles approved in Blair v. Commissioner, 300 U.S. 5, and applied in Helvering v. Horst, are controlling and call for affirmation of the judgment under review.

THE CHIEF JUSTICE and MR. JUSTICE ROBERTS concur in this opinion.

MOORE v. COMMISSIONER

Tax Court of the United States, 1968.
27 T.C.M. 536.

TIETJENS, JUDGE: The Commissioner determined a deficiency in income tax against the petitioners for the year 1962 in the amount of $1,567.93 and a negligence penalty under section 6653(a) of $78.40.

By stipulation the parties have settled all issues except one. The only question left for decision is whether petitioner Walter J. Moore must include in his income certain "royalties" based upon sales of an English edition of a book written by him entitled "Physical Chemistry," of which "royalties" he had purportedly made a valid and completed gift in 1958 to his children.

* * *

During the year 1950, petitioner Walter J. Moore's first book, entitled "Physical Chemistry," was published in the United States by Prentice–Hall, Inc. Royalties from that book aggregated approximately $4,000 per year.

[Moore's contract with Prentice–Hall provided that Moore would "set about writing and preparing for publication" a book about physical chemistry. The agreement granted all rights to the book—including the right to copyright it—to Prentice–Hall. The publisher agreed to publish the book and to pay royalties on copies sold. Prentice–Hall then sold its rights to publish the book in the British Commonwealth (except Canada) to Longmans, Green & Co., Ltd.

In 1958, Moore executed a "Certificate of Gift of Royalties," which assigned his entire interest in his author's royalties on the British edition of the book to his children.]

* * *

For the taxable year 1962, the "royalty" income attributable to the English edition of petitioner Walter J. Moore's book was $952.49 which was paid to petitioner's children.

The Commissioner determined that these "royalties" were includable in petitioners' gross income under section 61.

We sustain the Commissioner's determination.

Here, petitioner transferred no manuscript or literary production or copyright or royalty contract to his children. He did purport to give them a portion of his "royalties." Previous to his contract of July 26, 1948 with Prentice–Hall, Inc., no "literary property" was in existence. In essence, under that contract, petitioner simply agreed to "set about writing and preparing for publication a work." The contract contemporaneously "grants this work" (not yet in existence) and "exclusive rights" to it to Prentice–Hall, Inc., in return for certain "royalties," including an equal division of compensation which might in the future be paid to Prentice–Hall, Inc., for use by others of the yet to be created book, under arrangements to be made by Prentice–Hall, Inc. Subsequently, in 1954, such arrangements were made between Prentice–Hall, Inc., and Longmans, Green & Co., Ltd. The payments which were paid by Longmans thereunder were divided between Prentice–Hall, Inc., and petitioner. In 1958 petitioner gave, assigned, and transferred his share of these payments to his children.

To us this was a naked anticipatory assignment of future income by petitioner to his children. He cannot escape taxability of this income to him. The transactions did not transfer property rights in the book to the children. Petitioner had no such rights. He had already granted all of them to Prentice–Hall, Inc. All he ever had left was a right to compensation for his setting about "writing and preparing for publication a work." A portion of this compensation he gave to his children. That's all there was to it.

We do not think we have to decide questions of what are the consequences of how you "slice" or "cut" the tree and the fruit, whether vertically or horizontally. No matter what was sliced, or which way, it was still pure income, and nothing else. See Eustice & Lyons, "Assignment of Income: P.G. Lake and Beyond," 14th University of Southern California Tax Institute 47 (1962). We think the fundamental teachings of Helvering v. Eubank, 311 U.S. 122 (1940), and Harrison v. Schaffner, 312 U.S. 579 (1941), compel us to decide this case for the Commissioner.

Decision will be entered under Rule 50.

Problem, Note and Questions

1. *Copyrights, patents, and similar items.* If Moore had copyrighted his book himself and given the copyright away he would not have been taxed on the royalty income. Why the distinction? Is a transfer of a copyright or patent by an author or inventor distinguishable from the transfer in *Eubank*?

On facts substantially identical to those of *Moore*, the Service has ruled that an author's assignment of "contract rights" to a trust will be respected for tax purposes even though the contract, like Moore's, purports to call for the author's performance of services; Ltr Rul. 8337055. The ruling went on to characterize income attributable to the author's revising the book (after the assignment of the royalties) as earned income, taxable to the author despite the assignment. The extent to which payments to the trust after a revision of the book would be treated as earned income was described as a question of fact, on which the Service would not rule. Note that neither the *Moore* opinion nor Ltr Rul. 8337055 has any precedential value.

Sometimes the issue is whether a right has in fact been assigned. The Fourth Circuit held that purported assignments to an author's wife of half interests in stories written but not yet copyrighted or published lacked "economic reality" where the author (P.G. Wodehouse) alone dealt with the publisher. Wodehouse v. Commissioner, 178 F.2d 987 (4th Cir.1949). But on almost identical facts the Second Circuit went the other way, noting the absence of any evidence of an understanding between Wodehouse and his wife that Wodehouse was to retain control over the transferred stories. Wodehouse v. Commissioner, 177 F.2d 881 (2d Cir.1949).

2. *Problem.* Ownership of race horses is often divided. The owner of the "racing interest" has the right to race the horse and keep the winnings, while the owner of the "breeding interest" has all rights to the horse once he stops racing and is put out to stud. Suppose the owner of a horse assigns the racing interest to his children, retaining the breeding interest. Should the donor be taxed on race winnings on the theory that the racing interest is a "carved out" income interest, like the bond coupons in *Horst*? Or are race winnings income from services? If so, would it matter whether the donor trained the horse, chose the races, and selected the jockey? Compare Hogle v. Commissioner, 132 F.2d 66 (10th Cir.1942), in which the taxpayer, a stockbroker, engaged in extensive and profitable trading on margin for trusts he had established for his minor children. The court held that Hogle's devotion of time and effort to the trading activities made the gains from trading on margin (but not dividend or interest income) personal service income, taxable to Hogle.

3. TAXATION OF THE INCOME OF MINOR CHILDREN

Before 1987, the investment income of a child generally was taxed at the child's tax rates regardless of the parents' tax bracket. The child was usually in a lower tax bracket than the parents, and, even though the child was a dependent of the parents, the child could use the personal exemption to shelter investment income from tax.

The 1986 Act added § 1(g), which, in the case of a child under age 14, generally taxes investment income in excess of $1000 (ignoring inflation adjustments) at the parents' marginal tax rate. In addition, § 151(d)(2) denies a personal-exemption deduction to a taxpayer (regardless of age) for whom a dependency exemption is allowable to another. As a result of these measures, and ignoring inflation adjustments, the first $500 of the child's investment income is usually covered by the child's standard deduction,[b] the next $500 is taxed at the child's tax

---

b. Recall that § 63(c)(5) generally limits the standard deduction of a dependent taxpayer to the greater of (1) $500 or (2) the taxpayer's earned income plus $250.

rates, and investment income in excess of $1000 is taxed at the parent's tax rate.[c]

Under § 1(g)(7), the parents of a child under age 14 can sometimes elect to include the child's investment income in excess of $1000 in the parents' gross income. When an election is made, the first $500 of the child's investment income is still tax free, the next $500 is taxed to the parents at the 15% rate, and the amount in excess of $1000 is taxed to the parents at their marginal rate; see § 1(g)(7)(B)(ii). If an election is made, a return need not be filed for the child; § 1(g)(7)(A).

Generally speaking, a taxpayer can claim a dependency exemption for another only if the dependent's gross income for the year is less than the exemption amount; § 151(c)(1)(A). However, a parent can claim a dependency exemption for a child whom the parent supports if the child is under age 19, without regard to the amount of the child's gross income. And if the child is a full-time student, the parent can claim the exemption without regard to the child's income if the child is under 24; § 151(c)(1)(B).

Problems

Problem (1). H and W have two children, S, age 17, and D, age 12. H and W furnish all of the support for S and D, both of whom are full-time students. In the current year, both S and D receive income from investment securities held for them by W, as custodian under the Uniform Transfers to Minors Act.[d] (The children's grandparents had given the securities to the children in 2001. W accumulates all income received from the securities in a custodial account. No income or principal was used for the children's support during the year.) H and W have taxable income of $100,000 on their joint return. (In each case, use the rate tables in Appendix B unless your instructor directs otherwise.)

(a) S and D each receive $400 of income from the securities. What is the tax liability of each?

(b) Same as (a), except that each receives $900 of income from the securities.

(c) Same as (a), except that each receives $2000 of income from the securities.

(d) Same as (c), except that each also receives $2600 from a part-time job.

Problem (2). Using the rate tables for 2002–2003 in Appendix B, calculate the maximum amount of Federal income tax a parent in the

---

c. Even though the parent's marginal tax rate is used to determine the amount of tax due from the child, the tax liability remains the burden of the child.

d. Property held in a custodianship under the Uniform Transfers to Minors Act

legally belongs to the child. Thus, except to the extent used to discharge the parents' support obligation, income from the property is taxed to the child. Rev.Rul. 59–357, 1959–2 C.B. 212 (interpreting the Uniform Gifts to Minors Act).

35–percent bracket can save each year by transferring investment property to a custodian or trustee for the benefit of a dependent child who is:

(a) Under age 14?

(b) Not under age 14?

4. INCOME FROM PROPERTY PLACED IN TRUST

A common method of assigning property income to the taxpayer's children or other close relatives is to place income-producing property in trust. The income from the transferred property will ordinarily be taxed either to the beneficiaries to whom the trust's earnings are distributed or, if those earnings are accumulated, to the trust itself. Thus, if A transfers property in trust to pay all current income to B for life, with remainder to C, the trust's income will be taxed to B. If the trust distributes a portion of its income, keeping the rest, the distributed portion will be taxed to the beneficiary; the rest, less the trust's personal exemption of $100 or $300,[e] will be taxed to the trust itself. Sections 641–668 achieve these results by making the trust a taxpayer and then (1) requiring beneficiaries who receive (or who are entitled to receive) distributions to include some or all of the trust's income in their incomes, and (2) giving the trust a deduction

Using trusts enables donors to achieve important non-tax goals such as providing for relatives unable to manage property for themselves (children, for instance) and facilitating estate planning. Until 1986, using trusts could also provide major income-tax savings for wealthy taxpayers. Under a progressive income tax, the greater the number of taxpayers among whom a given amount of income is divided, the lower the tax: the tax on two incomes of $50,000 each is less than the tax on one income of $100,000. So a taxpayer owning property that produced $100,000 a year in taxable income might place the property in trust for her daughter, with half the trust's income being distributed to the daughter and the other half being accumulated. This would result in the $100,000 of income being taxed half to the trust, at its rates, and half to the daughter, at her rates, rather than entirely to the grantor, at her (usually high) rates. Furthermore, unless the grantor ran afoul of the grantor trust rules (below), the grantor could retain a fair amount of control over the trust property, unlike the case of an outright gift. (Even greater tax savings could once have been achieved by creating multiple trusts: instead of transferring the property in question to a single trust, the grantor might set up four trusts, each receiving one-fourth of the property, and each reporting income of only $25,000 less distributions. Section 643(f), effective as of 1984, now requires many "multiple trusts" like this to be taxed as if they were one trust.)

The Tax Reform Act of 1986 took away most of the income-tax advantages of trusts that accumulate income by compressing the rate

---

e. If the trust's governing instrument requires the trustee to distribute all of the trust's income (in the trust-accounting sense, not the tax sense) currently, the trust's personal exemption is $300; otherwise, it is $100; § 642(b).

brackets for trusts. Under § 1(e), only the first $1500 of a trust's taxable income is taxed at 15 percent, and the trust's highest bracket starts when taxable income exceeds $7500. (These figures, like the other rate brackets, are indexed for inflation: for 2002, a trust's 38.6–percent bracket starts with income over $9200.) Furthermore, if a trust's beneficiary is under the age of fourteen, most of the income distributed to that beneficiary will be taxed at the beneficiary's parents' rate (see p. 469). These measures make trusts much less attractive than they used to be. While a small amount of a trust's income can still be taxed at a lower rate than the grantor's or beneficiary's, the non-tax costs of creating and administering a trust may outweigh the tax savings.

Notes

1. *Grantor trusts.* The trust is a wonderfully flexible creation. A grantor can place property in trust while retaining substantial control over the transferred property or over the trust's distributions. To take an extreme case, suppose that a grantor places property in trust for the benefit of his grandchildren, but retains the right to terminate the trust at any time and get the property back, and to direct the trustee to pay the trust's earnings to someone other than the named beneficiaries. Although the trustee in this case holds "title" to the property, the grantor is in substance as much the owner of the property as before the transfer: the grandchildren will get nothing unless the grantor decides that they should.

Sections 671–679 provide for treating the grantor of a trust as "the owner" of trust property in a variety of situations in which the grantor's control over trust corpus or distributions is so great that it makes sense to treat the grantor as still owning the transferred property. Cases in which the grantor can terminate the trust, or can obtain the trust's income, or can exercise too much control over distributions, or retains a more-than-trivial reversionary interest are examples. If the grantor is "treated as the owner" under these grantor-trust provisions, the trust's income is taxed to the grantor, rather than to the trust and the beneficiaries (even if the income is actually retained by the trust or distributed).

Placing property in a grantor trust achieves no income-tax savings for the grantor but may be useful for a variety of non-tax reasons. For example, someone who owns a vacation home in a state other than that of his principal residence should normally hold the vacation home in trust, so as to avoid the necessity of probate in the vacation-home state when the owner dies. Furthermore, having a trust's income taxed to the grantor may be advantageous from the point of view of estate and gift taxation. Consider a grantor who transfers property in trust to her children, in such a way as to remove the property from her gross estate. If the income of the trust remains taxable to the grantor, the grantor's income-tax payments benefit the children, in the end, by enabling them to receive the trust's property and accumulated income free of income tax, yet the payments are not taxable gifts to the children because the grantor is paying "her own" tax. Estate planners call trusts that take the transferred assets out of the grantor's estate while leaving the grantor taxable on the income "defective trusts," though nothing about them is actually defective: they are designed to do precisely that.

2. *Mallinckrodt trusts.* Section 678 provides for taxing the income of certain trusts to a person other than the grantor or those who would be taxed under the "ordinary" trust rules of §§ 641–668. If, for example, A transfers property to B for life, remainder to C, and gives D a power to terminate the trust and get the corpus himself, or to have the income paid to himself, D rather than B will be taxed on the trust income. Furthermore, if D releases this power but keeps that degree of control that would make a grantor taxable under the grantor-trust provisions, D will be taxed on the income. These trusts are called "Mallinckrodt trusts," after Mallinckrodt v. Nunan, 146 F.2d 1 (8th Cir.1945), cert. denied 324 U.S. 871 (1945).

D. USING BUSINESS ENTERPRISES TO SHIFT INCOME: SECTION 482

The operation of § 482 can best be shown by example. Suppose a non-resident alien owns all the stock of two corporations, "Manufacturer" and "Distributor." Manufacturer is a domestic corporation, fully subject to U.S. income taxation. Distributor is a foreign corporation, not subject to any serious taxation. Manufacturer sells much of its output to Distributor, which packages the products and re-sells them. If the prices set by the parties were accepted at face value, there would be no reason for Manufacturer to pay any tax on account of its sales to Distributor, for prices could be set at a level so low as to produce no income for Manufacturer. Section 482 allows the Commissioner to "allocate" some of the gross income of Distributor to Manufacturer "in order to prevent evasion of taxes or clearly to reflect the income" of Manufacturer.

According to the regulations, § 1.482–1(b), the standard used for § 482 allocations is one of "arm's length dealing." Thus, if Manufacturer's products cost it $1.00 an item to make, and if it charges Distributor $1.10 an item but would have charged an unrelated buyer $1.30, the Commissioner could allocate 20 cents an item of Distributor's gross income to Manufacturer. The arm's length dealing standard of the regulations is extremely hard to apply in practice. If, for example, Manufacturer sells all of its output to Distributor, the arm's length price to be determined under § 482 is entirely hypothetical; it is not necessarily a price at which goods have ever changed hands. Sales of similar products between Manufacturer and unrelated buyers, or between other manufacturers of similar products and their customers, may help to suggest an appropriate transfer price, but many international transactions involve goods or services that are in some ways unique. Section 482 cases are time-consuming and expensive. The regulations provide several methods for establishing arm's length prices.

In an attempt to reduce litigation over hypothetical prices, the Service has established a mechanism by which it can reach "advance pricing agreements" (APAs) with taxpayers before goods or services are sold rather than contesting the prices used after the fact. APAs are agreements about the methods to be used for setting transfer prices in cases involving international transactions. Procedures for obtaining an APA are described in Rev.Proc. 91–22, 1991–1 C.B. 526. The Service charges a $5000 "user fee" for an APA, but this is a very minor part of the cost—it has been estimated that the legal and other costs of obtaining an agreement will range from $500,000 to several million dollars.

The relationship between § 482 and the assignment of income doctrine (often described as requiring "allocation of income under § 61") is unclear. Like the assignment of income doctrine, § 482 "rests on" the policy of taxing income to its earner; Philipp Bros. Chemicals, Inc. v. Commissioner, 435 F.2d 53, 57 (2d Cir.1970). Yet many cases have struggled with such questions as whether two trades or businesses are commonly controlled and whether a taxpayer is in a "trade or business" for purposes of § 482. Unless § 482 does something that the "common law" assignment of income doctrine does not do, litigation about the applicability of § 482 would be a waste of time.

COMMISSIONER v. FIRST SECURITY BANK OF UTAH

Supreme Court of the United States, 1972.
405 U.S. 394, 92 S.Ct. 1085, 31 L.Ed.2d 318.

Mr. Justice Powell delivered the opinion of the Court.

This case presents for review a determination by the Commissioner of Internal Revenue (Commissioner), pursuant to § 482, that the income of taxpayers within a controlled group should be reallocated to reflect the true taxable income of each. Deficiencies were assessed against respondents. The Tax Court affirmed the Commissioner's action, and respondents appealed to the Court of Appeals for the Tenth Circuit. That court reversed the decision of the Tax Court, 436 F.2d 1192 (1971), and we granted the Commissioner's petition for certiorari to resolve a conflict between the decision below and that in Local Finance Corp. v. Commissioner of Internal Revenue, 407 F.2d 629 (C.A.7), cert. denied, Commissioner of Internal Revenue v. Guardian Agency, Inc., 396 U.S. 956 (1969). We now affirm the decision of the Court of Appeals.

Respondents, First Security Bank of Utah, N.A., and First Security Bank of Idaho, N.A. (the Banks), are national banks that, during the tax years, were wholly owned subsidiaries of First Security Corp. (Holding Company). Other, non-bank, subsidiaries of the Holding Company, relevant to this case, were First Security Co. (Management Company), Ed. D. Smith & Sons, an insurance agency (Smith), and—from June 1954—First Security Life Insurance Company of Texas (Security Life). Beginning in 1948, the Banks offered to arrange for borrowers credit life, health, and accident insurance (credit life insurance). The Tax Court found that they did this "for several reasons," including (1) offering a service increasingly supplied by competing financial institutions, (2) obtaining the benefit of the additional collateral that credit insurance provides by repaying loans upon the death, injury, or illness of the borrower, and (3) providing an "additional source of income—part of the premiums from the insurance—to Holding Company or its subsidiaries."

Until 1954, any borrower who elected to purchase this insurance was referred by the Banks to two independent insurance companies. The premium rate charged was $1 per $100 of coverage per year, the rate commonly charged in the industry. The Insurance Commissioners of the States involved—Utah, Idaho, and Texas—accepted this rate. The Banks followed a routine procedure in making this insurance available to customers. The lending officer would explain the function and availability of credit insurance. If the customer desired the coverage, the necessary form was completed, a certificate of insurance was delivered, and the premium was collected or added to the customer's loan. The Banks then forwarded the completed forms and premiums to Management Company, which maintained records of the insurance purchased and forwarded the premiums to the insurance carrier. Management Company also processed claims filed under the policies. The cost to each of the Banks for the actual time devoted to explaining and processing the insurance was less than $2,000 per year, characterized by the courts below as "negligible." The cost to Management Company of the services rendered by it was also negligible, slightly in excess of $2,000 per year.

It was the custom in the insurance business (although not invariably followed), regardless of the cost of incidental paperwork, to pay a "sales commission"—ranging from 40% to 55% of net premiums collected—to a party who originated or generated the business. But the Banks had been advised by counsel that they could not lawfully conduct the business of an insurance agency or receive income resulting from their customers' purchase of credit life insurance. Neither the Banks nor any of their officers were licensed to sell insurance, and there is no question here of unlawfully acting as unlicensed agents. The Banks received no commissions or other income on or with respect to the credit insurance generated by them. During the period from 1948 to 1954 commissions were paid by the independent companies writing the insurance directly, to Smith, one of the wholly owned subsidiaries of Holding Company. These commissions were reported as taxable income, not by Smith, but by Management Company which had rendered the services above described. During this period (1948–1954), the Commissioner did not attempt to allocate the commissions to the Banks.

In 1954, Holding Company organized Security Life, a new wholly owned subsidiary licensed to engage in the insurance business. A new procedure was then adopted with respect to placing credit life insurance. It was referred by the Banks to, and written by an independent company, American National Insurance Company of Galveston, Texas (American National), at the same rate to the customer. American National then reinsured the policies with Security Life pursuant to a "treaty of reinsurance." For assuming the risk under the policies sold to the Banks' customers, Security Life retained 85% of the premiums. American National, which furnished actuarial and accounting services, received the remaining 15%. No sales commissions were paid. Under this new plan, the Banks continued to offer credit life insurance to their borrowers in the same manner as before.

Security Life was not a paper corporation. It commenced business in 1954 with an initial capital of $25,000, which was increased in 1956 to $100,000. Although it did not become a full-line insurance company (contemplated as a possibility when organized), its reinsurance business was substantial. The risks assumed by it had grown to $41,350,000 by the end of 1959, and it had paid substantial claims.

Security Life reported the entire amount of reinsurance premiums, 85% of the premiums charged, in its income for the years 1955–1959. Because the income of life insurance companies then was subject to a lower effective tax rate than that of ordinary corporations, the total tax liability for Holding Company and its subsidiaries was less than it would have been had Security Life paid a part of the premium to the Banks or Management Company as sales commissions. Pursuant to his § 482 power to allocate gross income among controlled corporations in order to reflect the actual incomes of the corporations, the Commissioner determined that 40% of Security Life's premium income was allocable to the Banks as compensation for originating and processing the credit life insurance. It is the Commissioner's view that the 40% of the premium income so allocated is the equivalent of commissions that the Banks earned and must be included in their "true taxable income."

The parties agree that § 482 is designed to prevent "artificial shifting, milking, or distorting of the true net incomes of commonly controlled enterprises." Treasury Regulations provide:

> "The purpose of section 482 is to place a controlled taxpayer on a tax parity with an uncontrolled taxpayer, by determining according to the standard of an uncontrolled taxpayer, the true taxable income from the property and business of a controlled taxpayer. * * * The standard to be applied in every case is that of an uncontrolled taxpayer dealing at arm's length with another uncontrolled taxpayer."

The question we must answer is whether there was a shifting or distorting of the Banks' true net income resulting from the receipt and retention by Security Life of the premiums above described.

We note at the outset that the Banks could never have received a share of these premiums. National banks are authorized to act as insurance agents when located in places having a population not exceeding 5,000 inhabitants, 12 U.S.C.A. § 92.[12] Although § 92 does not explic-

---

12. Section 92 of the National Bank Act was enacted in 1916. when the statutes were revised in 1918 and reenacted, § 92 was omitted. The revisers of the United States Code have omitted it from recent editions of the Code. However, the comp-

itly prohibit banks in places with a population of over 5,000 from acting as insurance agents, courts have held that it does so by implication. The Comptroller of the Currency has acquiesced in this holding, and the Court of Appeals for the Tenth Circuit expressed its agreement in the opinion below.

The penalties for violation of the banking laws include possible forfeiture of a bank's franchise and personal liability of directors. The Tax Court found that the Banks, upon advice of counsel, "held the belief that it would be contrary to Federal banking law * * * to receive income resulting from their customers' purchase of credit insurance" and, pursuant to this belief, "the two Banks have never received or attempted to receive commissions or reinsurance premiums resulting from their customers' purchase of credit insurance."

Petitioner does not contest this finding by the Tax Court or the holding in this respect of the Court of Appeals below. Accordingly, we assume for purposes of this decision that the Banks were prohibited from receiving insurance-related income, although this prohibition did not apply to non-bank subsidiaries of Holding Company.

We know of no decision of this Court wherein a person has been found to have taxable income that he did not receive and that he was prohibited from receiving. In cases dealing with the concept of income, it has been assumed that the person to whom the income was attributed could have received it. The underlying assumption always has been that in order to be taxed for income, a taxpayer must have complete dominion over it. "The income that is subject to a man's unfettered command and that he is free to enjoy at his own option may be taxed to him as his income, whether he sees fit to enjoy it or not." Corliss v. Bowers, 281 U.S. 376, 378 (1930).

It is, of course, well established that income assigned before it is received is nonetheless taxable to the assignor. But the assignment-of-income doctrine assumes that the income would have been received by the taxpayer had he not arranged for it to be paid to another. In Harrison v. Schaffner, 312 U.S. 579, 582 (1941), we said:

> "[O]ne vested with the right to receive income [does] not escape the tax by any kind of anticipatory arrangement, however skillfully devised by which he procures payment of it to another, since, by the exercise of his power to command the income, he enjoys the benefit of the income on which the tax is laid."

One of the Commissioner's regulations for the implementation of § 482 expressly recognizes the concept that income implies dominion or control of the taxpayer. It provides as follows:

> "The interests controlling a group of controlled taxpayers are assumed to have complete power to cause each controlled taxpayer so to conduct its affairs that its transactions and accounting records

troller of the currency considers § 92 to be effective and he still incorporates the provi- sion in his Regulations, 12 CFR §§ 2.1–2.5 (1971).

truly reflect the taxable income from the property and business of each of the controlled taxpayers."[18]

This regulation is consistent with the control concept heretofore approved by this court, although in a different context. The regulation, as applied to the facts in this case, contemplates that holding company—the controlling interest—must have "complete power" to shift income among its subsidiaries. It is only where this power exists, and has been exercised in such a way that the "true taxable income" of a subsidiary has been understated, that the Commissioner is authorized to reallocate under § 482. But Holding Company had no such power unless it acted in violation of federal banking laws. The "complete power" referred to in the regulations hardly includes the power to force a subsidiary to violate the law.

Apart from the inequity of attributing to the Banks taxable income that they have not received and may not lawfully receive, neither the statute nor our prior decisions require such a result. We are not faced with a situation such as existed in those cases, urged by the Commissioner, in which we held the proceeds of criminal activities to be taxable. Those cases concerned situations in which the taxpayer had actually received funds. Moreover, the illegality involved was the act that gave rise to the income. Here the originating and referring of the insurance, a practice widely followed, is acknowledged to be legal. Only the receipt of insurance commissions or premiums thereon by national banks is not. Had the Banks ignored the banking laws, thereby risking the loss of their charters and subjecting their officers to personal liability, the illegal-income cases would be relevant. But the Banks from the inception of their use of credit life insurance in 1948 were careful never to place themselves in that position. We think that fairness requires the tax to fall on the party that actually receives the premiums rather than on the party that cannot.

* * *

We conclude that the premium income received by Security Life could not be attributable to the Banks. Holding Company did not utilize its control over the Banks and Security Life to distort their true net incomes. The Commissioner's exercise of his § 482 authority was therefore unwarranted in this case. The judgment below is affirmed.

Affirmed.

MR. JUSTICE MARSHALL, dissenting.

* * *

Having implicitly rejected the argument that mere nonreceipt of money is sufficient to avoid taxation, the Court proceeds to accept respondents' second argument that in this case the taxpayer is legally barred from ever receiving money, and in this circumstance he cannot be

---

18. § 1.482–1(b)(1) (1971).

taxed on it. Respondents find a legal bar to receipt of the proceeds at issue herein 12 U.S.C.A. § 92 * * *.

* * *

But the crucial fact in this case is that under their own theory respondents have already violated the federal statute and regulations by soliciting insurance premiums. Title 12 U.S.C.A. § 92 was added to the federal banking laws in 1916 at the suggestion of John Skelton Williams, who was then Comptroller of the Currency. He wrote to Congress to recommend that national banks in small communities be permitted to associate with insurance companies, but that banks in larger communities be prohibited from doing the same:

> "It seems desirable from the standpoint of public policy and banking efficiency that this authority should be limited to banks in small communities. This additional income will strengthen them and increase their ability to make a fair return to their shareholders, while the new business is not likely to assume such proportions as to distract the officers of the bank from the principal business of banking. Furthermore in many small places the amount of insurance policies written * * * is not sufficient to take up the entire time of an insurance broker, and the bank is not therefore likely to trespass upon outside business naturally belonging to others.

> "I think it would be unwise and therefore undesirable to confer this privilege generally upon banks in large cities where the legitimate business of banking affords ample scope for the energies of trained and expert bankers. I think it would be unfortunate if any movement should be made in the direction of placing the banks of the country in the category of department stores. * * * " Letter of June 8, 1916, to Senate, 53 Cong.Rec. 11001.

There is nothing in the history of the provision to indicate that Congress was more concerned with banks' actually receiving money than with their performing the activities that generated the money. In fact, the history that is available indicates that it is the activities themselves that Congress wished to stop. Banks in large communities were simply not permitted to do anything that insurance agents might do, i.e., they were not permitted to solicit insurance.

Under respondents' theory of the case, the legal violation is thus a *fait accompli* and the respondents are taxable as if there had been no illegality. * * *

MR. JUSTICE BLACKMUN, with whom MR. JUSTICE WHITE joins, dissenting.

As I read the Court's opinion, I gain the impression that it chooses to link legality with taxability or, to put it better oppositely, that it ties illegality to receive with inability to tax. I find in the Internal Revenue Code no authority for the concoction of a restrictive connection of that kind. Because I think that the Commissioner's allocation of income here, under the auspices of § 482, and in the light of the established facts, was proper, I dissent.

1. Section 482 surely contemplates taxation of income without formal receipt of that income. That, indeed, is the scope and purport of the statute. It is directed at income distortion by a controlling interest among two or more of the controlled entities. I, therefore, am not convinced that the fact the income in question here did not flow through the Banks at any time—because it was deemed proscribed by the 1916 Act (if the pertinent portion thereof, 39 Stat. 753, is still in effect, a proposition which may not be free from doubt), and because the controlling interest routed it elsewhere—serves, in and of itself, to deny the efficacy of the statute.

2. Section 482 has a double purpose and a double target. It authorizes the Secretary or his delegate, that is, the Commissioner, to allocate whenever he determines it necessary so to do in order (a) "to prevent evasion of taxes" or (b) "clearly to reflect the income of any" of the controlled entities. The use of the statute, therefore, is not restricted to the intentional tax evasion. No evasion of tax, in the criminal sense, by these Banks is specifically suggested or at issue here. And I do not subscribe to my Brother Marshall's intimation that what the Banks were doing was otherwise illegal. The second alternative of the statute, however, is directed at something other than tax evasion or illegality. It is concerned with the proper reflection of income (or deductions, credits, or allowances) so as to place the controlled taxpayer on a tax parity with the uncontrolled taxpayer. It is designed to produce for tax purposes, and to recognize, economic realities and to have the tax consequences follow those realities and not some structured nonreality. This is the aspect of the statute with which the Commissioner and these respondents are here concerned. Thus, legality and illegality seem to me to be beside the point.

3. From this it follows that the Court's repetitive emphasis on the missing § 92 and the inability of these Banks legally to receive the insurance commissions give[s] undue emphasis to the first alternative of § 482, and seem[s] almost wholly to ignore the second.

4. The purpose of the controlling interest in structuring the several entities it controls is apparent and cannot be concealed. The Banks were wholly owned subsidiaries of Holding Company. The Tax Court found— and the respondents concede—that one of the purposes of the Banks' arranging for borrowers' credit life insurance was "to provide an additional source of income—part of the premiums from the insurance—to Holding Company or its subsidiaries." T.C.Memo 1967–256, p. 67–1453. For me, that means to provide an additional source of income for the group irrespective of the particular pocket into which that income might initially be routed.

* * *

10. Taxability, despite nonreceipt, is common in our tax law. It is present in a variety of contexts. For example, one has been held taxable,

under the applicable statute's general definition of gross income, for income or earnings assigned to another and never received; for the income from bond coupons, maturing in the future, assigned to another and never received; for dividends paid to the shareholders of a transferor corporation pursuant to a lease with no defeasance clause; for another's income from a short-term trust (until § 673, with its 10–year measure, came into the tax structure with the 1954 Code); for the employer's payment of income taxes on his employees' compensation; and for an irrevocable trust's income used to pay insurance premiums on the settlor's life, or, in the absence of particular state law provisions, distributed to a divorced wife in lieu of alimony (until § 215 came into the Code with the Revenue Act of 1942, 56 Stat. 817).

* * *

Problem, Notes and Questions

1. *Legality and taxability.* In Procter and Gamble Co. v. Commissioner, 95 T.C. 323 (1990), aff'd, 961 F.2d 1255 (6th Cir.1992), the Tax Court refused to allow an allocation of royalties from a wholly owned Spanish corporation to its United States parent. The subsidiary used the parent's patents, trademarks, and other intangible property, paying no royalties. Spanish law and administrative practice prohibited Spanish entities from paying royalties to residents of countries other than Spain. This prohibition was often waived for payments to unrelated entities, or to entities owning a less-than-controlling interest in the Spanish company, but Procter and Gamble, having been advised that a waiver in its case was unlikely, did not apply for one. The Tax Court rejected the Commissioner's contention that the restriction would have been removed if the taxpayer had made a serious attempt; Procter and Gamble, said the court, had "business reasons" for not seeking review.

The Commissioner also argued in *Procter and Gamble* that *First Security* was legally distinguishable. The bank in *First Security* was prohibited from receiving insurance premiums from any person, related or unrelated; in *Procter and Gamble,* the prohibition applied (in practice) only to related entities. That is, arm's length dealings between unrelated parties in the circumstances of *First Security* would not have led to payments, while arm's length dealings between unrelated parties comparable to Procter and Gamble and its subsidiary would have produced royalty payments. The court rejected this distinction on the ground that § 482 is concerned with attempts by taxpayers to distort income; here, it thought, the distortion was created by Spanish law, not by the taxpayer. Perhaps a court that viewed § 482 as a means of having income earned by a taxpayer taxed to that taxpayer would have found *First Security* distinguishable. For an argument that § 482 should be treated as a means of taxing income to its earner, rather than as punishment for those with "bad" motives, see Gunn, Tax Avoidance, 76 Mich.L.Rev. 733, 760–65 (1978).

2. *Section 482 and section 61.* Suppose the government had not relied on § 482 in *First Security,* but had simply argued that the bank, as the earner of the income in question, was the proper taxpayer under Lucas v. Earl. Would the case have gone the other way? If you think the answer is "yes," can you defend the distinction? If the answer is "no," is anything left of *Earl* after *First Security*? Fears that *First Security* had destroyed the assignment of income doctrine were allayed somewhat by United States v. Basye, 410 U.S. 441 (1973) (p. 436, above), in which the Court expressed renewed enthusiasm for the doctrine. *First Security* was distinguished on the ground that it had involved "a deflection of income imposed by law, not an assignment arrived at by the consensual agreement of two parties * * *." 410 U.S. at 453 n. 13.

3. *Problem.* F, a professor of law, earns about $20,000 a year proofreading novels for publishers. *F*'s marginal tax rate is 35 percent. In an attempt to reduce her taxes, *F* forms Proofreading, Inc., a C corporation, and informs the several publishers for whom she does proofreading that they should now send their requests to the corporation. *F* is Proofreading, Inc.'s only shareholder and its only employee. *F* receives a salary of only $500 a year from her corporation, which is very low, as the corporation's only source of income is the fees it receives from the publishers who pay for its services, all of which are actually performed by *F*. The balance of the money the corporation receives is invested; *F* plans to hold the stock until she dies, at which time she will leave it to her children, who (under provisions well beyond the scope of the basic tax course) will be able to liquidate the corporation and obtain the investments without serious tax consequences. The corporation's income, *F* reasons, will be taxed at 15 percent (a C corporation's tax rate on its first $50,000 of income).

Can the Commissioner invoke § 482 to tax *F* and the corporation as if the corporation had paid *F* a salary of around $20,000 a year?

Chapter Eight

INCOME FROM DEALINGS IN PROPERTY—GENERAL CONSIDERATIONS

Consider a taxpayer who purchases corporate stock in January at $40 and continues to hold the stock at the end of the year when the stock has appreciated to $100. The appreciation increases the taxpayer's wealth by $60, but the taxpayer does not include the increment in income because the stock has not been disposed of (that is, the gain has not been "realized"). Although Eisner v. Macomber, p. 99, held that the Sixteenth Amendment did not authorize the taxing of unrealized gains, few students of the tax law believe that *Macomber* is good law on this point today. Nevertheless, Congress has generally chosen not to take unrealized appreciation or depreciation into account because of the administrative and compliance difficulties that would result from requiring taxpayers to value their assets annually and to pay tax on their unrealized gains (or to deduct their unrealized losses).

You should begin the analysis of a property transaction by asking whether a sale, exchange, or other taxable event (a "realization event") has occurred. In most cases, the answer to this question will be apparent, though we will encounter some close cases. If a realization event has occurred, you should next determine the amount of the realized gain or loss (§ 1001(a)) by comparing the "amount realized" (§ 1001(b)) with the "adjusted basis" (§ 1011(b)) of the property disposed of.

Even a realized gain (or loss) is not included in gross income (or deducted) except to the extent that it is "recognized." Although § 1001(c) generally requires that realized gains and losses be taken into account (recognized) in the year in which realized, Congress has sometimes (for policy reasons) provided for "non-recognition" of the realized gain or loss. Thus, after determining the amount of gain or loss realized, you should ask to what extent the gain or loss is recognized. But even a recognized loss is deductible only to the extent that it is "allowable." Section 165(a) generally allows deductions for (recognized) losses "sustained" during the year, but § 165(c) prohibits non-corporate taxpayers from deducting losses other than (1) those incurred in a trade or business, (2) those incurred in a transaction entered into for profit, and (3) certain casualty losses with respect to personal-use property.

If you conclude that a gain is recognized (and hence includable in gross income) or a loss recognized and allowable (and hence tentatively deductible), your analysis is still not complete. You must next determine the "character" of the gain or loss as "ordinary" or "capital," for the Code sometimes prescribes different treatment for gain or loss depending upon its character. For example, capital losses can be used to offset capital gains, but they can be deducted against ordinary income only up to a maximum of $3000 a year; § 1211(b).

To summarize, you should begin the analysis of a property transaction by asking whether a realization event has occurred. If a realization event has occurred, what is the amount of realized gain or loss? To what extent is any realized gain or loss recognized? If a loss is recognized, to what extent is it allowable? What is the character (ordinary or capital) of the gain or loss? If the gain or loss is capital, must it be treated specially in making the tax computations for the year?

In this chapter, we examine in detail the taxable event and the concepts of basis and amount realized. This chapter also focuses on "tax shelters" (because their evolution depended in large measure upon the basis rules) and the congressional response to the tax-shelter problem. In Chapter 9, we turn to the issues of recognition and allowance, in Chapter 10 to the character (as ordinary or capital) of the recognized gain or allowed loss, and in Chapter 11 to the sale of property for deferred payments.

A. THE TAXABLE EVENT

COTTAGE SAVINGS ASS'N v. COMMISSIONER

Supreme Court of the United States, 1991.
499 U.S. 554, 111 S.Ct. 1503, 113 L.Ed.2d 589.

JUSTICE MARSHALL delivered the opinion of the Court.

The issue in this case is whether a financial institution realizes tax-deductible losses when it exchanges its interests in one group of residential mortgage loans for another lender's interests in a different group of residential mortgage loans. We hold that such a transaction does give rise to realized losses.

I

Petitioner Cottage Savings Association (Cottage Savings) is a savings and loan association (S & L) formerly regulated by the Federal Home Loan Bank Board (FHLBB). Like many S & L's, Cottage Savings held numerous long-term, low-interest mortgages that declined in value when interest rates surged in the late 1970's. These institutions would have benefited from selling their devalued mortgages in order to realize tax-deductible losses. However, they were deterred from doing so by FHLBB accounting regulations, which required them to record the losses on their books. Reporting these losses consistent with the then-effective FHLBB accounting regulations would have placed many S & L's at risk of closure by the FHLBB.

The FHLBB responded to this situation by relaxing its requirements for the reporting of losses. In a regulatory directive known as "Memorandum R–49," dated June 27, 1980, the FHLBB determined that S & L's need not report losses associated with mortgages that are exchanged for "substantially identical" mortgages held by other lenders.[2] The FHLBB's acknowledged purpose for Memorandum R–49 was to facilitate transactions that would generate tax losses but that would not substantially affect the economic position of the transacting S & L's.

This case involves a typical Memorandum R–49 transaction. On December 31, 1980, Cottage Savings sold "90% participation interests" in 252 mortgages to four S & L's. It simultaneously purchased "90% participation interests" in 305 mortgages held by these S & L's.[3] All of the loans involved in the transaction were secured by single-family homes, most in the Cincinnati area. The fair market value of the package of participation interests exchanged by each side was approximately $4.5 million. The face value of the participation interests Cottage Savings relinquished in the transaction was approximately $6.9 million. See 90 T.C. 372, 378–382 (1988).

On its 1980 federal income tax return, Cottage Savings claimed a deduction for $2,447,091, which represented the adjusted difference between the face value of the participation interests that it traded and the fair market value of the participation interests that it received. As permitted by Memorandum R–49, Cottage Savings did not report these losses to the FHLBB. After the Commissioner of Internal Revenue disallowed Cottage Savings' claimed deduction, Cottage Savings sought a redetermination in the Tax Court. The Tax Court held that the deduction was permissible. See 90 T.C. 372 (1988).

2. Memorandum R–49 listed 10 criteria for classifying mortgages as substantially identical.

"The loans involved must:

"1. involve single-family residential mortgages,

"2. be of similar type (e.g., conventionals for conventionals),

"3. have the same stated terms to maturity (e.g., 30 years),

"4. have identical stated interest rates,

"5. have similar seasoning (i.e., remaining terms to maturity),

"6. have aggregate principal amounts within the lesser of 2½% or $100,000 (plus or minus) on both sides of the transaction, with any additional consideration being paid in cash,

"7. be sold without recourse,

"8. have similar fair market values,

"9. have similar loan-to-value ratios at the time of the reciprocal sale, and

"10. have all security properties for both sides of the transaction in the same state." Record, Exh. 72–BT.

3. By exchanging merely participation interests rather than the loans themselves, each party retained its relationship with the individual obligors. Consequently, each S & L continued to service the loans on which it had transferred the participation interests and made monthly payments to the participation-interest holders. See 90 T.C. 372, 381 (1988).

On appeal by the Commissioner, the Court of Appeals reversed. 890 F.2d 848 (C.A.6 1989). The Court of Appeals agreed with the Tax Court's determination that Cottage Savings had realized its losses through the transaction. See id., at 852. However, the court held that Cottage Savings was not entitled to a deduction because its losses were not "actually" sustained during the 1980 tax year for purposes of § 165(a). See 890 F.2d, at 855.

Because of the importance of this issue to the S & L industry and the conflict among the Circuits over whether Memorandum R–49 exchanges produce deductible tax losses, we granted certiorari. * * * We now reverse.

II

Rather than assessing tax liability on the basis of annual fluctuations in the value of a taxpayer's property, the Internal Revenue Code defers the tax consequences of a gain or loss in property value until the taxpayer "realizes" the gain or loss. The realization requirement is implicit in § 1001(a), which defines "the gain [or loss] from the sale or other disposition of property" as the difference between "the amount realized" from the sale or disposition of the property and its "adjusted basis." As this Court has recognized, the concept of realization is "founded on administrative convenience." Helvering v. Horst, 311 U.S. 112, 116 (1940). Under an appreciation-based system of taxation, taxpayers and the Commissioner would have to undertake the "cumbersome, abrasive, and unpredictable administrative task" of valuing assets on an annual basis to determine whether the assets had appreciated or depreciated in value. See 1 B. Bittker & L. Lokken, Federal Taxation of Income, Estates and Gifts ¶ 5.2, p. 5–16 (2d ed. 1989). In contrast, "[a] change in the form or extent of an investment is easily detected by a taxpayer or an administrative officer." R. Magill, Taxable Income 79 (rev.ed. 1945).

Section 1001(a)'s language provides a straightforward test for realization: to realize a gain or loss in the value of property, the taxpayer must engage in a "sale or other disposition of [the] property." The parties agree that the exchange of participation interests in this case cannot be characterized as a "sale" under § 1001(a); the issue before us is whether the transaction constitutes a "disposition of property." The Commissioner argues that an exchange of property can be treated as a "disposition" under § 1001(a) only if the properties exchanged are materially different. The Commissioner further submits that, because the underlying mortgages were essentially economic substitutes, the participation interests exchanged by Cottage Savings were not materially different from those received from the other S & L's. Cottage Savings, on the other hand, maintains that any exchange of property is a "disposition of property" under § 1001(a), regardless of whether the property exchanged is materially different. Alternatively, Cottage Savings contends that the participation interests exchanged were materially different because the underlying loans were secured by different properties.

We must therefore determine whether the realization principle in § 1001(a) incorporates a "material difference" requirement. If it does, we must further decide what that requirement amounts to and how it applies in this case. We consider these questions in turn.

A

Neither the language nor the history of the Code indicates whether and to what extent property exchanged must differ to count as a "disposition of property" under § 1001(a). Nonetheless, we readily agree with the Commissioner that an exchange of property gives rise to a realization event under § 1001(a) only if the properties exchanged are "materially different." The Commissioner himself has by regulation construed § 1001(a) to embody a material difference requirement:

> "Except as otherwise provided * * * the gain or loss realized from the conversion of property into cash, *or from the exchange of property for other property differing materially either in kind or in extent,* is treated as income or as loss sustained." Treas.Reg. § 1.1001–1 (emphasis added).

Because Congress has delegated to the Commissioner the power to promulgate "all needful rules and regulations for the enforcement of [the Internal Revenue Code]," § 7805(a), we must defer to his regulatory interpretations of the code so long as they are reasonable, see National Muffler Dealers Assn., Inc. v. United States, 440 U.S. 472, 476–477 (1979).

We conclude that Treasury Regulation § 1.1001–1 is a reasonable interpretation of § 1001(a). Congress first employed the language that now comprises § 1001(a) in § 202(a) of the Revenue Act of 1924, ch. 234, 43 Stat. 253; that language has remained essentially unchanged through various reenactments. And since 1934, the Commissioner has construed the statutory term "disposition of property" to include a "material difference" requirement. As we have recognized, " 'Treasury regulations and interpretations long continued without substantial change, applying to unamended or substantially reenacted statutes, are deemed to have received congressional approval and have the effect of law.' "United States v. Correll, 389 U.S. 299, 305–306 (1967), quoting Helvering v. Winmill, 305 U.S. 79, 83 (1938).

Treasury Regulation § 1.1001–1 is also consistent with our landmark precedents on realization. In a series of early decisions involving the tax effects of property exchanges, this Court made clear that a taxpayer realizes taxable income only if the properties exchanged are "materially" or "essentially" different. See United States v. Phellis, 257 U.S. 156, 173 (1921); Weiss v. Stearn, 265 U.S. 242, 253–254 (1924); Marr v. United States, 268 U.S. 536, 540–542 (1925); see also Eisner v. Macomber, 252 U.S. 189, 207–212 (1920) (recognizing realization requirement). Because these decisions were part of the "contemporary legal context" in which Congress enacted § 202(a) of the 1924 Act, see Cannon v. University of Chicago, 441 U.S. 677, 698–699 (1979), and because Congress has left undisturbed through subsequent reenactments of the Code the principles of realization established in these cases, we may presume that Congress intended to codify these principles in § 1001(a), see Pierce v. Underwood, 487 U.S. 552, 567 (1988); Lorillard v. Pons, 434 U.S. 575, 580–581 (1978). The Commissioner's construction of the statutory language to incorporate these principles certainly was reasonable.

B

Precisely what constitutes a "material difference" for purposes of § 1001(a) is a more complicated question. The Commissioner argues that properties are "materially different" only if they differ in economic substance. To determine whether the participation interests exchanged in this case were "materially different" in this sense, the Commissioner argues, we should look to the attitudes of the parties, the evaluation of the interests by the secondary mortgage market, and the views of the FHLBB. We conclude that § 1001(a) embodies a much less demanding and less complex test.

Unlike the question *whether* § 1001(a) contains a material difference requirement, the question of *what constitutes* a material difference is not one on which we can defer to the Commissioner. For the Commissioner has not issued an authoritative, prelitigation interpretation of what property exchanges satisfy this requirement. Thus, to give meaning to the material difference test, we must look to the case law from which the test derives and which we believe Congress intended to codify in enacting and reenacting the language that now comprises § 1001(a). See Lorillard v. Pons, supra, at 580–581.

We start with the classic treatment of realization in Eisner v. Macomber, supra. In *Macomber,* a taxpayer who owned 2,200 shares of stock in a company received another 1,100 shares from the company as part of a pro rata stock dividend meant to reflect the company's growth in value. At issue was whether the stock dividend constituted taxable income. We held that it did not, because no gain was realized. See id., at 207–212. We reasoned that the stock dividend merely reflected the increased worth of the taxpayer's stock, see id., at 211–212, and that a taxpayer realizes increased worth of property only by receiving "something of exchangeable value *proceeding from* the property," see id., at 207.

In three subsequent decisions—United States v. Phellis, supra; Weiss v. Stearn, supra; and Marr v. United States, supra—we refined *Macomber*'s conception of realization in the context of property exchanges. In each case, the taxpayer owned stock that had appreciated in value since its acquisition. And in each case, the corporation in which the taxpayer held stock had reorganized into a new corporation, with the new corporation assuming the business of the old corporation. While the corporations in *Phellis* and *Marr* both changed from New Jersey to Delaware corporations, the original and successor corporations in *Weiss* both were incorporated in Ohio. In each case, following the reorganization, the stockholders of the old corporation received shares in the new corporation equal to their proportional interest in the old corporation.

The question in these cases was whether the taxpayers realized the accumulated gain in their shares in the old corporation when they received in return for those shares stock representing an equivalent proportional interest in the new corporations. In *Phellis* and *Marr,* we held that the transactions were realization events. We reasoned that because a company incorporated in one State has "different rights and powers" from one incorporated in a different State, the taxpayers in *Phellis* and *Marr* acquired through the transactions property that was "materially different" from what they previously had. United States v. Phellis; 257 U.S., at 169–173; see Marr v. United States, supra, at 540–542 (using phrase "essentially different"). In contrast, we held that no realization occurred in *Weiss.* By exchanging stock in the predecessor corporation for stock in the newly reorganized corporation, the taxpayer did not receive "a thing really different from what he theretofore had." Weiss v. Stearn, supra, at 254. As we explained in *Marr,* our determination that the reorganized company in *Weiss* was not "really different" from its predecessor turned on the fact that both companies were incorporated in the same State. See Marr v. United States, supra, at 540–542 (outlining distinction between these cases).

Obviously, the distinction in *Phellis* and *Marr* that made the stock in the successor corporations materially different from the stock in the predecessors was minimal. Taken together, *Phellis, Marr,* and *Weiss* stand for the principle that properties are "different" in the sense that is "material" to the Internal Revenue Code so long as their respective possessors enjoy legal entitlements that are different in kind or extent. Thus, separate groups of stock are not materially different if they confer "the same proportional interest of the same character in the same corporation." Marr v. United States, 268 U.S., at 540. However, they are materially different if they are issued by different corporations, id., at 541; United States v. Phellis, supra, at 173, or if they confer "different rights and powers" in the same corporation, Marr v. United States, supra, at 541. No more demanding a standard than this is necessary in order to satisfy the administrative purposes underlying the realization requirement in § 1001(a). See Helvering v. Horst, 311 U.S., at 116. For, as long as the property entitlements are not identical, their exchange will allow both the Commissioner and the transacting taxpayer easily to fix the appreciated or depreciated values of the property relative to their tax bases.

In contrast, we find no support for the Commissioner's "economic substitute" conception of material difference. According to the Commissioner, differences between properties are material for purposes of the Code only when it can be said that the parties, the relevant market (in this case the secondary mortgage market), and the relevant regulatory body (in this case the FHLBB) would consider them material. Nothing in

Phellis, Weiss, and *Marr* suggests that exchanges of properties must satisfy such a subjective test to trigger realization of a gain or loss.

Moreover, the complexity of the Commissioner's approach ill serves the goal of administrative convenience that underlies the realization requirement. In order to apply the Commissioner's test in a principled fashion, the Commissioner and the taxpayer must identify the relevant market, establish whether there is a regulatory agency whose views should be taken into account, and then assess how the relevant market participants and the agency would view the transaction. The Commissioner's failure to explain how these inquiries should be conducted further calls into question the workability of his test.

Finally, the Commissioner's test is incompatible with the structure of the Code. Section 1001(c) provides that a gain or loss realized under § 1001(a) "shall be recognized" unless one of the Code's nonrecognition provisions applies. One such nonrecognition provision withholds recognition of a gain or loss realized from an exchange of properties that would appear to be economic substitutes under the Commissioner's material difference test. This provision, commonly known as the "like kind" exception, withholds recognition of a gain or loss realized "on the exchange of property held for productive use in a trade or business or for investment * * * for property of like kind which is to be held either for productive use in a trade or business or for investment." § 1031(a)(1). If Congress had expected that exchanges of similar properties would not count as realization events under § 1001(a), it would have had no reason to bar recognition of a gain or loss realized from these transactions.

C

Under our interpretation of § 1001(a), an exchange of property gives rise to a realization event so long as the exchanged properties are "materially different"—that is, so long as they embody legally distinct entitlements. Cottage Savings' transactions at issue here easily satisfy this test. Because the participation interests exchanged by Cottage Savings and the other S & L's derived from loans that were made to different obligors and secured by different homes, the exchanged interests did embody legally distinct entitlements. Consequently, we conclude that Cottage Savings realized its losses at the point of the exchange.

The Commissioner contends that it is anomalous to treat mortgages deemed to be "substantially identical" by the FHLBB as "materially different." The anomaly, however, is merely semantic; mortgages can be substantially identical for Memorandum R–49 purposes and still exhibit "differences" that are "material" for purposes of the Internal Revenue Code. Because Cottage Savings received entitlements different from those it gave up, the exchange put both Cottage Savings and the Commissioner in a position to determine the change in the value of Cottage Savings' mortgages relative to their tax bases. Thus, there is no reason not to treat the exchange of these interests as a realization event, regardless of the status of the mortgages under the criteria of Memorandum R–49.

III

Although the Court of Appeals found that Cottage Savings' losses were realized, it disallowed them on the ground that they were not sustained under § 165(a). Section 165(a) states that a deduction shall be allowed for "any loss sustained during the taxable year and not compensated for by insurance or otherwise." Under the Commissioner's interpretation of § 165(a),

> "To be allowable as a deduction under section 165(a), a loss must be evidenced by closed and completed transactions, fixed by identifiable events, and, except as otherwise provided in section 165(h) and § 1.165–11, relating to disaster losses, actually sustained during the taxable year. Only a bona fide loss is allowable. Substance and not mere form shall govern in determining a deductible loss." Treas.Reg. § 1.165–1(b).

The Commissioner offers a minimal defense of the Court of Appeals' conclusion. The Commissioner contends that the losses were not sustained because they lacked "economic substance," by which the Commissioner seems to mean that the losses were not bona fide. We say "seems" because the Commissioner states the position in one sentence in a footnote in his brief without offering further explanation. See Brief for Respondent 34–35, n. 39. The only authority the Commissioner cites for this argument is Higgins v. Smith, 308 U.S. 473 (1940). See Brief for United States in No. 89–1926, p. 16, n. 11.

In *Higgins,* we held that a taxpayer did not sustain a loss by selling securities below cost to a corporation in which he was the sole shareholder. We found that the losses were not bona fide because the transaction was not conducted at arm's length and because the taxpayer retained the benefit of the securities through his wholly owned corporation. See Higgins v. Smith, supra, at 475–476. Because there is no contention that the transactions in this case were not conducted at arm's length, or that Cottage Savings retained de facto ownership of the participation interests it traded to the four reciprocating S & L's, *Higgins* is inapposite. In view of the Commissioner's failure to advance any other arguments in support of the Court of Appeals' ruling with respect to § 165(a), we conclude that, for purposes of this case, Cottage Savings sustained its losses within the meaning of § 165(a).

IV

For the reasons set forth above, the judgment of the Court of Appeals is reversed, and the case is remanded for further proceedings consistent with this opinion.

So ordered.

JUSTICE BLACKMUN, with whom JUSTICE WHITE joins, * * * dissenting * * *.

* * *

I dissent * * * from the Court's conclusion[ ] * * * that * * * Cottage Savings Association realized deductible losses for income tax purposes when [it] exchanged partial interests in one group of residential mortgage loans for partial interests in another like group of residential mortgage loans. I regard these losses as not recognizable for income tax purposes because the mortgage packages so exchanged were substantially identical and were not materially different.

* * *

It long has been established that gain or loss in the value of property is taken into account for income tax purposes only if and when the gain or loss is "realized," that is, when it is tied to a realization event, such as the sale, exchange, or other disposition of the property. Mere variation in value—the routine ups and downs of the marketplace—do not in themselves have income tax consequences. This is fundamental in income tax law.

In applying the realization requirement to an exchange, the properties involved must be materially different in kind or in extent. Treas. Reg. § 1.1001–1(a). * * *

That the mortgage participation partial interests exchanged in these cases were "different" is not in dispute. The materiality prong is the focus. A material difference is one that has the capacity to influence a decision. [Citations omitted.]

The application of this standard leads, it seems to me, to only one answer—that the mortgage participation partial interests released were not materially different from the mortgage participation partial interests received. Memorandum R–49, as the Court notes, Opinion in No. 89–1965, ante, at 2, n. 2, lists 10 factors that, when satisfied, as they were here, serve to classify the interests as "substantially identical." These factors assure practical identity; surely, they then also assure that any difference cannot be of consequence. Indeed, nonmateriality is the full purpose of the Memorandum's criteria. The "proof of the pudding" is in the fact of its complete accounting acceptability to the FHLBB. Indeed, as has been noted, it is difficult to reconcile substantial identity for financial accounting purposes with a material difference for tax accounting purposes. [Citations omitted.] Common sense so dictates.

This should suffice and be the end of the analysis. Other facts, however, solidify the conclusion: The retention by the transferor of 10% interests, enabling it to keep on servicing its loans; the transferor's continuing to collect the payments due from the borrowers so that, so far as the latter were concerned, it was business as usual, exactly as it had been; the obvious lack of concern or dependence of the transferor with the "differences" upon which the Court relies (as transferees, the taxpayers made no credit checks and no appraisals of collateral, [citations omitted]); the selection of the loans by computer programmed to match mortgages in accordance with the Memorandum R–49 criteria; the absence of even the names of the borrowers in the closing schedules attached to the agreements; Centennial's receipt of loan files only six years after its exchange, 682 F.Supp., at 1392, n.5; the restriction of the interests exchanged to the same State; the identity of the respective face and fair market values; and the application by the parties of common discount factors to each side of the transaction—all reveal that any differences that might exist made no difference whatsoever and were not material. This demonstrates the real nature of the transactions, including nonmateriality of the claimed differences.

We should be dealing here with realities and not with superficial distinctions. As has been said many times, and as noted above, in income tax law we are to be concerned with substance and not with mere form. When we stray from that principle, the new precedent is likely to be a precarious beacon for the future.

I respectfully dissent * * * .

Problem, Note and Question

1. *Modification of an existing note.* Although *Cottage Savings* involved an exchange of notes issued by different obligors, the economic differences between the notes given up and those received were minute. Was the difference in obligors essential to the Court's holding? Suppose, for example, that lender and borrower agree to modify the terms of an existing debt instrument. Might the transaction be viewed as an exchange of notes by the lender on which the lender realizes gain or loss? Treas. Reg. 1.1001–3, issued in response to the uncertainties arising from *Cottage Savings*, answers this question in the affirmative. It treats a "significant modification" in an instrument as a deemed exchange of the old instrument for the new. A "modification" comprises any alteration of a legal right or obligation of the issuer or holder, except for a change in terms that occurs by operation of the instrument itself. Thus, a variable-rate note on which the interest rate is annually adjusted to the market rate is not a modification since the interest-rate adjustment is called for by the original instrument. But if the parties negotiate a change in the interest rate payable on an existing loan, that constitutes a modification. If the modification is "significant," the holder of the note is deemed to have exchanged it. A change in rate is considered significant if it alters the yield by more than the greater of ¼ of one percent or five percent of the annual yield of the unmodified instrument.

2. *Problem.* In year 1, *S* sells real property to *B* for $100,000, payable $10,000 down and the balance due in five years with interest payable annually at 10%. *B* is personally liable on the note, and the deferred payments are secured by a mortgage against the property. In year 3, *B* sells the property to *C*, who assumes the mortgage and is substituted as obligor for *B*. Any tax consequences to *S* in year 3?

INTERNATIONAL FREIGHTING CORP., INC. v. COMMISSIONER

United States Court of Appeals, Second Circuit, 1943.
135 F.2d 310.

Before L. HAND, CHASE and FRANK, CIRCUIT JUDGES.

During the years 1933 to 1935, inclusive, E.I. duPont deNemours and Company, Inc., owned all of taxpayer's stock and during the year 1936 it owned two-thirds of taxpayer's stock, the balance being owned by the General Motors Corporation. During the years 1933 to 1936, inclusive, taxpayer informally adopted the bonus plan of the duPont Company as its own bonus plan. * * * Class B bonus awards (the only ones here involved) might be granted to those employees who, by their ability, efficiency and loyalty, had contributed most in a general way to the taxpayer's success, and were to be made from the portion of taxpayer's profits which its finance committee had set aside in the class B bonus fund. * * * Recommendations for bonuses were to be made by the president or the heads of departments and were to be acted on by the executive committee or the board of directors. It was not incumbent on the executive committee or the board of directors to distribute the entire amount available in the fund. The taxpayer reserved the right at any time to discontinue the awarding of any bonuses.

Bonuses were in the form of common stock of the duPont Company * * *.

* * *

* * * During the calendar year 1936 taxpayer paid over and distributed to the beneficiaries of its class B bonus award, certificates representing 150 shares of the common stock of the duPont Company, whose cost to taxpayer at the date of delivery was $16,153.36 and whose market value was then $24,858.75. Each of the employees receiving those shares in 1936 paid a tax thereon, computing the market value at the time of delivery as taxable income.

Taxpayer took a deduction of $24,858.75 in its income tax return for 1936 on account of the 150 shares of stock distributed in that year to its employees. In a notice of deficiency the Commissioner reduced the deduction from $24,858.75 to $16,153.35, a difference of $8,705.39, determining that, as the bonus was paid in property, "the basis for calculation of the amount thereof is the cost of such property and not its market value as claimed on the return." This was the only adjustment which the Commissioner made to taxpayer's return and, as a result, the Commissioner determined a deficiency in the amount of $2,156.76, in taxpayer's tax liability for the year. Taxpayer filed a petition with the Tax Court for a redetermination of the deficiency thus determined. By an amended answer, the Commissioner in the alternative, alleged that if it were held that taxpayer was entitled to a deduction in the amount of $24,858.75 on account of the payment of bonus in stock, then taxpayer realized a taxable profit of $8,705.39 on the disposition of the shares, and taxpayer's net taxable income otherwise determined should be increased accordingly.

The Tax Court held that taxpayer was entitled to a deduction for compensation paid in the year 1936 in the amount of $24,858.75. The Tax Court decided for the Commissioner, however, on the defense set forth in the Commissioner's amended answer, holding that taxpayer realized a gain of $8,705.39 in 1936 by paying the class B bonus in stock which had cost taxpayer $8,705.39 less than its market value when taxpayer transferred the stock to its employees. The deficiency resulting from this decision was $2,156.76. From that decision taxpayer seeks review.

FRANK, CIRCUIT JUDGE.

1. Up to the time in 1936 when the shares were delivered to the employees, the taxpayer retained such control of the shares that title had not passed to the employees. We think the Tax Court correctly held that the market value at the time of delivery was properly deducted by the taxpayer as an ordinary expense of the business under § [162(a)] because that delivery was an additional reasonable compensation for past services actually rendered. Cf. Lucas v. Ox Fibre Brush Co., 281 U.S. 115. The payment depleted the taxpayer's assets in an amount equal to that market value fully as much as if taxpayer had, at the time of delivery, first purchased those shares.

2. We turn to the question whether the transaction resulted in taxable gain to taxpayer. We think that the Tax Court correctly held that it did. The delivery of those shares was not a gift, else (1) it would have been wrongful as against taxpayer's stockholders, (2) the value of the shares could not have been deducted as an expense under § [162(a)] and (3) the employees as donees would not be obliged to pay, as they must, an income tax on what they received. It was not a gift precisely because it was "compensation for services actually rendered," i.e., because the taxpayer received a full quid pro quo. Accordingly, cases holding that one is not liable for an income tax when he makes a gift of shares are not in point. * * *

But, as the delivery of the shares here constituted a disposition for a valid consideration, it resulted in a closed transaction with a consequent realized gain. It is of no relevance that here the taxpayer had not been legally obligated to award any shares or pay any additional compensation to the employees; bonus payments by corporations are recognized as proper even if there was no previous obligation to make them; although then not obligatory, they are regarded as made for a sufficient consideration. Since the bonuses would be invalid to the extent that what was delivered to the employees exceeded what the services of the employees were worth, it follows that the consideration received by the taxpayer from the employees must be deemed to be equal at least to the value of the shares in 1936. Here then, as there was no gift but a disposition of shares for a valid consideration equal at least to the market value of the shares when delivered, there was a taxable gain equal to the difference between the cost of the shares and that market value.

For § [1001(a)] provides that the gain from "the sale or other disposition of property" shall be the excess of "the amount realized therefrom" over "the adjusted basis" provided in § [1011(a)], and § [1011(a)]—in light of § [1012]—makes the "basis" the cost of such property. True, § [1001(b)] provides that "the amount realized" is the sum of "any money received plus the fair market value of the property (other than money) received." Literally, where there is a disposition of stock for services, no "property" or "money" is received by the person who thus disposes of the stock. But, in similar circumstances, it has been held that "money's worth" is received and that such a receipt comes within § [1001(b)]. See Commissioner v. Mesta, 3 Cir., 123 F.2d 986, 988; cf. Commissioner v. Halliwell, 2 Cir., 131 F.2d 642; Kenan v. Commissioner, 2 Cir., 114 F.2d 217.

The taxpayer properly asks us to treat this case "as if there had been no formal bonus plan" and as if taxpayer "had simply paid outright 150 shares of duPont stock to selected employees as additional compensation." On that basis, surely there was a taxable gain. For to shift the equation once more, the case supposed is the equivalent of one in which the taxpayer in the year 1936, without entering into a previous contract fixing the amount of compensation, had employed a transposition expert for one day and, when he completed his work, had paid him 5 shares of duPont stock having market value at that time of $500 but which it had bought in a previous year for $100. There can be no doubt that, from such a transaction, taxpayer would have a taxable gain. And so here.

The order of the Tax Court is affirmed.

Problems

Problem (1). T, a cash-method taxpayer, owes an employee, E, $10,000 for services rendered in T's business. T satisfies the obligation by transferring to E property with an adjusted basis of $4000 and a value of $10,000. What result to T and E?

Problem (2). T made a legally enforceable pledge of $10,000 to the University Building Fund, which is an organization described in § 170(c)(2). T satisfies the pledge by transferring to the Fund stock with a basis of $4000 and a value of $10,000. What result to T?

Problem (3). D bequeathed $100,000 to B. D's executor satisfies the legacy by transferring to B stock with an adjusted basis of $80,000 and a value of $100,000. What result to the estate and to B?

Problem (4). G creates a trust to pay the income to B for life, remainder to C. In the current year, the trust has trust-accounting income of $20,000. The trustee satisfies B's right to income by transferring to B stock with an adjusted basis of $5000 and a value of $20,000. What result to the trust and to B?

LOUISIANA LAND & EXPLORATION
CO. v. COMMISSIONER

United States Court of Appeals, Fifth Circuit, 1947.
161 F.2d 842.

Before Sibley, Hutcheson, and Lee, Circuit Judges.

Lee, Circuit Judge.

* * *

* * * In 1936, the taxpayer, unable to obtain an oil and gas lease on the Rosedale Plantation, bought the plantation for $30,000 cash. At the date of the purchase, its surface value was $15,000 and its mineral value was $15,000. The taxpayer made an oil and gas lease to one Benedum. The lessee, after drilling unsuccessfully to 9017 feet, upon the advice of experienced geologists abandoned operation and forfeited the lease. The taxpayer in its 1942 return claimed a deduction of $18,000 (by agreement reduced to $15,000) for the cost of the mineral interest which became worthless during the year 1942. The Commissioner disallowed the deduction; the Tax Court, in sustaining the Commissioner, held that the taxpayer could not deduct any part of the purchase price as a loss because the retained fee had substantial value. The correctness of this holding is the only issue concerning the 1942 tax.

Section 19.23(e)–1[a] of Treasury Regulations 103 provides that losses must be evidenced by "closed completed transactions, fixed by identifiable events, bona fide and actually sustained during the taxable period for which allowed." The taxpayer contends that the drilling of a dry hole on the Rosedale Plantation in 1942 was a definite event which established the worthlessness of the minerals. In the case of real estate "the closed and completed transaction" must either be a transference of the real estate from the owner or his abandonment thereof. "Our study of comparable cases convinces us that where a loss is claimed by reason of abandonment of worthless property, it has been necessary in all cases to establish the absolute worthlessness of the claimant's interest in the property." For purpose of the computation of losses, the Tax Court considers claimant's fee interest as a unit and not as a bundle of many interests.

If the taxpayer could take a deduction for the loss of each use to which he put his fee, he would be taking a deduction for the shrinkage in value of his asset. In the words of the Tax Court:

> "* * * to permit such a deduction would be to allow the taxpayer to make one asset into as many as there were contemplated uses for it, and would have the effect in many cases of nullifying the established rule that mere shrinkage in the value of an asset prior to the closing of the transaction with respect thereto does not give rise to a deductible loss."

a. Compare Treas.Reg. § 1.165–1(b)—
Eds.

Since the taxpayer owns the entire fee, the cases where the taxpayer acquires only one interest in the land, as for instance an oil and gas lease, a royalty interest, or the whole or an undivided interest in the minerals, are not applicable. If the taxpayer had obtained any one of these single interests in Rosedale, the drilling of a dry hole would be an identifiable event that might permit a deduction for the worthlessness of the investment.

To be distinguished, also, are the cases where the courts permit the purchaser of a fee to allocate his cost between the surface interest and the mineral interests for the purpose of the computation of depletion or for the purpose of the computation of a gain or loss upon the dismemberment of the minerals from the fee by sale or other disposition.

* * *

Notes and Questions

1. *What is "the" property?* A taxpayer who owns land with a building on it does recognize loss when the building (but not the land) is abandoned; see Hanover v. Commissioner, 38 T.C.M. 1281 (1979) (holding that the taxpayer's partnership had abandoned a building when it boarded it up, cut off utilities, maintenance, and insurance, made no efforts to sell or lease it, and sought proposals for demolition). How does the situation in the principal case differ from that in the "abandoned building" cases?

The Court of Claims once allowed a deduction for the worthlessness of the minerals in land held by an estate. The decision was based on "the custom in oil-producing areas * * * to regard the mineral interest as a separate thing from the rest of the land" and on the government's having valued the mineral interest separately in assessing the estate's assets for estate-tax purposes. Pool v. United States, 119 F.Supp. 202 (Ct.Cl.1954). In Henley v. United States, 396 F.2d 956 (Ct.Cl.1968), the Court of Claims itself refused to follow *Pool* in a case in which the taxpayer had received separate deeds for the minerals and the surface in buying a tract of land. The *Henley* opinion limits *Pool* to cases in which the government itself "severed" the mineral and surface interests by valuing them separately for estate-tax purposes.

2. *When is a loss "sustained"?* As the materials above show, property need not be disposed of or completely destroyed to satisfy the "closed and completed transactions" requirement of Treas.Reg. § 1.165–1(b); a deduction for a loss on business or investment property is taken when the property "becomes worthless." This rule generates a good deal of litigation on the question of *when* a loss on property (or a bad debt) that concededly has become worthless occurred. One reason it matters is that the government may argue that property or a debt became worthless in a year that is closed because of the statute of limitations. Look at § 6511(d)(1).

building [illegible handwritten margin note: "moment of demolition"]

3. *Loss or capital expenditure?* If a taxpayer tears down an old business building to put up a new one, is the loss on the destruction of the building: (1) deductible, or (2) an addition to the basis of the land, or (3) an addition to the basis of the new building? See § 280B.

B. COMPUTATION OF REALIZED GAIN OR LOSS

1. THE BASIS OF PROPERTY ACQUIRED BY PURCHASE OR TAXABLE EXCHANGE

PHILADELPHIA PARK AMUSEMENT CO. v. UNITED STATES

United States Court of Claims, 1954.
126 F.Supp. 184.

Before JONES, CHIEF JUDGE, and LITTLETON, WHITAKER, MADDEN and LARAMORE, JUDGES.

LARAMORE, JUDGE.

* * *

[Taxpayer, the owner and operator of an amusement park, had a fifty-year franchise from the City of Philadelphia to operate a passenger railway in the park. It built the "Strawberry Bridge" to carry its streetcars and other traffic across the Schuylkill River. In 1934 the taxpayer conveyed the bridge to the City in exchange for a ten-year extension of its franchise. The issue was the cost basis of the franchise extension to the taxpayer under the predecessor of § 1012. The reason this basis was important was that the franchise was a depreciable asset under the predecessor of § 167. A high basis would give the taxpayer greater deductions for depreciation than a low basis.

In a portion of the opinion not reproduced here, the Court of Claims held that the 1934 exchange of the bridge for the franchise extension was a taxable event.]

This brings us to the question of what is the cost basis of the 10–year extension of taxpayer's franchise. Although defendant contends that Strawberry Bridge was either worthless or not "exchanged" for the 10–year extension of the franchise, we believe that the bridge had some value, and that the contract under which the bridge was transferred to the City clearly indicates that the one was given in consideration of the other. * * *

The gain or loss, whichever the case may have been, should have been recognized, and the cost basis under section [1012] of the Code, of the 10–year extension of the franchise was the cost to the taxpayer. The succinct statement in section [1012] that "the basis of property shall be the cost of such property" although clear in principle, is frequently difficult in application. One view is that the cost basis of property received in a taxable exchange is the fair market value of the property *given* in the exchange. The other view is that the cost basis of property received in a taxable exchange is the fair market value of the property *received* in the exchange. As will be seen from the cases and some of the Commissioner's rulings the Commissioner's position has not been altogether consistent on this question. The view that "cost" is the fair market value of the property given is predicated on the theory that the cost to the taxpayer is the economic value relinquished. The view that "cost" is the fair market value of the property received is based upon the theory that the term "cost" is a tax concept and must be considered in the light of the * * * prime role that the basis of property plays in determining tax liability. We believe that when the question is considered in the latter context that the cost basis of the property received in a taxable exchange is the fair market value of the property *received* in the exchange.

When property is exchanged for property in a taxable exchange the taxpayer is taxed on the difference between the adjusted basis of the property given in exchange and the fair market value of the property received in exchange. For purposes of determining gain or loss the fair market value of the property received is treated as cash and taxed accordingly. To maintain harmony with the fundamental purpose of these sections, it is necessary to consider the fair market value of the property received as the cost basis to the taxpayer. The failure to do so would result in allowing the taxpayer a stepped-up basis, without paying a tax therefor, if the fair market value of the property received is less than the fair market value of the property given, and the taxpayer would be subjected to a double tax if the fair market value of the property received is more than the fair market value of the property given. By holding that the fair market value of the property received in a taxable exchange is the cost basis, the above discrepancy is avoided and the basis of the property received will equal the adjusted basis of the property given plus any gain recognized, or that should have been recognized, or minus any loss recognized, or that should have been recognized.

Therefore, the cost basis of the 10–year extension of the franchise was its fair market value on August 3, 1934, the date of the exchange. The determination of whether the cost basis of the property received is its fair market value or the fair market value of the property given in exchange therefor, although necessary to the decision of the case, is generally not of great practical significance because the value of the two properties exchanged in an arms-length transaction are either equal in fact, or are presumed to be equal. The record in this case indicates that the 1934 exchange was an arms-length transaction and, therefore, if the value of the extended franchise cannot be determined with reasonable accuracy, it would be reasonable and fair to assume that the value of Strawberry Bridge was equal to the 10–year extension of the franchise. The fair market value of the 10–year extension of the franchise should be established but, if that value cannot be determined with reasonable certainty, the fair market value of Strawberry Bridge should be established and that will be presumed to be the value of the extended franchise. This value cannot be determined from the facts now before us since the case was prosecuted on a different theory.

* * *

Therefore, because we deem it equitable, judgment should be suspended and the question of the value of the extended franchise on August 3, 1934, should be remanded to the Commissioner of this court for the taking of evidence and the filing of a report thereon.

* * *

Jones, Chief Judge, and Madden, Whitaker and Littleton, Judges, concur.

Problems, Notes and Questions

1. *Basis of property acquired by exercise of an option.* Suppose a taxpayer pays $10,000 for an option to buy business real estate for $100,000 at any time during the next two years. When the taxpayer acquires the option, the property is worth $95,000. (Think about why someone might be willing to pay $10,000 for the option under these circumstances.) The taxpayer exercises the option at the end of the second year when the property is worth $115,000. The taxpayer recognizes no gain on the exercise of the option and obtains a basis of $110,000 ($10,000 paid for the option plus $100,000 paid upon exercise) for the property.

2. *Allocation of basis.* Consider a taxpayer who buys a 200–acre farm for $100,000 and later sells 50 acres for $40,000, retaining the rest of the farm (including the portion on which the house and barn are located). The taxpayer's amount realized is $40,000, but what is the basis of the property sold? Basis must be allocated between the portions sold and retained in proportion to the relative values of those portions at the time the property was purchased. See Treas.Reg. § 1.61–6(a) (Ex. 2).

The taxpayer in Inaja Land Co. v. Commissioner, 9 T.C. 727 (1947), owned land having a basis of $61,000, which became less valuable when the City of Los Angeles polluted its water. The city paid the taxpayer approximately $49,000 on account of the damage and for an easement to continue polluting. The court agreed with the taxpayer that allocation of part of the property's basis to the easement sold to the city would be "impracticable or impossible" and allowed the taxpayer to treat the entire $49,000 as a tax-free return of capital. What result in this case if the city had paid $70,000?

Does *Inaja Land* get it right? Suppose that before the pollution occurred the land was worth $98,000 and $49,000 after. If the easement reduced the value of the land by half, why not allocate half the basis to the property taken? Under that approach, the gain would be $18,500 ($49,000 amount realized less $30,500 adjusted basis allocable to the half interest disposed of).

3. *Problems.*

(1) *A* owns stock with a basis of zero and a value of $25,000. *B* owns stock with a value of $26,000. *A* and *B* exchange stock in a taxable, arm's-length exchange. What is *A*'s basis for the stock she acquired?

(2) *P* suffered physical injuries in an automobile accident resulting from *D*'s negligence. *P* filed suit against *D,* claiming $100,000 compensatory damages. *D* settled the suit by transferring to *P* land with a basis of $20,000 and a value of $50,000. What is *P*'s basis for the land? (And what result to *D*?)

(3) *T*, a cash-method taxpayer, is an attorney whose client owed her $10,000 for past legal services. Because the client was in financial difficulty, *T* agreed to accept $4000 in complete satisfaction of her claim. Can *T* deduct a $6000 loss? Would your answer differ if *T* had been an accrual-method taxpayer?

(4) Ten years ago, *F* bought a farm in upstate New York for $50,000. In the current year, much to *F*'s surprise, a valuable natural gas deposit is found beneath the farm. *F* sells the mineral rights for $100,000. How much gain does *F* realize on the sale?

BASIS AND THE STATUTE OF LIMITATIONS

As *Philadelphia Park* shows, the basis of property can depend upon the tax treatment of the transaction in which the taxpayer acquired the property. If, as often happens, the statute of limitations for the year of acquisition has run by the time the property's basis becomes important, a question arises as to whether erroneous reporting of the acquisition transaction should affect the property's basis. Consider, for instance, a case in which Smith receives stock as compensation from her employer in year 1. Smith files a return which reports gross income of $20,000 from the receipt of the stock. While this was a reasonable estimate of the stock's value (or at least a non-fraudulent estimate[b]), the true value of the stock was $50,000. In year 10, after the statute of limitations for year 1 has run, Smith sells the stock for $60,000. How, if at all, should Smith's underreporting of the income she recognized when she got the stock affect her right to use a $50,000 basis to calculate gain on the stock's sale?

In principle, there are three ways of dealing with the problem described above, and the tax system has used all three of them in some context:

> First, and most simply, one could say that Smith's erroneous reporting in year 1 is irrelevant to the determination of her income in some later year—the whole purpose of statutes of limitations is to prevent the correction of error after enough time has gone by. See Bennet v. Helvering, 137 F.2d 537, 538 (2d Cir.1943), in which Judge Learned Hand said, "statutes of limitations are passed to put

b. The statute of limitations never runs on a fraudulent return; § 6501(c)(1).

an end to the reconsideration of what has been once heard and decided; they presuppose that the original decision may have been erroneous.''

Second, Smith's taking a return position claiming a $20,000 value for the stock might estop her from later claiming that it had a higher value. This would mean that the basis of the stock could not be more than the $20,000, so her gain on the sale is $40,000 rather than the $10,000 it would have been if basis had been calculated correctly. For examples, see Continental Oil Co. v. Jones, 177 F.2d 508 (10th Cir.1949); Ashman v. Commissioner, 231 F.3d 541 (9th Cir.2000) (imposing a "duty of consistency" on the taxpayer).

While the estoppel doctrine serves the useful function of deterring taxpayers somewhat from taking optimistic positions, it can in some cases operate very harshly. Suppose, for instance, that underreporting the stock's value on receipt reduced Smith's taxes by only $100 because Smith had large losses from other sources in year 1, and that her gain on the sale in year 10 is taxed at 28 percent. An $8400 extra tax in year 10 seems a harsh penalty for underreporting year 1's tax by $100. The estoppel doctrine also results in treating more harshly taxpayers who underreport income received in the form of property than those who understate income received in the form of cash. If unreported cash is invested in property, the taxpayer obtains a cost basis for the property even though the cash receipt was not included in income.

Finally, Smith's use of the correct $50,000 basis figure in year 10 might be conditioned on reopening year 1. That is, if Smith calculates her year 10 gain using a $50,000 basis for the stock, her year 1 tax could be recalculated, using $50,000 rather than $20,000 as the income from her receipt of the stock. Today, the Code's "mitigation provisions" (§§ 1311–1314) permit limited reopening of closed years when the conditions of those provisions are satisfied. Among other requirements, reopening of closed years under the mitigation provisions usually requires that the taxpayer or the government have taken inconsistent positions, and that a "determination" (such as a court decision or a closing agreement with the Service) be reached in the later year.

2. TRANSACTIONS INVOLVING MORTGAGED PROPERTY

(a) Basis and Amount Realized

PARKER v. DELANEY

United States Court of Appeals, First Circuit, 1950.
186 F.2d 455, cert. denied 341 U.S. 926, 71 S.Ct. 797, 95 L.Ed. 1357 (1951).

Before MAGRUDER, CHIEF JUDGE, and WOODBURY and FAHY, CIRCUIT JUDGES.

FAHY, CIRCUIT JUDGE.

[In 1933, 1934, and 1936 Parker (the appellant) acquired four apartment houses from banks, which owned the properties as a result of foreclosure proceedings. He paid no money for the properties, and took them subject to mortgage liens totaling $273,000. He did not become personally liable for the mortgage debt. While holding the properties Parker deducted $45,280.48 as depreciation. He paid off $13,989.38 of principal on the mortgages. In 1945 the mortgages were in default, and Parker conveyed the properties to the banks.

On his 1945 return, Parker reported a $31,291.10 gain from the sale of the apartment properties to the banks. After thinking the matter over he sued for a refund, claiming that his "amount realized" under the predecessor of § 1001 was zero, since he "realized nothing when the properties were reconveyed to the banks in 1945 and so there was legally nothing to tax as a gain * * *."]

* * *

That there was a disposition of the properties by appellant in 1945 seems clear. * * * Appellant had regularly reported for tax purposes all income and had taken all deductions, including those for depreciation, to which he would be entitled as owner. The serious question is not whether there was a disposition within the meaning of § [1001], as to which we are clear, but whether a gain was realized from such disposition. * * *

* * * [W]e may conveniently consider first the question of the cost of the properties to appellant. During the years of his operation of them he took deductions for depreciation on a cost basis equal to the amount of the first mortgage liens. In this court he expressly disclaims any contention that their * * * [basis] for depreciation purposes was less than those liens. These mortgages represented the prices paid, or the consideration, for the properties. The properties became subject to these liens and appellant considered them as the cost in deducting depreciation. Nothing appears to the contrary and we must, as did the court below, accept these figures of cost used by appellant. Indeed we do not understand him to dispute this treatment of the cost question.

The depreciation deductions, taken on the basis discussed above, amounted to $45,280.48. We come to the time of disposition, therefore, with that amount having been set aside from gross income and put in capital account for replacement purposes, the justification for permitting depreciation deductions in computing taxable income. [Citations omitted.] The adjusted basis in 1945 accordingly was $273,000 less $45,280.48, or $227,719.52. The question is whether more than this was realized from disposition of the properties in that year. If so it was taxable gain * * *. It is here the real controversy arises. Appellant contends that he realized nothing or in any event nothing in excess of the adjusted basis of $227,719.52, though the amount of the mortgages then was $31,291.10 in excess of said adjusted basis. * * *

The burden of deciding whether or not the last named figure was gain we think has been assumed by Crane v. Commissioner, 331 U.S. 1. In that case there was a sale of improved real estate to a third party subject to the amount of the mortgage, plus $3,000 boot paid to the seller. The latter, like appellant here, was not personally liable on the mortgage. In the instant case the disposition was to the mortgagees instead of to a third party purchaser and no boot was paid.

In the *Crane* case the taxpayer contended that all she received was the boot, and that its amount, less expenses of the sale, was the amount of gain realized. But the Supreme Court held that the taxpayer received benefit in the amount of the mortgage as well as the boot. We see no logical or practical distinction which takes the present case out of the rationale of that decision. If the amount of the unassumed mortgage in the *Crane* case was properly included in the amount realized on the sale, the amounts of the unassumed mortgages should be held to have been realized on the disposition in this case. In both, such amounts had been considered in determining the unadjusted basis. Since in the *Crane* case taxpayer obtained the property by devise, the basis was the fair market value at the time of acquisition. § [1014]. In the case at bar the basis was cost. § [1012]. Depreciation had been computed and deducted on such amounts; and their relationship under § [1016] to the question of gain realized under § [1001] requires that account be taken of such value or cost in determining the realization on disposition. Furthermore, the property in the hands of appellant was relieved at the time of disposition of the mortgage liens and obligations. So far as appellant was concerned as owner these were paid even though he was not personally liable for them. The matter was so treated in the *Crane* case, 331 U.S. at page 13. The added factor there, not present here, that boot was paid over and above the mortgage, is not material so long as the value of the properties was not less than the liens. Boot served to show this in the *Crane* case, but the payment of boot is of course not the only means of showing whether or not value is equal to or more than the liens on the property disposed of.

This brings us to appellant's contention that in fact the value was less and the *Crane* doctrine accordingly does not apply. He points out that the Supreme Court, in such a situation, reserved decision: "Obviously, if the value of the property is less than the amount of the mortgage, a mortgagor who is not personally liable cannot realize a benefit equal to the mortgage. Consequently, a different problem might be encountered where a mortgagor abandoned the property or transferred it subject to the mortgage without receiving boot. That is not this case." Footnote 37, 331 U.S. at page 14.

This statement is predicated upon a situation where the value of the property when disposed of is less than the mortgage. There is no evidence to that effect in this case. The District Court treated the value as equal to the mortgages and we have no basis for doing otherwise. The critical point is that the value equaled the mortgages, not that it exceeded them, and on this factual matter we must on the record support the conclusion of the District Court.

Appellant also contends that the property was abandoned to the banks and accordingly that there could be no capital gain * * *. [I]t does not help appellant to term the transaction an abandonment if it was nevertheless a disposition within the meaning of § [1001] upon which a gain was realized and if, as we hold, it was then of a value equal to the first mortgage liens. In these circumstances the unpaid amount of the liens is carried forward, as it were, from the time of acquisition to the time of disposition. They are treated as cost at the earlier time and so must be treated as value at the later time. The result in the end is that the taxpayer accounts to the taxing authorities for the gain realized by his deductions for depreciation in excess of his own investment.

The judgment of the District Court is affirmed.

MAGRUDER, CHIEF JUDGE (concurring).

I concur. The logic of the court's opinion is inescapable, with Crane v. Commissioner, 331 U.S. 1, as the starting point.

As an original matter, I would have had some difficulty in understanding how the taxpayer in the *Crane* case realized more than $3,000 from her sale of the mortgaged property there involved, in view of the definition of "amount realized" in § [1001(b)]. By the same token in the case at bar, under the more natural and obvious reading of § [1001(b)], it would seem that the amount realized by the taxpayer herein was zero, when he caused his straw man to quitclaim to the banks, for no cash consideration, properties then subject to mortgages up to their full value, the taxpayer not being liable on the mortgage debt. To reach the conclusion that the taxpayer thereby "realized" the amount of the outstanding mortgage debt would seem to require a somewhat esoteric interpretation of the statutory language. Also, I do not clearly understand why the Treasury allowed the taxpayer deductions for depreciation, under § [167], in the total amount of $45,280.48, taking the taxpayer's original "cost" basis as the amount of the mortgages, though he made no cash investment in the properties upon acquisition, nor did he obligate himself on the mortgage debt. But that matter need not concern us here, because depreciation in the amount of $45,280.48 was in fact "allowed"; and under § [1016], the adjusted basis for determining gain or loss from the sale or other disposition of the property takes account of depreciation "to the extent allowed (but not less than the amount allowable)" under the income tax laws.

Perhaps the net result reached by the court here might be arrived at by another mode of computation with less strain upon the statutory language. Thus, the adjusted basis for determining gain or loss under § [1001(b)] might be computed as follows: Original cost, zero, plus $13,989.38, the total amount which taxpayer paid in reduction of the mortgage debt while he held the properties, minus $45,280.48, the amount of depreciation "allowed", which comes out to an adjusted basis of minus $31,291.10. Now, apply that adjusted basis of minus $31,291.10

to the computation of gain or loss under the formula in § [1001(a)]: The "amount realized" upon taxpayer's disposition of the properties, zero (as suggested above), minus the adjusted basis as computed under § [1016], or in other words, minus $31,291.10 subtracted from zero, comes out to a plus figure of $31,291.10, representing the amount of the taxpayer's gain, upon which the tax would be computed.

COMMISSIONER v. TUFTS

Supreme Court of the United States, 1983.
461 U.S. 300, 103 S.Ct. 1826, 75 L.Ed.2d 863.

JUSTICE BLACKMUN delivered the opinion of the Court.

Over 35 years ago, in Crane v. Commissioner, 331 U.S. 1 (1947), this Court ruled that a taxpayer, who sold property encumbered by a nonrecourse mortgage (the amount of the mortgage being less than the property's value), must include the unpaid balance of the mortgage in the computation of the amount the taxpayer realized on the sale. The case now before us presents the question whether the same rule applies when the unpaid amount of the nonrecourse mortgage exceeds the fair market value of the property sold.

I

[The taxpayers were the partners of a partnership which built and operated a 120–unit apartment complex in Duncanville, Texas. Construction of the building was financed by a $1,851,500 loan by the Farm & Home Savings Association. The loan was non-recourse; that is, it was secured only by a mortgage on the apartment complex and neither the partnership nor any partner assumed any personal liability.

By August, 1972, the partners found themselves unable to make payments on the mortgage. They had taken $439,972 in depreciation deductions, which reduced the property's adjusted basis to $1,455,740. They sold their partnership interests to Fred Bayles, an unrelated person. Bayles paid the partners no cash (except for a trivial "reimbursement" of their selling expenses); he took the property subject to the $1,851,500 mortgage.

The Court's discussion of an issue peculiar to the tax treatment of partnerships is omitted. For all practical purposes, the partners' sales of their partnership interests resulted in the same tax consequences as if they had borrowed the money themselves, built the apartment complex, and sold their interests in the complex to Bayles after deducting the depreciation.]

* * *

On the date of transfer, the fair market value of the property did not exceed $1,400,000. Each partner reported the sale on his federal income tax return and indicated that a partnership loss of $55,740 had been sustained.[1] The Commissioner of Internal Revenue, on audit, determined that the sale resulted in a partnership capital gain of approximately $400,000. His theory was that the partnership had realized the full amount of the nonrecourse obligation.[2]

Relying on Millar v. Commissioner, 577 F.2d 212, 215(CA3), cert. denied, 439 U.S. 1046 (1978), the United States Tax Court, in an unreviewed decision, upheld the asserted deficiencies. 70 T.C. 756 (1978). The United States Court of Appeals for the Fifth Circuit reversed. 651 F.2d 1058 (1981). That court expressly disagreed with the *Millar* analysis, and, in limiting Crane v. Commissioner, supra, to its facts, questioned the theoretical underpinnings of the *Crane* decision. We granted certiorari to resolve the conflict. 456 U.S. 960 (1982).

II

* * * Section 1001 governs the determination of gains and losses on the disposition of property. Under § 1001(a), the gain or loss from a sale or other disposition of property is defined as the difference between "the amount realized" on the disposition and the property's adjusted basis. Subsection (b) of § 1001 defines "amount realized": "The amount realized from the sale or other disposition of property shall be the sum of any money received plus the fair market value of the property (other than money) received." At issue is the application of the latter provision to the disposition of property encumbered by a nonrecourse mortgage of an amount in excess of the property's fair market value.

A

In Crane v. Commissioner, supra, this Court took the first and controlling step toward the resolution of this issue. Beulah B. Crane was the sole beneficiary under the will of her deceased husband. At his death in January 1932, he owned an apartment building that was then mortgaged for an amount which proved to be equal to its fair market value, as determined for federal estate tax purposes. The widow, of course, was not personally liable on the mortgage. She operated the building for nearly seven years, hoping to turn it into a profitable venture; during that period, she claimed income tax deductions for depreciation, property taxes, interest, and operating expenses, but did not make payments upon the mortgage principal. In computing her basis for the depreciation deductions, she included the full amount of the mortgage debt. In November 1938, with her hopes unfulfilled and the mortgagee threatening foreclosure, Mrs. Crane sold the building. The purchaser took the

---

1. The loss was the difference between the adjusted basis, $1,455,740, and the fair market value of the property, $1,400,000. On their individual tax returns, the partners did not claim deductions for their respective shares of this loss. In their petitions to the Tax Court, however, the partners did claim the loss.

2. The Commissioner determined the partnership's gain on the sale by subtracting the adjusted basis, $1,455,740, from the liability assumed by Bayles, $1,851,500. * * *

property subject to the mortgage and paid Crane $3,000; of that amount, $500 went for the expenses of the sale.

Crane reported a gain of $2,500 on the transaction. She reasoned that her basis in the property was zero (despite her earlier depreciation deductions based on including the amount of the mortgage) and that the amount she realized from the sale was simply the cash she received. The Commissioner disputed this claim. He asserted that Crane's basis in the property, under § [1014], was the property's fair market value at the time of her husband's death, adjusted for depreciation in the interim, and that the amount realized was the net cash received plus the amount of the outstanding mortgage assumed by the purchaser.

In upholding the Commissioner's interpretation of § [1014] the Court observed that to regard merely the taxpayer's equity in the property as her basis would lead to depreciation deductions less than the actual physical deterioration of the property, and would require the basis to be recomputed with each payment on the mortgage. 331 U.S., at 9–10. The Court rejected Crane's claim that any loss due to depreciation belonged to the mortgagee. The effect of the Court's ruling was that the taxpayer's basis was the value of the property undiminished by the mortgage. Id., at 11.

The Court next proceeded to determine the amount realized under § [1001(b)]. In order to avoid the "absurdity," see 331 U.S., at 13, of Crane's realizing only $2,500 on the sale of property worth over a quarter of a million dollars, the Court treated the amount realized as it had treated basis, that is, by including the outstanding value of the mortgage. To do otherwise would have permitted Crane to recognize a tax loss unconnected with any actual economic loss. The Court refused to construe one section of the Revenue Act so as "to frustrate the Act as a whole." Ibid.

Crane, however, insisted that the nonrecourse nature of the mortgage required different treatment. The Court, for two reasons, disagreed. First, excluding the nonrecourse debt from the amount realized would result in the same absurdity and frustration of the Code. Id., at 13–14. Second, the Court concluded that Crane obtained an economic benefit from the purchaser's assumption of the mortgage identical to the benefit conferred by the cancellation of personal debt. Because the value of the property in that case exceeded the amount of the mortgage, it was in Crane's economic interest to treat the mortgage as a personal obligation; only by so doing could she realize upon sale the appreciation in her equity represented by the $2,500 boot. The purchaser's assumption of the liability thus resulted in a taxable economic benefit to her, just as if she had been given, in addition to the boot, a sum of cash sufficient to satisfy the mortgage.

In a footnote, pertinent to the present case, the Court observed:

> "Obviously, if the value of the property is less than the amount of the mortgage, a mortgagor who is not personally liable cannot realize a benefit equal to the mortgage. Consequently, a different

problem might be encountered where a mortgagor abandoned the property or transferred it subject to the mortgage without receiving boot. That is not this case." Id., at 14, n. 37.

B

This case presents that unresolved issue. We are disinclined to overrule *Crane,* and we conclude that the same rule applies when the unpaid amount of the nonrecourse mortgage exceeds the value of the property transferred. *Crane* ultimately does not rest on its limited theory of economic benefit; instead, we read *Crane* to have approved the Commissioner's decision to treat a nonrecourse mortgage in this context as a true loan. This approval underlies *Crane*'s holdings that the amount of the nonrecourse liability is to be included in calculating both the basis and the amount realized on disposition. That the amount of the loan exceeds the fair market value of the property thus becomes irrelevant.

When a taxpayer receives a loan, he incurs an obligation to repay that loan at some future date. Because of this obligation, the loan proceeds do not qualify as income to the taxpayer. When he fulfills the obligation, the repayment of the loan likewise has no effect on his tax liability.

Another consequence to the taxpayer from this obligation occurs when the taxpayer applies the loan proceeds to the purchase price of property used to secure the loan. Because of the obligation to repay, the taxpayer is entitled to include the amount of the loan in computing his basis in the property; the loan, under § 1012, is part of the taxpayer's cost of the property. Although a different approach might have been taken with respect to a nonrecourse mortgage loan, the Commissioner has chosen to accord it the same treatment he gives to a recourse mortgage loan. The Court approved that choice in *Crane,* and the respondents do not challenge it here. The choice and its resultant benefits to the taxpayer are predicated on the assumption that the mortgage will be repaid in full.

When encumbered property is sold or otherwise disposed of and the purchaser assumes the mortgage, the associated extinguishment of the mortgagor's obligation to repay is accounted for in the computation of the amount realized. See United States v. Hendler, 303 U.S. 564, 566–567 (1938). Because no difference between recourse and nonrecourse obligations is recognized in calculating basis, *Crane* teaches that the Commissioner may ignore the nonrecourse nature of the obligation in determining the amount realized upon disposition of the encumbered property. He thus may include in the amount realized the amount of the nonrecourse mortgage assumed by the purchaser. The rationale for this treatment is that the original inclusion of the amount of the mortgage in basis rested on the assumption that the mortgagor incurred an obligation to repay. Moreover, this treatment balances the fact that the mortgagor originally received the proceeds of the nonrecourse loan tax-free on the same assumption. Unless the outstanding amount of the mortgage is deemed to be realized, the mortgagor effectively will have received untaxed income at the time the loan was extended and will have received an unwarranted increase in the basis of his property. The Commissioner's interpretation of § 1001(b) in this fashion cannot be said to be unreasonable.

C

The Commissioner in fact has applied this rule even when the fair market value of the property falls below the amount of the nonrecourse obligation. Treas.Reg. § 1.1001–2(b) (1982); Rev.Rul. 76–111, 1976–1 Cum.Bull. 214. Because the theory on which the rule is based applies equally in this situation, see Millar v. Commissioner, 67 T.C. 656, 660 (1977), aff'd on this issue, 577 F.2d 212, 215–216 (CA3), cert. denied, 439 U.S. 1046 (1978); Mendham Corp. v. Commissioner, 9 T.C. 320, 323–324 (1947); Lutz & Schramm Co. v. Commissioner, 1 T.C. 682, 688–689 (1943), we have no reason, after *Crane*, to question this treatment.[11]

Respondents received a mortgage loan with the concomitant obligation to repay by the year 2012. The only difference between that mortgage and one on which the borrower is personally liable is that the mortgagee's remedy is limited to foreclosing on the securing property.

---

11. Professor Wayne G. Barnett, as *amicus* in the present case, argues that the liability and property portions of the transaction should be accounted for separately. Under his view, there was a transfer of the property for $1.4 million, and there was a cancellation of the $1.85 million obligation for a payment of $1.4 million. The former resulted in a capital loss of $50,000, and the latter in the realization of $450,000 of ordinary income. Taxation of the ordinary income might be deferred under § 108 by a reduction of respondents' bases in their partnership interests.

Although this indeed could be a justifiable mode of analysis, it has not been adopted by the Commissioner. Nor is there anything to indicate that the Code requires the Commissioner to adopt it. We note that Professor Barnett's approach does assume that recourse and nonrecourse debt may be treated identically.

The Commissioner also has chosen not to characterize the transaction as cancellation of indebtedness. We are not presented with and do not decide the contours of the cancellation-of-indebtedness doctrine. We note only that our approach does not fall within certain prior interpretations of that doctrine. In one view, the doctrine rests on the same initial premise as our analysis here— an obligation to repay—but the doctrine relies on a freeing-of-assets theory to attribute ordinary income to the debtor upon cancellation. See Commissioner v. Jacobson, 336 U.S. 28, 38–40 (1949); United States v.

Kirby Lumber Co., 284 U.S. 1, 3 (1931). According to that view, when nonrecourse debt is forgiven, the debtor's basis in the securing property is reduced by the amount of debt canceled, and realization of income is deferred until the sale of the property. See Fulton Gold Corp. v. Commissioner, 31 B.T.A. 519, 520 (1934). Because that interpretation attributes income only when assets are freed, however, an insolvent debtor realizes income just to the extent his assets exceed his liabilities after the cancellation. Lakeland Grocery Co. v. Commissioner, 36 B.T.A. 289, 292 (1937). Similarly, if the nonrecourse indebtedness exceeds the value of the securing property, the taxpayer never realizes the full amount of the obligation canceled because the tax law has not recognized negative basis.

Although the economic benefit prong of *Crane* also relies on a freeing-of-assets theory, that theory is irrelevant to our broader approach. In the context of a sale or disposition of property under § 1001, the extinguishment of the obligation to repay is not ordinary income; instead, the amount of the canceled debt is included in the amount realized, and enters into the computation of gain or loss on the disposition of property. According to *Crane*, this treatment is no different when the obligation is nonrecourse: the basis is not reduced as in the cancellation-of-indebtedness context, and the full value of the outstanding liability is included in the amount realized. Thus, the problem of negative basis is avoided.

This difference does not alter the nature of the obligation; its only effect is to shift from the borrower to the lender any potential loss caused by devaluation of the property. If the fair market value of the property falls below the amount of the outstanding obligation, the mortgagee's ability to protect its interests is impaired, for the mortgagor is free to abandon the property to the mortgagee and be relieved of his obligation.

This, however, does not erase the fact that the mortgagor received the loan proceeds tax-free and included them in his basis on the understanding that he had an obligation to repay the full amount. See Woodsam Associates, Inc. v. Commissioner, 198 F.2d 357, 359 (C.A.2 1952); Bittker, 33 Tax L.Rev., at 284. When the obligation is canceled, the mortgagor is relieved of his responsibility to repay the sum he originally received and thus realizes value to that extent within the meaning of § 1001(b). From the mortgagor's point of view, when his obligation is assumed by a third party who purchases the encumbered property, it is as if the mortgagor first had been paid with cash borrowed by the third party from the mortgagee on a nonrecourse basis, and then had used the cash to satisfy his obligation to the mortgagee.

Moreover, this approach avoids the absurdity the Court recognized in *Crane.* Because of the remedy accompanying the mortgage in the nonrecourse situation, the depreciation in the fair market value of the property is relevant economically only to the mortgagee, who by lending on a nonrecourse basis remains at risk. To permit the taxpayer to limit his realization to the fair market value of the property would be to recognize a tax loss for which he has suffered no corresponding economic loss. Such a result would be to construe "one section of the Act * * * so as * * * to defeat the intention of another or to frustrate the Act as a whole." 331 U.S., at 13.

In the specific circumstances of *Crane,* the economic benefit theory did support the Commissioner's treatment of the nonrecourse mortgage as a personal obligation. The footnote in *Crane* acknowledged the limitations of that theory when applied to a different set of facts. *Crane* also stands for the broader proposition, however, that a nonrecourse loan should be treated as a true loan. We therefore hold that a taxpayer must account for the proceeds of obligations he has received tax-free and included in basis. Nothing in either § 1001(b) or in the Court's prior decisions requires the Commissioner to permit a taxpayer to treat a sale of encumbered property asymmetrically, by including the proceeds of the nonrecourse obligation in basis but not accounting for the proceeds upon transfer of the encumbered property. See Estate of Levine v. Commissioner, 634 F.2d 12, 15 (C.A.2 1980).

III

* * *

IV

When a taxpayer sells or disposes of property encumbered by a nonrecourse obligation, the Commissioner properly requires him to include among the assets realized the outstanding amount of the obligation. The fair market value of the property is irrelevant to this calculation. We find this interpretation to be consistent with Crane v. Commissioner, 331 U.S. 1 (1947), and to implement the statutory mandate in a reasonable manner. National Muffler Dealers Assn. v. United States, 440 U.S. 472, 476 (1979).

The judgment of the Court of Appeals is therefore reversed.

It is so ordered.

JUSTICE O'CONNOR, concurring.

I concur in the opinion of the Court, accepting the view of the Commissioner. I do not, however, endorse the Commissioner's view. Indeed, were we writing on a slate clean except for the *Crane* decision, I would take quite a different approach—that urged upon us by Professor Barnett as *amicus*.

Crane established that a taxpayer could treat property as entirely his own, in spite of the "coinvestment" provided by his mortgagee in the form of a nonrecourse loan. That is, the full basis of the property, with all its tax consequences, belongs to the mortgagor. That rule alone, though, does not in any way tie nonrecourse debt to the cost of property or to the proceeds upon disposition. I see no reason to treat the purchase, ownership, and eventual disposition of property differently because the taxpayer also takes out a mortgage, an independent transaction. In this case, the taxpayer purchased property, using nonrecourse financing, and sold it after it declined in value to a buyer who assumed the mortgage. There is no economic difference between the events in this case and a case in which the taxpayer buys property with cash; later obtains a nonrecourse loan by pledging the property as security; still later, using cash on hand, buys off the mortgage for the market value of the devalued property; and finally sells the property to a third party for its market value.

The logical way to treat both this case and the hypothesized case is to separate the two aspects of these events and to consider, first, the ownership and sale of the property, and, second, the arrangement and retirement of the loan. Under *Crane,* the fair market value of the property on the date of acquisition—the purchase price—represents the taxpayer's basis in the property, and the fair market value on the date of disposition represents the proceeds on sale. The benefit received by the taxpayer in return for the property is the cancellation of a mortgage that is worth no more than the fair market value of the property, for that is all the mortgagee can expect to collect on the mortgage. His gain or loss on the disposition of the property equals the difference between the proceeds and the cost of acquisition. Thus, the taxation of the transaction in property reflects the economic fate of the property. If the property has declined in value, as was the case here, the taxpayer recognizes a loss on the disposition of the property. The new purchaser then takes as his basis the fair market value as of the date of the sale. See, e.g., United States v. Davis, 370 U.S. 65, 72 (1962); Gibson Products

Co. v. United States, 637 F.2d 1041, 1045, n. 8 (C.A.5 1981) (dictum); see generally Treas.Reg. § 1.1001–2(a)(3) (1982); B. Bittker, 2 Federal Income Taxation of Income, Estates and Gifts, ¶ 41.2.2., at 41–10—41–11 (1981).

In the separate borrowing transaction, the taxpayer acquires cash from the mortgagee. He need not recognize income at that time, of course, because he also incurs an obligation to repay the money. Later, though, when he is able to satisfy the debt by surrendering property that is worth less than the face amount of the debt, we have a classic situation of cancellation of indebtedness, requiring the taxpayer to recognize income in the amount of the difference between the proceeds of the loan and the amount for which he is able to satisfy his creditor. § 61(a)(12). The taxation of the financing transaction then reflects the economic fate of the loan.

The reason that separation of the two aspects of the events in this case is important is, of course, that the Code treats different sorts of income differently. A gain on the sale of the property may qualify for capital gains treatment * * * while the cancellation of indebtedness is ordinary income, but income that the taxpayer may be able to defer. §§ 108, 1017. Not only does Professor Barnett's theory permit us to accord appropriate treatment to each of the two types of income or loss present in these sorts of transactions, it also restores continuity to the system by making the taxpayer-seller's proceeds on the disposition of property equal to the purchaser's basis in the property. Further, and most important, it allows us to tax the events in this case in the same way that we tax the economically identical hypothesized transaction.

Persuaded though I am by the logical coherence and internal consistency of this approach, I agree with the Court's decision not to adopt it judicially. We do not write on a slate marked only by *Crane*. The Commissioner's longstanding position, Rev.Rul. 76–111, 1976–1 C.B. 214, is now reflected in the regulations. Treas.Reg. § 1.1001–2 (1982). In the light of the numerous cases in the lower courts including the amount of the unrepaid proceeds of the mortgage in the proceeds on sale or disposition, see, e.g., Estate of Levine v. Commissioner, 634 F.2d 12, 15 (C.A.2 1980); Millar v. Commissioner, 577 F.2d 212 (C.A.3), cert. denied, 439 U.S. 1046 (1978); Estate of Delman v. Commissioner, 73 T.C. 15, 28–30 (1979); Peninsula Properties Co., Ltd. v. Commissioner, 47 B.T.A. 84, 92 (1942), it is difficult to conclude that the Commissioner's interpretation of the statute exceeds the bounds of his discretion. As the Court's opinion demonstrates, his interpretation is defensible. One can reasonably read § 1001(b)'s reference to "the amount realized *from* the sale or other disposition of property" (emphasis added) to permit the Commissioner to collapse the two aspects of the transaction. As long as his view is a reasonable reading of § 1001(b), we should defer to the regulations promulgated by the agency charged with interpretation of the statute. National Muffler Dealers Association v. United States, 440 U.S. 472, 488–489 (1979); United States v. Correll, 389 U.S. 299, 307 (1967); see also Fulman v. United States, 434 U.S. 528, 534 (1978).

Accordingly, I concur.

REVENUE RULING 90–16

1990–1 C.B. 12.

ISSUE

A taxpayer transfers to a creditor a residential subdivision that has a fair market value in excess of the taxpayer's basis in satisfaction of a debt for which the taxpayer was personally liable. Is the transfer a sale or disposition resulting in the realization and recognition of gain by the taxpayer under sections 1001(c) and 61(a)(3)?

FACTS

X was the owner and developer of a residential subdivision. To finance the development of the subdivision, *X* obtained a loan from an unrelated bank. *X* was unconditionally liable for repayment of the debt. The debt was secured by a mortgage on the subdivision.

X became insolvent (within the meaning of section 108(d)(3)) and defaulted on the debt. *X* negotiated an agreement with the bank whereby the subdivision was transferred to the bank and the bank released *X* from all liability for the amounts due on the debt. When the subdivision was transferred pursuant to the agreement, its fair market value was 10,000x dollars, *X*'s adjusted basis in the subdivision was 8,000x dollars, and the amount due on the debt was 12,000x dollars, which did not represent any accrued but unpaid interest. After the transaction *X* was still insolvent.

LAW AND ANALYSIS

Sections 61(a)(3) and 61(a)(12) provide that, except as otherwise provided, gross income means all income from whatever source derived, including (but not limited to) gains from dealings in property and income from discharge of indebtedness.

Section 108(a)(1)(B) provides that gross income does not include any amount that would otherwise be includible in gross income by reason of discharge (in whole or in part) of indebtedness of the taxpayer if the discharge occurs when the taxpayer is insolvent. Section 108(a)(3) provides that, in the case of a discharge to which section 108(a)(1)(B) applies, the amount excluded under section 108(a)(1)(B) shall not exceed the amount by which the taxpayer is insolvent (as defined in section 108(d)(3)).

[Treas.Reg. §] 1.61–6(a) provides that the specific rules for computing the amount of gain or loss from dealings in property under section 61(a)(3) are contained in section 1001 and the regulations thereunder.

* * *

[Treas.Reg. §] 1.1001–2(a)(1) provides that, except as provided in section 1.1001–2(a)(2) and (3), the amount realized from a sale or other disposition of property includes the amount of liabilities from which the transferor is discharged as a result of the sale or disposition. Section 1.1001–2(a)(2) provides that the amount realized on a sale or other disposition of property that secures a recourse liability does not include amounts that are (or would be if realized and recognized) income from the discharge of indebtedness under section 61(a)(12). Example (8) under section 1.1001–2(c) illustrates these rules as follows:

Example (8). In 1980, *F* transfers to a creditor an asset with a fair market value of $6,000 and the creditor discharges $7,500 of indebtedness for which *F* is personally liable. The amount realized on the disposition of the asset is its fair market value ($6,000). In addition, *F* has income from the discharge of indebtedness of $1,500 ($7,500 − $6,000).

In the present situation, *X* transferred the subdivision to the bank in satisfaction of the 12,000x dollar debt. To the extent of the fair market value of the property transferred to the creditor, the transfer of the subdivision is treated as a sale or disposition upon which gain is recognized under section 1001(c). To the extent the fair market value of the subdivision, 10,000x dollars, exceeds its adjusted basis, 8,000x dollars, *X* realizes and recognizes gain on the transfer. *X* thus recognizes 2,000x dollars of gain.

To the extent the amount of debt, 12,000x dollars, exceeds the fair market value of the subdivision, 10,000x dollars, *X* realizes income from the discharge of indebtedness. However, under section 108(a)(1)(B), the full amount of *X*'s discharge of indebtedness income is excluded from gross income because that amount does not exceed the amount by which *X* was insolvent.

If the subdivision had been transferred to the bank as a result of a foreclosure proceeding in which the outstanding balance of the debt was discharged (rather than having been transferred pursuant to the settlement agreement), the result would be the same. A mortgage foreclosure, like a voluntary sale, is a "disposition" within the scope of the gain or loss provisions of section 1001. See Helvering v. Hammel, 311 U.S. 504 (1941); Electro–Chemical Engraving Co. v. Commissioner, 311 U.S. 513 (1941); and Danenberg v. Commissioner, 73 T.C. 370 (1979), acq., 1980–2 C.B. 1.

HOLDING

The transfer of the subdivision by *X* to the bank in satisfaction of a debt on which *X* was personally liable is a sale or disposition upon which gain is realized and recognized by *X* under sections 1001(c) and 61(a)(3) to the extent the fair market value of the subdivision transferred exceeds *X*'s adjusted basis. Subject to the application of section 108, to the extent the amount of debt exceeds the fair market value of the subdivision, *X* would also realize income from the discharge of indebtedness.

Problems, Notes and Questions

1. *Inclusion of purchase-money mortgage in basis.* Chief Judge
Magruder's suggestion that the cost basis of purchased property should
not include the amount of a mortgage has never been followed. It is well
established that the principal amount of a purchase-money debt, even
without personal liability, is included in the property's basis. This rule is
subject to two qualifications. First, a purchase-money mortgage so greatly in excess of the property's value that the buyer is unlikely to pay it off
is almost certainly not included in basis.[c] Second, "contingent and
indefinite" obligations of the buyer are not included in the property's
depreciable basis.[d] Both exceptions represent judicial efforts "to validate
from objective criteria the assumption * * * that the obligation will be
paid."[e]

2. *Negative basis.* The Service and the courts have usually rejected
the "negative basis" idea propounded by Judge Magruder in Parker v.
Delaney. In the *Crane* case, the Tax Court held that the property's
unadjusted basis was zero, and that, "in the very nature of things," no
further adjustment for depreciation could be made; Crane v. Commissioner, 3 T.C. 585, 591 (1944). The taxpayer in Hall v. Commissioner,
595 F.2d 1059 (5th Cir.1979), had taken depreciation deductions in
excess of the property's basis. The Government conceded that gain on

c. E.g., Franklin's Estate v. Commissioner, 544 F.2d 1045, 1048 (9th Cir.1976)
(non-recourse obligation excluded from basis where it substantially exceeded value of
property; only a purchase at fair market
value "would rather quickly yield an equity
in the property which the purchaser could
not prudently abandon"); Odend'hal v.
Commissioner, 80 T.C. 588, 604–05 (1983),
affirmed 748 F.2d 908 (4th Cir.1984)
(same). In Pleasant Summit Land Corp. v.
Commissioner, 54 T.C.M. 566 (1987), the
taxpayer used non-recourse debt to purchase property at a price that greatly exceeded the property's value and which in
fact was never paid. The Tax Court, following the above decisions, excluded the indebtedness from the taxpayer's basis, and
the second circuit affirmed per curiam in
Estate of Isaacson v. Commissioner, 860
F.2d 55 (2d Cir.1988). But in an appeal by
another taxpayer in the case, the Third
Circuit allowed the taxpayer a basis equal
to the property's value; Pleasant Summit
Land Corp. v. Commissioner, 863 F.2d 263
(3d Cir.1988), rehearing denied 863 F.2d
277, cert. denied 493 U.S. 901 (1989). The
Third Circuit decision is examined in Jensen, The Unanswered Question in *Tufts:*
What Was the Purchaser's Basis?, 10 Va.
Tax Rev. 455 (1991), and in Johnson, The
Front End of the Crane Rule, 47 Tax Notes
593 (1990).

The Tax Reform Act of 1986 extended the
at-risk rules of § 465 to vendor-financed
real-estate investments. This should substantially diminish the temptation to inflate
the purchase price of vendor-financed real
estate. Section 465 is discussed at pp. 532–
533, below.

d. E.g., Albany Car Wheel Co., Inc. v.
Commissioner, 40 T.C. 831 (1963), affirmed
333 F.2d 653 (2d Cir.1964) (buyer's agreement to satisfy seller's obligation to pay
severance pay under a union contract not
included in basis because it was unclear
whether the buyer would have to make any
payments). Non-recourse obligations have
been excluded from basis where payment is
to be made from the proceeds of exploiting
the property. See, e.g., CRC Corp. v. Commissioner, 693 F.2d 281 (3d Cir.1982) (payment was contingent upon discovery of recoverable amounts of oil and gas); Gibson
Products Co. v. United States, 637 F.2d
1041 (5th Cir.1981) (same); Waddell v.
Commissioner, 86 T.C. 848, 898–904 (1986)
(obligation not included in basis, even
though adequately secured at inception of
loan, where obligation was payable only
from proceeds of exploiting the property).

e. Waddell v. Commissioner, 86 T.C.
848, 902 (1986).

the sale of the property could not exceed the amount realized because of the Service's "longstanding position" that property cannot have a negative basis. Rev.Rul. 75–451, 1975–2 C.B. 330, held that the taxpayer's basis could not be reduced below zero by percentage depletion deductions that exceeded the property's basis. But see Easson v. Commissioner, 294 F.2d 653 (9th Cir.1961) (property subject to mortgage in excess of its basis transferred to controlled corporation under § 351; transferor-shareholder obtained negative stock basis equal to the excess) (overturned by enactment of § 357(c)). Under the consolidated-return regulations, a parent corporation can obtain a negative basis (called an "excess loss account") in the stock of its subsidiary. See Treas.Reg. § 1.1502–32. For an argument that negative basis should sometimes be allowed, see Cooper, Negative Basis, 75 Harv.L.Rev. 1352 (1962).

3. *Cancellation-of-indebtedness aspects of the Crane rule.* Suppose a debtor transfers property with a basis of $5000 and a value of $6000 to a creditor in full satisfaction of a $7500 debt, which was secured by the property. If the debtor was personally liable on the indebtedness, he realizes a $1000 gain on the disposition of the property and, under Treas.Reg. § 1.1001–2(c), ex. (8), $1500 of discharge-of-indebtedness income;[f] Rev.Rul. 90–16, p. 515, above. If the debtor was not personally liable for the indebtedness, *Tufts* treats the full amount of the indebtedness as an amount realized on the transfer of the property to the lender, thus resulting in a $2500 gain.[g]

But what if the non-recourse borrower continues to hold the property after the discharge? Suppose in the above example that the debtor persuades the lender to accept $5000 cash in full discharge of the $7500 indebtedness. Since the encumbered property is not disposed of, there is no occasion to compute any amount realized. Does the debtor have $2500 of cancellation-of-indebtedness income? Some older cases said no; e.g., Fulton Gold Corp. v. Commissioner, 31 B.T.A. 519 (1934) (court applied the discount to reduce the basis of the property; United States v. Kirby Lumber Co., p. 123, above, was distinguished as involving "personal obligations"). More recently, however, Rev.Rul. 82–202, 1982–2 C.B. 36, held the discharge of non-recourse indebtedness taxable under *Kirby Lumber*. The ruling did not mention *Fulton Gold* or its progeny. Then, in Rev. Rul. 91–31, 1991–1 C.B. 19, the Service, contending that *Fulton Gold* was no longer good law, ruled that a solvent debtor realizes debt-discharge income upon the cancellation or reduction of a non-recourse debt. The Tax Court agreed in Parker Properties Joint Venture v. Commissioner, 71 T.C.M. 3195 (1996). The holding in *Parker Properties* had been foreshadowed by Gershkowitz v. Commissioner, 88 T.C. 984 (1987).

f. The $1000 gain on the disposition of the asset must be recognized even if the taxpayer is insolvent so that the $1500 of cancellation-of-indebtedness income is not recognized under § 108. See Rev. Rul. 90–16, p. 515, above.

g. Section 7701(g), enacted in 1984, "clarifies" that the value of property is to be treated as being not less than the amount of any non-recourse indebtedness to which the property is subject.

Under §§ 108(a)(1)(D) and 108(c), added in 1993, a taxpayer (other than a C corporation) can elect to exclude debt-discharge income from gross income whenever the forgiven debt was "qualified real property business indebtedness" (defined in § 108(c)(3)). The exclusion is limited to the amount by which (immediately before the discharge) the indebtedness exceeds the value of the property (reduced by any other qualified real property business indebtedness encumbering the property at that time). The amount excluded reduces the basis of the taxpayer's depreciable real property; §§ 108(c)(1); 1017(b)(1) & (3).

Consider the application of these rules to a solvent non-recourse debtor who pays a lender $5000 cash in full discharge of $7500 of qualified real property business indebtedness. (Assume that the real property was worth $6000 and had a basis of $5000.) Of the $2500 of indebtedness discharged, the borrower may elect to exclude $1500 from income and apply that amount against the basis of the property, thus reducing the basis to $3500. The regulations under § 1017 require that the basis reduction be applied first against the property that was encumbered by the discharged indebtedness; Treas. Reg. § 1.1017–1(c)(1).

4. *Problems.*

(1) In January, year 1, *T* purchased an apartment building for $275,000 (its fair market value). *T* paid $15,000 from his own funds and borrowed the remaining $260,000 from a bank. *T* gave the bank a promissory note for $260,000, payable $2000 on December 31 of each of years 1 through 10, with the balance due December 31, year 11. The note was secured by a mortgage against the building and bore interest (payable annually) at the market rate. *T* did not assume personal liability for payment of the note. Except as otherwise indicated, assume in each case that all principal and interest payments were made when due. Ignore the cost of the land, as if only the building were purchased and sold.

(a) What is *T*'s basis for the property immediately after the purchase?

(b) What is *T*'s depreciation deduction for year 1? See § 168.

(c) *T* makes the first $2000 annual payment on the mortgage on December 31, year 1. What is *T*'s adjusted basis for the property at the end of the year?

(d) In January, year 11, after properly deducting a total of $100,000 depreciation, *T* sold the building to *P*. *P* took subject to the $240,000 mortgage balance and paid *T* $40,000 cash.

(i) What is *T*'s realized gain or loss on the sale?

(ii) Would your answer differ if *T* had been personally liable on the note, *P* took subject to (but did not assume) the note, and *T* had therefore remained secondarily liable?

(e) What result if T had instead surrendered the building (then worth $220,000) to the lender in January, year 11?

(f) What result in (e) if the building was worth only $160,000 when T surrendered it to the lender?

(g) Suppose instead that T had originally assumed personal liability on the note.

    (i) What result in (e) and (f) if the lender had accepted the property in full satisfaction of T's liability and T was then solvent? Insolvent?

    (ii) What result in (e) and (f) if the property had been sold for fair market value at a foreclosure sale and the lender obtained a deficiency judgment against T for $20,000 (in (e)) or $80,000 (in (f))?

(2) B owns a building (used in B's business and with an adjusted basis of $10,000) which is subject to $60,000 of non-recourse indebtedness incurred in acquiring the property. The lender (who was not the seller of the property) has agreed to accept $40,000 in full satisfaction of the indebtedness. The building's value is $45,000. Except as otherwise indicated, B is solvent at all times.

(a) What result if B pays the lender $40,000 cash in satisfaction of the indebtedness?

(b) What result in (a) if B had been personally liable on the note but the lender had released B from liability upon payment of the $40,000?

(c) What result in each case if B was insolvent immediately after the transfer?

(3) E exchanges a yacht (adjusted basis $40,000 and value $100,000) for land worth $120,000 but which was subject to a mortgage of $20,000. Determine E's realized gain and her basis in the land.

5. *Non-purchase-money mortgages.* Suppose a taxpayer buys property for $50,000 cash, properly deducts $30,000 of depreciation thereon over the years, and then borrows $40,000 from a bank on a non-recourse note, using the property as security. Even though the loan proceeds exceed the property's basis, no gain is recognized. And since no gain is recognized, the basis of the property is not increased.[h] See Woodsam Associates, Inc. v. Commissioner, 198 F.2d 357 (2d Cir.1952), in which the owner of property having a low basis mortgaged it for $400,000, with no personal liability. In a dispute over the property's basis, the taxpayer (a corporation to which the owner had transferred the property) argued that the owner had recognized gain in the amount by which the mortgage debt exceeded the basis, and that the basis should have been increased by the amount of the gain (see § 1016). The court held that

h. This assumes that the taxpayer does not invest the loan proceeds in improving   the property.

gain had not been recognized because the owner had not disposed of the property to create a taxable event under § 1001.

What result in the above example if the taxpayer later deducted another $10,000 of depreciation, repaid $5000 of the debt, and then sold the property, the buyer taking subject to the mortgage and paying the taxpayer $25,000 cash?

6. *References.* Cunningham, Payment of Debt With Property—The Two–Step Analysis After *Commissioner v. Tufts,* 38 The Tax Lawyer 575 (1985); Andrews, On Beyond Tufts, 61 Taxes 949 (1983); Bittker, Tax Shelters, Nonrecourse Debt, and the *Crane* Case, 33 Tax L.Rev. 277 (1978).

(b) Who "Owns" the Property?

The tax advantages of depreciation on mortgaged property are useful only to *taxpayers* (as opposed to those with net operating loss carryovers in excess of income, or tax-exempt organizations). And because those advantages take the form of deductions, they are more useful to high-income taxpayers than to low-income ones. As a result, the tax system gives those with interests in property strong incentives to arrange things so that high-income people benefit from tax deductions, even though someone else may have stronger "economic" or non-tax connections with the property.

FRANK LYON CO. v. UNITED STATES

Supreme Court of the United States, 1978.
435 U.S. 561, 98 S.Ct. 1291, 55 L.Ed.2d 550.

MR. JUSTICE BLACKMUN delivered the opinion of the Court.

* * *

Lyon is a closely held Arkansas corporation engaged in the distribution of home furnishings, primarily Whirlpool and RCA electrical products. Worthen in 1965 was an Arkansas-chartered bank and a member of the Federal Reserve System. Frank Lyon was Lyon's majority shareholder and board chairman; he also served on Worthen's board. Worthen at that time began to plan the construction of a multistory bank and office building to replace its existing facility in Little Rock. * * *

* * *

[Arkansas and Federal statutes and regulations made it impossible for Worthen to finance and build the new building itself.]

Worthen therefore was forced to seek an alternative solution that would provide it with the use of the building, satisfy the state and federal regulators, and attract the necessary capital. In September 1967 it proposed a sale-and-leaseback arrangement. * * *

Worthen then obtained a commitment from New York Life Insurance Company to provide $7,140,000 in permanent mortgage financing on the building, conditioned upon its approval of the titleholder. At this point Lyon entered the negotiations and it, too, made a proposal.

* * *

[In September, 1967, Worthen began constructing the building. Later in 1967 Lyon, Worthen, and New York Life entered into agreements as follows:

    1. Worthen leased the construction site to Lyon for 76 years, 7 months (until November 30, 2044). Lyon paid $50 rent for the first 26 years, 7 months, of the lease and agreed to pay much larger sums for the remainder of the term.

    2. Lyon agreed to buy the building, piece by piece as it was constructed,[2] from Worthen. Lyon paid Worthen $7,640,000 for the building, which cost Worthen more than $10,000,000 to build.

    3. New York Life loaned $7,140,000 to Lyon for 25 years (from completion of the building) at 6¾ percent interest. The debt was secured by the property.

    4. Lyon leased the building to Worthen for a 25–year "primary term" (from completion of the building). Worthen had options to renew for eight additional 5–year terms.

During the "primary term" of the building lease, Worthen's payments of "rents" to Lyon were equal to Lyon's payments of principal and interest on its debt to New York Life. The lease was a "net lease," which obliged Worthen to pay all the costs of operating the building, including repairs, taxes, and insurance, and to keep the building in good condition.

After the primary term Worthen's net payments to Lyon (if Worthen exercised its options to extend the building lease) would have equalled the amount needed to repay Lyon's $500,000 out-of-pocket investment at 6–percent compound interest.

The building lease gave Worthen the option to repurchase the building in 1980, 1984, 1989, or 1994—in each case for an amount equal to "the sum of the unpaid balance of the New York Life mortgage, Lyon's $500,000 investment, and 6% interest compounded on that investment."

On its tax returns, Lyon reported rent received from Worthen as income and claimed deductions for depreciation, interest, and its costs in arranging the transaction.]

* * *

---

2. This arrangement appeared advisable and was made because purchases of materials by Worthen (which then had become a national bank) were not subject to Arkansas sales tax. See Ark.Stat.Ann. § 84–1904(1) (1960); First Agricultural Nat'l Bank v. State Tax Comm'n, 392 U.S. 339 (1968). Sales of the building elements to Lyon also were not subject to state sales tax, since they were sales of real estate. See Ark.Stat.Ann. § 84–1902(c) (Supp.1977). [Footnote by the Court.]

On audit of Lyon's 1969 return, the Commissioner of Internal Revenue determined that Lyon was "not the owner for tax purposes of any portion of the Worthen Building," and ruled that "the income and expenses related to this building are not allowable * * * for Federal income tax purposes." * * * In other words, the Commissioner determined that the sale-and-leaseback arrangement was a financing transaction in which Lyon loaned Worthen $500,000 and acted as a conduit for the transmission of principal and interest from Worthen to New York Life.

* * *

The United States Court of Appeals for the Eighth Circuit * * * held that the Commissioner correctly determined that Lyon was not the true owner of the building and therefore was not entitled to the claimed deductions. It likened ownership for tax purposes to a "bundle of sticks" and undertook its own evaluation of the facts. It concluded, in agreement with the Government's contention, that Lyon "totes an empty bundle" of ownership sticks. [536 F.2d] at 751. It stressed the following: (a) The lease agreements circumscribed Lyon's right to profit from its investment in the building by giving Worthen the option to purchase for an amount equal to Lyon's $500,000 equity plus 6% compound interest and the assumption of the unpaid balance of the New York Life mortgage. (b) The option prices did not take into account possible appreciation of the value of the building or inflation. (c) Any award realized as a result of destruction or condemnation of the building in excess of the mortgage balance and the $500,000 would be paid to Worthen and not Lyon. (d) The building rental payments during the primary term were exactly equal to the mortgage payments. (e) Worthen retained control over the ultimate disposition of the building through its various options to repurchase and to renew the lease plus its ownership of the site. (f) Worthen enjoyed all benefits and bore all burdens incident to the operation and ownership of the building so that, in the Court of Appeals' view, the only economic advantages accruing to Lyon, in the event it were considered to be the true owner of the property, were income tax savings of approximately $1.5 million during the first 11 years of the arrangement. Id., at 752–753. The court concluded, id., at 753, that the transaction was "closely akin" to that in Helvering v. Lazarus & Co., 308 U.S. 252 (1939). "In sum, the benefits, risks, and burdens which [Lyon] has incurred with respect to the Worthen building are simply too insubstantial to establish a claim to the status of owner for tax purposes. * * * The vice of the present lease is that all of [its] features have been employed in the same transaction with the cumulative effect of depriving [Lyon] of any significant ownership interest." 536 F.2d at 754.

* * *

This Court, almost 50 years ago, observed that "taxation is not so much concerned with the refinements of title as it is with actual command over the property taxed—the actual benefit for which the tax is paid." Corliss v. Bowers, 281 U.S. 376, 378 (1930). In a number of cases, the Court has refused to permit the transfer of formal legal title to shift the incidence of taxation attributable to ownership of property where the transferor continues to retain significant control over the property transferred. E.g., Commissioner of Internal Revenue v. Sunnen, 333 U.S. 591 (1948); Helvering v. Clifford, 309 U.S. 331 (1940). In applying this doctrine of substance over form, the Court has looked to the objective economic realities of a transaction rather than to the particular form the parties employed. The Court has never regarded "the simple expedient of drawing up papers," Commissioner of Internal Revenue v. Tower, 327 U.S. 280, 291 (1946), as controlling for tax purposes when the objective economic realities are to the contrary. "In the field of taxation, administrators of the laws and the courts are concerned with substance and realities, and formal written documents are not rigidly binding." Helvering v. Lazarus & Co., 308 U.S., at 255. See also Commissioner of Internal Revenue v. P.G. Lake, Inc., 356 U.S. 260, 266–267 (1958); Commissioner of Internal Revenue v. Court Holding Co., 324 U.S. 331, 334 (1945). Nor is the parties' desire to achieve a particular tax result necessarily relevant. Commissioner of Internal Revenue v. Duberstein, 363 U.S. 278, 286 (1960).

In the light of these general and established principles, the Government takes the position that the Worthen–Lyon transaction in its entirety should be regarded as a sham. The agreement as a whole, it is said, was only an elaborate financing scheme designed to provide economic benefits to Worthen and a guaranteed return to Lyon. The latter was but a conduit used to forward the mortgage payments, made under the guise of rent paid by Worthen to Lyon, on to New York Life as mortgagee. This, the Government claims, is the true substance of the transaction as viewed under the microscope of the tax laws. Although the arrangement was cast in sale-and-leaseback form, in substance it was only a financing transaction, and the terms of the repurchase options and lease renewals so indicate. It is said that Worthen could reacquire the building simply by satisfying the mortgage debt and paying Lyon its $500,000 advance plus interest, regardless of the fair market value of the building at the time; similarly, when the mortgage was paid off, Worthen could extend the lease at drastically reduced bargain rentals that likewise bore no relation to fair rental value but were simply calculated to pay Lyon its $500,000 plus interest over the extended term. Lyon's return on the arrangement in no event could exceed 6% compound interest (although the Government conceded it might well be less, Tr. of Oral Arg. 32). Furthermore, the favorable option and lease renewal terms made it highly unlikely that Worthen would abandon the building after it in effect had "paid off" the mortgage. The Government implies that the arrangement was one of convenience which, if accepted on its face, would enable Worthen to deduct its payments to Lyon as rent and would allow Lyon to claim a deduction for depreciation, based on the cost of construction ultimately borne by Worthen, which Lyon could offset against other income, and to deduct mortgage interest that roughly would offset the inclusion of Worthen's rental payments in Lyon's income. If, however, the Government argues, the arrangement was only a financing transaction under which Worthen was the owner of the building, Worthen's payments would be deductible only to the extent that they represented mortgage interest, and Worthen would be entitled to claim depreciation; Lyon would not be entitled to deductions for either mortgage interest or depreciation and it would not have to include Worthen's "rent" payments in its income because its function with respect to those payments was that of a conduit between Worthen and New York Life.

The Government places great reliance on Helvering v. Lazarus & Co., supra, and claims it to be precedent that controls this case. The taxpayer there was a department store. The legal title of its three buildings was in a bank as trustee for land-trust certificate holders. When the transfer to the trustee was made, the trustee at the same time leased the buildings back to the taxpayer for 99 years, with option to renew and purchase. The Commissioner, in stark contrast to his posture in the present case, took the position that the statutory right to depreciation followed legal title. The Board of Tax Appeals, however, concluded that the transaction between the taxpayer and the bank in reality was a mortgage loan and allowed the taxpayer depreciation on the buildings. This Court, as had the Court of Appeals, agreed with that conclusion and affirmed. It regarded the "rent" stipulated in the leaseback as a promise to pay interest on the loan, and a "depreciation fund" required by the lease as an amortization fund designed to pay off the loan in the stated period. Thus, said the Court, the Board justifiably concluded that the transaction, although in written form a transfer of ownership with a leaseback, was actually a loan secured by the property involved.

The *Lazarus* case, we feel, is to be distinguished from the present one and is not controlling here. Its transaction was one involving only two (and not multiple) parties, the taxpayer-department store and the trustee-bank. The Court looked closely at the substance of the agreement between those two parties and rightly concluded that depreciation was deductible by the taxpayer despite the nomenclature of the instrument of conveyance and the leaseback. See also Sun Oil Co. v. Commissioner of Internal Revenue, 562 F.2d 258 (C.A.3 1977) (a two-party case with the added feature that the second party was a tax-exempt pension trust).

* * *

There is no simple device available to peel away the form of this transaction and to reveal its substance. The effects of the transaction on all the parties were obviously different from those that would have resulted had Worthen been able simply to make a mortgage agreement with New York Life and to receive a $500,000 loan from Lyon. Then *Lazarus* would apply. Here, however, and most significantly, it was Lyon alone, and not Worthen, who was liable on the notes, first to City Bank, and then to New York Life. Despite the facts that Worthen had agreed to pay rent and that this rent equaled the amounts due from Lyon to New York Life, should anything go awry in the later years of the lease, Lyon was primarily liable. No matter how the transaction could have been devised otherwise, it remains a fact that as the agreements were placed in final form, the obligation on the notes fell squarely on Lyon. Lyon, an ongoing enterprise, exposed its very business well-being to this real and substantial risk.

The effect of this liability on Lyon is not just the abstract possibility that something will go wrong and that Worthen will not be able to make its payments. Lyon has disclosed this liability on its balance sheet for all the world to see. Its financial position was affected substantially by the presence of this long-term debt, despite the offsetting presence of the building as an asset. To the extent that Lyon has used its capital in this transaction, it is less able to obtain financing for other business needs.

* * *

It is not inappropriate to note that the Government is likely to lose little revenue, if any, as a result of the shape given the transaction by the parties. No deduction was created that is not either matched by an item of income or that would not have been available to one of the parties if the transaction had been arranged differently. While it is true that Worthen paid Lyon less to induce it to enter into the transaction because Lyon anticipated the benefit of the depreciation deductions it would have as the owner of the building, those deductions would have been equally available to Worthen had it retained title to the building. The Government so concedes. Tr. of Oral Arg. 22–23. The fact that favorable tax consequences were taken into account by Lyon on entering into the transaction is no reason for disallowing those consequences. We cannot ignore the reality that the tax laws affect the shape of nearly every business transaction. See Commissioner of Internal Revenue v. Brown, 380 U.S. 563, 579–580 (1965) (Harlan, J., concurring). Lyon is not a corporation with no purpose other than to hold title to the bank building. It was not created by Worthen or even financed to any degree by Worthen.

* * *

We recognize that the Government's position, and that taken by the Court of Appeals, is not without superficial appeal. One, indeed, may theorize that Frank Lyon's presence on the Worthen board of directors; Lyon's departure from its principal corporate activity into this unusual venture; the parallel between the payments under the building lease and the amounts due from Lyon on the New York Life mortgage; the provisions relating to condemnation or destruction of the property; the nature and presence of the several options available to Worthen; and the tax benefits, such as the use of double declining balance depreciation, that accrue to Lyon during the initial years of the arrangement, form the basis of an argument that Worthen should be regarded as the owner of the building and as the recipient of nothing more from Lyon than a $500,000 loan.

We however, as did the District Court, find this theorizing incompatible with the substance and economic realities of the transaction: * * * Worthen's undercapitalization; Worthen's consequent inability, as a matter of legal restraint, to carry its building plans into effect by a conventional mortgage and other borrowing; the additional barriers imposed by the state and federal regulators; * * * the three-party aspect of the transaction; Lyon's substantiality and its independence from Worthen; the fact that diversification was Lyon's principal motivation; Lyon's being liable alone on the successive notes to City Bank and New York Life; the reasonableness, as the District Court found, of the rentals and of the option prices; the substantiality of the purchase prices; Lyon's not being engaged generally in the business of financing; the presence of all building depreciation risks on Lyon; the risk borne by Lyon, that Worthen might default or fail, as other banks have failed; the facts that Worthen could "walk away" from the relationship at the end of the 25–year primary term, and probably would do so if the option price were more than the then-current worth of the building to Worthen; the inescapable fact that if the building lease were not extended, Lyon would be the full owner of the building, free to do with it as it chose; * * *—all convince us that Lyon has far the better of the case.

In so concluding, we emphasize that we are not condoning manipulation by a taxpayer through arbitrary labels and dealings that have no economic significance. Such, however, has not happened in this case.

In short, we hold that where, as here, there is a genuine multiple-party transaction with economic substance which is compelled or encouraged by business or regulatory realities, is imbued with tax-independent considerations, and is not shaped solely by tax-avoidance features that have meaningless labels attached, the Government should honor the allocation of rights and duties effectuated by the parties. Expressed another way, so long as the lessor retains significant and genuine attributes of the traditional lessor status, the form of the transaction adopted by the parties governs for tax purposes. What those attributes are in any particular case will necessarily depend upon its facts. It suffices to say that, as here, a sale-and-leaseback, in and of itself, does not necessarily operate to deny a taxpayer's claim for deductions.

The judgment of the Court of Appeals, accordingly, is reversed.

It is so ordered.

MR. JUSTICE WHITE dissents and would affirm the judgment substantially for the reasons stated in the opinion in the Court of Appeals for the Eighth Circuit. 536 F.2d 746 (1976).

MR. JUSTICE STEVENS, dissenting.

In my judgment the controlling issue in this case is the economic relationship between Worthen and petitioner, and matters such as the number of parties, their reasons for structuring the transaction in a particular way, and the tax benefits which may result, are largely irrelevant. The question whether a leasehold has been created should be answered by examining the character and value of the purported lessor's reversionary estate.

* * *

"It is fundamental that 'depreciation is not predicated upon ownership of property *but rather upon an investment in property.*' No such investment exists when payments of the purchase price in accordance with the design of the parties yield no equity to the purchaser." Estate of Franklin v. Commissioner, 544 F.2d 1045, 1049 (C.A.9 1976) (citations omitted; emphasis in original). Here, the petitioner has, in effect, been guaranteed that it will receive its original $500,000 plus accrued interest. But that is all. It incurs neither the risk of depreciation, nor the benefit of possible appreciation. Under the terms of the sale-leaseback, it will stand in no better or worse position after the 11th year of the lease— when Worthen can first exercise its option to repurchase—whether the property has appreciated or depreciated. And this remains true throughout the rest of the 25-year period.

Petitioner has assumed only two significant risks. First, like any other lender, it assumed the risk of Worthen's insolvency. Second, it assumed the risk that Worthen might *not* exercise its option to purchase at or before the end of the original 25-year term. If Worthen should exercise that right *not* to repay, perhaps it would *then* be appropriate to characterize petitioner as the owner and Worthen as the lessee. But speculation as to what might happen in 25 years cannot justify the *present* characterization of petitioner as the owner of the building. Until Worthen has made a commitment either to exercise or not to exercise its option, I think the Government is correct in its view that petitioner is not the owner of the building for tax purposes. At present, since Worthen has the unrestricted right to control the residual value of the property for a price which does not exceed the cost of its unamortized financing, I would hold, as a matter of law, that it is the owner.

I therefore respectfully dissent.

Notes and Questions

1. *Who is "the" owner?* Lyon's capital was surely "invested in the building" in the sense that it risked losing money if the building declined in value and Worthen became unable to pay "rent," but is this enough? How, if at all, did Lyon's risks and potential rewards differ from those of a typical mortgagee? Does the "three-party" nature of the transaction make Lyon less like a mortgagee?

Why was Worthen willing to spend over $10,000,000 to build a building which it had agreed to sell to Lyon for $7,640,000?

2. *Reference.* Wolfman, The Supreme Court in the *Lyon*'s Den: A Failure of Judicial Process, 66 Cornell L.Rev. 1075 (1981).

C. TAX SHELTERS

The *Crane* case and its progeny contributed significantly to the extensive use of "tax shelters" (that is, investments which are intended to generate deductible tax losses in excess of economic losses, with the tax losses being used to reduce ("shelter") the taxpayer's other income). In the case of the traditional real-estate tax shelter, for example, the inclusion of non-recourse purchase-money indebtedness in the taxpayer's basis enabled the taxpayer to generate depreciation deductions in excess of his cash investment. The resulting tax losses reduced taxes on the investor's income from activities other than real estate—dividends, interest, or salaries. As discussed below, the use of such shelters was substantially curtailed by the Tax Reform Act of 1986. Before examining the effect of the anti-tax-shelter legislation, however, we examine how tax shelters work.

1. HOW TAX SHELTERS WORK

(a) Deferral, Conversion, and Leverage

Whether an investment that generates a $1000 tax deduction and a $1000 economic loss is a tax shelter depends upon the timing of the deduction and the economic loss. If the deduction is allowed at the same time the taxpayer loses $1000 cash, and the highest tax rate is 50 percent (as was the case before 1987), the activity produces an after-tax loss of from $500 to $1000, depending upon the investor's tax bracket. But if the investor can arrange things so that the $1000 deduction can be taken many years before the $1000 cash expenditure, the activity can produce an after-tax gain. Consider a 50–percent–bracket taxpayer who could obtain an immediate $1000 deduction in exchange for having to give up $1000 cash in twelve years. The $1000 deduction saves the taxpayer $500 in taxes. This amount, invested for twelve years at an after-tax return of 7 percent, will grow to $1126. After twelve years, the investor can pay the $1000 and pocket $126.

If the investor in the above example had managed to break even and had had, as a result, $1000 income in the twelfth year,[i] the investment would have been even better. As above, the $1000 deduction would have enabled the taxpayer to accumulate $1126 in twelve years. At the end of the twelfth year, $500 would have been needed to pay the tax on the recognized gain. An investment which broke even economically, and which ("in the long run") produced an equal amount of income and deductions, would have given the taxpayer a $626 after-tax profit.

The above examples show the value of "deferral," which is the principal economic basis of most tax shelters. Now suppose that the

---

i. Recall that most of the tax rules you have encountered make the taxpayer's income and deductions work out right in the long run. For example, the taxpayer who depreciates an asset with a $1000 basis down to zero and then sells the asset for $1000 will have a $1000 gain on the sale to "make up for" the $1000 in deductions previously allowed. But see § 1014.

taxpayer's gain in the second example had been a "long-term capital gain" taxable at a maximum rate of 20 percent. The taxpayer would also have benefitted from "conversion" of ordinary income into capital gain, which occurred when a deduction that was taken against ordinary income (e.g., depreciation) was "made up for" by an income item (gain on the sale of the property) taxed as a capital gain. In that case, the taxpayer would pay no more than $200 tax on the $1000 gain, leaving an after-tax profit of at least $926.

In the absence of any statutory restriction, an investor could obtain deferral by making a cash investment in an asset that could be depreciated for tax purposes more rapidly than it actually declines in value. Buildings, which in some locations have not fallen in value at all in recent years, are one example. The resulting gain on the disposition of the asset is often taxed as long-term capital gain, thus permitting the investor also to obtain conversion. These advantages could be enhanced by using "leverage"—that is, by making part of the investment with borrowed funds.

Consider a 50–percent–bracket taxpayer who, after taking deferral and conversion into account, could make an annual after-tax profit of 7 percent on a cash investment of $100,000. If the taxpayer could borrow $900,000 at 12 percent, using the proceeds of the loan to make a larger investment, and deduct the interest paid each year, the rate of return would be much higher. The annual after-tax cost to a 50–percent–bracket taxpayer of borrowing $900,000 at 12 percent would be $54,000. If the taxpayer's million-dollar investment produced an annual after-tax profit of 7 percent, or $70,000 (ignoring the cost of borrowing), the annual after-tax profit with the interest cost taken into account would be $16,000, or 16 percent of the taxpayer's out-of-pocket investment.

(b) An Example of a Traditional Real–Estate Tax Shelter

Consider how a fairly typical real-estate tax shelter might have worked before the enactment of the Tax Reform Act of 1986. Before 1987, the highest individual tax rate was 50 percent, long-term capital gains were taxed at a maximum rate of 20 percent, and buildings could be depreciated over a recovery period of 19 years. Suppose that T, who is in the 50–percent bracket, buys a new apartment building for $1,000,000, paying $100,000 cash and taking subject to a $900,000 mortgage. Assume that: (1) 95 percent of the purchase price is allocable to the building; (2) the mortgage interest is $108,000 a year (12 percent); (3) the mortgage principal is payable in a single "balloon" payment in 20 years; (4) the building will generate $200,000 a year in rents; and (5) the current expenses of operating the building (property taxes, repairs, maintenance, and so on) are $92,000 a year. Assume further that T will be able to sell the property for $1,000,000 after ten years. But for taxes, an investment like this would make no sense, for it would tie up $100,000 of T's cash for ten years in exchange for no return. The effects of deferral, conversion and leverage, however, could make the investment profitable.

For each year, T would have a deductible loss of $50,000 if straight-line depreciation based on a 19–year recovery period was used:

Gross Income from Rents		$200,000
Less Expenses:		
Interest	$108,000	
Operating Expenses	92,000	
Depreciation [j]	50,000	
		250,000
Loss		($ 50,000)

Each year's $50,000 loss would save T $25,000 that would otherwise have been paid in taxes at the 50–percent rate on salary, dividend, or interest income. Thus, T's $100,000 investment would produce a cash flow (all from tax savings) of $25,000 a year for ten years.

Now suppose T sells the property for $1,000,000 ($100,000 cash plus the buyer's taking subject to the mortgage) at the end of year 10. T's gain on the sale would be $500,000 ($1,000,000 amount realized less $500,000 adjusted basis). (Notice that the gain is not a real economic gain but just "makes up" for T's having taken $500,000 of depreciation deductions when in fact the building was not declining in value at all.) Since the gain would be a long-term capital gain, it would be taxed at a maximum rate of 20 percent (at pre–1987 rates). Thus, the tax on the gain would be $100,000, which would consume all of the cash received by T on the sale. If invested at an after-tax return of 7 percent, T's annual cash return from the investment would have grown to approximately $345,411 by the end of the tenth year. Thus, an investment of $100,000 in a venture that just broke even, economically, would produce an after-tax profit of $245,411—an after-tax return of approximately 13 percent.

Congress has significantly reduced the benefits of these tax-sheltered investments by: (1) taxing "make-up" gains arising from the sale of buildings at a rate of 25 percent (versus 20 percent for most other capital gains), thus reducing the advantages of conversion; (2) cutting tax rates, thereby reducing the amount by which the taxpayer's cash flow can be increased by each dollar of tax loss; (3) lengthening the depreciation recovery period for buildings, which lessens the benefits of deferral and conversion; and (4) limiting (under § 469, which is discussed below) the deductibility of losses from activities in which the taxpayer is a passive investor, thus restricting the use of such investments to obtain deferral.

We turn now to the Commissioner's most potent weapons for combatting tax shelters—the "at-risk" rules of § 465 and the "passive-loss" rules of § 469.

j. Assume for simplicity that the annual depreciation deduction is $50,000 ($950,000/19).

2. TAX–SHELTER LEGISLATION

(a) The "At–Risk" Rules

The typical tax shelter uses depreciation on mortgaged property and other debt-financed expenses to generate large losses without large cash outlays in the venture's early years. The tax advantages of leverage do not depend upon the debt's being non-recourse but, in practice, few of those interested in buying tax deductions are willing to expose themselves to potentially ruinous financial losses by incurring personal liability.

Section 465, enacted in 1976, generally limits the deduction of losses (defined in § 465(d)) by individuals and closely held corporations[k] to the amount they have "at risk" with respect to the income-producing activity; § 465(a)(1). A loss disallowed by § 465 is carried forward to the following year and treated as a deduction allocable to the activity in that year; § 465(a)(2). A loss disallowed by § 465 is therefore not permanently barred from deduction, but rather is "suspended" until the taxpayer's amount at risk increases enough to absorb the suspended loss.

A taxpayer is considered "at risk" to the extent of (1) the amount of money (or the basis of property) contributed to the activity in question and (2) amounts borrowed, but (generally) only if the taxpayer is personally liable for repayment or has pledged property (other than property used in the activity) as security for the debt; §§ 465(b)(1) & (2). Borrowings from other investors in the activity usually do not put the taxpayer "at risk"; § 465(b)(3).

Although § 465 limits losses from the holding of real property, it contains an exception under which the investor is deemed to be at risk on "qualified nonrecourse financing"; § 465(b)(6). "Qualified nonrecourse financing" generally includes only non-recourse real-estate loans made by an unrelated[l] professional lender (other than one from whom the property was acquired) or the Federal, state or local government; §§ 465(b)(6)(B) & (D); 49(a)(1)(D)(iv). Section 465 thus does not prevent the taxpayer from deducting amounts exceeding that for which he is *economically* at risk with respect to real property. But since § 465 disallows losses based upon non-recourse financing provided by the vendor (and some non-recourse financing provided by persons related to the vendee), it helps to prevent the use of non-recourse financing to inflate the purchase price of the property (and hence the taxpayer's depreciation deductions).

---

k. Section 465 does not apply to (1) equipment leasing by closely held corporations that derive over half their gross receipts from that activity (§ 465(c)(4)); (2) active business activities of most closely held corporations (§ 465(c)(7)); or publicly held corporations (see § 465(a)(1)(B)).

l. A loan from a related person qualifies if the financing is "commercially reasonable and on substantially the same terms as loans involving unrelated persons"; § 465(b)(6)(D)(ii).

Problems

Problem (1). In year 1, *T*, an individual who uses the cash method of accounting, pays $10,000 cash to acquire a motion-picture film. The film is subject to a $90,000 non-recourse purchase-money mortgage. Before the application of § 465, *T* can deduct in year 1 $40,000 of depreciation and $10,000 of interest paid on the mortgage. The film earns $15,000 in (cash) gross income. There are no other expenses. (Ignore the effect of § 469.)

(a) How much can *T* deduct in year 1 after the application of § 465? (Assume that during year 1 *T* withdrew from the business the $5000 excess of cash income over the interest expense.)

(b) How much can *T* deduct in year 2 if income is $10,000, depreciation is $30,000, and *T* pays another $10,000 in mortgage interest?

(c) What are the tax consequences to *T* if, at the beginning of year 3, *T* transfers the film to the mortgagee in satisfaction of the $90,000 debt?

Problem (2). In year 1, *S*, an individual, purchases a piece of equipment for $50,000 cash and immediately leases the equipment to another. In years 1 through 3, the rental income equals *S*'s cash expenses with respect to the property, and *S* properly deducts a total of $25,000 of depreciation. At the beginning of year 4, *S* borrows $40,000 on a non-recourse note, pledging the equipment as security, and withdraws the $40,000 from the activity. The rental income for year 4 again equals *S*'s cash expenses, and, apart from § 465, *S* could deduct $10,000 of depreciation on the equipment. What result to *S*? See § 465(e).

(b) The Passive–Loss Rules

Most investors in tax shelters do not want to become actively involved in the management or operation of the activity that generates the tax losses. Therefore, the use of tax shelters can be curtailed by limiting the deductibility of losses from activities in which the taxpayer is a passive investor. In 1986, Congress adopted this approach by enacting § 469, which generally allows the taxpayer to offset passive deductions only against passive income.

Section 469 disallows a deduction for the taxpayer's "passive activity loss"; § 469(a)(1). The passive-activity loss is the amount by which the taxpayer's losses from "passive activities" exceed the income from such activities for the year; § 469(d)(1). Although this netting process permits the use of passive loss from one activity to offset passive income from another activity, passive loss generally cannot be used to shelter salaries or income from active business. And since passive income is defined to exclude "portfolio income" (interest, dividends, annuities, royalties, and gains from the sale of investment property) (§ 469(e)(1)), the taxpayer cannot shelter portfolio income with passive losses.

Losses are not permanently disallowed by § 469; instead they are "suspended" (that is, carried forward and treated as a deduction attributable to the passive activity in the next year); § 469(b). The suspended loss is finally allowed when the taxpayer disposes of the entire interest in the passive activity in a taxable transaction; § 469(g)(1). This treatment is premised upon the belief that many tax-shelter losses (for example, those based upon rapid depreciation of buildings) do not involve economic losses. When the taxpayer finally disposes of the interest in the activity, the actual economic loss (or gain) can be ascertained.

Credits from passive activities (for example, the low-income-housing and rehabilitation credits) are generally limited to the regular tax attributable to passive activities; §§ 469(d)(2) & (a)(1)(B). For example, an investor whose regular tax was $60,000 but whose tax would be only $50,000 if net passive income were excluded would be allowed up to $10,000 of passive-activity credits. If a taxpayer has a net loss from passive activities for the year, the passive-activity credits cannot be applied. They must be carried forward and treated as a credit attributable to the passive activity in the next year; § 469(b). Unlike a suspended loss, however, a suspended credit is not automatically allowed when the activity is disposed of. The taxpayer still applies the suspended credit only against the tax attributable to passive activities and carries forward any unused credit, subject to the same restriction.

Generally speaking, a "passive activity" is an activity involving the conduct of a trade or business[m] and in which the taxpayer does not "materially participate"; § 469(c)(1). To be a material participant, the taxpayer must participate in the operation of the business on a regular, continuous and substantial basis; § 469(h)(1). Temp.Treas.Reg. § 1.469–5T prescribes rules for determining whether an individual satisfies the material-participation test. Under one such test, for example, a taxpayer is considered to be a material participant if he devoted more than 500 hours to the activity during the year. Other tests may allow one to qualify as a material participant even though one devotes fewer than 500 hours to the activity. An activity conducted by an S corporation, limited-liability company or a partnership is considered passive with respect to a shareholder, member or partner who does not materially participate in the operation of the activity by the entity.[n] Since *limited* partners in a limited partnership cannot engage actively in the conduct of partnership business without sacrificing their limited liability (and since limited partnerships were extensively used as tax shelters under prior law),

m. The Treasury is empowered to prescribe regulations treating an activity with respect to which expenses are allowable under § 212 as a trade or business so as to bring it within the passive-activity definition; § 469(c)(6).

n. An "S corporation" is a corporation that elects (with the consent of its shareholders) not to be subject to tax under § 11. Its income and deductions are instead passed through to its shareholders in proportion to their interests. A corporation taxable under § 11 is called a "C corporation."

A partnership (other than a publicly traded partnership that is taxed as a C corporation) is also a "pass-through" entity; its various items of income and deduction are passed through to its partners for reporting on their returns. A limited-liability company is an unincorporated entity whose owners ("members") are not liable for the firm's debts; for tax purposes, a limited-liability company is treated as a partnership (unless it elects otherwise), so that its income and deductions pass through to its members.

limited partners are seldom treated as material participants with respect to their limited partnership interests; § 469(h)(2).

The widespread use of rental property as a tax shelter under prior law, and the low level of personal involvement necessary to conduct many rental activities, suggested that the effectiveness of § 469 could be seriously impaired if material participation in rental activities were sufficient to avoid its limits. S.Rep. No. 99–313, 99th Cong., 2d Sess. 718. Section 469(c) therefore treats the rental of tangible property as a passive activity regardless of whether the taxpayer materially participates;[o] §§ 469(c)(2) & (4). Nevertheless, real-estate professionals who materially participate in rental real estate can treat their rental real-estate activities as active income; § 469(c)(7). In order to qualify under this provision, taxpayers must devote more than half their total personal service (and more than 750 hours a year) to the real-estate business in which they materially participate. Under § 469(c), a real-estate broker who materially participates in the operation of an apartment building that she owns can apply losses from the apartment building to offset her income from other sources. A lawyer who owns and operates an apartment building on the side can deduct the rental losses only against her passive income. Does that make sense?

Under § 469(i), an individual (other than a limited partner) can deduct against non-passive income up to $25,000 of loss from rental real-estate activities in which he "actively participates." The active-participation standard, which is intended to be less stringent than the material-participation requirement, "can be satisfied without regular, continuous, and substantial involvement in operations, so long as the taxpayer participates, e.g., in the making of management decisions or arranging for others to provide services (such as repairs), in a significant and *bona fide* sense." S.Rep. No. 99–313, 99th Cong., 2d Sess. 737. The $25,000 allowance is phased out at the rate of $.50 for each dollar of adjusted gross income in excess of $100,000; § 469(i)(3).

Interest expense allocable to a passive activity is not treated as investment interest (nor is income or loss from a passive activity generally treated as investment income or loss) under § 163(d); §§ 163(d)(3)(B) & (d)(4)(D). Consider a taxpayer who takes out a home-equity loan and uses the proceeds to purchase a limited-partnership interest. Is the deduction for interest paid on the loan subject to § 469? See § 469(j)(7).

If both §§ 465 and 469 potentially apply, the taxpayer first applies § 465. If any loss is allowable after the application of § 465, it may still be disallowed by § 469. See Temp. Treas.Reg. § 1.469–2T(d)(6).

---

o. Even though it involves the receipt of payments for the use of property, an activity is not treated as a rental activity if significant services are rendered to the payers. For example, the renting of hotel rooms as lodging for transients is not considered to be rental activity if significant services (such as maid service) are provided to the guests. S.Rep. No. 99–313, 99th Cong., 2d Sess. 741–42.

Section 469 applies to individuals, estates, trusts, closely held C corporations, and personal-service corporations; § 469(a)(2). However, a closely held C corporation can use passive losses to offset active-business income (but not portfolio income); § 469(e)(2).

Keep in mind that § 469 was enacted in response to a particular problem—the tax shelter. No coherent principle of tax law requires disallowing deductions for legitimate expenses of earning income just because the taxpayer's investment is passive. But it was feared that many of these losses were not real economic losses because the properties were not declining in value as rapidly as they were being depreciated for tax purposes. Without question, § 469 has significantly curtailed the use of tax shelters.

Problems

Problem (1). In year 1, *A*, an individual, has a $10,000 loss (allowable but for § 469) passed through from a limited-partnership interest in rental housing (the partnership interest is not publicly traded), $4000 of business income passed through from a limited-liability company engaged in the clothing business (*A* does not materially participate in the business), and $8000 of dividend income from publicly held corporations.

(a) How much of the $10,000 loss can *A* deduct in year 1?

(b) In year 2, *A* has $2000 of loss (deductible but for § 469) passed through from the limited partnership and $7000 of business income passed through from the limited-liability company. What result to *A*?

Problem (2). On January 1, year 1, *T* purchased for $390,000 an office building to be held for rental income. *T* paid $70,000 from her own funds and borrowed the remaining $320,000 on a note (secured by the building) for which *T* was personally liable. *T* was required to pay only interest ($28,000 a year) on the note until December 31, year 5, when the entire principal was due.

The building was leased under "net" leases that required the tenants to pay all expenses of operation and maintenance and all property taxes. *T* delegates the management of the property to a property-management firm. Neither *T* nor the management firm renders any substantial services to the tenants.

(a) In year 1, *T* received $35,000 of rent, paid a $5000 fee to the property-management firm, and paid the $28,000 interest on the mortgage note. (Assume that the allowable depreciation deduction under § 168 is $10,000 a year.[p]) Apart from these items, *T* had adjusted gross income of $140,000 ($120,000 of income from active business and $20,000 of interest on corporate bonds). What result?

p. That is, ignore (1) the mid-month convention of § 168(d)(2) and (2) the cost of the land, as if *T* purchased only the building.

(b) How would your answer in (a) differ if the management firm handled day-to-day management of the building, but T's approval was required for new tenants and lease terms, capital expenditures, major repairs, and similar matters? See § 469(i).

(c) How would your answer in (a) differ if the building was owned by X Corp., a C corporation all of the stock of which is owned by T, and the data given pertained to X Corp.? See § 469(e)(2).

(d) Assume that T had the same amounts of income and expense for year 2 as given in (a) for year 1. On December 31, year 2, T sells the building for $380,000, the purchaser paying T $60,000 cash and taking subject to the $320,000 mortgage. In year 2, T also had a $10,000 loss (allowable apart from § 469) passed through from a limited partnership engaged in rental housing. (The partnership is not publicly traded.) What result?

(e) Same as (d), except that the building was sold for only $365,000, the purchaser paying $45,000 cash and taking subject to the $320,000 mortgage.

Problem (3). Individual S owns all of the stock of C Corporation (a C corporation) in whose business S materially participates. S also owns the building in which C's business is located. The building is leased to C under a rental arrangement that is very profitable to S. S also owns other rental properties that operate at a loss. Can S use her income from the C lease to offset her (passive) losses from the other rental properties? Consider § 469(c)(2) & (4), (*l*)(3); Temp. Treas. Reg. § 1.469–2T(f)(6).

References. Bankman, The Case Against Passive Investments: A Critical Appraisal of the Passive Loss Restrictions, 42 Stan L. Rev. 15 (1989); Zelenak, When Good Preferences Go Bad: A Critical Analysis of the Anti–Tax Shelter Provisions of the Tax Reform Act of 1986, 67 Texas L.Rev. 499 (1989); Johnson, Why Have Anti–Tax Shelter Legislation? A Response to Professor Zelenak, 67 Texas L.Rev. 591 (1989); Zelenak, Reply, 68 Texas L. Rev. 491 (1989); Peroni, A Policy Critique of the Section 469 Passive Loss Rules, 62 So.Cal.L.Rev. 1 (1988).

"ABUSIVE" TAX SHELTERS

Congress's decision in 1986 to eliminate most tax shelters was prompted by three considerations. First, by broadening the tax base, tax rates could be lowered. Second, tax shelters were encouraging investors to put their money into activities like motels and motion pictures, rather than into industries which could produce larger economic profits but which did not receive the considerable tax advantages accorded real estate and films. Finally, some promoters marketed "tax shelters" which bordered on (and in some cases amounted to) fraud: values of buildings and other properties were greatly exaggerated in the offering materials, and debt instruments were created which purported to impose personal liability but which in fact did not. In extreme cases, the "investments" being offered were complete shams; investors were sold interests in oil wells and similar properties which did not exist or which, even if they did exist, were worthless. Furthermore, the promotion of tax shelters, legitimate and otherwise, had become so blatant as to make the tax system look ridiculous (one widely advertised shelter was called "Gold for Tax Dollars"). The problem with "abusive" shelters was not so much that they would stand up to careful scrutiny in court, but rather that so many of them were being sold that investors were being defrauded and the Service's resources were being strained.

The story of abusive tax shelters is not one in which lawyers looked good. In order to give their offerings at least the appearance of legitimacy, promoters obtained opinion letters from lawyers which said, or appeared to say, that the investors had reasonable grounds for claiming deductions and credits on their returns. The promoters and buyers valued these letters not as assurances of the legitimacy of the deductions and credits but rather because they believed that their existence would prevent the imposition of penalties even if the investors' tax benefits were disallowed.

D. THE BASIS OF PROPERTY ACQUIRED BY GIFT

1. IN GENERAL

We saw in Chapter 3 that the recipient of a gift can exclude the gift from income under § 102(a). A donor who transfers property by gift usually recognizes no gain or loss on the transfer. Under § 1015(a), the donee generally assumes the donor's basis for the property.[q] (If the donee obtained a "cost" basis equal to the value of the property, as was the case for gifts made before 1921, any appreciation that occurred while the donor held the property would be exempted from tax.) Section 1015 may thus result in taxing the donee on gain attributable to appreciation that occurred while the donor held the property. The constitutionality of this approach was upheld in Taft v. Bowers, 278 U.S. 470 (1929).

If at the time of the gift the value of the property is less than the donor's adjusted basis, the donee must use that value (rather than the donor's basis) in computing the amount of loss realized on a disposition of the property.[r] This "lower-of-basis-or-value" rule was intended to prevent a donor who holds property with a value less than its basis from transferring the potential loss to a family member in a higher tax

---

q. In determining how long the property has been held by the donee (e.g., for capital-gains purposes), the donee can include ("tack on") the period during which the property was held by the donor if the property "has, for the purpose of determining gain or loss * * * the same basis in whole or in part" in the donee's hands as in the hands of the donor; § 1223(2). (The donee has "in part" the same basis as the donor even though the donee's basis may have been adjusted for depreciation, gift tax paid under § 1015(d), etc.)

r. When the donee uses the value of the property as the adjusted basis for computing loss, the donee's holding period does not include the donor's (since in that case the donee's adjusted basis is different from the donor's); Rev. Rul. 59–416, 1959–2 C.B. 159.

bracket. (Is that more objectionable than the donor's transferring appreciated property by gift to a lower-bracket taxpayer?)

Section 1015(d) sometimes permits the donee to increase the property's basis by gift tax paid on the transfer. For gifts made after 1976, the basis adjustment is limited to the portion of the gift tax attributable to the "net appreciation" in the property; § 1015(d)(6).

In a few instances the donor may be required to recognize gain or loss upon the transfer of property by gift.[s] In those cases the basis of the property in the hands of the donee is adjusted for the gain or loss recognized by the donor on the transfer.[t]

Problems

Problem (1). For several years *P* had owned stock with a basis of $10,000. Early this year, when the stock was worth $50,000, *P* gave the stock to his adult child, *C*. Five months later, *C* sold the stock for $60,000. What result to *C*?

Problem (2). Suppose in (1) that *P*'s basis in the stock was $100,000. What result to *C* if five months after the gift *C* sells the stock for:

    (a) $40,000?

    (b) $110,000?

    (c) $80,000?

Problem (3). What result in (1) and (2) if *P* had paid a gift tax of $20,000 on the transfer to *C*?

Problem (4). In the current year *P* also made a gift of depreciable business property (with an adjusted basis of $50,000) to *C*. At the time of the gift, the property was worth $30,000. The property remains depreciable business property in *C*'s hands. What is *C*'s basis for depreciation? See § 167(c). (Does your answer make sense in light of § 1015(a)?)

2. TRANSFERS IN CONNECTION WITH MARRIAGE AND DIVORCE

FARID–ES–SULTANEH v. COMMISSIONER

United States Court of Appeals, Second Circuit, 1947.
160 F.2d 812.

Before SWAN, CHASE, and CLARK, CIRCUIT JUDGES.

CHASE, CIRCUIT JUDGE.

The problem presented by this petition is to fix the cost basis to be used by the petitioner in determining the taxable gain on a sale she made in 1938 of shares of corporate stock. She contends that it is the adjusted value of the shares at the date she acquired them because her

---

    s. E.g., § 453B(a).   **t.** Rev.Rul. 87–112, 1987–2 C.B. 207; Rev.Rul. 79–371, 1979–2 C.B. 294.

acquisition was by purchase. The Commissioner's position is that she must use the adjusted cost basis of her transferor because her acquisition was by gift. The Tax Court agreed with the Commissioner and redetermined the deficiency accordingly.

* * *

In December 1923 when the petitioner, then unmarried, and S.S. Kresge, then married, were contemplating their future marriage, he delivered to her 700 shares of the common stock of the S.S. Kresge Company which then had a fair market value of $290 per share. The shares were all in street form and were to be held by the petitioner "for her benefit and protection in the event that the said Kresge should die prior to the contemplated marriage between the petitioner and said Kresge." The latter was divorced from his wife on January 9, 1924, and on or about January 23, 1924 he delivered to the petitioner 1800 additional common shares of S.S. Kresge Company which were also in street form and were to be held by the petitioner for the same purposes as were the first 700 shares he had delivered to her. On April 24, 1924, and when the petitioner still retained the possession of the stock so delivered to her, she and Mr. Kresge executed a written ante-nuptial agreement wherein she acknowledged the receipt of the shares "as a gift made by the said Sebastian S. Kresge, pursuant to this indenture, and as an ante-nuptial settlement, and in consideration of said gift and said ante-nuptial settlement, in consideration of the promise of said Sebastian S. Kresge to marry her, and in further consideration of the consummation of said promised marriage" she released all dower and other marital rights, including the right to her support to which she otherwise would have been entitled as a matter of law when she became his wife. They were married in New York immediately after the ante-nuptial agreement was executed and continued to be husband and wife until the petitioner obtained a final decree of absolute divorce from him on, or about, May 18, 1928. No alimony was claimed by, or awarded to, her.

The stock so obtained by the petitioner from Mr. Kresge had a fair market value of $315 per share on April 24, 1924, and of $330 per share on, or about May 6, 1924, when it was transferred to her on the books of the corporation. [Because of basis adjustments made necessary by intervening transactions, the taxpayer's basis when she sold the stock in 1938 would have been $10.66 per share if computed on the basis of fair market value when she obtained the stock. If computed under the predecessor of § 1015, her basis would have been $0.159091 per share.]
* * *

* * *

The Commissioner determined the deficiency on the ground that the petitioner's stock obtained as above stated was acquired by gift within the meaning of that word as used in § [1015], and, as the transfer to her was after December 31, 1920, used as the basis for determining the gain on her sale of it the basis it would have had in the hands of the donor.

This was correct if the just mentioned statute is applicable, and the Tax Court held it was on the authority of Wemyss v. Commissioner, 324 U.S. 303, and Merrill v. Fahs, 324 U.S. 308.

The issue here presented cannot, however, be adequately dealt with quite so summarily. The *Wemyss* case determined the taxability to the transferor as a gift, under §§ [2501 and 2512], and the applicable regulations, of property transferred in trust for the benefit of the prospective wife of the transferor pursuant to the terms of an antenuptial agreement. It was held that the transfer, being solely in consideration of her promise of marriage, and to compensate her for loss of trust income which would cease upon her marriage, was not for an adequate and full consideration in money or money's worth within the meaning of § [2512(b)] of the statute, the Tax Court having found that the transfer was not one at arm's length made in the ordinary course of business. But we find nothing in this decision to show that a transfer, taxable as a gift under the gift tax, is ipso facto to be treated as a gift in construing the income tax law.

In Merrill v. Fahs, supra, it was pointed out that the estate and gift tax statutes are in pari materia and are to be so construed. Estate of Sanford v. Commissioner of Internal Revenue, 308 U.S. 39, 44. * * *

We find in this decision no indication, however, that the term "gift" as used in the income tax statute should be construed to include a transfer which, if made when the gift tax were effective, would be taxable to the transferor as a gift merely because of the special provisions in the gift tax statute defining and restricting consideration for gift tax purposes. A fortiori, it would seem that limitations found in the estate tax law upon according the usual legal effect to proof that a transfer was made for a fair consideration should not be imported into the income tax law except by action of Congress.

In our opinion the income tax provisions are not to be construed as though they were in pari materia with either the estate tax law or the gift tax statutes. They are aimed at the gathering of revenue by taking for public use given percentages of what the statute fixes as net taxable income. Capital gains and losses are, to the required or permitted extent, factors in determining net taxable income. What is known as the basis for computing gain or loss on transfers of property is established by statute in those instances when the resulting gain or loss is recognized for income tax purposes and the basis for succeeding sales or exchanges will, theoretically at least, level off tax-wise any hills and valleys in the consideration passing either way on previous sales or exchanges. When Congress provided that gifts should not be treated as taxable income to the donee there was, without any correlative provisions fixing the basis of the gift to the donee, a loophole which enabled the donee to make a subsequent transfer of the property and take as the basis for computing gain or loss its value when the gift was made. Thus it was possible to exclude from taxation any increment in value during the donor's holding and the donee might take advantage of any shrinkage in such increment after the acquisition by gift in computing gain or loss upon a subsequent sale or exchange. It was to close this loophole that Congress provided that the donee should take the donor's basis when property was transferred by gift. Report of Ways and Means Committee (No. 350, p. 9, 67th Cong., 1st Sess.). This change in the statute affected only the statutory net taxable income. The altered statute prevented a transfer by gift from creating any change in the basis of the property in computing gain or loss on any future transfer. In any individual instance the change in the statute would but postpone taxation and presumably would have little effect on the total volume of income tax revenue derived over a long period of time and from many taxpayers. Because of this we think that a transfer which should be classed as a gift under the gift tax law is not necessarily to be treated as a gift income-tax-wise. Though such a consideration as this petitioner gave for the shares of stock she acquired from Mr. Kresge might not have relieved him from liability for a gift tax, had the present gift tax then been in effect, it was nevertheless a fair consideration which prevented her taking the shares as a gift under the income tax law since it precluded the existence of a donative intent.

Although the transfers of the stock made both in December 1923, and in the following January by Mr. Kresge to this taxpayer are called a gift in the ante-nuptial agreement later executed and were to be for the protection of his prospective bride if he died before the marriage was consummated, the "gift" was contingent upon his death before such marriage, an event that did not occur. Consequently, it would appear that no absolute gift was made before the ante-nuptial contract was executed and that she took title to the stock under its terms, viz: in consideration for her promise to marry him coupled with her promise to relinquish all rights in and to his property which she would otherwise acquire by the marriage. Her inchoate interest in the property of her affianced husband greatly exceeded the value of the stock transferred to her. It was a fair consideration under ordinary legal concepts of that term for the transfers of the stock by him. [Citations omitted.] She performed the contract under the terms of which the stock was transferred to her and held the shares not as a donee but as a purchaser for a fair consideration.

* * *

Decision reversed.

CLARK, CIRCUIT JUDGE (dissenting).

The opinion accepts two assumptions, both necessary to the result. The first is that definitions of gift under the gift and estate tax statutes are not useful, in fact are directly opposed to, definitions of gift under the capital-gains provision of the income tax statute. The second is that the circumstances here of a transfer of the stock some months before the marriage showed, contrary to the conclusions of the Tax Court, a purchase of dower rights, rather than a gift. The first I regard as doubtful; the second, as untenable.

It is true that Commissioner of Internal Revenue v. Wemyss, 324 U.S. 303, and Merrill v. Fahs, 324 U.S. 308, which would require the transactions here to be considered a gift, dealt with estate and gift taxes. But no strong reason has been advanced why what is a gift under certain sections of the Revenue Code should not be a gift under yet another section. As a matter of fact these two cases indicate that the donative intent of the common law is not an essential ingredient of a gift for tax purposes. Conversely love, affection, and the promise of future marriage will not be consideration adequate to avoid the gift tax. If that is so, it would seem that these should not be sufficient to furnish new and higher cost bases for computing capital gains on ultimate sale. The Congressional purpose would seem substantially identical—to prevent a gap in the law whereby taxes on gifts or on capital gains could be avoided or reduced by judicious transfers within the family or intimate group.

But decision on that point might well be postponed, since, to my mind, the other point should be decisive. Kresge transferred the stock to petitioner more than three months before their marriage. Part was given when Kresge was married to another woman. At these times petitioner had no dower or other rights in his property. If Kresge died before the wedding, she could never secure dower rights in his lands. Yet she would nevertheless keep the stock. Indeed the specifically stated purpose of the transfer was to protect her against his death prior to marriage. It is therefore difficult to perceive how her not yet acquired rights could be consideration for the stock. Apparently the parties themselves shared this difficulty, for in their subsequent instrument releasing dower rights they referred to the stock transfer as a gift and an antenuptial settlement.

If the transfer be thus considered a sale, as the majority hold, it would seem to follow necessarily that this valuable consideration (equivalent to one-third for life in land valued at one hundred million dollars) should have yielded sizable taxable capital gains to Kresge, as well as a capital loss to petitioner when eventually she sold. I suggest these considerations as pointing to the unreality of holding as a sale what seems clearly only intended as a stimulating cause to eventual matrimony. Since Judge Murdock in the Tax Court found this to be a gift, not a sale, and since this decision is based in part at least upon factual considerations, it would seem binding upon us. At any rate, it should be persuasive of the result we ought to reach.

Problems, Notes and Question

1. *The scope of Farid-Es-Sultaneh.* Does *Farid-Es-Sultaneh* hold that the taxpayer had income on account of the stock transfers, or is the decision limited to basis? Even if such transfers are not "gifts" under § 102, it does not necessarily follow that the recipients have income. Compare the material on the taxation of damages in Chapter 2. The problem is analogous to that of whether payments to a former spouse on account of divorce are taxable, an issue that will be considered below.

2. *The Davis case and § 1041*. In United States v. Davis, 370 U.S. 65 (1962), the taxpayer, a resident of a separate-property state, transferred appreciated stock to his former wife under a divorce property-settlement agreement. Rejecting the taxpayer's contention that the transfer was essentially a division of property between co-owners, as in the case of community property, the Court required the taxpayer to recognize gain to the extent that the value of the stock exceeded its basis. The taxpayer's wife obtained a cost basis equal to the value of the stock received.[u] In essence, the transaction was viewed as if the transferor had paid cash to his ex-wife, who had then used the cash to purchase the property.

The *Davis* decision created serious practical and legal difficulties. Many taxpayers (and their lawyers) were unaware of the rule taxing transfers of property upon divorce. A series of cases held that some states' "equitable distribution" statutes created interests sufficiently similar to community property to allow the parties to transfer property tax free at divorce. There was thus substantial uncertainty about whether *Davis* applied in those states. The government was sometimes subject to "whipsaw," with the spouse receiving appreciated property claiming a stepped-up basis on the theory that the transfer was taxable, while the transferor reported no gain.

In order to solve these problems, Congress in 1984 enacted § 1041, under which gain or loss is not recognized upon the transfer of property to the taxpayer's spouse or, in the case of transfers "incident to" divorce, to a former spouse. The exclusion for transfers incident to divorce covers all transfers within one year of the cessation of the marriage, as well as transfers "related to" that cessation.

Whenever § 1041(a) provides for non-recognition on the transfer of property between spouses or former spouses, the property is treated for income-tax (but not gift-tax) purposes as having been acquired by the transferee by gift; § 1041(b)(1). But § 1015(e) provides that § 1041(b)(2), rather than § 1015(a), governs the transferee's basis for the property. Under § 1041(b)(2), the transferee assumes the transferor's basis. The only practical difference between the basis rules of § 1041(b)(2) and § 1015(a) is that the former does not contain the lower-of-basis-or-value limitation.[v]

3. *Section 1041 and assignments of income*. In Rev.Rul. 87-112, 1987-2 C.B. 207, a cash-method taxpayer transferred United States Series E and EE savings bonds to a former spouse as part of a divorce property settlement. The taxpayer was required to include in gross income the interest that had accrued before the transfer. Section 1041(a) was held inapplicable to unrecognized "interest," as opposed to "gain."

---

u. Rev.Rul. 67-221, 1967-2 C.B. 63. The value of the property was not includable in the recipient's gross income.

v. If the basis rule of § 1015 does not apply, what is the significance of § 1041(b)(1)'s treating the property as having been acquired by gift? For one thing, it makes clear that the recipient has no income on account of the transfer; see § 102(a).

The transferee obtained a basis for the bonds equal to the sum of the transferor's basis and the amount of income recognized on the transfer.

The holding in Rev. Rul. 87–112 is not free from doubt; nonrecognition rules have sometimes been held to override assignment-of-income principles; e.g., Hempt Bros., Inc. v. United States, 490 F.2d 1172, cert. denied 419 U.S. 826 (1974).

4. *Problems.*

(1) As part of a divorce property settlement, *W* transferred to her former husband, *H*, stock with a basis of $10,000 and a value of $50,000. Five months later, *H* sold the stock for $60,000. What result to *W* and *H*?

(2) Suppose in (1) that *W*'s basis in the stock was $100,000. What result to *H* if five months after the transfer he sells the stock for $40,000?

(3) *C* and *D* are married but file separate returns. *C* makes a bona fide sale of stock with a basis of $10,000 to *D* for $50,000 cash. What result to *C* and *D*?

5. *Reference.* Asimow, The Assault on Tax–Free Divorce: Carryover Basis and Assignment of Income, 44 Tax L.Rev. 65 (1988).

3. PART–GIFT, PART–SALE TRANSACTIONS

DIEDRICH v. COMMISSIONER

Supreme Court of the United States, 1982.
457 U.S. 191, 102 S.Ct. 2414, 72 L.Ed.2d 777.

CHIEF JUSTICE BURGER delivered the opinion of the Court.

We granted certiorari to resolve a circuit conflict as to whether a donor who makes a gift of property on condition that the donee pay the resulting gift tax receives taxable income to the extent that the gift tax paid by the donee exceeds the donor's adjusted basis in the property transferred [citation omitted]. The United States Court of Appeals for the Eighth Circuit held that the donor realized income. 643 F.2d 499 (1981). We affirm.

I

A

Diedrich v. Com'r Internal Revenue

In 1972 petitioners Victor and Frances Diedrich made gifts of approximately 85,000 shares of stock to their three children, using both a direct transfer and a trust arrangement. The gifts were subject to a condition that the donees pay the resulting federal and state gift taxes. There is no dispute concerning the amount of the gift tax paid by the donees. The donors' basis in the transferred stock was $51,073; the gift tax paid in 1972 by the donees was $62,992. Petitioners did not include as income on their 1971 federal income tax returns any portion of the gift tax paid by the donees. After an audit the Commissioner of Internal

Revenue determined that petitioners had realized income to the extent that the gift tax owed by petitioners but paid by the donees exceeded the donors' basis in the property. Accordingly, petitioners' taxable income for 1972 was increased * * *.[1] Petitioners filed a petition in the United States Tax Court for redetermination of the deficiencies. The Tax Court held for the taxpayers, concluding that no income had been realized. [Citation omitted.]

B

United Mo. Bank of Kansas [City] v. Com'r Internal Revenue

In 1970 and 1971 Mrs. Frances Grant gave 90,000 voting trust certificates to her son on condition that he pay the resulting gift tax. Mrs. Grant's basis in the stock was $8,742.60; the gift tax paid by the donee was $232,620.09. As in *Diedrich*, there is no dispute concerning the amount of the gift tax or the fact of its payment by the donee pursuant to the condition.

Like the Diedrichs, Mrs. Grant did not include as income on her 1970 or 1971 federal income tax returns any portion of the amount of the gift tax owed by her but paid by the donee. After auditing her returns, the Commissioner determined that the gift of stock to her son was part gift and part sale, with the result that Mrs. Grant realized income to the extent that the amount of the gift tax exceeded the adjusted basis in the property. Accordingly, Mrs. Grant's taxable income was increased * * *.[2] Mrs. Grant filed a petition in the United States Tax Court for redetermination of the deficiencies. The Tax Court held for the taxpayer, concluding that no income had been realized. [Citation omitted.]

C

The United States Court of Appeals for the Eighth Circuit consolidated the two appeals and reversed, concluding that "to the extent the gift taxes paid by donees" exceeded the donors' adjusted bases in the property transferred, "the donors realized taxable income." 643 F.2d 499, 504 (1981). The Court of Appeals rejected the Tax Court's conclusion that the taxpayers merely had made a "net gift" of the difference between the fair market value of the transferred property and the gift taxes paid by the donees. The court reasoned that a donor receives a benefit when a donee discharges a donor's legal obligation to pay gift taxes. The Court of Appeals agreed with the Commissioner in rejecting the holding in Turner v. Commissioner, 49 T.C. 356 (1968), aff'd per curiam, 410 F.2d 752 (C.A.6 1969), and its progeny, and adopted the

---

1. Subtracting the stock basis of $51,073 from the gift tax paid by the donees of $62,992, the Commissioner found that petitioners had realized a long term capital gain of $11,919. * * *

2. The gift taxes were $232,630.09. Subtracting the adjusted basis of $8,742.60, the commissioner found that Mrs. Grant real-

ized a long term capital gain of $223,887.49. * * *

During pendency of this lawsuit, Mrs. Grant died and the United Missouri Bank of Kansas City, the decedent's executor, was substituted as petitioner.

approach of Johnson v. Commissioner, 59 T.C. 791 (1973), aff'd, 495 F.2d 1079 (CA6), cert. denied, 419 U.S. 1040 (1974), and Estate of Levine v. Commissioner, 72 T.C. 780 (1979), aff'd, 634 F.2d 12 (C.A.2 1980). We granted certiorari to resolve this conflict * * * and we affirm.

II

A

Pursuant to its Constitutional authority, Congress has defined "gross income" as income "from whatever source derived," including "[i]ncome from discharge of indebtedness." § 61. This Court has recognized that "income" may be realized by a variety of indirect means. In Old Colony Tr. Co. v. Commissioner, 279 U.S. 716 (1929), the Court held that payment of an employee's income taxes by an employer constituted income to the employee. Speaking for the Court, Chief Justice Taft concluded that "[t]he payment of the tax by the employer[ ] was in consideration of the services rendered by the employee and was a gain derived by the employee from his labor." Id., at 729. The Court made clear that the substance, not the form, of the agreed transaction controls. "The discharge by a third person of an obligation to him is equivalent to receipt by the person taxed." Ibid. The employee, in other words, was placed in a better position as a result of the employer's discharge of the employee's legal obligation to pay the income taxes; the employee thus received a gain subject to income tax.

The holding in *Old Colony* was reaffirmed in Crane v. Commissioner, 331 U.S. 1 (1947). In *Crane,* the Court concluded that relief from the obligation of a nonrecourse mortgage in which the value of the property exceeded the value of the mortgage constituted income to the taxpayer. The taxpayer in *Crane* acquired depreciable property, an apartment building, subject to an unassumed mortgage. The taxpayer later sold the apartment building, which was still subject to the nonrecourse mortgage, for cash plus the buyer's assumption of the mortgage. This Court held that the amount of mortgage was properly included in the amount realized on the sale, noting that if the taxpayer transfers subject to the mortgage,

> "the benefit to him is as real and substantial as if the mortgage were discharged, or as if a personal debt in an equal amount had been assumed by another." Id., at 14.

Again, it was the "reality," not the form, of the transaction that governed. Ibid. The court found it immaterial whether the seller received money prior to the sale in order to discharge the mortgage, or whether the seller merely transferred the property subject to the mortgage. In either case the taxpayer realized an economic benefit.

B

The principles of *Old Colony* and *Crane* control. A common method of structuring gift transactions is for the donor to make the gift subject to the condition that the donee pay the resulting gift tax, as was done in each of the cases now before us. When a gift is made, the gift tax liability falls on the donor under § 2502([c]).[6] When a donor makes a gift to a donee, a "debt" to the United States for the amount of the gift tax is incurred by the donor. Those taxes are as much the legal obligation of the donor as the donor's income taxes; for these purposes they are the same kind of debt obligation as the income taxes of the employee in *Old Colony,* supra. Similarly, when a donee agrees to discharge an indebtedness in consideration of the gift, the person relieved of the tax liability realizes an economic benefit. In short, the donor realizes an immediate economic benefit by the donee's assumption of the donor's legal obligation to pay the gift tax.

An examination of the donor's intent does not change the character of this benefit. Although intent is relevant in determining whether a gift has been made, subjective intent has not characteristically been a factor in determining whether an individual has realized income.[7] Even if intent were a factor, the donor's intent with respect to the condition shifting the gift tax obligation from the donor to the donee was plainly to relieve the donor of a debt owed to the United States; the choice was made because the donor would receive a benefit in relief from the obligation to pay the gift tax.[8]

Finally, the benefit realized by the taxpayer is not diminished by the fact that the liability attaches during the course of a donative transfer. It cannot be doubted that the donors were aware that the gift tax obligation would arise immediately upon the transfer of the property; the economic benefit to the donors in the discharge of the gift tax liability is indistinguishable from the benefit arising from discharge of a preexisting obligation. Nor is there any doubt that had the donors sold a portion of the stock immediately before the gift transfer in order to raise funds to pay the expected gift tax, a taxable gain would have been realized.

6. "The tax imposed by section 2501 shall be paid by the donor."

Section 6321 imposes a lien on the personal property of the donor when a tax is not paid when due. The donee is secondarily responsible for payment of the gift tax should the donor fail to pay the tax. § 6324(b). The donee's liability, however, is limited to the value of the gift. Ibid. This responsibility of the donee is analogous to a lien or security. Ibid. See also S.REP. No. 665, 72d Cong., 1st Sess. 42 (1932); H.R.Rep. No. 708, 72d Cong., 1st Sess. 30 (1932).

7. Several courts have found it highly significant that the donor intended to make a gift. Turner v. Commissioner, supra; Hirst v. Commissioner, supra. It is not enough, however, to state that the donor intended simply to make a gift of the amount which will remain after the donee pays the gift tax. As noted above, subjective intent has not characteristically been a factor in determining whether an individual has realized income. In Commissioner v. Duberstein, 363 U.S. 278, 286 (1960), the court noted that " * * * the donor's characterization of his action is not determinative * * *." See also Minnesota Tea Co. v. Helvering, 302 U.S. 609, 613 (1938) ("[a] given result at the end of a straight path is not made a different result because reached by following a devious path").

8. The existence of the "condition" that the gift will be made only if the donee assumes the gift tax consequences precludes any characterization that the payment of the taxes was simply a gift from the donee back to the donor.

A conditional gift not only relieves the donor of the gift tax liability, but also may enable the donor to transfer a larger sum of money to the donee than would otherwise be possible due to such factors as differing income tax brackets of the donor and donee.

§ 1001. The fact that the gift tax obligation was discharged by way of a conditional gift rather than from funds derived from a pregift sale does not alter the underlying benefit to the donors.

C

Consistent with the economic reality, the Commissioner has treated these conditional gifts as a discharge of indebtedness through a part gift and part sale of the gift property transferred. The transfer is treated as if the donor sells the property to the donee for less than the fair market value. The "sale" price is the amount necessary to discharge the gift tax indebtedness; the balance of the value of the transferred property is treated as a gift. The gain thus derived by the donor is the amount of the gift tax liability less the donor's adjusted basis in the entire property. Accordingly, income is realized to the extent that the gift tax exceeds the donor's adjusted basis in the property. This treatment is consistent with § 1001 of the Internal Revenue Code, which provides that the gain from the disposition of property is the excess of the amount realized over the transferor's adjusted basis in the property.

III

We recognize that Congress has structured gift transactions to encourage transfer of property by limiting the tax consequences of a transfer. See, e.g., § 102 (gifts excluded from donee's gross income). Congress may obviously provide a similar exclusion for the conditional gift. Should Congress wish to encourage "net gifts," changes in the income tax consequences of such gifts lie within the legislative responsibility. Until such time, we are bound by Congress' mandate that gross income includes income "from whatever source derived." We therefore hold that a donor who makes a gift of property on condition that the donee pay the resulting gift taxes realizes taxable income to the extent that the gift taxes paid by the donee exceed the donor's adjusted basis in the property.

The judgment of the United States Court of Appeals for the Eighth Circuit is

Affirmed.

JUSTICE REHNQUIST, dissenting.

It is a well-settled principle today that a taxpayer realizes income when another person relieves the taxpayer of a legal obligation in connection with an otherwise taxable transaction. See Crane v. Commissioner, 331 U.S. 1 (1947) (sale of real property); Old Colony Tr. Co. v. Commissioner, 279 U.S. 716 (1929) (employment compensation). In neither *Old Colony* nor *Crane* was there any question as to the existence of a taxable transaction; the only question concerned the amount of income realized by the taxpayer as a result of the taxable transaction. The Court in this case, however, begs the question of whether a taxable transaction has taken place at all when it concludes that "[t]he principles of *Old Colony* and *Crane* control" this case. * * *

In *Old Colony,* the employer agreed to pay the employee's federal tax liability as part of his compensation. The employee provided his services to the employer in exchange for compensation. The exchange of compensation for services was undeniably a taxable transaction. The only question was whether the employee's taxable income included the employer's assumption of the employee's income tax liability.

In *Crane,* the taxpayer sold real property for cash plus the buyer's assumption of a mortgage. Clearly a sale had occurred, and the only question was whether the amount of the mortgage assumed by the buyer should be included in the amount realized by the taxpayer. The Court rejected the taxpayer's contention that what she sold was not the property itself, but her equity in that property.

Unlike *Old Colony* or *Crane,* the question in this case is not the amount of income the taxpayer has realized as a result of a concededly taxable transaction, but whether a taxable transaction has taken place at all. Only *after* one concludes that a partial sale occurs when the donee agrees to pay the gift tax do *Old Colony* and *Crane* become relevant in ascertaining the amount of income realized by the donor as a result of the transaction. Nowhere does the Court explain why a gift becomes a partial sale merely because the donor and donee structure the gift so that the gift tax imposed by Congress on the transaction is paid by the donee rather than the donor.

In my view, the resolution of this case turns upon congressional intent: whether Congress intended to characterize a gift as a partial sale whenever the donee agrees to pay the gift tax. Congress has determined that a gift should not be considered income to the donee. § 102. Instead, gift transactions are to be subject to a tax system wholly separate and distinct from the income tax. See id. § 2501 et seq. Both the donor and the donee may be held liable for the gift tax. Id. §§ 2502([c]), 6324(b). Although the primary liability for the gift tax is on the donor, the donee is liable to the extent of the value of the gift should the donor fail to pay the tax. I see no evidence in the tax statutes that Congress forbade the parties to agree among themselves as to who would pay the gift tax upon pain of such an agreement being considered a taxable event for the purposes of the income tax. Although Congress could certainly determine that the payment of the gift tax by the donee constitutes income to the donor, the relevant statutes do not affirmatively indicate that Congress has made such a determination.

I dissent.

Problems

Problem (1). A owned stock with a basis of $40,000 and a value of $100,000. Intending to make a partial gift, A transferred the stock to her niece, N, for $50,000.

(a) What is the amount of A's recognized gain or loss? Treas. Reg. § 1.1001–1(e).

(b) What result if three months later *N* sells the stock for $110,000? Treas.Reg. § 1.1015–4.

(c) What result in (a) if *N* was a charitable organization? § 1011(b).

(d) What result in (a) and (b) if *A*'s basis for the stock was $60,000?

(e) What result in (a) and (b) if *A*'s basis for the stock was $120,000?

Problem (2). P owns property with an adjusted basis of $40,000 and a value of $100,000. The property is subject to a non-recourse mortgage of $50,000. *P* gives the property, subject to the mortgage, to his child, *C*. What result to *P?*

References. Freeland, Maxfield & Sawyer, Part Gift–Part Sale: An Income Tax Analysis with Policy Considerations, 47 Tax L. Rev. 407 (1992); Ward, Taxation of Gratuitous Transfers of Encumbered Property: Partial Sales and Section 677(a), 63 Iowa L.Rev. 823 (1978); Note, 63 Cornell L.Rev. 1074 (1978).

E. THE BASIS OF PROPERTY ACQUIRED BY BEQUEST OR INHERITANCE

1. IN GENERAL

(a) Present Law: Section 1014

Under present law, and continuing through 2009, the basis of inherited property (or property acquired by way of several substitutes for testamentary transfers) is usually the value of the property at the date of the decedent's death (or at the alternate valuation date of § 2032);[w] § 1014(a). Since the decedent is not required to recognize gain on the transfer of property at death (Rev. Rul. 73–183, 1973–1 C.B. 364), any appreciation that occurred during the decedent's life is exempted from tax. This tax-free "step-up"[x] in basis costs the Treasury more than $27 billion a year. It also distorts the investment decisions of older taxpayers, who may be "locked-in" to their investments by the prospect of a tax-free basis increase. Tax reformers have objected to § 1014 for many years, proposing instead either that appreciation on property transferred

---

w. Although the holding period for property acquired from a decedent begins at the decedent's death (Treas.Reg. § 1.1014–4(a)(2)), § 1223(11) provides an "automatic" long-term (i.e., more than one-year) holding period for property with a § 1014 basis. Section 1223(11) was enacted when Congress shortened the time for paying the Federal estate tax from fifteen to nine months after the decedent's death. Congress was concerned that the earlier pay-ment of the estate tax might force some estates to sell appreciated assets before establishing a long-term holding period, thus costing the estate the benefit of having the gain treated as *long-term* capital gain, which was taxed at a substantially lower rate than short-term capital gain.

x. This alchemy also works in reverse. The basis is "stepped-down" whenever the date-of-death value of the property is less than the decedent's basis.

at death be taxed or that the survivors take the property with a carryover basis as under § 1015.[y]

You can better understand the operation of § 1014 if you have at least a rudimentary grasp of the Federal estate tax. The Federal estate tax is an excise tax imposed upon the value of property transferred at death. Its purpose is to arrest the passing of large aggregations of wealth from one generation to the next. The Federal estate-tax base is the "taxable estate." To compute the taxable estate, you first determine the value of all items of property includable in the decedent's "gross estate," which is defined in § 2031. The gross estate includes not only property actually owned by the decedent at death (see § 2033), but other property passing by means of various testamentary substitutes that Congress has determined to be appropriate targets of estate taxation (for example, joint-tenancy property, discussed in notes 1 and 2 below); see §§ 2035–42. After determining the gross estate, you subtract various deductions to arrive at the taxable estate. Allowable deductions include funeral and administration expenses and estate obligations, and the value of property passing to charity or to a surviving spouse (the "marital deduction"). See § 2051.

The basis rules of § 1014 apply to "property acquired from a decedent"—a phrase that comprises all property includable in the decedent's gross estate for Federal estate-tax purposes. Any property passing from the decedent by means of a testamentary substitute (for example, joint-tenancy property) thus acquires a § 1014 basis in the hands of the recipient if the property was includable in the decedent's gross estate. Since such property is treated under the estate tax as if the decedent had owned the property at death, Congress thought the income-tax basis for the property should be determined under § 1014 as if the decedent had actually owned the property.

Today the estate tax usually applies only to decedents who have taxable estates in excess of an "exclusion amount" ($1,000,000 for 2002–2003 and gradually increasing until it reaches $3,500,000 in 2009); see § 2010. Yet, property transferred by bequest or inheritance or by means of one of the testamentary substitutes specified in §§ 2035–42 obtains a § 1014 basis even though the estate does not exceed the exclusion amount and hence owes no Federal estate tax.

Suppose that *D*'s executor files an estate-tax return reporting $500,000 as the value of Blackacre, a tract of real property left by *D*'s will to *H*. Five years later, *H* sells Blackacre for $900,000. In calculating gain on the sale, must *H* treat her § 1014(a) basis as being the $500,000 value reported on the estate-tax return, or is she free (if the facts support the contention) to argue that the real value of Blackacre at *D*'s

---

y. In 1976, Congress enacted § 1023, which prescribed a carryover basis for property acquired from a decedent. In response to complaints about § 1023's complexities and about the hardship to executors and heirs of establishing the decedent's basis for property acquired in the distant past, Congress postponed the effective date of § 1023 to January 1, 1980. The Crude Oil Windfall Profit Tax Act of 1980 then repealed § 1023 retroactively.

death was $750,000? In general, the answer seems to depend upon the degree to which *H* was involved in settling the estate. Where the taxpayer or the taxpayer's spouse has served as executor of the estate, the courts have generally held the taxpayer to be estopped from taking a position inconsistent with the estate-tax return; e.g., LeFever v. Commissioner, 100 F.3d 778 (10th Cir.1996); Cluck v. Commissioner, 105 T.C. 324 (1995); Hess v. United States, 537 F.2d 457 (Ct.Cl.1976). But where the selling taxpayer (or spouse) was not involved in preparing the estate-tax return and played no significant role in administering the estate, the taxpayer is not estopped from later challenging the valuation of the property on the estate-tax return. For example, Ford v. United States, 276 F.2d 17 (Ct.Cl.1960), held that the placing of a low value on stock for estate-tax purposes did not estop the heirs from claiming a higher value (and therefore a higher basis) in computing their gain on the sale of the stock. The heirs were the decedent's minor children who resided in Brazil and who had no knowledge of the representations made in the estate-tax return. See also Shook v. United States, 713 F.2d 662 (11th Cir.1983), refusing to estop heirs who had no role in settling an estate-tax dispute and who had made no representations upon which the United States had relied.

Problems and Notes

1. *Non-spousal joint-tenancy property.* Suppose that at the time of the decedent's death he owned property with another as joint tenants with right of survivorship. Since the decedent joint tenant's interest expires at death, § 2033 does not include the value of the joint property in the decedent's gross estate. But (where the joint tenants were not husband and wife) § 2040(a) may require inclusion under the "consideration-furnished" test. Under the consideration-furnished test, the decedent's gross estate includes that portion of the date-of-death value of the property determined by comparing the funds furnished by the decedent with the total amount paid for the property.

For example, *A* purchases securities for $10,000, taking title with *B* (who is not *A*'s spouse) as joint tenants with right of survivorship. *A* later dies, leaving *B* surviving. Even though *A*'s interest expires at death, the entire value of the securities at *A*'s death (say $15,000) is includable in *A*'s gross estate because *A* furnished the entire cost of the securities; § 2040(a). Since the value of the securities is includable in *A*'s gross estate, *B* obtains a $15,000 basis for the securities under §§ 1014(a) and (b)(9). Although *B* was the owner (in the property-law sense) of a half-interest in the securities before *A*'s death, *A* is treated as the sole owner of the securities for estate-tax purposes (that is, the full value of the securities is includable in *A*'s gross estate). At *A*'s death, when *B* becomes the fee owner of the securities, *B* gets a $15,000 basis, just as if *A* had been the fee owner of the securities and bequeathed them to *B*.

Now suppose that *A* furnished only $6000 of the $10,000 cost of the securities (and that *A* predeceased *B*). Three-fifths ($6000/$10,000) of the $15,000 date-of-death value of the jointly held securities, or $9000, is included in A's gross estate. After A's death, B's basis for the securities is $13,000. Since A is treated for estate-tax purposes as the owner of an undivided ⅗ interest, B gets a basis equal to the $9000 date-of-death value for that interest. B's basis for the undivided ⅖ interest of which she was regarded as the estate-tax owner is $4000 (her cost). So B's total basis for the securities is $13,000 ($9000 under § 1014 plus $4000 under § 1012).

2. *Spousal joint tenancies.* The consideration-furnished test does not apply to joint-tenancy property held by a married couple. Instead, § 2040(b) includes in the decedent spouse's gross estate only half of the value of the property regardless of which spouse furnished the funds for the purchase of the property.

For example, A purchases securities for $10,000, taking title with his wife, B, as joint tenants with right of survivorship, and A predeceases B. Only half the $15,000 date-of-death value of the securities is included in A's gross estate. B obtains a § 1014 basis for only an undivided half-interest in the securities. B's basis for the other undivided half-interest is the basis B got under § 1041(b) at the time the property was purchased. (It is as if A had purchased the securities for $10,000 and, immediately after the purchase, transferred a half-interest to B. B would assume A's $5000 basis for the half-interest acquired by her during A's life.) After A's death, B's total basis is therefore $12,500 ($7500 under § 1014, plus $5000 under § 1041).

Suppose that A furnished $6000 and B $4000 of the $10,000 cost of the securities. Still, only half of the $15,000 date-of-death value of the securities is includable in A's gross estate. B's basis for the securities is again $12,500. Now, B's fee ownership of the securities represents the accumulation of three separate interests:

(1) The one-half interest acquired at A's death, in which B obtains a basis of $7500 under § 1014.

(2) The ⁴⁄₁₀ interest acquired by B's contribution toward the purchase of the securities. Under § 1012, B has a $4000 basis in this interest.

(3) A ¹⁄₁₀ interest acquired by gift from A when the securities were purchased (recall that B paid for only a ⁴⁄₁₀ interest but acquired a ⁵⁄₁₀ interest at the time of purchase). Under § 1041(b), B assumes A's $1000 cost basis in this interest.

B's total basis is therefore $12,500 ($7500 under § 1014, plus $4000 under § 1012, plus $1000 under § 1041(b)).

3. *Property passing to a surviving spouse.* The primary target of the Federal estate tax is the *intergenerational* transmission of wealth. Accordingly, the transfer of property between spouses is usually tax free. This exemption for interspousal transfers is accomplished by § 2056, which allows a "marital deduction" for the value of property passing to a surviving spouse. For example, A, who resided with her husband B in a

separate-property state, owned Blackacre. *A* bequeathed Blackacre (which had an adjusted basis in *A*'s hands of $200,000 and a value at *A*'s death of $800,000) to *B*. Although the $800,000 value of Blackacre must be included in *A*'s gross estate for Federal estate-tax purposes, *A*'s estate gets an offsetting $800,000 marital deduction for the property passing to *B*. Thus, the value of Blackacre is not included in *A*'s *taxable* estate. But since the interest in Blackacre is includable in *A*'s *gross* estate, *B* obtains an $800,000 basis for the interest under § 1014.

Now suppose instead that Blackacre was held by *C* and *D* as community property. At *C*'s death, she owned only an undivided half-interest in Blackacre, the other half-interest having passed to *D* when the community property was acquired, and only *C*'s half-interest (valued at $400,000) is includable in her gross estate. If *C* bequeaths her half-interest to *D*, thus making *D* the sole owner of Blackacre, *D*'s situation closely resembles that of *B* in the preceding example. Yet, in the absence of a special rule, *D* would obtain a stepped-up basis for only the undivided half-interest included in *C*'s gross estate. Section 1014(b)(6) provides relief in this situation by treating the surviving spouse's interest in community property as property acquired from the decedent whenever at least one-half of the community interest in the property is includable in the decedent spouse's gross estate. All of Blackacre therefore qualifies as property acquired from a decedent (a half-interest under § 1014(b)(1) and a half-interest under § 1014(b)(6)), and *D* obtains an $800,000 basis for the property.

4. *The alternate valuation date.* Under the Federal estate tax, property includable in the gross estate is ordinarily valued at the date of death; § 2031(a). But if the aggregate value of the assets included in the gross estate is less on the "alternate valuation date" ("AVD") than on the date of death, the executor can elect to value the assets included in the gross estate on the AVD; § 2032(a). In that case, the property's basis is the value on the AVD;[z] § 1014(a)(2). In considering whether to make an AVD election, the executor must therefore weigh the potential estate-tax savings against the eventual income-tax cost of a lower basis. Because the lowest estate-tax bracket in which estate tax is actually paid (41 percent in 2002 and increasing to 45 percent in 2009) usually exceeds the maximum capital-gains tax rate, the executor of an estate subject to substantial estate tax should usually make an AVD election whenever the aggregate value of the assets has declined since the date of death.[a]

Although the AVD is usually the sixth-month anniversary of the decedent's death,[b] the AVD for an asset that is disposed of within six

z. Even if an AVD election is made, the holding period dates from the decedent's death rather than from the AVD; Treas.Reg. § 1.1014–4(a)(2). Nevertheless, § 1223(11) provides an automatic long-term (i.e., more than one-year) holding period.

a. In addition, the estate-tax savings will usually be realized before the income-tax detriment, which will be incurred only as the property is sold, depreciated, etc.

b. If there is no day in the sixth month following the decedent's death that corresponds numerically to the date of death, the

months after death is the date of disposition; §§ 2032(a)(1) & (2). Different assets may therefore have different AVDs. If an AVD election is made, all assets must be valued on the AVD; the executor cannot value some assets on the AVD and others on the date of death; Treas.Reg. § 20.2032–1(b)(2).

Consider an estate whose assets have increased in value between the date of death and the AVD. An AVD election would increase the income-tax basis of the assets, but would not necessarily increase the estate-tax liability (if, for example, the assets passed to a surviving spouse, thus qualifying for the marital deduction). To prevent this result, § 2032(c) forbids the executor from making an AVD election unless the election decreases both the value of the gross estate and the Federal estate tax due.

Under § 2032A, the executor can elect to value certain farm (and other) real property for estate-tax purposes at a figure that is often considerably lower than its actual value. Property covered by the election takes its § 2032A value, rather than its actual value on the date of death, as its basis; § 1014(a)(3). Section 1040 limits the recognition of gain by the estate when it transfers property covered by a § 2032A election to a beneficiary in satisfaction of a pecuniary bequest.

5. *Section 1014(e).* Suppose a donor gives appreciated property to a terminally ill person, who bequeaths the property back to the donor. In the absence of a special rule, the donor would obtain a stepped-up basis for the property under § 1014, even though the decedent's ownership of the property did not cause any increase in estate-tax liability (because of the exclusion amount or the marital deduction). Section 1014(e) denies the donor (or the donor's spouse) a stepped-up basis for property acquired from a decedent if the donor gave the property to the decedent within the one-year period ending on the decedent's death.

6. *Problems.*

Apply present (pre–2010) law in working the following problems.

(1) In year 1, *D* purchased corporate stock for $10,000. She died on March 31, year 4, specifically bequeathing the stock to *B*. The stock was worth $15,000 at *D*'s death. On September 30, year 4, the stock was worth $18,000. The executor distributed the stock to *B* on December 31, year 4, when it was worth $20,000. *B* sold the stock on March 31, year 5, for $25,000.

(a) What result to *B* and to *D*'s estate?

(b) What result in (a) if *D*'s executor elected under § 2032 to value the estate assets on the alternate valuation date?

(c) What result in (a) if instead of bequeathing the stock to *B*, *D* had left *B* a $20,000 legacy which *D*'s executor satisfied by transferring the stock (then valued at $20,000) to *B*?

AVD is the last day of the sixth month.
Rev.Rul. 74–260, 1974–1 C.B. 275.

(2) *D*'s will directed his executor to distribute to *B* $8000 worth, but no more than all, of the *X* Corp. stock owned by *D* at his death, the valuation to be made on the date of distribution. At the time of his death, *D* owned 300 shares of *X* Corp. stock with a value of $50 each. At the time of distribution, the stock was worth $100 a share, and the executor accordingly distributed 80 shares of the stock to *B*. What result to *B* and *D*'s Estate?

(3) For several years *A* and *B* owned *X* Corp. stock as joint tenants with right of survivorship. The cost of the stock was $40,000. *A* died in the current year, leaving *B* surviving. The stock was worth $100,000 at *A*'s death. What is *B*'s basis for the stock if:

 (a) *A* and *B* were parent and child and *A* paid the $40,000 cost of the stock?

 (b) *A* and *B* were parent and child and *A* paid $30,000 and *B* $10,000 of the cost of the stock?

 (c) *A* and *B* were husband and wife and *A* paid the $40,000 cost of the stock?

 (d) *A* and *B* were husband and wife and *A* paid $30,000 and *B* $10,000 of the cost of the stock?

(4) Several years ago *A* purchased a rental building (ignore the land) for $100,000, taking title with *B* (who is not *A*'s spouse) as joint tenants with right of survivorship. *A* died in the current year, leaving *B* surviving. The property was worth $150,000 at *A*'s death. Before *A*'s death, *A* and *B* had properly deducted $60,000 of depreciation ($30,000 each) on the property.

 (a) What is *B*'s basis for the property? See § 1014(b)(9).

 (b) How would your answer in (a) differ if *A* had paid $40,000 and *B* $60,000 of the original cost of the property?

 (c) How would your answers in (a) and (b) differ if *A* and *B* were husband and wife?

(5) *A* owned stock with a basis of $5000 and a value of $10,000. *A* gave the stock to his brother *B* on January 15. *B* died on December 15 of that year, when the stock was worth $12,000. What basis does the legatee of the stock take if *B* bequeathed the stock to:

 (a) *A*?

 (b) *A*'s wife, *W*?

 (c) *A*'s daughter, *D*?

(6) At her death *D* owned real estate with an adjusted basis of $20,000 and a value of $100,000, but which was subject to an $80,000 non-recourse mortgage. Does *D* recognize gain when she dies?

(7) At the time of his death, *P* owned an apartment building with an adjusted basis of $100,000. *P* had not actively participated in the management of the property. At the time of his death, $70,000 of passive-activity loss was "suspended" under the passive-loss rules of § 469.

(Review §§ 469(a) & (b).) *P* had no passive income or loss for the year of his death.

(a) How much of the loss can be deducted on *P*'s final return if the value of the property at the time of *P*'s death is $150,000? See § 469(g)(2).

(b) Same as (a), except that the value of the property at the time of *P*'s death is $180,000.

(b) The Law After Estate–Tax Repeal: Section 1022

In 2001 Congress repealed the estate tax for decedents dying after 2009. (The measure is to expire after one year, but further legislation is, of course, likely.) Initially, consideration was given to repealing the gift tax as well, but because the gift tax plays an important role in preventing avoidance of the income tax, it was ultimately retained. The elimination of the estate tax, coupled with the § 102 exclusion for bequests and the step-up in basis at death under § 1014, would mean that vast amounts of appreciation in the value of property would totally escape tax at the federal level.

To prevent the descendants of the very wealthiest decedents from escaping tax altogether, Congress enacted § 1022, which supersedes § 1014 in determining the basis for property acquired from a decedent dying after 2009. Section 1022(a) prescribes generally that the basis of property acquired from a decedent is the lesser of the decedent's adjusted basis or the value of the property at the date of the decedent's death. Although this might at first seem similar to the lower-of-basis-or-value rule of § 1015(a), discussed at p. 538, above, notice that the § 1022(a) basis rule applies in computing both gains and losses. Every estate can increase the basis of its assets by up to $1,300,000 (and by up to an additional $3,000,000 for property passing to the decedent's surviving spouse), though the basis of an asset cannot be increased to an amount exceeding its value on the date of death; §§ 1022(b), (c) & (d)(2). So, as a practical matter, the carryover-basis rule will apply only to the wealthiest decedents, and a stepped-up basis will continue to be the norm for most.

For example, suppose that *W*, a widow, died and bequeathed her estate (consisting of a single asset) to her son *S*. The asset had an adjusted basis of $100,000 and a value of $2,000,000 at the time of *W*'s death. *S* would acquire the asset with a basis of $1,400,000 ($100,000 carryover basis, plus $1,300,000 step-up under § 1022(b)(2)(B)).

Usually, of course, the estate consists of more than one asset, in which case the basis step-up is to be allocated among the decedent's assets as specified by the executor, who is required to file a return for this purpose under § 6018. For example, suppose that in the preceding example *W*'s estate consisted of two parcels of land:

	Blackacre	Whiteacre
W's Adjusted Basis	$ 40,000	$ 60,000
Value at *W*'s Death	$500,000	$1,500,000

W's executor can allocate the $1,300,000 basis increase between the parcels in any manner it chooses, so long as it does not allocate more than $460,000 of increased basis to Blackacre (since the adjusted basis of Blackacre cannot be increased to an amount that exceeds its $500,000 value at W's death). If, for example, the executor allocates $460,000 of additional basis to Blackacre and the remaining $840,000 to Whiteacre, the bases of the parcels will be $500,000 for Blackacre and $900,000 for Whiteacre.

The recipient's basis can be further augmented by the decedent's unused net-operating-loss or capital-loss carryovers[c] and by the amount of any unrealized depreciation in the decedent's assets at the time of death. For example, suppose that W, a widow, died owning two assets:

	Greenacre	Blueacre
W's Adjusted Basis	$500,000	$ 400,000
Value at W's Death	$100,000	$3,000,000

W also had an unused loss carryover of $200,000. W leaves both assets to her child C. C obtains a basis of $100,000 for Greenacre (its value at W's death) (§ 1022(a)) and $2,300,000 for Blueacre ($400,000 carryover basis, plus $400,000 unrealized loss on Greenacre, plus $200,000 loss carryover, plus $1,300,000 basis step-up); § 1022(b).

The step-up in basis is even more generous if the beneficiary is the decedent's spouse. "Qualified spousal property" qualifies for an additional $3,000,000 aggregate basis increase. For example, W dies owning two assets:

	Redacre	Yellowacre
W's Adjusted Basis	$1,000,000	$2,000,000
Value at W's Death	$2,000,000	$6,000,000

W leaves Redacre to her daughter D and Yellowacre to her husband H. W's executor allocates $1,000,000 of the general $1,300,000 basis increase to Redacre and allocates the $3,000,000 spousal step-up and the remaining $300,000 general step-up to Yellowacre. D obtains a $2,000,000 basis for Redacre ($1,000,000 carryover basis plus $1,000,000 increase), and H gets a basis of $5,300,000 for Yellowacre ($2,000,000 carryover basis, plus $3,000,000 spousal step-up, plus $300,000 balance of general step-up).

Qualified spousal property includes property transferred outright to the decedent's surviving spouse and also property transferred to a trust that is required to pay annually an amount equal to its income to the surviving spouse for life; §§ 1022(c)(4) & (5). Thus, if W in the preceding example had left Yellowacre in trust to pay the income to H annually for his life with remainder to D (and if the trustee allocated the basis increase as above), the trust's basis for Yellowacre would be $5,300,000.

c. The net-operating-loss carryover is discussed at p. 706, below, and the capital-loss carryover is discussed at p. 609, below.

The basis increases described above apply only for property "owned" by the decedent at the time of death; § 1022(d)(1). For the purpose of § 1022, special rules apply to determine the extent of the decedent's ownership of property held with another person as joint tenants with right of survivorship. If the decedent and the decedent's spouse owned the property as joint tenants, the decedent is deemed to own half the property, which, since it passes to the decedent's surviving spouse, qualifies for the additional spousal step-up in basis under § 1022(c). If the decedent's co-tenant was not the decedent's spouse, the decedent is deemed to own that portion of the property that is proportionate to the portion of the total consideration furnished by the decedent; § 1022(d)(1)(B)(i)(II) (which seems to incorporate the consideration-furnished test described at p. 553, above). The decedent is also deemed to own (1) any property transferred to a "qualified revocable trust" (defined in § 645(b)(1)) during his lifetime and (2) the surviving spouse's one-half share of the couple's community property (compare the present basis rule for community property, described at p. 555, above).

In the absence of a special rule, taxpayers might be tempted to transfer property to a decedent-to-be, who would then bequeath the property to the transferor with a stepped-up basis. (Compare the concern of present § 1014(e), discussed p. 556, above.) To prevent such mischief, § 1022(d)(1)(C) precludes a basis step-up for property gratuitously transferred *to* the decedent (other than transfers from the decedent's spouse) within the three years preceding the decedent's death.

What if the property transferred by the decedent at death is encumbered with liability in excess of basis? Recall that gain must be recognized if, during life, the taxpayer transfers property subject to a liability exceeding its basis. In the case of property acquired from a decedent, however, § 1022(g) provides that liabilities in excess of basis are to be disregarded.

Under general tax principles, property transferred by an executor to satisfy a fixed-dollar legacy is treated as having been sold by the estate for its value on the date of transfer. Any excess of the property's value over its basis is usually treated as gain realized by the estate. Under § 1040, however, the estate does not recognize gain on the distribution of carryover-basis property, except to the extent that the distribution exceeds the value of the property on the date of death.

Problem

D, a resident of a non-community-property state, died in 2010 owning the following assets:

    (a) Orangeacre, with adjusted basis of $500,000 and a value of $1,000,000, which was left to *D*'s son *S*.

    (b) Purpleacre, a tract of unimproved land, owned by *D* and *S* as joint tenants with right of survivorship. *D* had furnished $200,000 and *S* $50,000 of the cost of the property. Purpleacre was valued at $1,000,000 at *D*'s death.

(c) Grayacre, an apartment building owned by *D* and her husband *H* as joint tenants with right of survivorship. *H* had furnished the $1,100,000 cost of the building, which had been purchased nine years before *D*'s death. *D* and *H* had properly deducted $400,000 of depreciation with respect to Grayacre, which was valued at $1,000,000 at *D*'s death. The property was encumbered with an $800,000 recourse mortgage at *D*'s death.

(d) *X* Corp. stock purchased by *D* several years ago for $1,000,000. It was worth $4,450,000 at *D*'s death. She left it in trust to pay the income annually to *H* for life, remainder to *S*.

(e) Giftacre, undeveloped land which had been given to *D* by her brother *B* in 2009. *B*'s adjusted basis at the time of the gift was $1,000,000. (*D* had made no improvements and taken no deductions with respect to the property.) Giftacre was worth $1,500,000 at the time of the gift and $2,000,000 at *D*'s death. *D* bequeathed the property to her niece *N* (*B*'s daughter).

(f) Dismalacre, the unimproved family farm, which had been inherited by *D* at the death of her mother *M* in 2002. Immediately before her death, *M*'s adjusted basis had been $1,000,000. The farm was worth $600,000 at *M*'s death, and $200,000 at *D*'s death. *D* bequeathed the farm to *H*.

H, the executor of *D*'s estate, elects in accordance with the terms of *D*'s will to allocate any available basis increase first to the property passing to *S* to the extent permissible, then to the property passing to *N*, then to the property passing to him. What is the adjusted basis for each property immediately after *D*'s death?

2. INCOME IN RESPECT OF A DECEDENT

In order to understand the role of income in respect of a decedent (IRD), you must first reflect upon the treatment of the accrued, but uncollected, income of a taxpayer at the time of the taxpayer's death. Suppose, for example, that *D*, a calendar-year taxpayer, dies on March 1. At the time of *D*'s death, *D*'s employer owes her $1000 as compensation for services performed in February, and the employer pays the salary to *D*'s estate on June 1. *D*'s final taxable year ends on March 1 (the date of her death).

If *D* was an accrual-method taxpayer, the "all-events" test requires that the $1000 be included in gross income on her final return (since the services were performed before her death and the amount of the income can be determined with reasonable accuracy). The $1000 salary claim must also be included in *D*'s gross estate for Federal estate-tax purposes (under § 2033 since it represents intangible property owned by *D* at the time of her death). *D*'s executor obtains a basis for the claim equal to its estate-tax value (assumed to be $1000) under § 1014(a). *D*'s estate recognizes no income when it collects the salary payment because the $1000 amount realized upon the surrender of the claim is exactly offset by the estate's $1000 basis. Thus, if *D* was an accrual-method taxpayer, the $1000 of accrued salary is subject to both income tax (on D's final return) and estate tax.

Now suppose that D was a cash-method taxpayer. The $1000 claim for unpaid salary is includable in D's gross estate for estate-tax purposes, just as it would have been in the case of an accrual-method taxpayer. But the $1000 of salary is not includable on D's final income-tax return because payment was not received before her death. In the absence of a special rule, D's executor would obtain a basis in the claim under § 1014(a) equal to its $1000 estate-tax value. The estate would not recognize income when it collected the claim because the $1000 collected would be offset by the estate's $1000 basis in the claim surrendered. Thus, the accrued but uncollected salary would never be taxed as *income* either to D or to her estate.

Sections 1014(c) and 691 were enacted to mitigate this disparity in treatment between cash-method and accrual-method decedents. The key provision is § 1014(c), which denies D's successor-in-interest a stepped-up basis for items of IRD.[d] Section 691(a) requires that accrued (but uncollected) income be included in the gross income of the taxpayer's successor-in-interest who receives payment of the item. D's estate would therefore be required to include the $1000 in its income when it received payment.

The term "income in respect of a decedent" refers to:

> those amounts to which a decedent was entitled as gross income but which were not properly includible in computing his taxable income for the taxable year ending with the date of his death or for a previous taxable year under the method of accounting employed by the decedent; Treas.Reg. § 1.691(a)-(1)(b).

Notice how D's salary payment (in the above example) fits this definition. The $1000 was an amount earned by D before her death, but the amount was not includable in her income for the year of her death (or for any previous year) because she used the cash method of accounting.

As a practical matter, the IRD concept would be unnecessary if a decedent's successor did not receive a stepped-up basis for property acquired from a decedent. Given the decision to give heirs a stepped-up basis, is there any good reason to deny the benefits of that decision to those who receive rights to income in respect of a decedent? There is little difference between a taxpayer who gets paid on Monday and dies on Tuesday and one who dies on Monday and gets paid on Tuesday. Section 691 prevents drawing major lines according to accidents of timing and details of accounting methods. But, of course, this reasoning logically leads to carryover basis for all property, since there is no big difference between someone who sells stock on Monday and dies on

---

d. As discussed at p. 558, above, the basis of property acquired from a decedent dying after 2009 is determined by § 1022 instead of 1014. But § 1022, like its predecessor, does not apply to items of IRD; § 1022(f).

Tuesday and someone else who dies first and whose executor or beneficiary sells the stock.

Suppose that a cash-method taxpayer incurred business expenses, which are paid by his estate after his death. The taxpayer cannot deduct the expenses on his final return because the obligations were not paid before his death. Nor could the estate deduct the expenses under the usual rules; the liabilities were not incurred in carrying on the *estate's* business. Absent a special rule, therefore, no income-tax deduction would be allowed for the expenses. Under § 691(b), the estate (or another party on whom the obligation to pay the expenses devolves) can deduct specified expenses as deductions in respect of a decedent when it pays the expenses.

Problems, Notes and Question

1. *Rights to income from sales.* On January 1, D entered into a contract to sell land to B. The closing was scheduled for March 15. D died on February 5 after "substantial fulfillment of the prerequisites to consummation of the sale." D's executor completed the sale pursuant to the contract and transferred title and possession to B on March 15. Rev.Rul. 78–32, 1978–1 C.B. 198, holds that the gain recognized on the sale is IRD.

Suppose that D sells property for $100,000, payable $10,000 down and $10,000 a year (plus interest at the market rate) for the following nine years. D reports the gain on the sale under the installment method of § 453 (which is discussed in Chapter 11), but dies before receiving all of the payments. Under § 691(a), the post-death payments are IRD to the extent that D would have recognized gain had he lived to receive the payments.

2. *Investment income.* If the record date for a dividend precedes the date of death but payment is not received until after death, the dividend is taxable to a cash-method taxpayer's successor in interest as IRD. Interest accrued before death is IRD when received if the income was not includable on the decedent's return for a period preceding his death. Rev.Rul. 79–340, 1979–2 C.B. 320.

Suppose a decedent dies holding a "series E" bond on which no interest has been reported. Does the successor report all interest when the bond matures, or only interest accruing after the date of death? The successor must report all of the interest when the bond matures (rather than just that portion accruing after the date of death). The portion of the interest that accrued before the decedent's death is IRD; see Treas. Reg. § 1.691(a)–2(b) (Ex. 3). If the interest accruing before death were not treated as IRD, the successor would obtain a fair-market-value basis for the E bond at the time of the decedent's death, thus enabling him to avoid any income tax on the pre-death interest when the bond is redeemed. But since the accrued interest is characterized as IRD, the successor must assume the decedent's basis for the bond (1014(c)) and must include the pre-death interest in income when the bond is redeemed.

3. *The § 691(c) deduction.* We have seen that the major purpose of § 691 is to provide roughly equal treatment of cash-method and accrual-method decedents by making sure that income accrued at the decedent's death is taxed at some time regardless of the decedent's accounting method.

If the statute stopped there, a decedent who had used the accrual method might be treated more favorably than a cash-method decedent. Under the Federal estate tax, the accrual-method taxpayer's estate is reduced by the income tax attributable to the accrued income. Although the cash-method taxpayer's accrued income will eventually also be subject to income tax (as IRD), the income tax on that income is not imposed until after death; hence it is not deductible under the Federal estate tax. Congress might have eliminated this disparity by allowing the estate of a cash-method decedent an *estate-tax* deduction for the *income tax* payable on items of IRD when the income tax on the IRD is determined after death. This approach, however, was apparently thought to be unfeasible because of the possible delays in collecting the IRD and the difficulty of ascertaining the applicable income-tax rate when the IRD was collected by someone other than the estate. Section 691(c) instead allows the recipient of IRD an *income-tax* deduction for the *estate tax* attributable to the inclusion of the item of IRD in the gross estate. Under § 691(c), an item of IRD is subject to the same total tax burden as it would have borne if the income tax attributable to the IRD were deductible under the estate tax. But where the income and estate taxes are borne by different persons, § 691(c) may produce a different result than would an estate-tax deduction.

4. *Problems.* D, a cash-method taxpayer, died on June 30, year 1. Explain the tax treatment of the following items.

(1) *D*'s salary ($5000) for the month of June. The salary was collected by *D*'s executor in August, year 1.

(2) A bonus of $10,000 declared and paid by *D*'s employer (to *D*'s estate) in January, year 2. The employer had never before paid a bonus.

(3) A $1000 dividend from *X* Corp. on stock held by *D* and her child, *C*, as joint tenants with right of survivorship. *D* had paid for the stock from her funds. The dividend, declared on June 1, year 1, was payable on July 15 to shareholders of record on June 25. Payment was received by *C*.

(4) The $25,000 balance (representing $10,000 of original contributions and $15,000 of accumulated income) of *D*'s individual retirement account, which was distributed to *C*, the designated beneficiary, in August, year 1. *D* had deducted all contributions to the account when made.

(5) A $2500 state income-tax refund (for year 0) received by *D*'s executor on September 30, year 1. *D* had itemized deductions of $25,000 in year 0.

(6) $4000 of interest received by *D*'s executor on a six-month certificate of deposit that matured on September 30, year 1. (A substantial penalty would have been imposed for withdrawal before *D*'s death.)

(7) $40,000 of proceeds from the sale of investment real estate, received by the executor on July 10, year 1. On May 1, year 1, *D* had entered into a contract to sell the property, in which she had a basis of $100,000. Before her death, *D* had substantially fulfilled all conditions precedent to the closing. The transaction was closed by her executor.

(8) $5000 of interest, which had accrued before *D*'s death, on a mortgage covering *D*'s principal residence. The mortgage, in the amount of $125,000, had been taken out by *D* in year 1 to finance the purchase of a boat, which was used for recreation. (The residence was worth $250,000 at that time.) The interest was paid by the executor on July 15, year 1.

5. *References*. Brown, Income in Respect of a Decedent, 55 Cornell L.Rev. 211 (1970); Ferguson, Income and Deductions in Respect of Decedents and Related Problems, 25 Tax L.Rev. 5 (1969).

*

Chapter Nine

NON–RECOGNITION TRANSAC-
TIONS AND (DIS)ALLOW-
ANCE OF LOSSES

A realized gain is includable in gross income only to the extent that it is *recognized*. Similarly, a realized loss cannot be deducted unless it is recognized. (Even a recognized loss is deductible only to the extent that it is *allowable*. See pp. 584–601.) As a general rule, realized gain or loss must be recognized in the year in which realized; § 1001(c). As to some types of transactions, however, Congress has decided for policy reasons that immediate recognition of the realized gain or loss is inappropriate. It has therefore enacted a number of "non-recognition rules," which postpone the tax reckoning for certain types of transactions.

Suppose, for example, that the taxpayer exchanges one business building for another. The taxpayer realizes gain on the exchange to the extent that the value of the building acquired exceeds the adjusted basis of the building given up. Yet the general nature of the taxpayer's investment (a building) remains the same as before the exchange, the taxpayer receives no cash with which to pay tax, and the valuation of the property received in the exchange may pose administrative difficulties. In short, the taxpayer's position after the exchange is similar to what it would have been if no realization event had occurred. For these reasons Congress has provided that gain or loss should not be recognized in such an exchange; § 1031.

Because the notion underlying non-recognition is that the taxpayer generally should be treated as if no realization event had occurred, the taxpayer is not entitled to a cost basis for the property received. Instead, the taxpayer typically must transfer the basis of the property disposed of to the property acquired in the non-recognition transaction; e.g., § 1031(d). The gain or loss potential of the old property is thereby preserved for recognition when the new property is disposed of in a taxable transaction. Non-recognition thus usually results in *deferral* of the gain or loss rather than permanent exclusion of the gain or loss from the tax base.[a]

The Code contains a variety of non-recognition rules, many of which are covered in advanced courses in corporate and partnership taxation. In this chapter we examine two of the principal types of non-recognition rules: (1) tax-free exchanges, in which one item of property is *exchanged* for qualifying non-recognition property; and (2) tax-free rollovers, in which property is *sold* and qualifying replacement property is purchased by the taxpayer within some prescribed period of time.

A. TAX–FREE EXCHANGES

In a tax-free exchange, no gain or loss is recognized if property is *exchanged* for qualifying property. The basis of the property given up is usually transferred to the property acquired.[b] If the taxpayer receives cash or non-qualifying property ("boot") in the exchange, any realized gain usually must be recognized to the extent of the boot received. Even though boot is received, however, the taxpayer generally is not permitted to recognize loss. If the rule were otherwise, the taxpayer could recognize loss on an otherwise non-taxable exchange by having the transferee pay a small amount of boot.

1. LIKE–KIND EXCHANGES UNDER SECTION 1031

The operation of the exchange-type non-recognition provisions is typified by § 1031, which is the prototype for several of the Code's non-recognition rules. Section 1031 generally provides for non-recognition of gain or loss if business or investment property is exchanged solely for property of "like kind."

(a) Computations under Section 1031

Problems and Note

1. *Problems.*

(1) In each of these problems, assume that A qualifies for non-recognition of gain or loss on the exchange of buildings under § 1031(a) or § 1031(b). Compute A's: (1) realized gain or loss; (2) recognized gain or loss; and (3) basis for each item of property received in the exchange.

   (a) A exchanges a building with an adjusted basis of $40,000 and a value of $200,000 for a building with a value of $200,000.

   (b) A exchanges a building with an adjusted basis of $40,000 and a value of $200,000 for a building with a value of $170,000, plus $30,000 in cash.

---

a. Of course, the significance of deferral should not be underestimated. Recall that the appreciation on property held by the taxpayer until death generally escapes tax altogether.

b. In calculating the holding period of the new property, the taxpayer can usually include ("tack on") the holding period of the old property whenever the basis of the old property is transferred to the new; § 1223(1).

(c) Same as (b), except that the adjusted basis of *A*'s building is $210,000.

(d) Same as (b), except that *A*'s building is subject to a non-recourse mortgage in the amount of $30,000. The transferee takes subject to the mortgage and pays *A* no cash.

(e) *A* exchanges a building with an adjusted basis of $50,000 and a value of $140,000 for a building with a value of $200,000. The building acquired by *A* is encumbered by a $40,000 mortgage, to which *A* takes subject. *A* also pays $20,000 cash.

(f) *A* exchanges a building (adjusted basis $50,000, value $100,000) and a yacht (adjusted basis $10,000, value $40,000) for a building worth $140,000.

(2) How would your answer in problem (1)(a), above, differ if:

(a) *A*'s building was held for sale in the course of *A*'s business as a dealer in real estate?

(b) Instead of exchanging buildings, *A* exchanged *X* Corp. stock for *Y* Corp. stock?

(c) Instead of exchanging buildings, *A* exchanged a general partnership interest in the *XYZ* Partnership for an interest in the *ABC* Partnership? Each partnership held a business building as its only asset.

2. *Depreciation of property received in like-kind exchange.* In Notice 2000–4, 2000–3 I.R.B. 313, the Service provided guidance (pending the issuance of regulations under § 168) as to the depreciation of property acquired in a like-kind exchange. The property received is to be depreciated over the remaining recovery period of the property exchanged using the same convention and depreciation method as was used for the property exchanged. This rule applies only to the extent that the basis of the new property does not exceed the adjusted basis of the old. Any increase of the new property's basis over the adjusted basis of the old is treated as newly purchased property.

For example, suppose that in a qualifying § 1031 exchange the taxpayer exchanged a truck (adjusted basis $20,000) and $15,000 cash for a new truck. The basis of the new truck would be $35,000 ($20,000 adjusted basis of old truck, plus $15,000 additional cash invested). As to $20,000 of this basis, the taxpayer would compute depreciation using the method, convention and remaining recovery period of the old truck. The remaining $15,000 of basis would be depreciated as if a new truck had been purchased for that amount.

(b) The Requirement of an "Exchange"

REVENUE RULING 77–297

1977–2 C.B. 304.

Advice is requested whether the transaction described below is an exchange of property in which no gain or loss is recognized pursuant to section 1031(a).

A entered into a written agreement with *B* to sell *B* for 1,000*x* dollars a ranch (the "first ranch") consisting of land and certain buildings used by *A* in the business of raising livestock. Pursuant to the agreement, *B* placed 100*x* dollars into escrow and agreed to pay at closing an additional 200*x* dollars in cash, to assume a 160*x* dollar liability of *A,* and to execute a note for 540*x* dollars. The agreement also provided that *B* would cooperate with *A* to effectuate an exchange of properties should *A* locate suitable property. No personal property was involved in the transaction. *A* and *B* are not dealers in real estate.

A located another ranch (the "second ranch") consisting of land and certain buildings suitable for raising livestock. The second ranch was owned by *C. B* entered into an agreement with *C* to purchase the second ranch for 2,000*x* dollars. Pursuant to this agreement, *B* placed 40*x* dollars into escrow, agreed to pay at closing an additional 800*x* dollars, assume 400*x* dollars liability of *C,* and execute a note for 760*x* dollars. No personal property was involved in the transaction. *C* could not look to *A* for specific performance on the contract, thus, *B* was not acting as *A*'s agent in the purchase of the second parcel of property.

At closing, *B* purchased the second ranch as agreed. After the purchase, *B* exchanged the second ranch with *A* for the first ranch and assumed *A*'s liability of 160*x* dollars. With *C*'s concurrence, *A* assumed *C*'s 400*x* dollar liability and *B*'s note for 760*x* dollars. *C* released *B* from liability on the note. The escrow agent returned the 100*x* dollars to *B* that *B* had initially placed in escrow. This sum had never been available to *A,* since the conditions of the escrow were never satisfied.

Section 1031(a) provides that no gain or loss shall be recognized if property held for productive use in trade or business or for investment (not including stock in trade or other property held primarily for sale, nor stocks, bonds, notes, choses in action, certificates of trust or beneficial interest, or other securities or evidence of indebtedness or interest) is exchanged solely for property of a like kind to be held either for productive use in trade or business or for investment.

Section 1031(b) states that if an exchange would be within the provisions of subsection (a) if it were not for the fact that the property received in exchange consists not only of property permitted by such provisions to be received without the recognition of gain, but also of other property or money, then the gain, if any, to the recipient shall be recognized, but in an amount not in excess of the sum of such money and the fair market value of such other property.

[Treas.Reg. §] 1.1031(b)–1(c) states that consideration received in the form of an assumption of liabilities is to be treated as "other property or money" for the purpose of section 1031(b). However, if, on an exchange described in section 1031(b), each party to the exchange assumes a liability of the other party, then, in determining the amount of "other property or money" for purposes of section 1031(b), consideration given in the form of an assumption of liabilities shall be offset against consideration received in the form of an assumption of liabilities.

Ordinarily, to constitute an exchange, the transaction must be a reciprocal transfer of property, as distinguished from a transfer of property for a money consideration only.

In the instant case A and B entered into a sales agreement with an exchange option if suitable property were found. Before the sale was consummated, the parties effectuated an exchange. Thus, for purposes of section 1031, the parties entered into an exchange of property. See Alderson v. Commissioner, 317 F.2d 790 (9th Cir.1963), in which a similar transaction was treated as a like-kind exchange of property even though the original agreement called for a sale of the property. In addition, A's $160x$ dollar liability assumed by B was offset by B's liabilities assumed by A, pursuant to [Treas.Reg. §] 1.1031(b)–1(c).

Accordingly, as to A, the exchange of ranches qualifies for nonrecognition of gain or loss under section 1031. As to B, the exchange of ranches does not qualify for nonrecognition of gain or loss under section 1031 because B did not hold the second ranch for productive use in a trade or business or for investment. See Rev.Rul. 75–291, 1975–2 C.B. 332, in which it is held that the nonrecognition provisions of section 1031 do not apply to a taxpayer who acquired property solely for the purpose of exchanging it for like-kind property.

However, in the instant case, B did not realize gain or loss as a result of the exchange since the total consideration received by B of $2,160x$ dollars (fair market value of first ranch of $1,000x$ dollars plus B's liabilities assumed by A of $1,160x$ dollars) is equal to B's basis in the property given up of $2,000x$ dollars plus A's liability assumed by B of $160x$ dollars. See section 1001 and the applicable regulations thereunder.

Notes and Questions

1. *"Three-cornered" like-kind exchanges.* If the parties are careful about the formalities, and if the last step in the formalities consists of an exchange of properties, the Service is willing to accept the transaction as an "exchange." Shortcuts may lead to litigation. In Biggs v. Commissioner, 69 T.C. 905 (1978), the person who acquired the taxpayer's property never had title to the replacement property. Instead, he contracted to acquire that property, then assigned his contract right to the taxpayer. The court held that because the taxpayer's disposition of the old property and his acquisition of the new one were "part of an integrated plan," the transaction qualified as an "exchange" on "substance over form"

grounds. See also Redwing Carriers, Inc. v. Tomlinson, 399 F.2d 652 (5th Cir.1968), in which a trucking company tried unsuccessfully to avoid non-recognition of gain[c] when trading in old trucks for new ones by selling the old trucks to the dealer for cash and buying new trucks (from the same dealer). It is quite clear that a sale for cash followed by use of the sale proceeds to purchase new property from someone other than the buyer of the old property is not an "exchange" under § 1031. Taxpayers can, therefore, elect in fact to make taxable "sales" out of transactions that are "in substance" exchanges. In view of this fact, should the courts apply "substance over form" arguments to force non-recognition upon taxpayers who do not want that result and who have arranged transactions so as to avoid a formal exchange?

2. *Non-simultaneous exchanges.* Suppose that B in Rev.Rul. 77–297 had been unwilling to postpone the exchange until suitable property could be located for transfer to A. A might have transferred his property to B with the understanding that B would make a reciprocating transfer when suitable property was located. The Service usually argued that these non-simultaneous transfers did not qualify under § 1031 either because there was no "exchange" or because the property received in exchange was the promise of a future transfer, which was not property of like kind to that exchanged. The courts were more lenient, as illustrated by Starker v. United States, 602 F.2d 1341 (9th Cir.1979). In *Starker, S* transferred property to C under a contract requiring C to acquire suitable property of like kind and convey it to S. C had up to five years within which to find suitable property for exchange or to pay a specified amount of cash to S. The Ninth Circuit, rejecting the Commissioner's position, held that there was no requirement of simultaneity in a § 1031 exchange.

Congress responded in 1984 by amending § 1031 to limit non-simultaneous exchanges. Under the amendment, the property received by the taxpayer is treated as like-kind property only if two conditions are met: (1) The property is identified as property to be received in the exchange within forty-five days after the taxpayer's transfer; and (2) The taxpayer receives the property not more than 180 days after the taxpayer's transfer (or, if earlier, by the due date for the taxpayer's tax return for the year in which the taxpayer's transfer occurred); § 1031(a)(3). For the details, see Treas. Reg. § 1.1031(k)–1.

These regulations permit the taxpayer to hire a "qualified intermediary," who, for a fee, purchases replacement property from a third party (often using funds borrowed from the taxpayer), transfers the property to the taxpayer in exchange for the taxpayer's property, sells the taxpayer's former property for cash, and repays the loan to the taxpayer. Although the qualified intermediary is the taxpayer's agent under agency law, the regulations do not treat the intermediary as the

c. *Redwing* involved years before § 1245 took effect; the taxpayer wanted § 1231 gains followed by increased depreci- ation deductions. Sections 1245 and 1231 are discussed in Chapter 10.

taxpayer's agent for purposes of § 1031. So, even though the taxpayer's agent is selling the taxpayer's property for cash and making a cash purchase of replacement property for the taxpayer, the fiction that the taxpayer has engaged in a non-recognition exchange is preserved.

3. *Reverse-Starker transactions.* Suppose that T finds a piece of property (owned by S) that she would like to acquire, but she would like to exchange property that she owns for it. S wants to sell for cash. T hires A to acquire S's property for cash, often using funds borrowed from T (or a loan guaranteed by T). A acquires the property from S and holds it while T and A search for a party who would like to acquire T's property for cash. When a purchaser for T's property is found (U), A transfers the former S property to T in exchange for T's property, sells the former T property to U for cash, and repays the loan. Rev. Proc. 2000–37, 2000–4 I.R.B. 308, provides a method of qualifying these so-called "reverse-Starker exchanges" for § 1031 non-recognition to T, even though A is T's agent under agency principles.

4. *Policy considerations.* Compliance with these elaborate rules permits a taxpayer to preserve the fiction that property is being exchanged in transactions that essentially consist of the taxpayer's acting through an agent to sell one property and purchase another. The need for "qualified intermediaries" to hold the "parked" properties has spawned a new and lucrative industry. Rather than forcing taxpayers to incur the expense of hiring intermediaries (and tax advisors) and indulging in the elaborate fiction that property is being "exchanged," would it not be simpler and more efficient just to turn § 1031 into an elective rollover non-recognition rule? For a "yes" answer, see 2 Staff of the Joint Committee on Taxation, Study of the Overall State of the Federal Tax System and Recommendations for Simplification Pursuant to Section 8022(3)(B) of the Internal Revenue Code of 1986, 300–305 (2001).

JORDAN MARSH CO. v. COMMISSIONER

United States Court of Appeals, Second Circuit, 1959.
269 F.2d 453.

Before HINCKS, LUMBARD and MOORE, CIRCUIT JUDGES.

HINCKS, CIRCUIT JUDGE.

This is a petition to review an order of the Tax Court, which upheld the Commissioner's deficiency assessment of $2,101,823.39 in income and excess profits tax against the petitioner, Jordan Marsh Company. There is no dispute as to the facts, which were stipulated before the Tax Court and which are set forth in substance below.

The transactions giving rise to the dispute were conveyances by the petitioner in 1944 of the fee of two parcels of property in the city of Boston where the petitioner, then as now, operated a department store. In return for its conveyances the petitioner received $2,300,000 in cash which, concededly, represented the fair market value of the properties. The conveyances were unconditional, without provision of any option to repurchase. At the same time, the petitioner received back from the vendees leases of the same properties for terms of 30 years and 3 days, with options to renew for another 30 years if the petitioner-lessee should erect new buildings thereon. The vendees were in no way connected with the petitioner. The rentals to be paid under the leases concededly were full and normal rentals so that the leasehold interests which devolved upon the petitioner were of no capital value.

In its return for 1944, the petitioner, claiming the transaction was a sale under § [1001], sought to deduct from income the difference between the adjusted basis of the property and the cash received. The Commissioner disallowed the deduction, taking the position that the transaction represented an exchange of property for other property of like kind. Under § [1031] such exchanges are not occasions for the recognition of gain or loss; and even the receipt of cash or other property in the exchange of the properties of like kind is not enough to permit the taxpayer to recognize loss. Section [1031(c)]. Thus the Commissioner viewed the transaction, in substance, as an exchange of a fee interest for a long term lease, justifying his position by Treasury Regulation [§ 1.1031(a)–1(c)], which provides that a leasehold of more than 30 years is the equivalent of a fee interest. Accordingly the Commissioner made the deficiency assessment stated above. The Tax Court upheld the Commissioner's determination. Since the return was filed in New York, the case comes here for review. § 7482.

Upon this appeal, we must decide whether the transaction in question here was a sale or an exchange of property for other property of like kind within the meaning of § [1031] of the Internal Revenue Code cited above. If we should find that it is an exchange, we would then have to decide whether the Commissioner's regulation, declaring that a leasehold of property of 30 years or more is property "of like kind" to the fee in the same property, is a reasonable gloss to put upon the words of the statute. * * *

The controversy centers around the purposes of Congress in enacting § [1031], dealing with non-taxable exchanges. The section represents an exception to the general rule, stated in § [1001(c)], that upon the sale or exchange of property the entire amount of gain or loss is to be recognized by the taxpayer. The first Congressional attempt to make certain exchanges of this kind non-taxable occurred in Section 202(c), Revenue Act of 1921, c. 135, 42 Stat. 227. Under this section, no gain or loss was recognized from an exchange of property unless the property received in exchange had a "readily realizable market value." In 1924, this section was amended to the form in which it is applicable here. Discussing the old section the House Committee observed:

> "The provision is so indefinite that it cannot be applied with accuracy or with consistency. It appears best to provide generally that gain or loss is recognized from all exchanges, and then except specifically and in definite terms those cases of exchanges in which it is not desired to tax the gain or allow the loss. This results in

definiteness and accuracy and enables a taxpayer to determine prior to the consummation of a given transaction the tax liability that will result." (Committee Reports on Rev. Act of 1924, reprinted in Int.Rev.Cum.Bull. 1939–1 (Part 2), p. 250.)

Thus, the "readily realizable market value" test disappeared from the statute. A later report, reviewing the section, expressed its purpose as follows:

"The law has provided for 12 years that gain or loss is recognized on exchanges of property having a fair market value, such as stocks, bonds, and negotiable instruments; on exchanges of property held primarily for sale; or on exchanges of one kind of property for another kind of property; but not on other exchanges of property solely for property of like kind. In other words, profit or loss is recognized in the case of exchanges of notes or securities, which are essentially like money; or in the case of stock in trade; or in case the taxpayer exchanges the property comprising his original investment for a different kind of property; but *if the taxpayer's money is still tied up in the same kind of property* as that in which it was originally invested, he is not allowed to compute and deduct his theoretical loss on the exchange, nor is he charged with a tax upon his theoretical profit. The calculation of the profit or loss is deferred until it is realized in cash, marketable securities, or other property not of the same kind having a fair market value." (House Ways and Means Committee Report, reprinted in Int.Rev.Cum.Bull. 1939–1 (Part 2), p. 564.)

These passages lead us to accept as correct the petitioner's position with respect to the purposes of the section. Congress was primarily concerned with the inequity, in the case of an exchange, of forcing a taxpayer to recognize a paper gain which was still tied up in a continuing investment of the same sort. If such gains were not to be recognized, however, upon the ground that they were theoretical, neither should equally theoretical losses. And as to both gains and losses the taxpayer should not have it within his power to avoid the operation of the section by stipulating for the addition of cash, or boot, to the property received in exchange. These considerations, rather than concern for the difficulty of the administrative task of making the valuations necessary to compute gains and losses, were at the root of the Congressional purpose in enacting § [1031]. Indeed, if these sections had been intended to obviate the necessity of making difficult valuations, one would have expected them to provide for nonrecognition of gains and losses in all exchanges, whether the property received in exchanges were "of a like kind" or *not* of a like kind. And if such had been the legislative objective, § [1031(b)], providing for the recognition of gain from exchanges not wholly in kind, would never have been enacted.

* * *

In conformity with this reading of the statute, we think the petitioner here, by its unconditional conveyances to a stranger, had done more than make a change in the *form of ownership:* it was a change as to the *quantum* of ownership whereby, in the words just quoted, it had "closed out a losing venture." By the transaction its capital invested in the real estate involved had been completely liquidated for cash to an amount fully equal to the value of the fee. This, we hold, was a sale—not an exchange within the purview of § [1031].

The Tax Court apparently thought it of controlling importance that the transaction in question involved no change in the petitioner's possession of the premises: it felt that the decision in Century Electric Co. v. Commissioner of Internal Rev., [192 F.2d 155 (8th Cir.)], controlled the situation here. We think, however, that that case was distinguishable on the facts. For notwithstanding the lengthy findings made with meticulous care by the Tax Court in that case, 15 T.C. 581, there was no finding that the cash received by the taxpayer was the full equivalent of the value of the fee which the taxpayer had conveyed to the vendee-lessor, and no finding that the lease back called for a rent which was fully equal to the rental value of the premises. Indeed, in its opinion the Court of Appeals pointed to evidence that the fee which the taxpayer had "exchanged" may have had a value substantially in excess of the cash received. * * *

* * *

In ordinary usage, an "exchange" means the giving of one piece of property in return for another—not, as the Commissioner urges here, the return of a lesser interest in a property received from another. It seems unlikely that Congress intended that an "exchange" should have the strained meaning for which the Commissioner contends. For the legislative history states expressly an intent to correct the indefiniteness of prior versions of the Act by excepting from the general rule "specifically and in definite terms those cases of exchanges in which it is not desired to tax the gain or allow the loss."

But even if under certain circumstances the return of a part of the property conveyed may constitute an exchange for purposes of § [1031], we think that in this case, in which cash was received for the full value of the property conveyed, the transaction must be classified as a sale. Standard Envelope Manufacturing Co. v. C.I.R., 15 T.C. 41; May Department Stores Co. v. C.I.R., 16 T.C. 547.

Reversed.

Note

1. *Other "sale and leaseback" cases.* The Tax Court followed *Jordan Marsh* in Leslie Co. v. Commissioner, 64 T.C. 247 (1975) (Non-acq.), affirmed 539 F.2d 943 (3d Cir.1976), which involved facts very similar to those of *Jordan Marsh* except that the building was newly constructed. A taxpayer which spends $1,000,000 to construct a new building has no deductible loss simply because the building's market value is less than

$1,000,000 on completion.[d] But *Leslie Co.* enables the taxpayer to deduct immediately a cost of doing business over many years.

Judge Tannenwald's dissent in *Leslie Co.* noted that neither the Commissioner nor the taxpayer had addressed the question whether the transaction should have been characterized as a "mere financing arrangement," with the buyer-lessor being, in effect, a mortgagee. Compare Frank Lyon Co. v. United States, p. 521 above.

(c) "Like–Kind" Property

The Code does not define the expression "like kind," other than to indicate that (1) livestock of different sexes are not to be considered of like kind; § 1031(e); (2) foreign real property is not of like kind with real property located in the United States; § 1031(h); and (3) personal property used predominantly in the U.S. is not of like kind with personal property used predominantly outside the U.S.; id. Nor is the legislative history of § 1031 illuminating. Treas.Reg. § 1.1031(a)–1(b) provides some general guidance in determining whether properties are of like kind.

Treas. Reg. § 1.1031(a)–2 provides that items of personal property of "like class" are considered to be of like kind (though properties that do not satisfy the like-class test may still qualify under the more-general like-kind test). Under the regulation, items of tangible, depreciable personal property are of the same class if they are members of the same General Asset Class. (These General Asset Classes are the ones set forth in Rev. Proc. 87–56, pp. 251–253, which were our starting point in classifying assets for depreciation purposes.) If the assets are not classified within any General Asset Class, they may still be of like class if they belong to the same "Product Class" as listed in the Standard Industrial Identification Manual published by the Office of Management and Budget.

Treas. Reg. § 1.1031(j)–1 prescribes detailed rules for the exchange of multiple properties.

Problems

Consider which of the following qualify as exchanges of "like-kind" property under the regulations.

Problem (1). A fee interest in a New York City townhouse (held for rental) for a fee interest in undeveloped resort land in Colorado (to be held for investment);

Problem (2). A fee interest in a parcel of investment real estate for all of the stock of a corporation that holds as its only asset a virtually identical parcel of investment real estate;

---

d. It is fairly common for taxpayers who build buildings for their own use to spend more on construction than the building is worth upon completion. The building may include features that were custom-tailored to the needs of the taxpayer; a purchaser may not be willing to pay for such features and may even incur substantial additional costs in altering the building to fit its own needs.

Problem (3). An undivided interest as tenant in common in two parcels of land (held for investment) for sole ownership of a third parcel (to be held for use in business);

Problem (4). A used automobile for a new truck (both held for use in business);

Problem (5). All of the assets of one television station for all of the assets of another television station;

Problem (6). Numismatic gold coins issued by the United States for bullion-type South African Krugerrands.

Reference. Bogdanski, On Beyond Real Estate: The New Like–Kind Exchange Regulations, 48 Tax Notes 903 (1990).

2. OTHER EXCHANGE–TYPE NON–RECOGNITION RULES

Two important non-recognition rules patterned on § 1031 are §§ 351 and 721 (both of which are examined in detail in advanced tax courses). Consider first § 351. Suppose a sole proprietor decides to incorporate his business. In the absence of a special rule, the proprietor would recognize gain or loss upon the transfer of the proprietorship assets to the corporation in exchange for the corporation's stock. But the proprietor retains the indirect ownership of the assets after incorporation, the nature of the taxpayer's investment does not change much, and the taxpayer has not "cashed in" the investment. Imposition of a tax on the transfer may also be inconvenient: Valuation of the assets or stock of a closely held business is often difficult, and the shareholder usually receives no cash at the time of incorporation with which to pay tax. For these reasons, and because Congress wanted to lessen the influence of the tax law on the taxpayer's choice of business organization, Congress enacted § 351.

Under § 351(a), a shareholder recognizes no gain or loss upon the transfer of assets to a controlled corporation solely in exchange for the corporation's stock. Section 351(b), which is analogous to § 1031(b), requires the shareholder to recognize gain realized on the transfer to the extent of any boot received. The shareholder transfers the basis from the assets transferred to the stock received; § 358(a). The corporation recognizes no gain upon the issuance of its own stock in exchange for property (§ 1032) and generally assumes the shareholder's basis for the assets acquired; § 362(a).

Under § 721, a taxpayer recognizes no gain or loss upon the transfer of property to a partnership in exchange for an interest in the partnership; § 721. The partner obtains a basis for the partnership interest equal to the basis in the asset transferred; § 722. The partnership assumes the partner's basis for the property; § 723.

B. TAX–FREE ROLLOVERS

Under a rollover-type non-recognition rule, no gain or loss is recognized if the taxpayer disposes of property and, within prescribed time limits, purchases qualifying replacement property. As in the case of the exchange-type provisions, the new property usually takes the old property's basis. Gain must usually be recognized under a rollover-type provision to the extent that the amount realized on the disposition of the old property exceeds the cost of the replacement property.

1. INVOLUNTARY CONVERSIONS UNDER SECTION 1033

The operation of the rollover-type non-recognition rules is exemplified by § 1033(a)(2). That section provides that if (1) the taxpayer's property is involuntarily converted, and (2) within prescribed time limits the taxpayer purchases replacement property that is (generally) similar or related in service or use to the property involuntarily converted, then (at the taxpayer's election) the gain realized on the involuntary conversion is recognized only to the extent that the amount realized exceeds the cost of the replacement property; § 1033(a). The basis of the replacement property is its cost, less the amount of unrecognized gain on the involuntary conversion;[e] § 1033(b).

Problems and Notes

1. *Problems.* A owned a building (on leased land) with an adjusted basis of $40,000 and a value of $100,000. The building was completely destroyed by fire, and A received $100,000 of insurance proceeds. Assume in each of the following problems that A elected non-recognition and made a timely purchase of a qualifying replacement building under § 1033. Compute (1) A's realized gain; (2) A's recognized gain; (3) A's basis for the replacement building.

(1) A purchased the replacement building for $120,000.

(2) A purchased the new building for $90,000.

(3) The original building was subject to a non-recourse mortgage in the amount of $55,000. The insurer paid the $55,000 mortgage balance directly to the mortgagee and paid the $45,000 balance of the insurance proceeds to A. A purchased the replacement building for $45,000.

2. *"Similar or related in service or use."* In deciding whether a replacement for property owned by the taxpayer and leased to someone else satisfies the "similar or related in service or use" test of § 1033(a), the question arises whether the taxpayer's use or the lessee's use controls. The Service and some of the lower courts once took the position that the "functional use" or "end use" of the replacement property by the lessees had to be similar to the lessees' use of the converted property.

---

e. In determining the holding period for the replacement property, the taxpayer can include the period during which he held the converted property; § 1223(1).

Under this test, a replacement of an office building (leased by the taxpayer to tenants) by an apartment building would not qualify, since the "end use" of the buildings by the tenants differed. After losing several cases in the courts of appeals,[f] the Service issued Rev.Rul. 64–237, 1964–2 C.B. 319, adopting the "taxpayer-use" test (1964–2 C.B. at 320):

> In conformity with the appellate court decisions, in considering whether replacement property acquired by an investor is similar in service or use to the converted property, attention will be directed primarily to the similarity in the relationship of the services or uses which the original and replacement properties have to the taxpayer-owner. In applying this test, a determination will be made as to whether the properties are of a similar service to the taxpayer, the nature of the business risks connected with the properties, and what such properties demand of the taxpayer in the way of management, services and relations to his tenants.

> For example, where the taxpayer is a lessor, who rented out the converted property for a light manufacturing plant and then rents out the replacement property for a wholesale grocery warehouse, the nature of the taxpayer-owner's service or use of the properties may be similar although that of the end users change. The two properties will be considered as similar or related in service or use where, for example, both are rented and where there is a similarity in the extent and type of the taxpayer's management activities, the amount and kind of services rendered by him to his tenants, and the nature of his business risks connected with the properties.

> In modifying its position with respect to the involuntary conversion of property held for investment, the Service will continue to adhere to the functional test in the case of owner-users of property. Thus, if the taxpayer-owner operates a light manufacturing plant on the converted property and then operates a wholesale grocery warehouse on the replacement property, by changing his end use he has so changed the nature of his relationship to the property as to be outside the nonrecognition of gain provisions.

An example of the "taxpayer-use" test is Clifton Inv. Co. v. Commissioner, 312 F.2d 719 (6th Cir.1963), cert. denied 373 U.S. 921 (1963), holding that the replacement of an office building rented to tenants with stock of a company which operated a hotel failed to qualify under § 1033(a).

3. *Section 1033(g).* This section allows a taxpayer whose real property is condemned to qualify for non-recognition of gain by replacing the property with "like-kind" property, even if the replacement property fails the "similar or related in service or use" test. Section 1033(g) does not apply to involuntary conversions by casualty. If a replacement for condemned property satisfies the "similarity" test of § 1033(a), it is

---

f. For a list of the cases, see Davis v. United States, 589 F.2d 446, 449 n. 5 (9th Cir.1979).

immaterial whether it fails the "like-kind" test of § 1033(g); Rev.Rul. 71–41, 1971–1 C.B. 223.

2. SALE OF A PRINCIPAL RESIDENCE UNDER SECTION 121

Before its repeal by the Taxpayer Relief Act of 1997, § 1034 provided that a taxpayer who sold a principal residence and, within prescribed time limits, purchased and occupied another principal residence recognized no gain on the sale if the cost of the new residence equaled or exceeded the selling price of the old. If the selling price of the old residence exceeded the cost of the new residence, the taxpayer was required to recognize the realized gain to the extent of the excess. As usual under a non-recognition rule, the cost basis of the new residence was reduced by the amount of any unrecognized gain on the sale of the old. At least in theory, therefore, the unrecognized gain on the sale of the old residence would be recognized when the new residence was disposed of in a taxable transaction.[g]

For most taxpayers, the 1997 Act substituted exemption from tax under § 121 for the rollover non-recognition treatment of former § 1034. Section 121 excludes from gross income the first $250,000 ($500,000 on a joint return) of gain on the sale of the taxpayer's principal residence; § 121(a) & (b). The exclusion applies regardless of whether the taxpayer purchases a replacement residence and regardless of the taxpayer's age.

To qualify for the exclusion, the taxpayer must have owned the property (and used it as his principal residence) for at least two of the five years ending on the date of the sale; § 121(a). In general, the taxpayer can use the exclusion for only one sale in any two-year period; § 121(b)(3). But if the sale is occasioned by a change in place of employment or health, a proportionate part of the exemption can be used even though the taxpayer does not satisfy the two-year-ownership-and-occupancy test or the once-every-two-years requirement; § 121(c).

Realized gain in excess of the amount excluded must be recognized even if the taxpayer purchases a replacement residence.

Problems

Problem (1). A, a single person, had an adjusted basis of $60,000 for her principal residence, which she had owned and occupied for fifteen years. In the current year, she sold the property for $325,000. She paid a $10,000 brokerage commission on the sale. How much gain must A recognize?

Problem (2). Suppose instead that A had married B last year. B had sold his residence one month before marrying A and had used the § 121

---

g. In fact, however, the deferred gain often escaped recognition altogether because up to $125,000 of gain on the sale of the new residence by a taxpayer who had reached age 55 qualified for exemption from tax. Also, if the taxpayer held property acquired in a § 1034 transaction until death, the taxpayer's heirs or beneficiaries obtained a stepped-up basis for the property under § 1014. Thus, many residence sales were effectively exempt from tax under pre–1997 law.

exclusion on that sale (last year). Since the marriage, *B* has resided with *A* in her home. *A* and *B* file a joint return for the current year. How much gain must *A* recognize?

Problem (3). Five years ago *H* and *W* were divorced, and *H* moved out of the family home. Under the terms of the decree, *W* and the couple's child, *C*, continued to reside in the home, which was co-owned by *H* and *W* as tenants in common. The home was to be sold, and the sales proceeds divided equally between *H* and *W*, when *C* attained age 18. This year *C* reached 18, and the home was sold at a substantial gain. Can *H* use § 121 to exclude his share of the gain? Consider § 121(d)(3).

Problem (4). One year ago *D*, a single person, sold her home and excluded the gain from income under § 121. That same day she purchased a new home, which she has occupied since. Today she sold the new home at a gain of $20,000 and moved to another city 500 miles away, where she had been transferred by her employer. Can *D* exclude the gain from income?

Problem (5). *E*, who is single, had for many years owned and occupied as her principal residence a house in which she had a basis of $50,000 (for the house only). This year the house was completely destroyed by fire, and *E* received $400,000 of insurance proceeds. She promptly purchased a condominium for $120,000 and occupied it as her principal residence. How much gain must *E* recognize? (Consider the application of § 1033 and Prop. Treas. Reg. § 1.121–4(d).)

Problem (6). A married couple had resided for many years in a home that they owned as joint tenants with right of survivorship. The husband died earlier this year. The wife, as surviving joint tenant, sold the home for a $400,000 gain. Can the wife exclude the gain if:

> (a) The sale is made this year, and the wife and the executor of the husband's estate file a joint return for the year (note § 6013(a)(3))?

> (b) The sale is made next year?

Problem (7). Four years ago *F*, who is single, purchased a condominium and occupied it as his principal residence. After a year, he became incapable of caring for himself and moved in with his daughter in another city. (The condominium has since been unoccupied.) *F* sold the condominium today at a gain of $200,000.

> (a) Is the gain excludable under § 121?

> (b) Would your answer differ if instead of moving in with his daughter *F* had moved to a nursing home?

3. OTHER ROLLOVER NON–RECOGNITION PROVISIONS

Under § 1045, added in 1997, gain realized on the sale of "qualified small business stock" can, at the election of the taxpayer, be recognized only to the extent that the amount realized on the sale exceeds the amount reinvested in other such stock within sixty days of the sale. Any unrecognized gain is deferred for future recognition by an appropriate adjustment to the cost basis of the replacement stock. The term "qualified small business stock" is defined in § 1202, which is discussed at p. 607, below.

Under § 1044, an individual or C corporation can elect not to recognize gain on the sale of publicly traded securities if, within 60 days following the sale, the taxpayer purchases common stock of or a partnership interest in a "specialized small business investment company" (SSBIC). These are firms licensed by the Small Business Administration to invest in small businesses for the purpose of fostering ownership by persons whose participation in the free-enterprise system has been hampered by social or economic disadvantages. Gain must be recognized to the extent that the amount realized on the sale exceeds the amount invested in the SSBIC. The basis of the taxpayer's investment in the SSBIC must be reduced by the amount of gain not recognized on the sale of the publicly traded securities.

The maximum amount of gain that an individual can defer under § 1044 is $50,000 a year, with a lifetime maximum of $500,000. A C corporation can defer a maximum of $250,000 of gain a year, up to a total of $1,000,000 over the corporation's lifetime.

4. WASH SALES UNDER SECTION 1091

Section 1091 purports to "disallow" the deduction of a loss on a sale of stock or securities if, within thirty days preceding or following the sale, the taxpayer purchased stock or securities substantially identical to those sold. Section 1091(d) prescribes generally that the basis of the stock or securities purchased is the same as that of the stock or securities sold. Despite its "disallowance" language, § 1091 is a rollover non-recognition rule that postpones recognition of the loss on the sale until the new shares of stock or securities are sold.

Problems, Notes and Questions

1. *Problems.*

(1) On January 2, *T* buys a share of stock for $1000. On July 1, *T* buys an additional share of the same stock for $900. On July 10, *T* sells the share purchased on January 2 for $910. What is *T*'s basis in the stock purchased on July 1 after *T* sells the other share?

(2) Same as (1), except that *T* receives only $890 for the share sold on July 10.

2. *Gains.* Section 1091 does not apply to gains. Does this mean that a taxpayer who exchanges a share of appreciated General Motors preferred stock for another identical share of General Motors stock recognizes gain? See Treas.Reg. § 1.1001–1(a) (first sentence) and § 1036.

3. *Does § 1091 make sense?* Modern portfolio theory suggests that sophisticated investors operating in an efficient market are virtually

indifferent between one stock and another if the stocks have the same degree of risk:

> Investors don't buy a stock for its unique qualities; they buy it because it offers the prospect of a fair return for its risk. This means that stocks should be like *very* similar brands of coffee, almost perfect substitutes for each other. Therefore, the demand for one company's stock should be very elastic. If its prospective risk premium is lower relative to its risk than [that of] other stocks, *nobody* will want to hold that stock. If it is higher, *everybody* will want to hold it.

R. Brealey & S. Myers, Principles of Corporate Finance 278–79 (2d Ed. 1984).

Suppose the common shares of *X* Corp. and *Y* Corp. involve the same degree of risk and are therefore "almost perfect substitutes for each other." If the taxpayer sells *X* Corp. common at a loss and within thirty days repurchases shares of *X* Corp. common, § 1091 denies recognition of the loss. If the taxpayer instead repurchases shares of *Y* Corp., the loss on the sale of the *X* Corp. shares is recognized.

C. ALLOWANCE OF LOSSES

1. IN GENERAL

A recognized loss is deductible only if it is *allowable*. The Code uses the allowance (or disallowance) concept in two distinct senses. In the sense with which we are chiefly concerned in this chapter, a disallowed loss is permanently barred from deductibility. Examples are losses disallowed by §§ 165(c) and 267. Sometimes, however, a loss "disallowed" in one year may only be held in abeyance until a future year—usually a year in which the taxpayer has sufficient income of a specified character to match against the loss. For examples of losses that are disallowed in this sense, see §§ 1211 and 469. Disallowance in these cases may affect the timing of the deduction, but does not bar the deduction altogether. This type of disallowance is somewhat analogous to non-recognition of the loss.[h]

To determine the allowability of a recognized loss, begin with § 165. If the loss is not allowed by § 165, proceed no further; a deduction is permanently barred.[i] If the loss is allowable under § 165, then consider whether it is permanently disallowed by some other provision, such as § 267. If the loss still appears to be allowable, it must usually be characterized as ordinary or capital. Finally, if the loss is subject to some

---

h. To complicate matters further, the drafters of the code have sometimes been careless in their use of terminology. We have already seen that § 1091 purports to "disallow" losses sustained in wash sales even though the provision actually operates as a rollover non-recognition rule.

i. There is one exception: a bad-debt loss may be allowed under § 166 even though it is not described in § 165(c).

additional limit (such as the limit on the deductibility of capital losses under § 1211), apply the additional limit.

Section 165(a) generally allows as a deduction any loss sustained during the taxable year. For individual taxpayers, however, § 165(c) limits this general rule by restricting deductibility to: (1) losses incurred in a trade or business, (2) losses incurred in any transaction entered into for profit (investment losses), and (3) certain casualty losses to personal-use property. The limits of § 165(c) do not apply to corporate taxpayers.

Notes

1. *Capital losses.* Section 165(f) does *not* authorize a deduction for capital losses; it serves only as a cross reference to § 1211, which *limits* the deductibility of capital losses deductible under § 165. Therefore, an individual's loss from the sale or exchange of a capital asset not used in a trade or business or in an investment activity—a taxpayer's personal house or car, for example—cannot be deducted, even against capital gains, because the loss is not described in § 165. Put differently, the character of a loss does not matter if the loss is disallowed (in the sense of being permanently barred as a deduction). The treatment of capital losses is discussed in Chapter 10.

2. *Losses of corporations.* Nothing in § 165 expressly limits corporations' loss deductions to losses on business or investment property. International Trading Co. v. Commissioner, 484 F.2d 707 (7th Cir.1973), allowed a deduction for a corporation's loss on the sale of resort property neither used in business nor held for a profit-making purpose (the property was used for recreation by the corporation's shareholders). The Tax Court had denied a deduction, reasoning that "[i]f petitioner were now allowed a deduction for the loss accruing on the sale of the property, the effect would be to give it the benefit of a substantial portion of the depreciation which hitherto had not been deductible." The Seventh Circuit, in reversing, relied on the "plain meaning" of the words of the statute and cited, inter alia, "postage stamps commemorating the Boston Tea Party." Today, deductions for most losses like those involved in *International Trading* would be disallowed by § 274(a). See W.L. Schautz Co. v. United States, 567 F.2d 373 (Ct.Cl.1977).

2. CASUALTY LOSSES TO PERSONAL–USE PROPERTY

Section 165(c)(3) generally permits the taxpayer to deduct losses to personal-use property if the loss arises from "fire, storm, shipwreck, or other casualty, or from theft." Section 165(h)(1) imposes a $100 floor on the loss deduction for each occurrence, and § 165(h)(2) generally allows a deduction only for that portion of the net casualty loss which exceeds 10 percent of adjusted gross income. (The operation of the 10–percent floor is illustrated by the problems at p. 634.)

CHAMALES v. COMMISSIONER

United States Tax Court, 2000.
79 T.C.M. 1428.

NIMS, JUDGE.

Respondent determined a Federal income tax deficiency for petitioners' 1994 taxable year in the amount of $291,931. * * *

[The issue is whether petitioners are entitled to deduct a net casualty loss of $751,427.]

FINDINGS OF FACT

* * *

[In the spring of 1994] Gerald and Kathleen Chamales (petitioners) * * * became interested in purchasing a residence in Brentwood Park, an exclusive Los Angeles neighborhood. They were attracted to the beautiful, parklike setting and the quiet peacefulness of the area. * * * [O]n June 2, 1994, petitioners opened escrow on property located in Brentwood Park, at 359 North Bristol Avenue. * * *

At the time petitioners opened escrow, O.J. Simpson (Simpson) owned and resided at the property located directly west of and adjacent to that being purchased by petitioners. Simpson's address was 360 North Rockingham Avenue. Both parcels were corner lots, bounded on the north by Ashford Street. The rear or westerly side of petitioners' land abutted the rear or easterly side of the Simpson property.

During the escrow period, on June 12, 1994, Nicole Brown Simpson and Ronald Goldman were murdered at Ms. Brown Simpson's condominium in West Los Angeles. Simpson was arrested for these murders shortly thereafter. Following the homicides and arrest, the Brentwood Park neighborhood surrounding the Simpson property became inundated with media personnel and equipment and with individuals drawn by the area's connection to the horrific events. The media and looky-loos[1] blocked streets, trespassed on neighboring residential property, and flew overhead in helicopters in their attempts to get close to the Simpson home. Police were summoned to the area for purposes of controlling the crowds, and barricades were installed at various Brentwood Park intersections to restrict traffic. This police presence, however, had little practical effect. Significant media and public attention continued throughout 1994 and 1995. Although Simpson was acquitted on October 4, 1995, civil proceedings in 1996 reignited public interest.

Petitioners closed escrow on June 29, 1994, purchasing the residence on North Bristol Avenue for $2,849,000. Petitioners had consid-

---

1. As explained by petitioners' counsel, "looky-loo" is a term developed in Hollywood to describe individuals who gather at places and events in hopes of glimpsing celebrities. The phrase is apparently used in California to denote those who frequent a location not because of its status as a conventional tourist sight but because of its association with a famous or notorious person. * * *

ered canceling the escrow and had discussed this possibility with their attorney, but upon being advised that liability would result from a cancellation, they decided to go through with the transaction. Later that summer, as the crowds and disruption persisted, Gerald Chamales (petitioner) inquired of his broker Solton whether the value of his property had declined. Solton indicated that she estimated a decrease in value of 20 to 30 percent.

Petitioners' 1994 tax return was prepared by Ruben Kitay (Kitay), a certified public accountant. In the course of preparing this return, Kitay and petitioner discussed the possibility of claiming a deduction for casualty loss. After preliminary research in the regulations addressing casualty loss, Kitay spoke with two area real estate agents regarding the amount by which petitioners' property had decreased in value. The agents estimated the decline at 30 to 40 percent. Kitay and petitioner decided to use the more conservative 30 percent figure in calculating the deduction to be taken on petitioners' return. An expert appraisal was not obtained at this time, as Kitay felt that a typical appraisal based on values throughout the Brentwood Park area would be inconclusive as to the loss suffered by the few properties closest to the Simpson home.

Kitay and petitioner also recognized and discussed the fact that there existed a substantial likelihood of an audit focusing on petitioners' 1994 return. Hence, to clarify the position being taken and the reasons underlying petitioners' deduction, an explanatory supplemental statement labeled "Casualty Loss" was attached to the return. After indicating the location of petitioners' property in relation to that of Simpson, it stated that the casualty loss was premised on "the calamity of the murder & trial, which was sudden & unavoidable & which resulted in a permanent loss to value of property." A table enumerating instances of minor physical damage to petitioners' property, such as damage to lawn and sprinklers, was also attached to the return, but no valuation was placed upon the harm caused thereby.

At the time petitioners purchased their property, they were aware that the existing home required remodeling and repair. In the fall of 1994, petitioners demolished most of the house. Then, in March of 1995, they began a reconstruction project costing approximately $2 million. This reconstruction was completed in December of 1996, and petitioners moved into the residence. Petitioners continued to reside at 359 North Bristol Avenue up to and through the date of trial.

Other residents of Brentwood Park have undertaken similar reconstruction projects in recent years. The Nebekers, who own the property across Ashford Street from the former Simpson residence, are proceeding with a $1 million remodeling of their home. Likewise, the property owned by Simpson was sold after he moved out in 1998, the existing house was demolished, and a new residence is currently being constructed.

As of early 1999, the area surrounding the former Simpson home was no longer inundated with media personnel or equipment. The police barricades restricting traffic in the immediate vicinity of petitioners' property had been removed. Looky-loos, however, continued to frequent the neighborhood, often advised of the location of Simpson's former residence by its inclusion on "star maps" published for the Los Angeles area. Anniversaries of the murders were also typically accompanied by periods of increased media and public attention.

OPINION

We must decide whether petitioners are entitled to a casualty loss deduction based upon a postulated decline in the value of their residential property * * * .

Petitioners contend that the media and onlooker attention following the murders and focusing on Simpson's home has decreased the value of their adjacent property. They argue that because the homicides were a sudden, unexpected, and unusual event, and because aspects of the public interest precipitated thereby continued at least to the time of trial in this case, they have suffered a permanent casualty loss. Petitioners further allege that the proximity of their residence to that of Simpson has stigmatized their property and rendered it subject to permanent buyer resistance.

Conversely, respondent asserts that public attention over the course of a lengthy murder trial is not the type of sudden and unexpected event that will qualify as a casualty within the meaning of the Code. Respondent additionally contends that the Court of Appeals for the Ninth Circuit, to which appeal in this case would normally lie, has limited the amount that may be claimed as a casualty loss deduction to the loss suffered as a result of physical damage to property. According to respondent, since petitioners have failed to substantiate any such damage, they are entitled to no deduction. In respondent's view, any decline in market value represents merely a temporary fluctuation and not a permanent, cognizable loss.

We agree with respondent that petitioners have not established their entitlement to a casualty loss deduction. The difficulties suffered by petitioners as a consequence of their proximity to the Simpson residence do not constitute the type of damage contemplated by § 165(c)(3). * * *

* * *

* * * [Treas. Reg. § 1.165–1(b)] provide[s] that, to be allowable as a deduction, a loss must be both "evidenced by closed and completed transactions" and "fixed by identifiable events."

As interpreted by case law, a casualty loss within the meaning of § 165(c)(3) arises when two circumstances are present. First, the nature of the occurrence precipitating the damage to property must qualify as a casualty. * * * Second, the nature of the damage sustained must be such that it is deductible for purposes of § 165. * * * At issue here then are whether the events surrounding the alleged Simpson murders and affecting petitioners' property can properly be termed a casualty and whether the type of loss suffered by petitioners as a consequence of these events is recognized as deductible. We conclude that both inquiries must be answered in the negative.

A. Nature of Occurrence Constituting a Casualty

The word "casualty" as used in § 165(c)(3) has been defined, through application of the principle of ejusdem generis, by analyzing the shared characteristics of the specifically enumerated casualties of fire, storm, and shipwreck. * * * As explained by this Court:

> wherever unexpected, accidental force is exerted on property and the taxpayer is powerless to prevent application of the force because of the suddenness thereof or some disability, the resulting direct and proximate damage causes a loss which is like or similar to losses arising from the causes specifically enumerated in § 165(c)(3). * * *

Hence, casualty for purposes of the Code denotes " 'an undesigned, sudden and unexpected event,' " Durden v. Commissioner, [3 T.C. 1, 3 (1944)] (quoting Webster's New International Dictionary), or " 'an event due to some sudden, unexpected or unusual cause,' " (quoting Matheson v. Commissioner, 54 F.2d 537, 539 (2d Cir.1931), affg. 18 B.T.A. 674 (1930)). Conversely, the term " 'excludes the progressive deterioration of property through a steadily operating cause.' " Id. (quoting Fay v. Helvering, 120 F.2d 253, 253 (2d Cir.1941), affg. 42 B.T.A. 206 (1940)). The sudden and unexpected occurrence, however, is not limited to those events flowing from forces of nature and may be a product of human agency. See id. at 4.

Here, we cannot conclude that the asserted devaluation of petitioners' property was the direct and proximate result of the type of casualty contemplated by § 165(c)(3). While the stabbing of Nicole Brown Simpson and Ronald Goldman was a sudden and unexpected exertion of force, this force was not exerted upon and did not damage petitioners' property. Similarly, the initial influx of onlookers, although perhaps sudden, was not a force exerted on petitioners' property and was not, in and of itself, the source of the asserted decrease in the home's market value. Rather, petitioners base their claim of loss on months, or even years, of ongoing public attention. If neither media personnel nor looky-loos had chosen to frequent the Brentwood Park area after the murders, or if the period of interest and visitation had been brief, petitioners would have lacked grounds for alleging a permanent and devaluing change in the character of their neighborhood.

Hence, the source of their difficulties would appear to be more akin to a steadily operating cause than to a casualty. Press and media attention extending for months bears little similarity to a fire, storm, or shipwreck and is not properly classified therewith as an "other casualty."

B. Nature of Damage Recognized as Deductible

With respect to the requisite nature of the damage itself, this Court has traditionally held that only physical damage to or permanent abandonment of property will be recognized as deductible under § 165. * * * In contrast, the Court has refused to permit deductions based upon a temporary decline in market value.

For example, in Citizens Bank v. Commissioner, [28 T.C. 717, 720 (1957), aff'd, 407 F.2d 838 (9th Cir. 1969)], the Court stated that "physical damage or destruction of property is an inherent prerequisite in showing a casualty loss." When again faced with taxpayers seeking a deduction premised upon a decrease in market value, the Court further explained in Pulvers v. Commissioner, [48 T.C. 245, 249 (1967), aff'd, 407 F.2d 838 (9th Cir. 1969)], (quoting Citizens Bank v. Commissioner, 252 F.2d at 428): " 'The scheme of our tax laws does not, however, contemplate such a series of adjustments to reflect the vicissitudes of the market, or the wavering values occasioned by a succession of adverse or favorable developments.' " Such a decline was termed "a hypothetical loss or a mere fluctuation in value." Id. at 250.

Moreover, the Court of Appeals for the Ninth Circuit, to which appeal in the present case would normally lie, has adopted this rule requiring physical damage. See, e.g., Kamanski v. Commissioner, 477 F.2d at 452; Pulvers v. Commissioner, 407 F.2d 838, 839 (9th Cir.1969), affg. 48 T.C. 245 (1967). In Pulvers v. Commissioner, supra at 839, the Court of Appeals reviewed the specific casualties enumerated in § 165(c)(3) and concluded: "Each of those surely involves physical damage or loss of the physical property. Thus, we read 'or other casualty,' in para materia, meaning 'something like those specifically mentioned.' " Even more explicitly, the Court of Appeals based affirmance in Kamanski v. Commissioner, supra at 452, on the following grounds:

> The Tax Court ruled that the loss sustained was a nondeductible personal loss in disposition of residential property and not a casualty loss; that the drop in market value was not due to physical damage caused by the [earth]slide, but to "buyer resistance"; that casualty loss is limited to damage directly caused by the casualty. We agree.

* * *

In Caan v. United States, 99–1 USTC ¶ 50,349 (C.D.Cal.1999), the District Court dismissed for failure to state a claim the complaint of taxpayers alleging facts nearly identical to those at issue here. The Caans, residents of Brentwood Park, argued that they were entitled to a § 165(c)(3) casualty loss deduction for the decline in market value and permanent buyer resistance to which they asserted their property became subject as a result of the " 'O.J. Simpson double murders.' " Id. at ¶ 50,349, at 87,829 n.2. The court, however, reiterated that "the Ninth Circuit only recognizes casualty losses arising from physical damage caused by enumerated or other similar casualties" and held that "Because the Caans have not alleged any physical damage to their property due to the murders and subsequent media frenzy, they have not alleged a casualty loss that is a proper basis for a deduction." Id. at ¶ 50,349, at 87,829.

Given the above decisions, we conclude that petitioners here have failed to establish that their claimed casualty loss is of a type recognized as deductible for purposes of § 165(c)(3). They have not proven the extent to which their property suffered physical damage, and their attempt to base a deduction on market devaluation is contrary to existing law.

With respect to physical damage and assuming arguendo that petitioners' loss stemmed from an occurrence that could properly be deemed a casualty, they would be entitled to a deduction for physical harm to their property. Nonetheless, although petitioners attached to their return a list of minor instances of physical damage and mentioned several other items at trial, they have neither offered evidence of the monetary value of nor provided any substantiation for such losses. We therefore have no basis for determining what, if any, portion of the claimed deduction might be allowable, and we cannot sustain a $751,427 deduction on the grounds of damage to a lawn or a sprinkler system.

As regards decrease in property value, petitioners' efforts to circumvent the established precedent repeatedly rejecting deductions premised on market fluctuation, through reliance on Finkbohner v. United States, 788 F.2d 723 (11th Cir.1986), are misplaced. In Finkbohner v. United States, supra at 727, the Court of Appeals for the Eleventh Circuit permitted a deduction based on permanent buyer resistance in absence of physical damage. The Finkbohners lived on a cul-de-sac with 12 homes, and after flooding damaged several of the houses, municipal authorities ordered 7 of the residences demolished and the lots maintained as permanent open space. See id. at 724. Such irreversible changes in the character of the neighborhood were found to effect a permanent devaluation and to constitute a casualty within the meaning of § 165(c)(3). See id. at 727.

However, as explicated above, this Court has long consistently held that an essential element of a deductible casualty loss is physical damage or, in some cases, physically necessitated abandonment. Furthermore, under the rule set forth in Golsen v. Commissioner, 54 T.C. 742, 756–757 (1970), affd. 445 F.2d 985 (10th Cir.1971), we are in any event constrained to apply the law of the court in which an appeal would normally lie. Since the Court of Appeals for the Ninth Circuit has adopted and has not diverged from a requirement of physical damage for a section 165(c)(3) deduction, to hold otherwise would contravene *Golsen*.

Moreover, we further note that petitioners' circumstances do not reflect the type of permanent devaluation or buyer resistance which would be analogous to that held deductible in Finkbohner v. United States, supra. The evidence in the instant case reveals that media and onlooker attention has in fact lessened significantly over the years following the murders. Access to petitioners' property is no longer restricted by media equipment or police barricades. Residents of Brentwood Park have continued to invest substantial funds in remodeling and upgrading their homes. Hence, petitioners' difficulties are more akin to a temporary fluctuation in value, which no court has found to support a deduction under § 165(c)(3). We therefore hold that petitioners have failed to establish their entitlement to a casualty loss deduction. Respondent's determination of a deficiency is sustained.

* * *

Problem and Question

1. *Problem.* To what extent is T allowed a casualty-loss deduction as a result of each of the following calamities? (Ignore the 10–percent AGI floor.)

(1) T's personal car suffered $2000 damage (and another driver's car suffered $5000 damage) in a collision caused by T's negligent driving. T paid for the damage to both cars.

(2) Same as (1), except that T's insurance company would have paid for the damage to both cars had T filed a claim. But because T was concerned about an increase in his insurance rates, he decided not to file a claim. (See § 165(h)(4)(e).)

(3) T's personal residence, which had not been inspected for termites since he bought it ten years ago, was found to have suffered $8000 damage from termites.

(4) T's personal residence suffered $10,000 damage when the furnace exploded, knocking down a wall. (The explosion was caused by the failure of a valve, which had gradually worn out.)

(5) T's personal residence, which has a basis of $40,000 (for the house and land combined), suffered $10,000 damage from a tornado.

(6) Same as (5), except that the tornado caused a reduction in the value of the residence (basis $40,000) from $100,000 to $50,000.

(7) The tornado completely destroyed a piece of equipment used in T's business. Immediately before the casualty, the equipment had an adjusted basis of $20,000 and a value of $10,000. See Treas.Reg. § 1.165–7(b).

2. *Theft and disaster losses.* What purposes are served by §§ 165(e) and 165(i)?

3. CONVERSION OF PROPERTY FROM PERSONAL TO BUSINESS OR INVESTMENT USE

McAULEY v. COMMISSIONER

United States Tax Court, 1976.
35 T.C.M. 1236.

SCOTT, JUDGE: Respondent determined a deficiency in petitioners' Federal income tax for the calendar year 1971 in the amount of $1,598.09. The issues for decision are (1) whether petitioners are entitled to a deduction of a loss in the amount of $3,588.90 or any part thereof resulting from the sale of a house which they used as a personal residence until September 1, 1970, and (2) if petitioners are not entitled to the claimed loss deduction are they entitled to any deduction for the cost of maintenance and depreciation on the house in 1971.

Findings of Fact

[Petitioners moved from New Jersey to Binghamton, New York, in 1969. They bought a house on Leroy Street in Binghamton for $34,000, spent $2100 in improving it, and lived there from September 1, 1969, until September 1, 1970. In September, 1970, they bought a house on Riverside Drive in Binghamton. They planned to keep the Leroy Street house as investment rental property, but despite several attempts they were unable to find a tenant. The Leroy Street property was listed for sale in June, 1971, and was sold in July, 1971, for $33,800.]

* * *

Opinion

Section 165(a) provides for the allowance of a deduction for any loss sustained in the taxable year and not compensated by insurance or otherwise. However, section 165(c) limits such losses in the case of individuals to losses incurred in a trade or business or "losses incurred in any transaction entered into for profit, though not connected with a trade or business" and casualty losses. [Treas.Reg. §] 1.165–9(a), states that losses on the sale of residential property purchased or constructed and so used by a taxpayer up to the time of the sale are not deductible under section 165(a). [Treas.Reg. §] 1.165–9(b) provides that if property purchased or constructed by a taxpayer for use as a personal residence is prior to sale "rented or otherwise appropriated to income-producing purposes and is used for such purposes up to the time of its sale" a loss sustained on the sale of the property shall be allowed under section 165(a). The amount of the loss is the excess of the adjusted basis of the property for determining loss over the amount realized from the sale. The adjusted basis shall be the lesser of the cost of the property or its fair market value at the time of conversion with the necessary adjustments to such basis as prescribed in [Treas.Reg. §] 1.1011–1.

Respondent's position in this case is that since the Leroy Street property was not rented by petitioners prior to its sale and was not used by them at any time prior to its sale for income-producing purposes, the loss on its sale is a loss on the sale of residential property and therefore not deductible. Respondent in the alternative contends that petitioners have failed to show the fair market value of the house on Leroy Street as of September 1, 1970, when petitioners moved out of the house, and therefore even had there been a conversion of the property petitioners have failed to establish that any loss resulted from the sale of the property under the provisions of [Treas.Reg. §] 1.165–9(b).

Petitioners contend that when they offered the Leroy Street property for rent they effectively converted the property to business property so that they should be entitled to the claimed loss deduction and apparently further contend, though this is not clear, that in any event the loss on the sale of the property was a loss incurred in a transaction entered into for profit even though not connected with a trade or business and therefore is an allowable deduction under section 165(c). The cases petitioners rely on in support of their contention are all cases where property which had constituted a taxpayer's home had actually been rented for a fair rental by the taxpayer prior to the time the property was sold.

The facts here clearly show that petitioners' Leroy Street property was never at any time rented. In this type of situation we have consistently held that the former residence when it is sold is not business property and that the loss occurring on the sale of the property is not a loss in a transaction entered into for profit. The case of Allen L. Grammer, 12 T.C. 34 (1949), is not distinguishable factually from the instant case. In that case the taxpayer listed his former residence with a real estate broker for rent for a period of approximately a year and a half before listing the property for sale. In holding that the loss on the sale of the property was not deductible, we pointed out that the original acquisition there, as here, had been a personal one and "unless there has been a subsequent 'transaction' which was 'profit-inspired' "the loss would not be deductible. * * *

Petitioners in their argument in support of the contention that they should be allowed to deduct the loss on the sale of the Leroy Street house referred to certain cases which involved claimed deductions for expenses connected with property offered for rent but not rented and property offered for sale. These cases do not involve loss deductions under section 165 but rather expense deductions claimed under section 212, or depreciation deductions under section 167(a)(2). These sections allow a taxpayer to deduct all ordinary and necessary expenses paid or incurred during the taxable year for the "management, conservation, or maintenance of property held for the production of income," and depreciation with respect to property held for the production of income. The philosophy underlying these cases is that where property is held for rent by a taxpayer or held for investment to be later sold at a profit it may be held for production of income and therefore the expenses incurred in so holding the property may be deductible. In Frank A. Newcombe, 54 T.C. 1298 (1970), we discussed the cases and regulations dealing with the deduction of expenses in connection with property being held for the production of income. [Citations omitted.]

We recognize that the distinction between cases involving deductions of expenses and depreciation under sections 212 and 167 may seem difficult of comprehension to petitioners. However, this distinction has long been recognized.

The bona fide placement of property on the rental market has been held to be a sufficient holding of the property for production of income to justify the deduction of expenses paid by a taxpayer in connection with the holding of the property and depreciation incurred with respect to the property. In our view the facts show that petitioners had offered the property for rent with the bona fide intent to rent it if they had obtained an offer for an amount they considered an adequate rental payment. We therefore conclude that petitioners are entitled to a deduction in the year 1971 of the maintenance expenses of $306.25 and insurance expenses of $138 which they paid in that year in connection with holding the Leroy Street property for rent and the depreciation of $927.15 applicable to the property from January 1, 1971, up to the date of the sale of the property, if this issue has been properly presented to the Court.

* * *

Therefore we hold that petitioners are not entitled to any deduction under section 165 for loss on the sale of the Leroy Street house but are entitled to deduct the depreciation for the period from January 1, 1971, to the date of the sale of the house in 1971, and the maintenance and insurance expenses they paid with respect to the house in 1971 under section 167(a)(2) and section 212.

Decision will be entered under Rule 155.

Problems, Notes and Questions

1. *The effect of § 280A.* Deductions for depreciation and expenses in the case of a bona fide but unsuccessful attempt to rent would today be limited by § 280A(e), if the taxpayer has used the property for personal purposes at any time during the taxable year for which the deductions are claimed. Section 280A is discussed at pp. 369–376.

2. *Problems.* T purchases a house and lot for $70,000 (of which $20,000 is allocable to the lot), lives in the house for several years, and then rents it out to tenants.

(1) The house is worth $40,000 (and the lot $20,000) when first rented out. What is T's basis for depreciation?

(2) After properly deducting $10,000 of depreciation on the house, T sells the property for $45,000. What result to T?

(3) Same as (2), except that T sells the property for $65,000.

(4) Same as (2), except that T sells the property for $55,000.

3. *Denial of a deduction for a loss on the sale of personal assets.* Why should a taxpayer be denied a deduction for a loss on the sale of a personal residence? Does the no-deduction rule have as much appeal when applied to a loss on the sale of a house as it has when applied to a loss on the sale of a car?

4. *Property used partly for business.* Suppose a self-employed tax-payer pays $10,000 for a car, uses it 80 percent of the time for business

and 20 percent of the time for pleasure, and then sells it after two years for $6000. Assume that the taxpayer deducts straight-line depreciation based upon a five-year recovery period. If the car were used 100 percent of the time for business, the depreciation deduction for the first year would be $1000 (review § 168(d)(1)). But since it is used only 80 percent for business, the taxpayer can deduct only $800 (80% of $1000) of depreciation for the year. For the second year, the taxpayer can deduct depreciation of $1600 (80% of $2000). When the taxpayer sells the car at the end of the second year, he must fragment the transaction, treating it as if two separate assets (a business asset and a personal-use asset) had been purchased and sold. The business asset has an unadjusted basis of $8000 (80% of the $10,000 cost) and an adjusted basis of $5600 ($8000 unadjusted basis less $2400 depreciation). The personal-use asset has an unadjusted and adjusted basis of $2000 (because no depreciation is allowable with respect to personal-use property). The amount realized on the sale of the business asset is $4800 (80% of the total $6000 amount realized). Thus the taxpayer realizes a loss of $800 ($5600 adjusted basis less $4800 amount realized) on the disposition of this interest. The loss is recognized under § 1001(c) and allowed as a deduction by §§ 165(a) & (c)(1). On the disposition of the personal-use asset, the taxpayer realizes a loss of $800 ($2000 adjusted basis less $1200 amount realized). Although this loss is recognized under § 1001(c), it is disallowed as a deduction by § 165(c). Thus the taxpayer reports only a loss of $800 on the sale of the car.

What result if instead the taxpayer sells the car at the end of the second year for $8000?

5. *Reference.* Epstein, The Consumption and Loss of Personal Property Under the Internal Revenue Code, 23 Stan.L.Rev. 454 (1971).

4. LOSSES ON TRANSACTIONS BETWEEN RELATED PARTIES

Section 267(a)(1) disallows deductions for losses on the sale or exchange of property to a related person. The transferee acquires a cost basis for the property under § 1012. As a result, the transferee's basis for computing realized gain or loss on a subsequent disposition of the property is computed without regard to the loss previously disallowed to the transferor. A loss that has been disallowed to the transferor under § 267 cannot be deducted by the transferor even when the transferee sells the property to an unrelated party. In general, therefore, both the transferor and the transferee are denied any benefit from a loss disallowed by § 267. But if the transferee subsequently disposes of the property at a gain, § 267(d) limits the recognized gain to the amount in excess of the loss previously disallowed.

A number of decisions have held that § 267 disallows loss even on a bona fide sale to a related party; e.g., Englehart v. Commissioner, 30 T.C. 1013 (1958).

McWILLIAMS v. COMMISSIONER

Supreme Court of the United States, 1947.
331 U.S. 694, 67 S.Ct. 1477, 91 L.Ed. 1750.

Mr. Chief Justice Vinson delivered the opinion of the Court.

The facts of these cases are not in dispute. John P. McWilliams, petitioner in No. 945, had for a number of years managed the large independent estate of his wife, petitioner in No. 947, as well as his own. On several occasions in 1940 and 1941 he ordered his broker to sell certain stock for the account of one of the two and to buy the same number of shares of the same stock for the other, at as nearly the same price as possible. He told the broker that his purpose was to establish tax losses. On each occasion the sale and purchase were promptly negotiated through the Stock Exchange, and the identity of the persons buying from the selling spouse and of the persons selling to the buying spouse was never known. Invariably, however, the buying spouse received stock certificates different from those which the other had sold. Petitioners filed separate income tax returns for these years, and claimed the losses which he or she sustained on the sales as deductions from gross income.

The Commissioner disallowed these deductions on the authority of § [267(a)(1)] * * *.

On the taxpayers' applications to the Tax Court, it held § [267(a)(1)] inapplicable, following its own decision in Ickelheimer v. Commissioner, and expunged the Commissioner's deficiency assessments. The Circuit Court of Appeals reversed the Tax Court and we granted certiorari because of a conflict between circuits and the importance of the question involved.

Petitioners contend that Congress could not have intended to disallow losses on transactions like those described above, which, having been made through a public market, were undoubtedly bona fide sales, both in the sense that title to property was actually transferred, and also in the sense that a fair consideration was paid in exchange. They contend that the disallowance of such losses would amount, pro tanto, to treating husband and wife as a single individual for tax purposes.

In support of this contention, they call our attention to the pre–1934 rule, which applied to all sales regardless of the relationship of seller and buyer, and made the deductibility of the resultant loss turn on the "good faith" of the sale, i.e., whether the seller actually parted with title and control. They point out that in the case of the usual intra-family sale, the evidence material to this issue was peculiarly within the knowledge and even the control of the taxpayer and those amenable to his wishes, and inaccessible to the Government. They maintain that the only purpose of the provisions of the 1934 and 1937 Revenue Acts—the forerunners of § [267(a)(1)]—was to overcome these evidentiary difficulties by disallowing losses on such sales irrespective of good faith. It seems to be petitioners' belief that the evidentiary difficulties so contemplated were only those relating to proof of the parties' observance of the formalities of a sale and of the fairness of the price, and consequently that the legislative remedy applied only to sales made immediately from one member of a family to another, or mediately through a controlled intermediary.

We are not persuaded that Congress had so limited an appreciation of this type of tax avoidance problem. Even assuming that the problem was thought to arise solely out of the taxpayer's inherent advantage in a contest concerning the good or bad faith of an intra-family sale, deception could obviously be practiced by a buying spouse's agreement or tacit readiness to hold the property sold at the disposal of a selling spouse, rather more easily than by a pretense of a sale where none actually occurred, or by an unfair price. The difficulty of determining the finality of an intra-family transfer was one with which the courts wrestled under the pre–1934 law, and which Congress undoubtedly meant to overcome by enacting the provisions of § [267(a)(1)].

It is clear, however, that this difficulty is one which arises out of the close relationship of the parties, and would be met whenever, by prearrangement, one spouse sells and another buys the same property at a common price regardless of the mechanics of the transaction. Indeed, if the property is fungible, the possibility that a sale and purchase may be rendered nugatory by the buying spouse's agreement to hold for the benefit of the selling spouse, and the difficulty of proving that fact against the taxpayer, are equally great when the units of the property which the one buys are not the identical units which the other sells.

Securities transactions have been the most common vehicle for the creation of intra-family losses. Even if we should accept petitioners' premise that the only purpose of § [267(a)(1)] was to meet an evidentiary problem, we could agree that Congress did not mean to reach the transactions in this case only if we thought it completely indifferent to the effectuality of its solution.

Moreover, we think the evidentiary problem was not the only one which Congress intended to meet. Section [267(a)(1)] states an absolute prohibition—not a presumption—against the allowance of losses on any sales between the members of certain designated groups. The one common characteristic of these groups is that their members, although distinct legal entities, generally have a near-identity of economic interests. It is a fair inference that even legally genuine intra-group transfers were not thought to result, usually, in economically genuine realizations of loss, and accordingly that Congress did not deem them to be appropriate occasions for the allowance of deductions.

The pertinent legislative history lends support to this inference. * * *

We conclude that the purpose of § [267(a)(1)] was to put an end to the right of taxpayers to choose, by intra-family transfers and other designated devices, their own time for realizing tax losses on investments which, for most practical purposes, are continued uninterrupted.

We are clear as to this purpose, too, that its effectuation obviously had to be made independent of the manner in which an intra-group transfer was accomplished. Congress, with such purpose in mind, could not have intended to include within the scope of § [267(a)(1)] only simple transfers made directly or through a dummy, or to exclude transfers of securities effected through the medium of the Stock Exchange, unless it wanted to leave a loophole almost as large as the one it had set out to close.

* * *

Petitioners also urge that, whatever may have been Congress' intent, its designation in § [267(a)(1)] of sales "between" members of a family is not adequate to comprehend the transactions in this case, which consisted only of a sale of stock by one of the petitioners to an unknown stranger, and the purchase of different certificates of stock by the other petitioner, presumably from another stranger.

We can understand how this phraseology, if construed literally and out of context, might be thought to mean only direct intrafamily transfers. But petitioners concede that the express statutory reference to sales made "directly or indirectly" precludes that construction. Moreover, we can discover in this language no implication whatsoever that an indirect intra-family sale of fungibles is outside the statute unless the units sold by one spouse and those bought by the other are identical. Indeed, if we accepted petitioners' construction of the statute, we think we would be reading into it a crippling exception which is not there.

* * *

Affirmed.

Mr. Justice Burton took no part in the consideration or decision of these cases.

Problems, Notes and Questions

1. *The purpose of § 267.* An important purpose of § 267 is to disallow a deduction for ostensible losses resulting from the sale of property to related parties at a bargain price. A taxpayer dealing with an unrelated party is not likely to sell property for an amount less than its value in order to create (or increase) a tax loss. But a taxpayer dealing with a family member may be willing to make a partial gift by selling the property at a bargain price, especially if the bargain element can be deducted as a loss. Likewise, a shareholder might make a bargain sale of property to a controlled corporation for the purpose of creating or enhancing a tax loss, even though the bargain element really represents a contribution to the corporation's capital and thus enhances the value of the shareholder's stock. Although the Service could disallow the loss deduction in these cases under general tax principles if it determined that the sale was not bona fide, § 267 avoids the necessity of inquiring into the facts of each case. Section 267 does not preclude the Service

from disallowing deduction of a loss on a transaction not covered by § 267 if the transaction is determined not to be bona fide. And in Scully v. United States, 840 F.2d 478 (7th Cir.1988), the court relied upon § 165(a) in disallowing a loss on a good-faith sale of property between two trusts with identical fiduciaries and beneficiaries on the ground that the selling trust had not suffered a "genuine economic loss."

2. *McWilliams today.* Under § 1041, enacted in 1984, no loss (or gain) is recognized on transfers between spouses. See pp. 544–545. Under § 1041(a), would the wife in *McWilliams* be treated as having transferred the securities to her husband, so that no loss would be recognized? Keep in mind that § 1041(a), unlike § 267(a), does not expressly cover "indirect" transfers to a spouse. (But note Temp.Reg. § 1.1041–1T(a) (Ex. (3)) ("general tax principles, including the step-transaction doctrine," apply under § 1041)). Even if the transferor recognizes loss on a *McWilliams*-type transfer (because the transfer is not considered to be made to a spouse under § 1041), § 267, as interpreted in *McWilliams,* presumably continues to disallow the loss. Since one provision or the other prevents the transferor from deducting a loss in the *McWilliams* situation today, does the question of whether § 1041 or § 267 applies make any practical difference?

Problem. P sells stock in *X* Corp. at a loss. On the same day, and unknown to *P, P*'s adult child, *C,* purchases a like number of *X* Corp. shares. Both transactions were executed on a stock exchange. Does *McWilliams* require disallowance of *P*'s loss?

3. *Related parties.* Assume in these problems that all sales are bona fide sales of investment property at fair market value. Can the seller deduct a loss on the sale?

(1) *T* sold property at a loss to his daughter (*D*) and her husband (*H*). *D* and *H* took title to the property as tenants in common.

(2) *A, A*'s father *A–F, A*'s wife *A–W,* and an unrelated party (*U*) each own 25 of the 100 outstanding shares of *X* Corp. *A–F* sells property at a loss to *X* Corp.

(3) *B* owns 49% of the stock of *X* Corp., and a trust of which *B* is the sole beneficiary owns the remaining 51% of the stock. *B* sells property at a loss to *X* Corp.

(4) *B* owns 51% of the stock of *X* Corp., and a trust of which *B* is the sole beneficiary (and *B*'s father *F* is the grantor) owns the remaining 49% of the stock. The trust sells property to *X* Corp. at a loss.

(5) An estate sells property at a loss to one of its principal beneficiaries.

4. *Non-recognition under § 267(d). P* sells investment property to her child, *C,* for $60. *P* had an adjusted basis of $100 in the property. The sale is bona fide.

(1) What result to *P*? What result to *C* if *C* subsequently sells the property to an unrelated party for $40? for $90? for $110?

(2) Suppose instead that C gives the property (then worth $70) to her sister, S. S later sells the property for $90. What result to S?

(3) Suppose instead that C exchanges the property for property of like kind in a transaction qualifying under § 1031. What result to C if C later sells the property acquired in the exchange for $90?

5. *Relationship of § 267 to § 1091.* Suppose in *McWilliams* that more than thirty days had elapsed between the sale of stock at a loss by the husband and the repurchase of similar shares by the wife. Section 267 (or § 1041) probably should not apply in such a case because the husband could have repurchased substantially identical shares himself after thirty days without having his loss disallowed under § 1091.

A taxpayer who sells securities at a loss could be worse off if a related party buys similar securities within thirty days of the sale than if the taxpayer himself had bought similar securities. In either case the seller can take no immediate loss deduction. But if the transaction is treated as an indirect sale to a related party under § 267, the related party acquires a cost basis for the stock purchased, while the seller generally would obtain a basis equal to the basis of the stock sold under § 1091(d).

To illustrate, suppose P sells on the stock exchange for $50 X Corp. stock with an adjusted basis of $100. Within thirty days of the sale P purchases a like amount of X Corp. stock for $50. P's basis for the newly acquired shares of X Corp. stock is $100, the same as the basis in the stock sold; § 1091(d). If instead P's child C purchases X Corp. stock within thirty days of the sale by P, C would obtain a cost basis of $50 for the X Corp. stock; Treas.Reg. § 1.267(d)–1(a)(4). The purchaser therefore obtains a higher basis for the stock if P, rather than C, makes the purchase. (What result if *both* P and C purchase X Corp. stock within thirty days following P's sale?)

*

Chapter Ten

CAPITAL GAINS AND LOSSES

A. THE SIGNIFICANCE OF CHARACTERIZATION

Whenever a gain is recognized (or a loss allowed), it must be *characterized* as ordinary or capital. This is because the treatment of capital gains and losses differs from the treatment of ordinary gains and losses. The distinction between ordinary income and capital gain (and between ordinary loss and capital loss) has been immensely important in Federal tax law. For most of our income-tax history, long-term capital gains have been taxed more lightly than ordinary income. Although capital gains were taxed at the same rate as ordinary income from 1988 through 1990, the capital-gains preference was reinstated in 1990. Additional changes in recent years have made capital-gains-tax calculations grotesquely complex.

Capital losses are treated less favorably than ordinary losses: ordinary losses generally are fully deductible against ordinary income on a dollar-for-dollar basis; but only $3000 of ordinary income can be offset by capital loss in each year.[a]

When Are Gains and Losses Characterized?

Since *unrecognized* gains do not enter into the year's tax computations, we do not characterize them.[b] But *recognized* gains must usually be characterized in the year recognized.

The question of when a loss must be characterized is more complicated. Recall that even a recognized loss cannot be deducted unless it is also "allowable" as a deduction. But, depending on the context, a "disallowed" loss may be permanently barred from deductibility (under § 165 or § 267) or may be "suspended" temporarily but deducted in a future year (under, for example, § 1211, discussed below). A recognized

a. The character of gain or loss is important in a few other instances. E.g., §§ 170(b)(1)(C), (b)(1)(D) and (e)(1); 643(a). Capital and ordinary gains (and losses) are also treated differently under some state income-tax laws.

b. Note that capital gains are defined to include only those "taken into account in computing gross income" (that is, recognized gains); §§ 1222(1) & (3).

loss is usually characterized in the year in which it is "allowable" (in the sense of not being permanently barred as a deduction), even if the loss is temporarily "disallowed" (in the sense of being suspended as a deduction until a future year). For example, a recognized loss on an individual's sale of personal-use property (for which a deduction is permanently disallowed by § 165(c)) is not characterized. But a recognized loss from the sale of investment property must be characterized in the year in which recognized, even if § 1211 prohibits deduction of the loss in the year recognized.[c] If the loss is determined to be a capital loss, we turn (by way of § 165(f)) to § 1211 to see if the limits on the deductibility of capital losses apply.[d]

Definitions

Section 1222 defines "capital" gains and losses as gains and losses from the "sale or exchange" of "capital assets."[e] The term "capital asset," which is defined in § 1221, means "property," other than that excluded by §§ 1221(a)(1)–(8). Some everyday examples of capital assets are corporate securities, unimproved land held as an investment, and the taxpayer's personal residence. (Examine § 1221 carefully to be sure you understand why these are capital assets.)

To complicate matters further, Congress sometimes prescribes special characterization rules covering the disposition of certain assets. Thus, a Code provision may treat as ordinary a gain that would qualify as a capital gain under general characterization principles. Or a loss that appears to be ordinary under general principles may be treated as a capital loss because of a special characterization rule. We will examine several of these special characterization rules in this chapter.

Capital gains and losses are "long-term" or "short-term," depending upon the taxpayer's "holding period" for the asset sold or exchanged. The holding period is significant because only long-term gains get the benefit of the capital-gains preference.[f] A gain or loss is long-term if the asset was held for more than one year before being sold or exchanged; §§ 1222(3) & (4). A gain or loss is short-term if the asset was *not* held for more than one year; §§ 1222(1) & (2).

Section 1231

Section 1221(a)(2) excludes real and depreciable property used in the taxpayer's trade or business from the "capital-asset" definition. This

c. Capital losses include only losses "taken into account in computing taxable income" (that is, losses that are both recognized and allowed); §§ 1222(2) & (4). To avoid circularity, the regulations provide that, in determining whether a loss is taken into account in computing taxable income for this purpose, the limits on the deductibility of capital losses under § 1211 are to be disregarded; Treas.Reg. § 1.1222–1(a).

d. Sections 165(f) and 1211 do not authorize any deductions; they only impose limits on deductions allowed by other provisions (usually §§ 165(a) and (c)).

e. Compare the definitions of "ordinary income" (§ 64) and "ordinary loss" (§ 65). (We use the terms "ordinary income" and "ordinary gain" interchangeably.)

f. Two other provisions in which the holding period of property remains important are § 1231, discussed at pp. 629–632, and § 170(e), discussed at p. 640.

does not necessarily mean, however, that gains or losses from sales of such assets produce ordinary income or loss. These assets, if held for more than one year, are defined in § 1231(b) as "property used in the trade or business." (We call them "§ 1231 assets.") Under § 1231(a), gains and losses from the sale of § 1231 assets are netted (together with some gains or losses from involuntary conversions of capital and § 1231 assets). If the result of this netting process is a gain, the § 1231 gains and losses are treated as long-term capital gains and losses.[g] If the net result for the year is not a gain, the § 1231 gains and losses are ordinary. Section 1231 will be examined in detail in part D of this chapter.

The Mechanics of Capital Gains and Losses

Capital gains must be fully included in gross income; § 61(a)(3). If the taxpayer has both capital gains and losses, the gains are not netted against the losses in computing gross income; instead the losses are deducted (subject to the limits of § 1211) in computing adjusted gross income; § 62(a)(3).[h]

Understanding § 1(h), which provides the capital-gains preference, requires that you grasp the notion of "net capital gain" (NCG). The NCG is the excess of the net long-term capital gain (NLTCG) over the net short-term capital loss (NSTCL); § 1222(11). The NLTCG is the excess of the long-term capital gain (LTCG) over the long-term capital loss (LTCL); § 1222(7). The NSTCL is the excess of the short-term capital loss (STCL) over the short-term capital gain (STCG); § 1222(6). In other words, one computes the NCG by first netting all long-term transactions. If the LTCG exceeds the LTCL (the excess is the NLTCG), one next nets all short-term transactions. Any excess of STCL over STCG (that is, any NSTCL) is then subtracted from the NLTCG to arrive at the NCG.

For example, suppose a taxpayer has capital gains and losses as follows:

STCG	$ 5,000
STCL	$ 7,000
LTCG	$14,000
LTCL	$ 4,000

The taxpayer's NCG is $8000, computed as follows:

NLTCG = $14,000 (LTCG) − $4000 (LTCL) = $10,000;

NSTCL = $7000 (STCL) − $5000 (STCG) = $2000;

NCG = $10,000 (NLTCG) − $2000 (NSTCL) = $8000.

g. Thus, the sale of a non-capital asset can produce capital gain under § 1231. This is an example of a special characterization rule that sometimes trumps the general characterization principles of § 1222.

h. Does it matter whether gains are netted against losses in computing gross income or whether the statutory scheme is followed? See §§ 6012(a); 6501(e)(1); 151(c)(1).

It is the NCG that is subjected to the favorable capital-gains tax rates, and the NCG is the excess of NLTCG over NSTCL. So, the Code's rate favoritism is reserved for LTCG. Any excess of net short-term capital gain (NSTCG) (§ 1222(5)) over net long-term capital loss (NLTCL) (§ 1222(7)) is taxed at ordinary-income rates.

Conceptually, the capital-gains tax calculation is straightforward. Imagine that we live in a simple tax world in which all ordinary income is taxed at 35 percent and NCG is taxed at 20 percent. A taxpayer who had $120,000 of taxable income, of which $20,000 was NCG, would compute two partial taxes—one on ordinary income and one on NCG. Ordinary income would be the excess of taxable income over NCG. So, in this case, the taxpayer's ordinary income would be $100,000 ($120,000 taxable income less $20,000 NCG), and the tax on ordinary income would be $35,000 (35% of $100,000). The tax on the NCG would be $4000 (20% of $20,000 NCG). The total tax would be the sum of the two partial taxes ($39,000 in this case). The lower rate of tax on NCG saves the taxpayer $3000 (the difference between the 35–percent and 20–percent rates on $20,000 of NCG).

As in our conceptual model, § 1(h) provides generally for a maximum 20–percent tax rate on NCG, but a glance at § 1(h) reveals that the real tax world is much more complicated than our model. The complexity stems from several sources. First, unlike the assumption of our model, the rate schedules of §§ 1(a)-(e) do not tax ordinary income at a single rate but (when the 2001 tax changes are fully phased in) at rates varying from 10 percent to 35 percent. Congress perceived a need to provide relief for the capital gains of those taxpayers whose marginal tax rate on ordinary income is less than the usual 20 percent rate applicable to NCG. To provide relief in such cases, Congress created a 10–percent capital-gains tax rate (found in § 1(h)(1)(B)) that benefits those whose tax rate on ordinary income does not exceed 15 percent.

Additional complexity results from the use of different preferential rates for some categories of gain. The rate can be 28 percent (on "28–percent-rate gain"), 25 percent (on "unrecaptured § 1250 gain"), or 20 percent (on a residual category of NCG, called "adjusted net capital gain"). (Only the latter qualifies for the special 10–percent capital-gains rate described in the preceding paragraph.) The proliferation of rates prompts the need for a mechanism to allocate losses against different categories of gains, thus further complicating § 1(h). Moreover, the preferential rate that applies may vary depending upon the taxpayer's holding period for the property disposed of: Gain on the sale of property that has been held for more than five years may be taxed at a maximum of 18 percent (8 percent if the special 10–percent capital-gains rate would otherwise apply).[i]

i. The 18–percent (and 8–percent) rates apply only to gain that would otherwise be taxed at 20 percent (10 percent). In addition, the 18–percent rate applies only if the taxpayer's holding period for the property disposed of began after December 31, 2000; § 1(h)(2).

We now turn to the categories of gain that qualify for the various rates.

28–percent-rate gain. This category embraces (1) "collectibles gain" and (2) "section 1202 gain." Collectibles gain arises from the sale or exchange of collectibles (defined in § 408(m)), such as works of art, coins, stamps and gems), provided that the collectibles were capital assets (with a long-term holding period) in the hands of the taxpayer; § 1(h)(6).

Section 1202 gain arises from the sale or exchange of "qualified small business stock." To encourage investment in start-up companies that might have difficulty attracting equity financing, § 1202 permits a non-corporate taxpayer to exclude from gross income 50 percent of the gain from the sale or exchange of "qualified small business stock" held for more than five years; § 1202(a). The includable half of the gain is "section 1202 gain"; § 1(h)(8). Because the taxable half of the gain is a 28–percent rate gain taxable at a maximum rate of 28 percent, the maximum marginal tax rate on qualifying gains is 14 percent (that is, 28 percent of 50 percent). (Except where otherwise indicated, we assume in our examples and problems that the capital gains *do not* qualify for exclusion under § 1202.)

Qualified small business stock must be issued by a "qualified small business" and must be acquired by the taxpayer at its original issue; § 1202(c)(1). In order to be a qualified small business, the corporation must be a C corporation (that is, not a "pass-through" S corporation; see p. 534, at footnote n) with aggregate gross assets of no more than $50 million (as measured by the adjusted bases of the firm's assets immediately after the stock is issued); § 1202(d). At least 80 percent of the firm's assets must be used in an active business (§ 1202(e)(1)), other than (among others) banking, farming, mineral extraction, or the performing of services in the fields of health, law, accounting, consulting, athletics, or other businesses in which the principal asset is the reputation or skill of the firm's employees; § 1202(e)(3). In general, the investor cannot exclude more than a total of $10 million of gain on the stock of any one issuer; § 1202(b)(1)(A).

28–percent-rate gain is reduced by (1) loss on the sale or exchange of collectibles held for use in business or investment; (2) NSTCL for the year; and (3) any LTCL carried forward to the year under § 1212(b)(1)(B), discussed below; § 1(h)(5).

Unrecaptured § 1250 gain. Putting aside the technical details, which are considered at p. 640, below, this category of gain embraces the make-up gain on the sale of depreciable real property. Suppose a taxpayer purchases a rental building for $100,000, properly deducts $60,000 of straight-line depreciation, and then sells the building for $110,000. (Ignore the land, as if only the building had been bought and sold.) Assume that the $70,000 gain ($110,000 amount realized less $40,000 basis) is characterized as long-term capital gain. Notice that to the extent of $60,000 the gain just "makes up" for the over-depreciation of the building; the remaining $10,000 of gain represents real economic gain (that is, the excess of the $110,000 amount realized over the $100,000 original cost of the building). Under § 1(h)(7), the $60,000 make-up gain is treated as less-favored unrecaptured § 1250 gain, which is subject to tax at a maximum rate of 25 percent. The $10,000 economic gain qualifies for the 20–percent (and 10–percent) -rates.

Adjusted net capital gain (ANCG). The NCG, of course, includes the 28–percent-rate gain and the unrecaptured § 1250 gain. The ANCG is the residual amount of NCG after subtracting the 28–percent-rate gain and the unrecaptured § 1250 gain; § 1(h)(4). The ANCG qualifies for the 20–percent (and 10–percent) tax rates; §§ 1(h)(1)(B) & (C).

With considerable trepidation, we offer you the following guide through § 1(h). Be warned, though, that we are not attempting to describe every statutory nuance. You may find this intimidating. We do, too. Don't shoot the messenger.

Step 1: Characterize all recognized gains and allowable losses as (1) ordinary gain or loss, (2) short-term capital gain or loss, or (3) long-term capital gain or loss; see §§ 1222(1)-(4).

Step 2: Aggregate all long-term capital gains and losses. If LTCG exceeds LTCL, you have a NLTCG (§ 1222(7)). If LTCL exceeds LTCG, you have a NLTCL (§ 1222(8)).

Step 3: Aggregate all short-term capital gains and losses. If STCG exceeds STCL, you have a NSTCG (§ 1222(5)). If STCL exceeds STCG, you have a NSTCL (§ 1222(6)).

Step 4: If you have a NLTCG in step 2, compute the NCG (§ 1222(11)) by subtracting the NSTCL, if any, from the NLTCG. If you do not have a NCG, just use the regular § 1 rates to compute the tax. If you do have a NCG, continue on; § 1(h) may produce a lower tax.

Step 5: Compute the amount of gain that is taxable at a maximum rate of 28 percent (the "28–percent-rate gain") (defined by § 1(h)) in the following manner:

    a. Find the sum of the (1) collectibles gains (§ 1(h)(6)); and (2) § 1202 gain (§ 1(h)(8)).

    b. Find the sum of the (1) collectibles losses (§ 1(h)(6)); (2) NSTCL (if any); and (3) LTCL carried over to the year (if any).

    c. The excess of the gains over the losses is the 28–percent-rate gain. If the losses exceed the gains, the net loss is applied against the unrecaptured § 1250 gain in the next step.

Step 6: Determine the amount of the unrecaptured § 1250 gain (§ 1(h)(7)). Basically, this is the make-up gain that results from over-depreciating a building, less any loss from Step 5c. The unrecaptured § 1250 gain is subject to tax at a maximum rate of 25 percent.

Step 7: Determine the adjusted net capital gain (ANCG) (§ 1(h)(4)). The ANCG can be determined by subtracting from the NCG the sum of (1) the 28–percent-rate gain and (2) the unrecaptured § 1250 gain. The

ANCG is subject to tax at a maximum rate of 20 percent (10 percent in the case of taxpayers in the 15–percent bracket or below).

These seven steps give you the numbers that can be run through § 1(h)(1) to calculate the tax.

For example, suppose a married couple filing a joint return has ordinary taxable income of $140,000 and capital gains and losses as follows: LTCG of $35,000 (from the sale of securities held for 14 months) and STCL of $5,000. Their taxable income is $170,000.

To compute their tax liability, we first observe that they have a NSTCL of $5000 ($5000 STCL less 0 STCG); § 1222(6). They have a NLTCG of $35,000 ($35,000 LTCG less 0 LTCL); § 1222(7). They have a NCG of $30,000 ($35,000 NLTCG less $5000 NSTCL); § 1222(11). § 1(h)(5). Since there is no 28–percent-rate gain and no unrecaptured § 1250 gain, the ANCG is also $30,000; § 1(h)(4).

Turning to § 1(h)(1), we compute their tax as follows:

(1) The partial tax on ordinary income of $140,000 (taxable income of $170,000 less NCG of $30,000) is $34,297.50 (This is based on the statutory tax rates (§ 1(a)) for 2002 and 2003 (before inflation adjustments) as set forth in Appendix B, p. 803, below); § 1(h)(1)(A)(i);

(2) The tax on the ANCG is $6000 (20 percent of $30,000); § 1(h)(1)(C).

The total tax is therefore $40,297.50 ($34,297.50 + $6000).

If the tax on the couple's entire $170,000 taxable income had been calculated under § 1(a) (as set forth in Appendix B, p. 803, below), the couple's marginal tax rate would have been 35 percent, and their tax would have been $44,797.50, or $4500 more than the § 1(h) computation. The $4500 savings results from having the $30,000 ANCG taxed at 20 percent instead of 35 percent.

A corporation's NCG is taxed at the same rate as ordinary income. (Section 1(h) limits only the tax "imposed by this section [1]"; the corporate tax is imposed by § 11.)

A non-corporate taxpayer can use capital losses to offset capital gains, plus up to $3000 of ordinary income (on a dollar-for-dollar basis); § 1211(b). Capital losses that exceed the limit can be carried forward indefinitely; § 1212(b). A corporation can deduct capital losses only to the extent of its capital gains; § 1211(a). Unused corporate capital losses can be carried back three years and forward five years; § 1212(a).

Problems

Problem (1). In the current year, *T realized* gains and losses as follows:

(a) $5000 gain on the sale of business inventory;

(b) $12,000 loss on the sale of her personal residence;

(c) $5000 loss on the sale of General Motors stock held as an investment;

(d) $25,000 gain on the exchange of land (held as an investment) for property of like kind (*T* also received $10,000 boot);

(e) $2000 gain on the sale of *T*'s boat (used for recreational purposes);

(f) $6000 loss on the sale of business real estate. (

T had a long-term holding period for each asset. What is *T*'s net capital gain (§ 1222(11)) for the year?

Problem (2). *R*, a single person, is in the 35% bracket. What is the maximum rate of tax that would apply to *R*'s capital gains arising from the sale of:

(a) New York Stock Exchange-listed securities held for nine months?

(b) New York Stock Exchange-listed securities held for two years?

(c) New York Stock Exchange-listed securities purchased in 2001 and held for six years?

(d) Qualified small business stock (§ 1202) held for three years?

(e) Qualified small business stock (§ 1202) held for six years?

(f) *R*'s personal collection of fine wines purchased in 2001 and held for six years?

(g) *R*'s vacation home held for ten years?

Problem (3). For the current year, *S*, a single person (not a head of household or a surviving spouse), has ordinary taxable income of $115,000, $14,000 gain from the sale of securities held for four years, a short-term capital gain of $7000, and a short-term capital loss of $9000, for total taxable income of $127,000. What is *S*'s tax liability for the year? (Use the tax-bracket figures set forth in Appendix B, p. 803, below (without inflation adjustments), unless instructed otherwise.)

Problem (4). What result in (3) if *S* had had the capital gains and losses as indicated but had only $20,100 of ordinary taxable income for a total taxable income of $32,100?

Problem (5). For the current year, *T*, an individual, has ordinary gross income of $50,000 and has capital gains and losses in the amounts specified below. In each case, determine (i) *T*'s gross and adjusted gross income; and (ii) the amount and character of any capital-loss carryover to the next year. See §§ 1211(b) and 1212(b).

(a)	long-term capital gain	$ 4000
	long-term capital loss	$12,000
(b)	long-term capital loss	$ 4000
	short-term capital loss	$10,000
(c)	long-term capital loss	$10,000
	short-term capital gain	$ 8000

(d) long-term capital gain	$ 3000
long-term capital loss	$10,000
short-term capital gain	$ 5000
short-term capital loss	$ 6000

Problem (6). What is the purpose of the special rule of § 1212(b)(2)?

Problem (7). In the year 2003 *X* Corp. sustains a long-term capital loss of $12,000. In the preceding and following years (and before taking account of any carryovers), it had net capital gains (losses) as follows:

1999	$5000
2000	$3000
2001	$4000
2002	($6000)
2004	$2000
2005	($2000)
2006	$3000
2007	$4000

For what year(s) will the loss sustained in 2003 be allowed? See §§ 1211(a) and 1212(a).

POLICY CONSIDERATIONS IN THE TAXATION OF CAPITAL GAINS

Several reasons have been offered in support of taxing capital gains at lower rates than those on ordinary income.

(1) *The "income-averaging" rationale.* Some proponents argue that the lower rates of tax on capital gains are necessary to limit the tax resulting from the "bunching" in a single year of gains accrued over many years. For example, a taxpayer of modest income owns stock, which has gradually appreciated in value over the past twenty years. If the taxpayer now sells the stock, twenty years' appreciation may be taxed in a single year. This bunching of income may push the taxpayer into a higher tax bracket for the year of sale, after which she falls back into her customary low bracket.

Whatever the merit of this argument when tax rates were higher, it seems less compelling at today's lower, flatter rates. The possible unfairness of a "one-shot" jump in the taxpayer's marginal tax rate must be balanced against the advantage to the taxpayer of deferring tax on the appreciation until the year of sale. In fact, the above example may not be representative of the typical beneficiary of a capital-gains preference. At today's lower tax rates, many taxpayers who are consistently in the highest tax bracket, and who therefore cannot be hurt by bunching, derive substantial benefit from the lower rates of tax on capital gains. Indeed, for many taxpayers, the amount of realized capital gains probably does not fluctuate much from year to year. And since under present law an investor gets capital-gain treatment for an asset held for a year and a day, the gain does not necessarily represent many years' appreciation. See Andrews, A Consumption-type or Cash Flow Personal Income Tax, 87 Harv.L.Rev. 1113, 1131–33 (1974).

(2) *The "inflation" rationale.* Some argue for the lower rates of tax on capital gains because such gains may reflect inflation rather than real changes in economic value. Suppose, for example, that an asset has doubled in value during a period when the general price level has also doubled. Although the taxpayer has a *taxable* gain, he has no *real* gain whatsoever.

To be sure, this result is highly objectionable. But the concern about inflation does not seem to justify the lower rates of tax on long-term capital gains. Under present law, relief is not tied to the rate of inflation during the taxpayer's holding of the property. And what of the taxpayer whose property did not appreciate sufficiently to keep up with the rate of inflation? Although such a taxpayer has suffered an economic loss, he is required to pay tax (albeit at the capital-gains rates) on the nominal gain.[j] See Andrews, supra, at 1133.

(3) *The "locking-in" rationale.* A high rate of tax on capital gains may impede economic efficiency by deterring the taxpayer from making economically desirable sales and reinvestments. Consider a taxpayer with an asset worth $100,000, which is expected to produce income of $10,000 a year indefinitely. The taxpayer has an opportunity to invest in a comparably risky asset (with the same prospects for appreciation), but which will yield a 12–percent return. Were it not for the tax on the sale, the taxpayer would switch investments. But if the old asset's basis is $50,000, and the gain on its sale is subject to a 40–percent tax, the switch would leave the taxpayer with only $80,000 ($100,000 sales proceeds less $20,000 tax) to reinvest. Since the taxpayer could earn an annual return of only $9600 (12% of $80,000) on the reinvestment, the taxpayer probably would not switch investments. This "locking-in effect" on conversions does not depend in any way on whether the gain accumulated over a long time; indeed, it would exist even if the income tax were proportional rather than progressive.

The capital-gains preference can best be justified as an attempt to reduce this locking-in effect by mitigating the tax burden imposed on realized gains. The preference promotes economic efficiency by reducing the disincentive to investors of making those switches in investments that they would make in the absence of taxes. It also reduces the inequity of taxing realized but reinvested gains at ordinary-income rates while permitting unrealized gains to accumulate tax-free. See Andrews, supra, at 1133–34.

Even with lower capital-gains rates, however, older taxpayers will still be reluctant to realize gains so long as the Code permits a tax-free step-up in basis at death. (See pp. 551–561.) In fact, the imposition of a

j. For a discussion of the revisions that would be required to eliminate the effects of inflation on the income tax, see Note, Inflation and the Income Tax, 82 Yale L.J. 716 (1973).

capital-gains tax at death might be more apt to reduce the locking-in effect than will the lower capital-gains tax rates on sales during life.

Economists continue to debate whether the lower tax rates on capital gains will increase tax revenues. Some think that the lowering of rates will induce taxpayers to unlock their investments and realize their gains, thus increasing tax revenues. Others contend that, in the long run, the lower rates of tax on capital gains will reduce revenues. The empirical evidence is inconclusive.

(4) *The capital-formation rationale.* Pointing to our anemic national savings rate, some proponents of the capital-gains preference argue that it will promote savings and capital formation. With lower capital-gains rates, the argument goes, people will increase their investment in assets that produce capital gains. But though some consumption expenditures may be diverted to savings, the preference will probably result chiefly in the shifting of investments from those that produce disfavored returns (interest and dividends) to those that produce capital gains. Recall also that the lower rates of tax on capital gains apply even if the sales proceeds are spent on consumption rather than reinvested. And the Code generally provides no relief for other receipts (such as salaries, dividends and interest) that are saved rather than expended on consumption. Andrews, supra, at 1134–35. Carried to its logical conclusion, the capital-formation argument supports a shift from an income tax to a consumption tax. But it hardly justifies a capital-gains preference in an income tax.

Some proponents argue that the reduced rates of tax on capital gains will encourage investment in risky new ventures. Of course, the present preference is not limited to such investments. And in any event it seems unwise to try to promote economic growth by encouraging investment in projects that do not pass muster in the market.

(5) *Other considerations.* Most opponents of a capital-gains preference think it unfair. They stress that the preference benefits chiefly high-bracket taxpayers, who realize a disproportionately large share of reported capital gains. Although some of those taxpayers may be in a high bracket only because of a nonrecurring capital gain, it is surely true that many capital gains are reported by investors who are in the top tax bracket every year.

When capital gains are taxed more lightly than ordinary income, taxpayers and their advisors devote considerable energy and ingenuity to arranging transactions that result in capital gains rather than ordinary income. Opponents of a capital-gains preference suggest that these efforts might better be devoted to more-productive pursuits that would contribute to society's wealth.

You have already begun to encounter one unfortunate byproduct of the capital-gains preference: mind-numbing complexity. The tax law could be simplified considerably if the capital-ordinary distinction were abolished.

(6) *Rationale for limiting deductions for capital losses.* As we have seen, a corporation can deduct capital losses only against capital gains; an individual's capital losses in excess of capital gains are deductible only within the limits of § 1211(b). In part, the limits may stem from some sort of desire for symmetry: if capital gain is taxed more favorably than ordinary income, capital loss should be treated less favorably than ordinary loss. But it makes little sense to say that because successful investors get favorable treatment for their gains, the losses of unsuccessful investors should be limited.

A more-substantial reason for limiting the deductibility of capital losses against ordinary income is derived from the taxpayer's ability to control the timing of capital losses. Recall that it is only the *net* capital gain that is subject to preferred treatment. If a year's capital losses in excess of capital gains were fully deductible against ordinary income, a taxpayer could subvert the policy requiring netting of capital gains and losses by selling gain and loss assets in alternate years.

If capital losses were fully deductible, a taxpayer with a large ordinary income and with a stock portfolio steadily increasing in value might pay no tax simply by selling off enough loss stocks each year to wipe out ordinary income while retaining the gain stocks. See generally Warren, The Deductibility By Individuals of Capital Losses Under the Federal Income Tax, 40 U.Chi.L.Rev. 291 (1973).

References. Cunningham & Schenk, The Case for a Capital–Gains Preference, 48 Tax Law Review 319 (1993); Repetti, The Use of Tax Law to Stabilize the Stock Market: The Efficacy of Holding Period Requirements, 8 Va. Tax Rev. 591 (1989); Blum, A Handy Summary of the Capital Gains Arguments, 35 Taxes 247 (1957).

B. THE SALE–OR–EXCHANGE REQUIREMENT

In explaining the computation of realized gain or loss, § 1001(a) refers to the "sale or other disposition of property." Section 1222, however, limits *capital* gains and losses to those from the "sale or exchange" of capital assets. This difference in phrasing might be read as suggesting that there are taxable dispositions of property that are not "sales" or "exchanges," although § 1001(c)'s reference to recognition of "gain or loss, determined under this section, on the sale or exchange of property" might support the opposite conclusion. In any event, the language of § 1001 should not be overanalyzed, since the legislative history shows that Congress did not mean that section to have any real effect; it was enacted to spell out clearly how gains and losses always had been calculated and to make it clear that property-for-property exchanges are taxable, except as otherwise provided in the Code.[k]

Relying more on the "ordinary" meaning of "sale or exchange" than on subtle technical analysis of the statute, the courts have held that

k. See Kilbourn, Puzzling Problems in Property Settlements—The Tax Anatomy of Divorce, 27 Mo.L.Rev. 354, 380–83 (1962).

some taxable dispositions are not sales or exchanges and therefore do not result in capital gain or loss even if the property disposed of is a capital asset.

NAHEY v. COMMISSIONER

United States Tax Court, 1998.
111 T.C. 256 (1998), affirmed 196 F.3d 866 (7th Cir.1999).

JACOBS, JUDGE:

* * *

[Somewhat simplified, the facts are as follows: In 1983, Wehr Corporation, a manufacturer and distributor of industrial equipment, entered into a contract with Xerox Corporation for the installation of a sophisticated computer system, which it thought would give it a competitive edge in its marketplace. Although the contract required the installation to be completed by December 31, 1984, Xerox fell behind from the beginning and continually missed target dates. In 1985 Wehr filed suit against Xerox for breach of contract, fraud and misrepresentation. While the suit was pending, Xerox offered to settle the claim for up to $2 million, but Wehr rejected the offer. In 1986, the petitioners purchased the assets of Wehr, including Wehr's claim against Xerox, and continued Wehr's business. Although petitioners believed that the Xerox claim had substantial value (based upon the settlement offer), the petitioners' accountants refused to assign any part of the purchase price to the claim on the ground that it was "too speculative"; hence the claim had a zero basis in the petitioners' hands. In 1992 the parties settled the case for $6 million.]

The sole issue for decision herein is whether the proceeds received by the [petitioners] * * * from the settlement of Wehr's lawsuit against Xerox (the settlement proceeds) should be characterized as ordinary income or long-term capital gain. The resolution of this issue turns on whether the requirements for obtaining capital gain treatment are satisfied, including whether the settlement of Wehr's lawsuit against Xerox constitutes a "sale or exchange."

* * *

A sale or exchange is a prerequisite to the rendering of capital gain treatment. Sec. 1222; [other citations omitted.]. The phrase "sale or exchange" is not defined in section 1222, but we apply the ordinary meaning to those words. Helvering v. William Flaccus Oak Leather Co., 313 U.S. 247, 249 (1941).

It is well established that a compromise or collection of a debt is not considered a sale or exchange of property because no property or property rights passes to the debtor other than the discharge of the obligation. [Citations omitted.] In this regard, whatever property or property rights might have existed vanish as a result of the compromise or collection. Leh v. Commissioner, 27 T.C. 892, 898 (1957), affd. 260 F.2d 489 (9th Cir.1958).

On several occasions we have addressed the issue of whether a sale or exchange occurred on the payment of a judgment or the settlement of a claim. [Citations omitted.] In Fahey v. Commissioner, [16 T.C. 105 (1951)] supra, we held that where an attorney was assigned an interest in a contingent lawsuit fee in exchange for a cash payment, settlement of the lawsuit and payment of the fee to the attorney did not give rise to capital gain treatment because no sale or exchange occurred. In reaching our conclusion, we quoted from the opinion of the Court of Appeals for the District of Columbia in Hale v. Helvering, [85 F.2d 819 (D.C.Cir. 1936)] supra (relating to the compromise of a note for less than face value):

> There was no acquisition of property by the debtor, no transfer of property to him. Neither business men nor lawyers call the compromise of a note a sale to the maker. In point of law and in legal parlance property in the notes as capital assets was extinguished, not sold. In business parlance the transaction was a settlement and the notes were turned over to the maker, not sold to him. * * *

Fahey v. Commissioner, supra at 109.

In Hudson v. Commissioner, [20 T.C. 734 (1953)] supra, the taxpayers purchased a 50–percent interest in a judgment from the legatees of an estate, and subsequently the taxpayers settled the judgment with the debtor. The taxpayers reported the payment of the judgment as capital gain. We held that the payment should be characterized as ordinary income, explaining:

> We cannot see how there was a transfer of property, or how the judgment debtor acquired property as the result of the transaction wherein the judgment was settled. The most that can be said is that the judgment debtor paid a debt or extinguished a claim so as to preclude the execution on the judgment outstanding against him. In a hypothetical case, if the judgment had been transferred to someone other than the judgment debtor, the property transferred would still be in existence after the transaction was completed. However, as it actually happened, when the judgment debtor settled the judgment, the claim arising from the judgment was extinguished without the transfer of any property or property right to the judgment debtor. In their day-to-day transactions, neither businessmen nor lawyers would call the settlement of a judgment a sale; we can see no reason to apply a strained interpretation to the transaction before us. When petitioners received the $21,150 in full settlement of the judgment, they did not recover the money as a result of any sale or exchange but only as a collection or settlement of the judgment.

Id. at 736.

Despite these and other similar cases, petitioners contend that the passing of property or property rights to the debtor is not relevant in determining whether a sale or exchange occurred. In support of this argument, petitioners direct us to Commissioner v. Ferrer, 304 F.2d 125 (2d Cir.1962), revg. in part and remanding 35 T.C. 617 (1961). In *Ferrer*, the taxpayer acquired from an author the right to produce a play (based on the author's book) which included the right to prevent the author's transfer of film rights. Subsequently, the taxpayer surrendered his rights (the "lease") in exchange for the leading role in a film production. The issue arose as to whether the surrendering of the taxpayer's rights constituted a sale or exchange for purposes of the capital gain provisions. In holding that a sale or exchange of the surrendered lease occurred, the Court of Appeals for the Second Circuit stated that Congress was disenchanted with the "formalistic distinction" between a sale of property rights to third parties (which would give rise to capital gain or loss) and the release of those rights that results in their extinguishment (and which would not give rise to capital gain or loss). The court continued:

> In the instant case we can see no sensible business basis for drawing a line between a release of Ferrer's rights * * * and a sale of them[.] * * * Tax law is concerned with the substance, here the voluntary passing of "property" rights allegedly constituting "capital assets," not with whether they are passed to a stranger or to a person already having a larger "estate." * * *

Id. at 131.

Petitioners have misread *Ferrer* and its import. *Ferrer* (and the cases cited therein) can be factually distinguished from the instant case because in *Ferrer* the taxpayer's interest (or lease) to produce the play and prevent the author's transfer of film rights did not disappear but instead reverted to the author after the taxpayer surrendered the lease; whereas in the instant case, the [petitioners'] * * * rights in the lawsuit vanished both in form and substance upon the receipt of the settlement proceeds.

In the case herein, the [petitioners] * * * and Xerox settled the lawsuit originally brought by Wehr. The [petitioners] * * * received consideration of $6,345,183; Xerox received nothing other than the discharge of the liability that arose as the result of the lawsuit. We find no discernible distinction between the situation herein and the situations discussed in Fahey v. Commissioner, supra, or Hudson v. Commissioner, supra. In each case, the debtor made payment to the creditor or an assignee of the original creditor in exchange for the extinguishment of the claim. Whether the claim is reduced to judgment before payment is not relevant; ultimately the debtor receives nothing in the form of property or property rights which can later be transferred. Consequently, we hold that the settlement of the lawsuit between the [petitioners] * * * and Xerox does not constitute a sale or exchange and hence capital gain treatment is not warranted.

* * *

* * * Inasmuch as petitioners allocated no part of the purchase price for Wehr's assets to the Xerox lawsuit, they acquired no basis in the lawsuit. Thus, the entire settlement proceeds are includable in gross income.

Decision will be entered for respondent.

Notes and Questions

1. *Involuntary conversions.* In Helvering v. William Flaccus Oak Leather Co., 313 U.S. 247 (1941), the Supreme Court held that the burning of the taxpayer's factory and the taxpayer's receipt of insurance proceeds did not constitute a sale or exchange. Today, the character of the gain or loss on most involuntary conversions is determined under § 1231 or § 165(h), discussed at pp. 632–635.

Suppose that in *Sager Glove*, p. 134, the taxpayer had been able to establish that the settlement payment received by it was compensation for destruction of its goodwill (a capital asset with a basis of zero) instead of lost profits. Would the damage recovery have been treated as a capital gain? Big Four Industries, Inc. v. Commissioner, 40 T.C. 1055 (1963) (Acq.), treated a similar recovery as capital gain. Is *Big Four Industries* consistent with *William Flaccus Oak Leather Co.*?

The taking of the taxpayer's property by condemnation has been held to be a sale or exchange. Hawaiian Gas Products v. Commissioner, 126 F.2d 4 (9th Cir.1942), cert. denied 317 U.S. 653 (1942). Today, § 1231 prescribes the character of many condemnation gains and losses.

2. *Receipt by creditor in satisfaction of a claim.* As *Nahey* points out, receipt of payment by a creditor was not traditionally viewed as a sale or exchange because the obligation was extinguished by the payment. The amount received by the taxpayer was therefore characterized as ordinary income to the extent that it exceeded his basis in the claim. But the Code has long treated the retirement of an obligation by a corporate obligor as an exchange; § 1271(a). The predecessor of this provision was enacted during the depression to prevent the holders of bonds from claiming ordinary losses when their bonds were retired for less than the full principal amount. In 1997, Congress extended exchange treatment to satisfaction of debt instruments on which a natural person is obligor, thus overruling the *Hudson* case discussed in *Nahey*; see § 1271(b). Even if the debt instrument is a capital asset and § 1271 supplies the exchange, a gain may nevertheless be ordinary income under the market-discount rules discussed at p. 400, above.

3. *Transfer of property in satisfaction of debtor's obligation.* Suppose *D* owes *C* $100. To satisfy the claim, *D* transfers to *C* a capital asset with a basis of $40 and a value of $100. Does *D*'s $60 recognized gain arise from a sale or exchange? Yes. See, e.g., Peninsula Properties Co. Ltd. v. Commissioner, 47 B.T.A. 84 (1942) (Acq.); cf. Rev.Rul. 69–181, 1969–1 C.B. 196 (holding gain capital without discussion of the sale-or-exchange issue). Such cases can be thought of as involving the taxpayer's

sale of the property for cash and the transfer of the proceeds to the creditor. See also Kenan v. Commissioner, 114 F.2d 217 (2d Cir.1940) (estate's transfer of property in satisfaction of a pecuniary bequest was a sale or exchange by the estate).

4. *Conveyance of mortgaged property to mortgagee.* Suppose a mortgagor conveys the mortgaged property to the mortgagee. Where the mortgagor was not personally liable on the indebtedness, early cases held that the conveyance was not a sale or exchange by the mortgagor because the mortgagor received no consideration for the transfer.[*l*] More-recent cases and rulings hold that these conveyances of property subject to non-recourse indebtedness are sales or exchanges. See Freeland v. Commissioner, 74 T.C. 970 (1980) (overruling contrary decisions); Rev. Rul. 78–164, 1978–1 C.B. 264; cf. Yarbro v. Commissioner, 737 F.2d 479 (5th Cir.1984) (taxpayer's abandonment of property subject to non-recourse debt, followed by lender's foreclosure, treated as sale or exchange). A foreclosure sale is a sale within the meaning of § 1222, there being no intent on the part of Congress to differentiate between a forced sale and a voluntary one. Helvering v. Hammel, 311 U.S. 504 (1941).

5. *Statutory sales and exchanges.* In a number of instances the Code provides that transactions which normally would not (or might not) be "sales or exchanges" are to be treated as sales or exchanges. See, for example, § 331 (amount received by a shareholder in liquidation of a corporation); § 1241 (payment received by lessee or distributor of goods for cancellation of a lease or distributor's agreement); § 1271(a)(1) (amount received on retirement of debt instrument) (discussed above); § 165(g) (losses on worthless securities); § 166(d) (loss on non-business bad debt); § 1231 (certain gains and losses on involuntary conversions). In 1997, Congress added § 1234A (gain or loss on cancellation, lapse, expiration, or other termination of a right or obligation with respect to capital-asset property). If § 1234A had applied to the year in question in *Nahey*, would the case have come out the same way?

C.   CAPITAL ASSETS

1.   SECTIONS 1221(a)(1) AND 1231(b)(1)(A) & (B)

ESTATE OF SIMPSON v. COMMISSIONER

Tax Court of the United States, 1962.
21 T.C.M. 371.

BRUCE, JUDGE: [Josephine Clay, the owner of a 417–acre farm, died in 1920, leaving the property to her daughters for life, remainder to her

---

l. The courts have long held that, where the taxpayer is personally liable on the mortgage obligation, a transfer of the property to the mortgagee in settlement of the mortgage obligation is a sale or exchange. E.g., Stamler v. Commissioner, 145 F.2d 37 (3d Cir.1944). It was apparently easier to find that a sale or exchange had occurred in these cases because the taxpayer received consideration for the transfer in the form of a release from liability.

grandchildren. Upon the death of Josephine Clay's daughter Mary Anderson in 1930, Clay Simpson, Eugene E. Simpson, Josephine Clay Simpson, Henry Clay Anderson, and Matthew W. Anderson became the owners of the tract.]

* * *

This land had been actively farmed. After the death of Mary W. Anderson in 1930, the profits from farming operations were shared equally by the five heirs. The profits from farming were small in relation to the value of the property. Efforts were made by the five heirs to sell the entire tract. No satisfactory offer to purchase the entire tract was obtained. In 1934 or 1935, two pieces of the property, containing a total of approximately 10 acres, were sold to the Lexington School System. A little later, a lot containing approximately one-half acre was sold to an individual.

In about 1936, the five heirs orally agreed to subdivide a portion of the property into lots and sell the lots. Clay Simpson conducted the necessary business relative to such development and sale on behalf of all the heirs and received a commission of 5 percent of the gross sales prices of lots sold. The proceeds from the sales of lots, less specified expenses, were shared equally by the five heirs. During the period 1936 through 1945, Clay consulted with the other heirs with respect to improvements and "asking prices" on various lots.

In connection with the management of the development of the tract, Clay rented an office in the Blackstone Building in Lexington, obtained a telephone, hired a stenographer-bookkeeper, and established a bank account under the name "Clay Estate." Since 1936, Clay has held a real estate broker's license. Records were kept and deeds prepared under his supervision.

* * *

From 1936 through 1945, portions of the 417–acre tract were subdivided into lots and the lots sold. The name "Chevy Chase Subdivision" was given to the developed areas. From 1936 through 1945, 13 different plats of units of Chevy Chase Subdivision were approved by the Lexington–Fayette County City Planning and Zoning Commission. The general method of development was as follows: A small portion of the land was surveyed, improved, subdivided into lots and the lots sold. After the sale of these lots, the proceeds of sale, less expenses, were used to the extent necessary to survey, improve and subdivide another portion. The unused sales proceeds were divided equally among the five heirs. The development involved employing a surveyor for the platting and a contractor for the improvements. These improvements included blacktop street paving, generally curbs and gutters, water mains, sometimes storm sewers, sanitary sewers, and grading when needed. Also, electric and gas lines were made available by the utility companies. In most cases sidewalks were installed but not fire hydrants.

* * *

Prior to 1945 the five heirs had, on two occasions, divided among themselves small amounts of acreage in the 417–acre tract. In 1945 or 1946 the remaining undeveloped land in the 417–acre tract was divided among them. To accomplish this, the undeveloped land was surveyed and divided into three parcels. A parcel containing 152.33 acres and representing 60 percent in value was received by the Simpsons. The other parcels were transferred to the Anderson heirs. Deeds dated November 23, 1945, and February 14, 1946, were executed by the parties concerned to effect this division.

From 1946 through the taxable years, portions of the 152.33–acre tract which was received by the Simpsons have from time to time been developed, subdivided into lots, and the lots sold. The development has continued under the name "Chevy Chase Subdivision" and the manner of development has been similar to that which prevailed prior to 1946. The number of lots in Chevy Chase Subdivision sold, the total sales price of such lots, and the cost of the lots and improvements to the lots sold for each of the years 1936 through 1955 are as follows:

Year	Lots Sold	Total Sales Price	Total Cost of Land and Improvements
1936	13	$ 25,925.00	$13,945.49
1937	60	73,275.00	40,218.48
1938	57	77,115.00	36,341.79
1939	39	48,665.00	23,661.80
1940	29	53,096.00	25,750.58
1941	20	26,491.00	8,334.07
1942	8	10,316.00	3,648.86
1943	20	26,300.00	8,403.96
1944	7	9,342.00	3,211.40
1945	4	6,142.00	949.42
1946	17	29,850.00	12,906.27
1947	18	32,441.00	12,468.00
1948	15	36,302.50	14,668.25
1949	16	46,145.00	18,484.25
1950	37	102,765.50	39,516.00
1951	39	115,353.44	39,520.50
1952	19	63,330.00	17,559.25
1953	13	71,008.62	16,744.00
1954	14	77,962.50	16,179.80
1955	21	109,693.75	25,010.20

The proceeds from the sale of lots after 1945, less all expenses incurred in connection with the development of the property and sale of lots, including compensation for Clay and the office expenses, were shared equally by the Simpsons. During the period 1946 through 1955, 16 plats of units of the Chevy Chase Subdivision were approved by the Planning and Zoning Commission.

During the years 1936 through 1955, when land in Lexington, Fayette County, Kentucky, was subdivided, it was mandatory that the plats be approved and that specified improvements be made to the land before the lots were offered for sale. Streets had to meet specifications, as did sidewalks, sewers and drains, and water mains.

Most of the lots in the Chevy Chase Subdivision have been sold to home builders usually on terms of 10 percent of the purchase price down with the balance payable within 9 months with no interest on the unpaid balance. The other lots in the subdivision have been sold to individuals. In some instances, notes secured by mortgages on the property sold have been taken by the Simpsons in payment for lots sold to individuals. At various times, Clay, as agent for the Simpsons, has loaned money to contractors who purchased lots in the subdivision to enable them to construct houses on lots purchased, receiving notes for the amount of the loans. The interest rates provided for in the notes received by the Simpsons from purchasers of lots and contractors have been 5 to 6 percent.

In 1941 and 1942 Clay, as agent for the heirs, had six houses built on lots in Chevy Chase Subdivision. These houses were built primarily as a convenience to the contractors who constructed them, so that the contractors could keep their building crews employed and intact. In two cases, houses were built on lots which were not saleable otherwise. Profits on the sales of the houses were shared by the heirs and the contractors.

During the period 1936 through the present time, Lexington, Kentucky, has been an expanding city. Chevy Chase Subdivision, located on land which was a part of or adjacent to the original Clay estate and near "Ashland," the home of Henry Clay, is among the most desirable properties for residential purposes in the Lexington area. Subdivided, it has been readily saleable. There has been little or no advertising of the lots in Chevy Chase Subdivision. During all of the years here involved, Clay spent approximately two hours a day during the week at the office and approximately 10 to 12 hours a year in making sales of the lots. Usually the lots were sought out by prospective purchasers and Clay was required to exert little effort to sell. No other property was purchased by the Simpsons during the period 1936 through the present time for subdividing or selling.

* * *

Approximately 80 percent of the income of Eugene and Marguerite Simpson for the years 1953, 1954, and 1955 was derived from sources other than farming.

Respondent determined that total gains by petitioners on sales of land in the years noted constituted ordinary income and not capital gains as reported by petitioners.

The Simpsons did not hold the subject property primarily for sale to customers in the ordinary course of any business of theirs.

* * *

OPINION

The Simpson heirs and their cousins inherited a tract of farm land of about 417 acres in 1930. They sought to dispose of this property to their best advantage. When they found themselves unable to get satisfactory offers for purchase of the entire property or large parcels, they resorted to sale of it by lots. Clay Simpson, acting for all the heirs, attended to the subdividing, developing, and selling of portions of the property by lots. In 1945 the heirs arranged a division of the unsold property between the Andersons and the Simpsons. Thereafter, Clay Simpson carried on the liquidation of the part acquired by himself, his brother, and his sister, continuing with the process of subdividing and developing parts of it from time to time to make it saleable.

The respondent determined that the petitioners realized ordinary income from the sales of lots in the taxable years, holding that the lots were property held for sale to customers in the course of the business of the Simpson heirs. Section 117, Internal Revenue Code of 1939; section 1221, Internal Revenue Code of 1954. The petitioners contend that their sale of lots was the orderly liquidation of a capital asset, the inherited land, and that they were not in business in selling the lots.

Inherited real property, as such, is a capital asset. If it is sold as a unit, any gains realized by the heirs are generally regarded as capital gains. If it becomes necessary to sell in parts in order to realize a better price, that fact alone does not convert the parts into property held for sale to customers in a business of the heirs. Smith v. Dunn, 224 F.2d 353 (C.A.5, 1955); Camp v. Murray, 226 F.2d 931 (C.A.4, 1955); Allen Moore, 30 T.C. 1306 (1958). The heirs may engage an agent to develop and sell the property piecemeal, and although the agent is engaged in business, the heirs are not necessarily in business and holding the property for sale to their customers by virtue of the acts of the agent. Estate of William D. Mundy, 36 T.C. 703 (1961); Smith v. Dunn, supra.

The problem of whether real estate is held primarily for sale to customers in the ordinary course of business has been considered by the courts on numerous occasions. Criteria have been mentioned in the various opinions which may have weight in resolving the issue in a particular case. Among these have been the purpose or reason for the acquisition of the property; the number, frequency and volume of sales; the extent to which the owner or his agent engaged in sales activities, by developing, improving, and advertising the property; and whether the taxpayer continued to purchase more properties during the period as part of a basic plan of buying and selling real estate. Standards which may be significant in some settings, however, are of little aid in others. No single factor is necessarily controlling and each case turns upon its own facts. The issue here depends upon the intention of the heirs at the time of selling, whether it is to liquidate the property or to engage in the real estate business, using their land as stock held for sale. The heirs originally planned to liquidate. If the heirs changed their intention there must be evidence to show such a change. Their intent is to be deduced from all the facts and circumstances. In cases where it has been held that heirs were holding real property for sale to customers in the ordinary course of their trade or business, the evidence was regarded as showing that the heirs had changed their intention from that of liquidation to that of engaging in the real estate business for profit. Brown v. Commissioner, 143 F.2d 468 (C.A.5, 1944), affirming a Memorandum Opinion of this Court; Ehrman v. Commissioner, 120 F.2d 607 (C.A.9, 1941), affirming 41 B.T.A. 652 (1940), certiorari denied 314 U.S. 668 (1941).

The respondent contends that if a liquidating operation is conducted with the usual attributes of a business accompanied by frequent sales and a continuity of transactions, the operation is then a business and the proceeds of sales are taxable as ordinary income, and that the activities of the heirs in this case in disposing of the property amount to the carrying on of a trade or business. The respondent says that Clay Simpson, by agreement with all the heirs, has handled all the activities relative to development of the property and sale of lots since 1936, conducting the operation for a time as "Clay Estate" and later as "Simpson Realty Company," and that it is of no consequence that the other heirs did not actively participate as his activities are properly attributable to them. The argument is that sales have been frequent, continuous over a long period and in substantial amounts; that development of units prior to sale has been extensive and involved substantial expenditures; that maintaining an office, bookkeeper-stenographer, telephone listing, stationery with letterhead of "Simpson Realty Company," and broker's license all indicate a business operation; that Clay Simpson devoted much time and effort to the development and sale of lots; that partnership returns filed for the heirs listed "subdivision" or "sale of land" as the principal business of the partnership; and that sales promotion activities were extensive.

The fact that a liquidation of a capital asset consisting of real property may involve a number of sales of small parcels over a considerable period of time is not conclusive that the owners have changed their intent to that of engaging in business. In Chandler v. United States, 226 F.2d 403 (C.A.7, 1955), a corporation was liquidating from 1915 to 1950 its holdings of over a million acres of land and sold over 290,000 acres in the period from 1942 to 1950 in 536 transactions. This was held to warrant capital gains treatment. In Garrett v. United States, 120 F.Supp. 193 (Ct.Cl.1954), the taxpayers inherited certain beach property, previously divided into lots, and sought to liquidate the property. One of the heirs devoted most of his time to the property and the estate, maintained an office, placed signs on the property, and received fees as executor and commissions on the sale of lots for the benefit of the heirs, proceeds being deposited to the credit of the estate. The liquidation continued from 1925 to 1946. This was held to be a liquidating operation and the proceeds taxable as capital gains. In these cases the intent of the owners to liquidate was deemed established by the evidence.

The fact that sales were frequent and continuous is not conclusive that the owners were in a business. Fahs v. Crawford, 161 F.2d 315 (C.A.5, 1947); Delsing v. United States, 186 F.2d 59 (C.A.5, 1951).

It is apparent in the present case that the heirs had no purpose other than an orderly liquidation of the inherited farm land. The growth of the city of Lexington made this land suitable for potential home sites. The heirs had been unable to sell the entire property as a unit and unable to get offers for substantial parts at any price considered reasonable. The possibility of selling a part of it as lots suitable for residence purposes seemed the only practicable way of disposing of their land at its fair value. They did not then foresee the extent or duration of the liquidation. To subdivide and lay out in lots the entire property and install the facilities required by the local government to make it saleable was a large operation and might have overtaxed their resources. Hence, the platting of one small tract at a time and its sale appeared to be a proper step in an orderly liquidation.

Josephine was a homemaker and without business experience. Eugene was a farmer. Clay had been in the oil brokerage business, but gave that up on account of his health. He had no prior experience in real estate. He was able to give some of his time to serving as agent for all the heirs in the matter of disposing of the inherited land. He arranged with surveyors to lay out subdivisions from time to time and filed the plats as agent for the owners. He kept an office open for prospective purchasers and placed signs upon the property. He kept the records for the heirs and divided the receipts with them.

* * *

The development of subdivisions was not an extensive operation. There was no advertising. Builders asked for lots and bought two or three at a time. No sales effort was necessary. Development included surveying and laying out lots, a certain amount of leveling and clearing of the land, construction of streets, sidewalks, and curbs, installing sewers and water, and making available electric lines and gas lines. This was the minimum development essential to compliance with local ordinances and to make the lots saleable. Clay devoted only a few hours each year to the matter of negotiating sales and only a small part of his time to the other steps. His having a broker's license was a precaution to avoid any violation of local law.

The heirs never bought additional land for sale. They bought and operated a farm some eight miles from Lexington, and Josephine and Clay acquired another farm some miles away. Clay made a very few sales of land for other persons as agent in the period 1936 to 1952.

Considering all the facts of this case, we have found that the lots sold from the Chevy Chase Subdivision in the taxable years were not property held for sale to customers in a trade or business of the Simpson heirs.

* * *

Problem, Notes and Question

1. *The subdivision cases.* What result in *Simpson's Estate* if the heirs, in order to get a "reasonable" price for the land, had found it necessary to build houses on all the lots before selling them?

In Biedenharn Realty Co. v. United States, 526 F.2d 409 (5th Cir.1976), cert. denied 429 U.S. 819 (1976), the taxpayer bought land as an investment but decided to subdivide and sell when a nearby city expanded in the direction of the land. Because of the "substantiality and frequency of sales, improvements, solicitation and advertising efforts, and broker's activities," the majority found that the taxpayer was engaged in a trade or business and that the lots were disposed of in the ordinary course of that business. The court placed "greatest emphasis on the frequency and substantiality of sales over an extended time period," and also relied on the "vigorous" improvements made. The profits in *Biedenharn Realty* came from the sale of 38 lots over a three-year period; over a longer period the taxpayer had sold 208 lots from the tract in question and several hundred other lots. Five dissenting judges felt that the majority's emphasis on improvements and frequency of sales in a case in which the taxpayer's initial purpose was investment "discriminates irrationally against an investor who decides on liquidation but cannot locate purchasers interested in large acquisitions." Is the dissent's "discrimination" argument persuasive? Should a liquor store owner get capital-gain treatment on the sale of Scotch whisky to prevent "discrimination" in favor of those who hold bulk whisky as an investment?

The law applicable to the much-litigated "subdivision" cases was summarized in a luncheon talk by James L. Wood, reported in 35 Taxes 804, 806 (1957):

> If a client asks in any but an extreme case whether, in your opinion, his sale will result in capital gain, your answer should probably be "I don't know, and no one else in town can tell you."

2. *Section 1237.* Read § 1237, which was intended as a "safe harbor" provision for investors who find it necessary to subdivide land in order to sell it. Section 1237 has benefitted taxpayers very little because its requirements for avoiding ordinary-income treatment are usually more stringent than those imposed by case law.

3. *"Business" and "purpose" under § 1221(a)(1).* The threshold problem in determining whether property is "held by the taxpayer primarily for sale to customers in the ordinary course of his trade or business" is whether the taxpayer has a "trade or business." A taxpayer whose activities are so frequent or intensive that he is held to be in

"business" (in the rather literal sense of "busy-ness") is said to be a "dealer" in the property sold to that business's customers. Much of the real-estate litigation focuses on the question whether the taxpayer is a "dealer." If not, gains and losses will be capital. If so, does it necessarily follow that they will all be ordinary?

Problem. T is a dealer in real estate. In 1997, T purchased a tract of unimproved land for $50,000. T expected that the property would provide security for her old age because of its expected long-term appreciation. T never advertised the property for sale. In 2003, the property is condemned, and T receives $75,000 for her interest. (Assume that § 1033 does not apply and that T's gain is capital gain unless the property falls within § 1221(a)(1).) T also realizes $30,000 in stock-market losses in 2003. To what extent are the losses deductible?

4. *References.* Johnson, Seventeen Culls From Capital Gains, 48 Tax Notes 1285 (1990); Surrey, Definitional Problems in Capital Gains Taxation, 69 Harv.L.Rev. 985 (1956).

KEMON v. COMMISSIONER

Tax Court of the United States, 1951.
16 T.C. 1026 (Acq.).

[The Tax Court's findings of fact are omitted.]

OPINION

ARUNDELL, JUDGE: The respondent has determined that securities disposed of by Lilley & Co. during the years in question were not capital assets * * *. In support of his determination, the respondent argues that Lilley & Co. was a "dealer" holding the securities primarily for sale to customers in the ordinary course of business.

Whether or not securities are held primarily for sale to customers in the ordinary course of business is a question of fact, Stern Brothers & Co., 16 T.C. 295, in which the crucial phrase is "to customers." This phrase and the word "ordinary" were added to the definition of capital assets by Senate Amendment No. 66 in the Revenue Act of 1934 so that a speculator trading on his own account could not claim the securities he sold were other than capital assets. The theory of the amendment was that those who sell securities on an exchange have no "customers" and for that reason the property held by such taxpayers is not within the above quoted exclusionary clause. O.L. Burnett, 40 B.T.A. 605, 118 F.2d 659; Thomas E. Wood, 16 T.C. 213.

In determining whether a seller of securities sells to "customers," the merchant analogy has been employed. [Citations omitted.] Those who sell "to customers" are comparable to a merchant in that they purchase their stock in trade, in this case securities, with the expectation of reselling at a profit, not because of a rise in value during the interval of time between purchase and resale, but merely because they have or hope to find a market of buyers who will purchase from them at a price in excess of their cost. This excess or mark-up represents remuneration for their labors as a middle man bringing together buyer and seller, and performing the usual services of retailer or wholesaler of goods. [Citations omitted.] Such sellers are known as "dealers."

Contrasted to "dealers" are those sellers of securities who perform no such merchandising functions and whose status as to the source of supply is not significantly different from that of those to whom they sell. That is, the securities are as easily accessible to one as the other and the seller performs no services that need be compensated for by a mark-up of the price of the securities he sells. The sellers depend upon such circumstances as a rise in value or an advantageous purchase to enable them to sell at a price in excess of cost. Such sellers are known as "traders."

The securities sold by Lilley & Co. were held for widely varying lengths of time. Some were sold on the day of purchase; others were held for periods in excess of 3 years. We need not determine whether those held for not more than 6 months were capital assets. It may well be that as to them, the firm's status was that of a dealer holding securities primarily for sale to customers, but since the gains on their sale were reported in full and the losses were not in excess of these gains, the correctness of the asserted deficiency in nowise depends upon whether or not the securities were capital assets. Furthermore, the fact that the firm's status as to these securities was that of either a dealer or trader does not require a determination that the firm occupied the same status as to the remaining securities. Carl Marks & Co., 12 T.C. 1196. See I.T. 3891, 1948–1 C.B. 69.

But whatever the firm's status may be as to the securities held for not more than 6 months, the evidence taken as a whole clearly establishes that as to the remaining securities the firm was a trader holding them primarily for speculation or investment. Specific evidence has been submitted to show that a considerable number of the securities held for more than 6 months were accumulated as part of a program to force a reorganization and gain control of the issuing corporation, or for the realization of a gain when the issuing company redeemed them or issued liquidating dividends. Furthermore, as to these securities, it was the firm's practice to buy in small lots and dispose of them in large blocks. It did not acquire them "to create a stock of securities to take care of future buying orders in excess of selling orders," Schafer v. Helvering, [299 U.S. 171], or always sell to a class of persons different than those from whom it bought. Cf. Van Suetendael v. Commissioner, [152 F.2d 654]. It frequently refused to sell these securities which it was accumulating despite the fact that the bid price would have resulted in a profit. The activity of Lilley & Co. with regard to the securities in question conformed to the customary activity of a trader in securities rather than that of a dealer holding securities primarily for sale to customers.

Respondent has stressed other phases of the firm's activity in support of his argument that the firm is a dealer in securities. He points out that the firm has two regular places of business, is licensed by the State of Pennsylvania as a "dealer," advertises itself as a "dealer," transacts a large volume of business, and subscribes to certain services commonly used by brokers and dealers. These are all significant facts which weigh against petitioners' contention that the firm was a trader. But they are no more conclusive than are other facts which weigh just as heavily in favor of petitioners' contention, such as the fact that the firm had no salesmen, no "customers' men," no customers' accounts, no board room, and has never advertised itself or held itself out to the public as having on hand securities for sale.

After weighing all such factors and analyzing the activity previously referred to, we are of the opinion that Lilley & Co.'s status as to those securities held for more than 6 months was that of a trader holding them for speculation or investment. Therefore, those securities are capital assets and the gain upon their sale or exchange is taxable at capital gains rates.

* * *

Decisions Will Be Entered Under Rule 50.

Note

1. *"To customers."* As the principal case notes, Congress added the phrase "to customers" to the statute during the depths of the depression. Its purpose was to limit the deductibility of stock-market losses, and perhaps because of this narrow aim, sales of real estate in the ordinary course of a trade or business have never been held to produce capital gains or losses on the theory that the buyers were not "customers." Apparently, securities traders are the only people whose sales can be made "in the ordinary course of [a] trade or business" without being made "to customers." While real-estate sellers are either "dealers" or "investors," sellers of stock may be "dealers," or "traders," or "investors." A "trader" is someone who buys and sells securities on a large scale but whose gains and losses are capital because the sales are not "to customers."[m]

A dealer in securities may hold some securities for investment, and gains or losses on the sale of those securities can be capital just as gains or losses from the sale of a real-estate dealer's investment real estate can be capital. Section 1221(a)(1) classifies assets, not taxpayers. Section 1236(a) imposes a record-keeping requirement which must be satisfied if a dealer's gain from the sale of a security is to be a capital gain.

---

m. E.g., Swartz v. Commissioner, 54 T.C.M. 1153 (1987) (losses of full-time commodities trader, who traded through brokers, were capital because sales were not to "customers"). The distinction between "traders" and "investors" is irrelevant under the capital-gain and -loss sections, but matters elsewhere; for example, under § 1091, § 172, § 163(d) and § 62; see, e.g., Estate of Yaeger v. Commissioner, p. 294.

2. NON–CAPITAL ASSETS OTHER THAN INVENTORY

Section 1221(a)(2), as noted above, does not usually mandate ordinary-income treatment for gains on sales of the assets described; instead, it subjects them to § 1231, which is often even better for the taxpayer than capital-gain or-loss treatment.

Sections 1221(a)(3) through 1221(a)(8) exclude several categories of property from "capital-asset" classification. The assets thus excluded are also ineligible for § 1231 treatment, either because of the exclusions of §§ 1231(b)(1)(C) & (D) or because they are not real or depreciable property.

Section 1221(a)(3) reflects the notion that gains from labor are not capital gains. Note the absence of a reference to patents. Would a professional inventor's sale of a patent produce ordinary income because of § 1221(a)(1)? See § 1235(a). The original (1950) version of § 1221(a)(3), which did not include what is now § 1221(a)(3)(B), is called the "Eisenhower amendment." General Eisenhower's well-publicized 1948 sale of his memoirs received capital-gain treatment because he was an amateur author and because he retained no royalty. Sections 1221(a)(3)(B) and 170(e)(1)(A) operate to deny a charitable-contribution deduction to Presidents and others who donate their papers to the United States.

Section 1221(a)(4) deals with a problem faced by accrual-method taxpayers who sold goods or services for notes (or accounts receivable), took the amount of the notes into income, and subsequently realized losses on the sale of the notes. Unless the taxpayer was a dealer in such notes, the losses might have been capital although the income realized on receipt was ordinary. The taxpayer in Burbank Liquidating Corp. v. Commissioner, 39 T.C. 999 (1963), reversed in part on other grounds 335 F.2d 125 (9th Cir.1964), was a savings and loan association which argued that a loss on certain of its notes was ordinary because the notes were described in § 1221(a)(4), which requires that the notes be acquired for "services rendered or from the sale of property." The Tax Court, characterizing the business of a savings and loan association as "rendering the service" of making loans, upheld the taxpayer on this issue. *Burbank* was followed in Rev.Rul. 80–57, 1980–1 C.B. 157. But in Ardela, Inc. v. Commissioner, 28 T.C.M. 470 (1969), the Tax Court denied ordinary-loss treatment to an investment company which had loaned money and incurred losses on the sale of the notes evidencing the debts, observing that the "legislative history clearly indicates that section 1221[(a)](4) was directed to an entirely different problem * * *." The court also ruled that formal approval by the taxpayer's board of directors of all but one of the notes was "inconsistent with the idea that lending money was in the ordinary course of * * * business," so that the notes were not "acquired in the ordinary course of trade or business" as required by § 1221(a)(4).

Section 1221(a)(5) seems to have been aimed more at charitable contributions than at sales. The problem, in this case, was the claiming of deductions under § 170 for the value of free government publications contributed to charities. See § 170(e)(1)(A).

Section 1221(a)(6) is beyond the scope of the basic tax course.

Section 1221(a)(7) excludes hedging transactions from capital-asset treatment. For example, suppose that a manufacturer of products made from corn enters into a contract to deliver its product to a purchaser in six months at a set price. As it needs corn for processing, it buys corn in the local ("spot") market at the then-prevailing market price. That leaves the firm vulnerable to increases in the price of corn, because the price of its output is fixed. To protect itself, the firm buys corn-futures contracts (that is, contracts under which it is entitled to the delivery of corn at some specified future date) at harvest time each year when the price appears to be favorable. As it purchases corn in the spot market for its manufacturing operations, the firm sells the futures contracts. If the price of corn has risen, it will have to pay more in the spot market but will profit on the sale of the futures contracts. If the price of corn decreases, it will lose money on the sale of the futures contracts but make a correspondingly greater profit on the sale of its products. The futures transaction is a "hedge" because the firm uses the instruments primarily to manage the risk of price changes with respect to its ordinary (inventory) property; see § 1221(b)(2). Because § 1221(a)(7) says that the futures contracts are not capital assets in this situation, the resulting gains and losses are ordinary.

Taxpayers might be tempted to whipsaw the government in these transactions by claiming that their losses are ordinary (because resulting from a hedge) but their gains capital (because arising from speculation). Notice how § 1221(a)(7) forecloses that possibility by requiring that a hedging transaction be clearly identified as such on the day it is entered. (The taxpayer's classification, however, is not necessarily binding on the Commissioner; see § 1221(b)(2)(B).)

Treas. Reg. § 1.1221–2(a)(3) states that if a transaction is not a hedging transaction, "gain or loss from the transaction is not made ordinary on the grounds that property involved in the transaction is a surrogate for a noncapital asset" or "serves as insurance against a business risk * * *." This seems finally to put to rest the notion that loss on a sale of stock could be ordinary if the stock was purchased to ensure a source of raw materials; e.g., Booth Newspapers, Inc. v. United States, 303 F.2d 916 (Ct.Cl.1962); Rev. Rul. 58–40, 1958–1 C.B. 275. The authority of the "stock as source of supply" cases had already been seriously eroded by Arkansas Best Corp. v. Commissioner, 485 U.S. 212 (1988) (ordinary loss denied on the disposition of bank stock that the taxpayer claimed to have acquired for business rather than investment purposes). One can read *Arkansas Best* as precluding any extra-statutory exceptions to the capital-asset definition.

Section 1221(a)(8) makes clear that ordinary business supplies are not capital assets. The cost of supplies is usually deducted against ordinary income at the time the supplies are purchased; Treas. Reg.

§ 1.162–3. If the taxpayer deducts the cost of the supplies and then later sells the unconsumed portion, the gain should be ordinary to compensate for the ordinary deduction obtained when the supplies were purchased.

D. QUASI–CAPITAL GAINS AND LOSSES UNDER SECTION 1231

Section 1231 determines the character of gain or loss on three kinds of taxable dispositions of property:

(1) Sales or exchanges of "§ 1231 assets," that is, "property used in the trade or business" as defined in § 1231(b).[n] (Note that the definition of § 1231 assets requires a long-term holding period.)

(2) Condemnations (or dispositions under threat of condemnation) of § 1231 assets and long-term capital assets held in connection with business or investment activity.

(3) Involuntary conversions by destruction or theft of § 1231 assets and long-term capital assets held in connection with business or investment activity.

Section 1231(a)(3) defines the recognized gains from these dispositions as "section 1231 gains" and the allowable[o] losses as "section 1231 losses." Unlike the case of capital gains and losses, the character of § 1231 gains and losses cannot be determined on an asset-by-asset basis. Instead, gains and losses from these transactions are netted in "hotchpot" computations, and the character of the gains and losses depends upon whether the hotchpots produce net gain or loss.

In reading § 1231(a), it may be helpful to begin with § 1231(a)(4)(C), then go back to the beginning of § 1231(a). Section 1231(a)(4)(C) requires what is sometimes called the "firepot" computation. The taxpayer's gains and losses for the year from involuntary conversions due to "fire, storm, shipwreck or other casualty, or from theft" (but *not* condemnation) of § 1231 assets and long-term capital assets held for business or investment are netted. If the result is a net loss (that is, firepot losses exceed firepot gains), § 1231 does not apply to these firepot transactions, and all these gains and losses are ordinary.[p] If the "firepot" computations produce a net gain, the character of the

---

n. A warehouse used in a trade or business and held for more than the long-term holding period would be a § 1231 asset; self-developed goodwill of a business would not be (why?).

o. In determining whether a loss is allowable for this purpose, the limits on the deductibility of capital losses under § 1211 are necessarily disregarded. Until the loss is characterized as ordinary or capital, we do not know whether the limits of § 1211 apply.

p. Because of Helvering v. William Flaccus Oak Leather Co., 313 U.S. 247 (1941), which held that a taxpayer's gain from the destruction of its buildings and machinery and the receipt of insurance proceeds in excess of basis was ordinary income for lack of a "sale or exchange." (The assets were capital assets because the case involved a year before the enactment of what is now § 1221(a)(2).)

firepot gains and losses (as well as other § 1231 gains and losses) depends upon the outcome of the "hotchpot" computation.

The § 1231 "hotchpot" includes all gains and losses from the sale or exchange of § 1231 assets, all gains and losses from the condemnation of § 1231 assets and long-term business or investment capital assets, and all firepot gains and losses (*unless* the firepot computation produces a net loss). If the hotchpot produces a net gain, all of the hotchpot gains and losses are treated as long-term capital gains and losses. If the hotchpot does not produce a net gain, all the hotchpot gains and losses are ordinary.

Problems, Notes and Questions

1. *Problems.* Except as otherwise stated, assume in each of these problems that all assets have been held for more than the long-term holding period:

(1) *A* recognizes a $10,000 loss from the destruction by fire of an uninsured truck used in *A*'s business, a $30,000 gain from the condemnation of land held as an investment, and a $5000 loss from the sale of a warehouse used in the business. What is the character of each of these gains and losses?

(2) Same as (1), except that the loss on the sale of the warehouse was $50,000.

(3) Same as (1), except that the warehouse had been held for only five months before the sale.

(4) Same as (1), except that the $30,000 gain resulted from the condemnation of *A*'s vacation home.

2. *Recapture of loss under § 1231(c).* Before the enactment of § 1231(c) in 1984, business taxpayers could thwart the netting requirement of § 1231(a) by selling loss assets in one year and gain assets in the next. Under § 1231(c), a person who has $10,000 of § 1231 loss in year 1 and $12,000 of § 1231 gain in year 2 would have to treat $10,000 of the year-2 gain as ordinary.

Problem (1). S had § 1231 gains and losses as follows:

Year 1	$5000 loss
Year 2	$4000 gain
Year 3	$3000 gain

Characterize the gain or loss for each year as ordinary or capital.

Problem (2). In the current year *T* has realized $30,000 in stock-market losses. Near the end of the year, *T* considers the sale of two § 1231 assets, a tract of land that will produce a gain of $30,000 and a piece of machinery that will produce a loss of $30,000. How can *T* maximize the tax benefits from these sales?

3. *Background of §§ 1231 and 1221(a)(2).* Until 1938, land, buildings, and machinery were capital assets except when held for sale by a

dealer. Gains and losses on the sale (including condemnation) of such assets were, therefore, capital gains and losses, but gains or losses from their destruction were ordinary for lack of a sale or exchange under the *Flaccus Oak Leather* case. In 1938 Congress removed depreciable business assets from the capital-asset category in order to give ordinary-loss deductions to business taxpayers who sold such property. Capital-loss treatment discouraged sales of depreciable business property, since the taxpayer could get ordinary deductions by keeping the property and taking depreciation deductions.

When World War II broke out, "ordinary" treatment of gains on dispositions of depreciable business property, whether by sale, condemnation, or insured casualty, caused hardship. In 1942, Congress enacted the predecessor of § 1231 in order to: (1) continue ordinary treatment for losses on the sale of depreciable business property and on the destruction of business or capital assets, and (2) provide capital-gain treatment for gains from the sale or involuntary conversion of business or capital assets. Land used in a trade or business was removed from the capital-asset category and lumped together with depreciable business property, apparently to reduce the number of disputes over the allocation of purchase price when land and buildings were sold together.

4. *Business or investment?* T purchased a single-family residence for $70,000, resided in the house with his family for several years, and then, in 2000 (when the value of the residence was $85,000), moved out and rented it to a tenant. In 2005, T sells the property for $55,000. (At the time of the sale, the property has an adjusted basis of $62,000, as T had properly deducted $8000 of depreciation.) T practices law full time.

His involvement with the rental residence consisted of showing it to prospective tenants, preparing written leases, and arranging for maintenance work to be done. T had no other source of income other than his law practice and the rental property. What is the character of T's $7000 loss?

5. *Casualties to personal-use property.* Before its amendment in 1984, § 1231 also prescribed the character of gain and loss resulting from the destructive involuntary conversion (or theft) of capital assets held for personal (rather than business or investment) use. The characterization of these transactions is now governed by § 165(h).

If the personal casualty gains exceed the personal casualty losses for the year, all such gains and losses are treated as gains and losses from the sale or exchange of capital assets (either short-or long-term, depending upon their holding periods); § 165(h)(2)(B). Property held for personal use is a capital asset. How are personal casualty gains and losses characterized if the gains do not exceed the losses? Why?

Problems.

(1) In the current year, T sustains an uninsured flood loss of $20,000 to his home. T also receives a $10,000 insurance reimbursement for the theft of personal jewelry that had a basis of $5000. T had a long-

term holding period for both assets. *T*'s only other source of income is a salary of $100,000. Determine the amount and character of *T*'s casualty loss deduction. To what extent can *T* deduct the loss in computing adjusted gross income?

(2) What result in (1) if the flood loss is $5000 and *T* receives $25,000 of insurance proceeds for the stolen jewelry?

E. THE ARROWSMITH DOCTRINE

ARROWSMITH v. COMMISSIONER

Supreme Court of the United States, 1952.
344 U.S. 6, 73 S.Ct. 71, 97 L.Ed. 6.

MR. JUSTICE BLACK delivered the opinion of the Court.

This is an income tax controversy growing out of the following facts as shown by findings of the Tax Court. In 1937 two taxpayers, petitioners here, decided to liquidate and divide the proceeds of a corporation in which they had equal stock ownership. Partial distributions made in 1937, 1938, and 1939 were followed by a final one in 1940. Petitioners reported the profits obtained from this transaction, classifying them as capital gains. They thereby paid less income tax than would have been required had the income been attributed to ordinary business transactions for profit. About the propriety of these 1937–1940 returns, there is no dispute. But in 1944 a judgment was rendered against the old corporation and against Frederick R. Bauer, individually. The two taxpayers were required to and did pay the judgment for the corporation, of whose assets they were transferees. [Citations omitted.] Classifying the loss as an ordinary business one, each took a tax deduction for 100% of the amount paid. Treatment of the loss as a capital one would have allowed deduction of a much smaller amount. See § [1211]. The Commissioner viewed the 1944 payment as part of the original liquidation transaction requiring classification as a capital loss, just as the taxpayers had treated the original dividends as capital gains. Disagreeing with the Commissioner the Tax Court classified the 1944 payment as an ordinary business loss. 15 T.C. 876. Disagreeing with the Tax Court the Court of Appeals reversed, treating the loss as "capital." 2 Cir., 193 F.2d 734. This latter holding conflicts with the Third Circuit's holding in Commissioner of Internal Revenue v. Switlik, 184 F.2d 299. Because of this conflict, we granted certiorari. 343 U.S. 976.

[Section 1222] treats losses from sales or exchanges of capital assets as "capital losses" and § [331] requires that liquidation distributions be treated as exchanges. The losses here fall squarely within the definition of "capital losses" contained in these sections. Taxpayers were required to pay the judgment because of liability imposed on them as transferees of liquidation distribution assets. And it is plain that their liability as transferees was not based on any ordinary business transaction of theirs apart from the liquidation proceedings. It is not even denied that had this judgment been paid after liquidation, but during the year 1940, the losses would have been properly treated as capital ones. For payment during 1940 would simply have reduced the amount of capital gains taxpayers received during that year.

It is contended, however, that this payment which would have been a capital transaction in 1940 was transformed into an ordinary business transaction in 1944 because of the well-established principle that each taxable year is a separate unit for tax accounting purposes. United States v. Lewis, 340 U.S. 590; North American Oil Consolidated v. Burnet, 286 U.S. 417. But this principle is not breached by considering all the 1937–1944 liquidation transaction events in order properly to classify the nature of the 1944 loss for tax purposes. Such an examination is not an attempt to reopen and readjust the 1937 to 1940 tax returns, an action that would be inconsistent with the annual tax accounting principle.

The petitioner Bauer's executor presents an argument for reversal which applies to Bauer alone. He was liable not only by reason of being a transferee of the corporate assets. He was also held liable jointly with the original corporation, on findings that he had secretly profited because of a breach of his fiduciary relationship to the judgment creditor. Trounstine v. Bauer, Pogue & Co., D.C., 44 F.Supp. 767, 773; Id., 2 Cir., 144 F.2d 379, 382. The judgment was against both Bauer and the corporation. For this reason it is contended that the nature of Bauer's tax deduction should be considered on the basis of his liability as an individual who sustained a loss in an ordinary business transaction for profit. We agree with the Court of Appeals that this contention should not be sustained. While there was a liability against him in both capacities, the individual judgment against him was for the whole amount. His payment of only half the judgment indicates that both he and the other transferee were paying in their capacities as such. We see no reason for giving Bauer a preferred tax position.

Affirmed.

MR. JUSTICE DOUGLAS, dissenting.

I agree with Mr. Justice Jackson that these losses should be treated as ordinary, not capital, losses. There were no capital transactions in the year in which the losses were suffered. Those transactions occurred and were accounted for in earlier years in accord with the established principle that each year is a separate unit for tax accounting purposes. See United States v. Lewis, 340 U.S. 590. I have not felt, as my dissent in the *Lewis* case indicates, that the law made that an inexorable principle. But if it is the law, we should require observance of it—not merely by taxpayers but by the government as well. We should force each year to stand on its own footing, whoever may gain or lose from it in a particular case. We impeach that principle when we treat this year's losses as if they diminished last year's gains.

MR. JUSTICE JACKSON, whom MR. JUSTICE FRANKFURTER joins, dissenting.

This problem arises only because the judgment was rendered in a taxable year subsequent to the liquidation.

Had the liability of the transferor-corporation been reduced to judgment during the taxable year in which liquidation occurred, or prior thereto, this problem, under the tax laws, would not arise. The amount of the judgment rendered against the corporation would have decreased the amount it had available for distribution which would have reduced the liquidating dividends proportionately and diminished the capital gains taxes assessed against the stockholders. Probably it would also have decreased the corporation's own taxable income.

Congress might have allowed, under such circumstances, tax returns of the prior year to be reopened or readjusted so as to give the same tax results as would have obtained had the liability become known prior to liquidation. Such a solution is foreclosed to us and the alternatives left are to regard the judgment liability fastened by operation of law on the transferee as an ordinary loss for the year of adjudication or to regard it as a capital loss for such year.

This Court simplifies the choice to one of reading the English language, and declares that the losses here come "squarely within" the definition of capital losses contained within two sections of the Internal Revenue Code. What seems so clear to this Court was not seen at all by the Tax Court, in this case or in earlier consideration of the same issue; nor was it grasped by the Court of Appeals for the Third Circuit. Commissioner of Internal Revenue v. Switlik, 1950, 184 F.2d 299.

I find little aid in the choice of alternatives from arguments based on equities. One enables the taxpayer to deduct the amount of the judgment against his ordinary income which might be taxed as high as 87%, while if the liability had been assessed against the corporation prior to liquidation it would have reduced his capital gain which was taxable at only 25% (now 26%). The consequence may readily be characterized as a windfall (regarding a windfall as anything that is left to a taxpayer after the collector has finished with him).

On the other hand, adoption of the contrary alternative may penalize the taxpayer because of two factors: (1) since capital losses are deductible only against capital gains, plus $1,000, a taxpayer having no net capital gains in the ensuing five years would have no opportunity to deduct anything beyond $5,000; and (2) had the liability been discharged by the corporation, a portion of it would probably in effect have been paid by the Government, since the corporation could have taken it as a deduction, while here the total liability comes out of the pockets of the stockholders.

Solicitude for the revenues is a plausible but treacherous basis upon which to decide a particular tax case. A victory may have implications which in future cases will cost the Treasury more than a defeat. This might be such a case, for anything I know. Suppose that subsequent to liquidation it is found that a corporation has undisclosed claims instead of liabilities and that under applicable state law they may be prosecuted for the benefit of the stockholders. The logic of the Court's decision here, if adhered to, would result in a lesser return to the Government than if the recoveries were considered ordinary income. Would it be so clear that this is a capital loss if the shoe were on the other foot?

Where the statute is so indecisive and the importance of a particular holding lies in its rational and harmonious relation to the general scheme of the tax law, I think great deference is due the twice-expressed judgment of the Tax Court. In spite of the gelding of Dobson v. Commissioner, 320 U.S. 489, by [§ 7482(a)], I still think the Tax Court is a more competent and steady influence toward a systematic body of tax law than our sporadic omnipotence in a field beset with invisible boomerangs. I should reverse, in reliance upon the Tax Court's judgment more, perhaps, than my own.

Problem, Notes and Question

1. *The Arrowsmith doctrine.* What is the theoretically ideal treatment of the transactions in *Arrowsmith,* and how close does the Court's decision come to requiring that treatment?

A much-litigated issue concerns the treatment of payments by corporate "insiders" to their corporations pursuant to actions under § 16(b) of the Securities Exchange Act. Under that act, an "insider" who profits on short-term trading in his corporation's securities must pay an amount equal to his gain to the corporation. Several Tax Court cases have allowed such insiders ordinary deductions under § 162 for the repayments, but every court of appeals to consider the issue has reversed, applying the *Arrowsmith* doctrine to treat the repayments as capital losses. For example, in Cummings v. Commissioner, 506 F.2d 449 (2d Cir.1974), cert. denied 421 U.S. 913 (1975), the Second Circuit read *Arrowsmith* as requiring capital-loss treatment of deductions "sufficiently related to an earlier capital-gains transaction" and ruled that a "sufficient" relationship existed in an insider-profit case because the contrary result would give the taxpayer a "windfall" and frustrate "the policy of § 16(b) as well."

In cases involving taxpayer payments of damages on account of violations of securities laws other than § 16(b), even the Tax Court has applied *Arrowsmith.* See Smith v. Commissioner, 67 T.C. 570 (1976), treating a seller's payment of damages to a purchaser in settlement of an action under § 12(1) of the Securities Act of 1933 as a long-term capital loss. The court described the liabilities as arising out of the taxpayer's actions "as a prior shareholder," and said that the damages were not paid to protect the seller's "business reputation."

2. *Problem.* Three years ago *T* sold a piece of land used in his business at a gain of $10,000. The gain was a long-term capital gain under § 1231. In the current year, *T* paid $12,000 to the purchaser of the land in settlement of the purchaser's claim that *T* had induced the

purchase by misrepresentations in violation of state law. What result to *T*?

3. *References.* Rabinovitz, Effect of Prior Year's Transactions on Federal Income Tax Consequences of Current Receipts or Payments, 28 Tax L.Rev. 85 (1972); Lokken, Tax Significance of Payments in Satisfaction of Liability Arising Under Section 16(b) of the Securities Exchange Act of 1934, 4 Ga.L.Rev. 298 (1970).

F. DEPRECIATION RECAPTURE AND RELATED MATTERS

1. SECTIONS 1245 AND 1250

Suppose a taxpayer pays $10,000 for a truck, properly deducts $6000 in depreciation while using the truck in a business, and then sells the truck for $5500. The taxpayer's gain on the sale is $1500 ($5500 amount realized less $4000 adjusted basis). This gain can be viewed as a restoration of "excess" depreciation to income. In hindsight, it can be seen that the use of the truck over the years really cost the taxpayer $4500 (the difference between the $10,000 purchase price and the $5500 for which the truck was sold). Since the taxpayer was allowed $6000 in depreciation deductions, inclusion of $1500 in income on the truck's disposition is (very roughly) equivalent to allowing the taxpayer a total depreciation deduction of $4500 in the long run. That is, the $1500 is not a real economic gain but a "make-up" gain that just compensates for the excess depreciation deductions taken. (An *economic* gain results (ignoring inflation) where property is sold for more than its cost.)

If gain on the sale of the truck were a long-term capital gain and were taxed at a lower rate than ordinary income, the "restoration" of depreciation would be distorted. Suppose, for example, that ordinary income is taxed at a 40–percent rate, while long-term capital gain is taxed at only 20 percent. The $1500 "excess" depreciation would save the taxpayer $600 (40% of the $1500 of ordinary income that was offset by the excess depreciation); the restoration of the excess depreciation to income when the asset was sold would result in additional tax of only $300 (20% of the $1500 gain). The taxpayer would be $300 better off, even ignoring the time value of money, than a taxpayer who took $4500 of depreciation and realized no gain on the sale.

Section 1245 overrides[q] § 1222 and § 1231 to recapture as ordinary income the make-up gain on "section 1245 property" as defined in § 1245(a)(3). In the case of the truck in the above example, § 1245 would treat all the gain on the sale as ordinary income. (Work through § 1245 to see how this result is accomplished.)

Under the last sentence of § 1245(a)(1), depreciation recapture may occur even if the asset in question is disposed of in a non-recognition transaction. At the time § 1245 was enacted, there were several impor-

q. See § 1245(d).

tant non-recognition rules which were overridden by § 1245. Several of those non-recognition rules have since been repealed, so that today the exceptions of § 1245(b) cover most common non-recognition transactions. Most of the exceptions of § 1245(b) cover non-recognition transactions in which the basis of the section 1245 property is transferred to another item of section 1245 property (for example, § 1245(b)(4)) or to another person (for example, § 1245(b)(1)). The § 1245 gain in those cases does not permanently escape tax, but rather is deferred for future recognition when the property with the transferred basis is disposed of. (To see how this is accomplished, read § 1245(a)(2)(A) carefully.)

One important non-recognition provision that § 1245 does override is § 453,[r] which is discussed in Chapter 11. Section 453(i) requires that any § 1245 depreciation recapture be recognized in the year of sale rather than deferred under § 453.[s]

Section 1250, which governs depreciation recapture on most buildings, is easier on the taxpayer than § 1245. If "section 1250 property" (defined in § 1250(c)) has been held for more than one year, only "additional depreciation"—depreciation deductions in excess of those that would have been allowed under straight-line depreciation—is recaptured; § 1250(b)(1). Although buildings placed in service before 1987 could be depreciated under an accelerated method, § 168 generally requires that real property placed in service after 1986 be depreciated under the straight-line method. Section 1250 thus appears to apply chiefly to buildings placed in service before 1987.[t] But § 1245 usually applies to buildings that were placed in service from 1981 through 1986, except for (1) residential rental property and low-income housing and (2) other buildings that were depreciated on the straight-line method. Section 1250 therefore applies chiefly to the disposition of (1) real property placed in service before 1981 and (2) residential rental property and low-income housing placed in service after 1980 (and before 1987); in either case, however, § 1250 usually applies only if the property has been depreciated under an accelerated method.

Although § 1250(a) purports to override the Code's non-recognition rules, § 1250(d), like § 1245(b), provides exceptions for most of the important non-recognition rules. Again, however, § 453(i) provides for immediate recognition of recapture gain even though a sale of section 1250 property is reported on the installment method.

The make-up gain on the sale of a building that has been depreciated on the straight-line method is usually characterized as a long-term

r. Another is § 267(d), p. 596, above.

s. Section 453(i) was added in 1984. Why was it necessary to add § 453(i) when § 1245(a)(1) already provided for the recognition of the § 1245 gain "notwithstanding any other provision"? See Treas.Reg. § 1.1245–6(d), which was overturned by § 453(i).

t. One type of post–1986 real property to which § 1250 could apply is a non-resi-

dential farm building, such as a barn. A farm building can be depreciated over 20 years using 150–percent declining-balance depreciation. See § 168(b)(2). A farm building is not "nonresidential real property" for which straight-line depreciation must be used (§ 168(b)(3)) because it has a class life of less than 27.5 years (§ 168(e)(2)(B)).

capital gain, either under § 1222 (if the building was held for investment) or § 1231 (if it was held for business). This means that the gain is taxed at a lower rate of tax than that applicable to ordinary income (§ 1(h)). Section 1(h), however, taxes make-up gain on the sale of a building at 25 percent instead of the usual 20–percent rate applicable to most other long-term capital gains.

For example, suppose that in the current year the taxpayer sells for $500,000 a business building that she had purchased ten years before for $390,000. (Ignore the land, as if only the building had been bought and sold.) She had properly deducted $100,000 of straight-line depreciation on the building, leaving her with an adjusted basis of $290,000 and a realized and recognized gain of $210,000. The gain is composed of an economic gain of $110,000 ($500,000 selling price less $390,000 cost) and a make-up gain of $100,000 to compensate for the taking of depreciation deductions in excess of the property's decline in value. Section 1250 does not apply because the taxpayer used straight-line depreciation. Section 1231 characterizes the gain as long-term capital gain. But under § 1(h)(7) only the $110,000 of economic gain qualifies for the 20–percent tax rate of § 1(h); the $100,000 make-up gain is taxed at 25 percent; see § 1(h)(1)(D). (More technically, the "unrecaptured § 1250 gain" includes the amount that would be recaptured as ordinary income if § 1250 recaptured all depreciation (instead of just the excess of accelerated depreciation over the amount allowable under the straight-line method).)

When a corporation disposes of section 1250 property, § 291 requires that 20 percent of the excess of the amount that would have been treated as ordinary income under § 1245 (if § 1245 had applied) over the amount treated as ordinary income under § 1250 be treated as ordinary income. If the taxpayer in the preceding example had been a corporation, $20,000 (i.e., 20% of the $100,000 make-up gain) would be characterized as ordinary and $190,000 as § 1231 gain.

Problems

Problem (1). On January 1, year 1, *T* purchased for $10,000 a piece of equipment for use in her business.

(a) After properly deducting $4000 of depreciation, *T* sells the equipment on January 1, year 3 for $12,000. What result to *T*?

(b) What result in (a) if *T* had sold the equipment for $3000?

(c) What result in (a) if (instead of depreciating the equipment) *T* had elected under 179 to deduct the cost of the equipment in the year of purchase?

(d) What result in (a) if *T* had mistakenly deducted only $3000 of depreciation (instead of the $4000 she was entitled to)? See §§ 1016(a)(2) and 1245(a)(2)(B).

(e) What result in (a) if, instead of selling the equipment in year 3, *T* gave it to her son, *S*. *S* used the equipment for personal (non-profit-seeking) use until year 5, when he sold it for $8000. See § 1245(b)(1); Treas.Reg. § 1.1245–2(c)(2).

(f) What result if *T* died on January 1, year 3 (when the equipment was worth $12,000), the equipment passed to her estate, and the estate sold the equipment for $12,000. (Ignore any post-death depreciation.) See § 1245(b)(2); Treas.Reg. § 1.1245–2(c)(1)(iv).

(g) What result if on January 1, year 3 (when the equipment was worth $12,000 and had an adjusted basis of $6000), *T* exchanged it for $9000 worth of equipment of like kind to be used in the business and $3000 cash? See § 1245(b)(4); Treas.Reg. §§ 1.1245–4(d)(1) & (2); 1.1245–2(c)(4).

Problem (2). Five years ago *F* spent $80,000 to build a barn for use in his farming business. He sold it in the current year for $90,000. (Ignore the land, as if only the building had been sold.) Assume that over the five years, *F* properly deducted $26,000 of depreciation under the 150% declining-balance method. Straight-line depreciation would have been $20,000. The barn sale was *F*'s only transaction for the year. *F*'s tax rate on ordinary income is 35 percent. Determine the character of *F*'s recognized gain and the tax rate applicable to each component of the gain.

2. SECTION 1239

Sections 1245 and 1250 deal with the problem of ordinary depreciation deductions followed by closely related capital gains. Section 1239 deals with the similar problem of capital gain followed by depreciation deductions taken by a taxpayer closely related to the taxpayer who realized the gain. But for § 1239, a taxpayer who owned a depreciable asset with a basis of $2000 and a value of $10,000 could, at the cost of an $8000 capital gain, give his wholly owned corporation $8000 in additional depreciation deductions. This could result in a significant savings because the individual's capital gain is taxed at a much lower rate than the corporation's ordinary income which would be offset by the depreciation deduction. Section 1239, in effect, "recaptures" this additional depreciation before it is taken by making gains on the sale of depreciable property between "related persons" (as defined in § 1239(b)) ordinary income.

In determining whether taxpayers are "related persons" under § 1239(b), § 1239(c) incorporates and modifies the "constructive ownership" rules of § 267.

Problems

H purchased depreciable property for $20,000, properly deducted $12,000 of depreciation with respect to the property, and then sold it for $30,000 (its value at the time) to *Y* Corp. *H* owns all the stock of *Y* Corp.

(1) What is the character of *H*'s gain?

(2) Same as (1) except that *Y* Corp. was owned by *H*'s adult daughter.

(3) Suppose in (2) that *H* also recognized a $20,000 gain on the sale of land to *Y*. The land was a capital asset in *H*'s hands but was held by *Y* for sale to customers in the ordinary course of its business. What is the character of *H*'s gain?

3.   SECTION 1231 RECONSIDERED

Section 1231 is often criticized as a "heads the taxpayer wins, tails the government loses" provision, since § 1231 gains in excess of losses receive capital-gain treatment, while losses in excess of gains are fully deductible. Is this a valid objection? Consider § 1231 losses in light of depreciation recapture. Just as § 1245 requires ordinary-income treatment for gains attributable to the taxpayer's having taken "too much" depreciation, § 1231 can be viewed as allowing ordinary deductions for taxpayers who have taken "too little" depreciation (as determined after the fact). Under § 1231, a taxpayer who takes $6000 depreciation on a machine and sells the machine at a loss of $2000 is put in roughly the same long-run position as if he had taken $8000 depreciation and had no loss on the sale. Can this argument be used to support ordinary-loss treatment for land used in a business, or is land different from machinery because land is not depreciable?

G.   CAPITAL GAINS AND THE CHARITABLE– CONTRIBUTION DEDUCTION

Until 1969, the charitable-contribution deduction under § 170 was always the value of the property contributed, and the contribution was not a taxable event. Under this combination of rules, and the higher tax rates then applicable, some taxpayers were better off, after taxes, if they gave appreciated property to charity than if they had sold the property and kept the proceeds. Consider a 70–percent–bracket taxpayer who owned a fully depreciated (hence zero-basis) airplane worth $100,000. A sale of this airplane would have left the taxpayer with $30,000 to spend, assuming that the entire gain was subject to § 1245. A contribution of the plane to a qualified donee would have given the taxpayer $70,000 to spend, since the § 170 deduction would have shielded $100,000 of the taxpayer's other income from a 70–percent tax.

Non-recognition of gain on the contribution of appreciated property combined with the deduction for the full value of the property gave donors of property a "double benefit" as compared with the benefits given taxpayers who recognized income, paid tax, and donated cash. In 1969, Congress cut back somewhat by limiting the deduction under § 170 to the basis of ordinary-income and short-term capital-gain property. See § 170(e)(1)(A). Contributions of long-term capital assets and § 1231 assets are still deductible in full (except for recapturable depreciation), with the two exceptions described in § 170(e)(1)(B). Under § 170(b)(1)(C), an individual's annual limit on deductible contributions of most capital-gain property cannot exceed 30 percent of the contribution base (adjusted gross income). Deductions for excess contributions can be carried over for five years.

Problems

Problem (1). A, a professional artist, presented a painting (done by A and valued at $25,000) to the University Museum of Art. To what extent is A entitled to a charitable-contribution deduction? See § 1221(a)(3).

Problem (2). Suppose that several years ago A, the artist in (1), had given the painting to her child, C, who is not an artist. In the current year, C donates the painting (valued at $25,000) to the museum. To what extent is C entitled to a deduction?

Problem (3). T donated a boat valued at $50,000 to the University. T had purchased the boat for $40,000, used it in his business for several years, and properly deducted $25,000 of depreciation thereon. The University sold the boat and used the proceeds for scholarships. To what extent is T entitled to a charitable deduction?

Problem (4). Same as (3), except that the University kept the boat for use by its marine biology department.

H. BAD DEBTS AND WORTHLESS SECURITIES

PUTNAM v. COMMISSIONER

Supreme Court of the United States, 1956.
352 U.S. 82, 77 S.Ct. 175, 1 L.Ed.2d 144.

MR. JUSTICE BRENNAN delivered the opinion of the Court.

The petitioner, Max Putnam, in December 1948, paid $9,005.21 to a Des Moines, Iowa, bank in discharge of his obligation as guarantor of the notes of Whitehouse Publishing Company. That corporation still had a corporate existence at the time of the payment but had ceased doing business and had disposed of its assets eighteen months earlier. The question for decision is whether, in the joint income tax return filed by Putnam and his wife for 1948, Putnam's loss is fully deductible as a loss "incurred in [a] transaction * * * for profit, though not connected with [his] trade or business" within the meaning of § [165(c)] or whether it is nonbusiness bad debt within the meaning of § [166(d)], and therefore deductible only as a short-term capital loss.

The Commissioner determined that the loss was a nonbusiness bad debt to be given short-term capital loss treatment. The Tax Court and the Court of Appeals for the Eighth Circuit sustained his determination. Because of an alleged conflict with decisions of the Courts of Appeals of other circuits, we granted certiorari.

Putnam is a Des Moines lawyer who in 1945, in a venture not

connected with his law practice,[7] organized Whitehouse Publishing Company with two others, a newspaperman and a labor leader, to publish a labor newspaper. Each incorporator received one-third of the issued capital stock, but Putnam supplied the property and cash with which the company started business. He also financed its operations, for the short time it was in business, through advances and guarantees of payment of salaries and debts. Just before the venture was abandoned, Putnam acquired the shares held by his fellow stockholders and in July 1947, as sole stockholder, wound up its affairs and liquidated its assets. The proceeds of sale were insufficient to pay the full amount due to the Des Moines bank on two notes given by the corporation and guaranteed by Putnam for moneys borrowed in August 1946 and March 1947.

The familiar rule is that, *instanter* upon the payment by the guarantor of the debt, the debtor's obligation to the creditor becomes an obligation to the guarantor, not a new debt, but, by subrogation, the result of the shift of the original debt from the creditor to the guarantor who steps into the creditor's shoes. Thus, the loss sustained by the guarantor unable to recover from the debtor is by its very nature a loss from the worthlessness of a debt. This has been consistently recognized in the administrative and the judicial construction of the Internal Revenue laws which, until the decisions of the Courts of Appeals in conflict with the decision below, have always treated guarantors' losses as bad debt losses. The Congress recently confirmed this treatment in the Internal Revenue Code of 1954 by providing that a payment by a noncorporate taxpayer in discharge of his obligation as guarantor of certain noncorporate obligations "shall be treated as a debt."[11]

There is, then, no justification or basis for consideration of Putnam's loss under the general loss provisions of § [165(c)], i.e., as an ordinary nonbusiness loss sustained in a transaction entered into for profit. Congress has legislated specially in the matter of deductions of nonbusiness bad debt losses, i.e., such a loss is deductible only as a short-term capital loss by virtue of the special limitation provisions contained in § [166(d)]. * * *

* * *

The decisions of the Courts of Appeals in conflict with the decision below turn upon erroneous premises. It is said that the guarantor

---

7. Petitioners abandoned in this court the alternative contention made below that the loss was deductible in full as a business bad debt under § [166(a)].

11. "§ 166. Bad debts

* * *

"(f) Guarantor of certain noncorporate obligations.—A payment by the taxpayer (other than a corporation) in discharge of part or all of his obligation as a guarantor, endorser, or indemnitor of a noncorporate obligation the proceeds of which were used in the trade or business of the borrower shall be treated as a debt becoming worthless within such taxable year for purposes of this section (except that subsection (d) shall not apply), but only if the obligation of the borrower to the person to whom such payment was made was worthless (without regard to such guaranty, endorsement, or indemnity) at the time of such payment." 68A Stat. 50. And see 65 Yale L.J. 247. [This provision has since been repealed— Eds.]

taxpayer who involuntarily acquires a worthless debt is in a position no different from the taxpayer who voluntarily acquires a debt known by him to be worthless. The latter is treated as having acquired no valid debt at all. The situations are not analogous or comparable. The taxpayer who voluntarily buys a debt with knowledge that he will not be paid is rightly considered not to have acquired a debt but to have made a gratuity. In contrast the guarantor pays the creditor in compliance with the obligation raised by the law from his contract of guaranty. His loss arises not because he is making a gift to the debtor but because the latter is unable to reimburse him.

Next it is assumed * * * that a new obligation arises in favor of the guarantor upon his payment to the creditor. From that premise it is argued that such a debt cannot "become" worthless but is worthless from its origin, and so outside the scope of § [166]. This misconceives the basis of the doctrine of subrogation, apart from the fact that, if it were true that the debt did not "become" worthless, the debt nevertheless would not be regarded as an ordinary loss under § [165] * * *. Under the doctrine of subrogation, payment by the guarantor, as we have seen, is treated not as creating a new debt and extinguishing the original debt, but as preserving the original debt and merely substituting the guarantor for the creditor. The reality of the situation is that the debt is an asset of full value in the creditor's hands because backed by the guaranty. The debtor is usually not able to reimburse the guarantor and in such cases that value is lost at the instant that the guarantor pays the creditor. But that this instant is also the instant when the guarantor acquires the debt cannot obscure the fact that the debt "becomes" worthless in his hands.

* * *

The objectives sought to be achieved by the Congress in providing short-term capital loss treatment for non-business bad debts are also persuasive that § [166(d)] applies to a guarantor's nonbusiness debt losses. The section was part of the comprehensive tax program enacted by the Revenue Act of 1942 to increase the national revenue to further the prosecution of the great war in which we were then engaged. It was also a means for minimizing the revenue losses attributable to the fraudulent practices of taxpayers who made to relatives and friends gifts disguised as loans. Equally, however, the plan was suited to put nonbusiness investments in the form of loans on a footing with other nonbusiness investments. The proposal originated with the Treasury Department, whose spokesman championed it as a means "to insure a fairer reflection of taxable income," and the House Ways and Means Committee Report stated that the objective was "to remove existing inequities and to improve the procedure through which bad-debt deductions are taken." We may consider Putnam's case in the light of these revealed purposes. His venture into the publishing field was an investment apart from his law practice. The loss he sustained when his stock became worthless, as well as the losses from the worthlessness of the loans he made directly to the corporation, would receive capital loss treatment; the 1939 Code so provides as to nonbusiness losses both from worthless stock investments and from loans to a corporation, whether or not the loans are evidenced by a security. It is clearly a "fairer reflection" of Putnam's 1948 taxable income to treat the instant loss similarly. There is no real or economic difference between the loss of an investment made in the form of a direct loan to a corporation and one made indirectly in the form of a guaranteed bank loan. The tax consequences should in all reason be the same, and are accomplished by § [166(d)]. The judgment is

Affirmed.

MR. JUSTICE HARLAN, dissenting.

Being unreconciled to the Court's decision, which settles a conflict on this tax question among the Courts of Appeals and thus has an impact beyond the confines of this particular case, I must regretfully dissent.

* * *

Upon analysis, the Government's argument comes down to this: when the petitioner honored his guaranty obligation his payment was offset by the acquisition of the creditor Bank's rights against the Company on its indebtedness; in the Bank's hands those rights were worth full value, since the Company's indebtedness was secured by the guaranty; therefore petitioner's loss should be attributed to the subrogation debt, which became worthless in his hands because no longer so secured.

This argument would have substance in a case where the principal debtor was not insolvent at the time the guaranty was fulfilled; for in such a case it could be said that the acquired debt was not without value in the guarantor's hands, and hence he should not be allowed a tax deduction until the debt turns out to be worthless. But when, as here, the debtor is insolvent at the very time the guarantor meets his obligation, it defies reality to attribute the guarantor's loss to anything other than the discharge of his guaranty obligation. To attribute that loss to the acquired debt in such a case requires one to conceive of the debt as having value at the moment of acquisition, but as withering to worthlessness the moment the guarantor touches it. That the same debt in the same millisecond can have both of these antagonistic characteristics is, for me, too esoteric a concept to carry legal consequences, even in the field of taxation.

* * *

Problems, Notes and Questions

1. *Is subrogation necessary?* If, under the local law of suretyship, Putnam's payment of Whitehouse's debt had not created a (worthless) obligation on the part of Whitehouse to reimburse Putnam, would

Putnam's loss still have been subject to § 166 rather than § 165?[u] As a practical matter, the question whether a right of subrogation exists will often lack non-tax significance, either because the debtor has no assets or because the debtor is (as in *Putnam*) a corporation controlled by the guarantor. Several cases have held that subrogation is irrelevant; e.g., In re Vaughan, 719 F.2d 196 (6th Cir.1983); Stratmore v. United States, 420 F.2d 461 (3d Cir.1970), cert. denied 398 U.S. 951 (1970); Martin v. Commissioner, 52 T.C. 140 (1969), aff'd per curiam 424 F.2d 1368 (9th Cir.1970), cert. denied 400 U.S. 902 (1970). The House Ways and Means Committee's report on the Tax Reform Act of 1976 (H.R.Rep. No. 94–658, 94th Cong., 1st Sess. 177 (1975)) says:

> The Committee also wishes to make it clear that in the case of a guarantor of a corporation [sic] obligation, any payment * * * must be deducted (if at all) as a * * * debt, regardless of whether there is any right of subrogation * * *.

The 1976 Act did not contain any provision purporting to enact the Ways and Means Committee's views on the effects of subrogation.

2. *"Debt" or "gift"?* The House Report on the 1976 Act had this to say about the deductibility of losses resulting from loans between family members (H.R.Rep. No. 94–658 at 177):

> Generally, in the case of a direct loan, the transaction is entered into for profit by the lender, who hopes to realize interest on the loan. However, this may not be true in the case of loans made between friends or family members, and in these cases the Internal Revenue Service will generally treat any loss resulting from such a "loan" as a gift with respect to which no bad debt deduction is available. (Reg. § 1.166–1(c)).

Did the Committee read the regulations correctly? The courts have routinely allowed a non-business bad-debt deduction for worthless intra-family debt when convinced that the parties intended to create a true debtor-creditor relationship. E.g., Shirar v. Commissioner, 54 T.C.M. 698 (1987) (husband and wife allowed non-business bad-debt deduction for amounts lent to his brother).

The report goes on to say that a guarantor can take no deduction under § 166 unless the guaranty was entered into as part of the guarantor's business, or for profit, so that a guarantor who received no compensation or business benefit (for example, a parent who guaranteed a loan for a child for nominal consideration) can get no deduction under § 166. The only effect of the 1976 Act on the language of § 166 was the repeal of former § 166(f), which gave "business" bad-debt treatment to non-corporate guarantors who guaranteed non-corporate obligations, the proceeds of which were used in the borrower's business. Treas.Reg. § 1.166–9(e)(1) adopts the House Report's position.

---

u. Such cases may arise, for example, because only part of a debt is paid (since subrogation might interfere with the credi-tor's right to collect the rest of the debt); see Restatement (Third) of Suretyship and Guaranty § 27, comment (b) (1996).

Section 271 denies deductions for the worthlessness of most debts owed by political parties to taxpayers other than banks. Compare § 276, which disallows deductions for specified payments which may well be disguised campaign contributions.

3. *Other "debt" vs. "loss" cases.* Although the mutual exclusivity of §§ 166 and 165 has been established for many years,[v] the borderline between bad-debt losses and other losses remains unclear. Does a loss from theft, casualty, or breach of contract become a bad-debt loss if the taxpayer who suffers it sues the person who caused the loss and obtains a worthless judgment? Why does it matter? United States v. Kyle, 242 F.2d 825 (4th Cir.1957), held that a taxpayer who sued a buyer for breach of a contract to buy the taxpayer's house and got an uncollectible judgment for the difference between the contract price and the market price had a non-deductible loss, not a deductible bad debt. See Note, Bad Debt Deductions for Capital Lost Through Breach of Contract, 67 Yale L.J. 492 (1958).

4. *Problems.*

(1) Three years ago *M*, a cash-method taxpayer, lent $50,000 to her child, *C*, to assist *C* in a new business venture. The loan bore interest at the market rate. The business failed in the current year, *C* was adjudicated bankrupt, and *M* was therefore unable to collect the $50,000 principle and $5,000 of accrued interest. What is the amount and character of any deduction to which *M* is entitled? (What additional information might you need?)

(2) Would your answer in (1) differ if *M* had lent the $50,000 to *C* without interest?

(3) Suppose that, instead of lending the funds to *C*, *M* had guaranteed a $50,000 loan to *C* from a bank. *C* paid *M* $5000 for acting as guarantor. When *C* was adjudicated bankrupt in the current year, *M*, as guarantor, was required to pay the $50,000 and was subrogated to the bank's rights against *C*.

(4) Would your answer in (3) differ if *M* had served as guarantor for no fee?

(5) *T* made a $5000 deposit with a contractor who agreed to build a personal residence for *T*. The contractor became insolvent and discontinued business without beginning construction of the residence. *T* was unable to recover the $5000. What is the amount and character of any deduction to which *T* is entitled?

(6) Would your answer in (5) differ if, instead of becoming insolvent, the contractor had absconded with the $5000? See § 165(c).

(7) What is the purpose of § 6511(d)(1)?

---

v. Spring City Foundry Co. v. Commissioner, 292 U.S. 182, 189 (1934): "The making of the specific provision as to debts indicates that these were to be considered as a special class and that losses on debts were not to be regarded as falling under the * * * general provision [of § 165]."

5. *Reference.* Brown, Putnam v. Commissioner—The Reimbursable Outlay Under the Tax Law, 6 Buffalo L.Rev. 283 (1957).

UNITED STATES v. GENERES

Supreme Court of the United States, 1972.
405 U.S. 93, 92 S.Ct. 827, 31 L.Ed.2d 62.

MR. JUSTICE BLACKMUN delivered the opinion of the Court.

A debt a closely held corporation owed to an indemnifying shareholder-employee became worthless in 1962. The issue in this federal income tax refund suit is whether, for the shareholder-employee, that worthless obligation was a business or a nonbusiness bad debt within the meaning and reach of §§ 166(a) and (d) and of the implementing Regulations § 1.166–5.

* * *

In determining whether a bad debt is a business or a nonbusiness obligation, the Regulations focus on the relation the loss bears to the taxpayer's business. If, at the time of worthlessness, that relation is a "proximate" one, the debt qualifies as a business bad debt and the aforementioned desirable tax consequences then ensue.

The present case turns on the proper measure of the required proximate relation. Does this necessitate a "dominant" business motivation on the part of the taxpayer or is a "significant" motivation sufficient?

* * *

I

The taxpayer as a young man in 1909 began work in the construction business. His son-in-law, William F. Kelly, later engaged independently in similar work. During World War II the two men formed a partnership in which their participation was equal. The enterprise proved successful. In 1954 Kelly–Generes Construction Co., Inc., was organized as the corporate successor to the partnership. It engaged in the heavy-construction business, primarily on public works projects.

The taxpayer and Kelly each owned 44% of the corporation's outstanding capital stock. The taxpayer's original investment in his shares was $38,900. The remaining 12% of the stock was owned by a son of the taxpayer and by another son-in-law. Mr. Generes was president of the corporation and received from it an annual salary of $12,000. Mr. Kelly was executive vice-president and received an annual salary of $15,000.

The taxpayer and Mr. Kelly performed different services for the corporation. Kelly worked full time in the field and was in charge of the day-to-day construction operations. Generes, on the other hand, devoted no more than six to eight hours a week to the enterprise. He reviewed bids and jobs, made cost estimates, sought and obtained bank financing, and assisted in securing the bid and performance bonds that are an essential part of the public-project construction business. Mr. Generes, in addition to being president of the corporation, held a full-time position as president of a savings and loan association he had founded in 1937. He received from the association an annual salary of $19,000. The taxpayer also had other sources of income. His gross income averaged about $40,000 a year during 1959–1962.

Taxpayer Generes from time to time advanced personal funds to the corporation to enable it to complete construction jobs. He also guaranteed loans made to the corporation by banks for the purchase of construction machinery and other equipment. In addition, his presence with respect to the bid and performance bonds is of particular significance. Most of these were obtained from Maryland Casualty Co. That underwriter required the taxpayer and Kelly to sign an indemnity agreement for each bond it issued for the corporation. In 1958, however, in order to eliminate the need for individual indemnity contracts, taxpayer and Kelly signed a blanket agreement with Maryland whereby they agreed to indemnify it, up to a designated amount, for any loss it suffered as surety for the corporation. Maryland then increased its line of surety credit to $2,000,000. The corporation had over $14,000,000 gross business for the period 1954 through 1962.

In 1962 the corporation seriously underbid two projects and defaulted in its performance of the project contracts. It proved necessary for Maryland to complete the work. Maryland then sought indemnity from Generes and Kelly. The taxpayer indemnified Maryland to the extent of $162,104.57. In the same year he also loaned $158,814.49 to the corporation to assist it in its financial difficulties. The corporation subsequently went into receivership and the taxpayer was unable to obtain reimbursement from it.

In his federal income tax return for 1962 the taxpayer took his loss on his direct loans to the corporation as a nonbusiness bad debt. He claimed the indemnification loss as a business bad debt and deducted it against ordinary income. Later he filed claims for refund for 1959–1961, asserting net operating loss carrybacks under § 172 to those years for the portion, unused in 1962, of the claimed business bad debt deduction.

In due course the claims were made the subject of the jury trial refund suit in the United States District Court for the Eastern District of Louisiana. At the trial Mr. Generes testified that his sole motive in signing the indemnity agreement was to protect his $12,000–a–year employment with the corporation. The jury, by special interrogatory, was asked to determine whether taxpayer's signing of the indemnity agreement with Maryland "was proximately related to his trade or business of being an employee" of the corporation. The District Court charged the jury, over the Government's objection, that *significant* motivation satisfies the Regulations' requirement of proximate relationship. The court refused the Government's request for an instruction that the applicable standard was that of *dominant* rather than significant motivation.

After twice returning to the court for clarification of the instruction given, the jury found that the taxpayer's signing of the indemnity agreement was proximately related to his trade or business of being an employee of the corporation. Judgment on this verdict was then entered for the taxpayer.

The Fifth Circuit majority approved the significant-motivation standard so specified and agreed with a Second Circuit majority in Weddle v. Commissioner of Internal Revenue, 325 F.2d 849, 851 (1963), in finding comfort for so doing in the tort law's concept of proximate cause. Judge Simpson dissented, 427 F.2d, at 284. He agreed with the holding of the Seventh Circuit in Niblock v. Commissioner of Internal Revenue, 417 F.2d 1185 (1969), and with Chief Judge Lumbard, separately concurring in *Weddle,* 325 F.2d, at 852, that dominant and primary motivation is the standard to be applied.

II

A. The fact responsible for the litigation is the taxpayer's dual status relative to the corporation. Generes was both a shareholder and an employee. These interests are not the same, and their differences occasion different tax consequences. In tax jargon, Generes' status as a shareholder was a nonbusiness interest. It was capital in nature and it was composed initially of tax-paid dollars. Its rewards were expectative and would flow, not from personal effort, but from investment earnings and appreciation. On the other hand, Generes' status as an employee was a business interest. Its nature centered in personal effort and labor, and salary for that endeavor would be received. The salary would consist of pre-tax dollars.

Thus, for tax purposes it becomes important and, indeed, necessary to determine the character of the debt that went bad and became uncollectible. Did the debt center on the taxpayer's business interest in the corporation or on his nonbusiness interest? * * *

* * *

III

We conclude that in determining whether a bad debt has a "proximate" relation to the taxpayer's trade or business, as the Regulations specify, and thus qualifies as a business bad debt, the proper measure is that of dominant motivation, and that only significant motivation is not sufficient. We reach this conclusion for a number of reasons:

A. The Code itself carefully distinguishes between business and nonbusiness items. It does so, for example, in § 165 with respect to losses, in § 166 with respect to bad debts, and in § 162 with respect to expenses. It gives particular tax benefits to business losses, business bad debts, and business expenses, and gives lesser benefits, or none at all, to nonbusiness losses, nonbusiness bad debts, and nonbusiness expenses. It does this despite the fact that the latter are just as adverse in financial consequence to the taxpayer as are the former. But this distinction has been a policy of the income tax structure ever since the Revenue Act of 1916, § 5(a), 39 Stat. 759, provided differently for trade or business losses than it did for losses sustained in another transaction entered into for profit. And it has been the specific policy with respect to bad debts since the Revenue Act of 1942 incorporated into § 23(k) of the 1939 Code the distinction between business and nonbusiness bad debts. 56 Stat. 820.

The point, however, is that the tax statutes have made the distinction, that the Congress therefore intended it to be a meaningful one, and that the distinction is not to be obliterated or blunted by an interpretation that tends to equate the business bad debt with the nonbusiness bad debt. We think that emphasis upon the significant rather than upon the dominant would have a tendency to do just that.

B. Application of the significant-motivation standard would also tend to undermine and circumscribe the Court's holding in *Whipple*[, 373 U.S. 193 (1963),] and the emphasis there that a shareholder's mere activity in a corporation's affairs is not a trade or business. As Chief Judge Lumbard pointed out in his separate and disagreeing concurrence in *Weddle,* supra, 325 F.2d, at 852–853, both motives—that of protecting the investment and that of protecting the salary—are inevitably involved, and an inquiry whether employee status provides a significant motivation will always produce an affirmative answer and result in a judgment for the taxpayer.

C. The dominant-motivation standard has the attribute of workability. It provides a guideline of certainty for the trier of fact. The trier then may compare the risk against the potential reward and give proper emphasis to the objective rather than to the subjective. As has just been noted, an employee-shareholder, in making or guaranteeing a loan to his corporation, usually acts with two motivations, the one to protect his investment and the other to protect his employment. By making the dominant motivation the measure, the logical tax consequence ensues and prevents the mere presence of a business motive, however small and however insignificant, from controlling the tax result at the taxpayer's convenience. This is of particular importance in a tax system that is so largely dependent on voluntary compliance.

D. The dominant-motivation test strengthens and is consistent with the mandate of § 262 of the Code that "no deduction shall be allowed for personal, living, or family expenses" except as otherwise provided. It prevents personal considerations from circumventing this provision.

E. The dominant-motivation approach to § 166(d) is consistent with that given the loss provisions in § 165(c)(1), see, for example, Imbesi v. Commissioner, 361 F.2d 640, 644 (C.A.3 1966), and in § 165(c)(2), see Austin v. Commissioner, 298 F.2d 583, 584 (C.A.2 1962). In these related areas, consistency is desirable. See also, Commissioner v. Duberstein, 363 U.S. 278, 286 (1960).

* * *

G. The Regulations' use of the word "proximate" perhaps is not the most fortunate, for it naturally tempts one to think in tort terms. The temptation, however, is best rejected, and we reject it here. In tort law factors of duty, of foreseeability, of secondary cause, and of plural liability are under consideration, and the concept of proximate cause has been developed as an appropriate application and measure of these factors. It has little place in tax law where plural aspects are not usual, where an item either is or is not a deduction, or either is or is not a business bad debt, and where certainty is desirable.

The conclusion we have reached means that the District Court's instructions, based on a standard of significant rather than dominant motivation, are erroneous and that, at least, a new trial is required. We have examined the record, however, and find nothing that would support a jury verdict in this taxpayer's favor had the dominant-motivation standard been embodied in the instructions. Judgment n.o.v. for the United States, therefore, must be ordered. See Neely v. Martin K. Eby Construction Co., 386 U.S. 317 (1967).

* * *

The judgment is reversed and the case is remanded with direction that judgment be entered for the United States.

It is so ordered.

MR. JUSTICE POWELL and MR. JUSTICE REHNQUIST took no part in the consideration or decision of this case.

MR. JUSTICE MARSHALL, concurring.

[Omitted.]

MR. JUSTICE WHITE, with whom MR. JUSTICE BRENNAN joins.

While I join Parts I, II, and III of the Court's opinion and its judgment of reversal, I would remand the case to the District Court with directions to hold a hearing on the issue of whether a jury question still exists as to whether taxpayer's motivation was "dominantly" a business one in the relevant transactions under §§ 166(a) and (d). * * *

MR. JUSTICE DOUGLAS, dissenting.

[Omitted.]

Problem, Notes and Questions

1. *Worthless "securities."* Section 165(g) governs the treatment of losses from worthless "securities." The term "security" includes (1) stock and (2) registered or coupon bonds issued by corporations or Governments; § 165(g)(2). Although a bond is a debt instrument, losses on the worthlessness of bonds that are "securities" are deductible under § 165 rather than § 166. What difference does that make?

What is the purpose of § 165(g)(3)?

2. *Section 1244 stock.* Section 1244 sometimes overrides § 165(g) to permit ordinary-loss treatment upon the disposition (or worthlessness) of "section 1244 stock." An individual (or partnership) who was the original holder of § 1244 stock can deduct up to $50,000 ($100,000 on a joint return) of ordinary loss each year. "Section 1244 stock" includes only stock issued by a "small business corporation" that receives limited amounts of passive income.

3. *Advances to corporations: debt or equity?* "Loans" by shareholders to their corporations may be treated for tax purposes as giving the shareholders "equity" rather than "debt" interests, even if the advances create debt under local law. Investors in closely held corporations have a strong incentive to call their instruments "debt" in order to obtain an interest deduction. If the purported debt is found to be equity, no interest deduction is allowed. (Recall that a corporation cannot deduct dividends paid.) Classification as "equity" rather than "debt" may also affect the character of a loss on worthlessness. If the debt is held to be true debt (but not a "security") the loss may qualify as a short-term capital loss under § 166(d) rather than as a long-term capital loss under § 165(g).

The classification issue may also arise when the corporation repays the "debt." Amounts received by a shareholder as repayment of a debt are treated as a return of capital to the extent of the shareholder's basis in the debt. Except as provided in the market-discount rules of § 1276, the excess of the amount received over the shareholder's basis is usually capital gain since the debt is usually a capital asset in the hands of the shareholder. (Recall that § 1271(a) treats the retirement of debt as an exchange.) If the purported debt is held to be equity, the amount received in redemption thereof is often treated as a dividend. In that case, the shareholder must treat the amount received (without any offset for the basis of the stock redeemed) as ordinary income.

Treatment of purported debt as "equity" is likely if the corporation has an unusually high ratio of debt to equity; if debt is held by shareholders in proportion to their holdings of stock; if shareholder debt is subordinated to the debts of outside creditors; and if the corporation fails to pay interest and principal on schedule. Section 385, enacted in 1969, authorizes the Treasury Department to issue regulations on classifying interests as debt or equity. Proposed regulations under § 385 were issued in 1980, but were withdrawn in 1983 after encountering considerable criticism.

4. *Problem.* For several years *P,* a cash-method taxpayer, has been the sole shareholder of *X* Corp., a real-estate broker. *P* also served as a full-time officer of the firm at a salary of $40,000 a year. *P*'s *X* Corp. stock has a basis of $20,000. (The firm has never paid a dividend.) From time to time *P* also made unsecured advances to *X* Corp. In the current year, *X* Corp became hopelessly insolvent. *P* is unable to collect $30,000 of cash advanced to *X* Corp. and $3000 of interest on those advances. What result to *P*?

5. *Reference.* Plumb, The Federal Income Tax Significance of Corporate Debt: A Critical Analysis and a Proposal, 26 Tax L.Rev. 369 (1971).

I. THE SALE OF A GOING BUSINESS

Suppose a potential purchaser is attempting to decide how much to offer for a going business. The potential purchaser might attempt to evaluate each asset of the business and then offer an amount equal to the aggregate value of the assets. But evaluating each identifiable asset of a large business is usually unfeasible (and unreliable in measuring the value of a going concern). A more-common approach to valuation of a business is the *capitalization-of-earnings* method. Under this method, the potential purchaser attempts to estimate the future earnings of the business. (The future earnings are usually extrapolated from the firm's past earnings, as adjusted for factors, such as improved efficiency, that might accompany the shift in control.) The purchaser then determines the rate of return required on the investment by assessing the likelihood that the projected earnings will materialize (that is, the degree of risk). For example, *T* estimates that a small hardware store will earn $100,000 a year for the indefinite future. If *T* could earn a 20–percent annual return on investments involving the same degree of risk as the hardware store, *T* would be willing to buy the business for some amount (*X*), which when multiplied by 20 percent equals $100,000 (that is, $20\% \times X = \$100,000$). *T* would thus be willing to pay up to $500,000 ($100,000/20%) for the business as a going concern.

When a business is sold for a lump-sum purchase price, how are the amount and character of the seller's gain or loss to be determined? If the business is incorporated, a sale by the shareholders of their stock usually results in capital gain or loss since the stock is usually a capital asset. The sale of a sole proprietorship might in principle have been treated like a sale of corporate stock, with the seller computing the amount and character of gain or loss as if a single capital asset (the business) had been sold. But because a sole proprietorship is not an entity apart from its owner, the proprietor is considered to be selling each of the assets. The courts have therefore required that the sale be "fragmented," and the amount and character of gain or loss on each of the business's assets (including goodwill) determined separately.[w] The leading case is Williams v. McGowan, 152 F.2d 570 (2d Cir.1945), in which the Second Circuit treated the sale of a hardware business as a sale of cash, accounts receivable, fixtures, and inventory.[x] The *Williams* rule requires fragmen-

---

w. Section 741 recognizes the capital-asset status of a partnership interest, but § 751 requires that amounts received on the sale of a partnership interest be treated as amounts realized on the sale of ordinary-income assets to the extent attributable to the partnership's "unrealized receivables" and "inventory items." Because § 751 defines "unrealized receivables" and "inven-

tory items" very broadly, many sales of partnership interests are fragmented in much the same way as sales of proprietorship interests.

x. The Supreme Court approved of *Williams* in Watson v. Commissioner, 345 U.S. 544 (1953).

tation in the case of an individual sole proprietor's sale of an unincorporated business and in the case of a sale of a corporate business by the corporation.

When a business is purchased as a going concern, the value of the business may exceed the sum of the values of each of the firm's identifiable assets taken separately. For example, in the hardware-store example above, the aggregate values of the inventory, equipment, fixtures and other such assets may be only $400,000. But, valued as a going concern, the firm is worth $500,000. This is the market's way of telling us that even if we were to assemble the identifiable *assets* owned by the firm, we would not have *the firm*. The $100,000 excess of the value of the firm over the sum of the values of its identifiable tangible and intangible assets is "goodwill" or "going-concern" value.[y] Goodwill arises from the firm's having an established clientele, a favorable business reputation, and so forth. Although self-developed goodwill has a zero basis (because the costs incurred in developing the goodwill are deducted as expenses when paid or incurred), the purchaser of a business obtains a cost basis for the goodwill. Under § 197, goodwill, going-concern value, and other intangible assets acquired as part of the acquisition of a business must be amortized over a period of 15 years.

When a proprietorship is sold for a lump-sum amount, the allocation of the purchase price among the assets is important to both seller and purchaser. The allocation determines the character of the seller's gain or loss and the purchaser's basis for each asset acquired. The allocation thus affects the purchaser's depreciation or amortization deductions and the amount and character of gain or loss to the seller.

Section 1060 requires that the consideration be allocated among the assets in the same manner as under § 338(b)(5), which in turn empowers the Treasury to issue regulations prescribing the method of allocation. The Treasury has used that authority to promulgate Treas.Reg. §§ 1.1060–1 and 1.338–6, under which the purchase price is first reduced by any cash acquired from the seller. Speaking very generally, the remaining purchase price is then allocated among several classes of other identifiable tangible and intangible assets in a descending order of liquidity. That is, the consideration is allocated among the assets of one class to the extent of their value, with the balance of the consideration then allocated to the assets of the next class to the extent of their value, etc. Any remaining excess is allocated to § 197 intangibles (other than goodwill and going-concern value) to the extent of their value, and the residue is allocated to goodwill and going-concern value; Treas. Reg. § 1.338–6(b). (This approach is called the "residual method" of allocating consideration to the goodwill.)

Suppose that the purchase agreement provides for an allocation of the purchase price among the assets of the business. Is that allocation

---

y. Although Treas. Reg. § 1.1060–1(b)(2) attempts to distinguish "goodwill" from "going-concern value," practitioners usually use the terms interchangeably. So do we.

dispositive of the values of the assets for purposes of the § 1060 regulations? Or can one of the parties to the agreement, or the Commissioner, successfully challenge an allocation made in the purchase agreement? If the buyer and the seller agree in writing as to the allocation, a party can refute the allocation only by satisfying the standard set forth in Commissioner v. Danielson, 378 F.2d 771 (3d Cir.), cert. denied 389 U.S. 858 (1967), which requires a showing that the party's assent was based upon fraud, mistake, or duress; Treas. Reg. § 1.1060–1(c)(4). The Commissioner, however, can always challenge an allocation agreed to by the parties; id. In practice, the Government will usually accept an allocation reached in arm's length negotiation between parties who have adverse tax interests in making the allocation. See Treas.Reg. §§ 1.1245–1(a)(5).

Since long-term capital gain is usually taxed at a substantially lower rate than ordinary income, the buyer and seller often have conflicting interests in allocating the purchase price. For example, a seller would usually prefer a larger allocation to land used in the business (a § 1231 asset) and a smaller allocation to inventory (an ordinary-income asset). The buyer would usually prefer a larger allocation to the inventory and a smaller allocation to the land. (Why?)

Before the enactment of § 197 in 1993, purchased goodwill was not amortizable. But the seller's covenant not to compete was amortizable over the period covered by the covenant. The buyer and seller therefore sometimes had conflicting interests in allocating a portion of the purchase price to goodwill or a covenant not to compete. Consider the sale of a business for a price exceeding the value of the business's tangible assets by $100,000. If the $100,000 premium was treated as for goodwill having a zero basis, the seller had a capital gain of $100,000, and the buyer had spent that amount on a nonamortizable asset. But if the $100,000 was treated as payment for the seller's covenant not to compete, the seller had $100,000 ordinary income and the buyer had acquired an amortizable asset.

Because § 197 requires both goodwill and non-compete covenants to be amortized over fifteen years, there will be no difference in tax treatment as far as the purchaser is concerned. The seller, however, may still prefer to characterize the payment as one for goodwill so as to obtain capital-gain treatment.

Problems

For several years, *S* has operated University Cleaners, a sole proprietorship engaged in the laundry business in University City. On December 31 of the current year, *S* sells the business to *P* for $150,000 cash and the assumption of $40,000 of the firm's liabilities (a mortgage on the land and building). The adjusted basis and value of the firm's identifiable assets are as follows.

Asset	Basis	Value	Notes
Accounts receivable	$ 0	$ 10,000	(a)
Supplies	0	5000	(b)
Equipment	5000	20,000	(c)
Delivery truck	10,000	5000	
Building	40,000	70,000	(d)
Land	20,000	30,000	
	$75,000	$140,000	

Notes.

(a) *S* uses the cash method of accounting.

(b) *S* deducted the $10,000 cost of the supplies in the preceding year.

(c) *S* purchased the equipment for $15,000 and properly deducted $10,000 of depreciation thereon.

(d) *S* paid $60,000 for the building (exclusive of the land) and has properly deducted $20,000 of straight-line depreciation.

Questions.

(1) What result to *S* and *P*?

(2) How would your answer to (1) differ if *S* also paid *P* $30,000 for a covenant by *S* not to compete with *P* in the laundry business in University City for a period of five years?

J. SALES OF RIGHTS TO INCOME

HORT v. COMMISSIONER

Supreme Court of the United States, 1941.
313 U.S. 28, 61 S.Ct. 757, 85 L.Ed. 1168.

MR. JUSTICE MURPHY delivered the opinion of the Court.

We must determine whether the amount petitioner received as consideration for cancellation of a lease of realty in New York City was ordinary gross income as defined in § [61], and whether in any event, petitioner sustained a loss through cancellation of the lease which is recognized in § [165].

Petitioner acquired the property, a lot and ten-story office building, by devise from his father in 1928. At the time he became owner, the premises were leased to a firm which had sublet the main floor to the Irving Trust Co. In 1927, five years before the head lease expired, the Irving Trust Co. and petitioner's father executed a contract in which the latter agreed to lease the main floor and basement to the former for a term of fifteen years at an annual rental of $25,000, the term to commence at the expiration of the head lease.

In 1933, the Irving Trust Co. found it unprofitable to maintain a branch in petitioner's building. After some negotiations, petitioner and the Trust Co. agreed to cancel the lease in consideration of a payment to petitioner of $140,000. Petitioner did not include this amount in gross income in his income tax return for 1933. On the contrary, he reported a loss of $21,494.75 on the theory that the amount he received as consideration for the cancellation was $21,494.75 less than the difference between the present value of the unmatured rental payments and the fair rental value of the main floor and basement for the unexpired term of the lease. He did not deduct this figure, however, because he reported other losses in excess of gross income.

The Commissioner included the entire $140,000 in gross income, disallowed the asserted loss, made certain other adjustments not material here, and assessed a deficiency. The Board of Tax Appeals affirmed. 39 B.T.A. 922. The Circuit Court of Appeals affirmed per curiam on the authority of Warren Service Corp. v. Helvering, 2 Cir., 110 F.2d 723. 2 Cir., 112 F.2d 167. Because of conflict with Commissioner v. Langwell Real Estate Corp., 7 Cir., 47 F.2d 841, we granted certiorari limited to the question whether, "in computing net gain or loss for income tax purposes, a taxpayer [can] offset the value of the lease canceled against the consideration received by him for the cancellation". 311 U.S. 641.

Petitioner apparently contends that the amount received for cancellation of the lease was capital rather than ordinary income and that it was therefore subject to * * * [the provisions governing] capital gains and losses. Further, he argues that even if that amount must be reported as ordinary gross income he sustained a loss which § [165] authorizes him to deduct. We cannot agree.

The amount received by petitioner for cancellation of the lease must be included in his gross income in its entirety. Section [61] expressly defines gross income to include "gains, profits, and income derived from * * * rent, * * * or gains or profits and income from any source whatever". Plainly this definition reached the rent paid prior to cancellation just as it would have embraced subsequent payments if the lease had never been canceled. It would have included a prepayment of the discounted value of unmatured rental payments whether received at the inception of the lease or at any time thereafter. Similarly, it would have extended to the proceeds of a suit to recover damages had the Irving Trust Co. breached the lease instead of concluding a settlement. Compare United States v. Safety Car Heating Co., 297 U.S. 88; Burnet v. Sanford & Brooks Co., 282 U.S. 359. That the amount petitioner received resulted from negotiations ending in cancellation of the lease rather than from a suit to enforce it cannot alter the fact that basically the payment was merely a substitute for the rent reserved in the lease. So far as the application of § [61] is concerned, it is immaterial that petitioner chose to accept an amount less than the strict present value of the unmatured rental payments rather than to engage in litigation, possibly uncertain and expensive.

The consideration received for cancellation of the lease was not a return of capital. We assume that the lease was "property", whatever that signifies abstractly. Presumably the bond in Helvering v. Horst, 311 U.S. 112, and the lease in Helvering v. Bruun, 309 U.S. 461, were also "property", but the interest coupon in *Horst* and the building in *Bruun* nevertheless were held to constitute items of gross income. Simply because the lease was "property" the amount received for its cancellation was not a return of capital, quite apart from the fact that "property" and "capital" are not necessarily synonymous in the Revenue Act of 1932 or in common usage. Where, as in this case, the disputed amount was essentially a substitute for rental payments which § [61] expressly characterizes as gross income, it must be regarded as ordinary income, and it is immaterial that for some purposes the contract creating the right to such payments may be treated as "property" or "capital".

For the same reasons, that amount was not a return of capital because petitioner acquired the lease as an incident of the realty devised to him by his father. Theoretically, it might have been possible in such a case to value realty and lease separately and to label each a capital asset. Compare Maass v. Higgins, 312 U.S. 443, decided March 3, 1941; Appeal of Farmer, 1 B.T.A. 711. But that would not have converted into capital the amount petitioner received from the Trust Co. since § [102] would have required him to include in gross income the rent derived from the property, and that section, like § [61], does not distinguish rental payments and a payment which is clearly a substitute for rental payments.

We conclude that petitioner must report as gross income the entire amount received for cancellation of the lease without regard to the claimed disparity between that amount and the difference between the present value of the unmatured rental payments and the fair rental value of the property for the unexpired period of the lease. The cancellation of the lease involved nothing more than relinquishment of the right to future rental payments in return for a present substitute payment and possession of the leased premises. Undoubtedly it diminished the amount of gross income petitioner expected to realize, but to that extent he was relieved of the duty to pay income tax. Nothing in § [165] indicates that Congress intended to allow petitioner to reduce ordinary income actually received and reported by the amount of income he failed to realize. * * *

The judgment of the Circuit Court of Appeals is affirmed.

Problems, Notes and Question

1. *Basis aspects*. Recall that a taxpayer who buys an asset like a tract of land and later sells part of that asset computes gain by allocating the basis of the asset between the portion sold and the portion retained; Treas.Reg. § 1.61–6(a). If Hort had sold a half interest in his building, his gain would have been the amount realized less half the building's basis. Why, then, could he not use part of the property's basis to reduce gain on the "sale" of his right to hold the Irving Trust Co. to its lease?

Suppose Hort had sold his rights as lessor to a third party, retaining all other interests in the property; would a basis offset have been appropriate?

In Estate of Camden v. Commissioner, 47 B.T.A. 926 (1942) (Non-acq.), affirmed mem., 139 F.2d 697 (6th Cir.1943), the Board of Tax Appeals allowed a basis offset to the owner of real estate who sold a life interest in the property to her husband. The court answered the Commissioner's argument that the transfer should be treated as a lease by saying that "the conveyance was in form a plain grant of a life estate and no tax evasion motive [existed]."

2. *Capital gain.* Does the Court's description of the amount Hort received as "a substitute for rent" justify treating the gain as ordinary income? Consider a taxpayer who buys an apartment building for $100,000, and who sells it for $150,000 after an increase in demand for housing drives up rents. The sale price is surely a "substitute for rent," yet just as surely the gain is a capital (or § 1231) gain.

3. *Problems.*

(1) In 1990 *L* leased a building to *T* under a lease running through 2009 at a fixed rent.

    (a) What result to *L* if in 2003 *T* pays *L* $100,000 for a cancellation of the lease?

    (b) What result to *T* if in 2003 *L* pays *T* $100,000 for a cancellation of the lease? See § 1241.

(2) Suppose that in 2001 *T* had sublet the building to *S* under a sublease that ran through 2009. In 2003 *S* pays $100,000 to *T* in consideration of *T*'s canceling the sublease and transferring the primary lease to *S*. What result to *T*?

McALLISTER v. COMMISSIONER
United States Court of Appeals, Second Circuit, 1946.
157 F.2d 235, cert. denied 330 U.S. 826, 67 S.Ct. 864, 91 L.Ed. 1276 (1947).

Before SWAN, CLARK, and FRANK, CIRCUIT JUDGES.

CLARK, CIRCUIT JUDGE.

This petition for review presents the question whether the sum of $55,000 received by petitioner on "transfer" or "surrender" of her life interest in a trust to the remainderman constitutes gross income under [§ 61] or receipts from the sale of capital assets as defined in [§ 1221]. As we shall see, some significance seemingly is attached to a choice between the two words set in quotation marks as a description of the transaction. Petitioner contends that the life estate was a capital asset, the transfer of which resulted in a deductible capital loss, leaving her with no taxable income for the year. A majority of the Tax Court agreed with the Commissioner that the receipt in question was merely an advance payment of income, while four judges dissented, Judges Opper and Disney writing the opposing opinions. 5 T.C. 714.

* * *

[Upon the death of another income beneficiary, the taxpayer became entitled to a life income interest in a trust established by the will of Richard McAllister, her father-in-law. The remainderman was one of Richard McAllister's sons. The taxpayer sold her interest to the remainderman, reporting a capital loss in the amount by which the cash she received was exceeded by her basis (which was determined in accordance with actuarial tables in a manner similar to that described in Note 1, p. 665). The Commissioner disallowed a deduction for the loss.]

The issue, as stated by the Tax Court and presented by the parties, reduces itself to the question whether the case is within the rule of Blair v. Commissioner of Internal Revenue, 300 U.S. 5, or that of Hort v. Commissioner of Internal Revenue, 313 U.S. 28. In the *Blair* case, the life beneficiary of a trust assigned to his children specified sums to be paid each year for the duration of the estate. The Supreme Court held that each transfer was the assignment of a property right in the trust and that, since the tax liability attached to ownership of the property, the assignee, and not the assignor, was liable for the income taxes in the years in question. The continued authority of the case was recognized in Helvering v. Horst, 311 U.S. 112, 118, 119, although a majority of the Court thought it not applicable on the facts, and in Harrison v. Schaffner, 312 U.S. 579, 582, where the Court very properly distinguished it from the situation where an assignor transferred a portion of his income for a single year. We think that its reasoning and conclusion support the taxpayer's position here. It has been relied upon by other cases cited below which we find indistinguishable from the present case.

Petitioner's right to income for life from the trust estate was a right in the estate itself. Had she held a fee interest, the assignment would unquestionably have been regarded as the transfer of a capital asset; we see no reason why a different result should follow the transfer of the lesser, but still substantial, life interest. As the Court pointed out in the *Blair* case, the life tenant was entitled to enforce the trust, to enjoin a breach of trust, and to obtain redress in case of breach. The proceedings in the state chancery court [by which she sold her interest] completely divested her of these rights and of any possible control over the property. The case is therefore distinguishable from that of Hort v. Commissioner of Internal Revenue, supra, where a landlord for a consideration cancelled a lease for a term of years, having still some nine years to run. There the taxpayer surrendered his contractual right to the future yearly payments in return for an immediate payment of a lump sum. The statute expressly taxed income derived from rent, [§ 61], and the consideration received was held a substitute for the rent as it fell due. It was therefore taxed as income.

What we regard as the precise question here presented has been determined in the taxpayer's favor on the authority of the *Blair* case by the Eighth Circuit in Bell's Estate v. Commissioner of Internal Revenue, 8 Cir., 137 F.2d 454, reversing 46 B.T.A. 484. * * *

The Tax Court and the government have attempted to distinguish both the *Bell* and the *Blair* cases on grounds which seem to us to lack either substance or reality. The principal ground seems to be the form the transaction assumed between the parties. Thus the Court says that petitioner received the payment for "surrendering" her rights to income payments, and "she did not assign her interest in the trust, as did petitioners in the *Bell* case." But what is this more than a distinction in words? Both were cases where at the conclusion of the transaction the remaindermen had the entire estate and the life tenants had a substantial sum of money. There surely cannot be that efficacy in lawyers' jargon that termination or cancellation or surrender carries some peculiar significance vastly penalizing laymen whose counsel have chanced to use them. * * *

* * *

Setting the bounds to the area of tax incidence involves the drawing of lines which may often be of an arbitrary nature. But they should not be more unreal than the circumstances necessitate. Here the line of demarcation between the *Blair* and the *Hort* principles is obviously one of some difficulty to define explicitly or to establish in borderline cases. Doubtless all would agree that there is some distinction between selling a life estate in property and anticipating income for a few years in advance. It is the kind of distinction stressed in Harrison v. Schaffner, supra, 312 U.S. 579, 583, where the Court said: "Nor are we troubled by the logical difficulties of drawing the line between a gift of an equitable interest in property for life effected by a gift for life of a share of the income of the trust and the gift of the income or a part of it for the period of a year as in this case." The distinction seems logically and practically to turn upon anticipation of income payments over a reasonably short period of time and an out-and-out transfer of a substantial and durable property interest, such as a life estate at least is. See 57 Harv.L.Rev. 382; 54 Harv.L.Rev. 1405; 50 Yale L.J. 512, 515. Where the line should be finally placed we need not try to anticipate here. But we are clear that distinctions attempted on the basis of the various legal names given a transaction, rather than on its actual results between the parties, do not afford a sound basis for its delimitation. More rationally, to accept the respondent's contention we ought frankly to consider the *Blair* case as overruled, 50 Yale L.J. 512, 518, a position which, as we have seen, the Supreme Court itself has declined to take.

The parties are in conflict as to the valuation of the life estate; and we are returning the case to the Tax Court for computation, without, of course, assuming that there will necessarily be some tax.

Reversed and remanded.

FRANK, CIRCUIT JUDGE (dissenting).

[Omitted.]

Problems, Notes and Question

1. *Basis.* Under Treas.Reg. §§ 1.1014–4 and 1.1015–1(b), the basis of property acquired from a decedent or by gift is apportioned between the life tenant and the remainderman. Each party's share of the "uniform basis" is adjusted with the passage of time, so that eventually (if the property is not sold) the remainderman ends up with all the basis.

For example, suppose that *D* bequeaths Blackacre to *A* for life, remainder to *B*. Assume that at the date of *A*'s death Blackacre is worth $100,000. If at that time the actuarial present value[z] of *A*'s life interest represents 60% of the total value of Blackacre, *A*'s basis for her income interest at that time is $60,000 (60% of $100,000) and *B*'s basis is $40,000.

If ten years later the actuarial present value of *A*'s income interest represents only 30% of the value of the entire property, then she is allocated 30% (and *B* 70%) of the property's basis. At *A*'s death, 100% of the property's basis is allocated to *B*.

Section 273 makes a life (or term) interest acquired by gift, bequest, or inheritance non-depreciable. Compare § 102(b)(2). Therefore, McAllister's share of the uniform basis would have done her no good if she had not sold her interest.

Section 1001(e) overrules that portion of the *McAllister* opinion dealing with the amount of gain or loss; today, McAllister would not be allowed to offset her basis against the amount realized on the sale.

2. *Capital gain.* What is the distinction between *McAllister* and *Hort*? Rev.Rul. 72–243, 1972–1 C.B. 233, announced that the Service will follow *McAllister* on the capital-gain issue.

3. *Problems.* *D* dies, bequeathing real property to *A* for life, remainder to *B*. The property is worth $100,000 on the applicable estate-tax valuation date. The actuarial value of *A*'s interest on the date of *D*'s death is $70,000.

(1) Can *A* amortize her interest over her remaining life expectancy?

(2) Suppose that immediately after *D*'s death *A* sells her interest to *P* for its $70,000 actuarial value. What result to *A* and *P*?

(3) Would your answer in (2) differ if *A* and *B* had simultaneously sold their interests to *P*, who paid *A* $70,000 and *B* $30,000?

4. *Reference.* Plumb, Tax Effects of Sales of Life Interests in Trusts, 9 Tax L.Rev. 39 (1953).

---

z. As the life tenant, *A* is entitled to the rents from Blackacre as long as she lives. The value of *A*'s interest is determined by discounting to present value that stream of future payments. This present-value figure is called the *actuarial* present value when the number of future payments to be received is estimated upon the basis of *A*'s life expectancy, as determined from actuarial tables.

STRANAHAN'S ESTATE v. COMMISSIONER

United States Court of Appeals, Sixth Circuit, 1973.
472 F.2d 867.

Before CELEBREZZE, PECK and KENT, CIRCUIT JUDGES.

PECK, CIRCUIT JUDGE.

This appeal comes from the United States Tax Court, which partially denied appellant estate's petition for a redetermination of a deficiency in the decedent's income tax for the taxable period January 1, 1965 through November 10, 1965, the date of decedent's death.

The facts before us are briefly recounted as follows: On March 11, 1964, the decedent, Frank D. Stranahan, entered into a closing agreement with the Commissioner of Internal Revenue Service (IRS) under which it was agreed that decedent owed the IRS $754,815.72 for interest due to deficiencies in federal income, estate and gift taxes regarding several trusts created in 1932. Decedent, a cash-basis taxpayer, paid the amount during his 1964 tax year. Because his personal income for the 1964 tax year would not normally have been high enough to fully absorb the large interest deduction, decedent accelerated his future income to avoid losing the tax benefit of the interest deduction. To accelerate the income, decedent executed an agreement dated December 22, 1964, under which he assigned to his son, Duane Stranahan, $122,820 in anticipated stock dividends from decedent's Champion Spark Plug Company common stock (12,500 shares). At the time both decedent and his son were employees and shareholders of Champion. As consideration for this assignment of future stock dividends, decedent's son paid the decedent $115,000 by check dated December 22, 1964. The decedent thereafter directed the transfer agent for Champion to issue all future dividend checks to his son, Duane, until the aggregate amount of $122,820 had been paid to him. Decedent reported this $115,000 payment as ordinary income for the 1964 tax year and thus was able to deduct the full interest payment from the sum of this payment and his other income. During decedent's taxable year in question, dividends in the total amount of $40,050 were paid to and received by decedent's son. No part of the $40,050 was reported as income in the return filed by decedent's estate for this period. Decedent's son reported this dividend income on his own return as ordinary income subject to the offset of his basis of $115,000, resulting in a net amount of $7,282 of taxable income.

Subsequently, the Commissioner sent appellant (decedent's estate) a notice of deficiency claiming that the $40,050 received by the decedent's son was actually income attributable to the decedent. After making an adjustment which is not relevant here, the Tax Court upheld the deficiency in the amount of $50,916.78. The Tax Court concluded that decedent's assignment of future dividends in exchange for the present discounted cash value of those dividends "though conducted in the form of an assignment of a property right, was in reality a loan to [decedent] masquerading as a sale and so disguised lacked any business purpose; and, therefore, decedent realized taxable income in the year 1965 when the dividend was declared paid."

As pointed out by the Tax Court, several long-standing principles must be recognized. First, under Section 451(a), a cash basis taxpayer ordinarily realizes income in the year of receipt rather than the year when earned. Second, a taxpayer who assigns future income for consideration in a bona fide commercial transaction will ordinarily realize ordinary income in the year of receipt. Commissioner v. P.G. Lake, Inc., 356 U.S. 260 (1958); Hort v. Commissioner, 313 U.S. 28 (1941). Third, a taxpayer is free to arrange his financial affairs to minimize his tax liability[2]; thus, the presence of tax avoidance motives will not nullify an otherwise bona fide transaction.[3] We also note there are no claims that the transaction was a sham, the purchase price was inadequate or that decedent did not actually receive the full payment of $115,000 in tax year 1964. And it is agreed decedent had the right to enter into a binding contract to sell his right to future dividends. 12 Ohio Jur.2d, Corporations, Sec. 604.

The Commissioner's view regards the transaction as merely a temporary shift of funds, with an appropriate interest factor, within the family unit. He argues that no change in the beneficial ownership of the stock was effected and no real risks of ownership were assumed by the son. Therefore, the Commissioner concludes, taxable income was realized not on the formal assignment but rather on the actual payment of the dividends.

It is conceded by taxpayer that the sole aim of the assignment was the acceleration of income so as to fully utilize the interest deduction. Gregory v. Helvering, 293 U.S. 465 (1935), established the landmark principle that the substance of a transaction, and not the form, determines the taxable consequences of that transaction. See also Higgins v. Smith, 308 U.S. 473 (1940). In the present transaction, however, it appears that both the form and the substance of the agreement assigned the right to receive future income. What was received by the decedent was the present value of that income the son could expect in the future. On the basis of the stock's past performance, the future income could have been (and was[5]) estimated with reasonable accuracy. Essentially,

2. "Any one may so arrange his affairs that his taxes shall be as low as possible; he is not bound to choose that pattern which will best pay the treasury; there is not even a patriotic duty to increase one's taxes." Helvering v. Gregory, 69 F.2d 809, 810 (2d Cir.1934) (Hand, J. Learned), aff'd 293 U.S. 465 (1935).

3. "As to the astuteness of taxpayers in ordering their affairs so as to minimize taxes, we have said that 'the very meaning of a line in the law is that you intentionally may go as close to it as you can if you do not pass it.' Superior Oil Co. v. Mississippi,

280 U.S. 390, 395–396. This is so because 'nobody owes any public duty to pay more than the law demands: taxes are enforced exactions, not voluntary contributions.' "Atlantic Coast Line v. Phillips, 332 U.S. 168, 172–173 (Frankfurter, J.).

5. It was determined that with the current dividend payment rate at that time of 50 cents per share per quarter, $115,000 represented the present value of the right to receive the assigned dividends of $4.60 per share discounted at the then prevailing interest rate of five percent.

decedent's son paid consideration to receive future income. Of course, the fact of a family transaction does not vitiate the transaction but merely subjects it to special scrutiny. Helvering v. Clifford, 309 U.S. 331 (1940).

We recognize the oft-stated principle that a taxpayer cannot escape taxation by legally assigning or giving away a portion of the income derived from income producing property retained by the taxpayer. Lucas v. Earl, 281 U.S. 111 (1930); Helvering v. Horst, 311 U.S. 112 (1940); Commissioner v. P.G. Lake, Inc., supra. Here, however, the acceleration of income was not designed to avoid or escape recognition of the dividends but rather to reduce taxation by fully utilizing a substantial interest deduction which was available. As stated previously, tax avoidance motives alone will not serve to obviate the tax benefits of a transaction. Further, the fact that this was a transaction for good and sufficient consideration, and not merely gratuitous, distinguishes the instant case from the line of authority beginning with Helvering v. Horst, supra.

* * *

Accordingly, we conclude the transaction to be economically realistic, with substance, and therefore should be recognized for tax purposes even though the consequences may be unfavorable to the Commissioner. The facts establish decedent did in fact receive payment. Decedent deposited his son's check for $115,000 to his personal account on December 23, 1964, the day after the agreement was signed. The agreement is unquestionably a complete and valid assignment to decedent's son of all dividends up to $122,820. The son acquired an independent right against the corporation since the latter was notified of the private agreement. Decedent completely divested himself of any interest in the dividends and vested the interest on the day of execution of the agreement with his son.

* * *

The judgment is reversed and the cause remanded for further proceedings consistent with this opinion.

Notes and Questions

1. *Assignment-of-income considerations.* The cases on gratuitous assignments of income from property establish that income from property is taxed to the property's owner (Chapter 7). Is the Sixth Circuit's attempt to distinguish those cases convincing? Should the assignment-of-income cases be read as establishing some arbitrary rule for donative assignments only, or do they teach us something basic about income?

Hydrometals, Inc. v. Commissioner, 31 T.C.M. 1260 (1972), affirmed mem. 485 F.2d 1236 (5th Cir.1973), cert. denied 416 U.S. 938 (1974), held that an assignment of a fraction of the taxpayer's manufacturing revenues up to a stated maximum figure (plus interest) was a loan.

2. *Sales of remainder interests.* Suppose A owns securities, or land, with a value of $100,000 and a basis of $90,000. The property generates fully taxable revenues of $10,000 a year (dividends, interest, or rent). A sells the right to three years' income for $24,868 (the present value of $10,000, payable at the end of each of the next three years, discounted at 10%). Under *Stranahan,* A has $24,868 income in the year of sale; under the Service's "loan" theory, A has borrowed $24,868 and is taxed on the property's income when earned (less interest).

Now suppose A keeps a right to three years' income and sells the rest of his interest in the property to B for $75,132. The tax treatment of this transaction is far from settled. Four possibilities worth considering are:

(1) Under the "loan" theory rejected in *Stranahan, B,* as the property's owner, would be taxed on the $10,000 annual income. A would be treated as having sold the property for $100,000 ($75,132 cash plus a $24,868 purchase-money mortgage), and so would have a $10,000 gain on the sale and $5132 interest income.

(2) A might be treated as having sold the entire property at a $10,000 gain; the theory here being that A's amount realized is the $75,132 cash plus property (the right to receive three years' earnings) worth $24,868. See Steinway & Sons v. Commissioner, 46 T.C. 375 (1966) (Acq.). This approach resembles the "loan" theory but does not require characterizing A's interest as a mortgage.

(3) A might be viewed as having sold property (the remainder) with a basis of $90,000 (since, under *Hort,* no basis is allocable to the income interest) for an amount realized of $75,132, producing a $14,868 loss. A has kept zero-basis property which will produce $30,000 income over three years.

(4) Despite *Hort,* A might allocate the property's $90,000 basis between the interest sold and the interest retained. If this were done, the basis of the interest sold would be $67,618 ($75,132/$100,000 of $90,000); that of the retained interest would be $22,382 ($24,868/$100,000 of $90,000). A would have a gain on the sale of $7514, and taxable income of $7618 ($30,000 minus $22,382) over three years from the retained interest. This method was applied in Hunter v. Commissioner, 44 T.C. 109 (1965), and Rev.Rul. 77–413, 1977–2 C.B. 298. (Today, however, § 167(e) prohibits amortization of the retained term interest if the remainder is held by a related party.)

No matter which of the above methods is followed, A's income in the long run will be $15,132 (if the purchaser is not related to A). The stakes involve timing and character.

3. *Depreciation of a term interest.* In Richard Hansen Land, Inc. v. Commissioner, 65 T.C.M. 2869 (1993), the taxpayer purchased a thirty-year term interest in land. Its controlling shareholder purchased the remainder. The Tax Court allowed the taxpayer to amortize its basis over thirty years. Today, § 167(e) forbids amortization of a term interest

whenever the remainder is held by a related person (within the meaning of § 267).

4. *"Remainder interest"* in a coupon bond. Under § 1286, the owner of a coupon bond who strips the coupons from the bond and then sells the bond, without the coupons, must include in income interest accrued up to the time of disposal. The basis of the bond and coupons is increased by the amount of accrued interest recognized, and the basis, as increased, is then allocated between the bond and the coupons according to their fair market values. In effect, § 1286 adopts the treatment described in (4) (note 2, above), if the property is a coupon bond.

COMMISSIONER v. PHILLIPS

United States Court of Appeals, Fourth Circuit, 1960.
275 F.2d 33.

Before SOBELOFF, CHIEF JUDGE, BOREMAN, CIRCUIT JUDGE, and HOFFMAN, DISTRICT JUDGE.

WALTER E. HOFFMAN, DISTRICT JUDGE.

By this appeal we are called upon to consider the tax status of a transaction wherein the taxpayer, admittedly motivated by a desire to minimize taxes, sold an endowment policy twelve (12) days prior to its maturity, and thereafter treated the excess received by him, over and above the cost of said policy, as a capital gain. The Commissioner contends that the questioned transaction was merely a transfer of the right to receive ordinary income taxable as such. The Tax Court concluded the issue favorably to the taxpayer. * * *

The taxpayer is an attorney specializing in tax matters. In 1931 The Connecticut Mutual Life Insurance Company insured taxpayer's life for the sum of $27,000. * * *

As of March 7, 1952, the cost of the policy to the taxpayer was $21,360.49, and the cash surrender value was $26,973.78. As noted, twelve days thereafter the policy matured in the face amount of $27,000.00.

On March 7, 1952, taxpayer assigned and transferred all of his right, title and interest in and to said policy to his two partners, Barker and Reid, for a cash consideration of $26,750, which amount was received and deposited in taxpayer's checking account on the same date. The assignment was executed on a form provided by the insurance company and, as we view the case, it is not essential that we refer to the contents thereof. Suffice it to say, it admittedly and irrevocably transferred any and all of taxpayer's interest in the policy.

* * *

Admittedly, had this policy been surrendered by the taxpayer, either at maturity for its face amount or earlier for its cash surrender value, it would not be considered a sale or exchange and the excess of the proceeds over taxpayer's cost basis would have been taxable as ordinary income. [Citations omitted.] By the means of a sale prior to maturity, may the excess of proceeds over cost be considered a capital gain?

* * *

We have no hesitancy in agreeing with the Tax Court on certain basic principles. The legal right of the taxpayer to decrease the amount of his taxes, or altogether to avoid them, by means which the law permits, cannot be doubted. [Citations omitted.] If, upon careful scrutiny, the transaction has real substance and is not a sham, it matters not whether the taxpayer's aim was "to avoid taxes, or to regenerate the world". Chisholm v. Commissioner, 2 Cir., 79 F.2d 14, 15. The sale must be real and bona fide with no vestige of control retained over the policy or its transferees by means of utilizing wholly owned corporations and like devices which follow the line of cases relied upon by the Commissioner. The Tax Court held that there had been full compliance with the requirements of a real and bona fide sale, and the fact that the purchase by the transferees may have been one of accommodation does not affect the nature of the transaction as a sale. John D. McKee, et al., Trustees, 35 B.T.A. 239. Disregarding the motive and accommodation factors, as we must for this purpose, it necessarily follows that the Tax Court was correct in concluding that the transaction represented an unequivocal and bona fide sale.

Taxpayer urges that the endowment policy constituted "property" and, as such, was only subject to capital gains treatment. This argument does not necessarily follow. That it was "property" in the broad sense of the word does not satisfy the requirements of the law for capital gain purposes. In Hort v. Commissioner, 313 U.S. 28, a fifteen year lease was held to be "property", but when cancelled by the lessor and lessee under an agreement wherein the lessor received a lump sum payment, the consideration received was not, for the purposes of internal revenue laws, deemed to be a return of capital, the court noting (313 U.S. 31):

> "Where, as in this case, the disputed amount was essentially a substitute for rental payments which § [61] expressly characterizes as gross income, it must be regarded as ordinary income, and it is immaterial that for some purposes the contract creating the right to such payments may be treated as 'property' or 'capital.'"

This brings us to a consideration of the principal argument advanced in this court by the Commissioner. Reliance is placed upon the recent decisions in Commissioner of Internal Revenue v. P.G. Lake, Inc., 356 U.S. 260, and Arnfeld v. United States, [163 F.Supp. 865], the latter being an opinion of the Court of Claims decided subsequent to the present case.

In accepting the theory advanced by the Commissioner we recognize that the line of demarcation is not clear. There are, of course, factual differences in *Lake* and *Arnfeld* which the taxpayer insists afford an opportunity to distinguish the principles there invoked. We believe, however, that we are required to adopt the view that since the amounts receivable upon maturity or surrender of the endowment policy unquestionably would have been taxable as ordinary income, the taxpayer may not convert such income into capital gain by a bona fide sale of the contract which is the means of producing such ordinary income. The cash value of the policy was equivalent to the reserve value which, in turn, was computed on the basis of three percent compound interest. The sale of the policy was, as said by Mr. Justice Douglas in *Lake,* "essentially a substitute for what would otherwise be received at a future time as ordinary income." Manifestly, the consideration paid by taxpayer's partners was "not for an increase in the value of income-producing property." [356 U.S. 260.] The policy had a face value of $27,000, and its cash surrender value as of March 7, 1952 (the date of the assignment), was $26,973.78. The increased value had already accrued, and we cannot accept the suggestion that the assignees would pay out $26,750 merely to receive an increase in value of $26.22. While the tax-saving motive is not to be considered in ascertaining the bona fides of the sale or assignment, we think that it may play some part in determining whether or not the consideration was paid for an increase in the value of income-producing property, and whether the amount so received was essentially a substitute for what would have otherwise been received as ordinary income in a matter of twelve days.

If we could revert to 1938 and determine the status of the property at the time of taxpayer's conversion of the policy into an endowment contract, we could then give serious consideration to the myriad economic factors which are determinative of the dividend paid over a period of years. We believe, however, that the test to be applied with respect to a contract of insurance is the status of the same at the time the transaction in controversy may have occurred. Under ordinary circumstances in situations involving an insurance contract, whenever an amount receivable under the policy is in excess of the cost, the excess of the amount received, whether through the medium of sale, assignment or surrender, would be tantamount to the right to receive ordinary income.[3]

* * *

For the foregoing reasons the decision of the Tax Court is Reversed.

Notes and Questions

1. *Donative transactions.* If Phillips had given the policy away just before maturity, would the gain have been taxed to him or to the donee?

2. *The "substitute for ordinary income" doctrine reconsidered.* As noted above (p. 662), cases like *Hort* and *Phillips* cannot be explained

---

3. On reargument, counsel for the Commissioner conceded that there may be exceptional circumstances requiring a modification of this rule. For example, if a policyholder had an amount receivable thereunder which was in excess of his cost, but policyholder was afflicted with a disease which would result in his death in the near future, he could, if in need of cash, assign his policy for an amount in excess of that receivable under the policy and, as to such excess, treat the same as a capital gain.

simply by saying that gain on a sale is ordinary if the sale proceeds are a "substitute for ordinary income." This argument, if accepted, would leave nothing of the capital-gains provisions since, at least if "imputed income" is viewed as ordinary income of a sort, all capital gains are substitutes for ordinary income. Furthermore, the common rationales for favorable treatment of capital gains expressly recognize that this is so. Can you devise a more refined version of the "substitute" theory—a version that will explain *Hort, McAllister,* and *Phillips?*

3. *References.* Popkin, The Deep Structure of Capital Gains, 33 Case W.Res.L.Rev. (1983); Note, A Spreading of Receipts Formula for Creating a Capital Gains/Ordinary Income Brightline: Contract Terminations and Business–Versus–Investment Assets, 84 Yale L.J. 729 (1978); Del Cotto, "Property" in the Capital Asset Definition: Influence of "Fruit and Tree," 15 Buffalo L.Rev. 1 (1965); Note, The *P.G. Lake* Guides to Ordinary Income: An Appraisal in Light of Capital Gains Policies, 14 Stan.L.Rev. 551 (1962); Note, Distinguishing Ordinary Income from Capital Gain Where Rights to Future Income Are Sold, 69 Harv.L.Rev. 737 (1956).

*

Chapter Eleven

DEFERRED–PAYMENT SALES

A. THE INSTALLMENT METHOD

1. IN GENERAL

Suppose a taxpayer sells property in exchange for a cash down payment and the purchaser's obligation to make additional payments on the purchase price in the future. In the absence of a special rule, a cash-method taxpayer would usually recognize in the year of sale gain or loss equal to the difference between the amount realized (the cash received plus the value of the purchaser's obligation to make future payments) and the adjusted basis of the property sold; §§ 1001(a) & (b). An accrual-method taxpayer would have to include the face amount of the purchaser's obligation in the amount realized.[a] Under either accounting method, a taxpayer would be required to pay tax on the gain before receiving a substantial portion of the sales price in cash. Section 453 avoids this inconvenience by permitting a deferred-payment seller to recognize a portion of the gain as each payment is received.[b]

Unless the taxpayer elects to recognize the gain in the year of sale[c], *gain*[d] from an *installment sale* is to be reported under the *installment method;* § 453(a). Generally speaking, an installment sale is "a disposition of property where at least 1 payment is to be received after the close of the taxable year in which the disposition occurs";[e] § 453(b)(1). Under the installment method, the taxpayer recognizes as gain for each year that proportion of the (principal) *payments* received during the year which the *gross profit* (realized or to be realized when payment is completed) bears to the *contract price;* § 453(c). The ratio of the gross profit to the contract price is known as the *gross-profit ratio;* Temp. Treas.Reg. § 15a.453–1(b)(2)(i). Thus the taxpayer recognizes in each

---

a. E.g., George L. Castner Co. v. Commissioner, 30 T.C. 1061 (1958).

b. Legislation enacted in 1999 prohibited use of the installment method by accrual-method taxpayers. The 1999 provision was retroactively repealed in 2000.

c. Section 453(d) permits taxpayers to opt out of the installment method.

d. Section 453 does not apply to losses. Rev.Rul. 70–430, 1970–2 C.B. 51.

e. But under §§ 453(b)(2) & (*l*), a sale of property by a dealer generally does not qualify as an installment sale and therefore cannot be reported on the installment method.

year an amount equal to the product of the payments received during the year and the gross-profit ratio.

The gross profit is the *selling price* less the adjusted basis of the property sold; Temp.Treas.Reg. § 15a.453–1(b)(2)(v). The selling price means the gross selling price without reduction for selling expenses or mortgages on the property; Temp.Treas.Reg. § 15a.453–1(b)(2)(ii). Interest, whether stated or unstated, is not considered to be part of the selling price; id. Commissions and other selling expenses are added to the basis for the purpose of determining the gross profit; Temp.Treas.Reg. § 15a.453–1(b)(2)(v).

The contract price is the selling price reduced by any *qualifying indebtedness* assumed, or taken subject to, by the buyer, except to the extent that the qualifying indebtedness exceeds the seller's basis; Temp. Treas.Reg. § 15a.453–1(b)(2)(iii). Qualifying indebtedness is discussed at pp. 682–684.

For example, in a sale qualifying under § 453 T sells nondepreciable property (adjusted basis $75,000) for $160,000, payable $40,000 down and $40,000 (plus market-rate interest) in each of the following three years. T pays her broker a $5000 sales commission on the transaction. T's gross profit is $80,000 ($160,000 selling price less $80,000 adjusted basis, which includes the $5000 broker's commission). The gross-profit ratio is ½ ($80,000 gross profit ÷ $160,000 contract price). As each payment is received, T must recognize $20,000 (½ of $40,000) as gain; the balance of each payment is a return of basis. (Notice how the entire $80,000 of realized gain is recognized over the four-year period (at the rate of $20,000 a year).) The interest received is ordinary income to T.

The character of the gain recognized as payments are received on an installment obligation is usually determined in accordance with the character and holding period of the asset sold. Thus, if the installment obligation was received in the sale of a nondepreciable capital asset with a long-term holding period, the gain recognized each year is long-term capital gain. If the asset sold was a § 1231 asset, the gain is § 1231 gain. Whether the § 1231 gain is ultimately characterized as long-term capital gain or ordinary gain depends upon the outcome of the § 1231 hotchpot for the year in which the payment is received (since that is when the gain is *recognized*).

Whenever the property sold is subject to depreciation recapture under § 1245 or § 1250, § 453(i) requires that the recapture income be recognized in the year of sale. Any remaining gain can be recognized under the installment method. In applying § 453 to the remaining gain, the adjusted basis of the property is increased by the amount of the recapture income to prevent that portion of the gain from being recognized a second time as payments are received. The upward adjustment to basis causes a reduction in the gross profit and the gross-profit ratio. Then the taxpayer recognizes gain (beginning in the year of sale if a year-of-sale payment is received) in an amount equal to the product of the gross-profit ratio and the amount of the payment received.

Suppose, for example, that in the preceding illustration the property was business equipment (§ 1245 property) and T's adjusted basis reflected depreciation deductions of $60,000. In the year of sale, T must recapture as ordinary income the $60,000 of § 1245 gain. In computing T's gross profit, the adjusted basis is increased by the $60,000 to prevent the recognition of that gain a second time under the installment method. So, T's gross profit is $20,000 ($160,000 selling price less $140,000 adjusted basis, as increased by the amount of § 1245 gain recaptured), and T's gross-profit ratio is ⅛ ($20,000 gross profit ÷ $160,000 contract price). In addition to the $60,000 of ordinary income, T recognizes $5000 of § 1231 gain (⅛ of $40,000) in the year of sale and $5000 of § 1231 gain when each subsequent payment is received. Whether the § 1231 gain is ultimately characterized as ordinary income or long-term capital gain will depend upon the outcome of T's § 1231 hotchpot each year.

Since capital gains are taxed at a substantially lower rate than interest income, a deferred-payment seller may be tempted to increase the selling price for the property and decrease the interest rate on the deferred portion of the purchase price. Although the pre-tax present value of the future payments may remain the same, the after-tax present value could be increased if interest income could be transmuted into capital gain in this way. Sections 483 and 1274 prevent this mischief by recharacterizing a portion of the ostensible purchase price as interest in most cases in which the parties' agreement fails to provide for interest at the market rate.

Problems and Notes

1. *Problems.*

(1) Unless otherwise indicated, assume in each of the following problems that (1) S (not a dealer) sells to P a nondepreciable capital asset with a basis of $40,000; (2) the contract of sale provides for adequate stated interest on any deferred balance of the sale price; (3) S and P are not related; and (4) S makes no election under § 453(d). How will S be taxed in each case if all payments are made on schedule?

(a) In year 1 S sells the property to P for $10,000 down and $10,000 a year in each of years 2 through 10. P's $90,000 deferred-payment obligation has a value of $81,000 at the time of the sale.

(b) Same as (a), except that S incurs a $5000 brokerage commission on the sale.

(c) Same as (a), except that the property is § 1245 property and S's adjusted basis reflects $30,000 of depreciation deductions. See § 453(i).

(d) Same as (a), except that the property is depreciable property (not subject to recapture) and the purchaser is P Corp., all of the stock of which is owned by S. See § 453(g).

(e) Same as (a), except that P transferred to S in year 1 $10,000 cash and a promissory note issued by T with a principal balance and value of $36,000. The *T* note was payable $4000 a year in years 2 through 10. *P* gave his $54,000 promissory note, payable $6000 a year in years 2 through 10, for the balance of the purchase price. See Temp.Treas.Reg. § 15a.453–1(b)(3).

(f) Same as (a), except that *P*'s note was secured by an irrevocable standby letter of credit issued by *P*'s bank. See § 453(f)(3) and Temp.Treas.Reg. § 15a.453–1(b)(3).

(g) Same as (a), except that the sales contract did not provide for interest on the deferred payments. Note §§ 483 and 1274. (State your answer in general terms without making specific calculations.)

(2) In an exchange qualifying under § 1031, *T* (not a dealer) transferred to *P* land with a basis of $70,000 and a value of $100,000. *P* transferred to *T* land worth $60,000 and agreed to pay *T* $20,000 cash (plus adequate stated interest) in each of the following two years. How does *T* report the gain on the transaction if *P* makes the payments on schedule? See § 453(f)(6) and Prop.Treas.Reg. § 1.453–1(f)(1). What is *T*'s basis for the land received in the exchange?

2. *Installment sales to related taxpayers.* Consider an installment sale by a parent to his adult child, followed by the child's sale of the property for cash to an unrelated buyer. If the parent were allowed to use installment reporting, these transactions would achieve for the family, considered as a unit, the tax advantages of installment reporting without the non-tax disadvantage of having to wait for the sales proceeds. The courts had considerable difficulty in denying the benefits of installment reporting to these sale-and-resale transactions before the enactment of § 453(e). That provision, which was added to the Code in 1980, requires a taxpayer who has made an installment sale to a "related person" to recognize gain if the related person disposes of the property before the taxpayer has reported all of the gain.

This rule applies only if the second disposition occurs within two years of the first; § 453(e)(2). Exceptions are provided for certain dispositions described in § 453(e)(6) and for cases in which neither disposition "had as one of its principal purposes the avoidance of Federal income tax"; § 453(e)(7). If the "evil" at which § 453(e) is directed is the achievement by an economic unit of the tax advantages of an installment sale and the non-tax advantages of a cash sale, the exception for transactions not motivated by "tax avoidance" makes little sense.

Problem. In year 1, *S* (not a dealer) made a bona fide sale of a nondepreciable capital asset (adjusted basis $40,000) to her adult child, *C*, for $100,000, payable $10,000 down and $10,000 (plus adequate stated interest) in each of years 2 through 10. In year 2 (before making the principal payment to *S* for that year), *C* resold the property to an unrelated party for $110,000 cash. *C* remained liable on the indebtedness to *S* and made timely payments thereon in years 2 through 10. what result to *S* and *C*?

3. *Contingent-payment sales.* Before the enactment of the Installment Sales Revision Act of 1980, the Commissioner took the position that the installment method could not be used in sales in which the purchase price was not fixed. The Act added § 453(j)(2), which directs the Treasury to prescribe by regulation for the installment reporting of contingent-payment sales. In response to that directive, the Treasury has promulgated Temp.Treas.Reg. § 15a.453–1(c).

Problem. S sells closely held corporate stock (adjusted basis $40,000) to *P*. *P* agrees to pay *S* $10,000, plus an amount equal to 20% of the corporation's profits, in each of years 1 through 5. Assume that *S* receives the following amounts (plus adequate stated interest):

Year	Fixed Payment	Contingent Payment
1	$10,000	$ 5000
2	10,000	5000
3	10,000	10,000
4	10,000	30,000
5	10,000	20,000

How does *S* report the gain under the installment method?

4. *Publicly traded property.* Section 453(k) prohibits taxpayers from using the installment method for the sale of securities that are traded on an established securities market. In addition, § 453(k) authorizes the Treasury to issue regulations forbidding the use of installment reporting for other property that is regularly traded on an established market. Property that can easily be sold for cash does not present the liquidity problem that § 453 is intended to alleviate. See Joint Committee on Taxation, General Explanation of the Tax Reform Act of 1986 at pp. 490–91.

When securities are sold through a stock exchange, cash settlement of the transaction usually occurs three business days after the date on which the trade is executed. The legislative history of § 453(k) suggests that taxpayers who sell securities through an exchange must recognize their gain or loss on the day the trade is executed rather than on the settlement date. See S.Rep. No. 99–313, 99th Cong., 2d Sess. 131 (1986). Rev. Rul. 93–84, 1993–2 C.B. 225, agrees. The taxpayer's holding period is based upon the trade dates, excluding the day on which the security was acquired and including the day on which it was sold; Rev. Rul. 66–97, 1966–1 C.B. 190. So, a taxpayer who purchases stock on June 2 and sells it on the following June 2 has a short-term capital gain because the holding period is *exactly* (not more than) one year; Anderson v. Commissioner, 33 T.C.M. 234 (1974).

5. *Another characterization issue.* Even when the gain on the sale of a building is characterized as long-term capital gain, the portion of the gain that "makes up" for depreciation taken is usually taxed at a maximum rate of 25% rather than the usual capital-gains rate of 20%; § 1(h) (discussed p. 605, above). This make-up gain is called the "unre-

captured § 1250 gain"; § 1(h)(7). When gain on the sale of the building is recognized under the installment method, how is the gain apportioned each year between the unrecaptured § 1250 gain and other gain? Treas. Reg. § 1.453–12(a) requires that the unrecaptured § 1250 gain be taken into account before the other (20%-rate) gain.

For example, *T* sells a building (without the land) for $100,000, payable $10,000 down and $10,000 (plus market-rate interest) for each of the following nine years. *T*'s adjusted basis for the building is $35,000, which basis reflects $40,000 of straight-line depreciation deductions. On the sale, *T* realizes gain of $65,000 ($100,000 amount realized less $35,000 adjusted basis), of which $40,000 just makes up for T's having taken $40,000 of depreciation deductions even though the building did not decline in value. That portion of the gain is the unrecaptured § 1250 gain. The other $25,000 of gain (representing the excess of the $100,000 selling price over *T*'s original cost of $75,000) is real economic gain. Assume that the building is a § 1231 asset and that the § 453 gain recognized each year is *T*'s only § 1231 transaction for that year. As each $10,000 payment is received, *T* must recognize $6500 of § 1231 gain, which is characterized as long-term capital gain in the § 1231 hotchpot. The first $40,000 so recognized is unrecaptured § 1250 gain. So, the unrecaptured § 1250 gain comprises the $6500 recognized in each of years 1 through 6 (a total of $39,000) and $1000 of the gain recognized in year 7. Those gains are subject to tax at a maximum rate of 25%. The other $5500 of gain recognized in year 7 and the $6500 of gain recognized in each of years 8 through 10 qualifies for the 20% rate.

Now suppose that in the year of sale *T* also recognized (and was allowed) $8000 of loss from the sale of another § 1231 asset. Since the § 1231 loss ($8000) exceeds the § 1231 gain ($6500), both the loss and the gain are characterized as ordinary. Nevertheless, in determining the amount of unrecaptured § 1250 gain remaining to be taken into account in future years, *T*'s $6500 of ordinary gain for year 1 reduces the unrecaptured § 1250 gain. (What result if *T*'s only § 1231 gain or loss in year 2 is the $6500 of gain recognized from the installment sale? Before answering, review § 1231(c).)

Keep in mind also that any capital gain on the sale of the land on which the building sits qualifies for the 20% rate. So, one must begin by apportioning the consideration received between the land and the building and computing the gain realized on each. As the gains are recognized under § 453, the gain on the building must be treated in the manner described above.

6. *Section 453 and the time-value of money.* The purpose of § 453 is to match the recognition of gain with the receipt of cash. Unlike most other non-recognition provisions, however, § 453 permits the deferral of gain even though the nature of the asset disposed of (for example, real estate or closely held corporate stock) differs drastically from that of the property received in exchange (the purchaser's obligation to make future payments). Critics of § 453 argue that deferral gives the deferred-

payment seller an unwarranted advantage over the seller who receives cash.

Consider, for example, a taxpayer (not a dealer) who owns land with a basis of $20,000 and value of $100,000. Assume the taxpayer wishes to sell the land and invest the proceeds in a five-year certificate of deposit yielding 10–percent interest. If the taxpayer sells the land for cash, he must recognize a gain of $80,000 in the year of sale. If the tax rate is 40 percent, the tax on the gain would be $32,000, the taxpayer would have $68,000 ($100,000 sale proceeds less $32,000 tax) to reinvest, and the annual yield on the investment would be $6800 (10% of $68,000).

Now suppose instead that the taxpayer sold the land for $100,000, payable after five years with annual interest at 10 percent. Assume that payment of the deferred balance is secured by an irrevocable standby letter of credit issued by a bank.[f] Since § 453 defers recognition of the $80,000 realized gain, the taxpayer can earn interest of $10,000 a year (10% of $100,000) during the five-year deferral period.

Deferral under § 453 is particularly suspect where the seller borrows against the security of the installment obligations. In those cases, the taxpayer may have effectively "cashed in" on the installment obligations so that deferral of the gain is no longer appropriate.

Over time, Congress has restricted deferral under § 453 in several ways:

> (1) Most sales by dealers no longer qualify for installment reporting; §§ 453(b)(2) & (*l*).

> (2) If the face amount of installment obligations arising during the year exceeds $5,000,000, the seller generally must pay annual interest on the deferred tax attributable to installment obligations in excess of that amount; §§ 453A(a)(1), (b), & (c).

> (3) If the seller pledges an obligation as security for a loan, the loan proceeds are treated as a constructive payment on the installment note; §§ 453A(a)(2) & (d).

Rules (2) and (3) apply to installment obligations arising from sales in which the sales price exceeds $150,000, except for sales of personal-use property or farm property (§ 453A(b)(3)) and time shares and residential lots with respect to which an interest charge is imposed on the deferred tax by § 453(*l*); § 453A(b)(4).

7. *References.* Note, Fairness and Tax Avoidance in the Taxation of Installment Sales, 100 Harv.L.Rev. 403 (1986); Ginsburg, Rethinking the Tax Law in the New Installment Sale World, 59 Taxes 886 (1981);

---

f. We make this assumption so that the seller's risk will approximate that of investing in a government-insured bank certificate of deposit. In reality, the taxpayer would assume somewhat greater risk in a deferred-payment sale in which the future payments were secured by a bank letter of credit because the letter of credit would not be backed by the government. The taxpayer would therefore probably insist upon a rate of interest higher than that on five-year certificates of deposit.

Emory, The Installment Method of Reporting Income: Its Election, Use, and Effect, 53 Cornell L.Rev. 181 (1968).

2. SALES OF MORTGAGED PROPERTY

The treatment of liabilities encumbering property sold in an installment sale poses difficulties because, depending on the origin of the liability, the purchaser's assumption of the liability (or the transfer of the property subject to the liability) may or may not be tantamount to a cash payment by the purchaser to the seller. Consider a taxpayer who purchases land for $100,000, paying $20,000 cash down and agreeing to pay the $80,000 balance of the purchase price (with adequate stated interest) in a subsequent year. Payment of the deferred portion of the purchase price is secured by a mortgage on the land. Before making any principal payments on the mortgage, the taxpayer sells the property subject to the mortgage for $120,000, the $40,000 due the taxpayer for the equity being payable $10,000 cash down and $10,000 a year (plus adequate stated interest) for each of the following three years. Although the *Crane* doctrine (pp. 503–521, above) requires the inclusion of the liability in the taxpayer's amount realized, the policy underlying § 453 suggests that the $80,000 of liability relief should not be treated as a payment received by the taxpayer for the purpose of computing the gain recognized in the year of sale. In essence, the taxpayer has made a deferred-payment sale of the equity in the property.

Now suppose the taxpayer owns unencumbered property with a basis of $100,000 and value of $120,000. In anticipation of selling the property, the taxpayer obtains an $80,000 loan against the security of the property and uses the loan proceeds for purposes unrelated to the property. The taxpayer then sells the property, subject to the $80,000 encumbrance, receiving $10,000 cash down and $10,000 a year (plus adequate stated interest) for each of the subsequent three years. This resembles the situation where the seller does not encumber the property before the sale and the purchaser makes an additional $80,000 down payment.

Under the Temporary Regulations, *qualifying indebtedness* is not treated as part of either the payments or the contract price, except to the extent that the liability exceeds the property's basis; Temp.Treas.Reg. §§ 15a.453–1(b)(2) & (3). Non-qualifying indebtedness is included in the contract price and treated as a payment received by the seller in the year in which the assumption of (or acquisition of the property subject to) the liability occurs; Temp.Treas.Reg. § 15a.453–1(b)(2).

The term "qualifying indebtedness" is defined in Temp.Treas.Reg. § 15a.453–1(b)(2)(iv):

> The term "qualifying indebtedness" means a mortgage or other indebtedness encumbering the property and indebtedness, not secured by the property but incurred or assumed by the purchaser incident to the purchaser's acquisition, holding, or operation in the ordinary course of business or investment, of the property. The term

"qualifying indebtedness" does not include an obligation of the taxpayer incurred incident to the disposition of the property (e.g., legal fees relating to the taxpayer's sale of the property) or an obligation functionally unrelated to the acquisition, holding, or operation of the property (e.g., the taxpayer's medical bill). Any obligation created subsequent to the taxpayer's acquisition of the property and incurred or assumed by the taxpayer or placed as an encumbrance on the property in contemplation of disposition of the property is not qualifying indebtedness if the arrangement results in accelerating recovery of the taxpayer's basis in the installment sale.

Problems, Notes and Question

1. *Problems.*

(1) *S* (not a dealer) owns a nondepreciable capital asset with a basis of $40,000 and value of $100,000. The property is subject to a $20,000 mortgage incurred by *S* in purchasing the property. *S* sells the property to *P*. *P* assumes the $20,000 mortgage and pays *S* $10,000 down and $10,000 a year in each of years 2–8. (The contract of sale provides for adequate stated interest on the deferred payments.) How will *S* be taxed if all payments are made on schedule?

(2) Same as (1), except that *S* incurs the mortgage liability in anticipation of the sale to *P*.

(3) Same as (1), except that the amount of the mortgage encumbering the property is $60,000, and *P* pays *S* $5000 cash in each of years 1–8.

2. *An alternative approach.* Suppose in problem (1) (note 1, above) that *P*'s payments on the $20,000 assumed mortgage (say $10,000 a year) were treated as payments to *S* and included in *S*'s contract price. *S*'s gain would still be $60,000 in the long run, but the deferral period would be longer than under the computations required by the regulations. Under this approach, *S* would be treated as receiving payments of $20,000 each year for two years, and $10,000 a year for the next six years. Sixty percent of each payment would be taxable. Why are the computations specified by the regulations preferable to this alternative? The regulations' approach was held valid in Burnet v. S & L Building Corp., 288 U.S. 406 (1933).

3. *Wrap-around mortgages.* The parties to a sale may wish to leave in place an existing mortgage against the property (perhaps because the mortgage note bears interest at a rate favorable to the borrower). In most such sales, the purchaser either *assumes* the existing indebtedness (in which case the lender can proceed against the purchaser personally if a default occurs) or the purchaser acquires the property *subject to* the indebtedness (in which case the lender cannot obtain a personal judgment against the purchaser in case of default). Under either approach, it is understood that the purchaser (rather than the seller) is to make the mortgage payments.

Occasionally, however, the parties agree instead that the purchaser will make payments only to the seller and that the seller will continue to service the existing mortgage. In these cases, the purchaser customarily gives the seller a mortgage against the property to secure the purchaser's obligation to make future payments to the seller. The mortgage running from the purchaser to the seller is called a "wrap-around" mortgage; the original mortgage is referred to as the "underlying" or "wrapped" indebtedness. The seller typically must make payments on the wrapped indebtedness regardless of whether the purchaser makes the required payments to the seller on the wrap-around mortgage.

The Treasury once attempted to treat sales in which the buyer gives the seller a wrap-around mortgage the same as sales in which the buyer assumes or takes subject to an existing mortgage. If the seller retained liability for servicing an existing ("wrapped") indebtedness, with the buyer giving the seller a wrap-around mortgage, Temp.Treas.Reg. § 15a.453–1(b)(3) & (5) would have computed the seller's gain as if the buyer had acquired the property subject to the wrapped indebtedness. This would have reduced the seller's contract price under § 453 and accelerated the seller's gain. This portion of the regulations was held invalid in Professional Equities, Inc. v. Commissioner, 89 T.C. 165 (1987), and the Commissioner has acquiesced in the decision; 1988–2 C.B. 1.

To illustrate the approach of *Professional Equities*, which the Commissioner has now accepted, consider the following example. *S* (not a dealer) owned land with a basis of $60,000 and a value of $120,000. The property was subject to an underlying mortgage in the amount of $40,000. In year 1, *S* sold the property to *P* for $120,000, payable $20,000 down and $20,000 a year (plus adequate stated interest) in each of years 2 through 6. *P* neither assumed nor took subject to the underlying mortgage. Instead, *S* continued to make all payments on the mortgage. *P*'s obligation to *S* was secured by a wrap-around mortgage.

Under the Tax Court's approach in *Professional Equities*, the wrapped indebtedness is disregarded, the selling price and contract price are $120,000, the gross profit is $60,000 ($120,000 selling price less $60,000 basis), and the gross-profit ratio is ½ ($60,000 gross profit divided by $120,000 contract price). As *S* receives each $20,000 payment, he recognizes $10,000 (½ of $20,000) as gain.

3. THE DISPOSITION OF INSTALLMENT OBLIGATIONS

What if the seller disposes of an installment obligation, the gain on which is being reported under § 453, before receiving all of the installment payments? Section 453B prescribes generally that the holder must recognize gain or loss if the obligation is "satisfied at other than face value or distributed, transmitted, sold, or otherwise disposed of * * *."

In the case of a sale or exchange of an installment obligation, § 453B(a) requires, as one would expect, that the taxpayer recognize gain or loss equal to the difference between the amount realized and the adjusted basis of the obligation. As to an obligation satisfied at other than its face amount, § 453B(a) treats the transaction like a sale of the obligation. Section 453B(a) goes further, however, to require the taxpayer to recognize gain when an installment obligation is distributed, transmitted, or otherwise disposed of—events, such as gifts, that would not usually cause the recognition of gain or loss if other types of property were involved. In these cases, § 453B(a) codifies assignment-of-income principles: Gain from a sale made by the taxpayer cannot be diverted to another by reporting the sale on the installment method and transferring the installment obligations.

Problems and Notes

1. *Problems.* In year 1, *S* sold a nondepreciable capital asset with a basis of $40,000 to *P* for $100,000, payable $10,000 cash down in year 1 and $10,000 (plus adequate stated interest) in each of years 2 through 10.

(1) What is *S*'s basis in the $90,000 installment obligation? See § 453B(b).

(2) What result if later in year 1 *S* sells the installment obligation for $80,000? for $95,000? What is the character of *S*'s gain on the sale of the obligation?

(3) What result if later in year 1 *S* gives the installment obligation (value $80,000) to her child, *C*? What result to *C* as *C* receives payments on the obligation?

(4) What result in (3) if *C* is the obligor on the installment obligation (that is, *C* is the purchaser of the property)? See § 453B(f).

(5) What result if later in year 1 *S* dies and bequeaths the obligation to *C*? What result as *C* receives payments on the obligation? See §§ 453B(c) and 691.

(6) What result in (5) if *C* is the obligor on the installment obligation (that is, if *C* is the purchaser of the property)? See § 691(a)(5).

2. *Non-recognition transactions.* Despite the broad language of § 453B(a), Treas.Reg. § 1.453–9 permits the transfer of installment obligations in some non-recognition transactions without the recognition of gain or loss. These transactions include, among others, transfers to a partnership by a partner under § 721 and transfers to a controlled corporation under § 351.

3. *Modification of obligation.* The Commissioner has frequently argued that a modification of the terms of an installment obligation is a taxable "satisfaction" or "disposition" under § 453B. The courts' acceptance of this theory reached its apogee in Burrell Groves, Inc. v. Commissioner, 223 F.2d 526 (5th Cir.1955). In *Burrell Groves, T* sold property to *A*, receiving a cash down payment and a fifteen-year installment mortgage note bearing interest at four percent. Two years later *A* sold the property to *B*, who assumed the obligation for the unpaid

portion of the purchase price by executing a new note and mortgage in favor of T. The terms of the note given by B increased the interest rate to five percent and reduced the schedule for principal payments by eight years. A was released from liability on the original note. Because the obligor, the maturities, and the interest rates were changed, the Fifth Circuit held that T had made a taxable disposition of the original note, even though the amount of the debt, the obligee, and the security remained the same.

Rev.Rul. 82–122, 1982–1 C.B. 80, comes close to repudiating the government's victory in *Burrell Groves*. In the ruling, T held an installment note secured by a mortgage, arising from the sale of property to A. The note provided for annual interest at thirteen percent and equal monthly payments on principal for a period of ten years. It also provided that, unless T consented, the note would become fully due and payable if A sold the property before paying off the note. Prior to paying off the note, A sold the property to B, who, with T's consent, assumed the mortgage held by T. T and B agreed to increase the interest rate to fifteen percent, the monthly payments were increased to reflect the higher rate of interest, and A was released from further liability on the note. The Service ruled that the substitution of B as obligor on the note and the increase in the interest rate did not constitute a taxable satisfaction or disposition of the note under § 453B(a). The switch of obligors, however, would be a realization event to T under Treas. Reg. § 1.1001–3, discussed at p. 493, above. This possible conflict between § 453 and Treas. Reg. § 1.1001–3 has yet to be resolved.

4. *Reference.* Emory & Hjorth, Installment sales act, part II: cost recovery, 337 liquidations, related parties, dispositions, 54 J.Tax'n 130 (1981).

B. SALES NOT ON THE INSTALLMENT METHOD

1. NO FIXED PURCHASE PRICE

BURNET v. LOGAN

Supreme Court of the United States, 1931.
283 U.S. 404, 51 S.Ct. 550, 75 L.Ed. 1143.

MR. JUSTICE MCREYNOLDS delivered the opinion of the Court.

These causes present the same questions. One opinion, stating the essential circumstances disclosed in No. 521, will suffice for both.

Prior to March, 1913, and until March 11, 1916, respondent, Mrs. Logan, owned 250 of the 4,000 capital shares issued by the Andrews & Hitchcock Iron Company. It held 12% of the stock of the Mahoning Ore & Steel Company, an operating concern. In 1895 the latter corporation procured a lease for 97 years upon the "Mahoning" mine and since then has regularly taken therefrom large, but varying, quantities of iron ore—

in 1913, 1,515,428 tons; in 1914, 1,212,287 tons; in 1915, 2,311,940 tons; in 1919, 1,217,167 tons; in 1921, 303,020 tons; in 1923, 3,029,865 tons. The lease contract did not require production of either maximum or minimum tonnage or any definite payments. Through an agreement of stockholders (steel manufacturers) the Mahoning Company is obligated to apportion extracted ore among them according to their holdings.

On March 11, 1916, the owners of all the shares in Andrews & Hitchcock Company sold them to Youngstown Sheet & Tube Company, which thus acquired, among other things 12% of the Mahoning Company's stock and the right to receive the same percentage of ore thereafter taken from the leased mine.

For the shares so acquired the Youngstown Company paid the holders $2,200,000 in money and agreed to pay annually thereafter for distribution among them 60 cents for each ton of ore apportioned to it. Of this cash Mrs. Logan received 250/4000ths—$137,500; and she became entitled to the same fraction of any annual payment thereafter made by the purchaser under the terms of sale.

Mrs. Logan's mother had long owned 1100 shares of the Andrews & Hitchcock Company. She died in 1917, leaving to the daughter one-half of her interest in payments thereafter made by the Youngstown Company. This bequest was appraised for federal estate tax purposes at $277,164.50.

During 1917, 1918, 1919 and 1920 the Youngstown Company paid large sums under the agreement. Out of these respondent received on account of her 250 shares $9,900.00 in 1917, $11,250.00 in 1918, $8,995.50 in 1919, $5,444.30 in 1920—$35,589.80. By reason of the interest from her mother's estate she received $19,790.10 in 1919, and $11,977.49 in 1920.

Reports of income for 1918, 1919 and 1920 were made by Mrs. Logan upon the basis of cash receipts and disbursements. They included no part of what she had obtained from annual payments by the Youngstown Company. She maintains that until the total amount actually received by her from the sale of her shares equals their value on March 1, 1913, no taxable income will arise from the transaction. Also that until she actually receives by reason of the right bequeathed to her a sum equal to its appraised value, there will be no taxable income therefrom.

On March 1, 1913, the value of the 250 shares then held by Mrs. Logan *exceeded* $173,089.80—the total of all sums actually received by her prior to 1921 from their sale ($137,500.00 cash in 1916 plus four annual payments amounting to $35,589.80). That value also exceeded original cost of the shares. The amount received on the interest devised by her mother was less than its valuation for estate taxation; also less than the value when acquired by Mrs. Logan.

The Commissioner ruled that the obligation of the Youngstown Company to pay 60 cents per ton had a fair market value of

$1,942,111.46 on March 11, 1916; that this value should be treated as so much cash and the sale of the stock regarded as a closed transaction with no profit in 1916. He also used this valuation as the basis for apportioning subsequent annual receipts between income and return of capital. His calculations, based upon estimates and assumptions, are too intricate for brief statement. He made deficiency assessments according to the view just stated and the Board of Tax Appeals approved the result.

The Circuit Court of Appeals held that, in the circumstances, it was impossible to determine with fair certainty the market value of the agreement by the Youngstown Company to pay 60 cents per ton. Also, that respondent was entitled to the return of her capital—the value of 250 shares on March 1, 1913, and the assessed value of the interest derived from her mother—before she could be charged with any taxable income. As this had not in fact been returned, there was no taxable income.

We agree with the result reached by the Circuit Court of Appeals.

The 1916 transaction was a sale of stock—not an exchange of property. We are not dealing with royalties or deductions from gross income because of depletion of mining property. Nor does the situation demand that an effort be made to place according to the best available data some approximate value upon the contract for future payments. This probably was necessary in order to assess the mother's estate. As annual payments on account of extracted ore come in they can be readily apportioned first as return of capital and later as profit. The liability for income tax ultimately can be fairly determined without resort to mere estimates, assumptions and speculation. When the profit, if any, is actually realized, the taxpayer will be required to respond. The consideration for the sale was $2,200,000.00 in cash and the promise of future money payments wholly contingent upon facts and circumstances not possible to foretell with anything like fair certainty. The promise was in no proper sense equivalent to cash. It had no ascertainable fair market value. The transaction was not a closed one. Respondent might never recoup her capital investment from payments only conditionally promised. Prior to 1921 all receipts from the sale of her shares amounted to less than their value on March 1, 1913. She properly demanded the return of her capital investment before assessment of any taxable profit based on conjecture.

"In order to determine whether there has been gain or loss, and the amount of the gain, if any, we must withdraw from the gross proceeds an amount sufficient to restore the capital value that existed at the commencement of the period under consideration." Doyle v. Mitchell Bros. Co., 247 U.S. 179, 184, 185. Rev.Act 1916, § 2, 39 Stat. 757, 758; Rev.Act 1918, c. 18, 40 Stat. 1057. Ordinarily, at least, a taxpayer may not deduct from gross receipts a supposed loss which in fact is represented by his outstanding note. Eckert v. Commissioner of Internal Revenue, [283 U.S. 140 (1931)]. And, conversely, a promise to pay indeterminate sums of money is not necessarily taxable income. "Generally speaking, the income tax law is concerned only with realized losses, as with realized gains." Lucas v. American Code Co., 280 U.S. 445, 449.

From her mother's estate Mrs. Logan obtained the right to share in possible proceeds of a contract thereafter to pay indefinite sums. The value of this was assumed to be $277,164.50 and its transfer was so taxed. Some valuation—speculative or otherwise—was necessary in order to close the estate. It may never yield as much, it may yield more. If a sum equal to the value thus ascertained had been invested in an annuity contract, payments thereunder would have been free from income tax until the owner had recouped his capital investment.[g] We think a like rule should be applied here. The statute definitely excepts bequests from receipts which go to make up taxable income. See Burnet v. Whitehouse, [283 U.S. 148 (1931)].

The judgments below are affirmed.

Notes and Questions

1. *The estate-tax comparison.* As the Court notes, the rights involved in *Logan* had to be valued, however inaccurately, for purposes of the estate tax. Although the administrative considerations requiring immediate valuation for estate-tax purposes do not apply with equal force under the income tax, it is also true that the consequences of a mistake about value are permanent under the estate tax. Under the income tax, by contrast, the amount reported in the long run will be correct, even if a time-of-sale valuation is wrong. The main benefit of the *Logan* doctrine is that it makes some disputes about value unnecessary (except in cases involving losses).

2. *"Rare and extraordinary cases."* Treas.Reg. § 1.1001–1(a) provides that "[o]nly in rare and extraordinary cases does property have no fair market value." Whether this statement is an accurate description of the caselaw is questionable. See, e.g., McShain v. Commissioner, 71 T.C. 998 (1979) (value of second-mortgage note received on sale of real estate not ascertainable). In any event, Burnet v. Logan certainly does not stand for the proposition that any sale for an indefinite price stays "open." See Bernice Patton Testamentary Trust v. United States, 2001–1 U.S.T.C. ¶ 50,332 (Fed.Cl.2001).

3. *Further computations in the case of closed transactions.* Suppose the right to receive royalties in *Logan* had been valued at $150,000. Since the seller would in almost all cases have received either more or less than $150,000 eventually, further gains or losses would have had to be reported in order to produce the right long-run income figure. Should a taxpayer whose transaction has been closed using a value of $150,000, and who expects to receive $200,000 over the life of the contract, report one-fourth of each payment as additional income, or should each payment be treated as non-taxable until the seller has recovered $150,000 and as fully taxable thereafter? The practice was to treat payments as a

g. See p. 113.—Eds.

tax-free return of capital until an amount equal to the value placed on the right had been recovered, and to treat further payments as income in full. Today, however, each payment would usually be treated in part as an interest payment, unless the contract provides for adequate stated interest (which would be a rarity in a sale for contingent consideration).

4. *Open and closed transactions compared.* Suppose that in year 1 *T* sells to an individual a nondepreciable capital asset with an adjusted basis of $100,000. The purchaser pays $40,000 in year 1 and is to make contingent payments (including, for simplicity, adequate stated interest) over the following four years. In years 2 through 5 *T* receives contingent payments as follows:

Year	Amount
2	$20,000
3	25,000
4	15,000
5	25,000

First assume that the transaction is treated as closed in year 1 with the right to contingent payments valued at $70,000. If *T* does not use installment reporting under § 453, *T* would recognize $10,000 gain ($110,000 amount realized less $100,000 basis) in year 1. *T*'s basis in the contingent-payment obligation would be $70,000, the amount which was included in *T*'s amount realized. The $60,000 in contingent payments received by *T* in years 2 through 4 and $10,000 of the amount received in year 5 would be treated as a return of basis in the contingent-payment obligation, thus reducing *T*'s basis to zero. The remaining $15,000 received in year 5 would be characterized as long-term capital gain arising from the "exchange" of *T*'s right to contingent payments. (Under a 1997 amendment to § 1271, receipt of payment on an individual's debt is treated as an "exchange."[h])

If instead the transaction is treated as open, *T* treats the $100,000 of payments received in years 1 through 4 as a return of basis, thus exhausting *T*'s basis in the property sold. The $25,000 gain in year 5 is considered to have arisen from the sale in year 1, which was held open, and therefore is characterized as capital gain.

h. See p. 618. This assumes that the obligation arose after June 8, 1997; see § 1271(b)(1)(A).

SUMMARY

		Closed Transaction		Open Transaction	
Year	Amount Received	Income	Character	Income	Character
1	$40,000	$10,000	capital gain	None	—
2	20,000	None	—	None	—
3	25,000	None	—	None	—
4	15,000	None	—	None	—
5	25,000	15,000	capital gain	$25,000	capital gain
		$25,000		$25,000	

5. *Burnet v. Logan today.* The House Report on the Installment Sales Revision Act of 1980 had this to say about the current status of the *Logan* doctrine (H.R.Rep. No. 96–1042, 96th Cong., 2d Sess. 21 (1980)):

> The creation of a statutory deferred payment option for all forms of deferred payment sales significantly expands the availability of installment reporting to include situations where it has not previously been permitted. By providing an expanded statutory installment reporting option, the Committee believes that in the future there should be little incentive to devise convoluted forms of deferred payment obligations to attempt to obtain deferred reporting. In any event, the effect of the new rules is to reduce substantially the justification for treating transactions as "open" and permitting the use of the cost-recovery method sanctioned by Burnet v. Logan, 283 U.S. 404 (1931). Accordingly, it is the Committee's intent that the cost-recovery method not be available in the case of sales for a fixed price (whether the seller's obligation is evidenced by a note, contractual promise, or otherwise), and that its use be limited to those rare and extraordinary cases involving sales for a contingent price where the fair market value of the purchaser's obligation cannot reasonably be ascertained.

The Temporary Regulations under the Installment Sales Revision Act provide:

> Under no circumstances will an installment sale for a fixed amount obligation be considered an "open" transaction * * *.

> * * *

> * * * Only in those rare and extraordinary cases involving sales for a contingent payment obligation in which the fair market value of the obligation * * * cannot reasonably be ascertained will the taxpayer be entitled to assert that the transaction is "open."

Temp.Treas.Reg. § 15a.453–1(d)(2)(iii).

For an example of post–1980 use of *Logan*, see Rev. Rul. 85–48, 1985–1 C.B. 126.

2. FIXED PURCHASE PRICE

WARREN JONES CO. v. COMMISSIONER

United States Court of Appeals, Ninth Circuit, 1975.
524 F.2d 788.

Before ELY and HUFSTEDLER, CIRCUIT JUDGES, and TAYLOR, SENIOR DISTRICT JUDGE.

ELY, CIRCUIT JUDGE:

During its taxable year ending on October 31, 1968, the Warren Jones Company, a cash basis taxpayer, sold an apartment building for $153,000. In return, the taxpayer received a cash downpayment of $20,000 and the buyer's promise in a standard form real estate contract, to pay $133,000, plus interest, over the following fifteen years. The Tax Court held, with three judges dissenting, that the fair market value of the real estate contract did not constitute an "amount realized" by the taxpayer in the taxable year of sale under section 1001(b) of the Internal Revenue Code. Warren Jones Co., 60 T.C. 663 (1973) (reviewed by the full Court). The Commissioner of Internal Revenue has appealed, and we reverse.

I. BACKGROUND

On May 27, 1968, the taxpayer, a family-held corporation chartered by the State of Washington, entered into a real estate contract for the sale of one of its Seattle apartment buildings, the Wallingford Court Apartments, to Bernard and Jo Ann Storey for $153,000. When the sale closed on June 15, 1968, the Storeys paid $20,000 in cash and took possession of the apartments. The Storeys were then obligated by the contract to pay the taxpayer $1,000 per month, plus 8 percent interest on the declining balance, for a period of fifteen years. The balance due at the end of fifteen years is to be payable in a lump sum. The contract was the only evidence of the Storeys' indebtedness, since no notes or other such instruments passed between the parties. Upon receipt of the full purchase price, the taxpayer is obligated by the contract to deed the Wallingford Apartments to the Storeys.

The Tax Court found, as facts, that the transaction between the taxpayer and the Storeys was a completed sale in the taxable year ending on October 31, 1968, and that in that year, the Storeys were solvent obligors. The court also found that real estate contracts such as that between the taxpayer and the Storeys were regularly bought and sold in the Seattle area. The court concluded, from the testimony before it, that in the taxable year of sale, the taxpayer could have sold its contract, which had a face value of $133,000, to a savings and loan association or a similar institutional buyer for approximately $117,980. The court found, however, that in accordance with prevailing business practices, any potential buyer for the contract would likely have required the taxpayer to deposit $41,000 of the proceeds from the sale of the contract in a savings account, assigned to the buyer, for the purpose of securing the first $41,000 of the Storeys' payments. Consequently, the court found that in the taxable year of sale, the contract had a fair market value of only $76,980 (the contract's selling price minus the amount deposited in the assigned savings account.)

On the sale's closing date, the taxpayer had an adjusted basis of $61,913 in the Wallingford Apartments. In determining the amount it had realized from the sale, the taxpayer added only the $20,000 down-payment and the portion of the $4,000 in monthly payments it had received that was allocable to principal. Consequently, on its federal income tax return for the taxable year ending October 31, 1968, the taxpayer reported no gain from the apartment sale. The taxpayer's return explained that the corporation reported on the cash basis and that under the Tax Court's holding in Nina J. Ennis, 17 T.C. 465 (1951), it was not required to report gain on the sale until it had recovered its basis. The return also stated, however, that in the event the taxpayer was required to report gain in the taxable year of the sale, it elected to do so on the installment basis (I.R.C. § 453).

The Commissioner disagreed with the taxpayer's assertion that it had realized no gain on the sale, but he conceded that the sale qualified as an installment sale. Consequently, the Commissioner recalculated the taxpayer's gain in accordance with section 453 and notified the taxpayer that it had recognized an additional $12,098 in long term capital gain. The taxpayer then petitioned the Tax Court for a redetermination of its liability.

* * * The question presented is whether section 1001(b) requires the taxpayer to include the fair market value of its real estate contract with the Storeys in determining the "amount realized" during the taxable year of the sale.

Holding that the fair market value of the contract was not includable in the amount realized from the sale, the Tax Court majority relied on the doctrine of "cash equivalency." Under that doctrine, the cash basis taxpayer must report income received in the form of property only if the property is the "equivalent of cash." [Citation omitted.]

The Tax Court majority adopted the following as its definition of the phrase, "equivalent of cash":

> * * * if the promise to pay of a solvent obligor is unconditional and assignable, not subject to set-offs, and is of a kind that is frequently transferred to lenders or investors at a discount not substantially greater than the generally prevailing premium for the use of money, such promise is the equivalent of cash * * *

Warren Jones Co., supra at 668–69, quoting, Cowden v. Commissioner, 289 F.2d 20, 24 (5th Cir.1961). Applying the quoted definition, the tax court held that the taxpayer's contract, which had a face value of $133,000, was not the "equivalent of cash" since it had a fair market value of only $76,980. Had the taxpayer sold the contract, the discount from the face value, approximately 42 percent, would have been "substantially greater than the generally prevailing premium for the use of money."[4]

The Tax Court observed that requiring the taxpayer to realize the fair market value of the contract in the year of the sale could subject the taxpayer to substantial hardships. The taxpayer would be taxed in the initial year on a substantial portion of its gain from the sale of the property, even though it had received, in cash, only a small fraction of the purchase price. To raise funds to pay its taxes, the taxpayer might be forced to sell the contract at the contract's fair market value, even though such a sale might not otherwise be necessary or advantageous. Most importantly in the Tax Court's view, if the taxpayer were required to realize the fair market value of the contract in the year of the sale, the sale transaction would be closed for tax purposes in that year; hence, the taxpayer's capital gain on the transaction would be permanently limited to the difference between its adjusted basis and the contract's fair market value plus the cash payments received in the year of sale. If the taxpayer did retain the contract, so as to collect its face value, the amounts received in excess of the contract's fair market value would constitute ordinary income. The Tax Court also noted that requiring the cash basis taxpayer to realize the fair market value of the real estate contract would tend to obscure the differences between the cash and accrual methods of reporting.

The Commissioner does not dispute the Tax Court's conclusion that the taxpayer's contract with the Storeys had a fair market value of $76,980, or any other of the court's findings of fact. Rather, the Commissioner contends that since, as found by the Tax Court, the contract had a fair market value, section 1001(b) requires the taxpayer to include the amount of that fair market value in determining the amount realized.[6]

II. Statutory Analysis

The first statutory predecessor of section 1001(b) was section 202(b) of the Revenue Act of February 24, 1919, which stated:

> When property is exchanged for other property, the property received in exchange shall for the purpose of determining gain or loss

---

4. The taxpayer's argument on appeal that to be a cash equivalent, a debt instrument must be negotiable is untenable. See, e.g., Heller Trust v. Comm'r, 382 F.2d 675, 681 (9th Cir.1967); Cowden v. Comm'r, 289 F.2d 20, 24 (5th Cir.1961).

6. The Commissioner's theoretical approach to the result for which he contends is not altogether clear. He may be rejecting the doctrine of cash equivalency altogether, cf. *Warren Jones Co.,* supra at 673–74 (Quealy, J., dissenting), or he may be contending that any property with a fair market value is the equivalent of cash in the

amount of its fair market value. See Comment, the Doctrine of Cash Equivalency, [22 U.C.L.A. L.Rev. 219 (1974)] at 225–26; but see M. Levine, Real Estate Transactions, Tax Planning and Consequences § 731 (1973). Since as to a cash basis taxpayer, with which we are here concerned, both theories would achieve the same result, we need not distinguish between them.

The taxpayer contends that the basic question before us is one of fact. We disagree. The question is essentially one of statutory construction and it therefore presents an issue of law.

be treated as the equivalent of cash to the amount of its fair market value, if any * * *.

Ch. 18, § 202(b), 40 stat. 1060. We have no doubt that under that statute, the taxpayer would have been required to include the fair market value of its real estate contract as an amount realized during the taxable year of sale.

Only three years later, however, in the Revenue Act of November 23, 1921, Congress replaced the language of the statute enacted in 1919 with the following:

> On an exchange of property, real, personal or mixed, for any other such property, no gain or loss shall be recognized unless the property received in exchange has a readily realizable market value * * *.

Ch. 136, § 202(c), 42 Stat. 230. The original statute had created "a presumption in favor of taxation." H.R.Rep. No. 350, 67th Cong., 1st Sess. (1921), reproduced at 1939–1 Cum.Bull. (part 2) 168, 175. In the 1921 Act, Congress doubtless intended a policy more favorable to the taxpayer. Interpreting the 1921 statute, the Treasury regulations provided that

> [p]roperty has a readily realizable market value if it can be readily converted into an amount of cash or its equivalent substantially equal to the fair value of the property.

Treas.Reg. 62, Art. 1564 (1922 ed.). The law established in 1921 appears to have been substantially in accord with the position taken in this case by the Tax Court majority.

Notwithstanding the foregoing, in the Revenue Act of 1924, ch. 234, § 202(c), 43 Stat. 256, Congress again changed the law, replacing the 1921 statute with the language that now appears in section 1001(b) of the current Code. Of the 1921 statute, and its requirement of a "readily realizable market value," the Senate Finance Committee wrote in 1924:

> The question whether, in a given case, the property received in exchange has a readily realizable market value is a most difficult one, and the rulings on this question in given cases have been far from satisfactory. * * * The provision can not be applied with accuracy or consistency.

S.Rep. No. 398, 68th Cong., 1st Sess. (1924), reproduced at 1939–1 Cum.Bull. (Part 2) 266, 275. See also H.R.Rep. No. 179, 68th Cong., 1st Sess. (1924), reproduced at 1939–1 Cum.Bull. (Part 2) 241, 251. Under the 1924 statute, "where income is realized in the form of property, the measure of the income is the fair market value of the property at the date of its receipt." H.R.Rep. No. 179, supra, 1939–1 Cum.Bull. (Part 2) at 250; S.Rep. No. 398, supra, 1939–1 Cum.Bull. (Part 2) at 275.

There is no indication whatsoever that Congress intended to retain the "readily realizable market value" test from the 1921 statute as an unstated element of the 1924 Act. Indeed, as noted above, Congress sharply criticized that test. We cannot avoid the conclusion that in 1924

Congress intended to establish the more definite rule for which the Commissioner here contends and that consequently, if the fair market value of property received in an exchange can be ascertained, that fair market value must be reported as an amount realized.

Congress clearly understood that the 1924 statute might subject some taxpayers to the hardships discussed by the Tax Court majority. In the Revenue Act of 1926, ch. 27, § 212(d), 44 Stat. 23, Congress enacted the installment basis for reporting gain that is now reflected in section 453 of the current Code. Under section 453, a taxpayer who sells real property * * * may elect to report as taxable income in any given year only

> that proportion of the installment payments actually received in that year which the gross profit, realized or to be realized when payment is completed, bears to the total contract price.

[§ 453(c).]

By providing the installment basis, Congress intended " * * * to relieve taxpayers who adopted it from having to pay an income tax in the year of sale based on the full amount of anticipated profits when in fact they had received in cash only a small portion of the sales price." Commissioner v. South Texas Lumber Co., 333 U.S. 496, 503 (1948). For sales that qualify, the installment basis also eliminates the other potential disadvantages to which the Tax Court referred. Since taxation in the year of the sale is based on the value of the payments actually received, the taxpayer should not be required to sell his obligation in order to meet his tax liabilities. Furthermore, the installment basis does not change the character of the gain received. If gain on an exchange would otherwise be capital, it remains capital under section 453. Finally, the installment basis treats cash and accrual basis taxpayers equally.

We view section 453 as persuasive evidence in support of the interpretation of section 1001(b) for which the Commissioner contends. The installment basis is Congress's method of providing relief from the rigors of section 1001(b). In its report on the Revenue Act of 1926, the Senate Finance Committee expressly noted that in sales or exchanges not qualifying for the installment basis, "deferred-payment contracts"

> * * * are to be regarded as the equivalent of cash if such obligations have a fair market value. In consequence, that portion of the initial payment and of the fair market value of such obligations which represents profit is to be returned as income as of the taxable year of the sale.

S.Rep. No. 52, 69th Cong., 1st Sess. (1926), reproduced at 1939–1 Cum.Bull. (Part 2) 332, 347.

[In an omitted portion of the opinion, the court rejected the taxpayer's argument that Congress intended to treat as the equivalent of cash only those instruments described in the predecessor of §§ 453(f)(4) and (5).]

III. Case Law

The prior decisions of our own court support the conclusion we have reached. On several occasions, we have held that if the fair market value of a deferred payment obligation received in a sale or other exchange can be ascertained, that fair market value must be included as an amount realized under section 1001(b). Most recently, in In re Steen, 509 F.2d 1398, 1404–05 (9th Cir.1975), we held that the fair market value of an installment payment contract received in exchange for shares of stock was ascertainable and that, consequently, that fair market value was an amount realized in the year of the sale. In Heller Trust v. Commissioner, 382 F.2d 675, 681 (9th Cir.1967), our court affirmed a Tax Court decision requiring a taxpayer to include the fair market value of real estate contracts as an amount realized in the year of a sale, even though the fair market value of the contracts there involved was only 50 percent of their face value. [Other citations omitted.][9]

There are, of course, "rare and extraordinary" situations in which it is impossible to ascertain the fair market value of a deferred payment obligation in the year of sale. See Treas.Reg. § 1.1001–1(a). The total amount payable under an obligation may be so speculative, or the right to receive any payments at all so contingent, that the fair market value of the obligation cannot be fixed. See Burnet v. Logan, 283 U.S. 404 (1931). [Other citations omitted.] If an obligation is not marketable, it may be impossible to establish its fair market value. See Willhoit v. Commissioner, 308 F.2d 259 (9th Cir.1962) (uncontradicted testimony that there was no market for high risk contracts); Phillips v. Frank, 295 F.2d 629 (9th Cir.1961) (uncontradicted testimony that highly speculative contracts could not have been sold in the year of sale). But see United States v. Davis, 370 U.S. 65, 71–74 (1962) (wife's release of her marital rights in a property settlement agreement held to have a fair market value equal to the value of property that her husband transferred to her in exchange); Gersten v. Commissioner, [267 F.2d 195, 197 (9th Cir.1959)] ("It is not necessary to find any actual sales of like articles to establish a fair market value.")

The Tax Court found, as a fact, that the taxpayer's real estate contract with the Storeys had a fair market value of $76,980 in the

9. * * *

The Tax Court adopted as its definition of "cash equivalency" certain language from the opinion in Cowden v. Comm'r, 289 F.2d 20 (5th Cir.1961). In our view, the holding in *Cowden* does not conflict with the prior decisions of our court or with our present decision. In *Cowden,* the Fifth Circuit held that the Tax Court had overemphasized one of its findings of fact in reaching its decision and remanded the case for the Tax Court's reconsideration. The language adopted by the Tax Court appears within the context of the Fifth Circuit's discussion, in *Cowden,* of the taxpayer's contention that the deferred payment obligation he had received in exchange for an oil and gas lease could have no realizable value because it was not negotiable. In rejecting the taxpayer's contention, the *Cowden* court appears to have written the language adopted by the Tax Court principally as a description of the obligation involved in that case. See Dennis v. Comm'r, 473 F.2d 274, 285 (5th Cir.1973), in which the Fifth Circuit, citing *Cowden,* states that when property received in a sale or exchange has a fair market value, that value constitutes an amount realized.

taxable year of sale. Consequently, the taxpayer must include $76,980 in determining the amount realized under section 1001(b). As previously noted, however, the Commissioner has conceded that the taxpayer is eligible to report on the installment basis and has calculated the taxpayer's deficiency accordingly.

* * *

Reversed and remanded, with directions.

Notes and Questions

1. *The demise of the cash-equivalency doctrine.* Before the Ninth Circuit's decision in *Warren Jones*, the courts often said that a cash-method seller does not recognize gain upon "receipt" of nothing more than the purchaser's "promise to pay." Since the rejection of the cash-equivalency doctrine in *Warren Jones,* the courts generally have not permitted a cash-method seller to use the cost-recovery method where the value of the property received by the seller can be ascertained. The Temporary Regulations under the Installment Sales Revision Act also reject the cash-equivalency doctrine:

> Receipt of an installment obligation shall be treated as a receipt of property, in an amount equal to the fair market value of the installment obligation, whether or not such obligation is the equivalent of cash. An installment obligation is considered to be property and is subject to valuation * * * without regard to whether the obligation is embodied in a note, an executory contract, or any other instrument, or is an oral promise enforceable under local law.

> * * * A taxpayer using the cash receipts and disbursements methods [sic] of accounting shall treat as an amount realized in the year of sale the fair market value of the installment obligation [if § 453 does not apply].

Temp.Treas.Reg. § 15a.453–1(d)(2).

Treas. Reg. § 1.1001–1(g) (issued in 1996) implies that, if the deferred-payment obligation bears adequate stated interest, the seller's amount realized is the face amount of the obligation. If the obligation doesn't bear adequate stated interest, the principal amount of the obligation is recalculated to exclude imputed interest and the recalculated principal is the seller's amount realized. Is the regulation consistent with § 1001(b)? Is it possible that an obligation could bear adequate stated interest but still not be worth its face amount? In view of these rules, few taxpayers will want to opt out of § 453.

2. *Accrual-method taxpayers.* The Temporary Regulations under § 453 say that an accrual-method taxpayer who does not elect installment reporting "shall treat as an amount realized in the year of sale the total amount payable under the installment obligation"; Temp.

Treas.Reg. § 15a.453–1(d)(2)(ii)(A). This approach is consistent with prior law; e.g., Western Oaks Building Corp. v. Commissioner, 49 T.C. 365 (1968); George L. Castner Co. v. Commissioner, 30 T.C. 1061 (1958); Rev.Rul. 79–292, 1979–2 C.B. 287. Is it consistent with § 1001(b)? Treas. Reg. § 1.1001–1(g), which supersedes the 453 regulations in this respect, does not distinguish between cash-and accrual-method taxpayers.

*

Chapter Twelve

TIMING OF INCOME AND DEDUCTIONS

This chapter will examine the rules of tax accounting—that is, the rules governing *when* an income or deduction item is taken into account. Generally speaking, these rules respond to two concerns. The first is administrative convenience. Suppose a taxpayer makes a deductible charitable contribution by signing a pledge on October 1 and mailing a check to the charity on December 10. The charity receives the check on December 20 and deposits it in a bank account on January 5; funds are withdrawn from the taxpayer's bank account on January 12. Which of these dates is "the" date of the contribution? The tax system must furnish clearcut, easily applied answers to questions like this, not because they raise important issues of "fairness" or "public policy" but simply to avoid disputes over questions that are trivial on an overall basis but important in particular cases. A second concern has to do with the time-value of money. A taxpayer who can deduct an expense long before it has been incurred, in an economic sense, receives a substantial benefit, as does someone who can postpone reporting income until long after receiving money or property. Until the 1980s, Congress showed little concern for time-value problems, but times have changed.

A. "ANNUAL" vs. "TRANSACTIONAL" ACCOUNTING

Income must be reported, and tax must be paid, at regular intervals. Income is "computed on the basis of the taxpayer's taxable year" (§ 441(a)), which may be a calendar year, a fiscal year ending on the last day of a month other than December, or a 52–53 week taxable year.[a] Under certain circumstances, the most common of which involves a taxpayer who dies during a year, § 443 requires a return for a "short period." Section 442 prohibits a change of taxable year without the Commissioner's consent.

---

a. This is a taxable year which always ends on the same day of the week; it may be more convenient than a calendar or fiscal year for taxpayers having weekly payrolls. See § 441(f).

Individuals almost always report on a calendar-year basis. Most of us failed to keep fiscal-year books as children, so we became calendar-year taxpayers under § 441(g), and the Commissioner would surely deny us permission to change to a different year. Most partnerships, S corporations, personal-service corporations, and trusts must use a calendar year (or a 52–53 week year ending sometimes in the last week of December and sometimes in the first week of January); §§ 706(b), 1378, 441(i), 444.

Although computing income on an annual basis is at least as convenient as any conceivable alternative, a strict annual accounting requirement can cause hardship. If, for example, a taxpayer earned $100,000 in year one and lost $200,000 in year two, strict annual accounting would impose a substantial income tax, even though the taxpayer's income is negative over a two-year period. Taxpayers subjected to hardship because of annual accounting often ask Congress or the courts for relief; sometimes they get it.

1. UNUSABLE DEDUCTIONS

BURNET v. SANFORD & BROOKS CO.

Supreme Court of the United States, 1931.
282 U.S. 359, 51 S.Ct. 150, 75 L.Ed. 383.

Mr. Justice Stone delivered the opinion of the Court.

In this case certiorari was granted, 281 U.S. 707, to review a judgment of the Court of Appeals for the Fourth Circuit, 35 F.2d 312, reversing an order of the Board of Tax Appeals, 11 B.T.A. 452, which had sustained the action of the Commissioner of Internal Revenue in making a deficiency assessment against respondent for income and profits taxes for the year 1920.

From 1913 to 1915, inclusive, respondent, a Delaware corporation engaged in business for profit, was acting for the Atlantic Dredging Company in carrying out a contract for dredging the Delaware River, entered into by that company with the United States. In making its income tax returns for the years 1913 to 1916, respondent added to gross income for each year the payments made under the contract that year, and deducted its expenses paid that year in performing the contract. The total expenses exceeded the payments received by $176,271.88. The tax returns for 1913, 1915 and 1916 showed net losses. That for 1914 showed net income.

In 1915 work under the contract was abandoned, and in 1916 suit was brought in the Court of Claims to recover for a breach of warranty of the character of the material to be dredged. Judgment for the claimant, 53 Ct.Cls. 490, was affirmed by this Court in 1920. United States v. Atlantic Dredging Co., 253 U.S. 1. It held that the recovery was upon the contract and was "compensatory of the cost of the work, of which the government got the benefit." From the total recovery, petitioner received in that year the sum of $192,577.59, which included the $176,271.88 by which its expenses under the contract had exceeded receipts from it, and accrued interest amounting to $16,305.71. Respondent having failed to include these amounts as gross income in its tax returns for 1920, the Commissioner made the deficiency assessment here involved, based on the addition of both items to gross income for that year.

The Court of Appeals ruled that only the item of interest was properly included, holding, erroneously as the government contends, that the item of $176,271.88 was a return of losses suffered by respondent in earlier years and hence was wrongly assessed as income. Notwithstanding this conclusion, its judgment of reversal and the consequent elimination of this item from gross income for 1920 were made contingent upon the filing by respondent of amended returns for the years 1913 to 1916, from which were to be omitted the deductions of the related items of expenses paid in those years. Respondent insists that as the Sixteenth Amendment and the Revenue Act of 1918, which was in force in 1920, plainly contemplate a tax only on net income or profits, any application of the statute which operates to impose a tax with respect to the present transaction, from which respondent received no profit, cannot be upheld.

If respondent's contention that only gain or profit may be taxed under the Sixteenth Amendment be accepted without qualification, see Eisner v. Macomber, 252 U.S. 189, Doyle v. Mitchell Brothers Co., 247 U.S. 179, the question remains whether the gain or profit which is the subject of the tax may be ascertained, as here, on the basis of fixed accounting periods, or whether, as is pressed upon us, it can only be net profit ascertained on the basis of particular transactions of the taxpayer when they are brought to a conclusion.

All the revenue acts which have been enacted since the adoption of the Sixteenth Amendment have uniformly assessed the tax on the basis of annual returns showing the net result of all the taxpayer's transactions during a fixed accounting period, either the calendar year, or, at the option of the taxpayer, the particular fiscal year which he may adopt. Under §§ 230, 232 and 234(a) of the Revenue Act of 1918, 40 Stat. 1057, respondent was subject to tax upon its annual net income, arrived at by deducting from gross income for each taxable year all the ordinary and necessary expenses paid during that year in carrying on any trade or business, interest and taxes paid, and losses sustained, during the year. By §§ 233(a) and 213(a) gross income "includes * * * income derived from * * * businesses * * * or the transaction of any business carried on for gain or profit, or gains or profits and income derived from any source whatever." The amount of all such items is required to be included in the gross income for the taxable year in which received by the taxpayer, unless they may be properly accounted for on the accrual basis under § 212(b). See United States v. Anderson, 269 U.S. 422; Aluminum Castings Co. v. Routzahn, [282 U.S. 92 (1930)].

That the recovery made by respondent in 1920 was gross income for that year within the meaning of these sections cannot, we think, be doubted. The money received was derived from a contract entered into in the course of respondent's business operations for profit. While it equalled, and in a loose sense was a return of, expenditures made in performing the contract, still, as the Board of Tax Appeals found, the expenditures were made in defraying the expenses incurred in the prosecution of the work under the contract, for the purpose of earning profits. They were not capital investments, the cost of which, if converted, must first be restored from the proceeds before there is a capital gain taxable as income. See Doyle v. Mitchell Brothers Co., supra, p. 185.

That such receipts from the conduct of a business enterprise are to be included in the taxpayer's return as a part of gross income, regardless of whether the particular transaction results in net profit, sufficiently appears from the quoted words of § 213(a) and from the character of the deductions allowed. Only by including these items of gross income in the 1920 return would it have been possible to ascertain respondent's net income for the period covered by the return, which is what the statute taxes. The excess of gross income over deductions did not any the less constitute net income for the taxable period because respondent, in an earlier period, suffered net losses in the conduct of its business which were in some measure attributable to expenditures made to produce the net income of the later period.

Bowers v. Kerbaugh–Empire Co., 271 U.S. 170, on which respondent relies, does not support its position. In that case the taxpayer, which had lost, in business, borrowed money, which was to be repaid in German marks, and which was later repaid in depreciated currency, had neither made a profit on the transaction, nor received any money or property which could have been made subject to the tax.

But respondent insists that if the sum which it recovered is the income defined by the statute, still it is not income, taxation of which without apportionment is permitted by the Sixteenth Amendment, since the particular transaction from which it was derived did not result in any net gain or profit. But we do not think the amendment is to be so narrowly construed. A taxpayer may be in receipt of net income in one year and not in another. The net result of the two years, if combined in a single taxable period, might still be a loss; but it has never been supposed that that fact would relieve him from a tax on the first, or that it affords any reason for postponing the assessment of the tax until the end of a lifetime, or for some other indefinite period, to ascertain more precisely whether the final outcome of the period, or of a given transaction, will be a gain or a loss.

The Sixteenth Amendment was adopted to enable the government to raise revenue by taxation. It is the essence of any system of taxation that it should produce revenue ascertainable, and payable to the government, at regular intervals. Only by such a system is it practicable to produce a regular flow of income and apply methods of accounting, assessment, and collection capable of practical operation. It is not suggested that there has ever been any general scheme for taxing income on any other basis. The computation of income annually as the net result of all transactions within the year was a familiar practice, and taxes upon income so arrived at were not unknown, before the Sixteenth Amendment. See Bowers v. Kerbaugh–Empire Co., supra, p. 174; Pacific Insurance Co. v. Soule, 7 Wall. 433; Pollock v. Farmers' Loan & Trust Co., 158 U.S. 601, 630. It is not to be supposed that the amendment did not contemplate that Congress might make income so ascertained the basis of a scheme of taxation such as had been in actual operation within the United States before its adoption. While, conceivably, a different system might be devised by which the tax could be assessed, wholly or in part, on the basis of the finally ascertained results of particular transactions, Congress is not required by the amendment to adopt such a system in preference to the more familiar method, even if it were practicable. It would not necessarily obviate the kind of inequalities of which respondent complains. If losses from particular transactions were to be set off against gains in others, there would still be the practical necessity of computing the tax on the basis of annual or other fixed taxable periods, which might result in the taxpayer being required to pay a tax on income in one period exceeded by net losses in another.

Under the statutes and regulations in force in 1920, two methods were provided by which, to a limited extent, the expenses of a transaction incurred in one year might be offset by the amounts actually received from it in another. One was by returns on the accrual basis under § 212(b), which provides that a taxpayer keeping accounts upon any basis other than that of actual receipts and disbursements, unless such basis does not clearly reflect its income, may, subject to regulations of the Commissioner, make its return upon the basis upon which its books are kept. See United States v. Anderson, and Aluminum Castings Co. v. Routzahn, supra. The other was under Treasury Regulations (Art. 121 of Reg. 33 of Jan. 2, 1918, under the Revenue Acts of 1916 and 1917; Art. 36 of Reg. 45, Apr. 19, 1919, under the Revenue Act of 1918) providing that in reporting the income derived from certain long term contracts, the taxpayer might either report all of the receipts and all of the expenditures made on account of a particular contract in the year in which the work was completed, or report in each year the percentage of the estimated profit corresponding to the percentage of the total estimated expenditures which was made in that year.

The Court of Appeals said that the case of the respondent here fell within the spirit of these regulations. But the court did not hold, nor does respondent assert, that it ever filed returns in compliance either with these regulations, or § 212(b), or otherwise attempted to avail itself of their provisions; nor on this record do any facts appear tending to support the burden, resting on the taxpayer, of establishing that the Commissioner erred in failing to apply them. See Niles Bement Pond Co. v. United States, 281 U.S. 357, 361.

The assessment was properly made under the statutes. Relief from their alleged burdensome operation which may not be secured under these provisions, can be afforded only by legislation, not by the courts.

Reversed.

Problems and Notes

1. *Net operating loss carrybacks and carryovers.* The hardship suffered by taxpayers like Sanford & Brooks is not limited to cases in which the income and deductions are produced by the same "transaction" or activity: someone who lost $1,000,000 in 1916 and earned $500,000 in a different transaction in 1920 would also have been taxed too heavily. Section 172 now provides relief by allowing net operating losses to be carried back for (usually) two years and forward for (usually) twenty years.

2. *Problems.*

(1) *X* Corp. can deduct $280,000 in 2002; its 2002 gross income is $200,000. This gives *X* a net operating loss of $80,000 for 2002. *X*'s taxable income for the two years before 2002 was as follows:

Year	Income
2000	$30,000
2001	$10,000

(a) How does *X*'s 2002 net operating loss affect its tax liability for 2000 and 2001?

(b) How much taxable income will it have for 2003 if it has $100,000 in 2003 gross income and $30,000 in 2003 deductions (other than its net operating loss carryover)? See §§ 172(a) and 172(b).

(2) *T*, a single person with no dependents, is engaged in the laundry business. In the current year, *T* had the following income and deductions:

Income:
gross income from business	$50,000
capital gain on sale of investment	2,000
dividends	1,000

Deductions:
business expense deductions	$80,000
net operating loss carryover from preceding year	8,000
loss on sale of business property	10,000
capital loss on sale of investment	6,000
property taxes on personal residence	1,500
alimony	10,000
personal exemption	3,000

What is the amount of *T*'s net operating loss for the year? See §§ 172(c) & (d).

3. *Income averaging.* The net-operating-loss provisions relieve only the most extreme hardships caused by annual accounting. Under a progressive tax system, someone with an annual income of $40,000 pays less tax than someone whose income alternates between $0 and $80,000 each year. For many years before 1987, the "income averaging" provisions of the Code eased the burden on many individuals whose taxable incomes increased sharply. The Tax Reform Act of 1986 repealed income averaging. Section 1301, added in 1997, permits farmers to average income.

2.   THE TAX BENEFIT RULE

CONTINENTAL ILLINOIS NATIONAL BANK & TRUST CO. v. COMMISSIONER

United States Tax Court, 1977.
69 T.C. 357 (Acq.).

WILBUR, JUDGE: [Taxpayer had an interest in mortgages and conditional sales contracts guaranteed by three corporations: Tastee Freez, Allied Business Credit Corp., and Carrols, Inc. In 1963 these corporations filed petitions under Chapter XI of the Bankruptcy Act. In the bankruptcy proceedings, taxpayer received two ten-year subordinated Tastee Freez debentures and some Tastee Freez common stock. Taxpayer valued these assets at $3.00 and in 1964 took a bad debt deduction of $593,972.30, the difference between its basis in the conditional sales contracts and mortgages and the value of the stock and debentures received in the bankruptcy proceedings. In 1968, taxpayer exchanged its Tastee Freez debentures for more Tastee Freez common stock and then contributed all its Tastee Freez stock, which had risen in value to $660,435.75, to a charity. The Commissioner argued that the taxpayer, having recovered a debt previously deducted as worthless, had to include the recovery in income to the extent that the earlier deduction reduced its taxable income.]

* * *

Respondent contends that, to the extent petitioner received debentures of Tastee Freez pursuant to the chapter XI proceedings, the debtor-creditor relationship was simply modified, and that "a technical debtor-creditor relationship" actually continued to exist. To the extent petitioner received Tastee Freez stock, respondent claims, "a part of its debt was connected in the *form* of an equity investment." Focusing on the underlying economic facts, regardless of the form, the argument proceeds, petitioner in 1964 wrote off as lost the $593,972.30, and in "1968 the corpse was resurrected, (as part of the larger charitable deduction of $660,435.75) and again utilized to reduce petitioner's otherwise taxable 1968 income."

Respondent argues that the receipt of the securities by petitioner is a normal, ongoing phase of petitioner's day-to-day banking operations; that its disposition, following a chargeoff of the original debt, is inevitably "the practical equivalent of a double deduction," condemned in United States v. Skelly Oil Co., 394 U.S. 678 (1969); and this should "always" be viewed as relating back to the prior bad debt chargeoff with sufficient vitality "to invoke the tax-benefit rule."

Petitioner, not surprisingly, has an entirely different view of the matter. Petitioner contends that the substitution of the debentures and stock for the original guarantee of the chattel mortgages and conditional sales contracts closed the transaction, and required computation of gain or loss. Any subsequent gain was attributable to appreciation of the securities, a new and different investment involving quite different risks, and should be neither excludable if the prior loss was deducted without tax benefit, nor includable as ordinary income if the prior loss was deducted with tax benefit. Petitioner asserts that this argument has particular vigor in the present circumstances, since pursuant to the bankruptcy proceedings, the securities received were in satisfaction of the original obligation; Tastee Freez and Allied were discharged from their initial liability; and petitioner could no longer sue thereon.

While hardly free from doubt, we agree with petitioner. We begin by emphasizing what is *not* at issue. Respondent concedes that the deduction for the contribution of the appreciated stock "is not in controversy, either as to its propriety or amount." Similarly, petitioner concedes that assuming the other elements of the tax benefit rule are here present, there was a "recovery." See First Wisconsin Bankshares Corp. v. United States, 369 F.Supp. 1034 (E.D.Wis.1973). Cf. Tennessee Carolina Transportation, Inc. v. Commissioner, 65 T.C. 440 (1975), [aff'd, 582 F.2d 378 (6th Cir.1978), cert. denied, 440 U.S. 909].

The narrow issue before us, therefore, is simply whether the appreciation of the Tastee Freez stock must be related back for purposes of the tax benefit rule to the original conditional sales contracts and chattel mortgages guaranteed by Tastee Freez and Allied or is attributable to a new investment in securities acquired pursuant to the bankruptcy proceedings that closed out the prior transaction for tax purposes. The parties have extensively analyzed Allen v. Trust Co. of Georgia, 180 F.2d 527 (5th Cir.1950), cert. denied 340 U.S. 814 (1950), and Waynesboro Knitting Co. v. Commissioner, 23 T.C. 404 (1954), affd. 225 F.2d 477 (3d Cir.1955), which we believe to be the controlling precedents. In Allen v. Trust Co. of Georgia, the taxpayer made a $400,000 loan to the Tom Huston Corp., which was secured by 60,000 shares of stock in the Tom Huston Peanut Co., a third corporation controlled by the borrower. In 1932, as a result of the debtor's poor financial condition, the taxpayer took the pledged shares of stock "in full satisfaction and complete cancellation" of the debt. The bank sustained a loss of $220,000 on the transaction, but only $58,455.37 of this loss produced a tax benefit.

In 1940, the bank sold its remaining shares for $537,500 realizing a gain of $376,250. Although the bank reported the gain, it argued in its suit for refund that part of the gain should be excluded from income as a recovery on a bad debt for which it received no tax benefit. The court rejected this argument, finding that no debt existed in 1940 which could be recovered. The court reasoned as follows:

> Moreover, this income did not arise from a payment by the debtor or from a sale of the debt. The pledged shares of stock had no more relation to the debt than the shares of *some totally unrelated* corporation would have had. the acquisition of the stock in satisfaction of the debt was not the summation or integration of two specified values, but it was a total termination of the debt and the beginning of a new and separate transaction. The shares of stock so acquired had their own independent basis for future gain or loss, which was the fair market value on the date of acquisition. [180 F.2d at 528. Citations omitted; emphasis added.]

This Court made a similar finding in *Waynesboro Knitting Co., supra.* * * *

Similarly, petitioner herein originally purchased obligations secured by conditional sales contracts and chattel mortgages, with the promise of the primary obligor guaranteed by Tastee Freez and its subsidiaries. Petitioner filed claims against the guarantors in the chapter XI proceedings and salvaged what it could by selling some of the mobile units pursuant to the contracts involved. Petitioner began with an interest in individual obligations secured by conditional sales contracts, chattel mortgages, and guarantees, and ended up with debt and equity securities in Tastee Freez and Allied. These obligations were acquired pursuant to proceedings under the Bankruptcy Act that discharged Tastee Freez and its subsidiaries, and clearly precluded petitioner from suing on their original obligation. By virtue of these proceedings, "there was a total termination of the debt and the beginning of a new and separate transaction." The debt and equity securities "so acquired had their own independent basis for future gain or loss, which was the fair market value on the date of acquisition." Allen v. Trust Co. of Georgia, supra at 528.

We believe that Allen v. Trust Co. of Georgia states the settled rule in this area as it has existed for nearly 3 decades. Indeed, in Rev.Rul. 66–320, 1966–2 C.B. 37, 38, respondent, citing only Allen v. Trust Co. of Georgia, succinctly restates and reaffirms the principle of that case, as follows:

> X was indebted to Y in the amount of $5,000. In 1961, Y acquired property with a fair market value of $3,000 from X in partial satisfaction of the indebtedness due. The unsatisfied portion of the indebtedness ($2,000) was properly deducted as a bad debt by Y in 1961 without tax benefit. Y sold the property in 1965 for $5,000, realizing a gain of $2,000, and wishes to exclude the $2,000 from gross income under section 111 of the Code, on the ground that

it represents the recovery of a bad debt deducted in 1961 without tax benefit.

* * *

Under the above circumstances, the acquisition by the creditor of the property in partial satisfaction of the indebtedness is separate and distinct from the subsequent sale of such property, and the gain realized on such sale does not represent income attributable to a recovery of the unsatisfied portion of the original indebtedness. The tax result is the same as if the debtor, instead of giving the creditor the property, had paid the creditor $3,000 in cash, and the creditor had used this $3,000 to purchase other property. Clearly, section 111 of the Code would not be applicable to gain realized on the creditor's subsequent sale of such other property. See Allen v. Trust Company of Georgia, 180 F.2d 527 (5th 1950), reversing 84 F.Supp. 944 (M.D.Ga.1949).

Accordingly, a creditor who sells property acquired in partial satisfaction of an indebtedness, cannot, under section 111 of the Code, exclude from gross income gain from such sale as representing income attributable to the recovery of a bad debt previously deducted without tax benefit.

Respondent accepts these principles but attempts, at two different points in his brief, to distinguish them with the following argument:

It should also be noted that the statutory provision with respect to tax benefit, as embodied in present *Code* section 111, is an *exclusionary* provision, enacted as a remedial measure to protect a taxpayer from being required to include in income amounts which were previously deducted *without* tax benefit. It does not purport to limit the includibility of any recovery of an item deducted *with* tax benefit. In Allen v. Trust Co. of Georgia, supra, the taxpayer, seeking to rely upon a specific statutory provision, failed because it could not bring itself squarely within its terms and intent.

We reject this analysis for two very good reasons. First, the tax benefit rule is a two-way street, sometimes favoring petitioner, sometimes respondent. Respondent's argument would make both lanes run in his favor. Secondly, the argument is predicated on a clearly erroneous understanding of the tax benefit rule. The tax benefit rule is both a rule of inclusion and of exclusion: the previously deducted item must be *included* in income in the year of its recovery but that portion of the recovery not resulting in a prior tax benefit is *excluded*. Whether a transaction is open or closed for tax benefit purposes does not in any manner depend on which aspect of the rule is in issue. The exclusionary aspect of the rule has no real existence apart from the inclusionary aspect, but merely acts as a limitation on the amount included. So integrated are these aspects of the tax benefit rule, in fact, that the statutory articulation of the rule in section 111 recites only its exclusionary aspect, and assumes the inclusion. As we recently stated on this specific point:

> The tax benefit rule is both a rule of inclusion and exclusion: recovery of an item previously deducted must be *included* in income; that portion of the recovery not resulting in a prior tax benefit is *excluded*. The rule in both aspects evolved judicially and administratively. The rule has been codified as to certain items in sec. 111. While focusing on the second aspect (exclusion), sec. 111 is predicated on the validity of the first aspect (inclusion). Although the rule has been partly absorbed in the statute, it has been expressly stated that the unabsorbed portion of the rule continues to apply. Dobson v. Commissioner, 320 U.S. 489, 506 (1943); Alice Phelan Sullivan Corp. v. United States, 381 F.2d 399 (Ct.Cl.1967); [further citations omitted].

Respondent also cites Bear Mill Manufacturing Co. v. Commissioner, 15 T.C. 703 (1950), and Birmingham Terminal Co. v. Commissioner, 17 T.C. 1011 (1951). But in both of these cases it is clear that the precise debt or charge that was previously written off was being repaid, and the payment was for precisely the identical amount—down to the penny—of the previously deducted item.

Finally, respondent eloquently embellishes his argument at several points with admonitions from United States v. Skelly Oil Co., 394 U.S. 678 (1969), and Arrowsmith v. Commissioner, 344 U.S. 6 (1952), about the evils of a double deduction. But this simply begs the question, assuming that we have one integrated transaction rather than two separate transactions in two different tax years, which is the very point at issue. We have, for the reasons set out above, decided this point against the respondent.[12]

* * *

Problem and Notes

1. *The tax benefit rule.* The phrase "tax benefit rule" is used to describe: (1) cases in which an item must be included in income because of some prior year's transaction and (2) cases in which all or part of a receipt is *not* included in income because an earlier year's transaction did not produce a tax benefit. To illustrate, consider a taxpayer who receives a $1000 refund of a state income tax paid the year before. If the

---

12. Parading out the pejorative term "double deduction" effects an avoidance ambience that fails to compensate for the substantive inadequacies of respondent's case. One could as easily say that the closed transaction rule applied in Rev.Rul. 66–320, 1966–2 C.B. 37, imposes a tax on a return of capital or requires a "double inclusion" of income. As we have consistently noted, this is a two-way street we are negotiating. The avoidance ambience in this case is real-ly centered on the ability to contribute appreciated property without including the gain in income, a problem no different in this than in cases not involving the tax benefit rule at all. As we noted earlier * * * congress carefully considered this problem in 1969. We see no reason to provide the equivalent of retroactive application of the new provisions added in 1969 by misapplying the tax benefit rule to a closed transaction.

payment reduced the taxpayer's Federal taxable income in the first year by $1000, the refund is taxable, even though a tax refund is normally not income. In a sense, taxing the refund makes up for allowing too large a deduction in the earlier year. If the taxpayer received no tax benefit on account of the state tax payment in the earlier year (if, for example, he claimed the standard deduction), the refund would not be taxable.

Inclusion of an item in gross income matters not just because gross income is the first step in calculating taxable income, but for other reasons. For instance, whether a state tax refund is includable in gross income will affect the taxpayer's adjusted gross income (and, often, some form of "modified adjusted gross income"), which in turn may affect deductions, phaseouts, and the like. Back when the tax benefit rule was being developed, these secondary effects of the gross-income determination seldom mattered; today, it is a rare taxpayer for whom they do not matter. As traditionally applied, the tax benefit rule ignores this problem. For examples and a proposal for refining the rule, see Barrett, Determining an Individual's Federal Income Tax Liability When the Tax Benefit Rule Applies: A Fifty–Year Checkup Brings a New Prescription for Calculating Gross, Adjusted Gross, and Taxable Incomes, 1994 B.Y.U.L.Rev. 1.

2. *Problem.* In year 1, *A* claimed a deduction for state income-tax payments of $2000. *A*'s Federal taxable income for year 1 was $40,000; her total itemized deductions for year 1 amounted to $4900. Her standard deduction for year 1 would have been $4700. How much income does *A* have to report for year 2 if she receives a state tax refund of: (1) $200, or (2) $300? See § 111.

3. *The tax benefit rule and basis.* Some cases which can be seen as illustrating the "inclusionary" aspect of the tax benefit rule really involve no more than basis adjustments. Suppose, for example, that a bank lends a customer $10,000, that the debt becomes worthless, and that the bank takes a deduction for the bad debt, with full tax benefit (i.e., assume that the deduction reduces the bank's taxable income by $10,000). In a later year, the debtor comes into some money and repays the debt. The repayment is fully includable in the bank's income. One could say that the tax benefit rule overrides the usual principle that the repayment of a debt is not income to the creditor, but this is unnecessarily complex. The no-income-on-repayment rule is simply a manifestation of the fact that someone who lends $10,000 has a basis of $10,000 for the right to repayment, and so repayment is not normally income because it does not exceed basis. On deducting the debt, however, the bank must adjust the basis of the debt downward to zero under § 1016; therefore, the repayment is taxable because it exceeds the bank's basis.

The kind of case in which the inclusionary tax benefit rule amounts to more than an application of the rules for basis adjustments is that in which the taxpayer receives no "recovery" of the item deducted. The opinion which follows provides an illustration.

HILLSBORO NAT. BANK v. COMMISSIONER

Supreme Court of the United States, 1983.
460 U.S. 370, 103 S.Ct. 1134, 75 L.Ed.2d 130.

JUSTICE O'CONNOR delivered the opinion of the Court.

These[b] consolidated cases present the question of the applicability of the tax benefit rule to [a] corporate tax situatio[n]: * * * the distribution of expensed assets in a corporate liquidation. We conclude that, unless a nonrecognition provision of the Internal Revenue Code prevents it, the tax benefit rule ordinarily applies to require the inclusion of income when events occur that are fundamentally inconsistent with an earlier deduction. * * *

[Bliss Dairy, a cash-method corporation engaged in the business of farming, bought cattle feed during its fiscal year ending June 30, 1973, and deducted the cost of the feed. During the first month of its next taxable year, Bliss Dairy adopted a plan of liquidation and distributed all of its assets—including a "substantial portion" of the feed—to its shareholders. Under § 336, as it then read, a corporation recognized no gain or loss when it distributed property in liquidation, except for depreciation recapture and other specified items.

The government argued that the value of the feed distributed to the shareholders should be included in the corporation's income under the tax benefit rule because distribution of the feed was inconsistent with the previous year's deduction. The taxpayer contended that the tax benefit rule did not apply because there was no "recovery" in the later year.]

* * *

II

The Government * * * relies solely on the tax benefit rule—a judicially developed principle[8] that allays some of the inflexibilities of the annual accounting system. An annual accounting system is a practical necessity if the federal income tax is to produce revenue ascertainable and payable at regular intervals. Burnet v. Sanford & Brooks Co., 282 U.S. 359, 365 (1931). Nevertheless, strict adherence to an annual accounting system would create transactional inequities. * * *

The taxpayers and the Government * * * propose different formulations of the tax benefit rule. The taxpayers contend that the rule requires the inclusion of amounts *recovered* in later years, and they do not view the events in these cases as "recoveries." The Government, on the other hand, urges that the tax benefit rule requires the inclusion of

---

b. We have included only the Court's discussion of United States v. Bliss Dairy, Inc. The Court's discussion of Hillsboro National Bank v. Commissioner is omitted.— Eds.

8. Although the rule originated in the courts, it has the implicit approval of Congress, which enacted § 111 as a limitation on the rule.

amounts previously deducted if later events are inconsistent with the deductions; it insists that no "recovery" is necessary to the application of the rule. Further, it asserts that the events in these cases are inconsistent with the deductions taken by the taxpayers. We are not in complete agreement with either view.

An examination of the purpose and accepted applications of the tax benefit rule reveals that a "recovery" will not always be necessary to invoke the tax benefit rule. The purpose of the rule is not simply to tax "recoveries." On the contrary, it is to approximate the results produced by a tax system based on transactional rather than annual accounting. [Citations omitted.] It has long been accepted that a taxpayer using accrual accounting who accrues and deducts an expense in a tax year before it becomes payable and who for some reason eventually does not have to pay the liability must then take into income the amount of the expense earlier deducted. [Citations omitted.] The bookkeeping entry canceling the liability, though it increases the balance sheet net worth of the taxpayer, does not fit within any ordinary definition of "recovery." Thus, the taxpayers' formulation of the rule neither serves the purposes of the rule nor accurately reflects the cases that establish the rule. Further, the taxpayers' proposal would introduce an undesirable formalism into the application of the tax benefit rule. Lower courts have been able to stretch the definition of "recovery" to include a great variety of events. For instance, in cases of corporate liquidations, courts have viewed the corporation's receipt of its own stock as a "recovery," reasoning that, even though the instant that the corporation receives the stock it becomes worthless, the stock has value as it is turned over to the corporation, and that ephemeral value represents a recovery for the corporation. See, e.g., Tennessee–Carolina Transportation, Inc. v. Commissioner, 582 F.2d, at 382 (alternative holding). Or, payment to another party may be imputed to the taxpayer, giving rise to a recovery. See First Trust and Savings Bank of Taylorville v. United States, 614 F.2d, at 1146 (alternative holding). Imposition of a requirement that there be a recovery would, in many cases, simply require the Government to cast its argument in different and unnatural terminology, without adding anything to the analysis.

The basic purpose of the tax benefit rule is to achieve rough transactional parity in tax, * * * and to protect the Government and the taxpayer from the adverse effects of reporting a transaction on the basis of assumptions that an event in a subsequent year proves to have been erroneous. Such an event, unforeseen at the time of an earlier deduction, may in many cases require the application of the tax benefit rule. We do not, however, agree that this consequence invariably follows. Not every unforeseen event will require the taxpayer to report income in the amount of his earlier deduction. On the contrary, the tax benefit rule will "cancel out" an earlier deduction only when a careful examination shows that the later event is indeed fundamentally inconsistent with the premise on which the deduction was initially based. That is, if that event had occurred within the same taxable year, it would have foreclosed the deduction. In some cases, a subsequent recovery by the taxpayer will be the only event that would be fundamentally inconsistent with the provision granting the deduction. In such a case, only actual recovery by the taxpayer would justify application of the tax benefit rule. For example, if a calendar-year taxpayer made a rental payment on December 15 for a 30–day lease deductible in the current year under § 162(a)(3), * * * the tax benefit rule would not require the recognition of income if the leased premises were destroyed by fire on January 10. The resulting inability of the taxpayer to occupy the building would be an event not fundamentally inconsistent with his prior deduction as an ordinary and necessary business expense under § 162(a). The loss is attributable to the business and therefore is consistent with the deduction of the rental payment as an ordinary and necessary business expense. On the other hand, had the premises not burned and, in January, the taxpayer decided to use them to house his family rather than to continue the operation of his business, he would have converted the leasehold to personal use. This would be an event fundamentally inconsistent with the business use on which the deduction was based. In the case of the fire, only if the lessor—by virtue of some provision in the lease—had refunded the rental payment would the taxpayer be required under the tax benefit rule to recognize income on the subsequent destruction of the building. In other words, the subsequent recovery of the previously deducted rental payment would be the only event inconsistent with the provision allowing the deduction. It therefore is evident that the tax benefit rule must be applied on a case-by-case basis. A court must consider the facts and circumstances of each case in the light of the purpose and function of the provisions granting the deductions.

* * *

Justice Stevens * * * suggests that we err in recognizing transactional equity as the reason for the tax benefit rule. It is difficult to understand why even the clearest recovery should be taxed if not for the concern with transactional equity. Nor does the concern with transactional equity entail a change in our approach to the annual accounting system. Although the tax system relies basically on annual accounting, see Burnet v. Sanford & Brooks Co., 282 U.S., at 365, the tax benefit rule eliminates some of the distortions that would otherwise arise from such a system. * * *

IV

* * * Bliss took a deduction under § 162(a), so we must begin by examining that provision. Section 162(a) permits a deduction for the "ordinary and necessary expenses" of carrying on a trade or business. The deduction is predicated on the consumption of the asset in the trade or business. * * * If the taxpayer later sells the asset rather than consuming it in furtherance of his trade or business, it is quite clear that he would lose his deduction, for the basis of the asset would be zero, see, e.g., Spitalny v. United States, 430 F.2d 195 (C.A.9 1970), so he would

recognize the full amount of the proceeds on sale as gain. See §§ 1001(a), (c). In general, if the taxpayer converts the expensed asset to some other, nonbusiness use, that action is inconsistent with his earlier deduction, and the tax benefit rule would require inclusion in income of the amount of the unwarranted deduction. That nonbusiness use is inconsistent with a deduction for an ordinary and necessary business expense is clear from an examination of the Code. While § 162(a) permits a deduction for ordinary and necessary business expenses, § 262 explicitly denies a deduction for personal expenses. * * * Thus, if a corporation turns expensed assets to the analog of personal consumption, as Bliss did here—distribution to shareholders—it would seem that it should take into income the amount of the earlier deduction.

That conclusion, however, does not resolve this case, for the distribution by Bliss to its shareholders is governed by a provision of the Code that specifically shields the taxpayer from recognition of gain—[former] § 336. We must therefore proceed to inquire whether this is the sort of gain that goes unrecognized under [former] § 336. Our examination of the background of [former] § 336 and its place within the framework of tax law convinces us that it does not prevent the application of the tax benefit rule.

* * *

V

Bliss paid the assessment on an increase of $60,000 in its taxable income. In the District Court, the parties stipulated that the value of the grain was $56,565, but the record does not show what the original cost of the grain was or what portion of it remained at the time of liquidation. The proper increase in taxable income is the portion of the cost of the grain attributable to the amount on hand at the time of liquidation. In *Bliss*, then, we remand for a determination of that amount. * * *

It is so ordered.

JUSTICE BRENNAN, concurring in [*Bliss*] and dissenting in [*Hillsboro*].

[Omitted.]

JUSTICE STEVENS, with whom JUSTICE MARSHALL joins, concurring in the judgment in [*Hillsboro*] and dissenting in [*Bliss*].

* * *

Today the Court declares that the purpose of the tax benefit rule is "to approximate the results produced by a tax system based on transactional rather than annual accounting." Whereas the rule has previously been used to determine the character of a current wealth-enhancing event, when viewed in the light of past deductions, the Court now suggests that the rule requires a study of the propriety of earlier deductions, when viewed in the light of later events. The Court states that the rule operates to "cancel out" an earlier deduction if the premise on which it is based is "fundamentally inconsistent" with an event in a later year.

The Court's reformulation of the tax benefit rule constitutes an extremely significant enlargement of the tax collector's powers. In order to identify the groundbreaking character of the decision, I shall review the history of the tax benefit rule. I shall then discuss the *Bliss Dairy* case in some detail, to demonstrate that it fits comfortably within the class of cases to which the tax benefit rule has not been applied in the past. Finally, I shall explain why the Court's adventure in lawmaking is not only misguided but does not even explain its inconsistent disposition of these two similar cases.

I

What is today called the "tax benefit rule" evolved in two stages, reflecting the rule's two components. The "inclusionary" component requires that the recovery within a taxable year of an item previously deducted be included in gross income. The "exclusionary component," which gives the rule its name, allows the inclusionary component to operate only to the extent that the prior deduction benefited the taxpayer.

The inclusionary component of the rule originated in the Bureau of Internal Revenue in the context of recoveries of debts that had previously been deducted as uncollectible. The Bureau sensed that it was inequitable to permit a taxpayer to characterize the recovery of such a debt as "return of capital" when in a prior year he had been allowed to reduce his taxable income to compensate for the loss of that capital. As one commentator described it, "the allowance of a deduction results in a portion of gross income not being taxed; when the deducted item is recouped, the recovery stands in the place of the gross income which had not been taxed before and is therefore taxable."[3] This principle was quickly endorsed by the Board of Tax Appeals and the courts. See Excelsior Printing Co. v. Commissioner, 16 B.T.A. 886 (1929); Putnam National Bank v. Commissioner, 50 F.2d 158 (C.A.5 1931).

The exclusionary component was not so readily accepted. The Bureau first incorporated it during the Great Depression as the natural equitable counterweight to the inclusionary component. G.C.M. 18525, 1937–1 Cum.Bull. 80. It soon retreated, however, insisting that a recovery could be treated as income even if the prior deduction had not benefited the taxpayer. G.C.M. 22163, 1940–2 Cum.Bull. 76. The Board of Tax Appeals protested, e.g., Corn Exchange National Bank & Trust Co. v. Commissioner, 46 B.T.A. 1107 (1942), but the Circuit Courts of Appeals sided with the Bureau. Helvering v. State–Planters Bank & Trust Co., 130 F.2d 44 (C.A.4 1942); Commissioner v. United States & International Securities Corp., 130 F.2d 894 (C.A.3 1942). At that point,

---

3. Plumb, The Tax Benefit Rule Today, 57 Harv.L.Rev. 129, 131, n. 10 (1943). Accord, Estate of Collins v. Commissioner, 46 B.T.A. 765, 769 (1942), rev'd *sub nom.* Har- wick v. Commissioner, 133 F.2d 732 (CA8), rev'd *sub nom.* Dobson v. Commissioner, 320 U.S. 489 (1943).

Congress intervened for the first and only time. It enacted the forerunner of § 111 of the present Code, ch. 619, Title I, § 116(a), Act of Oct. 21, 1942, 56 Stat. 812, using language that by implication acknowledges the propriety of the inclusionary component by explicitly mandating the exclusionary component.

The most striking feature of the rule's history is that from its early formative years, through codification, until the 1960's, Congress, the Internal Revenue Service, courts, and commentators, understood it in essentially the same way. They all saw it as a theory that appropriately characterized certain recoveries of capital as income. Although the rule undeniably helped to accommodate the annual accounting system to multi-year transactions, I have found no suggestion that it was regarded as a generalized method of approximating a transactional accounting system through the fabrication of income at the drop of a fundamentally inconsistent event. An inconsistent event was always a necessary condition, but with the possible exception of the discussion of the Board of Tax Appeals in Barnett v. Commissioner, 39 B.T.A. 864, 867 (1939), inconsistency was never by itself a sufficient reason for applying the rule. Significantly, the first case from this Court dealing with the tax benefit rule emphasized the role of a recovery.[11] And when litigants in this Court suggested that a transactional accounting system would be more equitable, we expressly declined to impose one, stressing the importance of finality and practicability in a tax system.[12]

* * *

II

In the *Bliss Dairy* case, the Court today reaches a result contrary to that dictated by a recovery theory. One would not expect such a break with the past unless it were apparent that prior law would produce a

---

11. In Dobson v. Commissioner, 320 U.S. 489 (1943), the taxpayer had bought stock, sold it at a loss, and then claimed a deductible loss on his tax return. Eight years later, the taxpayer had sued for rescission of the stock purchase, claiming fraud; he settled the suit and received approximately $30,000 for the stock on which he had sustained the loss. We upheld the Tax Court's determination that the $30,000 recovery did not need to be reported as income, since the earlier deductible losses had not reduced the taxpayer's taxes in the year he had claimed them. For present purposes, the holding in *Dobson* was less significant than the way it endorsed the Tax Court's analysis:

"The Tax Court has not attempted to revise liability for earlier years closed by the statute of limitation, nor used any expense, liability, or deficit of a prior year to reduce the income of a subsequent year. *It went to prior years only to determine the nature of the recovery, whether return of capital or income.*" Id., at 493 (emphasis added).

The tax benefit question was not one of inconsistent events, but whether a recovery should be characterized as return of capital or as income.

12. Burnet v. Sanford & Brooks Co., 282 U.S. 359 (1931), was a mirror image of this case. The taxpayer argued that a recovery of previously deducted funds should not be income because, seen from a transactional view, no net profits had been realized. The Court framed the issue as whether net profits are to be determined "on the basis of fixed accounting periods, or * * * on the basis of particular transactions of the taxpayer when they are brought to a conclusion." Id., at 363. The answer was unanimous and unflinching: [See Burnet v. Sanford & Brooks Co., p. 702, above, requiring annual accounting.—Eds.]

palpable inequity—a clear windfall for the taxpayer. Yet that is not the case in *Bliss Dairy*. * * *

Three statutory provisions, as interpreted by the Commissioner, interact in *Bliss Dairy*. First, pursuant to § 162(a), the Commissioner allowed the corporation to deduct the entire cost of all grain purchased in 1972. That deduction left it with a basis of zero in that grain. Second, under the terms of § 336, the corporation was not required to recognize any gain or loss when it went through a § 333 liquidation in 1973. And third, pursuant to the regulations implementing § 334, the shareholders were allowed to assign some portion of their basis in the corporation's stock to the grain they received in the liquidation. Admittedly, this combination of provisions could in some cases cause a "step-up" in the grain's basis that is not reflected in the income of either the corporation or the shareholders. That possibility figured strongly in the decision of the Court of Appeals for the Sixth Circuit to endorse an inconsistent-event theory in a precursor of this case. See Tennessee–Carolina Transportation, Inc. v. Commissioner, 582 F.2d 378, 382, and n. 14 (1978). And it is stressed by the Solicitor General in his argument in this case. Yet close analysis reveals that the potential untaxed step-up is not the sort of extraordinary and inequitable windfall that calls for extraordinary measures in *this* case.

As a factual matter, the record does not include the tax returns of Bliss Dairy's shareholders. We have no indication of how much, if any, step-up in basis actually occurred. And as a legal matter, a § 333 liquidation expressly contemplates steps-up in basis that are not reflected in income. Thus, even if the corporation had behaved as the Court believes it should have and had fed all the grain to the cows before liquidating, whatever shareholder stock basis was assigned to the grain in this case would have been used to step up the basis of some other asset that passed to the shareholders in the liquidation.

* * *

III

Because tax considerations play such an important role in decisions relating to the investment of capital, the transfer of operating businesses, and the management of going concerns, there is a special interest in the orderly, certain, and consistent interpretation of the Internal Revenue Code. Today's decision seriously compromises that interest. It will engender uncertainty, it will enlarge the tax gatherer's discretionary power to reexamine past transactions, and it will produce controversy and litigation.

Any inconsistent-event theory of the tax benefit rule would make the tax system more complicated than it has been under the recovery theory. Inconsistent-event analysis forces a deviation from the traditional pattern of calculating income during a given year: identify the transactions in which the taxpayer was made wealthier, determine from the history of those transactions which apparent sources of enrichment should be characterized as income, and then determine how much of that income must be recognized. Of course, in several specific contexts, Congress has already mandated deviations from that traditional pattern, and the additional complications are often deemed an appropriate price for enhanced tax equity. But to my knowledge Congress has never even considered so sweeping a deviation as a general inconsistent-event theory.

Nonetheless, a general inconsistent-event theory would surely give more guidance than the vague hybrid established by the Court today. The dimensions of the Court's newly fashioned "fundamentally inconsistent event" version of the tax benefit rule are by no means clear. It obviously differs from both the Government's "inconsistent event" theory and the familiar "recovery" theory, either of which would require these two cases to be decided in the same way. I do not understand, however, precisely why the Court's theory distinguishes between these cases, or how it is to be applied in computing the 1973 taxes of Bliss Dairy, Inc.

The Government describes its test as whether "subsequent events eliminate the factual premise on which the deduction was originally claimed." The Court describes its test as whether "the later event is indeed fundamentally inconsistent with the premise on which the deduction was initially based." One might infer that the difference between these tests is a difference between "inconsistent events" and "fundamentally inconsistent events." The Court attempts to place the line more precisely "between merely unexpected events and inconsistent events." I am afraid the attempt fails because, however it is described, the line does not cleanly and predictably separate the Court's position from the Government's.

* * *

IV

Neither history nor sound tax policy supports the Court's abandonment of its interpretation of the tax benefit rule as a tool for characterizing certain recoveries as income. If Congress were dissatisfied with the tax treatment that I believe Bliss Dairy should be accorded under current law, it could respond by changing any of the three provisions that bear on this case. It could modify the manner in which deductions are authorized under § 162. It could legislate another statutory exception to the annual accounting system, much as it did when it made the depreciation recapture provisions, §§ 1245, 1250, apply to § 336 liquidations. Or it could modify the manner in which basis is allocated under § 334. But in the absence of legislative action, I cannot join in the Court's attempt to achieve similar results by distorting the tax benefit rule.

* * *

Justice Blackmun, dissenting.

[JUSTICE BLACKMUN argued that when the year in which the deduction was taken is open at the time of the later event, the deduction should be disallowed. If the earlier year was closed because of the statute of limitations, the "resolution might well be different."]

* * *

Problem and Notes

1. *Drawing the line.* Rojas v. Commissioner, 901 F.2d 810 (9th Cir.1990), presented a fact situation one step removed from that of *Bliss Dairy.* In *Rojas,* a farming corporation deducted the costs of seed and fertilizer used to produce crops and then, before the crops were sold, liquidated, distributing the crops to its shareholders. The government argued that the tax benefit rule required the corporation to recognize gain on the distribution of the crops; distribution (rather than sale) of the crops was, it reasoned, "fundamentally inconsistent" with deducting the costs of producing those crops. The Ninth Circuit declined to extend the tax benefit rule that far; it distinguished *Bliss Dairy* by saying that the corporation in *Rojas* had "consumed" its seed and fertilizer by turning them into crops. While the line between *Bliss Dairy* and *Rojas* is fine indeed, a line must be drawn somewhere.

The particular question of when the tax benefit rule will override the nonrecognition rule of § 336 has been made moot by statutory developments. Today, most corporations recognize gains when they distribute appreciated assets to their shareholders.[c] Under current law, the taxpayer corporations in *Bliss Dairy* and *Rojas* would have to recognize the gains in question simply because they disposed of appreciated property. Whether that disposition was "fundamentally inconsistent" with taking deductions in the first place no longer matters.

2. *Problem.* T buys stock for $50,000 and then properly claims a $50,000 deduction for the worthlessness of the stock. T keeps the stock certificates as souvenirs. Much to everyone's surprise, the corporation in question revives, and the stock increases in value to $80,000, at which time T contributes it to a charity, claiming an $80,000 deduction. Must T include $50,000 in income?

3. *Statutory tax benefit rules.* Section 186 provides an exclusion for recoveries of damages on account of certain business losses which were deducted without tax benefit. See also the exception to the exclusion of § 104(a) for recoveries of previously deducted medical expenses.

For historical reasons, the tax benefit rule does not exclude gains on the sale of property even if the property's basis reflects adjustments for depreciation deductions which produced no tax benefit. There is one statutory exception: a taxpayer who claimed depreciation in excess of the

---

c. § 336(a). Under § 337, a subsidiary that is liquidated does not recognize gains upon distributing property to its parent. But in that case, the parent takes the distributed property with the subsidiary's basis, so the gain in question will eventually be recognized by the parent.

amount properly allowable need not reduce basis by more than the amount allowable if the excess did not reduce taxes; § 1016(a)(2).

4. *References.* White, An Essay on the Conceptual Foundations of the Tax Benefit Rule, 82 Mich.L.Rev. 486 (1983); Blum, The Role of the Supreme Court in Federal Income Tax Controversies—*Hillsboro National Bank* and *Bliss Dairy, Inc.,* 61 Taxes 363 (1983).

3. SECTION 1341

VAN CLEAVE v. UNITED STATES

United States Court of Appeals, Sixth Circuit, 1983.
718 F.2d 193.

Before ENGEL and KRUPANSKY, CIRCUIT JUDGES and BROWN, SENIOR CIRCUIT JUDGE.

BAILEY BROWN, SENIOR CIRCUIT JUDGE.

This appeal involves a claim of favorable income tax treatment under § 1341 by a taxpayer who in a subsequent year paid back excessive compensation to the corporation which employed him. The taxpayer included this excessive compensation in his return for the year the compensation was received. The government concedes that taxpayer is entitled to a deduction in the subsequent year. Taxpayer contends, however, that he should be allowed, pursuant to Section 1341, more favorable tax treatment by in effect excluding the excessive compensation from his income in the year received, thereby reducing his tax liability for that year and receiving a credit against his tax liability for the subsequent year. The district court, after a bench trial, entered judgment for the government in taxpayer's refund action and taxpayer appealed. We reverse and hold that taxpayer is entitled to the benefit of Section 1341.

BACKGROUND

The taxpayer, Eugene Van Cleave, was president and majority stockholder of Van–Mark Corporation throughout the time in question. In 1969, the corporation adopted a by-law requiring corporate officers who received from the corporation income determined by the Internal Revenue Service (IRS) to be excessive—and so not deductible by the corporation as a business expense—to pay back the amount determined to be excessive to the corporation. In addition, Mr. Van Cleave entered into a separate agreement requiring him to reimburse the corporation for nondeductible compensation.

Mr. Van Cleave received $332,000 in salary and bonuses in 1974. During 1975, the IRS audited the corporation's return, determined that $57,500 of Mr. Van Cleave's salary was excessive, and disallowed that portion of his salary as a deduction to the corporation. In December, 1975, pursuant to the corporation's by-law and the agreement between

Mr. Van Cleave and the corporation, Mr. Van Cleave repaid the nondeductible $57,500.

Mr. Van Cleave reported the full compensation on his calendar year 1974 income tax return. On his 1975 return, prepared with the repayment to the corporation in mind, he calculated his tax liability by using § 1341. The IRS audited the return, and allowed a deduction for 1975 but disallowed use of Section 1341, resulting in a tax deficiency of $5,987.34. Mr. Van Cleave paid this deficiency and brought this action for a refund.

This case turns on the interpretation of Section 1341 of the Internal Revenue Code. * * *

Section 1341 was enacted by Congress to mitigate the sometimes harsh result of the application of the "claim of right" doctrine. United States v. Skelly Oil Co., 394 U.S. 678 (1969); H.R.Rep. No. 1337, 83d Cong., 2d Sess., 86–87 * * *. Under the claim of right doctrine, a taxpayer must pay tax on an item in the year in which he receives it under a claim of right even if it is later determined that his right to the item was not absolute and he is required to return it. The taxpayer, however, is allowed to deduct the amount of the item from his income in the year of repayment. This result was held to be required because income and deductions are determined on an annual basis. *Skelly* at 681. But, as pointed out by the Supreme Court in *Skelly,* it is possible for a taxpayer to benefit less from the deduction in the year of repayment than he would benefit if he had been able to deduct the amount repaid from his income in the year of receipt. Id. This result of the claim of right doctrine could occur when, as was the case with Mr. Van Cleave, the taxpayer had been in a higher tax bracket in the year of receipt than he was in the year of repayment.

Section 1341 allows the taxpayer to choose the more favorable alternative * * *.

I.

The district court held that Section 1341 treatment was not available to Mr. Van Cleave because it determined that his repayment was voluntary. The district court determined that it was voluntary because Mr. Van Cleave owned a substantial majority of the stock and in that sense controlled the corporation. On appeal, however, the government does not contend that Section 1341 is inapplicable because the repayment was voluntary and indeed does not contend that the repayment in fact was voluntary.

The district court also seemed to be persuaded by the argument that, if Mr. Van Cleave were allowed Section 1341 treatment under these circumstances, this would open the door to tax avoidance in that taxpayers who controlled corporations could "test the waters" in setting their compensation without risk of an adverse tax result. We believe, however, that such possibility of tax avoidance is not a proper consideration in applying this statute, and that the consideration is a legislative rather than a judicial consideration. Moreover, as Mr. Van Cleave suggests, the possibility of tax avoidance could be reduced by requiring the corporation and recipient of compensation to state in their returns that such compensation was paid subject to an obligation to reimburse in the event a deduction is disallowed to the corporation.

II.

The leading case on the claim of right tax doctrine is North American Oil Consolidated v. Burnet, 286 U.S. 417 (1932). *North American Oil* involved a dispute over the year in which income, earned on property held by a receiver during a title dispute between the taxpayer and the government, was to be taxed. The possibilities were 1916, the year in which the income was earned; 1917, the year in which the district court ruled in favor of the taxpayer and the money was paid to the taxpayer; or 1922, the year the litigation was finally terminated in the taxpayer's favor. In an opinion by Justice Brandeis, the Court determined that 1917 was the year that the income must be reported and set forth the claim of right doctrine as follows:

> If a taxpayer receives earnings under a claim of right and without restriction as to its disposition, he has received income which he is required to return, even though it may still be claimed that he is not entitled to retain the money, and even though he may still be adjudged liable to restore its equivalent. Id. at 424.

* * *

As previously noted, Section 1341 was enacted to alleviate the effect of the claim of right doctrine * * *. The government argues, however, that Section 1341 is not available to the taxpayer in the instant case. The government points out that Section 1341 provides for taxpayer relief only if "it *appeared* that the taxpayer had an unrestricted right" (emphasis added) to the excess salary and "it was established after the close of such prior taxable year * * * that the taxpayer did not have an unrestricted right to such item." Section 1341(a)(1) and (2). The government argues that Mr. Van Cleave had more than an *appearance* of an unrestricted right to the excess compensation in the year in which it was received, and that the right to the compensation became restricted only upon the occurrence of the IRS audit and determination in a subsequent year. The government maintains that, since Mr. Van Cleave had an unrestricted right to the compensation in the year of receipt, contingent only upon the happening of an event in a subsequent year, Section 1341 is not available to him.

We reject this argument and hold that Section 1341 is available to Mr. Van Cleave. The fact that his ultimate right to the compensation was not determined until the occurrence of a subsequent event does not mean that Mr. Van Cleave had, in the statutory sense, an unrestricted right to the compensation when he received it. In Prince v. United States, 610 F.2d 350 (1980), the Fifth Circuit reversed a district court decision that the estate of a taxpayer was not entitled to Section 1341 tax adjustment. A state court had ruled that the decedent, a trust beneficiary, had received trust funds—and paid federal income tax on them—that should have gone to the trustee as part of its fee. The state court required the decedent's estate to return these funds to the trustee. The government's position in that case was identical to its stance in this case: Section 1341 was not available to the taxpayer's estate because the taxpayer had an unrestricted right to the income in the year of receipt, not just the appearance of a right. Id. at 352. In rejecting the government's argument, the court said:

> The Alabama judgment established, whether expressly or by implication, that the deductions from the trust income for the ten year fee had been miscalculated. As a result, [decedent] had received more income from the trust than she was entitled to receive. This income had to be returned. The requirements of Section 1341 were thus clearly satisfied. [Decedent] appeared to have an unrestricted right to the income when she received it; it was established in a taxable year after she received it that she did not have such a right. Id.

We agree with the Fifth Circuit's reading of Section 1341 and hold that the fact that a restriction on a taxpayer's right to income does not arise until a year subsequent to the time of receipt does not affect the availability of Section 1341 tax adjustment. Therefore, Section 1341 tax adjustment is available to a taxpayer in this situation if the other requirements of the section are met. We are aided in this conclusion by our examination of cases involving the application of the claim of right doctrine, the effect of which the section was designed to alleviate. [Citations omitted.] Acceptance of the government's reading of the statute would thwart the ameliorative purpose intended by Congress in enacting the section. [Citations omitted.] * * *

The judgment of the district court is reversed and the case is remanded for proceedings consistent with this opinion.

Problems, Notes and Questions

1. *The problem.* Section 1341 was enacted to ease the "inequity" of cases like United States v. Lewis, 340 U.S. 590 (1951). Lewis received a $22,000 bonus from his employer in 1944 and reported it as income. Litigation in the state courts then established that the bonus had been improperly computed, and in 1946 Lewis repaid approximately $11,000. The Court of Claims held that the "excess" portion of the bonus, received under a "mistake of fact," was not income for 1944, but the Supreme Court reversed, relying on the "claim of right" doctrine of North American Oil Consolidated v. Burnet, p. 753, below. The taxpayer, therefore, could deduct the repayment in 1946, but could not reduce his 1944 income by the amount of the payment. The supposed inequity arose because the tax saved by the 1946 deduction of $11,000 was less than the tax paid as a result of including the $11,000 in income in 1944. Work through § 1341 to see how it helps people like Lewis.

Would Van Cleave have been allowed to use § 1341 if the agreement requiring repayment had been made after Van Cleave had received the payment?

2. *Section 1341 and the Arrowsmith doctrine.* The Service has ruled that § 1341 can be used in cases like Arrowsmith v. Commissioner, p. 635, above, if the amount of the repayment exceeds $3000; Rev.Rul. 78–25, 1978–1 C.B. 270. What if a repayment characterized as a capital loss by the *Arrowsmith* doctrine exceeds $3000 but the taxpayer's deduction for the year of repayment is limited to $3000 by § 1211(b)? See Treas. Reg. § 1.1341–1(c).

3. *Embezzlers.* McKinney v. United States, 574 F.2d 1240 (5th Cir.1978), cert. denied 439 U.S. 1072 (1979), held that an embezzler who reported his loot as income in 1966 and repaid his victim in 1969 could not use § 1341 (the government conceded that he was entitled to a deduction in 1969—why?). Since it did not appear to the embezzler that he had "*any* right to the funds, much less 'an unrestricted right' to them," § 1341(a) was not satisfied. Does this decision unduly emphasize matters of wording that are essentially stylistic?

McKinney is criticized in Newman, Of Time and Up the River: Criminal Restitution and the Annual Accounting System, 56 Taxes 420 (1978).

4. *Problems.*

(1) Under the terms of *E*'s employment contract with *X* Corp., *E* receives a stated salary plus an annual bonus based upon *X*'s profits. Under this agreement, *X* paid *E* a $20,000 bonus in year 1. In year 2, *X* Corp. notified *E* that the bonus had been erroneously calculated, that it should have been only $10,000, and that *E* should repay the $10,000 excess. *E* repaid the $10,000 in year 2. *E*, a single person with no dependents, had taxable income of $75,000 for year 1 (and would have had taxable income of $65,000 but for inclusion of the $10,000 excess bonus). In year 1, *E*'s 30–percent tax bracket began at a taxable income of $60,000. Her income for year 2 was $30,000 (and would have been $40,000 but for the $10,000 deduction for the repayment of the excess bonus). Under the year-2 rate schedule, the top $10,000 of an income of $40,000 would be taxed at 27 percent. What result to *E* under § 1341?

(2) Same as (1), except that *E*'s taxable income for year 1 was $40,000 (and would have been $30,000 but for inclusion of the excess bonus) and *E*'s taxable income for year 2 was $65,000 (and would have been $75,000 without the deduction for the repayment of the excess bonus). The top $10,000 of a $40,000 income is taxable at 27 percent in year 1; the top $10,000 of a $75,000 income is taxable at 30 percent in year 2.

B. AN INTRODUCTION TO TAX ACCOUNTING

Most taxpayers report income and deductions on either the "cash method" of accounting or on some variation of the "accrual method."

Under the cash method, income and deductions are normally reported for the period in which the taxpayer "receives" (actually or constructively) an income item or "pays" a deductible amount. Under an accrual method, timing questions are usually said to turn upon whether "all the events" giving rise to a right to receive or an obligation to make a payment have occurred.

Generally speaking, a taxpayer starting a new business is free to adopt either the cash method or an accrual method, if the taxpayer's books are kept in the same way; § 446. However, Treas.Reg. § 1.446–1(c)(2)(i) requires taxpayers who must use inventories to account for sales of goods under an accrual method. This rule may be a relic of pre-computer days, when opening and closing inventories were determined by a physical count of stock on hand.[d] Section 448, which was adopted in 1986, denies the use of the cash method to most C corporations, partnerships which have C corporations as partners, and tax shelters. Special rules for some farming corporations and partnerships are provided by § 447. Notice 2001–76, 2001–52 I.R.B. 613, presents a proposal for a Revenue Procedure that would allow "qualifying small business taxpayers" having gross receipts of less than $10 million a year to use the cash method, even if they sell goods.

Some Code sections authorizing deductions or requiring inclusions in income provide that deductions are allowed for items "paid" or that income includes amounts "received"; these provisions put all taxpayers on the cash method with respect to those items. Examples include § 71(a) (alimony "received"), § 170(a) (charitable contributions "payment of which is made within the taxable year"), and § 213(a) (medical expenses "paid during the taxable year").

Although it is common practice to refer to "cash-method taxpayers" and "accrual-method taxpayers,"[e] accounting methods are attributes of activities, not of taxpayers: a taxpayer can adopt different methods for different businesses. References in this book to "cash-method taxpayers" or "accrual-method taxpayers" should be understood as references to taxpayers who use those methods for reporting the items under discussion.

d. If inventories are determined by a physical count, the cost of all inventory items shipped will be included in cost of goods sold. Accurate calculation of gain or loss in such a case would require that revenues attributable to all items shipped be included in gross receipts from sales, whether or not those revenues have been received; this, in turn, would require accrual accounting. But computerized record-keeping could allow inventory shipped but not yet paid for to be counted as still being on hand.

Another possible justification for requiring those who use inventories to use accrual accounting is that businesses with inventory accounting should be sophisticated enough to use an accrual method.

e. Sometimes the phrases "cash basis" and "accrual basis" are used; this terminology can cause confusion, as "basis" is itself a technical tax term. References to the "cash basis method" or the "accrual basis method" should be avoided. A common periphrasis is "cash receipts and disbursements method" for "cash method."

1. THE CASH METHOD

(a) Actual or Constructive Receipt of Cash or an "Economic Benefit"

DAVIS v. COMMISSIONER

United States Tax Court, 1978.
37 T.C.M. 42.

DAWSON, JUDGE: * * *

The first issue for decision is whether petitioner constructively received her severance pay in 1974. The evidentiary facts related to this issue are not disputed. Although petitioner did not expect to receive the severance pay until 1975, the Railway mailed it to her in late December via certified mail, return receipt requested. A postal employee attempted delivery on December 31, 1974, but petitioner was not at home. Petitioner arrived home after the post office had closed and she saw the notice of attempted delivery of certified mail which she expected to be a notice of increase in her rent. Petitioner picked up the letter when the post office reopened on January 2, 1975, and discovered the certified mail to be her severance pay.

Respondent contends that petitioner constructively received the pay in 1974 since the severance payment was unqualifiedly committed to petitioner on December 31, 1974, and the checks were made available to petitioner at the post office after three o'clock p.m. on the same date. Petitioner argues, on the other hand, that there was no constructive receipt since the check was mailed in the ordinary course of business, was not actually received until 1975, and was not intentionally delayed in transit by petitioner. We agree with petitioner.

The Federal income tax is based on a computation period which is the taxable year. Section 451(a) provides the general rule that "any item of gross income shall be included in the gross income for the taxable year in which received by the taxpayer, unless, under the method of accounting used in computing taxable income, such amount is to be properly accounted for as of a different period." Since petitioner is on the cash receipts and disbursements method based on a calendar taxable year of accounting, income is taxable to her in the year the item is actually or constructively received. [Treas. Reg. §§ 1.446–1(c)(1)(i) & 1.451–1(a)]. Petitioner did not actually receive the severance pay in 1974, so the issue is whether she constructively received it in that year.

The doctrine of constructive receipt is based on the principle that income is received or realized by cash method taxpayers "when it is made subject to the will and control of the taxpayer and can be, except for his own action or inaction, reduced to actual possession." Loose v. United States, 74 F.2d 147, 150 (8th Cir.1934), affg. 4 F.Supp. 375 (W.D.Mo.1933). The regulations provide that:

> Income although not actually reduced to a taxpayer's possession is constructively received by him in the taxable year during which it is credited to his account, set apart for him, or otherwise made available so that he may draw upon it at any time, or so that he could have drawn upon it during the taxable year if notice of intention to withdraw had been given. However, income is not constructively received if the taxpayer's control of its receipt is subject to substantial limitations or restrictions. [Treas. Reg. § 1.451–2(a)]

Although these general principles are well-settled and easily stated, each case necessarily turns on its facts and the doctrine of constructive receipt should be applied sparingly. [citations omitted.] "It is only in unique circumstances and a clear case that the invoking of this doctrine will be approved." Roach v. Commissioner, 20 B.T.A. 919, 925 (1930). The facts of petitioner's situation here do not present such a case.

Respondent is correct in his contention that the Railway had unqualifiedly committed the funds to petitioner by December 31, 1974, but such a commitment is not sufficient in itself to cause constructive receipt. The funds must be made available to the taxpayer without substantial limitations, [Treas. Reg. § 1.451–2(a)]. Implicit in availability is notice to the taxpayer that the funds are subject to his will and control. Such notice is lacking here.

Petitioner had no expectation that she would receive the payment in 1974. The Railway had told her it would take months to process her severance pay and that she would not receive the checks until 1975. We see no reason to charge her with constructive receipt simply because she received a notice of attempted delivery of certified mail on December 31, 1974. Petitioner had no inkling that the certified mail was her severance pay; she thought it was a notice of rent increase. Receipt for tax purposes did not effectively occur until January 2, 1975, at which time petitioner actually received the letter and discovered it to be her pay.

Respondent argues that petitioner should be charged with constructive receipt since she would have actually received the payment in 1974 but for the fact that she chose not to be at home on December 31, 1974. We find this argument unpersuasive. It is true that case law has consistently held that any delay in receipt, any substantial limitation or any restriction cannot be of the taxpayer's unilateral making. [Citations omitted.] Those cases, however, dealt with situations where the taxpayer knew he could have receipt in the earlier year and took steps specifically designed to prevent actual receipt. The error in respondent's logic lies in equating petitioner's choice to be absent from home with a conscious choice not to receive the severance pay until the following year. In fact, petitioner's absence here was not procured to prevent actual receipt. Under these circumstances application of the doctrine of constructive receipt is inappropriate. "[I]n general, income should not be construed to have been received prior to the date of actual receipt except where a taxpayer turns his back upon income or does not choose to receive income which he could have if he chose." Adams v. Commissioner, [20 B.T.A.] at 246.

Respondent's reliance on McEuen v. Commissioner, 196 F.2d 127 (5th Cir.1952), revg. a Memorandum Opinion of this Court; Loose v. United States, supra; and Kahler v. Commissioner, 18 T.C. 31 (1952), is misplaced. In the *McEuen* case the Fifth Circuit concluded that, although not actually received until 1944, a check mailed to the taxpayer at his request in 1943 was constructively received in the year of request. The holding turned on the fact that the payment was at the direction of the taxpayer and the taxpayer could have picked up the check personally but for the geographical distance separating him from the payor. In the instant case the payment time was not subject to petitioner's direction. Furthermore, there is no indication that petitioner could have picked up the check in person; the normal procedure for the Railway was to mail the severance pay after processing the claim.

In Loose v. United States, supra, constructive receipt was found despite the fact that the taxpayer had suffered a stroke which rendered him unable to personally avail himself of actual receipt. *Loose* is distinguishable from the instant case, however, since there the taxpayer had actual notice of the availability of the income via the cashing of interest coupons which already were in the taxpayer's possession. Moreover, his wife had a power of attorney for access to the coupons and apparently could have cashed them except for her desire to stay with her ill husband. Here petitioner had no actual knowledge or expectation that the income would be available to her in 1974.

Respondent cites *Kahler,* supra, for the proposition that constructive receipt may be found despite no expectation of income in the earlier year. In *Kahler,* however, although the taxpayer did not expect to receive the check, he actually received it sometime after five p.m. on December 31 of the earlier year. Petitioner here had no actual receipt until 1975. *Kahler* is therefore inapposite.

In our judgment the facts in the instant case are inappropriate for the application of the doctrine of constructive receipt. Accordingly, we hold that the severance pay is not taxable to petitioner in the calendar year 1974.

* * *

Problems, Notes and Questions

1. *What barriers prevent constructive receipt?* Most courts have held that mere physical inability to obtain cash (or a check) does not prevent constructive receipt. Loose v. United States (discussed in the principal case) is one example. Likewise, the ability to get cash immediately does not put a taxpayer in constructive receipt if the payor has not met the setting-aside requirements of the regulation. The taxpayer in Hyland v. Commissioner, 175 F.2d 422 (2d Cir.1949), was the president and con-

trolling shareholder of a corporation. The corporation's board of directors had voted Hyland a $40,000 salary payment for 1942. Although Hyland could have directed the corporation's financial officers to pay him this amount at any time, he did not do so, and so he was held not to be in receipt of his 1942 salary until it was paid to him. Rev. Rul. 73–99, 1973–1 C.B. 412, holds that a check is generally includable in income in the year received rather than the year mailed, but also held that the taxpayer would be in constructive receipt if he could have picked the check up from his employer by year's end.

What if the taxpayer would have to travel a substantial distance to pick up the check? Baxter v. Commissioner, 816 F.2d 493 (9th Cir.1987), held that a taxpayer was not in constructive receipt of a check for commissions because he would have had to drive 40 miles to pick up the check on December 30 and could not have cashed it until January 2. Unlike Davis, Baxter knew that the check was available. If this is the law, maybe employees on year-end vacations far from work will not have to report their last paycheck(s) for the year as income until the following year, even though their employers will routinely report and withhold on the amounts as income for the first year. A test turning upon whether it would make practical sense in particular cases for taxpayers to turn their rights into cash might be very difficult to administer. Other cases where a lack of geographical proximity was a factor precluding constructive receipt include Hornung v. Commissioner, 47 T.C. 428, 434 (1967) (taxpayer was awarded a Corvette for being most valuable player in National Football League championship game played on December 31 in Green Bay, Wisconsin; car was at dealership in New York City and dealership was closed for weekend; held, no constructive receipt); Paul v. Commissioner, 64 T.C.M. 955 (1992) (winner of New Jersey Lottery not in constructive receipt of winnings in December even though he could have collected by driving 68 miles to Trenton).

Aldrich Ames, a CIA employee who spied for the Soviet Union, was told in 1985 by a Soviet agent that $2 million had been "set aside" for him in Russia and that he could draw on this money. He was told that the money was not in a bank account but was held "by the Soviet Union." In 1989 through 1992, Ames received some $320,000 in cash for his services. In response to the government's argument that these payments were income to Ames when received, Ames argued that he had constructively received most of these payments in 1985. The Tax Court held that Ames had not constructively received payment in 1985; Ames v. Commissioner, 112 T.C. 304 (1999). Before he could get any money from his "account," Ames would have had to contact his employers, using a complex set of signals, and they would have had to transfer the cash to the United States and leave it in a secret location for Ames to pick up. Furthermore, there was "no practical or legal way" for Ames to make the Soviets pay him if they became dissatisfied with his work.

2. *The "economic benefit" doctrine.* A taxpayer who receives property or services as compensation has income even though the receipt does not take the form of cash: the phrase "cash method" should not be

taken literally. (See § 83 for the tax treatment of compensatory transfers of property.) One important qualification to this rule is that a promise to pay is not regarded as "property" in applying the cash method of accounting, even though the promise has value and even though it is surely property in the constitutional sense.

3. *Receipt by an agent.* Alsop v. Commissioner, 290 F.2d 726 (2d Cir.1961), held that an author was not in receipt of amounts paid to her agent and embezzled by the agent without the taxpayer's ever learning of the payments. Ordinarily, however, payments to the taxpayer's agent are treated as payments to the taxpayer; Maryland Cas. Co. v. United States, 251 U.S. 342 (1920).

4. *Bank accounts and certificates of deposit.* A cash-method depositor who buys a certificate of deposit is not in constructive receipt of interest which cannot be withdrawn without a substantial penalty. However, if the CD matures more than one year from the date of purchase, the taxpayer will have to report interest as it accrues under the original-issue-discount rules of § 1272. See § 1272(a)(2)(C), exempting debt instruments which mature "not more than 1 year from the date of issue" from the OID rules. Because tax deferral—which is valuable— is lost when maturity exceeds one year, banks must pay higher interest on CDs with a one-year-and-one-day maturity date than on one-year certificates.

5. *Problems.* L, a cash-method taxpayer, leases a house (located a few blocks from L's residence) to T for a monthly rent of $1000, payable on the last day of each month. In each of the following cases, determine the year in which L must include in income the rent due on December 31, year 1.

(1) In accordance with the parties' customary practice, T mailed a check to L on December 31. L received the check in January, year 2. If L had called upon T and asked for the check on December 31, T would have given it to him, but L had never done that.

(2) Same as (1), except that L resided in New York and T resided in California, and it would have been extremely inconvenient for L to travel to California to pick up the check on December 31.

(3) L usually called upon T (T's house again being located a short distance from L's residence) on the last day of the month to pick up the rent. When L called upon T on December 31 (to wish T a Happy New Year), T took out her checkbook and offered to pay the rent. But L said "please wait until next week; I'd rather report the income next year than this year," and T complied.

(4) L usually called upon T on the last day of the month to pick up the rent, but on December 31 L was hospitalized with a serious illness. L picked up the December 31 check in January after his release from the hospital.

REVENUE RULING 60–31

1960–1 C.B. 174.

Advice has been requested regarding the taxable year of inclusion in gross income of a taxpayer, using the cash receipts and disbursements method of accounting, of compensation for services received under the circumstances described below.

(1) On January 1, 1958, the taxpayer and corporation X executed an employment contract under which the taxpayer is to be employed by the corporation in an executive capacity for a period of five years. Under the contract, the taxpayer is entitled to a stated annual salary and to additional compensation of $10x$ dollars for each year. The additional compensation will be credited to a bookkeeping reserve account and will be deferred, accumulated, and paid in annual installments equal to one-fifth of the amount in the reserve as of the close of the year immediately preceding the year of first payment. The payments are to begin only upon (a) termination of the taxpayer's employment by the corporation; (b) the taxpayer's becoming a part-time employee of the corporation; or (c) the taxpayer's becoming partially or totally incapacitated. Under the terms of the agreement, corporation X is under a merely contractual obligation to make the payments when due, and the parties did not intend that the amounts in the reserve be held by the corporation in trust for the taxpayer.

The contract further provides that if the taxpayer should fail or refuse to perform his duties, the corporation will be relieved of any obligation to make further credits to the reserve (but not of the obligation to distribute amounts previously contributed); but, if the taxpayer should become incapacitated from performing his duties, then credits to the reserve will continue for one year from the date of the incapacity, but not beyond the expiration of the five-year term of the contract. There is no specific provision in the contract for forfeiture by the taxpayer of his right to distribution from the reserve; and, in the event he should die prior to his receipt in full of the balance in the account, the remaining balance is distributable to his personal representative at the rate of one-fifth per year for five years, beginning three months after his death.

(2) The taxpayer is an officer and director of corporation A, which has a plan for making future payments of additional compensation for current services to certain officers and key employees designated by its board of directors. This plan provides that a percentage of the annual net earnings (before Federal income taxes) in excess of $4,000x$ dollars is to be designated for division among the participants in proportion to their respective salaries. This amount is not currently paid to the participants; but, the corporation has set up on its books a separate account for each participant and each year it credits thereto the dollar amount of his participation for the year, reduced by a proportionate part

of the corporation's income taxes attributable to the additional compensation. Each account is also credited with the net amount, if any, realized from investing any portion of the amount in the account.

Distributions are to be made from these accounts annually beginning when the employee (1) reaches age 60, (2) is no longer employed by the company, including cessation of employment due to death, or (3) becomes totally disabled to perform his duties, whichever occurs first. The annual distribution will equal a stated percentage of the balance in the employee's account at the close of the year immediately preceding the year of first payment, and distributions will continue until the account is exhausted. However, the corporation's liability to make these distributions is contingent upon the employee's (1) refraining from engaging in any business competitive to that of the corporation, (2) making himself available to the corporation for consultation and advice after retirement or termination of his services, unless disabled, and (3) retaining unencumbered any interest or benefit under the plan. In the event of his death, either before or after the beginning of payments, amounts in an employee's account are distributable in installments computed in the same way to his designated beneficiaries or heirs-at-law. Under the terms of the compensation plan, corporation A is under a merely contractual obligation to make the payments when due, and the parties did not intend that the amounts in each account be held by the corporation in trust for the participants.

(3) On October 1, 1957, the taxpayer, an author, and corporation Y, a publisher, executed an agreement under which the taxpayer granted to the publisher the exclusive right to print, publish and sell a book he had written. This agreement provides that the publisher will (1) pay the author specified royalties based on the actual cash received from the sale of the published work, (2) render semiannual statements of the sales, and (3) at the time of rendering each statement make settlement for the amount due. On the same day, another agreement was signed by the same parties, mutually agreeing that, in consideration of, and notwithstanding any contrary provisions contained in the first contract, the publisher shall not pay the taxpayer more than $100x$ dollars in any one calendar year. Under this supplemental contract, sums in excess of $100x$ dollars accruing in any one calendar year are to be carried over by the publisher into succeeding accounting periods; and the publisher shall not be required either to pay interest to the taxpayer on any such excess sums or to segregate any such sums in any manner.

* * *

[Treas. Reg. §] 1.451–1(a) provides in part as follows:

Gains, profits, and income are to be included in gross income for the taxable year in which they are actually or constructively received by the taxpayer unless includible for a different year in accordance with the taxpayer's method of accounting. * * *

And, with respect to the cash receipts and disbursements method of accounting, section 1.446–1(c)(1)(i) provides in part—

> Generally, under the cash receipts and disbursements method in the computation of taxable income, all items which constitute gross income (whether in the form of cash, property, or services) are to be included for the taxable year in which actually or constructively received. * * *.

As previously stated, the individual concerned in each of the situations described above, employs the cash receipts and disbursements method of accounting. Under that method, as indicated by the above-quoted provisions of the regulations, he is required to include the compensation concerned in gross income only for the taxable year in which it is actually or constructively received. Consequently, the question for resolution is whether in each of the situations described the income in question was constructively received in a taxable year prior to the taxable year of actual receipt.

A mere promise to pay, not represented by notes or secured in any way, is not regarded as a receipt of income within the intendment of the cash receipts and disbursements method. See United States v. Christine Oil & Gas Co., 269 Fed. 458; William J. Jackson v. Smietanka, 272 Fed. 970 (1921); and E.F. Cremin v. Commissioner, 5 B.T.A. 1164, acquiescence, C.B. VI–1, 2 (1927). Also C. Florian Zittel v. Commissioner, 12 B.T.A. 675, in which, holding a salary to be taxable when received, the Board said: "Taxpayers on a receipts and disbursements basis are required to report only income actually received no matter how binding any contracts they may have to receive more."

This should not be construed to mean that under the cash receipts and disbursements method income may be taxed only when realized in cash. For, under that method a taxpayer is required to include in income that which is received in cash or cash equivalent. W.P. Henritze v. Commissioner, 41 B.T.A. 505. And, as stated in the above-quoted provisions of the regulations, the "receipt" contemplated by the cash method may be actual or constructive.

With respect to the constructive receipt of income, [Treas. Reg. §] 1.451–2(a) (which accords with prior regulations extending back to, and including, Article 53 of Regulations 45 under the Revenue Act of 1918) provides, in part, as follows:

> Income although not actually reduced to a taxpayer's possession is constructively received by him in the taxable year during which it is credited to his account or set apart for him so that he may draw upon it at any time. However, income is not constructively received if the taxpayer's control of its receipt is subject to substantial limitations or restrictions. Thus, if a corporation credits its employees with bonus stock, but the stock is not available to such employees until some future date, the mere crediting on the books of the corporation does not constitute receipt.

Thus, under the doctrine of constructive receipt, a taxpayer may not deliberately turn his back upon income and thereby select the year for which he will report it. The Hamilton National Bank of Chattanooga, as Administrator of the Estate of S. Strang Nicklin, Deceased, v. Commissioner, 29 B.T.A. 63. Nor may a taxpayer, by a private agreement, postpone receipt of income from one taxable year to another. James E. Lewis v. Commissioner, 30 B.T.A. 318.

However, the statute cannot be administered by speculating whether the payor would have been willing to agree to an earlier payment. See, for example, J.D. Amend, et ux., v. Commissioner, 13 T.C. 178, acquiescence, C.B. 1950–1, 1; and C.E. Gullett, et al., v. Commissioner, 31 B.T.A. 1067, in which the court, citing a number of authorities for its holding, stated:

> It is clear that the doctrine of constructive receipt is to be sparingly used; that amounts due from a corporation but unpaid, are not to be included in the income of an individual reporting his income on a cash receipts basis unless it appears that the money was available to him, that the corporation was able and ready to pay him, that his right to receive was not restricted, and that his failure to receive resulted from exercise of his own choice.

Consequently, it seems clear that in each case involving a deferral of compensation a determination of whether the doctrine of constructive receipt is applicable must be made upon the basis of the specific factual situation involved.

Applying the foregoing criteria to the situations described above, the following conclusions have been reached:

(1) The additional compensation to be received by the taxpayer under the employment contract concerned will be includible in his gross income only in the taxable years in which the taxpayer actually receives installment payments in cash or other property previously credited to his account. To hold otherwise would be contrary to the provisions of the regulations and the court decisions mentioned above.

(2) For the reasons in (1) above, it is held that the taxpayer here involved also will be required to include the deferred compensation concerned in his gross income only in the taxable years in which the taxpayer actually receives installment payments in cash or other property previously credited to his account.

In arriving at this conclusion and the conclusion reached in case "(1)," consideration has been given to [Treas. Reg. §] 1.402(b)–1 and to Revenue Ruling 57–37, C.B. 1957–1, 18, as modified by Revenue Ruling 57–528, C.B. 1957–2, 263. Section 1.402(b)–1(a)(1) provides in part, with an exception not here relevant, that any contribution made by an employer on behalf of an employee to a trust during a taxable year of the employer which ends within or with a taxable year of the trust for which the trust is not exempt under section 501(a) of the Code, shall be included in income of the employee for his taxable year during which the contribution is made if his interest in the contribution is nonforfeitable at the time the contribution is made. Revenue Ruling 57–37, as modified by Revenue Ruling 57–528, held, *inter alia,* that certain contributions conveying fully vested and nonforfeitable interests made by an employer into separate independently controlled trusts for the purpose of furnishing unemployment and other benefits to its eligible employees constituted additional compensation to the employees includible, under section 402(b) of the Code and [Treas. Reg. §] 1.402(b)–1(a)(1), in their income for the taxable year in which such contributions were made. These Revenue Rulings are distinguishable from cases "(1)" and "(2)" in that, under all the facts and circumstances of these cases, no trusts for the benefit of the taxpayers were created and no contributions are to be made thereto. Consequently, section 402(b) of the Code and [Treas. Reg. §] 1.402(b)–1(a)(1) are inapplicable.

(3) Here the principal agreement provided that the royalties were payable substantially as earned, and this agreement was supplemented by a further concurrent agreement which made the royalties payable over a period of years. This supplemental agreement, however, was made before the royalties were earned; in fact, it was made on the same day as the principal agreement and the two agreements were a part of the same transaction. Thus, for all practical purposes, the arrangement from the beginning is similar to that in (1) above. Therefore, it is also held that the author concerned will be required to include the royalties in his gross income only in the taxable years in which they are actually received in cash or other property.

* * *

Problems, Notes and Questions

1. *Agreement to defer made after work performed.* In each of the cases discussed in Rev.Rul. 60–31, the agreement for deferred compensation was made before the taxpayer performed the services (or, in situation 3, at the time the author granted exclusive rights to the publisher). Suppose an employee entitled to payment in December for work done during the year agrees with the employer, after the work has been performed but before payment is due, to defer part of the payment until the following year. Do the reasons given in the ruling for allowing deferral apply to this case? In Commissioner v. Oates, 207 F.2d 711 (7th Cir.1953), retired insurance agents entitled to renewal commissions on policies they had sold negotiated a revision of their contract with the insurance company. The revised contract, which each agent had the option of accepting, provided for more deferral, under certain circumstances, than did the original agreement. Finding "no reason why full legal effect should not be accorded the second agreement," the court held that an agent was not in constructive receipt of the excess of amounts that would have been payable under the first agreement over the amounts payable under the second. The Service announced its acquiescence in *Oates* in Rev.Rul. 60–31.

Despite its acquiescence in *Oates,* the Service will ordinarily issue advance rulings on unfunded deferred-compensation plans only if any election to defer compensation must be made before the services in question are performed. This is so even if the arrangement contains forfeiture provisions. There are exceptions for some cases involving newly established deferred-compensation plans and employees newly eligible to participate in a plan. See Rev.Proc. 92–65, 1992–2 C.B. 428.

2. *Rabbi trusts.* The deferred-compensation arrangements approved in Rev.Rul. 60–31 were "unfunded" in the sense that the recipients had only contractual rights to payment. If an employer transfers funds to an irrevocable trust for the benefit of an employee, the employee will be taxed on the value of the interest in the trust (see §§ 402(b) and 83) unless the plan is "qualified" under § 401. As a sort of compromise between mere promises to pay (which provide tax deferral but little security for employees) and transfers to trusts for the benefit of employees (which provide security but no deferral), employers sometimes pay deferred compensation to trusts created in such a way that the trusts' assets remain subject to the claims of the employers' general creditors. Because funds have actually been set aside, this kind of arrangement may make employees feel somewhat sure of receiving their money; because the money remains subject to the claims of the employers' creditors, the arrangements are "unfunded" for tax purposes. The Service will issue favorable rulings on these "rabbi trusts" (so called because the first favorable ruling involved the deferred compensation of a rabbi). Rabbi trusts are grantor trusts, so their income and deductions are taken into account in computing the employers' incomes.

Revenue Procedure 92–64, 1992–2 C.B. 422, contains a model trust for use as a rabbi trust. Except in "rare and unusual" cases, the Service will rule on deferred-compensation plans involving trusts only if this model trust is used.

3. *"Individual option" to defer.* Under Prop.Treas.Reg. § 1.61–16 (1978), a taxpayer with an "individual option" to defer some or all "basic or regular compensation fixed by contract, statute, or otherwise" would have been taxed currently on the amount that would have been received but for the exercise of the option. This rule would have applied even if deferred payments became forfeitable because of the exercise of the option to defer payment. Section 132(a) of the Revenue Act of 1978 provides:

> The taxable year of inclusion in gross income of any amount covered by a private deferred compensation plan shall be determined in accordance with the principles set forth in regulations, rulings, and judicial decisions relating to deferred compensation which were in effect on February 1, 1978.

This provision prevents the Treasury Department from applying proposed Treas.Reg. § 1.61–16, which was published in the Federal Register on February 3, 1978.

4. *Constructive receipt and lottery winnings.* State lotteries typically offer winners a choice between a lump-sum payment and a series of payments over a period of years, as do some casinos in the case of big winners at the slots. (For consideration of which option a winner should choose, see Appendix A. Although the total amount of payments to a winner who elects installments will be greater than if a lump-sum payment is chosen, the lump sum will sometimes be the better choice, depending on the discount rate.) Section 451(h) provides that the existence of a "qualified prize option" does not put a cash-method winner who chooses installments in constructive receipt of the amount that could have been taken as a lump sum. Among other things, a qualified prize option must be exercisable not later than 60 days after the winner has become entitled to a prize.

Query whether § 451(h) adds much, if anything, to the law. If a state lottery allows the holder of a winning ticket to choose between $100,000 and payments of $10,000 a year for twenty years ($200,000 total), would a cash-method winner who chose the installments have been in constructive receipt of $100,000 in the year of the drawing under *Davis*, Rev.Rul. 60–31, and the regulations, even without § 451(h)?

5. *The employer's deduction.* Review the materials at pp. 71–72, above, for an illustration of the substantial tax benefits that could be obtained if an accrual-method employer could deduct deferred compensation as a business expense long before a cash-method employee had to include the compensation in income. In the case of non-qualified plans "deferring the receipt of compensation," § 404(a)(5) denies employers deductions for contributions until the contributions are includable in the employees' incomes. Section 404(d) extends this treatment to deferred-compensation plans for independent contractors.

Suppose an employer who could receive a salary of $100,000 for year 1 agrees with the employer to take only $90,000 for year 1 in exchange for getting more in year 10. (This is, in substance, what goes on under any deferred-compensation agreement.) Unless the parties are irrational, the employee will ask for, and the employer will agree to pay, more than $10,000 in year 10—say, $25,000. Unless the deferral occurs under a qualified pension or profit-sharing plan, the employer cannot deduct the $10,000 deferred compensation until year 10, when the employee receives the money and includes it in income, because of § 404(a)(5). But what of the other $15,000? This part of the payment is, in substance, interest, and it may even be labelled "interest" (though it seldom is, in practice). Does § 404(a), which delays deductions for "contributions to" and "compensation paid or accrued under" a non-qualified deferred-compensation plan, delay the employer's deduction for the whole $25,000 until the employee gets paid, or is the interest portion of the payment deductible as it accrues?

In Albertson's Inc. v. Commissioner, 12 F.3d 1529 (9th Cir.1993), the Ninth Circuit allowed a deduction, despite § 404(a)(5), for the "interest" accrued by the employer. On rehearing, however, the court changed its mind and disallowed current deductions even for the accrued interest. It reasoned that Congress could have had no reason for delaying deductions for the compensation itself, but not for the interest, as that pattern would give non-qualified plans most of the tax benefits of qualified plans, without the burdens; 42 F.3d 537 (9th Cir.1994). The version of § 404(a) that applied in *Albertson's* delayed deductions only for amounts that would otherwise have been deductible *under § 162 or § 212*; interest, if deductible at all, is deductible under § 163. The original *Albertson's* outcome was, therefore, more appealing on "plain meaning" grounds than the opinion on rehearing. Whether the "plain meaning" outcome was the one the court should have reached has been hotly contested. Compare Geier, Interpreting Tax Legislation: The Role of Purpose, 2 Fla.Tax Rev. 492, 517–519 (1995), arguing that the structure of the Code's "matching provisions" for non-qualified deferred compensation was undermined by the original *Albertson's* decision, with Zelinsky, Text, Purpose, Capacity and *Albertson's*, 2 Fla.Tax Rev. 717 (1996), arguing that the second decision may have overruled a policy decision made by Congress as well as setting aside the statutory language.

For years beginning in 1984, section 404(a) has been amended to remove its references to §§ 162 and 212. This change makes clear that the result of the second *Albertson's* opinion is the law today, even if it was wrong for the years in question. See Zelinsky, The Ninth Circuit's *Albertson's* Decision: Wrong for 1983, Right for Today, 63 Tax Notes 231 (1994).

6. *Problems.* Under *E*'s employment contract with *X* Corp., *E* is to receive a stated annual salary plus a bonus of 1 percent of *X*'s annual profits. Except as otherwise indicated below, the bonus for each calendar year (the "bonus year") is payable to *E* on the following March 31. In each case, determine when the bonus will be taxable to *E* (who uses the cash method) and deductible by *X* Corp. (which uses the accrual method).

(1) *E* can elect before the beginning of the bonus year to have the bonus paid to him at age 65. If *E* elects to so defer his bonus, *X* Corp. will increase the amount payable to *E* at age 65 by interest at 8 percent a year. If the bonus is deferred, the bonus and interest are reflected by entries on *X*'s books, but no specific assets are set aside for *E* until he turns 65. Before the bonus year begins, *E* elects to defer the bonus.

(2) Same as (1), except that instead of crediting the deferred amount with interest, *X* Corp. will, at *E*'s election, credit the deferred amount to a bookkeeping account, invest an amount equal to the account balance in publicly traded securities as directed by *E*, and credit (or charge) the account with any gains (or losses) and earnings from the investments. When *E* reaches age 65, *X* will pay *E* an amount equal to the value of the account. The investments remain the property of *X; E* acquires no property interest in the securities as such. *E* elects to have the deferred bonus so invested.

(3) Same as (1), except that E can elect to defer the bonus at any time during the first nine months of the bonus year, and E so elects on September 30 of the bonus year.

(4) Same as (1), except that X Corp. transfers the deferred bonus to a revocable trust for investment. E will be entitled to the trust assets at age 65. Until then, the trust assets theoretically remain subject to the claims of X Corp.'s general creditors, but there is little likelihood that X Corp.'s creditors will ever have to resort to the trust assets.

(b) Checks, Notes, and Credit–Card Charges

COMMISSIONER v. BRADLEY

United States Court of Appeals, Sixth Circuit, 1932.
56 F.2d 728.

Before HICKS and HICKENLOOPER, CIRCUIT JUDGES, and TUTTLE, DISTRICT JUDGE.

TUTTLE, DISTRICT JUDGE.

[On June 25, 1926, Bradley, a cash-method taxpayer, paid some county real-estate taxes by having his check for $47,383.51 delivered to the county treasurer. The next day, Bradley died. Nearly three months later, the county presented Bradley's check to the bank on which it was drawn, and the bank paid the check. Although Bradley's estate could have challenged the bank's payment, it did not.

The Commissioner argued that the real-estate taxes could be deducted only by Bradley's estate because those taxes were paid after Bradley's death. The taxpayer took the position that the taxes were paid on June 25, when the check was delivered to the county, so that the deduction was properly taken on Bradley's final return. The Board of Tax Appeals ruled in favor of the taxpayer.]

* * *

We think it entirely clear that the decision of the Board was correct. It cannot be doubted that the delivery and acceptance of this check as payment of the taxes in question constituted a conditional payment, by the deceased, of such taxes, as of the time of such delivery and acceptance, subject only to a condition subsequent that such check would be promptly paid on presentation thereof to the drawee. Second National Bank of Saginaw v. United States (Ct.Cl.) 42 F.(2d) 344. When, therefore, the check was paid promptly on such presentation, the condition to which this payment was subject was performed, and what had been, at the time of the acceptance of the check, a conditional payment by the deceased, became an absolute payment by him as of that time.

The fact that the death of the drawer of the check before its presentation revoked the authority of the drawee to pay it did not affect the validity or effect of such check as between the drawer and the payee, at least after its payment by the drawee, but merely subjected the latter to possible liability to the estate of the deceased for such unauthorized payment. As, however, neither the estate nor the county is complaining of such payment, but both have acquiesced therein, the legal situation as between the taxpayer and the government appears to be, in all substantial respects, the same as if the check had been presented and paid during the life of the deceased.

We conclude that the Board of Tax Appeals reached the correct result, and its decision is affirmed.

Problems and Notes

1. *"The check rule."* Note that in both *Bradley* and *Davis* (p. 728, above), the face amount of the check is treated as deductible or includable in income when the check is delivered or received, as the case may be. This is so even if the check's value at the time is less than its face amount; the check rule is not, therefore, an application of the "economic benefit" doctrine. Nor is the rule based on the theory that the recipient of a check has constructively received cash. As *Bradley* shows, however, payment by check is disregarded if the check is not honored when presented for payment.

The treatment given checks is usually justified on one or more of these grounds: (1) taxpayers think of themselves as receiving or paying when they get or deliver checks; (2) treatment of checks as conditional payment corresponds to their treatment under the law of commercial paper; and (3) the rule is easier to understand and apply than any conceivable alternative. See Note, Checks and Notes as Income When Received by a Cash–Basis Taxpayer, 73 Harv.L.Rev. 1199 (1960).

2. *Payment by mailing a check.* A cash-method taxpayer is treated as having delivered a check when the check is placed in the mail (if the check arrives and is cashed); Witt's Estate v. Fahs, 160 F.Supp. 521 (S.D.Fla.1956).

3. *Problems.* T, a cash-method taxpayer, rents a business office from L for $1000 a month, payable on the last day of the month. In the following problems, determine the year in which T can deduct the rent payable on December 31, year 1.

(1) T mails a check (dated December 31) to L on December 31. The check is received and cashed by L in January, year 2.

(2) Same as (1), except that (unknown to L) T did not have sufficient funds in his account on December 31 to cover the check. T made a covering deposit on January 2, and the check cleared T's account in due course on January 5.

REVENUE RULING 76–135
1976–1 C.B. 114.

An individual issued and delivered a negotiable promissory note to a lawyer who accepted the note in payment for legal services rendered to the individual as operator of a small business. The cost of the legal services was an ordinary and necessary business expense. Upon receipt of the note from the individual, the lawyer immediately discounted the note at a local bank. Both the lawyer and the client file their Federal income tax returns on a calendar year basis and use the cash receipts and disbursements method of accounting.

The note in the instant case was issued in 1973 in the face amount of $50x$ dollars, bearing interest at six percent per annum. By its terms the note called for payment of one-half of its face value plus interest in 1974 and the remaining one-half with interest in 1975. It stipulated that default of the first payment or of the interest would result in the full amount of the note and interest becoming immediately due and payable. The bank discounted the note, and the lawyer received $47x$ dollars for it in 1973. The client made payments to the bank in the years 1974 and 1975 as required by the note.

Held, for purposes of section 451, which relates to the taxable year for which items of gross income are included, the fair market value of the note ($47x$ dollars) accepted by the lawyer in 1973 as payment for legal services and discounted at a bank for cash was income includible in the lawyer's 1973 Federal income tax return. Section 1.61–2(d)(4) of the Income Tax Regulations.

Held further, for purposes of section 461 of the Code, which relates to the taxable year for which deductions may be taken, the same note was not a "payment" deductible on the client's 1973 Federal income tax return. See Helvering v. Price, 309 U.S. 409 (1940), 1940–1 C.B. 134.

However, the client's payment to the bank of one-half of the face value of the note plus interest in 1974, and the payment of the remaining one-half with interest in 1975, are the actual payments of cash required as a basis for any deductions allowable to the individual as a cash basis taxpayer. Accordingly, amounts paid by the client to the bank as principal and interest on the note are deductible by the individual as business expenses and as interest on the Federal income tax returns for 1974 and 1975, respectively.

A.R.M. 201, II–1 C.B. 86 (1923), is hereby superseded since the position set forth therein is updated and restated under the current statute and regulations in this Revenue Ruling.

Problem and Question

1. *Problem.* When would the lawyer in Rev.Rul. 76–135 have had income if he had waited until 1974 to discount the note to the bank?

2. *Checks and notes compared.* What justifies treating the giving and receiving of notes differently from the giving and receiving of checks?

REVENUE RULING 78–38

1978–1 C.B. 68.

The Internal Revenue Service has given further consideration to Rev.Rul. 71–216, 1971–1 C.B. 96, which holds that a taxpayer who used a bank credit card to contribute to a qualified charity may not deduct any part of the contribution under section 170(a)(1) until the year the cardholder makes payment of the amount of the contribution to the bank.

Rev.Rul. 71–216 cites section 1.170–2(a)(1) of the Income Tax Regulations (predecessor to current section 1.170A–1(a)(1) of the regulations) which provides that a deduction is only allowable to an individual under section 170 of the Code for charitable contributions "actually paid" during the taxable year, regardless of when pledged and regardless of the method of accounting employed by the taxpayer in keeping books and records.

In Rev.Rul. 71–216 the assumption was made that a charitable contribution made by a taxpayer by use of a credit card was tantamount to a charitable contribution made by the issuance and delivery of a debenture bond or a promissory note by the obligor to a charitable organization, as discussed in Rev.Rul. 68–174, 1968–1 C.B. 81, which holds that, under the facts presented, the issuance of a debenture bond or a promissory note represents a mere promise to pay at some future date, and delivery of the bond or note to a charitable organization is not "payment" under section 170 of the Code.

Upon further study, it has been concluded that there are major distinctions between contributions made by the use of credit cards and contributions made by debenture bonds and promissory notes. In Rev. Rul. 68–174, the charitable organization that received the debenture bond or promissory note from the obligor received no more than a mere promise to pay. Conversely, the credit card holder in Rev.Rul. 71–216, by using the credit card to make the contribution, became immediately indebted to a third party (the bank) in such a way that the cardholder could not thereafter prevent the charitable organization from receiving payment. The credit card draft received by the charitable organization from the credit card holder in Rev.Rul. 71–216 was immediately creditable by the bank to the organization's account as if it were a check.

Since the cardholder's use of the credit card creates the cardholder's own debt to a third party, the use of a bank credit card to make a charitable contribution is equivalent to the use of borrowed funds to make a contribution.

The general rule is that when a deductible payment is made with borrowed money, the deduction is not postponed until the year in which the borrowed money is repaid. Such expenses must be deducted in the year they are paid and not when the loans are repaid. Granan v. Commissioner, 55 T.C. 753 (1971).

Accordingly, the taxpayer discussed in Rev.Rul. 71–216, who made a contribution to a qualified charity by a charge to the taxpayer's bank credit card, is entitled to a charitable contribution deduction under section 170(a) of the Code in the year the charge was made and the deduction may not be postponed until the taxpayer pays the indebtedness resulting from such charge.

Pursuant to the authority contained in section 7805(b) of the Code, contributions made by credit card use before January 1, 1978, may be deducted either in the year in which the contribution is charged or in accordance with Rev.Rul. 71–216.

Rev.Rul. 68–174 is distinguished; Rev.Rul. 71–216 is revoked.

Problems

Problem (1). In year 1, *C*, a cash-method taxpayer, purchased business supplies from a department store. *C* charged the supplies on her bank credit card. *C* paid the credit-card bill in year 2. In which year is the expense deductible by *C*?

Problem (2). Same as (1), except that the credit card had been issued by the department store.

2. ACCRUAL ACCOUNTING

(a) *The All–Events Test*

Accrual-method taxpayers recognize receipts of income items and expenditures of deductible items according to the "all events test." Income items are treated as received when "all the events have occurred which fix the right to receive such income and the amount thereof can be determined with reasonable accuracy"; Treas.Reg. § 1.451–1(a). An expense is deductible when "all the events have occurred which determine the fact of the liability and the amount thereof can be determined with reasonable accuracy"; Treas.Reg. § 1.461–1(a)(2); United States v. Anderson, 269 U.S. 422 (1926).

Section 461(h), which was added to the Code in 1984, provides (with some exceptions) that the all-events test cannot be satisfied with respect to an outlay by the taxpayer "any earlier than when economic performance with respect to such item occurs"; this provision will be examined in more detail below. The case which follows involved taxable years before the enactment of the "economic performance" requirement.

UNITED STATES v. HUGHES PROPERTIES, INC.

Supreme Court of the United States, 1986.
476 U.S. 593, 106 S.Ct. 2092, 90 L.Ed.2d 569.

JUSTICE BLACKMUN delivered the opinion of the Court.

This case concerns the deductibility for federal income tax purposes, by a casino operator utilizing the accrual method of accounting, of amounts guaranteed for payment on "progressive" slot machines but not yet won by playing patrons.

I

A

There is no dispute as to the relevant facts; many of them are stipulated. Respondent Hughes Properties, Inc., is a Nevada corporation. It owns Harolds Club, a gambling casino, in Reno, Nev. It keeps its books and files its federal income tax returns under the accrual method of accounting. During the tax years in question (the fiscal years that ended June 30 in 1973 to 1977, inclusive), respondent owned and operated slot machines at its casino. Among these were a number of what are called "progressive" machines. A progressive machine, like a regular one, pays fixed amounts when certain symbol combinations appear on its reels. But a progressive machine has an additional "progressive" jackpot, which is won only when a different specified combination appears. The casino sets this jackpot initially at a minimal amount. The figure increases, according to a ratio determined by the casino, as money is gambled on the machine. The amount of the jackpot at any given time is registered on a "payoff indicator" on the face of the machine. That amount continues to increase as patrons play the machine until the jackpot is won or until a maximum, also determined by the casino, is reached.

The odds of winning a progressive jackpot obviously are a function of the number of reels on the machine, the number of positions on each reel, and the number of winning symbols. The odds are determined by the casino, provided only that there exists a possibility that the winning combination of symbols can appear.[1]

The Nevada Gaming Commission closely regulates the casino industry in the State, including the operation of progressive slot machines. In September 1972, the Commission promulgated § 5.110 of the Nevada Gaming Regulations. This section requires a gaming establishment to record at least once a day the jackpot amount registered on each progressive machine. § 5.110.5. Furthermore,

> "[N]o payoff indicator shall be turned back to a lesser amount, unless the amount by which the indicator has been turned back is actually paid to a winning player or unless the change in the indicator reading is necessitated through a machine malfunction, in which case an explanation must be entered on the daily report as required in subsection 5." § 5.110.2.

The Regulation is strictly enforced. Nevada, by statute, authorizes the commission to impose severe administrative sanctions, including license

---

1. A 1976 study of the 24 4–reel progressive machines then in operation at respondent's casino revealed that the average period between payoffs was approximately 4 ½ months, although one machine had been in operation for 13 months and another for 35 months without a payoff as of September 1, 1976. The payoff frequency of the other 22 machines ranged from a high of 14.3 months to a low of 1.9 months.

revocation, upon any casino that wrongfully refuses to pay a winning customer a guaranteed jackpot. See Nev.Rev.Stat. § 463.310 (1986).

It is respondent's practice to remove the money deposited by customers in its progressive machines at least twice every week and also on the last day of each month. The Commission does not regulate respondent's use of the funds thus collected, but, since 1977, it has required that a casino maintain a cash reserve sufficient to provide payment of the guaranteed amounts on all its progressive machines available to the public. Nev. Gaming Regs. § 5.110(3).

B

At the conclusion of each fiscal year, that is, at midnight on June 30, respondent entered the total of the progressive jackpot amounts shown on the payoff indicators as an accrued liability on its books. From that total, it subtracted the corresponding figure for the preceding year to produce the current tax year's increase in accrued liability. On its federal income tax return for each of its fiscal years 1973, 1974, 1975, and 1977, respondent asserted this net figure as a deduction under § 162(a) as an ordinary and necessary expense "paid or incurred during the taxable year in carrying on any trade or business." There is no dispute as to the amounts so determined or that a progressive jackpot qualifies for deduction as a proper expense of running a gambling business.

On audit, the Commissioner of Internal Revenue disallowed the deduction. He did so on the ground that, under Treas.Reg. § 1.461–1(a)(2), an expense may not be deducted until "all the events have occurred which determine the fact of the liability and the amount thereof can be determined with reasonable accuracy." In his view, respondent's obligation to pay a particular progressive jackpot matures only upon a winning patron's pull of the handle in the future. According to the Commissioner, until that event occurs, respondent's liability to pay the jackpot is contingent and therefore gives rise to no deductible expense. Indeed, until then, there is no one who can make a claim for payment. Accordingly, the Commissioner determined deficiencies in respondent's income taxes for the years in question in the total amount of $433,441.88, attributable solely to the denial of these progressive jackpot deductions. Respondent paid the asserted deficiencies and filed timely claims for refund. When the claims were denied, respondent brought this suit for refunds in the Claims Court.

C

Each side moved for summary judgment. * * *

The Claims Court denied the Government's motion for summary judgment but granted respondent's motion. * * *

* * *

II

* * *

For a number of years, the standard for determining when an expense is to be regarded as "incurred" for federal income tax purposes has been the "all events" test prescribed by the Regulations. See Treas.Reg. § 1.446–1(c)(1)(ii) (accruals in general); § 1.451–1(a) (accrual of income); and § 1.461–1(a)(2) (accrual of deductions). This test appears to have had its origin in a single phrase that appears in this Court's opinion in United States v. Anderson, 269 U.S. 422, 441 (1926) ("it is also true that in advance of the assessment of a tax, all the events may occur which fix the amount of the tax and determine the liability of the taxpayer to pay it"). Since then, the Court has described the "all events" test "established" in Anderson, as "the 'touchstone' for determining the year in which an item of deduction accrues," and as "a fundamental principle of tax accounting." United States v. Consolidated Edison, Co. 366 U.S. 380, 385 (1961) (citing cases).

Under the Regulations, the "all events" test has two elements, each of which must be satisfied before accrual of an expense is proper. First, all the events must have occurred which establish the fact of the liability. Second, the amount must be capable of being determined "with reasonable accuracy." Treas.Reg. § 1.446–1(c)(1)(ii). This case concerns only the first element, since the parties agree that the second is fully satisfied.

III

The Court's cases have emphasized that "a liability does not accrue as long as it remains contingent." Brown v. Helvering, 291 U.S. 193, 200 (1934); accord, Dixie Pine Co. v. Commissioner, 320 U.S. 516, 519 (1944). Thus, to satisfy the all-events test, a liability must be "final and definite in amount," Security Flour Mills Co. v. Commissioner, 321 U.S. 281, 287 * * * (1944), must be "fixed and absolute," Brown v. Helvering, 291 U.S., at 201, and must be "unconditional," Lucas v. North Texas Lumber Co., 281 U.S. 11, 13 (1930). And one may say that "the tax law requires that a deduction be deferred until 'all the events' have occurred that will make it fixed and certain." Thor Power Tool Co. v. Commissioner, 439 U.S. 522, 543 (1979).

A

The Government argues that respondent's liability for the progressive jackpots was not "fixed and certain," and was not "unconditional" or "absolute," by the end of the fiscal year, for there existed no person who could assert any claim to those funds. It takes the position, quoting Nightingale v. United States, 684 F.2d [611 (9th Cir.1982)] at 614, that the indispensable event "is the winning of the progressive jackpot by some fortunate gambler." It says that, because respondent's progressive jackpots had not been won at the close of the fiscal year, respondent had not yet incurred liability. Nevada law places no restriction on the odds set by the casino, as long as a possibility exists that the winning combination can appear. Thus, according to the Government, by setting very high odds respondent can defer indefinitely into the future the time when it actually will have to pay off the jackpot. The Government argues that if a casino were to close its doors and go out of business, it would not owe the jackpots to anyone. Similarly, if it were to sell its business, or cease its gaming operations, or go into bankruptcy, or if patrons were to stop playing its slot machines, it would have no obligation.

B

We agree with the Claims Court and with the Federal Circuit and disagree with the Government for the following reasons:

1. The effect of the Nevada Gaming Commission's regulations was to fix respondent's liability. * * * That an extremely remote and speculative possibility existed that the jackpot might never be won, did not change the fact that, as a matter of state law, respondent had a fixed liability for the jackpot which it could not escape. The effect of Nevada's law was equivalent to the situation where state law requires the amounts of the jackpot indicators to be set aside in escrow pending the ascertainment of the identity of the winners. The Government concedes that, in the latter case, the liability has accrued, even though the same possibility would still exist that the winning pull would never occur.

2. The Government misstates the need for identification of the winning player. That is, or should be, a matter of no relevance for the casino operator. The obligation is there, and whether it turns out that the winner is one patron or another makes no conceivable difference as to basic liability.

3. The Government's heavy reliance on Brown v. Helvering, 291 U.S. 193 (1934), in our view, is misplaced. That case concerned an agent's commissions on sales of insurance policies, and the agent's obligation to return a proportionate part of the commission in case a policy was canceled. The agent sought to deduct from gross income an amount added during the year to his reserve for repayment of commissions. This Court agreed with the Commissioner's disallowance of the claimed deduction because the actual event that would create the liability—the cancellation of a particular policy in a later year—"[did] not occur during the taxable year," id., at 200, but rather occurred only in the later year in which the policy was in fact canceled. Here, however, the event creating liability, as the Claims Court recognized, was the last play of the machine before the end of the fiscal year, since that play fixed the jackpot amount irrevocably. 5 Cl.Ct., at 645. That event occurred during the taxable year.

4. The Government's argument that the fact that respondent treats unpaid jackpots as liabilities for financial accounting purposes does not justify treating them as liabilities for tax purposes is unpersuasive. Proper financial accounting and acceptable tax accounting, to be sure, are not the same. Justice Brandeis announced this fact well over 50

years ago: "The prudent business man often sets up reserves to cover contingent liabilities. But they are not allowable as deductions." Lucas v. American Code Co., 280 U.S. 445, 452 (1930). See also Brown v. Helvering, 291 U.S., at 201–202, and Lucas v. Structural Steel Co., 281 U.S. 264, 269 (1930). The Court has long recognized "the vastly different objectives that financial and tax accounting have." Thor Power Tool Co. v. Commissioner, 439 U.S., at 542 * * *

Granting all this—that the Commissioner has broad discretion, that financial accounting does not control for tax purposes, and that the mere desirability of matching expenses with income will not necessarily sustain a taxpayer's deduction, * * *—the Commissioner's disallowance of respondent's deductions was not justified in this case. As stated above, these jackpot liabilities were definitely fixed. A part of the machine's intake was to be paid out, that amount was known, and only the exact time of payment and the identity of the winner remained for the future. But the accrual method itself makes irrelevant the timing factor that controls when a taxpayer uses the cash receipts and disbursements method.

5. The Government suggests that respondent's ability to control the timing of payouts shows both the contingent nature of the claimed deductions and a potential for tax avoidance. It speaks of the time value of money, of respondent's ability to earn additional income upon the jackpot amounts it retains until a winner comes along, of respondent's "virtually unrestricted discretion in setting odds," and of its ability to transfer amounts from one machine to another with the accompanying capacity to defer indefinitely into the future the time at which it must make payment to its customers. All this, the Government says, unquestionably contains the "potential for tax avoidance." See Thor Power Tool Co. v. Commissioner, 439 U.S., at 538. And the Government suggests that a casino operator could put extra machines on the floor on the last day of the tax year with whatever initial jackpots it specifies and with whatever odds it likes, and then, on the taxpayer's theory, could take a current deduction for the full amount even though payment of the jackpots might not occur for many years, citing *Nightingale*, 684 F.2d, at 615.

None of the components that make up this parade of horribles, of course, took place here. * * *

6. There is always a possibility, of course, that a casino may go out of business, or surrender or lose its license, or go into bankruptcy, with the result that the amounts shown on the jackpot indicators would never be won by playing patrons. But this potential nonpayment of an incurred liability exists for every business that uses an accrual method, and it does not prevent accrual. See, e.g., Wien Consolidated Airlines, Inc. v. Commissioner, 528 F.2d 735 (C.A.9 1976). "The existence of an absolute liability is necessary; absolute certainty that it will be discharged by payment is not." Helvering v. Russian Finance & Constr. Corp., 77 F.2d 324, 327 (C.A.2 1935). And if any of the events hypothesized by the

Government should occur, the deducted amounts would qualify as recaptured income subject to tax. Treas.Reg. § 1.461–1(a)(2).

7. Finally, the result in United States v. Anderson, 269 U.S. 422 (1926), a case to which the Government makes repeated reference, is itself instructive. The issue there was the propriety of the accrual of a federal munitions tax prior to its actual assessment. The assessment was required before the tax became due. The Government's position, in contrast to its position in the present case, was that the tax liability accrued before assessment. The Court held that the absence of the assessment did not prevent accrual of the tax. It recognized that the taxpayer's "true income for the year * * * could not have been determined without deducting * * * the * * * expenses attributable to the production of that income during the year." Id., at 440. One of the expenses that necessarily attended the production of munitions income was the commitment of a particular portion of the revenue generated to a "reserve for munitions taxes." Ibid. Similarly, one of the expenses that necessarily attends the production of income from a progressive slot machine is the commitment of a particular portion of the revenue generated to an irrevocable jackpot. Respondent's true income from its progressive slot machines is only that portion of the money gambled which it is entitled to keep.

The judgment of the Court of Appeals is affirmed.

It is so ordered.

JUSTICE STEVENS, with whom THE CHIEF JUSTICE joins, dissenting.

Unlike the Court, I believe that the distinction between the nonpayment of an existing obligation and the nonexistence of an obligation is of controlling importance in this case.

It is common ground that the taxpayer can accrue as a deduction the jackpots in its progressive slot machines only if "all the events have * * * occurred which fix the liability." [Citations omitted.] The question is whether an "obligation" created by the rules of a state gaming commission and defeasible at the election of the taxpayer is "fixed" within the meaning of the Treasury Regulation. To me, the answer is clearly "no."

"Under Nevada law," if the taxpayer in this case "were to surrender its gaming license, it would no longer be subject to the gaming laws and regulations and could thus avoid the payment of the liability." Thus, "the bankruptcy of the [taxpayer], or the surrender of its gaming license could relieve it of its obligation."

On these facts, the taxpayer has no present liability to accrue.

* * *

Problems and Notes

1. *What are "all" the events?* The taxpayer in United States v. General Dynamics Corp., 481 U.S. 239 (1987), had a plan under which it was obliged to pay for medical treatment given its employees. It claimed deductions which included amounts which it estimated it would have to pay to employees who had received medical treatment, but who had not submitted claims for reimbursement before the end of the taxable year. The Supreme Court held that the all-events test was not satisfied until the employees submitted claim forms, even though General Dynamics could make reasonable estimates of the amounts that would be claimed. Justice O'Connor's dissent viewed the filing of a claim as a formality, argued that the possibility of nonpayment was no more remote than in *Hughes Properties,* and noted that denial of deductions "unnecessarily burdens taxpayers by * * * expanding the differences between tax and business accounting methods without a compelling reason to do so." Both Justice Blackmun, the author of the *Hughes Properties* opinion, and Justice Stevens, who dissented in that case, joined Justice O'Connor's dissent in *General Dynamics.*

That accrual accounting amounts to more than a mechanical determination of liability is shown by Treas.Reg. § 1.446–1(c)(1)(ii), which lists a number of points at which an accrual-method manufacturer can account for sales of goods. Within limits, accrual in such a case depends upon how the taxpayer keeps its books, not upon whether the formalities of the all-events test have been satisfied.

2. *Matching of costs and revenues.* A major objective of *financial* accounting is to "match" revenues with the costs of earning them by reporting income and related expenses in the same accounting period. Although the Supreme Court described matching as desirable for tax purposes in both United States v. Anderson and *Hughes Properties,* the law as actually applied in those and other cases does not always further matching. Under the all-events test, a cost of earning revenues received this year cannot be deducted this year if the obligation to pay is contingent. If the matching principle were applied as often as it is invoked, taxpayers would be allowed to deduct reserves for estimated future expenses related to current income; as Brown v. Helvering (discussed in *Hughes Properties*) shows, they are not. Note also that *Hughes Properties* itself does not necessarily further matching: a jackpot entered on a machine late in December is currently deductible even though it is largely a cost of earning income the following year.

3. *Problems.*

(1) In year 1 X Corp., an accrual-method taxpayer, earned a profit, on which it is required to pay state income tax. The amount of tax was computed by X's accountants in February, year 2, and paid by X in March, year 2. In what year is the state income tax deductible by X?

(2) On December 31, year 1, X also owed its employees $10,000 for work performed by them during the last week of year 1. (X pays its

employees biweekly.) It paid the $10,000 in January, year 2. In what year is the compensation deductible by X?

(3) In what year can X deduct the FICA (Social Security) taxes paid with respect to the wages described in (2)?

4. *Reference.* Jensen, The Supreme Court and the Timing of Deductions for Accrual–Basis Taxpayers, 22 Georgia L.Rev. 229 (1988).

(b) Disputed or Uncertain Items

NORTH AMERICAN OIL CONSOLIDATED v. BURNET

Supreme Court of the United States, 1932.
286 U.S. 417, 52 S.Ct. 613, 76 L.Ed. 1197.

MR. JUSTICE BRANDEIS delivered the opinion of the Court.

The question for decision is whether the sum of $171,979.22 received by the North American Oil Consolidated in 1917, was taxable to it as income of that year.

The money was paid to the company under the following circumstances. Among many properties operated by it in 1916 was a section of oil land, the legal title to which stood in the name of the United States. Prior to that year, the Government, claiming also the beneficial ownership, had instituted a suit to oust the company from possession; and on February 2, 1916, it secured the appointment of a receiver to operate the property, or supervise its operations, and to hold the net income thereof. The money paid to the company in 1917 represented the net profits which had been earned from that property in 1916 during the receivership. The money was paid to the receiver as earned. After entry by the District Court in 1917 of the final decree dismissing the bill, the money was paid, in that year, by the receiver to the company. United States v. North American Oil Consolidated, 242 Fed. 723. The Government took an appeal (without supersedeas) to the Circuit Court of Appeals. In 1920, that Court affirmed the decree. 264 Fed. 336. In 1922, a further appeal to this Court was dismissed by stipulation. 258 U.S. 633.

The income earned from the property in 1916 had been entered on the books of the company as its income. It had not been included in its original return of income for 1916; but it was included in an amended return for that year which was filed in 1918. Upon auditing the company's income and profits tax returns for 1917, the Commissioner of Internal Revenue determined a deficiency based on other items. The company appealed to the Board of Tax Appeals. There, in 1927 the Commissioner prayed that the deficiency already claimed should be increased so as to include a tax on the amount paid by the receiver to the company in 1917. The Board held that the profits were taxable to the receiver as income of 1916; and hence made no finding whether the company's accounts were kept on the cash receipts and disbursements basis or on the accrual basis. 12 B.T.A. 68. The Circuit Court of Appeals held that the profits were taxable to the company as income of 1917, regardless of whether the company's returns were made on the cash or on the accrual basis. 50 F.2d 752. This Court granted a writ of certiorari. 284 U.S. 614.

It is conceded that the net profits earned by the property during the receivership constituted income. The company contends that they should have been reported by the receiver for taxation in 1916; that if not returnable by him, they should have been returned by the company for 1916, because they constitute income of the company accrued in that year; and that if not taxable as income of the company for 1916, they were taxable to it as income for 1922, since the litigation was not finally terminated in its favor until 1922.

* * *

Second. The net profits were not taxable to the company as income of 1916. For the company was not required in 1916 to report as income an amount which it might never receive. See Burnet v. Logan, 283 U.S. 404, 413. Compare Lucas v. American Code Co., 280 U.S. 445, 452; Burnet v. Sanford & Brooks Co., 282 U.S. 359, 363. There was no constructive receipt of the profits by the company in that year, because at no time during the year was there a right in the company to demand that the receiver pay over the money. Throughout 1916 it was uncertain who would be declared entitled to the profits. It was not until 1917, when the District Court entered a final decree vacating the receivership and dismissing the bill, that the company became entitled to receive the money. Nor is it material, for the purposes of this case, whether the company's return was filed on the cash receipts and disbursements basis, or on the accrual basis. In neither event was it taxable in 1916 on account of income which it had not yet received and which it might never receive.

Third. The net profits earned by the property in 1916 were not income of the year 1922—the year in which the litigation with the Government was finally terminated. They became income of the company in 1917, when it first became entitled to them and when it actually received them. If a taxpayer receives earnings under a claim of right and without restriction as to its disposition, he has received income which he is required to return even though it may still be claimed that he is not entitled to retain the money, and even though he may still be adjudged liable to restore its equivalent. See Board v. Commissioner, 51 F.(2d) 73, 75, 76. Compare United States v. S.S. White Dental Mfg. Co., 274 U.S. 398, 403. If in 1922 the Government had prevailed, and the company had been obliged to refund the profits received in 1917, it would have been entitled to a deduction from the profits of 1922, not from those of any earlier year. Compare Lucas v. American Code Co., supra.

Affirmed.

Problems and Notes

1. *Uncertain rights and uncertain amounts.* The degree of uncertainty needed to prevent accrual of an income item not yet received depends upon whether what is uncertain is the right to a receipt or the amount to be received. Under Treas.Reg. §§ 1.446–1(c)(1)(ii) and 1.451–1(a), the "right" to the receipt must be "fixed," while the amount need only be determinable "with reasonable accuracy." Uncertainty over the amount of damages to be paid a successful plaintiff in a patent infringement case prevented accrual until the report of a special master was issued in Blake v. Commissioner, 67 T.C. 7 (1976). But in Continental Tie & Lumber Co. v. United States, 286 U.S. 290 (1932), accrual of an award under a statute providing for payment to railroads controlled by the government during World War I was required although the Interstate Commerce Commission had to resolve both legal and factual questions before the amount of the award could be determined. The Court felt that the "general principles" set forth in the statute authorizing the ICC action were enough to enable the taxpayer to estimate the amount owed "within reasonable limits."

2. *Claim of right.* One way to look at *North American Oil* (as applied to an accrual-method taxpayer) is to say that the taxpayer reports income when it has either a fixed right to payment or the actual payment, whichever comes first. This rule is much easier to apply than either of the plausible alternatives. Accrual before receipt of disputed payments would often entail subsequent adjustments to reflect eventual nonpayment and would raise a question—with no obvious answer—of just how likely receipt was: should a taxpayer with a one-percent chance of receiving a payment have to accrue the amount? If the taxpayer has received cash, however, a rule that no accrual is required until the dispute was resolved would encourage taxpayers to delay taxation by prolonging disputes, and would generate tax controversies about whether disputes in fact remained active.

3. *Deductions.* Just as a dispute over whether one is entitled to a receipt prevents accrual of that receipt, a dispute over whether one must pay a deductible outlay bars accrual of the deduction; Dixie Pine Products Co. v. Commissioner, 320 U.S. 516 (1944). If an accrual-method taxpayer pays an amount in dispute and sues for a refund, § 461(f) allows accrual of a deduction upon payment. Section 461(f) does not itself require that the payment be made to the taxpayer's adversary; a payment into an escrow account is enough. However, § 461(h) (p. 769, below) will often delay deductions for accrued items until the other party to the transaction receives the payment, and § 461(h) overrides § 461(f).

4. *Problems.* W Corp. supplies water to University City. In year 1, C Corp., one of W's customers, filed suit against W challenging the calculation of its bill. The total bill for year 1 was $40,000. While the suit was pending, C paid W only 50 percent of the amount that W alleged was

due each month (a total of $20,000 for the year). Both *C* and *W* are accrual-method taxpayers.

(1) The litigation is still pending at the end of year 1.

    (a) Must *W* include the disputed $20,000 in income?

    (b) Can *C* deduct the $20,000?

(2) In year 2, the trial court held for *W* Corp., and, although *C* appealed the judgment, it paid the additional $20,000 to *W*. What is the tax effect of these events?

(3) In year 3, the appeals court affirmed the judgment of the trial court. Any further tax consequences?

3. TRANSACTIONS BETWEEN CASH–METHOD AND ACCRUAL–METHOD TAXPAYERS: SECTION 267(a)(2) AND SECTION 467

We have examined several situations in which a transaction between an accrual-method taxpayer and a cash-method taxpayer could generate substantial tax benefits if the ordinary tax-accounting rules applied. For example, if an accrual-method employer could take a current deduction for salary accrued today but not payable for many years, with the cash-method employee reporting no income until payment, the employer's tax benefit could exceed the non-tax cost of paying the salary.[f] Section 404(a)(5) responds to this problem by postponing the employee's deduction until the year in which the employee has income, and § 404(d) extends this treatment to cases in which the person receiving compensation is an independent contractor, rather than an employee.

The "tax float" problem described above can arise in situations not involving the performance of services. For instance, if an accrual-method tenant, *A*, accrues (but does not pay) deductible rent to be paid to a cash-method landlord, *C*, allowing *A* a deduction before *C* reports income would produce a tax benefit which would not exist if both parties used the same accounting method. Two provisions which respond to this kind of problem are § 267(a)(2) and § 467.

Section 267(a)(2) delays an accrual-method taxpayer's deductions for expenses and interest until the time when the cash-method recipient of the payments has income, but only if the payor and recipient are related persons as defined in § 267(b). Under this section, an accrual-method individual who becomes obliged to pay interest or a business expense to a family member (as defined in § 267(c)(4)) can deduct the interest or expense in the year of accrual only if the other party must report income in that year.

The main shortcoming of § 267(a)(2) is that it applies only to taxpayers who are "related" in the statutory sense. The benefits of creating a tax float do not depend upon the payor's being related to the payee, except that related taxpayers may be more willing than others to

---

f. See pp. 71–72, above.

allow large debts to remain outstanding for a long time. In 1984, Congress responded to the problem by enacting § 467. Among other things, this section puts many lessors and lessees on the accrual method with respect to rental payments if the total amount of rentals under a lease agreement exceeds $250,000.

In addition to requiring consistency between lessor and lessee, § 467 deals with cases in which interest has been disguised as rent. Consider a lease which provides for payment and accrual of rent according to the following schedule.

Year	Payment
1	$ 10,000
2	20,000
3	30,000
4	40,000
5	100,000
6	150,000
7	500,000

Absent highly unusual circumstances,[g] it is reasonable to think that some of the large payments in the later years of the lease are in fact being made for the use of the property in earlier years. That is, the large payments in the later years are likely in fact to consist of delayed payments for earlier years' use of the property, plus enough interest to compensate the lessor for the delay.

The kind of "stepped rent" schedule illustrated above was likely to exist when the lessee was in a lower bracket than the lessor—the extreme case being that of a tax-exempt lessee. By shifting rental payments to later years, the parties could save taxes for the lessor by delaying payment of the rent. To be sure, this reduction in the lessor's taxes was purchased at the cost of an increase in the lessee's taxes because the lessee's deductions were delayed. But, if the lessor paid taxes at a higher rate than the lessee, the lessor's tax advantage would outweigh the lessee's tax disadvantage.

A simple way to look at the stepped-rent problem is to view it as an arrangement for leaving money in the hands of whichever party is taxed at a lower rate. Money in the hands of a zero-bracket or low-bracket taxpayer will grow more rapidly—after tax—than it would have grown in the hands of a high-bracket taxpayer. Under a stepped-rent arrangement, the total amount of money available to both parties in the long run can be greater than if rents were paid as the use of the property occurred.

An examination of the mechanics of § 467 as applied to the stepped-rent problem is probably beyond the scope of a basic course. Briefly, and ignoring details and qualifications, § 467 requires that rentals be accrued as the use of the property occurs and that part of the later, larger

g. So unusual that your editors are unable to think of a plausible example.

payments be treated as interest. In effect, the stepped-rent transaction is translated into an economically equivalent arrangement under which rentals are treated as having been paid earlier than the agreement called for, and the payments are then lent by the lessor to the lessee, at interest.

If, as is commonly the case, the income-producing potential of an asset declines as it ages, even equal rent for each year distorts; the rent should decline as the asset ages. See Mundstock, Taxation of Business Rent, 11 Va. Tax Rev. 683 (1992).

Problem and Notes

1. *Decreasing rental payments.* If the lessor is in a lower tax bracket than the lessee, the advantage of putting the money in question into the hands of the low-bracket taxpayer can be achieved by requiring large payments in the early years of the lease, with lower payments in later years. Instead of spelling out the solution to this decreasing-stepped-rent problem in the Code, Congress enacted § 467(f), which directs the Treasury Department to prescribe regulations "comparable to" the rules of § 467 for cases in which rentals decrease over the term of the agreement.

2. *Stepped payments for services.* Section 467(g) authorizes regulations to characterize portions of some large, late payments for services as interest. In principle, the stepping problem is not limited to rents. Section 467 focuses upon rents because the abuses called to the attention of Congress arose in that context.

3. *Problem.* All of the stock of *X* Corp. is owned by *A*. *X* leases a business building from *D* and *H*, who hold title to the property as joint tenants with right of survivorship. *D* is *A*'s daughter, and *H* is *D*'s husband. *X* uses the accrual method and *D* and *H* use the cash method. *X* pays the year–1 rent ($100,000) to *D* and *H* on January 2, year 2. In what year can *X* deduct the rent?

4. *Reference.* Halperin, Interest in Disguise: Taxing the "Time Value of Money," 95 Yale L.J. 506 (1986).

C. CLEAR REFLECTION OF INCOME AND RELATED PROBLEMS

Section 446 requires that a taxpayer's accounting method "clearly reflect income." This means that a taxpayer will not always be able to deduct a business or investment outlay when the amount in question is paid or, in the case of an accrual-method taxpayer, when the all-events test is met. For example, the purchase price of a building cannot be deducted upon payment or accrual. Similarly, an accrual-method lender with a fixed right to receive interest over several years does not have to accrue and report all of that income upon making the loan, even though the all-events test may be satisfied at that time. See Security Flour Mills Co. v. Commissioner, 321 U.S. 281 (1944).

Treas.Reg. § 1.446–1(a)(2) says that a taxpayer's accounting method is acceptable only if it clearly reflects income "in the opinion of the Commissioner,"[h] and the Supreme Court has agreed on several occasions; e.g., Thor Power Tool Co. v. Commissioner, 439 U.S. 522, 531–32 (1979). Therefore, clear-reflection litigation does not raise the question whether a method in fact reflects income clearly; instead, the issue is always whether the Commissioner's insistence upon a particular method was an abuse of discretion.

1. PREPAID EXPENSES

U.S. FREIGHTWAYS CORP. v. COMMISSIONER

United States Court of Appeals, Seventh Circuit, 2001.
270 F.3d 1137.

Before BAUER, MANION, and DIANE P. WOOD, CIRCUIT JUDGES.

DIANE P. WOOD, CIRCUIT JUDGE

This is an appeal from the United States Tax Court's decision affirming the Commissioner's determination that U.S. Freightways Corp. (Freightways) improperly deducted certain expenses during the 1993 tax year. Although we acknowledge that * * * we owe some deference to the Commissioner's interpretation of his own regulations, we conclude here that the lack of any sound basis behind the Commissioner's interpretation, coupled with a lack of consistency on the Commissioner's own part, compels us to rule in favor of Freightways. Because the Tax Court did not reach the Commissioner's alternative argument that Freightways' method of accounting for the expenses in question did not clearly reflect its income, we remand for the limited purpose of allowing that court to consider this issue in the first instance.

I

* * * Every year [Freightways] is required to purchase a large number of permits and licenses and to pay significant fees and insurance premiums in order legally to operate its fleet of vehicles. These items are referred to collectively as FLIP expenses in the record, and we will follow that convention. During the 1993 tax year, Freightways' FLIP expenses totaled $5,399,062. None of the licenses and permits at issue was valid for more than twelve months, nor did the benefits of any of the fees and insurance premiums paid extend beyond a year from the time the expense was incurred. But because the various FLIP expenses were incurred at different times during the tax year, Freightways enjoyed the benefits of a substantial portion of them in more than one tax year. According to Freightways' own accounting, $2,984,197, or approximately 55%, of the FLIP expenses it incurred in 1993 actually benefitted the company during 1994.

---

h. Section 446 itself refers to "the opinion of the Secretary," but only in the context of determining what method may be used if the taxpayer's method "does not clearly reflect income."

Despite the subsequent tax year benefits of its FLIP expenses, Freightways, which otherwise uses the accrual accounting method for bookkeeping and tax reporting purposes, deducted the entire $5,399,062 in FLIP expenses on its 1993 federal income tax return. This had been its common practice for a number of years. After auditing Freightways' tax return, the Commissioner concluded that Freightways should have capitalized its 1993 FLIP expenses and deducted them ratably over the 1993 and 1994 tax years. Freightways disputed this conclusion and petitioned the Tax Court for a redetermination of the IRS's proposed judgment. The Tax Court sided with the Commissioner, concluding that under the relevant provisions of the tax code, Freightways, as an accrual method taxpayer, was required to capitalize these expenses. Given this holding, the court declined to reach the Commissioner's alternative argument that Freightways' use of the accrual accounting method did not fairly reflect its income.

II

The [Tax Court] recognized that whether Freightways could properly deduct its FLIP expenses in full depends on whether they are ordinary and necessary business expenses as defined by § 162(a), or capital expenditures covered by § 263(a). Citing INDOPCO, Inc. v. Commissioner, 503 U.S. 79 (1992), the court explained, accurately, that the essential reason behind the need to distinguish between currently deductible expenses and those that are subject to capitalization is "to match expenses with the revenues of the taxable period to which they are properly attributable, thereby resulting in a more accurate calculation of net income for tax purposes." 503 U.S. at 84. Some mismatching is inevitable: it is not necessary to count every pencil on hand at the end of a tax year to determine whether it will be useful in the next tax year and, if so, to treat it as a capital asset. The critical consideration in determining whether an expense should be treated as a capital expenditure is whether the expenditure produces more than an incidental future benefit or, as the Treasury Regulations put it, whether a benefit for the taxpayer extends "substantially beyond the tax year." See, e.g., Treas. Regs. §§ 1.263(a)–2, 1.461–1(a)(2).

* * *

* * * [T]he Tax Court understood Freightways to be arguing that it should be allowed to deduct its FLIP expenses in full under a "one-year rule" permitting the deduction of any current expense with a benefit that extends less than 12 months into the subsequent tax year. * * * The Tax Court rejected Freightways' reliance on a one-year rule for two reasons. First, it questioned whether such rule was, in fact, well established in the case law. Second, it found that Freightways had a "more fundamental problem," namely the fact that "even if such a 1–year rule were widely recognized, it would be inapplicable to an accrual method taxpayer." On these two grounds, and without further explanation, the court affirmed the Commissioner's deficiency judgment.

III

* * *

A.

* * *

* * * [The] regulations provide that expenditures producing nothing more than an "incidental" future benefit are eligible for current year deductions, while expenditures whose benefits extend "substantially" beyond the tax year must be capitalized. See Treas. Regs. §§ 1.263(a)–2, 1.461–1(a)(2). But this is not a case where the regulations themselves fully answer the question before us. Instead, another layer of interpretation has been laid on top of the regulations: the Commissioner has informed the courts throughout the course of this litigation that the term "substantially" as used in the regulations should be interpreted to cover anything that extends more than a few days, or perhaps a month, into the second tax year. This is so regardless of the implications for the capitalization decision of the other factors normally used to draw the line between ordinary and capital expenses.

* * *

In the present case, * * * no one is arguing that the regulations the Commissioner has promulgated are invalid or that they are inconsistent with the text of the Code. The issue is instead whether the Commissioner's interpretation of his own regulations is a reasonable one. And as to that, there is no question but that the interpretive methodologies he has used have been informal. The interpretation with which we are concerned has emerged inferentially in the way the IRS has applied the rules to different cases and it has appeared through the litigating positions the Service has taken.

B.

One reason the Tax Court gave for accepting the Commissioner's disallowance of Freightways' deductions was that, even if there is some kind of one-year rule for deductible expenses, accrual taxpayers are never entitled to it. This, we conclude, is an unsustainable position. * * *

* * *

In our view, the decision whether to expense or capitalize a particular item should not turn on whether the taxpayer uses the cash or accrual basis of accounting. As Freightways points out, even the Treasury Regulation on which the Commissioner has relied here, Treas. Reg. § 1.461–1(a), uses identical language in subpart (1) (relating to cash basis taxpayers) and in subpart (2) (relating to accrual basis taxpayers): both must capitalize an expenditure that results in the creation of an asset having a useful life which extends substantially beyond the close of the tax year. The mere fact that Freightways is an accrual method taxpayer thus does not disqualify it from expensing the short-term items at issue here.

C.

We turn thus to the central reason the Commissioner, as affirmed by the Tax Court, gave: that no matter what other characteristics an expenditure has, if it is made in one tax year and its useful life extends "substantially" (an undefined term) beyond the close of that year, then it must be capitalized. Perhaps this rule works in some simple cases. It relies on an implicit spectrum between things that are consumed immediately and those that last well beyond a year. Consumable office supplies, such as paper and pens, might not be thought to have a useful life that will extend substantially beyond a given year, even if they are acquired late in the year (though it depends on the pen—some disposable pens bought in November might well be functioning four or five months into the new year). Something like computers or furniture, on the other hand, predictably will last beyond one tax year. The problem is that many things fall somewhere in the middle of this hypothetical spectrum. Some employers, for example, pay for employee training seminars, which surely create human capital that lasts for many years. Are the training expenses one-year deductible items? Must they be capitalized? What about a light bulb that the company expected would last for eight months, but turned out to be burning brightly after 14—or anything else whose useful life was estimated at approximately a year, but that might have failed sooner or lasted longer? The license fees, permit fees, and insurance premiums Freightways pays are, in a sense, easier to characterize as deductible expenses than the pens or the light bulbs because the issuing entities and insurance companies have strictly defined the useful life of the item to be exactly one year—not a minute more or less. The only reason that the FLIP expenses are also in the middle range of the spectrum is because the twelve-month period each one covers will usually lap across two tax years.

Looking at the language of Treas. Reg. § 1.263(a)–2, we find two somewhat contradictory clues. On the one hand, there is the simple word "substantially," which the Commissioner seems to interpret as meaning at least a month (or maybe two, three, or four months?) into a second tax year. We do not wish to quibble about the number of months because even Freightways appears to concede that nine, ten, or eleven months into a second year would qualify as "substantially," and some of the FLIP expenses might fit this pattern. Indeed, "substantially" could be defined instead as a ratio between the benefit in the year of deduction and the subsequent tax year. But, on the other side, Treas. Reg. § 1.263(a)–2 certainly suggests that the FLIP expenses are not similar to the kinds of expenditures that the IRS itself thinks must be capitalized. The most pertinent subsection of that regulation indicates that "the cost of acquisition, construction, or erection of buildings, machinery and equipment, furniture and fixtures, and similar property having a useful life substantially beyond the tax year" should be capitalized. Id. at

§ 1.263(a)–2(a). Followers of the interpretive maxim expressio unius est exclusio alterius would argue that the enumeration of items all of which seem to have a multiple-year life span implies that something that will expire or wear out in exactly a year should not be capitalized. We further note that these examples are all of expenses that become part of the basis of a capital good. There is no such capital good attached to the FLIP expenses. In this sense, Freightways' position is even more compelling than that of the petitioner in the leading case of PNC Bancorp, Inc. v. Commissioner, 212 F.3d 822 (3d Cir.2000). *PNC Bancorp* relied on the language of §§ 162(a) and 263(a) and the regulations enacted thereunder to hold that ordinary and necessary expenses incurred in the origination of loans could be deducted under § 162(a). It explained that recurring, administrative expenses that are necessary to the business activity of the petitioner fall too far "from the heartland of the traditional capital expenditure (a 'permanent improvement or betterment')," id. at 835, to require capitalization. That permanence is precisely what the FLIP expenses lack.

The regulation itself, it is evident, does not resolve this issue one way or the other. We turn then to the way the IRS has applied the regulation. It is not particularly useful in this connection to focus on whether some kind of "one-year" rule exists: it is clear that no such rule has been promulgated using notice-and-comment or other formal procedures, and thus at most we would be deciding whether it could be discerned in agency practice. The Commissioner denies that there is any such rule. Freightways, for its part, points to numerous Revenue Rulings, decisions of the Tax Court, and judicial opinions in which deductions have been allowed for expenditures whose value is limited to twelve months, even if two tax years are covered. See, e.g., Rev. Rul. 59–239, 1959–2 C.B. 55 (deduction allowed for cost of tires and tubes with average useful life of one year or less); Rev. Rul. 69–81, 1969–1 C.B. 137 (deduction allowed for cost of towels, garments, and gloves with useful life of one year or less); Mennuto v. Commissioner, 56 T.C. 910, 924 (1971) (deduction allowed for costs of installing leaching pit designed to last for one year); Bell v. Commissioner, 13 T.C. 344, 348 (1949) (current deduction allowed for insurance expense where policy covered part of 1945 and part of 1946); Encyclopedia Britannica v. Commissioner, 685 F.2d 212, 217 (7th Cir.1982) (stating that a capital expenditure is anything that yields income beyond a period, typically one year, in which the expenditure is made); Clark Oil and Ref. Corp. v. United States, 473 F.2d 1217, 1219–20 (7th Cir.1973) (also mentioning a useful life of one year as the normal dividing line between a capital expense and an ordinary expense).

* * *

Freightways' final point is that perfection in temporal matching comes at too high a price for these kinds of expenses. At some point the "administrative costs and conceptual rigor" of achieving a more perfect match become too great. *Encyclopedia Britannica*, 685 F.2d at 216. Here, there is a considerable administrative burden that Freightways and any similarly situated taxpayer will bear if it must always allocate one-year expenses to two tax years, year in and year out. It argues that the gain in precision for the taxing authorities is far outweighed by the administrative burden it will bear in performing this task. The Commissioner responds that, as an accrual taxpayer, Freightways is already reflecting on its financial accounting records precisely the allocation the Commissioner wants for tax purposes. But it is well known that financial accounting and tax accounting need not be handled in exactly the same way. See, e.g., United States v. Hughes Properties, Inc., 476 U.S. 593, 603 (1986) ("Proper financial accounting and acceptable tax accounting, to be sure, are not the same.... The Court has long recognized the vastly different objectives that financial and tax accounting have."). See also Peoples Bank and Trust Co. v. Commissioner, 415 F.2d 1341, 1343 (7th Cir.1969). The kind of change in the company's tax accounting system for which the Commissioner is arguing will impose an administrative burden regardless of the way its financial accounts are kept.

We conclude that, for the particular kind of expenses at issue in this case—fixed, one-year items where the benefit will never extend beyond that term, that are ordinary, necessary, and recurring expenses for the business in question—the balance of factors under the statute and regulations cuts in favor of treating them as deductible expenses under I.R.C. § 162(a). We therefore reverse the Tax Court's ruling to the contrary.

IV

One final point remains to be decided. The Commissioner argued before the Tax Court that Freightways' method of accounting did not clearly reflect its income. When the Commissioner has made such a determination, he can require computation of taxable income under an alternative method that will accurately reflect income. § 446(b). See *Hughes Properties,* 476 U.S. at 603. Freightways concedes that the Tax Court did not reach this point, but it urges that we should decide as a matter of law that its method of accounting did clearly reflect its income. The Commissioner, however, possesses broad discretion in this area, and we are reluctant to decide the case as a matter of law on the state of the record as it now stands. We will instead remand the case to the Tax Court for the limited purpose of considering this alternative ground for the Commissioner's decision.

The judgment of the Tax Court is REVERSED, and the case is REMANDED to the Tax Court for further proceedings consistent with this opinion.

Problems, Notes and Questions

1. *Importance of the taxpayer's method of accounting.* Whether the answer to problems like that presented in the principal case varies according to the taxpayer's accounting method has never received a

definitive answer. Although neither cash-method nor accrual-method taxpayers can take current deductions for capital expenditures, one can safely say that less-than-ideal methods are more likely to "clearly reflect income" if the taxpayer is on the cash method than if accrual accounting is involved. This is not to say that cash-method taxpayers can always deduct prepayments.

The prepaid-expense decisions have a somewhat ad hoc quality, perhaps because of a feeling that denying a deduction to a cash-method taxpayer who has prepaid an expense conflicts with the cash method. Except for prepaid rent, for which the cases uniformly require capitalization, authorities can usually be found on both sides, at least if the prepayment period is short.

Section 461(g) solves the prepaid-interest problem by requiring capitalization of prepaid interest (except for "points" on some home-mortgage loans). Suppose someone buys a house, taking out a large mortgage. Five years later, when home-mortgage interest rates have dropped, the buyer refinances by replacing the original mortgage with a new one at a lower rate. If the buyer pays points on the new mortgage, does § 461(g) preclude an immediate deduction for those points? The Tax Court has held that § 461(g) unambiguously denies an immediate deduction, but the Eighth Circuit disagrees, at least in a case in which the refinancing was clearly contemplated when the original mortgage was taken out; Huntsman v. Commissioner, 91 T.C. 917 (1988), reversed 905 F.2d 1182 (8th Cir.1990). Further litigation can be expected.

In the much-litigated area of farmers' prepaid feed expenses, the cases tend to allow the deduction unless the "prepayment" was in fact a deposit. Section 447, added to the Code in 1976, requires corporations (and partnerships with a corporate partner) engaged in farming to use accrual accounting. Exceptions are provided for some small and family-controlled farming corporations. See also § 464, limiting prepaid feed or supplies deductions in the case of "farming syndicates" and some other farmers.

In Fort Howard Paper Co. v. Commissioner, 49 T.C. 275, 283 (1967), the court described §§ 263 and 446 as "inextricably intertwined." See generally Gunn, The Requirement That a Capital Expenditure Create or Enhance an Asset, 15 B.C.Ind. & Comm.L.Rev. 443, 452–65 (1974).

2. *A possible solution?* Announcement 2002–9, 2002–7 I.R.B. 536, says that the Service and the Treasury Department expect to propose regulations under which capitalization will not be required for prepaid expenses and the costs of acquiring certain other intangible rights "unless that expenditure created or enhanced intangible rights or benefits for the taxpayer that extend beyond the earlier of (i) 12 months after the first date on which the taxpayer realizes the rights or benefits attributable to the expenditure, or (ii) the end of the taxable year following the taxable year in which the expenditure is incurred." Whether the proposed safe-harbor would preclude an attack on current deductions under clear-reflection-of-income principles is unclear.

3. *Problems.*

(1) On October 1, year 1, *T*, a calendar-year, cash-method taxpayer, pays $1200 for insurance on business property for the 12–month period beginning on the date of payment. When can *T* deduct the $1200?

(2) What result in (1) if the $1200 had instead been paid as interest on a business loan for the 12–month period beginning on the date of payment?

4. *References.* Ward, Tax Postponement and the Cash Method Farmer: An Analysis of Revenue Ruling 75–152, 53 Texas L.Rev. 1119 (1975); Schapiro, Prepayments and Distortion of Income Under Cash Basis Tax Accounting, 30 Tax L.Rev. 117 (1974); Asimow, Principle and Prepaid Interest, 16 U.C.L.A. L.Rev. 36 (1968).

2. UNUSUALLY LONG DEFERRALS: THE "ECONOMIC PERFORMANCE" REQUIREMENT

MOONEY AIRCRAFT, INC. v. UNITED STATES

United States Court of Appeals, Fifth Circuit, 1969.
420 F.2d 400.

Before THORNBERRY and SIMPSON, CIRCUIT JUDGES, and CASSIBRY, DISTRICT JUDGE.

CASSIBRY, DISTRICT JUDGE.

* * *

This is yet another case in the continuing conflict between commercial accounting practice and the federal income tax. The facts, as accepted by the parties for the purpose of the motion for summary judgment, may be summarized as follows:

During the years 1961 through 1965 taxpayer was in the business of manufacturing and selling single-engine, executive aircraft. The taxpayer's practice was to sell exclusively to regional distributors throughout the United States and Canada. These distributors sold to more localized dealers who in turn sold to the ultimate consumers.

During the fiscal years ending October 31, 1961, 1963, 1964 and 1965 taxpayer issued, with each aircraft which it manufactured and sold, a document captioned "Mooney Bond" setting out an unconditional promise that taxpayer would pay to the bearer the sum of $1,000 when the corresponding aircraft should be permanently retired from service. By far the great majority of the "Mooney Bonds" issued by the taxpayer were retained by the distributors to whom they were originally issued, or by persons related to such distributors as the result of reorganizations, liquidations, etc. By October 31, 1965 many distributors had accumulated quite large holdings in the certificates; one distributor, for example, held no fewer than 122.

Taxpayer seeks to exclude or deduct from gross income the face value of either all Mooney Bonds, or those Mooney Bonds which it is estimated will ultimately be redeemed, in the year the instruments were issued. It is the Government's position that the Mooney Bonds may be deducted only in the year the aircraft to which they relate are in fact permanently retired from service. The Government has alleged, and the taxpayer has not denied, that perhaps 20 or more years may elapse between issuance of the Bonds and retirement of the aircraft. The district court sustained the Government's position and, for the reasons to be discussed, we affirm the judgment of the district court.

* * *

[The portion of the court's opinion holding that Mooney had satisfied the all-events test is omitted. The court held that "retirement of the aircraft" was not a contingency because retirement had to occur eventually. Compare United States v. Hughes Properties, Inc., p. 745, above.]

The "all events test," however, is not the only basis upon which the Commissioner can disallow a deduction. Under § 446(b) he has discretion to disallow any accounting method which does not clearly reflect income. As previously stated, the Commissioner has often relied on the "claim of right test" * * * to disallow a deduction or a deferral of income in cases where the taxpayer's receipt of the funds was unrestricted. He appears to be doing so here, for the Government says in its brief, "Taxpayer received the full economic benefit of these proceeds, without any restriction as to use or enjoyment, and without any duty to return or transfer any part of these proceeds." The claim of right doctrine, however, has not enjoyed universal acceptance in the courts, see e.g., Schuessler v. Commissioner of Internal Revenue, 230 F.2d 722 (5th Cir.1956); Beacon Publishing Co. v. Commissioner of Internal Revenue, 218 F.2d 697 (10th Cir.1955), and in two recent major decisions in this area, American Automobile Assn. v. United States, 367 U.S. 687 (1961) (hereafter *AAA*) and Schlude v. Commissioner of Internal Revenue, 372 U.S. 128 (1963) (hereafter *Schlude*), the Supreme Court seems to have placed little if any reliance on the doctrine.

* * *

The question remains: Was there reasonable basis for the Commissioner's action in this case? It appears to us there was ample basis.

The most salient feature in this case is the fact that many or possibly most of the expenses which taxpayer wishes to presently deduct will not actually be paid for 15, 20 or even 30 years (the taxpayer has not attempted to deny this). In no other case coming to our attention have we found anything even comparable to the time span involved in this case. In virtually all these other cases, even though a taxpayer may have received money under "claim [of] right" and had unrestricted use of the funds, there was still some relationship between those funds and related expenses which, more or less proximately, had to be borne. If there were no actual strings there were at least invisible strings attached to the money. Taxpayers could not use the money without at least an eye to the upcoming expenses or services to be performed. In this case, however, the related expenditure is so distant from the time the money is received as to completely attenuate any relationship between the two. For all practical purposes the revenue taxpayer received from the sale of the planes is his to use as he pleases. Rather than being set up as a reserve to pay an impending expense it is far more probable that the money will be used as capital to expand the business. In what sense, then, is it an accurate reflection of income to regard it as an expense of doing business in the current year? To so regard it is to let an accounting fiction obscure the business and fiscal realities that are the heart of this case. In exercising his discretion the Commissioner need not close his eyes to these realities. We feel that from both a business and tax standpoint the accounting systems rejected by the Supreme Court in *Schlude* and *AAA* were much more reasonable than the one involved here, and that to allow a present deduction in this case would distort rather than reflect income. We therefore find no difficulty in concluding that the Commissioner had a reasonable basis for disallowing the deduction as not clearly reflecting income.

* * *

Problems and Notes

1. *Clear reflection of income and cash flow.* In everyday cases the difference between cash and accrual accounting is likely to be fairly small. The income of a lawyer who deducts expenses as incurred and reports income as services are performed will, on the average, be close to that of another lawyer doing the same things at the same costs, but reporting on the cash method. In cases involving a long delay between obligation and payment, however, the disparities between cash accounting and accrual accounting could be spectacular. The present value of $1000 in 20 years is about $150 at a discount rate of ten percent.

If *Mooney Aircraft* had gone the other way, the taxpayer would have been in a position in which a sale of an airplane for a given price with the issuance of a bond could have been preferable to a sale for the same price without a bond. To illustrate, suppose that Mooney Aircraft's income is taxed at a rate of forty percent. Issuing a $1000 bond would have saved the taxpayer $400 in taxes in the year of the sale. This $400, invested to earn an after-tax return of five percent, would increase to $1061 in twenty years, at which time the taxpayer could pay the holder of the bond $1000 and have $61 left over. The agreement to pay an immediately deductible item on a date far in the future would have made the taxpayer better off after taxes than if it had never become liable to make the payment.

Despite the economic absurdity of allowing a deduction for the full face amount of the liability in cases involving substantial delays between accrual and payment, the government did not press its victory in *Mooney*

Aircraft.[i] Instead, it relied on technical arguments that the all-events test was not satisfied in particular cases, and it often lost. In 1984, Congress dealt with the "premature accrual" problem by enacting § 461(h), which in many cases provides that the all-events test will not be treated as being satisfied until "economic performance" of the obligation in question has occurred.

2. *Premature accruals and § 461(h).* A problem similar in economic terms to that posed by *Mooney Aircraft* involves accrued liabilities to pay tort judgments or workers' compensation claims. In some cases, actual payment of these liabilities will stretch out over a period of many years. If the payor could deduct the face amount of the deferred payments in the year in which the liability is fixed, the value of the tax deduction might exceed the present value of the payments, making the payor better off than if it had never become liable (so much for deterrence!).

Section 461(h), which was adopted in 1984, provides that the all-events test cannot be treated as met any earlier than the time when "economic performance" with respect to an item has taken place. In the case of workers' compensation and tort liabilities incurred by the taxpayer, § 461(h)(2)(C) defines economic performance as payment by the taxpayer. The regulations extend this rule to all damages arising out of "breach of contract, or violation of law"; Treas. Reg. § 1.461–4(g)(2). In general, though, "economic performance" can occur before the taxpayer pays; see §§ 461(h)(2)(A) and 461(h)(2)(B). Section 461(h)(3) makes the economic-performance requirement inapplicable to some "recurring" items if economic performance will occur within 8½ months after the close of the year in which the items were accrued.

3. *Economic performance in Mooney Aircraft and Hughes Properties.* Nothing in the language of § 461(h) seems to affect the outcome of cases like *Mooney Aircraft* and *Hughes Properties* (p. 745). Indeed, because the Code specifies two particular cases in which payment does constitute economic performance, most observers had read § 461(h) as meaning that economic performance did not wait for payment in other

---

i. The one exception is Ford Motor Co. v. Commissioner, 102 T.C. 87 (1994), aff'd, 71 F.3d 209 (6th Cir.1995). *Ford* presented a *Mooney Aircraft* problem involving structured tort settlements—funded at least in part by Ford's buying annuity contracts—made in years before the effective date of § 461(h). Ford claimed immediate deductions for the total amounts it would pay under its agreements with the plaintiffs, although many of the payments would not be made for a long time. The Commissioner determined that Ford's deduction should be limited to the amount Ford had actually paid for annuity contracts. (The contracts did not release Ford from liability in the event the companies which sold the annuities defaulted.) The Tax Court held that the Commissioner's determination was not an abuse of discretion. It noted that current deductions could make Ford better off than if it had never become liable at all. (On appeal, the Sixth Circuit found an error in this calculation, but ruled the error immaterial: an undeserved tax benefit was present even if the benefit was not so great as to completely offset the taxpayer's payment.)

Because Ford had purchased annuity contracts, at a cost equal to the present value of the liabilities, the Tax Court's holding gave the taxpayer a current deduction equal in amount to the present value of its future obligation. Query whether, if Ford had simply agreed to make future payments to the claimants, the Commissioner and the court would have allowed it to deduct the present value of its obligation.

cases. Furthermore, the Joint Committee Staff's "General Explanation" of the 1984 legislation said that the term "property" in § 461(h)(2)(B) does not include money. Nevertheless, the regulations under § 461 provide that economic performance in the case of jackpots occurs only when the winner cashes in, and an example seems to cover the *Mooney Aircraft* situation as well. See Treas. Reg. §§ 1.461–4(g)(4) and 1.461–4(g)(8) (Ex. 5) (jackpots); 1.461–4(g)(8) (Ex. 3) (sellers' rebates to buyers).

4. *Problems.*

(1) In year 1, *H* Corp. hires a contractor, *R* Corp., to repair *H*'s hotel building. *R* makes the repairs in year 2 and bills *H* for $120,000. *H*, an accrual-method taxpayer, pays the bill in year 3. When does *H* deduct the $120,000? See § 461(h)(2).

(2) Same as (1) except that *H* pays *R* $100,000 in year 1, before *R* does the work.

(3) In year 1, *S* sells a machine to *B* under a contract which requires *S* to repair the machine if it breaks down within ten years. In year 5, the machine breaks down and *S* hires *K* Corp. to fix it. *K* Corp. does the work in year 5 and sends *S* a bill for $40,000; *S* pays the bill in year 6. When does *S*, an accrual-method taxpayer, deduct the $40,000?

5. *Reference.* Jensen, The Deduction of Future Liabilities by Accrual–Basis Taxpayers: Premature Accruals, the All Events Test, and Economic Performance, 37 U.Fla.L.Rev. 443 (1985).

ACCRUAL OF PRESENT VALUE AS AN ALTERNATIVE TO § 461(h)

One reason why traditional accrual accounting sometimes leads to economically absurd results is that the all-events test ignores the time-value of money. Although a liability to pay $1000 in 20 years bears much more lightly on the payor than a liability to pay the same amount tomorrow, pre–1984 accounting practice generally treated the two cases as being identical. In cases involving tort and workers' compensation claims, § 461(h) responds to this problem by delaying the deduction until payment. Another possible response would be to treat the deferred payment as the equivalent of a present payment (of a smaller amount) plus interest. For example, a taxpayer who agrees to pay $1000 in the future could be treated as having paid the present value of $1000—say $200—today, and as paying the difference—$800 on these figures—as interest. If this were done, the payor would deduct $200 immediately and $800 as interest under the original-issue-discount rules.

A reason for preferring the approach of § 461(h) in the case of tort and workers' compensation claims is that treating part of the deferred payments as interest would be inconsistent with the tax treatment of the recipient of the payments, who can exclude all payments from income under § 104(a). Actual interest payments are usually deducted by the payor and taxed to the recipient; "imputed interest" on deferred deductible personal-injury payments would be deducted by the payor and taxed to no one (unless § 104 were amended). See generally Cunningham, A Theoretical Analysis of the Tax Treatment of Future Costs, 40 Tax L.Rev. 577 (1985).

3. PREPAID INCOME, DEPOSITS, AND OPTIONS

SCHLUDE v. COMMISSIONER

Supreme Court of the United States, 1963.
372 U.S. 128, 83 S.Ct. 601, 9 L.Ed.2d 633.

MR. JUSTICE WHITE delivered the opinion of the Court.

This is still another chapter in the protracted problem of the time certain items are to be recognized as income for the purposes of the federal income tax. The Commissioner of Internal Revenue increased the 1952, 1953 and 1954 ordinary income of the taxpayers by including in gross income for those years amounts received or receivable under contracts executed during those years despite the fact that the contracts obligated taxpayers to render performance in subsequent periods. These increases produced tax deficiencies which the taxpayers unsuccessfully challenged in the Tax Court on the ground that the amounts could be deferred under their accounting method. On appeal, the Court of Appeals for the Eighth Circuit agreed with the taxpayers and reversed the Tax Court, 283 F.2d 234, the decision having been rendered prior to ours in American Automobile Assn. v. United States, 367 U.S. 687. Following the *American Automobile Association* case, certiorari in this case was granted, the judgment of the lower court vacated, 367 U.S. 911, and the cause remanded for further consideration in light of *American Automobile Association*. 368 U.S. 873. In a *per curiam* opinion, the Court of Appeals held that in view of *American Automobile Association,* the taxpayers' accounting method "does not, for income tax purposes, clearly reflect income" and affirmed the judgment for the Commissioner, 296 F.2d 721. We brought the case back once again to consider whether the lower court misapprehended the scope of *American Automobile Association*. 370 U.S. 902.

Taxpayers, husband and wife, formed a partnership to operate ballroom dancing studios (collectively referred to as "studio") pursuant to Arthur Murray, Inc., franchise agreements. Dancing lessons were offered under either of two basic contracts. The cash plan contract required the student to pay the entire down payment in cash at the time the contract was executed with the balance due in installments thereafter. The deferred payment contract required only a portion of the down payment to be paid in cash. The remainder of the down payment was due in stated installments and the balance of the contract price was to be paid as designated in a negotiable note signed at the time the contract was executed.

Both types of contracts provided that (1) the student should pay tuition for lessons in a certain amount, (2) the student should not be relieved of his obligation to pay the tuition, (3) no refunds would be made, and (4) the contract was noncancelable. The contracts prescribed a specific number of lesson hours ranging from five to 1,200 hours and some contracts provided lifetime courses entitling the student additionally to two hours of lessons per month plus two parties a year for life. Although the contracts designated the period during which the lessons had to be taken, there was no schedule of specific dates, which were arranged from time to time as lessons were given.

Cash payments received directly from students and amounts received when the negotiable notes were discounted at the bank or fully paid were deposited in the studio's general bank account without segregation from its other funds. The franchise agreements required the studio to pay to Arthur Murray, Inc., on a weekly basis, 10% of these cash receipts as royalty and 5% of the receipts in escrow, the latter to continue until a $20,000 indemnity fund was accumulated. Similarly, sales commissions for lessons sold were paid at the time the sales receipts were deposited in the studio's general bank account.

The studio, since its inception in 1946, has kept its books and reported income for tax purposes on an accrual system of accounting. In addition to the books, individual student record cards were maintained showing the number of hours taught and the number still remaining under the contract. The system, in substance, operated as follows. When a contract was entered into, a "deferred income" account was credited for the total contract price. At the close of each fiscal period, the student record cards were analyzed and the total number of taught hours was multiplied by the designated rate per hour of each contract. The resulting sum was deducted from the deferred income account and reported as earned income on the financial statements and the income tax return. In addition, if there had been no activity in a contract for over a year, or if a course were reduced in amount, an entry would be made canceling the untaught portion of the contract, removing that amount from the deferred income account, and recognizing gain to the extent that the deferred income exceeded the balance due on the contract, i.e., the amounts received in advance. The amounts representing lessons taught and the gains from cancellations constituted the chief sources of the partnership's gross income. The balance of the deferred income account would be carried forward into the next fiscal year to be increased or decreased in accordance with the number of new contracts, lessons taught and cancellations recognized.

Deductions were also reported on the accrual basis except that the royalty payments and the sales commissions were deducted when paid irrespective of the period in which the related receipts were taken into income. Three certified public accountants testified that in their opinion the accounting system employed truly reflected net income in accordance with commercial accrual accounting standards.

The Commissioner included in gross income for the years in question not only advance payments received in cash but the full face amounts of notes and contracts executed during the respective years. The Tax Court and the Court of Appeals upheld the Commissioner, but the United States in this Court has retreated somewhat and does not now claim the includibility in gross income of future payments which were not evidenced by a note and which were neither due by the terms of the contract nor matured by performance of the related services. The question remaining for decision, then, is this: Was it proper for the Commissioner, exercising his discretion under § 41, 1939 Code, and § 446(b), 1954 Code, to reject the studio's accounting system as not clearly reflecting income and to include as income in a particular year advance payments by way of cash, negotiable notes and contract installments falling due but remaining unpaid during that year? We hold that it was since we believe the problem is squarely controlled by *American Automobile Association*, 367 U.S. 687.

The Court there had occasion to consider the entire legislative background of the treatment of prepaid income. The retroactive repeal of § 452 of the 1954 Code, "the only law incontestably permitting the practice upon which [the taxpayer] depends," was regarded as reinstating long-standing administrative and lower court rulings that accounting systems deferring prepaid income could be rejected by the Commissioner.

> "[T]he fact is that § 452 for the first time specifically declared petitioner's system of accounting to be acceptable for income tax purposes, and overruled the long-standing position of the Commissioner and courts to the contrary. And the repeal of the section the following year, upon insistence by the Treasury that the proposed endorsement of such tax accounting would have a disastrous impact on the Government's revenue, was just as clearly a mandate from the congress that petitioner's system was not acceptable for tax purposes." 367 U.S., at 695.

Confirming that view was the step-by-step approach of Congress in granting the deferral privilege to only limited groups of taxpayers while exploring more deeply the ramifications of the entire problem.

Plainly, the considerations expressed in *American Automobile Association* are apposite here. We need only add here that since the *American Automobile Association* decision, a specific provision extending the deferral practice to certain membership corporations was enacted, § 456, 1954 Code, added by § 1, Act of July 26, 1961, 75 Stat. 222, continuing, at least so far, the congressional policy of treating this problem by precise provisions of narrow applicability. Consequently, as in the *American Automobile Association* case, we invoke the "long-established policy of the Court in deferring, where possible, to congressional procedures in the tax field," and, as in that case, we cannot say that the Commissioner's rejection of the studio's deferral system was unsound.

The *American Automobile Association* case rested upon an additional ground which is also controlling here. Relying upon Automobile Club of Michigan v. Commissioner, 353 U.S. 180, the Court rejected the taxpayer's system as artificial since the advance payments related to services which were to be performed only upon customers' demands without relation to fixed dates in the future. The system employed here suffers from that very same vice, for the studio sought to defer its cash receipts on the basis of contracts which did not provide for lessons on fixed dates after the taxable year, but left such dates to be arranged from time to time by the instructor and his student. Under the contracts, the student could arrange for some or all of the additional lessons or could simply allow their rights under the contracts to lapse. But even though the student did not demand the remaining lessons, the contracts permitted the studio to insist upon payment in accordance with the obligations undertaken and to retain whatever prepayments were made without restriction as to use and without obligation of refund. At the end of each period, while the number of lessons taught had been meticulously reflected, the studio was uncertain whether none, some or all of the remaining lessons would be rendered. Clearly, services were rendered solely on demand in the fashion of the *American Automobile Association* and *Automobile Club of Michigan* cases.

Moreover, percentage royalties and sales commissions for lessons sold, which were paid as cash was received from students or from its note transactions with the bank, were deducted in the year paid even though the related items of income had been deferred, at least in part, to later periods. In view of all these circumstances, we hold the studio's accrual system vulnerable under § 41 and § 446(b) with respect to its deferral of prepaid income. Consequently, the Commissioner was fully justified in including payments in cash or by negotiable note in gross income for the year in which such payments were received. If these payments are includible in the year of receipt because their allocation to a later year does not clearly reflect income, the contract installments are likewise includible in gross income, as the United States now claims, in the year they become due and payable. For an accrual basis taxpayer "it is the *right* to receive and not the actual receipt that determines the inclusion of the amount in gross income," Spring City Co. v. Commissioner, 292 U.S. 182, 184; Commissioner v. Hansen, 360 U.S. 446, and here the right to receive these installments had become fixed at least at the time they were due and payable.

We affirm the Court of Appeals insofar as that court held includible the amounts representing cash receipts, notes received and contract installments due and payable. Because of the Commissioner's concession, we reverse that part of the judgment which included amounts for which services had not yet been performed and which were not due and payable during the respective periods and we remand the case with directions to return the case to the Tax Court for a redetermination of the proper income tax deficiencies now due in light of this opinion.

It is so ordered.

MR. JUSTICE STEWART, with whom MR. JUSTICE DOUGLAS, MR. JUSTICE HARLAN, and MR. JUSTICE GOLDBERG join, dissenting.

[Omitted.]

Notes

1. *The American Automobile Association case.* In American Auto. Ass'n v. United States, 367 U.S. 687 (1961), upon which the *Schlude* Court relied, the taxpayer received membership dues, payment of which entitled the member to services during the year of membership (often not a calendar year). At first the taxpayer reported as income that portion of a year's dues received which corresponded to the number of months remaining in that calendar year. In 1954 it changed to a convention of reporting half of each receipt of dues in the year of receipt and half in the following year, a system which produced virtually the same result as the earlier monthly proration method. The Court characterized the Association's method as "artificial" because it failed to match the reporting of a particular member's dues with performance of services to that member. Relying heavily on the repeal of § 452 and § 462, which would have allowed deferral of prepaid income and deductions of reserves for estimated future expenses, the Court held that "the exercise of the Commissioner's discretion in rejecting the Association's accounting system was not unsound." Congress overruled *American Auto. Ass'n* by enacting § 456.

2. *Tax accounting and financial accounting.* For financial-accounting purposes, prepaid income like that in the principal case must be deferred. Allowing it to show up on the taxpayer's financial statements when received, especially with no offset for the costs of earning it, would mislead prospective investors and creditors, who want to know "income" in order to estimate the business's chances of future success. If prepaid income were included in the income statement, a failing business could be made to look profitable simply by arranging for some of its customers to pay early. Financial accounting must "match" income and related deductions so that the performance of the company's employees, and thus the prospects of continued success, can be estimated. Tax accounting, on the other hand, need not concern itself with whether the taxpayer is likely to prosper next year. The use of income as the tax base is usually supported on the ground that income is a satisfactory measure of "ability to pay," a concept more linked to the past and present than to the future.

3. *Reserves.* Some cases have allowed accrual-method taxpayers who have received income not fully earned to deduct additions to a "reserve for estimated future expenses." For example in Schuessler v. Commissioner, 230 F.2d 722 (5th Cir.1956), a taxpayer who sold furnaces was allowed to deduct his estimated costs of satisfying guarantees to turn each of the furnaces on and off each year for five years. The court felt that allowing the reserve would "most accurately [reflect] the taxpayer's income on an annual accounting basis." Section 461(h) now solves the "reserves" problem for cases in which the taxpayer must

furnish property or services in the future because economic performance will not occur until the taxpayer provides the property or services.

SCHAPIRO, TAX ACCOUNTING FOR PREPAID INCOME AND RESERVES FOR FUTURE EXPENSES

2 Tax Revision Compendium 1133, 1142–43.
(House Comm. on Ways and Means 1959).

(1) Arguments in Support of Continuing the Strict Tax Rule for Taxing Prepaid Income

The principal arguments in favor of the strict tax accounting rule of not permitting deferment of prepaid income can be outlined as follows:

(*a*) The strict tax rule protects the revenues by levying a tax at a time when the taxpayer has the funds with which to pay the tax. This conforms to a general policy of gearing tax collections to dollars in taxpayer's hands. This general policy, of course, at times works in the taxpayer's favor. For example, unrealized appreciation (even in readily marketable securities) is not taxed; and the installment method of reporting in general correlates tax collections with the receipt of money.

(*b*) The commercial accounting rule, under which recognition of prepaid income is deferred until the products or services are supplied, may in some cases be further from the mark of the "intuitively correct" computation of net income than the strict tax rule. Where the future costs of supplying the product or service are relatively small compared with the price received, a "fairer" reckoning of net income (and one probably closer to the businessman's mental calculations) might result from taking the full proceeds into income and deducting a reserve for future expenses. To illustrate, suppose a taxpayer leases land on a net basis and receives the fifth year's net cash rent in advance. Why is it more accurate or fairer to postpone the incidence of the tax until the fifth year? Also, under commercial practice, which tend[s] toward conservatism in showing net income, many costs incurred in the current year are related to prepaid income (e.g., selling expenses) but are nevertheless deducted when incurred, thus violating the theory of the matching of related income and expenses.

(*c*) The strict tax rule is easier to administer because it involves fewer subjective judgments and estimates and produces a more uniform result among different taxpayers. To draw illustrations from two recent cases:

(*i*) How should prepaid income received by an automobile club be prorated where the taxpayer agrees to provide a variety of services such as towing, bail bond and travel service for a fixed period and, in addition, where a portion of the receipts are expended in the discretion of the auto club for the solution of safety and traffic problems, and promotion of certain laws favorable to motorists?

(*ii*) How should income be prorated where it is received in advance for a television service contract which includes both installation of the set and continuing service visits?

Questions such as those posed above cannot be answered automatically by reference to generally accepted accounting principles. Reasonable men, accountants included, can and do differ in their answers to questions involving allocation of revenue to particular accounting periods. The pivotal point of commercial accounting—no matter how the question of allocation may be decided in a particular case—is that it attempts to match revenues of a particular accounting period with the expenses which pertain to such revenues. Generally accepted accounting principles sanction different procedures for allocating income and deductions to various accounting periods which, in the above illustrations, may produce substantially different calculations of net income in any particular period. Commercial accounting practice cannot and does not supply a single answer to the allocation problems inherent in segmenting business operations into accounting periods.

* * *

Problem and Notes

1. *Tax accounting, financial accounting, and the Supreme Court.* The *Schlude* opinion represents a midpoint in the development of the law of tax accounting. In United States v. Anderson, 269 U.S. 422 (1926), the Court had described financial-accounting principles as "scientific," thereby implying that there is one "true" measure of "income" for all purposes and that the accountants had found it. The Court later retreated from this position, holding in Old Colony R. Co. v. Commissioner, 284 U.S. 552 (1932), that financial-accounting rules are not necessarily applicable in tax cases, even when the rules are imposed upon the taxpayer by a regulatory agency. The opinions in *American Auto. Ass'n* and *Schlude,* while not allowing the use of the particular methods in question, did not say that financial accounting has no place in determining tax liability, but went off on criticisms (sometimes far-fetched) of details of the methods before the Court. Furthermore, in Commissioner v. Idaho Power Co., 418 U.S. 1 (1974), the Court supported its decision that depreciation on construction equipment used in building an asset had to be capitalized as part of the cost of that asset by observing that financial-accounting principles required capitalization.

The Court's failure to give any general reason for rejecting rules borrowed from financial accounting in *American Auto. Ass'n* and *Schlude,* and its own use of financial-accounting wisdom in *Idaho Power,* encouraged many people to think, or hope, that financial-accounting principles were at least presumptively correct in tax cases. Justice

Blackmun's opinion for a unanimous Court in Thor Power Tool Co. v. Commissioner, 439 U.S. 522 (1979), flatly rejects this view. The Court held that a taxpayer could not write down its inventory to scrap value under circumstances in which financial-accounting principles might have permitted the writedown. It noted that Treas.Reg. § 1.446–1(a)(2) provides that "no" accounting method is acceptable unless it is acceptable to the Commissioner, and read the prepaid-income cases as supporting this interpretation of the regulation. For the first time, the Court squarely faced the question whether "generally accepted accounting principles" are presumptively correct in tax cases (439 U.S. at 542–544):

> [T]he presumption petitioner postulates is insupportable in light of the vastly different objectives that financial and tax accounting have. The primary goal of financial accounting is to provide useful information to management, shareholders, creditors, and others properly interested; the major responsibility of the accountant is to protect these parties from being misled. The primary goal of the income tax system, in contrast, is the equitable collection of revenue; the major responsibility of the Internal Revenue Service is to protect the public fisc. Consistently with its goals and responsibilities, financial accounting has as its foundation the principle of conservatism, with its corollary that "possible errors in measurement [should] be in the direction of understatement rather than overstatement of net income and net assets." In view of the Treasury's markedly different goals and responsibilities, understatement of income is not destined to be its guiding light. Given this diversity, even contrariety, of objectives, any presumptive equivalency between tax and financial accounting would be unacceptable.
>
> This difference in objectives is mirrored in numerous differences of treatment. Where the tax law requires that a deduction be deferred until "all the events" have occurred that will make it fixed and certain, United States v. Anderson, 269 U.S. 422, 441 (1926), accounting principles typically require that a liability be accrued as soon as it can reasonably be estimated. Conversely, where the tax law requires that income be recognized currently under "claim of right," "ability to pay," and "control" rationales, accounting principles may defer accrual until a later year so that revenues and expenses may be better matched. Financial accounting, in short, is hospitable to estimates, probabilities, and reasonable certainties; the tax law, with its mandate to preserve the revenue, can give no quarter to uncertainty. This is as it should be. Reasonable estimates may be useful, even essential, in giving shareholders and creditors an accurate picture of a firm's overall financial health; but the accountant's conservatism cannot bind the Commissioner in his efforts to collect taxes. "Only a few reserves voluntarily established as a matter of conservative accounting," Mr. Justice Brandeis wrote for the Court, "are authorized by the Revenue Acts." Brown v. Helvering, 291 U.S., at 201–202.

Finally, a presumptive equivalency between tax and financial accounting would create insurmountable difficulties of tax administration. Accountants long have recognized that "generally accepted accounting principles" are far from being a canonical set of rules that will ensure identical accounting treatment of identical transactions. "Generally accepted accounting principles," rather, tolerate a range of "reasonable" treatments, leaving the choice among alternatives to management. Such, indeed, is precisely the case here. Variances of this sort may be tolerable in financial reporting, but they are questionable in a tax system designed to ensure as far as possible that similarly situated taxpayers pay the same tax. If management's election among "acceptable" options were dispositive for tax purposes, a firm, indeed, could decide unilaterally—within limits dictated only by its accountants—the tax it wished to pay. Such unilateral decisions would not just make the Code inequitable; they would make it unenforceable.

2. *Cases in which deferral of prepaid income is allowed.* Section 455 allows accrual-method (but not cash-method) taxpayers to elect deferral of prepaid receipts for subscriptions to newspapers and magazines. Section 456, overruling *American Auto. Ass'n,* allows accrual-method taxpayers to defer prepaid dues income. Two broader exceptions to the rules taxing prepaid income when received have been carved out by administrative action. Treas.Reg. § 1.451–5 provides for deferral of advance payment for goods at the election of an accrual-method taxpayer. Under this provision, advance payments for goods to be sold can be included in gross receipts when the goods are shipped, but deferral cannot delay inclusion beyond the end of the second taxable year following the year in which advance payments are received if the goods sold are inventory. Revenue Procedure 71–21, 1971–2 C.B. 549, allows deferral of prepaid income for services until the services are performed if the accrual-method taxpayer is to perform the services by the end of the year following the year in which payment was received. Neither Treas. Reg. § 1.451–5 nor Rev.Proc. 71–21 allows deferral of prepaid interest or rent, and neither allows deferral for more than a relatively short period.

Sellers of consumer goods sometimes sell "service warranty contracts" with their goods, and some of those sellers then pay another company to insure the risks they have assumed. This practice can create a cash-flow problem for the sellers, because the income they get by selling the warranty contracts is taxable in the year of the sale, while the amounts they pay for insurance are capital expenditures, recoverable over the lives of the policies. Suppose, for example, that a seller charges $100,000 for six years of warranty protection on goods and pays an insurer $99,000 to cover its risks. Under the usual rules, the seller would have $100,000 of gross income in the year of the sale and no deductions (except for whatever portion of the $99,000 is allocable to the year of sale). In this kind of case, the seller's tax liability in the year of the sale could exceed the amount of money it could receive that year (net of the payments to the insurer) from those sales. In response to this problem, the Service has issued a ruling which, in substance, allows sellers faced with this problem to delay the tax payments, with interest to make up for the delay. Revenue Procedure 97–38, 1997–2 C.B. 479, gives the sellers an election to report the income from sales of service contracts over the life of the service contracts or six years, whichever is shorter. Taxpayers who make this election must agree to report additional amounts of income in the later years, with the total amount of income being calculated so that its present value (as of the year of the sale) equals the amount of income that would have been taxed in that year. In substance, the tax payments on the "extra" income serve as interest on the rest of the payments.

Because the Supreme Court's prepaid-income cases have never said in so many words that the Commissioner's discretion extends to prohibiting deferral of prepaid income in every case, some courts have allowed deferral. See Artnell Co. v. Commissioner, 400 F.2d 981 (7th Cir.1968) (income from selling season tickets to baseball games deferred because dates of performance were fixed); Boise Cascade Corp. v. United States, 530 F.2d 1367 (Ct.Cl.1976), cert. denied 429 U.S. 867 (1976) (services income deferred because Commissioner's method "would appear to the ordinary mind to distort income instead of clearly reflecting it"). In RCA Corp. v. United States, 664 F.2d 881 (2d Cir.1981), the Second Circuit cited the Supreme Court's reference in *Thor* to the "vastly different objectives" of tax and financial accounting and refused to allow deferral.

3. *Problem.* F Corp., a professional football club, sells tickets (for cash) in December for a playoff game to be played in the following January. *F* is a calendar-year, accrual-method taxpayer. In which year should *F* include the income from the ticket sales?

4. *The payor's tax position.* People who pay in advance for goods or services may get a tax benefit, especially when the costs of buying those goods or services are not deductible. Consider, for instance, a consumer who plans to buy a $1000 item five years from today. The consumer has cash of $700 on hand. One way to handle the purchase would be for the consumer to invest the $700, let it grow to $1000 in five years[j], and buy the item. This approach would, however, subject the consumer to income tax on the $300 investment return as it was earned, leaving less than $1000 to make the purchase. Therefore, $700 today would not be enough to finance the purchase. If the consumer buys the good by paying $700 now, and if the seller is exempt from income taxation (or pays tax at a rate much lower than the consumer), a $700 payment would suffice.

An everyday, though very minor, example of prepayments used as described above is magazine subscriptions. Magazines encourage their subscribers to pay years in advance by offering low rates; this is, in substance, a way of giving the subscribers a tax-free investment return. An example involving considerably more money is found in the practices

---

j. This is the amount to which $700 would grow in five years at an interest rate of about six percent.

of some retirement communities which charge in advance for residents' entire stays (or for a portion of the costs of those stays).

In the absence of legislation solving the prepaid-income problem in a comprehensive, economically sound way, the strongest argument for immediate taxation of the recipient may be that this serves in some cases to offset the tax advantages to the payor.

5. *References.* Gunn, Matching of Costs and Revenues as a Goal of Tax Accounting, 4 Va.Tax Rev. 1 (1984); Oberdorfer & Michelman, A Commentary on Tax Administration and Accrual Accounting, 12 Am. U.L.Rev. 135 (1963).

COMMISSIONER v. INDIANAPOLIS POWER & LIGHT CO.

Supreme Court of the United States, 1990.
493 U.S. 203, 110 S.Ct. 589, 107 L.Ed.2d 591.

JUSTICE BLACKMUN delivered the opinion of the Court.

Respondent Indianapolis Power & Light Company (IPL) requires certain customers to make deposits with it to assure payment of future bills for electric service. Petitioner Commissioner of Internal Revenue contends that these deposits are advance payments for electricity and therefore constitute taxable income to IPL upon receipt. IPL contends otherwise.

I

IPL is a regulated Indiana corporation that generates and sells electricity in Indianapolis and its environs. It keeps its books on the accrual and calendar year basis. During the years 1974 through 1977, approximately 5% of IPL's residential and commercial customers were required to make deposits "to insure prompt payment," as the customers' receipts stated, of future utility bills. These customers were selected because their credit was suspect. Prior to March 10, 1976, the deposit requirement was imposed on a case-by-case basis. IPL relied on a credit test but employed no fixed formula. The amount of the required deposit ordinarily was twice the customer's estimated monthly bill. IPL paid 3% interest on a deposit held for six months or more. A customer could obtain a refund of the deposit prior to termination of service by requesting a review and demonstrating acceptable credit. The refund usually was made in cash or by check, but the customer could choose to have the amount applied against future bills.

In March 1976, IPL amended its rules governing the deposit program. See Title 170, Ind. Admin. Code 4–1–15 (1988). Under the amended rules, the residential customers from whom deposits were required were selected on the basis of a fixed formula. The interest rate was raised to 6% but was payable only on deposits held for 12 months or more. A deposit was refunded when the customer made timely payments for either nine consecutive months, or for 10 out of 12 consecutive months so long as the two delinquent months were not themselves consecutive. A customer could obtain a refund prior to that time by satisfying the credit test. As under the previous rules, the refund would be made in cash or by check, or, at the customer's option, applied against future bills. Any deposit unclaimed after seven years was to escheat to the State. See Ind. Code section 32–9–1–6(a) (1988).

IPL did not treat these deposits as income at the time of receipt. * * * Customer deposits were not physically segregated in any way from the company's general funds. They were commingled with other receipts and at all times were subject to IPL's unfettered use and control. It is undisputed that IPL's treatment of the deposits was consistent with accepted accounting practice and applicable state regulations.

Upon audit of respondent's returns for the calendar years 1974 through 1977, the Commissioner asserted deficiencies. * * * The Commissioner took the position that the deposits were advance payments for electricity and therefore were taxable to IPL in the year of receipt. He contended that the increase or decrease in customer deposits outstanding at the end of each year represented an increase or decrease in IPL's income for the year. IPL disagreed and filed a petition in the United States Tax Court for redetermination of the asserted deficiencies.

In a reviewed decision, with one judge not participating, a unanimous Tax Court ruled in favor of IPL. 88 T.C. 964 (1987). The court followed the approach it had adopted in City Gas Co. of Florida v. Commissioner of Internal Revenue, 74 T.C. 386 (1980), rev'd, 689 F.2d 943 (C.A.11 1982). It found it necessary to "continue to examine all of the circumstances," 88 T.C., at 976, and relied on several factors in concluding that the deposits in question were properly excluded from gross income. It noted, among other things, that only 5% of IPL's customers were required to make deposits; that the customer rather than the utility controlled the ultimate disposition of a deposit; and that IPL consistently treated the deposits as belonging to the customers, both by listing them as current liabilities for accounting purposes and by paying interest. Id., at 976–978.

The United States Court of Appeals for the Seventh Circuit affirmed the Tax Court's decision. 857 F.2d 1162 (1988). The court stated that "the proper approach to determining the appropriate tax treatment of a customer deposit is to look at the primary purpose of the deposit based on all the facts and circumstances. * * *" Id., at 1167. The court appeared to place primary reliance, however, on IPL's obligation to pay interest on the deposits. It asserted that "as the interest rate paid on a deposit to secure income begins to approximate the return that the recipient would be expected to make from 'the use' of the deposit amount, the deposit begins to serve purposes that comport more squarely with a security deposit." Id., at 1169. Noting that IPL had paid interest on the customer deposits throughout the period in question, the court upheld, as not clearly erroneous, the Tax Court's determination that the principal purpose of these deposits was to serve as security rather than as prepayment of income. Id., at 1170.

Because the Seventh Circuit was in specific disagreement with the Eleventh Circuit's ruling in *City Gas Co. of Florida,* supra, we granted certiorari to resolve the conflict. 490 U.S. 1033 (1989).

II

We begin with the common ground. IPL acknowledges that these customer deposits are taxable as income upon receipt if they constitute *advance payments* for electricity to be supplied.[3] The Commissioner, on his part, concedes that customer deposits that secure the performance of nonincome-producing covenants—such as a utility customer's obligation to ensure that meters will not be damaged—are not taxable income. And it is settled that receipt of a loan is not income to the borrower. See Commissioner v. Tufts, 461 U.S. 300, 307 (1983) ("Because of [the repayment] obligation, the loan proceeds do not qualify as income to the taxpayer"); James v. United States, 366 U.S. 213, 219 (1961) (accepted definition of gross income "excludes loans"); Commissioner v. Wilcox, 327 U.S. 404, 408 (1946). IPL, stressing its obligation to refund the deposits with interest, asserts that the payments are similar to loans. The Commissioner, however, contends that a deposit which serves to secure the payment of future income is properly analogized to an advance payment for goods or services. See Rev. Rul. 72–519, 1972–2 Cum. Bull. 32, 33 ("[W]hen the purpose of the deposit is to guarantee the customer's payment of amounts owed to the creditor, such a deposit is treated as an advance payment, but when the purpose of the deposit is to secure a property interest of the taxpayer the deposit is regarded as a true security deposit").

In economic terms, to be sure, the distinction between a loan and an advance payment is one of degree rather than of kind. A commercial loan, like an advance payment, confers an economic benefit on the recipient: a business presumably does not borrow money unless it believes that the income it can earn from its use of the borrowed funds will be greater than its interest obligation. See Illinois Power Co. v. Commissioner of Internal Revenue, 792 F.2d 683, 690 (C.A.7 1986). Even though receipt of the money is subject to a duty to repay, the borrower must regard itself as better off after the loan than it was before. The economic benefit of a loan, however, consists entirely of the opportunity to earn income on the use of the money prior to the time the loan must be repaid. And in that context our system is content to tax these earnings as they are realized. The recipient of an advance payment, in contrast, gains both immediate use of the money (with the chance to

---

3. This Court has held that an accrual-basis taxpayer is required to treat advance payments as income in the year of receipt. See Schlude v. Commissioner, 372 U.S. 128 (1963); American Automobile Assn. v. United States, 367 U.S. 687 (1961); Automobile Club of Michigan v. Commissioner, 353 U.S.

180 (1957). These cases concerned payments—nonrefundable fees for services—that indisputably constituted income; the issue was *when* that income was taxable. Here, in contrast, the issue is whether these deposits, as such, are income at all.

realize earnings thereon) *and* the opportunity to make a profit by providing goods or services at a cost lower than the amount of the payment.

The question, therefore, cannot be resolved simply by noting that respondent derives some economic benefit from receipt of these deposits. Rather, the issue turns upon the nature of the rights and obligations that IPL assumed when the deposits were made. In determining what sort of economic benefits qualify as income, this Court has invoked various formulations. It has referred, for example, to "undeniable accessions to wealth, clearly realized, and over which the taxpayers have complete dominion." Commissioner v. Glenshaw Glass Co., 348 U.S. 426, 431 (1955). It also has stated: "When a taxpayer acquires earnings, lawfully or unlawfully, without the consensual recognition, express or implied, of an obligation to repay and without restriction as to their disposition, 'he has received income. * * * ' "James v. United States, 366 U.S., at 219, quoting North American Oil Consolidated v. Burnet, 286 U.S. 417, 424 (1932). IPL hardly enjoyed "complete dominion" over the customer deposits entrusted to it. Rather, these deposits were acquired subject to an express "obligation to repay," either at the time service was terminated or at the time a customer established good credit. So long as the customer fulfills his legal obligation to make timely payments, his deposit ultimately is to be refunded, and both the timing and method of that refund are largely within the control of the customer.

The Commissioner stresses the fact that these deposits were not placed in escrow or segregated from IPL's other funds, and that IPL therefore enjoyed unrestricted use of the money. That circumstance, however, cannot be dispositive. After all, the same might be said of a commercial loan; yet the Commissioner does not suggest that a loan is taxable upon receipt simply because the borrower is free to use the funds in whatever fashion he chooses until the time of repayment. In determining whether a taxpayer enjoys "complete dominion" over a given sum, the crucial point is not whether his use of the funds is unconstrained during some interim period. The key is whether the taxpayer has some guarantee that he will be allowed to keep the money. IPL's receipt of these deposits was accompanied by no such guarantee.

Nor is it especially significant that these deposits could be expected to generate income greater than the modest interest IPL was required to pay. Again, the same could be said of a commercial loan, since, as has been noted, a business is unlikely to borrow unless it believes that it can realize benefits that exceed the cost of servicing the debt. A bank could hardly operate profitably if its earnings on deposits did not surpass its interest obligations; but the deposits themselves are not treated as income. Any income that the utility may earn through use of the deposit money of course is taxable, but the prospect that income will be generated provides no ground for taxing the principal.

The Commissioner's advance payment analogy seems to us to rest upon a misconception of the value of an advance payment to its recipient. An advance payment, like the deposits at issue here, concededly protects the seller against the risk that it would be unable to collect money owed it after it has furnished goods or services. But an advance payment does much more: it protects against the risk that the purchaser will back out of the deal before the seller performs. From the moment an advance payment is made, the seller is assured that, so long as it fulfills its contractual obligation, the money is its to keep. Here, in contrast, a customer submitting a deposit made no commitment to purchase a specified quantity of electricity, or indeed to purchase any electricity at all. IPL's right to keep the money depends upon the customer's purchase of electricity, and upon his later decision to have the deposit applied to future bills, not merely upon the utility's adherence to its contractual duties. Under these circumstances, IPL's dominion over the fund is far less complete than is ordinarily the case in an advance-payment situation.

The Commissioner emphasizes that these deposits frequently will be used to pay for electricity, either because the customer defaults on his obligation or because the customer, having established credit, chooses to apply the deposit to future bills rather than to accept a refund. When this occurs, the Commissioner argues, the transaction, from a cash-flow standpoint, is equivalent to an advance payment. In his view this economic equivalence mandates identical tax treatment.

Whether these payments constitute income when received, however, depends upon the parties' rights and obligations *at the time the payments are made*. The problem with petitioner's argument perhaps can best be understood if we imagine a loan between parties involved in an ongoing commercial relationship. At the time the loan falls due, the lender may decide to apply the money owed him to the purchase of goods or services rather than to accept repayment in cash. But this decision does not mean that the loan, when made, was an advance payment after all. The lender in effect has taken repayment of his money (as was his contractual right) and has chosen to use the proceeds for the purchase of goods or services from the borrower. Although, for the sake of convenience, the parties may combine the two steps, that decision does not blind us to the fact that in substance two transactions are involved. It is this element of choice that distinguishes an advance payment from a loan. Whether these customer deposits are the economic equivalents of advance payments, and therefore taxable upon receipt, must be determined by examining the relationship between the parties at the time of the deposit. The individual who makes an advance payment retains no right to insist upon the return of the funds; so long as the recipient fulfills the terms of the bargain, the money is its to keep. The customer who submits a deposit to the utility, like the lender in the previous hypothetical, retains the right to insist upon repayment in cash; he may *choose* to apply the money to the purchase of electricity, but he assumes no obligation to do so, and the utility therefore acquires no unfettered ''dominion'' over the money at the time of receipt.

When the Commissioner examines privately structured transactions, the true understanding of the parties, of course, may not be apparent. It may be that a transfer of funds, though nominally a loan, may conceal an unstated agreement that the money is to be applied to the purchase of goods or services. We need not, and do not, attempt to devise a test for addressing those situations where the nature of the parties' bargain is legitimately in dispute. * * *

Our decision is also consistent with the Tax Court's longstanding treatment of lease deposits—perhaps the closest analogy to the present situation. The Tax Court traditionally has distinguished between a sum designated as a prepayment of rent—which is taxable upon receipt—and a sum deposited to secure the tenant's performance of a lease agreement. See, e.g., J. & E. Enterprises, Inc. v. Commissioner, 26 TCM 944 (1967). In fact, the customer deposits at issue here are less plausibly regarded as income than lease deposits would be. The typical lease deposit secures the tenant's fulfillment of a contractual obligation to pay a specified rent throughout the term of the lease. The utility customer, however, makes no commitment to purchase any services at all at the time he tenders the deposit.

We recognize that IPL derives an economic benefit from these deposits. But a taxpayer does not realize taxable income from every event that improves his economic condition. A customer who makes this deposit reflects no commitment to purchase services, and IPL's right to retain the money is contingent upon events outside its control. We hold that such dominion as IPL has over these customer deposits is insufficient for the deposits to qualify as taxable income at the time they are made.

The judgment of the Court of Appeals is affirmed.

It is so ordered.

Problems and Notes

1. *Deposits as interest-free loans.* The Conference Committee Report on the Tax Reform Act of 1984 says that some deposits may be treated as interest-free loans under § 7872. However, Prop.Treas.Reg. § 1.7872–2(b)(1) provides that *non-refundable* deposits are not loans.

2. *Options.* Suppose that A, who is interested in buying Blackacre from B for use in A's business, pays B $10,000 for an option to buy the property for $200,000. If A does not exercise the option, A will have a $10,000 deduction and B will have $10,000 ordinary income. If A does exercise the option, the $10,000 will be included in A's basis for Blackacre and in B's amount realized. If the parties do not know in the year in which A bought the option whether it will be exercised, how should they report the transaction? According to Virginia Iron, Coal & Coke Co. v. Commissioner, 99 F.2d 919 (4th Cir.1938), cert. denied 307 U.S. 630 (1939), a "wait-and-see" rule applies. The transaction has no tax effect until the option either lapses or is exercised.

3. *Problems. L* owned investment property which he leased to *T* in year 1 for a five-year term at $10,000 a year. *T* also had an option (exercisable not later than January 31, year 2) to purchase the property for $80,000. The terms of the lease required *T* to pay *L* $5000 (in addition to the first year's rent in advance) to secure *T*'s performance under the lease. The $5000 was to be credited against the rent for the last six months of the lease term if *T* had performed his obligations under the lease until that time. If *T* exercised the option to purchase the property, the $5000 was to be credited toward the purchase price. In January, year 2, *T* exercised the option, paying *L* $75,000 cash. *L* had a basis of $80,000 for the property at that time.

(1) What result to *L?*

(2) What is *T*'s basis for the property?

THE CODE AND THE TIME–VALUE OF MONEY: AN OVERVIEW

Recent tax legislation shows that Congress has become much more aware of time-value issues than it used to be. So far, though, the time-value provisions of the Code have little in common. Congress has not addressed the problems in a systematic way; instead, it has responded to "abuses" by enacting legislation to deal with the problems on an ad hoc basis. These measures take five different approaches to taxpayer exploitation of timing rules:

(1) *Arbitrary reductions in or elimination of tax preferences.* One example of this technique is § 291, which reduces specified "tax preferences" of corporations by 20 or 30 percent. Some of the preferences covered by § 291 are timing provisions. Another example is the passive-loss rules (Chapter 8), which respond to tax shelters—most of which depend on favorable timing rules—by limiting deductibility of losses.

(2) *Requiring consistent treatment of the parties to a transaction.* Sections 267(a)(2), 467, 404(a)(5), and 404(d) are examples of this technique.

(3) *Delaying deductions.* By denying deductions to accrual-method taxpayers until "economic performance" has occurred, § 461(h) limits (without eliminating) some of the advantages accrual-method taxpayers used to get by accruing items not currently payable. Section 419 uses a somewhat similar technique in the case of employer contributions to funded employee-benefit plans.

(4) *Identifying interest and requiring that interest be accounted for accurately.* Sections 7872 (interest-free and low-interest loans), § 1272 (original-issue discount), and § 467 (as applied to the interest component of "stepped rents") operate by recharacterizing arrangements that are economically equivalent to payment of interest on a regular basis. Section 483, which identifies one form of dis-

guised interest but falls short of treating that interest on a constant-rate basis, is a sort of halfway measure.

(5) *Endorsing, and even expanding, the abuse.* Section 529 (p. 71) originally allowed those who prepaid college tuition to defer taxes on the prepayments' investment returns until the tuition was actually paid. Under today's version of that section, the earnings from the prepayments are not taxed at all.

Taxpayer efforts to identify and exploit weaknesses in the timing rules will continue to trigger congressional responses. Today's set of timing provisions is "not the last word, only the latest."[k]

k. Brown, C.J., in Parr v. United States, 469 F.2d 1156, 1159 (5th Cir.1972).

Appendix A

AN INTRODUCTION TO THE CONCEPTS OF PRESENT AND FUTURE VALUE

In order to understand business and investment transactions, one must have a grasp of the concepts of present and future value. Consider, for example, a person who is deciding whether to make a particular investment. The investor will enter into the deal only if the expected benefits of entering the transaction exceed its costs (both measured in dollars). But it is difficult to compare costs and benefits if the costs are incurred today while the benefits will not be received for several years (or vice versa). Because of the time-value of money, a dollar in hand is more valuable than the promise of a dollar to be received at some time in the future, even if the future receipt is assured. In order to make comparisons of costs and benefits across time, we need a means of expressing future cash flows in terms of their present value—a means of comparing apples with apples rather than with oranges.

This Appendix is intended to aid you in making comparisons of costs and benefits across time by substituting present values for expectations about the future. We begin with the calculation of future value. We then use that material as an aid in developing the concept of present value.

FUTURE VALUE

Most of us are accustomed to thinking in terms of future value. Suppose we invest one dollar today at 10% annual interest. After one year, we will have $1.10 (our original $1.00 "principal" and $.10 "interest" on that principal). That is, the value of $1.00 after one period at 10% interest is $1.10.

We can generalize this result by the following formula:

$$f_1 = p + rp = p\,(1 + r),$$

where f_1 is the value after one period of p invested at interest rate r, with r expressed as a decimal.

If p equals \$1.00 and r equals 10% (that is, .10), the above formula yields:

$$f_1 = \$1.00\ (1 + .10) = \$1.00 \times 1.10 = \$1.10.$$

Now suppose that at the end of the first year we reinvest the \$1.10 for another year at 10% interest. At the end of the second year we will have \$1.21, which represents the \$1.10 with which we began the second year and the \$.11 interest (10% of \$1.10) that we earn for the second year. Notice that in the second year we earn interest of \$.10 on our original one dollar of principal, and we also earn \$.01 interest on the first year's interest of \$.10. The process of earning interest on previous periods' interest is called "compounding" of interest. In this case, the interest is compounded annually.

Notice also that the balance at the end of the second period (f_2) is just the balance with which we began the second period (f_1) multiplied by $(1 + r)$:

$$f_2 = f_1\ (1 + r).$$

Since we know that the balance at the end of the first period (f_1) is equal to the sum with which we began the first period (p) multiplied by $(1 + r)$, it follows that:

$$f_2 = f_1\ (1 + r) = [p\ (1 + r)]\ (1 + r) = p\ (1 + r)^2.$$

By similar reasoning we can establish that the future value (f_3) of some amount p invested at interest rate r for three periods is:

$$f_3 = f_2\ (1 + r) = [p\ (1 + r)^2]\ (1 + r) = p\ (1 + r)^3.$$

And, more generally, the future value (f) of a present sum p invested for n periods at interest rate r is:

$$f = p\ (1 + r)^n.$$

Remember that in each case the interest rate r must be expressed as a decimal.

Notice that the factor $(1 + r)^n$ is a constant for each given value of r and n. Table I lists the values of this future-value factor for various values of r and n. You can think of Table I as setting forth the amount (in dollars) to which \$1.00 will grow if invested for n periods at r percent interest.

For example, suppose that we invest \$1.00 at 8% annual interest for 20 years, with each year's interest to be reinvested in the fund at the 8% rate. How much will we have in the fund after 20 years? From Table I, we infer that \$1.00 invested at 8% for 20 years will cumulate to approximately \$4.66. (To find the factor for $r = 8\%$ and $n = 20$, go down the 8% column to the point at which it intersects the 20–period row. The factor is 4.66096.[a] Thus, \$1.00 invested at 8% (compounded annually) for 20 years will grow to \$4.66096.)

---

a. That is, $(1.08)^{20}$. One can easily calculate future and present values by use of a financial calculator. Working with the ta- bles, however, will help you grasp the conceptual underpinnings of future and present values. We therefore urge you to work

If instead of investing $1 we had initially invested $10,000, the fund would cumulate to $46,609.60 ($10,000 × 4.66096) (that is, if $1.00 would cumulate to $4.66096, $10,000 would cumulate to an amount 10,000 times greater).

In applying the formula $f = p (1 + r)^n$, it is important to keep in mind that n refers to the number of periods over which the interest is compounded and that r refers to the interest rate for the compounding period. If the interest is compounded annually, the period is one year, as in the preceding example. But what if the interest is to be compounded semiannually?

For example, we invest $10,000 for one year at 8% compounded semiannually. This means that after six months we have earned $400 of interest ($10,000 × 8% × ½), thus increasing our fund to $10,400. We then earn interest of $416 ($10,400 × 8% × ½) for the second six-month period. By the end of the year, the fund has increased to $10,816. To obtain this result from Table I, we use $n = 2$ (because there are two semiannual compounding periods in one year) and $r = 4\%$ (because we earn 4% (= ½ of 8%) in each semiannual period). The factor is 1.08160[b], and the value of our $10,000 fund after one year is $10,816 ($10,000 × 1.08160).

Notice that the result in this case is the same as if we had earned 8.16% compounded annually. If we invest $10,000 at 8.16% compounded annually, we will have $10,816 ($10,000 × 1.08160) after one year. In other words, 8% interest compounded semiannually is economically equivalent to 8.16% interest compounded annually. The 8.16% figure in this example is referred to as the *effective* annual interest rate. In this case, 8% is the *nominal* annual rate. If the interest is compounded more frequently than annually, the effective rate exceeds the nominal rate.

Suppose you are given a nominal annual interest rate and told that the interest will be compounded m times each year. To find the appropriate future-value factor in Table I (or to apply the future-value formula), you must divide the nominal rate by m and multiply by m the number of years during which the fund will be invested. For example, suppose you are going to invest $1.00 for two years at 12% a year compounded monthly. The nominal rate (12%) must be divided by 12 to find the rate for each (monthly) compounding period (12%/12 = 1%). The investment will be compounded for 24 periods (2 years × 12 months/year). The future-value factor is therefore 1.26973 (from Table I, with $r = 1\%$ and $n = 24$ periods), and the $1.00 investment will grow to approximately $1.27 ($1.00 × 1.26973) after two years.

When you compare interest rates, you must always consider the frequency of compounding. The more frequently the interest is compounded, the higher the effective annual rate. Thus, after one year, a $10,000 fund at 8% compounded annually cumulates to $10,800; at 8%

with the tables until you become comfortable with these concepts.   **b.**   That is, $(1.04)^2$.

compounded semiannually, it grows to $10,816; at 8% compounded quarterly, it grows to $10,824.30; at 8% compounded semiquarterly, it grows to $10,828.60, etc. (Make sure you understand how these figures are derived from Table I.)[c]

Problems

Except where otherwise indicated, assume that interest is compounded annually.

(1) *A* invests $100,000 in a five-year certificate of deposit. The issuer will pay interest on the funds at 10%. What will the balance in the fund be at the end of five years if *A* permits the interest to accumulate?

(2) What result in (1) if the interest rate is 10% compounded *semiannually*? (Why is the future value greater when the compounding is more frequent?)

(3) *B* Corp. has $100,000 to invest today. It anticipates needing $200,000 five years from now for a building project. At what rate of interest must the $100,000 be invested today in order to accumulate a fund of $200,000 in five years?

(4) *C* Corp. has $100,000 to invest today. It can invest that sum at 9%. For how many periods must the fund be invested in order to increase to $200,000?

FUTURE VALUE OF AN ANNUITY

Suppose we wish to know how much we can accumulate if we put aside a constant amount each year. For example, suppose we are going to put aside one dollar at the end of this year and another dollar at the end of next year. Assume that we can earn a return of 10% on the funds so put aside. How much will we have in the fund at the end of next year?

At the end of the first year, we put one dollar aside. By the end of the second year, that dollar has earned $.10 interest, giving us a total of $1.10 at the end of the second year with respect to the first dollar put aside. We also put aside one more dollar at the end of the second year. But that dollar will have earned no interest by the end of the second year because it has just been set aside. Thus, our total set aside (plus interest) by the end of the second year is $2.10.

We can think of this as the future value of an "annuity" of $1 a year for two years at ten percent. (The term "annuity" here refers to a series of equal contributions to be made at regular intervals.) Again, because

---

c. Interest can be compounded monthly, weekly, daily or even hourly. Indeed, by the use of calculus, one can derive a formula for the future value of a sum that is compounded every instant ("continuous compounding"). The formula is $f = pe^{rn}$, where p is the principal amount, r is the nominal annual interest rate (expressed as a decimal), n is the number of years for which the sum is invested and e is the base of the natural logarithm (a constant with a value approximately equal to 2.718). Thus, $10,000 invested for one year at 12% compounded continuously grows to approximately $11,275. The effective annual rate is 12.75% ($1275/$10,000).

the future value of an annuity of $1 is a constant for any given values of r and n, we can construct a table (Table III) that provides the appropriate factor for the future value of an annuity.

An important caveat: In constructing a table for the future value of an annuity, the usual convention is to assume that the annuity payment is to be made at the end rather than at the beginning of the period. We have followed that convention in preparing Table III. (Technically, Table III sets forth the factors for an "annuity in arrears." We discuss below the use of the table to value an "annuity in advance," in which the payment is assumed to be made at the beginning of each period.)

To illustrate the computation under Table III, assume that on January 1, year 1, we decide to invest $10,000 on December 31, year 1, and a like sum on each subsequent December 31 through year 5. We can earn 10% (compounded annually) on the fund. How much will we have in the fund at the end of the fifth year? Table III provides the factor for the future value of an annuity for five periods at an interest rate of 10%: 6.10510. Therefore, we will have $61,051 ($10,000 × 6.10510) in the fund after five years.

Suppose that in this example we made each annual payment on January 1 instead of December 31 (an annuity in advance). What would be the value of the fund at the end of the fifth year? In that case, the value of the fund at the *beginning* of year 5 would be $61,051 ($10,000 × 6.10510). By the *end* of year 5, the fund would increase to $67,156 ($61,051 × 1.10) (1.10 being the factor from Table I for $n = 1$, $r = 10\%$). Alternatively, we could determine the factor for an annuity in arrears for *six* periods and subtract 1.00. Under this approach, the factor for the five-year annuity in advance would be 6.71561 (7.71561 − 1.0000), and the value of the annuity would be $67,156 ($10,000 × 6.71561).

Problems

(1) *A* plans to accumulate a college fund for her newborn child *C* by investing $3000 on each of *C*'s first 18 birthdays. *A* expects to earn a return of 7% on the investment. What will the value of the fund be immediately after *C*'s 18th birthday?

(2) What result in (1) if *A* makes the first contribution to the fund at *C*'s birth and then makes a contribution on each of *C*'s first 17 birthdays?

PRESENT VALUE

Suppose we offer to pay you one dollar one year from today. What would you be willing to pay us today for that promise? You might check our credit rating and find that it is impeccable, have a binding promissory note drafted, etc. Yet, you would not pay us a dollar for our promise to pay you a dollar in one year because of the time-value of money. If you have a dollar today, you can invest it in a government-guaranteed savings account, earn a year's interest, and have more than a dollar one year from now. You would therefore be willing to pay for our promise some amount p, which, when added to the amount of one year's interest on p ($p \times r$), is equal to one dollar:

$p + (p \times r) = \$1.00$, or

$p(1 + r) = \$1.00$, or

$p = \$1.00/(1 + r)$.

If you know the rate of interest that you can earn on an investment involving a comparable degree of risk, you can determine how much you would be willing to pay for our promise to pay you a dollar one year from now. Suppose, for example, that you could earn 10% (compounded annually) on a comparably risky one-year investment. Then you would presumably be willing to pay today approximately \$.91 for the right to receive one dollar in one year (that is, $p = \$1.00/1.10 = \$.90909$). In other words, \$.90909 is the *present value* of the right to receive \$1.00 discounted for one year at 10%.

Recall the formula for the amount (f) to which a present sum (p) will cumulate after n periods of compounding at interest rate r:

$f = p(1 + r)^n$

If we solve this equation for p, we get:

$p = f/(1 + r)^n$,

which enables us to compute the present value (p) of the right to receive some amount f discounted at rate r for n periods. (As always, r must be expressed as a decimal.) By setting f equal to \$1.00 in the formula, we get $p = 1/(1 + r)^n$. The latter is a constant for any given r and n, a fact that allows us to construct a table of present-value factors (Table II).

Notice in Table II that the present value of the right to receive one dollar discounted for one year at 10% is \$.90909.)

Now suppose we offer to pay you \$10,000 after four years. What would you be willing to pay for this promise if you can earn 12% (compounded annually) on a comparably risky investment? From Table II, we see that the present-value factor ($n = 4$, $r = 12\%$) is .63552. This means that the present value of \$1.00 discounted for four periods at 12% is \$.63552. Therefore, the present value of the right to receive the \$10,000 payment is \$6355.20 (\$10,000 × .63552).

As in the case of the future-value calculation, we must take into account the frequency of compounding. If in the preceding example the appropriate discount rate had been 12% compounded semiannually, we would have used $n = 8$ (because 4 years include 8 semiannual compounding periods) and $r = 6\%$ (12% × ½) to determine the present-value factor (.62741). The present value of \$10,000 discounted at 12% (compounded semiannually) for four years would thus be \$6274.10. (Notice that this figure is smaller than in the case where interest was compounded annually. To see why this should be so, recall that more-frequent compounding increases the *effective* interest rate. The higher the effective interest rate, the smaller the present value of a future sum.)

Problems

Unless otherwise indicated, assume that the appropriate interest rate is 10% compounded annually.

(1) *D* sells property for $100,000, payable (without interest) five years after the date of sale. What is the equivalent cash selling price for the property? (What result if the interest rate is 10% compounded semiannually?)

(2) *K* makes a $100,000 interest-free loan to her child for a term of one year. To what extent should *K* be deemed to have made a gift to the child?

(3) *E* bequeaths $100,000 in trust to pay the income to *F* for life, remainder to *G*. *F* has a life expectancy of 15 years. What is the present value of *G*'s remainder interest? Of *F*'s income interest?

PRESENT VALUE OF AN ANNUITY

Suppose we promise to pay you one dollar one year from today and one dollar two years from today. What would you be willing to pay for that promise, assuming that you can earn 10% in comparably risky investments? It seems clear that you would pay an amount equal to the sum of (1) the present value of the right to receive one dollar one year from now (discounted at 10%), and (2) the present value the right to receive one dollar two years from now (discounted at 10%). That is, you would be willing to pay $.90909 for the right to receive the payment due in one year (Table II), and $.82645 for the right to receive the payment due in two years (Table II), or a total of $1.73554 for the right to the two payments. Recall that a stream of periodic payments is called an annuity. In this case, the annuity is for a term of two years. Again, we can construct a table that will tell us the present value of the right to receive an annuity of $1 whenever we know (1) the appropriate discount rate and (2) the number of periods for which the annuity payments will be received. Table IV is such a table.

To illustrate the application of Tables II and IV, consider the problem of valuing a $10,000 *X* Corp. bond which bears interest (payable at the end of each year) at 10% and which will become due at the end of the fifth year. Assume that an investor could earn 10% interest by investing in corporate bonds that involve a comparable degree of risk. How much would an investor pay for the *X* Corp. bond?

The purchaser of the bond acquires two separate rights: (1) the right to the annual interest payment of $1000 (10% of $10,000); and (2) the right to the return of the $10,000 bond principal at maturity—in this case, after five years. The value of the bond is just the sum of the present values of these two rights to future cash payments.

To evaluate the right to receive the $10,000 principal payment after five years, we turn to Table II. With $n = 5$ and $r = 10\%$, the present-value factor is .62092. The present value of the right to receive the $10,000 principal payment is therefore $6209.20 ($10,000 $\times$ .62092).

To evaluate the stream of five annual interest payments of $1000 each, we turn to Table IV. With $n = 5$ and $r = 10\%$, the factor for the present value of an annuity is 3.79079. The present value of the right to the interest payments is therefore $3790.79 ($1000 $\times$ 3.79079).

The value of the bond is therefore $10,000 (rounded), the sum of the present values of the rights to the interest and principal payments.

In this example, the bond sells for an amount equal to its face amount ("par") because the contractual (or "coupon") interest rate of 10% is the same as the *market* rate that an investor can earn on comparably risky bonds. But suppose an investor can earn a 12% annual return by investing in comparably risky bonds. At what price would the 10% bond sell in that case?

The bondholder's *contractual* rights are the same as before: (1) a right to $1000 of annual interest; and (2) a right to the $10,000 principal after five years. But if the *market* is now offering a 12% annual return on comparable bonds, the bondholder's right to the future payments must be discounted at the 12% market rate. Thus, the present value of the interest payments is $3604.78 ($1000 $\times$ 3.60478) (the factor is obtained from Table IV, with $n = 5$, $r = 12\%$). The present value of the principal payment is $5674.30 ($10,000 $\times$ .56743) (the factor is from Table II, with $n = 5$, $r = 12\%$). The bond will therefore sell for $9279.08 ($3604.78 + $5674.30), a price that brings the effective yield on the bond into congruence with the market rate of interest.

How much would you pay today for the right to receive $1000 a year *forever*? Such arrangements are called perpetuities. If comparably risky investments yield 10%, we can say that we would be willing to pay some amount, X, where 10% of X equals $1000, from which it follows that $X = $1000/.10 = $10,000. More generally, the value of a perpetuity (V) is equal to the amount of the annual annuity payment (A) provided by the perpetuity divided by the discount rate (r) (expressed as a decimal):

$V = A/r$.

Compare the value of the perpetuity ($10,000) with the present value of a 100–year annuity of $1000 discounted at 10%. We can infer from Table IV that the 100–year annuity is worth $9,999.27. The present value of the payments from year 101 through Armageddon is only 73 cents!

The formula for valuing a perpetuity is useful in valuing a going business. As explained in Chapter 10, businesses are usually valued by discounting their anticipated earnings or cash flow to present value. If we expect a firm to generate net income of $250,000 a year indefinitely, and if the expected return on comparably risky investments is 20%, we can value the business as a perpetuity of $250,000:

$V = A/r = \$250,000/.20 = \$1,250,000.$

Problems

Unless otherwise indicated, assume that interest is compounded annually.

(1) *T* recently won $3,000,000 (payable $100,000 at the end of each year for 30 years) in the state lottery. A newspaper story described the winner as the state's "newest millionaire." Do you agree? (The applicable discount rate is 10%.)

(2) *H* Corp. is negotiating a ten-year lease of property for use in its business. The lessor is demanding an annual rent of $100,000, payable at the end of each year. However, the lessor is willing instead to accept $500,000 total rent if the entire $500,000 is paid at the inception of the lease. *H* Corp. can earn 15% on its investments. Which rental arrangement should it accept?

(3) *J* Corp. wishes to borrow $100,000 for ten years at 10% interest. The lender will require amortization (repayment) of the loan by means of equal annual payments due at the end of each of the ten years, each payment being credited first to accrued interest and then to principal. What annual payment will *J* Corp. be required to make?

(4) *L* represents a plaintiff in a personal-injury suit. The defendant has offered three alternative settlement arrangements. If the appropriate discount rate is 10%, which settlement arrangement should *L* recommend?

   (a) $250,000 payable immediately;

   (b) $400,000 payable after four years;

   (c) $80,000 payable at the end of each of the next four years.

(5) A bond in the principal amount of $10,000 is due on December 31, year 10. It bears interest at 10%, payable semiannually. If the market interest rate on comparable bonds is 12% compounded semiannually, at what price would you expect the bond to be trading in the market at the beginning of year 1?

(6) *M* wishes to set aside $2000 a year for the college education of her child, *C*. The first contribution to the fund is made on *C*'s first birthday. The last contribution will be made on *C*'s seventeenth birthday. *M* can earn an after-tax return of 10% on the investment. *M* expects *C* to make four equal annual withdrawals from the fund to pay for her college education. The first withdrawal is to be made on *C*'s eighteenth birthday. What amount will *C* be able to withdraw from the fund each year?

(7) *P* wishes to purchase a thriving laundry business in University City. She expects the firm to generate an annual cash flow of $1,000,000 into the indefinite future. She estimates that she can earn a return of 25% in comparably risky investments. Approximately how much should she expect to pay for the business?

Table I

Future Value of $1.00

$f = p \ (1 + r)^n$, where r = interest rate; n = number of compounding periods; p = $1.00.

Periods = n	1%	2%	3%	4%	5%	6%	7%	8%	9%	10%	12%	15%
1	1.01000	1.02000	1.03000	1.04000	1.05000	1.06000	1.07000	1.08000	1.09000	1.10000	1.12000	1.15000
2	1.02010	1.04040	1.06090	1.08160	1.10250	1.12360	1.14490	1.16640	1.18810	1.21000	1.25440	1.32250
3	1.03030	1.06121	1.09273	1.12486	1.15763	1.19102	1.22504	1.25971	1.29503	1.33100	1.40493	1.52087
4	1.04060	1.08243	1.12551	1.16986	1.21551	1.26248	1.31080	1.36049	1.41158	1.46410	1.57352	1.74901
5	1.05101	1.10408	1.15927	1.21665	1.27628	1.33823	1.40255	1.46933	1.53862	1.61051	1.76234	2.01136
6	1.06152	1.12616	1.19405	1.26532	1.34010	1.41852	1.50073	1.58687	1.67710	1.77156	1.97382	2.31306
7	1.07214	1.14869	1.22987	1.31593	1.40710	1.50363	1.60578	1.71382	1.82804	1.94872	2.21068	2.66002
8	1.08286	1.17166	1.26677	1.36857	1.47746	1.59385	1.71819	1.85093	1.99256	2.14359	2.47596	3.05902
9	1.09369	1.19509	1.30477	1.42331	1.55133	1.68948	1.83846	1.99900	2.17189	2.35795	2.77308	3.51788
10	1.10462	1.21899	1.34392	1.48024	1.62889	1.79085	1.96715	2.15892	2.36736	2.59374	3.10585	4.04556
11	1.11567	1.24337	1.38423	1.53945	1.71034	1.89830	2.10485	2.33164	2.58043	2.85312	3.47855	4.65239
12	1.12683	1.26824	1.42576	1.60103	1.79586	2.01220	2.25219	2.51817	2.81266	3.13843	3.89598	5.35025
13	1.13809	1.29361	1.46853	1.66507	1.88565	2.13293	2.40985	2.71962	3.06580	3.45227	4.36349	6.15279
14	1.14947	1.31948	1.51259	1.73168	1.97993	2.26090	2.57853	2.93719	3.34173	3.79750	4.88711	7.07571
15	1.16097	1.34587	1.55797	1.80094	2.07893	2.39656	2.75903	3.17217	3.64248	4.17725	5.47357	8.13706
16	1.17258	1.37279	1.60471	1.87298	2.18287	2.54035	2.95216	3.42594	3.97031	4.59497	6.13039	9.35762
17	1.18430	1.40024	1.65285	1.94790	2.29202	2.69277	3.15882	3.70002	4.32763	5.05447	6.86604	10.76126
18	1.19615	1.42825	1.70243	2.02582	2.40662	2.85434	3.37993	3.99602	4.71712	5.55992	7.68997	12.37545
19	1.20811	1.45681	1.75351	2.10685	2.52695	3.02560	3.61653	4.31570	5.14166	6.11591	8.61276	14.23177
20	1.22019	1.48595	1.80611	2.19112	2.65330	3.20714	3.86968	4.66096	5.60441	6.72750	9.64629	16.36654
22	1.24472	1.54598	1.91610	2.36992	2.92526	3.60354	4.43040	5.43654	6.65860	8.14027	12.10031	21.64475
24	1.26973	1.60844	2.03279	2.56330	3.22510	4.04893	5.07237	6.34118	7.91108	9.84973	15.17863	28,62518
26	1.29526	1.67342	2.15659	2.77247	3.55567	4.54938	5.80735	7.39635	9.39916	11.91818	19.04007	37.85680
28	1.32129	1.74102	2.28793	2.99870	3.92013	5.11169	6.64884	8.62711	11.16714	14.42099	23.88387	50.06561
30	1.34785	1.81136	2.42726	3.24340	4.32194	5.74349	7.61226	10.06266	13.26768	17.44940	29.95992	66.21177
32	1.37494	1.88454	2.57508	3.50806	4.76494	6.45339	8.71527	11.73708	15.76333	21.11378	37.58173	87.56507
34	1.40258	1.96068	2.73191	3.79432	5.25335	7.25103	9.97811	13.69013	18.72841	25.54767	47.14252	115.8048
36	1.43077	2.03989	2.89828	4.10393	5.79182	8.14725	11.42394	15.96817	22.25123	30.91268	59.13557	153.1519
38	1.45953	2.12230	3.07478	4.43881	6.38548	9.15425	13.07927	18.62528	26.43668	37.40434	74.17966	202.5433
40	1.48886	2.20804	3.26204	4.80102	7.03999	10.28572	14.97446	21.72452	31.40942	45.25926	93.05097	267.8635
50	1.64463	2.69159	4.38391	7.10668	11.46740	18.42015	29.45703	46.90161	74.35752	117.3909	289.0022	1,083.66
100	2.70481	7.24465	19.21863	50.50495	131.5013	339.3021	867.7163	2,199.76	5,529.04	13,780.6	83,522.3	117×10^4

Table II

Present Value of $1.00

$p = f/(1 + r)^n$, where r = discount (interest) rate; n = number of periods until payment; f = \$1.00.

Periods = n	1%	2%	3%	4%	5%	6%	7%	8%	9%	10%	12%	15%
1	.99010	.98039	.97087	.96154	.95238	.94340	.93458	.92593	.91743	.90909	.89286	.86957
2	.98030	.96117	.94260	.92456	.90703	.89000	.87344	.85734	.84168	.82645	.79719	.75614
3	.97059	.94232	.91514	.88900	.86384	.83962	.81630	.79383	.77218	.75131	.71178	.65752
4	.96098	.92385	.88849	.85480	.82270	.79209	.76290	.73503	.70843	.68301	.63552	.57175
5	.95147	.90573	.86261	.82193	.78353	.74726	.71299	.68058	.64993	.62092	.56743	.49718
6	.94205	.88797	.83748	.79031	.74622	.70496	.66634	.63017	.59627	.56447	.50663	.43233
7	.93272	.87056	.81309	.75992	.71068	.66506	.62275	.58349	.54703	.51316	.45235	.37594
8	.92348	.85349	.78941	.73069	.67684	.62741	.58201	.54027	.50187	.46651	.40388	.32690
9	.91434	.83676	.76642	.70259	.64461	.59190	.54393	.50025	.46043	.42410	.36061	.28426
10	.90529	.82035	.74409	.67556	.61391	.55839	.46319	.46319	.42241	.38554	.32197	.24718
11	.89632	.80426	.72242	.64958	.58468	.52679	.47509	.42888	.38753	.35049	.28748	.21494
12	.88745	.78849	.70138	.62460	.55684	.49697	.44401	.39711	.35553	.31863	.25668	.18691
13	.87866	.77303	.68095	.60057	.53032	.46884	.41496	.36770	.32618	.28966	.22917	.16253
14	.86996	.75788	.66112	.57748	.50507	.44230	.38782	.34046	.29925	.26333	.20462	.14133
15	.86135	.74301	.64186	.55526	.48102	.41727	.36245	.31524	.27454	.23939	.18270	.12289
16	.85282	.72845	.62317	.53391	.45811	.39365	.33873	.29189	.25187	.21763	.16312	.10686
17	.84438	.71416	.60502	.51337	.43630	.37136	.31657	.27027	.23107	.19784	.14564	.09293
18	.83602	.70016	.58739	.49363	.41552	.35034	.29586	.25025	.21199	.17986	.13004	.08081
19	.82774	.68643	.57029	.47464	.39573	.33051	.27651	.23171	.19449	.16351	.11611	.07027
20	.81954	.67297	.55368	.45639	.37689	.31180	.25842	.21455	.17843	.14864	.10367	.06110
22	.80340	.64684	.52189	.42196	.34185	.27751	.22571	.18394	.15018	.12285	.08264	.04620
24	.78757	.62172	.49193	.39012	.31007	.24698	.19715	.15770	.12640	.10153	.06588	.03493
26	.77205	.59758	.46369	.36069	.28124	.21981	.17220	.13520	.10639	.08391	.05252	.02642
28	.75684	.57437	.43708	.33348	.25509	.19563	.15040	.11591	.08955	.06934	.04187	.01997
30	.74192	.55207	.41199	.30832	.23138	.17411	.13137	.09938	.07537	.05731	.03338	.01510
32	.72730	.53063	.38834	.28506	.20987	.15496	.11474	.08520	.06344	.04736	.02661	.01142
34	.71297	.51003	.36604	.26355	.19035	.13791	.10022	.07305	.05339	.03914	.02121	.00864
36	.69892	.49022	.34503	.24367	.17266	.12274	.08754	.06262	.04494	.03235	.01691	.00653
38	.68515	.47119	.32523	.22529	.15661	.10924	.07646	.05369	.03783	.02673	.01348	.00494
40	.67165	.45289	.30656	.20829	.14205	.09722	.06678	.04603	.03184	.02209	.01075	.00373
50	.60804	.37153	.22811	.14071	.08720	.05429	.03395	.02132	.01345	.00852	.00346	.00092
100	.36971	.13803	.05203	.01980	.00760	.00295	.00115	.00045	.00018	.00007	.00001	.00000

Table III

Future Value of Annuity of $1.00 in Arrears

$$F = [(1 + r)^n - 1]/r, \text{ where } r = \text{interest rate}; \ n = \text{number of payments.}$$

No. of Payments = n	1%	2%	3%	4%	5%	6%	7%	8%	9%	10%	12%	15%
1	1.00000	1.00000	1.00000	1.00000	1.00000	1.00000	1.00000	1.00000	1.00000	1.00000	1.00000	1.00000
2	2.01000	2.02000	2.03000	2.04000	2.05000	2.06000	2.07000	2.08000	2.09000	2.10000	2.12000	2.15000
3	3.03010	3.06040	3.09090	3.12160	3.15250	3.18360	3.21490	3.24640	3.27810	3.31000	3.37440	3.47250
4	4.06040	4.12161	4.18363	4.24646	4.31013	4.37462	4.43994	4.50611	4.57313	4.64100	4.77933	4.99338
5	5.10101	5.20404	5.30914	5.41632	5.52563	5.63709	5.75074	5.86660	5.98471	6.10510	6.35285	6.74238
6	6.15202	6.30812	6.46841	6.63298	6.80191	6.97532	7.15329	7.33593	7.52333	7.71561	8.11519	8.75374
7	7.21354	7.43428	7.66246	7.89829	8.14201	8.39384	8.65402	8.92280	9.20043	9.48717	10.08901	11.06680
8	8.28567	8.58297	8.89234	9.21423	9.54911	9.89747	10.25980	10.63663	11.02847	11.43589	12.29969	13.72682
9	9.36853	9.75463	10.15911	10.58280	11.02656	11.49132	11.97799	12.48756	13.02104	13.57948	14.77566	16.78584
10	10.46221	10.94972	11.46388	12.00611	12.57789	13.18079	13.81645	14.48656	15.19293	15.93742	17.54874	20.30372
11	11.56683	12.16872	12.80780	13.48635	14.20679	14.97164	15.78360	16.64549	17.56029	18.53117	20.65458	24.34928
12	12.68250	13.41209	14.19203	15.02581	15.91713	16.86994	17.88845	18.97713	20.14072	21.38428	24.13313	29.00167
13	13.80933	14.68033	15.61779	16.62684	17.71298	18.88214	20.14064	21.49530	22.95338	24.52271	28.02911	34.35192
14	14.94742	15.97394	17.08632	18.29191	19.59863	21.01507	22.55049	24.21492	26.01919	27.97498	32.39260	40.50471
15	16.09690	17.29342	18.59891	20.02359	21.57856	23.27597	25.12902	27.15211	29.36092	31.77248	37.27971	47.58041
16	17.25786	18.63929	20.15688	21.82453	23.65749	25.67253	27.88805	30.32428	33.00340	35.94973	42.75328	55.71747
17	18.43044	20.01207	21.76159	23.69751	25.84037	28.21288	30.84022	33.75023	36.97370	40.54470	48.88367	65.07509
18	19.61475	21.41231	23.41444	25.64541	28.13238	30.90565	33.99903	37.45024	41.30134	45.59917	55.74971	75.83636
19	20.81090	22.84056	25.11687	27.67123	30.53900	33.75999	37.37896	41.44626	46.01846	51.15909	63.43968	88.21181
20.	22.01900	24.29737	26.87037	29.77808	33.06595	36.78559	40.99549	45.76196	51.16012	57.27500	72.05244	102.4436
22	24.47159	27.29898	30.53678	34.24797	38.50521	43.39229	49.00574	55.45676	62.87334	71.40275	92.50258	137.6316
24	26.97346	30.42186	34.42647	39.08260	44.50200	50.81558	58.17667	66.76476	76.78981	88.49733	118.1552	184.1678
26	29.52563	33.67091	38.55304	44.31174	51.11345	59.15638	68.67647	79.95442	93.32398	109.1818	150.3339	245.7120
28	32.12910	37.05121	42.93092	49.96758	58.40258	68.52811	80.69769	95.33883	112.9682	134.2099	190.6989	327.1041
30	34.78489	40.56808	47.57542	56.08494	66.43885	79.05819	94.46079	113.2832	136.3075	164.4940	241.3327	434.7451
32	37.49407	44.22703	52.50276	62.70147	75.29883	90.88978	110.2182	134.2135	164.0370	201.1378	304.8477	577.1005
34	40.25770	48.03380	57.73018	69.85791	85.06696	104.1838	128.2588	158.6267	196.9823	245.4767	384.5210	765.3654
36	43.07688	51.99437	63.27594	77.59831	95.83632	119.1209	148.9135	187.1021	236.1247	299.1268	484.4631	1,014.35
38	45.95272	56.11494	69.15945	85.97034	107.7095	135.9042	172.5610	220.3159	282.6298	364.0434	609.8305	1,343.62
40	48.88637	60.40198	75.40126	95.02552	120.7998	154.7620	199.6351	259.0565	337.8824	442.5926	767.0914	1,779.09
50	64.46318	84.57940	112.7969	152.6671	209.3480	290.3359	406.5289	573.7702	815.0836	1,163.91	2,400.02	7,217.72
100	170.4814	312.2323	607.2877	1,237.62	2,610.03	5,638.37	12,381.7	27,484.5	61,422.7	137,796	696,011	783×10^4

Table IV

Present Value of Annuity of $1.00 in Arrears

$P = (1 - 1/[1 + r]^n)/r$, where r = discount (interest) rate; n = number of payments.

No. of Payments = n	1%	2%	3%	4%	5%	6%	7%	8%	9%	10%	12%	15%
1	.99010	.98039	.97087	.96154	.95238	.94340	.93458	.92593	.91743	.90909	.89286	.86957
2	1.97040	1.94156	1.91347	1.88609	1.85941	1.83339	1.80802	1.78326	1.75911	1.73554	1.69005	1.62571
3	2.94099	2.88388	2.82861	2.77509	2.72325	2.67301	2.62432	2.57710	2.53129	2.48685	2.40183	2.28323
4	3.90197	3.80773	3.71710	3.62990	3.54595	3.46511	3.38721	3.31213	3.23972	3.16987	3.03735	2.85498
5	4.85343	4.71346	4.57971	4.45182	4.32948	4.21236	4.10020	3.99271	3.88965	3.79079	3.60478	3.35216
6	5.79548	5.60143	5.41719	5.24214	5.07569	4.91732	4.76654	4.62288	4.48592	4.35526	4.11141	3.78448
7	6.72819	6.47199	6.23028	6.00205	5.78637	5.58238	5.38929	5.20637	5.03295	4.86842	4.56376	4.16042
8	7.65168	7.32548	7.01969	6.73274	6.46321	6.20979	5.97130	5.74664	5.53482	5.33493	4.96764	4.48732
9	8.56602	8.16224	7.78611	7.43533	7.10782	6.80169	6.51523	6.24689	5.99525	5.75902	5.32825	4.77158
10	9.47130	8.98259	8.53020	8.11090	7.72173	7.36009	7.02358	6.71008	6.41766	6.14457	5.65022	5.01877
11	10.36763	9.78685	9.25262	8.76048	8.30641	7.88687	7.49867	7.13896	6.80519	6.49506	5.93770	5.23371
12	11.25508	10.57534	9.95400	9.38507	8.86325	8.38384	7.94269	7.53608	7.16073	6.81369	6.19437	5.42062
13	12.13374	11.34837	10.63496	9.98565	9.39357	8.85268	8.35765	7.90378	7.48690	7.10336	6.42355	5.58315
14	13.00370	12.10625	11.29607	10.56312	9.89864	9.29498	8.74547	8.24424	7.78615	7.36669	6.62817	5.72448
15	13.86505	12.84926	11.93794	11.11839	10.37966	9.71225	9.10791	8.55948	8.06069	7.60608	6.81086	5.84737
16	14.71787	13.57771	12.56110	11.65230	10.83777	10.10590	9.44665	8.85137	8.31256	7.82371	6.97399	5.95423
17	15.56225	14.29187	13.16612	12.16567	11.27407	10.47726	9.76322	9.12164	8.54363	8.02155	7.11963	6.04716
18	16.39827	14.99203	13.75351	12.65930	11.68959	10.82760	10.05909	9.37189	8.75563	8.20141	7.24967	6.12797
19	17.22601	15.67846	14.32380	13.13394	12.08532	11.15812	10.33560	9.60360	8.95011	8.36492	7.36578	6.19823
20	18.04555	16.35143	14.87747	13.59033	12.46221	11.46992	10.59401	9.81815	9.12855	8.51356	7.46944	6.25933
22	19.66038	17.65805	15.93692	14.45112	13.16300	12.04158	11.06124	10.20074	9.44243	8.77154	7.64465	6.35866
24	21.24339	18.91393	16.93554	15.24696	13.79864	12.55036	11.46933	10.52876	9.70661	8.98474	7.78432	6.43377
26	22.79520	20.12104	17.87684	15.98277	14.37519	13.00317	11.82578	10.80998	9.92897	9.16095	7.89566	6.49056
28	24.31644	21.28127	18.76411	16.66306	14.89813	13.40616	12.13711	11.05108	10.11613	9.30657	7.98442	6.53351
30	25.80771	22.39646	19.60044	17.29203	15.37245	13.76483	12.40904	11.25778	10.27365	9.42691	8.05518	6.56598
32	27.26959	23.46833	20.38877	17.87355	15.80268	14.08404	12.64656	11.43500	10.40624	9.52638	8.11159	6.59053
34	28.70267	24.49859	21.13184	18.41120	16.19290	14.36814	12.85401	11.58693	10.51784	9.60857	8.15656	6.60910
36	30.10751	25.48884	21.83225	18.90828	16.54685	14.62099	13.03521	11.71719	10.61176	9.67651	8.19241	6.62314
38	31.48466	26.44064	22.49246	19.36786	16.86789	14.84602	13.19347	11.82887	10.69082	9.73265	8.22099	6.63375
40	32.83469	27.35548	23.11477	19.79277	17.15909	15.04630	13.33171	11.92461	10.75736	9.77905	8.24378	6.64178
50	39.19612	31.42361	25.72976	21.48218	18.25593	15.76186	13.80075	12.23348	10.96168	9.91481	8.30450	6.66051
100	63.02888	43.09835	31.59891	24.50500	19.84791	16.61755	14.26925	12.49432	11.10910	9.99927	8.33323	6.66666

*

Appendix B

STATUTORY TAX RATES
FOR 2002 AND 2003

Section 1(i), adopted in 2001, creates a ten-percent bracket for individual taxpayers and provides for a schedule of reductions in the 28–percent, 31–percent, 36–percent, and 39.6–percent rates for individuals, trusts, and estates. Sections 1(a) through 1(e) as they would read for 2002 and 2003 after application of the adjustments of § 1(i) appear below. Note that, except for the ten-percent bracket, the dollar amounts of §§ 1(a) through 1(e) are adjusted for inflation; these adjustments are not incorporated in this presentation.

§ 1. Tax imposed

(a) Married individuals filing joint returns and surviving spouses.—There is hereby imposed on the taxable income of—

(1) every married individual (as defined in section 7703) who makes a single return jointly with his spouse under section 6013, and

(2) every surviving spouse (as defined in section 2(a)), a tax determined in accordance with the following table:

If taxable income is	The tax is:
Not over $12,000	10% of taxable income.
Over $12,000 but not over $36,900	$1,200, plus 15% of the excess over $12,000.
Over $36,900 but not over $89,150	$4,935, plus 27% of the excess over $36,900.
Over $89,150 but not over $140,000	$19,042.50, plus 30% of the excess over $89,150.
Over $140,000 but not over $250,000	$34,297.50, plus 35% of the excess over $140,000.
Over $250,000	$72,797.50, plus 38.6% of the excess over $250,000.

(b) Heads of households.—There is hereby imposed on the taxable income of every head of a household (as defined in section 2(b)) a tax determined in accordance with the following table:

If taxable income is:	The tax is:
Not over $10,000	10% of taxable income.
Over $10,000 but not over $29,600	$1,000, plus 15% of the excess over $10,000.
Over $29,600 but not over $76,400	$3,940, plus 27% of the excess over $29,600.
Over $76,400 but not over $127,500	$16,576, plus 30% of the excess over $76,400.
Over $127,500 but not over $250,000	$31,906, plus 35% of the excess over $127,500.
Over $250,000........................	$74,781, plus 38.6% of the excess over $250,000.

(c) Unmarried individuals (other than surviving spouses and heads of households).—There is hereby imposed on the taxable income of every individual (other than a surviving spouse as defined in section 2(a) or the head of a household as defined in section 2(b)) who is not a married individual (as defined in section 7703) a tax determined in accordance with the following table:

If taxable income is:	The tax is:
Not over $6,000	10% of taxable income.
Over $6,000 but not over $22,100	$600, plus 15% of the excess over $6,000.
Over $22,100 but not over $53,500	$3,015, plus 27% of the excess over $22,100.
Over $53,500 but not over $115,000	$11,493, plus 30% of the excess over $53,500.
Over $115,000 but not over $250,000	$29,943, plus 35% of the excess over $115,000.
Over $250,000........................	$77,193, plus 38.6% of the excess over $250,000.

(d) Married individuals filing separate returns.—There is hereby imposed on the taxable income of every married individual (as defined in section 7703) who does not make a single return jointly with his spouse under section 6013, a tax determined in accordance with the following table:

If taxable income is:	The tax is:
Not over $6,000	10% of taxable income.
Over $6,000 but not over $18,450	$600, plus 15% of the excess over $6,000.
Over $18,450 but not over $44,575	$2,467.50, plus 27% of the excess over $18,450.
Over $44,575 but not over $70,000	$9,521.25, plus 30% of the excess over $44,575.
Over $70,000 but not over $125,000	$17,148.75, plus 35% of the excess over $70,000.
Over $125,000........................	$36,398.75, plus 38.6% of the excess over $125,000.

(e) Estates and trusts.—There is hereby imposed on the taxable income of—

(1) every estate, and

(2) every trust,

taxable under this subsection a tax determined in accordance with the following table:

If taxable income is:	The tax is:
Not over $1,500	15% of taxable income.
Over $1,500 but not over $3,500	$225, plus 27% of the excess over $1,750.
Over $3,500 but not over $5,500	$765, plus 30% of the excess over $4,050.
Over $5,500 but not over $7,500	$1,365, plus 35% of the excess over $6,200.
Over $7,500	$2,065, plus 38.6% of the excess over $8,450.

For 2004 and 2005, each rate higher than 15% is scheduled to drop another one percentage point, and a further reduction is scheduled for 2006. In addition, the ten-percent bracket of § 1(a) will increase to $14,000 in 2008 and, beginning in that year, the ten-percent bracket for single taxpayers and married taxpayers filing separate returns will increase. The ten-percent bracket is to be indexed for inflation starting with 2009. Finally, the 15–percent bracket for married taxpayers will be expanded in the years 2005 to 2008.

SOME NOTES ON INFLATION ADJUSTMENTS

Many of the Code's dollar amounts, including nearly all of the dollar amounts in the rate tables, are adjusted annually for inflation. For example, according to the statute the highest marginal rate (38.6 percent) for unmarried taxpayers and for married taxpayers filing joint returns applies to the excess of taxable income over $250,000. For 2002, the actual starting point for the 38.6–percent bracket is $307,500; Rev.Proc. 2001–59, I.R.B. 2001–52, 623. Other examples of 2002 inflation-adjusted dollar amounts are:

Personal Exemptions and Standard Deductions

The statutory personal-exemption amount of $2000 (§ 151(d)(1)) applied for 1989. The 2002 figure is $3000. The inflation-adjusted basic standard deduction amounts for 2002 are as follows:

Joint return or surviving spouse (§ 63(c)(2)(A)): $7850

Head of household (§ 63(c)(2)(B)): $6900

Unmarried (§ 63(c)(2)(C)): $4700

Married filing separately (§ 63(c)(2)(D)): $3925

The "additional amounts" referred to in § 63(f) are $900 (§§ 63(f)(1) & (2)) and $1150 (§ 63(f)(3)).

The $500 figure in § 63(c)(5)(A) is $750 for 2002. The $250 figure in § 63(c)(5)(B) is still $250.

Selected Phaseouts

The Code contains so many phaseouts that a list of all of the inflation-adjusted figures would be very cumbersome. We present here a selection of the more-important phaseouts for 2002.

Section 68 (itemized deductions). The 2002 phaseout begins at AGI of $137,300, except for married taxpayers filing separately, for whom it is half that amount.

Section 151(d) (personal exemptions). The 2002 phaseout begins at AGI of $137,300 for unmarried taxpayers generally, at $171,650 for heads of households, and at $206,000 for married taxpayers filing jointly.

The earned-income credit for a married couple with at least one qualifying child begins to phase out at AGI of $14,520 for 2002. For unmarried taxpayers with one or more qualifying children, the phaseout begins at $13,520. (Note the substantial marriage penalty here.)

Social Security Tax Earnings Limit

The FICA tax (Social Security and Medicare) is 7.65 percent of wages. This tax is imposed on both the employer and the employee, so in fact it is 15.3 percent. The 7.65 percent FICA tax consists of the Social Security tax (6.2 percent) and the Medicare tax (1.45 percent). The Social Security portion of the tax is imposed on wages only up to the statutory limit. For 2002, this limit is $84,900. There is no limit on wages subject to the Medicare tax.

Index

References are to pages